SIXTH EDITION

FUNDAMENTALS OF ENGINEERING DRAWING

for design, communication, and numerical control

FUNDAMENTALS OF ENGINEERING DRAWING
for design, communication, and numerical control
SIXTH EDITION

by Warren J. Luzadder, P.E.

© 1971, 1965, 1959, 1952, 1946, 1943
BY PRENTICE-HALL, INC., ENGLEWOOD CLIFFS, NEW JERSEY

All rights reserved. No part of this book
may be reproduced in any form or by any means
without permission in writing from the publisher.

Library of Congress Catalog Card No.: 78-137983
Printed in the United States of America

13-338376-8

Current printing (last digit):
10   9   8   7

OTHER BOOKS BY THE AUTHOR:

Basic Graphics for Design, Analysis, Communications and the Computer, 2nd ed., Prentice-Hall, Inc., 1968.

Fundamentos De Dibujo Para Ingenieros, 2nd ed., Compania Editoria Continental, 1967.

Graphics for Engineers, Prentice Hall of India Private Limited, 1964.

Technical Drafting Essentials, 2nd ed., Prentice-Hall, Inc., 1956.

Problems in Engineering Drawing, 6th ed., Prentice-Hall, Inc., 1971.

Engineering Graphics Problems for Design, Analysis and Communications, Prentice-Hall, Inc., 1968.

Problems in Drafting Fundamentals, Prentice-Hall, Inc., 1956.

Purdue University Engineering Drawing Films, with J. Rising et al.

PRENTICE-HALL INTERNATIONAL, INC., LONDON
PRENTICE-HALL OF AUSTRALIA, PTY. LTD., SYDNEY
PRENTICE-HALL OF CANADA, LTD., TORONTO
PRENTICE-HALL OF INDIA PRIVATE LIMITED, NEW DELHI
PRENTICE-HALL OF JAPAN, INC., TOKYO

FUNDAMENTALS
OF
ENGINEERING DRAWING

Warren J. Luzadder, P.E.
Purdue University

PRENTICE-HALL, INC., ENGLEWOOD CLIFFS, NEW JERSEY

Preface

The rapid absorption of new scientific knowledge into the engineering sciences coupled with the phenomenal advances made in automation and computer control of production processes has increased the need for the clear and concise presentation of technical information. The need for the preparation of engineering drawings to convey much of this information has not diminished in these days of the so-called second industrial revolution and now more drawings are required than in the past. The future appears bright for the young person who selects a career as a draftsman, technical-aid, or as a member of one of the new branches of applied engineering, now being developed, that will require four years of study for a degree.

This sixth edition of FUNDAMENTALS OF ENGINEERING DRAWING has been reorganized and expanded to fulfill the present day needs of curriculums of technical institutes and schools of applied engineering of a new era of education. An era in which engineers have found it necessary to broaden their knowledge of the sciences so as to be competent to bring to the people of the world the benefits of new scientific discoveries.

With engineers now having their attention centered mainly on the creation and development of new products, American industry has found it necessary and desirable to assign much of the traditional work done by engineers in the past to technically trained persons known as engineering technologists. Engineers, technologists, draftsmen, and technical aides taken together form the complete engineering team. The great demand for draftsmen and technical aids, that has as yet not been satisfied, has led to a tremendous growth of our technical institutes. Persons being trained for this type of semi-professional work are usually in a two-year associate degree program.

The newest member of the engineering team, the technologist, has need for a somewhat broader education that may require four years of study. To satisfy the demand of industry for this type of highly trained professional, a number of our colleges and larger universities have created schools of technology or are in the process of doing so. The educational goal of these schools has been to give an up-dated type of technical training similar to that given to engineering students in the late Forties and early Fifties. This may be said to be a return to applied engineering which necessarily requires considerable training in engineering drawing and practical design accompanied by a working knowledge of the production and construction processes.

Although this text is intended for use primarily in schools of technology and technical institutes, it will be found suitable for use in some of the creative design courses now being offered in our engineering colleges. These courses may be thought of as providing an introduction to design in that they afford the student the opportunity to develop ideas through sketching as well as on the drawing board. The inclusion of design in graphics courses gives a beginning student an insight into engineering as a career. Furthermore, design experience leads to the discovery that both the engineer and technologist are constantly being called upon to use logical, analytic, and creative thought processes to arrive at conclusions and make necessary decisions.

Although the professional engineer is no longer interested in the art of preparation of engineering drawings, he does find it necessary to read engineering drawings with full understanding and to expand or alter them by means of his own sketches. He can hardly be expected to do this effectively unless he himself is thoroughly familiar with the graphical methods for problem solving and graphical communication. Legally and ethically an engineer usually must assume full responsibility for the final system (mechanism or structure) that he has conceived. In assuming such responsibility the experienced person comes to realize that full and complete communication without error is as important in engineering as in law and medicine. This fact being true, an up-to-date engineering drawing text should be at hand in an engineer's collection of reference books.

The principal reasons for making a revision of this text are (1) to bring existing material up to date and make all illustrations, written material, and tables conform with the latest American National Standards Institute Manual ANS Y14; (2) to improve both the written material and the graphic presentations where deemed desirable; (3) to add new material to old chapters, and (4) to add five new chapters for which a need has developed. Two of these five chapters present material that has not appeared in any standard drawing text up to this time.

This sixth edition has been arranged for convenience into six main parts: Part I, Basic Graphical Techniques; Part II, Spatial Graphics; Part III, Graphics for Design and Communication; Part IV, Computer Graphics and Numerical Control; Part V, Design and Communication Drawing in Specialized Fields; and Part VI, Reproduction of Drawings. Within this framework the five new chapters are: Chapter 10 (Part II) Spatial Geometry for Design and Analysis (descriptive geometry & vector geometry); Chapter 13 (Part III) Introduction to Design; Chapter 18 (Part IV) Computer-aided Design and Automated Drafting; Chapter 19 (Part IV) Numerically Controlled Machine Tools; and Chapter 28 (Part V) Graphic Methods for Engineering Communication and Computation (graphs, charts, empirical equations, and alignment charts).

In the decade ahead, changes of procedure will be forced upon engineers and technologists by the developing techniques of computer-aided design that make possible computer-plotter prepared drawings and graphical solutions to engineering problems. However, since the computerization of engineering design is based upon the fundamental principles of orthographic projection (multiview drawing) and the concepts of descriptive geometry, basic courses in engineering drawing will assume a greater importance in technical education. Even now one can not ignore the fact that graphics, as presented in this text, has become a language for communication between man and computer (see Chapter 18). Special image processors are in use that permit a computerized system to both read and generate a permanent copy of a drawing as revised under new design concepts. Control tapes for automatic drafting machines or machine tools may be produced as required. In order to use these new techniques the engineer, technologist, and draftsman must all have a deeper knowledge of engineering drawing than in the past.

Computerized design and automated drafting will not eliminate manual design and the use of graphical constructions for the solution of engineering problems. Work at drafting tables will continue and the need for professional personnel with a full knowledge of engineering drawing will increase. This is true because there has not been a single new development that has made thinking obsolete. Furthermore, even out "on-a-cloud" dreamers have come to realize that it is not economically feasible to use a million dollar computer and a one hundred and fifty thousand dollar plotter to make all of the drawings required for the ordinary products that are produced for the consumer market by American industry.

The chapter covering numerically controlled machine tools has been included in this text so that the student may be able to understand the possible implications of this new kind of machine-tool. During this decade, students now using this text will be faced with changes in drafting practices, manufacturing procedures, and quality control that have been brought about by numerical control (see Chapter 19). It is recommended that an instructor make his students aware of the fact that the use of these numerically controlled machine tools will eventually bring changes in our dimensioning practices.

In this sixth edition, the material on sketching has been rearranged in order to relate it to creative design as the subject is now being presented in our basic courses in engineering graphics. Descriptive geometry, because of its recognized importance to design, has been expanded and organized into a new chapter that also includes vector geometry. Material covering technical illustrations has been added to the chapter on pictorial drawing and the chapter on piping has been expanded to include the use of models for the design and construction of chemical processing plants. Finally, since designers and draftsmen have a need for a working knowledge of graphic methods that are useful for deriving equations and making graphical computations, new sections have been added covering empirical equations and the construction of alignment charts (Chapter 28).

A sincere effort has been made to bring this book into the era of the space age and abreast of recent technological developments. Leading industrial organizations have generously assisted the author towards this end by supplying illustrations that were deemed of value in developing specific subjects. Every commercial illustration supplied by American industry has been identified using a courtesy credit line. The author deeply appreciates the kindness of each and every busy person who found the time needed to select these drawings and illustrations.

The author reaffirms his indebtedness to Professor George Shiers of Santa Barbara City College and Mr. William J. Hornung, Director of Long Island Technical School at Hicksville, New York. The chapter on electronic drawing, that was prepared by Professor Shiers for the previous edition, has been used in this edition with minor changes. Mr. Hornung prepared the chapter on architectural drawing.

Special appreciation must be expressed for the assistance of Mr. Thomas J. Heeg of the Major Tool and Machine Company at Indianapolis, Indiana. Mr. Heeg prepared the two programs that produced the computer print-outs in the chapter covering numerically controlled machine tools.

He read the material presented in this chapter for technical accuracy and made several valuable suggestions.

The author is particularly grateful to Professor K. E. Botkin, who willingly served as an advisor during the entire time that the manuscript for this edition was in preparation.

Finally, it is fitting to acknowledge a continued indebtedness to Professors R. L. Airgood, F. W. Duff, O. D. Lascoe, and R. P. Thompson all of Purdue University. Their many excellent suggestions have been incorporated in this edition.

W. J. L.
Purdue University

Contents

1 Introduction *1*

I BASIC GRAPHICAL TECHNIQUES *5*

2 Freehand Technical Lettering *7*
3 Drawing Equipment and Use of Instruments *25*
4 Engineering Geometry *51*

II SPATIAL GRAPHICS: SHAPE DESCRIPTION AND SPATIAL RELATIONSHIPS *75*

5 Theory of Projection *77*
6 Multiview Representation, Revolution, and Conventional Practices *83*
      A. MULTIVIEW DRAWING 83
      B. REVOLUTION 101
      C. CONVENTIONAL PRACTICES 105

7 Freehand Technical Drawing—Basic Techniques *125*
      A. MULTIVIEW SKETCHES 125
      B. SKETCHES IN ISOMETRIC AND OBLIQUE 133

8 Sectional Views *143*

9 Auxiliary Views *163*
       A. PRIMARY AUXILIARY VIEWS   163
       B. SECONDARY AUXILIARY VIEWS   173

10 Basic Spatial Geometry for Design and Analysis *185*
       A. BASIC DESCRIPTIVE GEOMETRY   185
       B. VECTOR GEOMETRY   197

11 Developments and Intersections *215*
       A. DEVELOPMENTS   216
       B. INTERSECTIONS   228

12 Pictorial Presentation *249*
       A. AXONOMETRIC PROJECTION   250
       B. OBLIQUE PROJECTION   263
       C. PERSPECTIVE PROJECTION   269
       D. INDUSTRIAL ILLUSTRATION   279

III GRAPHICS FOR DESIGN AND COMMUNICATION *289*

13 Introduction to Design: Sketching and Creative Thinking *291*

14 Shop Processes and Shop Terms *311*

15 Representation and Specification of Threads, Fasteners and Springs *327*
       A. SCREW THREADS   327
       B. FASTENERS   337
       C. SPRINGS   345

16 Size Description: Dimensions and Specifications *353*
       A. FUNDAMENTALS AND TECHNIQUES   353
       B. GENERAL DIMENSIONING PRACTICES   357
       C. LIMIT DIMENSIONING AND GEOMETRIC TOLERANCING   369

17 Design and Communication Drawings *391*

IV COMPUTER GRAPHICS AND NUMERICAL CONTROL *433*

18 Computer-aided Design and Automated Drafting *435*
- A. COMPUTER-AIDED DESIGN 435
- B. AUTOMATED DRAFTING 445
- C. AUTOMATED PHOTO-DRAFT SYSTEMS 461

19 Numerically Controlled Machine Tools *465*

V DESIGN AND COMMUNICATION DRAWING IN SPECIALIZED FIELDS *477*

20 Machine Elements *479*

21 Piping, Drawings and Models *491*
- A. PIPING DRAWINGS 491
- B. PROCESS MODELS 499

22 Welding Drawings *505*

23 Tool Design and Tool Drawings *513*

24 Electronic Drawings *529*

25 Structural Drawings *547*

26 Architectural Drawings *565*

27 Topographic and Engineering Map Drawings *583*

28 Graphic Methods for Engineering Communication and Computation *595*
- A. GRAPHS AND CHARTS 595
- B. EMPIRICAL EQUATIONS 607
- C. ALIGNMENT CHARTS 609

29 Patent Office Drawings *627*

xi

VI REPRODUCTION OF DRAWINGS *633*

30 Reproduction and Duplication of Engineering Drawings *635*

APPENDIX *645*

Symbols *647*

Tables *650*

Abbreviations *686*

American National Standards *687*

Bibliography *689*

INDEX *694*

FUNDAMENTALS
OF
ENGINEERING DRAWING

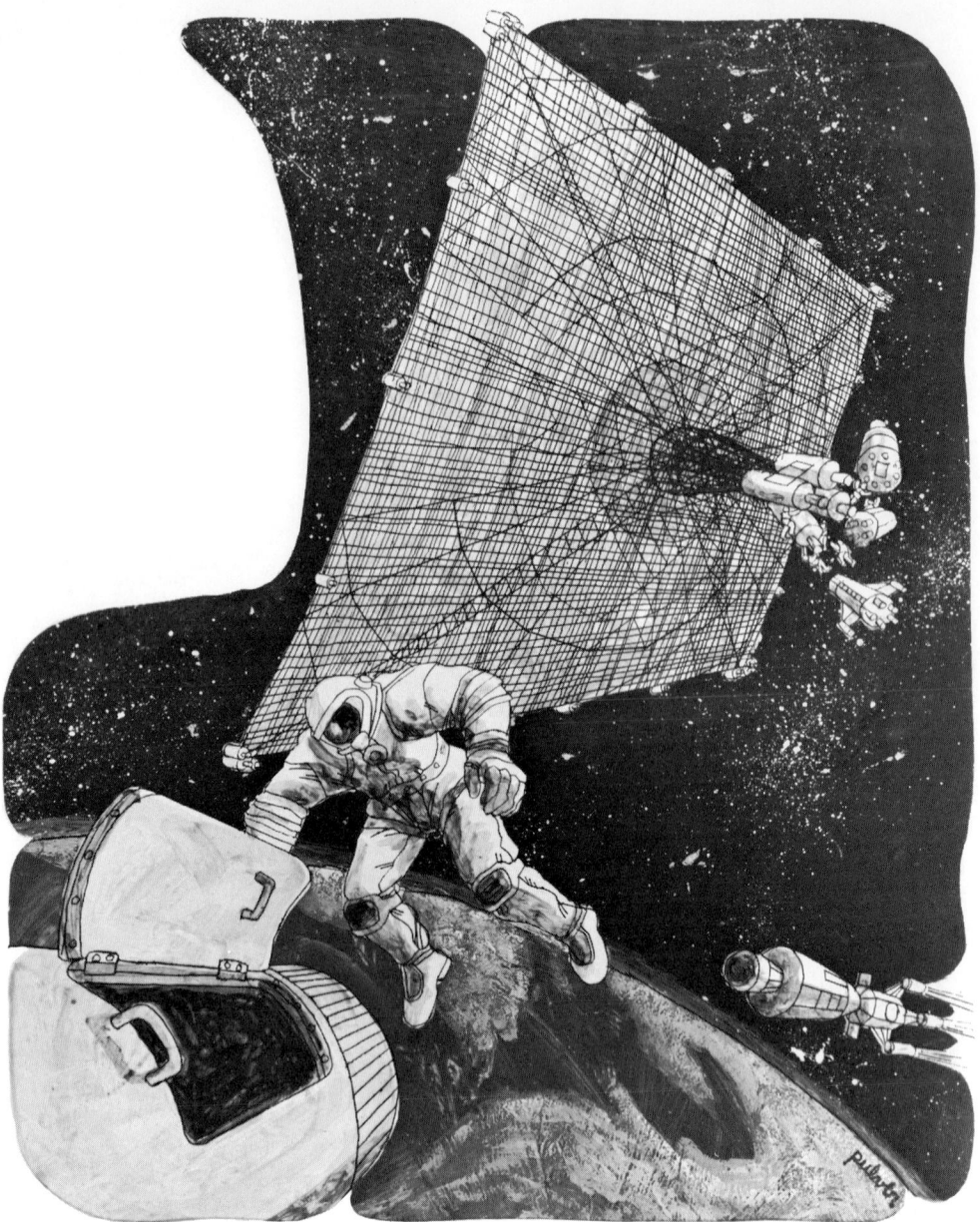

In the decade ahead man will establish orbiting stations around the earth. Some of these will be observatories from which he can study his own solar system and reach out across boundless space to search his own galaxy and galaxies beyond having billions of other suns. Unmanned satellites will roam our solar system. In the planning stage are grand-tour missions that will fly by Jupiter, Saturn, Uranus, Neptune, and far-away Pluto.

The development of these space stations and satellites will require enormous numbers of drawings and sketches. Most of these will be prepared by well-trained designers and draftsmen. Other drawings will be prepared by plotters operating on-line with computers. Thus we reach outward into space in this age of the computer and numerical control.

(*Courtesy 3M Company.*)

Introduction

1.1

Engineering drawing is a graphic language that is used universally by design engineers, engineering technologists, and draftsmen to describe the shape and size of structures and mechanisms. It has developed through the centuries, much as have various spoken and written languages, until at the present time its fundamental principles are understood by trained persons in all civilized nations. If an engineering technologist, who is assigned in the related fields of either design or production, is not to be an illiterate member of his or her profession, he or she must understand not only the theory of projection and dimensioning as related to working drawings but must be familiar with the idioms and conventions as well.

Even though the attention of a designer may be said to be centered mainly on the problems that arise in design and development (Fig. 1.1), he must have a complete working knowledge of communication drawing, for it is often his responsibility to direct the preparation of the final drawings. These follow the preliminary design drawings and instructive sketches that he and his aids have prepared in accordance with the basic principles underlying the preparation of working drawings.

For a full and complete exchange of ideas with others, the engineering technologist must be proficient in the three means of communication that are at his disposal: (1) English, both written and oral; (2) symbols, as used in the basic sciences; and (3) engineering drawing.

As a member of the engineering team, the draftsman must be fully capable of preparing the final drawings that will convey the information about size and shape needed to fabricate the parts and assemble the structure. This must be done in accordance with company practices and with the practices recommended in the publications of the American National Standards Institute.* It is expected that the draftsman keep up-to-date with the changes in standards that are constantly being made by standards engineers employed by his company and by the committees working under the sponsorship of the American National Standards Institute.

Engineering technicians, assigned to production areas or to the engineering department to aid the engineers, must have considerable knowledge of engineer-

---

*Formerly the American Standards Association.

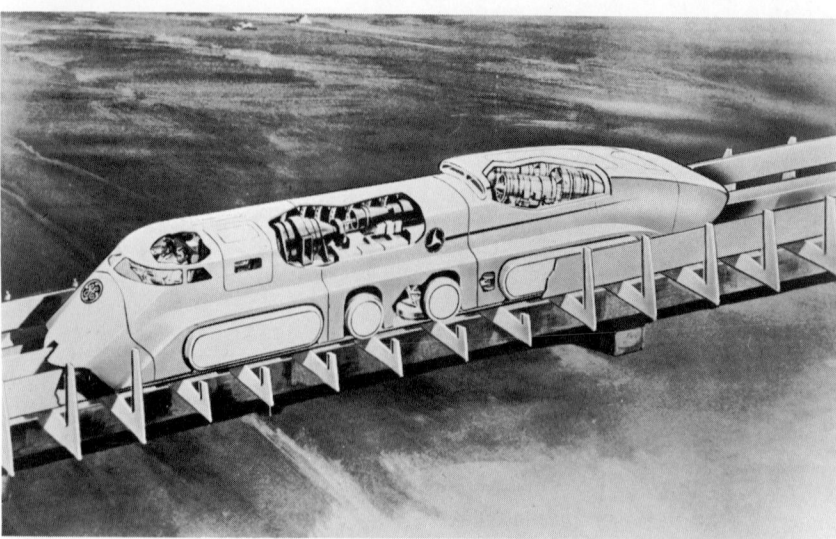

FIG. 1.1. The 300-mph TACRV (tracked air cushion research vehicle) shown could be in passenger service as early as 1975 to meet the greatly increased intercity transportation needs. It is designed to be supported one-half inch above a channel-shaped guideway. Hundreds of drawings will be required to produce this vehicle. (*Courtesy General Electric Company.*)

ing drawing. Those closely assisting a design engineer or technologist may be called on to solve problems graphically, to prepare design layouts, and to make working sketches relating to mechanisms, electrical circuits, and structural systems.

1.2
The purpose of this text is to present the grammar and composition of drawing so that those students in engineering colleges and technical institutes who conscientiously study the basic principles will eventually be able to prepare satisfactory industrial drawings and, after some practical experience, be capable of directing the work of others. To facilitate study, the subject matter has been separated into its various component parts: engineering, geometry, multiview drawing, dimension-

ing, pictorial drawing, sketching, and so forth. Later chapters discuss the preparation of working drawings, both detail and assembly, the preparation of topographic drawings, and the construction of charts and graphs. The major portion of the material presented leads up to the preparation of machine drawings, which the prospective members of some of the other branches of engineering technology think is not of interest to them. Since the methods used in the preparation of machine drawings, however, are the same methods used in the preparation of drawings in other fields, a thorough understanding of machine drawing assures a good foundation for later study in some specialized field, such as structural drawing. For those interested in specific types of drawing, some material has been presented with the assumption that the student already possesses a working knowledge of projection and dimensioning.

Proficiency in applying the principles of orthographic projection leads to easy graphical methods of solving space problems such as the determination of the clearance distance between members of a structure, the distance from a point to a plane, or the true angle between plane surfaces.

1.3

The graphic language has become a means for an intimate and continuous conversational style of interchange between man and computer in the process of creative design. At present, computer systems have been developed that are in daily use and that interact with a human partner using the designers' own graphic language (Fig. 18.3). In bringing the computational power of the digital computer to bear on graphical design, special image processing systems have been built that allow the computer to both read and generate drawings (General Motors DAC-1). Chapter 18 covers computer graphics in considerable detail.

1.4

This is a period of revolutionary change in the field of communication technology. At the present time, we are integrating new methods with the stylized methods of the past, using each method where it would seem to be best suited for the production of technical communications. We will continue to draw graphical representations manually and print out dimensions, notes, lists of materials, and so forth for the foreseeable future. However, plotters used on-line with computers or off-line directed by tapes will continue to gain wider utilization. Plotters are used in particular by aircraft and aerospace companies that produce products having complex contours. They are used also to a limited extent for the preparation of ordinary drawings of machine parts, for printed circuitry, for structural steel drawings, for highway route plans, and for determining the tool paths of milling (NC) machine tapes. Computer-aided design and automated drafting are discussed in Chapter 18. Information on the use and programming of numerically controlled machine tools is presented in Chapter 19.

Since nothing has happened to alter the fact that we communicate with others best in the graphic language, the greatest advance that has come about in the use of computers has been the development of computer graphics—that is, the development of the hardware and the software that enable the computer to accept, understand, analyze, and produce engineering design data in graphic form. The graphic language has thus assumed a new importance and the designer and the draftsman of the future will find it necessary both to have a deeper knowledge of projection, as presented in this text, and to know more about the preparation of communication drawings than in the past. In addition, persons who are responsible for the preparation of technical representations must become familiar with programming and with the use of both the computer and the plotter. These are their newest design and drafting tools. Although plotters are somewhat sophisticated as well as expensive, they save the designer and draftsman hours of tedious manual labor.

No new developments appear on the immediate horizon that will relieve the designer of the task of thinking out his design or the draftsman of the responsibility of applying the knowledge of his trade. Furthermore, recent technological breakthroughs have served to extend, rather than supplant, the direct application of the principles of engineering drawing by designers and draftsmen. The

FIG. 1.2. An entirely new concept for the electronic control of automobiles is illustrated above by an artist's rendering. Many additional drawings of a more conventional type will be needed to make the idea a reality.

The trailing car is equipped with a transmitter (at left) which projects an invisible beam at the car ahead. Tail lights of the car in front, which does not have to be specially equipped, reflect the beam back to a receiver (right). A computer "reads" the signal and adjusts brakes and accelerator automatically so that a pre-set safe following distance will be maintained. (*Courtesy Ford Motor Company.*)

technical field needs the graphic language in all of its many forms.

As technology advances to meet the rising expectations of people all around the world, more and more drawings and other forms of graphical representation will be required. Most of these, as might be expected, will continue to be prepared manually.

Automation has already entered the field of communication technology and therefore must be accepted by those persons now in the field and by those about to enter. The only question that either a student or a technically trained man now at work can ask himself is whether or not he can adjust to new knowledge, new methods, and different requirements during his career.

1.5

Engineering drawing offers students an insight into the methods of attacking engineering problems. Its lessons teach the principles of accuracy, exactness, and positiveness with regard to the information necessary for the production of a nonexisting structure. Finally, it develops the engineering imagination that is so essential to the creation of successful design (Fig. 1.2).

BASIC GRAPHICAL TECHNIQUES

Several styles of letters.

Freehand Technical Lettering

2.1
Introduction. To impart to the men in the shops all the necessary information for the complete construction of a machine or structure, the shape description, which is conveyed graphically by the views, must be accompanied by size descriptions and instructive specifications in the form of figured dimensions and notes (Fig. 2.1).

All dimensions and notes should be lettered freehand in a plain, legible style that can be rapidly executed. Poor lettering detracts from the appearance of a drawing and often impairs its usefulness, regardless of the quality of the line work.

2.2
Single-stroke Letters (Reinhardt). Single-stroke letters are now used universally for technical drawings. This style is suitable for most purposes because it possesses the qualifications necessary for legibility and speed. On commercial drawings it appears in slightly modified forms, however, since each person finally develops a style that reflects his own individuality.

The expression "single-stroke" means that the width of the straight and curved lines that form the letters are the same width as the stroke of the pen or pencil.

2.3
The General Proportions of Letters. Although there is no fixed standard for the proportions of the letters, certain definite rules must be observed in their design if one wishes to have his lettering appear neat and pleasing. The recognized characteristics of each letter should be carefully studied and then thoroughly learned through practice.

It is advisable for the beginner, instead of relying on his untrained eye for proportions, to follow the fixed proportions given in this chapter. Otherwise, his lettering will most likely be displeasing to the trained eye of the professional man. Later, after he has thoroughly mastered the art of lettering, his individuality will be revealed naturally by slight variations in the shapes and proportions of some of the letters.

It is often desirable to increase or decrease the width of letters in order to make a word or group of words fill a certain space. Letters narrower than normal letters of the same height are called *compressed letters;* those that are wider are called *extended letters* (Fig. 2.2).

2.4
Lettering Pencils and Pens. Pencil lettering is usually done with a medium-soft

8 PART I / BASIC GRAPHICAL TECHNIQUES

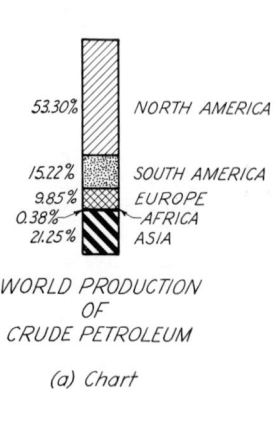

(a) Chart

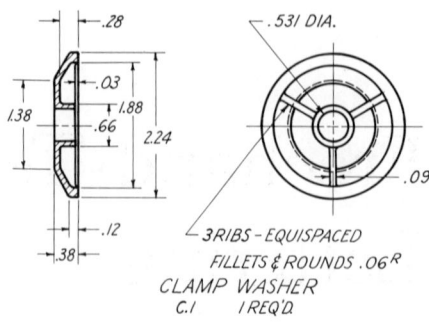

(b) Machine Drawing

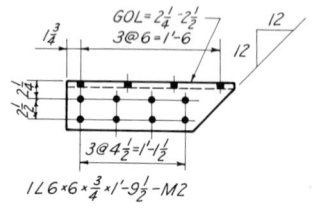

(c) Structural Drawing

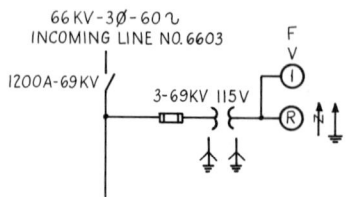

(d) Electrical Diagram
From ASA Y32.2-1954

FIG. 2.1. Technical drawings.

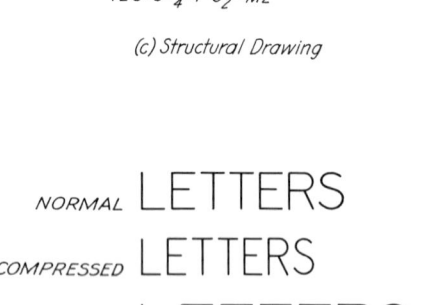

FIG. 2.2. Compressed and extended letters.

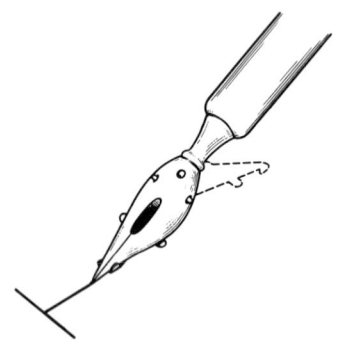

FIG. 2.3. Henry tank pen.

A very flexible point should never be used for lettering. Such a point is apt to shade the downward stem strokes as well as the downward portions of curved strokes. A good point has enough resistance to normal pressure to permit the drawing of curved and stem strokes of uniform width.

There are ordinary steel pen points with special ink-holding devices that make them especially suitable for lettering. The *Henry tank* pen, for example, shown in Fig. 2.3, has an ink reservoir that holds the ink above the point so that it feeds down the slit in an even flow. This device further assists in maintaining a uniform line by preventing the point from spreading.

Four of the many special pens designed for single-stroke letters are illustrated in Fig. 2.4. The *Barch–Payzant pen* (a) is available in graded sizes from No. 000 (very coarse) to No. 8 (very fine). The very fine size is suitable for lettering $1/8$–$3/16$ in. high on technical drawings. The *Edco* (b) has a patented holder into which any one of a graded set of lettering nibs (ranging in sizes from No. 0 to No. 6) may be screwed. The tubular construction of the point makes it possible to draw uniform lines regardless of the direction of the stroke. Also of tubular construction is the *Leroy* (c). The *Speedball* (d) may be obtained in many graded sizes.

pencil. Since the degree of hardness of the lead required to produce a dark opaque line will vary with the type of paper used, a pencil should be selected only after drawing a few trial lines. In order to obtain satisfactory lines, the pencil should be sharpened to a long conical point and then rounded slightly on a piece of scratch paper. To keep the point symmetrical while lettering, the pencil should be rotated a partial revolution before each new letter is started.

The choice of a type of pen point for lettering depends largely upon the personal preference and characteristics of the individual. The beginner can learn only from experience which of the many types available are best suited to him.

A pen that makes a heavy stroke should be used for bold letters in titles, and so forth, while a light-stroke pen is required for the lighter letters in figures and notes.

2.5

Devices for Drawing Guide Lines and Slope Lines. Devices for drawing guide lines (Fig. 2.5) are available in a variety of forms. The two most popular are the *Braddock lettering triangle* (Fig. 2.6), and the *Ames lettering instrument* (Fig. 2.7).

The Braddock lettering triangle is provided with sets of grouped countersunk holes that may be used to draw guide lines by inserting a sharp-pointed pencil (4H or 6H) into the holes and sliding the triangle

CHAP. 2 / FREEHAND TECHNICAL LETTERING 9

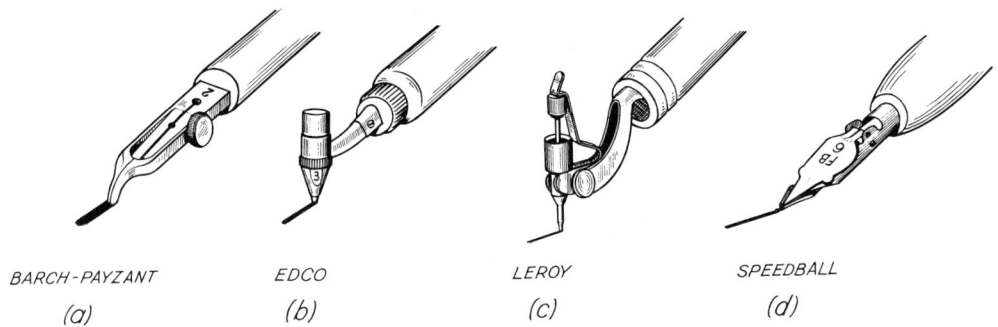

BARCH-PAYZANT EDCO LEROY SPEEDBALL
(a) (b) (c) (d)

FIG. 2.4. Special lettering pens.

back and forth along the guiding edge of a T-square or a triangle supported by a T-square (Fig. 2.6). The holes are grouped to give guide lines for capitals and lowercase letters. The numbers below each set indicate the height of the capitals in thirty-seconds of an inch. For example, the No. 3 set is for capitals $3/32$ in. high, the No. 4 set is for capitals $1/8$ in. high, the No. 5 is for capitals $5/32$ in. high, and so on.

To draw seven guide lines for a $1/8$-in. whole number and a fraction, use the countersunk holes indicated with black centers in Fig. 2.8. The height of a fraction numeral will be three-fourths the height of the whole number, and the total height of the fraction will be twice that of the whole number. If this useful combination is analyzed, it can be observed that the middle hole of the lower group in No. 3 and the top hole of the lower group in No. 6 give the guide lines for the whole number. The upper hole of the lower group in No. 4 gives the fraction bar, while the top and bottom holes in the two lower groups in No. 3 give the guide lines for the numerator and denominator (Fig. 2.9).

2.6
Uniformity in Lettering. Uniformity in height, inclination, spacing, and strength of line is essential for good lettering (Fig. 2.10). Professional appearance depends

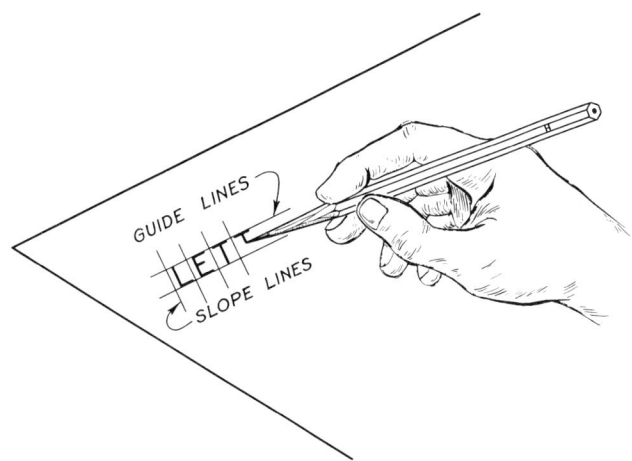

FIG. 2.5. Guide lines and slope lines.

as much on uniformity as on the correctness of the proportion and shape of the individual letters. Uniformity in height and inclination is assured by the use of guide lines and slope lines and uniformity in weight and color, by the skillful use of the pencil and proper control of the pressure of its point on the paper. The ability to space letters correctly becomes easy after continued thoughtful practice.

2.7
Composition. In combining letters into words, the spaces for the various combinations of letters are arranged so that the

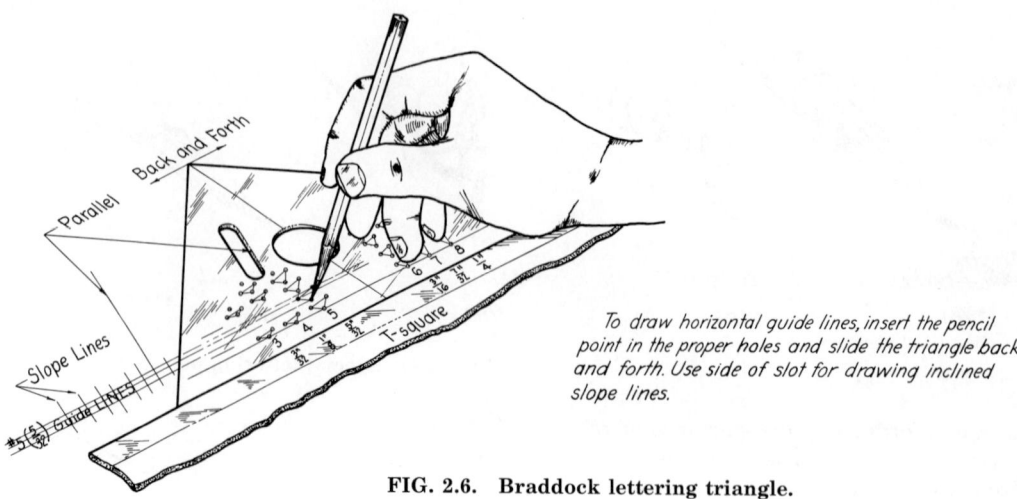

FIG. 2.6. Braddock lettering triangle.

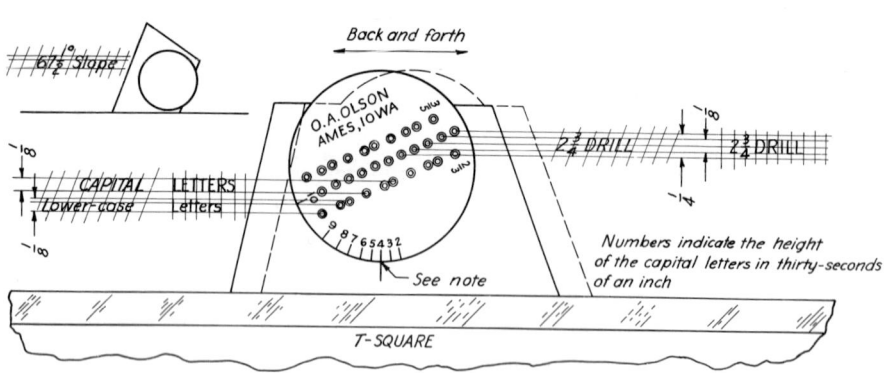

FIG. 2.7. Ames lettering instrument.

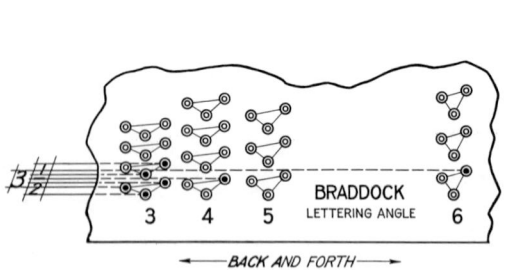

FIG. 2.8. Guide lines for fractions.

FIG. 2.9. Lettering numerals and fractions.

areas appear to be equal (Fig. 2.11). For standard lettering, this area should be about equal to one-half the area of the letter M. If the adjacent sides are stems, this area is obtained by making the distance between the letters slightly greater than one-half the height of a letter, and a smaller amount depending on the contours, for other combinations. Examples of good and poor composition are shown in Fig. 2.11.

The space between words should be equal to or greater than the height of a letter but not more than twice the height. The space between sentences should be somewhat greater. The distance between lines of lettering may vary from one-half the height of the capitals to $1\frac{1}{2}$ times their height.

2.8
Stability. If the areas of the upper and lower portions of certain letters are made equal, an optical illusion will cause them to appear to be unstable and top-heavy. To overcome this effect, the upper portions of the letters B, E, F, H, K, S, X, and Z and the figures 2, 3, and 8 must be reduced slightly in size.

An associated form of illusion is the phenomenon that a horizontal line drawn across a rectangle at the vertical center will appear to be below the center. Since the letters B, E, F, and H are particularly subject to this illusion, their central horizontal strokes must be drawn slightly above the vertical center in order to give them a more balanced and pleasing appearance.

The letters K, S, X, Z and the figures 2, 3, and 8 are stabilized by making the width of the upper portion less than the width of the lower portion.

2.9
The Technique of Freehand Lettering. Any prospective engineer can learn to letter if he practices intelligently and is persistent

UNIFORMITY IN HEIGHT, INCLINATION, AND STRENGTH OF LINE IS ESSENTIAL FOR GOOD LETTERING

FIG. 2.10. Uniformity in lettering.

FIG. 2.11. Letter areas.

in his desire to improve. The necessary muscular control, which must accompany the knowledge of lettering, can be developed only through constant repetition.

Pencil letters should be formed with strokes that are dark and sharp, never with strokes that are gray and indistinct. Beginners should avoid the tendency to form letters by sketching, as strokes made in this manner vary in color and width.

When lettering with ink, the results obtained depend largely on the manner in which the pen is used. Many beginners complain that the execution of good freehand lettering is impossible with an ordinary pen point, although their own incorrect habits may have resulted in the inability to make strokes of uniform width. This lack of uniformity may be due to one of four causes: (1) excessive pressure on the pen point; (2) an accumulation of lint, dirt, or dried ink on the point; (3) tilting the point while forming a stroke; or (4) fresh ink on the point. The latter cause requires some explanation, since very few persons know the proper method of "inking" the pen. The pen should be wiped

FIG. 2.12. "Inking" the pen.

INK ON POINT

FIG. 2.13

FIG. 2.14. Holding the pen.

thoroughly clean, and the ink should be deposited on the underside over the slot, well above the point (Fig. 2.12). When the pen is filled in this manner, the ink feeds down the slit in an even flow, making possible the drawing of uniform curved and straight lines. If ink is placed on the point or allowed to run to the point, an excessive amount of ink will be deposited on the first letters made, and the width of the strokes will be somewhat wider than the strokes of, say, the sixth or seventh letter (Fig. 2.13).

When lettering, the pen is held as shown in Fig. 2.14. It should rest so loosely between the fingers that it can be slid up and down with the other hand.

The thin film of oil on a new point must be removed by wiping before the point is used.

2.10
Inclined and Vertical Capital Letters. The letters shown in Figs. 2.15 and 2.16 have been arranged in related groups. In laying out the characters, the number of widths has been reduced to the smallest number consistent with good appearance; similarities of shape have been emphasized and minute differences have been eliminated. Each letter is drawn to a large size on a cross-section grid that is 2 units wider, to facilitate the study of its characteristic shape and proportions. Arrows with numbers indicate the order and direction of the strokes. The curves of the inclined capital letters are portions of ellipses, while the curves of the vertical letters are parts of circles.

The I, T, L, E, and F. The letter I is the basic or stem stroke. The horizontal stroke of the T is drawn first, and the stem starts at the exact center of the bar. The L is 5 units wide, but it is often desirable to reduce this width when an L is used in combination with such letters as A and T. It should be observed that the letter L consists of the first two strokes of the E. The middle bar of the E is $3\frac{1}{2}$ units long and is placed slightly above the center for stability. The top bar is $\frac{1}{2}$ unit shorter than the bottom bar. The letter F is the E with the bottom bar omitted.

The H and N. Stroke 3 of the H should be slightly above the center, for stability. The outside parallel strokes of the N are drawn first to permit an accurate estimate of its width. The inclined stroke should intersect these accurately at their extremities.

The Z and X. The top of the Z should be 1 unit narrower than the bottom, for stability. In the smaller sizes, this letter may be formed without lifting the pen. The X is similar to the Z in that the top is made 1 unit narrower than the bottom. The inclined strokes cross slightly above center.

The A, V, M, and W. The horizontal bar of the A is located up from the bottom a distance equal to one-third the height of the letter. The V is the letter A inverted without the crossbar, and is the same width. The letters M and W are the widest letters of the alphabet. The outside strokes of the M are drawn first, so that its width may be judged accurately. The inside strokes of this letter meet at the center of the base. The W is formed by two modified V's. Alternate strokes are parallel.

The K and Y. The top of the letter K should be made 1 unit narrower than the bottom, for stability. Stroke 2 intersects the stem one-third up from the bottom. Stroke 3 is approximately perpendicular to stroke 2, and, if extended, would touch the stem at the top. The strokes of the Y meet at the center of the enclosing parallelogram or square.

CHAP. 2 / FREEHAND TECHNICAL LETTERING **13**

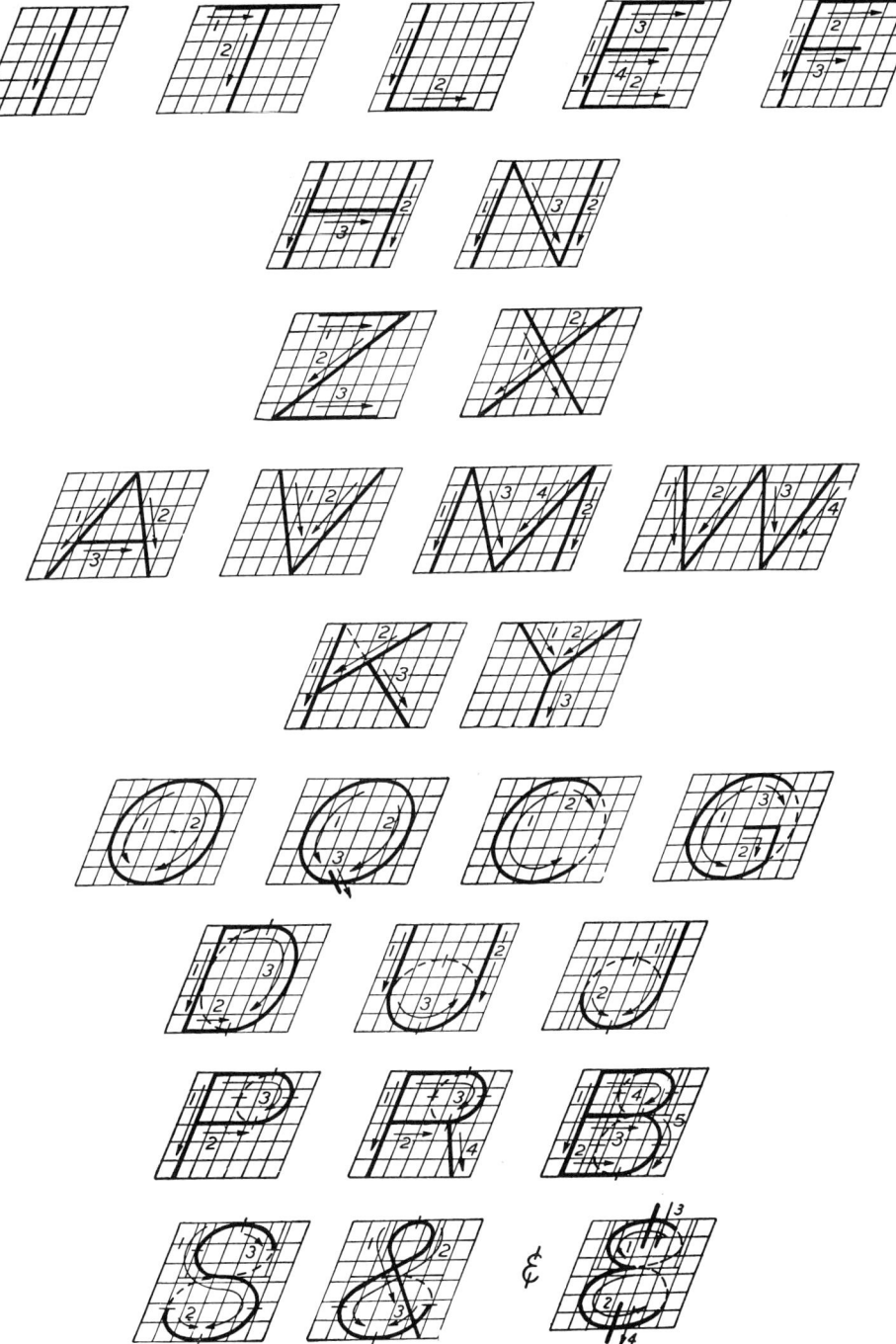

FIG. 2.15. Inclined capital letters.

PART I / BASIC GRAPHICAL TECHNIQUES

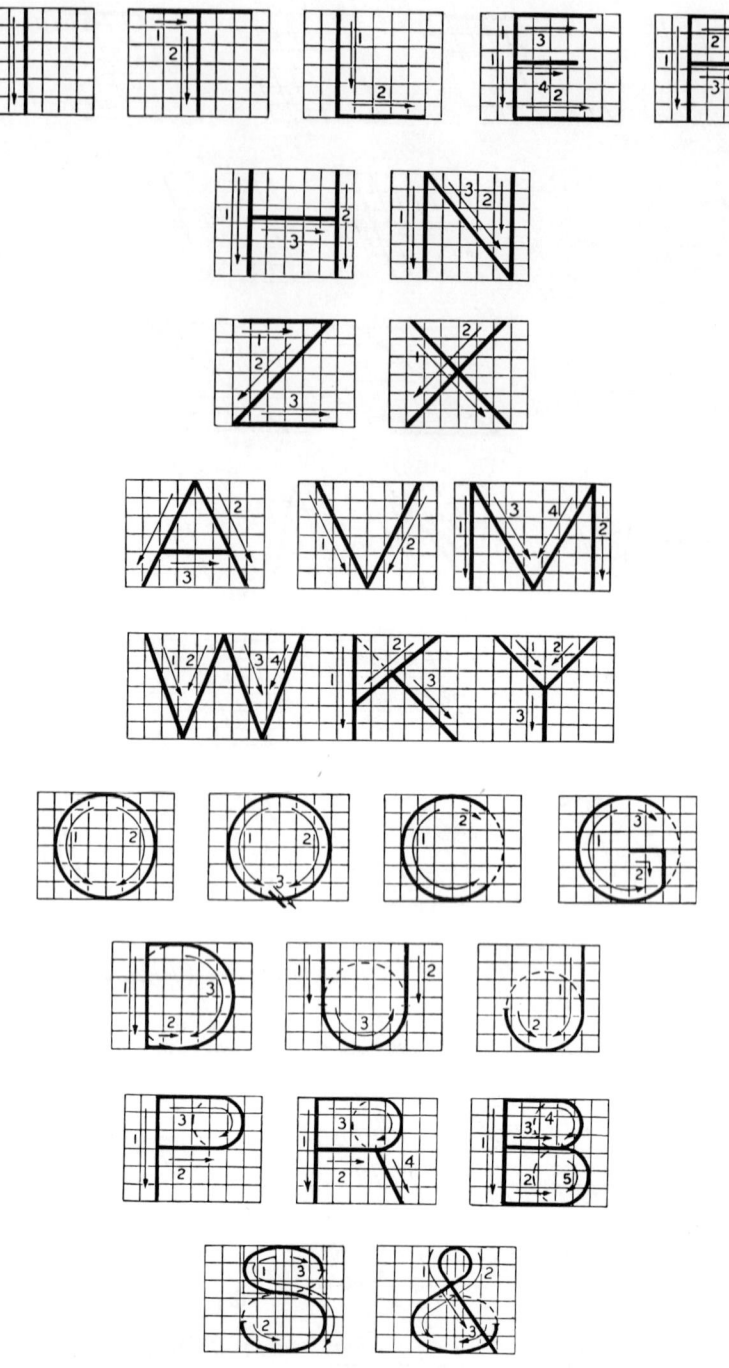

FIG. 2.16. Vertical capital letters.

The O, Q, C, and G. Stroke 1 of the letter O starts just to the right of the top and continues to the left around the side to a point beyond the bottom. Thus stroke 1 forms more than half of the ellipse or circle. The Q is the letter O with the added kern, which is a straight line located near the bottom tangent point. The C is based on the O, but since it is not a complete ellipse or circle, it is narrower than either the O or Q. The top extends 1 unit down and the bottom 1 unit up on the right side. G is similar to C. The horizontal portion of stroke 2 starts at the center.

The D, U, and J. The first two strokes of the D form an incomplete letter L. Stroke 3 starts as a horizontal line. The bottom third of the U is one-half of an ellipse or circle. J is similar to the letter U.

The P, R, and B. The middle horizontal bar of the P is located at the center of stroke 1. The curved portion of stroke 3 is one-half of a perfect ellipse or circle. The R is constructed similarly to the P. The tail joins at the point of tangency of the curve and middle bar. To stabilize the letter B, the top is made $\frac{1}{2}$ unit narrower than the bottom and the middle bar is placed slightly above the center. The curves are halves of ellipses or circles.

The S and &. The upper and lower portions of the S are perfect ellipses with one-quarter removed. The top ellipse should be made $\frac{1}{2}$ unit narrower than the lower one, for stability. In the smaller sizes this letter may be made with one or two strokes, depending upon its size. The true ampersand is made with three strokes. Professional men, however, usually represent an ampersand with a character formed by using portions of the upper and lower ellipses of the numeral 8 with the addition of two short bars (Fig. 2.15).

Although many favor the inclined letters, recent surveys indicate that vertical letters are used more generally.

2.11
Inclined and Vertical Numerals. The numerals shown in Figs. 2.17 and 2.18 have been arranged in related groups in accordance with the common characteristics that can be recognized in their construction.

The 1, 7, and 4. The stem stroke of the 4 is located 1 unit in from the right side. The bar is $1\frac{1}{2}$ units above the base. The stem of the 7 terminates at the center of the base.

The 0, 6, and 9. The cipher, which is 1 unit narrower than the letter O, is the basic form for this group. In the figure 6, the right side of the large ellipse ends 1 unit down from the top, and the left side ends at the center of the base. The small loop is slightly more than three-fourths of an ellipse. The 9 is the 6 inverted.

The 8, 3, and 2. Each of these figures is related to the letter S, and the same rule of stability should be observed in their construction. The top portion of the figure 8 is shorter and $\frac{1}{2}$ unit narrower than the lower portion. Each loop is a perfect ellipse. The figure 3 is the 8 with the lower-left quarter of the upper loop and the upper-left quarter of the lower loop omitted. The 2 is simply three-quarters of the upper loop of the 8 and the upper-left quarter of the lower loop of the 8 with straight lines added.

The 5. This figure is a modification of the related groups previously described. The top is $\frac{1}{2}$ unit narrower than the bottom, for stability. The curve is a segment of a perfect ellipse, ending one unit up from the bottom.

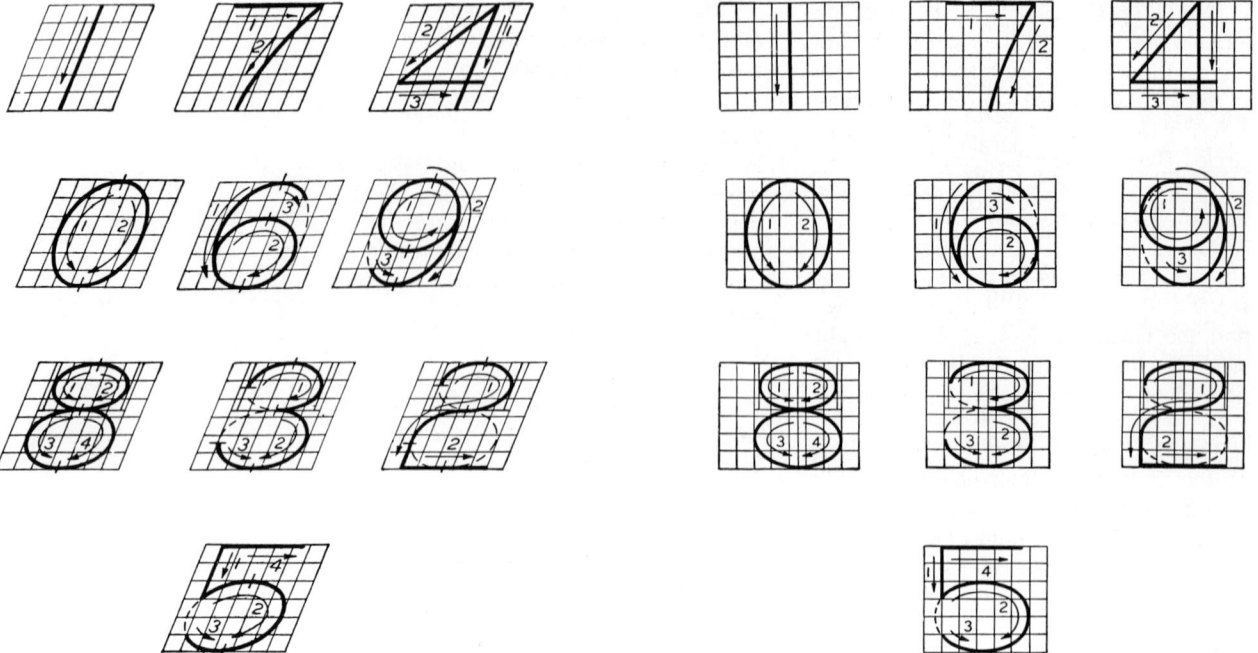

FIG. 2.17. Inclined numerals.

FIG. 2.18. Vertical numerals.

2.12
Single-stroke Lowercase Letters. Single-stroke lowercase letters, either vertical or inclined, are commonly used on map drawings, topographic drawings, structural drawings, and in survey field books. They are particularly suitable for long notes and statements because, first, they can be executed much faster than capitals and, second, words and statements formed with them can be read more easily.

The construction of inclined lowercase letters (Fig. 2.19) is based on the straight line and the ellipse. This basic principle of forming letters is followed more closely for lowercase letters than for capitals. The body portions are two-thirds the height of the related capitals. As shown in Fig. 2.20, ascenders extend to the cap line, and descenders descend to the drop line. For lowercase letters based on a capital letter 6 units high, the waistline is 2 units down from the top and the drop line 2 units below the base line.

The order of stroke, direction of stroke, and formation of the letters follow the same principles as for the capitals. The letters are presented in family groups having related characteristics, to enable the beginner to understand their construction. The vertical lowercase letters, illustrated in Fig. 2.21, are constructed in the same manner as inclined letters.

The i, l, k, and t. All letters of this group are formed by straight lines of standard slope. The i is drawn four units high, and the dot is placed halfway between the waistline and cap line. Stroke 2 of the k starts at the waistline and intersects stroke 1 at a point 2 units above the base. Stroke 3, extended should intersect stroke 1 at the top. The t is 5 units high, and the crossbar is on the waistline.

The v, w, x, and z. All of these letters are similar to the capitals. Alternate strokes of the w are parallel. The width of the top of both the x and the z is made ½ unit less than the width across the bottom, for stability.

The o, a, b, d, p, and q. The bodies of the letters in this group are formed by the letter o, and they differ only in the position and length of the stem stroke. The o is made with two strokes, and the first stroke should form more than half of the character.

The g. The g is related to the letters o and y. Stroke 3 starts at the waistline and ends slightly beyond the point of tangency of the curve with the drop line.

The c and e. The c is a modified letter o. It is not a complete form, and therefore, its width is less than its height. Stroke 1 ends 1 unit up on the right side, stroke 2 ends 1 unit down. The e is similarly constructed, except for the fact that stroke 2 continues as a curve and finishes as a horizontal line that terminates at the middle of the back.

The h, n, r, and m. The curve of the h is the upper portion of the letter o. Stroke 2 starts 2 units above the bottom of the stem and finishes parallel to stroke 1. The n differs from the h in that the stem stroke extends only from the waistline to the base line. The r is a portion of the letter n, stroke 2 ending 1 unit down from the top. The m consists of two modified letter n's. The straight portions of strokes 2 and 3 are parallel to stroke 1.

The u and y. The letter u is an inverted n, and the curve is a portion of the letter o. It should be noted that stroke 2 extends to the base line. The y is a partial combination of the letters u and g.

The j and f. The portion of the j above the base line is the letter i. The curve is the same as that which forms the tail of

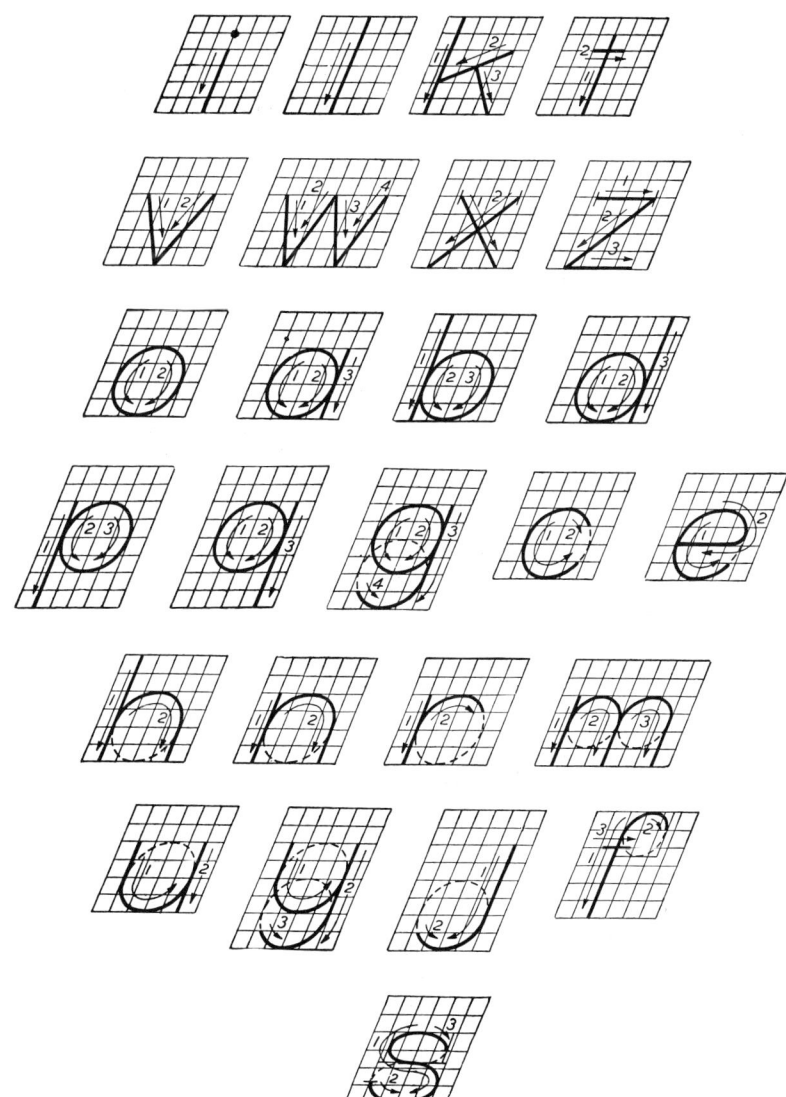

FIG. 2.19. Inclined lower-case letters.

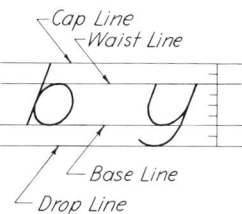

FIG. 2.20

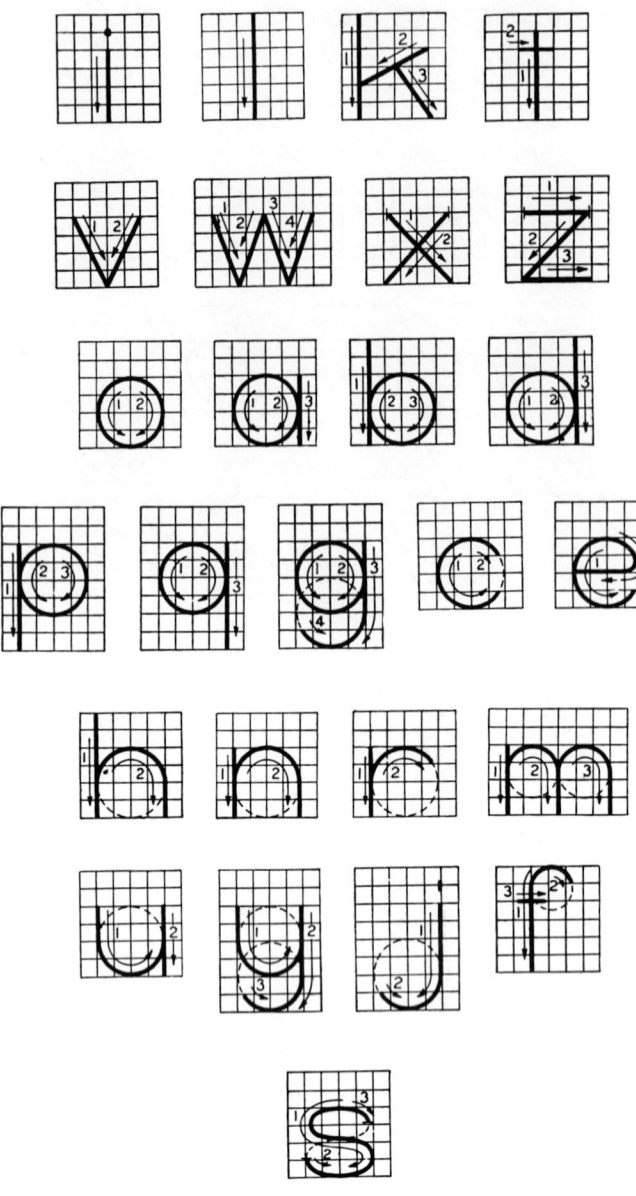

FIG. 2.21. Vertical lower-case letters.

the g. The curved portion of the letter f is 2½ units wide, stroke 1 starting slightly to the right of the point of tangency with the cap line.

The s. The lowercase s is almost identical to the capital S.

2.13
Fractions. The height of the figures in the numerator and denominator is equal to three-fourths the height of the whole number, and the total height of the fraction is twice the height of the whole number. The division bar should be horizontal and centered between the fraction numerals, as shown in Fig. 2.22. It should be noted that the sloping center line of the fraction bisects both the numerator and denominator and is parallel to the sloping center line of the whole number.

2.14
Large Caps and Small Caps in Combination. Many commercial draftsmen use a combination of large caps and small caps in forming words, as illustrated in Fig. 2.23. When this style is used, the height of the small caps should be approximately three-fifths the height of the first capital letter of the word.

2.15
Titles. Every drawing, sketch, graph, chart, or diagram has some form of descriptive title to impart certain necessary information and to identify it. On machine drawings, where speed and legibility are prime requirements, titles are usually single-stroke. On display drawings, maps, and so on, which call for an artistic effect, the titles are usually composed of "built-up" ornate letters.

Figure 2.24 shows a title block that might be used on a machine drawing. It should be noted that the important items are made more prominent by the use of larger letters formed with heavier lines. Less important data, such as the scale, date, drafting information, and so on, are given less prominence.

To be pleasing in appearance, a title should be symmetrical about a vertical center line and should have some simple geometric form. An easy way to insure the symmetry of a title is first to count the letter and word spaces, then, working to the left and right from the middle space or letter on the vertical center line, to sketch the title lightly in pencil, before lettering it in finished form. An alternate method is to letter a trial line along the edge of a piece of scrap paper and place it in a balanced position just above the location of the line to be lettered.

2.16
Mechanical Lettering Devices and Templates. Although mechanical lettering devices produce letters that may appear stiff to an expert, they are used in many drafting rooms for the simple reason that they enable even the unskilled to do satisfactory lettering with ink. The average draftsman rightly prefers stiff uniformity to wavy lines and irregular shapes. One of the oldest instruments of this sort on the market is the Wrico outfit. With a satisfactory set of Wrico pens and templates, letters ranging in size from $3/32$–$1/2$ in. in height may be executed. The letters are formed by a stylographic pen that is guided around the sides of openings in a template made of transparent pyralin.

The *Leroy* device, shown in Fig. 2.25, is possibly even more efficient than the Wrico, for it does not require the sliding of a template to complete a letter.

2.17
Commercial Gothic (Fig. 2.26). Gothic letters are comparatively easy to construct. They are drawn first in outline, in skeleton form and then filled in with a ball-point pen. This style, from which the single-stroke engineering letters are derived, is used to some extent for titles on machine drawings, but more frequently it appears on maps, charts, and graphs that are prepared for display purposes.

2.18
Modern Roman. The Modern Roman letters shown in Fig. 2.27 are used extensively by engineers for names and titles on maps. Students should be familiar with this alphabet, for it appears in all modern publications. As in the case of the Gothic style, these letters must be drawn first in outline, in skeleton form, and then filled in with a ball-point or wide-line pen. The straight lines are usually drawn with a ruling pen. The curved lines, except for the serifs, may be formed either mechanically or freehand. When attempting to construct this type of letter it is wise to bear in mind the following facts: (1) All vertical strokes are heavy except those forming the letters M, N, and U. (2) All horizontal strokes are light. (3) The width of the heavy strokes may vary from one-eighth to one-sixth the height of the letter.

Roman letters may be drawn either extended or compressed, depending on the area to be covered or the space restrictions determined by other lettering, such as on maps. If a draftsman using the Roman-style letter would have his work look professional, he must pay particular attention to detail. Care must be taken to keep the proportions of a letter appearing more than once in a name or title identical.

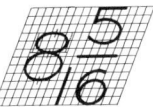

FIG. 2.22

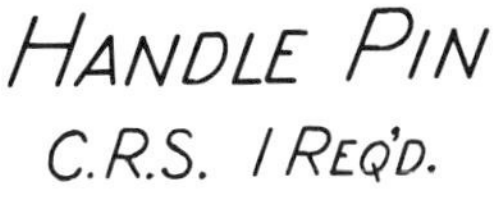

HANDLE PIN
C.R.S. 1 REQ'D.

FIG. 2.23. Use of large and small caps.

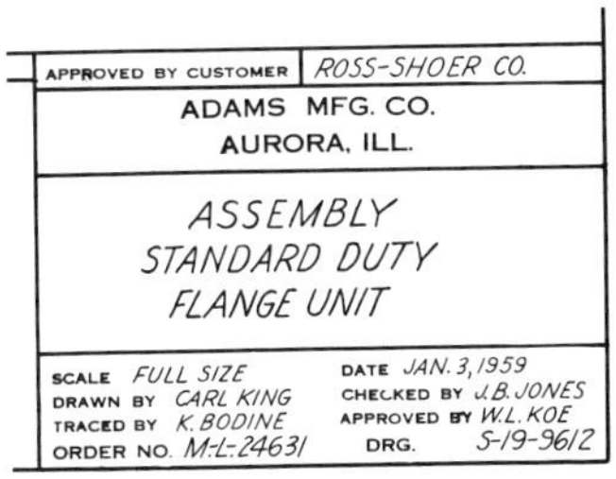

FIG. 2.24. A machine-drawing title block.

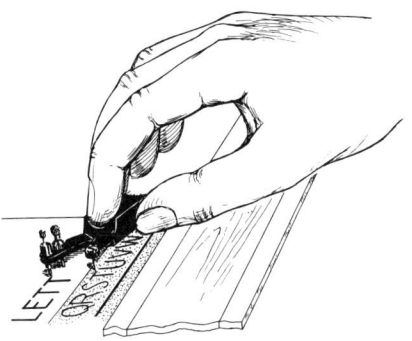

FIG. 2.25. Leroy lettering device.

20 PART I / BASIC GRAPHICAL TECHNIQUES

ABCDEFG
HIJKLMN
OPQRSTU
VWXYZ &
1234567
890

FIG. 2.26. Gothic letters and numerals.

ABCDEFG
HIJKLMN
OPQRSTU
VWXYZ &
12345678
90

abcdefghijk
lmnopqrstu
vwxyz

FIG. 2.27. Modern roman letters and numerals.

EXERCISES

It should be noted that while these exercises are offered to give the student practice in letter forms and word composition, they also contain statements of important principles of drawing, shop notes, and titles with which every engineer should be familiar. Each lettering exercise should be submitted to the instructor for severe criticism before the student proceeds to the next. Section 2.3 should be reread before starting the first exercise.

1. Letter the statement given in Fig. 2.28 in $5/32$-in. capital letters using an appropriate pencil that is suited to the type of paper being used and that will produce uniform opaque lines. The necessary guide lines should be drawn with a hard pencil.

2–3. Letter the statements given in Figs. 2.29 and 2.30 in $1/8$-in. capital letters using an appropriate pencil that is suited to the type of paper being used and that will produce uniform opaque lines. The necessary guide lines should be drawn with a hard pencil.

4. Letter the statement given in Fig. 2.31 in $5/32$-in. capital letters using an appropriate pencil that is suited to the type of paper being used and that will produce uniform opaque lines. The necessary guide lines should be drawn with a hard pencil.

5–6. Letter the statements given in Figs. 2.32 and 2.33 in $1/8$-in. capital letters using an appropriate pencil that is suited to the type of paper being used and that will produce uniform opaque lines. The necessary guide lines should be drawn with a hard pencil.

7–13. Letter the following statements in $1/8$-in. capital letters using an appropriate pencil that is suited to the type of paper being used and that will produce uniform opaque lines. The necessary guide lines should be drawn with a hard pencil.

7. A GOOD STUDENT REALIZES THE IMPORTANCE OF NEAT AND ATTRACTIVE LETTERING.

POOR LETTERING DETRACTS FROM THE APPEARANCE OF A DRAWING

FIG. 2.28

IN LEARNING TO LETTER, CERTAIN DEFINITE RULES OF FORM & DESIGN MUST BE OBSERVED

FIG. 2.29

WHEN LETTERING WITH INK, THE INK SHOULD BE WELL ABOVE THE TIP OF THE POINT

FIG. 2.30

#26 (.1470) DRILL AND REAM FOR #1×1 TAPER PIN WITH PC #41 IN POSITION

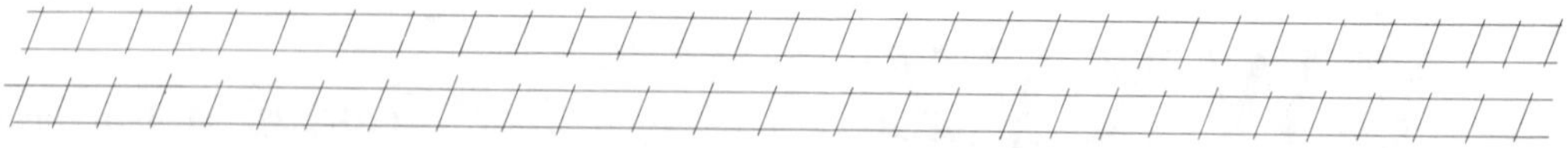

FIG. 2.31. Lettered statement. Draw guide lines as shown.

CHAP. 2 / FREEHAND TECHNICAL LETTERING   23

S.A.E. 1020 - COLD DRAWN STEEL BAR
1-12UNF-2B   1-8UNC-2A   1-5 SQUARE
BREAK ALL SHARP CORNERS UNLESS OTHERWISE SPECIFIED

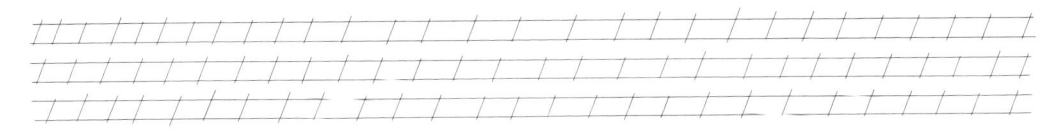

FIG. 2.32. Lettered statement. Draw guide lines as shown.

NECK $\frac{1}{8}$ WIDE × $\frac{1}{16}$ DEEP $\frac{1}{8}$ ×45° CHAMFER   TAPER $1\frac{1}{2}$ PER FT.

$\frac{5}{16}$ DRILL - $\frac{3}{8}$-16 UNC-2A $\frac{21}{32}$ DRILL - C'BORE $\frac{29}{32}$ D × $\frac{7}{8}$ DEEP - 2 HOLES

FIG. 2.33. Lettered statement. Draw guide lines as shown.

8. THE POSITION OF THE VIEWS OF AN ORTHOGRAPHIC DRAWING MUST BE IN STRICT ACCORDANCE WITH THE UNIVERSALLY RECOGNIZED ARRANGEMENT ILLUSTRATED IN FIG. 6.6.

9. THE VIEWS OF AN ORTHOGRAPHIC DRAWING SHOULD SHOW THE THREE DIMENSIONS: WIDTH, DEPTH, AND HEIGHT.

10. AN INVISIBLE LINE SHOULD START WITH A SPACE WHEN IT FORMS AN EXTENSION OF A SOLID LINE.

11. THE FRONT VIEW OF AN ORTHOGRAPHIC DRAWING SHOULD BE THE VIEW THAT SHOWS THE CHARACTERISTIC SHAPE OF THE OBJECT.

12. AN AUXILIARY VIEW SHOWS THE TRUE SIZE AND SHAPE OF AN INCLINED SURFACE.

13. A SECTIONAL VIEW SHOWS THE INTERIOR CONSTRUCTION OF AN OBJECT.

14. Draw horizontal and inclined guide lines and letter the following detail titles. Use $\frac{5}{32}$-in. capitals for the part names and $\frac{1}{8}$-in. capitals for the remainder of the titles.

     BASE   BUSHING
C.I. 1 REQ'D   BRO.   1 REQ'D
             SPINDLE
       C.R.S.   1 REQ'D

15–19. Using a hard pencil, draw two or more sets of horizontal and inclined guide lines for $\frac{5}{32}$-in. letters; then letter the following exercises in lowercase letters.

15. The front and top views are always in line vertically.

16. The front and side views are in line horizontally.

17. The depth of the top view is the same as the depth of the side view.

18. If a line is perpendicular to a plane of projection, its projection will be a point.

19. If a line is parallel to a plane of projection, its projection on the plane is exactly the same length as the true length of the line.

A draftsman discusses part of the design of the TF-41 jet engine with his supervisor.
(*Courtesy Allison Division, General Motors Corp.*).

Drawing Equipment and Use of Instruments

3.1
Introduction. The instruments and materials needed for making ordinary engineering drawings are shown in Fig. 3.1. The instruments in the plush-lined case should be particularly well made, for with inferior ones it is often difficult to produce accurate drawings of professional quality.

3.2
List of Equipment and Materials. The following list is a practical selection of equipment and materials necessary for making pencil drawings and ink tracings.

1. Case of drawing instruments
2. Drawing board
3. T-square
4. 45° triangle*
5. 10-in. 30°–60° triangle
6. French curve
7. Scales (Sec. 3.19)
8. Drawing pencils
9. Pencil pointer (file or sandpaper pad)

10. Thumbtacks, brad machine, or Scotch tape
11. Pencil eraser
12. Cleaning eraser
13. Erasing shield
14. Dusting brush
15. Bottle of black waterproof drawing ink
16. Pen wiper
17. Penholder

*A 6-in. 45° Braddock lettering triangle, which may be used as either a triangle or a lettering instrument, may be substituted for this item.

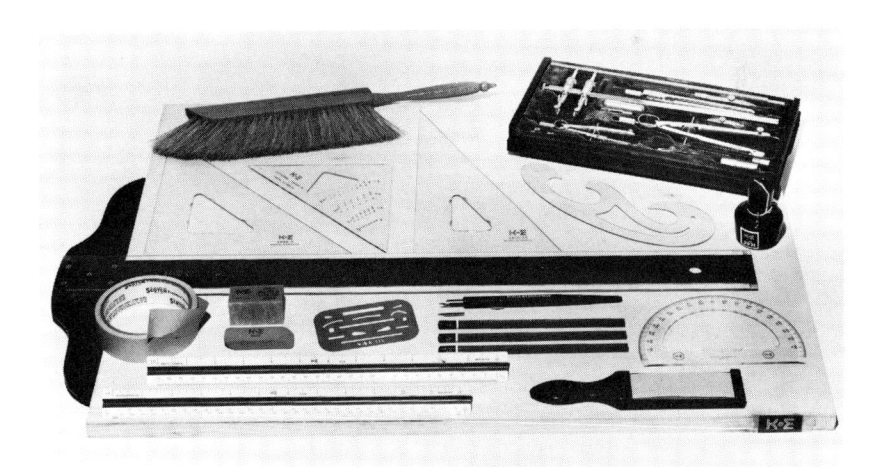

FIG. 3.1. Essential drafting equipment.

26 PART I / BASIC GRAPHICAL TECHNIQUES

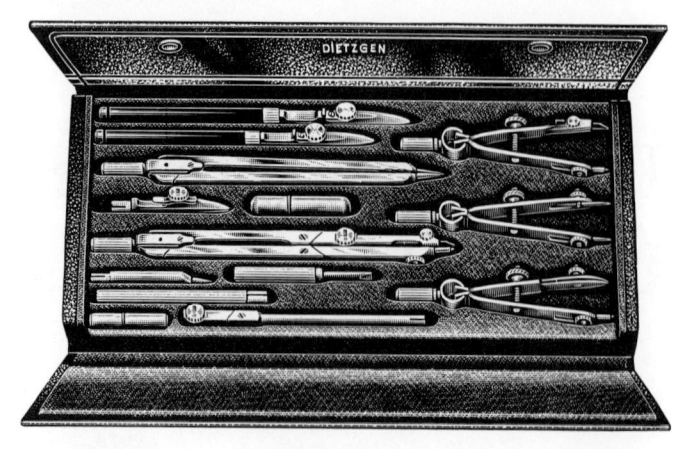

FIG. 3.2. A standard set of drawing instruments.

18. Lettering pens
19. Protractor
20. Pad of sketching paper (plain or ruled)

21. Drawing paper
22. Tracing paper
23. Tracing cloth

To these may be added the following useful items:

24. Piece of soapstone
25. Ink-bottle holder
26. Tack lifter
27. Slide rule

3.3

The Set of Instruments. A standard set of drawing instruments in a velvet-lined case and a large-bow set, which is capable of fulfilling the needs of most engineers and draftsmen, are shown in Figs. 3.2 and 3.3, respectively.

Large-bow sets are preferred by many persons, especially in the aircraft and automotive fields. A complete set might include the following large bow (compass), beam compass with an extension bar for drawing very large circles, dividers, small bow, and a slip-handle ruling pen. Since the large bow (Fig. 3.4) is particularly

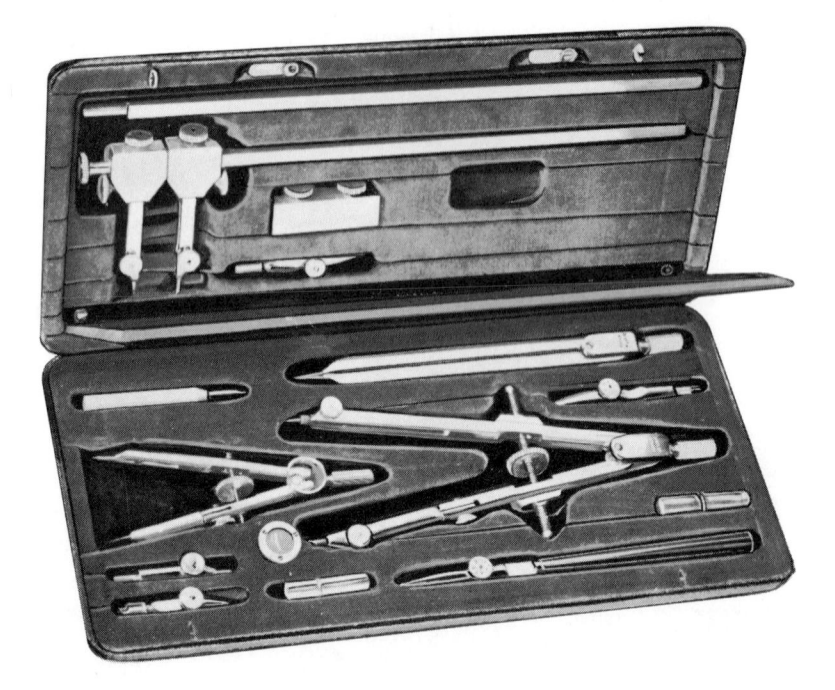

FIG. 3.3. The Purdue Riefler set.

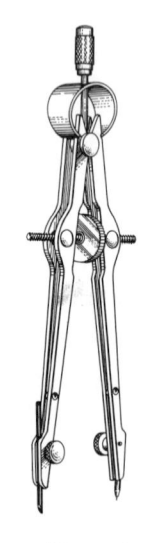

FIG. 3.4. Large bow (Vemco).

suited for drawing circles of very small size up to 10 in. in diameter, its range covers that of both the bow instruments and the compass (without the extension bar) of the standard set (Fig. 3.2).

The large bow is preferred by its advocates because its sturdy construction permits the draftsman to exert the pressure necessary to secure black, opaque lines on pencil drawings that are to be used for making prints.

3.4
The Protractor. The protractor (Fig. 3.5) is used for measuring and laying off angles.

3.5
Special Instruments and Templates. A few of the many special instruments and templates that are convenient for drawing are shown in Figs. 3.6–3.14.

Because of the time consumed in cutting back the wood to repoint an ordinary drawing pencil, some draftsmen favor the use of artist's automatic pencils (Fig. 3.6). Separate leads for these pencils may be purchased in any of the 17 degrees of hardness obtainable for regular drawing pencils.

Although it is not widely used, the protractor angle (Fig. 3.7) is a useful device. It is hinged in such a manner that it may be substituted for a protractor and a set of triangles.

FIG. 3.5. Protractor.

One of several types of special triangles that may be used for drawing the end views of standard bolt heads is shown in Fig. 3.8.

FIG. 3.7. Protractor angle.

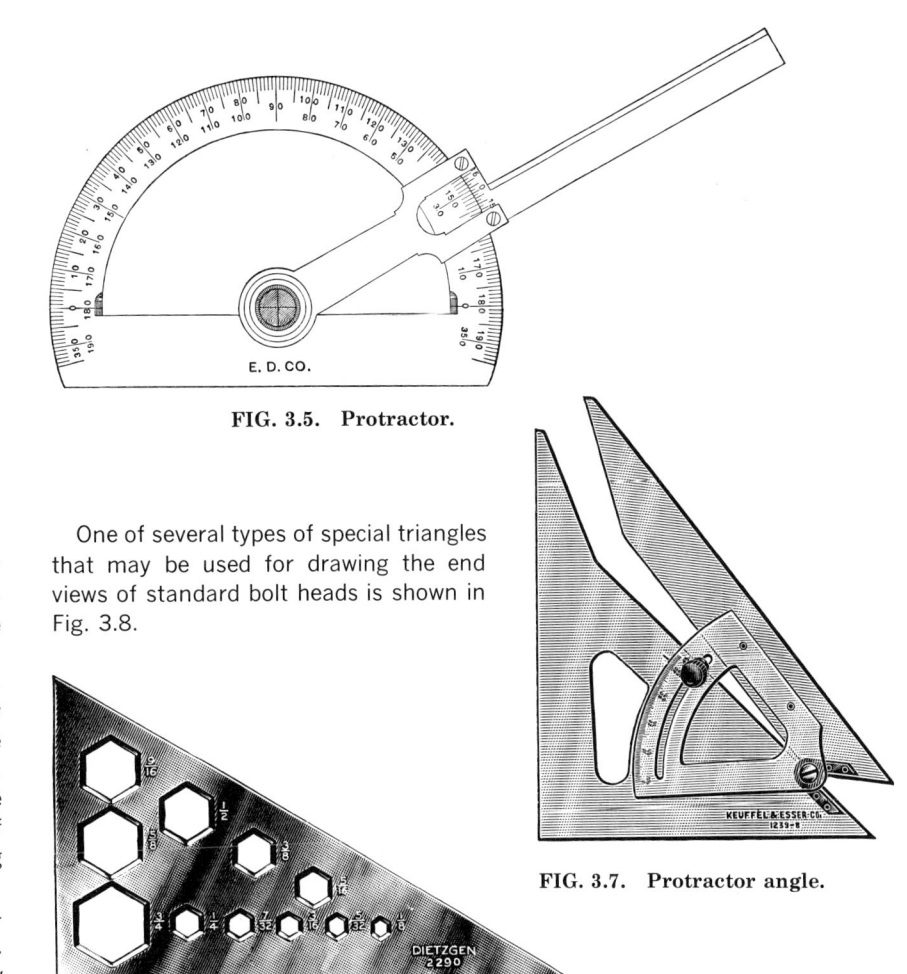

FIG. 3.8. Wrico triangle (*Courtesy Eugene Dietzgen Co.*).

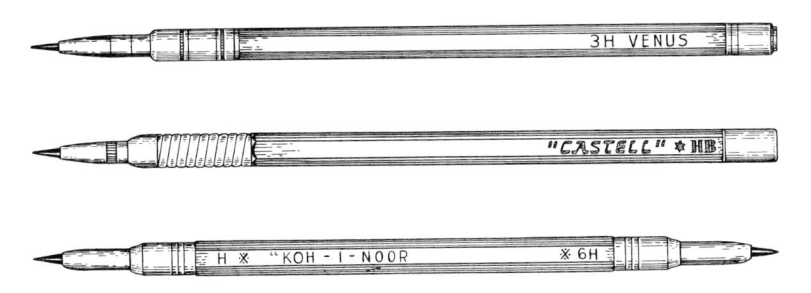

FIG. 3.6. Artist's pencils.

The flexible curves shown in Fig. 3.9, because of their limitless variations, are extremely convenient. The type shown in (*a*) is a lead bar enclosed in rubber. The more desirable one shown in (*b*) has a steel ruling edge attached to a spring with a lead core.

The drop pen (pencil) (Fig. 3.10) is designed for repeated drawing of circles of small diameter, such as the circles representing rivet heads.

The electric erasing machine (Fig. 3.11) saves valuable drafting time of those persons who prepare reproductions in ink and

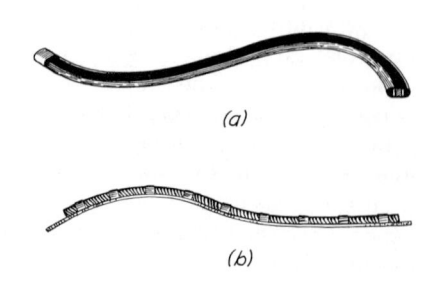

FIG. 3.9. Flexible curves.

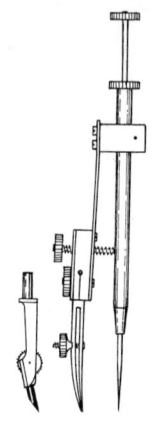

FIG. 3.10. Drop pen (pencil).

FIG. 3.11. Erasing machine.

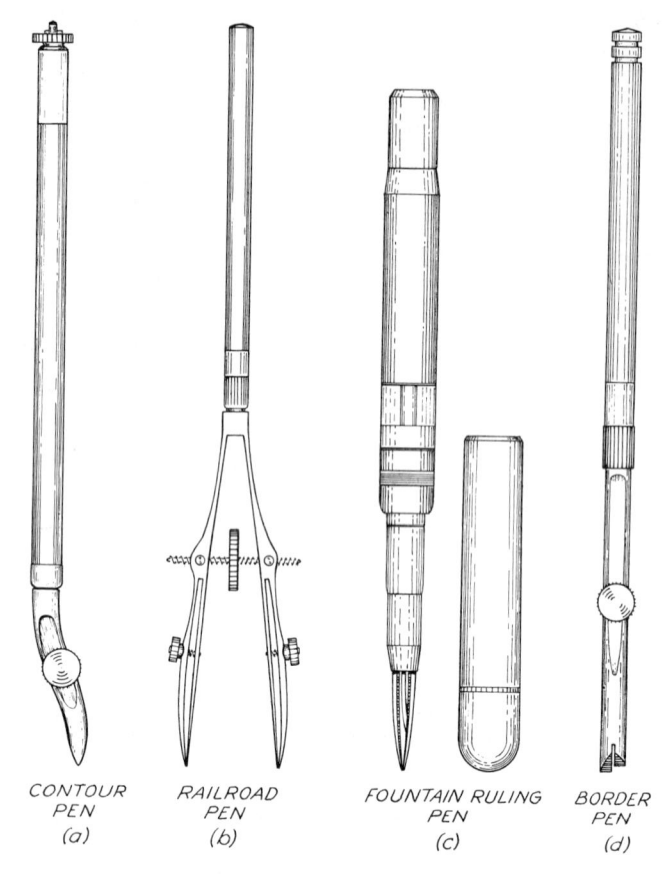

FIG. 3.12. Special ruling pens.

CONTOUR PEN (a)   RAILROAD PEN (b)   FOUNTAIN RULING PEN (c)   BORDER PEN (d)

who find it necessary to make frequent erasures.

Several of a number of special ruling pens that are available are shown in Fig. 3.12. The contour pen (*a*) is used freehand for tracing contours on a map. The inking leg is free to swivel in the handle. The railroad pen (*b*) draws parallel lines that may represent roads or railroad tracks. The fountain ruling pen (*c*) is useful when much inking is to be done. It does not require frequent filling. The border pen (*d*) draws a line of fixed width. It is desirable to have a set of these pens available, since a separate pen is required for each different line width.

Proportional dividers (Fig. 3.13) are used to reproduce distances to a reduced or an enlarged scale.

The use of templates (Fig. 3.14) can save valuable time in the drawing of standard figures and symbols on plans and drawings.

3.6
The Drafting Machine. The drafting machine (Fig. 3.15) is designed to combine the functions of the T-square, triangles, scale, and protractor. Drafting machines are used extensively in commercial drafting rooms because it has been estimated that their use leads to a 25–50% saving in time.

3.7
Tracing Paper and Tracing Cloth. White lightweight tracing paper, on which pencil drawings can be made and from which blueprints can be produced, is used in most commercial drafting rooms in order to keep labor costs at a minimum.

The two general types of cloth available are ink cloth and pencil cloth. The cloth used for ink is clear and transparent, dull on one side and glossy on the other. Pencil cloth is a white cloth with a surface specially prepared to take pencil marks readily.

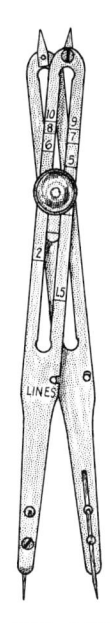

FIG. 3.13. Proportional dividers.

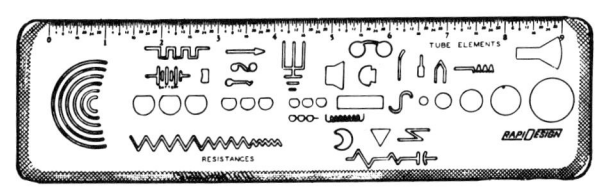

ELECTRO SYMBOL TEMPLATE

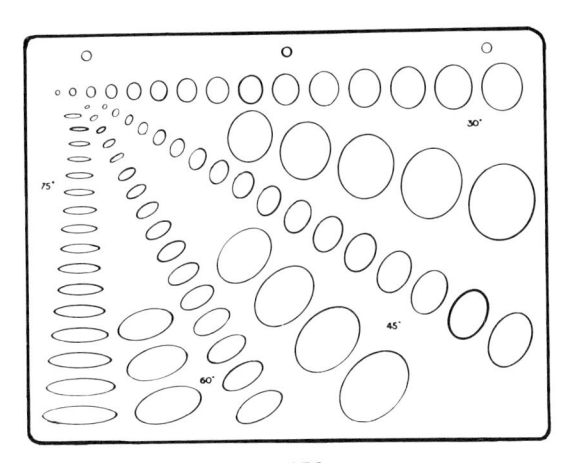

ELLIPSES

TOOLING TEMPLATE

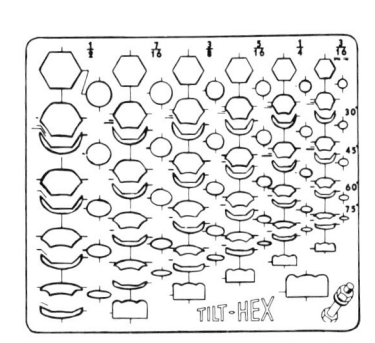

TILT-HEX DRAFTING TEMPLATE

FIG. 3.14. Special templates (*Courtesy Frederick Post Co.*).

3.8
Pencils. The student and professional man should be equipped with a selection of good, well-sharpened pencils with leads of various degrees of hardness, such as 9H, 8H, 7H, and 6H (hard); 5H and 4H (medium hard); 3H and 2H (medium); and H and F (medium soft).

The grade of pencil to be used for various purposes depends on the type of line desired, the kind of paper employed, and the humidity, which affects the surface of the paper. Standards for line quality usually will govern the selection. As a minimum, however, the student should have available a 6H pencil for the light construction lines in layout work where accuracy is required, a 4H for repenciling light finished lines (dimension lines, center lines, and invisible object lines), a 2H for visible object lines, and an F or H for all lettering and freehand work.

FIG. 3.15. Drafting machine (*Courtesy Keuffel & Esser Co.*).

3.9
Pointing the Pencil. Many persons prefer the conical point for general use (Fig. 3.16), while others find the wedge point more suitable for straight-line work, as it requires less sharpening and makes a denser line (Fig. 3.17).

When sharpening a pencil, the wood should be cut away (on the unlettered end) with a knife or a pencil sharpener equipped with draftsman's cutters. About $\frac{3}{8}$ in. of the lead should be exposed and should form a cut, including the wood, about $1\frac{1}{2}$ in. long. The lead then should be shaped to a conical point on the pointer (file or sandpaper pad). This is done by holding the file stationary in the left hand and drawing the lead toward the handle while rotating the pencil against the movement (Fig. 3.16). All strokes should be made in the same manner, a new grip being taken each time so that each stroke starts with the pencil in the same rotated position as at the end of the preceding stroke.

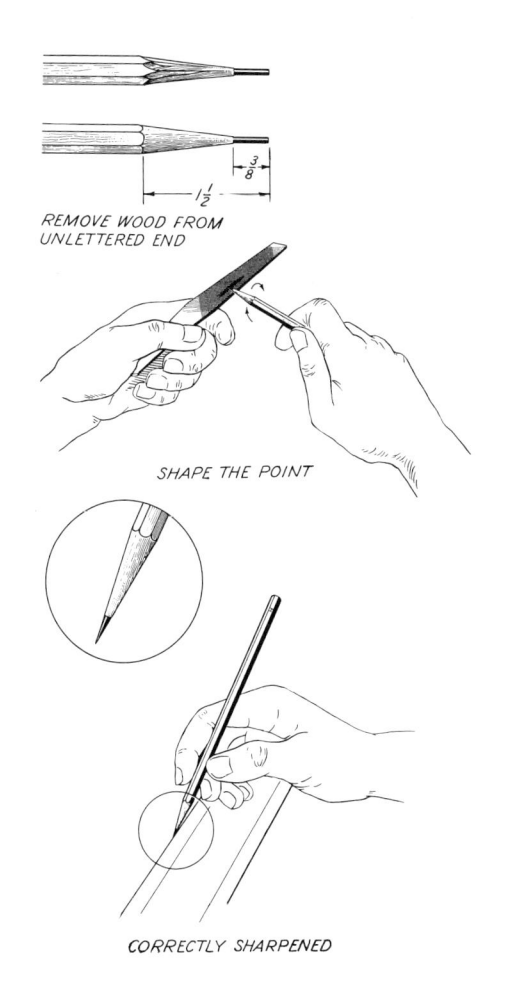

FIG. 3.16. Conical point.

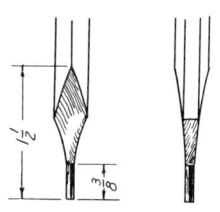

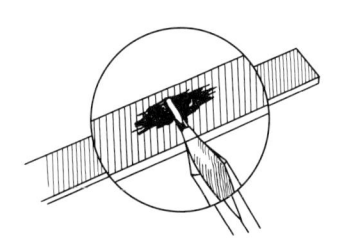

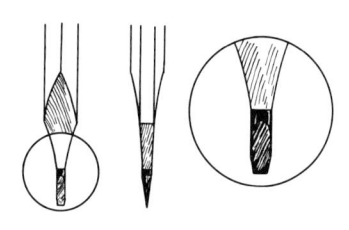

FIG. 3.17. Wedge point.

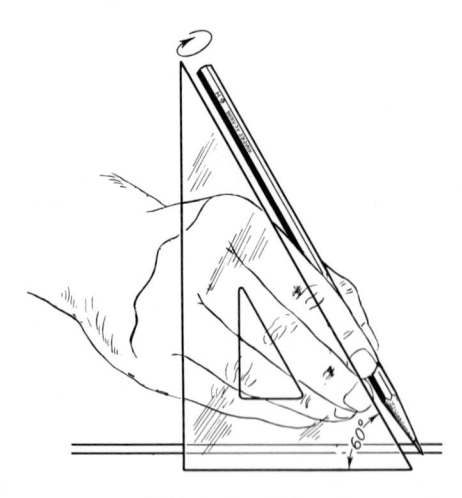

FIG. 3.18. Using the pencil.

3.10
Drawing Pencil Lines. Pencil lines should be sharp and uniform along their entire length and sufficiently distinct to fulfill their ultimate purposes. Construction lines (preliminary lines) should be drawn *very* lightly so that they may be easily erased. Finished lines should be made boldly and distinctly, so that there will be definite contrast between visible and invisible object lines and auxiliary lines, such as dimension lines, center lines, and section lines. To give this contrast, which is necessary for clearness and ease in reading, object lines should be of medium width and very black, invisible lines black and not so wide, and auxiliary lines dark and thin.

When drawing a line, the pencil should be inclined slightly (about 60°) in the direction in which the line is being drawn (Fig. 3.18). The pencil should be "pulled" (never pushed) at the same inclination for the full length of the line. If it is rotated (twirled) slowly between the fingers as the line is drawn, a symmetrical point will be maintained and a straight uniform line will be insured.

3.11
Placing and Fastening the Paper. For accuracy and ease in manipulating the T-square, the drawing paper should be located well up on the board and near the left-hand edge. The lower edge of the sheet (if plain) or the lower border line (if printed) should be aligned along the working edge of the T-square before the sheet is fastened down at all four corners with thumbtacks, Scotch tape, or staples.

3.12
The T-square. The T-square is used primarily for drawing horizontal lines and for guiding the triangles when drawing vertical and inclined lines. It is manipulated by sliding the guiding edge (inner face) of the head along the left edge of the board [Fig. 3.19(a)] until the blade is in the required

(a)

(b)

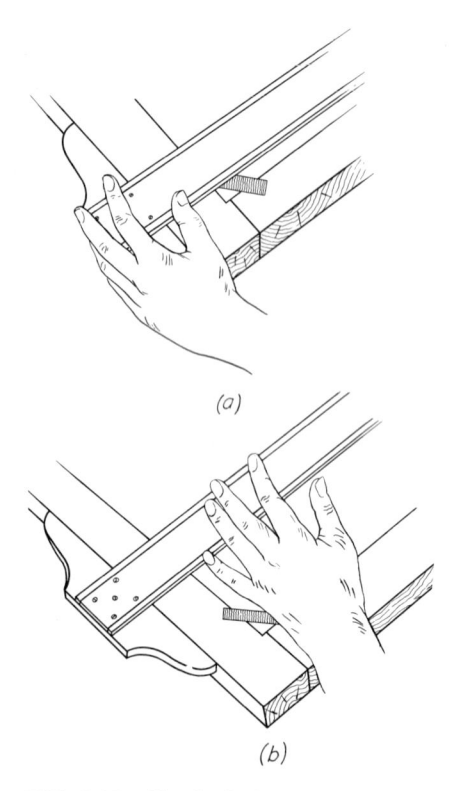

FIG. 3.19. Manipulating the T-square.

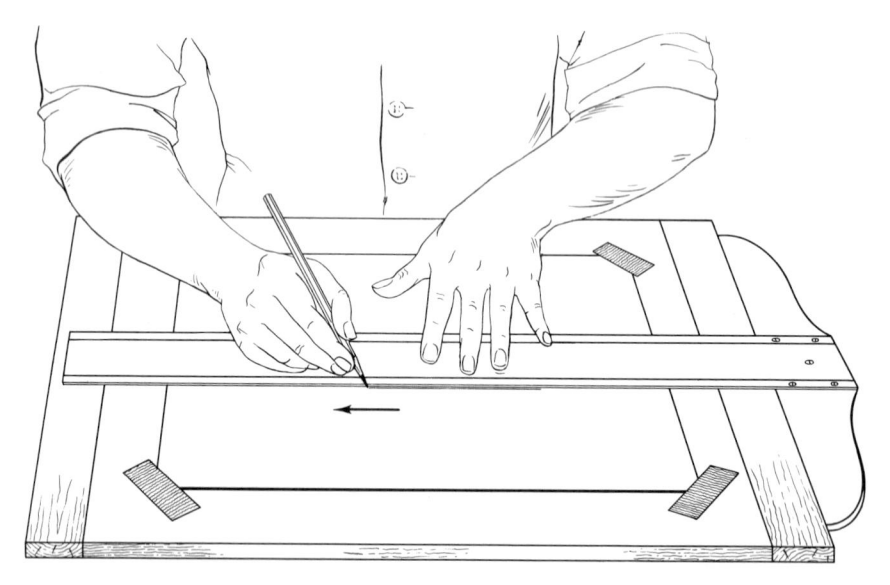

FIG. 3.20. Drawing horizontal lines.

position. The left hand then should be shifted to a position near the center of the blade to hold it in place and to prevent its deflection while drawing the line. Experienced draftsmen hold the T-square, as shown in Fig. 3.19(*b*), with the fingers pressing on the blade and the thumb on the paper. Small adjustments may be made with the hand in this position by sliding the blade with the fingers.

Horizontal lines are drawn from left to right along the upper edge of the T-square (Fig. 3.20). (*Exception:* Left-handed persons should use the T-square head at the right side of the board and draw from right to left.) While drawing the line, the ruling hand should slide along the blade on the little finger.

3.13
The Triangles. The 45° and the 30° × 60° triangles (Fig. 3.21) are the ones commonly used for ordinary work. A triangle may be checked for nicks by sliding the thumbnail along the ruling edges, as shown in Fig. 3.22.

3.14
Vertical Lines. Vertical lines are drawn upward along the vertical leg of a triangle whose other (horizontal) leg is supported and guided by the T-square blade. The blade is held in position with the palm and thumb of the left hand, and the triangle is adjusted and held by the fingers, as shown in Fig. 3.23. In the case of a right-handed person, the triangle should be to the right of the line to be drawn.

Either the 30° × 60° or the 45° triangle may be used since both triangles have a right angle. However, the 30° × 60° is generally preferred because it usually has a longer perpendicular leg.

3.15
Inclined Lines. Triangles also are used for drawing inclined lines. Lines that make angles of 30°, 45°, or 60° with the horizontal may be drawn with the 30° × 60° or the 45° triangle in combination with the T-square, as shown in Fig. 3.24. If the two triangles are combined, lines that make 15° or a multiple of 15° may be drawn

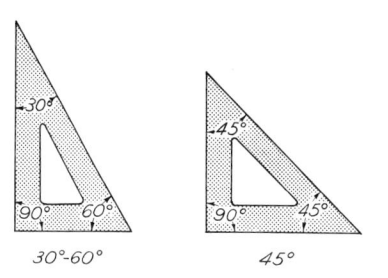

FIG. 3.21. Triangles.

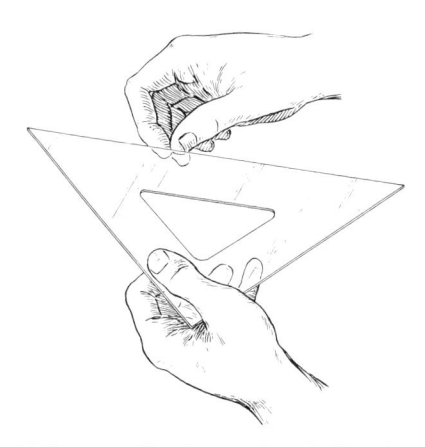

FIG. 3.22. Testing a triangle for nicks.

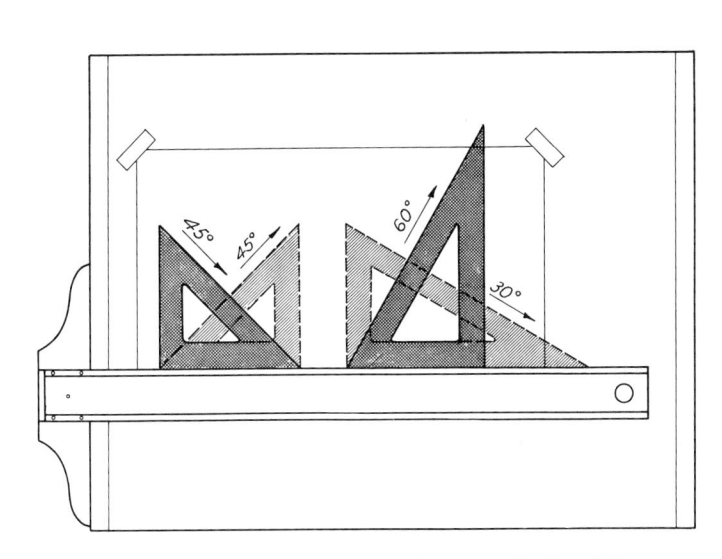

FIG. 3.24. Inclined lines.

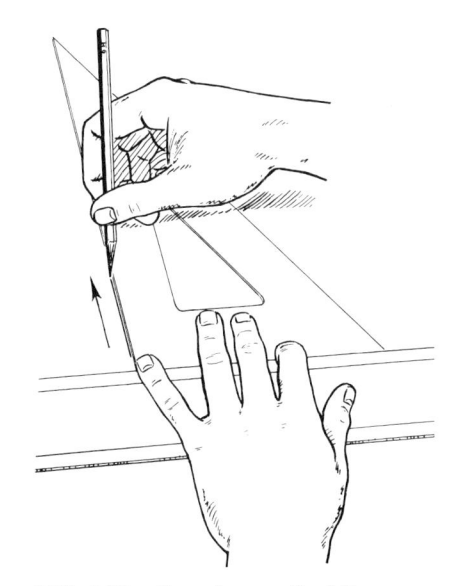

FIG. 3.23. Drawing vertical lines.

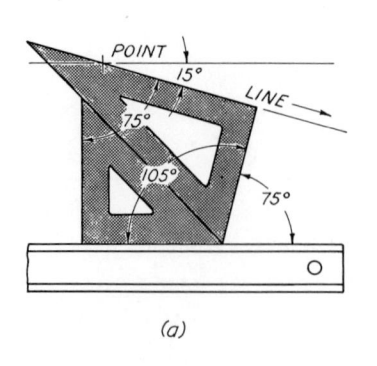

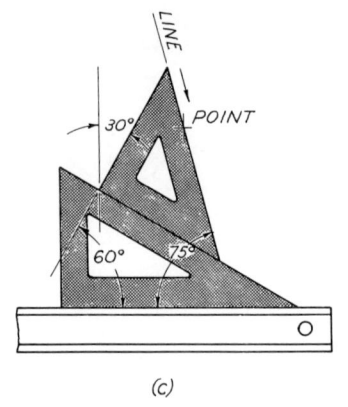

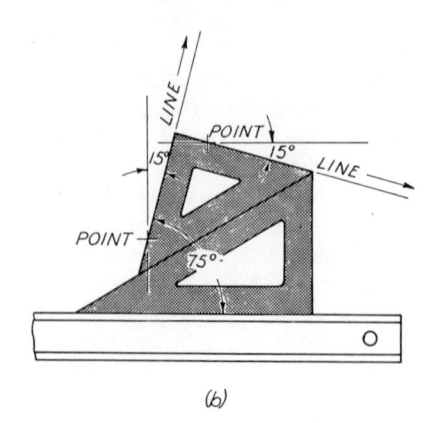

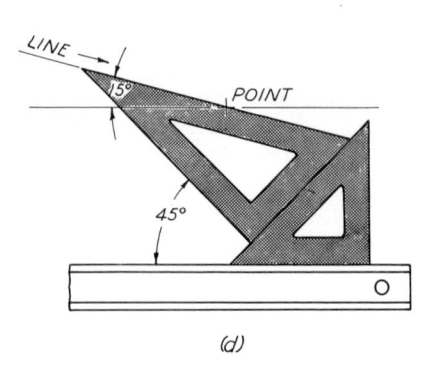

FIG. 3.25. Drawing inclined lines with triangles.

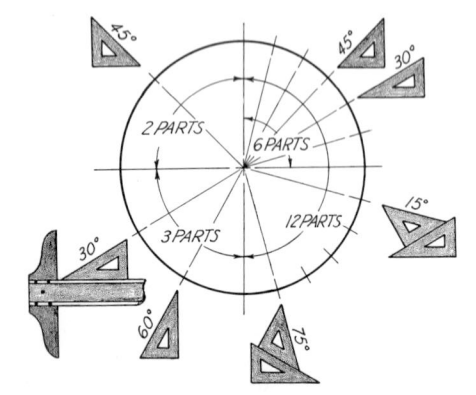

FIG. 3.26. To divide a circle into four, six, eight, twelve, or twenty-four equal parts.

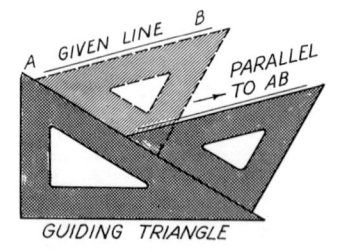

FIG. 3.27. To draw a line parallel to a given line.

with the horizontal. Several possible arrangements and the angles that result are shown in Fig. 3.25.

The triangles used singly or in combination offer a useful method for dividing a circle into 4, 6, 8, 12, or 24 equal parts (Fig. 3.26). For angles other than those divisible by 15, a protractor must be used.

3.16

Parallel Lines. The triangles are used in combination to draw a line parallel to a given line. To draw such a line, place a ruling edge of a triangle, supported by a T-square or another triangle, along the given line; then slip the triangle, as shown in Fig. 3.27, to the required position and draw the parallel line along the same ruling edge that previously coincided with the given line.

3.17

Perpendicular Lines. Either the sliding triangle method [Fig. 3.28(a)] or the revolved triangle method [Fig. 3.28(b)] may be used to draw a line perpendicular to a given line. When using the sliding triangle method, adjust to the given line a side of a triangle that is adjacent to the right angle. Guide the side opposite the right angle with a second triangle, as shown in Fig. 3.28(a); then slide the first triangle along the guiding triangle until it is in the required position for drawing the perpendicular along the other edge adjacent to the right angle.

Although the revolved triangle method [Fig. 3.28(b)] is not so quickly done, it is widely used. To draw a perpendicular using this method, align along the given line the hypotenuse of a triangle, one leg of which is guided by the T-square or another triangle; then hold the guiding member in position and revolve the triangle about the right angle until the other leg is against the guiding edge. The new position of the hypotenuse will be perpendicular to its previous location along the given line and, when moved to the required position, may be used as a ruling edge for the desired perpendicular.

3.18
Inclined Lines Making 15°, 30°, 45°, 60°, or 75° With an Oblique Line. A line making an angle with an oblique line equal to any angle of a triangle may be drawn with the triangles. The two methods previously discussed for drawing perpendicular lines are applicable with slight modifications. To draw an oblique line using the revolved triangle method [Fig. 3.29(a)], adjust along the given line the edge that is opposite the required angle; then revolve the triangle about the required angle, slide it into position, and draw the required line along the side opposite the required angle.

To use the sliding triangle method [Fig. 3.29(b)], adjust to the given line one of the edges adjacent to the required angle, and guide the side opposite the required angle with a straight edge; then slide the triangle into position and draw the required line along the other adjacent side.

To draw a line making 75° with a given line, place the triangles together so that the sum of a pair of adjacent angles equals 75°, and adjust one side of the angle thus formed to the given line; then slide the triangle, whose leg forms the other side of the angle, across the given line into position, and draw the required line, as shown in Fig. 3.30(a).

To draw a line making 15° with a given line, select any two angles whose difference is 15°. Adjust to the given line a side adjacent to one of these angles, and guide the side adjacent with a straight edge. Remove the first triangle and substitute the other so that one adjacent side of the angle to be subtracted is along the guiding edge, as shown in Fig. 3.30(b); then slide it into position and draw along the other adjacent side.

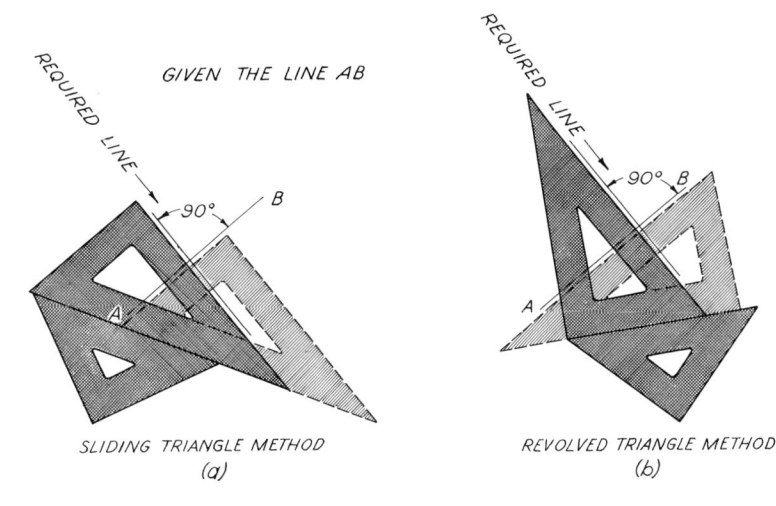

FIG. 3.28. To draw a line perpendicular to another line.

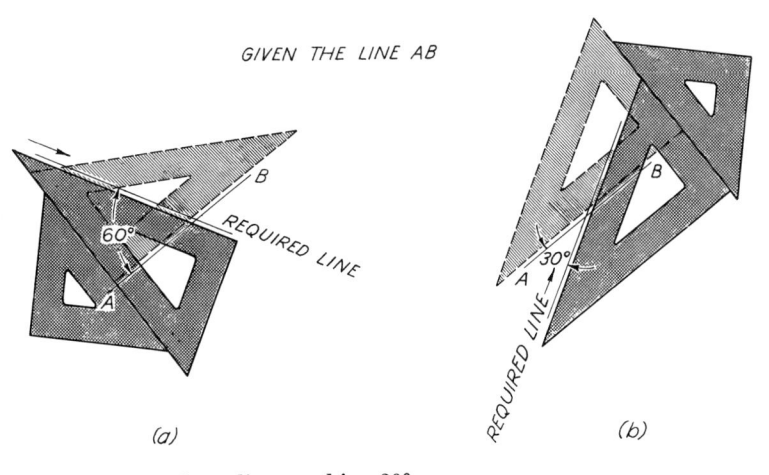

FIG. 3.29. To draw lines making 30°, 45°, or 60° with a given line.

3.19
Scales. A number of kinds of scales are available for varied types of engineering design. For convenience, however, all scales may be classified according to their use as mechanical engineers' scales (both fractional and decimal), civil engineers' scales, architects' scales, or metric scales.

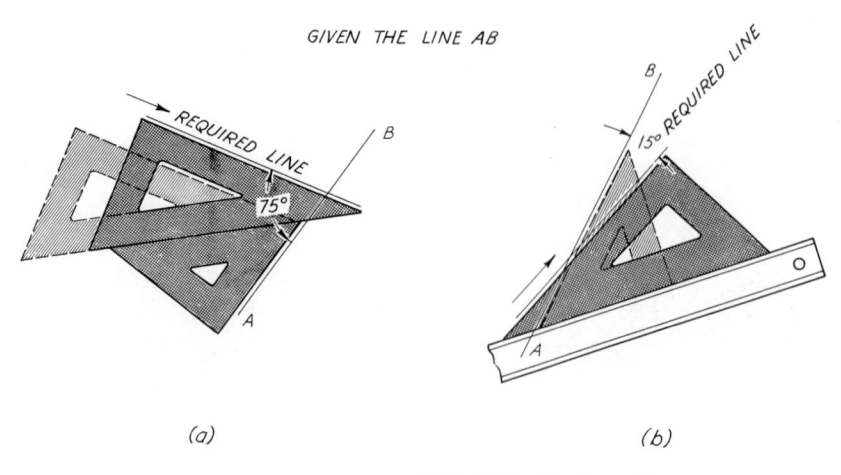

FIG. 3.30. To draw lines making 15° or 75° with a given line.

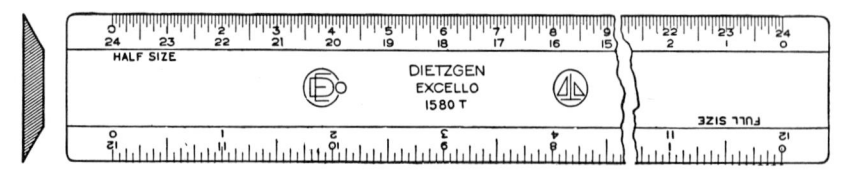

FIG. 3.31. Mechanical engineers' scale. Full-divided.

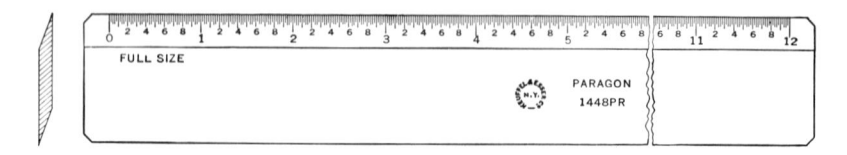

FIG. 3.32. Engineers' decimal scale.

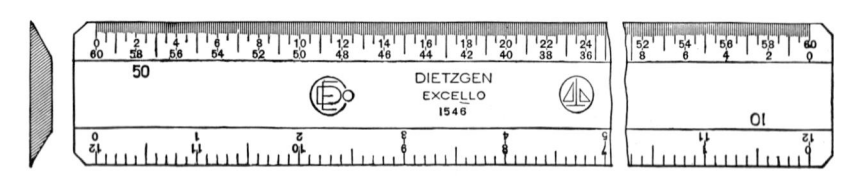

FIG. 3.33. Civil engineers' scale.

The mechanical engineers' scales are generally of the full-divided type, graduated proportionally to give reductions based on inches. On one form (Fig. 3.31) the principal units are divided into the common fractions of an inch (4, 8, 16, and 32 parts). The scales are indicated on the stick as eighth size (1½ in. = 1 ft), quarter size (3 in. = 1 ft), half size (6 in. = 1 ft), and full size.

Since the decimal system, employed in automotive design for nearly 40 years and in aircraft design since World War II, has been rapidly spreading into other fields in recent years, decimals of an inch may soon replace the use of fractions in most of the divisions of American industry. In any case, the use of decimal scales has become so widespread that the American National Standards Institute found it desirable to establish the standard ANS Z75.1–1955 for markings on scales used with decimal-inch dimensioning. The full-size scale (Fig. 3.32), which has the principal units (inches) divided into fiftieths, is particularly suited for use with the two-place decimal system. The half-size, three-eighths size, and quarter-size scales (Fig. 3.35) have the principal units divided into tenths.

The civil engineers' (chain) scales (Fig. 3.33) are full-divided, and are graduated in decimal parts, usually 10, 20, 30, 40, 50, 60, 80, and 100 divisions to the inch.

Architects' scales (Fig. 3.34) differ from mechanical engineers' scales in that the divisions represent a foot, and the end units are divided into inches, half-inches, quarter-inches, and so forth (6, 12, 24, 48, or 96 parts). The usual scales are ⅛ in. = 1 ft, ¼ in. = 1 ft, ⅜ in. = 1 ft, ½ in. = 1 ft, 1 in. = 1 ft, 1½ in. = 1 ft, and 3 in. = 1 ft.

The sole purpose of the scale is to reproduce the dimensions of an object full-size on a drawing or to reduce or enlarge them to some regular proportion, such as eighth-size, quarter-size, half-size, or double-size. The scales of reduction most frequently used are as follows:

FRACTIONAL

Mechanical engineers' scales

Full-size	($1'' = 1''$)
Half-size	($\frac{1}{2}'' = 1''$)
Quarter-size	($\frac{1}{4}'' = 1''$)
Eighth-size	($\frac{1}{8}'' = 1''$)

Architects' or mechanical engineers' scales

Full-size	($12'' = 1'\text{-}0$)
Half-size	($6'' = 1'\text{-}0$)
Quarter-size	($3'' = 1'\text{-}0$)
Eighth-size	($1\frac{1}{2}'' = 1'\text{-}0$)
$1'' = 1'\text{-}0$	$\frac{1}{4}'' = 1'\text{-}0$
$\frac{3}{4}'' = 1'\text{-}0$	$\frac{3}{16}'' = 1'\text{-}0$
$\frac{1}{2}'' = 1'\text{-}0$	$\frac{1}{8}'' = 1'\text{-}0$
$\frac{3}{8}'' = 1'\text{-}0$	$\frac{3}{32}'' = 1'\text{-}0$

DECIMAL

Mechanical engineers' scales

Full-size	($1.00'' = 1.00''$)
Half-size	($0.50'' = 1.00''$)
Three-eighths-size	($0.375'' = 1.00''$)
Quarter-size	($0.25'' = 1.00''$)

Civil engineers' scales

10 scale: $1'' = 1'$; $1'' = 10'$; $1'' = 100'$; $1'' = 1000'$
20 scale: $1'' = 2'$; $1'' = 20'$; $1'' = 200'$; $1'' = 2000'$
30 scale: $1'' = 3'$; $1'' = 30'$; $1'' = 300'$; $1'' = 3000'$
40 scale: $1'' = 4'$; $1'' = 40'$; $1'' = 400'$; $1'' = 4000'$
50 scale: $1'' = 5'$; $1'' = 50'$; $1'' = 500'$; $1'' = 5000'$
60 scale: $1'' = 60'$; etc.
80 scale: $1'' = 80'$; etc.

The first four scales, full-size, half-size, quarter-size, and eighth-size, are the ones most frequently selected for drawing machine parts, although other scales can be used. Since objects drawn by structural draftsmen and architects vary from small to very large, scales from full-size to $\frac{3}{32}$ in. = 1 ft ($\frac{1}{128}$-size) are commonly encountered. For maps, the civil engineers'

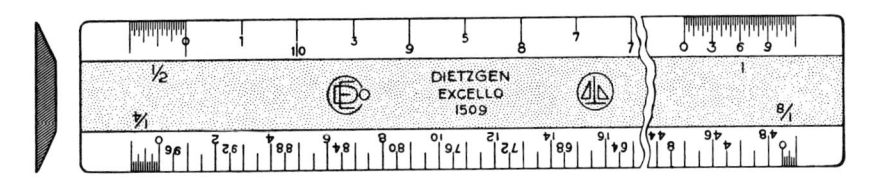

FIG. 3.34. Architects' scale. Open-divided.

decimal scales having 10, 20, 30, 40, 50, 60, and 80 divisions to the inch are used to represent 10, 20, 30 ft, and so forth, to the inch.

On a machine drawing, it is considered good practice to omit the inch ('') marks in a scale specification. For example, a scale may be specified as: FULL SIZE, 1.00 = 1.00, or 1 = 1; HALF SIZE, .50 = 1.00, or $\frac{1}{2}$ = 1; and so forth.

The decimal scales shown in Fig. 3.35

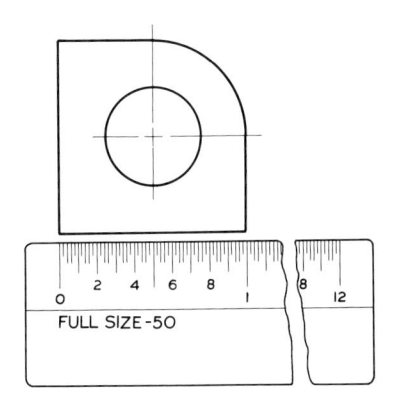

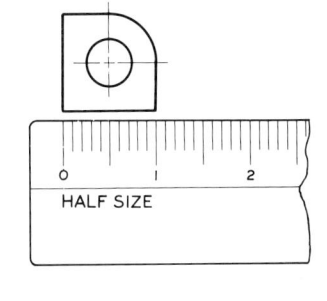

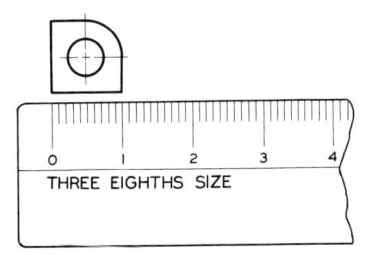

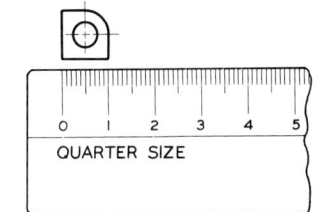

FIG. 3.35. Decimal scales.

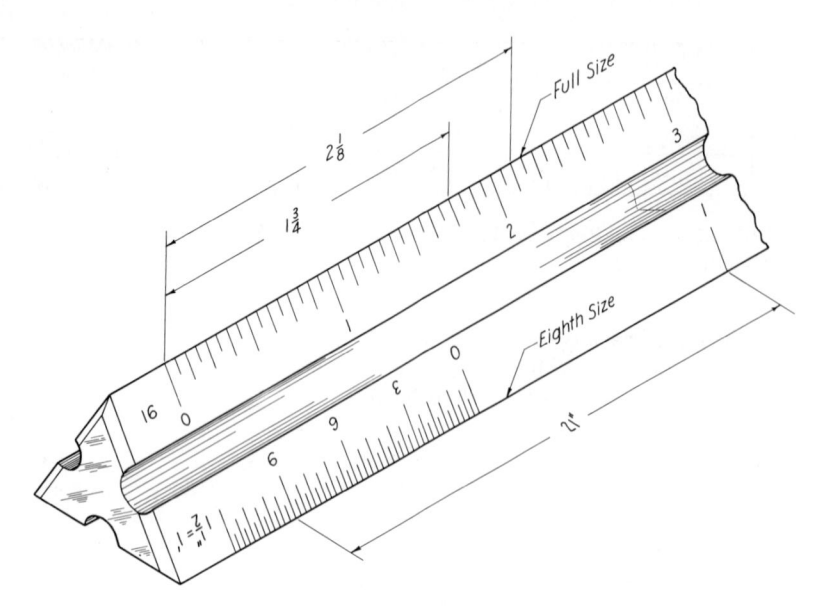

FIG. 3.36. Reading a scale.

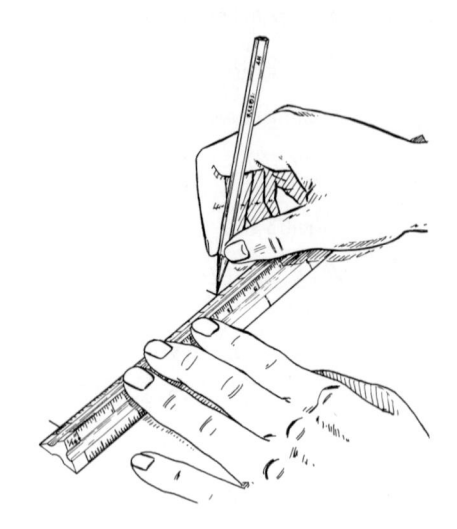

FIG. 3.37. To lay off a measurement.

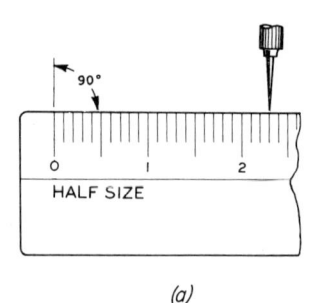

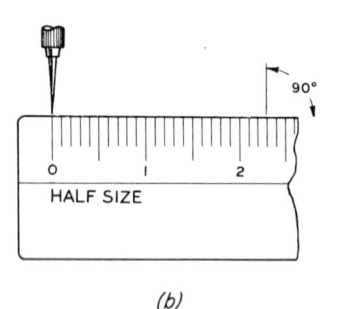

FIG. 3.38. To lay off a measurement-decimal scale.

have been approved by the American National Standards Institute for making machine drawings when the decimal system is used.

It is essential that a draftsman always think and speak of each dimension as full-size when scaling measurements, because the dimension figures given on the finished drawing indicate full-size measurements of the finished piece, regardless of the scale used.

The reading of an open-divided scale is illustrated in Fig. 3.36 with the eighth-size (1½ in. = 1 ft) scale shown. The dimension can be read directly as 21 in., the 9 in. being read in the divided segment to the left of the cipher. Each long open division represents 12 in. (1 ft).

To lay off a measurement, using a scale starting at the left of the stick, align the scale in the direction of the measurement with the zero of the scale being used toward the left. After it has been adjusted to the correct location, make short marks opposite the divisions on the scale that

establish the desired distance (Fig. 3.37). For ordinary work most men use the same pencil used for the layout. When extreme accuracy is necessary, however, it is better practice to use a pricker and make slight indentations (not holes) at the required points. If a regular pricker is not available, the dividers may be opened to approximately 60° and the point of one leg used as a substitute.

To ensure accuracy, place the eye directly over the division to be marked, hold the marking instrument perpendicular to the paper directly in front of the scale division, and mark the point. Always check the location of the point before removing the scale. If a slight indentation is made, it will be covered by the finished line; if a short mark is made and it is *very* light, it will be unnoticeable on the finished drawing.

To set off a measurement (say 2.30 in.) to half-size, the scale indicated either as half-size (Fig. 3.38) or 20 should be used. If the measurement is to be made from

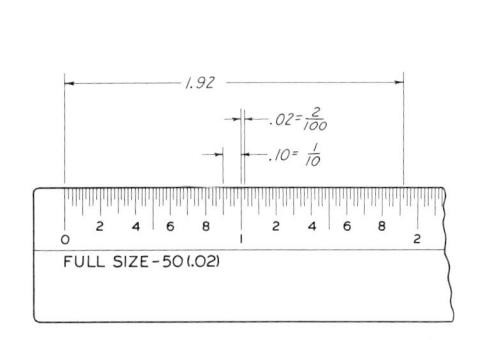

CHAP. 3 / DRAWING EQUIPMENT AND USE OF INSTRUMENTS 39

FIG. 3.39. Reading the decimal scale.

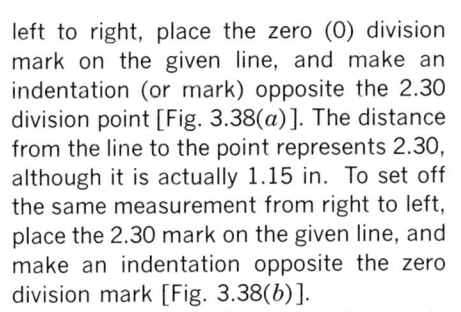

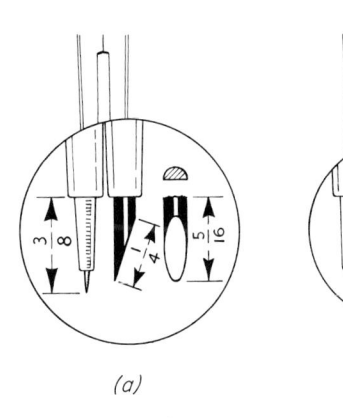

FIG. 3.40. Shaping the compass lead.

left to right, place the zero (0) division mark on the given line, and make an indentation (or mark) opposite the 2.30 division point [Fig. 3.38(a)]. The distance from the line to the point represents 2.30, although it is actually 1.15 in. To set off the same measurement from right to left, place the 2.30 mark on the given line, and make an indentation opposite the zero division mark [Fig. 3.38(b)].

The reading of the full-size decimal scale is illustrated in Fig. 3.39. The largest division indicated in the illustration represents one inch, which is subdivided into tenths and fiftieths (.02 in.). In Fig. 3.35, the largest divisions on the half size, three eighths size, and quarter size decimal scales represent one inch.

3.20
The Compass or Large Bow. The compass or large bow is used for drawing circles and circle arcs. For drawing pencil circles, the style of point illustrated in Fig. 3.40(c) should be used because it gives more accurate results and is easier to maintain than most other styles. This style of point is formed by first sharpening the outside of the lead on a file (Fig. 3.41) or sandpad to a long flat bevel approximately $\frac{1}{4}$ in. long [Fig. 3.40(a)] and then finishing it [Fig. 3.40(b)] with a slight rocking motion to reduce the width of the point. Although a hard lead (4H–6H) will maintain a point longer without resharpening, it gives a finished object line that is too light in color. Soft lead (F or H) gives a darker line but quickly loses its edge and, on larger circles, gives a thicker line at the end than at the beginning. Some draftsmen have found that a medium-grade (2H–3H) lead is a satisfactory compromise for ordinary working drawings. For design drawings, layout work, and graphical solutions, however, a harder lead will give better results.

The needle point should have the shouldered end out and should be adjusted approximately $\frac{3}{8}$ in. beyond the end of the split sleeve (Fig. 3.42).

3.21
Using the Compass or Large Bow. To draw a circle, it is first necessary to draw two intersecting center lines at right angles and mark off the radius. The pivot point should be guided accurately into position at the center. After the pencil point has been adjusted to the radius mark, the circle is drawn in a clockwise direction, as shown in Fig. 3.43. While drawing the circle, the instrument should

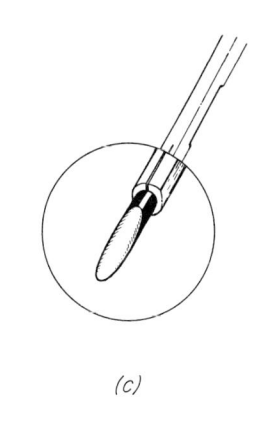

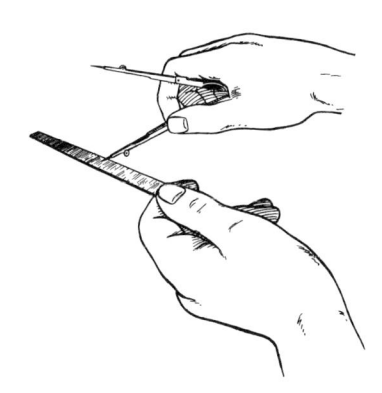

FIG. 3.41. Sharpening the compass lead.

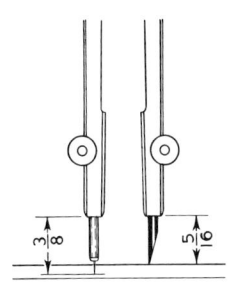

FIG. 3.42. The adjustment of the needle point.

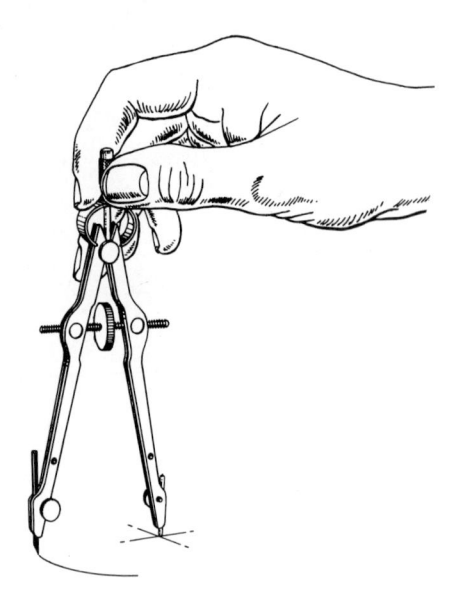

FIG. 3.43. Using the large bow (Vemco).

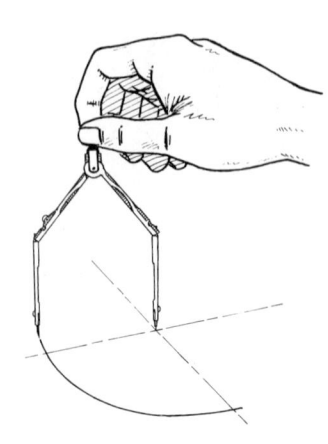

FIG. 3.44. Using the compass (legs bent).

be inclined slightly forward. If the pencil line is not dark enough, it may be drawn around again.

When using a compass for a radius larger than 2 in., the legs should be bent at the knee joints to stand approximately perpendicular to the paper (Fig. 3.44). It is particularly important that this adjustment be made when drawing ink circles, otherwise both nibs will not touch the paper. For circles whose radii exceed 5 in., the lengthening bar should be used to increase the capacity.

The beam compass is manipulated by steadying the instrument at the pivot leg with one hand while rotating the marking leg with the other (Fig. 3.45).

3.22
The Dividers. The dividers are used principally for dividing curved and straight lines into any number of equal parts and for transferring measurements. If the instrument is held with one leg between the forefinger and second finger, and the other leg between the thumb and third finger, as illustrated in Fig. 3.46, an adjustment may be made quickly and easily with one hand. The second and third fingers are used to "open out" the legs, and the thumb and forefinger to close them. This method of adjusting may seem awkward to the beginner at first, but with practice absolute control can be developed.

3.23
Use of the Dividers. The trial method is used to divide a line into a given number of equal parts (Fig. 3.47). To divide a line into a desired number of equal parts, open the dividers until the distance between the points is estimated to be equal to the

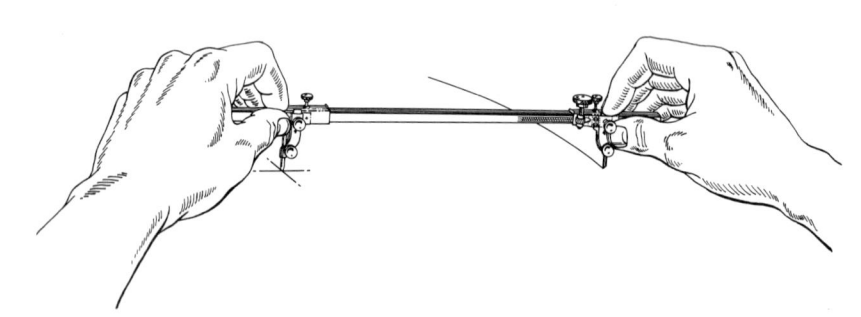

FIG. 3.45. Drawing large circles (Vemco beam compass).

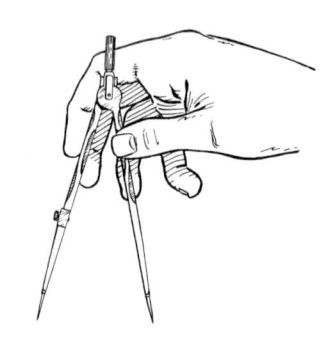

FIG. 3.46. To adjust the large dividers.

length of a division, and step off the line *lightly*. If the last prick mark misses the end point, increase or decrease the setting by an amount estimated to be equal to the error divided by the number of divisions, before lifting the dividers from the paper. Step off the line again. Repeat this procedure until the dividers are correctly set, then space the line again and indent the division points. When stepping off a line, the dividers are rotated alternately in an opposite direction on either side of the line, each half-revolution, as shown in Fig. 3.47.

Although the dividers are used to transfer a distance on a drawing, they should never be used to transfer a measurement from the scale, as the method is slow and inaccurate and results in serious damage to the graduation marks. Care should be taken to avoid pricking large unsightly holes with the divider points. It is the common practice of many expert draftsmen to draw a small freehand circle around a very light indentation to establish its location.

3.24
Use of the Bow Instruments. The bow pen and bow pencil are convenient for drawing circles having a radius of 1 in. or less (Fig. 3.48). The needle points should be adjusted slightly longer than the marking points, as in the case of the compass.

Small adjustments are made by the fingers of the hand holding the instrument, with the pivot point in position at the center of the required circle or arc.

3.25
Use of the French Curve. A French curve is used for drawing irregular curves that are not circle arcs. After sufficient points have been located, the French curve is applied so that a portion of its ruling edge passes through at least three points, as shown in Fig. 3.49. It should be so placed

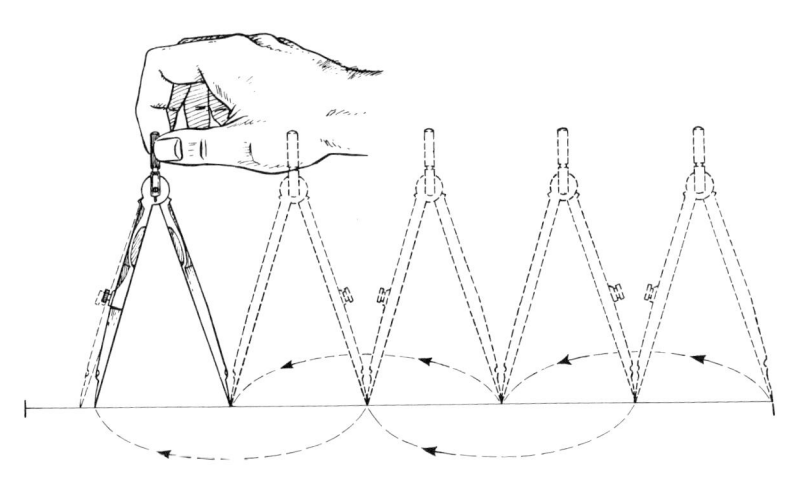

FIG. 3.47. Use of the dividers.

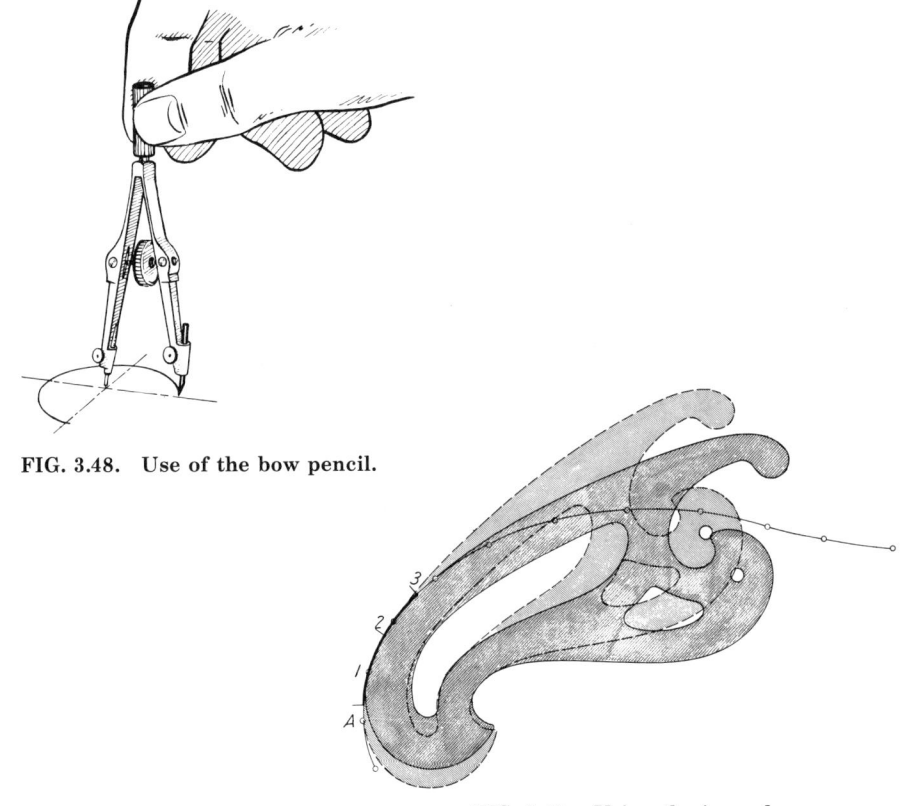

FIG. 3.48. Use of the bow pencil.

FIG. 3.49. Using the irregular curve.

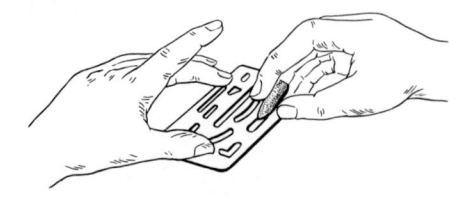

FIG. 3.50. Using the erasing shield.

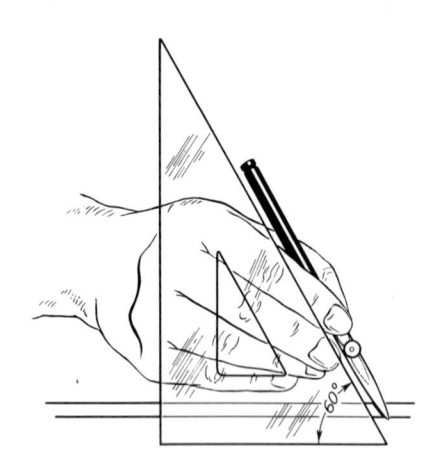

FIG. 3.51. Holding the pen.

that the increasing curvature of the section of the ruling edge being used follows the direction of that part of the curve which is changing most rapidly. To ensure that the finished curve will be free of humps and sharp breaks, the first line drawn should start and stop short of the first and last points to which the French curve has been fitted. Then the curve is adjusted in a new position with the ruling edge coinciding with a section of the line previously drawn. Each successive segment should stop short of the last point matched by the curve. In Fig. 3.49, the curve fits the three points, A, 1, and 2. A line is drawn from between point A and point 1 to between point 1 and point 2. Then, the curve is shifted, as shown, to fit again points 1 and 2 with an additional point 3, and the line is extended to between point 2 and point 3.

Some people sketch a smooth continuous curve through the points in pencil before drawing the mechanical line. This procedure makes the task of drawing the curve less difficult, since it is easier to adjust the ruling edge to segments of the freehand curve than to the points.

3.26
Use of the Erasing Shield and Eraser. An erasure is made on a drawing by placing an opening in the erasing shield over the work to be erased and rubbing with a pencil eraser (never an ink eraser) until it is removed (Fig. 3.50). Excessive pressure should not be applied to the eraser because, although the lines will disappear more quickly, the surface of the paper is likely to be permanently damaged. The fingers holding the erasing shield should rest partly on the drawing paper to prevent the shield from slipping.

3.27
Use of the Ruling Pen. The ruling pen is used to ink mechanical lines. It is always guided by the working edge of a T-square, triangle, or French curve and is never used freehand.

When ruling a line, the pen should be in a vertical plane and inclined slightly (approximately 60°) in the direction of the movement. It is held by the thumb and forefinger, as illustrated in Fig. 3.51, with the blade against the second finger and the adjusting screw on the outside away from the ruling edge. The third and fourth fingers slide along the T-square blade and help control the pen. Short lines are drawn with a hand movement, long lines with a free arm movement that finishes with a finger movement. While drawing, the angle of inclination and speed must remain constant to obtain a line of uniform width and straightness. Particular attention should be given to the position of the pen, as practically all faulty lines are due to incorrect inclination or to leaning the pen so that the point is too close to the straightedge or too far away from it. The correct position of the pen for drawing a satisfactory line is illustrated in Fig. 3.51.

If the pen is held so that it leans outward, as shown in Fig. 3.52(a), the point will be against the straightedge, and ink will run under and cause a blot; or, if it leans inward, as in Fig. 3.52(b), the outer nib will not touch the paper and the line will be ragged.

Unnecessary pressure against the straightedge changes the distance between the nibs, which in turn may either reduce the width of the line along its entire length or cause its width to vary, as in Fig. 3.52(d).

It will not take any beginner long to discover that care must be taken when removing a T-square or triangle away from a wet ink line [Fig. 3.52(c)].

The ruling pen is filled by inserting the quill or dropper device of the stopper between the nibs. Care must be taken, while filling, to see that there is enough ink to finish the line and that none of the ink from the filler gets on the outside of the blades. No more than $\frac{1}{4}$ in. should ever be put in; there is a danger of blotting if the pen is used with a greater amount.

The special ink-bottle holder and filler shown in Fig. 3.53 is a convenience that saves time when filling a pen, because only one hand is needed to raise the stopper and insert the ink.

The width of a line is determined by the distance between the nibs, which is regulated by the adjusting screw. When setting the pen, a series of test lines should be drawn with a straightedge on a small piece of the same kind of paper or cloth to establish the setting for the desired width of the line. The draftsman's line gauge, shown in Fig. 3.54, is convenient for testing the widths of trial lines as illustrated. If the first trial line is not of the desired width, another and another should be drawn until the final one agrees with the selected width as given on the gauge.

If the ink refuses to flow when the pen is touched to the paper, either the ink has thickened or the opening between the nibs has become clogged. To start it flowing, draftsmen often touch the point to the back of a finger or pinch the blades together. Whenever this fails to produce an

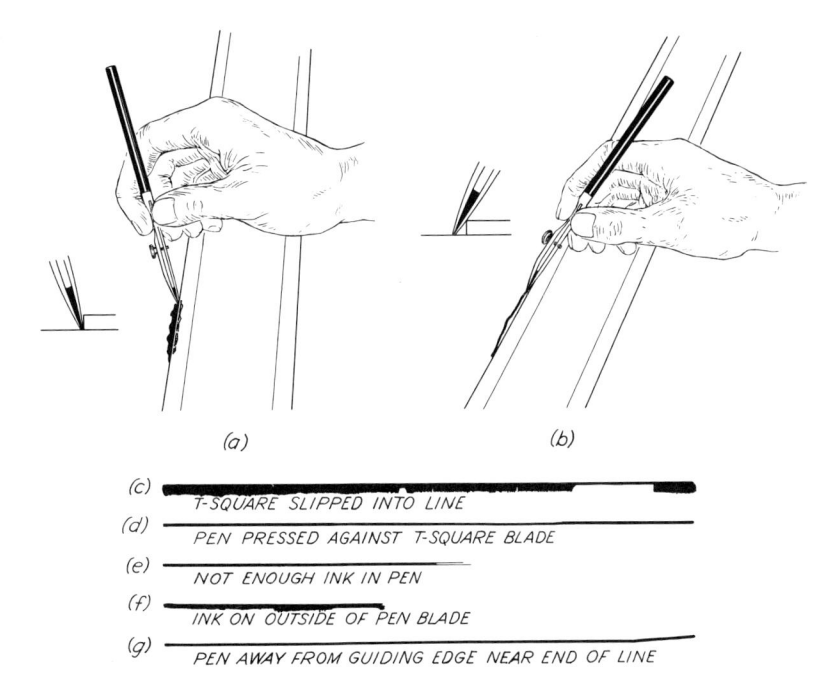

FIG. 3.52. Common faults in handling a ruling pen.

FIG. 3.53. Special ink bottle holder and filler.

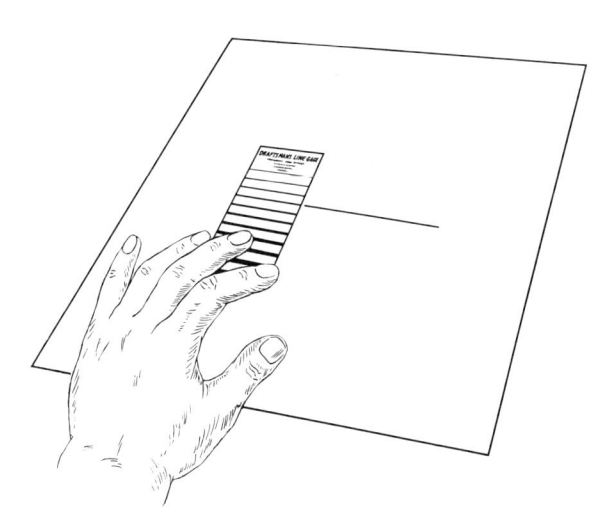

FIG. 3.54. Testing a trial line on a "try sheet."

immediate flow, the pen should be cleaned and refilled.

A dirty pen in which the ink has been allowed to thicken will not draw any better than a dull one. To avoid changing the setting of the pen when cleaning it, fold the pen wiper twice at 90° and draw the corner of the fold between the ends of the blades (Fig. 3.55).

3.28

Tracing. Often, when it is necessary to make duplicate copies (blueprints) of important drawings for a machine or structure, the original pencil drawings are traced in ink on a tracing medium, usually tracing cloth. Contrary to the practice of old-time draftsmen and the intention of the early manufacturers of this medium, the dull side is now almost universally used for the inking surface instead of the slick side because it produces less light glare, will take both pencil and ink lines better, and will withstand more erasing. The fact that the dull side will take pencil lines is important because, on some occasions, in order to save time, drawings are made directly on the cloth and then traced. On completion of the tracing, all pencil lines including the guide lines and slope lines for the lettering may be removed by wiping the surface of the cloth with a rag moistened with a small amount of gasoline, benzine, or cleaning fluid.

When the tracing cloth has been fastened down over the drawing, a small quantity of tracing cloth powder may be sprinkled over the surface to make it take the ink evenly and smoothly. After it has been well rubbed in, the excess must be thoroughly removed by wiping with a clean cloth, for even a small amount of loose powder left on the surface can cause clogging of the pen. Powder is also used by some persons over a spot where an erasure has been made; but a better practice is to use a piece of soapstone, which will put a smooth, slick finish over the damaged area. In applying the soapstone, rub the spot and then wipe a finger over it a few times. Following this treatment, the erased area will take ink almost as well as the original surface.

Since ink lines are made much wider than pencil lines, in order to get a good contrast on a blueprint, they should be carefully centered over the pencil lines when tracing. The center of an ink line should fall directly on the pencil line, as shown correctly in Fig. 3.56. For ink work it might be said that ink lines are tangent when their center lines touch. In this same illustration, note the poor junctures obtained when ink lines are not centered so that their center lines are tangent.

Figure 3.57(a) shows the filled-in corner effect that frequently appears to the disgust of the draftsman, when an ink line is drawn from or to another previously drawn line that is still wet.

When a working drawing is traced in ink on either paper or cloth, the lines should be "inked" in a definite order. Otherwise, the necessity of waiting for the ink to dry after every few lines not only wastes time but often results in a line here and there being left out. Furthermore, hit-and-miss inking may produce lines of unequal

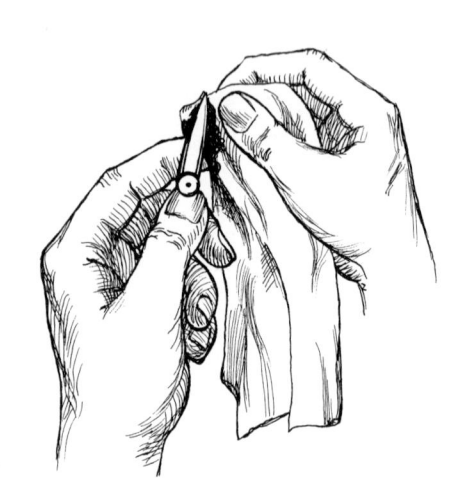

FIG. 3.55. Cleaning the ruling pen.

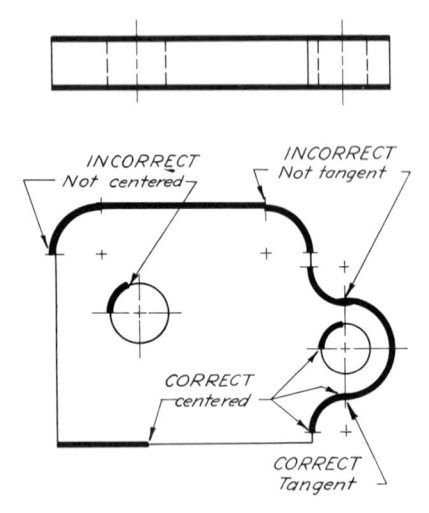

FIG. 3.56. Inking over pencil lines.

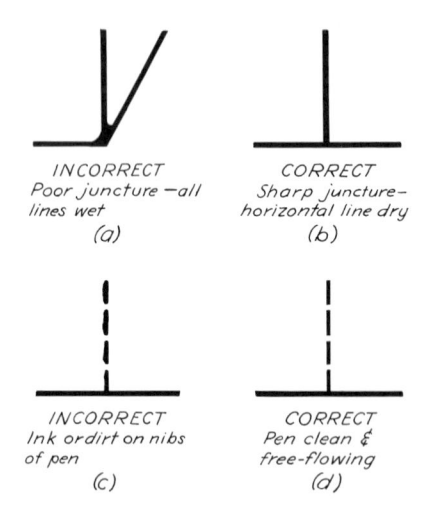

FIG. 3.57. Ink lines.

width. It is therefore recommended that the student make a conscientious attempt to follow the order of inking suggested in this chapter.

After the paper or cloth has been fastened down over the drawing, and before the inking is begun, each tangent point should be marked and all centers should be indented.

ORDER OF INKING

1. Curved lines
    a. Circles and circle arcs (small circles first) in the order of 1, 2, and 3 below.
        (1) Visible
        (2) Invisible
        (3) Circular center lines and dimension lines
    b. Irregular curves
        (1) Visible
        (2) Invisible
2. Straight lines
    a. Visible
        (1) Horizontal, from the top of the sheet down
        (2) Vertical, from the left side of the sheet to the right
        (3) Inclined, from the left to the right
    b. Invisible
        (1) Horizontal
        (2) Vertical
        (3) Inclined
    c. Auxiliary (center, extension, dimension lines, etc.)
        (1) Horizontal
        (2) Vertical
        (3) Inclined
        (4) Section lines
3. Arrowheads and dimension figures
4. Notes and titles
5. Border

3.29

Sharpening a Ruling Pen. Ruling pens, whether they have been used continuously or intermittently, eventually show signs of wear. When a pen's nibs have lost their elliptical shape and have become so dull that the ink spreads under their tips, fine lines cannot be drawn until the pen has been sharpened. The way to detect this condition is to examine the tips. If bright spots may be seen on the tips, the pen is too dull for satisfactory work. An example of a worn point is illustrated in Fig. 3.58(*a*).

Since even new pens are seldom sharpened properly and often require retouching, every draftsman should be able to reshape and sharpen his own pen.

Incorrectly sharpened points are illustrated in Fig. 3.58(*b*) and (*c*). Points shaped as shown in either (*b*) or (*c*) are aggravating, because if a point is rounded, as in (*b*), the ink flows too freely; if it is too pointed, as in (*c*), the ink cups up and the flow is difficult to start. Only a pen that is correctly shaped and sharpened, as shown in Fig. 3.58(*d*), will give the results that should be expected.

Although blades should be sharpened to a thin edge, care should be taken not to make them sharp enough to cut the surface of the paper. A pen should never be sharpened, even the slightest amount, on the inside of the blades.

A fine-grained Arkansas oilstone is the best all-purpose stone for sharpening a

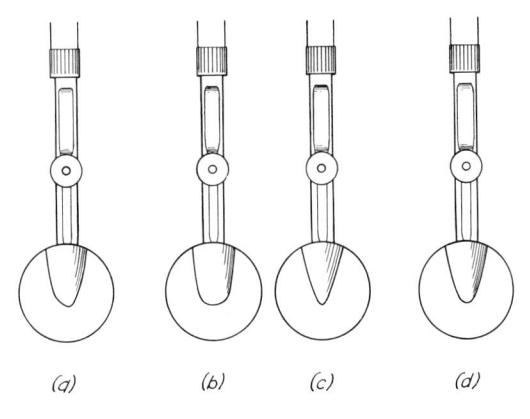

(*a*)   (*b*)   (*c*)   (*d*)

FIG. 3.58. Worn, incorrectly shaped, and correctly shaped blades.

ruling pen. The first step in sharpening is to equalize the length of the nibs and correct their shape. This may be done by bringing the blades together so that they barely touch and then drawing them lightly back and forth across the stone while swinging the pen through an arc of approximately 120° each stroke (Fig. 3.59). During this operation, it is essential that the pen be held in a vertical plane and that an even pressure be maintained against the stone. When an inspection, under a magnifying glass, reveals that the nibs have been restored to their correct shape, the blades should be opened and each nib sharpened all around the outside to a thin edge. A blade is sharpened by holding the pen as shown in Fig. 3.60 and sliding it back and forth across the stone with a slight rolling motion to preserve its original convex shape. The pen should be examined from time to time so that the sharpening can be stopped as soon as the bright point disappears.

Finally, a test should be made by filling the pen and drawing a series of lines of various weights on a piece of tracing paper or tracing cloth. If the instrument is capable of drawing satisfactory lines of any weight, particularly very fine lines, it has been correctly sharpened.

FIG. 3.59. Shaping the nibs.

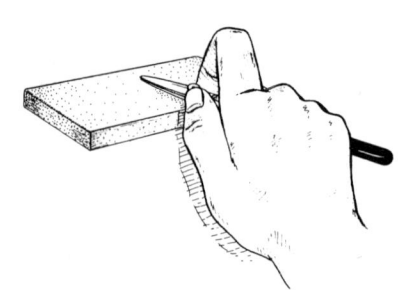

FIG. 3.60. Sharpening the blades.

3.30
Conventional Line Symbols. Symbolic lines of various weights are used in making technical drawings. The recommendations of the American National Standards Institute, as given in ANS Y14.2–1957, are the following:

Three widths of lines—thick, medium, and thin—are recommended for use on drawings (Fig. 3.61). Pencil lines in general should be in proportion to the ink lines except that the thicker pencil lines will be necessarily thinner than the corresponding ink lines but as thick as practicable for pencil work. Exact thicknesses may vary according to the size and type of drawing. For example, where lines are close together, the lines may be slightly thinner.

Pencil lines may be further simplified, if desired, to two widths of lines: *medium-thick* for visible, hidden, cutting-plane, and short-break lines; and *thin* for section, center, extension, dimension, long-break, and phantom lines.

The lines illustrated in Fig. 3.61 are shown full-size. When symbolic lines are used on a pencil drawing they should not vary in color. For example, center lines, extension lines, dimension lines, and section lines should differ from object lines only in width. The resulting contrast makes a drawing easier to read. All lines, except construction lines, should be very dark and bright to give the drawing the "snap" that is needed for good appearance. If the drawing is on tracing paper the lead must be "packed on" so that a satisfactory print can be obtained. Construction lines should be drawn *very* fine so as to be unnoticeable on the finished drawing. The lengths of the dashes and spaces shown in Figs. 6.32 and 8.23 are recommended for the hidden lines, center lines, and cutting-plane lines on average-size drawings.

EXERCISES IN INSTRUMENTAL DRAWING

The following elementary exercises have been designed to offer experience in the use of the drafting instruments. The designs should be drawn *lightly* with a hard pencil. After making certain that all constructions shown on a drawing are correct, the lines forming the designs

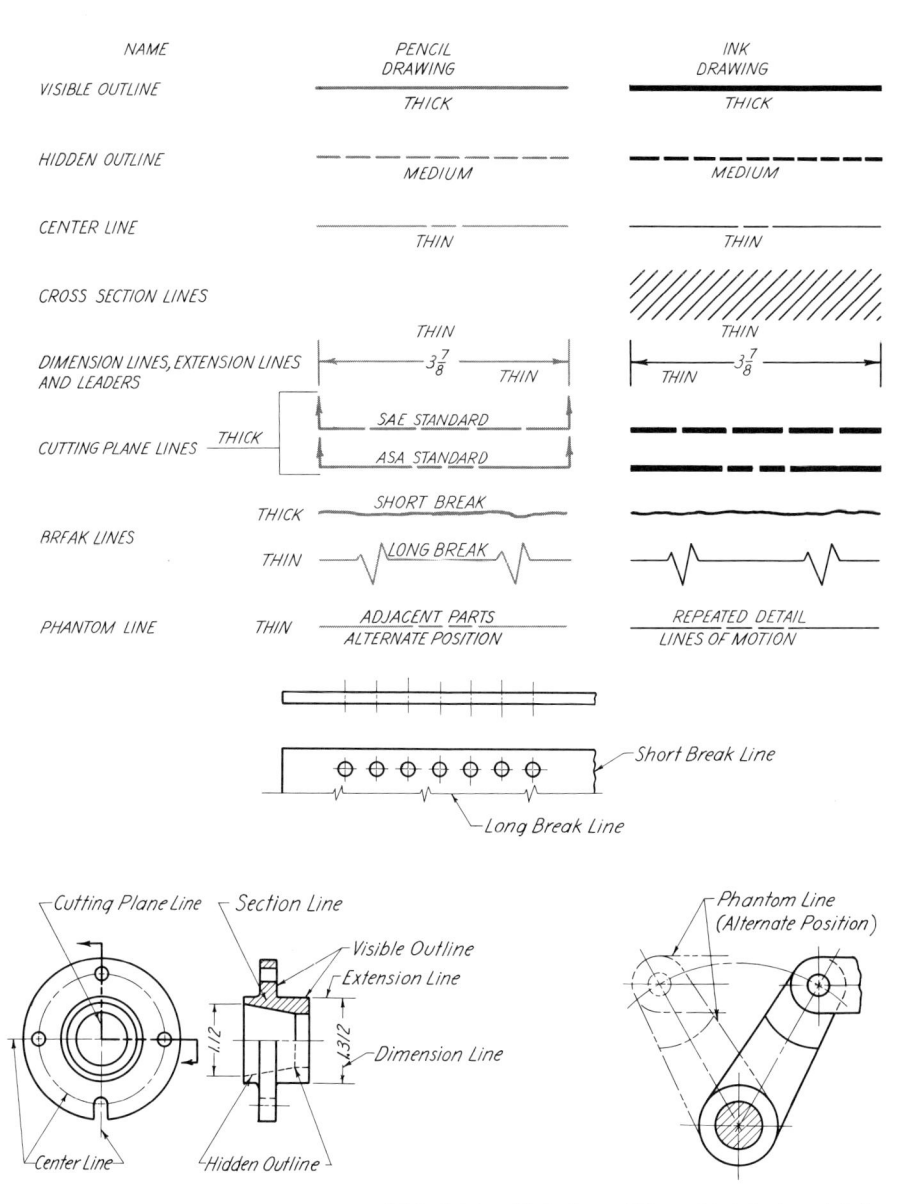

FIG. 3.61. Alphabet of lines (finished weight).

should be heavied with a medium-hard pencil. The light construction lines need not be erased if the drawing is relatively clean.

1. (Fig. 3.62). On a sheet of drawing paper reproduce the line formations shown. If the principal border lines have not been printed on the sheet, they may be drawn first so that the large $5\frac{1}{2} \times 8\frac{1}{4}$-in. rectangle can be balanced horizontally and vertically within the border. To draw the inclined lines, first draw the indicated measuring lines through the lettered points at the correct angle, and mark off $\frac{1}{4}$-in. dis-

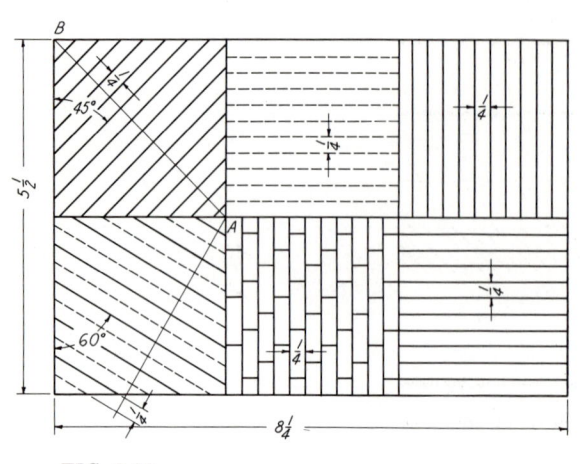

FIG. 3.62

FIG. 3.63

tances. These division points establish the locations of the required lines of the formation. The six squares of the formation are equal in size.

2. (Fig. 3.63). Reproduce the line formations shown, following the instructions given for Exercise 1.

3. (Fig. 3.64). This exercise is designed to give the student practice with the bow pencil and compass by drawing some simple geometric figures. The line work within each large circle may be reproduced with only the knowledge that the diameter is 3¼ in. All circles and circle arcs are to be made finished-weight when they are first drawn, since retracing often produces a double line. Do not "overrun" the straight lines or stop them too short.

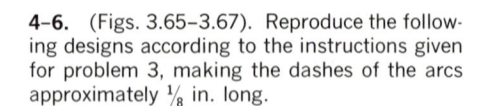

4–6. (Figs. 3.65–3.67). Reproduce the following designs according to the instructions given for problem 3, making the dashes of the arcs approximately ⅛ in. long.

7–9. (Figs. 3.68–3.70). Reproduce the line work within each square, using the dimensions given. (The dimensions shown, however, are for

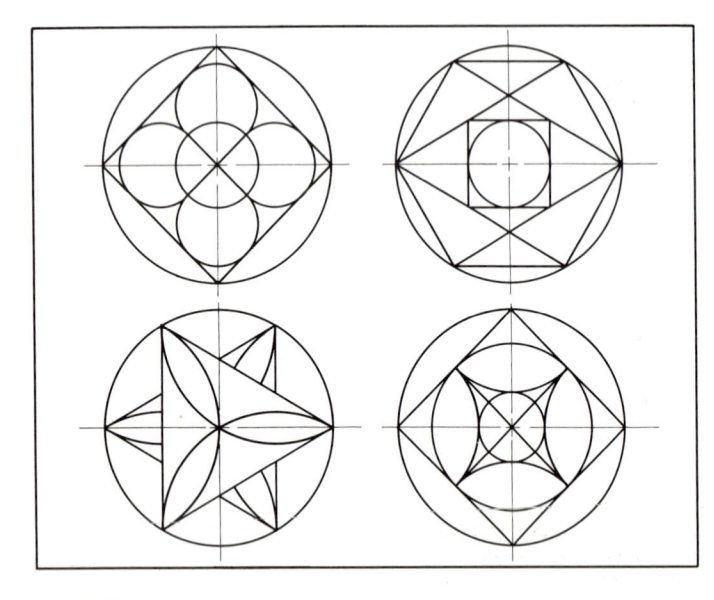

FIG. 3.64

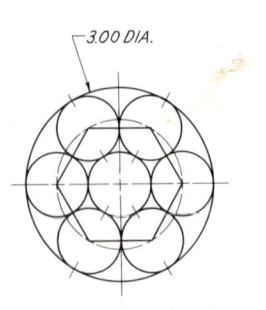

FIG. 3.65

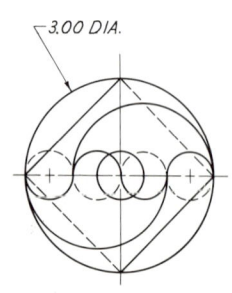

FIG. 3.66

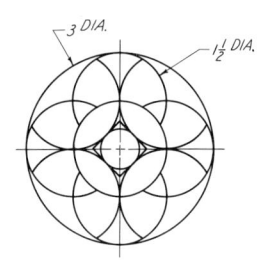

CHAP. 3 / DRAWING EQUIPMENT AND USE OF INSTRUMENTS   49

FIG. 3.67

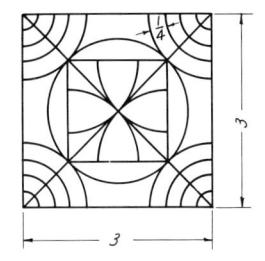

FIG. 3.68

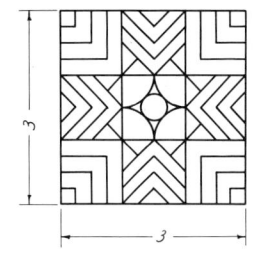

FIG. 3.69

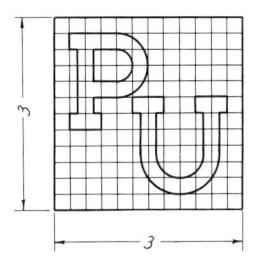

FIG. 3.70

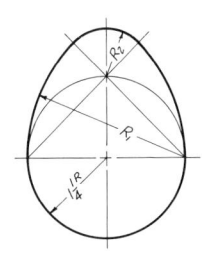

FIG. 3.71. Oval.

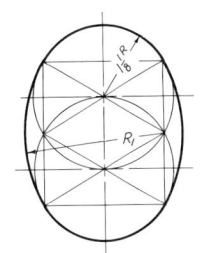

FIG. 3.72. Ellipse (approximate).

the student's use only and should not appear on the finished drawing.) Arcs should be made finished-weight when first drawn. The straight lines of each design may be drawn with a hard pencil and later heavied with a softer pencil. Do not erase the construction lines.

10–13. (Figs. 3.71–3.74). Reproduce the geometric shapes.

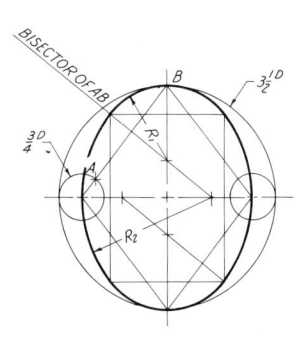

FIG. 3.73. Ellipse (approximate).

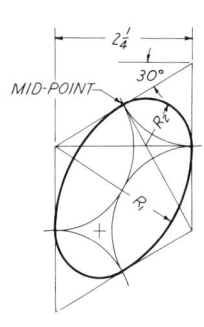

FIG. 3.74. Ellipse (pictorial).

The design of highway interchanges has been a principle application of X-Y plotters that feature digital input with an analog drive system. Up-to-date plotting systems include character printers, multiple line drawing pens, origin and scale controls, and input controlled paper advance. These systems are of solid state modular design. See Chapter 18.
(Extracted from Computer Yearbook and Directory. Courtesy American Data Processing, Inc.)

Engineering Geometry

4.1
Introduction. The simplified geometrical constructions presented in this chapter are those with which an engineer should be familiar, for they frequently occur in engineering drawing. The methods are applications of the principles found in textbooks on plane geometry. The constructions have been modified to take advantage of time-saving methods made possible by the use of drawing instruments.

Since a study of the subject of plane geometry should be a prerequisite for a course in engineering drawing, the mathematical proofs have been omitted intentionally. Geometric terms applying to lines, surfaces, and solids, however, are given in Figs. 4.60 and 4.61 for the purpose of review.

4.2
To Bisect a Straight Line (Fig. 4.1).

(*a*) With A and B as centers, strike the intersecting arcs as shown using any radius greater than one-half of AB. A straight line through points C and D bisects AB.

(*b*) Draw either 60° or 45° lines through E and F. Through their intersection draw the perpendicular GH that will bisect EF.

The use of the dividers to divide or bisect a line by the trial method is explained in Sec. 3.23.

4.3
To Trisect a Straight Line (Fig. 4.2). Given the line AB. Draw the lines AO and OB making 30° with AB. Similarly, draw CO and OD making 60° with AB. AC equals CD equals DB.

4.4
To Bisect an Angle (Fig. 4.3).

(*a*) Given the angle BAC. Use any radius with the vertex A as a center, and strike an arc that intersects the sides of the angle at D and E. With D and E as centers and a radius larger than one-half of DE, draw intersecting arcs. Draw AF. Angle BAF equals angle FAC.

(*b*) Given an angle formed by the lines KL and MN having an inaccessible point

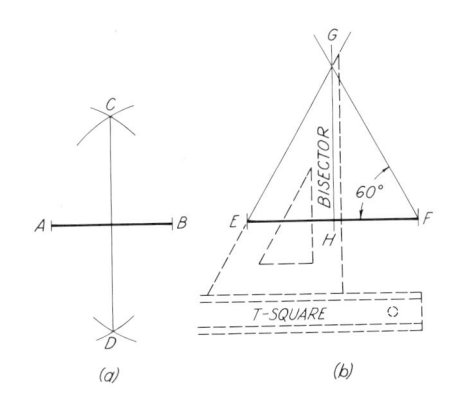

FIG. 4.1. To bisect a straight line.

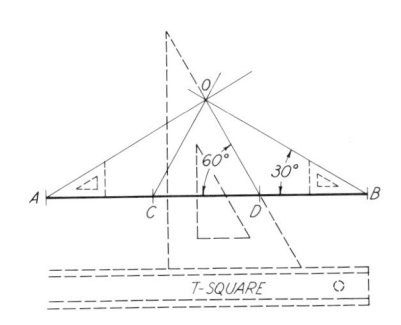

FIG. 4.2. To trisect a straight line.

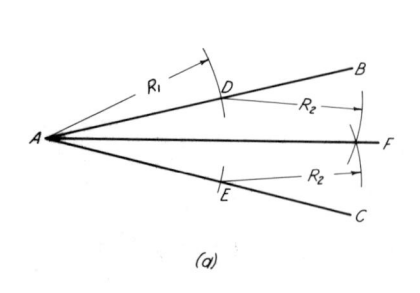

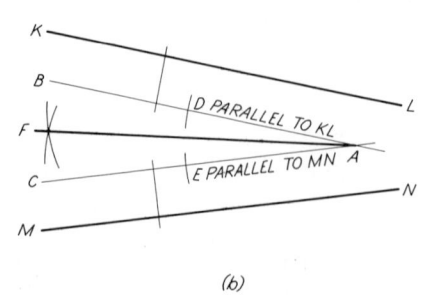

FIG. 4.3. To bisect an angle.

of intersection. Draw BA parallel to KL and CA parallel to MN at the same distance from MN as BA is from KL. Bisect angle BAC using the method explained in part (a). The bisector FA of angle BAC bisects the angle between the lines KL and MN.

4.5
To Draw Parallel Curved Lines About a Curved Center Line (Fig. 4.4). Draw a series of arcs having centers located at random along the given center line AB. Using the French curve, draw the required curved lines tangent to these arcs.

4.6
To Trisect an Angle (Fig. 4.5). Given the angle BAC. Lay off along AB any conven-

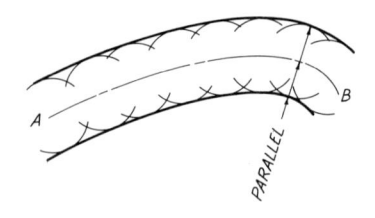

FIG. 4.4. To draw parallel curved lines.

ient distance AD. Draw DE perpendicular to AC and DF parallel to AC. Place the scale so that it passes through A with a distance equal to twice AD intercepted between the lines DE and DF. Angle HAC equals one-third of the angle BAC.

4.7
To Divide a Straight Line into a Given Number of Equal Parts (Fig. 4.6). Given the line LM, which is to be divided into five equal parts.

(a) Step off, with the dividers, five equal divisions along a line making any convenient angle with LM. Connect the last point P with M, and through the remaining points draw lines parallel to MP intersecting the given line. These lines divide LM into five equal parts.

(b) Some commercial draftsmen prefer a modification of this construction known as the scale method. For the first step, draw a vertical PM through point M. Place the scale so that the first mark of five equal divisions is at L and the last mark falls on PM. Locate the four intervening division points, and through these draw verticals intersecting the given line. The verticals will divide LM into five equal parts.

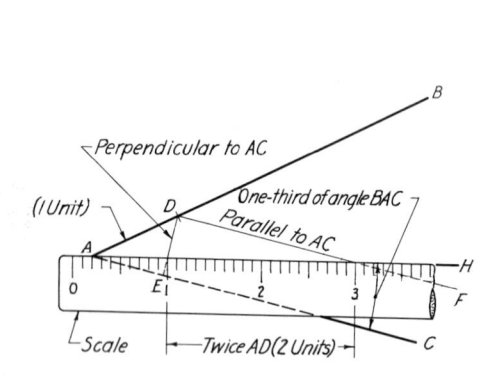

FIG. 4.5. To trisect an angle.

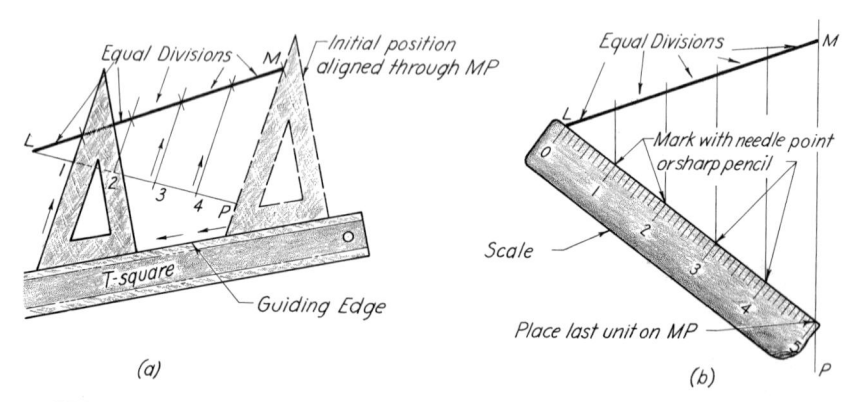

FIG. 4.6. To divide a straight line into a number of equal parts.

4.8
To Divide a Line Proportionally (Fig. 4.7). Given the line AB. Draw BC perpendicular to AB. Place the scale across A and BC so that the number of divisions intercepted is equal to the sum of the numbers representing the proportions. Mark off these proportions and draw lines parallel to BC to divide AB as required. The proportions in Fig. 4.7 are 1:2:3.

4.9
To Construct an Angle Equal to a Given Angle (Fig. 4.8). Given the angle BAC and the line $A'C'$ that forms one side of the transferred angle. Use any convenient radius with the vertex A as a center, and strike the arc that intersects the sides of the angle at D and E. With A' as a center, strike the arc intersecting $A'C'$ at E'. With E' as a center and the chord distance DE as a radius, strike a short intersecting arc to locate D'. $A'B'$ drawn through D' makes angle $B'A'C'$ equal angle BAC.

4.10
To Draw a Line Through a Given Point and the Inaccessible Intersection of Two Given Lines (Fig. 4.9). Given the lines KL and MN, and the point P. Construct any triangle, such as PQR, having its vertices falling on the given lines and the given point. At some convenient location construct triangle STU similar to PQR, by drawing SU parallel to PR, TU parallel to QR, and ST parallel to PQ. PS is the required line.

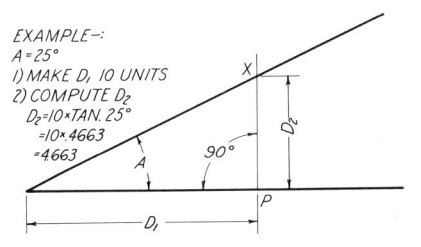

4.11
To Construct an Angle, Tangent Method (Fig. 4.10). Draftsmen often find it necessary to draw long lines having an angle between them that is not equal to an angle of a triangle. Such an angle may be laid off with a protractor, but it should be remembered that as the lines are extended any error is multiplied. To avoid this situation, the tangent method may be used. The tangent method involves trigonometry but, since it is frequently used, a discussion of it here is pertinent. (See Table 31 of the Appendix.)

In this method, a distance D_1 is laid off along a line that is to form one side of the angle, and a distance D_2, equal to D_1 times the natural tangent of the angle, is marked off along a perpendicular through point P. A line through point X is the required line, and angle A is the required angle. In laying off the distance D_1, unnecessary multiplication will be eliminated if the distance is arbitrarily made 10 in. When the use of 10 in. for D_1 makes P fall off the drawing, a temporary auxiliary sheet will furnish space needed to carry out the construction. However, in order to keep the construction on the drawing, the draftsman may decide to lay off the 10-in. length D_1 using either the half-size or quarter-size scale.

This method is also used for angles formed by short lines whenever a protractor is not available.

4.12
To Construct an Angle, Chord Method (Fig. 4.11). Engineers and draftsmen frequently select the chordal method for constructing an angle accurately. This method, as applied in laying out a given angle, involves the use of an easily determined chord length for a selected length

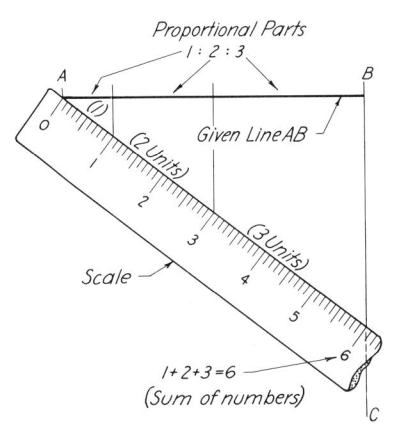

FIG. 4.7. To divide a line proportionally.

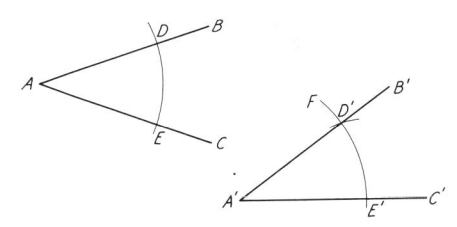

FIG. 4.8. To construct an angle equal to a given angle.

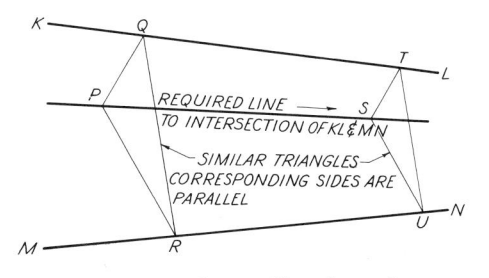

FIG. 4.9. To draw a line through a given point and the inaccessible intersection of two given lines.

FIG. 4.10. To construct an angle, tangent method.

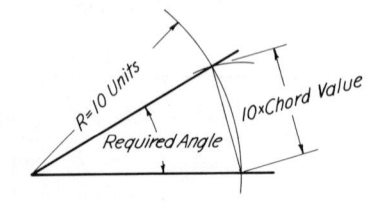

FIG. 4.11. To construct an angle, chord method.

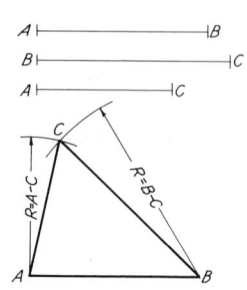

FIG. 4.12. To construct a triangle, given its three sides.

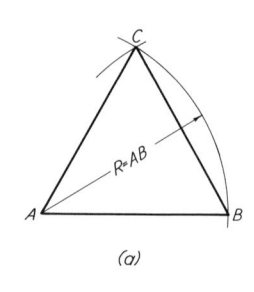

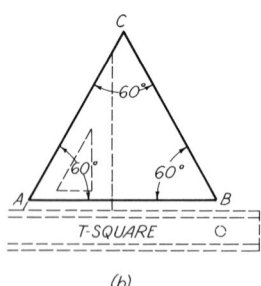

FIG. 4.13. To construct an equilateral triangle.

of radius laid off in units. Given the angle (say, 29°), the procedure is as follows: First, lay off any convenient distance, usually 10 in., along a line that is to form one side of the angle and strike an arc of indefinite length using this distance as a radius. Second, obtain the unit chord value for the given angle from Table 32 of the Appendix (29° = .5008) and multiply this value by 10. With the compass or dividers lay off the chord length (.5008 × 10 = 5.008) along the arc from the starting line and complete the angle.

When a table of chords is not available, the chord length for a 1-in. radius may be calculated for a given angle by taking the sine of one-half the angle and multiplying by 2. For example, one-half of 29° = 14°30′. The sine of 14°30′ multiplied by 2 is .2504 × 2 = .5008.

4.13
To Construct a Triangle, Given Its Three Sides (Fig. 4.12). Given the three sides AB, AC, and BC. Draw the side AB in its correct location. Using its end points A and B as centers and radii equal to AC and BC, respectively, strike the two intersecting arcs locating point C. ABC is the required triangle. This construction is particularly useful for developing the surface of a transition piece by triangulation.

4.14
To Construct an Equilateral Triangle (Fig. 4.13). Given the side AB.

(a) Using the end points A and B as centers and a radius equal to the length of AB, strike two intersecting arcs to locate C. Draw lines from A to C and C to B to complete the required equilateral triangle.

(b) Using a 30°–60° triangle, draw through A and B lines that make 60° with the given line. If the line AB is inclined, the 60° lines should be drawn as shown in Fig. 3.29.

4.15
To Transfer a Polygon (Fig. 4.14). Given the polygon $ABCDE$.

(a) Enclose the polygon in a rectangle. Draw the "enclosing rectangle" in the new position and locate points A, B, C, D, and E along the sides by measuring from the corners of the rectangle. A compass may be used for transferring the necessary measurements.

(b) To transfer a polygon by the triangle method, divide the polygon into triangles and, using the construction explained in Sec. 4.13, reconstruct each triangle in its transferred position.

4.16
To Construct a Square (Fig. 4.15).

(a) Given the side AB. Using a T-square and a 45° triangle, draw perpendiculars to line AB through points A and B. Locate point D at the intersection of a 45° construction line through A and the perpendicular from B. Draw CD parallel

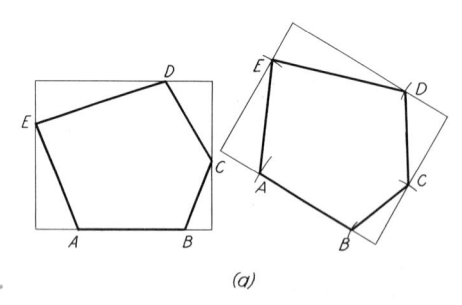

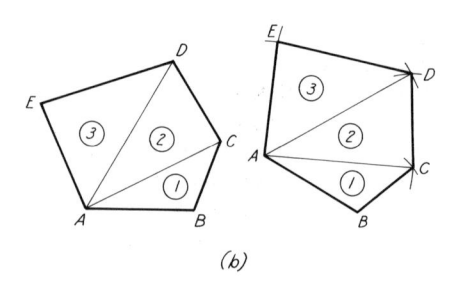

FIG. 4.14. To transfer a polygon.

FIG. 4.15. To construct a square.

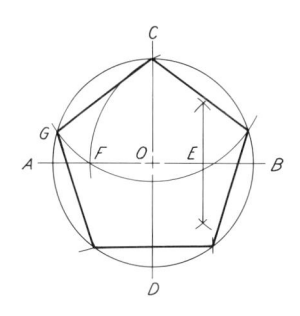

FIG. 4.16. To construct a regular pentagon.

to AB through D to complete the square. To eliminate unnecessary movements the lines should be drawn in the order indicated.

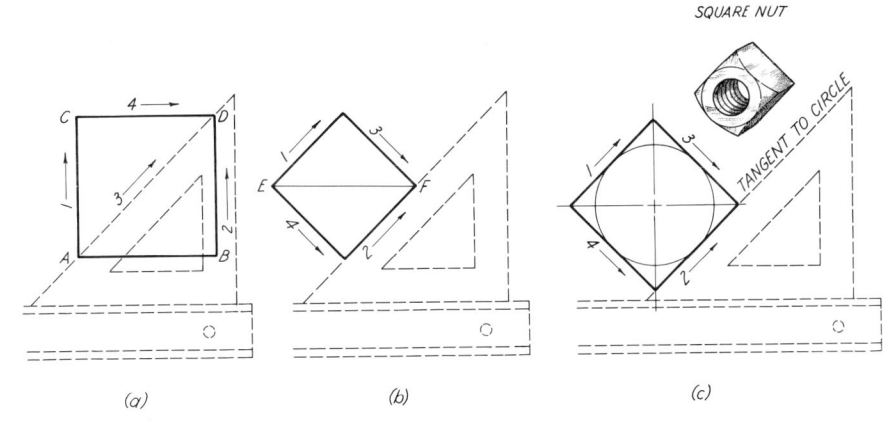

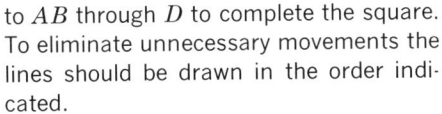

(b) Given the diagonal length EF. Using a T-square and a 45° triangle, construct the square by drawing lines through E and F at an angle of 45° with EF in the order indicated.

(c) The construction of an inscribed circle is the first step in one method for drawing a square when the location of the center and the length of one side are given.

Using a T-square and a 45° triangle, draw the sides of the square tangent to the circle. This construction is used in drawing square bolt heads and nuts.

4.17
To Construct a Regular Pentagon (Fig. 4.16). Given the circumscribing circle. Draw the perpendicular diameters AB and CD. Bisect OB and, with its mid-point E as a center and EC as a radius, draw the arc CF. Using C as a center and CF as a radius, draw the arc FG. The line CG is one of the equal sides of the required pentagon. Locate the remaining vertices by striking off this distance around the circumference.

If the length of one side of a pentagon is given, the construction described in Sec. 4.20 should be used.

4.18
To Construct a Regular Hexagon (Fig. 4.17).
(a) Given the distance AB across corners. Draw a circle having AB as a diameter. Using the same radius and with points A and B as centers, strike arcs intersecting the circumference. Join these points to complete the construction.

(b) Given the distance AB across corners. Using a 30°-60° triangle and a T-square, draw the lines in the order indicated by the numbers on the figure.

(c) Given the distance across flats. Draw a circle whose diameter equals the distance across flats. Using a 30°-60° triangle and a T-square, as shown, draw the tangents that establish the sides and vertices of the required hexagon.

This construction is used in drawing hexagonal bolt heads and nuts.

4.19
To Construct a Regular Octagon (Fig. 4.18).
(a) Given the distance across flats. Draw the circumscribed square and its

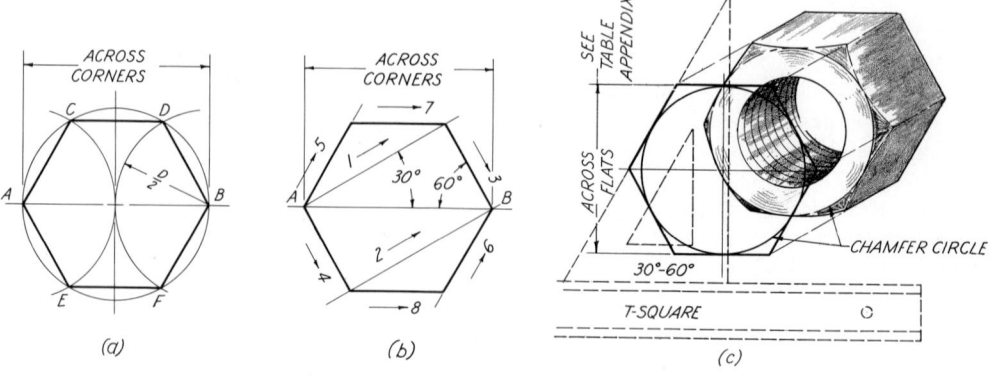

FIG. 4.17. To construct a regular hexagon.

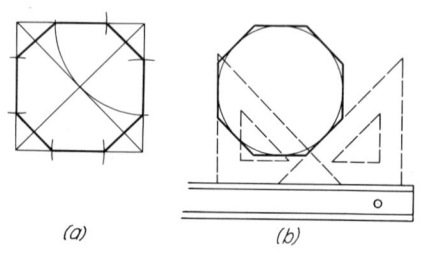

FIG. 4.18. To construct a regular octagon.

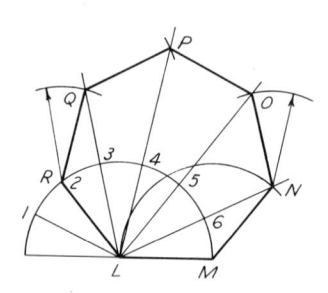

FIG. 4.19. To construct any regular polygon, given one side.

diagonals. Using the corners as centers and one-half the diagonal as a radius, strike arcs across the sides of the square. Join these points to complete the required octagon.

(b) Given the distance across flats. Draw the inscribed circle; then, using a 45° triangle and T-square, draw the tangents that establish the sides and vertices of the required octagon.

4.20
To Construct Any Regular Polygon, Given One Side (Fig. 4.19). Given the side LM. With LM as a radius, draw a semicircle and divide it into the same number of equal parts as the number of sides needed for the polygon. Suppose the polygon is to be seven-sided. Draw radial lines through points 2, 3, and so forth. Point 2 (the second division point) is always one of the vertices of the polygon, and line $L2$ is a side. Using point M as a center and LM as a radius, strike an arc across the radial line $L6$ to locate point N. Using the same radius with N as a center, strike another arc across $L5$ to establish O on $L5$. Although this procedure may be continued with point O as the next center, more accurate results will be obtained if point

R is used as a center for the arc to locate Q, and Q as a center for P.

4.21
To Divide the Area of a Triangle or Trapezoid into a Given Number of Equal Parts (Fig. 4.20).

(a) Given the triangle ABC. Divide the side AC into (say, five) equal parts, and draw a semicircle having AC the diameter. Through the division points (1, 2, 3, and 4) draw perpendicular lines to points of intersection with the semicircle (5, 6, 7, and 8). Using C as a center, strike arcs through these points (5, 6, 7, and 8) that will cut AC. To complete the construction, draw lines parallel to AB through the points (9, 10, 11, and 12) at which the arcs intersect the side AC.

(b) Given the trapezoid $DEBA$. Extend the sides of the trapezoid to form the triangle ABC and draw a semicircle on AC with AC as a diameter. Using C as a center and CD as a radius, strike an arc cutting the semicircle at point P. Through P draw a perpendicular to AC to locate point Q. Divide QA into the same number of equal parts as the number of equal areas required (in this case, four), and proceed using the construction explained

CHAP. 4 / ENGINEERING GEOMETRY   57

in (a) for dividing the area of a triangle into a given number of equal parts.

4.22
To Find the Center of a Circle Through Three Given Points Not in a Straight Line (Fig. 4.21). Given the three points A, B, and C. Join the points with straight lines (which will be chords of the required circle), and draw the perpendicular bisectors. The point of intersection O of the bisectors is the center of the required circle, and OA, OB, or OC is its radius.

4.23
Tangent Circles and Arcs. Figure 4.22 illustrates the geometry of tangent circles. In (a) it can be noted that the locus of centers for circles of radius R tangent to AB is a line that is parallel to AB at a distance R from AB. The locus of centers for circles of the same radius tangent to CD is a line that is parallel to CD at distance R (radius) from CD. Since point O at which these lines intersect is distance R from both AB and CD, a circle of radius R with center at O must be tangent to both AB and CD.

In (b) the locus of centers for circles of radius R_3 that will be tangent to the circle with a center at O and having a radius R_1 is a circle that is concentric with the given circle at distance R_3. The radius of the locus of centers will be $R_1 + R_3$. In the case of the circle with center at point P, the radius of the locus of centers will be $R_2 + R_3$. Points Q and Q_1 where these arcs intersect are points that are distance R_3 from both circles. Therefore, circles of radius R_3 that are centered at Q and Q_1 will be tangent to both circles with centers at O and P.

4.24
To Draw a Circular Arc of Radius R Tangent to Two Lines (Fig. 4.23).

(a) Given the two lines AB and CD at right angles to each other, and the radius of the required arc R. Using their point of intersection X as a center and R as a radius, strike an arc cutting the given lines at T_1 and T_2 (tangent points). With T_1 and T_2 as centers and the same radius, strike the intersecting arcs locating the center O of the required arc.

(b),(c) Given the two lines AB and CD, not at right angles, and the radius R. Draw lines EF and GH parallel to the given lines at a distance R. Since the point of intersection of these lines is distance R from both given lines, it will be the center

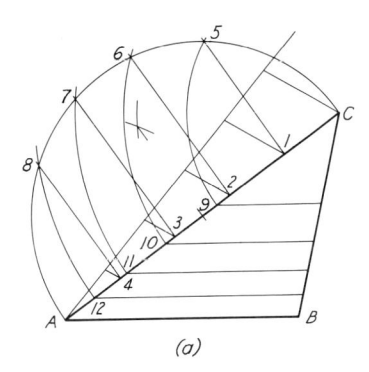

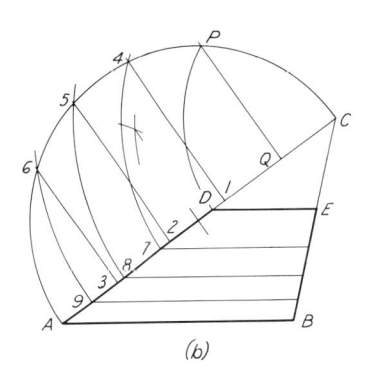

FIG. 4.20. To divide the area of a triangle or trapezoid into a given number of equal parts.

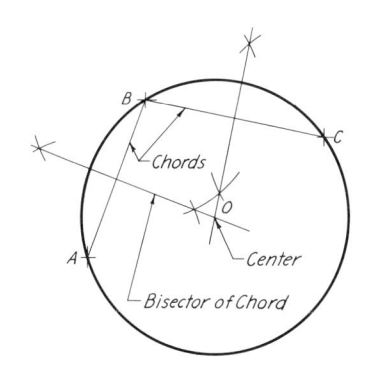

FIG. 4.21. To find the center of a circle through three points.

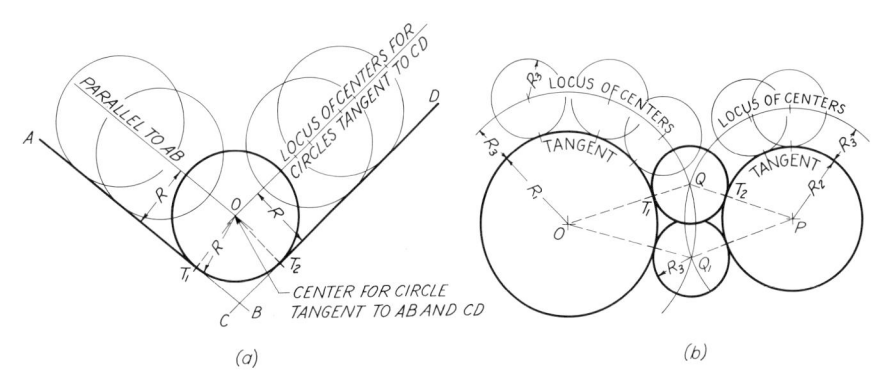

FIG. 4.22. Tangent circles.

O of the required arc. Mark the tangent points T_1 and T_2 that lie along perpendiculars to the given lines through O.

These constructions are useful for drawing fillets and rounds on views of machine parts.

4.25
To Draw a Circular Arc of Radius R_1 Tangent to a Given Circular Arc and a Given Straight Line (Fig. 4.24). Given the line AB and the circular arc with center O.

(a),(b) Draw line CD parallel to AB at a distance R_1. Using the center O of the given arc and a radius equal to its radius plus or minus the radius of the required arc (R_2 plus or minus R_1), swing a parallel arc intersecting CD. Since the line CD and the intersecting arc will be the loci of centers for all circles of radius R_1, tangent respectively to the given line AB and the given arc, their point of intersection P will be the center of the required arc. Mark the points of tangency T_1 and T_2. T_1 lies along a perpendicular to AB through the center P, and T_2 along a line joining the centers of the two arcs.

This construction is also useful for drawing fillets and rounds on views of machine parts.

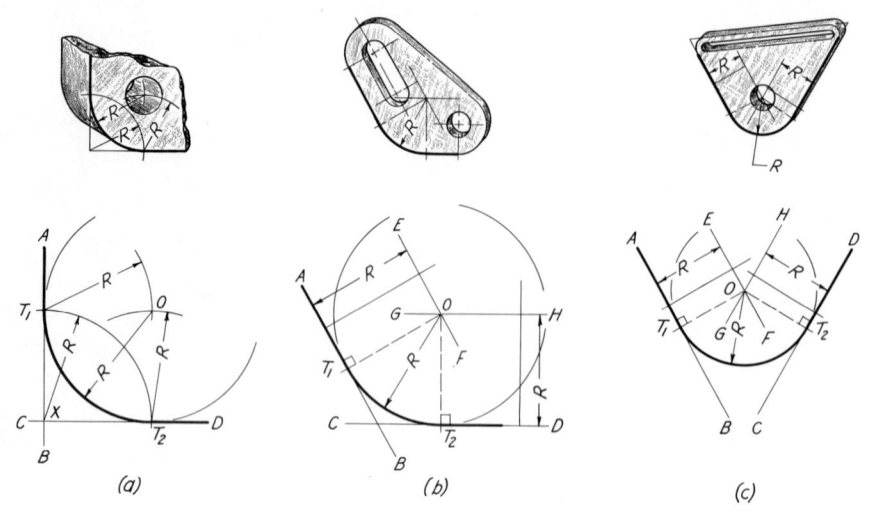

FIG. 4.23. To draw a circular arc tangent to two lines.

4.26
To Draw a Circular Arc of a Given Radius R_1 Tangent to Two Given Circular Arcs (Fig. 4.25). Given the circular arcs AB and CD with centers O and P, and radii R_2 and R_3, respectively.

(a) Using O as a center and R_2 plus R_1 as a radius, strike an arc parallel to AB. Using P as a center and R_3 plus R_1 as a radius, strike an intersecting arc parallel to CD. Since each of these intersecting arcs is the locus of centers for all circular arcs of radius R_1 tangent to the given arc to which it is parallel, their point of intersection S will be the center for the required arc that is tangent to both. Mark the

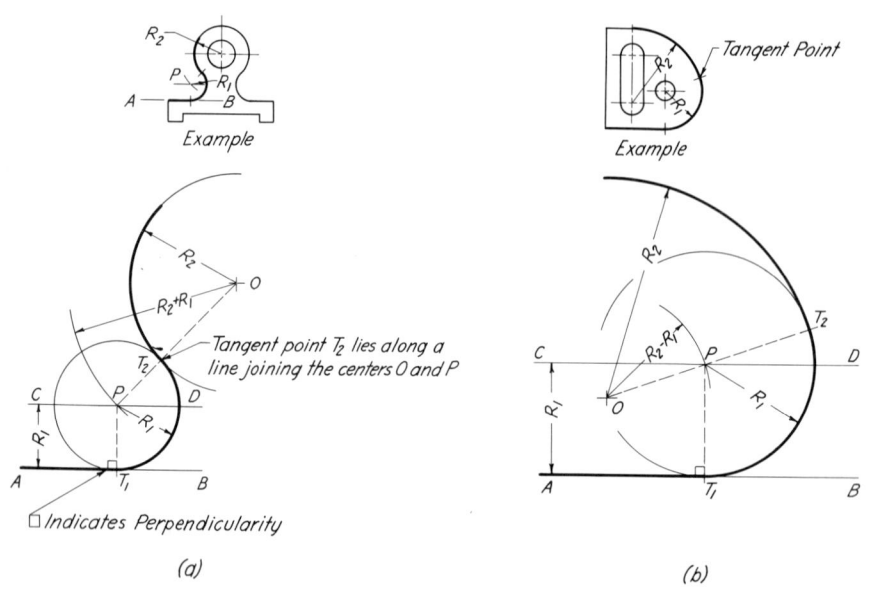

FIG. 4.24. To draw a circular arc tangent to a given circular arc and a line.

points of tangency T_1 and T_2 that lie on the lines of centers PS and OS.

(b) Using O as a center and R_2 plus R_1 as a radius, strike an arc parallel to AB. Using P as a center and R_3 minus R_1 as a radius, strike an intersecting arc parallel to CD. The point of intersection of these arcs is the center for the required arc.

4.27
To Draw a Reverse (Ogee) Curve (Fig. 4.26).

(a) *Reverse (ogee) curve connecting two parallel lines.* Given the two parallel lines AB and CD. At points B and C, the termini and tangent points of the reverse curve, erect perpendiculars. Join B and C with a straight line and assume a point E as the point at which the curves will be tangent to each other. Draw the perpendicular bisectors of BE and EC. Since an arc tangent to AB at B must have its center on the perpendicular BP, the point of intersection P of the bisector and the perpendicular is the center for the required arc that is to be tangent to the line at B and the other required arc at point E. For the same reason, point Q is the center for the other required arc.

This construction is useful to engineers in laying out center lines for railroad tracks, pipe lines, and so forth.

(b) *Reverse (ogee) curve connecting two nonparallel lines.* Given the two nonparallel lines AB and CD. At points B and C, the termini and tangent points, erect perpendiculars. Along the perpendicular at B lay off the given (or selected) radius R and draw the arc having P as its center. Then draw a construction line through point P perpendicular to CD to establish the location of point X. With the position of X known, join points X and C with a straight line along which will lie the chords of the arcs forming the ogee curve between points X and C. The broken line XY (not a part of the construction) has been added to show that the procedure to

be followed in completing the required curve will be as previously explained for drawing a reverse curve joining two parallel lines. In this case the parallel lines are XY and CD, instead of the lines AB and CD as in (a).

An alternate method for establishing the

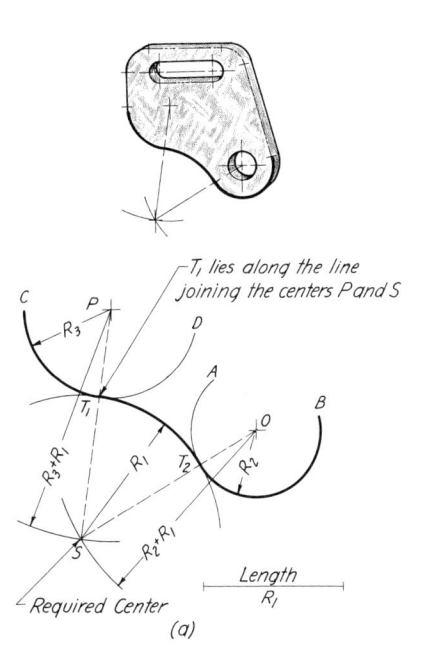

FIG. 4.25. To draw a circular arc tangent to two given arcs.

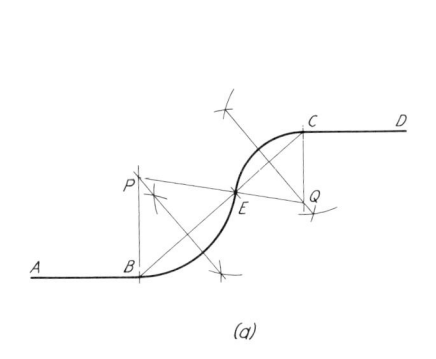

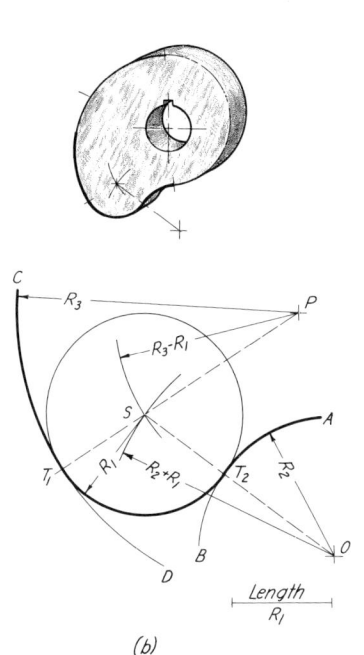

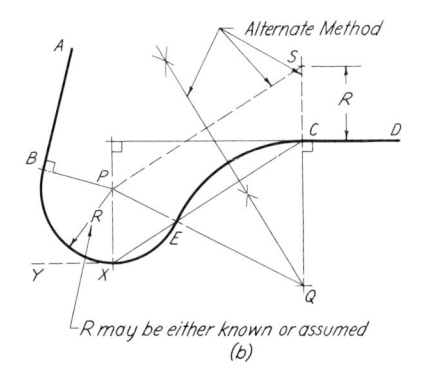

FIG. 4.26. To draw a reverse curve.

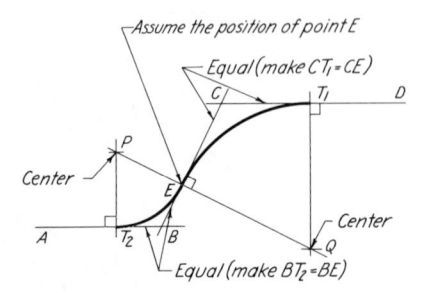

FIG. 4.27. To draw a reverse curve tangent to three lines.

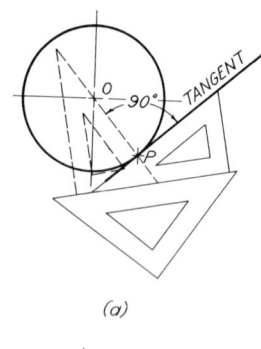

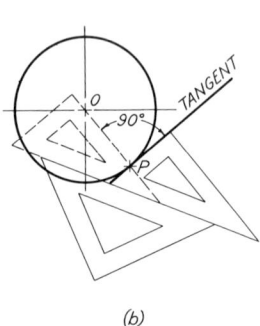

FIG. 4.28. To draw a line tangent to a circle at a point on the circumference.

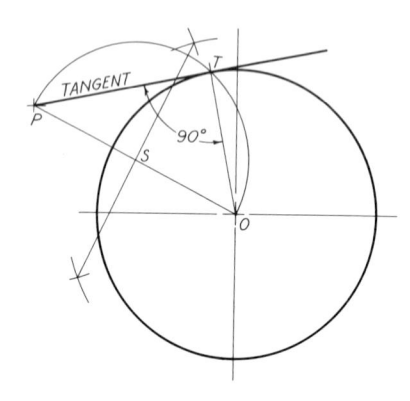

FIG. 4.29. To draw a line tangent to a circle through a given point outside.

needed center for the required arc has been added to the illustration in (b). In this method the radius distance R is laid off upward along a perpendicular to CD through C. With point S established by this measurement, the line PS, as drawn, becomes the chord of an arc (not shown) that will have the same center as the required arc EC. The intersection of the perpendicular bisector of PS with the perpendicular erected downward from C will establish the position of point Q, the center of concentric arcs having chords PS and EC.

4.28
To Draw a Reverse Curve Tangent to Three Given Lines (Fig. 4.27). Given the lines AB and CD that are intersected by a third line BC at points B and C. Assume the position of point E (point of tangency) along BC and locate the termini points T_1 and T_2 by making CT_1 equal to CE and BT_2 equal to BE. The intersections of the perpendiculars erected at points T_1, E, and T_2 establish the centers P and Q of the arcs that form the reversed curve.

4.29
To Draw a Line Tangent to a Circle at a Given Point on the Circumference (Fig. 4.28). Given a circle with center O and point P on its circumference. Place a triangle supported by a T-square or another triangle in such a position that one side passes through the center O and point P. When using the method illustrated in (a), align the hypotenuse of one triangle on the center of the circle and the point of tangency; then, with the guiding triangle held in position, revolve the triangle about the 90° angle and slide into position for drawing the required tangent line.

Another procedure is shown in (b). To draw the tangent by this method, align one leg of a triangle, which is adjacent to the 90° angle, through the center of the circle and the point of tangency; then slide it along the edge of a guiding triangle into position.

This construction satisfies the geometric requirement that a tangent must be perpendicular to a radial line drawn to the point of tangency.

4.30
To Draw a Line Tangent to a Circle Through a Given Point Outside the Circle (Fig. 4.29). Given a circle with center O and an external point P. Join the point P and the center O with a straight line, and bisect it to locate point S. Using S as a center and SO (one-half PO) as a radius, strike an arc intersecting the circle at point T (point of tangency). Line PT is the required tangent.

4.31
To Draw a Tangent Through a Point P on a Circular Arc Having an Inaccessible Center (Fig. 4.30). Draw the chord PB; then erect a perpendicular bisector. With point P as a center swing an arc through point C where the perpendicular bisector cuts the given arc. With C as a center and a radius equal to the chord distance CE, draw an arc to establish the location of point F. A line drawn through points P and F is the required tangent.

4.32
To Draw a Line Tangent to a Circle Through a Given Point Outside the Circle (Fig. 4.31). Place a triangle supported by a T-square or another triangle in such a position that one leg passes through point P tangent to the circle, and draw the tangent. Slide the triangle along the guiding edge until the other leg coincides with the center O, and mark the point of tangency. Although this method is not as accurate as the geometric one explained in Sec. 4.30, it is frequently employed by commercial draftsmen.

4.33
To Draw a Line Tangent to Two Given Circles (Fig. 4.32). Given two circles with centers O and P and radii R_1 and R.

(a) *Open belt.* Using P as a center and a radius equal to R minus R_1, draw an arc. Through O draw a tangent to this arc using the method explained in Sec. 4.30. With the location of tangent point T established, draw line PT and extend it to locate T_1. Draw OT_2 parallel to PT_1. The line from T_2 to T_1 is the required tangent to the given circles.

(b) *Crossed belt.* Using P as a center and a radius equal to R plus R_1, draw an arc. With the location of tangent point T determined through use of the method shown in Fig. 4.29, locate tangent point T_1 on line TP and draw OT_2 parallel to PT. The line T_1T_2, drawn parallel to OT, is the required tangent.

4.34
To Approximate a Curve With Tangent Circular Arcs (Fig. 4.33). Draftsmen often find it desirable to approximate a noncircular curve with a series of tangent arcs. If the curve consists of a number of points, a pleasing curve should be sketched lightly through these points before starting to draw the arcs. The centers and radii are selected by trial, but it must be remembered after the first arc has been drawn (as far as it coincides with the sketched curve) that when arcs are tangent, the centers are on a common normal through their point of tangency. Sometimes draftsmen use this method to draw curves in ink instead of using a French curve.

4.35
To Lay Off the Approximate Length of the Circumference of a Circle (Fig. 4.34). Draw a line through point A tangent to the circle and lay off along it a distance AB equal to three times the diameter $(3D)$. Using point E on the circumference as a center and a radius equal to the

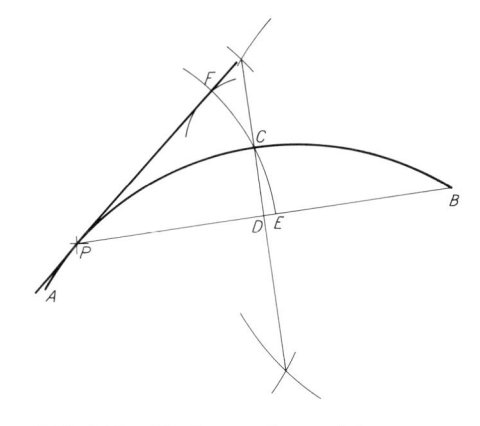

FIG. 4.30. To draw a tangent to a circular arc having an inaccessible center.

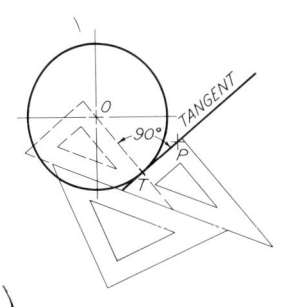

FIG. 4.31. To draw a line tangent to a circle through a given point outside.

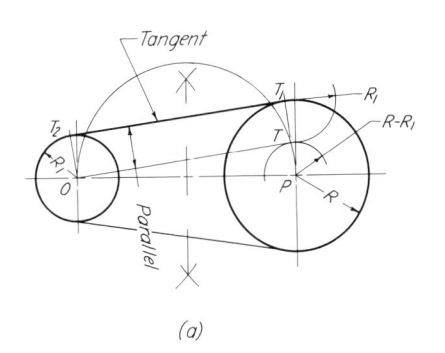

FIG. 4.32. To draw a line tangent to two given circles.

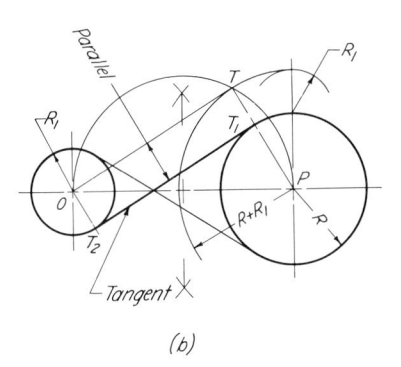

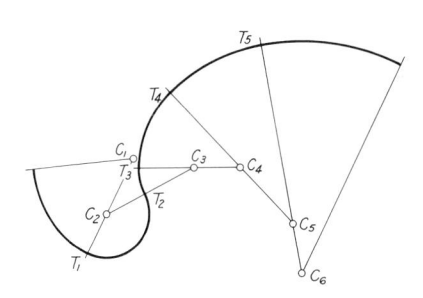

FIG. 4.33. To approximate a curve with tangent circular arcs.

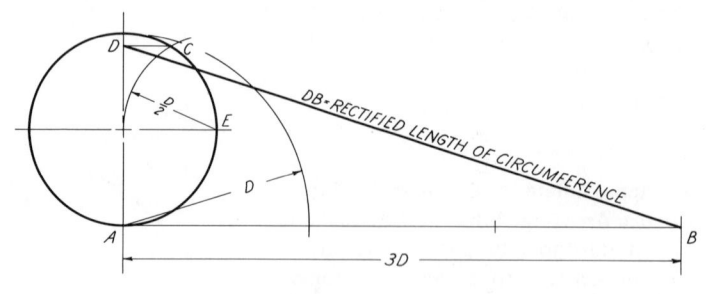

FIG. 4.34. To lay off the approximate length of the circumference of a circle.

radius of the circle strike an arc to establish the location of point C. Draw CD perpendicular to the vertical center line through point A. DB is the rectified length of the circumference; however, it is slightly longer than the true circumference by a negligible amount (approximate error 1/21,800).

4.36
To Lay Off the Approximate Length of a Circular Arc on Its Tangent (Fig. 4.35). Given the arc AB.

(a) Draw the tangent through A, and extend the chord BA. Locate point C by laying off AC equal to one-half the length of the chord AB. With C as a center and a radius equal to CB, strike an arc intersecting the tangent at D. The length AD along the tangent is slightly shorter than the true length of the arc AB by an amount that may be disregarded, for when the angle is less than 60°, the length of AD differs from the true length of the arc AB by less than 6 ft in 1 mile; when 30°, the error is $4\frac{1}{2}$ in. in 1 mile.

(b) Draw the tangent through A. Using the dividers, start at B and step off equal chord distances around the arc until the point nearest A is reached. From this point (without raising the dividers) step off along the tangent an equal number of distances to locate point C. If the point nearest A is indented into the tangent instead of the arc, the almost negligible error in the length of AC will be still less.

Since the small distances stepped off are in reality the chords of small arcs, the length AC will be slightly less than the true length of the arc. For most practical purposes the difference may be disregarded.

When the central angle (θ) and the radius of an arc are known, the length of the arc may be computed by the formula $L = 2\pi R(\theta/360°) = 0.01745R\theta$.

4.37
To Lay Off a Specified Length Along a Given Circle Arc (Fig. 4.36). On the tangent to the arc, lay off the distance DE representing the specified length of arc. Divide DE into four equal parts. Then, using point 1 as a center and with the length 1–E as the radius R, strike an arc intersecting the given arc at F. The arc DF is approximately equal in length to the line DE. For large angles, it is advisable to make the construction for one-half of DE.

4.38
Conic Sections (Fig. 4.37). When a right circular cone of revolution is cut by planes at different angles, four curves of intersection are obtained that are called *conic sections*.

When the intersecting plane is perpen-

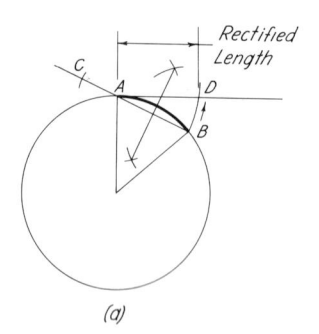

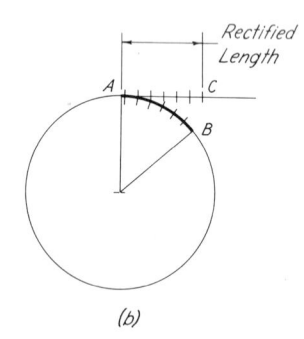

FIG. 4.35. To lay off the approximate length of a circular arc on its tangent.

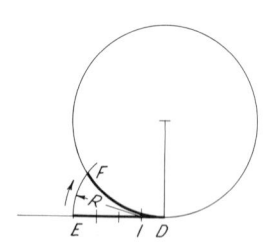

FIG. 4.36. To lay off a specified length along an arc.

dicular to the axis, the resulting curve of intersection is a *circle*.

If the plane makes a greater angle with the axis than do the elements, the intersection is an *ellipse*.

If the plane makes the same angle with the axis as the elements, the resulting curve is a *parabola*.

Finally, if the plane makes a smaller angle with the axis than do the elements or is parallel to the axis, the curve of intersection is a *hyperbola*.

The geometric methods for constructing the ellipse, parabola, and hyperbola are discussed in succeeding sections.

4.39
The Ellipse (Fig. 4.37). Mathematically the ellipse is a curve generated by a point moving so that at any position the sum of its distances from two fixed points (foci) is a constant (equal to the major diameter). It is encountered very frequently in orthographic drawing when holes and circular forms are viewed obliquely. Ordinarily, the major and minor diameters are known.

4.40
To Construct an Ellipse, Foci Method (Fig. 4.38). Draw the major and minor axes (AB, CD) and locate the foci F_1 and F_2 by striking arcs, centered at C and having a radius equal to OA (one-half of the major diameter). The construction is as follows: Determine the number of points needed along the circumference of each quadrant of the ellipse for a relatively accurate layout (say, four) and mark off this number of division points (P, Q, R, and S) between O and F_1 on the major axis. In many cases it may be desirable to use additional points spaced closer together nearer F_1 in order to form accurately the sharp curvature at the end of the ellipse. Next, with F_1 and F_2 as centers and the distances AP and BP as radii, respectively, strike intersecting arcs to locate P' on the circumference of the ellipse. Distances AQ amd BQ are radii for locating points Q'. Locate points R' and S' in a similar manner and complete the ellipse using a French curve.

This method is sometimes known as the definition method, since it is based on the mathematical definition of the ellipse as given in Sec. 4.39.

4.41
To Construct an Ellipse, Trammel Method (Fig. 4.39). Given the major axis AB and the minor axis CD. Along the straight edge of a strip of paper or cardboard, locate the points O, C, and A, so that the distance OA is equal to one-half the length of the major axis, and the distance OC is equal to one-half the length of the minor axis. Place the marked edge across the axes so that point A is on the minor axis and point C is on the major axis. *Point O will fall on the circumference of the ellipse.* Move the strip, keeping A on the minor axis and C on the major axis, and mark at least five other positions of O on the ellipse in each quadrant. Using a French curve, complete the ellipse by drawing a smooth curve through the points. The ellipsograph, which draws ellipses mechanically, is based on this same principle. The trammel method is an accurate method.

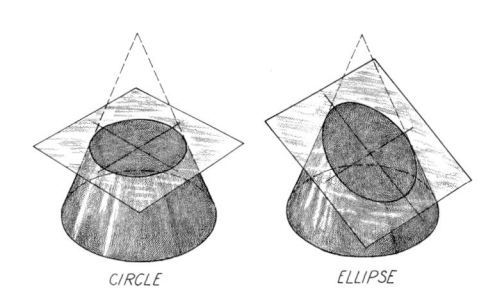

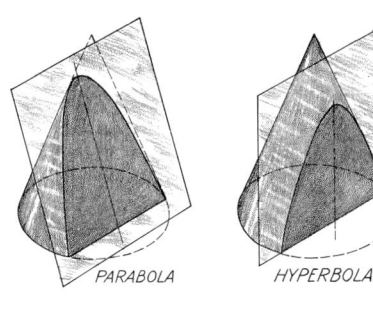

FIG. 4.37. Conic sections.

FIG. 4.38. To construct an ellipse, foci (definition) method.

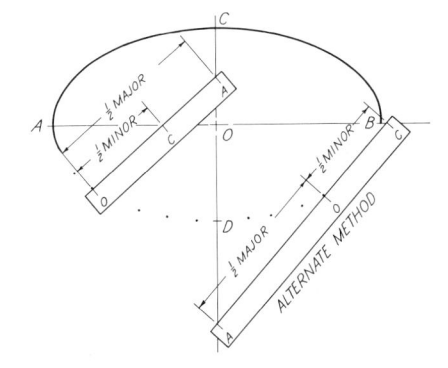

FIG. 4.39. To construct an ellipse, trammel method.

An alternate method for marking off the location of points A, O, and C is given in Fig. 4.39.

4.42
To Construct an Ellipse, Concentric Circle Method (Fig. 4.40). Given the major axis AB and the minor axis CD. Using the center of the ellipse (point O) as a center, describe circles having the major and minor axes as diameters. Divide the circles into equal central angles and draw diametrical lines such as P_1P_2. From point P_1 on the circumference of the larger circle, draw a line parallel to CD, the minor axis, and from point P_1' at which the diameter P_1P_2 intersects the inner circle, draw a line parallel to AB, the major axis. The point of intersection of these lines, point E, is on the required ellipse. At points P_2 and P_2' repeat the same procedure and locate point F. Thus, two points are established by the line P_1P_2. Locate at least five points in each of the four quadrants. The ellipse is completed by drawing a smooth curve through the points.

This is one of the most accurate methods used to form ellipses.

4.43
To Construct an Ellipse, Four-Center Method (Fig. 4.41). Given the major axis AB and the minor axis CD. Draw the line AC. Using the center of the ellipse O as a center and OC as a radius, strike an arc intersecting OA at point E. Using C as a center and EA as a radius, strike an arc intersecting the line AC at F. Draw the perpendicular bisector of the line AF. The points G and H, at which the perpendicular bisector intersects the axes AB and CD (extended), are the centers of two of the arcs forming the ellipse. Locate the other two centers, J and K, by laying off OJ equal to OH and OK equal to OG. To determine the junction points (tangent points), T, T_1, T_2, and T_3, for the arcs, draw lines through the centers of the tangent arcs. The figure thus formed by the four circle arcs approximates a true ellipse. When an accurate ellipse is required, this method should not be used.

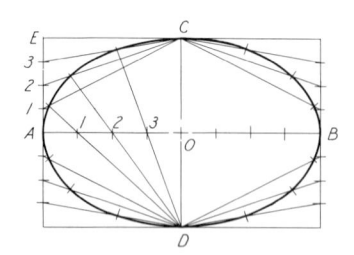

4.44
To Construct an Ellipse, Parallelogram Method (Fig. 4.42). Given the major axis AB and the minor axis CD. Construct the circumscribing parallelogram. Divide AO and AE into the same number of equal parts (say, four) and number the division points from A. From C draw a line through point 3 on line AE, and from D draw a line through point 3 on line AO. The point of intersection of these lines is on the required ellipse. Similarly, the intersections of lines from C and D through points numbered 1 and 2 are on the ellipse. A similar construction will locate points in the other three quadrants of the ellipse. Use of a French curve will permit a smooth curve to be drawn through the points.

Had the circumscribing parallelogram not been a rectangle as in Fig. 4.42, the completed construction would appear as in Fig. 4.43, and AB and CD would be conjugate axes. To establish the major and minor axes, draw a semicircle on CD as a diameter, intersecting the ellipse at E. FG, running parallel to CE through the center of the ellipse, will be the required minor axis. HK, running through

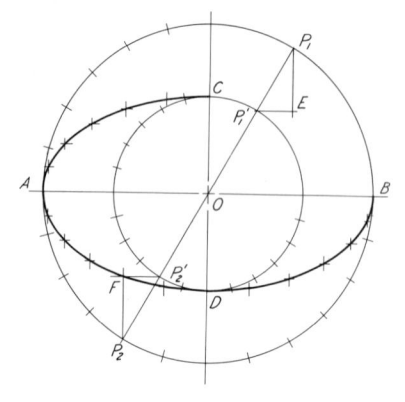

FIG. 4.40. To construct an ellipse, concentric circle method.

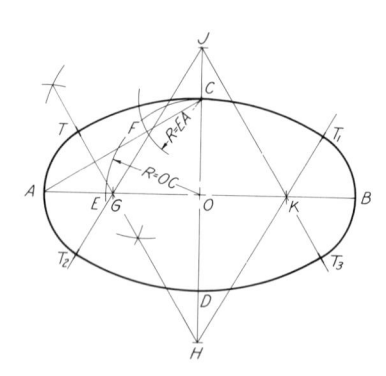

FIG. 4.41. To construct an ellipse, center method.

FIG. 4.42. To construct an ellipse, parallelogram method.

the center of the ellipse parallel to *DE* and perpendicular to *FG*, will be the major axis.

4.45
To Draw a Tangent to an Ellipse at Any Given Point (Fig. 4.44). Given any point, such as *P*, on the perimeter of the ellipse *ABCD*. Using *C* as a center and a radius equal to *OA* (one-half the major diameter), strike arcs across the major axis at F_1 and F_2. From these points, which are foci of the ellipse, draw F_1P and F_2G. The bisector of the angle GPF_1 is the required tangent to the ellipse.

4.46
To Draw a Tangent to an Ellipse From a Given Point P Outside the Ellipse (Fig. 4.45). With the end of the minor axis as a center and a radius *R* equal to one-half the length of the major axis, strike an arc to find the foci F_1 and F_2. With point *P* as a center and the distance PF_2 as a radius, draw an arc. Using F_1 as a center and the length *AB* as a radius, strike arcs cutting the arc with center *P* at points *G* and *H*. Draw lines GF_1 and HF_1 to establish the location of the tangent points T_1 and T_2. Draw the required tangent.

4.47
The Parabola (Fig. 4.37). Mathematically the parabola is a curve generated by a point moving so that at any position its distance from a fixed point (the focus) is always exactly equal to its distance to a fixed line (the directrix). The construction shown in Fig. 4.46 is based on this definition.

In engineering design, the parabola is used for parabolic sound and light reflectors, for vertical curves on highways, and for bridge arches.

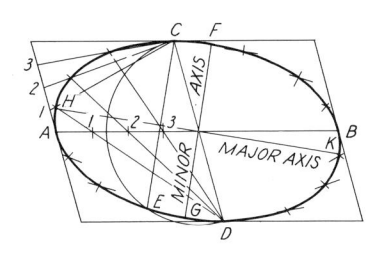

FIG. 4.43. To draw the major and minor axes of an ellipse, given the conjugate diameters.

4.48
To Construct a Parabola (Fig. 4.46). Given the focus *F* and the directrix *AB*. Draw the axis of the parabola perpendicular to the directrix. Through any point on the axis, for example, point *C*, draw a line parallel to the directrix *AB*. Using *F* as a center and the distance *OC* as a radius, strike arcs intersecting the line at points P_4 and P_4'. Repeat this procedure until a sufficient number of additional points have been located to determine a smooth curve. The vertex *V* is located at a point midway between *O* and *F*.

To construct a tangent to a parabola, say, at point P_6, draw the line P_6D parallel to the axis; then bisect the angle DP_6F. The bisector of the angle is the required tangent.

4.49
To Construct a Parabola, Tangent Method (Fig. 4.47). Given the points *A* and *B* and the distance *CD* from *AB* to the vertex. Extend the axis *CD*, and set off *DE* equal to *CD*. *EA* and *EB* are tangents to the parabola at *A* and *B*, respectively.

Divide *EA* and *EB* into the same number of equal parts (say, six), and number the division points as shown. Connect the corresponding points 1 and 1, 2 and 2, 3 and 3, and so forth. These lines, as tangents of the required parabola, form its envelope. Draw the tangent curve.

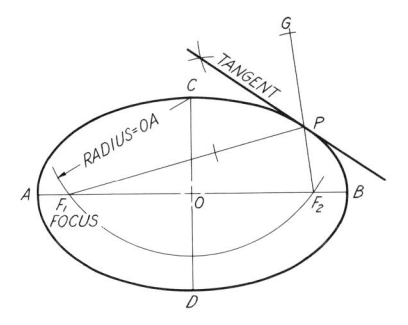

FIG. 4.44. To draw a tangent to an ellipse.

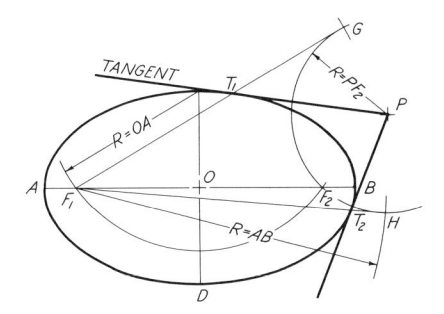

FIG. 4.45. To draw a tangent to an ellipse through a point outside the ellipse.

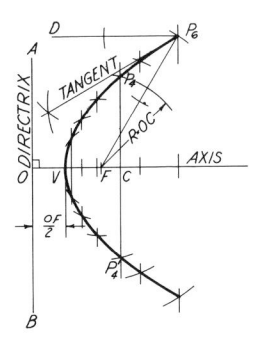

FIG. 4.46. To construct a parabola.

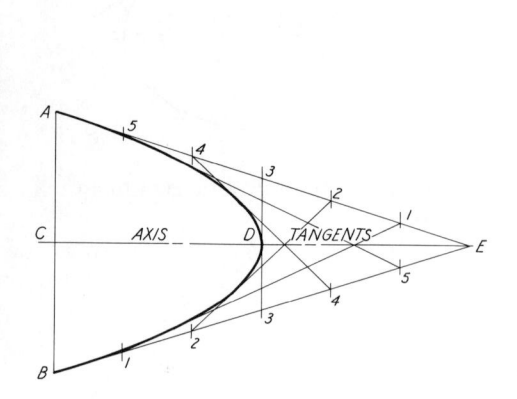

FIG. 4.47. To construct a parabola, tangent method.

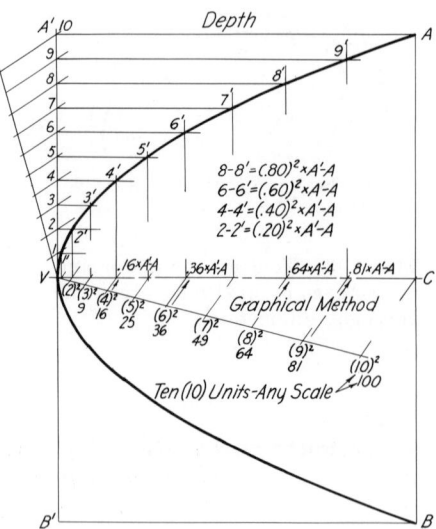

FIG. 4.48. To construct a parabola, offset method.

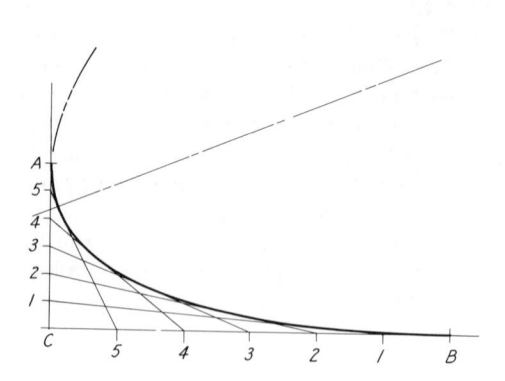

FIG. 4.49. To construct a curve of parabolic form.

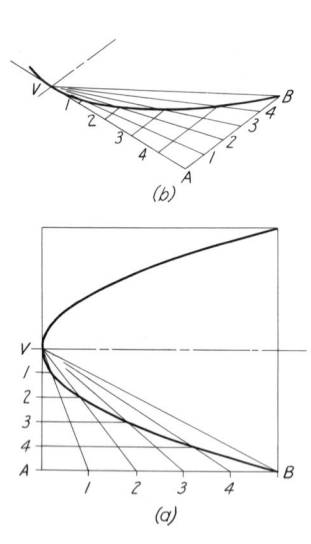

FIG. 4.50. To construct a parabola, parallelogram method.

4.50
To Construct a Parabola, Offset Method (Fig. 4.48). Given the enclosing rectangle $A'ABB'$. Divide VA' into any number of equal parts (say, ten) and draw from the division points the perpendiculars parallel to VC, along which offset distances are to be laid off. The offsets vary as the square of their distances from V. For example, since V to 2 is two-tenths of the distance from V to A', 2-2' will be $(.2)^2$ or .04 of $A'A$. Similarly, 6-6' will be $(.6)^2$ or .36 of $A'A$; and 8-8' will be .64 of $A'A$. To complete the parabola, lay off the computed offset values along the perpendiculars and form the figure with a French curve.

The entire construction can be done graphically (as illustrated) by first calculating the values for the squared distances and then dividing the depth distance (along the axis) proportionally using these values. The graphical method shown in Fig. 4.7 was used.

The offset method is preferred by civil engineers for laying out parabolic arches and computing vertical curves for highways. The parabola shown in Fig. 4.48 could represent a parabolic reflector.

4.51
To Construct a Curve of Parabolic Form Through Two Given Points (Fig. 4.49). Given the points A and B. Assume a point C. Draw the tangents CA and CB, and construct the parabolic curve using the tangent method shown in Fig. 4.47. This method is frequently used in machine design to draw curves that are more pleasing than circular arcs.

4.52
To Construct a Parabola, Parallelogram Method. Since the dimensions for a parallelogram that will enclose a given parabola are generally known, a parabola may be constructed by the parallelogram method illustrated in Fig. 4.50. With the enclosing rectangle drawn to the given width and depth dimensions, divide VA and AB into the same number of equal divisions (say, five) and number the divi-

sion points as shown in (a). Draw light construction lines from point V to each of the division points along AB. Then draw lines parallel to the axis from points 1, 2, 3, and 4 on VA. The intersection of the construction lines from points numbered 1 is on the parabola.

Likewise, the intersection of the lines from points numbered 2 is on the parabola. The complete parabolic outline passes through the additional points at the intersection of the lines from points numbered 3 and the lines from points numbered 4. The method as explained for a parabola enclosed in a rectangle may be applied to a nonrectangular shape, as shown in (b).

4.53
To Locate the Directrix and Focus of a Given Parabolic Curve (Fig. 4.51). With the location of the axis known [see (a)] draw the tangent PY by locating point Y on the axis extended at a distance D_1 from the vertex V. Draw PX parallel to the axis and construct angle FPY equal to YPX. The point at which the line forming the newly constructed angle cuts the given axis is the focus F. The directrix through O is perpendicular to the axis at the same distance from the vertex V as the focus F.

When the position of the axis is not known the procedure illustrated in (b) will establish the location of the axis, focus, and directrix. As the initial step, draw two parallel chords at random and locate the midpoint of each, points R and S. Draw line RS to establish the direction of the axis that will be parallel to RS. Next, draw a chord perpendicular to RS at any location and through the midpoint M draw the axis of the parabola as required. The position of the vertex is now known and one might follow the procedure given in (a) to locate the focus and directrix. However, the position of the directrix may be found easily and quickly merely by drawing a tangent to the parabola at 45° with the axis. The directrix passes through O at the intersection of the tangent and the axis extended.

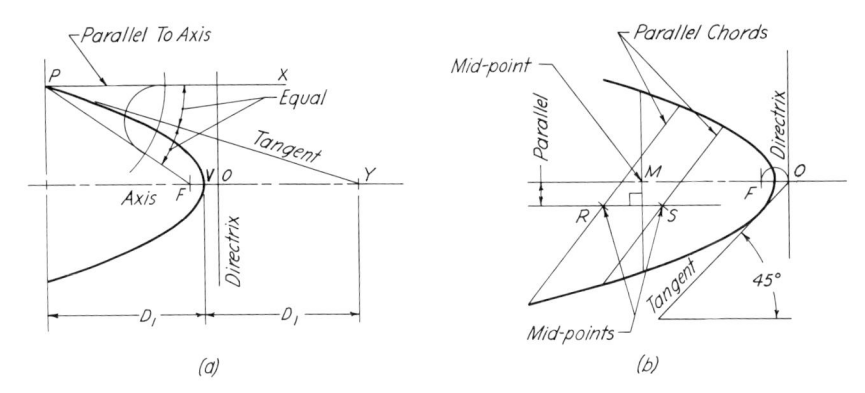

FIG. 4.51. To locate the directrix and focus of a given parabolic curve.

4.54
The Hyperbola (Fig. 4.37). Mathematically the hyperbola can be described as a curve generated by a point moving so that at any position the difference of its distances from two fixed points (foci) is a constant (equal to the transverse axis of the hyperbola). This definition is the basis for the construction shown in Fig. 4.52.

4.55
To Construct a Hyperbola (Fig. 4.52). Given the foci F_1 and F_2, and the transverse axis AB. Using F_1 and F_2 as centers, and any radius R_1 greater than F_1B, strike arcs. With these same centers and a radius equal to R_1-AB, strike arcs intersecting the first arcs. These intersecting arcs establish the positions of four symmetrically located points (P_1, P_2, P_3, and P_4) using a single pair of radii. Additional sets of four points are obtained by assuming a different initial radius each time. Repeat this procedure, as outlined, until a sufficient number of points have been located to determine a smooth curve.

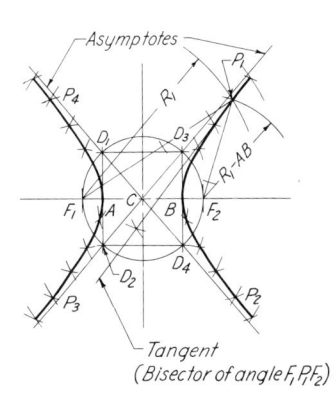

FIG. 4.52. To construct a hyperbola.

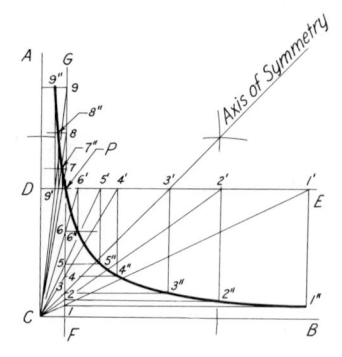

FIG. 4.53. To construct an equilateral hyperbola.

(a)

(b)

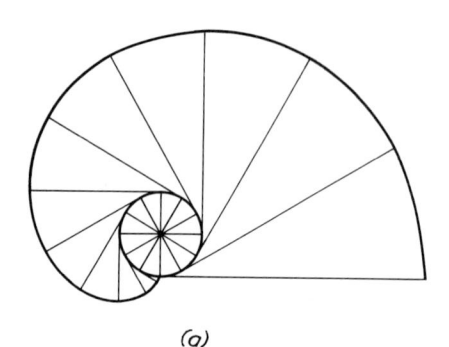

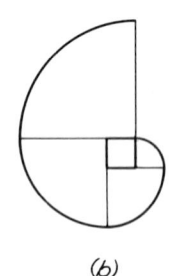

FIG. 4.54. The involute.

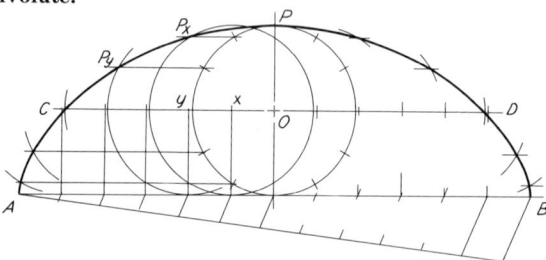

FIG. 4.55 A cycloid.

The tangent to the hyperbola at any point, such as P_1, is the bisector of the angle between the focal radii F_1P_1 and F_2P_1.

As hyperbolic curves extend towards infinity they gradually approach two straight lines known as *asymptotes*. These may be located by drawing a circle having the distance F_1-F_2 as a diameter and erecting perpendiculars to the transverse axis through points A and B. The points at which these perpendicular lines intersect the circle are points (D_1, D_2, D_3, and D_4) on the asymptotes.

4.56
To Construct an Equilateral, or Rectangular, Hyperbola Through a Given Point P—Asymptotic to Given Axes (Fig. 4.53). Given the asymptotes CA and CB and any point P on the curve. Bisect the angle ACB to establish the position of the axis of symmetry of the hyperbola. Then, through point P draw the lines PD and PF perpendicular to CA and CB, respectively. Along PF extended, mark off points 1, 2, 3, 4, and so forth, as needed. Through these points draw rays converging at C and intersecting DE (DP extended) at points 1', 2', 3', 4', 5', and so forth. From each of the numbered points along DE draw perpendiculars to DP and through the numbered points along FG draw perpendiculars to PF. The intersections of corresponding lines (perpendiculars) establish the location of the points 1″, 2″, 3″, 4″, and so forth along the required curve.

4.57
An Involute. The spiral curve traced by a point on a chord as it unwinds from around a circle or a polygon is an *involute curve*. Figure 4.54 (*a*) shows an involute of a circle, while (*b*) shows that of a square. The involute of a polygon is obtained by extending the sides and drawing arcs using the corners, in order, as centers. The circle in (*a*) may be considered to be a polygon having an infinite number of sides.

4.58
To Draw an Involute of a Circle [Fig. 4.54(a)]. Divide the circumference into a number of equal parts. Draw tangents through the division points. Then, along each tangent, lay off the rectified length of the corresponding circular arc, from the starting point to the point of tangency. The involute curve is a smooth curve through these points. The involute of a circle is used in the development of tooth profiles in gearing.

4.59
To Draw the Involute of a Polygon [Fig. 4.54(b)]. Extend the sides of the polygon as shown in (*b*). With the corners as centers, in order around the polygon, draw arcs terminating on the extended sides. The first radius is equal to the length of one side of the polygon. The radius of each successive arc is the distance from the center to the terminating point of the previous arc.

4.60
A Cycloid. A cycloid is the curve generated by a point on the circumference of a moving circle when the circle rolls in a plane along a straight line, as shown in Fig. 4.55.

4.61
To Draw a Cycloid (Fig. 4.55). Draw the generating circle and the line AB tangent

to it. The length AB should be made equal to the circumference of the circle. Divide the circle and the line AB into the same number of equal parts. With this much of the construction completed, the next step is to draw the line of centers CD through point O and project the division points along AB to CD by drawing perpendiculars. Using these points as centers for the various positions of the moving circle, draw circle arcs. For the purpose of illustration, assume the circle is moving to the left. When the circle has moved along CD to x, point P will have moved to point P_x. Similarly, when the center is at y, P will be at P_y. To locate positions of P along the cycloidal curve, project the division points of the divided circle in their proper order, across to the position circles. A smooth curve through these points will be the required cycloid.

4.62
An Epicycloid (Fig. 4.56). An epicycloid is the curve generated by a point on the circumference of a circle that rolls in a plane on the outside of another circle. The method used in drawing an epicycloid is similar to the one used in drawing the cycloid.

4.63
A Hypocycloid (Fig. 4.57). A hypocycloid is the curve generated by a point on the circumference of a circle that rolls in a plane on the inside of another circle. The method used to draw a hypocycloid is similar to the method used to draw the cycloid.

Additional information on the use of cycloidal curves to form the outlines of cycloidal gear teeth may be found in the chapter on gears (Chapter 20).

4.64
Spiral of Archimedes. Archimedes' spiral is a plane curve generated by a point moving uniformly around and away from a fixed point. In order to define this curve more specifically, it can be said that it is generated by a point moving uniformly along a straight line while the line revolves with uniform angular velocity about a fixed point.

The definition of the spiral of Archimedes is applied in drawing this curve as illustrated in Fig. 4.58. To find a sufficient number of points to allow the use of an irregular curve for drawing the spiral it is the practice to divide the given circle into a number of equal parts (say, 12) and draw radical lines to the division points. Next, divide a radial line into the same number of equal parts as the circle and number the division points on the circumference of the circle beginning with the radial line adjacent to the divided one. With the center of the circle as a center draw concentric arcs that in each case will start at a numbered division point on the divided radial line and will end at an intersection with the radial line that is numbered correspondingly. The arc starting at point 1 gives a point on the curve at its intersection with radial line 1, the arc starting at 2 gives an intersection point on radial line 2, etc. The spiral is a smooth curve drawn through these intersection points.

4.65
The Helix (Fig. 4.59). The cylindrical helix is a space curve that is generated by a point moving uniformly on the surface of a cylinder. The point must travel parallel to the axis with uniform linear velocity while at the same time it is moving with uniform angular velocity around the axis. The curve can be thought of as being generated by a point moving uniformly along a straight line while the line is revolving with uniform angular velocity around the axis of the given cylinder. Study the pictorial drawing, Fig. 4.59.

The first step in drawing a cylindrical helix is to lay out the two views of the

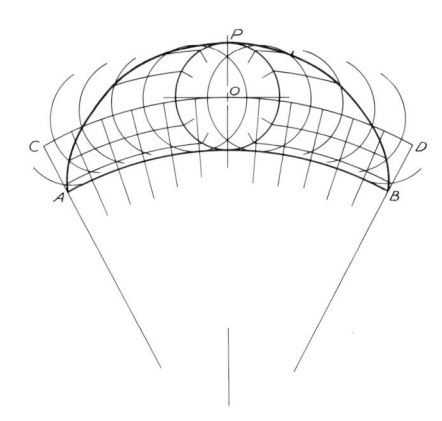

FIG. 4.56 An epicycloid.

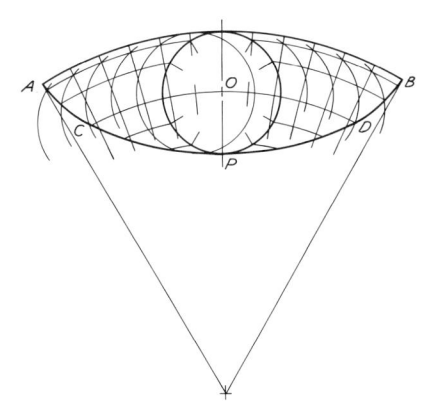

FIG. 4.57. A hypocycloid

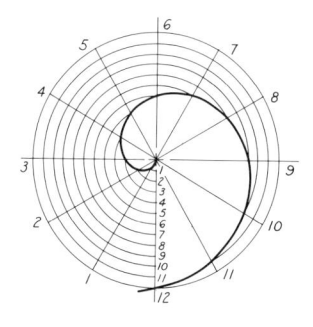

FIG. 4.58. Spiral of Archimedes.

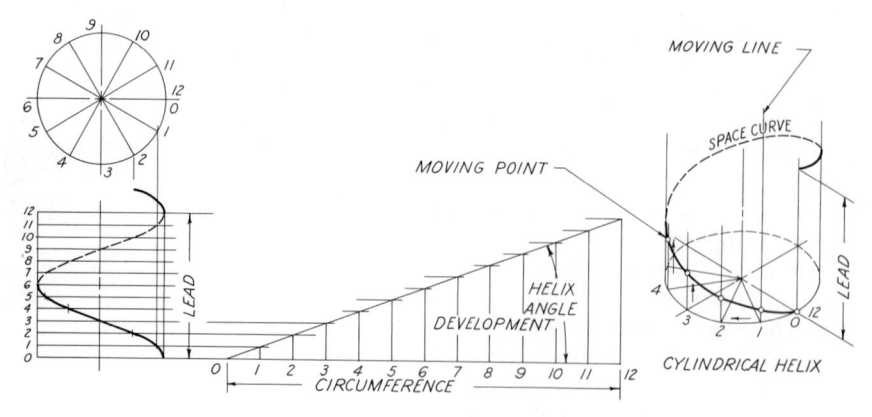

FIG. 4.59. The helix.

cylinder. Next, the lead should be measured along a contour element and divided into a number of equal parts (say, 12). Divide the circular view of the cylinder into the same number of parts and number the division points.

The division lines of the lead represent the various positions of the moving point as it travels in a direction parallel to the axis of the cylinder along the moving line. The division points on the circular view are the related position of the moving line. For example, when the line has moved from the 0 to the 1 position, the point has traveled along the line a distance equal to one twelfth of the lead; when the line is in the 2 position, the point has traveled one-sixth of the lead. (See pictorial drawing, Fig. 4.59.) In constructing the curve the necessary points are found by projecting from a numbered point on the circular view to the division line of the lead that is numbered similarly.

A helix may be either right-hand or left-hand. The one shown in Fig. 4.59 is a left-hand helix.

When the cylinder is developed, the helix becomes a straight line on the development, as shown. It is inclined to the base line at an angle known as the "helix angle." A screw thread is an example of a practical application of the cylindrical helix.

PROBLEMS

The following exercises not only require the student to study and use certain common geometric constructions but also furnish additional practice in applying good line technique to the drawing of instrumental figures and practical designs. All work should be very accurately done. Tangent points should be indicated by a light, short dash across the line.

1. Draw a line $3\frac{1}{8}$ in. long. Divide it proportionally in the ratio 1:2:3. Use the method shown in Fig. 4.7.

2. Construct a regular hexagon having a $2\frac{1}{2}$-in. distance across flats. Select the most practical procedure.

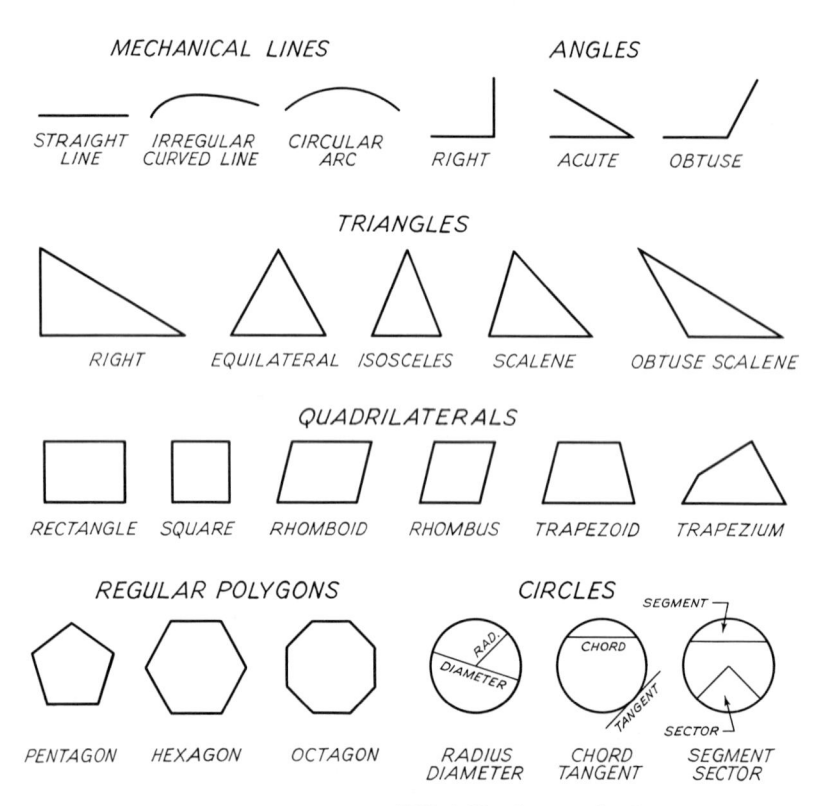

FIG. 4.60. Geometric shapes.

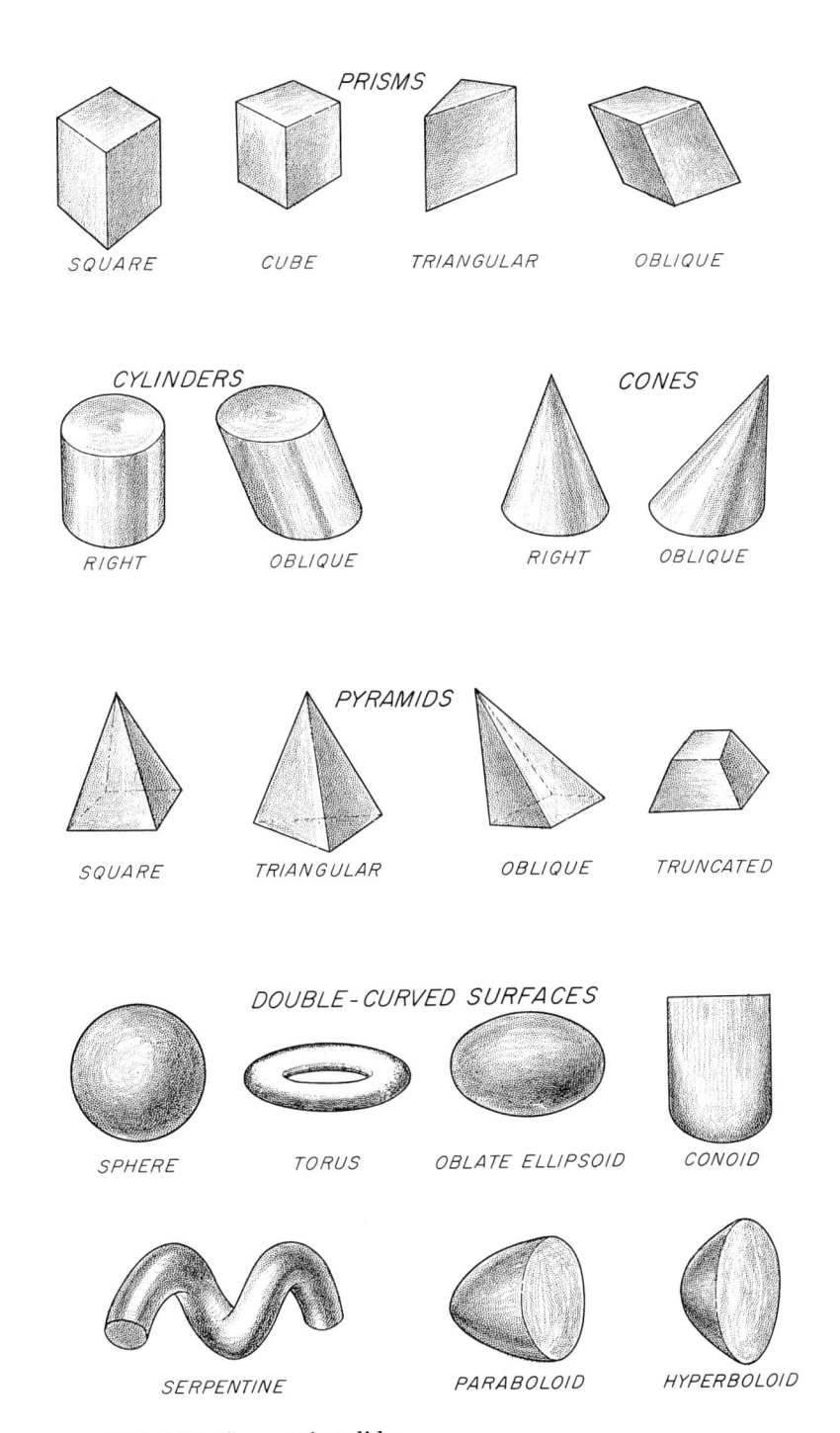

FIG. 4.61. Geometric solids.

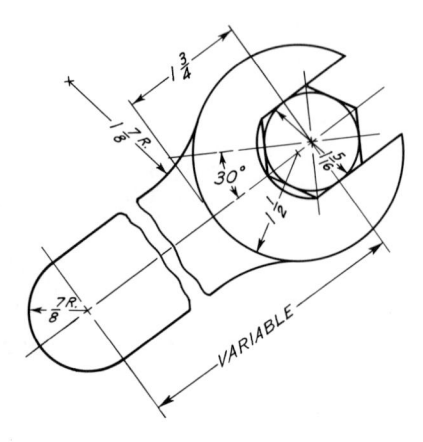

FIG. 4.62. Wrench.

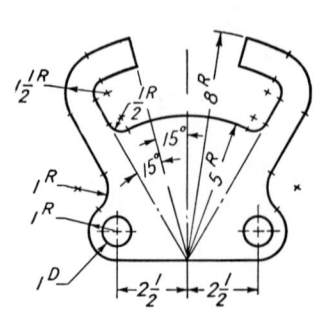

FIG. 4.63. Slotted guide.

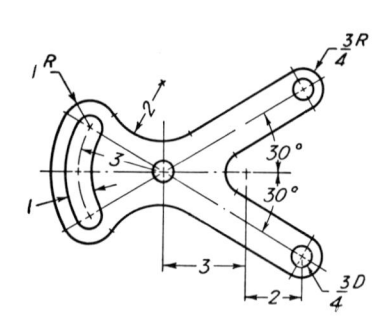

FIG. 4.64. Adjustable Y-clamp.

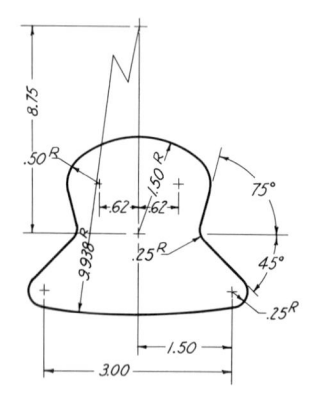

FIG. 4.65. End view-dolly block.

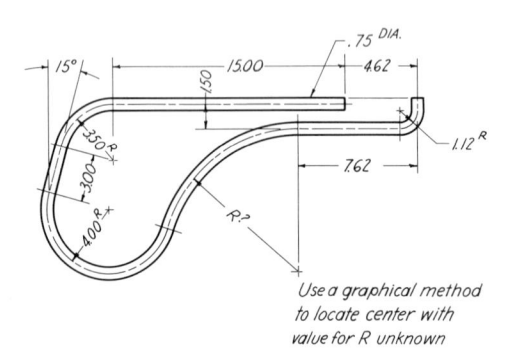

FIG. 4.66. Electrode.

the concentric circle method illustrated in Fig. 4.40. Find a sufficient number of points to obtain a smooth curve.

8. Construct a parabola with vertical axis. Make the focus 3/4 in. from the directrix. Select a point on the curve and draw a line tangent to the parabola. Study Sec. 4.48 and Fig. 4.46.

9. Construct a hyperbola having a transverse axis of 1 in. and foci 1 5/8 in. apart. Study Sec. 4.55 and Fig. 4.52.

10. Construct the involute of an equilateral triangle with 1-in. sides. Study Secs. 4.57 and 4.59.

11. Construct the cycloid generated by a 1 1/2-in. circle. Study Sec. 4.61 and Fig. 4.55.

12. Construct the epicycloid generated by a 1 1/2-in. circle rolling on a 5-in. circle. Study Sec. 4.62 and Fig. 4.56.

13. Construct the hypocycloid generated by a 1 1/2-in. circle rolling on a 4 1/2-in. circle. Study Sec. 4.63 and Fig. 4.57.

14. Reconstruct the view of the wrench and hexagonal nut shown in Fig. 4.62. Mark all tangent points with short lines.

15. Construct the shape of the slotted guide shown in Fig. 4.63. Show all construction for locating centers, and mark points of tangency.

16. Construct the adjustable Y-clamp shown in Fig. 4.64. Show all construction for locating centers and mark points of tangency.

17. Reconstruct the end view of the dolly block shown in Fig. 4.65.

18. Reconstruct the view of the electrode shown in Fig. 4.66.

19. Reconstruct the plat of a land survey shown in Fig. 4.67. Use the tangent method, as explained in Sec. 4.11, to determine the direction of the center line of State Road 26. The triangles used in combination will produce the other angles.

20. Reconstruct the view of the spline plate shown in Fig. 4.68.

21. Reconstruct the view of the adjustment plate shown in Fig. 4.69.

3. Construct a regular hexagon having a 3 1/4-in. distance across corners. Select the most practical method.

4. Construct a regular pentagon having 1 1/4-in. sides. Use the method illustrated in Fig. 4.19.

5. Draw two horizontal lines 2 in. apart. Locate two points 3 in. apart horizontally, one on each line. Draw an ogee curve tangent to these lines. Study the procedure illustrated in Fig. 4.26(a).

6. Construct an ellipse having a major diameter of 4 1/4 in. and a minor diameter of 2 3/4 in. Use the trammel method illustrated in Fig. 4.39.

7. Construct an ellipse having a major diameter of 4 in. and a minor diameter of 2 3/4 in. Use

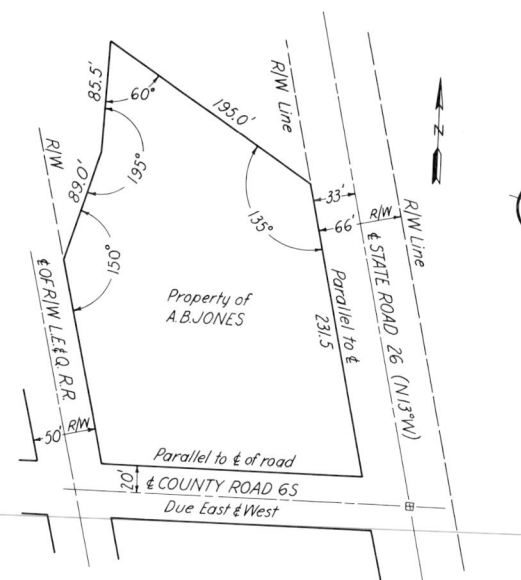

CHAP. 4 / ENGINEERING GEOMETRY   73

FIG. 4.67. A plate of a land survey.

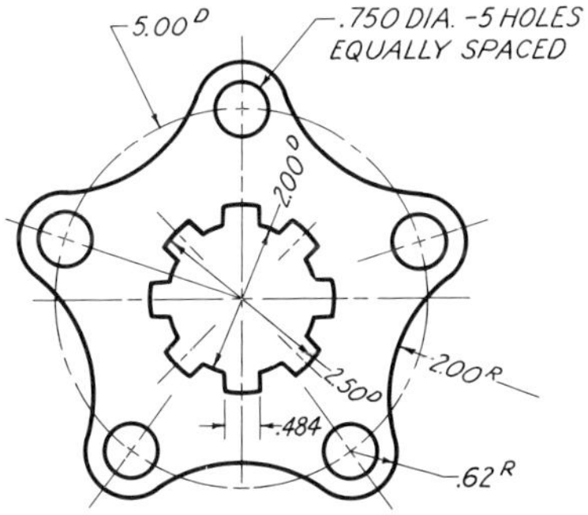

FIG. 4.68. Spline plate.

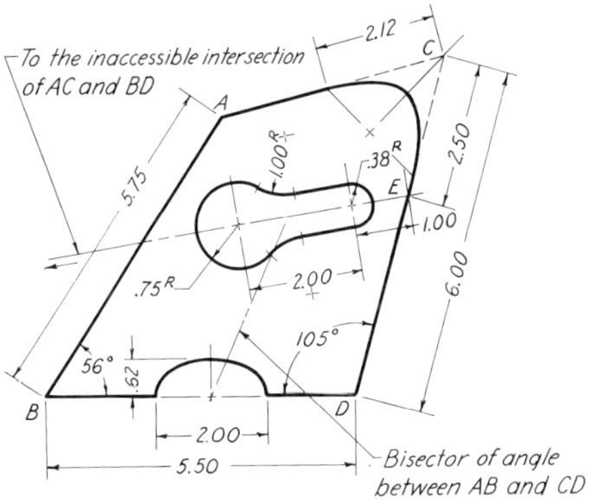

FIG. 4.69. Adjustment plate.

22. (Fig. 4.70). Part A is free to pivot about a shaft. If this part should be revolved in a counterclockwise direction as indicated by the arrows, it would contact surface C. Reproduce the drawing as given and show part A revolved until it is in contact with surface C. Use the symbolic line for showing an alternate position for part A in this new position. Show all geometric constructions clearly and do not erase construction lines.

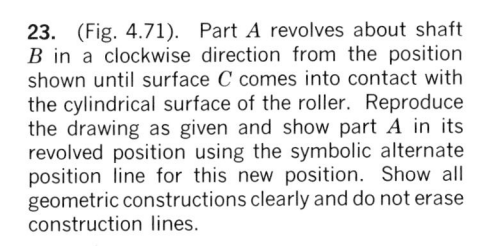

23. (Fig. 4.71). Part A revolves about shaft B in a clockwise direction from the position shown until surface C comes into contact with the cylindrical surface of the roller. Reproduce the drawing as given and show part A in its revolved position using the symbolic alternate position line for this new position. Show all geometric constructions clearly and do not erase construction lines.

24. (Fig. 4.72). Draw the top of the arch through point C. Use an exact method. Scale and record the rise of the arch (one-half the length of the minor axis). Locate the foci. Show all construction.

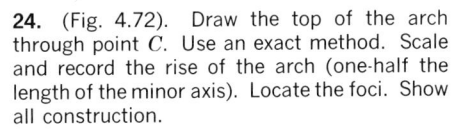

25. (Fig. 4.73). The design of a counterweight system is such that point A (pivot point) of the counterweight and point C (end view of the axis

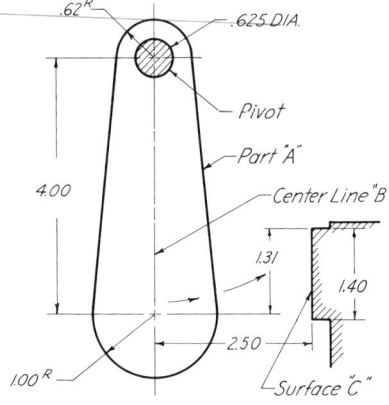

FIG. 4.70. Geometric construction.

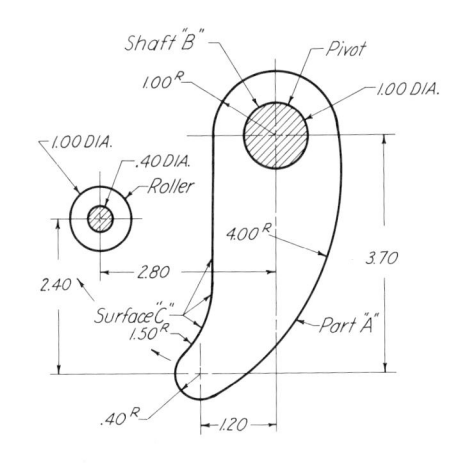

FIG. 4.71. Geometric construction.

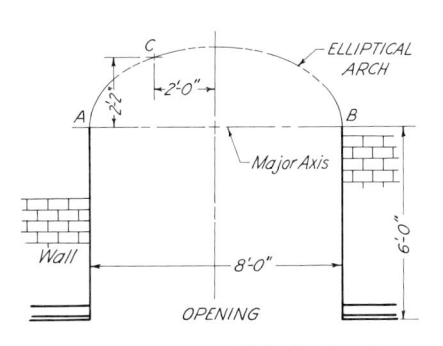

FIG. 4.72. Elliptical arch.

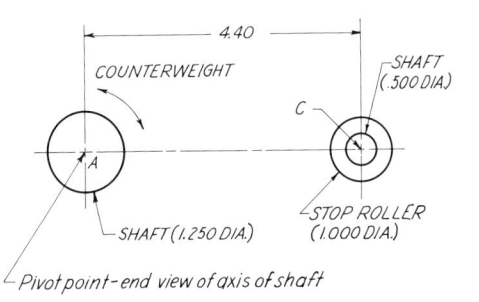

FIG. 4.73. Design of a counterweight system.

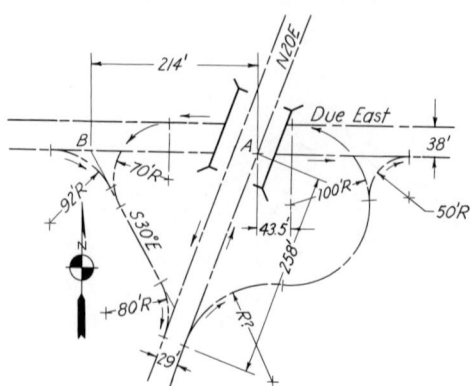

FIG. 4.74. Highway interchange.

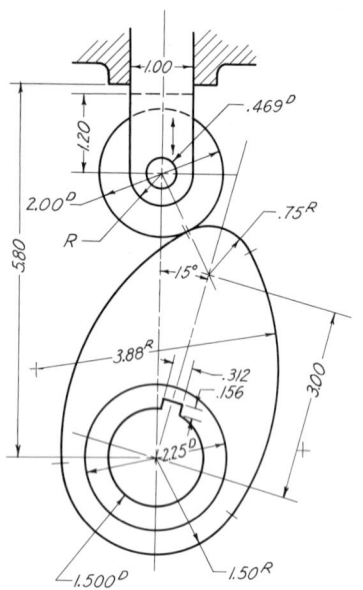

FIG. 4.75. Cam and follower.

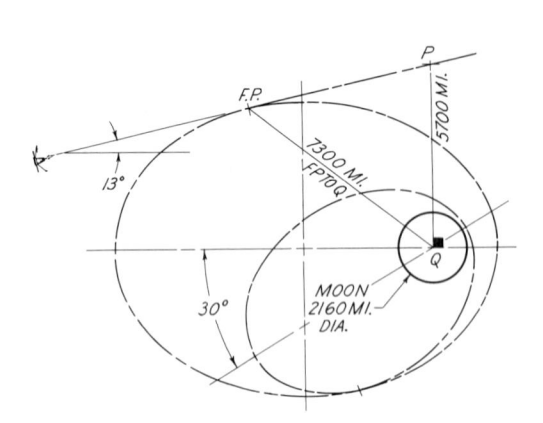

FIG. 4.76. Elliptical lunar orbits.

line of the counterweight. Complete the upper part of the outline by drawing a reverse curve tangent to the top of the 1.00 and 1.60 arcs. The radius of the curve tangent to the 1.60 arc is to be 43 percent of the total length of the two chords of the reverse curve. Using geometry, determine the location of the point of tangency of the counterweight and roller when the counterweight swings clockwise into contact with the outside surface of the stop-roller.

26. Prepare a plan view drawing showing the center lines of the highway interchange (Fig. 4.74). Select a suitable scale.

27. It is desired to know the angular displacement of the center line of the cam (Fig. 4.75) when the follower moves to a position .74 below the position shown. Show the cam and follower in their new positions in phantom outline. Use only an approved geometrical method to find the location of the centers of the arcs. A trial and error method is not acceptable. Show all construction and mark all points of tangency.
Determine the angle through which the center line of the cam has moved. Dimension the angle between the center lines.

28. (Fig. 4.76). It is desired to construct the elliptical lunar trajectories of an unmanned lunar spacecraft after it has been fired into space by an Atlas–Agena D. rocket. As it approaches along the path indicated, its control rockets are fired at firing-point FP (on the tangent) in such a manner as to place the spacecraft in an elliptical orbit, which has the center of the moon as one focus and the major axis in the direction shown by the center line. After exactly one and one-half orbits, the control rockets are fired again to place the spacecraft in a smaller orbit, which also has the center of the moon as one focus. The major axis of the smaller orbit makes an angle of 30° with the major diameter of the first orbit. Plot the first orbit using the foci method and plot the second orbit by the trammel method. Determine the location of the second firing.

of the shaft and roller) are in line horizontally. A point *B* on the counterweight is 4.12 from *A* on a line making an angle of 41° with *AC* through *A*. Points *A* and *B* are the centers of 1.60R and 1.00R arcs respectively.
Draw an arc of 3.20R tangent to the 1.00 and 1.60 arcs to form the lower portion of the out-

SPATIAL GRAPHICS: SHAPE DESCRIPTION AND SPATIAL RELATIONSHIPS

II

Earth-orbiting space stations with nuclear shuttle craft from the earth to the stations and then onward to the moon may be a reality late in this decade. Such stations would have fully equipped living quarters.

Shown floating at the bottom left is a concept of a 120-inch telescope. A ferry and resupply craft is shown approaching the telescope. The center section of the space station has a hanger. A small satellite is shown being taken in for maintenance.

Many of the problems that arise in the development of projects of this type are solved by projection methods.
(*Courtesy National Aeronautics and Space Administration*)

The Theory of Projection

5.1
Introduction. Since engineers are confronted with the task of recording the shapes and sizes of three-dimensional objects on the plane of a sheet of drawing paper, it is obvious that recognized procedures must be followed if their drawings and sketches are to be easily understood. Size description and shape description are equally important, but, in order to simplify the presentation of the fundamentals of making drawings and sketches, this chapter is concerned entirely with the methods commonly employed in describing shape. A later chapter will discuss size description.

Each of the different methods—axonometric, oblique, and orthographic—is based on some form of projection. The theory governing a method should be understood thoroughly before it is used.

5.2
Perspective (Scenographic) Projection. In perspective projection, the projecting lines (visual rays) converge to a point, as shown in Fig. 5.1. The representation on the transparent picture plane may be considered the view that would be seen by one eye located at a definite point in space. The picture is established on the imaginary plane by the piercing points of the projecting lines from the eye to the object. The size of the view depends on the distance from the observer to the plane and the distance from the plane to the object.

Perspective projection is not suitable for working drawings because a perspective view does not reveal exact size and shape. It is used to some extent by engineers in preparing preliminary sketches.

5.3
Orthographic Projection (Parallel Projection). If the observer in Fig. 5.1 moves straight back from the picture plane until he is an infinite distance from it, the projecting lines (projectors) from the eye to the object become parallel to each other and perpendicular to the picture plane. The resulting projection (Fig. 5.2) will then be the same shape and size as the front surface of the object. From a practical viewpoint, the projection may be thought of as being formed by perpendicular pro-

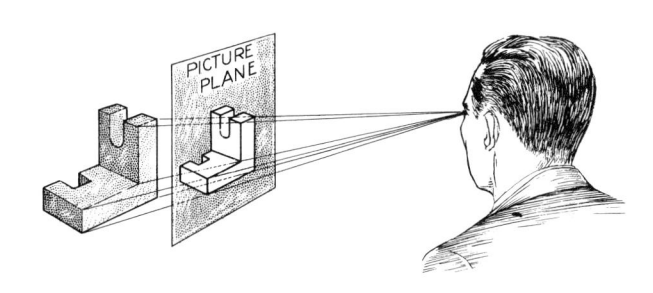

FIG. 5.1. Perspective projection.

77

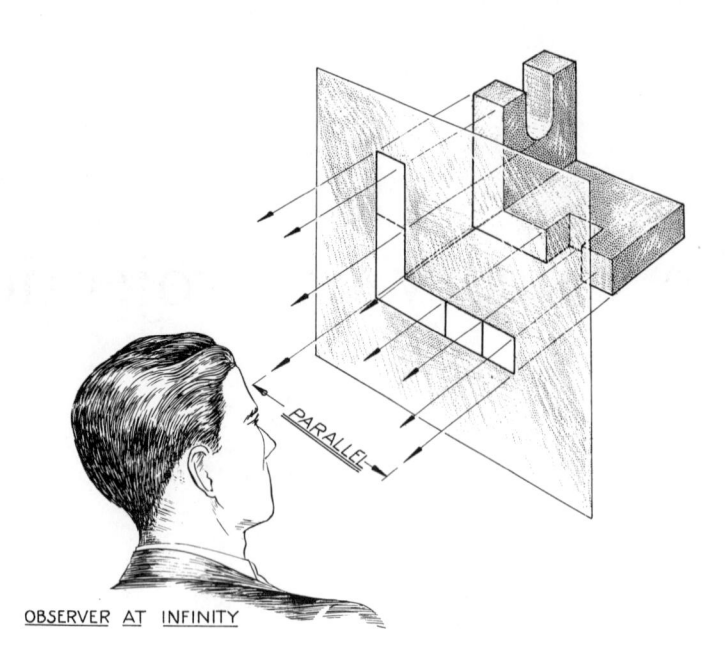

FIG. 5.2. Orthographic projection.

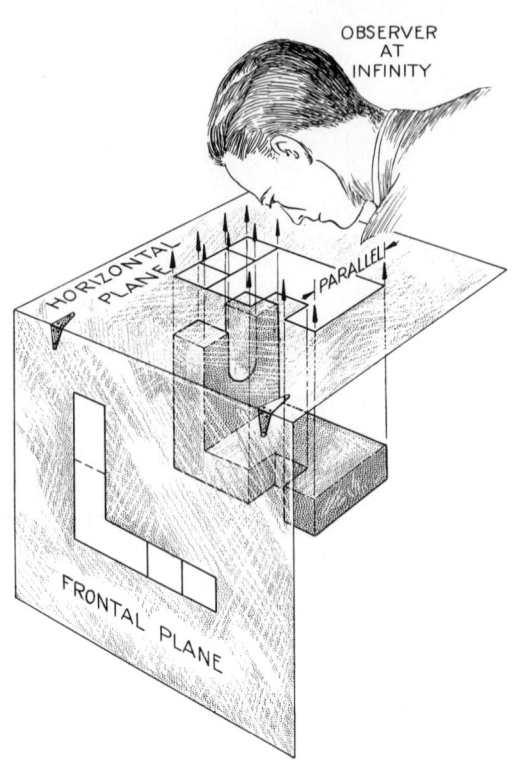

FIG. 5.3. Planes of projection.

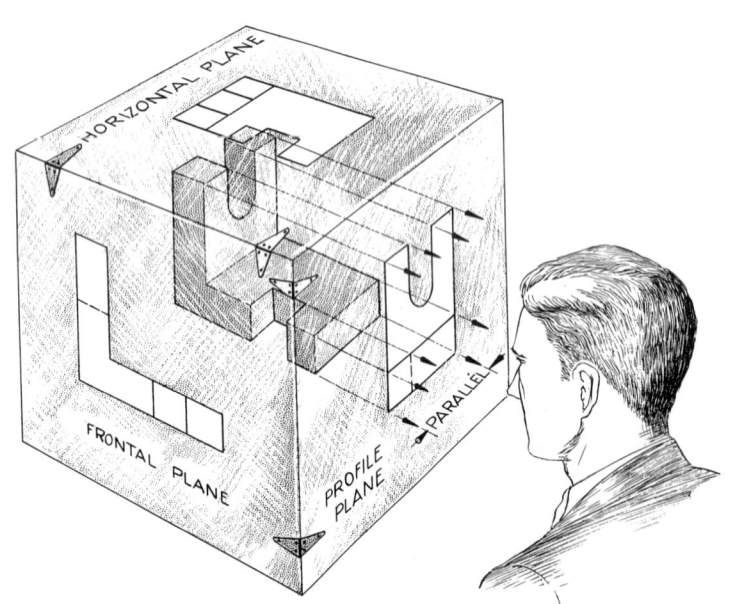

FIG. 5.4. Planes of projection.

jectors extended from the object to the plane. The view is called an *orthographic projection*.

Since the view shown in Fig. 5.2 does not reveal the thickness of the object, one or more additional projections (Fig. 5.3) are necessary to complete the description. Two projections are usually sufficient to describe simple objects, but three or more are necessary for complicated ones.

The picture planes are customarily called the *principal* or *coordinate* planes of projection, and the perpendiculars, *projectors*. In engineering drawing, the planes are usually arranged as shown in Fig. 5.4. Since all three are mutually perpendicular, they are called the horizontal, frontal, and profile coordinate planes. To maintain this mutual relationship when laying out views, it is the usual practice to consider the frontal plane as lying in the plane of the paper and the horizontal and profile planes as being revolved into position (Fig. 5.6). Note in Fig. 5.5 the manner in which the planes are revolved. This theoretical treatment of the coordinate planes establishes an absolute relationship between the views. Visualizing an object would be considerably more difficult than it is, if it were not for this fixed relationship, for it would be impossible to determine quickly the direction of sight for a particular view.

5.4

One-plane Projection. If the object is turned and then tilted so that three faces are inclined to the plane of projection, the resulting projection is a special type of orthographic projection known as *axonometric projection*. Figure 5.7 illustrates an axonometric projection of a cube. Note that the projectors from the object to the plane are perpendicular to the plane. The three recognized subdivisions of axonometric projection, namely, isometric, dimetric, and trimetric, are explained in Chapter 12.

Another form of one-plane projection is known as *oblique projection*. This form differs from orthographic projection in that, although one face is imagined to be parallel to the plane of projection, the projectors make an angle other than 90° with it (Fig. 5.8). Obviously an infinite number of different views are possible, depending on the angle the parallel projectors make with the plane of projection (picture plane). The various subdivisions are cavalier projection, cabinet projection, and clinographic projection (Chapter 12).

Axonometric projection, oblique projection, and perspective projection may all be classed together as *one-plane pictorial projection*.

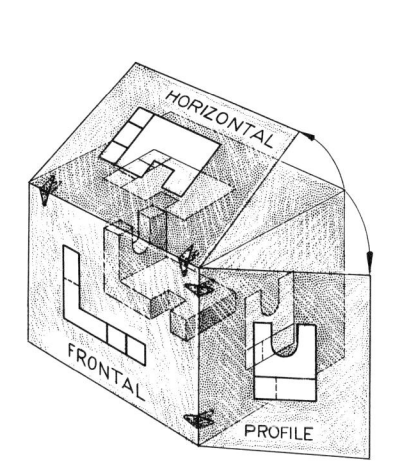

FIG. 5.5. The revolution of the planes of projection.

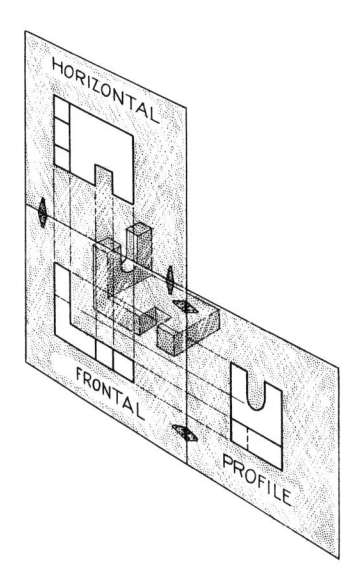

FIG. 5.6. The planes resolved into the plane of the paper.

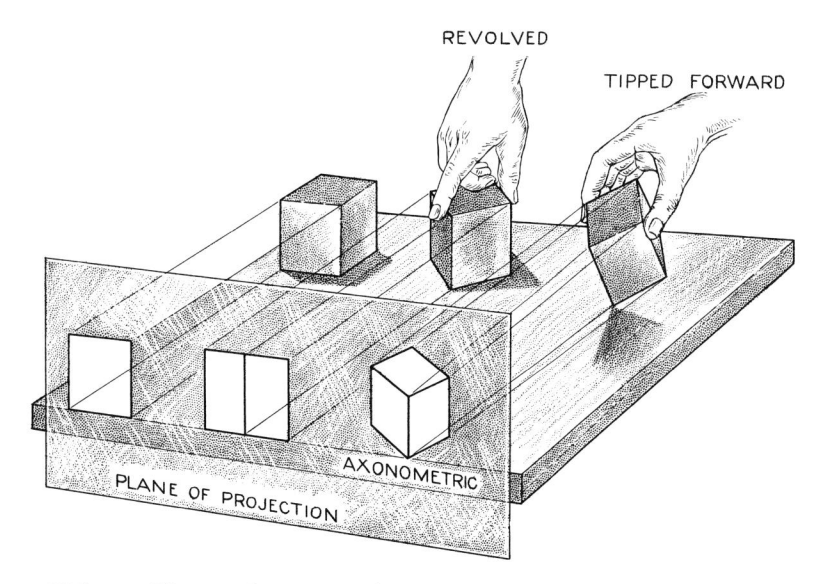

FIG. 5.7. Theory of axonometric projection.

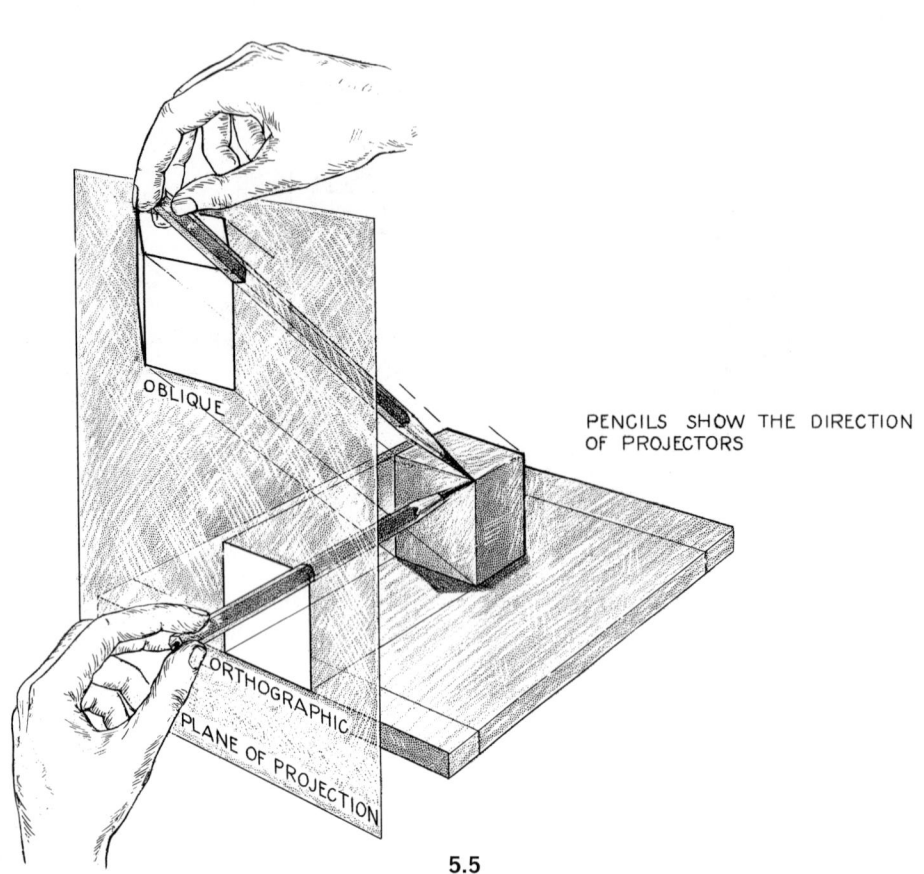

FIG. 5.8. Oblique projection.

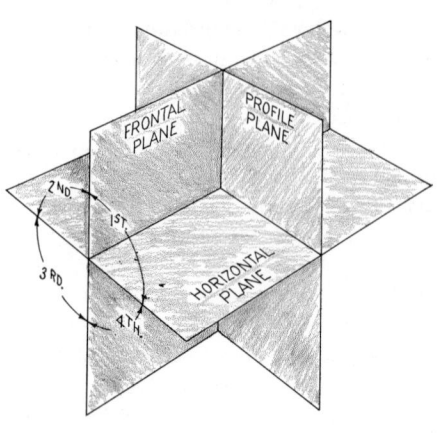

PENCILS SHOW THE DIRECTION OF PROJECTORS

FIG. 5.9. Planes of projection.

5.5

First- and Third-angle Projection. If the horizontal and frontal planes are assumed to extend indefinitely on one side of the profile plane, four dihedral angles are formed and are designated as the *first, second, third,* and *fourth* angles (Fig. 5.9). The lines of intersection of these planes are called coordinate axes. Their point of intersection is called the origin. In this discussion of first- and third-angle projection, it should be remembered that no matter in which angle the object is placed, the observer views it from in front of the frontal plane and from above the horizontal plane. To avoid misunderstandings, the directions for revolving the horizontal and profile planes into the frontal plane are illustrated in Fig. 5.10. Note that the first and third quadrants are "opened" and the second and fourth are "closed" in revolving the horizontal plane into the frontal plane.

If an object, such as the one shown in Fig. 5.10, is placed so that its main faces are parallel to the principal planes, the respective projections on each plane will show the true size and shape of all surfaces that are parallel to that principal plane. Theoretically, the object could have been shown in any one of the four quadrants. It has been placed in the third quadrant simply because engineering custom in the United States dictates the use of the third. This quadrant is used because the views, when revolved into the frontal plane, are in their natural positions. That is, the top view appears *above* the front view, as is expected, and the profile view, showing the *right side*, falls on the *right* of the front view.

In most foreign countries, "first-angle projection" is used for working drawings (study Fig. 5.11). Observe that the top view is projected on the horizontal plane and the front view on the frontal plane. For this reason, the top view falls below the front view when the coordinate planes are revolved.

In this country, the use of first-angle projection for working drawings was abandoned by engineering draftsmen some fifty years ago, although it is still used by architects and structural designers.

5.6
Systems of Projection. The different systems of projection may be conveniently classified as follows:

CONVERGENT PROJECTION
(*Converging projectors*)

- LINEAR
  - Parallel (One-point)
  - Angular (Two-point)
  - Oblique (Three-point)
- AERIAL

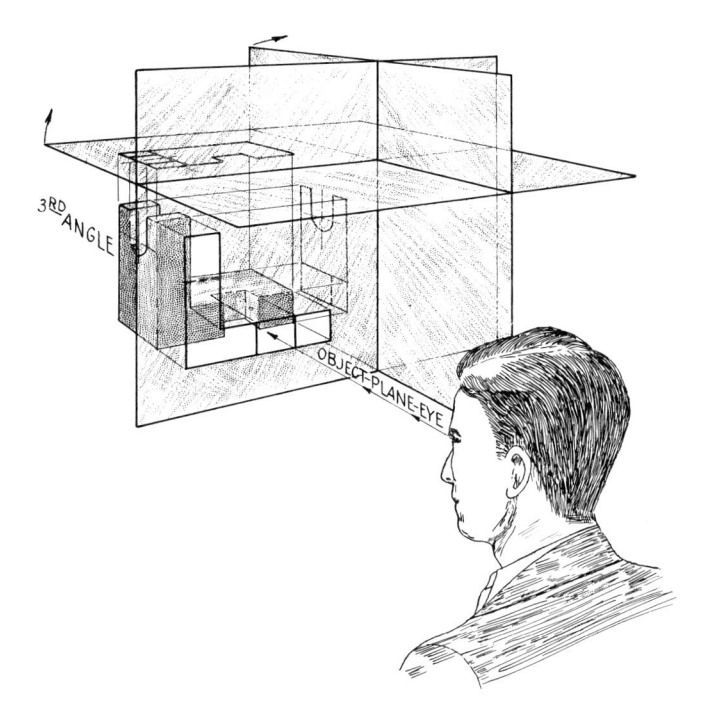

FIG. 5.10. Third-angle projection.

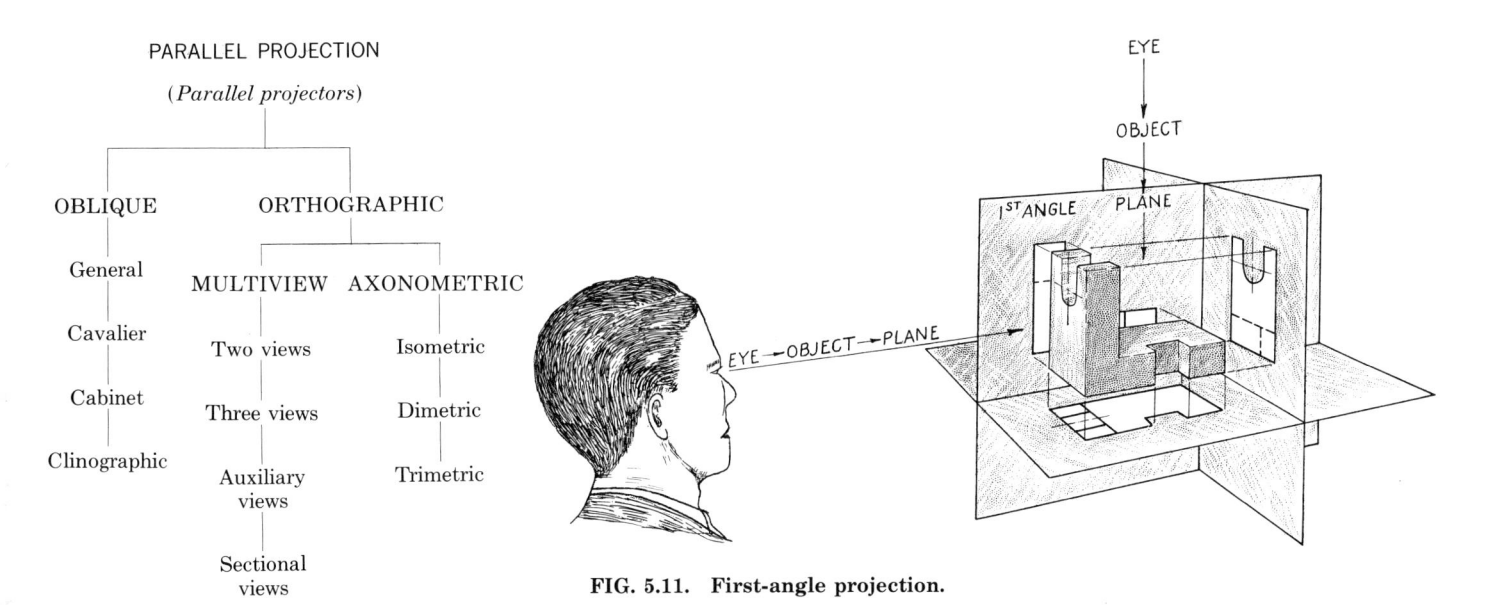

PARALLEL PROJECTION
(*Parallel projectors*)

- OBLIQUE
  - General
  - Cavalier
  - Cabinet
  - Clinographic
- ORTHOGRAPHIC
  - MULTIVIEW
    - Two views
    - Three views
    - Auxiliary views
    - Sectional views
  - AXONOMETRIC
    - Isometric
    - Dimetric
    - Trimetric

FIG. 5.11. First-angle projection.

300 MPH Tracked-Air-Cushion-Vehicle (TACV). The General Electric Company's Transportation Systems Division has been awarded a contract by the Department of Transportation's Office of High Speed Ground Transportation to make a preliminary design study for the TACV shown. This high-speed vehicle will "fly" at about ¾-inch above and between a fixed guideway. The TACV is expected to receive community acceptability for intercity passenger service because of excellent ride quality and quietness of operation.
(*Courtesy General Electric Company*)

Multiview Representation, Revolution, and Conventional Practices

A: MULTIVIEW DRAWING

6.1
Introduction. Engineers use the orthographic system of projection for describing the shape of machine parts and structures (Fig. 6.1). Practical application of this method of describing an object results in a drawing consisting of a number of systematically arranged views that reproduce the object's exact shape. It was explained in Chapter 5, Sec. 5.3 that a set of views showing the object from different positions is always taken. These views, positioned in strict accordance with the universally recognized arrangement, must show the three dimensions, width, height, and depth. Although three views (Fig. 6.2) are usually required to describe an ordinary object, only two may be needed for a particularly simple one. A very complicated object may require four or more views. A view projected on an auxiliary plane also may be desirable (p. 164). Such a view often makes possible the elimination of one of the principal views. Therefore, it is up to the individual to determine the number and type of views needed to produce a satisfactory drawing. He will soon develop a knack for this, if he bears in mind that the number of views required depends entirely on the complexity of the shape to be described.

6.2
Definition. Multiview (multiplanar) projection is a method by means of which the exact shape of an object can be represented by two or more separate views produced on projection planes that are usually at right angles to each other.

6.3.
Methods of Obtaining the Views. The views of an object may be obtained by either of two methods: (1) the natural method; (2) the "glass box" method.

Since the resulting views will be the same in either case, the beginner should adopt the method he finds the easiest to understand. Both methods are explained here in detail.

6.4
The Natural Method. In using this method, each of the necessary views is obtained by looking directly at the particular side of the object the view is to represent.

Figure 6.2 shows three of the principal views of an object, the front, top, and side views. They were obtained by looking directly at the front, top, and right side, respectively. In the application of this method, some consider the position of the object as fixed and the position of the observer as shifted for each view; others find it easier to consider the observer's position as fixed and the position of the object as changed for each view (Fig. 6.2).

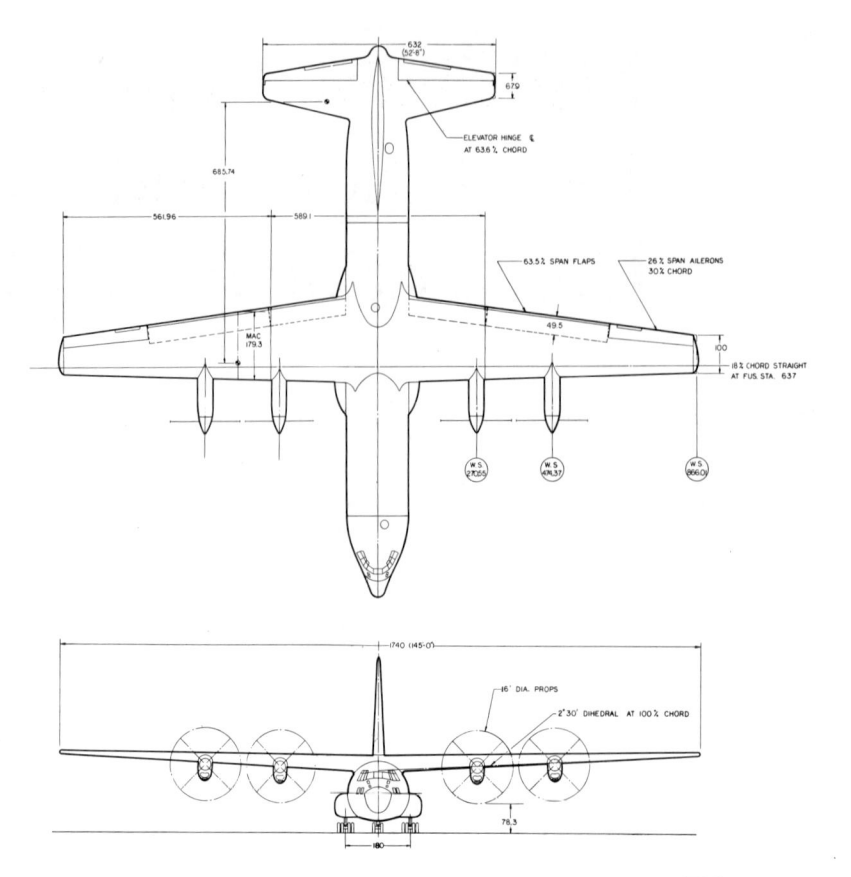

FIG. 6.1. A multiview drawing. *(Courtesy of Lockheed, Georgia Division)*

Regardless of which procedure is followed, the top and side views must be arranged in their natural positions relative to the front view.

Figure 6.3 illustrates the natural relationship of views. Note that the top view is *vertically above* the front view, and the side view is *horizontally in line with* the front view. In both of these views *the front of the block is toward the front view.*

6.5
The "Glass Box" Method. An imaginary "glass box" is used widely by instructors to explain the arrangement of orthographic views. An explanation of this scheme can best be made by reviewing the use of planes of projection (Chapter 5). It may be considered that planes of projection placed parallel to the six faces of an object form an enclosing "glass box" (Fig. 6.4). The observer views the enclosed object from the outside. The views are obtained by running projectors from points on the object to the planes. This procedure is in accordance with the theory of orthographic projection explained in Sec. 5.3, as well as the definition in Sec. 6.2. The top, front, and right side of the box represent the H (horizontal), F

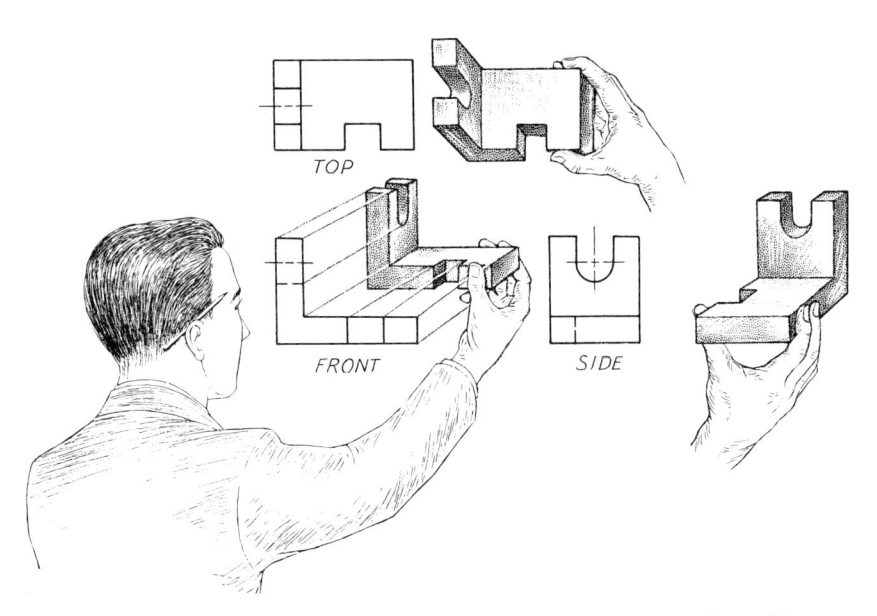

CHAP. 6 / MULTIVIEW REPRESENTATION, REVOLUTION, AND CONVENTIONAL PRACTICES 85

FIG. 6.2. Obtaining three views of an object.

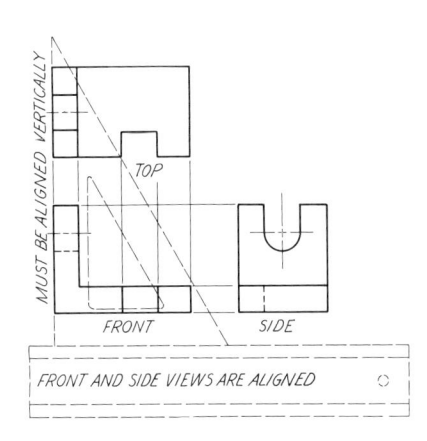

FIG. 6.3. Position of views.

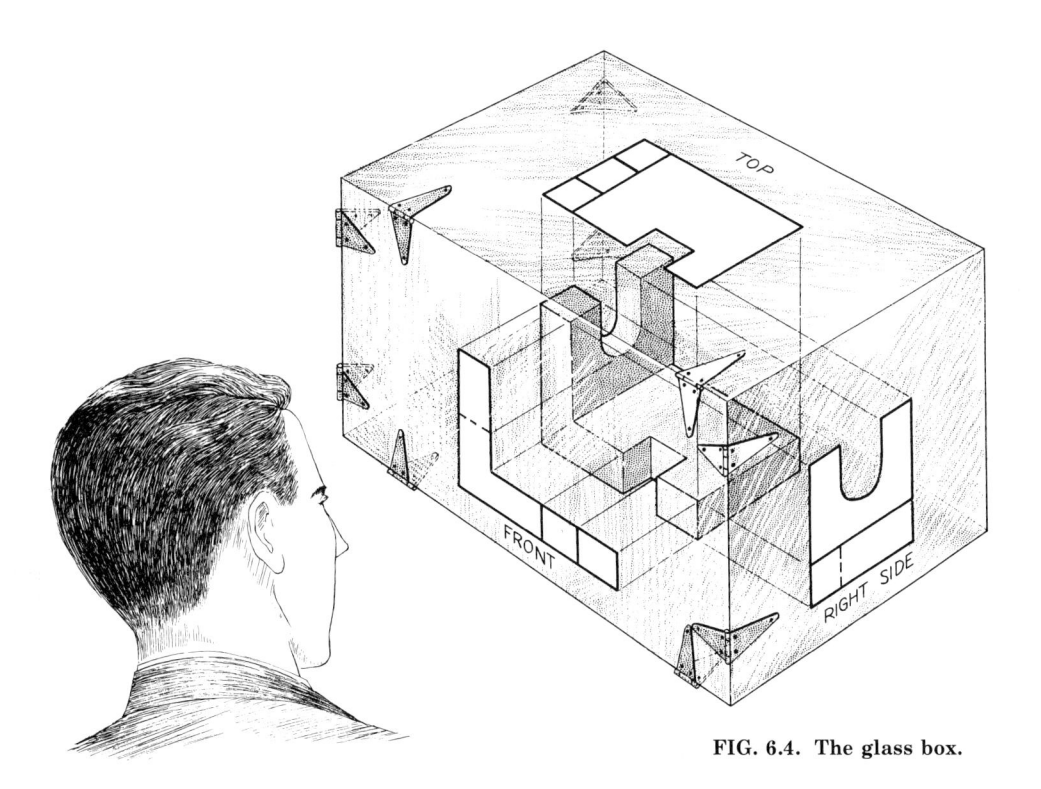

FIG. 6.4. The glass box.

(frontal), and P (profile) projection planes.

Since the projections on the sides of the three-dimensional transparent box are to appear on a sheet of drawing paper, it must be assumed that the box is hinged (Fig. 6.5) so that, when it is opened outward into the plane of the paper, the planes assume the positions illustrated in Figs. 6.5 and 6.6. Note that all of the planes, except the back one, are hinged to the frontal plane. In accordance with this universally recognized assumption, the top projection must take a position directly above the front projection, and the right-side projection must lie horizontally to the right of the front projection. To identify the separate projections, engineers call the one on the frontal plane the *front view* or *front elevation*, the one on the horizontal plane the *top view* or *plan*, and the one on the side or profile plane the *side view, side elevation,* or *end view*. Figure 6.6 shows the six views of the same object as they would appear on a sheet of drawing paper. Ordinarily, only three of these views are necessary (front, top, and right side). A bottom or rear view will be required in comparatively few cases.

6.6
The "Second Position." Sometimes, especially in the case of a broad, flat object, it is desirable to hinge the sides of the box to the horizontal plane so that the side view will fall to the right of the top view, as illustrated in Fig. 6.7. This arrangement conserves space on the paper and gives the views better balance.

6.7
The Principles of Multiview Drawing. The following principles should be studied carefully and understood thoroughly before any attempt is made to prepare an orthographic drawing:

1. The front and top views are *always* in line vertically (Fig. 6.3).

2. The front and side views are in line horizontally, except when the second position is used (Fig. 6.3).

3. The front of the object in the top view faces the front view (Fig. 6.5).

4. The front of the object in the side view faces the front view (Fig. 6.5).

5. The depth of the top view is the same as the depth of the side view (or views) (see Fig. 6.8).

6. The width of the top view is the same as the width of the front view (Fig. 6.8).

7. The height of the side view is the same as the height of the front view (Fig. 6.8).

8. A view taken from above is a top view and *must* be drawn above the front view (Fig. 6.6).

9. A view taken from the right, in relation to the selected front, is a right-side view and *must* be drawn to the right of the front view (Fig. 6.6).

10. A view taken from the left is a left-side view and *must* be drawn to the left of the front view (Fig. 6.6).

11. A view taken from below is a bottom view and *must* appear below the front view (Fig. 6.6).

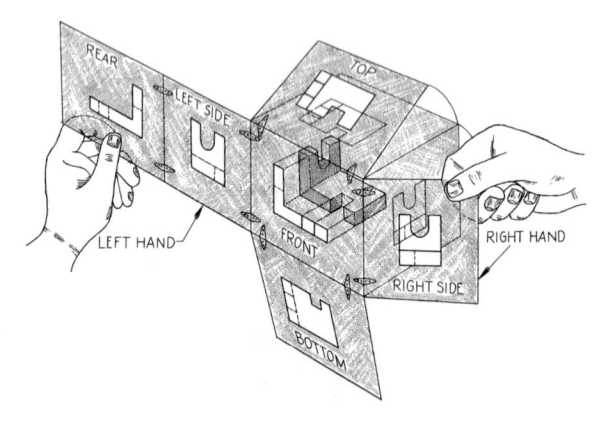

FIG. 6.5. Opening the glass box.

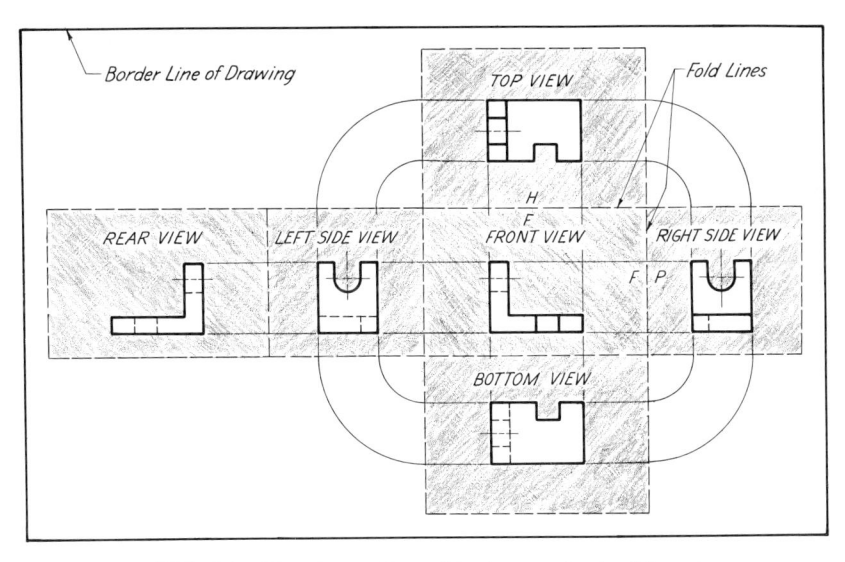

CHAP. 6 / MULTIVIEW REPRESENTATION, REVOLUTION, AND CONVENTIONAL PRACTICES   87

FIG. 6.6. Six views of an object on a sheet of drawing paper.

6.8
Projection of Lines. A line may project either in true length, foreshortened, or as a point in a view depending on its relationship to the projection plane on which the view is projected (see Fig. 6.9). In the top view, the line projection $a^H b^H$ shows the true length of the edge AB (see pictorial) because AB is parallel to the horizontal plane of projection. Looking directly at the frontal plane, along the line, AB projects as a point ($a^F b^F$). Lines, such as CD, that are inclined to one of the planes of projection, will show a foreshortened projection in the view on the projection plane to which the line is inclined and true length in the view on the plane of projection to which the line is parallel. The curved line projection $e^F f^F$ shows the true length of the curved edge.

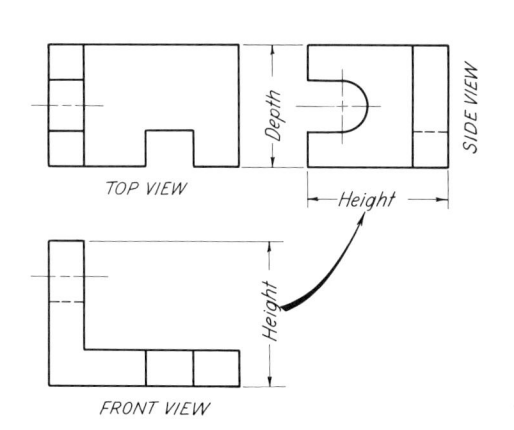

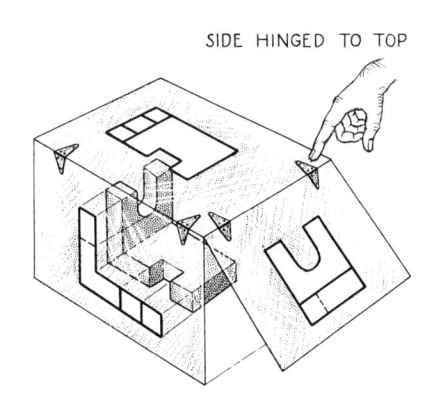

FIG. 6.7. The "second position" for the side view.

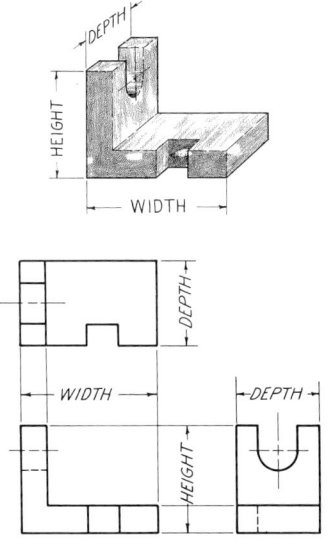

FIG. 6.8. View terminology.

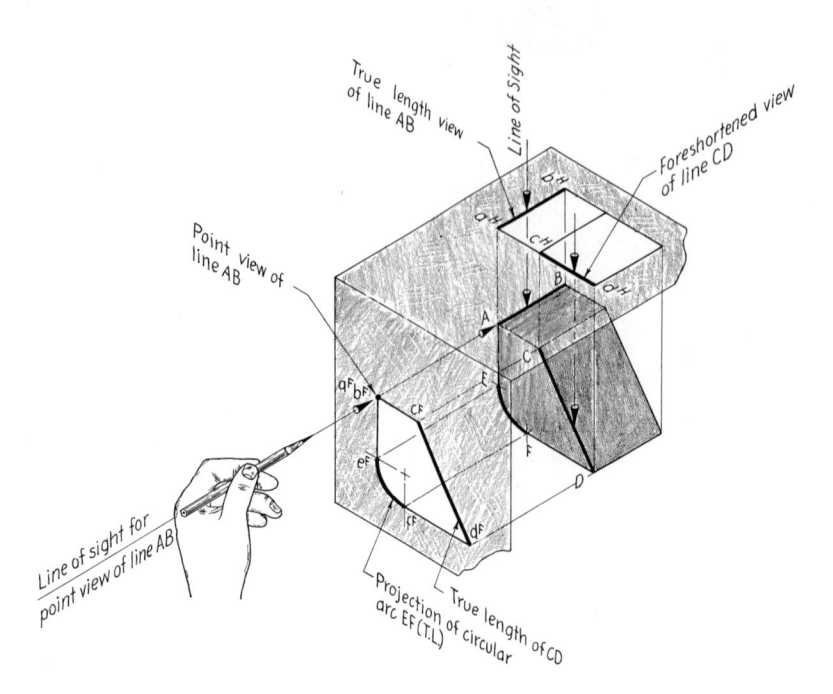

FIG. 6.9. Projected views of lines.

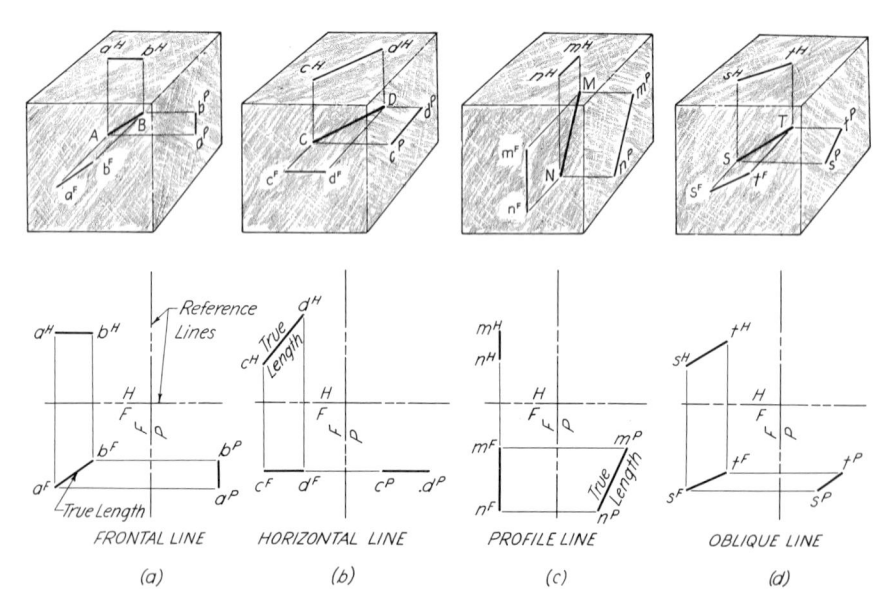

FIG. 6.10. Some typical line positions.

The student should study Fig. 6.10 and attempt to visualize the space position of each of the given lines. It is very necessary both in preparing and reading graphical representations to recognize the position of a point, line, or plane and to know whether the projection of a line is true length or foreshortened, and whether the projection of a plane shows the true size and shape. The indicated reference lines may be thought of as representing the edges of the glass boxes shown. The projections of a line are identified as being on either a frontal, horizontal, or profile plane by the use of the letters F, H, or P with the lowercase letters that identify the endpoints of the line. For example, in Fig. 6.10 (a), $a^H b^H$ is the horizontal projection of line AB, $a^F b^F$ is the frontal projection, and $a^P b^P$ is the profile projection.

It is suggested that the student hold a pencil before him and move it into the following typical line positions to observe the conditions under which the pencil representing a line, appears in true length.

1. *Vertical line.* The vertical line is perpendicular to the horizontal and will therefore appear as a point in the H (top) view. It will appear in true length in the F (frontal) view and in the P (profile) view.

2. *Horizontal line* [Fig. 6.10(b)]. The horizontal line will appear in true length when viewed from above because it is parallel to the H-plane of projection and its endpoints are theoretically equidistant from an observer looking downward.

3. *Inclined line* [Fig. 6.10(c)]. The inclined line is any line not vertical or horizontal that is parallel to either the frontal plane or the profile plane of projection. An inclined line will show true length in the F (frontal) view or P (profile) view.

4. *Oblique line* [Fig. 6.10(d)]. The oblique line will not appear in true length in any of the principal views because it is inclined to all of the principal planes of projection. It should be apparent in viewing the pencil alternately from the directions used to obtain the principal views, namely, from the front, above, and side, that one end of the pencil is always farther away from the observer than the other. Only when looking directly at the pencil from such a position that the endpoints are equidistant from the observer can the true length be seen. On a drawing, the true length projection of an oblique line will appear in a supplementary A (auxiliary) view projected on a plane that is parallel to the line (Sec. 10.7).

6.9
Meaning of Lines. On a multiview drawing a visible or invisible line may represent either the intersection of two surfaces, the edge view of a surface, or it may be the limiting element of a surface. These three different meanings of a line are illustrated in Fig. 6.11. In the top view, the curved line is an edge view of surface C, while a straight line is the edge view of surface A. The full circle in the front view may be considered as the edge view of the cylindrical surface of the hole. In the side view, the top line, representing the contour element of the cylindrical surface, indicates the limits for the surface and therefore can be thought of as being a surface limit line. The short vertical line in this same view represents the intersection of two surfaces. In reading a drawing, one can be sure of the meaning of a line on a view only after an analysis of the related view or views. All views must be studied carefully.

6.10
Projection of Surfaces. The components of most machine parts are bounded by

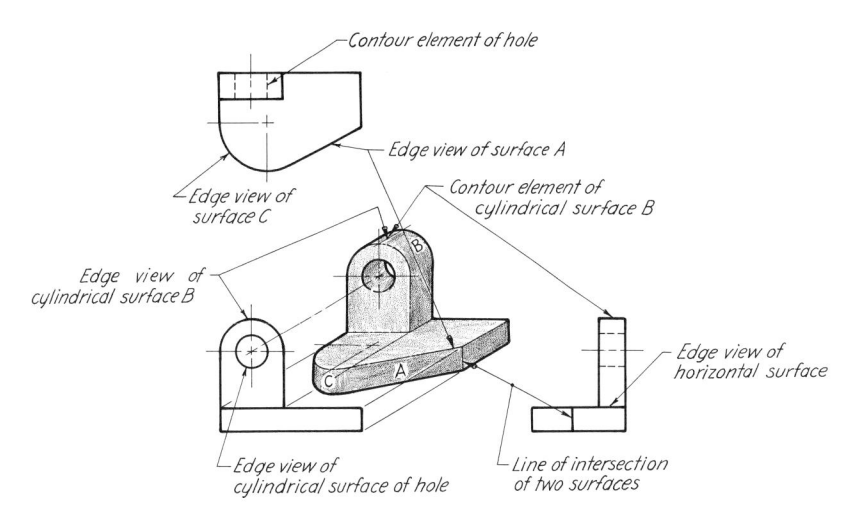

FIG. 6.11. The meaning of lines.

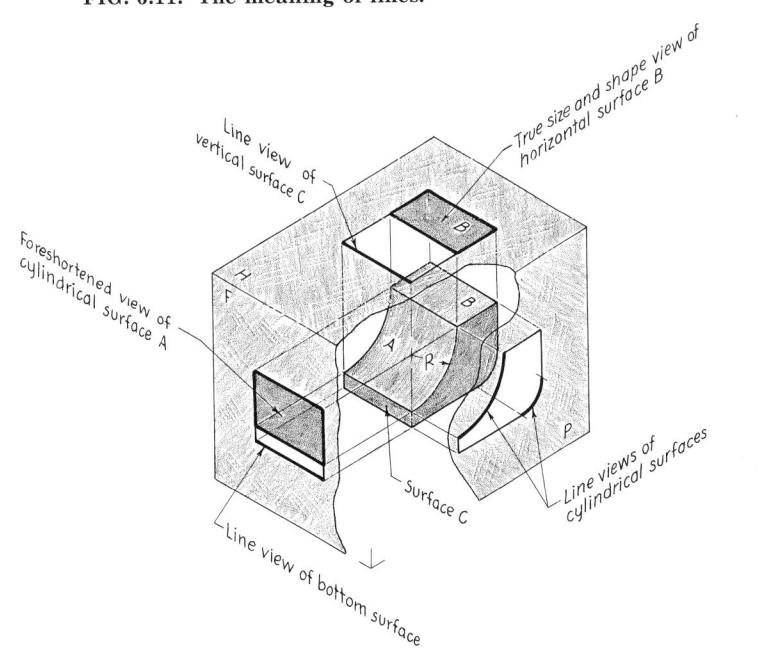

FIG. 6.12. Projected views of surfaces.

either plane or single-curved surfaces. Plane surfaces bound cubes, prisms, and pyramids, while single-curved surfaces, ruled by a moving straight line, bound cylinders and cones. The projected repre-

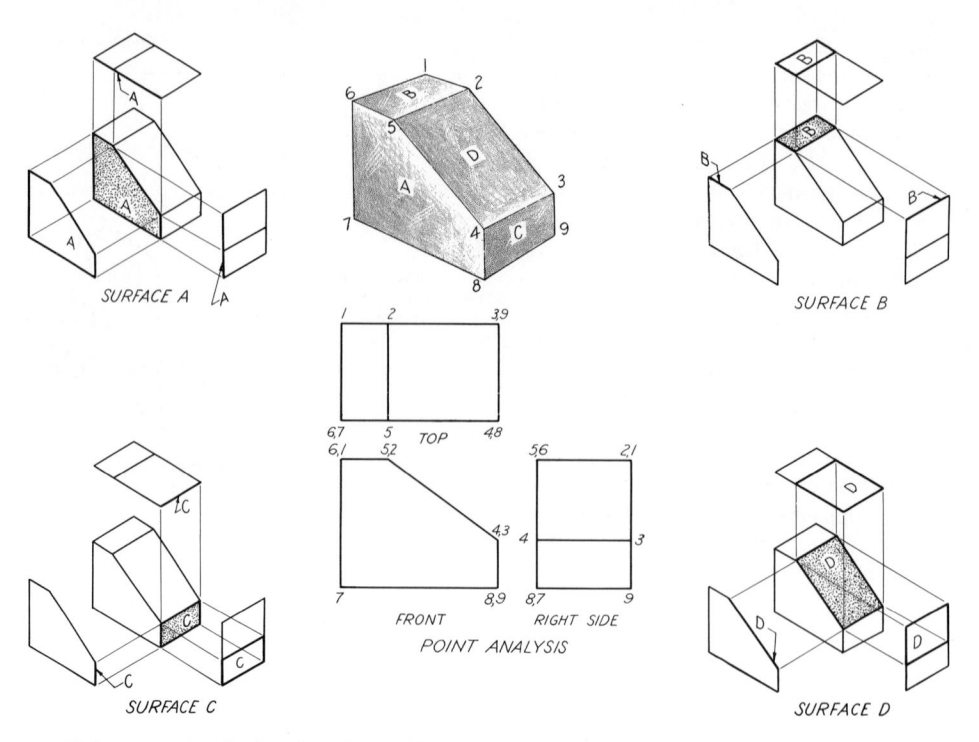

FIG. 6.13. Analysis of surfaces, lines, and points.

sentations (lines or areas) of both plane and single-curved surfaces are shown in Fig. 6.12. From this illustration the student should note that (1) when a surface is parallel to a plane of projection, it will appear in true size in the view on the plane of projection to which it is parallel; (2) when it is perpendicular to the plane of projection, it will project as a line in the view; and (3) when it is positioned at an angle, it will appear foreshortened. A surface will always project either as a line or an area on a view. The area representing the surface may be either a full-size or foreshortened representation.

In Fig. 6.12 the cylindrical surface A appears as a line in the side (profile) view and as an area in the top and front views. Surface B shows true size in the top view and as a line in both the front and side views. Surface C, a vertical surface, will appear as a line when observed from above.

6.11

Analysis of Surfaces, Lines, and Points in Three Principal Views. An analysis of the representation of the surfaces of a mutilated block is given pictorially in Fig. 6.13. It can be noted that each of the surfaces A, B, and C appears in true size and shape in one view and as a line in each of the other two related views. Surface D, which is inclined, appears with foreshortened length in the top and side views and as an inclined line in the front view.

Three views of each of the visible points are shown on the multiview drawing. At the very beginning of an elementary course in drawing, a student will often find it helpful to number the corners of an object in all views.

6.12
The Selection of Views. Careful study should be given to the outline of an object before the views are selected (Fig. 6.14); otherwise there is no assurance that the object will be described completely from the reader's viewpoint (Fig. 6.15). Only those views that are necessary for a clear and complete description should be selected. Since the repetition of information only tends to confuse the reader, superfluous views should be avoided.

Although some objects, such as cylinders, bushings, bolts, and so forth, require only two views (front and side), more complicated pieces may require an auxiliary or sectional view in addition to the ordinary three views.

The space available for arranging the views often governs the choice between the use of a top or side view. The difference between the descriptive values of the two frequently is not great. For example, a draftsman often finds that the views of a long object will have better balance if a top view is used [see Fig. 6.16(a)]; while in the case of a short object [see (b)], the use of a side view may make possible a more pleasing arrangement. It should be remembered that the choice of views for many objects is definitely fixed by the contour alone, and no choice is offered as far as spacing is concerned. It is more important to have a set of views that describes an object clearly than one that is artistically balanced.

Often there is a choice between two equally important views, such as between a right-side and left-side view (Fig. 6.17) or between a top and bottom view (Fig. 6.18). In such cases, one should adhere to the following rule: *A right-side view should be used in preference to a left-side view and a top view in preference to a bottom view.* When this rule is applied to irregular objects, the front (contour) view should be drawn so that the most irregular outline is toward the top and right side.

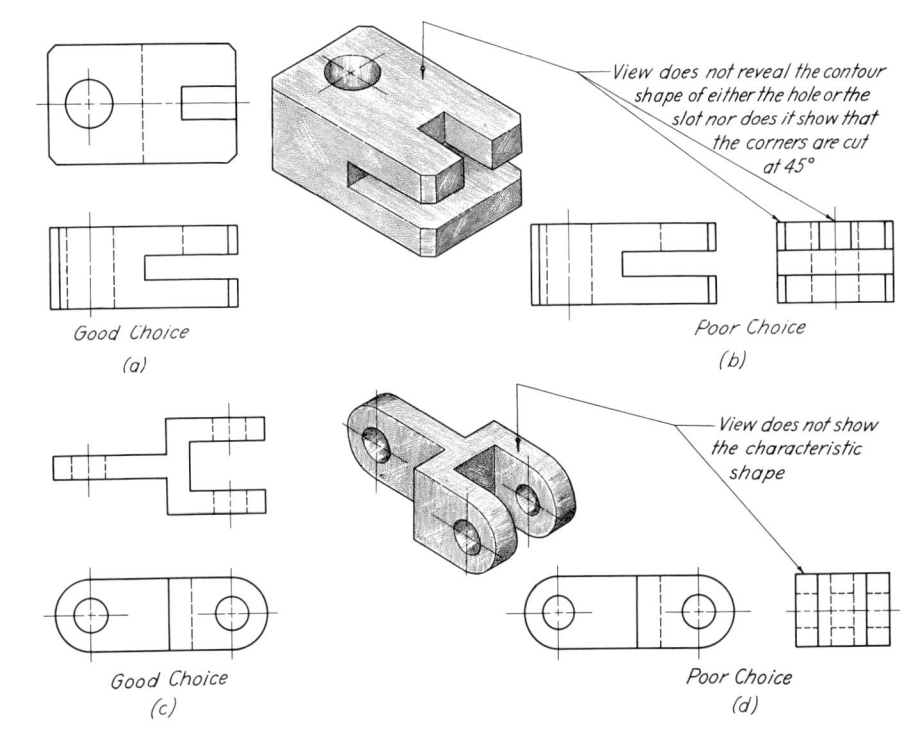

FIG. 6.14. Choice of views.

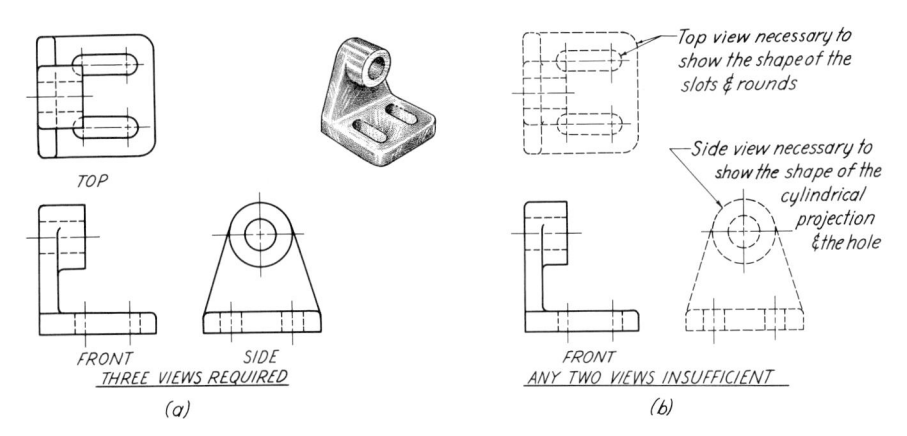

FIG. 6.15. Choice of views.

Another rule, one that must be considered in selecting the front view, is as follows: *Place the object to obtain the smallest number of hidden lines.*

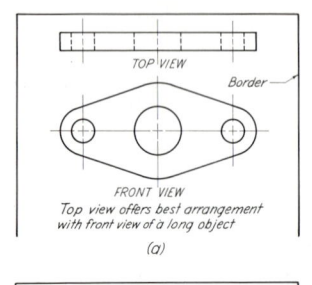

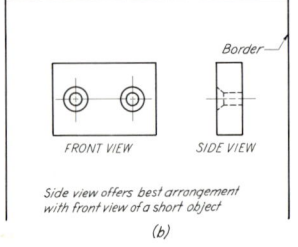

FIG. 6.16. Choice of views.

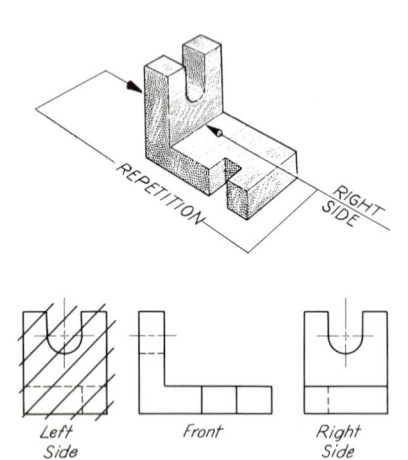

FIG. 6.17. The preferred side view.

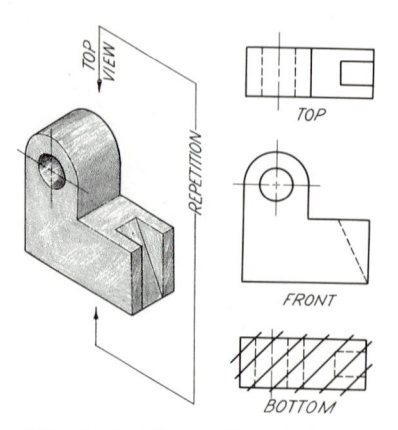

FIG. 6.18. The preferred choice of a top view.

6.13
The Principal (Front) View. The principal view is the one that shows the characteristic contour of the object [see Fig. 6.19(a) and (b)]. Good practice dictates that this be used as the front view on a drawing. It should be clearly understood that the view of the natural front of an object is not always the principal view, because frequently it fails to show the object's characteristic shape. Therefore, another rule to be followed is: *Ordinarily, select the view showing the characteristic contour shape as the front view, regardless of the normal or natural front of the object.*

When an object does have a definite normal position, however, the front view should be in agreement with it. In the case of most machine parts, the front view can assume any convenient position that is consistent with good balance.

6.14
Invisible Lines. Dotted lines are used on an external view of an object to represent surfaces and intersections invisible at the point from which the view is taken. In Fig. 6.20(a), one invisible line represents a line

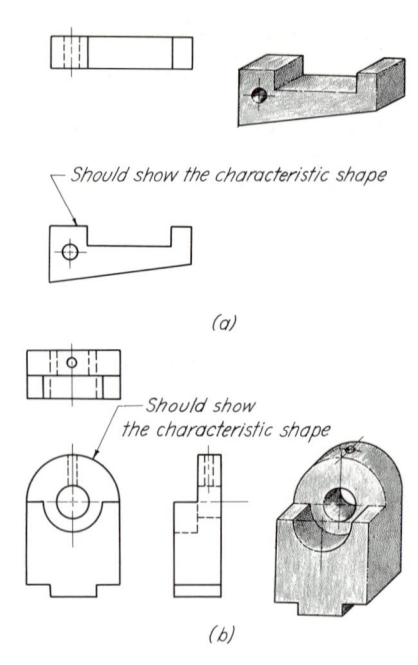

FIG. 6.19. The principal view of an object.

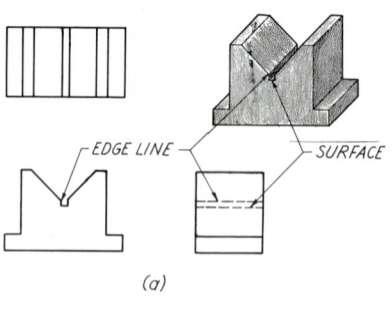

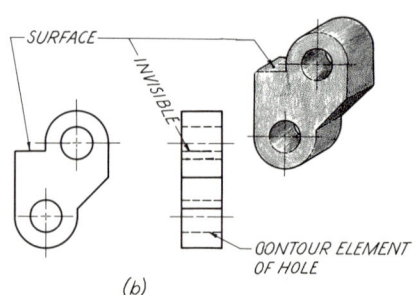

FIG. 6.20. Invisible lines.

of intersection or edge line, while the other invisible line may be considered to represent either the surface or lines of intersection. On the side view in (*b*) there are invisible lines, which represent the contour elements of the cylindrical holes.

6.15
Treatment of Invisible Lines. The short dashes that form an invisible line should be drawn carefully in accordance with the recommendations in Sec. 6.24. An invisible line always starts with a dash in contact with the object line from which it starts, unless it forms a continuation of a visible line. In the latter case, it should start with a space, in order to establish at a glance the exact location of the endpoint of the visible line (see Fig. 6.21*C*). Note that the effect of definite corners is secured at points *A*, *B*, *E*, and *F*, where, in each case, the end dash touches the intersecting line. When the point of intersection of an invisible line and another object line does not represent an actual intersection on the object, the intersection should be open as at points *C* and *D*. An open intersection tends to make the lines appear to be at different distances from the observer.

Parallel invisible lines should have the breaks staggered.

The correct and incorrect treatment for starting invisible arcs is illustrated at *G* and *G'*. Note that an arc should start with a dash at the point of tangency. This treatment enables the reader to determine the exact end points of the curvature.

6.16
Omission of Invisible Lines. Although it is common practice for commercial draftsmen to omit hidden lines when their use tends to confuse further an already overburdened view or when the shape description of a feature is sufficiently clear in another view, it is not advisable for a beginning student to do so. The beginner,

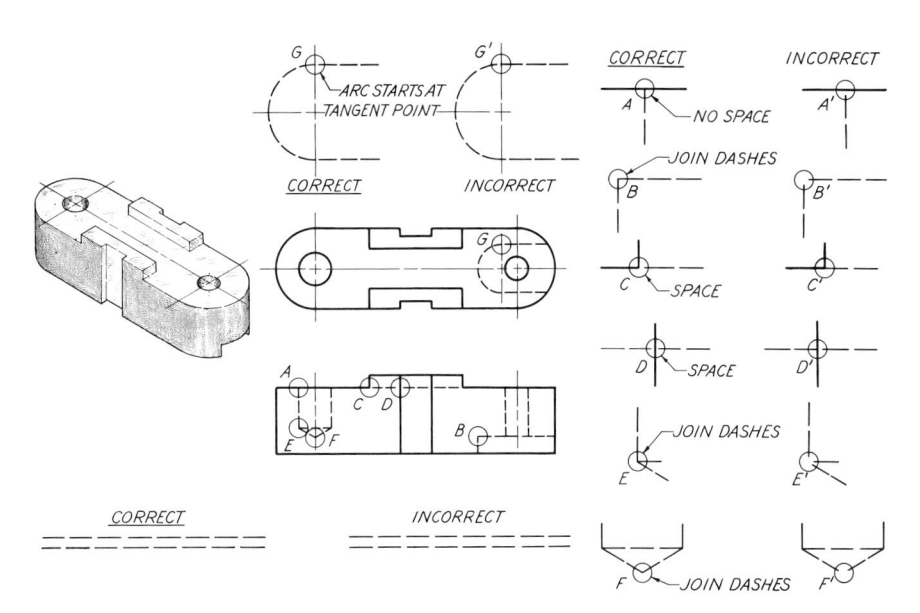

FIG. 6.21. Correct and incorrect junctures of invisible outlines.

until he has developed the discrimination that comes with experience, will be wise to show all hidden lines.

6.17
Precedence of Lines. When one discovers in making a multiview drawing that two lines coincide, the question arises as to which line should be shown or, in other words, which line must have precedence if the drawing is to be read intelligently. For example, as revealed in Fig. 6.22, a solid line may have the same position as an invisible line representing the contour element of a hole, or an invisible line may occur at the same place as a center line for a hole. In these cases the decision rests on the relative importance of each of the two lines that can be shown. The precedence of lines is as follows:

Solid lines (visible object lines) take precedence over all other lines.

Dashed lines (invisible object lines) take precedence over center lines, although

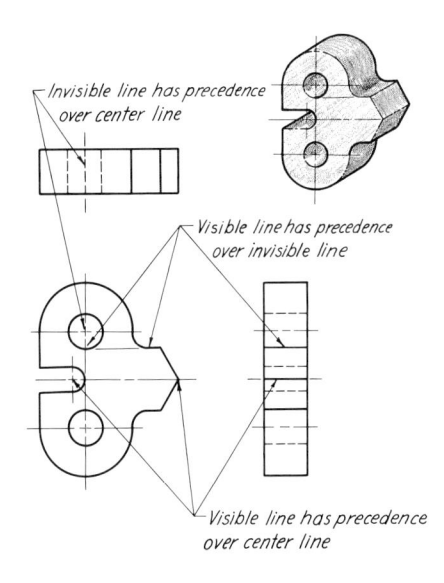

FIG. 6.22. Precedence of lines.

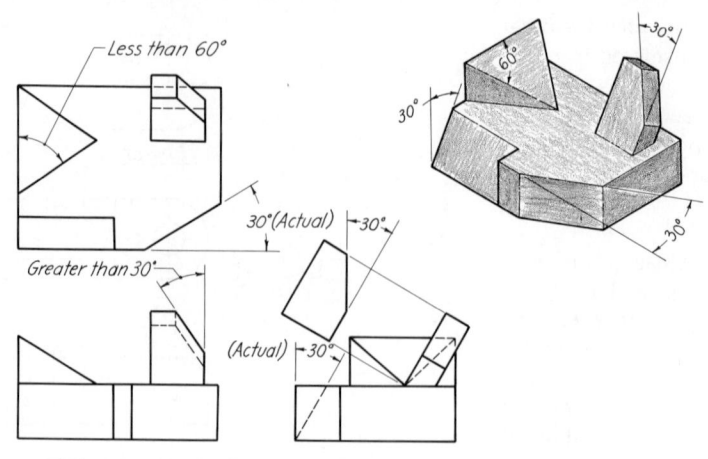

FIG. 6.23. Projection of angles.

evidence of center lines may be indicated as shown in both the top and side views of Fig. 6.22.

A *cutting-plane line* takes precedence over a center line where it is necessary to indicate the position of a cutting plane.

6.18
Projection of Angles. When an angle lies in a plane that is parallel to one of the planes of projection, the angle will show in true size in the view on that particular plane of projection to which the angle is parallel. In Fig. 6.23 those angles indicated as actual show in their true size. The 60° angle, which lies in a surface that is not parallel to the *H*-plane, appears at less than 60° in the top view. The 30° angle for the sloping line on the component portion that is inclined backwards projects at greater than 30° in the front view. It may be said that, except for a 90° angle having one leg as a normal line, angles lying on inclined planes will project either larger or smaller than true size, depending on the position of the plane in which the angle lies. A 90° angle always projects in true size, even on an inclined plane, if the line forming one side of the angle is parallel to the plane of projection and a normal view of the line results. The normal view of a line is any view of a line that is obtained with the direction of sight perpendicular to the line.

What has been stated concerning angles on inclined surfaces can be easily verified by the student if he will observe what happens to the angles of a 30° × 60° triangle resting on the long leg, as it is revolved from a vertical position downward onto the surface of his desk top.

6.19
Treatment of Tangent Surfaces. When a curved surface is tangent to a plane surface, as illustrated in several ways on the pictorial drawing in Fig. 6.24, no line should be shown as indicated at *A* and *B* in the top view and as noted for the front and side views. At *C* in the top view the line represents a small vertical surface that must be shown even though the upper and lower lines for this surface may be omitted in the front view, depending on the decision of the draftsman. In the top view a line has been drawn to represent the intersection of the inclined and horizontal surfaces at the rear, even though they meet in a small round instead of a sharp edge. The presence of this line emphasizes the fact that there are two

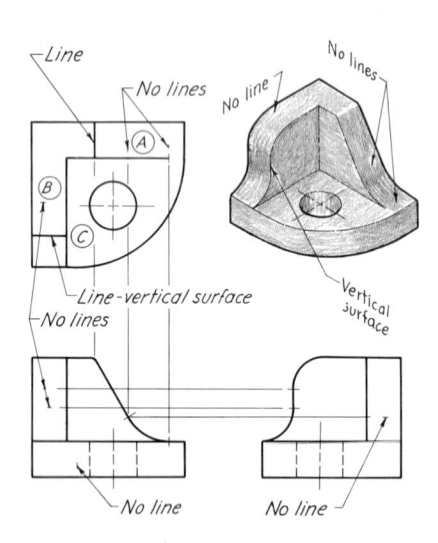

FIG. 6.24. Treatment of tangent surfaces.

surfaces meeting here that are at a definite angle, one to the other. Several typical examples of tangencies and intersections have been illustrated in Fig. 6.25.

6.20
Parallel Lines. When parallel surfaces are cut by a plane, the resulting lines of intersection will be parallel, as shown by the pictorial drawing in Fig. 6.26(b), where the near corner of the object has been removed by the oblique plane ABC. It can be observed from the multiview drawing in (c) that "when two lines are parallel in space, their projections will be parallel in all of the views," even though at times both lines may appear as points in one view.

In Fig. 6.26, three views are to be drawn that show the block after the near front corner has been removed [see (b)]. Several of the required lines of intersection can be readily established through the given points A, B, and C that define the oblique plane. For example, $c^F b^F$ can be drawn in the front view and the line through a^F can be drawn parallel to it. In the top view, $a^H b^H$ should be drawn first and the intersection line through c^H should then be drawn parallel to this H-view of AB. The drawing can now be completed by working back and forth from view to view while applying the rule that a plane intersects parallel planes along lines of intersection that are parallel. The remaining lines are thus drawn parallel to either AB or CB [see the pictorial in (b)].

6.21
Plotting an Elliptical Boundary. The actual intersection of a circular cylinder or cylindrical hole with a slanting surface (inclined plane) is an ellipse (Fig. 6.27). The elliptical boundary in (a) appears as an ellipse in the top view, as a line in the front view, and as a semicircle in the side view. The ellipse was plotted in the top view by projecting selected points (such as points A and B) from the circle arc in the side

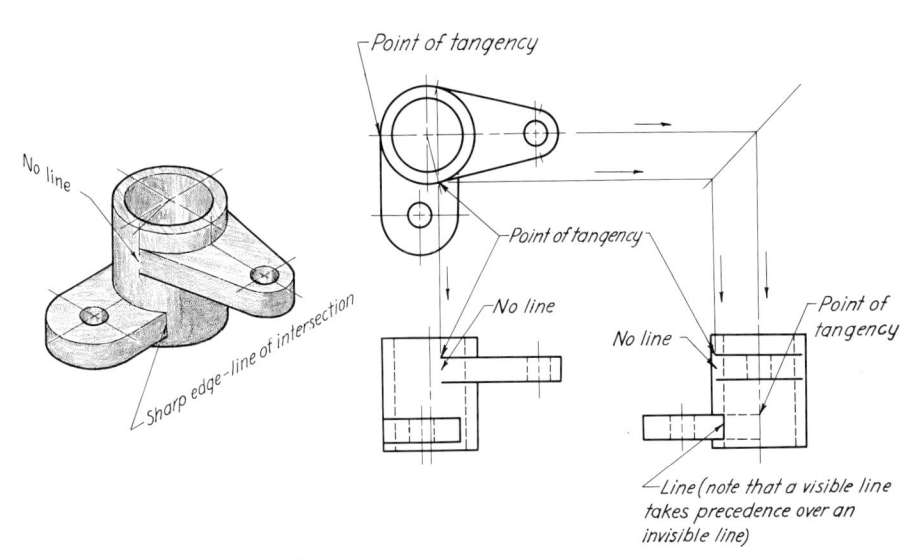

FIG. 6.25. Treatment of tangent surfaces.

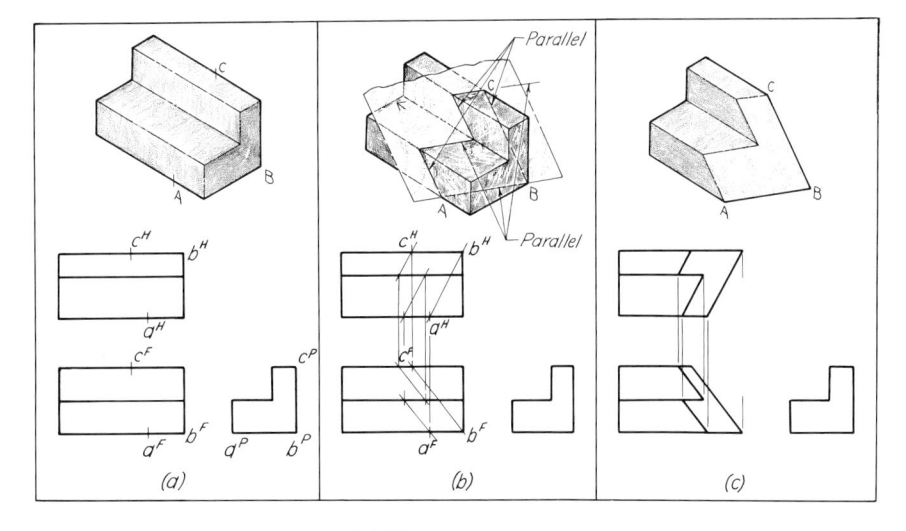

FIG. 6.26. Parallel lines.

view, as shown. For example, point A was projected first to the inclined line in the front view and then to the top view. The mitre line shown was used to project the depth distance for A in the top view for illustrative purposes only. Ordinarily, dividers should be used to transfer measurements to secure great accuracy.

In (b) the intersection of the hole with the sloping surface is represented by an ellipse in the side view. Points selected around the circle in the top view (such as points C and D) projected to the side view as shown permit the draftsman to form the elliptical outline. It is recommended that a smooth curve be sketched freehand through the projected points before the French curve is applied to draw the finished ellipse, because it is easier to fit a curved ruling edge to a line than to scattered points.

6.22
Projecting a Curved Outline (Space Curve). When a boundary curve lies in an inclined plane, the projection of the curve may be found in another view by projecting points along the curve, as illustrated in Fig. 6.28. In the example, points selected along the arcs forming the curve in the top view were first located in the side view, using distances taken from the top view, as shown by the X and Y measurements. Then the front view positions of these points, through which the front view of the curve must pass, were established by projecting horizontally from the side view and downward from the top view.

6.23
Treatment of Intersecting Finished and Unfinished Surfaces. Figure 6.29 illustrates the removal of material when machining surfaces, cutting a slot, and drilling a hole in a small part. The italic f on

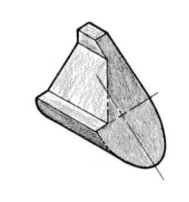

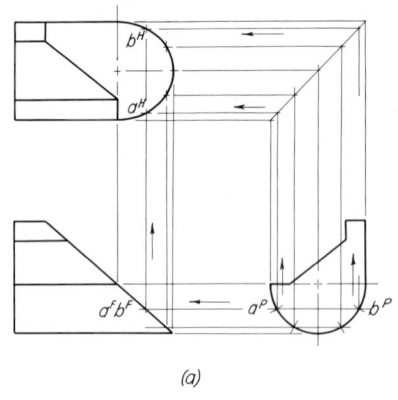

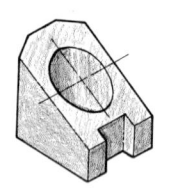

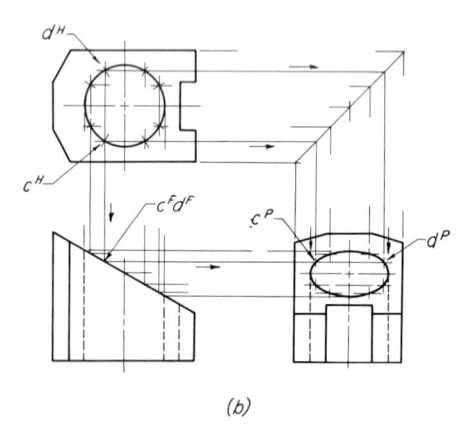

FIG. 6.27. Representation of an elliptical boundary.

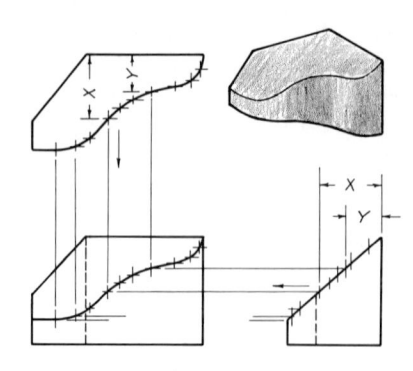

FIG. 6.28. Projecting a space curve.

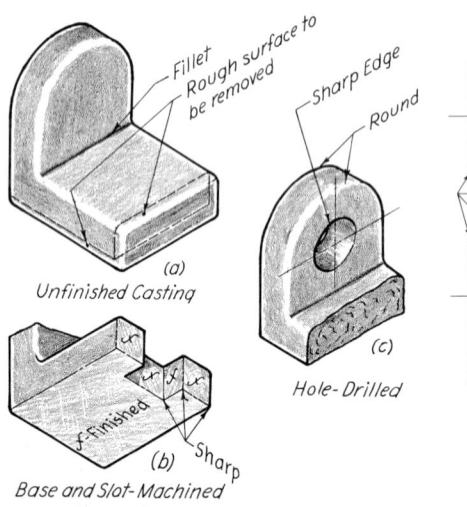

FIG. 6.29. Rough and finished surfaces on a casting.

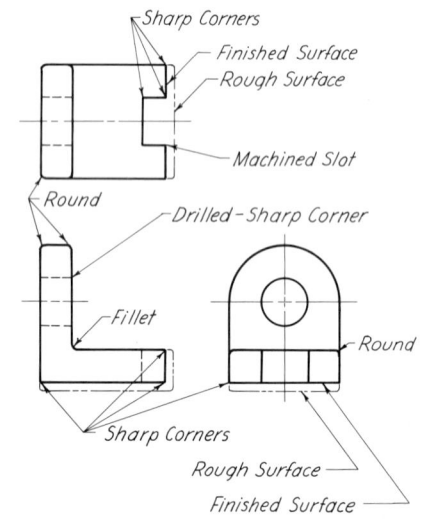

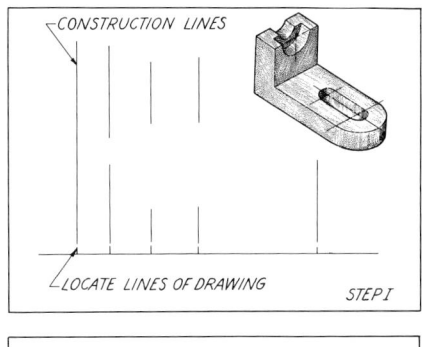

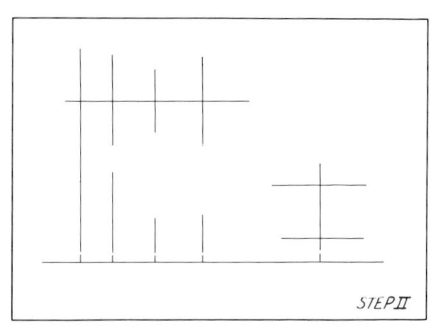

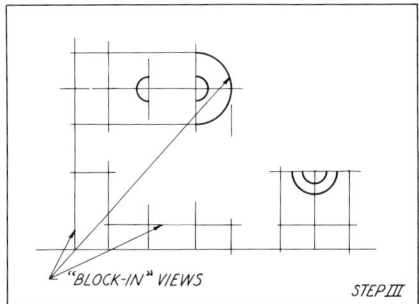

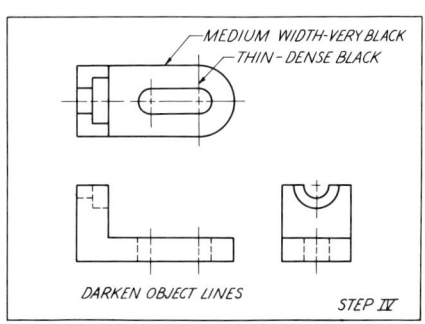

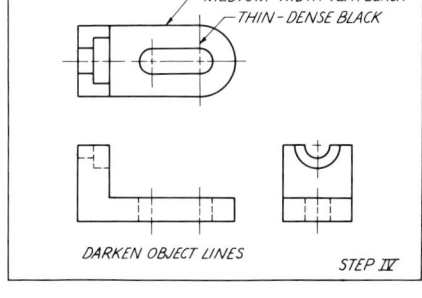

CHAP. 6 / MULTIVIEW REPRESENTATION, REVOLUTION, AND CONVENTIONAL PRACTICES   97

FIG. 6.30. Steps in making a three-view drawing of an object.

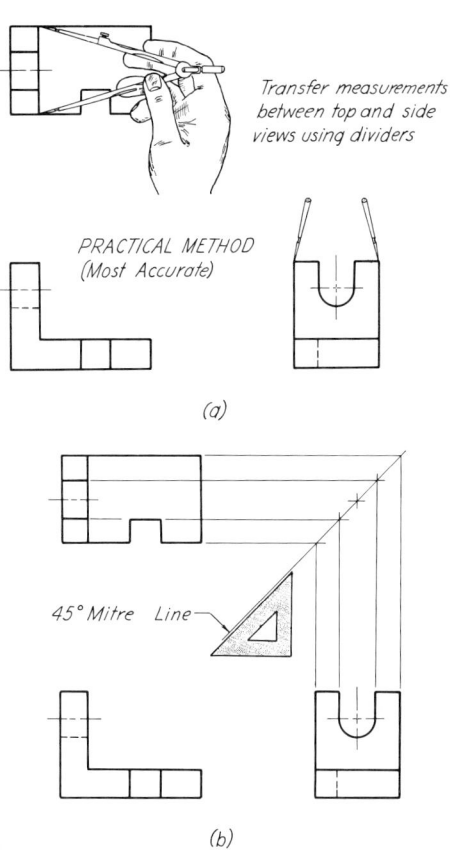

FIG. 6.31. Methods for transferring depth dimensions.

a surface of a pictorial drawing indicates that the surface has been machined. The location of sharp and rounded corners, as illustrated in (b) and (c), are noted on the multiview drawing. A discussion covering rounded internal and external corners is given in Sec. 6.44.

6.24
To Make an Orthographic Drawing. The location of all views should be determined before a drawing is begun. This will ensure balance in the appearance of the finished drawing. The contour view is usually started first. After the initial start, the draftsman should construct his views simultaneously by projecting back and forth from one to the other. It is poor practice to complete one view before starting the others, as much more time will be required to complete the drawing. Figure 6.30 shows the procedure for laying out a three-view drawing. The general outline of the views first should be drawn lightly with a hard pencil and then heavied with a medium-grade pencil. Although experienced persons sometimes deviate from this procedure by drawing in the lines of known length and location in finished weight while constructing the views, it is not recommended that beginners do so (see Fig. 6.30, step III).

Although a 45° mitre line is sometimes used for transferring depth dimensions from the top view to the side view, or vice versa, as shown in Fig. 6.31(b), it is better practice to use dividers, as in (a). Continuous lines need not be drawn between the views and the mitre line, as in the illustration, for one may project from short dashes across the mitre line. The location of the mitre line may be obtained by extending the construction lines representing the front edge of the top view and the front edge of the side view to an intersection.

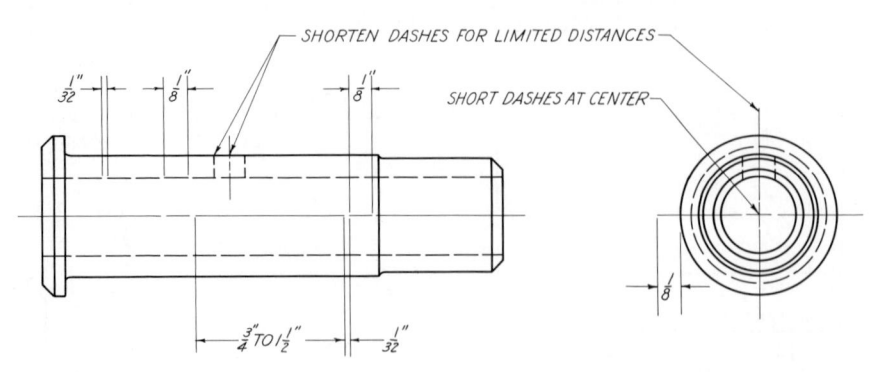

FIG. 6.32. Invisible lines and center lines.

When making an orthographic drawing in pencil, the beginner should endeavor to use the line weights recommended in Sec. 3.30. The object lines should be made very dark and bright, to give snap to the drawing as well as to create the contrast necessary to cause the shape of the object to stand out. Special care should be taken to gauge the dashes and spaces in invisible object lines. On ordinary drawings, $\frac{1}{8}$-in. dashes and $\frac{1}{32}$-in. spaces are recommended (Fig. 6.32).

Center lines consist of alternate long and short dashes. The long dashes are from $\frac{3}{4}$ to $1\frac{1}{2}$ in. long, the short dashes $\frac{1}{8}$ in., and the spaces $\frac{1}{32}$ in. (Fig. 6.32). The following technique is recommended in drawing center lines:

1. Where center lines cross, the short dashes should intersect symmetrically (Fig. 6.32). (In the case of very small circles the breaks may be omitted.)

2. The breaks should be so located that they will stand out and allow the center line to be recognized as such.

3. Center lines should extend approximately $\frac{1}{8}$ in. beyond the outline of the part whose symmetry they indicate (Fig. 6.32).

4. Center lines should not end at object lines.

5. Center lines that are aligned with object lines should have not less than a $\frac{1}{16}$-in. space between the end of the center line and the object line.

For a finished drawing to be pleasing in appearance, all lines of the same type must be uniform, and each type must have proper contrast with other symbolic types. The contrast between the types of pencil lines is similar to that of ink lines (Fig. 3.61), except that pencil lines are never as wide as ink lines (read Sec. 3.30). On commercial drawings, the usual practice is to "burn in" the object lines by applying heavy pressure.

If reasonable care is taken not to soil a drawing, it will not be necessary to clean any part of it with an eraser. Since the practice in most commercial drawing rooms is not to erase construction lines if they have been drawn lightly, the student, at the very beginning of his first course, should try to acquire habits that insure cleanliness.

When constructing a two-view drawing of a circular object, the pencil work must start with the drawing of the center lines, as shown in Fig. 6.33. This is necessarily the first step, because the construction of the circular (contour) view is based on a horizontal and a vertical center line. The horizontal object lines of the rectangular view are projected from the circles.

6.25

Visualizing an Object from Given Views. Most students in elementary graphics courses find it difficult to visualize an object from two or more views. This trouble is largely due to the lack of systematic procedure for analyzing complex shapes.

The simplest method of determining shape is illustrated pictorially in Fig. 6.34. This method of "breaking down" may be applied to any object, since all objects may be thought of as consisting of elemental geometric forms, such as prisms, cylinders, cones, and so on. These imaginary component parts may be additions in the form of projections or subtractions in the form of cavities. Following such a detailed geometric analysis, a clear picture of an entire object can be obtained by mentally assembling a few easily visualized forms.

It should be realized, when analyzing component parts, that it is impossible ordinarily to determine whether a form is an addition or a subtraction by looking at one view. For example, the small circles in the top view in Fig. 6.34 indicate a cylindrical form, but they do not reveal whether the form is a hole or a projection. By consulting the front view, however, the form is shown to be a hole (subtracted cylinder).

The graphic language is similar to the written language in that neither can be read at a glance. A drawing must be read patiently by referring systematically back and forth from one view to another. At the same time the reader must imagine a three-dimensional object and not a two-dimensional flat projection.

A student usually will find that a pictorial sketch will clarify the shape of a part that is difficult to visualize. The method for preparing quick sketches in isometric is explained in Secs. 7.16 and 7.17.

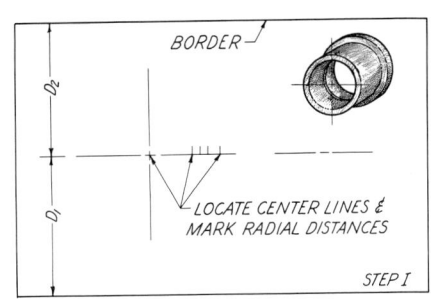

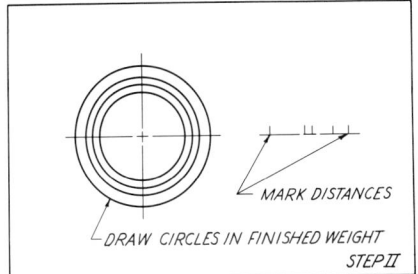

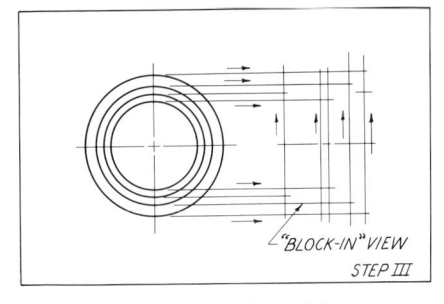

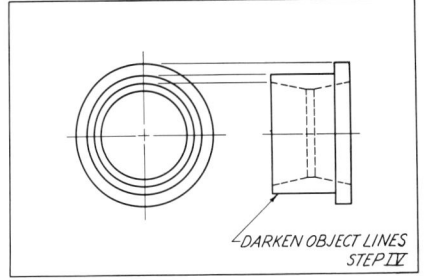

FIG. 6.33. Steps in making a two-view drawing of a circular object.

6.26

Interpretation of Adjacent Areas of a View.
To obtain a full understanding of the true geometric shape of a part, all the areas on a given view must be carefully analyzed, because each area represents a surface on the part. For example, in

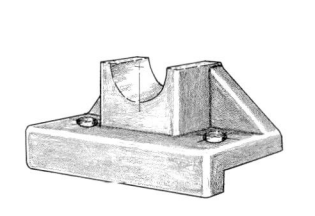

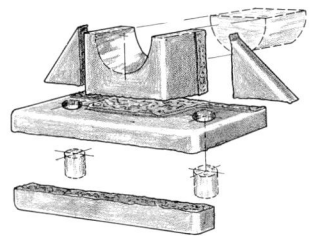

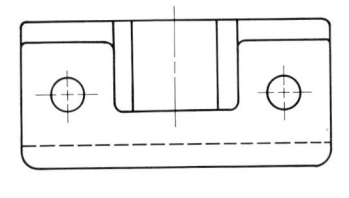

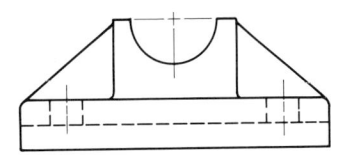

FIG. 6.34. "Breaking down" method.

(a) (b) (c) (d) (e)

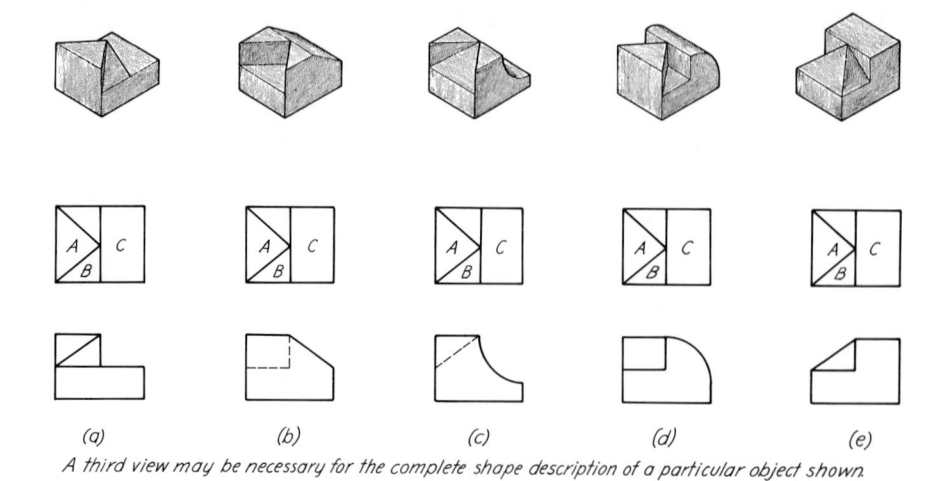

A third view may be necessary for the complete shape description of a particular object shown.

FIG. 6.35. Meaning of areas.

of possibilities in that it may be either low and horizontal (a), sloping (b), cylindrical [(c) and (d)], or high and horizontal (e).

The student must realize at this point that since there are infinite possibilities for the shape, position, and arrangement of surfaces that form objects, he must learn to study tediously the views of any object with which he is not familiar until he is sure of the exact shape. Multiview drawings cannot be read with the ease of our written language, which lists all the components in a dictionary.

Figure 6.36 shows a pictorial drawing and a three-view orthographic drawing of a mutilated block. The accompanying table gives an orderly analysis of the reading of the three views of the object. A table similar to this one may be prepared by a student to facilitate study of a particular drawing.

All lines and surfaces are numbered at random on the orthographic drawing so that the student may take each surface designated on the pictorial drawing and identify it by a different number on each of the three views. For example, surface 1 on the pictorial view appears as a surface in the top view and is identified by the number 5. The same surface appears as surface 24 in the front view and as line 4 in the end view.

reading a drawing it must be determined whether a particular area in a top view represents a surface that is inclined or horizontal and whether the surface is higher or lower than adjacent ones. Five distinctly different objects are shown in Fig. 6.35, all having the same top view. In determining the actual shape of these objects, memory and previous experience can be a help, but one can easily be misled if he does not approach the analysis with an open mind, for it is only by trial and error effort and by referring back and forth from view to view that a drawing can be read. In considering area A in (a) it might be thought that the triangular surface could be high and horizontal, which would be correct because of the arrangement of lines in the front view. However, in considering the top view alone A could be either sloping, as in (c) and (e) or low and horizontal, as in (b). An analysis of the five parts reveals that the surface represented by area B can also be either sloping, high and horizontal, or low and horizontal. Area C offers even a wider variety

6.27

True-length Lines. Students who, lacking a thorough understanding of the principles of projection (Sec. 6.8), find it difficult to determine whether or not a projection of a line in one of the principal views shows the true length of the line, should study carefully the following facts:

1. If the projection of a line shows the true length of the line, one of the other projections must appear as a horizontal line, a vertical line, or a point, on one of the other views of the drawing.

CHAP. 6 / MULTIVIEW REPRESENTATION, REVOLUTION, AND CONVENTIONAL PRACTICES **101**

2. If the top and front views of a line are horizontal, then both views show the true length.

3. If the top view of a line is a point, the front and side views show the true length.

4. If the front view of a line is a point, the top and side views show the true length.

5. If the top and front views of a line are vertical, the side view shows the true length.

6. If the side projection of a line is a point, the top and front views show the true length.

7. If the front view of a line is horizontal and the top view is inclined, the top inclined view shows the true length.

8. If the top view of a line is horizontal and the front view is inclined, the front inclined view shows the true length.

6.28
Representation of Holes. In preparing drawings of parts of mechanisms, a draftsman finds it necessary to represent machined holes, which most often are either drilled, drilled and reamed, drilled and countersunk, drilled and counterbored, or drilled and spotfaced. Graphically, a hole is represented to conform with the finished form. The form may be completely specified by a note attached to the view showing the circular contour (Fig. 6.37). The shop note, as prepared by the draftsman, usually specifies the several shop operations in the order that they are to be performed in the shop. For example, in (d) the hole, as specified, is drilled before it is counterbored. When depth has not been given in the note for a hole, it is understood to be a through hole; that is, the holes goes entirely through the piece [(a), (c), (d), and (e)]. A hole that does not go through is known as a "blind

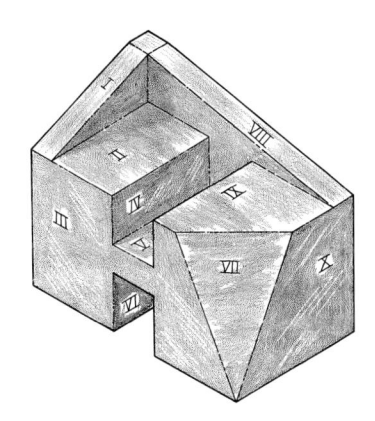

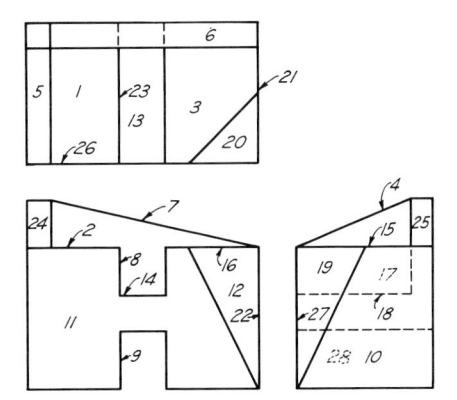

FIG. 6.36. Lines and surfaces.

hole" (b). For such holes, depth is the length of the cylindrical portion. Drilled, bored, reamed, cored, or punched holes are always specified by giving their diameters, never their radii. Drill diameters for number- and letter-size drills are given in Table 29 in the Appendix.

In drawing the hole shown in (a), which must be drilled before it is reamed, the limits are ignored and the diameter is scaled to the nearest regular fractional or decimal size. In (b) the 30° × 60° triangle is used to draw the approximate representation of the conical hole formed by the drill point. In (c) a 45° triangle has been used to draw an approximate representation of the outline of the conical

SURFACE NUMBER ON PICTORIAL	PROJECTS AS LINE OR SURFACE		
	NUMBER ON TOP VIEW	NUMBER ON FRONT VIEW	NUMBER ON END VIEW
I	5	24	4
II	1	2	15
III	26	11	27
IV	23	8	17
V	13	14	18
VI	23	9	28
VII	20	12	19
VIII	6	7	25
IX	3	16	15
X	21	22	10

102 PART II / SPATIAL GRAPHICS: SHAPE DESCRIPTION AND SPATIAL RELATIONSHIPS

FIG. 6.37. Representation of holes.

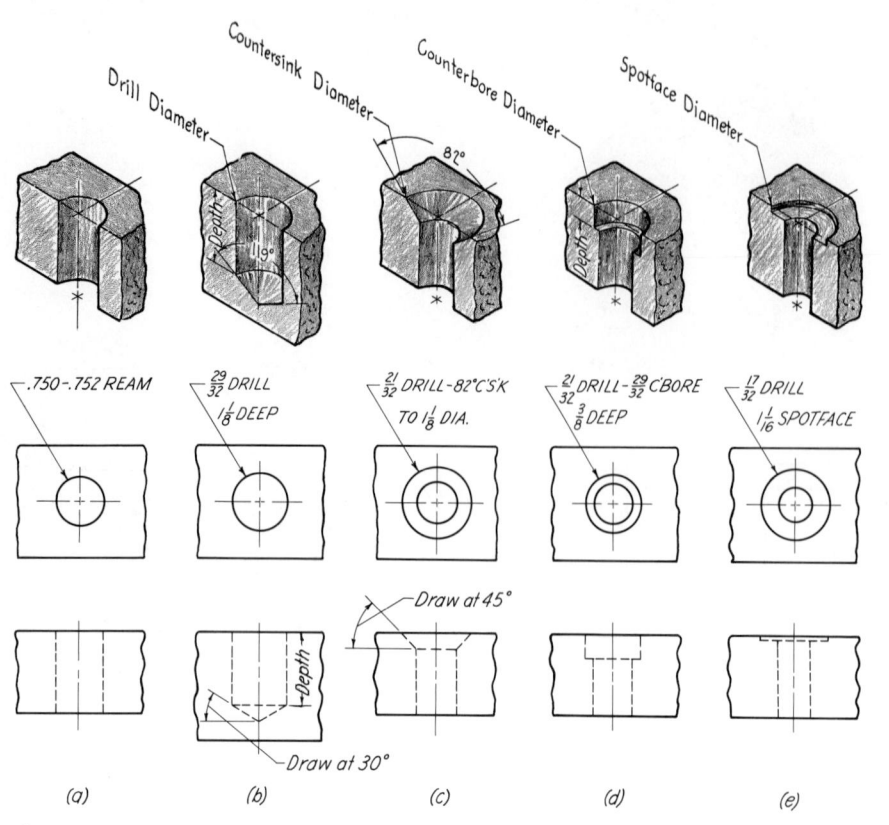

(For representations of threaded holes see chapter covering screw threads and fasteners)

enlargement. The actual angle of 82° is ignored in order to save time in drawing. The spotface in (e) is most often cut to a depth of $\frac{1}{16}$ in.; however, the depth is usually not specified.

The beginner should now scan the several sections in the chapter on shop processes to obtain some general information on the production of holes. Complete information on the preparation of shop notes for holes may be found in Chapters 14, 15, and 16.

B: REVOLUTION

6.29

To Find the True Length of a Line by Revolution. In engineering drafting, it is frequently necessary to determine the true length of a line when constructing the development of a surface (Chapter 11). The true lengths must be found of those lines that are not parallel to any coordinate plane and therefore appear foreshortened in all the principal views. (See Sec. 6.8, "Projection of lines.") The practical as well as theoretical procedure is to revolve any such oblique line into a position parallel to a coordinate plane such that its projection on that particular plane will be the same length as the line. In Fig. 6.38(a), this is illustrated by the edge AB

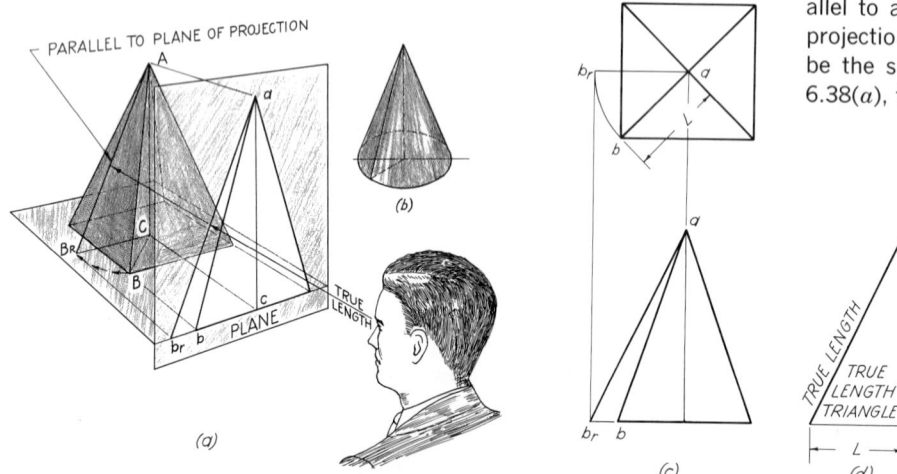

FIG. 6.38. True length of a line, revolution method.

on the pyramid. AB is oblique to the coordinate planes, and its projections are foreshortened. If this edge line is imagined to be revolved until it becomes parallel to the frontal plane, then the projection ab_r in the front view will be the same length as the true length of AB.

A practical application of this method is shown in Fig. 6.38(c). The true length of the edge AB in Fig. 6.38(a) would be found by revolving its top projection into the position ab_r, representing AB revolved parallel to the frontal plane, and then projecting the end point b_r down into its new position along a horizontal line through b. The horizontal line represents the horizontal plane of the base, in which the point B travels as the line AB is revolved.

Commercial draftsmen who are unfamiliar with the theory of coordinate planes find the true-length projection of a line by visualizing the line's revolution. They think of an edge as being revolved until it is in a plane perpendicular to the line of sight of an observer stationed an infinite distance away (Figs. 11.10, 11.11, and 11.12). The process corresponds to that used in drawing regular orthographic views (Sec. 6.4). Usually this method is more easily understood by a student.

Note in Fig. 6.38(a) and (b) that the true length of a line is equal to the hypotenuse of a right triangle whose altitude is equal to the difference in the elevation of the end points and whose base is equal to the top projection of the line. With this fact in mind, many draftsmen determine the true length of a line by constructing a true-length triangle similar to the one illustrated in Fig. 6.38(d).

6.30
Revolution of an Object. Although in general the views on a working drawing represent a machine part satisfactorily when shown in a natural position, it is sometimes desirable to revolve an element until it is parallel to a coordinate plane in order to improve the representation or to reveal the true size and shape of a principal surface, or true length of a line.

The distinguishing difference between this method and the method of auxiliary projection (Chapter 9) is that, in the procedure of revolution, the observer turns (revolves) the object with respect to the customary planes of projection, instead of shifting his viewing position with respect to either an inclined or an oblique surface of the object.

Despite the fact that the revolution of an entire object, as illustrated in Fig. 6.39, rarely has a practical application in industry, the making of such a drawing provides excellent drill in projection.* Therefore, since the several articles that follow are intended primarily for training students, the practical applications have been omitted, while the procedures for revolving simple objects are explained in detail.

6.31
Simple (Single) Revolution. When the regular views are given, an object may be shown in another position, as may be required, by imagining it to be revolved about an axis perpendicular to one of the principal (horizontal, frontal, or profile) planes. A single revolution about such an axis is known as a "simple revolution." The three general cases are shown in Fig. 6.39, spaces II, III, and IV.

6.32
To Determine the True-shape Projection (Normal View) of a Plane Surface—Revolution Method. If a surface is parallel to one of the principal planes of projection, its projection on that plane will

---

*Practical applications of revolution may be found in the chapter covering descriptive geometry in the author's text, *Basic Graphics for Design, Analysis, Communications, and the Computer*, 2nd ed., Prentice-Hall, Inc., Englewood Cliffs, N.J., 1968.

show its true shape, as has been explained in Sec. 6.10. In Fig. 6.39, space I, the inclined surface $ABCD$ appears as a line ($a^F b^F c^F d^F$) in the front view and is shown foreshortened in the top and side views. Line $A-B$ was taken as the axis of rotation and the surface was revolved into a position parallel to the H-plane, as shown by the pictorial drawing ($ABC_R D_R$). First, the edge view of the surface, as represented by the line $a^F b^F c^F d^F$, was revolved about $a^F b^F$ into a horizontal position, as shown by the line $a^F b^F c_r^F d_r^F$. The complete H-view ($a^H b^H c_r^H d_r^H$) of the surface as revolved shows the true shape of $ABCD$.

6.33
Revolution About a Vertical Axis Perpendicular to the Horizontal Plane. A simple revolution about an axis perpendicular to the horizontal plane is illustrated in Fig. 6.39, space II. The object is first revolved about the assumed imaginary axis until it is in the desired position (see pictorial). The views of the part in its revolved position then are obtained by orthographic projection, as in the case of any ordinary multiview drawing. Since the top view will not be changed in shape by the revolution, it must be drawn first in its revolved position (at 30° in this case) and the front and side views should be projected from it. Since the heights to all of the points on the object also remain unchanged by the revolution, height distances could be conveniently projected from the initial views in I.

The top view may be drawn directly in revolved position, without first drawing the usual orthographic views. If this procedure is followed, the height distances for the front and side views may be set off to known dimensions.

6.34
Revolution About a Horizontal Axis Perpendicular to the Frontal Plane. If an object is revolved about an imaginary axis perpendicular to the frontal plane, as shown in Fig. 6.39, space III, the front view changes in position but not in shape. The front view, therefore, should be drawn first in its revolved position, and the top and side views should be projected from it. The depth of the top view and the side view remain unchanged since the depth distance is parallel to the axis. If the usual unrevolved views are not drawn first, the front view may be drawn directly in its revolved position and depth distances can then be laid off to known dimensions.

6.35
Revolution About a Horizontal Axis Perpendicular to the Profile Plane. A single revolution of an object about an axis perpendicular to the profile plane is illustrated in Fig. 6.39, space IV. Since in this case

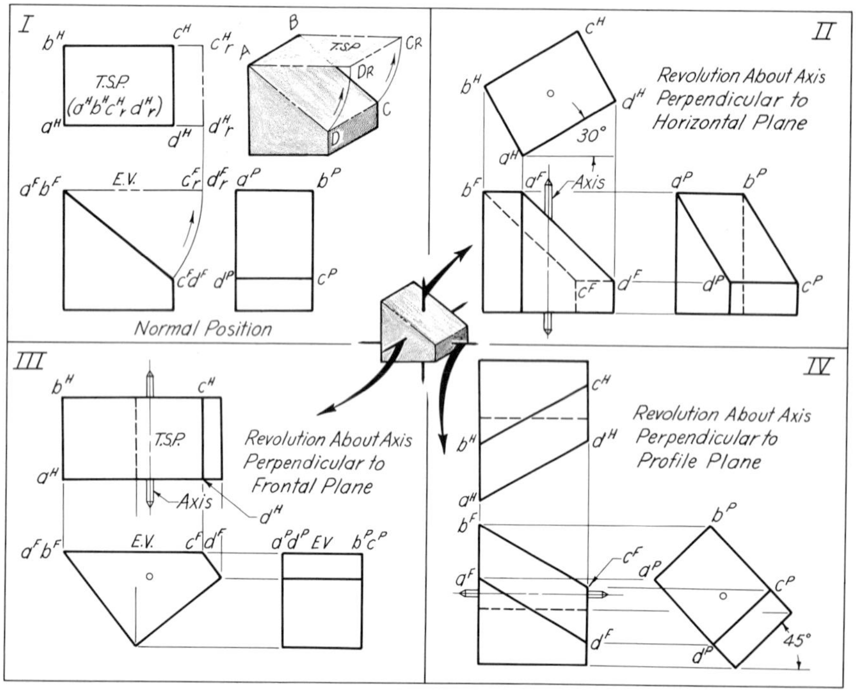

FIG. 6.39. A single revolution about an axis perpendicular to a principal (horizontal, frontal, or profile) plane.

it is the side view that is perpendicular to the axis and revolves parallel to the coordinate plane of projection, it is the side view that remains unchanged in its shape. The width of the top and front views is not affected by the revolution. Therefore, horizontal dimensions for these views may be set off by using known measurements.

From these general cases of simple revolution, two principles have emerged that can be stated as follows:

1. The view that is perpendicular to the axis of revolution changes only in position.

2. The lengths of the lines parallel to the axis do not change during the revolution and, therefore, may be either laid off to known measurements or projected from the usual orthographic views of the object.

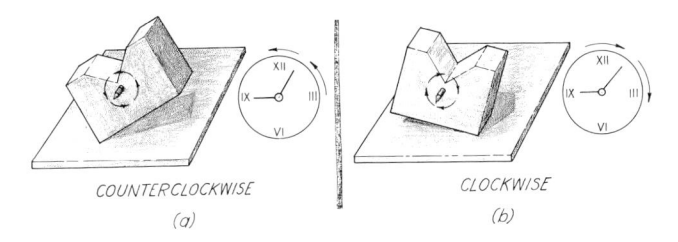

FIG. 6.40. Direction of revolution.

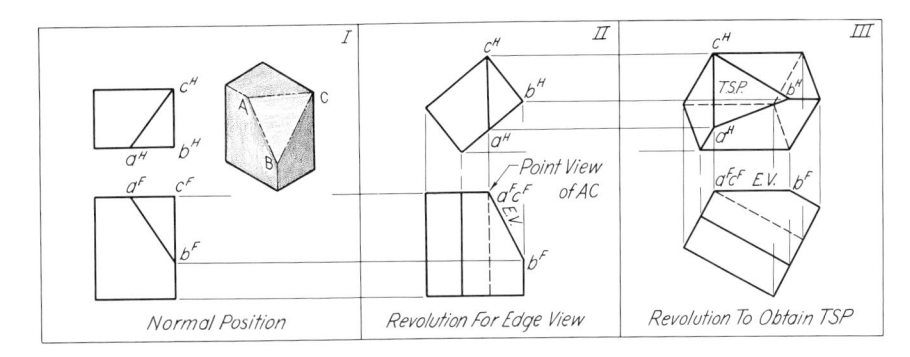

FIG. 6.41. Successive revolution to show the true shape (TSP) of an oblique surface.

6.36
Clockwise and Counterclockwise Revolution. An object may be revolved either clockwise or counterclockwise about an axis of revolution. The direction is indicated by the view to which the axis is perpendicular. For example, front views, when revolved as in Fig. 6.40(b), show a clockwise revolution. When revolved as in (a), their revolution is counterclockwise. Top views show a clockwise revolution when revolved to the right. Right-side views indicate a clockwise direction of revolution when they have been revolved to the right and a counterclockwise direction when revolved to the left.

6.37
Successive (Multiple) Revolution. Since it is possible to show an object in any position relative to the coordinate planes of projection, it can be drawn as may be required by making a series of successive simple revolutions. Usually such a series is limited to three or four stages. Figure 6.41 shows an object revolved successively about two separate axes. The usual orthographic views of the given object are shown at the left in space I. In space II, the object has been revolved (counterclockwise) about a vertical axis to obtain an edge view (EV) of the oblique surface ABC (see pictorial). Note that the line AC projects as a point ($a^F c^F$) in the front view. The identification of each corner may not be necessary in the case of a simple object. However, if the object is in the least complex, possible confusion is avoided if each corner point is either numbered or identified by a letter, as was done for the oblique surface in the illustration. In space III at the right, the object is represented after it has been revolved from its previous position in space II. In this case, since the edge view (EV) of surface ABC is now horizontal, a true-shape projection (TSP) of the surface will appear in the top view.

A convenient method of copying a view in a new revolved position is first to trace it on a small piece of tracing paper and then to place the traced view in correct position and draw the new view. An alternative method is to place the traced view in correct position and prick the corner points, using the dividers opened out. With the traced view removed, the revolved view on the final drawing may be completed by joining the prick-points.

C: CONVENTIONAL PRACTICES

6.38

To reduce the high cost of preparing engineering drawings and at the same time to convey specific and concise information without a great expenditure of effort, some generally recognized systems of symbolic representation and conventional practices have been adopted by American industry.

A standard symbol or conventional representation can express information that might not be understood from a true-line representation unless accompanied by a lettered statement. In many cases, even though a true-line representation would convey exact information, very little more would be gained from the standpoint of better interpretation. Some conventional practices have been adopted for added clearness. For instance, they can eliminate awkward conditions that arise from strict adherence to the rules of projection.

These idioms of drawing have slowly developed with the graphic language until at the present time they are universally recognized and observed and appear in the various standards of the American National Standards Institute.

Professional men and skilled workmen have learned to accept and respect the use of the symbols and conventional practices, for they can interpret these representations accurately and realize that their use saves valuable time in both the drawing room and the shop.

6.39

Half Views and Partial Views. When the available space is insufficient to allow a satisfactory scale to be used for the representation of a symmetrical piece, it is considered good practice to make one view either a half view or a partial view, as shown in Fig. 6.42. The half view, however, must be the top or side view and not the front view, which shows the characteristic contour. The half view should be the front half of the top or side view. In the case of the partial view shown in (b), a break line is used to limit the view.

6.40

Accepted Violations of True Projection in the Representation of Boltheads, Slots, and Holes for Pins. A departure from true projection is encountered in representing a bolthead. For example, on a working drawing, it is considered the best practice to show the head across corners in both views, regardless of the fact that in true projection one view would show "across flats." This method of treatment eliminates the possibility of a reader's interpreting a hexagonal head to be a square head (Fig. 6.43). Furthermore, the show-

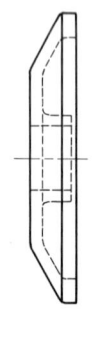

Half view
(a)

Partial view
(b)

FIG. 6.42. Half views and partial views.

ing of a head the "long way" in both views clearly reveals the space needed for proper clearance.

In the case of the slotted head fasteners, the slots are shown at 45° in the end views in order to avoid placing a slot on a center line, where it is usually difficult to draw so that the center line passes accurately through the center (Fig. 6.44). This practice does not affect the descriptive value of the drawing, because the true size and shape of the slot is shown in the front view. The hole for a pin is shown at 45° for the same reason. In such a position it may be more quickly observed.

6.41

The Treatment of Unimportant Intersections. The conventional methods of treating various unimportant intersections are shown in Fig. 6.45. To show the true line of intersection in each case would add little to the value of the drawing. Therefore, in the views designated as preferred, true projection has been ignored in the interest of simplicity. On the side views, in (a) and (b), for example, there is so little difference between the descriptive values of the true and approximate representations of the holes that the extra labor necessary to draw the true representation is unwarranted.

6.42

Aligned Views. Pieces that have arms, ribs, lugs, or other features at an angle are shown aligned or "straightened out" in one view, as illustrated in Fig. 6.46. By this method, it is possible to show the true shape as well as the true position of such features. In Fig. 6.47, the front view has been drawn as though the slotted arm had been revolved into alignment with the element projecting outward to the left. This practice is followed to avoid drawing an element—that is at an angle—in a foreshortened position.

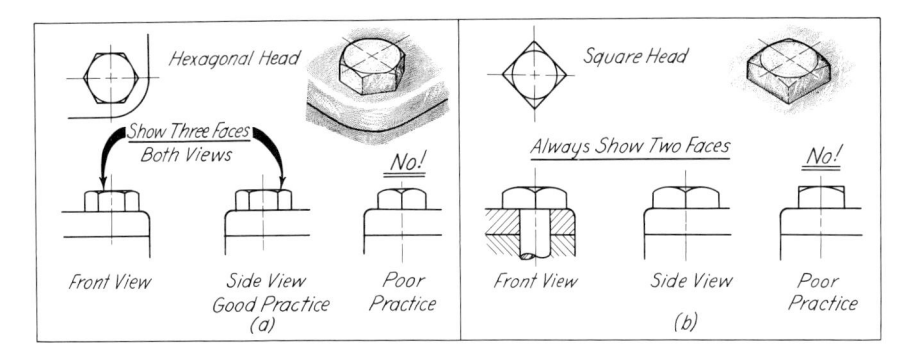

FIG. 6.43. Treatment of bolt heads.

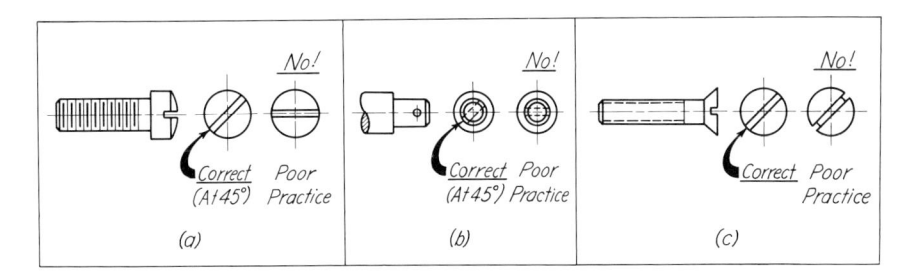

FIG. 6.44. Treatment of slots and holes in fasteners and pins.

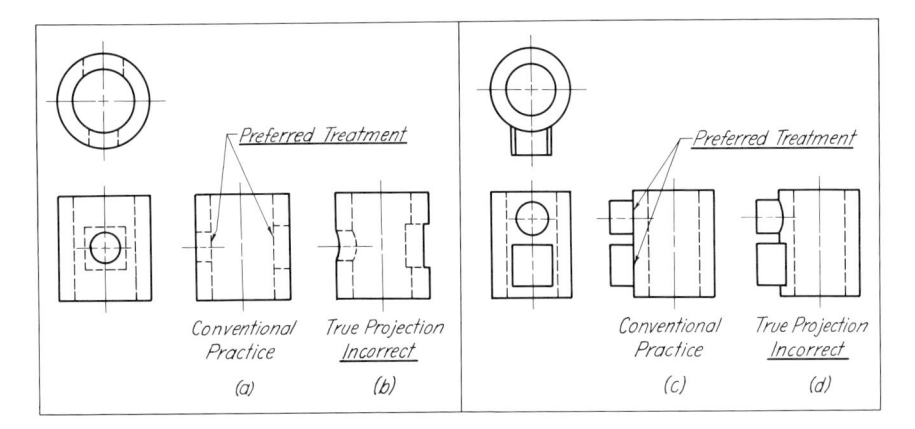

FIG. 6.45. Treatment of unimportant intersections.

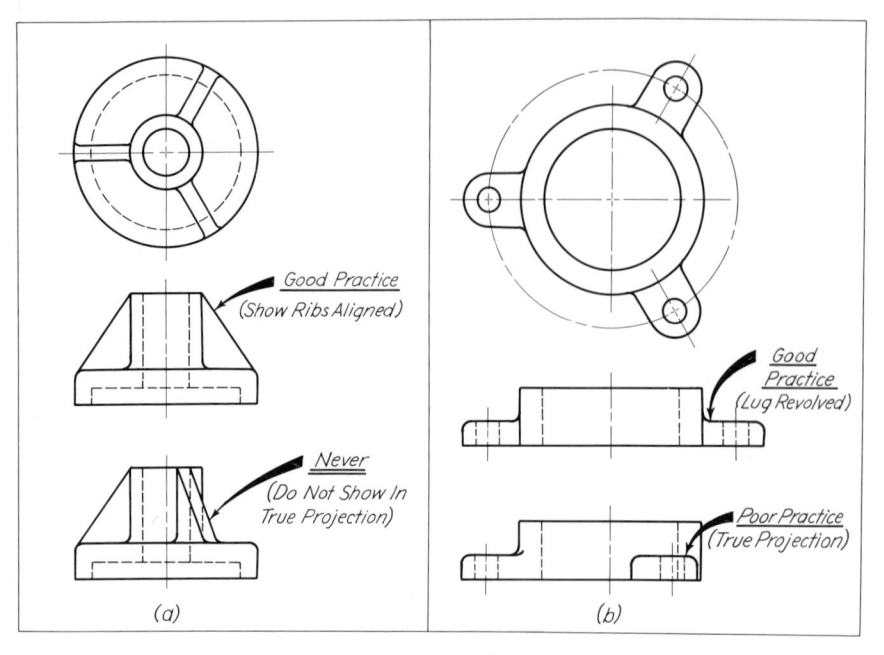

FIG. 6.46. Conventional practice of representing ribs and lugs.

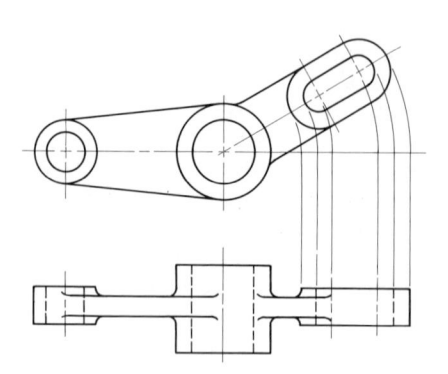

FIG. 6.47 Aligned views.

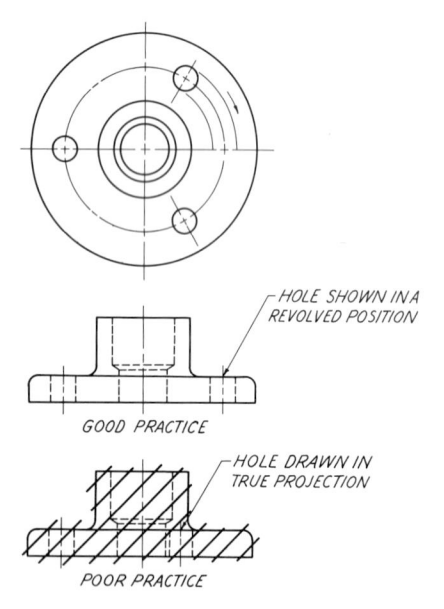

FIG. 6.48. Radially arranged holes.

6.43
Conventional Treatment of Radially Arranged Features. Many objects that have radially arranged features may be shown more clearly if true projection is violated, as in Fig. 6.46(b). Violation of true projection in such cases consists of intentionally showing such features swung out of position in one view to present the idea of symmetry and show the true relationship of the features at the same time. For example, while the radially arranged holes in a flange (Fig. 6.48) should always be shown in their true position in the circular view, they should be shown in a revolved position in the other view in order to show their true relationship with the rim.

Radial ribs and radial spokes are similarly treated [Fig. 6.46(a)]. The true projection of such features may create representations that are unsymmetrical and misleading. The preferred conventional method of treatment, by preserving symmetry, produces representations that are more easily understood and that at the same time are much simpler to draw. Figure 6.49 illustrates the preferred treatment for radial ribs and holes.

6.44
Representations of Fillets and Rounds. Interior corners, which are formed on a casting by unfinished surfaces, always are filled in (filleted) at the intersection in order to avoid possible fracture at that point. Sharp corners are also difficult to obtain and are avoided for this reason as well. Exterior corners are rounded for appearance and for the comfort of persons

who must handle the part when assembling or repairing the machine on which the part is used. A rounded internal corner is known as a *fillet;* a rounded external corner is known as a *round* (Fig. 6.50).

When two intersecting surfaces are machined, however, their intersection will become a sharp corner. For this reason, all corners formed by unfinished surfaces should be shown "broken" by small rounds, and all corners formed by two finished surfaces, or one finished surface and one unfinished surface, should be shown "sharp." Although in the past it has been the practice to allow patternmakers to use their judgment about the size of fillets and rounds, many present-day companies require their designers and draftsmen to specify their size even though their exact size may not be important.

Since fillets and rounds eliminate the intersection lines of intersecting surfaces, they create a special problem in orthographic representation. To treat them in the same manner as they would be treated if they had large radii results in views that are misleading. For example, the true-projection view in Fig. 6.51(c) confuses the reader, because at first glance it does not convey the idea that there are abrupt changes in direction. To prevent such a probable first impression and to improve the descriptive value of the view, it is necessary to represent these theoretically nonexisting lines. These characteristic lines are projected from the approximate intersections of the surfaces, with the fillets disregarded.

Figure 6.52 illustrates the accepted conventional method of representing the "run-out" intersection of a fillet in cases where a plane surface is tangent to a cylindrical surface. Although run-out arcs such as these are usually drawn freehand, a French curve or a bow instrument may be used. If they are drawn with the bow instrument, a radius should be used that

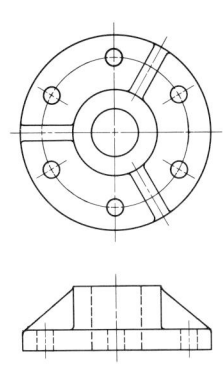

FIG. 6.49. Conventional treatment of radially arranged ribs.

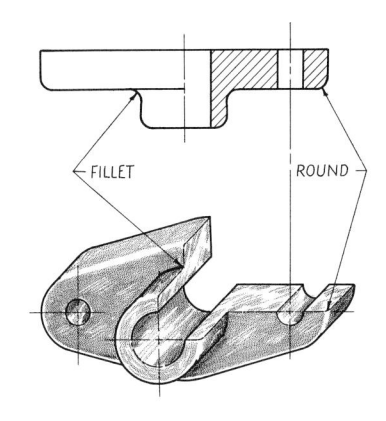

FIG. 6.50. Fillets and rounds.

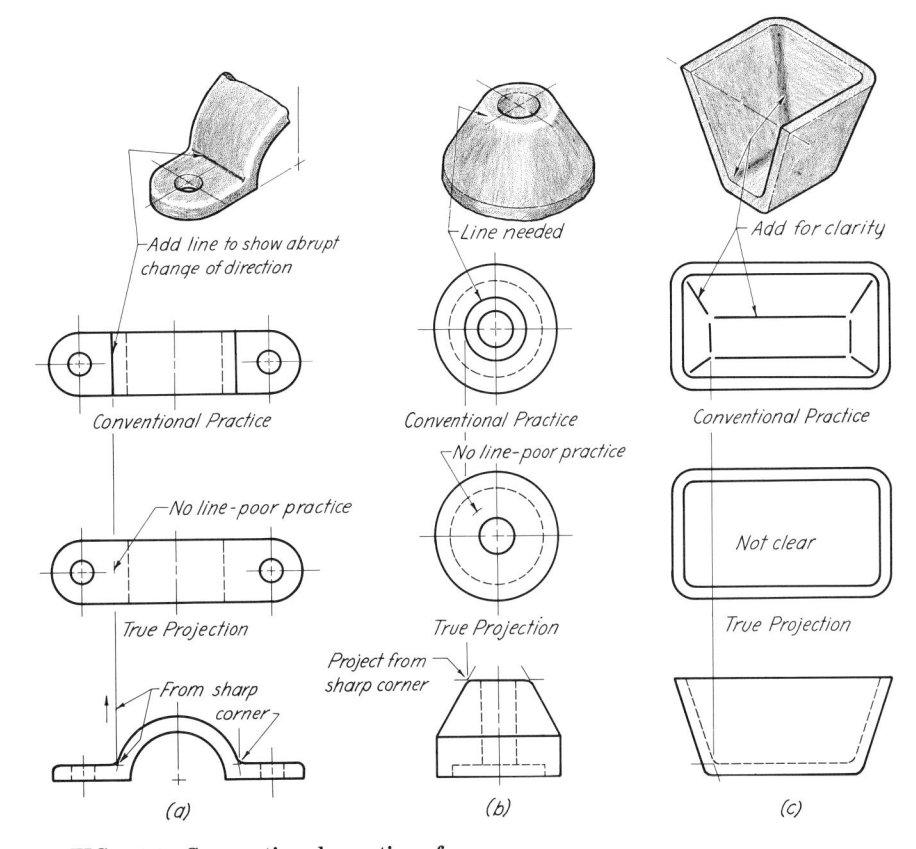

FIG. 6.51. Conventional practice of representing nonexisting lines of intersection.

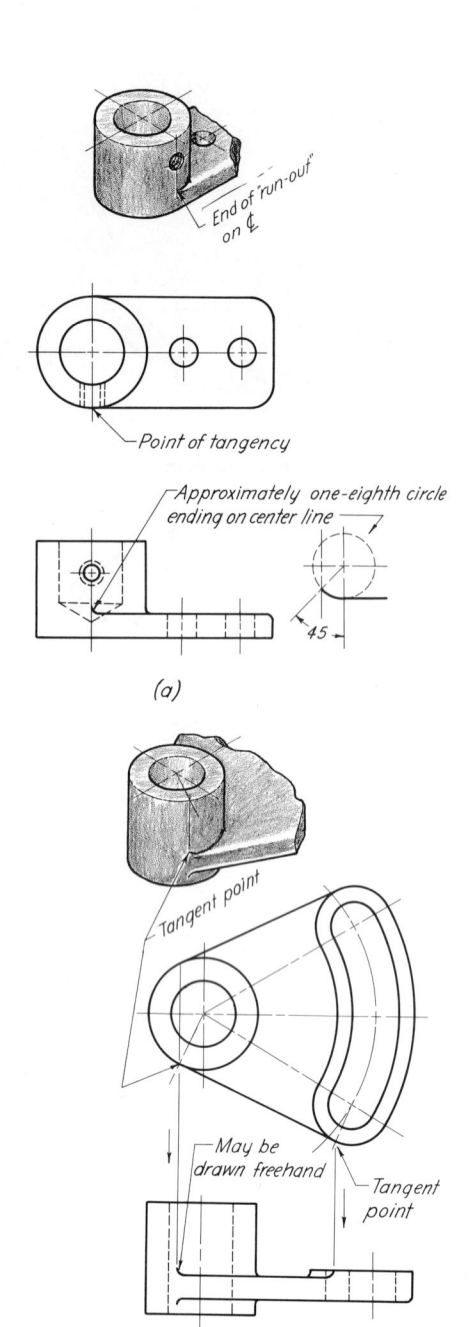

FIG. 6.52. The conventional treatment for fillets.

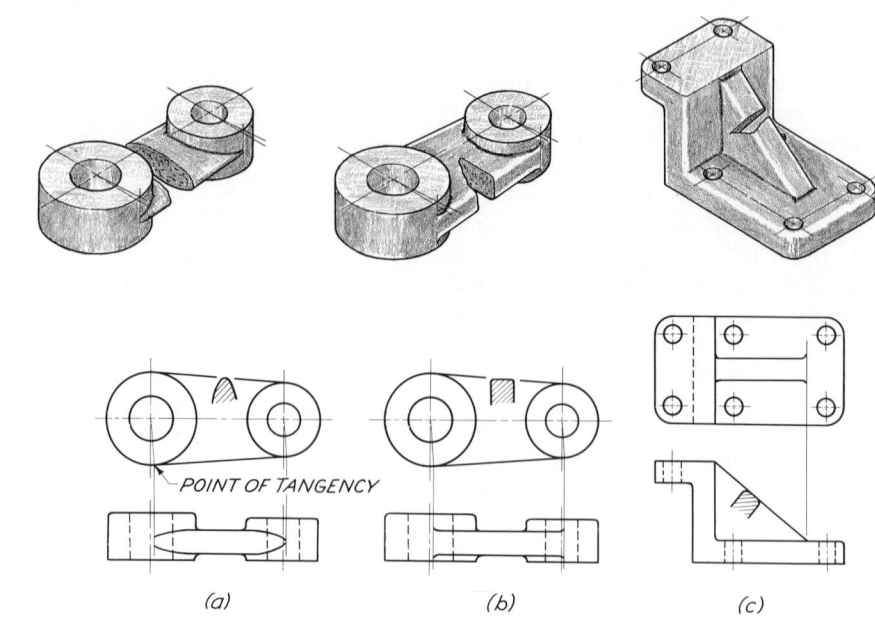

FIG. 6.53. The approximate methods of representing run-outs for intersecting fillets and rounds.

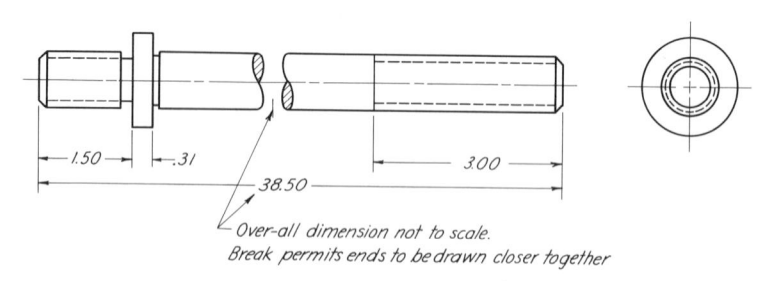

FIG. 6.54. A broken-out view.

is equal to the radius of the fillet, and the completed arc should form approximately one-eighth of a circle.

The generally accepted methods of representing intersecting fillets and rounds are illustrated in Fig. 6.53. The treatment, in each of the cases shown, is determined by the relationship existing between the sizes of the intersecting fillets and rounds.

6.45
Conventional Breaks. A relatively long piece of uniform section may be shown to a larger scale, if a portion is broken out so that the ends can be drawn closer together (Fig. 6.54). When such a scheme is employed, a conventional break is used to indicate that the length of the representation is not to scale. The American National Standard conventional breaks,

FIG. 6.55. Conventional breaks.

FIG. 6.56. Ditto lines.

FIG. 6.57. Alternate positions.

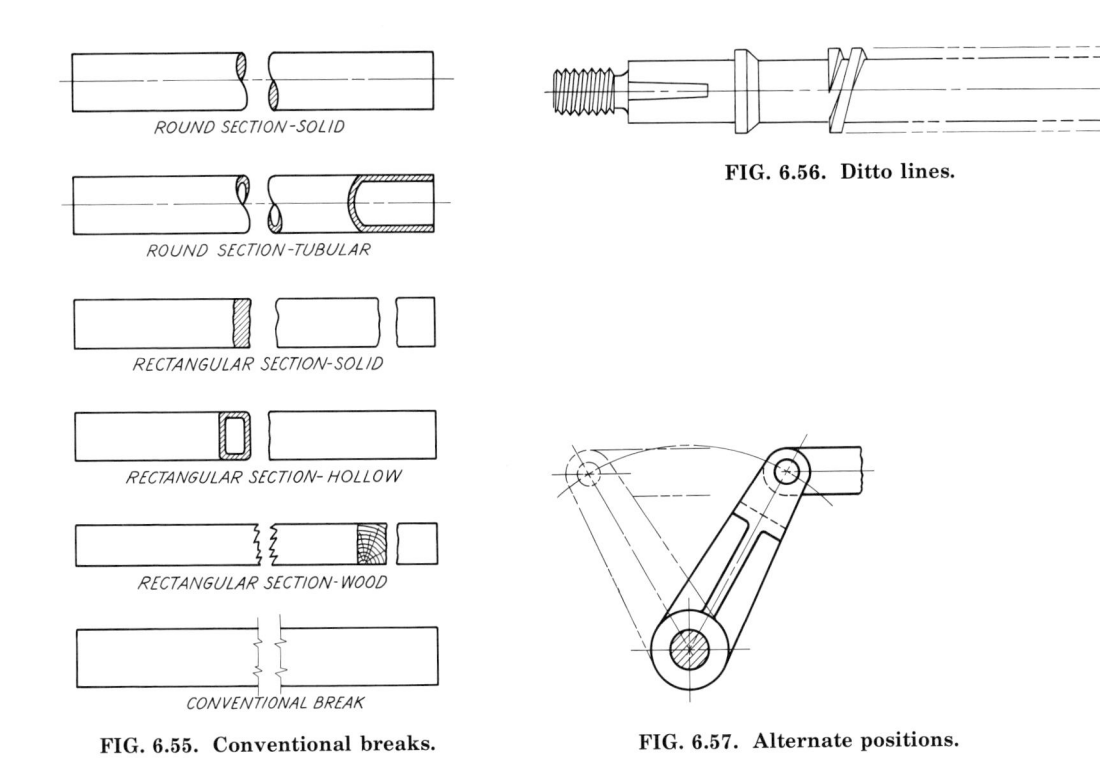

shown in Fig. 6.55, are used on either detail or assembly drawings. The break representations for indicating the broken ends of rods, shafts, tubes, and so forth, are designed to reveal the characteristic shape of the cross section in each case. Although break lines for round sections may be drawn freehand, particularly on small views, it is better to draw them with either an irregular curve or a bow instrument. The breaks for wood sections, however, always should be drawn freehand.

6.46
Ditto Lines. When it is desirable to minimize labor in order to save time, ditto lines may be used to indicate a series of identical features. For example, the threads on the shaft shown in Fig. 6.56 are just as effectively indicated by ditto lines as by a completed profile representation. When ditto lines are used, a long shaft of this type may be shortened without actually showing a conventional break.

6.47
A Conventional Method for Showing a Part in Alternate Positions. A method frequently used for indicating an alternate position of a part or a limiting position of a moving part is shown in Fig. 6.57. The dashes forming the object lines of the view showing the alternate position should be of medium weight. The phantom line shown in Fig. 3.61 is recommended for representing an alternate position.

6.48
Conventional Representation. Symbols are used on topographic drawings, archi-

tectural drawings, electrical drawings, and machine drawings. No engineer serving in a professional capacity can very well escape their use.

Most of the illustrations that are shown in Fig. 6.58 should be easily understood. However, the crossed-lines (diagonals) symbol has two distinct and different meanings. First, this symbol may be used on a drawing of a shaft to indicate the position of a surface for a bearing or, second, it may indicate that a surface perpendicular to the line of sight is flat. These usages are illustrated with separate examples.

PROBLEMS

The problems that follow are intended primarily to furnish study in multiview projection through the preparation of either sketches or instrumental drawings. Many of the problems in this chapter, however, may be prepared in more complete form. Their views may be dimensioned as are the views of working drawings, if the student will study carefully the beginning of the chapter covering dimensioning before attempting to record size description (Chapter 16). All dimensions should be placed in accordance with the general rules of dimensioning. The problems given at the end of

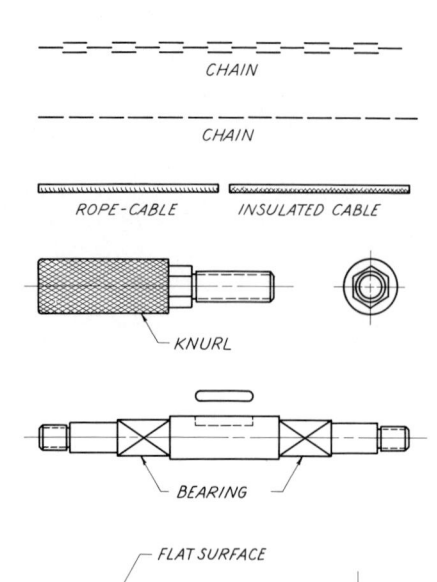

FIG. 6.58. Conventional symbols.

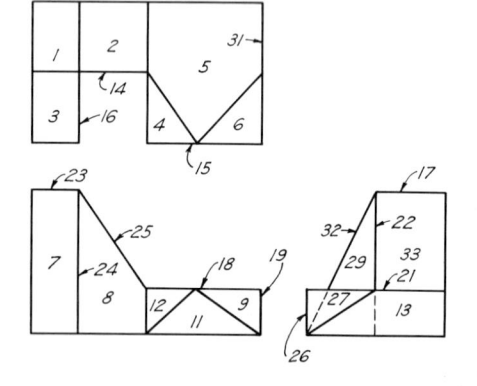

FIG. 6.59. Reading exercise.

Chapter 7 offer further study in multiview representation.

The views shown in a sketch or drawing should be spaced on the paper with aim for balance within the borderlines. Ample room should be allowed between the views for the necessary dimensions. If the views are not to be dimensioned, the distance between them may be made somewhat less than would be necessary otherwise.

Before starting to draw, the student should reread Sec. 6.24 and study Fig. 6.30, which shows the steps in making a multiview drawing. The preparation of a preliminary sketch always proves helpful to the beginner.

All construction work should be done in light lines with a sharp hard pencil. A drawing should be checked by an instructor before the lines are "heavied in," unless the preliminary sketch was checked beforehand.

1. (Fig. 6.59). Draw a table similar to that shown in Fig. 6.36 and fill in the required information for each of the surfaces designated on the pictorial drawing by a Roman numeral. Draw the necessary guide lines and letter the column headings and information in $\frac{1}{8}$-in. capitals.

2. (Fig. 6.60). Add the missing line or lines in one view of each of the three-view drawings. When the missing line or lines have been determined, the three views of each object will be consistent with one another.

3. (Fig. 6.61). Draw or sketch the third view for each of the given objects.

4–7. (Figs. 6.62–6.65). Reproduce the given views and draw the required view. Show all hidden lines.

8. (Fig. 6.66). Make an orthographic drawing or sketch of the bench stop. The views may be dimensioned. The shaft portion that fits into the hole in the bench top is $\frac{3}{4}$ in. in diameter and 2 in. long.

9–40. (Figs. 6.67–6.98). Make multiview drawings of the given objects. The views of a drawing may or may not be dimensioned.

41. (Fig. 6.99). Make a complete orthographic drawing of the anchor bracket.

42. (Fig. 6.100). Make a complete orthographic drawing of the tube holder.

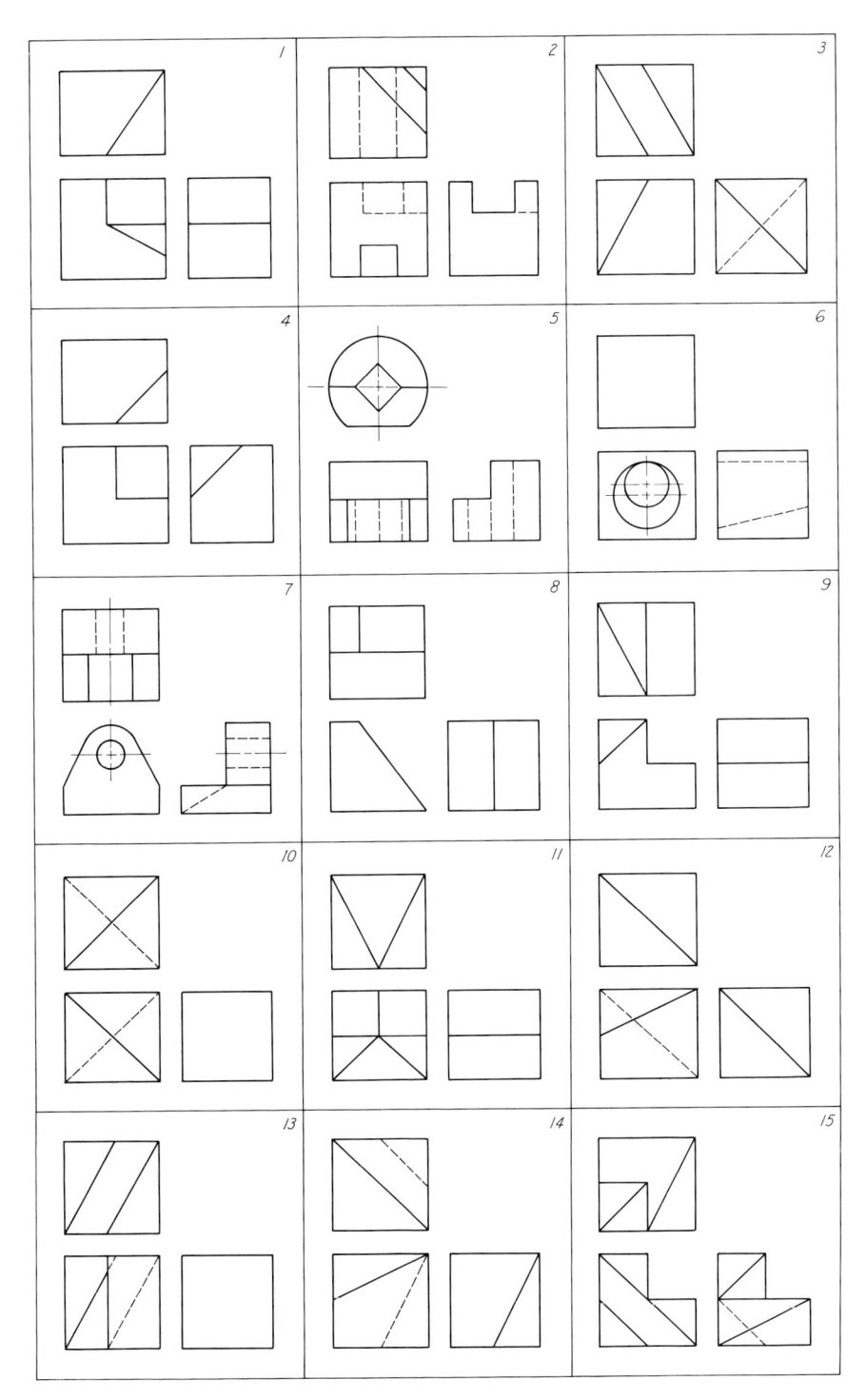

FIG. 6.60. Missing-line (or lines) exercises.

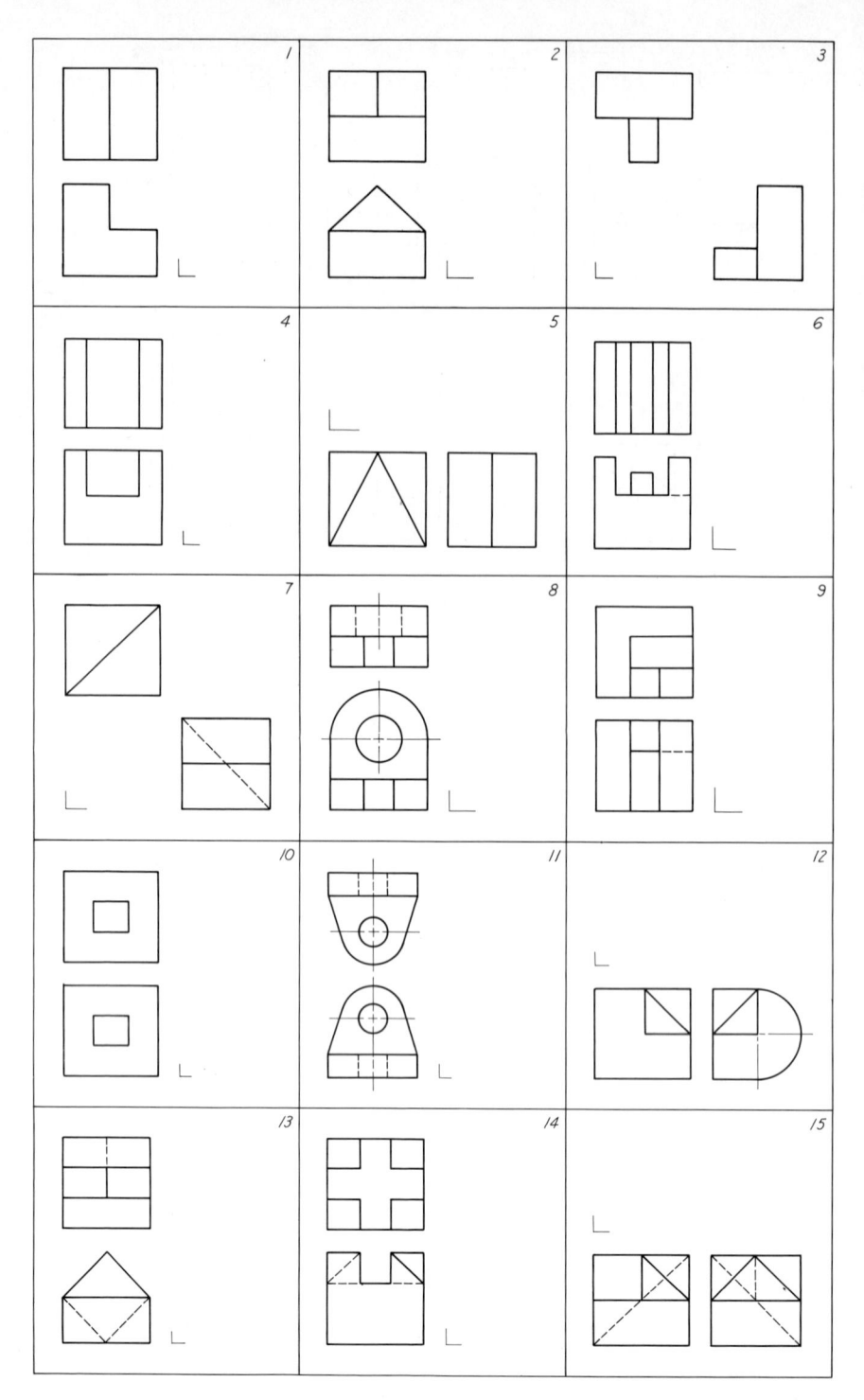

FIG. 6.61. Third-view problems.

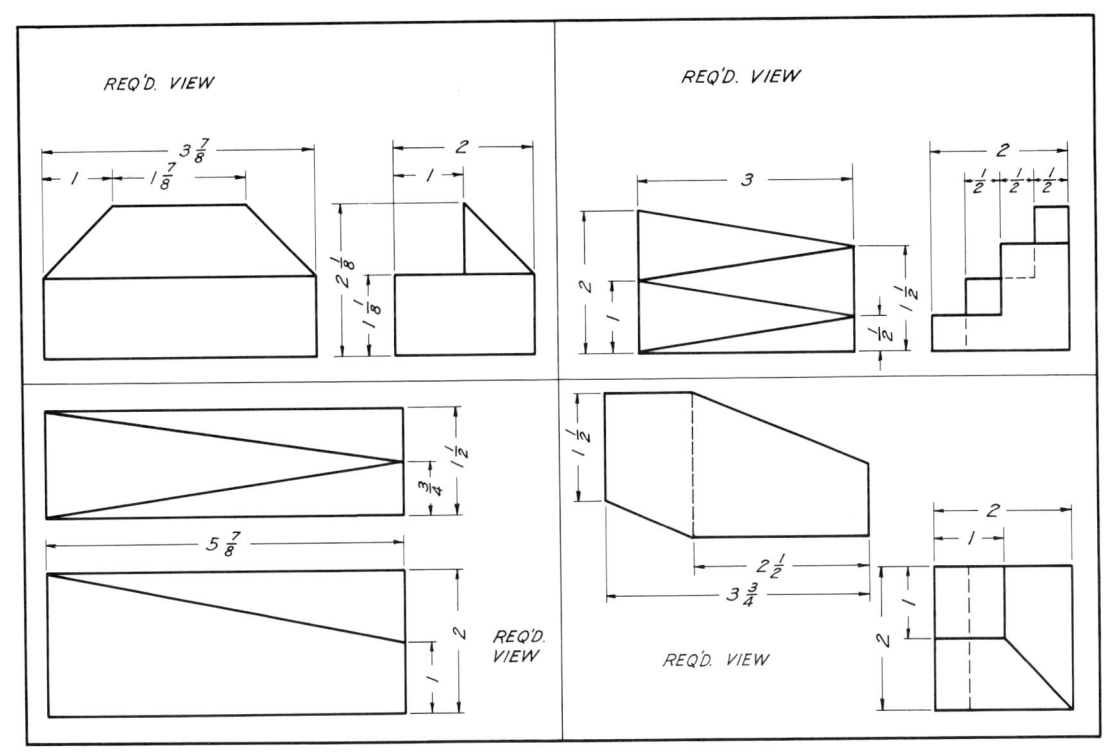

FIG. 6.62.

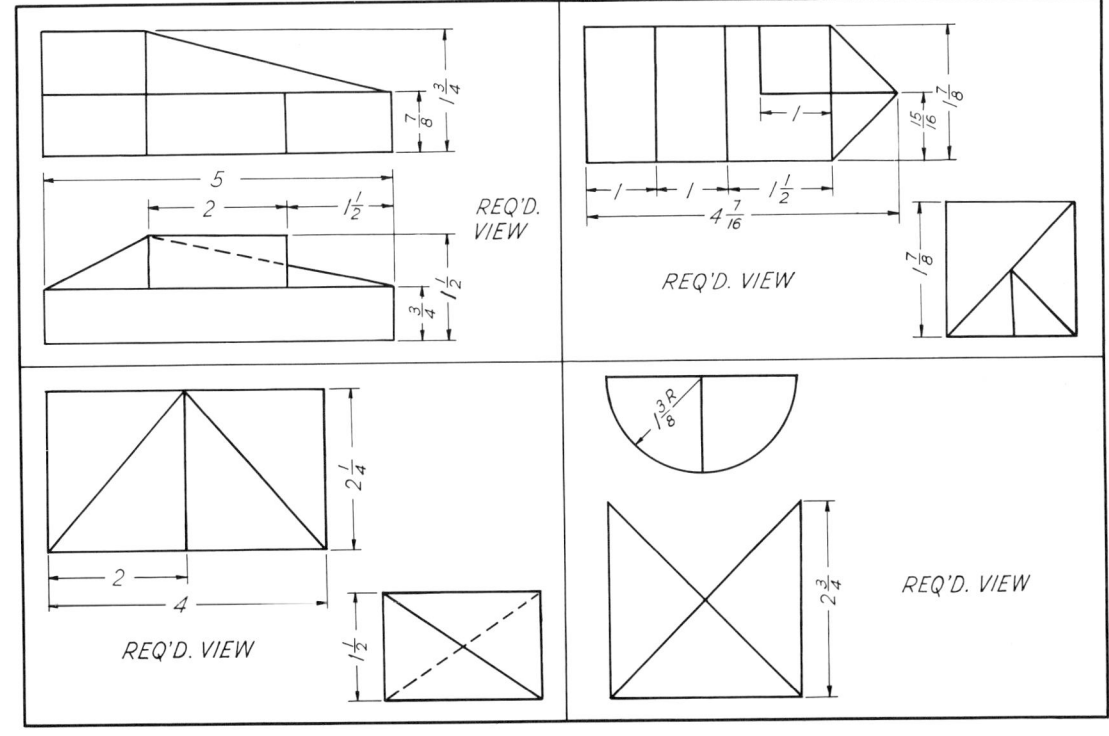

FIG. 6.63.

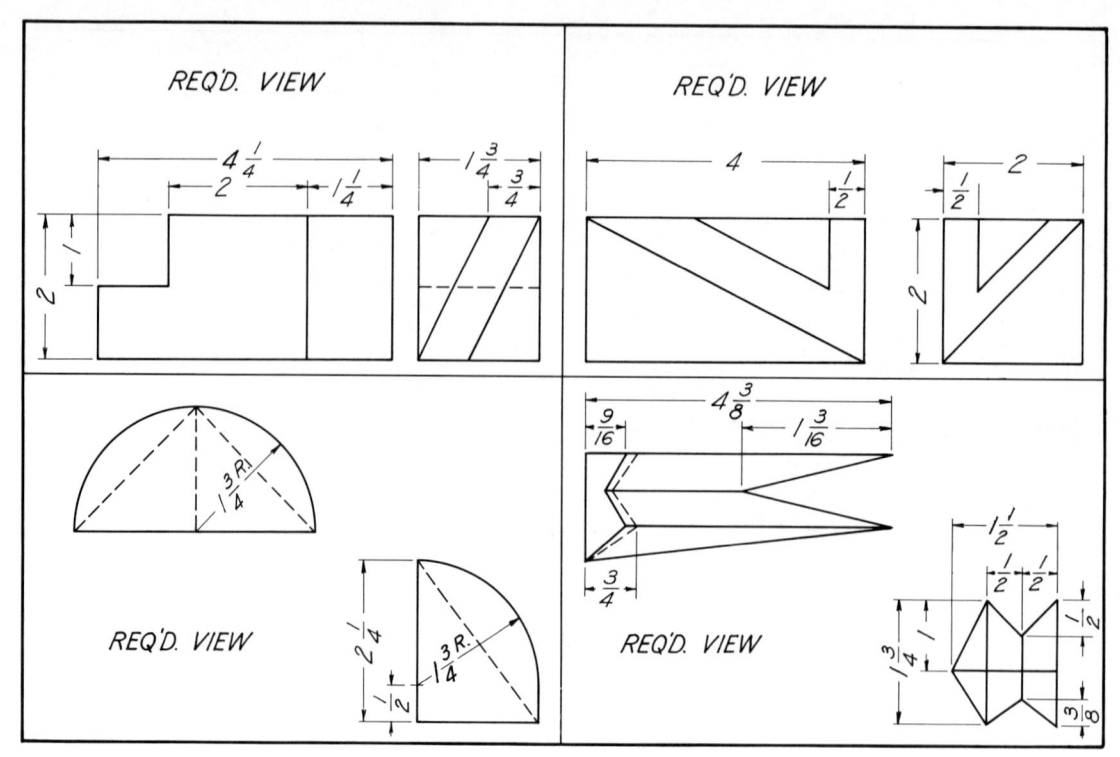

FIG. 6.64.

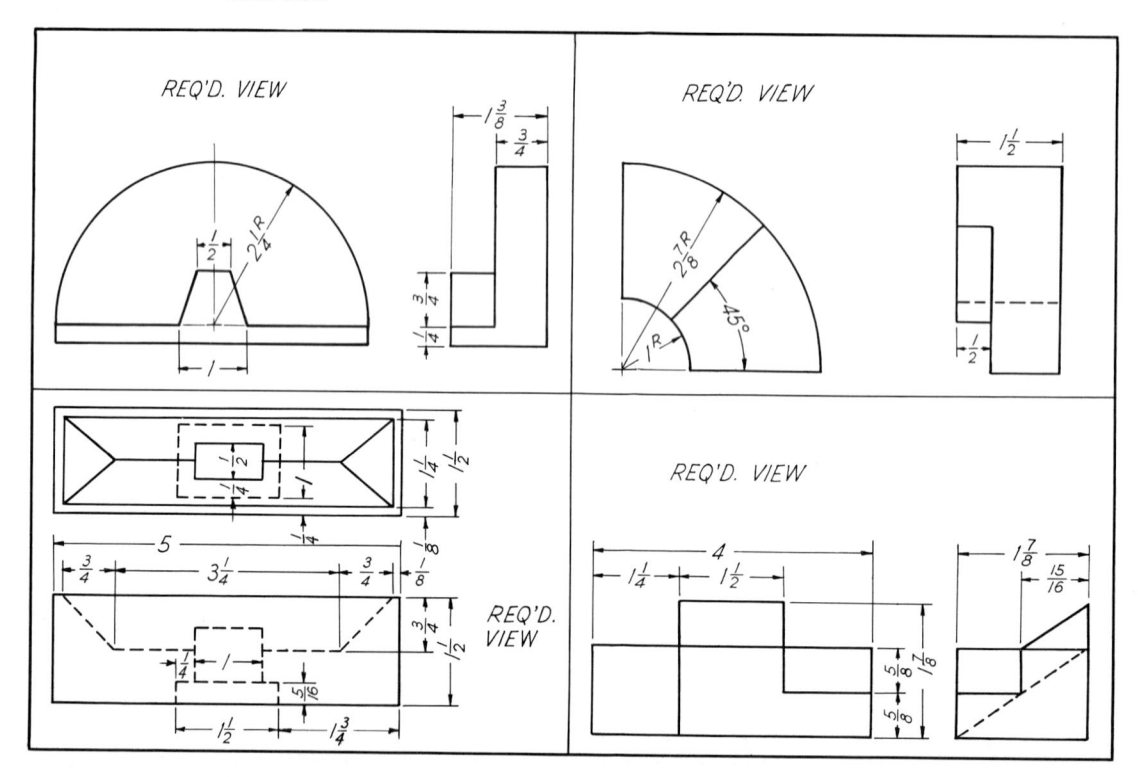

FIG. 6.65.

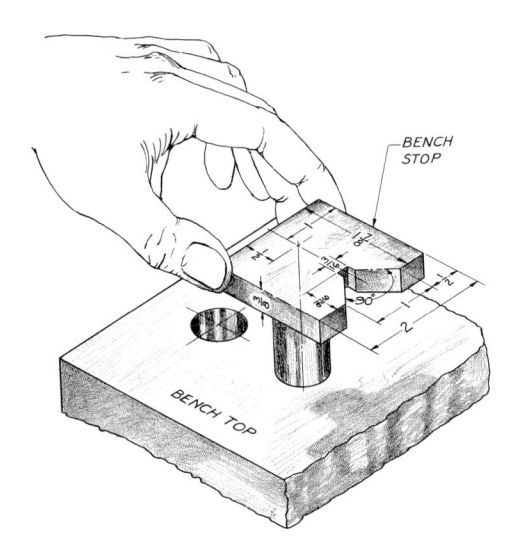

CHAP. 6 / MULTIVIEW REPRESENTATION, REVOLUTION, AND CONVENTIONAL PRACTICES 117

FIG. 6.66. Bench stop.

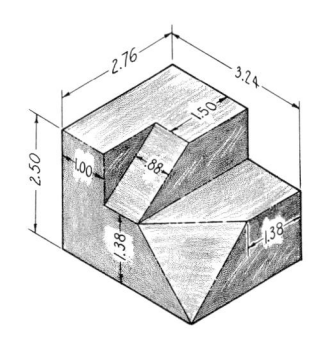

FIG. 6.67. Corner block.

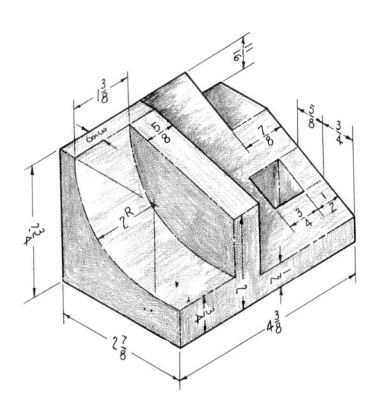

FIG. 6.68. Stop block.

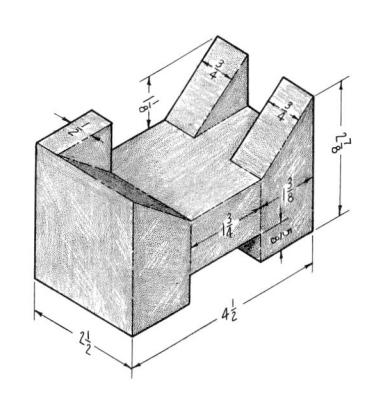

FIG. 6.69. Rest block.

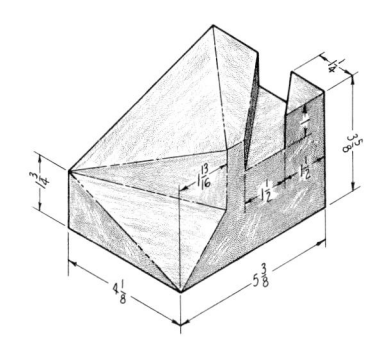

FIG. 6.70. Adjustment block.

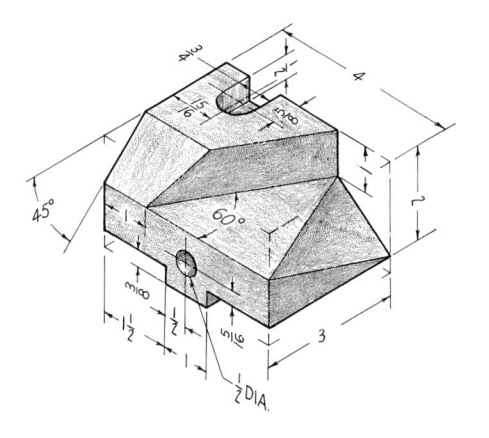

FIG. 6.71. Locating block.

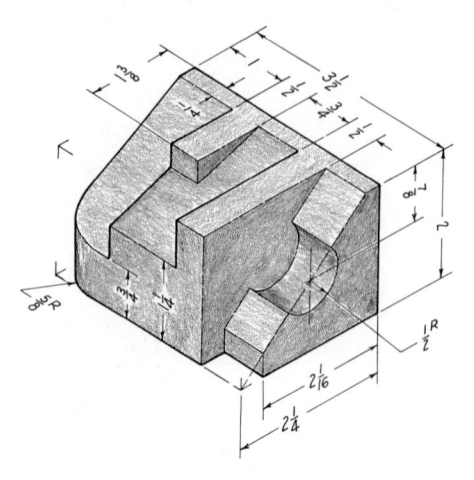

FIG. 6.72. Safety block.

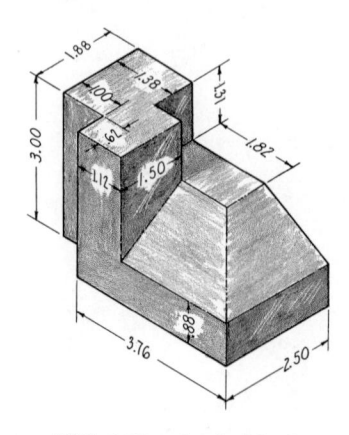

FIG. 6.73. Angle block.

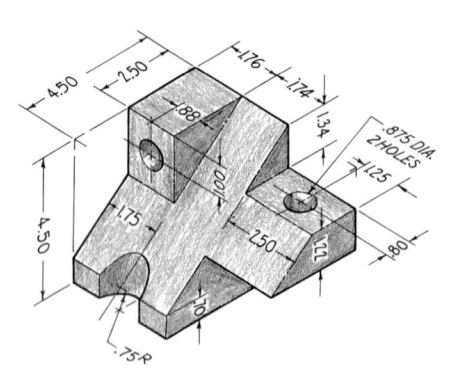

FIG. 6.74. Cross stop.

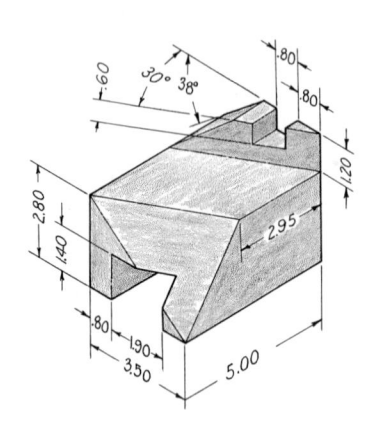

FIG. 6.75. End block.

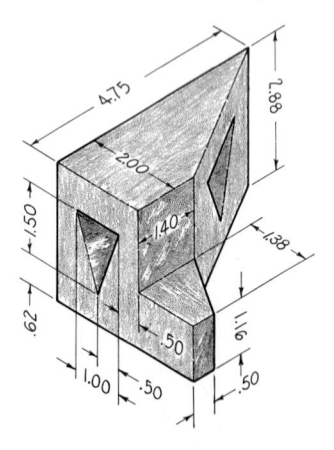

FIG. 6.76. Bevel block.

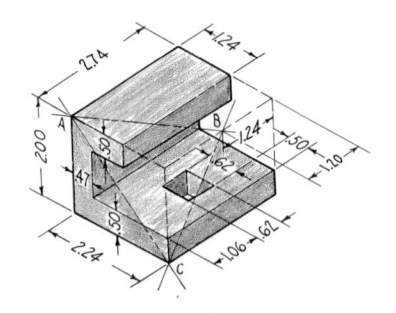

FIG. 6.77. Stabilizer block.

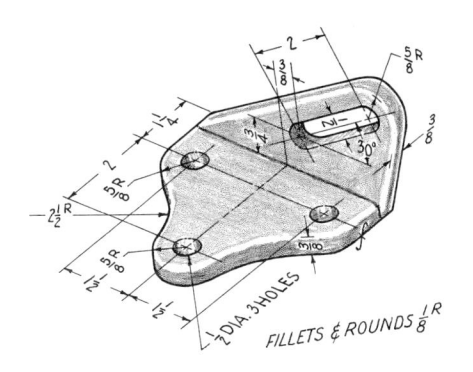

CHAP. 6 / MULTIVIEW REPRESENTATION, REVOLUTION, AND CONVENTIONAL PRACTICES 119

FIG. 6.78. Mounting bracket.

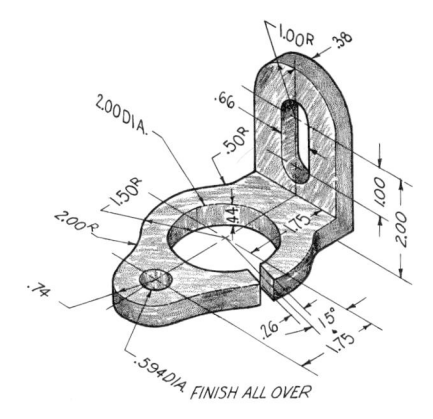

FIG. 6.79. Index guide.

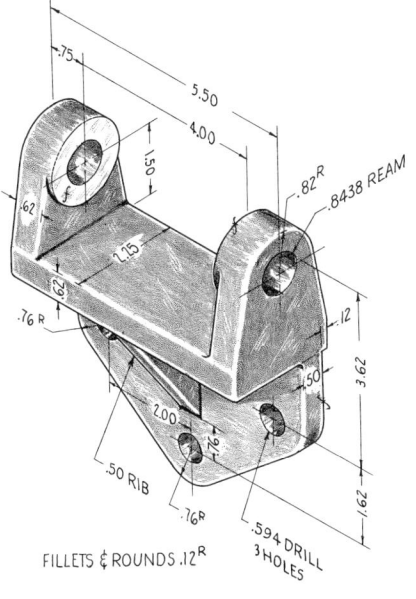

FIG. 6.80. Guide bracket.

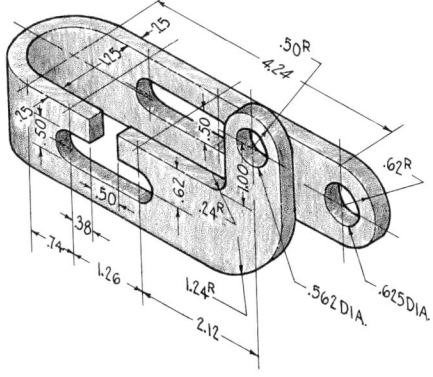

FIG. 6.81. Control guide.

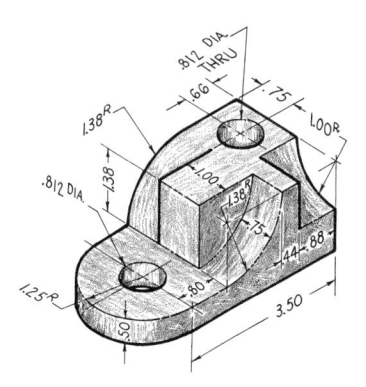

FIG. 6.82. Shoe block.

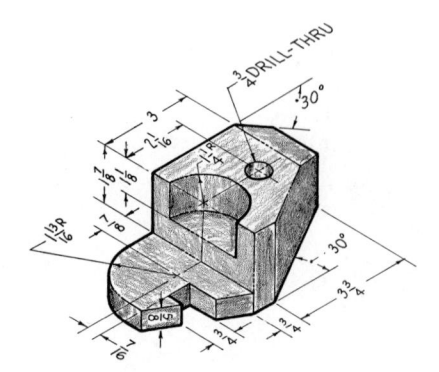

FIG. 6.83. Holder block.

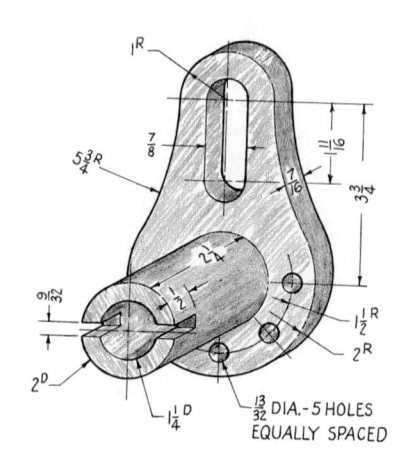

FIG. 6.84. Slotted guide.

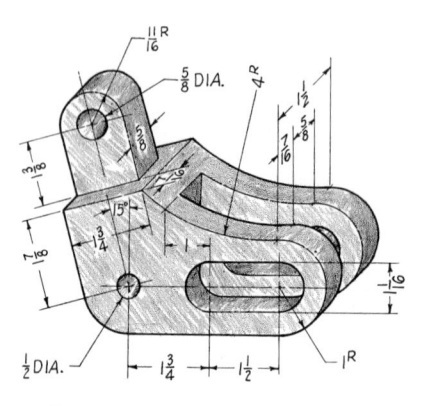

FIG. 6.85. Pivot guide.

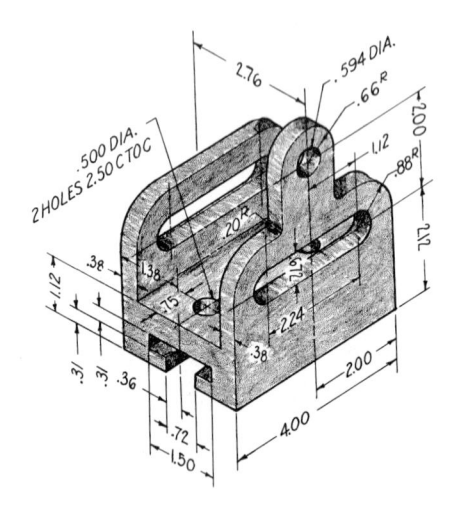

FIG. 6.86. Control guide.

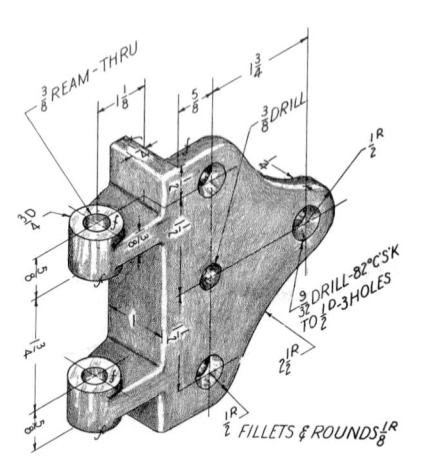

FIG. 6.87. Corner bracket.

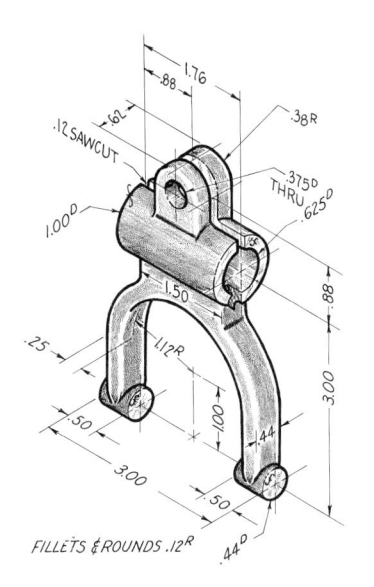

CHAP. 6 / MULTIVIEW REPRESENTATION, REVOLUTION, AND CONVENTIONAL PRACTICES 121

FIG. 6.88. Auxiliary fork.

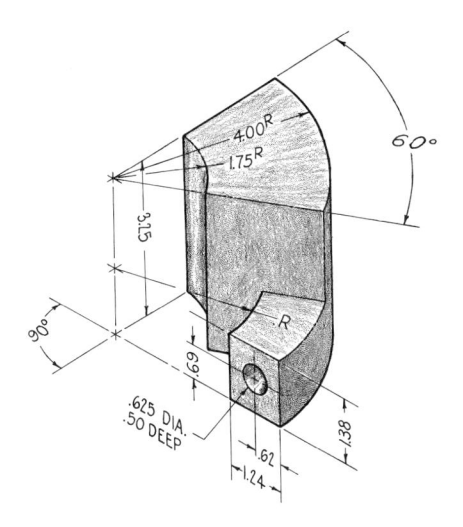

FIG. 6.89. Jaw block.

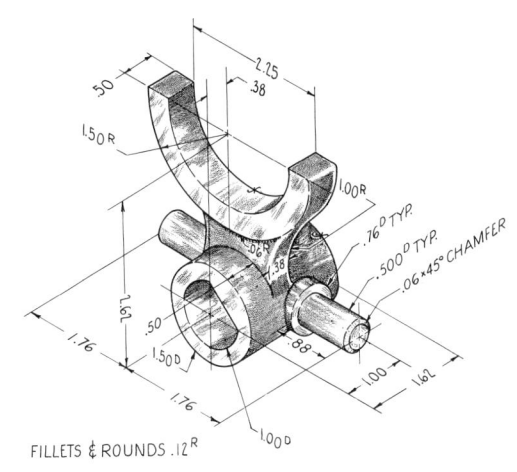

FIG. 6.90. Shifter.

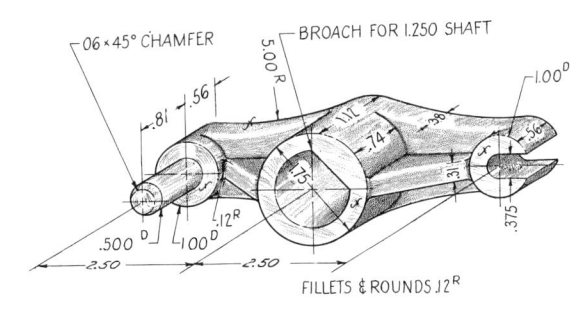

FIG. 6.91. Stud guide.

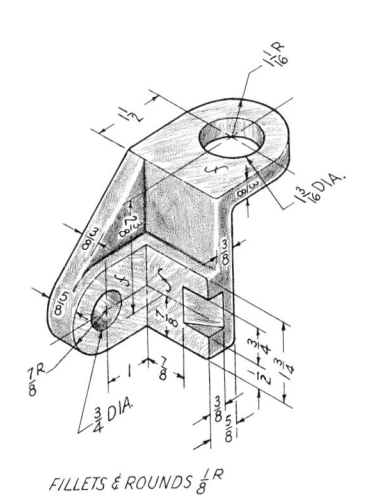

FIG. 6.92. Ejector bracket.

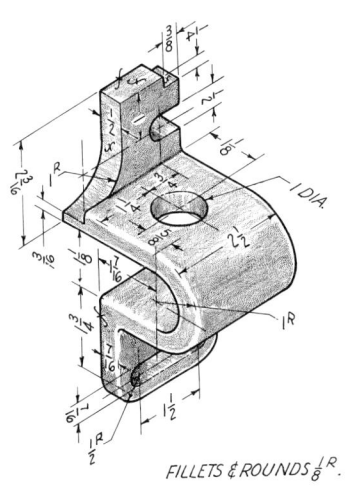

FIG. 6.93. Guide clip.

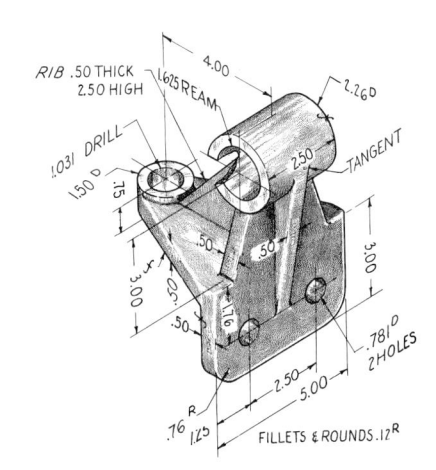

FIG. 6.94. Control rod guide.

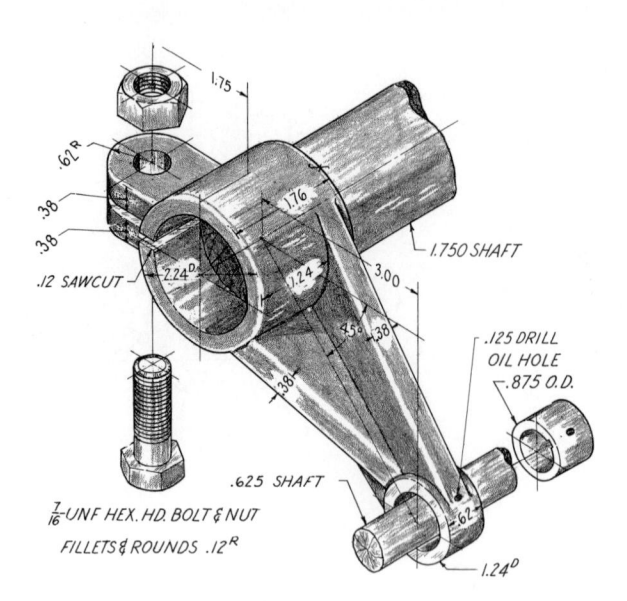

FIG. 6.95. Shaft bracket.

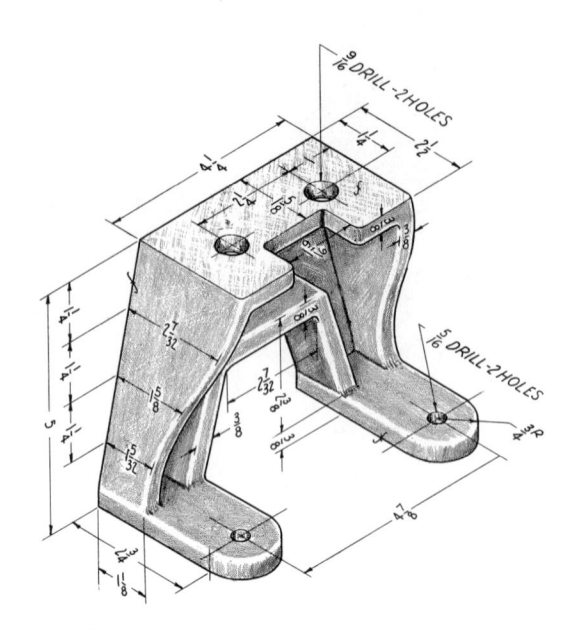

FIG. 6.96. Lathe leg.

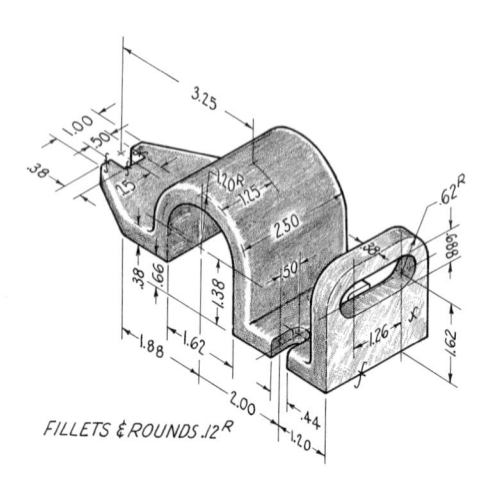

FIG. 6.97. Feed guide.

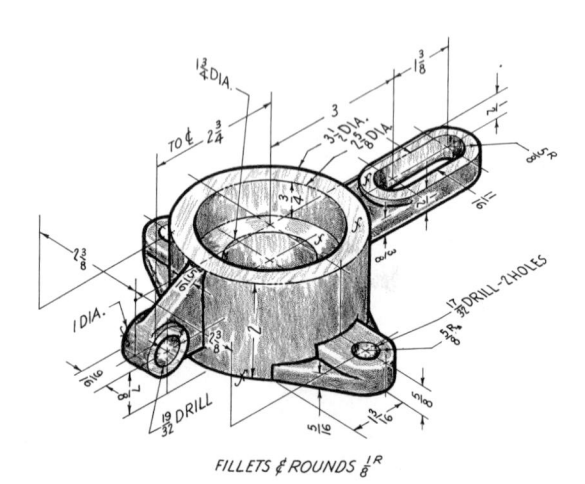

FIG. 6.98. Control bracket.

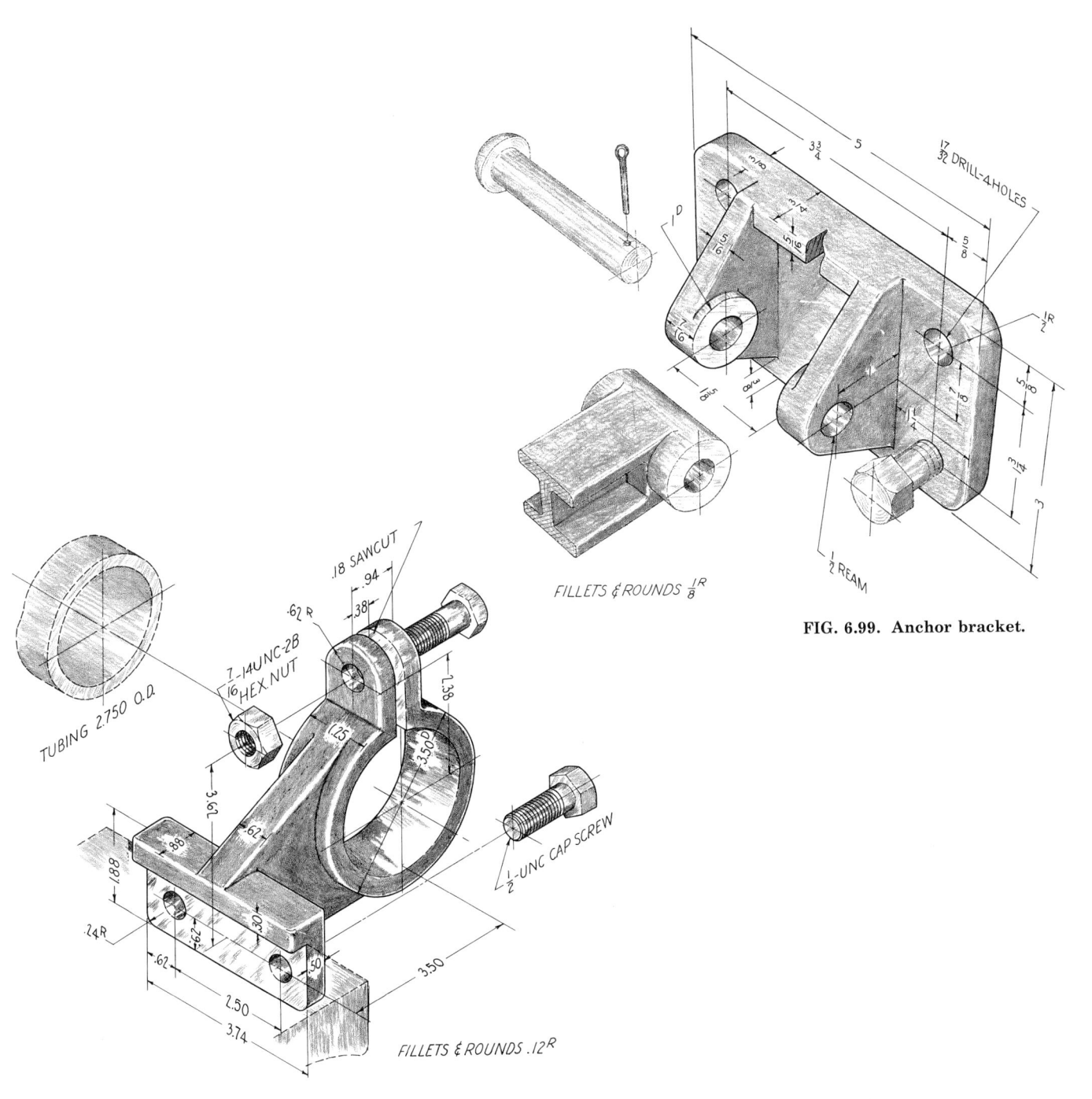

CHAP. 6 / MULTIVIEW REPRESENTATION, REVOLUTION, AND CONVENTIONAL PRACTICES **123**

FIG. 6.99. Anchor bracket.

FIG. 6.100. Tube holder.

self contained crane

Bulk plastic tanks re-supply by air-drop

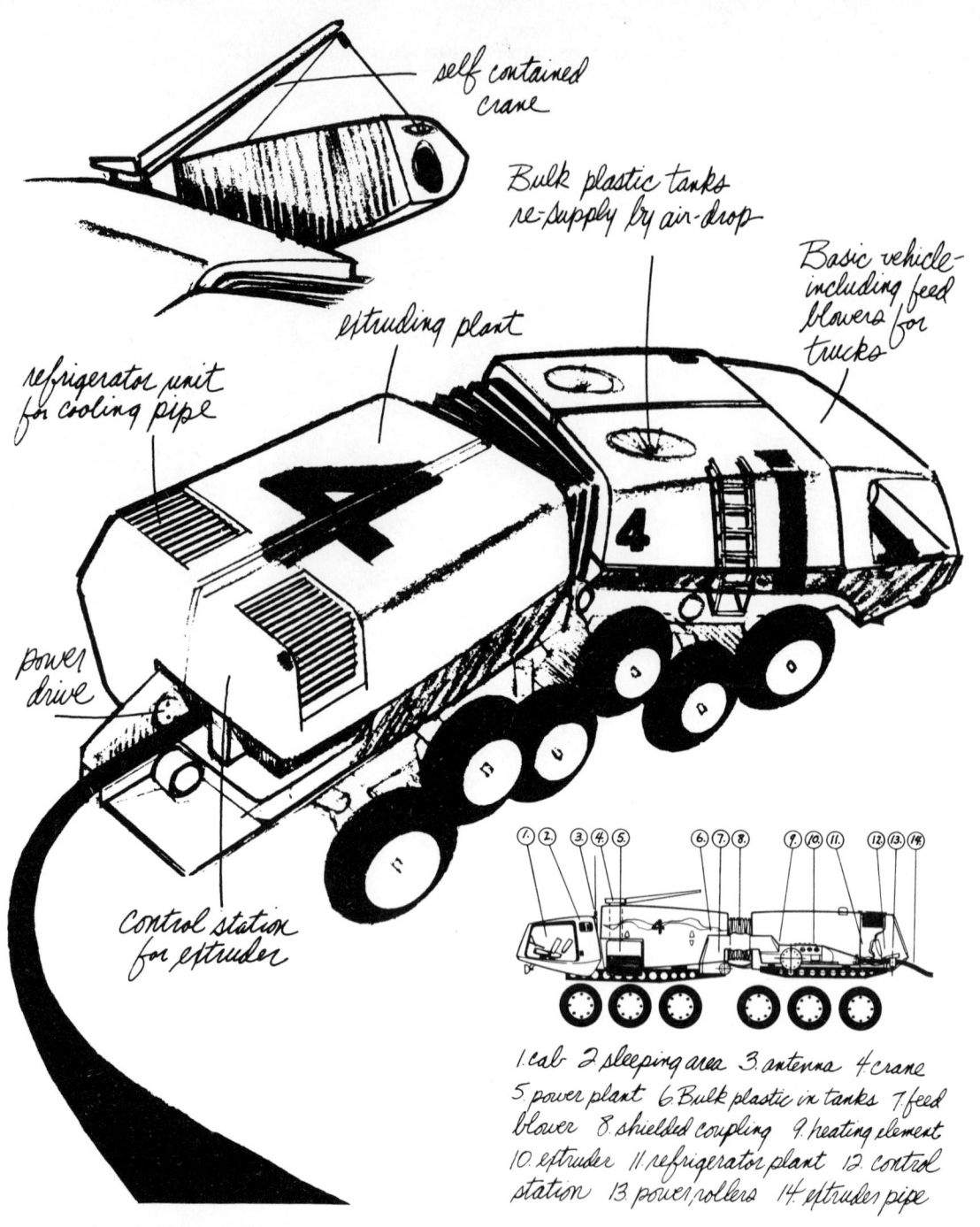

Basic vehicle including feed blowers for trucks

extruding plant

refrigerator unit for cooling pipe

power drive

control station for extruder

1. cab 2. sleeping area 3. antenna 4. crane
5. power plant 6. Bulk plastic in tanks 7. feed blower 8. shielded coupling 9. heating element
10. extruder 11. refrigerator plant 12. control station 13. power rollers 14. extruder pipe

The design of a self-contained pipelayer which could be in use in 1985. It is intended to facilitate irrigation of large tracts of desert land. The equipment as designed is capable of transporting sufficient bulk plastic to lay approximately two miles of plastic pipe from each pair of storage tanks. Tanks are to be discarded when empty and replaced by air drop.
(Courtesy of Donald Desky Associates, Inc., and Charles Bruning Company.)

Freehand Technical Drawing—Basic Techniques

A: MULTIVIEW SKETCHES

7.1
Value of Freehand Drawing. Freehand technical drawing is primarily the language of those in responsible charge of the development of technical designs and plans. Chief engineers, chief draftsmen, designers, and squad bosses have found that the best way to present their ideas for either a simple or complex design is through the medium of sketches. Sketches may be schematic, as are those that are original expressions of new ideas (Fig. 7.1), or they may be instructional, their purpose being to convey ideas to draftsmen or shopmen. Some sketches, especially those prepared for the manufacture of parts that are to replace worn or broken parts on existing machines, may resemble complete working drawings (Fig. 7.2).

Since the importance of freehand drawing is often underestimated, the purpose of this discussion is to amplify training in this phase. A person preparing for a career in the field of design should understand, when beginning his studies, that sketching may be his ultimate form of expression and that he must be able to prepare complete sketches that will present his ideas and decisions to subordinates in an understandable manner.

7.2
Sketching Materials. For the type of sketching discussed here, the required materials are an F pencil, a soft eraser, and some paper. In the industrial field, men who have been improperly trained in sketching often use straightedges and cheap pocket compasses that they could well dispense with if they would adopt the correct technique. Preparing sketches with instruments consumes much unnecessary time.

For the person who cannot produce a satisfactory sketch without guide lines, cross-section paper is helpful. Ordinarily, the ruling on this paper forms 1-in. squares, which are subdivided into $\frac{1}{8}$-, $\frac{1}{4}$-, or $\frac{1}{10}$-in. squares. Such paper is especially useful when sketching to scale is desirable (Fig. 7.3).

7.3
Projections. Although freehand drawing lacks the refinement given by mechanical instruments, it is based on the same principles of projection and conventional practices that apply to multiview, pictorial, and the other divisions of mechanical drawing. For this reason, one must be thoroughly familiar with projection, in all its many forms, before he is adequately trained to prepare sketches.

7.4
Technique of Lines. Freehand lines quite naturally will differ in their appearance

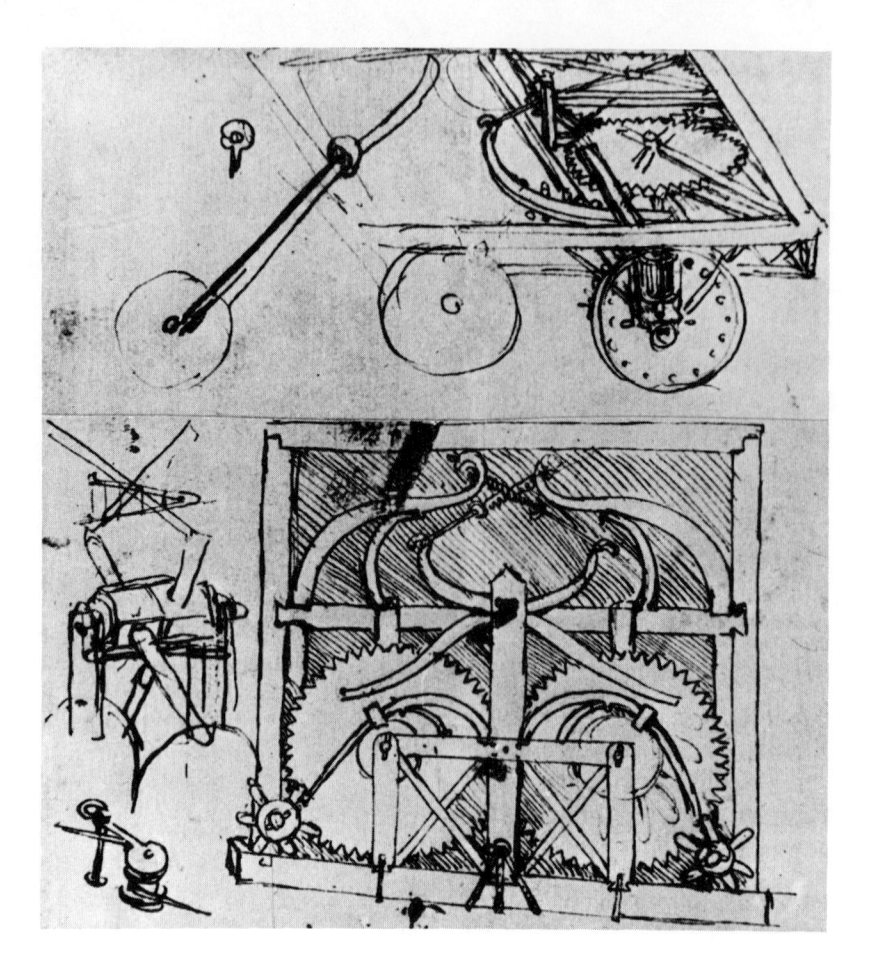

126   PART II / SPATIAL GRAPHICS: SHAPE DESCRIPTION AND SPATIAL RELATIONSHIPS

FIG. 7.1. An idea sketch prepared by Leonardo da Vinci (1452–1519). *(From Collections of Fine Arts Department, International Business Machines Corp.)*

FIG. 7.2. A freehand sketch for the manufacture of a part.

from mechanical ones. A well-executed freehand line will never be perfectly straight and absolutely uniform in weight, but an effort should be made to approach *exacting uniformity*. As in the case of mechanical lines, they should be black and clear, not broad and fuzzy (Fig. 7.4).

7.5

Sharpening the Sketching Pencil. A sketching pencil should be sharpened on a file or piece of sandpaper to a conical point. The point then should be rounded slightly, on the back of the sketch pad or on another sheet of paper, to the correct

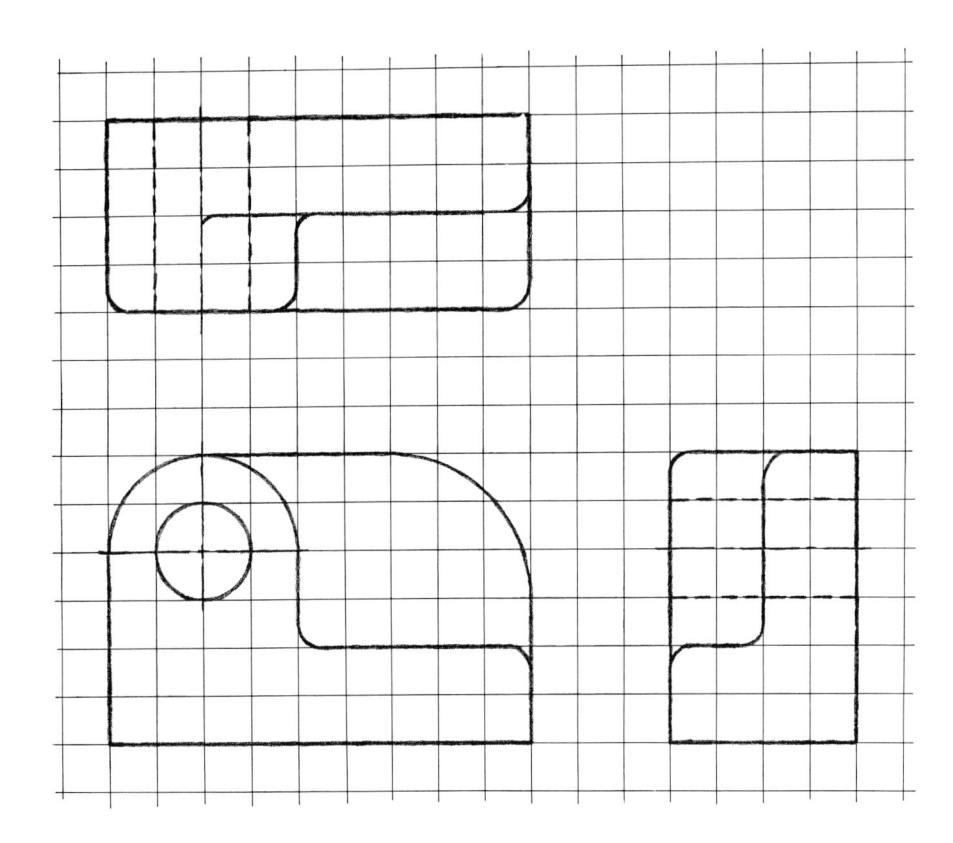

FIG. 7.3. Sketch actual size on one-quarter inch grid.

degree of dullness. When rounding the point, the pencil should be rotated to prevent the formation of sharp edges.

7.6
Straight Lines. The pencil should rest on the second finger and be held loosely by the thumb and index finger about $1\text{-}1\frac{1}{2}$ in. above the point.

Horizontal lines are sketched from left to right with an easy arm motion that is pivoted about the muscle of the forearm. The straight line thus becomes an arc of infinite radius. When sketching a straight line, it is advisable first to mark the end points with light dots or small crosses (Fig. 7.5).

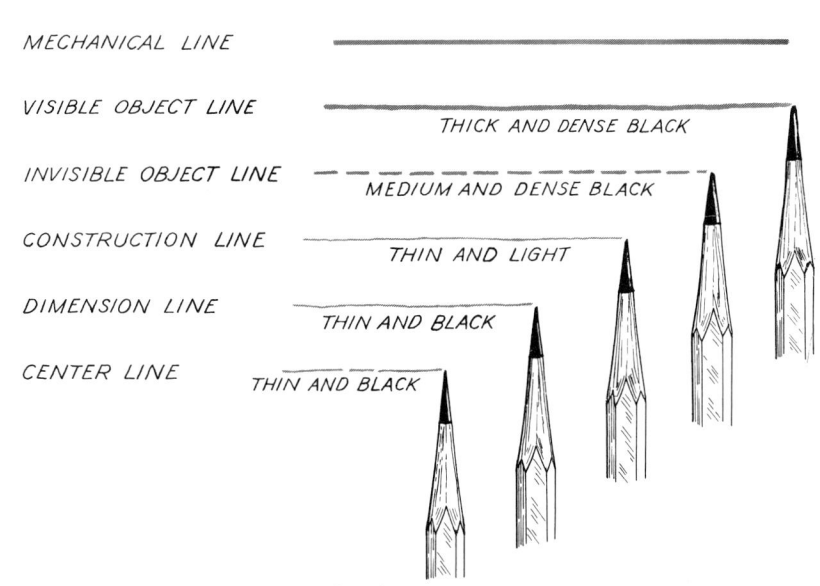

FIG. 7.4. Pencil points and sketch lines.

FIG. 7.5. Steps in sketching a straight line.

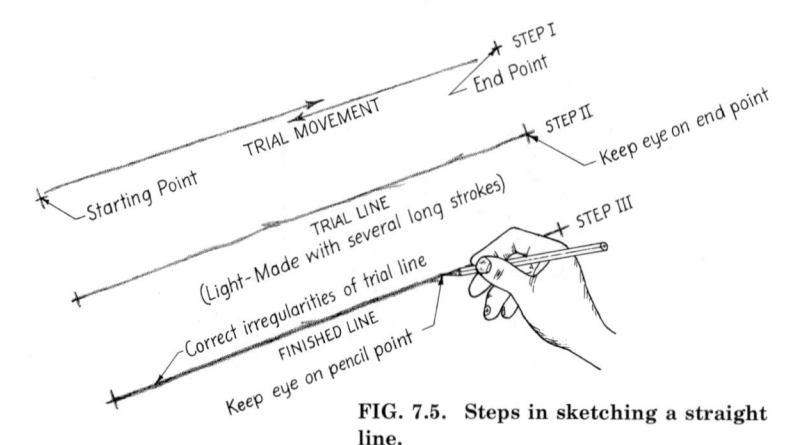

The complete procedure for sketching a straight line is as follows:

1. Mark the end points.

2. Make a few trial motions between the marked points to adjust the eye and hand to the contemplated line.

3. Sketch a *very* light line between the points by moving the pencil in two or three sweeps. When sketching the trial line, the eye should be on the point toward which the movement is directed. With each stroke, an attempt should be made to correct the most obvious defects of the stroke preceding, so that the finished trial line will be relatively straight.

4. Darken the finished line, keeping the eye on the pencil point on the trial line. The final line, replacing the trial line, should be distinct, black, uniform, and straight.

It is helpful to turn the paper through a *convenient angle* so that the horizontal and vertical lines assume a slight inclination (Fig. 7.6). A horizontal line, when the paper is in this position, is sketched to the right and upward, thus allowing the arm to be held slightly away from the body and making possible a free arm motion.

Short vertical lines may be sketched either downward or upward, without changing the position of the paper. When sketching downward, the arm is held slightly away from the body and the movement is toward the sketcher (Fig. 7.7). To sketch vertical lines upward, the arm is held well away from the body. By turning the paper, a long vertical line may be made to assume the position of a horizontal line and can be sketched with the same general movements used for the latter.

Inclined lines running upward from lower left to upper right may be sketched upward with the same movements used for horizontal lines, but those running downward from upper left to lower right are sketched with the general movements used for either horizontal or vertical lines, depending on their inclination (Fig. 7.8). Inclined lines may be more easily sketched by turning the paper to make them conform to the direction of horizontal lines.

7.7

Circles. Small circles may be sketched by marking radial distances on perpendicular center lines. When additional points are needed, the distances can be marked off either by eye or by measuring with a marked strip of paper (Fig. 7.9). Larger circles may be constructed more accurately by sketching two or more diagonals, in addition to the center lines, and by sketching short construction lines perpendicular to each, equidistant from the center. Tangent to these lines, short arcs are drawn perpendicular to the radii. The circle is completed with a light construction line, and all defects are corrected before darkening (Fig. 7.10).

The beginner will find the graphical method illustrated in Fig. 7.11(*a*) useful in establishing the locations of points through which he can sketch the line representation of a circle. The steps in using this method are the following:

CHAP. 7 / FREEHAND TECHNICAL DRAWING—BASIC TECHNIQUES **129**

FIG. 7.6. Sketching horizontal lines.

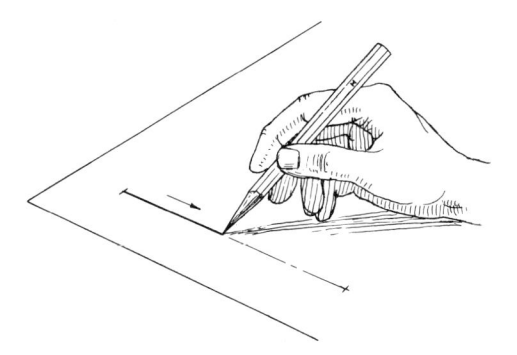

FIG. 7.7. Sketching vertical lines.

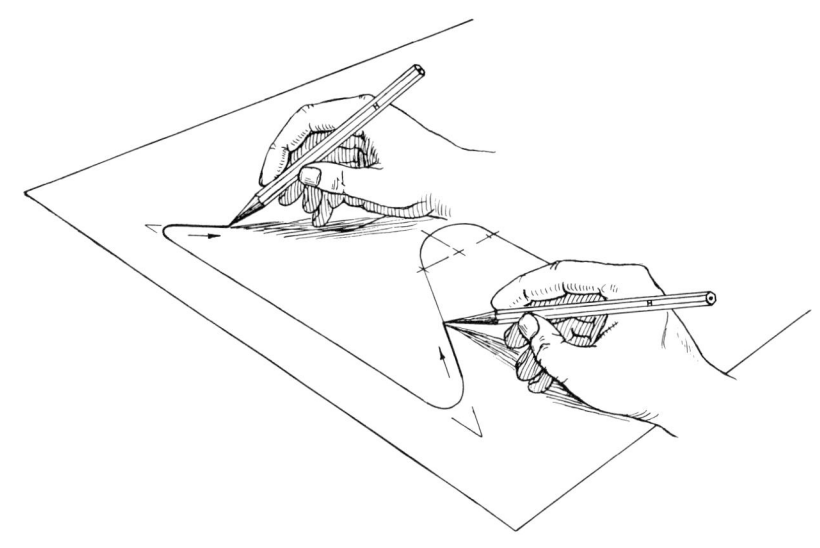

FIG. 7.8. Sketching inclined lines.

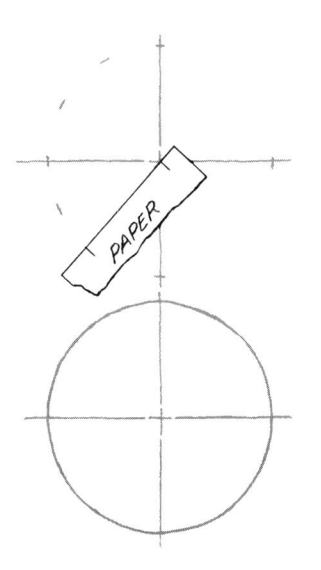

FIG. 7.9. Marking off radial distances.

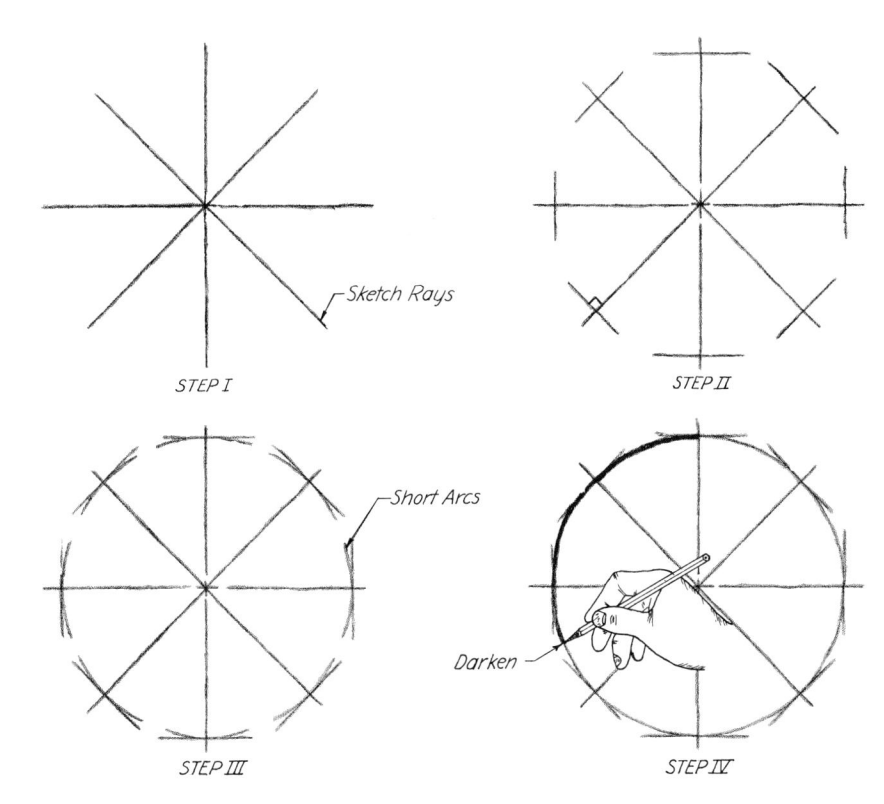

FIG. 7.10. Sketching large circles.

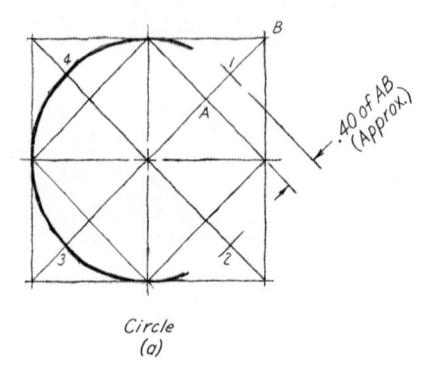

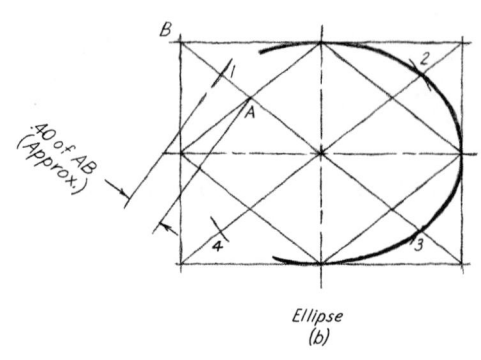

FIG. 7.11. Sketching circles and ellipses, graphical method.

Step I. Sketch the center lines and the enclosing square at an estimated size.

Step II. Sketch the diagonals of the enclosing square.

Step III. Sketch the short diagonals in each quadrant.

Step IV. Mark the locations of points 1, 2, 3, and 4 on the long diagonals. In each quadrant, the point on the circle is at a distance from the intersection of the diagonals that is approximately equal to four-tenths the distance from the intersection to the corner of the enclosing square. For example, point 1 will be four-tenths the length of AB from A. This is an estimated distance that is determined by the eye.

Step V. Form the circle initially with a light line and then sketch the finished circle using a bold black line.

7.8
Ellipses. The graphical method, as explained in Sec. 7.7 for sketching a circle, may be applied for sketching an ellipse [Fig. 7.11(b)]. The step procedure is the same except that the enclosing quadrilateral in this case will be a rectangle instead of a square.

7.9
Making a Multiview Sketch. When making orthographic working sketches a systematic order should be followed, and all the rules and conventional practices used in making working drawings should be applied. The following procedure is recommended:

1. Examine the object, giving particular attention to detail.

2. Determine which views are necessary.

3. "Block-in" the views, using light construction lines.

4. Complete the detail and darken the object lines.

5. Sketch extension lines and dimension lines, including arrowheads.

6. Complete the sketch by adding dimensions, notes, title, date, sketcher's name or initials, and so on.

7. Check the entire sketch carefully to see that no dimensions have been omitted.

The progressive steps in making a sketch of an object are shown in Fig. 7.12.

7.10
Proportions. The beginner must recognize the importance of being able to estimate comparative relationship between

the width, height, and depth of an object being sketched. The complete problem of proportioning a sketch also involves relating the estimated dimensions for any component parts, such as slots, holes, and projections, to the over-all dimensions of the object. It is not the practice to attempt to estimate actual dimensions, for sketches are not usually made to scale. Rather one must decide, for example, that the width of the object is twice its height, that the width of a given slot is equal to one-half the width of the object, and that its depth is approximately one-fourth the overall height.

To become proficient at sketching one must learn to recognize proportions and be able to compare dimensions "by eye." Until he is able to do so, he can not really "think with his pencil." Some people can develop a keen eye for proportion with only a limited amount of practice and can maintain these estimated proportions when making the views of sketch. Others have alternately discouraging and encouraging experiences. Discouragement comes when one's knowledge of sketching is ahead of his ability and he has not had as much practice as he needs. The many who find it difficult to make the proportions of the completed sketch agree with the estimated proportions of the object may begin by using the graphical method shown in Fig. 7.13(a), (b), and (c). This method is based on the fact that a rectangle (enclosing a view) may be divided to obtain intermediate distances along any side that are in such proportions to the total length as one-half, one-fourth, one-third, and so on. Those who start with this rectangle method as an aid in proportioning should abandon its use when they have developed their eye and sketching skills so that it is no longer needed.

Sketching must be done rapidly, and the addition of unnecessary lines consumes much valuable time. Furthermore, the addition of construction lines distracts the reader, and it is certain that they do not contribute to the neatness of the sketch.

The midpoint of a rectangle is the point of intersection of the diagonals, as shown in Fig. 7.13(a). A line sketched through this point that is perpendicular to any side

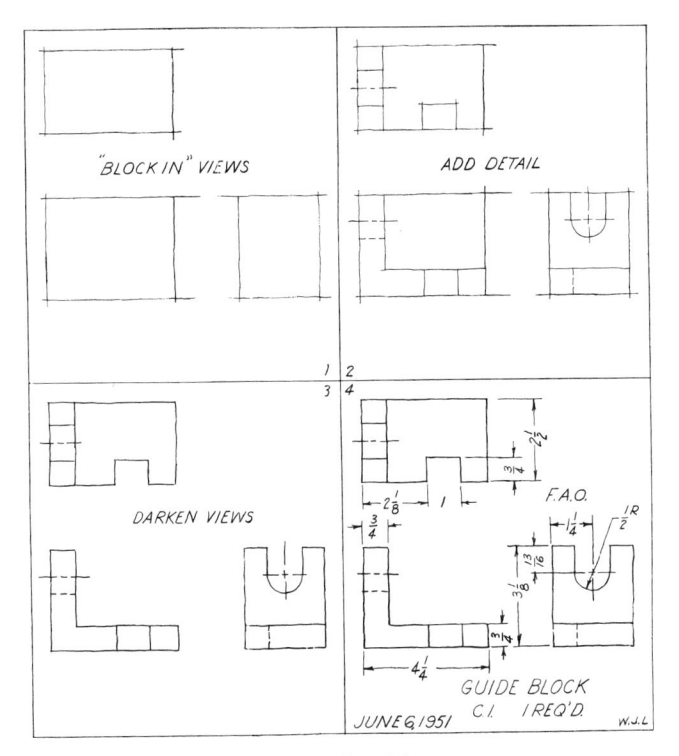

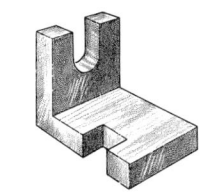

FIG. 7.12. Steps in sketching.

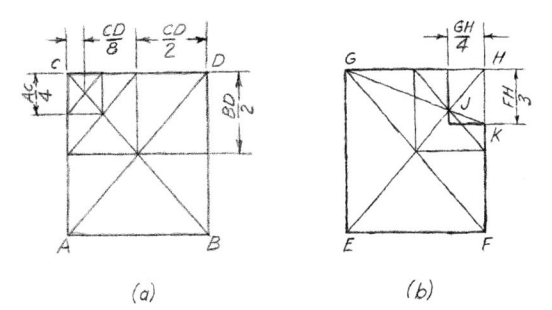

FIG. 7.13. Methods of proportioning a rectangle representing the outline of a view.

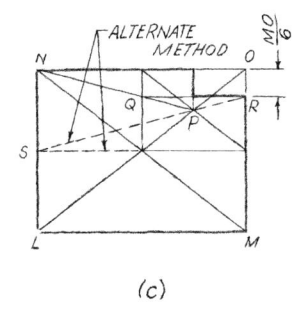

will establish the midpoint of that side. Should it be necessary to determine a distance that is equal to one-fourth the length of a side, (say, AC), the quarter-point may be located by repeating this procedure for the small rectangle representing the upper left hand quarter of $ABCD$.

With the midpoint J located by the intersecting diagonals of the small rectangle [representing one-fourth of the larger rectangle $EFGH$, as in (b)], the one-third point along FH may be located by sketching a line from point G through J and extending it to line FH. The point K at the intersection of these lines establishes the needed one-third distance.

To determine one-sixth the length of a side of a rectangle, as in (c), sketch a line from N through point P, as was done in (b), to determine a one-third distance. Point Q at which the line NP crosses the center line of the rectangle establishes the one-sixth distance along the center line.

Figure 7.14 shows how this method for dividing the sides of a rectangle might be used to proportion an orthographic sketch.

The square may be used to proportion a view after one dimension for the view has been assumed. In this method, additional squares are added to the initial one having the assumed length as one side (Fig. 7.15). As an example, suppose that it has been estimated that the front view of an object should be three times as long as it is high. In Fig. 7.15 the height of the view has been represented by the line AB sketched to an assumed length. The first step in making the construction is to sketch the initial square $ABCD$ and extend AC and BD to indefinite length, being certain that the overall length from A and B will be slightly greater than three times the length of AB. Then the center line must be sketched through the intersection of AD and BC. Now BX extended to E locates EF to form the second square, and DY extended to point G locates the line GH. Line AG will be three times the length of AB.

7.11

Making Sketches of Parts for the Purpose of Replacement and Repair. It is quite frequently necessary to make working-drawing sketches of broken or worn parts. Such sketches are used instead of mechanical drawings because they can be made and sent to the shop in a much shorter time. The procedure given in Sec. 7.9 should be followed carefully when making sketches to be used by workmen in the shops.

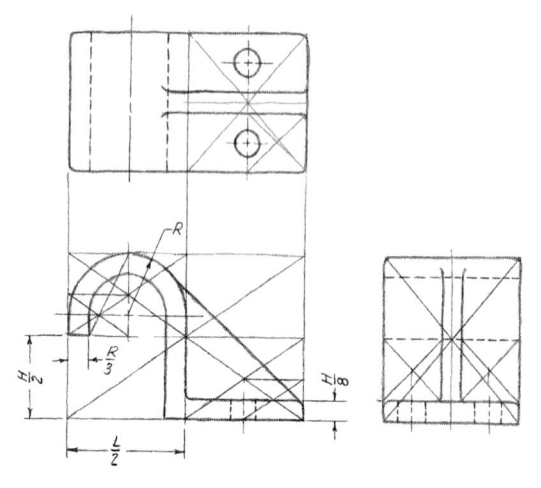

FIG. 7.14. The rectangle method applied in making an orthographic sketch.

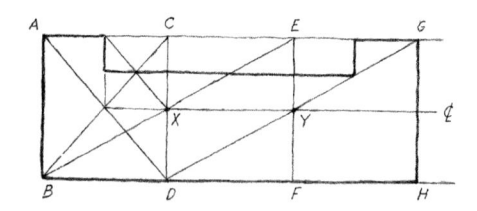

FIG. 7.15. The build-up method.

7.12

Measurements and Measuring Instruments. If a sketch is to serve as a working drawing, it must contain all the necessary dimensions and instructional notes needed by the workmen. If a sketch is for the manufacture of a part that is to replace a worn or broken part in an existing machine, measurements must be taken from the original part with the same general types of measuring devices to be used in manufacturing the new part. The instrument selected for each particular detail should be of a type that will allow measurements to be made with the correct degree of accuracy. For some machine parts, a steel scale and a set of inside and outside calipers will prove sufficient. When more accurate measurements are necessary, a micrometer must be used (Fig. 7.16). In any case, the selection of the instrument for a measurement should be determined by exercising good judgment backed by practical shop experience. Figure 7.17 shows how the outside calipers are used to take measurements from an object. Figure 7.18 shows the use of the inside calipers for measuring the diameter of a hole.

When taking measurements, certain practices are recommended. For example, to obtain the distance between holes (shown on the sketch as between centers), measure the distance between corresponding edges. To locate other features and to take off size dimensions, measure from a finished surface whenever possible, for a finished surface is usually a mating surface. The man in the shop must work from such a surface if he is to produce a part accurate enough to function in the existing machine.

7.13

The Title. A title is far more important on a sketch than many persons realize. It serves to identify the sketch and usually contains such valuable additional information as (1) the type of material, (2) the number required, (3) the name or initials of the sketcher, and (4) the date (Fig. 7.12).

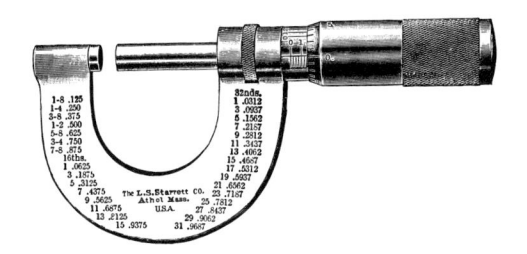

FIG. 7.16. A micrometer.

B: SKETCHES IN ISOMETRIC AND OBLIQUE

7.14

Pictorial Sketching Students may employ pictorial sketches to advantage as an aid in visualizing and organizing problems. Sales engineers may frequently include pictorial sketches with orthographic sketches when preparing field reports on the needs and suggestions of the firm's customers.

With some training anyone can prepare pictorial sketches that will be satisfactory for all practical purposes. Artistic ability is not needed. This fact is important, for many persons lack only the necessary confidence to start making pictorial sketches.

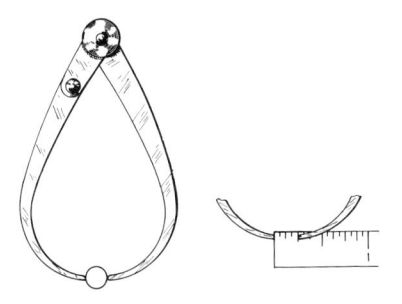

FIG. 7.17. Outside calipers.

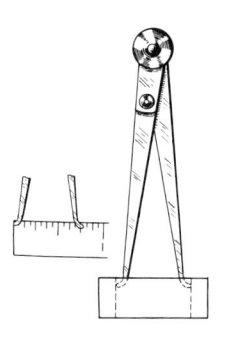

FIG. 7.18. Inside calipers.

7.15

Mechanical Methods of Sketching. Many engineers have found that they can produce satisfactory pictorial sketches by using one of the so-called mechanical methods. They rely on these methods because of their familiarity with the procedures used in making pictorial drawings with instruments.

It has been assumed that the student has read part A covering multiview sketching, for the techniques discussed there apply to pictorial sketching.

The practices presented in Chapter 12 for the mechanical methods, axonometric, oblique, and perspective, are followed generally in pictorial sketching, except that angles are assumed and lengths are estimated. For this reason, one must develop an eye for good proportion before he will be able to create a satisfactory pictorial sketch that will be in no way misleading.

A student having difficulty in interpreting a multiview drawing usually will find that a pictorial sketch, prepared as illustrated in Fig. 7.19, will clarify the form that he is trying to visualize, even before the last lines of the sketch have been drawn.

7.16

Isometric Sketching. Isometric sketching starts with three isometric lines, called axes, which represent three mutually perpendicular lines. One of these axes is sketched vertically, the other two at 30° with the horizontal. In Fig. 7.19 (step I), the near front corner of the enclosing box lies along the vertical axis, while the two visible receding edges of the base lie along the axes receding to the left and to the right.

If the object is of simple rectangular form, as in Fig. 7.19, it may be sketched by drawing an enclosing isometric box (step I) on the surfaces of which the orthographic views may be sketched (step II). Care must be taken in assuming lengths and distances so that the finished view (step III) will have relatively correct proportions. In constructing the enclosing box (step I), the vertical edges are parallel to the vertical axis, and edges receding to the right and to the left are parallel to the right and left axes, respectively.

Objects of more complicated construction may be "blocked in," as shown in Fig. 7.20. Note that the projecting cylindrical features are enclosed in "isometric" prisms and that the circles are sketched within isometric squares. The procedure in Fig. 7.20 is the same as in Fig. 7.19, except that three enclosing isometric boxes are needed in the formation of the final representation instead of one.

In sketching an ellipse to represent a circle pictorially, an enclosing "isometric square" (rhombus) is drawn having sides equal approximately to the diameter of the true circle (step I, Fig. 7.21). The ellipse is formed by first drawing arcs tangent to the midpoints of the sides of the isometric square in light sketchy pencil lines (step II). In finishing the ellipse (step III) with a dark heavy line, care must be taken to obtain a nearly elliptical shape.

Figure 7.22 shows the three positions for an isometric circle. Note that the

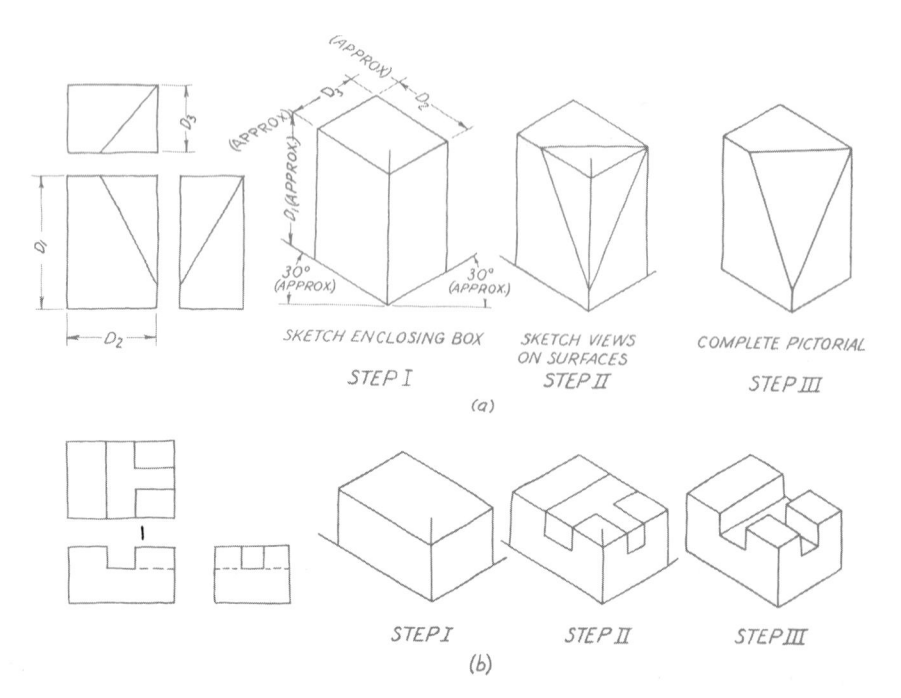

FIG. 7.19. Steps in isometric sketching.

major axis is horizontal for an ellipse on a horizontal plane (I).

The construction procedure shown in Fig. 7.11(b) may be used to construct a pictorial circle freehand. (See also Fig. 7.22, III.)

7.17

Proportioning. As stated in Sec. 7.10, one should eventually be able to judge lengths and recognize proportions. Until this ultimate goal has been reached, the graphical method presented in Fig. 7.13 may be used with pictorial sketching (Fig. 7.23). The procedures as used are identical, the only recognizable difference being that the rectangle in the first case now becomes a rhomboid. Figure 7.24 illustrates how the method might be applied in making a sketch of a simple object. The enclosing box was sketched first with light lines, and then the graphical method was applied as shown to locate the points at one-quarter and one-half of the height. To establish the line of the top surface that is at a distance equal to one-third of the length from the end, a construction line was sketched from A to the midpoint B to locate C at the point of intersection of AB with the diagonal. Point C will fall on the required line.

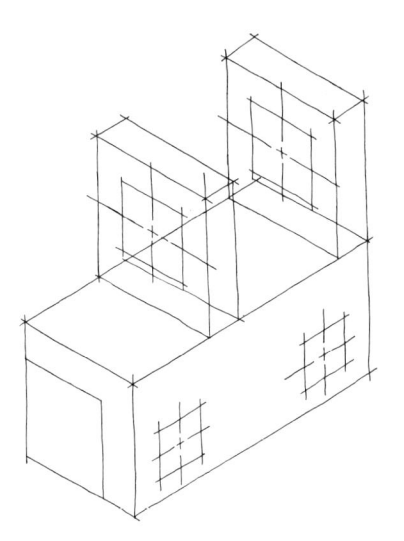

FIG. 7.20. Blocking in an isometric sketch.

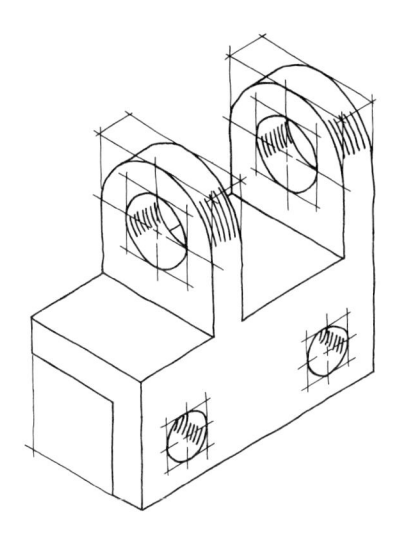

FIG. 7.21. Isometric circles.

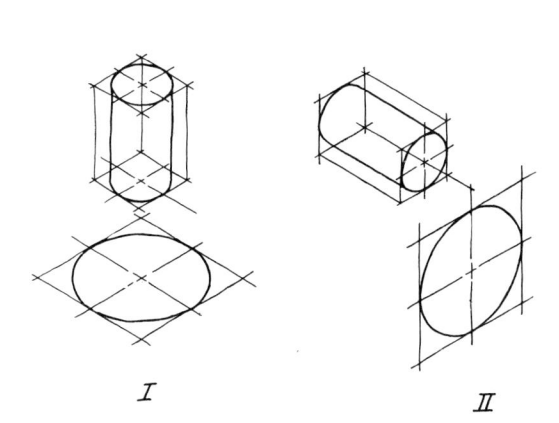

FIG. 7.22. Isometric circles.

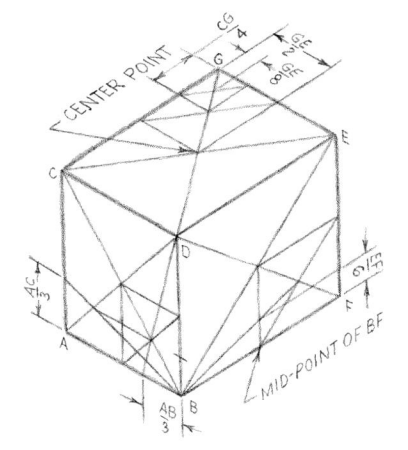

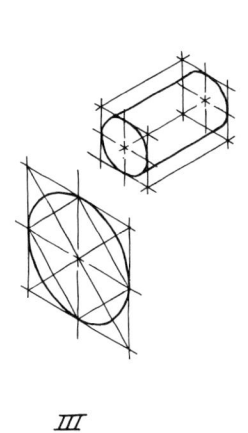

FIG. 7.23. Method for proportioning a rhomboid.

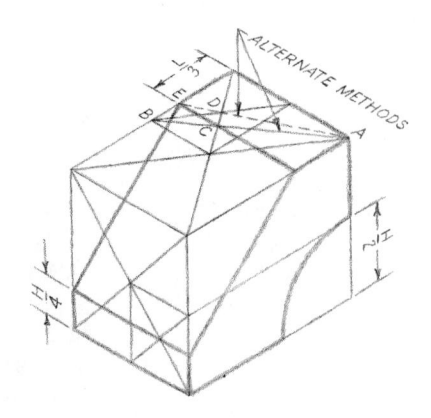

FIG. 7.24. Proportioning method applied.

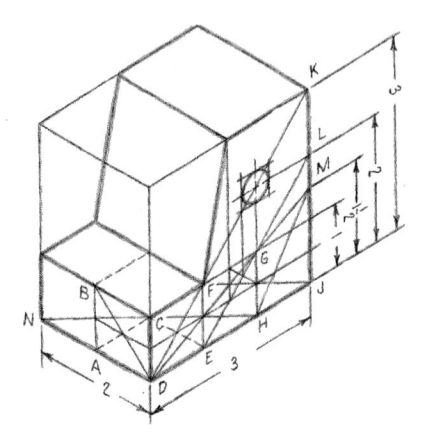

FIG. 7.25. The build-up method.

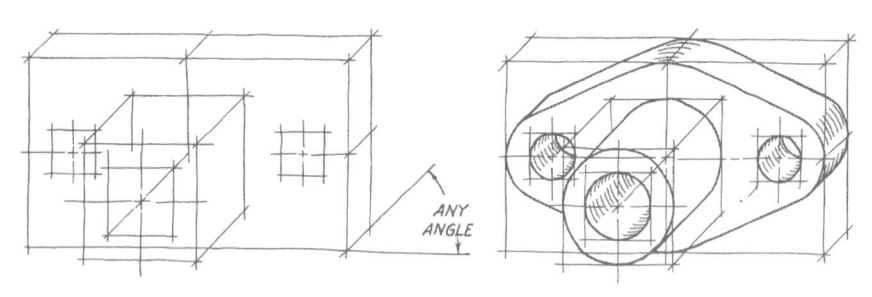

FIG. 7.26. Blocking in an oblique sketch.

One might also use the build-up method (Fig. 7.15) to lay off the estimated proportions of an object. This method is particularly easy to apply when using an approximation of isometric. Suppose that the proportions are to be as shown in Fig. 7.25, and that the axes have been sketched through point D, one being vertical while the other two are at 30° upward to the right and to the left.

A start is made by drawing the two rhombuses $ABCD$ and $CDEF$. The interesting facts that can be observed are as follows:

1. A horizontal line through point C intersects the inclined axes at points H and N, the lower corner points of adjacent rhombuses.

2. A horizontal line through point F intersects the right-hand axis at point J, the far corner of the third rhombus.

3. Line DF extended locates point K. Line KJ is equal in length to the sum of the lengths of the sides of three of the isometric squares (rhombuses).

4. Line EG extended locates point L at two units above DJ.

5. Line DG extended locates the midpoint M of line KJ.

After this means of proportioning has been used a few times, a student will discover the possibilities that are offered by this method of building up an object, and he will become aware that there are varied ways of locating the needed points.

The object shown in Fig. 7.25 can also be thought of as being built up of cubes. The hidden lines at the lower corner complete the outline of the initial cube. More will be written about the use of cubes when sketching in perspective is presented in Chapter 13.

7.18
Sketches in Oblique. A sketch in oblique shows the front face without distortion, in its true shape. It has this one advantage over a representation prepared in isometric, even though the final result usually will not present so pleasing an appearance. It is not recommended for objects having circular or irregularly curved features on any but the front plane or in a plane parallel to it.

The beginner who is familiar with axonometric sketching will have very little difficulty in preparing a sketch in oblique, for, in general, the methods of preparation presented in the previous sections apply to both. The principal difference between these two forms of sketching is in the position of the axes, oblique sketching being unlike the isometric in that two of the axes are at right angles to each other. The third axis may be at any convenient angle, as indicated in Fig. 7.26.

Figure 7.27 shows the steps in making an oblique sketch using the proportioning methods previously explained for dividing a rectangle and a rhomboid. The receding lines are made parallel when a sketch is made in oblique projection.

The distortion and illusion of extreme elongation in the direction of the receding axis may be minimized by foreshortening to obtain proportions that are more realistic to the eye and by making the receding lines converge slightly. The resulting sketch will then be in a form of pseudo-perspective, which resembles parallel perspective to some extent.

PROBLEMS

The problems presented with this chapter have been selected to furnish practice in freehand drawing. The individual pieces that appear in pictorial form have been taken from a wide variety of mechanisms used in different fields of engineering. The student may be required to prepare complete working sketches of these parts if his instructor desires. Such an assignment, however, would presuppose an understanding of the fundamentals of dimensioning as they are presented in the beginning sections of Chapter 16.

The two one-view working sketches were selected to provide practice in lettering and sketching.

Finally, the problems presented in Figs. 7.47–7.54 were selected to give practice in preparing pictorial sketches—isometric and oblique. In addition to developing proficiency in sketching, these problems offer the student further opportunity to gain experience in reading drawings. Additional problems that are suitable for pictorial sketching may be found in Chapter 12.

1–2. (Figs. 7.28–7.29). Reproduce an assigned one-view sketch on a sheet of sketching paper.

3–6. (Figs. 7.30–7.33). Sketch, freehand, the necessary views of the given objects as assigned. The selected length for the unit will determine the size of the views. Assume any needed dimensions that are not given in units.

7–16. (Figs. 7.34–7.43). These problems are designed to give the student further study in multiview representation and, at the same time, offer him the opportunity to apply good line technique to the preparation of sketches.

Only the necessary views on which all of the hidden lines are to be shown should be drawn.

If dimensions are to be given, ample space

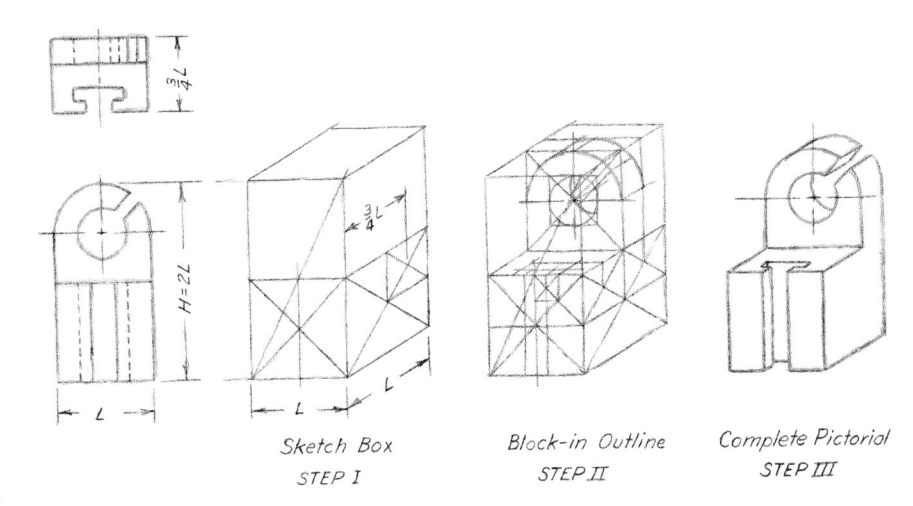

FIG. 7.27. Steps in oblique sketching.

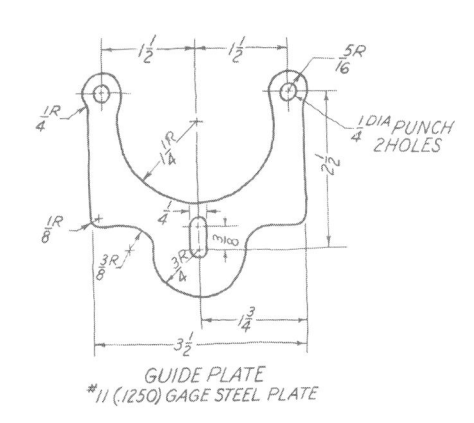

FIG. 7.28.

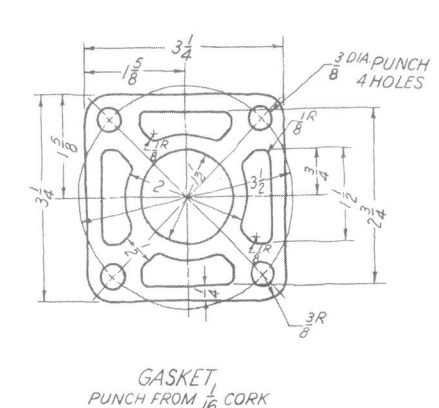

FIG. 7.29.

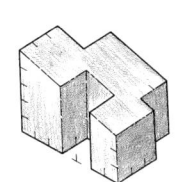

FIG. 7.30. Support block.

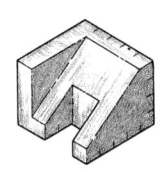

FIG. 7.31. Wedge block.

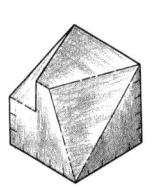

FIG. 7.32. End block.

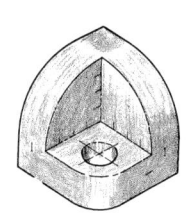

FIG. 7.33. Corner block.

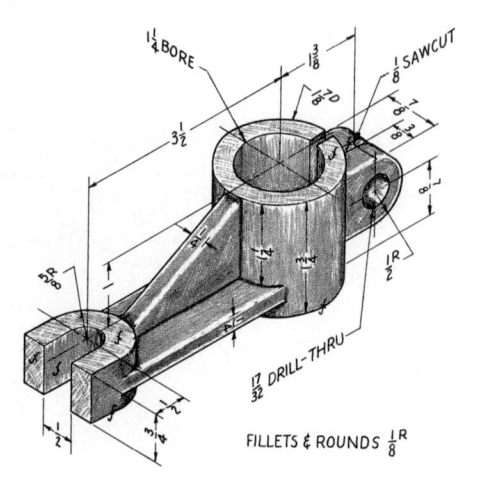

FIG. 7.34. Shifter.

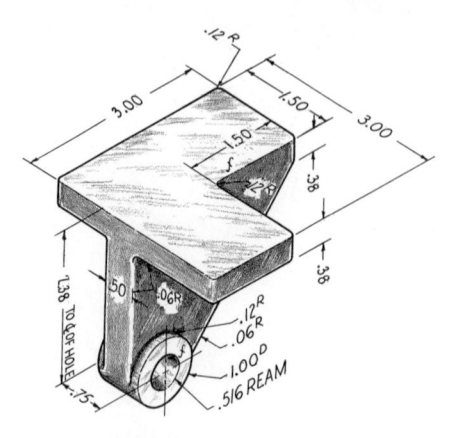

FIG. 7.35. Tool rest.

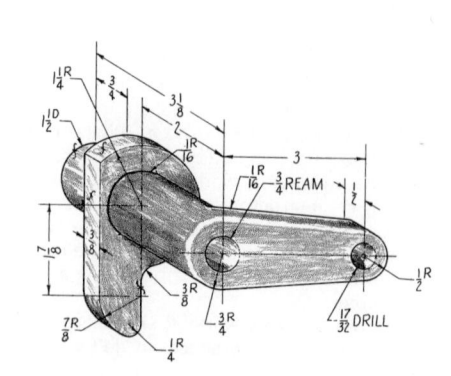

FIG. 7.36. Offset trip lever.

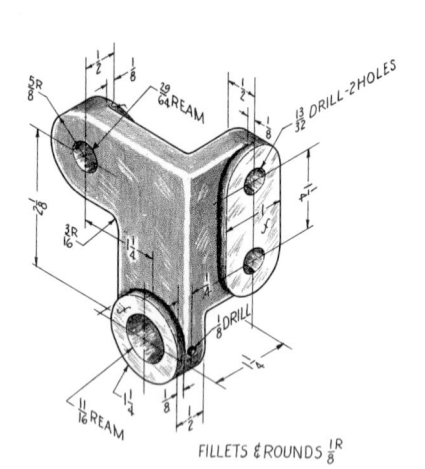

FIG. 7.37. Link.

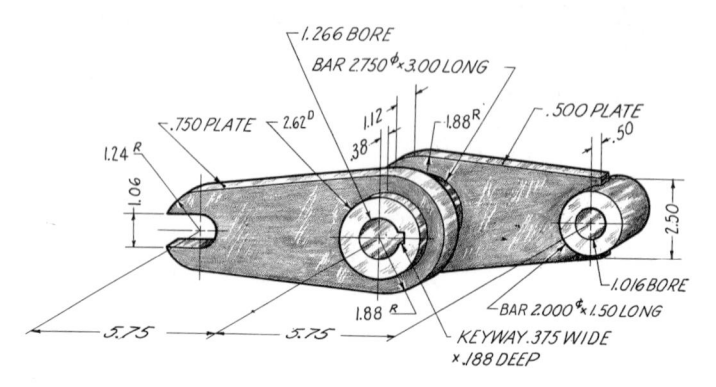

FIG. 7.38. Idler lever (weldment).

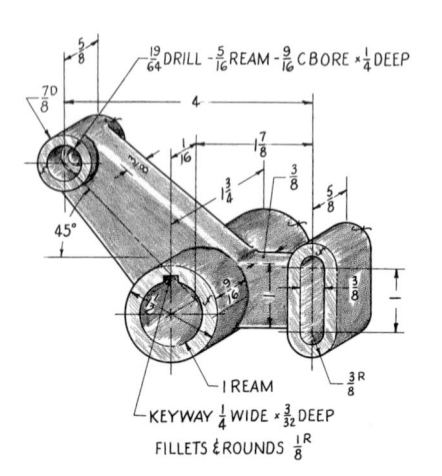

FIG. 7.39. Control bracket.

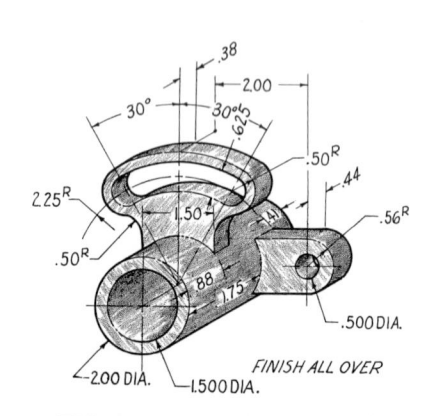

FIG. 7.40. Index guide.

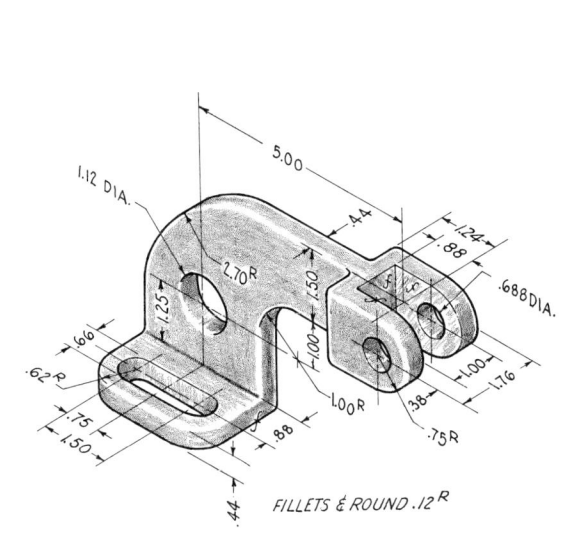

CHAP. 7 / FREEHAND TECHNICAL DRAWING—BASIC TECHNIQUES   139

FIG. 7.41. Arm bracket.

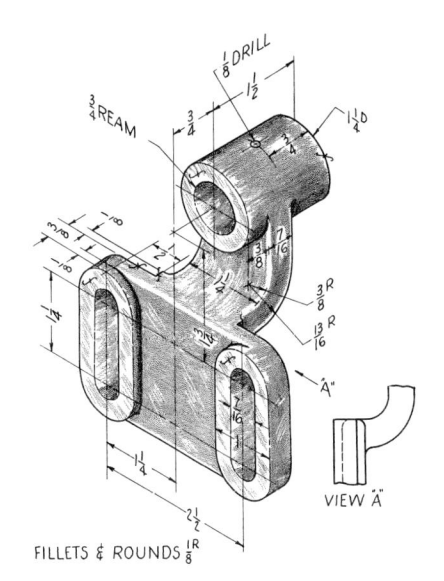

FIG. 7.42. Bearing bracket.

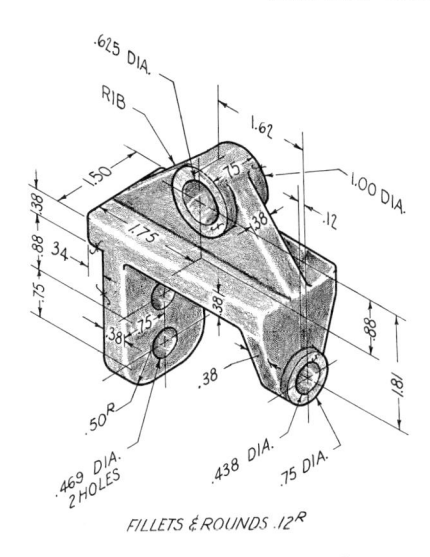

FIG. 7.43. Rear support bracket.

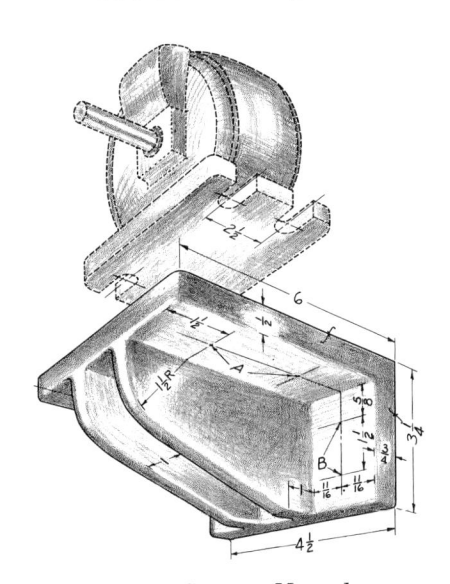

FIG. 7.44. Motor base.

must be allowed between the views for their placement. The beginning sections of Chapter 16 present the basic principles of size description.

17. (Fig. 7.44). Make a complete three-view sketch of the motor base. The ribs are $\frac{3}{8}$ in. thick. At points A, four holes are to be drilled for $\frac{1}{2}$-in. bolts that are to be $2\frac{1}{2}$ in. center to center in one direction and $3\frac{1}{8}$ in. in the other. At points B four holes are to be drilled for $\frac{1}{2}$-in. bolts that fasten the motor base to a steel column. Fillets and rounds are $\frac{1}{8}R$.

18. (Fig. 7.45). Make a three-view orthographic sketch of the motor bracket.

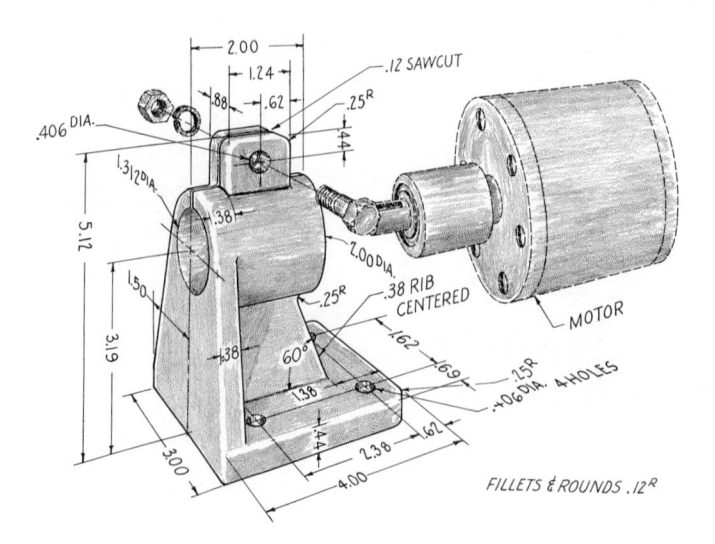

FIG. 7.45. Motor bracket.

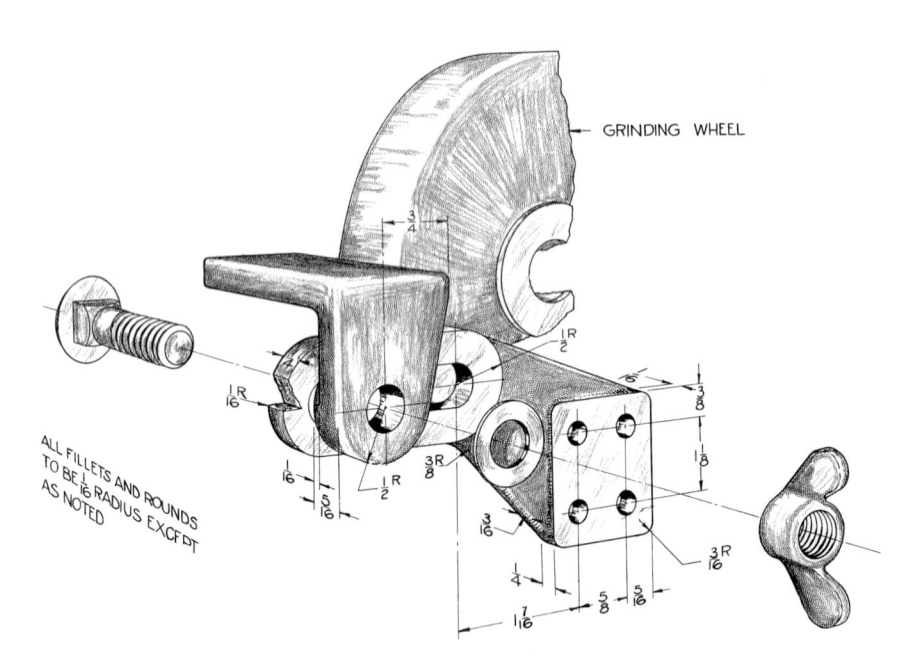

FIG. 7.46. Tool rest and tool rest bracket.

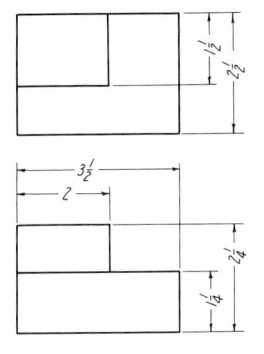

CHAP. 7 / FREEHAND TECHNICAL DRAWING—BASIC TECHNIQUES   **141**

FIG. 7.47.

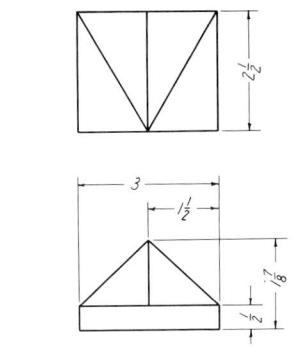

FIG. 7.48.

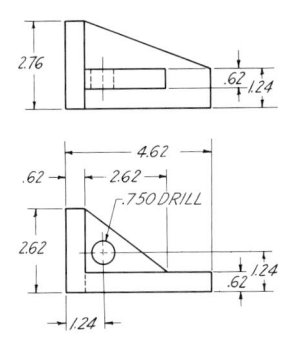

FIG. 7.49.

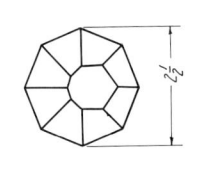

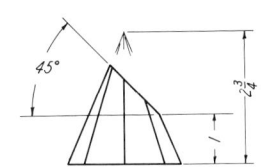

FIG. 7.50.

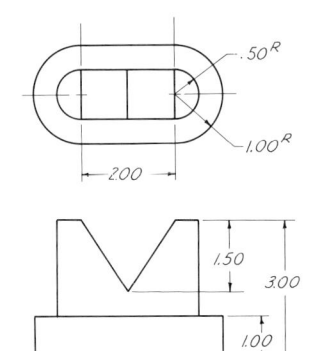

FIG. 7.51.

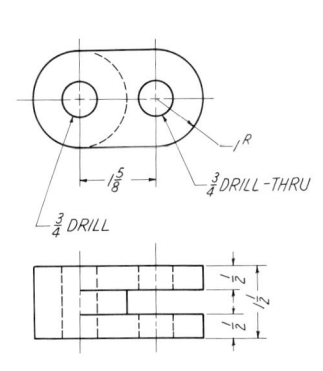

FIG. 7.52.

19. (Fig. 7.46). Make a complete three-view sketch of the tool rest and/or the tool rest bracket. The rectangular top surface of the tool rest is to be 1⅛ in. above the center line of the hole for the ⁷⁄₁₆-in. bolt. The overall dimensions of the top are 1¼ × 2½ in. It is to be ¼ in. thick. The overall dimensions of the rectangular pad of the bracket are 1¼ × 1⅞ in. The center line of the adjustment slot is ⁹⁄₁₆ in. above the center line of the top holes in the rectangular pad and the distance from center line to center line of the slot is 1⅜ in. The bracket is to be fastened to a housing with ¼-in. roundhead machine screws.

20–25. (Figs. 7.47–7.52). Make freehand isometric sketches of the objects as assigned.

26–29. (Figs. 7.51–7.54). Make freehand oblique sketches of the objects as assigned.

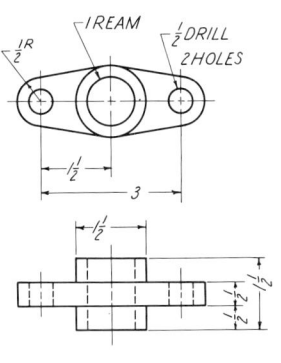

FIG. 7.53.

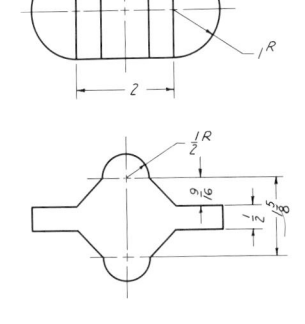

FIG. 7.54.

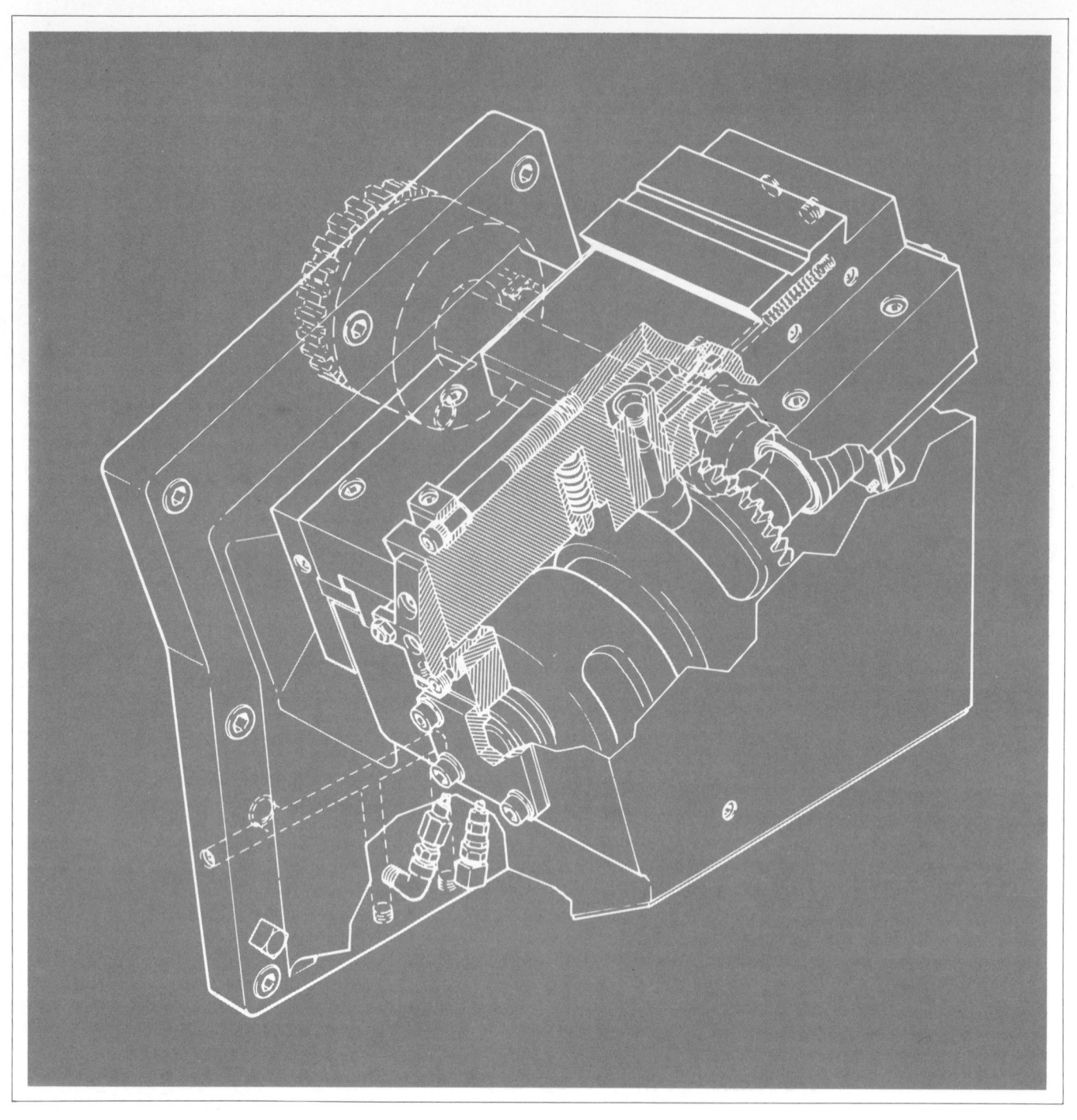

Pictorial sections are used in instruction manuals and catalogs and are prepared very often for display applications. They are easier to read and understand than conventional assembly drawings. The various related parts (cross slide, base, and cam drive) of the unit shown above can be easily recognized.
(*Courtesy Warner and Swasey Company.*)

Sectional Views

8.1

Sectional Views (Fig. 8.1). Although the invisible features of a simple object usually may be described on an exterior view by the use of hidden lines, it is unwise to depend on a perplexing mass of such lines to describe adequately the interior of a complicated object or an assembled mechanism. Whenever a representation becomes so confused that it is difficult to read, it is customary to make one or more of the views "in section" (Fig. 8.2). A view "in section" is one obtained by imagining the object to have been cut by a cutting plane, the front portion being removed to reveal clearly the interior features. Figure 8.3(*a*) illustrates the use of an imaginary cutting plane. The resulting section (front) view, accompanied by a top view,

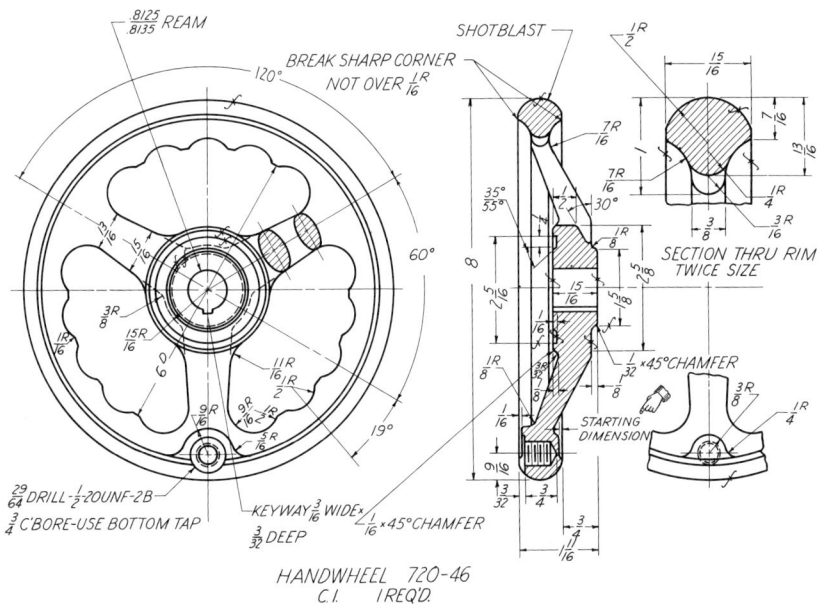

FIG. 8.1. A working drawing with sectional views. (*Courtesy Warner and Swasey Co.*)

143

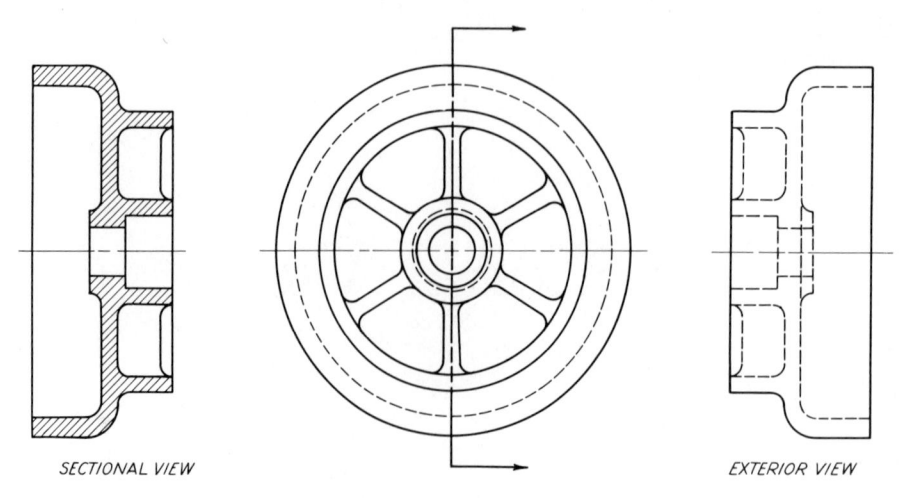

FIG. 8.2. A sectional view.

is shown in Fig. 8.3(c). At this point it should be understood that a portion is shown removed only in a sectional view, not in any of the other views [Fig. 8.3(c)].

When the cutting plane cuts an object lengthwise, the section obtained is commonly called a longitudinal section; when crosswise, it is called a cross section. It is designated as being either a full section, a half section, or a broken section. If the plane cuts entirely across the object, the section represented is known as a *full section*. If it cuts only halfway across a symmetrical object, the section is a *half section*. A *broken section* is a partial one, which is used when less than a half section is needed.

On a completed sectional view, fine sec-

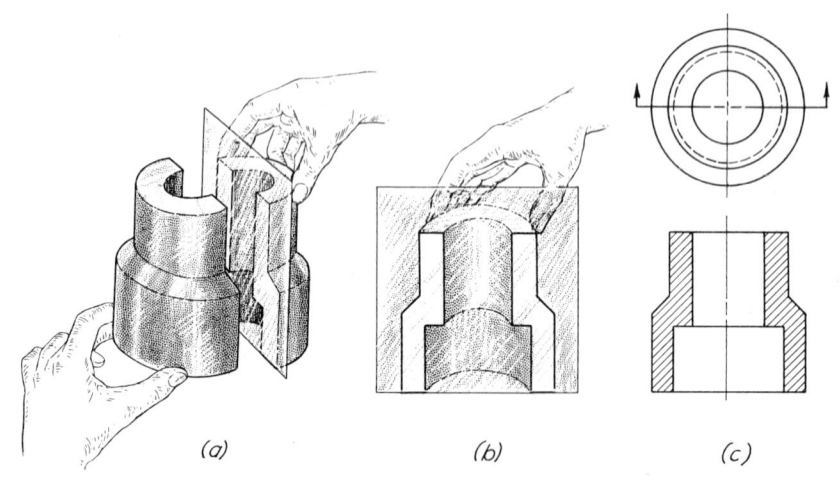

FIG. 8.3. The theory of the construction of a sectional view.

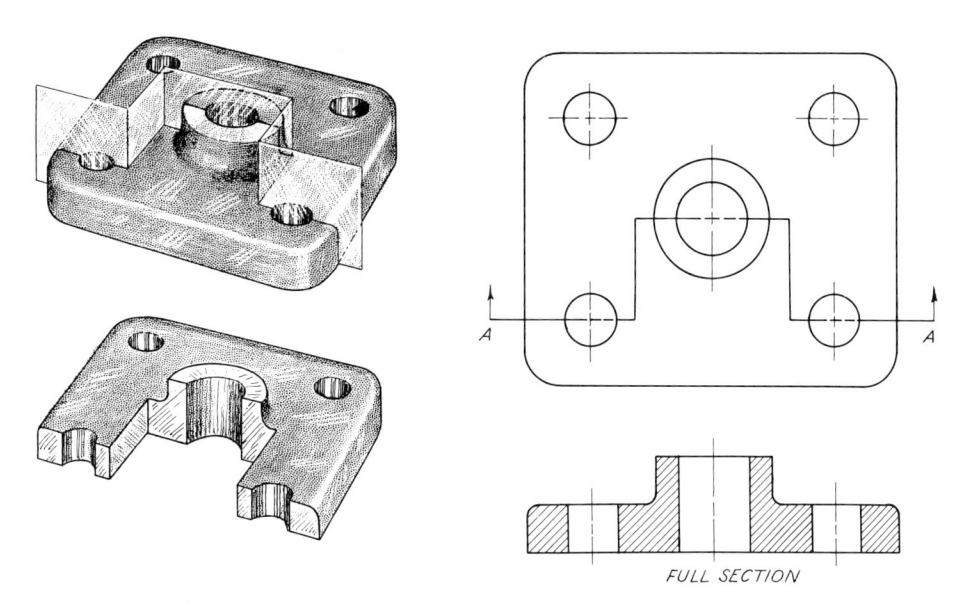

FIG. 8.4. An offset cutting plane.

tion lines are drawn across the surface cut by the imaginary plane, to emphasize the contour of the interior (see Sec. 8.8).

8.2
A Full Section. Since a cutting plane that cuts a full section passes entirely through an object, the resulting view will appear as illustrated in Fig. 8.3(c). Although the plane usually passes along the main axis, it may be offset (Fig. 8.4) to reveal important features.

A full-sectional view, showing an object's characteristic shape, usually replaces an exterior front view; however, one of the other principal views, side or top, may be converted to a sectional view if some interior feature thus can be shown to better advantage or if such a view is needed in addition to a sectioned front view.

The procedure in making a full-sectional view is simple, in that the sectional view is an orthographic one. The imaginary cut face of the object simply is shown as it would appear to an observer looking directly at it from a point an infinite distance away. In any sectional view, it is considered good practice to omit all invisible lines unless such lines are necessary to clarify the representation. Even then they should be used sparingly.

8.3
A Half Section. The cutting plane for a half section removes one-quarter of an object. The plane cuts halfway through to the axis or center line so that half the finished sectional view appears in section and half appears as an external view (Fig. 8.5). This type of sectional view is used when a view is needed showing both the exterior and interior construction of a

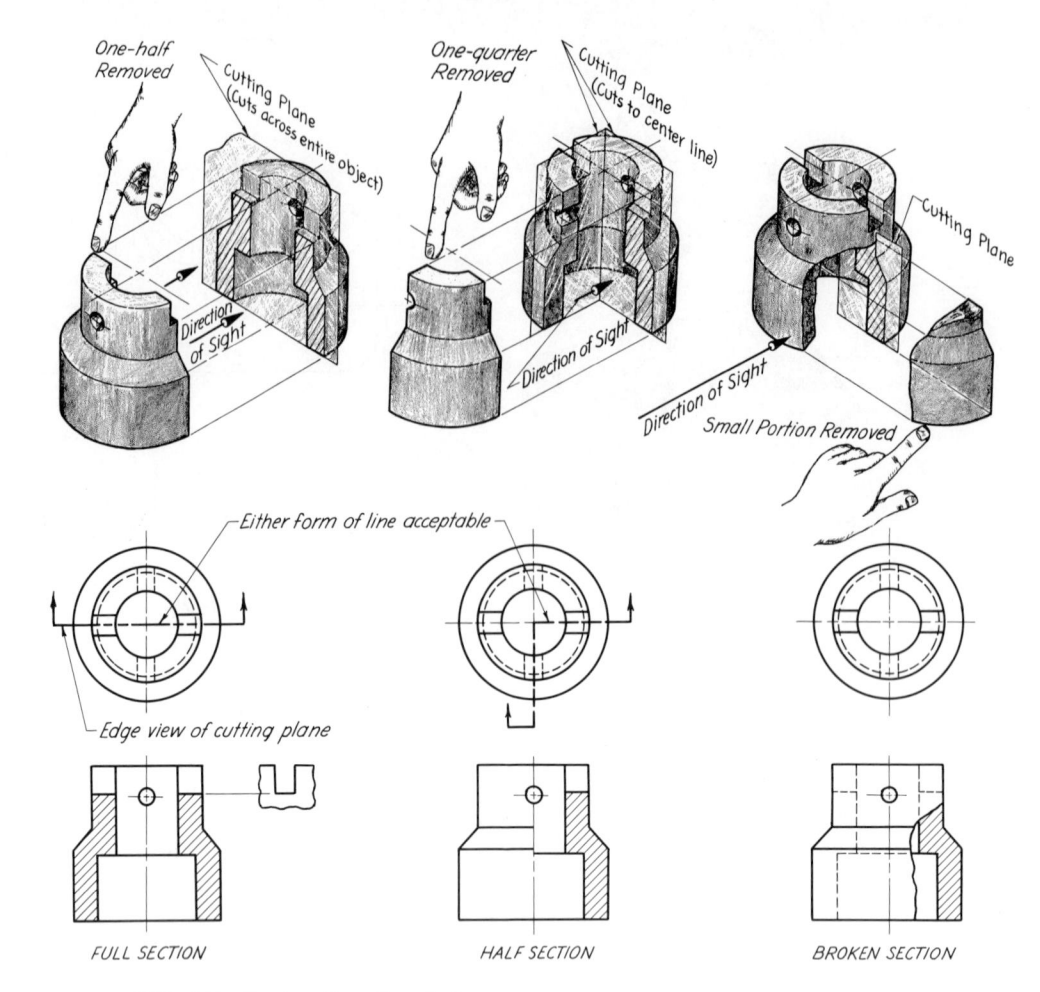

FIG. 8.5. Types of sectional views.

FIG. 8.6. A half section.

(a) SOLID LINE ASA STANDARD
(b) CENTER LINE ASA STANDARD

symmetrical object. Good practice dictates that hidden lines be omitted from both halves of the view unless they are absolutely necessary for dimensioning purposes or for explaining the construction. Although the use of a solid object line to separate the two halves of a half section has been approved by the Society of Automotive Engineers and has been accepted by the American National Standards Institute [Fig. 8.6(a)], many draftsmen prefer to use a center line, as shown in Fig. 8.6(b). They reason that the removal of a quarter of the object is theoretical and imaginary and that an actual edge, which would be implied by a solid line, does not exist. The center line is taken as denoting a theoretical edge.

8.4

A Broken Section. A broken or partial section is used mainly to expose the interior of objects so constructed that less than a half section is required for a satisfactory description (Fig. 8.7). The object theoretically is cut by a cutting plane and the front portion is removed by breaking it away. The "breaking away" gives an irregular boundary line to the section.

8.5
A Revolved Section. A revolved section is useful for showing the true shape of the cross section of some elongated object, such as a bar, or some feature of an object, such as an arm, spoke, or rib (Figs. 8.1 and 8.8).

To obtain such a cross section, an imaginary cutting plane is passed through the member perpendicular to the longitudinal axis and then is revolved through 90° to bring the resulting view into the plane of the paper (Fig. 8.9). When revolved, the section should show in its true shape and in its true revolved position, regardless of the location of the lines of the exterior view. If any lines of the view interfere with the revolved section, they should be omitted (Fig. 8.10). It is sometimes advisable to provide an open space for the section by making a break in the object (Fig. 8.8).

8.6
Removed (Detail) Sections. A removed section is similar to a revolved section, except that it does not appear on an external view but instead is drawn "out of place" and appears adjacent to it (Fig. 8.11). There are two good reasons why detail sections frequently are desirable. First, their use may prevent a principal view of an object, the cross section of which is not uniform, from being cluttered with numerous revolved sections (Fig. 8.12). Second, they may be drawn to an enlarged scale in order to emphasize detail and allow for adequate dimensioning (Fig. 8.13).

Whenever a detail section is used, there must be some means of identifying it. Usually this is accomplished by showing the cutting plane on the principal view and

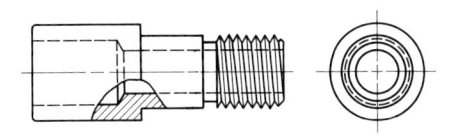

FIG. 8.7. A broken section.

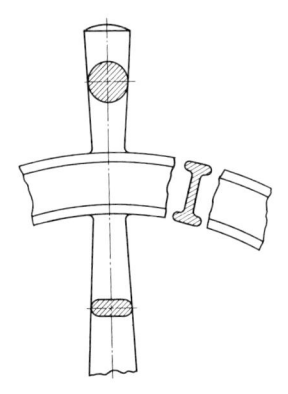

FIG. 8.8. A revolved section.*

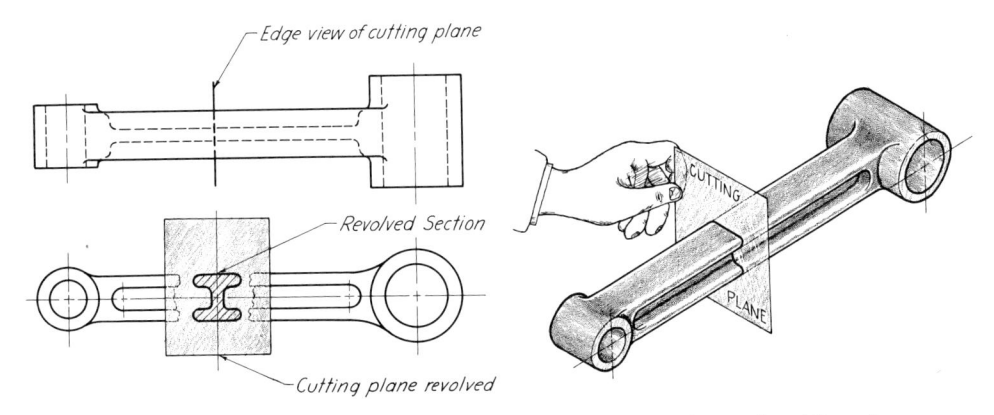

FIG. 8.9. A revolved section and cutting plane.

*ANS (ASA) Y14.2-1957.

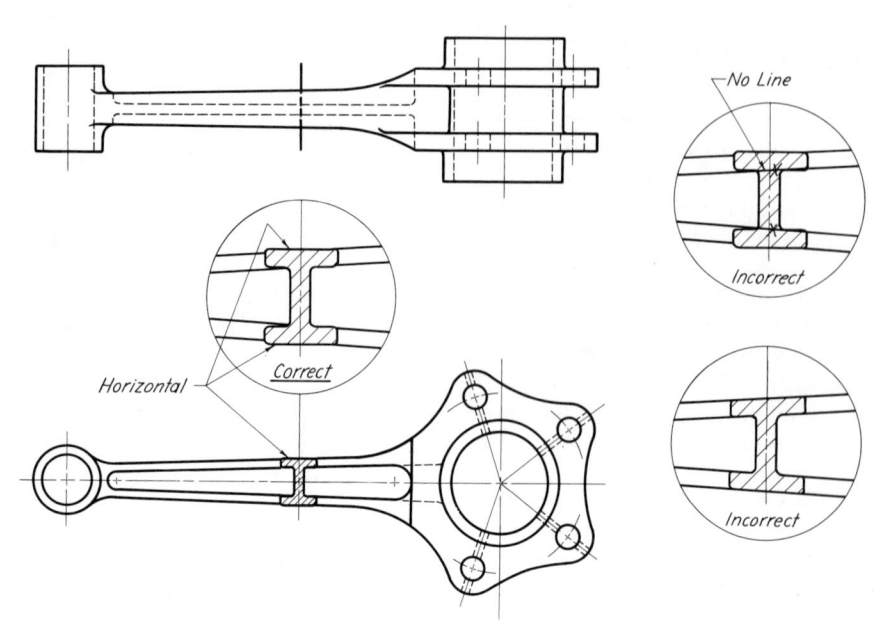

FIG. 8.10. Correct and incorrect treatment of a revolved section.

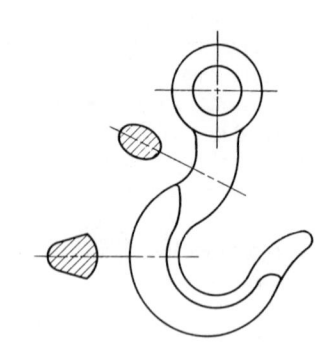

FIG. 8.11. Removed Sections*

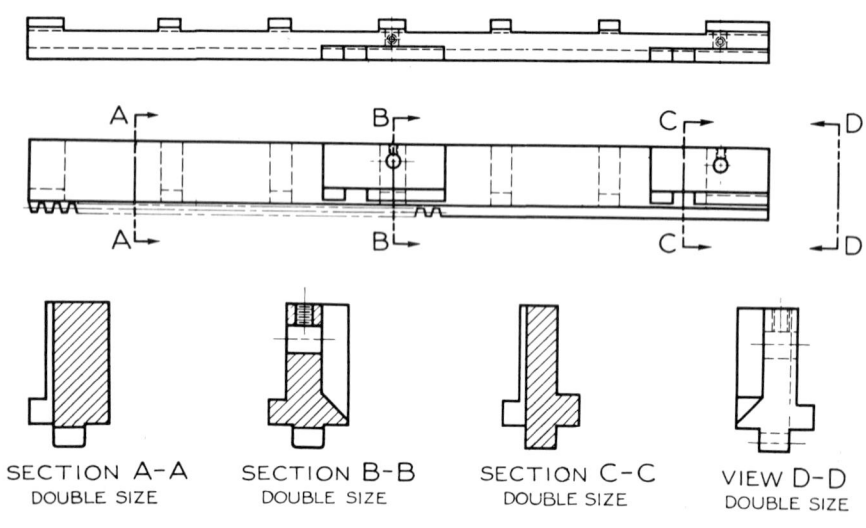

FIG. 8.12. Removed sections.*

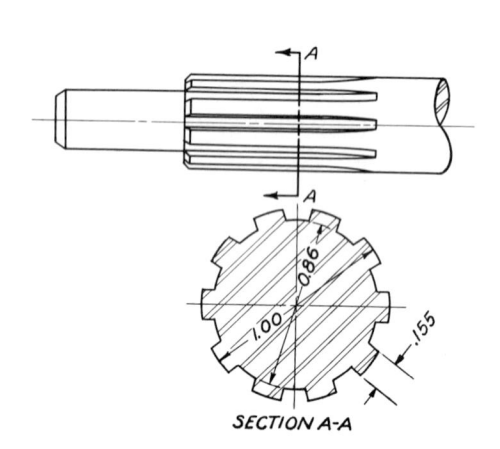

FIG. 8.13. A detail section enlarged for dimensioning.

*ANS (ASA) Y14.2-1957.

then labeling both the plane and the resulting view, as shown in Fig. 8.13.

8.7
Phantom Sections. A phantom or hidden section is a regular exterior view on which the interior construction is emphasized by crosshatching an imaginary cut surface with dotted section lines (Fig. 8.14). This type of section is used only when a regular section or a broken section would remove some important exterior detail, or, in some instances, to show an accompanying part in its relative position with regard to a particular part (Fig. 8.15). Instead of using a broken line with dashes of equal length, the phantom line shown in Fig. 3.61 could have been used to represent the outline of the adjacent parts shown in Fig. 8.15.

8.8
Section Lining. Section lines are light continuous lines drawn across the imaginary cut surface of an object for the purpose of emphasizing the contour of its interior. Usually they are drawn at an angle of 45° except in cases where a number of adjacent parts are shown assembled (Fig. 8.19).

To be pleasing in appearance, these lines must be correctly executed. While on ordinary work they are spaced about $\frac{3}{32}$ in. apart, there is no set rule governing their spacing. They simply should be spaced to suit the drawing and the size of the areas to be crosshatched. For example, on small views having small areas, the section lines may be as close as $\frac{1}{32}$ in., while on large views having large areas they may be as far apart as $\frac{1}{8}$ in. In the case of very thin plates, the cross section is shown "solid black" (Fig. 8.16).

The usual mistake of the beginning student is to draw the lines too close together. This, plus the unavoidable slight variations, causes the section lining to appear streaked. Although several forms

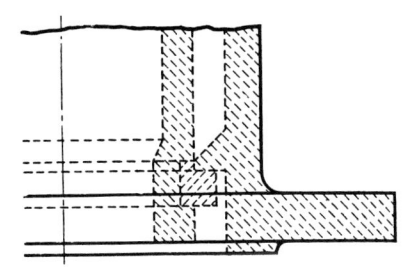

FIG. 8.14. A phantom section.

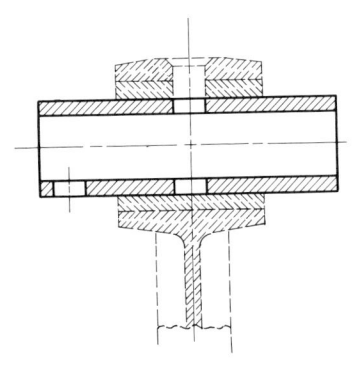

FIG. 8.15. Phantom sectioning—adjacent parts.

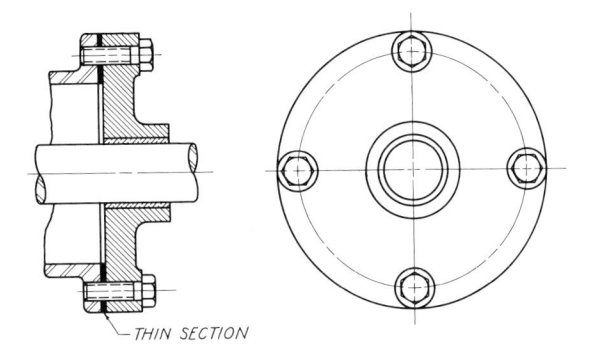

FIG. 8.16. Thin sections.

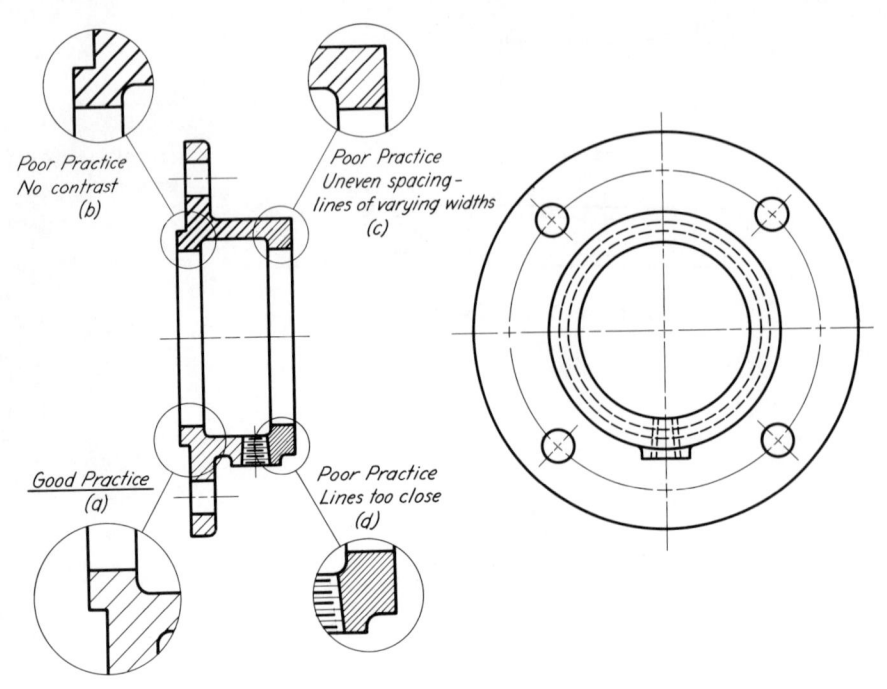

FIG. 8.17. Faults in section lining.

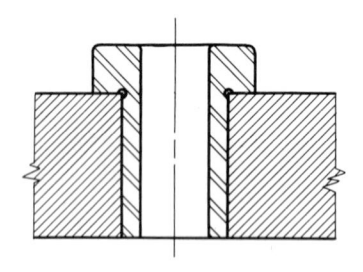

FIG. 8.18. Two adjacent pieces.

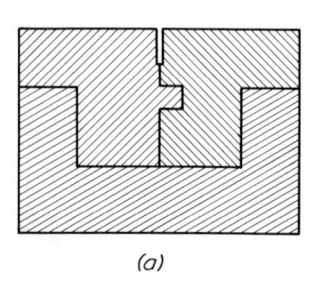

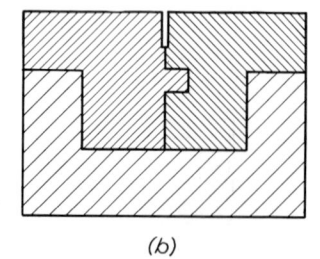

FIG. 8.19. Three adjacent pieces.

of mechanical section liners are available, most draftsmen do their spacing by eye. The student is advised to do likewise, being careful to see that the initial pitch, as set by the first few lines, is maintained across the area. To accomplish this, he should check back from time to time to make sure there has been no slight general increase or decrease in the spacing. An example of correct section lining is shown in Fig. 8.17(a), and, for comparison, examples of faulty practice may be seen in Fig. 8.17(b), (c), and (d). Experienced draftsmen realize that nothing will do more to ruin the appearance of a drawing than carelessly executed section lines.

As shown in Fig. 8.18, the section lines on two adjacent pieces should slope at 45° in opposite directions. If a third piece adjoins the two other pieces, as in Fig. 8.19(a), it ordinarily is section-lined at 30°. An alternate treatment that might be used would be to vary the spacing without changing the angle. On a sectional view showing an assembly of related parts, *all portions of the cut surface of any part must be section-lined in the same direction,* for a change would lead the reader to consider the portions as belonging to different parts. Furthermore, to allow quick identification, each piece (and all identical pieces) in every view of the assembly drawing should be section-lined in the same direction.

Shafts, bolts, rivets, balls, and so on, whose axes lie in the plane of section, are not treated the same as ordinary parts. Having no interior construction to be shown, they are drawn in full and thus tend to make the adjacent sectioned parts stand out to better advantage (Fig. 8.20).

Whenever section lines drawn at 45° with the horizontal are parallel to part of the outline of the section (see Fig. 8.21), it is advisable to draw them at some other angle (say, 30° or 60°). Those drawn as in (a) and (c) produce an unusual appearance that is contrary to what is expected. Note the more natural effect obtained in (b) and (d) by sloping the lines at 30° and 75°.

8.9
Outline Sectioning. Very large surfaces may be section-lined around the bounding outline only, as illustrated in Fig. 8.22.

CHAP. 8 / SECTIONAL VIEWS   **151**

POOR PRACTICE
(a)

PREFERRED
(b)

POOR PRACTICE
(c)

PREFERRED
(d)

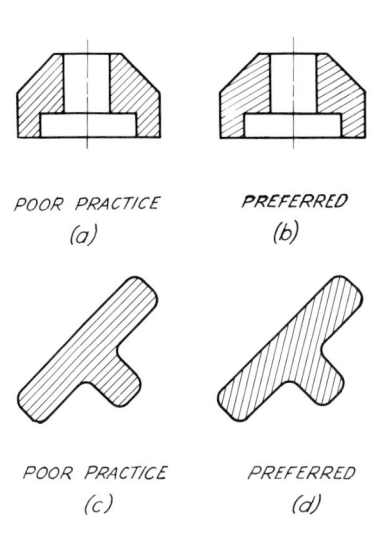

FIG. 8.21. Section lining at 30°, 60°, or 75°.

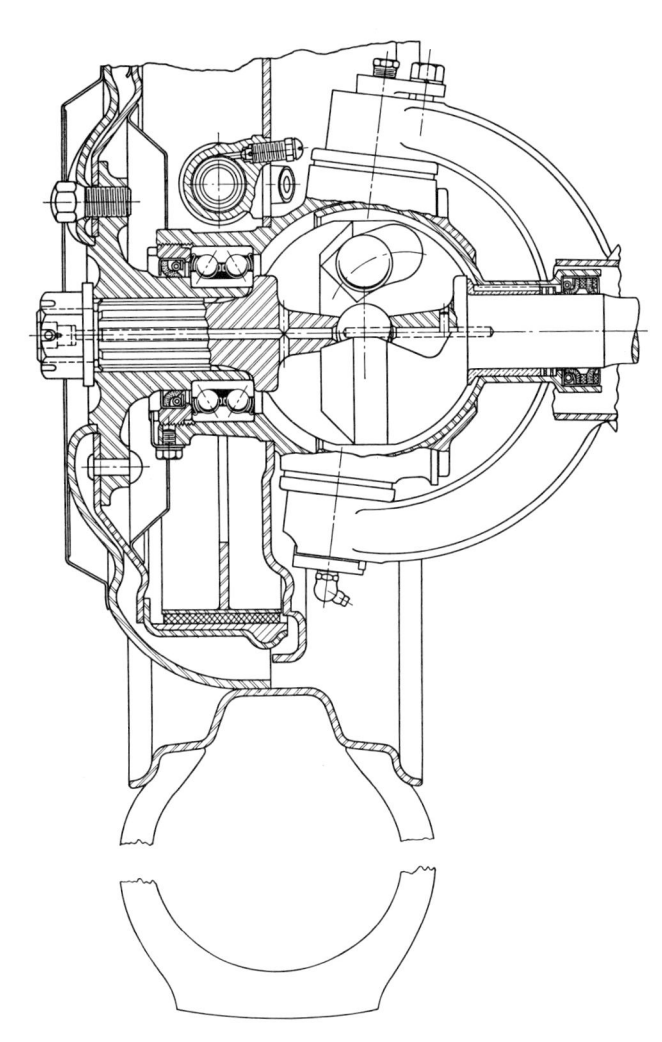

FIG. 8.20. Treatment of shafts, fasteners, ball bearings, and other parts. *(Courtesy New Departure, Division General Motors Corp.)*

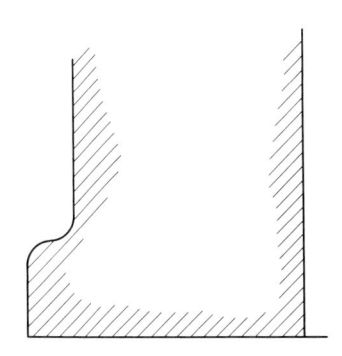

FIG. 8.22. Outline sectioning.

8.10
The Symbolic Representation for a Cutting Plane. The symbolic lines that are used to represent the edge view of a cutting plane are shown in Fig. 8.23. The line is as heavy as an object line and is composed of either alternate long and short dashes or a series of dashes of equal length. The latter form is used in the automobile industry and has been approved by the SAE (Society of Automotive Engineers) and the American National Standards Institute. On drawings of ordinary size, when alternate long and short dashes are used for the cutting-plane line, the long dashes are $\tfrac{3}{4}$ in. long, the short dashes $\tfrac{1}{8}$ in. long, and the spaces $\tfrac{1}{32}$ in. wide. When drawn in ink, the dashes are $\tfrac{1}{40}$–$\tfrac{1}{32}$ in. wide, depending on the size of the drawing. When drawn in pencil on manila paper, they are made with a medium pencil.

Arrowheads are used to show the direction in which the imaginary cut surface is viewed, and reference letters are added to identify it (Fig. 8.24).

Whenever the location of the cutting plane is obvious, it is common practice to omit the edge-view representation, particularly in the case of symmetrical objects. But if it is shown, and coincides with a center line, it takes precedence over the center line.

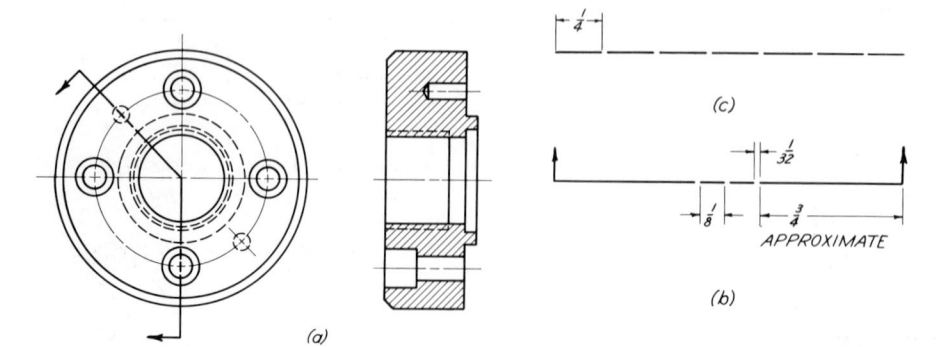

FIG. 8.23. Cutting plane lines (AN Standard).

8.11
Summary of the Practices of Sectioning.

1. A cutting plane may be offset in order to cut the object in such a manner as to reveal an important detail that would not be shown if the cutting plane were continuous (Fig. 8.4).

2. All visible lines beyond the cutting plane for the section are usually shown.

3. Invisible lines beyond the cutting plane for the section are usually not shown, unless they are absolutely necessary to clarify the construction of the piece. In a half section, they are omitted in the unsectioned half, and either a center line or a solid line is used to separate the two halves of the view (Figs. 8.5 and 8.6).

4. On a view showing assembled parts, the section lines on adjacent pieces are drawn in opposite directions at an angle of 45° (Fig. 8.18).

5. On an assembly drawing, the portions of the cut surface of a single piece in the same view or different views always should be section-lined in the same direction, with the same spacing (Fig. 8.20).

6. The symbolic line indicating the location of the cutting plane may be omitted if the location of the plane is obvious (Fig. 8.1).

7. On a sectioned view showing assembled pieces, an exterior view is preferred for shafts, rods, bolts, nuts, rivets, and so forth, whose axes are in the plane of section (Fig. 8.20).

8.12
Auxiliary Sections. A sectional view, projected on an auxiliary plane, is sometimes necessary to show the shape of a surface cut by a plane or to show the cross-sectional shape of an arm, rib, and so forth, inclined to any two or all three of the principal planes of projection (Fig. 8.25). When a cutting plane cuts an object, as in Fig. 8.25, arrows should show the direction in which the cut surface is viewed. Auxiliary sections are drawn by the usual method for drawing auxiliary views. When the bounding edge of the

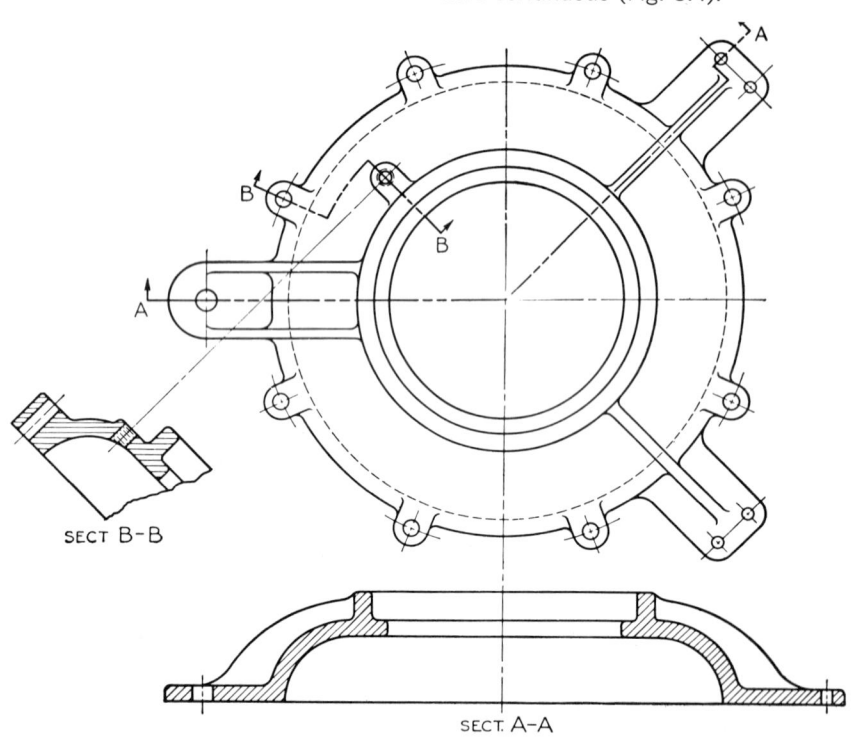

FIG. 8.24. A sectional view.*

*ANS (ASA) Y14.2-1957.

CHAP. 8 / SECTIONAL VIEWS   **153**

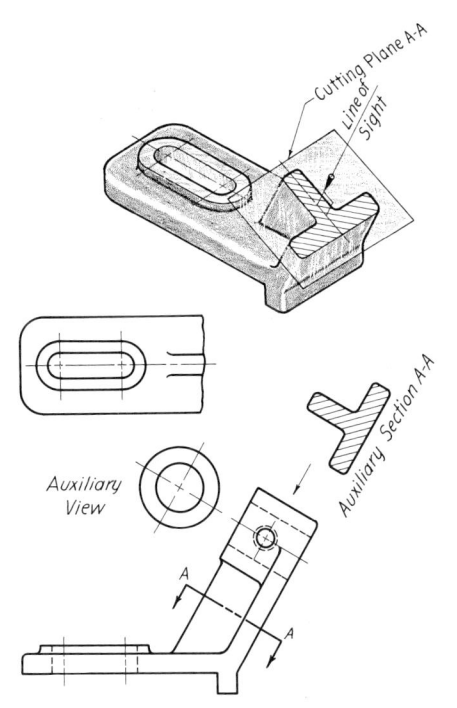

FIG. 8.25. An auxiliary section.

Poor Practice
(a)

Poor Practice
(b)

Preferred
(c)

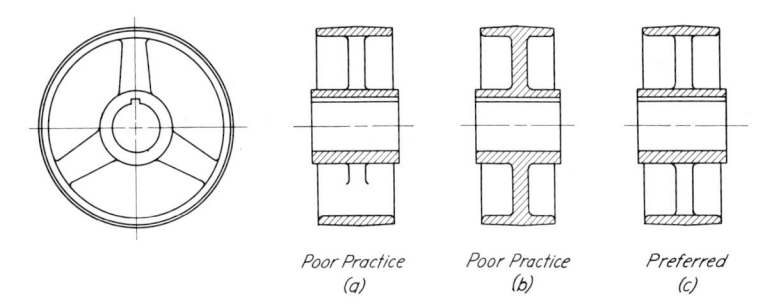

FIG. 8.26. Conventional treatment of spokes in section.

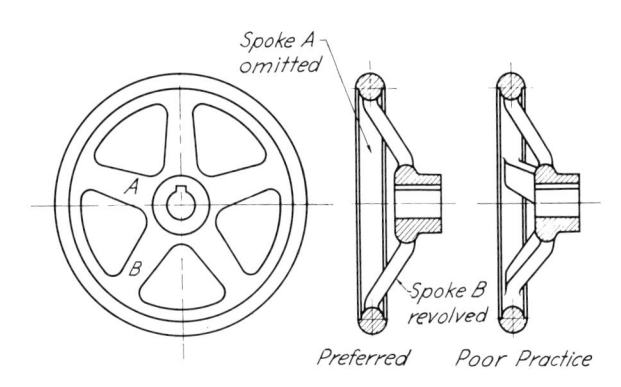

FIG. 8.27. Spokes in section.*

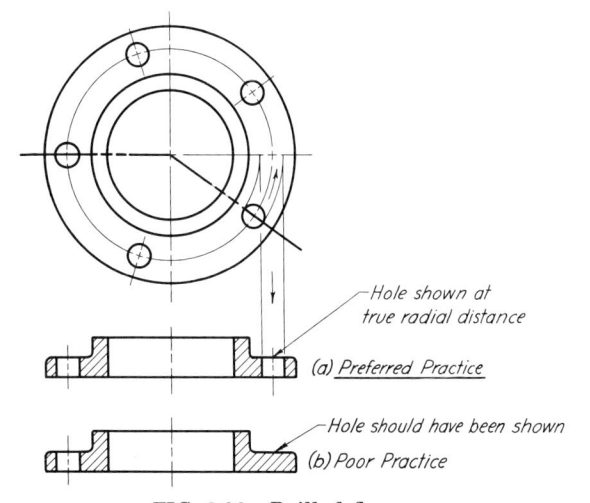

FIG. 8.28. Drilled flanges.

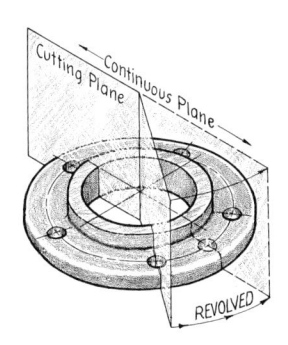

section is a curve, it is necessary to plot enough points to obtain a smooth one. Section 9.11 explains in detail the method for constructing the required view. A section view of this type usually shows only the inclined cut surface.

8.13
Conventional Sections. Sometimes a less confusing sectioned representation is obtained if certain of the strict rules of projection are violated, as explained in Chapter 6. For example, an unbalanced and confused view results when the sectioned view of the pulley shown in Fig. 8.26 is drawn in true projection, as in (*a*). It is better practice to preserve symmetry by showing the spokes as if they were aligned into one plane, as in (*c*). Such treatment of unsymmetrical features is not misleading, since their actual arrangement is revealed in the circular view. The spokes are not sectioned in the preferred view. If they

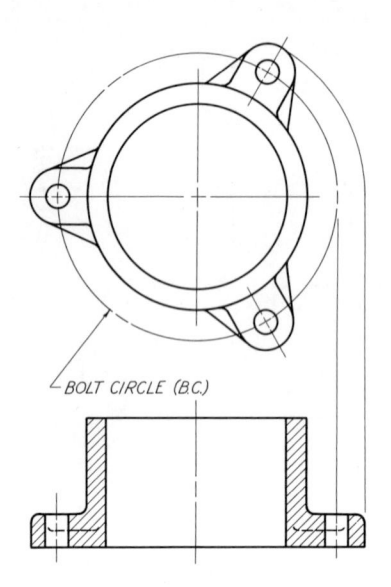

FIG. 8.29. Revolution of a portion of an object.

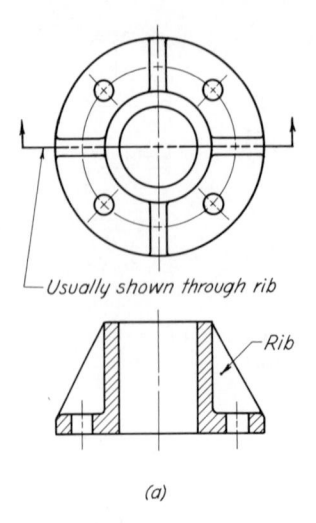

FIG. 8.30. Conventional treatment of ribs in section.

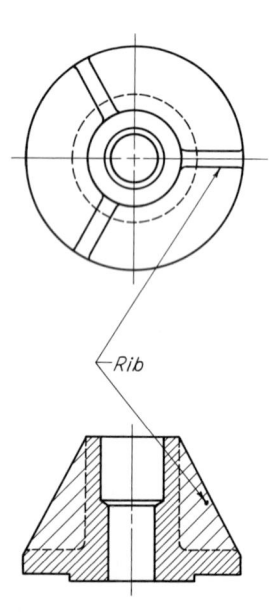

FIG. 8.31. Alternate treatment of ribs in section.

were, the first impression would be that the wheel had a solid web (*b*) (see Fig. 8.27).

When there are an odd number of holes in a flange, as is the case with the part in Fig. 8.28, they should be shown aligned in the sectioned view to reveal their true location with reference to the rim and the axis of the piece. To secure the so-called aligned section, one usually considers the cutting plane to be bent to pass through the angled hole, as shown in the pictorial drawing. Then, the bent portion of the plane (with the hole) is imagined to be revolved until it is aligned with the other portion of the cutting plane. As straightened out, the imaginary continuous plane produces the preferred section view shown in (*a*).

Figure 8.29 shows another example of conventional representation. The sectional view is drawn as though the upper projecting lug had been swung until the portion of the cutting plane through it formed a continuous plane with the other portion (Sec. 6.43). It should be noted that the hidden lines in the sectioned view are necessary for a complete description of the construction of the lugs.

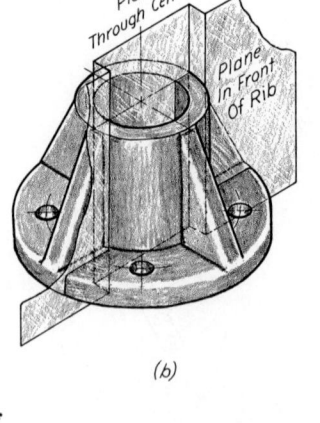

8.14
Ribs in Section. When a machine part has a rib cut by a plane of section (Fig. 8.30), a "true" sectional view taken through the rib would prove to be false and misleading, because the crosshatching on the rib would cause the object to appear "solid." The preferred treatment is to omit arbitrarily the section lines from the rib, as illustrated by Fig. 8.30(*a*). The resulting sectional view may be considered the view that would be obtained if the plane were offset to pass just in front of the rib (*b*).

An alternative conventional method, approved but not used as frequently, is illustrated in Fig. 8.31. This practice of omitting alternate section lines sometimes is adopted when it is necessary to emphasize a rib that might otherwise be overlooked.

8.15
Half Views. When the space available is insufficient to allow a satisfactory scale to

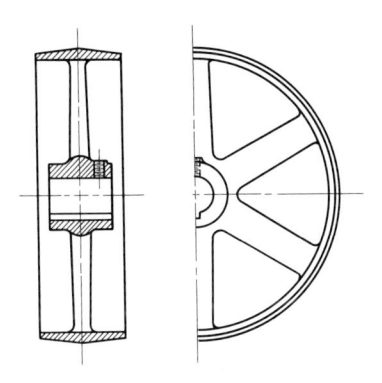

CHAP. 8 / SECTIONAL VIEWS   **155**

FIG. 8.32. A half view.

be used for the representation of a symmetrical piece, it is considered good practice to make one view a half view, as shown in Fig. 8.32. The half view, however, must be the top or side view and not the front view, which shows the characteristic contour. The half view should be the rear half.

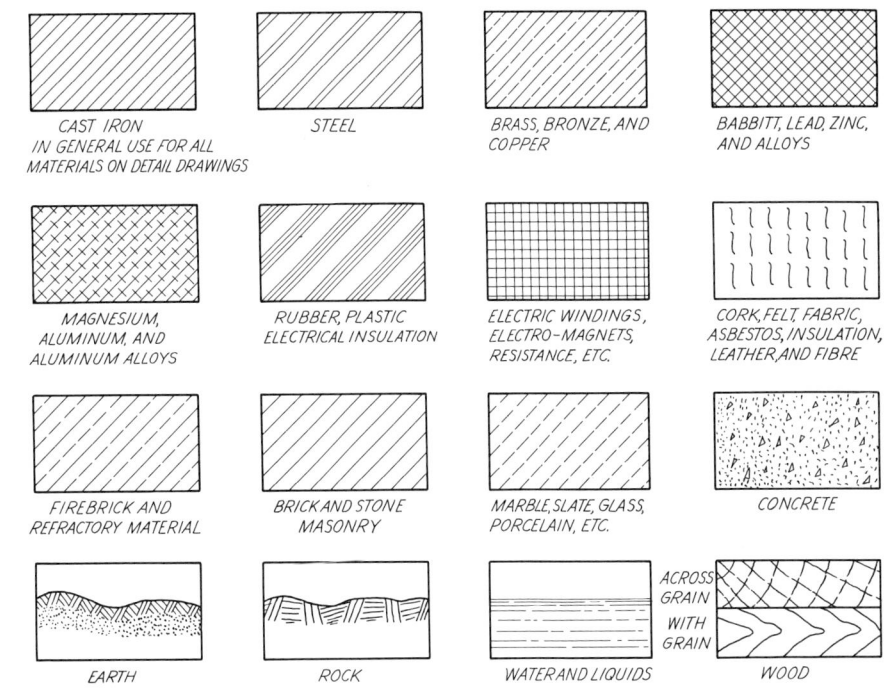

8.16
Material Symbols. The section-line symbols recommended by the American National Standards Institute for indicating various materials are shown in Fig. 8.33. Code section lining ordinarily is not used on a working (detail) drawing of a separate part. It is considered unnecessary to indicate a material symbolically when its exact specification must be given as a note. For this reason, and in order to save time as well, the easily drawn symbol for cast iron is commonly used on detail drawings for all materials. Contrary to this general practice, however, some few chief draftsmen insist that symbolic section lining be used on all detail drawings prepared under their supervision.

Code section lining usually is employed on an assembly section showing the various parts of a unit in position, because a distinction between the materials causes the parts to "stand out" to better advantage. Furthermore, a knowledge of the type of material of which an individual part is composed often helps the reader to identify it more quickly and understand its function.

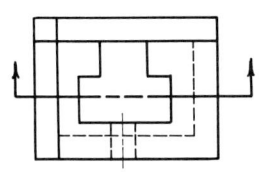

FIG. 8.33. Material symbols (AN Standard).

PROBLEMS

The following problems were designed to emphasize the principles of sectioning. Those drawings that are prepared from the pictorials of objects may be dimensioned if the elementary principles of dimensioning (Chapter 16) are carefully studied.

1. (Fig. 8.34). Reproduce the top view and change the front view to a full section view in accordance with the indicated cutting plane.

2. (Fig. 8.35). Reproduce the top view and

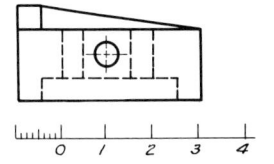

FIG. 8.34. Mutilated block.

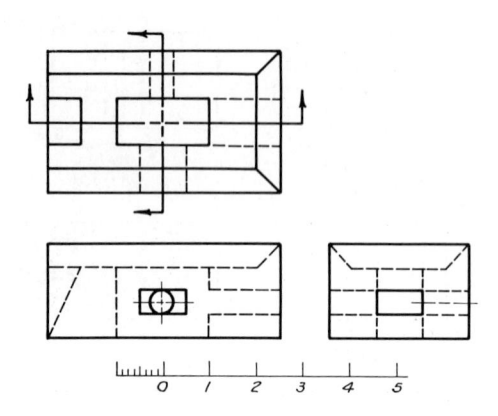

FIG. 8.35. Mutilated block.

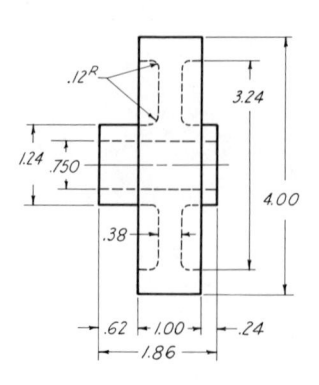

FIG. 8.36. Pulley.

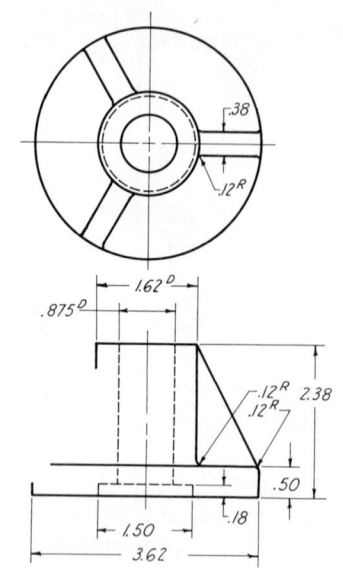

FIG. 8.37. Rod support.

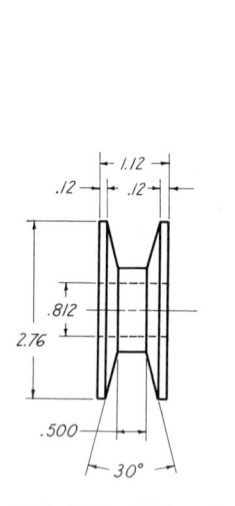

FIG. 8.38. "V" pulley.

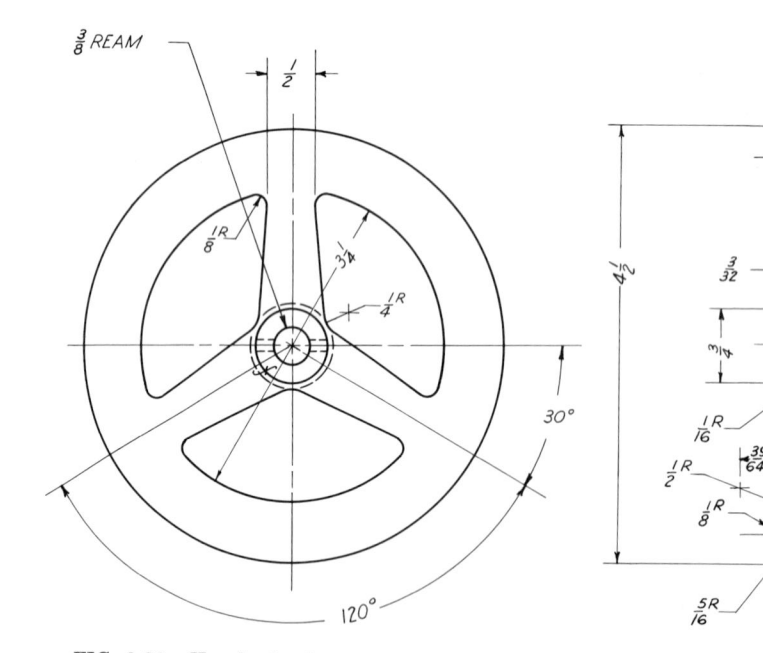

FIG. 8.39. Hand wheel.

CHAP. 8 / SECTIONAL VIEWS 157

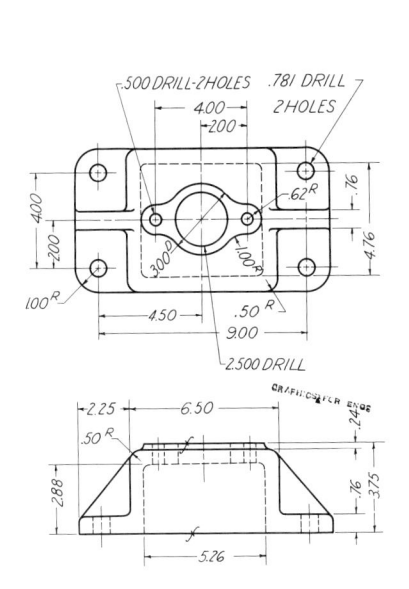

FIG. 8.40. Control housing cover.

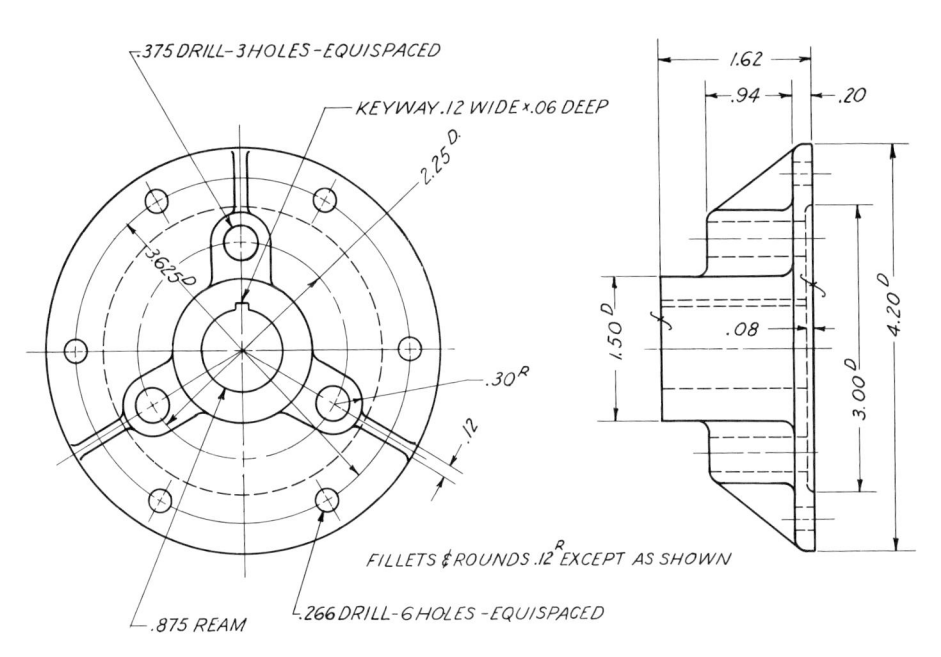

FIG. 8.41. Pump cover.

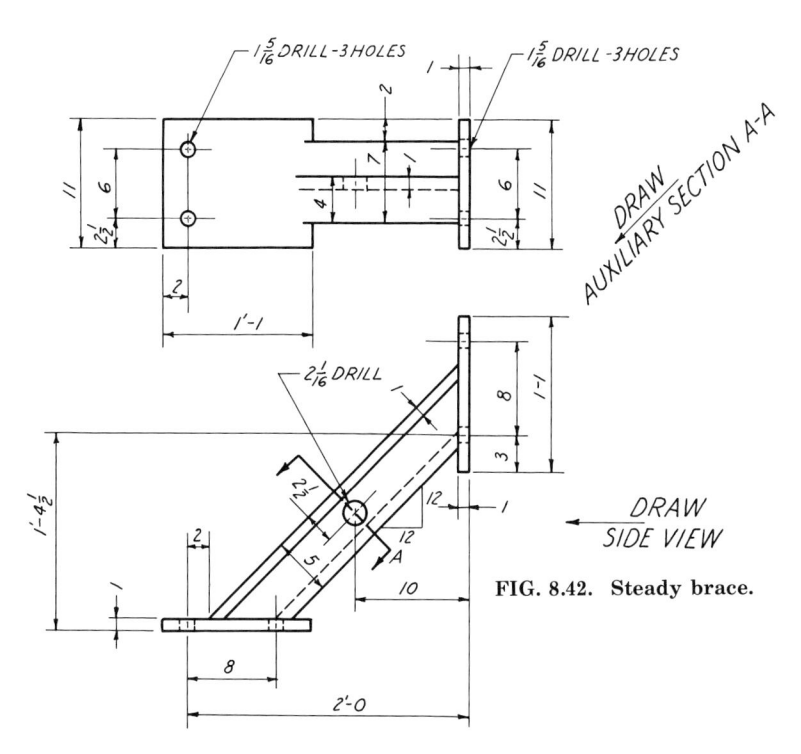

change the front and side views to sectional views that will be in accordance with the indicated cutting planes.

3. (Fig. 8.36). Draw a front view of the pulley (circular view) and a side view in full section.

4. (Fig. 8.37). Reproduce the top view of the rod support and draw the front view in full section. Read Sec. 6.43 before starting to draw.

5. (Fig. 8.38). Draw a front view of the "V"-pulley (circular view) and a side view in full section.

6. (Fig. 8.39). Reproduce the two views of the hand wheel and change the right-side view to a full section.

7. (Fig. 8.40). Reproduce the top view of the control housing cover and convert the front view to a full section.

8. (Fig. 8.41). Reproduce the circular front view of the pump cover and convert the right-side view to a full section.

9. (Fig. 8.42). Reproduce the front and top views of the steady brace. Complete the top

FIG. 8.42. Steady brace.

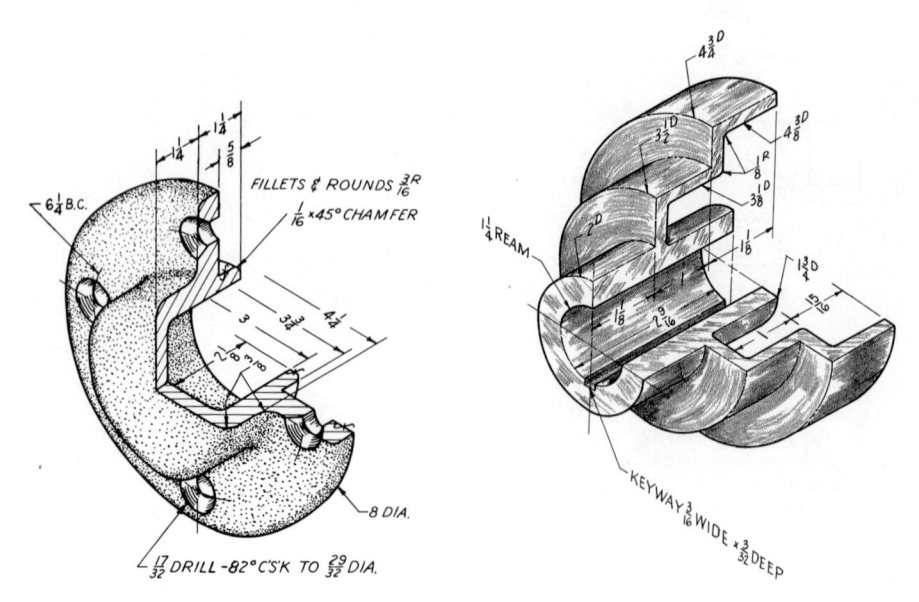

FIG. 8.43. Cover.   **FIG. 8.44.** Cone pulley.

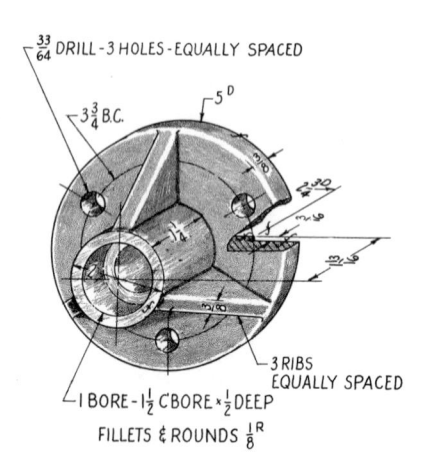

FIG. 8.45. Rod yoke.

view and draw the required side view and auxiliary section. Since this is a structural drawing, the figure giving the value of a distance appears above an unbroken dimension line in accordance with the custom in this field of engineering. The slope (45°) of the inclined member to which the plates are welded is indicated by a slope triangle with 12-in. legs.

This problem has been designed to make it necessary for the student to test his power of visualization if he is to determine the shape of the inclined structural member. Good judgment must be exercised in determining the location of the third hole in each plate. All hidden object lines should be shown.

10-19. (Figs. 8.43–8.52). These problems may be dimensioned, as are working drawings. For each object, the student should draw all the views necessary for a working drawing of the part. Good judgment should be exercised in deciding whether the sectional view should be a full section or a half section. After the student has made his decision, he should consult his class instructor.

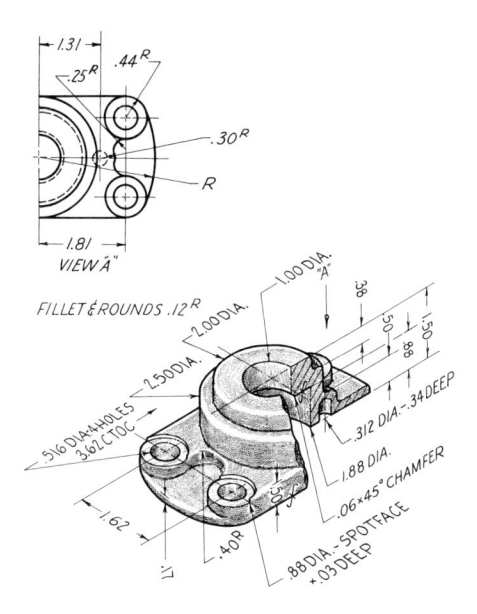

FIG. 8.46. Control housing cover.

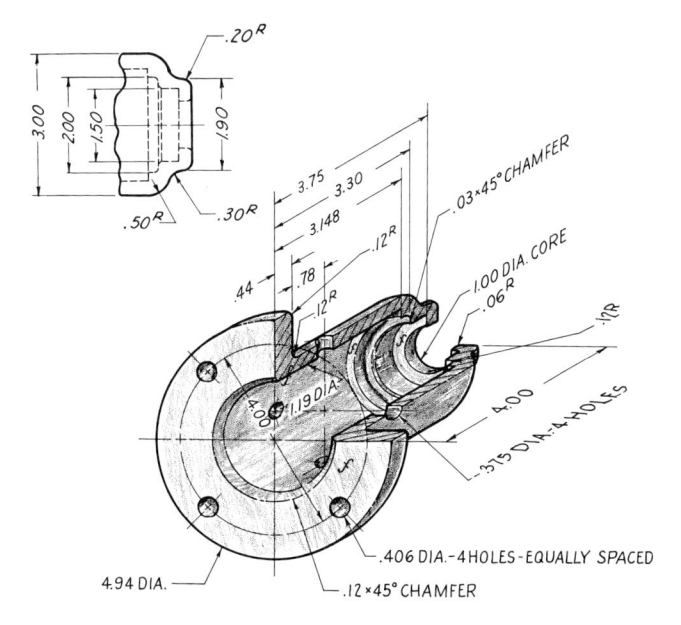

FIG. 8.47. Centering bearing.

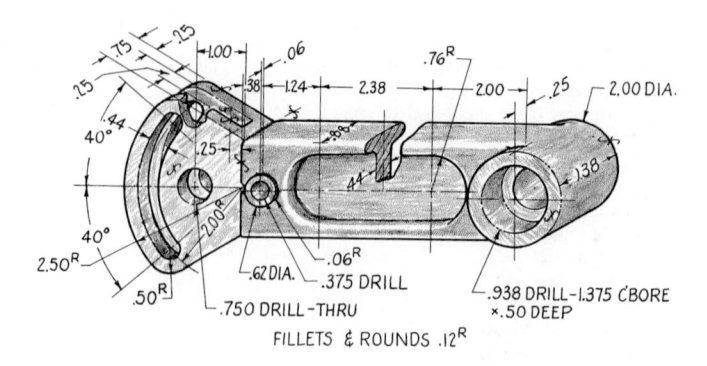

FIG. 8.48. Slotted guide link.

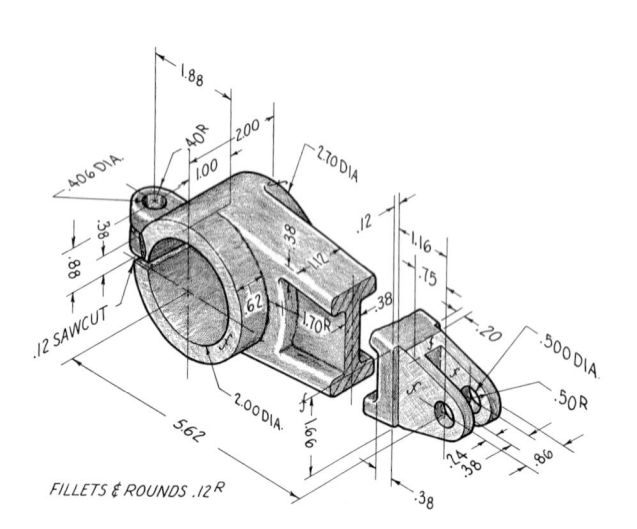

FIG. 8.49. Shifter link.

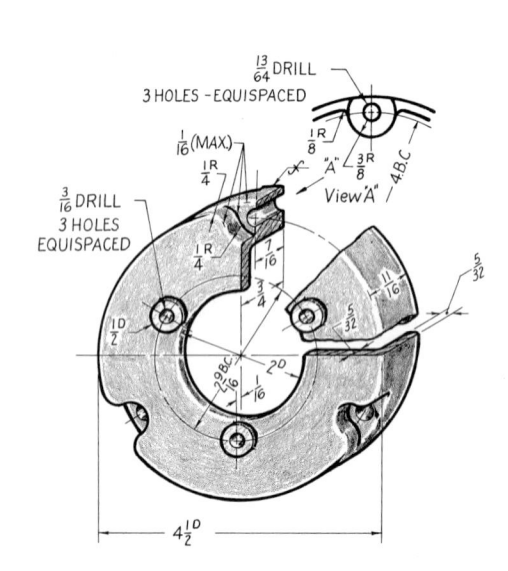

FIG. 8.50. Cover.

CHAP. 8 / SECTIONAL VIEWS **161**

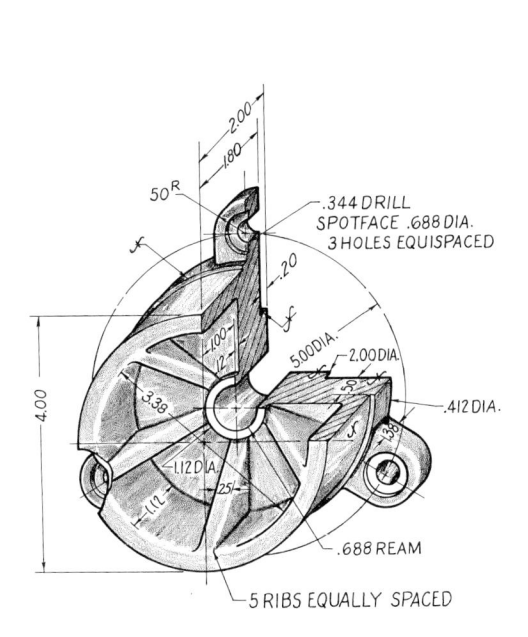

FIG. 8.51. End guide.

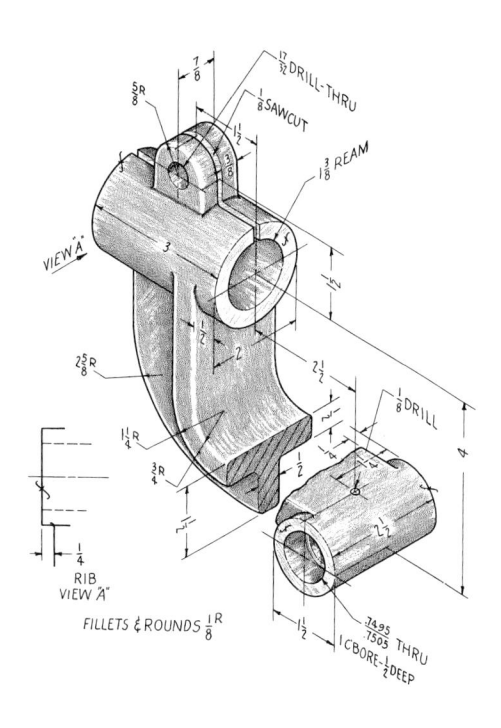

FIG. 8.52. Hanger bracket.

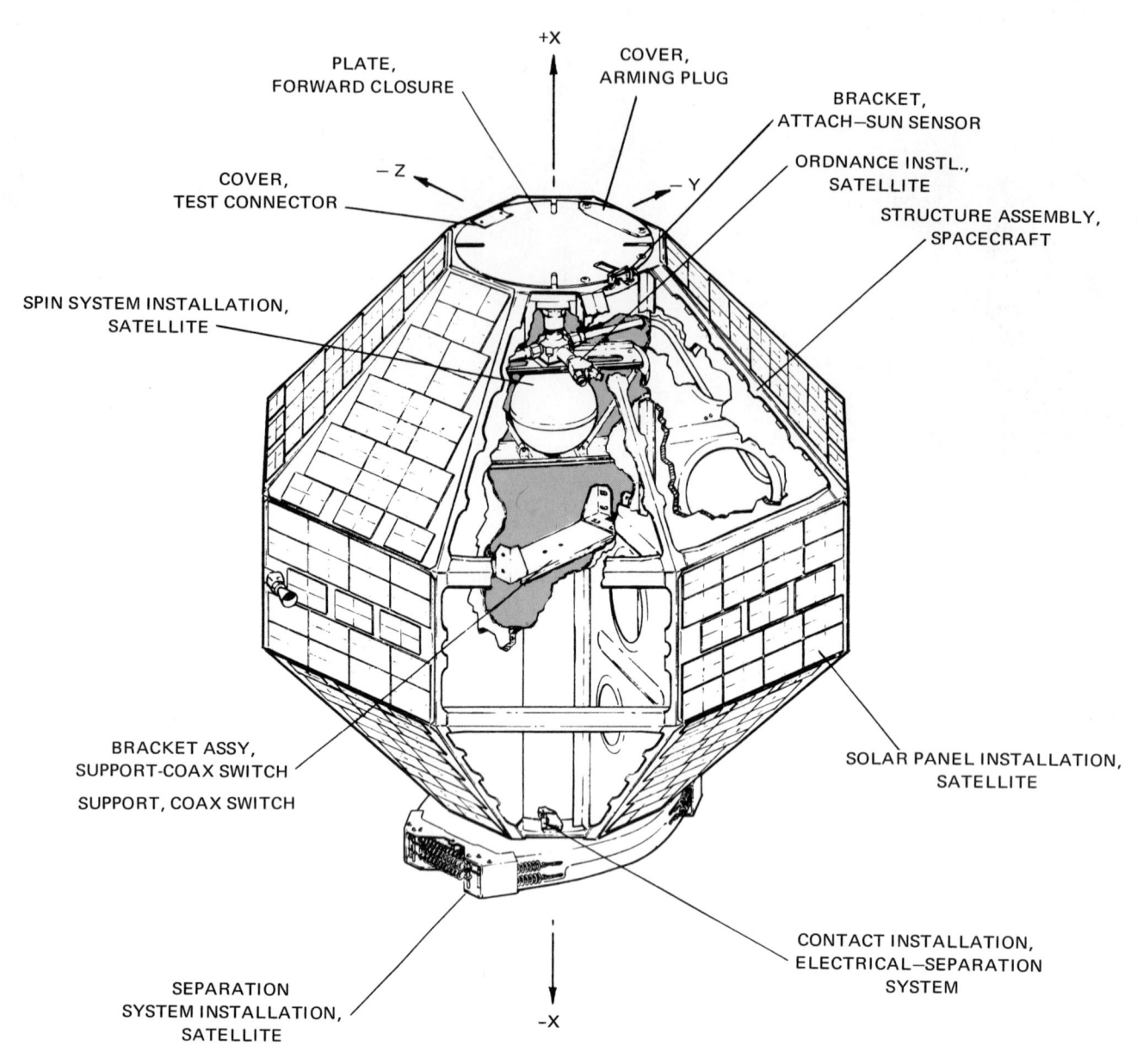

The pictorial representation above shows the solar panel installation for a research satellite. As can be observed, these panels have angular relationships that must be specified. These angles may be determined and other problems involving size and space position may be solved graphically by using appropriate auxiliary view methods that are explained in Chapters 9 and 10 that follow.
(*Courtesy TRW Systems Group Space Technology Laboratories.*)

Auxiliary Views

A: PRIMARY AUXILIARY VIEWS

9.1
Introduction. When it is desirable to show the true size and shape of an irregular surface, which is inclined to two or more of the coordinate planes of projection, a view of the surface must be projected on a plane parallel to it. This imaginary projection plane is called an *auxiliary plane,* and the view obtained is called an *auxiliary view* (Fig. 9.1).

The theory underlying the method of projecting principal views applies also to auxiliary views. In other words, an auxiliary view shows an inclined surface of an object as it would appear to an observer stationed an infinite distance away (Fig. 9.2).

9.2
The Use of Auxiliary Views. In commercial drafting, an auxiliary view ordinarily is a partial view showing only an inclined surface. The reason for this is that a projection showing the entire object adds very little to the shape description. The added lines are likely to defeat the intended purpose of an auxiliary view. For example, a complete drawing of the casting in Fig. 9.3 must include an auxiliary view of the inclined surface in order to show the true shape of the surface and the location of the holes. Compare the views in (*a*) and (*b*) and note the confused appearance of the view in (*b*). In technical schools, some instructors require that an auxiliary view show the entire object, including all invisible lines. Such a requirement, though impractical commercially, is justified in the classroom, for the construction of a complete auxiliary view furnishes excellent practice in projection.

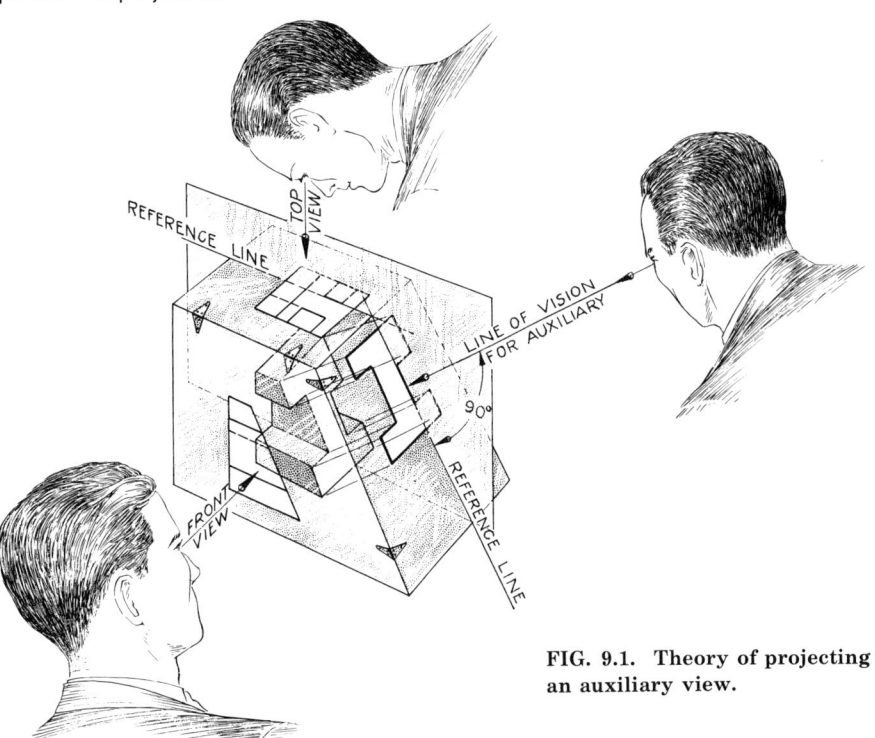

FIG. 9.1. Theory of projecting an auxiliary view.

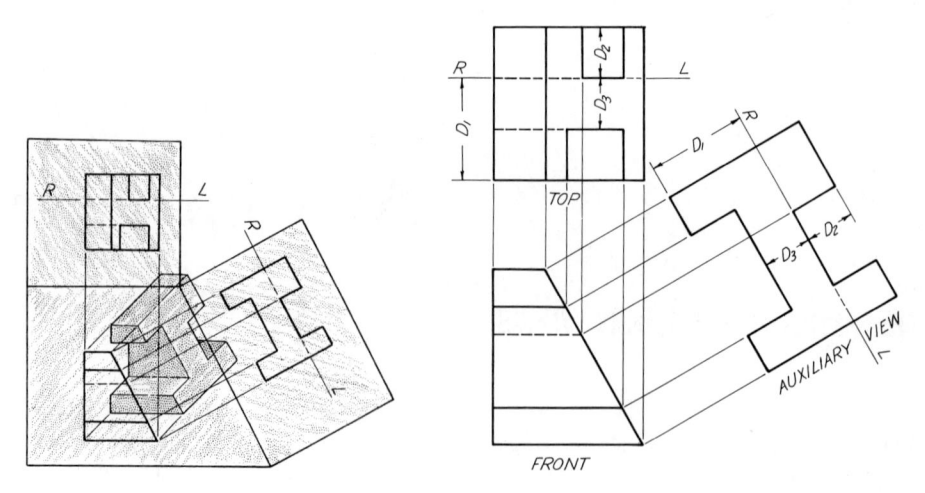

FIG. 9.2. An auxiliary view.

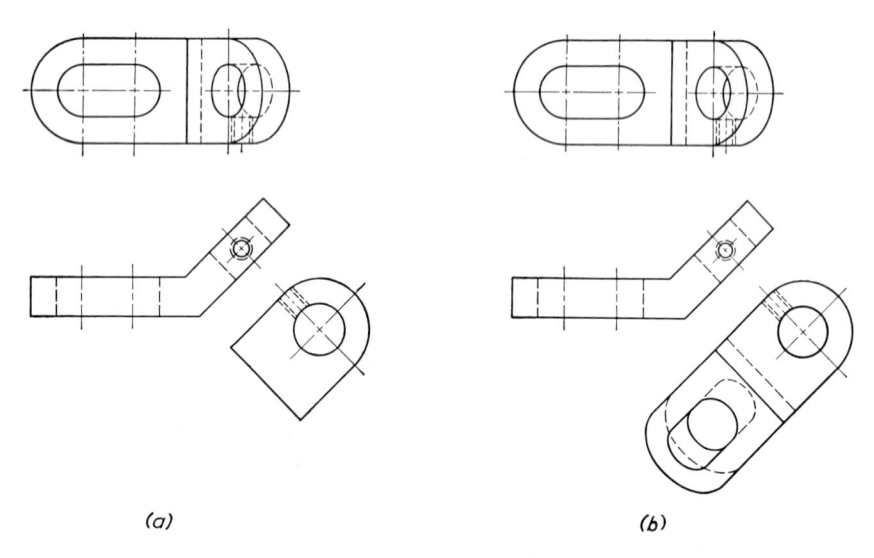

(a)   (b)

FIG. 9.3. Partial and complete auxiliary views.

A partial auxiliary view often is needed to complete the projection of a foreshortened feature in a principal view. This second important function of auxiliary views is illustrated in Fig. 9.16 and explained in Sec. 9.13.

9.3
Types of Auxiliary Views. Although auxiliary views may have an infinite number of positions in relation to the three principal planes of projection, primary auxiliary views may be classified into three general types in accordance with position relative to the principal planes. Figure 9.4 shows the first type, where the auxiliary plane is perpendicular to the frontal plane and inclined to the horizontal plane of projection. Here the auxiliary view and top view have one dimension that is common to both: the depth. Note that the auxiliary plane is hinged to the frontal plane and that the auxiliary view is projected from the front view.

In Fig. 9.5 the auxiliary plane is perpendicular to the horizontal plane and inclined

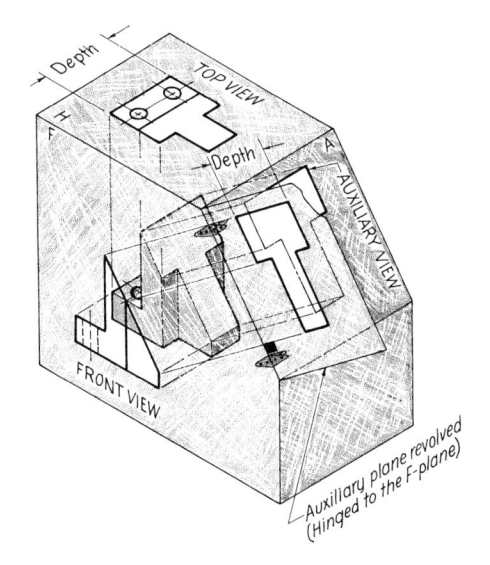

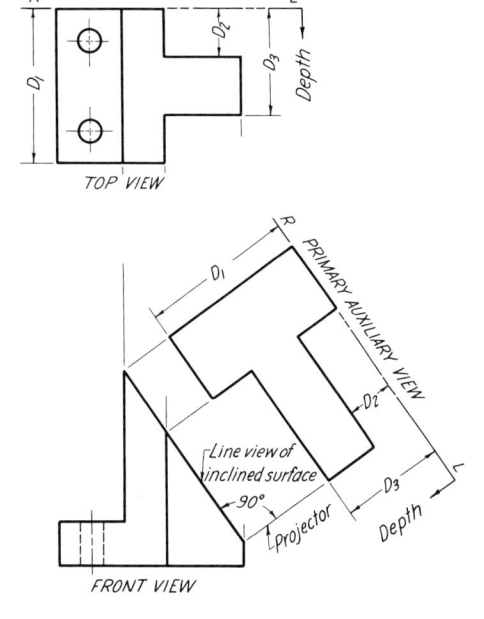

FIG. 9.4. Auxiliary view projected from front view.

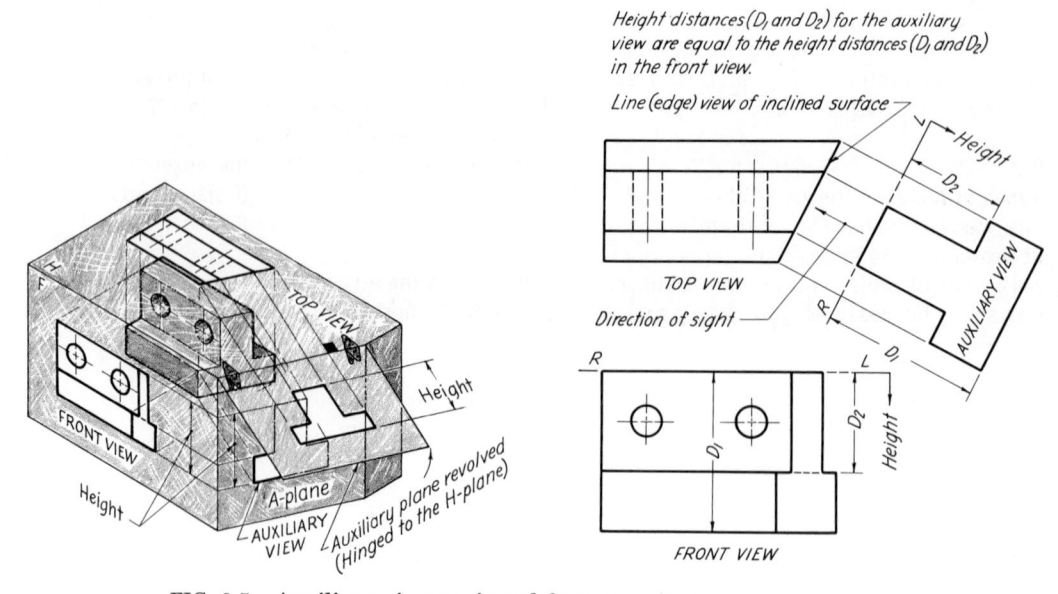

FIG. 9.5. Auxiliary view projected from top view.

to the frontal and profile planes of projection. The auxiliary view is projected from the top view, and its height is the same as the height of the front view.

The third type of auxiliary view, as shown in Fig. 9.6, is projected from the side view and has a common dimension with both the front and top views. To construct it, distances may be taken from either the front or top view.

All three types of auxiliary views are constructed similarly. Each is projected from the view that shows the slanting surface as a line, and the distances for the view are taken from the other principal view that has a common dimension with the auxiliary. A careful study of the three illustrations will reveal the fact that the inclined auxiliary plane is always hinged to the principal plane to which it is perpendicular.

9.4

Symmetrical and Unsymmetrical Auxiliary Views. Since auxiliary views are either symmetrical or unsymmetrical about a center line or reference line, they may be termed (1) symmetrical, (2) unilateral, or (3) bilateral, according to the degree of symmetry. A symmetrical view is drawn symmetrically about a center line, the unilateral view entirely on one side of a reference line, and the bilateral view on both sides of a reference line.

9.5

To Draw a Symmetrical Auxiliary View. When an inclined surface is symmetrical, the auxiliary view is "worked" from a center line (Fig. 9.7). The first step in drawing such a view is to draw a center line parallel to the inclined line that represents an edge view of the surface. If the object is assumed to be enclosed in a glass box, this center line may be considered the line of intersection of the auxiliary plane and an imaginary vertical center plane. There are professional draftsmen who, not acquainted with the "glass" box, proceed without theoretical explanation. Their method is simply to draw a working center line for the auxiliary view and a corresponding line in one of the principal views.

Although theoretically, this working center line may be drawn at any distance from the principal view, actually it should be so located to give the whole drawing a balanced appearance. If not already shown, it also must be drawn in the principal view showing the true width of the inclined surface.

The next step is to draw projection lines from each point of the sloping face, remembering that the projectors make an angle of 90° with the inclined line representing the surface. With the projectors drawn, the location of each point in the auxiliary can be established by setting the dividers to each point's distance from the center line in the principal view and transferring the distance to the auxiliary view. For example, point X is projected to the auxiliary by drawing a projector from point X in the front view perpendicular to the center line. Since its distance from the center line in the top view is the same as it is from the center line in the auxiliary view, the point's location along the projector may be established by using the distance taken from the top view. In the case of point X, the distance is set off from the center line toward the front view. Point Y is set off from the center line away from the front view. A careful study of Fig. 9.7 reveals the fact that if a point lies between the front view and the center line of the top view, it will lie between the front view and the center line of the auxiliary view, and, conversely, if it lies away from the front view with reference to the center line of the top view, it will lie away from the front view with reference to the center line of the auxiliary view.

FIG. 9.6. Auxiliary view projected from side view.

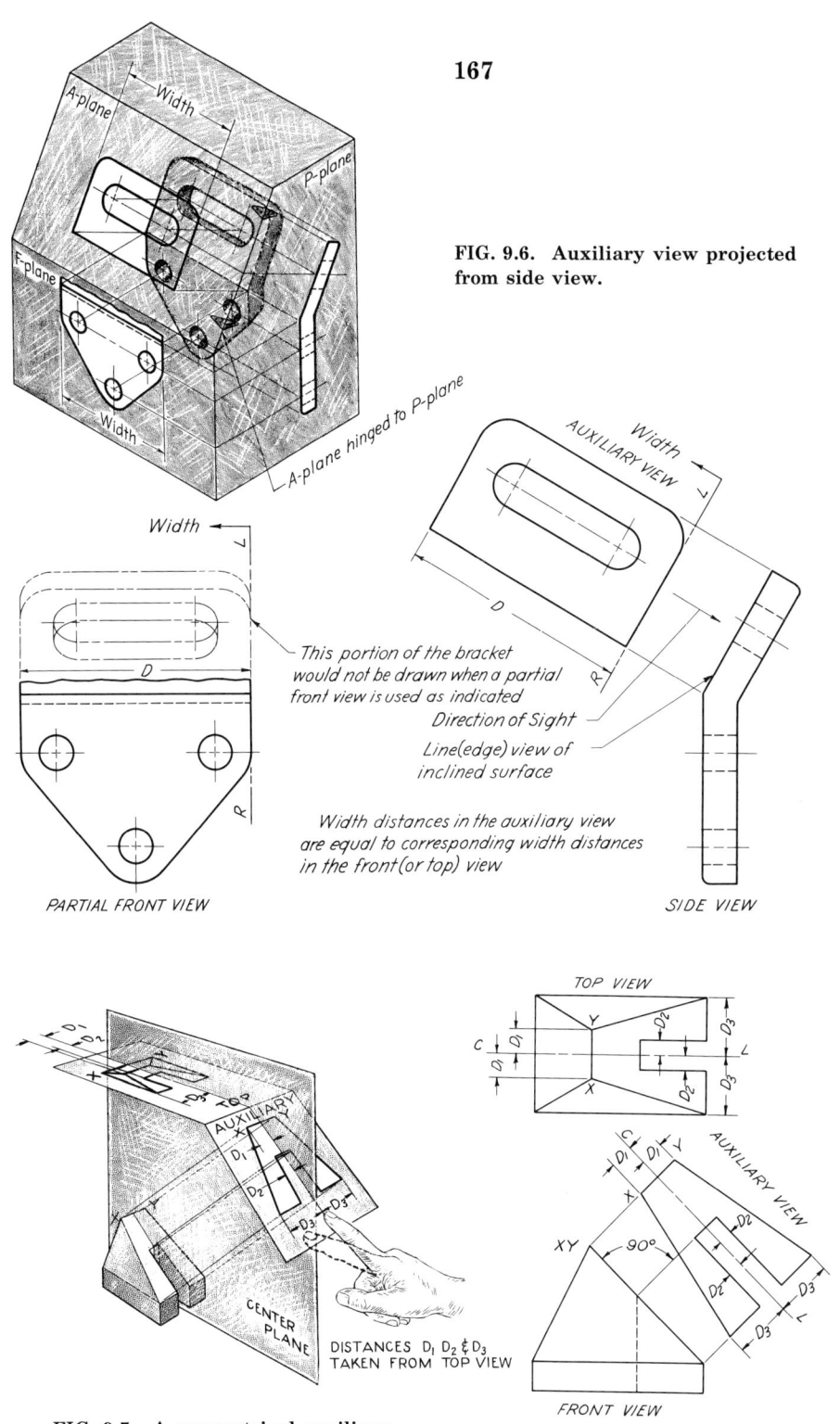

FIG. 9.7. A symmetrical auxiliary view of an inclined surface.

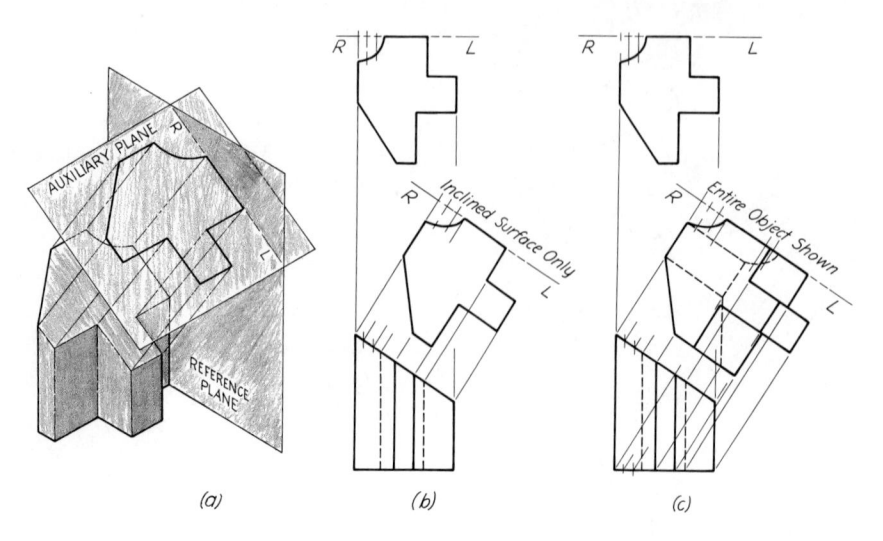

168   PART II / SPATIAL GRAPHICS: SHAPE DESCRIPTION AND SPATIAL RELATIONSHIPS

FIG. 9.8. A unilateral auxiliary view.

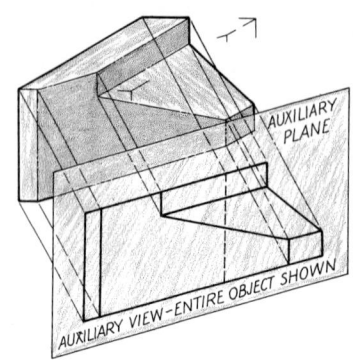

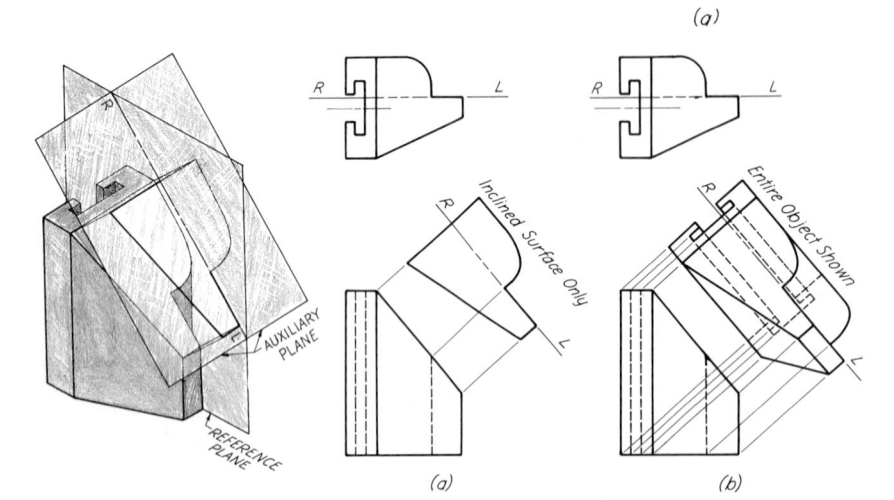

FIG. 9.9. An auxiliary view of an object.

FIG. 9.10. A bilateral auxiliary view.

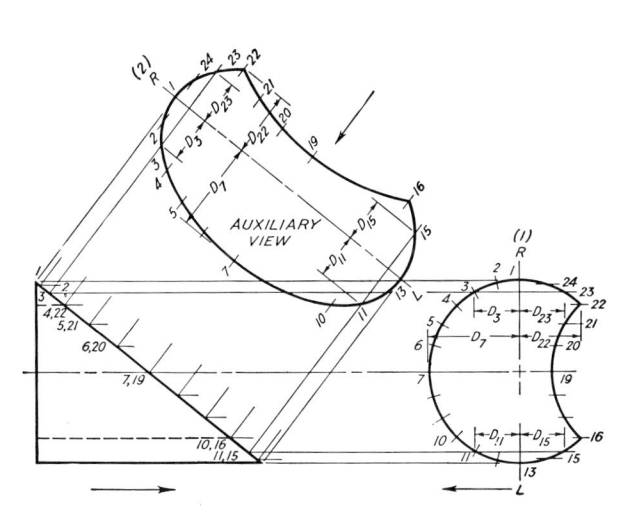

FIG. 9.11. Curved line auxiliary view.

9.6
Unilateral Auxiliary Views. When constructing a unilateral auxiliary view, it is necessary to work from a reference line that is drawn in a manner similar to the working center line of a symmetrical view. The reference line for the auxiliary view may be considered to represent the line of intersection of a reference plane, coinciding with an outer face, and the auxiliary plane (Fig. 9.8). The intersection of this plane with the top plane establishes the reference line in the top view. All the points are projected from the edge view of the surface, as in a symmetrical view, and it should be noted in setting them off that they all fall on the same side of the reference line.

Figure 9.9 shows an auxiliary view of an entire object. In constructing such a view, it should be remembered that the projectors from all points of the object are perpendicular to the auxiliary plane, since the observer views the entire figure by looking directly at the inclined surface. The distances perpendicular to the auxiliary reference line were taken from the front view.

9.7
Bilateral Auxiliary Views. The method of drawing a bilateral view is similar to that of drawing a unilateral view, the only difference being that in a bilateral view the inclined face lies partly on both sides of the reference plane, as shown in Fig. 9.10.

9.8
Curved Lines in Auxiliary Views. To draw a curve in an auxiliary view, the draftsman must plot a sufficient number of points to ensure a smooth curve (Fig. 9.11). The points are projected first to the inclined line representing the surface in the front view and then to the auxiliary view. The distance of any point from the center line in the auxiliary view is the same as its distance from the center line in the end view.

9.9
Projection of a Curved Boundary. In Fig. 9.11, the procedure is illustrated for plotting the true size and shape of an inclined surface bounded by a curved outline. A similar procedure can be followed to plot a curve, such as the one on the left end

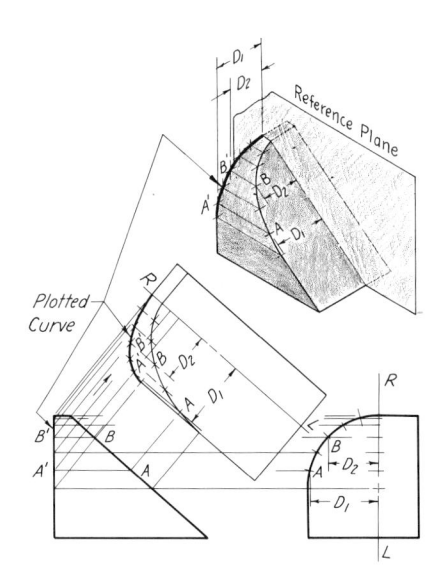

FIG. 9.12. Plotted boundary curves.

of the object shown in Fig. 9.12, in an auxiliary view. Since the points on the curved outline of the vertical surface are being viewed from the same direction as those on the curved boundary of the inclined surface, the projectors from points on both surfaces will be parallel. From the pictorial drawing, it can be observed that points A and A' and B and B' lie on elements of the cylindrical surface. Also it should be noted that A and A' are the same distance from the reference plane as are B and B'. It is for this reason that point A' in the auxiliary view is at the intersection of the projector from A' in the front view and a line through A in the auxiliary view, drawn parallel to the reference line RL.

9.10
Dihedral Angles. Frequently, an auxiliary view may be needed to show the true size of a dihedral angle—that is, the true size of the angle between two planes. In Fig. 9.13, it is desirable to show the true size of the angle between the planes forming the V-slot by means of a partial auxiliary view, as shown. The direction of sight (see pictorial) must be taken parallel to the edge lines 1–2 and 3–4 so that these lines will appear as points and the surfaces forming the dihedral angle will project as line views in the auxiliary view. The reference line for the partial auxiliary view would necessarily be drawn perpendicular to the lines 1–2 and 3–4 in the top view. Since the plane on which the auxiliary view is projected is a vertical one, height dimensions were used—that is, distances in the direction of the dimension D in the auxiliary view, were taken from the front view.

9.11
To Construct an Auxiliary View, Practical Method. The usual steps in constructing an auxiliary view are shown in Fig. 9.14. The illustration should be studied carefully, as each step is explained in the drawing.

9.12
Auxiliary and Partial Views. Often the use of an auxiliary view allows the elimination of one of the principal views (top or side) or makes possible the use of a partial principal view. The shape description furnished by the partial views shown in Fig. 9.15 is sufficient for a complete understanding of the shape of the part. The use of partial views simplifies the drawing, saves valuable drafting time, and tends to make the drawing easier to read.

A break line is used at a convenient location to indicate an imaginary break for a partial view.

9.13
The Use of an Auxiliary View to Complete a Principal View. As previously stated, it is frequently necessary to project a fore-

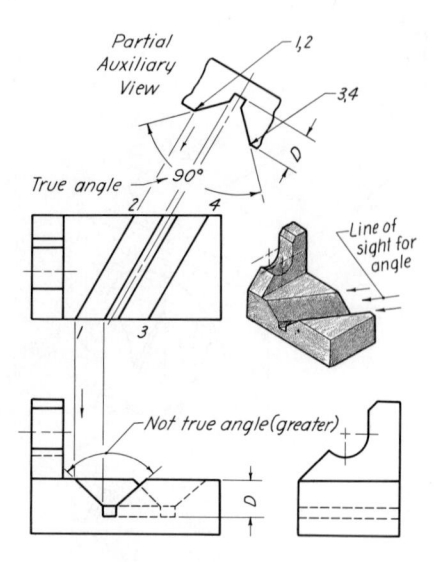

FIG. 9.13. To determine the true dihedral angle between inclined surfaces.

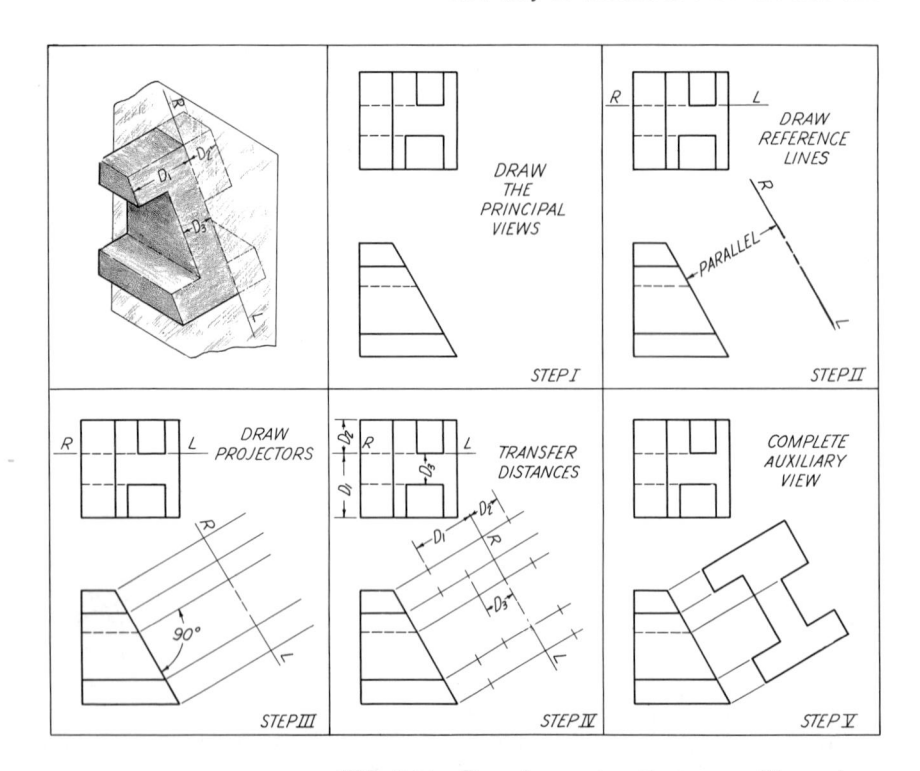

FIG. 9.14. Steps in constructing an auxiliary view.

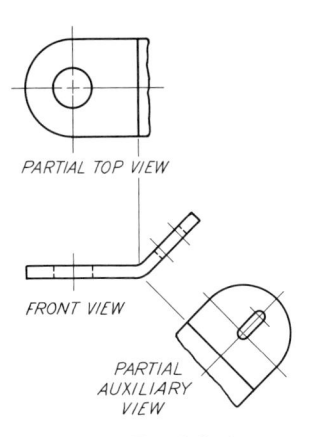

FIG. 9.15. Partial views.

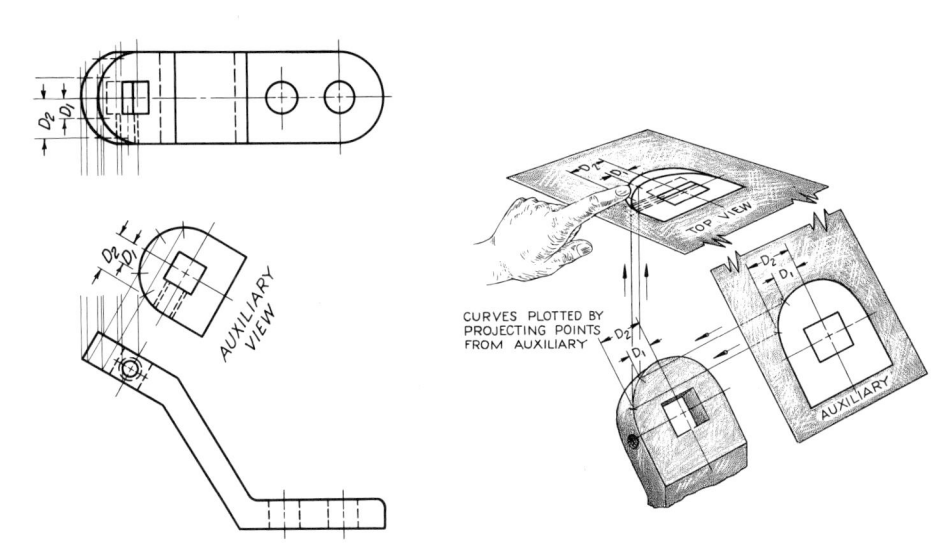

FIG. 9.16. Use of auxiliary to complete a principal view.

shortened feature in one of the principal views from an auxiliary view. In the case of the object shown in Fig. 9.16, the foreshortened projection of the inclined face in the top view can be projected from the auxiliary view. The elliptical curves are plotted by projecting points from the auxiliary view to the front view and from there to the top view. The location of these points in the top view with respect to the center line is the same as their location in the auxiliary view with respect to the auxiliary center line. For example, the distance D_1 from the center line in the top view is the same as the distance D_1 from the auxiliary center line in the auxiliary view.

The steps in preparing an auxiliary view and using it to complete a principal view are shown in Fig. 9.17.

9.14

Line of Intersection. It is frequently necessary to represent a line of intersection between two surfaces when making a multiview drawing involving an auxiliary view. Figure 9.18 shows a method for

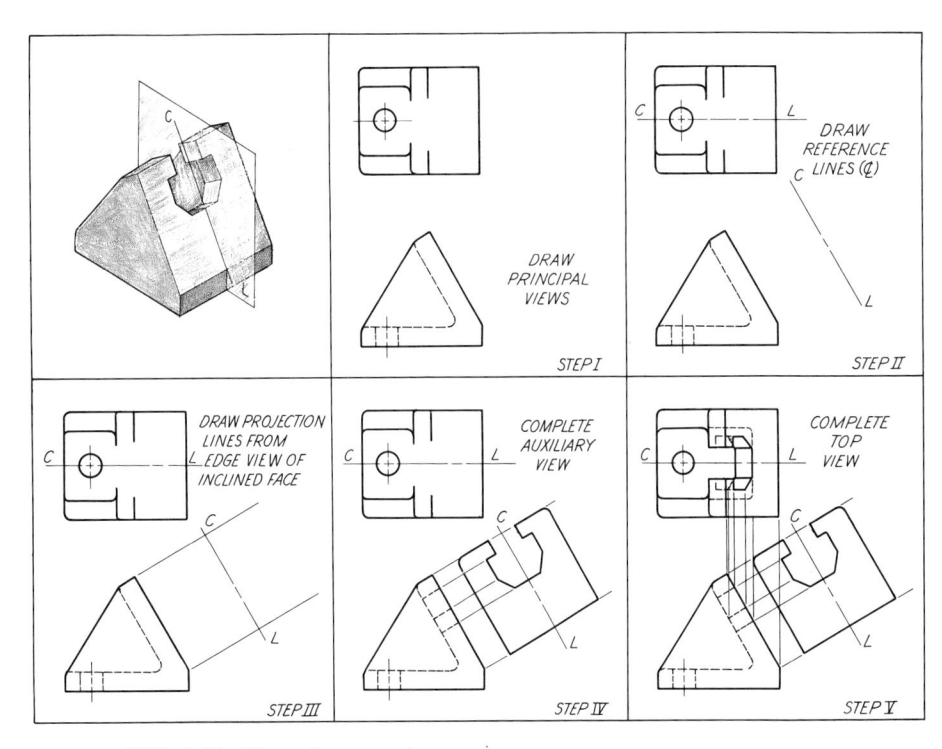

FIG. 9.17. Steps in preparing an auxiliary view and completing a principal view.

drawing the line of intersection on a principal view. In this case the scheme commonly used for determining the intersection involves the use of elements drawn on the surface of the cylindrical portion of the part, as shown on the pictorial drawing. These elements, such as AB, are common to the cylindrical surface. Point B, where the element pierces the flat surface, is a point that is common to both surfaces and therefore lies on the line of intersection.

On the orthographic views, element AB appears as a point on the auxiliary view and as a line on the front view. The location of the projection of the piercing point on the front view is visible upon inspection. Point B is found in the other principal view by projecting from the front view and setting off the distance D taken from the auxiliary view. The distance D of point B from the center line is a true distance for both views. The center line in the auxiliary view and side view can be considered as the edge view of a reference plane or datum plane from which measurements can be made.

9.15
True Length of a Line. The true length of an oblique line may be determined either by means of an auxiliary view or by revolution of the line. Separate discussions of the procedure to be followed in the application of these methods are given in Chapters 6 and 10. To determine the true length of a line by revolution, see Sec. 6.29. To find the true length through the use of an auxiliary view, read Sec. 10.7.

B: SECONDARY AUXILIARY VIEWS

9.16
Secondary (Oblique) Auxiliary Views. Frequently an object will have an inclined face that is not perpendicular to any one of the principal planes of projection. In such cases it is necessary to draw a primary auxiliary view and a secondary auxiliary or oblique view (Fig. 9.19). The primary auxiliary view is constructed by projecting the figure on a primary auxiliary plane that is perpendicular to the inclined surface and one of the principal planes. This plane may be at any convenient location. In the illustration, the primary auxiliary plane is perpendicular to the frontal plane. Note that the inclined face appears as a straight line in the primary auxiliary view. Using this view as a regular view, the secondary auxiliary view may be projected on a plane parallel to the in-

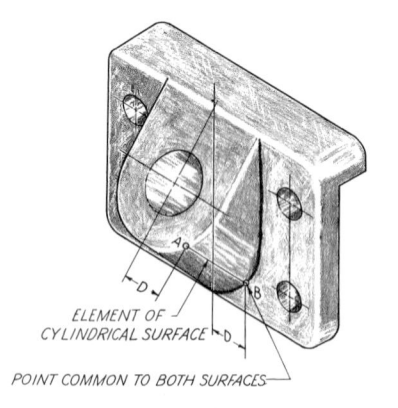

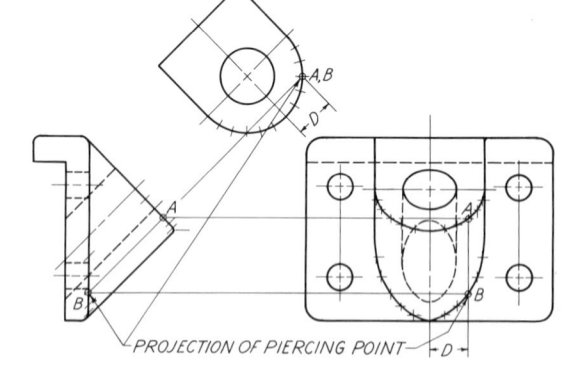

FIG. 9.18. Line of intersection.

clined face. Figure 9.19(b) shows a practical application of the theoretical principles shown pictorially in (a).

It is suggested that the student read Sec. 10.14 in which the procedure for drawing the normal (true-shape) view of an oblique surface is presented step by step.

Figure 9.20 shows the progressive steps in preparing and using a secondary auxiliary view of an oblique face to complete a principal view. Reference planes have been used as datum planes from which to take the necessary measurements. Step II shows the partial construction of the primary auxiliary view in which the inclined surface appears as a line. Step III shows the secondary auxiliary view projected from the primary view and completed, using the known measurements of the lug. The primary auxiliary view is finished by projecting from the secondary auxiliary view. Step IV illustrates the procedure for projecting from the secondary auxiliary view to the top view through the primary auxiliary in order to complete the foreshortened view of the lug. It should be noted that distance D_1 taken from reference R_2P_2 in the secondary auxiliary is transferred to the top view because both views show the same width distances in true length. A sufficient number of points should be obtained to allow the use of an irregular curve. Step V shows the projection of these points on the curve to the front view. In this case the measurements are taken from the primary auxiliary view because the height distances from reference plane R_1P_1 are the same in both views.

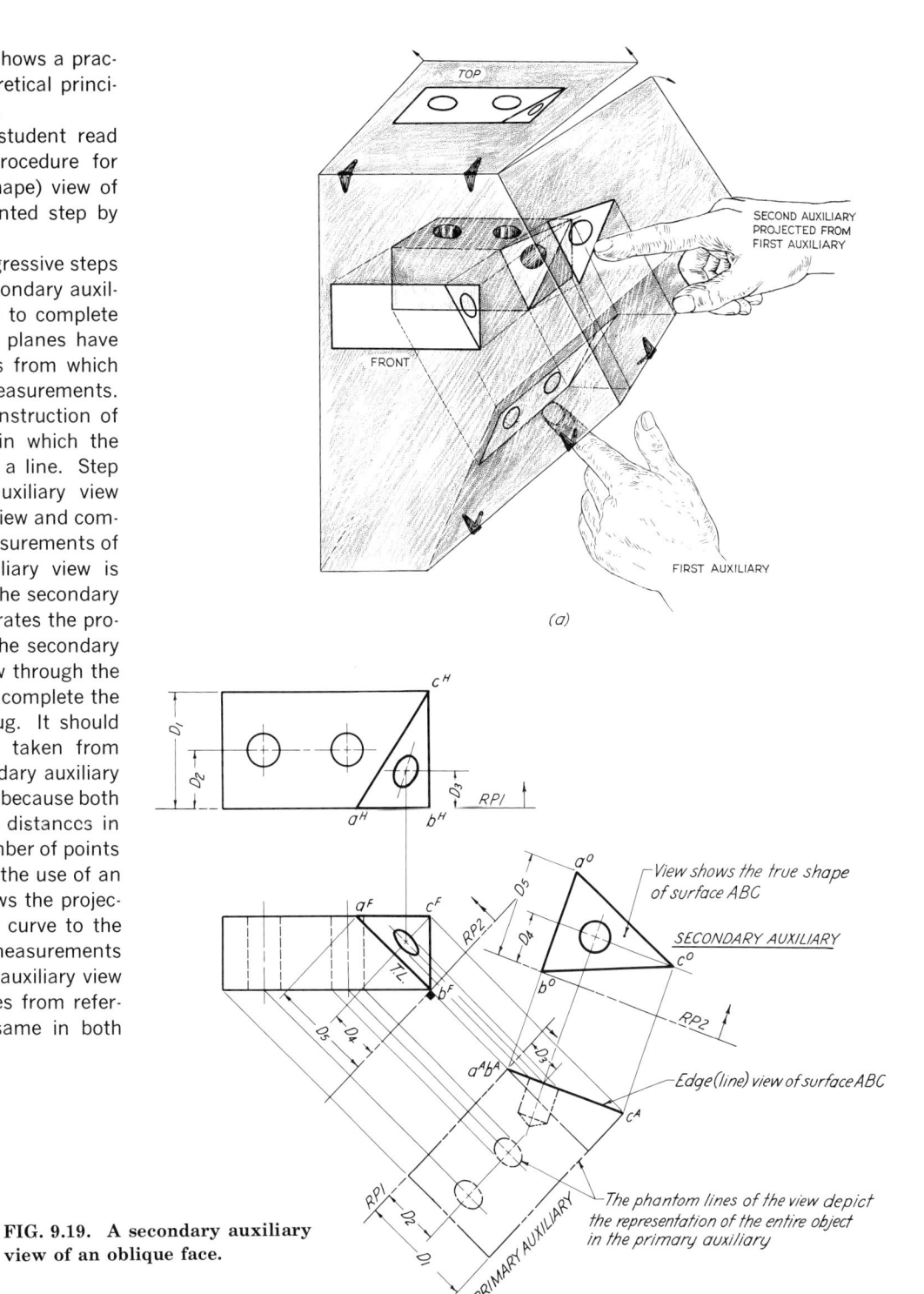

FIG. 9.19. A secondary auxiliary view of an oblique face.

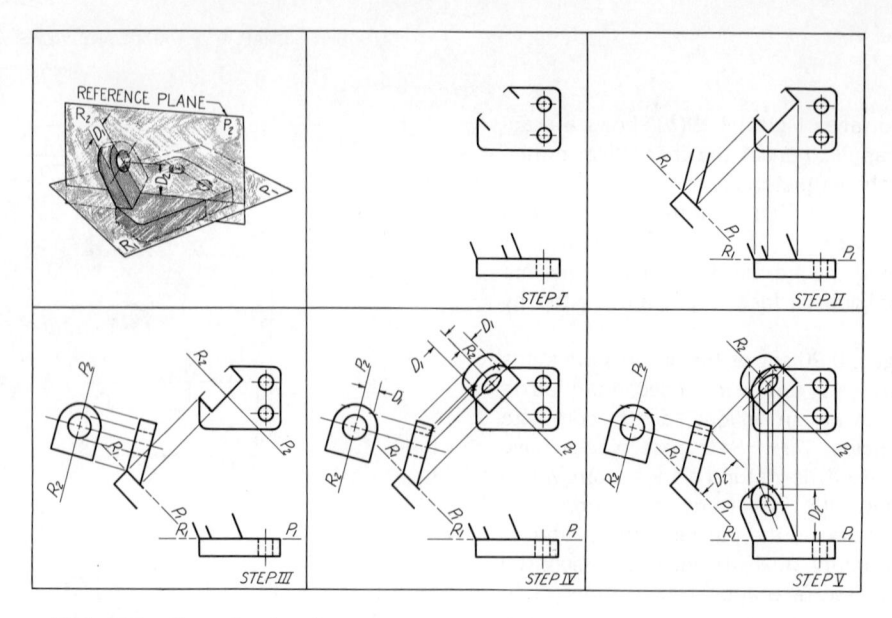

FIG. 9.20. Steps in drawing a secondary auxiliary view and using it to complete a principal view.

PROBLEMS

The problems shown in Fig. 9.21 are designed to give the student practice in constructing auxiliary views of the inclined surfaces of simple objects formed mainly by straight lines. They will provide needed drill in projection if, for each of the objects in Fig. 9.21, an auxiliary is drawn showing the entire object. Complete drawings may be made of the objects shown in Figs. 9.22–9.30. If the views are to be dimensioned, the student should adhere to the rules of dimensioning given in Chapter 16 and should not take too seriously the locations for the dimensions on the pictorial representations.

1. (Fig. 9.21). Using instruments, reproduce the given views of an assigned object and draw an auxiliary view of its inclined surface.

2. (Fig. 9.22). Draw the views that would be necessary on a working drawing of the dovetail bracket.

3. (Fig. 9.23). Draw the necessary views of the anchor bracket. Make partial views for the top and end views.

CHAP. 9 / AUXILIARY VIEWS **175**

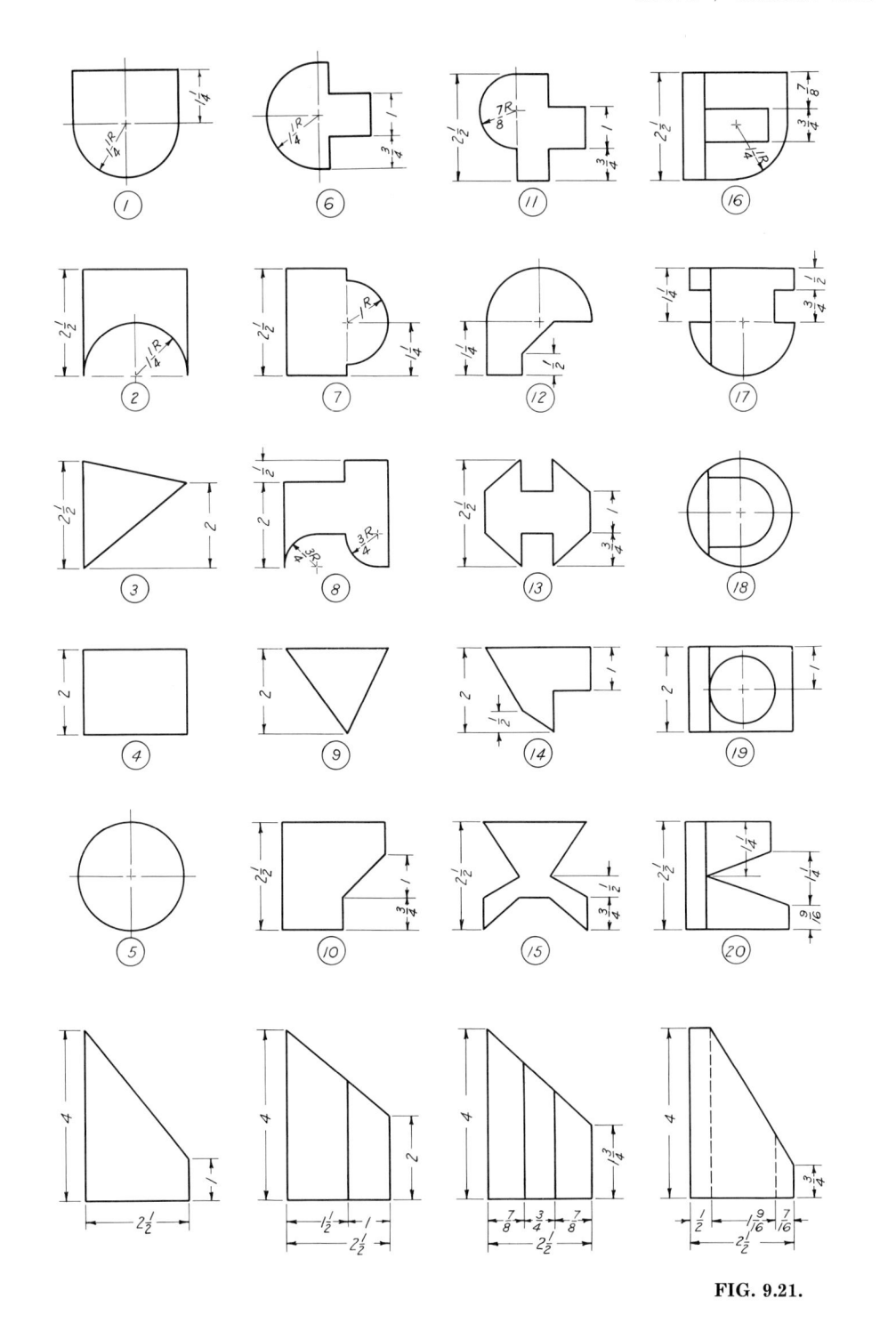

FIG. 9.21.

FIG. 9.22. Dovetail bracket.

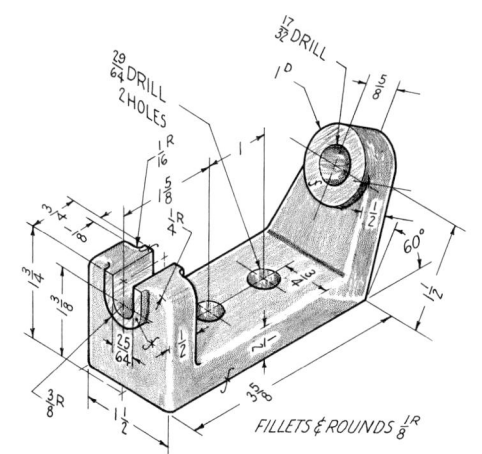

FIG. 9.23. Anchor bracket.

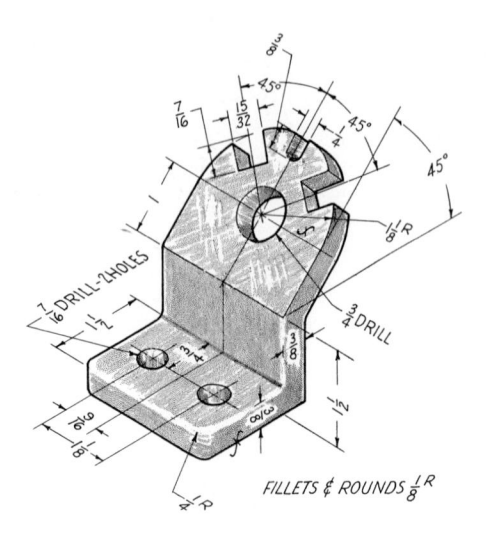

FIG. 9.24. Feeder bracket.

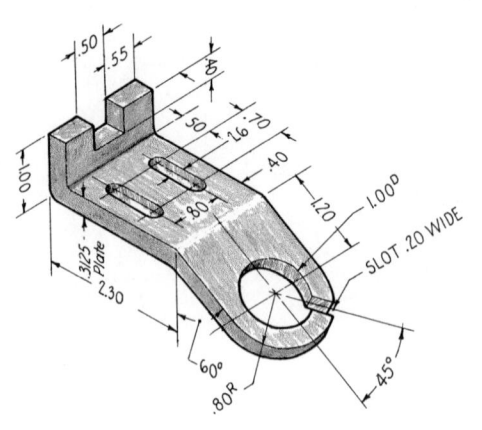

FIG. 9.25. Anchor clip.

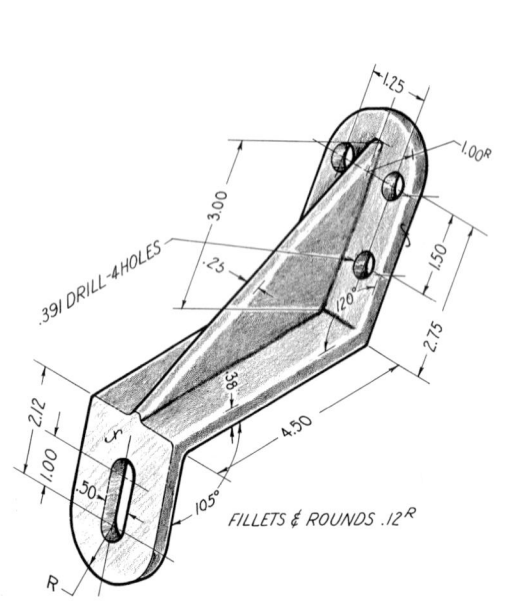

FIG. 9.26. Angle bracket.

4. (Fig. 9.24). Draw the views that would be necessary on a working drawing of the *feeder bracket*.

5. (Fig. 9.25). Draw the necessary views of the anchor clip. It is suggested that the top view be a partial one and that the auxiliary view show only the inclined surface.

6. (Fig. 9.26). Draw the views that would be necessary on a working drawing of the angle bracket. Note that two auxiliary views will be required.

CHAP. 9 / AUXILIARY VIEWS **177**

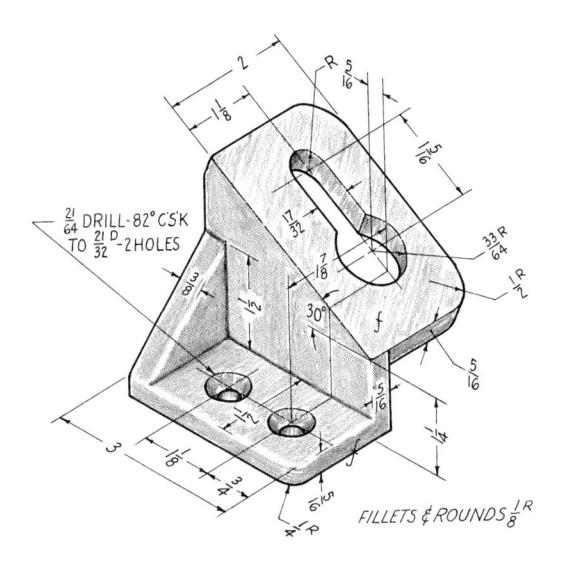

FIG. 9.27. Offset guide.

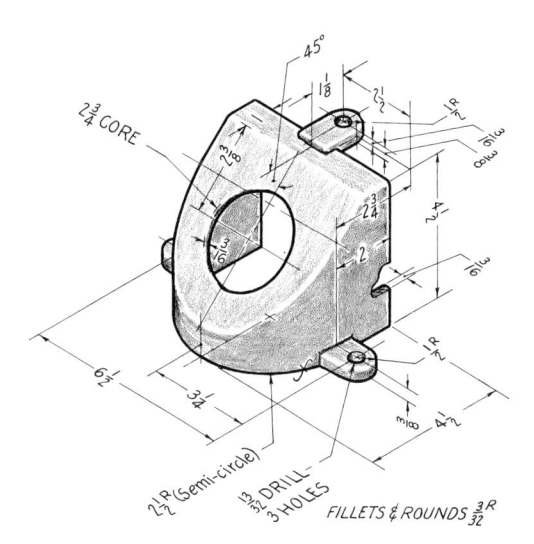

FIG. 9.28. Gear cover.

7. (Fig. 9.27). Draw the necessary views of the offset guide. It is suggested that partial views be used, except in the view where the inclined surface appears as a line.

8. (Fig. 9.28). Draw the views that would be needed on a working drawing of the gear cover. The opening on the inclined face is circular.

9. (Fig. 9.29). Draw the necessary views of the cutoff clip.

10. (Fig. 9.30). Draw the necessary views of the ejector clip.

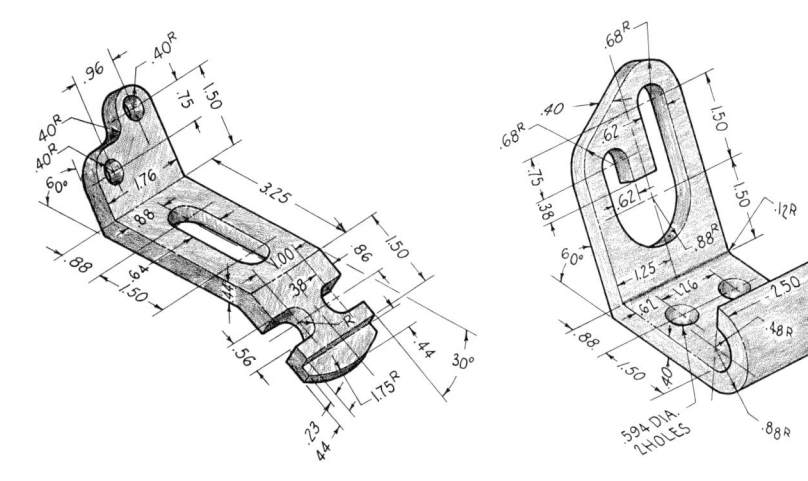

FIG. 9.29. Cut-off clip.

FIG. 9.30. Ejector clip.

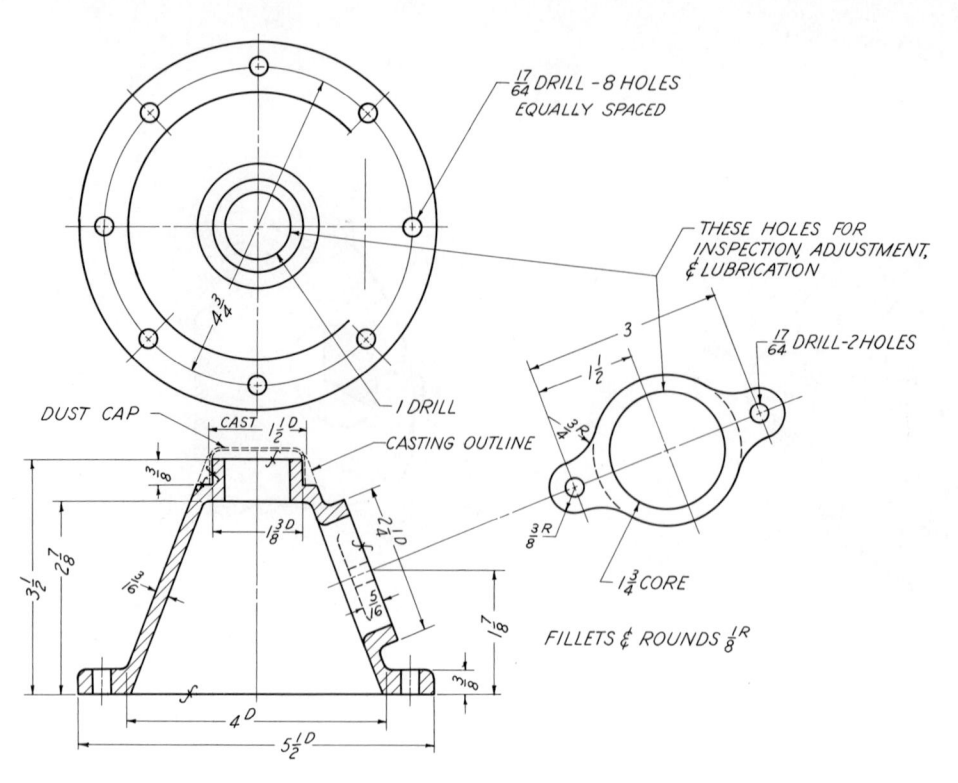

FIG. 9.31. Housing cover.

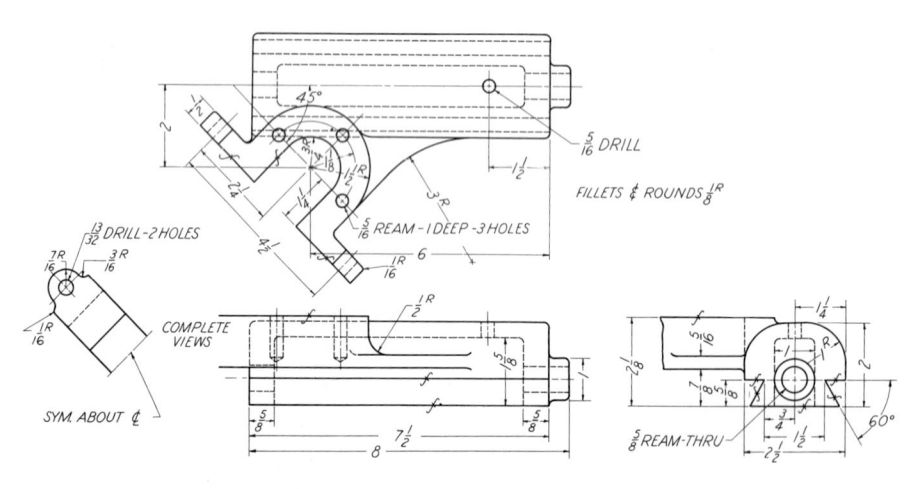

FIG. 9.32. Sliding tool base.

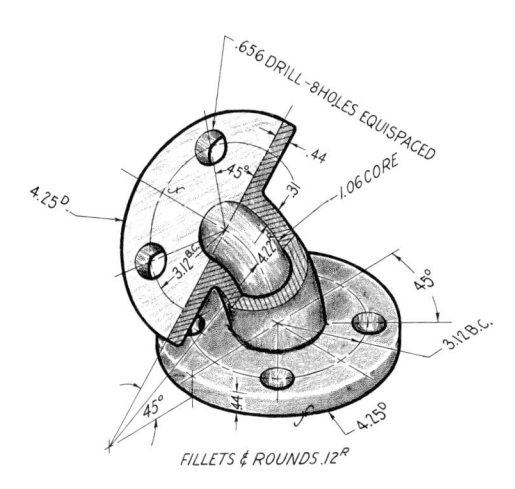

FIG. 9.33. 45° elbow.

11. (Fig. 9.31). Draw the views as given. Complete the top view.

12. (Fig. 9.32). Draw the views as given. Complete the auxiliary view and the front view.

13. (Fig. 9.33). Draw the views that would be necessary on a working drawing of the 45° elbow.

14. Make a multiview drawing of the airplane engine mount shown in Fig. 9.34. The engine mount is formed of three pieces of steel plate welded to a piece of steel tubing. The completed drawing is to consist of four views. It is suggested that the front view be the view obtained by looking along and parallel to the axis of the tube. The remaining views that are needed are an auxiliary view showing only the inclined lug, a side view that should be complete with all hidden lines shown, and a partial top view with the inclined lug omitted.

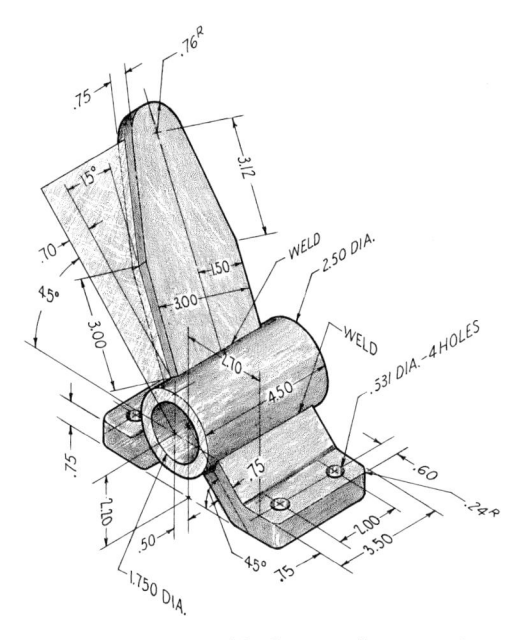

FIG. 9.34. Airplane engine mount.

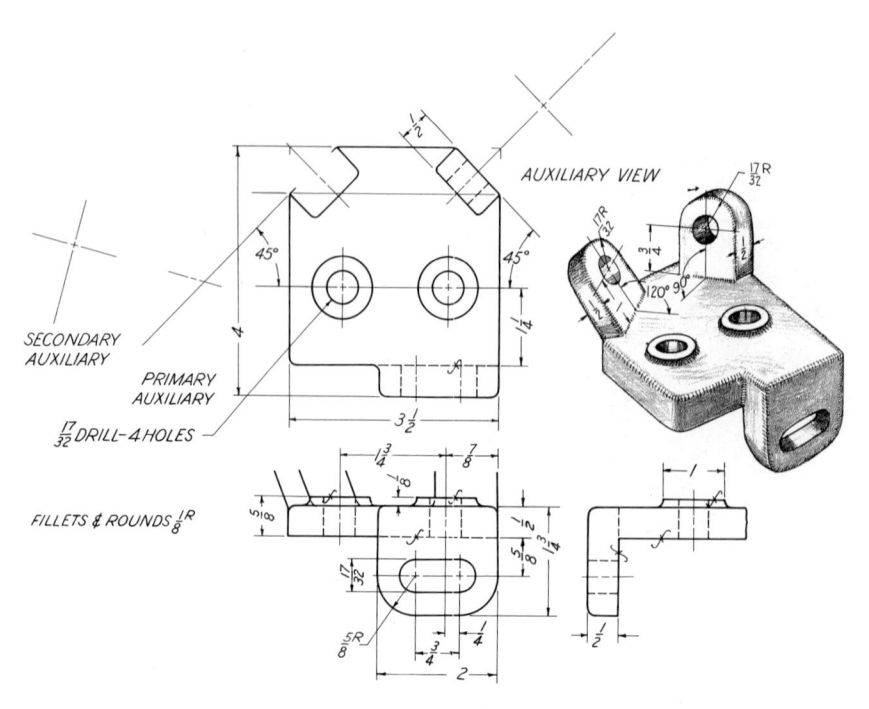

FIG. 9.35. Cross anchor.

15. (Fig. 9.35). Draw the views given and add the required primary and secondary auxiliary views.

16. (Fig. 9.36). Draw the necessary views of the tool holder.

17. (Fig. 9.37). Draw the necessary views of the angle block. One view should be drawn to show the true·size and shape of the oblique surface.

18. (Fig. 9.38). Draw the necessary views of the locating slide.

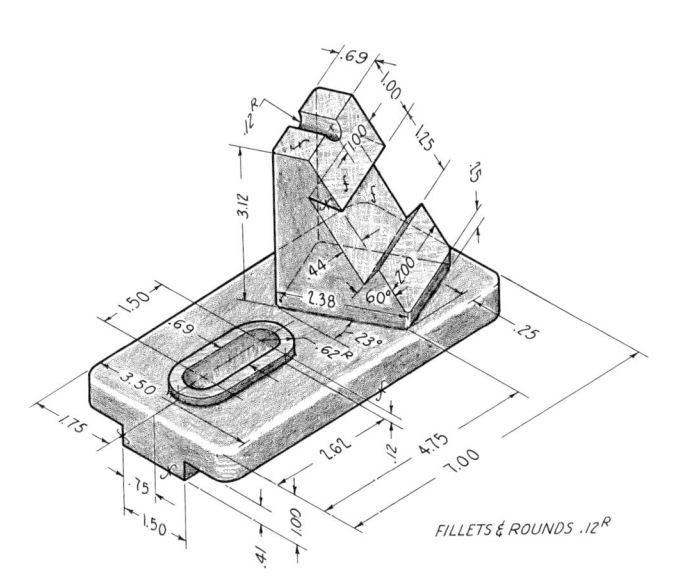

FIG. 9.36. Tool holder.

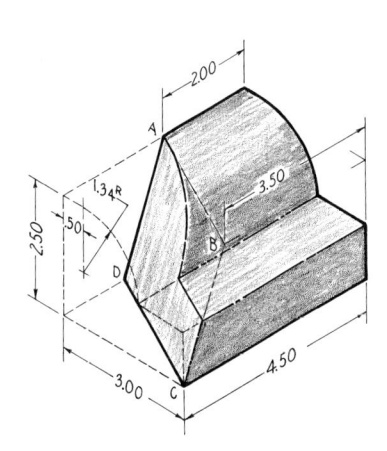

FIG. 9.37. Angle block.

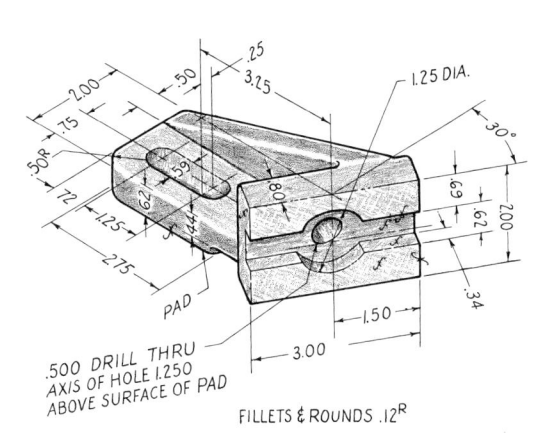

FIG. 9.38. Locating slide.

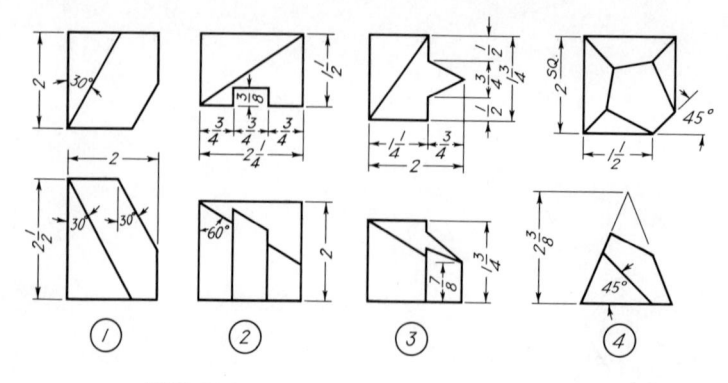

182 PART II / SPATIAL GRAPHICS: SHAPE DESCRIPTION AND SPATIAL RELATIONSHIPS

FIG. 9.39.

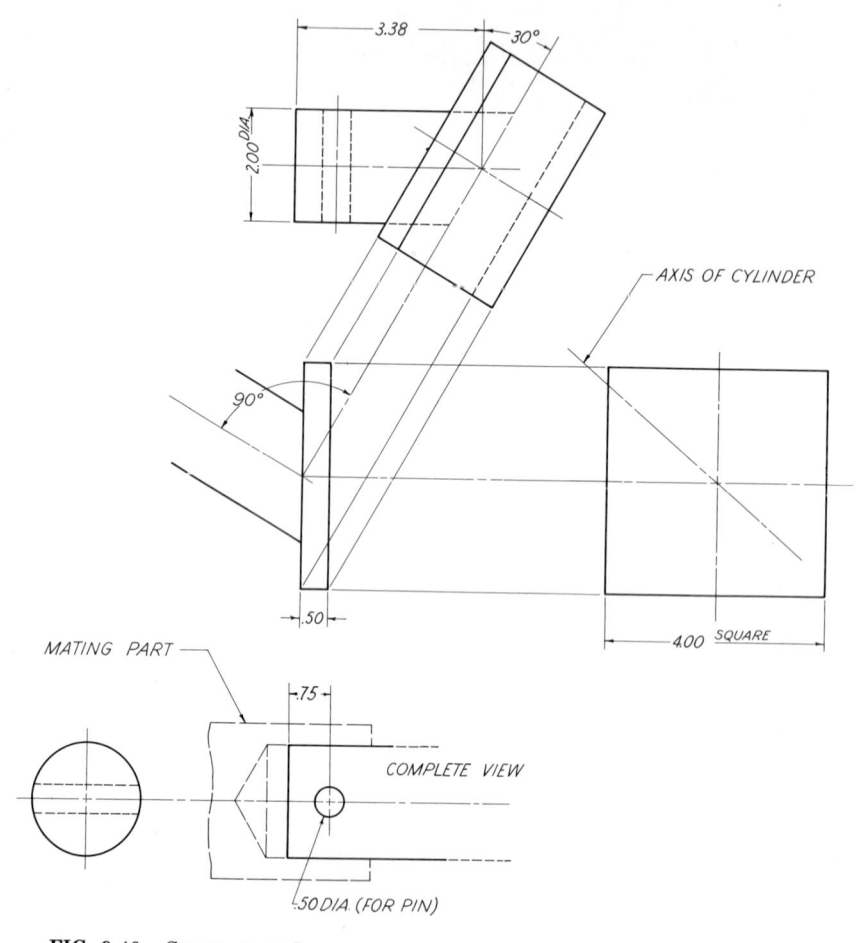

FIG. 9.40. Support anchor.

19. (Fig. 9.39). Using instruments, draw a secondary auxiliary view that will show the true size and shape of the inclined surface of an assigned object. The drawing must also show the given principal views.

20. (Fig. 9.40). Draw the layout for the support anchor as given and then, using the double auxiliary view method, complete the views as required.

The plate and cylinder are to be welded. Since the faces of the plate show as oblique surfaces in the front and top views, double auxiliary views are necessary to show the thickness and the true shape.

Start the drawing with the auxiliary views that are arranged horizontally on the paper, then complete the principal views. The inclined face of the cylinder will show as an ellipse in top and front views; but do not show this in the auxiliary view that shows the true shape of the square plate.

How would you find the view that shows the true angle between the inclined face and the axis of the cylinder?

The air-cushion vehicle shown skims along over the water on a cushion of air and docks on land. It could not have been designed successfully without the application of descriptive geometry methods.

At the present time ACV's are sweeping across the English Channel, three times faster than regular ships, carrying more than 250 passengers and thirty cars at each crossing.

(*Courtesy Aluminum Corporation of America.*)

Basic Spatial Geometry for Design and Analysis

A: BASIC DESCRIPTIVE GEOMETRY

10.1
Introduction. On many occasions, problems arise in engineering design that may be solved quickly by applying the basic principles of orthographic projection.

If one thoroughly understands the solution for each of the problems presented, he should find it easy, at a later time, to analyze and solve almost any of the practical problems he may encounter.

It should be pointed out at the very beginning that to solve most types of problems one must apply the principles and methods used to solve a few basic problems, such as: (1) to find the true length of a line, (2) to find the point projection of a line, and (3) to find the true size and shape of a surface (Fig. 10.1). To find information such as the angle between surfaces, the angle between lines, or the clearance between members of a structure, one must use, in proper combination, the methods of solving these basic problems. Success in solving problems by projection depends largely on the complete understanding of the principles of projection, the ability to visualize space conditions, and the ability to analyze a given situation. Since the ability to analyze and to visualize are of utmost importance in engineering design, the student is urged to develop these abilities by resisting the temptation to memorize step procedures.

10.2
The Projection of a Point. Figure 10.2(a) shows the projection of point S on the three principal planes of projection and a supplementary plane A. The notation used is as explained in Sec. 6.8. Point s^F is the view of point S on the frontal plane; s^H is the view of S on the horizontal plane; and s^P is its view on the profile plane. For convenience and ease in recog-

FIG. 10.1. The frame of this satellite could not have been designed without the application of descriptive geometry methods. (*Courtesy TRW Systems Group*)

185

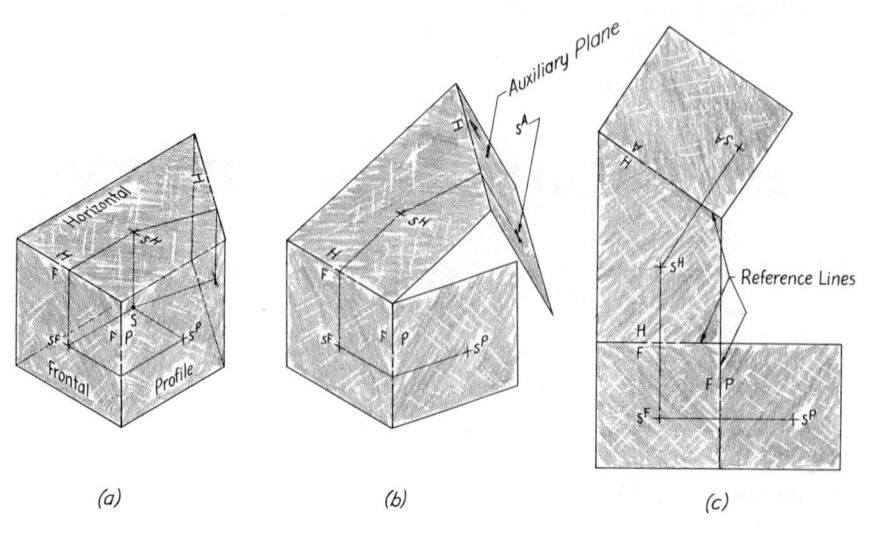

186 PART II / SPATIAL GRAPHICS: SHAPE DESCRIPTION AND SPATIAL RELATIONSHIPS

FIG. 10.2. Frontal, horizontal, profile, and auxiliary views of a point S.

nizing the projected view of a point on a supplementary plane, the supplementary planes are designated as *A*-planes and *O*-planes. *A* (auxiliary) planes are always

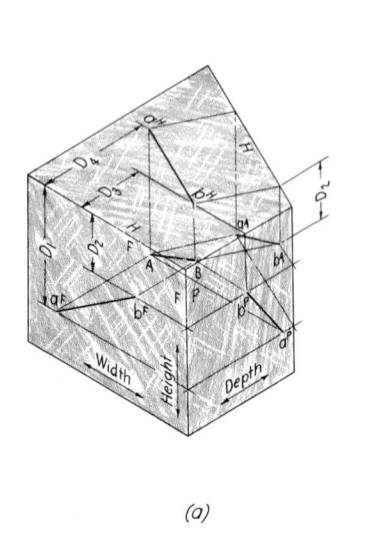

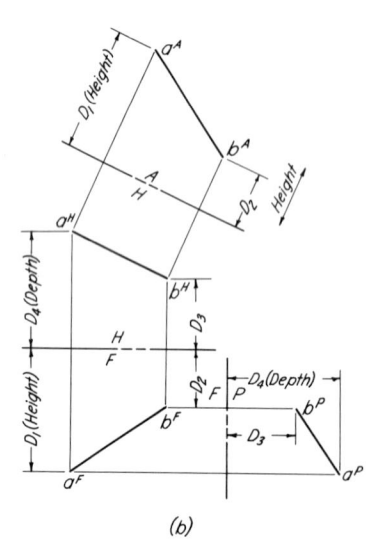

FIG. 10.3. The line in space and in successive views.

perpendicular to one of the principal planes. Point s^A is the view of S on the *A*-plane. The view of S on an O (oblique) plane would be designated s^O. Additional *O*-planes are identified as O_1, O_2, O_3, etc., in the order that they follow the first *O*-plane.

Since it is necessary to represent on one plane (the working surface of our drawing paper) the views of point S that lie on mutually perpendicular planes of projection, the planes are assumed to be hinged so that they can be revolved, as shown in Fig. 10.2(*b*), until they are in a single plane, as in (*c*). The lines about which the planes of projection are hinged are called *reference lines*. A reference line is identified by the use of capital letters representing the adjacent planes, as *FH*, *FP*, *FA*, *HA*, *AO*, and so forth (see Fig. 10.2).

It is important to note in (*c*) that the projections s^F and s^H fall on a vertical line, s^F and s^P lie on a horizontal line, and s^H and s^A lie on a line perpendicular to the reference line *HA*. In each case this results from the fact that point S and its projections on adjacent planes lie in a plane perpendicular to the reference line for those planes [Fig. 10.2(*a*)]. This important principal of projection determines the location of views when the relationship of lines and planes form the problem.

10.3
The Projection of a Straight Line. Capital letters are used for designating the end points of the actual line in space. In the projected views, these points are identified as shown in Fig. 10.3. The student should read Sec. 6.8, which presents the principles of multiview drawing. In particular, he should study the related illustration, which shows some typical line positions.

10.4
Projection of a Plane in Space. Theoretically, a plane is considered to be flat and unlimited in extent. A plane can be deline-

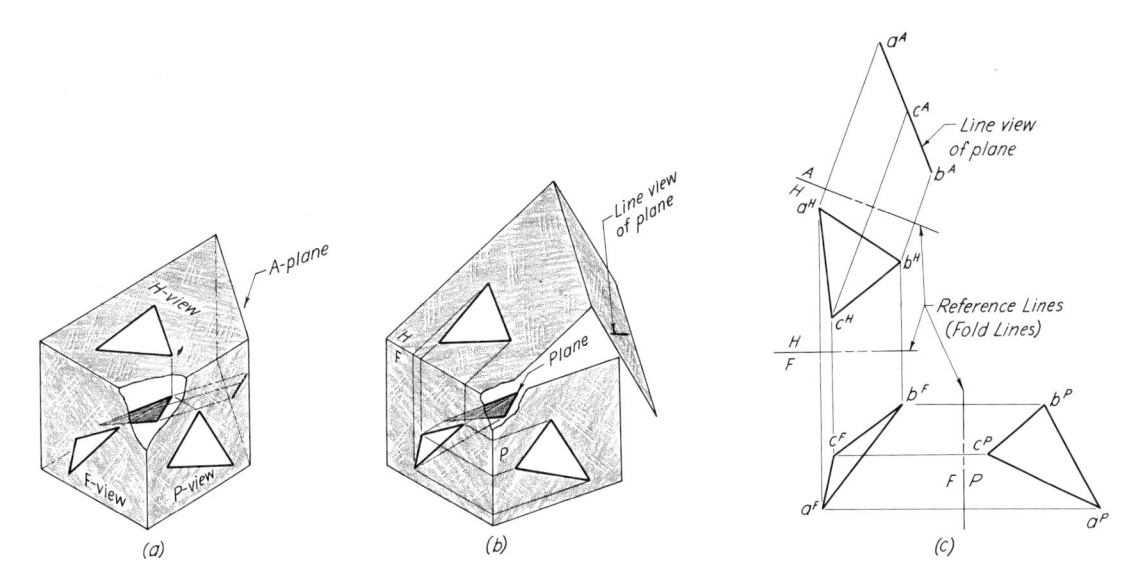

CHAP. 10 / BASIC SPATIAL GEOMETRY FOR DESIGN AND ANALYSIS   187

FIG. 10.4. The plane in space and in successive views.

ated graphically by: (1) two intersecting lines, (2) a line and a point not on the line, (3) two parallel lines, and lastly, (4) three points not on a straight line. For graphical purposes and to facilitate the solution of space problems as presented in this chapter, planes will be bounded and usually triangular. The space picture and multiview representation of a plane ABC are given in Fig. 10.4. The pictorial at the left in (a) shows the projected views on the principal planes of projection. In (b) the planes are shown being opened outward to be in the plane of the paper, as in (c). It should be noted that plane ABC projects as a line (edge view) on the auxiliary plane. The three points A, B, and C of the plane are projected in the same manner as the single point S in Fig. 10.2 and are identified similarly (a^F, a^H, a^P, a^A, etc.).

10.5
Parallel Lines. Any two lines in space must be either (1) parallel, (2) intersecting, or (3) nonintersecting and nonparallel (called *skew lines*). Figure 10.18 shows intersecting lines, while Fig. 10.17 shows skew lines. Parallel lines are shown in Fig. 10.5.

It might be stated as a rule of projection, with one exception, that when two lines are parallel their projections will be parallel in every view (Fig. 10.5). In other words the lines will appear to be parallel in every view in which both appear. This is true even though in specific views they may appear as points or their projections may coincide. In either case they are still parallel because both conditions indicate that the lines have the same direction. The exception that has been mentioned occurs when the F- and H-projections of two inclined profile lines are shown. For proof of parallelism a supplementary view should be drawn, which may or may not be the profile view.

The true or shortest distance between two parallel lines can be determined on the view that will show these lines as

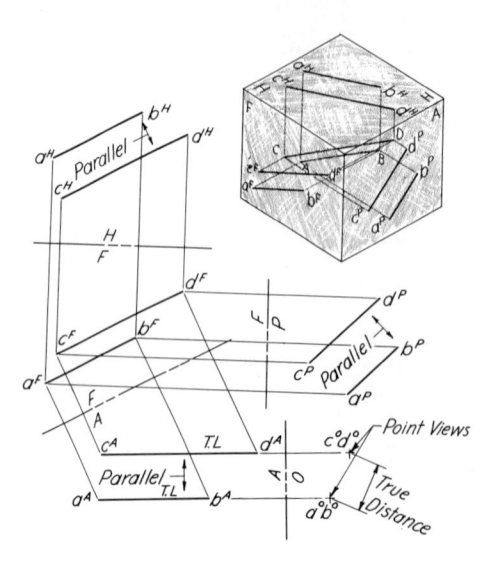

FIG. 10.5. Parallel lines.

points. The true distance can be measured between the points (Fig. 10.5).

10.6

To Determine the True Length of a Line. An observer can see the true length of a line when he looks in a direction perpendicular to it. It is suggested that the student hold a pencil before him and move it into the following typical line positions to observe the conditions under which the pencil, representing a line, appears in true length.

 1. *Vertical line.* The vertical line is perpendicular to the horizontal and will therefore appear as a point in the H (top) view. It will appear in true length in the F (frontal) view, in true length in the P (profile) view, and in true length in any auxiliary view that is projected on an auxiliary plane that is perpendicular to the horizontal plane of projection.

 2. *Horizontal line.* The horizontal line will appear in true length when viewed from above because it is parallel to the H-plane of projection and its end points are theoretically equidistant from an observer looking downward.

 3. *Inclined line.* The inclined line will show true length in the F-view or P-view, for by definition (Sec. 6.8) an inclined line is one that is parallel to either the F-plane or the P-plane of projection. However, it cannot be parallel to both planes of projection at the same time.

 4. *Oblique line.* The oblique line will not appear in true length in any of the principal views because it is inclined to all of the principal planes of projection. It should be apparent, in viewing the pencil alternately from the directions used to obtain the principal views, namely, from the front, above, and side, that one end of the pencil is always farther away from the observer than the other. Only when looking directly at the pencil from such a position that the end points are equidistant from the observer can the true length be seen. On a drawing, the true length projection of an oblique line will appear in a supplementary A (auxiliary) view on a plane that is parallel to the line.

10.7

To Determine the True Length of an Oblique Line. In order to find the true length of an oblique line, it is necessary to select an auxiliary plane of projection that will be parallel to the line (Figs. 10.6 and 10.7).

GIVEN: The F (frontal) view $a^F b^F$ and the H (top) view $a^H b^H$ of the oblique line AB (Fig. 10.6).

SOLUTION: (1) Draw the reference line HA parallel to the projection $a^H b^H$. The A-plane for this reference line will be parallel to AB and perpendicular to the H-plane (see pictorial drawing). (2) Draw lines of projection from points a^H and b^H perpendicular to the reference line. (3) Transfer height measurements from the

F-view to the A-view to locate a^A and b^A. In making this transfer of measurements, the students should attempt to visualize the space condition for the line and understand that, since the F-view and A-view both show height and because the planes of projection for these views are perpendicular to the H-plane, the perpendicular distance D_1 from the reference line HF to point a^F must be the same as the distance D_1 from the reference line HA to point a^A.

The projection $a^A b^A$ shows the true length of the line AB.

It was not necessary to use an auxiliary plane perpendicular to the H-plane to find the true length of line AB in Fig. 10.6. The auxiliary plane could just as well have been perpendicular to either the F- or P-planes. Figure 10.7 shows the use of an auxiliary plane perpendicular to the frontal plane to find the true length of the line. In this case the auxiliary view has depth distances in common with the top view, as indicated.

10.8
Perpendicular Lines. Lines that are perpendicular in space will have their projections perpendicular in any view that shows either or both of the lines in true length. A second rule of perpendicularity might be that, when a line is perpendicular to a plane, it will be perpendicular to every line in that plane. A careful study of Fig. 10.8 will verify these rules. For instance, it should be noted that the lines AB and CD lie in a plane that is outlined with broken lines and that $e^H f^H$ is perpendicular to $a^H b^H$ because $a^H b^H$ shows the true length of the line AB. In the A-view, we see that $e^A f^A$ is perpendicular to the line view of the plane and is therefore perpendicular to both AB and CD. The O-view shows the true shape (TSP) of the plane and the line EF as a point. This again verifies the fact that EF is perpendicular to the plane and to lines AB and CD. Otherwise line

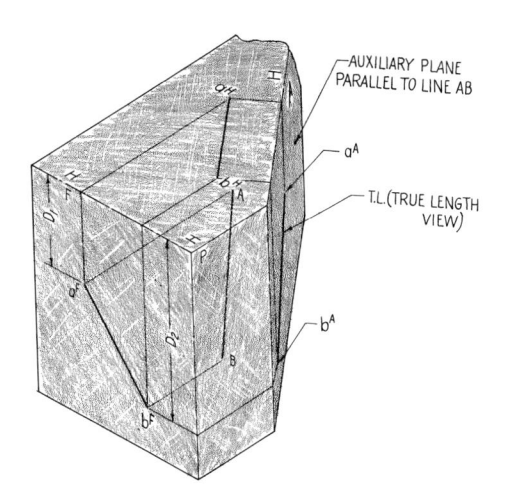

FIG. 10.6. To find the true length of an oblique line.

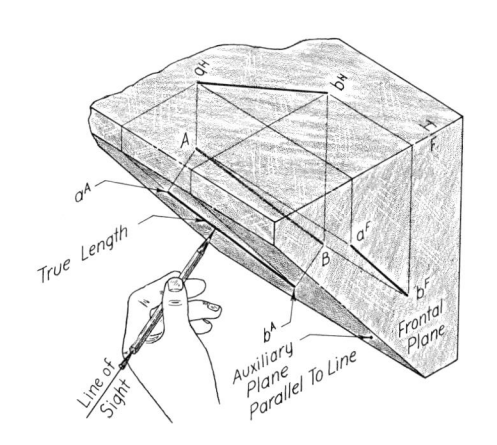

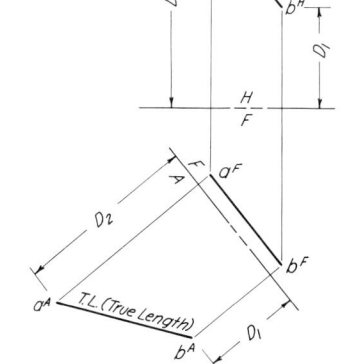

FIG. 10.7. To find the true length of a line.

EF would not appear as a point. Note also that the O-view shows the true length (TL) of AB and CD.

10.9
Bearing of a Line. The bearing of a line is the horizontal angle between the line

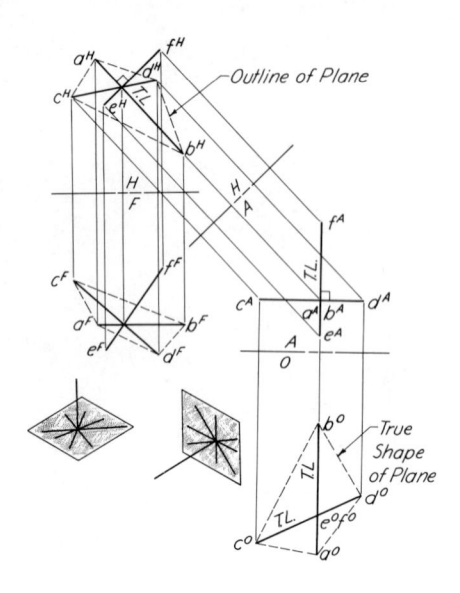

FIG. 10.8. Perpendicular lines.

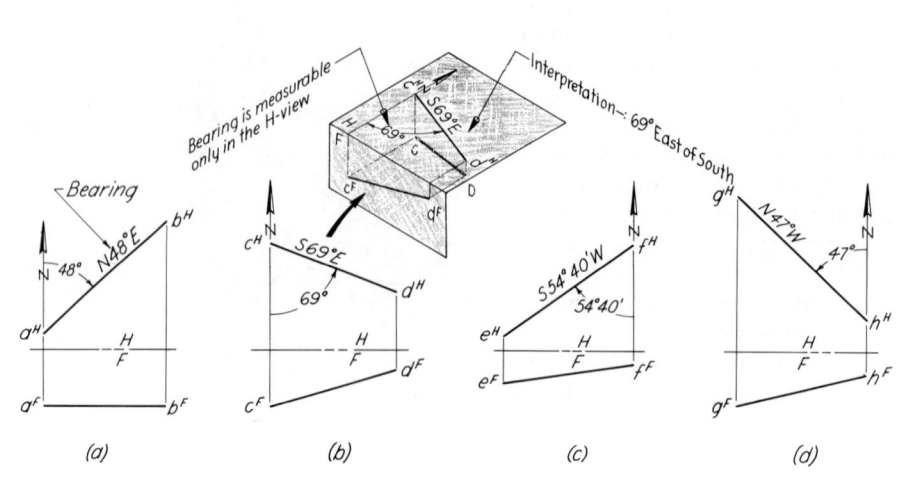

FIG. 10.9. The bearing of a line.

FIG. 10.10. The point view of a line.

and a north–south line. A bearing is given in degrees with respect to the meridian and is measured from 0° to 90° from either north (N) or south (S). The bearing reading indicates the quadrant in which the line is located by use of the letters N and E, S and E, S and W, or N and W, as N 48° E or S 54° 40′ W. The bearing of a line is measured in the *H*-view (Fig. 10.9).

10.10

Point View of a Line (Fig. 10.10). It was pointed out in the first section of this chapter that the solutions of many types of problems depend on an understanding of a few basic constructions. One of these basic constructions involves the finding of the view showing the point view or point projection of a line. For instance, this construction is followed when it is necessary to determine the dihedral angle between two planes, for the true size of the angle will appear in the view that shows the line common to the two planes as a point.

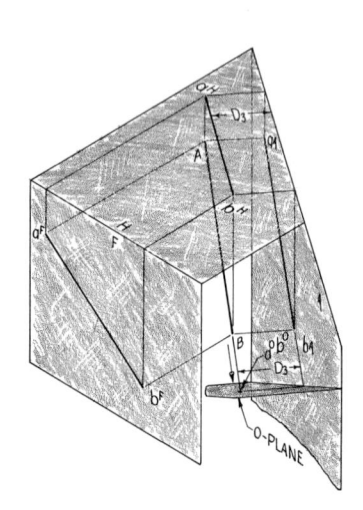

A line will show as a point on a projection plane that is perpendicular to the line. The observer's direction of sight must be along and parallel to the line. When a line appears in true length on one of the principal planes of projection, only an auxiliary view is needed to show the line as a point. However, in the case of an oblique line both an auxiliary and an oblique view are required, for a point view must always follow a true-length view. In other words, the plane of projection for the view showing the line as a point must be adjacent to the plane for the true view and be perpendicular to it.

GIVEN: The F-view $a^F b^F$ and the H-view $a^H b^H$ of the oblique line AB (Fig. 10.10).

SOLUTION: (1) Draw the view showing the TL (true length) of AB. This is an auxiliary view drawn, as explained in Sec. 10.7. (2) Draw reference line AO perpendicular to the true-length projection $a^A b^A$. This reference line is for an O-plane that is perpendicular to the A-plane. (3) Draw a projection line from $a^A b^A$ and transfer the distance D_3 from the H-view to the O-view. It should be noted from the pictorial drawing that the distance D_3 is common to both of these views, and that points a^o and b^o coincide to give a point or end view of line AB.

10.11
To Find the Shortest Distance from a Point to a Line. The shortest distance between a given point and a given straight line must be measured along a perpendicular drawn from the point to the line. Since lines that are perpendicular will have their projections show perpendicular in any view showing either or both lines in true length (Sec. 10.8), the perpendicular must be drawn in the view showing the given line in true length.

GIVEN: The F- and H-views of the line AB and point C (Fig. 10.11).

SOLUTION: (1) Draw the A(auxiliary) view showing the true-length view $a^A b^A$ of line AB and view c^A of point C. (2) Draw $c^A x^A$ perpendicular to $a^A b^A$. Line $c^A x^A$ is a view of the required perpendicular from

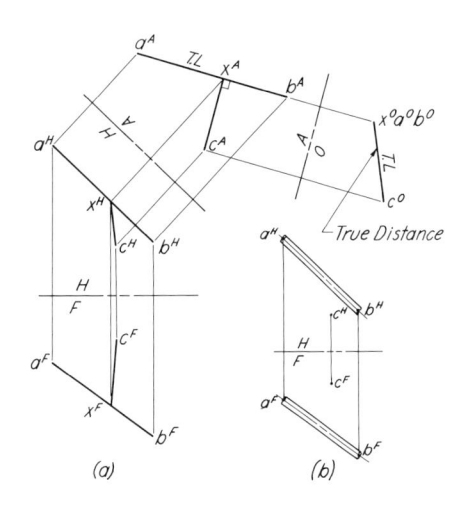

FIG. 10.11. To find the shortest distance from a point to a line.

point C to its juncture with line AB at point X. (3) Draw reference line AO parallel to $c^A x^A$. This reference line locates an O-plane, which will be parallel to the perpendicular CX and perpendicular to the A-plane. The O-view will show the true length of CX. Line CX does not show true length in any of the other views.

10.12
The Principal Lines of a Plane (Fig. 10.12). Those lines that are parallel to the principal planes of projection are the *principal lines of a plane*. A principal line may be either a horizontal line, a frontal line, or a profile line. Principal lines are true-length lines and one such line may be drawn in any plane to appear true length in any one of the principal views, as desired. This is an important principle that is the basis for the solution of many problems involving lines and planes.

10.13
To Obtain the Edge View of a Plane. When a plane is vertical, an edge view of it will be seen from above and it will be represented by a line in the top view. Should

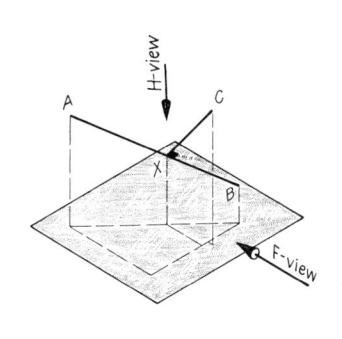

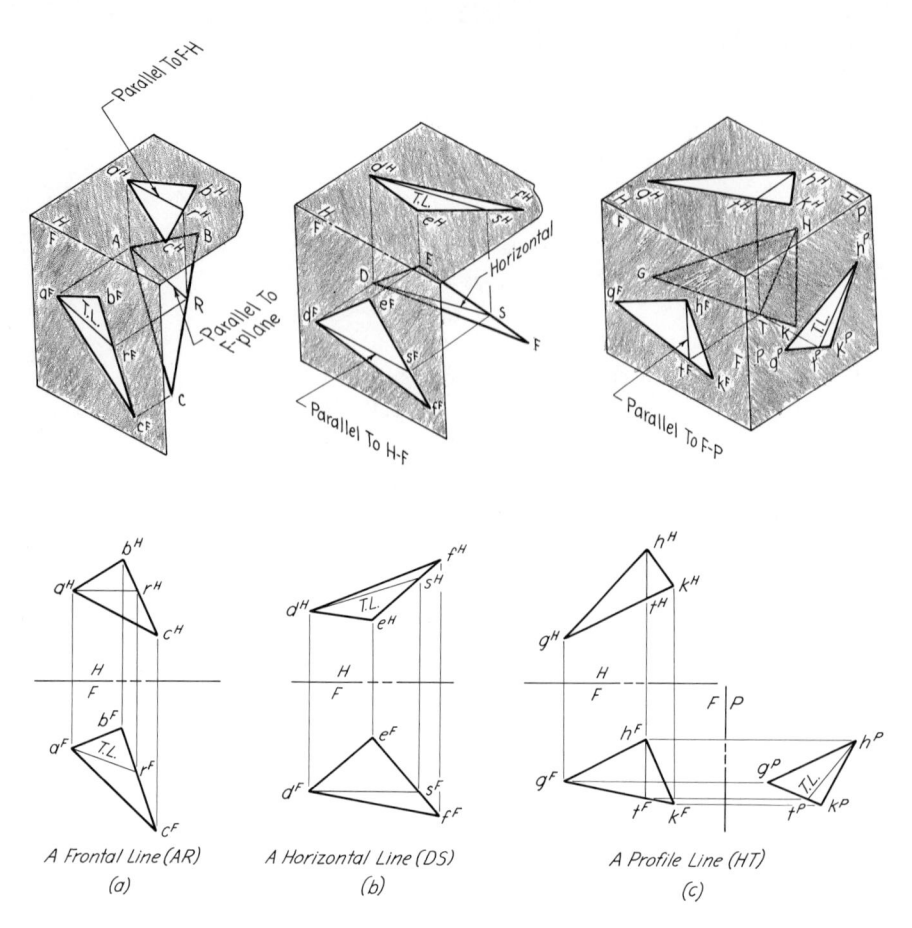

FIG. 10.12. The location of a principal line in a plane.

(a) A Frontal Line (AR)
(b) A Horizontal Line (DS)
(c) A Profile Line (HT)

and to establish the location at which a line pierces a plane.

The edge view of an oblique plane can be obtained by viewing the plane with direction of sight parallel to it. The edge view will then appear in an auxiliary view. When the auxiliary view shows height, the slope of the plane is shown (Fig. 10.13).

GIVEN: The F- and H-views of plane ABC.

SOLUTION: (1) Draw the horizontal line AX in the plane. Because AX is parallel to the horizontal, $a^F x^F$ will be horizontal and must be drawn before the position of $a^H x^H$ can be established. (2) Draw reference line HA perpendicular to $a^H x^H$. (3) Construct the A-view, which will show the plane ABC as a straight line. Since the F-view and A-view have height as a common dimension, the distances used in constructing the A-view were taken from the F-view. It should be noted by the reader that an edge view found by projecting from the front view will show the angle that the plane makes with the F-plane. Similarly, the edge view found by projecting from the side view will show the angle with the P-plane.

10.14
To Find the True Shape (TSP) of an Oblique Plane. Finding the true shape of a plane by projection is another of the basic constructions that the student must understand, for it is used to determine the solution of two of the problems that are to follow. In a way, the construction shown in Fig. 10.14 is a repetition of that shown in Fig. 9.19. However, repetition in the form of another presentation should help even those students who feel they understand the method for finding the true shape of an oblique surface of an object.

To see the true size and shape of an oblique plane an observer must view it with a line of sight perpendicular to it. To do this he must, as the first step in the con-

a plane be horizontal, it will appear as an edge in the frontal view. However, planes are not always vertical or horizontal; frequently they are inclined or oblique to the principal planes of projection.

Finding the edge view of a plane is a basic construction that is used to determine the slope of a plane (dip), to determine clearance, and to establish perpendicularity. The method presented here is part of the construction used to obtain the true size and shape of a plane, to determine the angle between a line and plane,

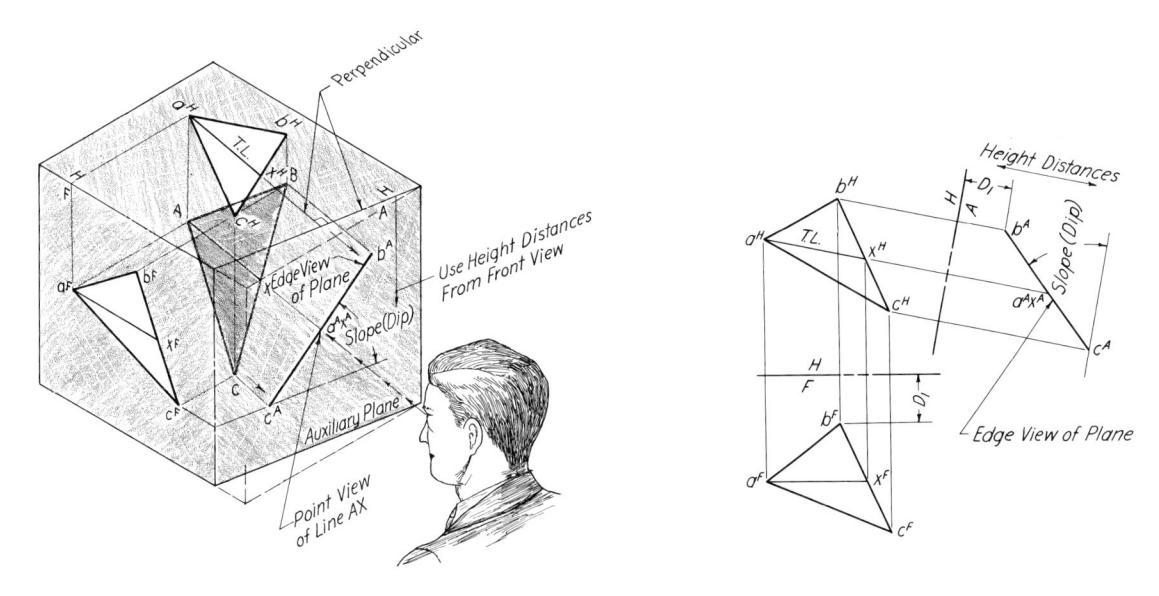

CHAP. 10 / BASIC SPATIAL GEOMETRY FOR DESIGN AND ANALYSIS   193

FIG. 10.13. To find the edge view of a plane.

struction, obtain an edge view of the plane. An O-view taken from the A-view will then show the true shape of the plane.

GIVEN: The F- and H-views of plane ABC.

SOLUTION: (1) Draw a frontal line CD in plane ABC. (2) Draw reference line FA perpendicular to $c^F d^F$ and construct the A-view showing the edge view of the plane. The auxiliary view has depth in common with the H-view. (3) Draw reference line AO parallel to the edge view in the A-view and construct the O-view, which will show the true size and shape of plane ABC. The needed distances from the reference line to points in the O-view are found in the F-view.

10.15
To Find the Piercing Point of a Line and a Plane. Determining the location of the point where a line pierces a plane is another fundamental operation with which one must be familiar. A line, if it is not parallel to a plane, will intersect the plane

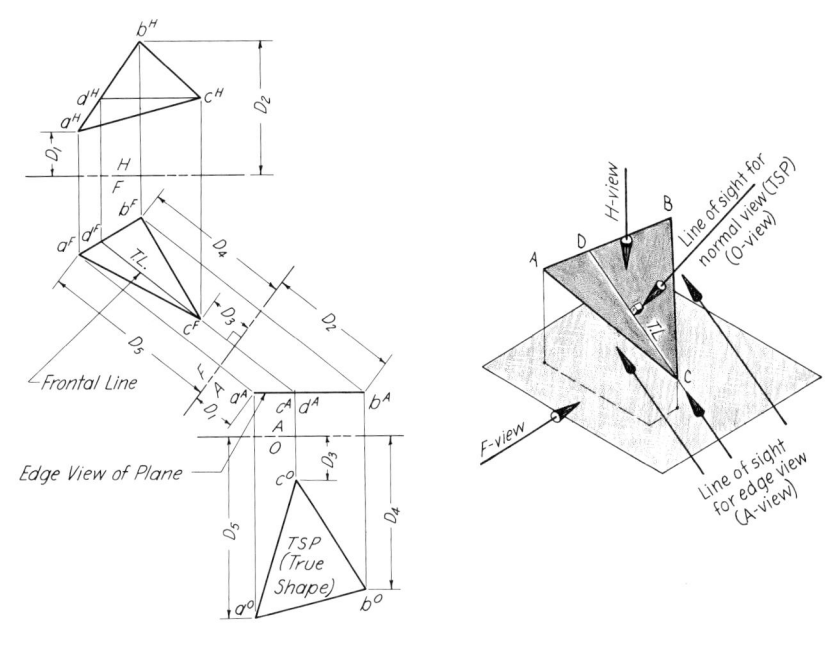

FIG. 10.14. To find the true shape (TSP) of an oblique plane.

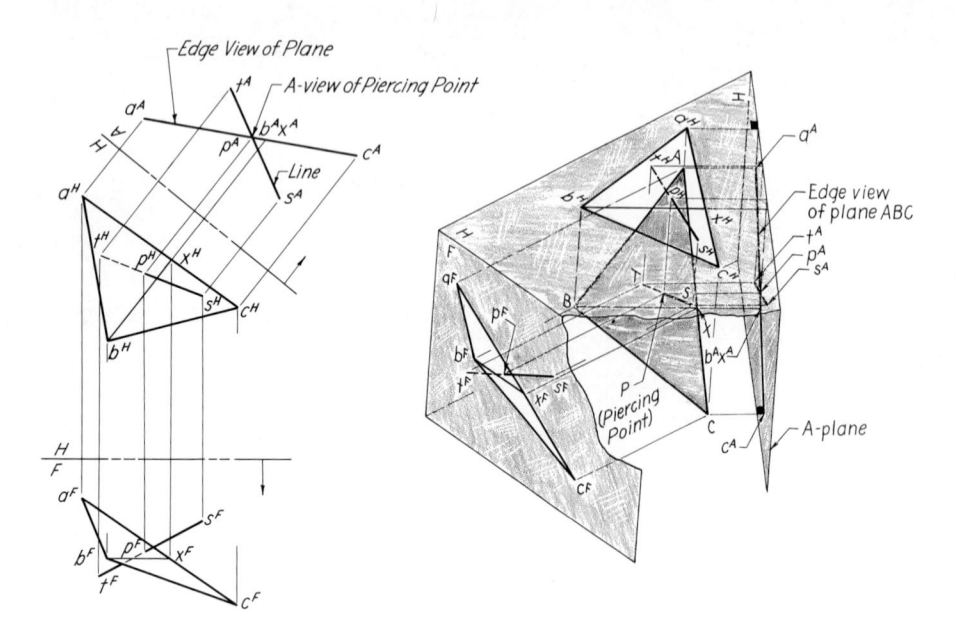

FIG. 10.15. To find the piercing point of a line and a plane.

at a point that is common to both. In a view showing the plane as an edge, the piercing point appears where the line intersects (cuts) the edge view. This method is known as the edge-view method to distinguish it from the cutting-plane method, which may be found in Chapter 11.

The simple cases occur when the plane appears as an edge in one of the principal views. The general case, for which we use an oblique plane, is given in Fig. 10.15.

GIVEN: Plane ABC and line ST.

SOLUTION: (1) Draw the horizontal line BX in ABC. (2) Draw reference line HA perpendicular to $b^H x^H$ and construct the A-view showing an edge view of the plane as line $a^A b^A c^A$ and the view of the line $s^A t^A$. Point p^A where the line cuts the edge view of the plane is the A-view of the piercing point. (3) Project point P back from the A-view first to the H-view and then to the F-view.

10.16

To Determine the Angle Between a Line and a Given Plane. The true angle between a given line and a given plane will be seen

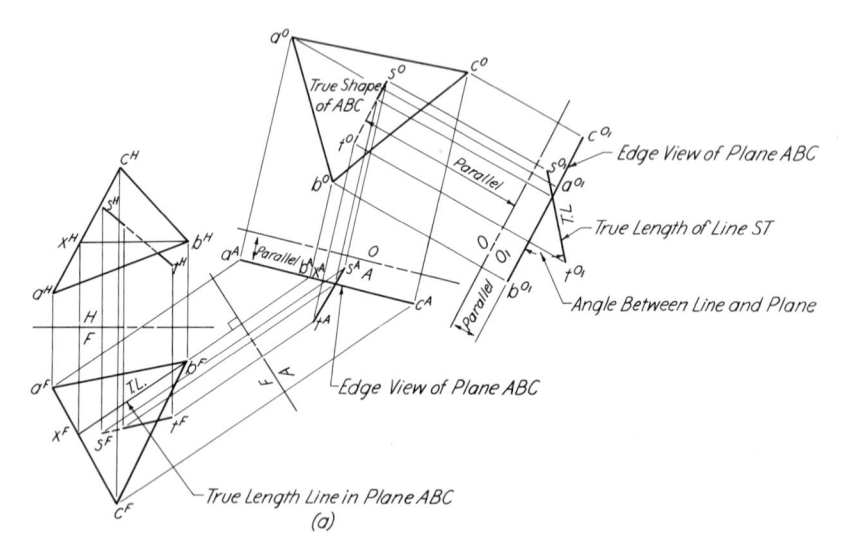

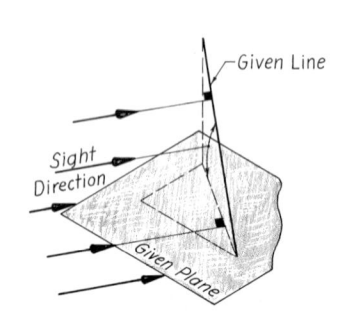

FIG. 10.16. To find the angle between a line and a plane.

in the view that shows the plane as an edge (a line) and the line in true length. The solution shown in Fig. 10.16 is based on this premise. The solution as presented might be called the *edge-view method.*

GIVEN: The F- and H-views of plane ABC and line ST.

SOLUTION: (1) Draw the frontal line BX in the plane ABC. (2) Draw reference line FA perpendicular to $x^F b^F$ and construct the A-view. This view will show plane ABC as line ($a^A b^A c^A$); however, since this view does not show ST in true length, the true angle is not shown. (3) Draw reference line AO parallel to the edge view of the plane and construct the O-view that will show line ST viewed obliquely and plane ABC in its true size and shape. (4) Draw reference line OO_1 parallel to $s^o t^o$ and construct the second oblique view.

Line $s^{O_1} t^{O_1}$ will show the true length of ST in this second oblique view. Plane ABC will be seen again as an edge (line), for it now appears on an adjacent view taken perpendicular to the view showing true shape (TSP). The required angle can now be measured between the true-length view of line ST and the edge view of plane ABC.

In the illustration of Fig. 10.16 three supplementary views were required to obtain the true angle. If the plane had appeared as an edge in one of the given views, only two supplementary views would have been needed; if it had appeared in true shape in a given view only one additional view, properly selected to show the plane as an edge and the line in true length, would be needed.

10.17
To Determine the Angle Between Two Nonintersecting (Skew) Lines. The angle between two nonintersecting lines is measurable in a view that shows both lines in true length. The analysis and construction that might be followed to obtain the needed view is shown in Fig. 10.17.

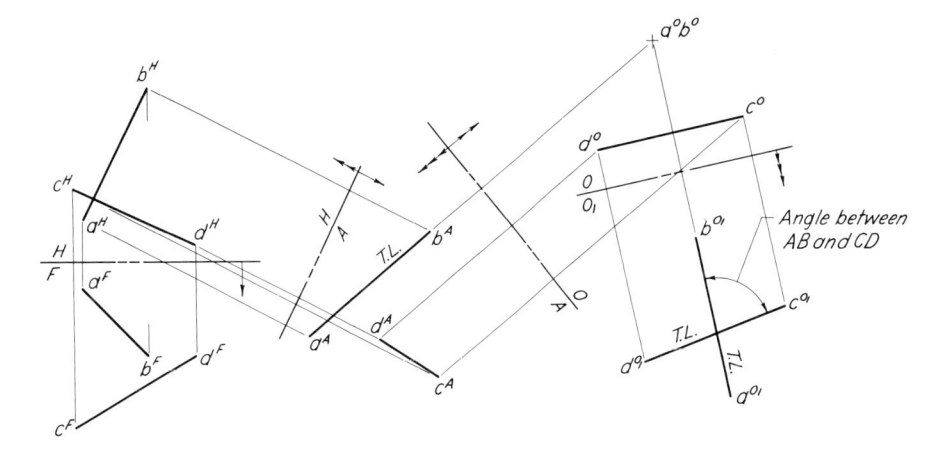

FIG. 10.17. To find the angle between two skew lines.

GIVEN: The two nonintersecting lines AB and CD.

SOLUTION: (1) Draw the reference line HA parallel to $a^H b^H$ and construct the A-view that shows AB in true length and the view of the line CD. (2) Draw reference line AO perpendicular to $a^A b^A$ and draw the O-view in which the line AB will appear as a point ($a^o b^o$). (3) Draw reference line OO_1, parallel to $c^o d^o$ and construct the O-view showing the true length of CD. Line AB must also show true length in this view since AB, showing as a point in the O-view, is parallel to the OO_1-plane. With both lines shown in true length in the O_1-view, the required angle may be measured in this view.

10.18
To Determine the True Angle Between Two Intersecting Oblique Lines. Since, as previously stated, two intersecting lines establish a plane, the true angle between the intersecting lines may be seen in a true-shape view of a plane containing the lines (Fig. 10.14). In Fig. 10.18 line AC com-

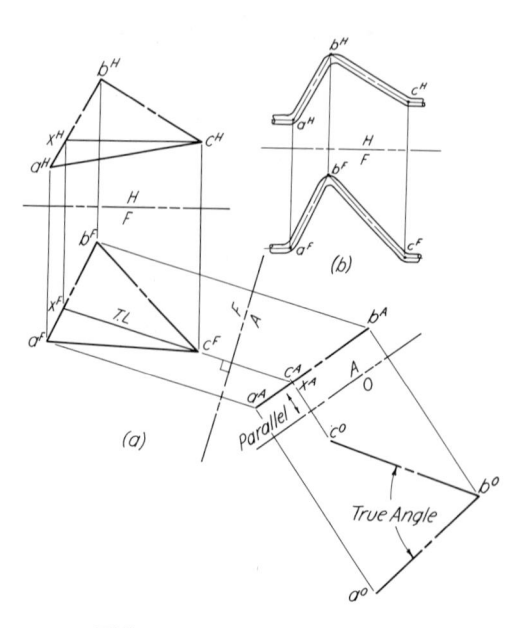

FIG. 10.18. To find the true angle between two intersecting lines.

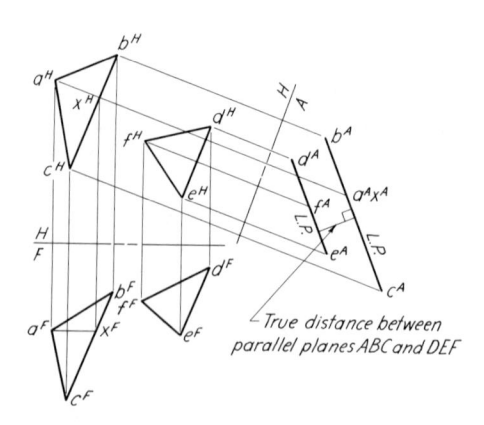

FIG. 10.19. Distance between parallel planes.

FIG. 10.20. To find the dihedral angle between two planes.

pletes plane *ABC* containing the given lines *AB* and *BC*. It is necessary to find the true angle between *AB* and *BC*.

SOLUTION: (1) Draw the frontal line *XC*. (2) Draw reference line *FA* perpendicular to $c^F x^F$ and construct the *A*-view showing an edge view of plane *ABC*. (3) Draw reference line *AO* parallel to the edge view $a^A c^A b^A$ and construct the *O*-view, which will show the TSP of plane *ABC*. In this view it is desirable to show only the given lines. The true angle between *AB* and *BC* is shown by $a^O b^O c^O$. As a practical application this method might be used to determine the angle between two adjacent sections of bent rod, as shown in (*b*).

10.19
The Distance Between Two Parallel Planes. When two planes are parallel their edge views will appear as parallel lines in the same view. The clearance or perpendicular distance between them can be measured in this view (Fig. 10.19). The existence of planes as parallel lines in a view is another proof that they are parallel.

10.20
To Find the Dihedral Angle Between Two Planes. The angle between two planes is known as a *dihedral angle*. The true size of this angle between intersecting planes may be seen in a plane that is perpendicular to both. For this condition as set forth, the intersecting planes will appear as edges and the line of intersection of the two planes as a point. The true angle may be measured between the edge views of the planes (Fig. 10.20).

GIVEN: The intersecting planes *ABCD* and *CDEF*. The line of intersection is line *CD*, as shown in the pictorial drawing.

SOLUTION: (1) Draw reference line *FA* parallel to $c^F d^F$ and construct the *A*-view.

This view will show CD in true length ($c^A d^A$). (2) Draw reference line AO perpendicular to $c^A d^A$ and construct the adjacent O-view. Since this view was taken looking along line CD, points C and D are coincident and appear as a single point identified as $c^o d^o$. The intersecting planes show as edge views and the true angle between the given planes may be measured between these edge-view lines. When two planes are given that do not intersect, the dihedral angle may be found after the line of intersection has been determined.

10.21
To Find the Shortest Distance Between Two Skew Lines. As was stated in Sec. 10.5, any two lines that are not parallel and do not intersect are called *skew lines*. The shortest distance between any such lines must be measured along one line and only one line that can be drawn perpendicular to both. This common perpendicular can be drawn in a view that is taken to show one line as a point. Its projection will be perpendicular to the view of the other line and will show in true length (Fig. 10.21).

GIVEN: The F- and H-views of two skew lines AB and CD.

SOLUTION: (1) Draw an A-view adjacent to the H-view to show line AB in true length ($a^A b^A$). Line CD should also be shown in this same view ($c^A d^A$). (2) Draw reference line AO perpendicular to $a^A b^A$ and draw the O-view in which line AB will appear as a point ($a^o b^o$). It is in this view that the exact location of the required perpendicular can be established. (3) Draw the line $e^o f^o$ through point $a^o b^o$ perpendicular to $c^o d^o$. The shortest distance between the skew lines now appears in true distance as the length of $e^o f^o$. Although the CD does not appear in true length in the O-view, $e^o f^o$ does, and hence $c^o d^o$ and $e^o f^o$ will appear perpendicular. (4) Complete the A-view by first locating point e^A on $c^A d^A$ and then draw $e^A f^A$ parallel to reference line AO. (5) Locate points E and F in the H- and F-views remembering that point E is located on line CD and point F on line AB.

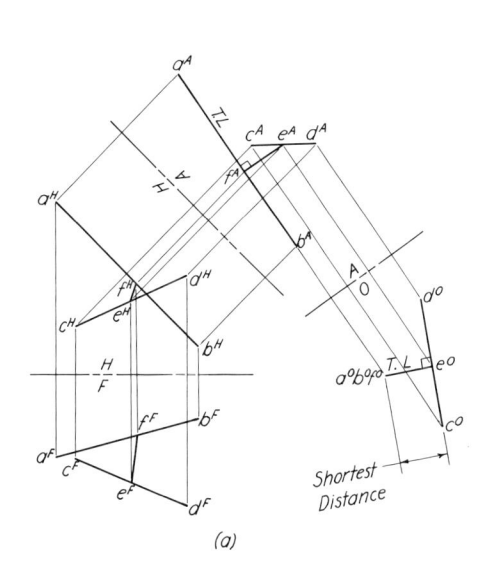

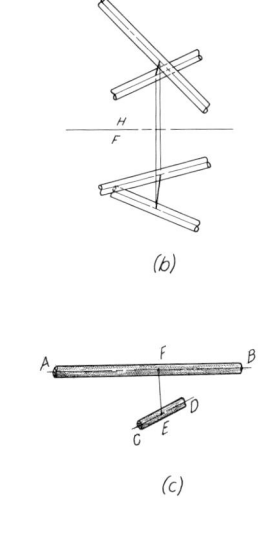

In engineering design an engineer frequently has to locate and find the length of the shortest line between two skewed members in order to determine clearance or the length of a connecting member. In underground construction work one might use this method to locate a connecting tunnel.

In Fig. 10.21(b) and (c) we see the two rods for which the clearance distance was determined in (a). Lines AB and CD represent the center lines of the rods.

FIG. 10.21. To find the shortest distance between two skew lines.

B: VECTOR GEOMETRY

10.22
Vector Methods. In order to be successful in solving some types of problems that

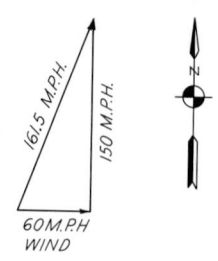

FIG. 10.22. A vector problem.

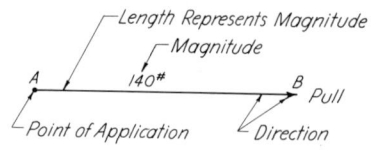

FIG. 10.23. A vector.

arise in design, a well-trained technologist should have a working knowledge of "vector geometry." The methods presented in this chapter should furnish the student with some background knowledge for solving force problems as they appear in the study of mechanics, strength of materials, and design. Through discreet use of the methods of vector geometry, as well as mathematical methods, it is possible to solve engineering problems quickly within a fully acceptable range of accuracy. Since any quantity having both magnitude and direction may be represented by a fixed or rotating vector, vector operations are commonly used for problems in the design of frame structures, problems dealing with velocities in mechanisms, and for problems arising in the study of electrical properties. Because a student in a beginning course in engineering graphics should have basic principles rather than specialized cases presented to him, the methods given in this chapter for solving both two-dimensional and three-dimensional force problems deal mainly with static structures or, in other words, structures with forces acting so as to be in equilibrium. In a study of physics, graphical methods are useful for the composition and resolution of forces.

It is hoped that as a student progresses through his other undergraduate courses, he will desire to learn more about the use of vector methods for solving problems, and that he will become able to recognize the cases where he may have a choice between a graphical and an algebraic method. The graphical method is the better for many cases because it is much quicker and can be checked more easily.

An example of a vector addition is shown in Fig. 10.22. An airplane is flying north with a cross wind from the west. If the speed of the plane is 150 mph (miles per hour) and the wind is blowing toward the east at 60 mph, the plane will be flying NE (northeast) at 161.5 mph. Vectors can be used for problems of this type because forces acting on a body have both magnitude and direction.

10.23

A Force. In our study of vector methods, a force may be defined as a cause which tends to produce motion in an object.

A force has four characteristics which determine it. First, a force has "magnitude." The value of this magnitude may be expressed in terms of some standard unit. It is usually given in pounds. Second, a force has a "line of action." This is the line along which the force acts. Third, a force has "direction." This is the direction in which it tends to move the object upon which it acts. Fourth, and last, a force has a "point of application." This is the place at which it acts upon the object, often assumed to be a point at the center of gravity.

10.24

A Vector. A force can be represented graphically by a straight line segment with an arrowhead at one end. Such an arrow when used for this purpose is known as a "vector" (Fig. 10.23). The position of the body of the arrow represents the line of action of the force while the arrowhead points out the direction. The magnitude is represented to some selected scale by the overall length of the arrow itself.

When a force acts in a two-dimensional plane, only one view of the vector is needed. However, if the force is in space, two views of the vector must be given.

10.25

Addition of Vector Forces—Two Forces. For a thorough understanding of the principles of vector addition, two simple examples will be considered first.

If one of two men who find it necessary to move a supply cabinet pushes on it with 60 lb force while the other pushes in the same direction with 40 lb force, the total force exerted to move the cabinet is 100 lb. The representation of two or more such forces in the manner shown in Fig. 10.24 amounts to a vector addition. Should these men be in a prankish mood and decide to push in opposite directions, as illustrated in Fig. 10.25, the cabinet might move provided the 20 lb resultant force were sufficient to overcome friction. The 20 lb resultant comes from a graphical addition.

Now let it be supposed that force A represented by F_A and force B represented by F_B in Fig. 10.26 act from a point P, the point of application. The resultant force on the body will not now be the sum of forces A and B, but instead will be the graphical addition of these forces as represented by the diagonal of a parallelogram having sides equal to the scaled length of the given forces. This single force R of 105.5 lb would produce an effect upon the body that would be equivalent to the combined forces F_A and F_B. The single force which could replace any given force system, is known as the *resultant* (R) for the force system.

Figure 10.26 shows that the resultant R divides the parallelogram into two equal triangles. Therefore, R could have been found just as well by constructing a single triangle as shown in Fig. 10.27 provided that the vector F_B is drawn so that its tail-end touches the tip-end of F_A, and R is drawn with its arrow-end to the tip-end of F_B. Since either of the triangles shown in Fig. 10.26 could have been drawn to determine R, it should be obvious the resultant is the same regardless of the order in which the vectors are added. However, it is important that they be added tip-end to tail-end and that the vector arrows show the true direction for the action of the concurrent forces in the given system.

To find the resultant of two forces, which are applied as shown in Fig. 10.28, it is first necessary to move the vector arrows along their lines of action to the intersection point P before one can apply the parallelogram method.

The forces of a system whose lines of action all lie in one plane are called *coplanar forces*. Should the lines of action pass through a common point, the point of application, the forces are said to be *concurrent*. Figure 10.29 shows a system of forces that are both concurrent and coplanar.

**10.26
Addition of Vectors—Three or More Forces.** The parallelogram method may be used to determine the resultant for a system of three or more forces that are concurrent and coplanar. In applying this method to three or more forces, it is necessary to draw a series of parallelograms, the number depending upon the number of vector quantities that are to be added graphically. For example, in Fig. 10.30 two parallelograms are required to determine the resultant R for system. The resultant R_1 for forces F_A and F_B is determined by the first parallelogram to be drawn, and

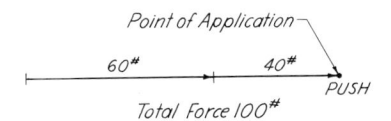

FIG. 10.24. A vector addition.

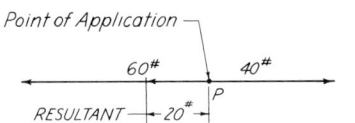

FIG. 10.25. Forces in opposite directions.

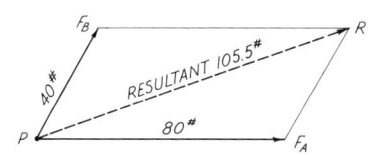

FIG. 10.26. Parallelogram of forces.

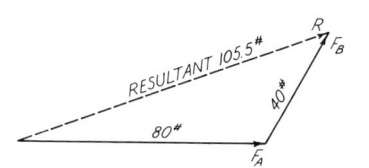

FIG. 10.27. A vector triangle.

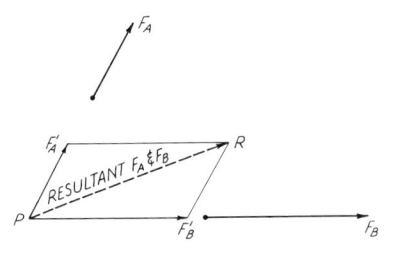

FIG. 10.28. Resultant of two forces.

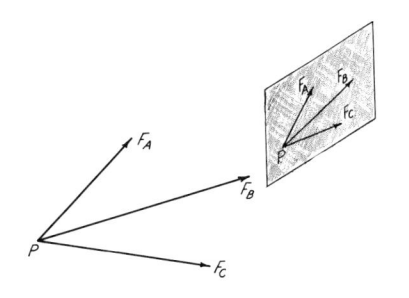

FIG. 10.29. Coplanar, concurrent forces.

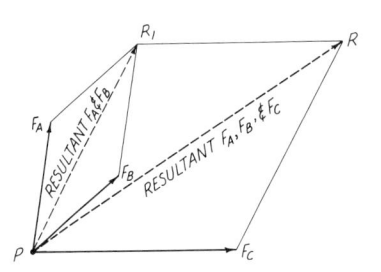

FIG. 10.30. Resultant of three or more forces with a common point of application (parallelogram method).

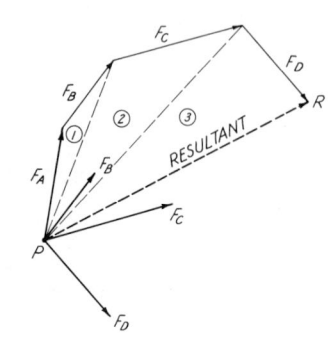

FIG. 10.31. Resultant of forces (polygon of forces).

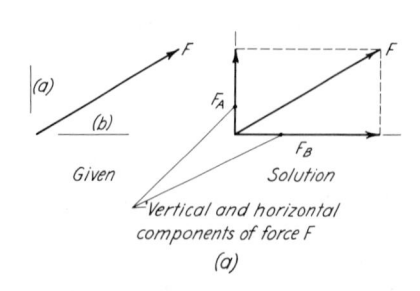

FIG. 10.32. Components.

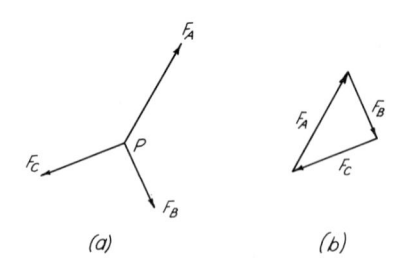

FIG. 10.33. Forces in equilibrium.

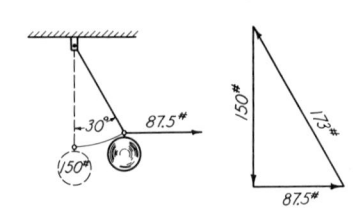

FIG. 10.34. Determination of forces (graphically).

then R_1 is combined in turn with F_C by forming the second and larger parallelogram. By combining the forces in this way R becomes the resultant for the complete system.

Where a considerable number of vectors form a system, a somewhat less complicated diagram results, and less work is required when the triangle method is extended and applied to the formation of a vector diagram such as the one shown in Fig. 10.31. In this case the diagram is formed by three vector triangles, one adjacent to the other, and the resultant of forces F_A and F_B is combined with F_C to form the second triangle. Finally, by combining the resultant of the three forces F_A, F_B, and F_C with F_D, the vector R is obtained, which represents the magnitude and direction of the resultant of the four forces. In the construction F_B, F_C, and F_D in the diagram must be drawn so as to be parallel respectively to their lines of action in the system. However, the order in which they are placed in the diagram is optional as long as one vector joins another tip to tail.

10.27
Vector Components. A component may be defined as one of two or more forces into which an original force may be resolved. The components, which together have the same action as the single force, are determined by a reversal of the process for vector addition, that is, the original force is resolved using the parallelogram method (see Fig. 10.32). The resolution of a plane vector into two components, horizontal and vertical, is illustrated in (a). In (b), the resolution of a force into components of specified direction is shown.

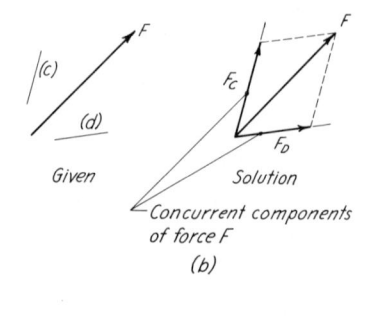

10.28
Forces in Equilibrium. A body is said to be in equilibrium when the opposing forces acting upon it are in balance. In such a state the resultant of the force system will be zero. The concurrent and coplanar force system shown in Fig. 10.33 is in a state of equilibrium, for the vector triangle closes and each vector follows the other tip to tail.

An "equilibrant" is the force which will balance two or more forces and produce equilibrium. It is a force that would equal the resultant of the system but would necessarily have to act in an opposite direction.

Figure 10.34 shows a weight supported by a short steel cable. The force to be determined is that needed to hold the weight in a state of equilibrium when it is swung from the position indicated by the broken lines into the position shown by solid lines.

This may be done by drawing a vector

triangle with the forces in order from tip to tail. The 87.5 lb force vector represents the equilibrant, the force that will balance the 150 lb force and the 173 lb tension force now in the cable. The reader may wonder at the increase in the tension force in the cable from a 150 lb force when hanging straight down to a 173 lb force when the cable is at an angle of 30° with the vertical. It might help to realize that as the weight is swung outward towards a position where the cable will be horizontal, both the tension force and the equilibrant will increase. Theoretically it would require forces infinitely large to hold the system in equilibrium with the cable in a horizontal position.

In solving a force system graphically it is possible to determine two unknowns in a coplanar system.

Now suppose that it is desired to determine the forces acting in the members of a simple truss as shown in Fig. 10.35(a). To determine these forces graphically, one should isolate the joint supporting the weight and draw a diagram, known as a free-body diagram to show the forces acting at the joint (b). Although the lines of this diagram may have any length, they must be parallel to the lines in the space diagram in (a). Since the boom will be in compression, a capital letter C has been placed along the line that represents the boom in the diagram. A letter T has been placed along the line for the cable because it will be in tension. Although the diagram may not have been essential in this particular case, such a diagram does play an important part in solving more complex systems.

In constructing the force polygon, it is necessary to start by drawing the vertical vector, for the load is the only force having a known magnitude and direction. After this vertical vector has been drawn to a length representing 1200 lb, using a selected scale, the force polygon (triangle) may be completed by drawing the remaining lines representing the unknown forces parallel to their known lines of action as shown in (a). The force polygon will close since the force system is in equilibrium.

The magnitude of the unknown forces in the members of the truss can now be determined by measuring the lines of the diagram using the same scale selected to lay out the length of the vertical vector. This method might be used to determine the forces acting in the members at any point in a truss.

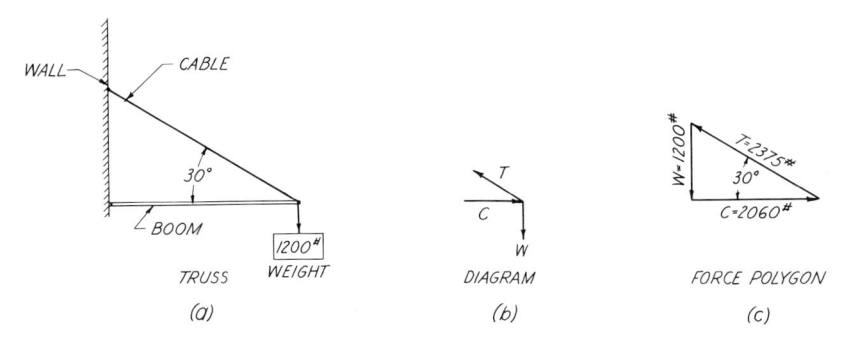

FIG. 10.35. Determination of the forces at the joint of a simple truss.

10.29
Coplanar, Noncurrent Force Systems. Forces in one plane having lines of action that do not pass through a common point are said to be *coplanar, nonconcurrent forces* (Fig. 10.36).

10.30
Two Parallel Forces. When two forces are parallel and act in the same direction, their resultant will have a line of action that is parallel to the lines of action of the given forces and it will be located between them. The magnitude of the resultant will be equal to the sum of the two forces [Fig. 10.37(a)], and it will act through a point that divides any perpendicular line joining the lines of action of the given forces inversely as the forces.

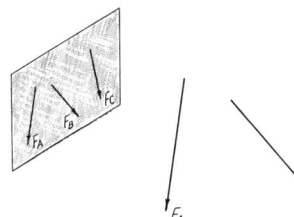

FIG. 10.36. Coplanar, nonconcurrent forces.

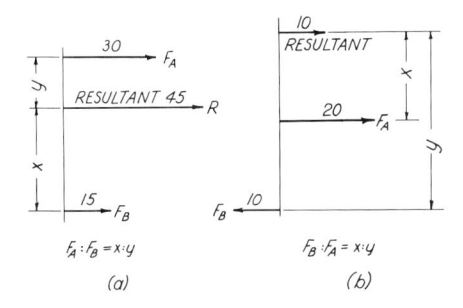

FIG. 10.37. Parallel forces.

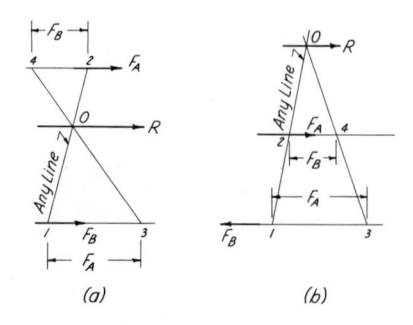

FIG. 10.38. Determination of the position of the resultant of parallel forces (graphical method).

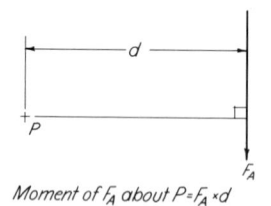

FIG. 10.39. Moment of a force.

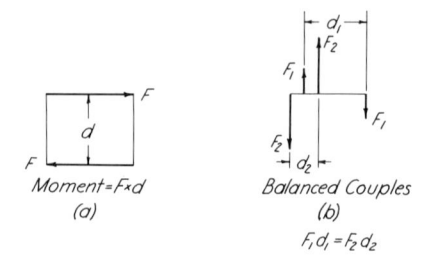

FIG. 10.40. Force couples.

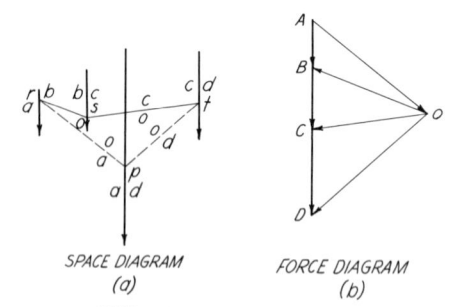

FIG. 10.41. Resultant of parallel forces—Bow's notation.

Should the two forces act in opposite directions, as shown in (b), the resultant will be located outside of them and will have the same direction as the greater force. Its magnitude will be equal to the difference between the two given forces. The proportion shown with the illustration in (b) may be used to determine the location of the point of application of the resultant. Those who prefer to determine graphically the location of the line of action for the resultant may use the method illustrated in Fig. 10.38. This method is based on well known principles of geometry.

With the two forces F_A and F_B given, any line 1–2 is drawn joining their lines of action. From this line two distances must be laid off along the lines of action of the given forces. If the given forces act in the same direction, then the distances are laid off in opposite directions from the line 1–2, (a). If they act in opposite directions, the distances must be laid off on the same side of line 1–2, (b). In Fig. 10.38(a), a length equal by scale to F_A was laid off from point 1 on the line of action of F_B. Then from point 2 a length equal to F_B was marked off in an opposite direction. These measurements located points 3 and 4, the end-points of the line intersecting line 1–2 at point O. Point O is on the line of action of the resultant R. In Fig. 10.38(b) this method has been applied to establish the location of the resultant for two forces acting in opposite directions.

10.31
Moment of a Force. The "moment of a force" with respect to a point is the product of the force and the perpendicular distance from the given point to the line of action of the force. In the illustration, Fig. 10.39, the moment of the force F_A about point P is Mom. $= F_A \times d$. The perpendicular distance d is known as the lever arm of the force. Should the distance d be measured in inches and the force be given in pounds, the moment of the force will be in inch-pounds.

10.32
Force Couples (Fig. 10.40). Two equal forces that act in opposite directions are known as a "couple." A couple does not have a resultant, and no single force can counteract tendency to produce rotation. The measurement of this tendency is the moment of the couple that is the product of one of the forces and the perpendicular distance between them.

To prevent the rotation of a body that is acted upon by a couple, it is necessary to use two other forces that will form a second couple. The body acted upon by these couples will be in equilibrium if each couple tends to rotate the body in opposite directions and the moment of one couple is equal to the other.

10.33
String Polygon—Bow's Notation. A system for lettering space and force diagrams, known as "Bow's notation," is widely used by technical authors. Its use in this chapter will tend to simplify the discussions which follow.

In the space diagram, shown in Fig. 10.41(a), each space from the line of action of one force to the line of action of the next one is given a lower-case letter such as a, b, c, and d in alphabetical order. Thus the line of action for any particular force can be designated by the letters of the areas on each side of it. For example, in Fig. 10.43 the line of action for the 1080 lb force, acting downward on the beam, would be designated as line of action bc. On the force diagram, corresponding capital letters are used at the ends of the vectors. In Fig. 10.41(b), AB represents the magnitude of ab in the space diagram and BC represents the magnitude of bc.

To find the resultant of three or more

parallel forces graphically, the "funicular" or "string polygon" is used. The magnitude and direction of the required resultant for the system shown in Fig. 10.41 are known. The magnitude, representing the algebraic sum of the given forces, appears as the heavy line AD of the force polygon. It is required to determine the location of its line of action. With the forces located in the space diagram and the force polygon drawn, the steps for the solution are as follows:

1. Assume a pole point O and draw the rays OA, OB, OC, and OD. Each of the triangles formed is regarded as a vector triangle with one side representing the resultant of the forces represented by the other two sides. For example: If we consider AB to be a resultant force, then OA and OB are two component forces that could replace AB. For the second vector triangle, OB and BC have OC as their resultant. OC, when combined with CD, will have OD as the resultant. OA and OD combine with AD, the final resultant of the system.

2. Draw directly on the space diagram the corresponding strings of the funicular polygon. The funicular polygon may be started at any selected point r along the line of action ab. The string ob will then be parallel to OB of the force polygon. From point s, where ob intersects bc, draw oc parallel to OC. The line oc extended to cd establishes the location of point t. Line od drawn parallel to OD and line oa drawn parallel to OA intersect at point p. Point p is a point on the line of action of force ad, the resultant force AD for the given force system.

When one or more of a system of parallel forces are directed oppositely from the others, the magnitude and direction of the resultant will be equal to the algebraic sum of the original forces.

**10.34
Coplanar, Nonconcurrent, Nonparallel Forces.** In further study of coplanar and nonconcurrent forces it might be supposed that it is necessary to determine the magnitude, direction, and line of action of the one force that will establish a state of equilibrium when combined with the given forces AB, BC, and CD of the force system shown in Fig. 10.42. The direction and line of action of the original forces are given in both the space diagram in (a) and the force polygon in (b). The magnitude and direction of the force that will produce equilibrium is represented by DA, the force needed to close the force polygon. With the force polygon completed, the next step is to assume a pole point O and draw the rays OA, OB, OC, and OD. Now OA and OB are component forces of AB, and AB might be replaced by these forces. To clarify this statement; each of the four triangles may be considered to be a vector triangle, and in the case of vector triangle OAB, AB can be regarded as the resultant for the other two forces OA and OB. It should be noted that component force OB of the vector triangle OBC must be equal and opposite in direction to component force OB of OAB.

All that remains to be done is to determine the line of action of the required force DA by drawing the string diagram as explained in Sec. 10.33, remembering that point r may be any point along the line of action of ab. The intersection point p for strings oa and od is a point along the line of action da of force DA. Although lines of action ab, bc, cd, and da were drawn to a length representing their exact magnitude in Fig. 10.42(a), they could have been drawn to a convenient length to allow for the construction of the string polygon, for these lines merely rep-

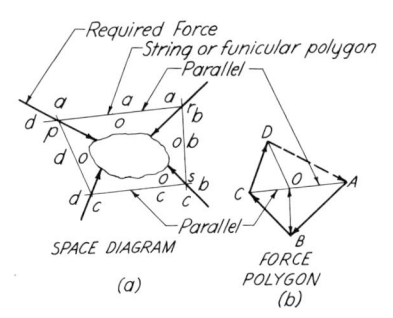

FIG. 10.42. Funicular or string polygon.

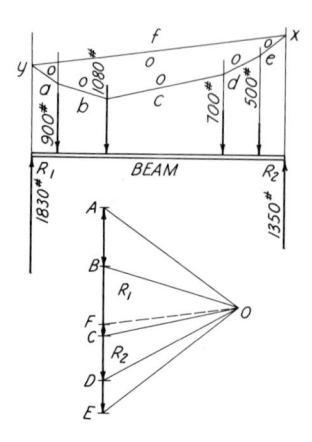

FIG. 10.43. To determine the reaction forces of a loaded beam.

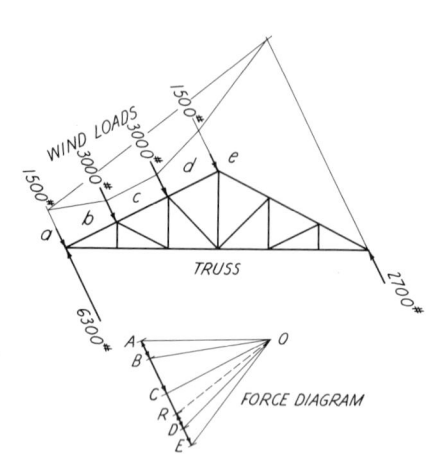

FIG. 10.44. The determination of the reactions for wind loads.

resent lines of action for the forces AB, BC, CD, and DA. The lines were presented in scaled length for illustrative purposes.

10.35
Equilibrium of Three or More Coplanar Parallel Forces. When a given system, consisting of three or more coplanar forces, is in equilibrium, both the force polygon and the funicular polygon must close. If the force polygon should close and the funicular polygon not close, the resultant of the given system will be found to be a force couple.

Two unknown forces of a parallel coplanar force system may be determined graphically by drawing the force and funicular polygons as shown in Fig. 10.43, since the forces are known to be in equilibrium, and all are vertical. Although one may be aware that the sum of the two reaction forces R_1 and R_2 is equal to the sum of forces AB, BC, CD, and DE, the magnitude of R_1 and R_2 as single forces is unknown. The location of point F in the force polygon, which is needed if one is to determine the magnitudes of R_1 and R_2, may be found by fulfilling the requirement that the funicular polygon be closed.

The funicular polygon is started at any convenient point along the known line of action of R_1, and successive strings are drawn parallel to corresponding rays of the force polygon. In area b the string will be parallel to OB, in area c the string will be parallel to OC and so on, until the string that is parallel to OE has been drawn. String of may then be added to close the funicular polygon. This closing line from point x to the starting point y determines the position of OF in the force polygon, for ray OF must be parallel to the string of. The magnitude of the reaction R_1 is represented to scale by vector FA, and R_2 is represented by the vector FE.

The graphical method for determining the values of wind load reactions for a roof truss having both ends fixed is shown in Fig. 10.44. The solution given is practically identical with the solution applied to the beam in Fig. 10.43.

10.36
Concurrent, Noncoplanar Force Systems. Up to this point in our study of force systems, the student's attention has been directed solely to systems lying in one plane in order that the graphical methods dealing with the composition and resolution of forces could be presented in a clear and simple manner, free from the thinking needed for understanding force systems involving the third dimension.

In dealing with noncoplanar forces it is necessary to use at least two views to represent a structure in space. Although the methods as applied to coplanar force systems for solving problems may be extended to noncoplanar systems, the vector diagram for noncoplanar forces must have two views instead of one view as in the case of coplanar forces. If the student is to understand the discussions that are to follow he must grasp the idea that for the composition and resolution of noncoplanar forces he will work with two distinct and separate space representations, the space diagram for the given structure and the related vector diagram (force polygon). Figure 10.45 shows two views of a concurrent, noncoplanar force system not in equilibrium.

There are a few basic relationships that exist between a space diagram and its related vector diagram, which must be kept in mind when solving noncoplanar force problems. These relationships are: (1) in corresponding views (H-view and H-view, or F-view and F-view), each vector in the vector diagram will be parallel to its corresponding representation in the space diagram, (2) if a system of concurrent, noncoplanar forces is in equilibrium, the force polygon in space closes and the projection on each plane will close, and

(3) the true magnitude of a force can be measured only in the vector diagram when it appears in true length or is made to do so.

10.37
Determination of the Resultant of a Force System of Concurrent, Noncoplanar Forces. The parallelogram method for determining the resultant of concurrent forces as explained in Sec. 10.26 may be employed to find the resultant of the three forces *OA*, *OB*, and *OC* in Fig. 10.46. Any number of given concurrent, noncoplanar forces can be combined into their resultant by this method. In the illustration, forces *OA* and *OB* were combined into their resultant, which is the diagonal of the smaller parallelogram, then this resultant in turn was combined with the third force *OC* to obtain the final resultant *R* for the given system. Since the true magnitude of *R* can be scaled only in a view showing its true length, an auxiliary view was projected from the front view. The true length of *R* could also have been determined by revolution.

Since the single force needed to hold a force system in balance, known as the *equilibrant*, is equal to the resultant in magnitude but is opposite in direction, this method might be used to determine the equilibrant for a system of concurrent, noncoplanar forces.

In presenting this problem and the two problems that follow, it has been assumed that the student has read the previous sections of this chapter and that his knowledge of the principles of projection is sufficient for him to find the true length, having two views given, and to draw the view of a plane so that it will appear as an edge.

10.38
To Find the Three Unknown Forces of a Simple Load-Bearing Frame—Special Case. In dealing with the simple load-bearing frame in Fig. 10.47, it should be realized that this is a special case rather than a general one, for two of the truss members appear as a single line in the frontal view of the space diagram. This condition considerably simplifies the task of finding the unknown forces acting in the members, and it is this particular spatial situation that makes this a special case. However, it should be pointed out now that this condition must exist or be set up in a projected view when a vector solution is to be applied to any problem involving a system of concurrent, noncoplanar forces. More will be said about the necessity for having two unknown forces coincide in one of the views in the discussion in Sec. 10.40.

After the space diagram has been drawn to scale, the steps toward the final solution are as follows:

1. Draw a free-body diagram showing the joint at *A*, the joint at which the load is applied. The lines of this diagram may be of any length, but each line in it must be parallel respectively to a corresponding line in the view of the space diagram to which the free-body diagram is related. In this case, it is the horizontal (top) view. A modified form of Bow's notation was used for convenience in identifying the forces. The vertical load has been shown pulled to one side in order that this force can be made to fall within the range of the notation. This diagram is important to the solution of this problem, for it enables one to see and note the direction of all of the forces that the members exert upon the joint (note arrowheads). Capital letters were used on the free-body diagram to identify the spaces between the forces, rather than lower-case letters as is customary, so that lower-case letters could be used for the ends of the views of the vectors in the vector diagram.

2. Using a selected scale, start the two

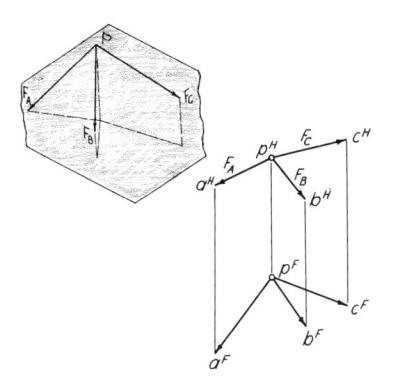

FIG. 10.45. Concurrent, noncoplanar forces.

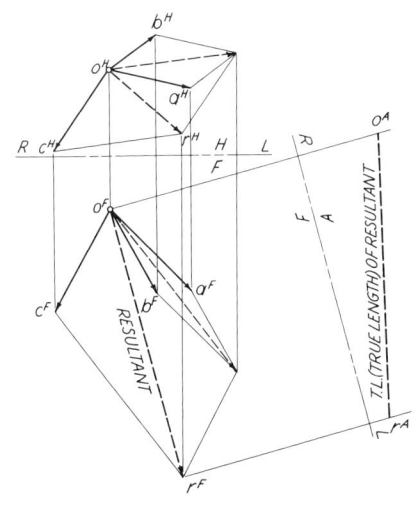

FIG. 10.46. Determination of the resultant of concurrent, noncoplanar forces.

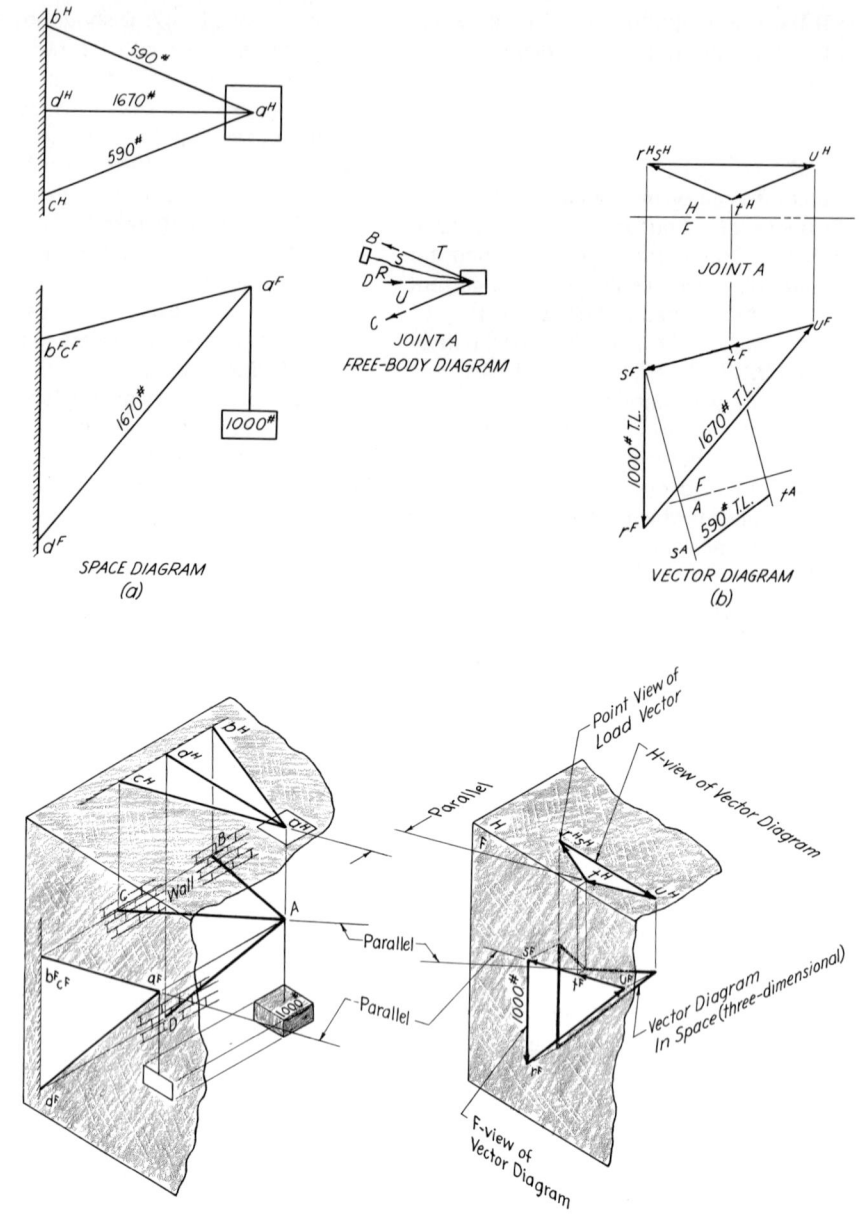

FIG. 10.47. Solution of a concurrent, noncoplanar force system—special case.

views of the vector diagram (b) by laying out vector RS representing the only known force, in this case the 1000 lb load. Since RS is a force acting in a vertical direction $r^F s^F$ will be in true length in the F-view and will appear as point $r^H s^H$ in the H-view.

3. Complete the H- and F-views of the vector diagram. Since each vector line in the top view must be parallel to a corresponding line in the top view of the space diagram, $s^H t^H$ must be drawn parallel to $a^H b^H$, $t^H u^H$ parallel to $a^H c^H$, and $u^H r^H$ parallel to $a^H d^H$. Since the forces acting at joint A are in equilibrium, the vector triangle will close and the vectors will appear tip to tail.

In the frontal view of the vector diagram, $s^F t^F$ will be parallel to $a^F b^F$, $t^F u^F$ will be parallel to $a^F c^F$, and $r^F u^F$ will be parallel to $d^F a^F$.

4. Determine the magnitude of the forces acting on joint A. Since vector RU shows its true length in the F-view, the true magnitude of the force represented may be determined by scaling $r^F u^F$ using the same scale used to lay out the length of $r^F s^F$. Although it is known that vectors ST and TU are equal in magnitude, it is necessary to find the true length representation of one or the other of these vectors by some approved method before scaling to determine the true value of the force.

An arrowhead may now be added to the line of action of each force in the free-body diagram to indicate the direction of the action. Since the free-body diagram was related to the top view of the space diagram, the arrowhead for each force will point in the same direction as does the arrowhead on the corresponding vector in the H-view of the vector diagram. These arrowheads show that the forces in members AB and AC are acting away from joint A and are therefore *tension forces*. The

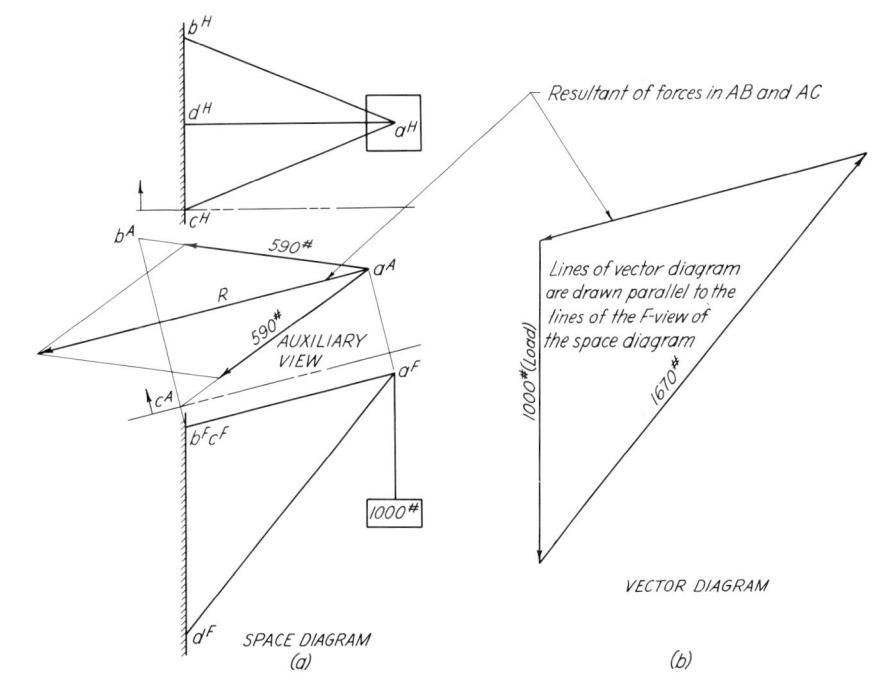

FIG. 10.48. To determine the three unknown forces of a simple load-bearing frame-composition method.

force in AD acts toward A and thus is a *compression force*.

10.39

To Find the Three Unknown Forces of a Simple Load-Bearing Frame—Composition Method (Fig. 10.48). Since the forces in AB and AC lie in an inclined plane that appears as an edge in the F-view, they may be composed into a single force that will have the same effect in the force system as the forces it replaces. This replacement force along with the force in AD and the load now become the forces that would be acting in a simple load-bearing truss (See Fig. 10.35). After the vertical vector of this concurrent coplanar force system has been drawn to a selected scale, the triangular force polygon in (b) may be completed by drawing the remain-

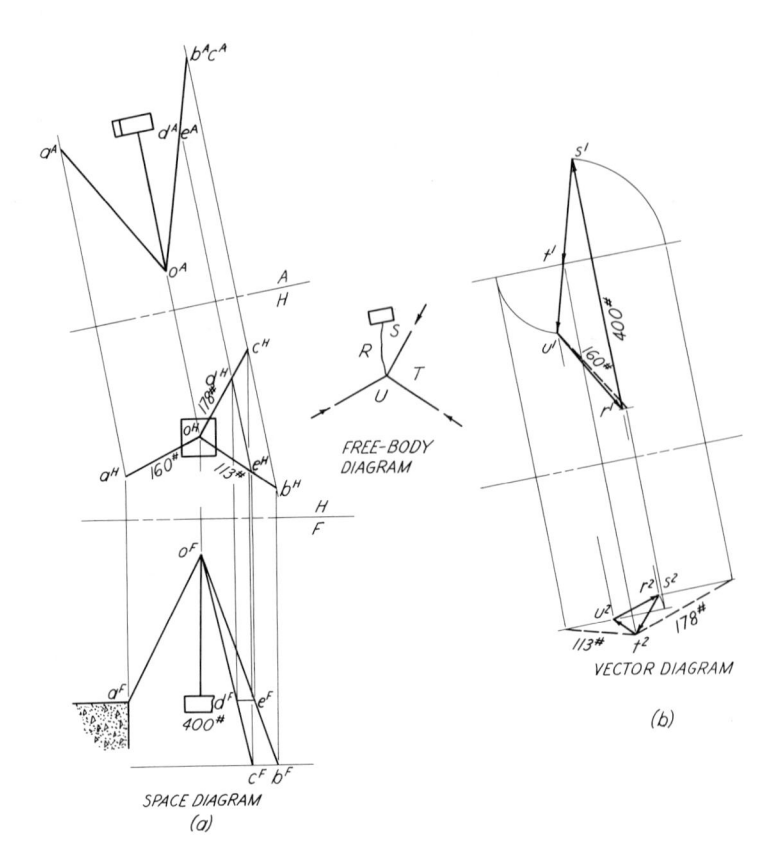

208   PART II / SPATIAL GRAPHICS: SHAPE DESCRIPTION AND SPATIAL RELATIONSHIPS

FIG. 10.49. Solution of a concurrent, noncoplanar force system—general case.

the known force is in a vertical position as in the previous problem, but no two of the three unknown forces appear conincident in either of the two given views. For this reason, it is necessary at the very start to add a complete auxiliary view to the space diagram that will combine with the existing top view to give a point view of one member and a line view of two of the three unknown forces. To obtain this desired situation, one should start with the following steps, which will transform the general case into the special case with which one should now be familiar.

Step 1. Draw a true length line in the plane of two of the members. In Fig. 10.49(a) this line is DE, which appears in true length (TL) in the H-view.

Step 2. Draw the needed auxiliary view, taken so that DE will appear as a point ($d^A e^A$) and OB and OC will be coincident (line $o^A b^A c^A$). This construction involves finding the edge view of a plane (see Sec. 10.13). In this particular case, the auxiliary view has height in common with the frontal view.

Step 3. Draw the two views of the vector diagram by assuming the H-view and the A-view to be the given views of the special case. Proceed by the steps set forth for the special case in Sec. 10.38.

Step 4. Determine the magnitude of the forces and add arrowheads to the free-body diagram to show the direction of action of the forces acting on point O.

ing lines representing the forces in AD and the resultant R. These lines are drawn parallel to their known lines of action as shown in the F-view of the space diagram in (a). Finally, the true length view of R must be transferred to the auxiliary view in (a) and resolved into its component forces, acting in AB and AC, that collectively have the same action as the resultant R.

10.40
To Find the Three Unknown Forces of a Simple Load-Bearing Truss—General Case. For the general case shown in Fig. 10.49,

10.41
In practice, engineers and technologists find wide use for methods that solve problems through the use of three-dimensional vector diagrams, for any quantity having both magnitude and direction may be represented by a vector. And, although the examples used in the chapter dealt

with static structures, which are in the field of the structural engineer, vector diagram methods are used frequently by the electrical engineer for solving problems arising in his field and by the mechanical engineer for problems dealing with bodies in motion. The student will without doubt encounter some of these methods in a textbook for a later course or will have them presented to him by his instructor.

PROBLEMS—DESCRIPTIVE GEOMETRY

Problems 1 through 5 have been selected and arranged to offer the student an opportunity to apply basic principles of descriptive geometry.
The problems can be reproduced to a suitable size by transferring the needed distances from the drawing to the scale that has been provided for each group of problems.

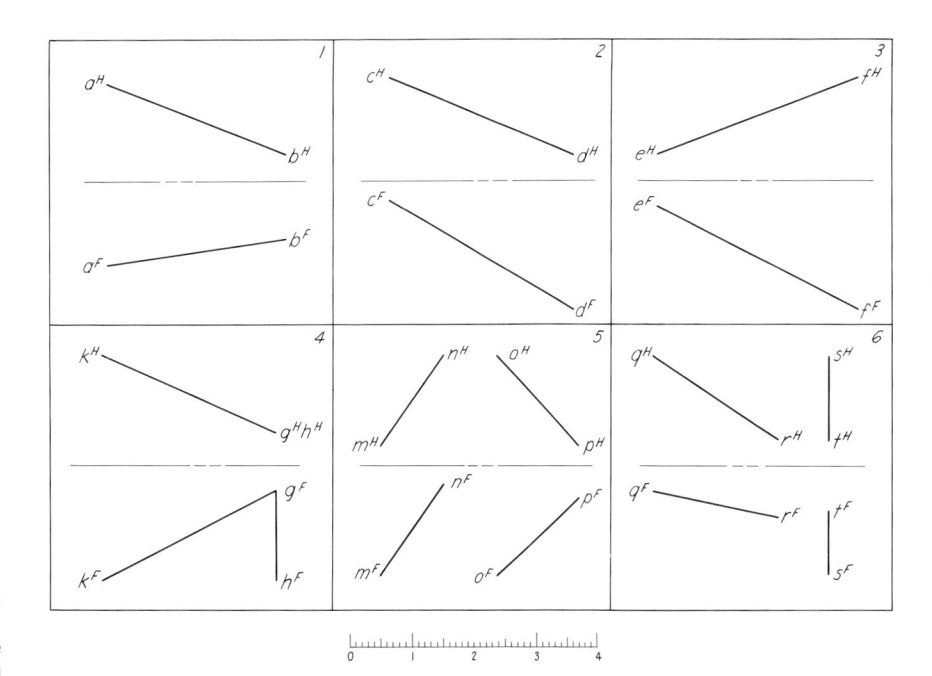

FIG. 10.50. True length of a line.

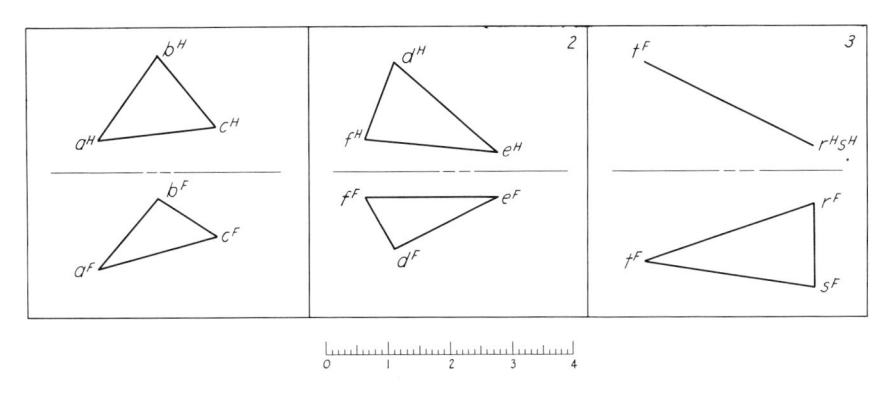

FIG. 10.51. True size and shape of a plane.

1. (Fig. 10.50). Reproduce the given views of the line or lines of a problem as assigned and determine the true length or lengths using the auxiliary view method explained in Sec. 10.7. A problem may be reproduced to a suitable size by transferring the needed distances from the drawing to the given scale to determine values. The distances, as they are determined, should be laid off on the drawing paper using a full-size scale.

2. (Fig. 10.51). Reproduce the given views of the plane of a problem as assigned and draw the view showing the true size and shape. Use the method explained in Sec. 10.14. Determine needed distances by transferring them from the drawing to the accompanying scale, by means of the dividers.

3. (Fig. 10.52). These problems are intended to give some needed practice in manipulating views to obtain certain relationships of points and lines. Determine needed distances by transferring them from the drawing to the accompanying scale, by means of the dividers.

1. Determine the distance between points A and B.
2. Draw the H- and F-views of a $\frac{1}{2}$-in. perpendicular erected from point N of the line MN.
3. Draw the H-view of the $3\frac{3}{4}$-in. line ST.
4. Draw the H- and F-views of a plane represented by an equilateral triangle and containing line AB as one of the edges. The added plane ABC is to be at an angle of 30° with plane $ABDE$.
5. If the figure $MNOP$ is a plane surface, an edge view of the surface would appear as a line. Draw such a view to determine whether or not $MNOP$ is a plane.
6. A vertical pole with top O is held in place by three guy wires. Determine the slope in tangent value of the angle for the guy wire that has a bearing of N 23° W.

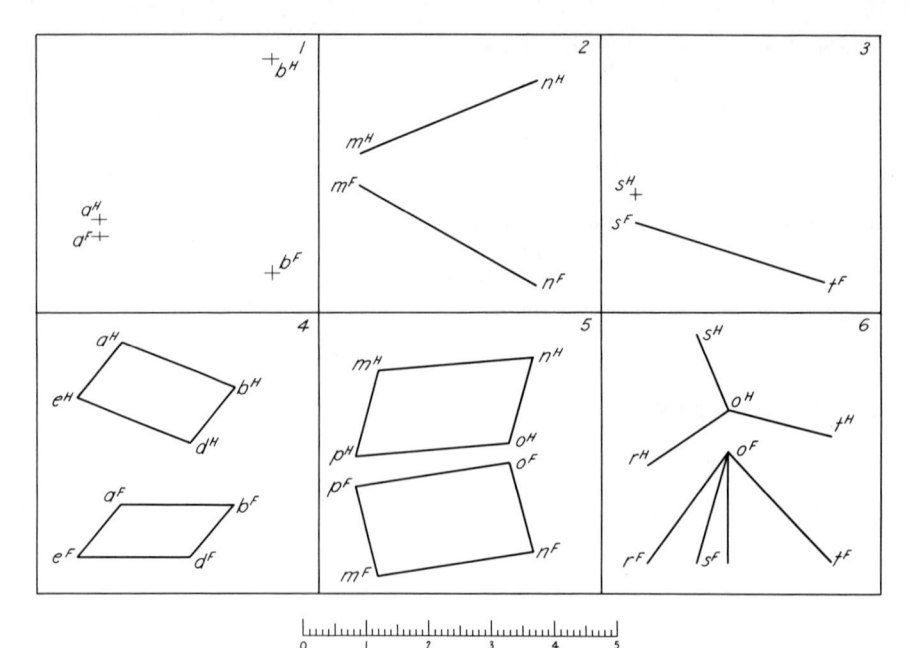

FIG. 10.52. Relationships of points and lines.

4. (Fig. 10.53). In this group of problems it is required to determine the shortest distance between skew lines and the angle formed by intersecting lines.

1. Show proof that the plane $ABCD$ is an oblique plane.
2. Determine the shortest distance between the lines MN and ST.
3. Through point K on line GH draw the F- and H-views of a line that will be perpendicular to line EF.
4. Determine the angle between line AB and a line intersecting AB and CD at the level of point E.
5. Through a point on line MN that is $1\frac{1}{4}$ in. from point N, draw the F- and H-views of a line that will be perpendicular to line ST.
6. Erect a 1-in. perpendicular at point K in the plane $EFGH$. Connect the outer end point L of the perpendicular with F. Determine the angle between LF and KF.

5. (Fig. 10.54). These problems require that the student determine the angle between a line and a plane and the angle between two given planes.

1. Determine the angle between the planes $MNQP$ and RST.
2. Determine the angle between the line ST and
   (a) The H-plane.
   (b) The F-plane.
3. The line EF has a bearing of N 53° E. What angle does this line make with the P-plane?
4. Draw the F- and H-views of a line through point K that forms an angle of 35° with plane $MNQR$.
5. The top and front views of planes ABC and RST are partially drawn.
   (a) Complete the views including the line of intersection.
   (b) Determine the angle between the line of intersection and the H-plane of projection.
6. Two views of a plane RST and the top view of an arrow are shown. The arrow, pointing downward and toward the left, is in a plane that forms an angle of 68° with plane RST. The arrow point is $\frac{1}{4}$ in. from the place RST.
   (a) Draw the front view of the arrow.
   (b) Draw the top and front views of the line of intersection of the 68° plane and plane RST.

211

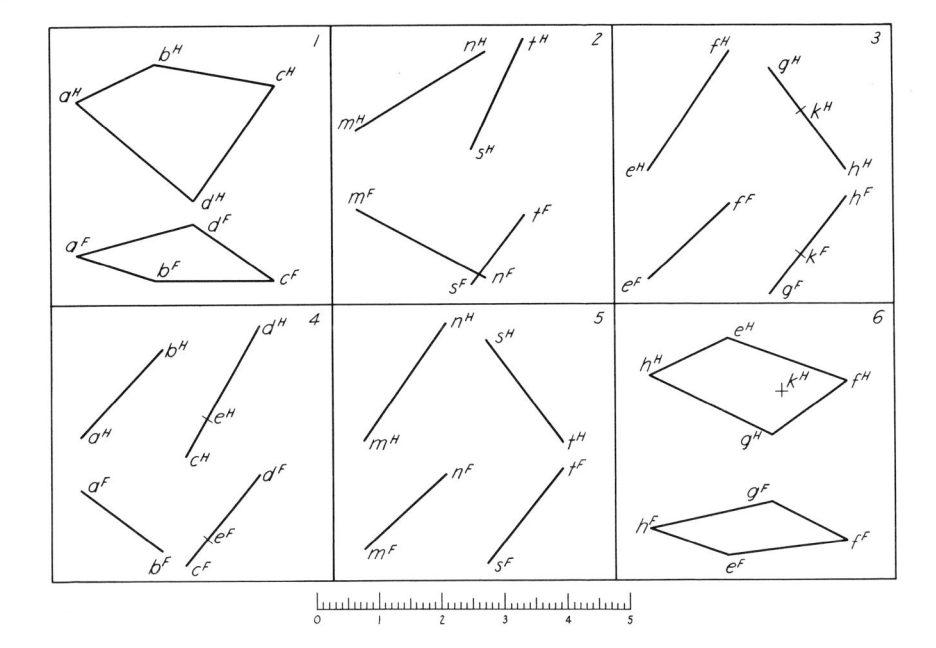

FIG. 10.53. Shortest distance between skew lines and the angle formed by intersecting lines.

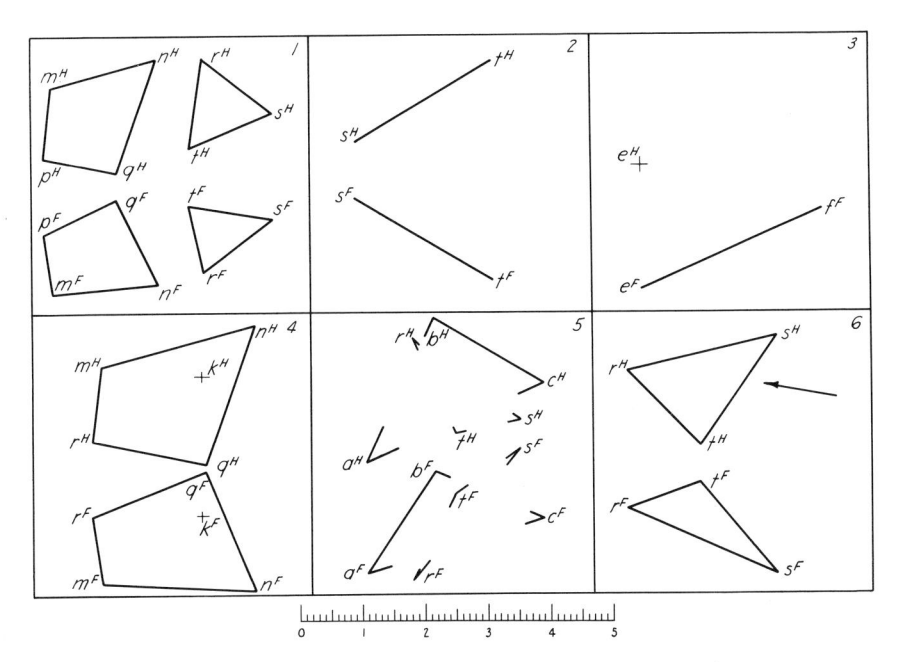

FIG. 10.54. Angle between a line and a plane and the angle between two planes.

PROBLEMS— VECTOR GEOMETRY

The following problems have been selected to emphasize the basic principles underlying vector geometry. By solving a limited number of the problems presented, the student should find that he has a working knowledge of some vector methods that are useful for solving problems in design that involve the determination of the magnitude of forces as well as their composition and resolution. The student is to select his own scale remembering that a drawing made to a large scale usually assures more accurate results.

1. (Fig. 10.55). A force of 900 lb acts downward at an angle of 60° with the horizontal. Determine the vertical and horizontal components of this force.

2. (Fig. 10.56). Determine the resultant force for the given coplanar, concurrent force system.

3. (Fig. 10.57). Determine the magnitude of the force F_C and the angle that the resultant force R makes with the horizontal for the given coplanar, concurrent force system.

4. (Fig. 10.58). Determine the magnitude and direction of the equilibrant for the given coplanar, concurrent force system.

5. (Fig. 10.59). A block weighing 45 lb is to be pulled up an inclined plane sloping at an angle of 30° with the horizontal. If the frictional resistance is 16 lb, what is the magnitude of the force F_M that is required to move the block uniformly up the plane?

6. (Fig. 10.60). A horizontal beam AB is hinged at B as shown. The end of the beam at A is connected by a cable to a hook in the wall at C. The load at A is 250 lb. Using the dimensions as given, determine the tension force in the cable and the reaction on the hinge at B. The weight of the beam is to be neglected.

7. (Fig. 10.61). A 600 lb load is supported by cables as shown. Determine the magnitude of the tension in the cables.

8. (Fig. 10.62). A ship that is being pulled through the entrance of a harbor is headed due

FIG. 10.55.

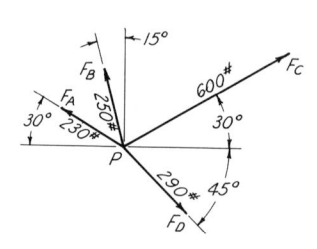

FIG. 10.56.

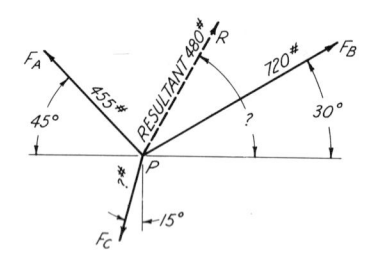

FIG. 10.57.

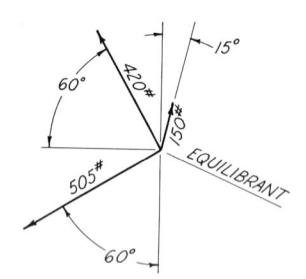

FIG. 10.58.

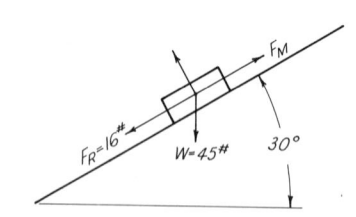

FIG. 10.59.

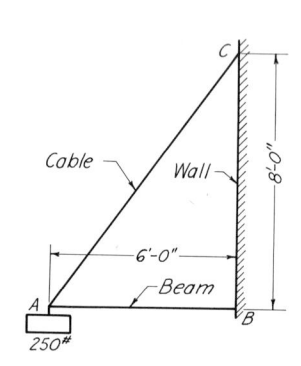

FIG. 10.60.

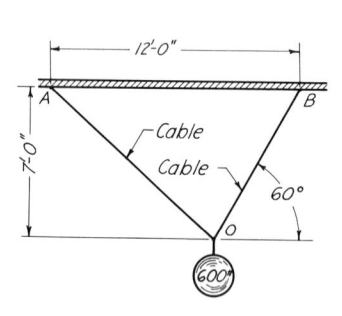

FIG. 10.61.

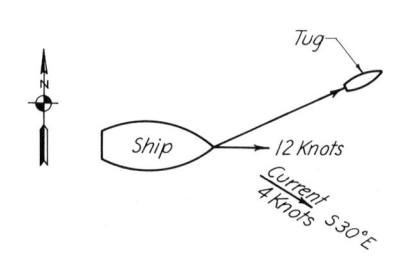

FIG. 10.62.

east through a cross current moving at 4 knots as shown. If the ship is moving at 12 knots, what is the speed of the tug boat?

9. (Fig. 10.63). Determine the magnitude of the reactions R_1 and R_2 of the beam with loads as shown.

10. (Fig. 10.64). Determine the magnitude of the reactions R_1 and R_2 of the beam.

11. (Fig. 10.65). Determine the magnitude of the reactions R_1 and R_2 for the roof truss shown. Each of the six panels is of the same length.

12. (Fig. 10.66). Determine the magnitude of the reactions R_1 and R_2 to the wind loads acting on the roof truss as shown.

13. (Fig. 10.67). A tripod with an 85 lb load is set up on a level floor as shown. Determine the stresses in the three legs due to the vertical load on the top.

14-15. (Figs. 10.68–10.69). Determine the stresses in the members of the space frame shown.

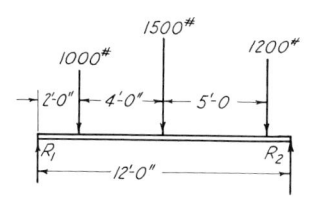

FIG. 10.63.

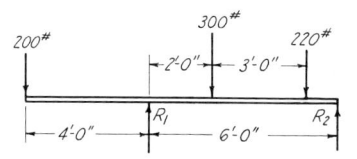

FIG. 10.64.

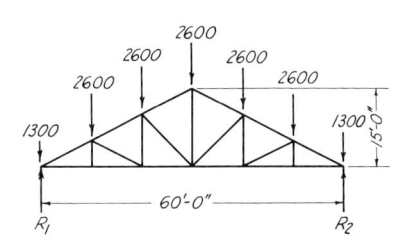

FIG. 10.65.

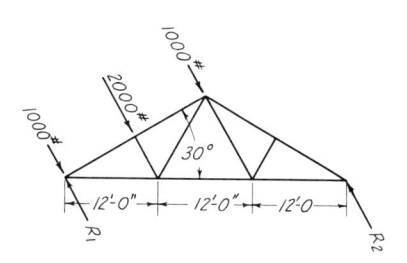

FIG. 10.66.

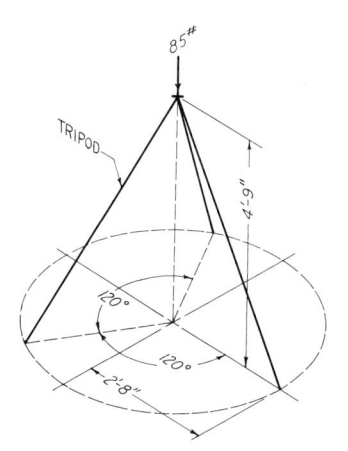

FIG. 10.67.

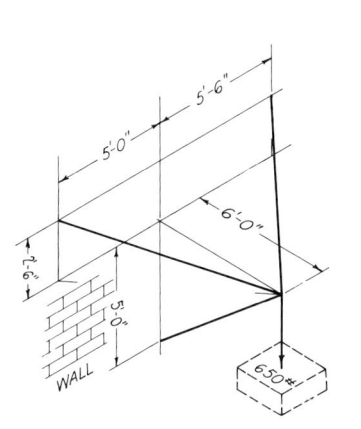

FIG. 10.68.

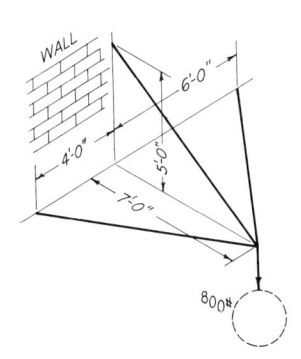

FIG. 10.69.

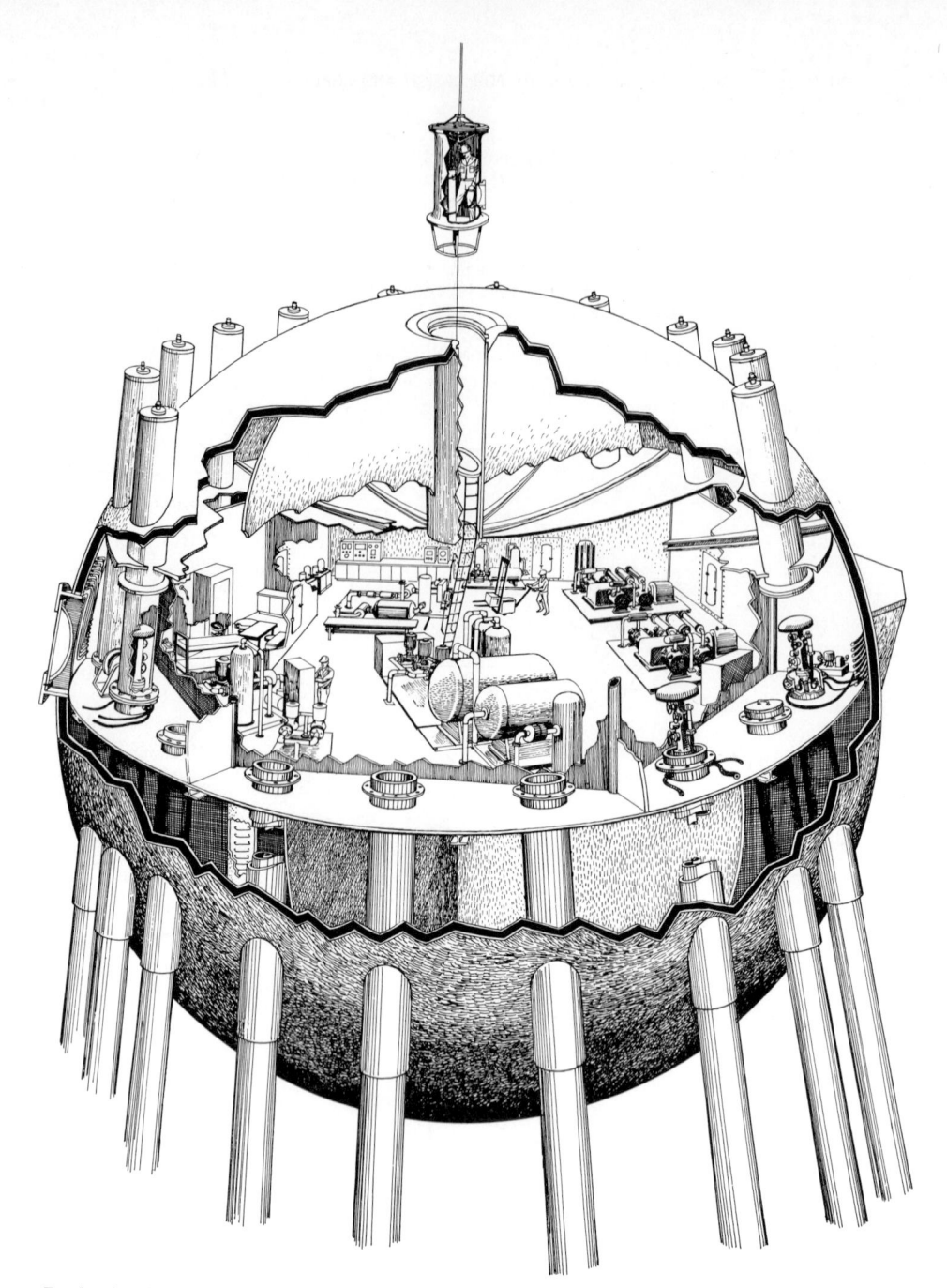

The Underwater Production System illustrated above represents a new approach to solving the critical problems of offshore oil recovery. This system is being developed by Ocean Systems, Inc., for rather deep water (over 300 feet). The pictorial representation shows a personnel-transfer capsule being lowered into the 80-foot sphere.

In the development of the spherical capsule and its related components, many of the problems involving intersections between geometric shapes may be solved by the graphical methods of projection that have been presented in Chapter 11. (*Courtesy of Design News and Ocean Systems, Inc. an affiliate of Union Carbide Corp.*)

Developments and Intersections

11.1
Introduction. Intersections and developments are logically a part of the subject of descriptive geometry. A few of the many applications that can be handled without advanced study in projection, however, are presented in this chapter.

Desired lines of intersection between geometric surfaces may be obtained by applying the principles of projection with which the student is already familiar. Although developments are laid out and are not drawn by actual projection in the manner of exterior views, their construction nevertheless requires the application of orthographic projection in finding the true lengths of elements and edges.

11.2
Geometric Surfaces. A geometric surface is generated by the motion of a geometric line, either straight or curved. Surfaces that are generated by a moving straight line are known as *ruled surfaces,* and those generated by a curved line are known as *double-curved surfaces.* Any position of the generating line, known as a *generatrix,* is called an *element of the surface.*

Ruled surfaces include planes, single-curved surfaces, and warped surfaces. A *plane* is generated by a straight line moving in such a manner that one point touches another straight line as it moves parallel to its original position.

A *single-curved surface* is generated by a straight line moving so that in any two of its near positions it is in the same plane.

A *warped surface* is generated by a straight line moving so that it does not lie in the same plane in any two near positions.

Double-curved surfaces include surfaces that are generated by a curved line moving in accordance with some mathematical law.

11.3
Geometric Objects. Geometric solids are bounded by geometric surfaces. They may be classified as follows:

1. Solids bounded by plane surfaces: Tetrahedron, cube, prism, pyramid, and others.

2. Solids bounded by single-curved surfaces: Cone and cylinder (generated by a moving straight line).

3. Solids bounded by warped surfaces: Conoid, cylindroid, hyperboloid of one nappe, and warped cone.

4. Solids bounded by double-curved surfaces: Sphere, spheroid, torus, paraboloid, hyperboloid, and so on (surfaces of revolution generated by curved lines).

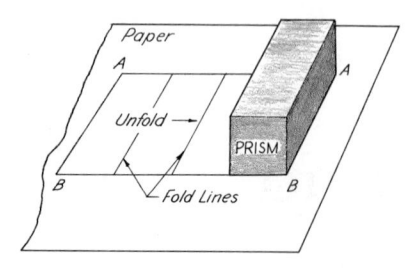

FIG. 11.1. The development of a prism.

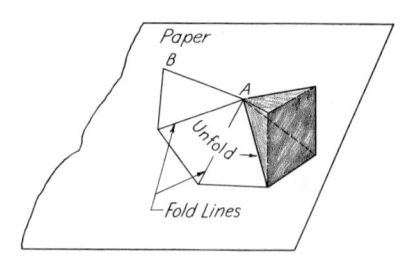

FIG. 11.2. The development of a pyramid.

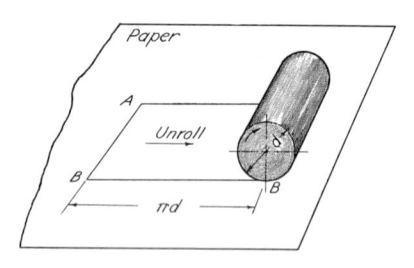

FIG. 11.3. The development of a cylinder.

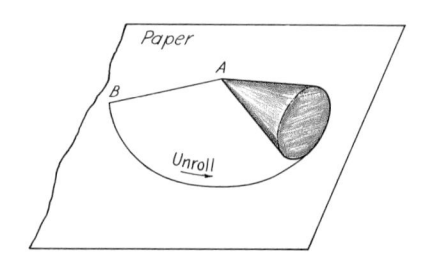

FIG. 11.4. The development of a cone.

A: DEVELOPMENTS

11.4
Introduction. A layout of the complete surface of an object is called a *development* or *pattern*. The development of an object bounded by plane surfaces may be thought of as being obtained by turning the object, as illustrated in Figs. 11.1 and 11.2, to unroll the imaginary enclosing surface on a plane. Practically, the drawing operation consists of drawing the successive surfaces in their true size with their common edges joined.

The surfaces of cones and cylinders also may be unrolled on a plane. The development of a right cylinder (Fig. 11.3) is a rectangle having a width equal to the altitude of the cylinder and a length equal to the cylinder's computed circumference (πd). The development of a right circular cone (Fig. 11.4) is a sector of a circle having a radius equal to the slant height of the cone and an arc length equal to the circumference of its base.

Warped and double-curved surfaces cannot be developed accurately, but they may be developed by some approximate method. Ordinarily, an approximate pattern will prove to be sufficiently accurate for practical purposes if the material of which the piece is to be made is somewhat flexible.

Plane and single-curved surfaces (prisms, pyramids, cylinders, and cones), which can be accurately developed, are said to be developable. Warped and double-curved surfaces, which can be only approximately developed, are said to be nondevelopable.

11.5
Practical Developments. On many industrial drawings, a development must be shown to furnish the necessary information for making a pattern to facilitate the cutting of a desired shape from sheet metal. Because of the rapid advance of the art of manufacturing an ever-increasing number of pieces by folding, rolling, or pressing cut sheet-metal shapes, one must have a broad knowledge of the methods of constructing varied types of developments. Patterns also are used in stonecutting as guides for shaping irregular faces.

A development of a surface should be drawn with the inside face up, as it theoretically would be if the surface were unrolled or unfolded, as illustrated in Figs. 11.1–11.4. This practice is further justified because sheet-metal workers must make the necessary punch marks for folding on the inside surface.

Although in actual sheet-metal work extra metal must be allowed for lap at seams, no allowance will be shown on the developments in this chapter. Many other practical considerations have been purposely ignored, as well, in order to avoid confusing the beginner.

11.6
To Develop a Right Truncated Prism. Before the development of the lateral surface of a prism can be drawn, the true lengths of the edges and the true size of a right section must be determined. On the right truncated prism, shown in Fig. 11.5, the true lengths of the prism edges are shown in the front view and the true size of the right section is shown in the top view.

The lateral surface is "unfolded" by first drawing a "stretch-out line" and marking off the widths of the faces (distances 1–2, 2–3, 3–4, and so on, from the top view) along it in succession. Through these points light construction lines are then drawn perpendicular to the line $1_D 1_D$, and the length of the respective edge is set off on each by projecting from the front view. When projecting edge lengths to the development, the points should be taken in a clockwise order around the perimeter, as indicated by the order of the numbers in the top view. The outline of the devel-

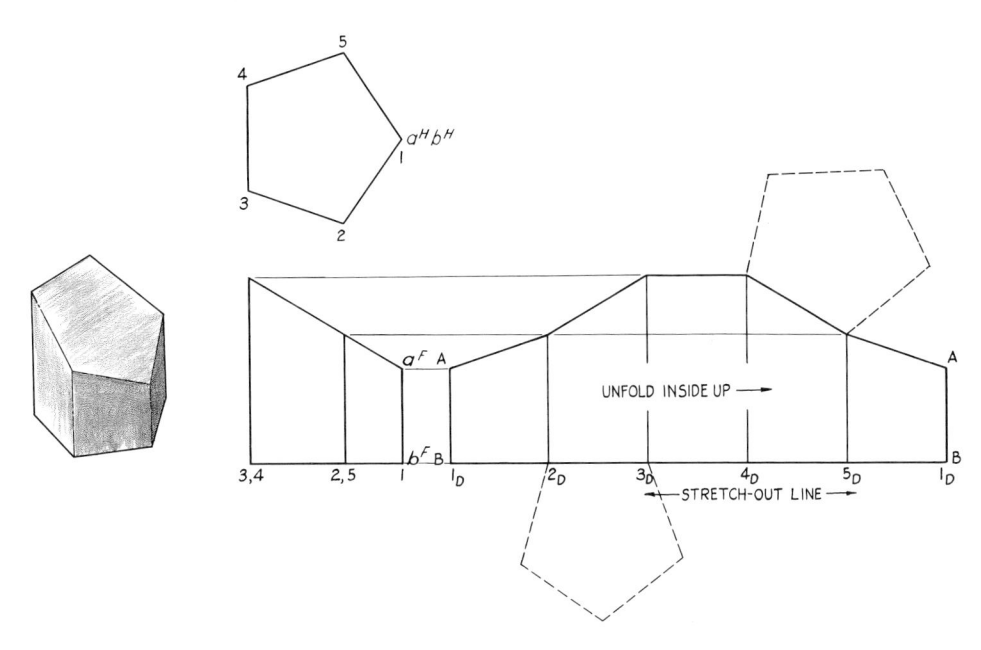

FIG. 11.5. The standard method of developing the lateral surface of a right prism.

opment is completed by joining these points. Thus far, nothing has been said about the lower base or the inclined upper face. These may be joined to the development of the lateral surface, if so desired.

In sheet-metal work, it is usual practice to make the seam on the shortest element in order to save time and conserve solder or rivets.

11.7
To Develop an Oblique Prism. The lateral surface of an oblique prism, such as the one shown in Fig. 11.6, is developed by the same general method used for a right prism. Similarly, the true lengths of the edges are shown in the front view, but it is necessary to find the true size of the right section by auxiliary plane construction. The widths of the faces, as taken from the auxiliary right section, are set off along the stretch-out line, and perpendicular construction lines representing the edges are drawn through the division points. The lengths of the portions of each respective edge, above and below plane XX, are transferred to the corresponding line in development. Distances above plane XX are laid off above the stretch-out line, and distances below XX are laid off below it. The development of the lateral surface is then completed by joining the end points of the edges by straight lines. Since an actual fold will be made at each edge line when the prism is formed, it is the usual practice to heavy these edge (fold) lines on the development.

The stretch-out line might well have been drawn in a position perpendicular to the edges of the front view, so that the length of each edge might be projected to the development (as in the case of the right prism).

11.8
To Develop a Right Cylinder. When the lateral surface of a right cylinder is rolled

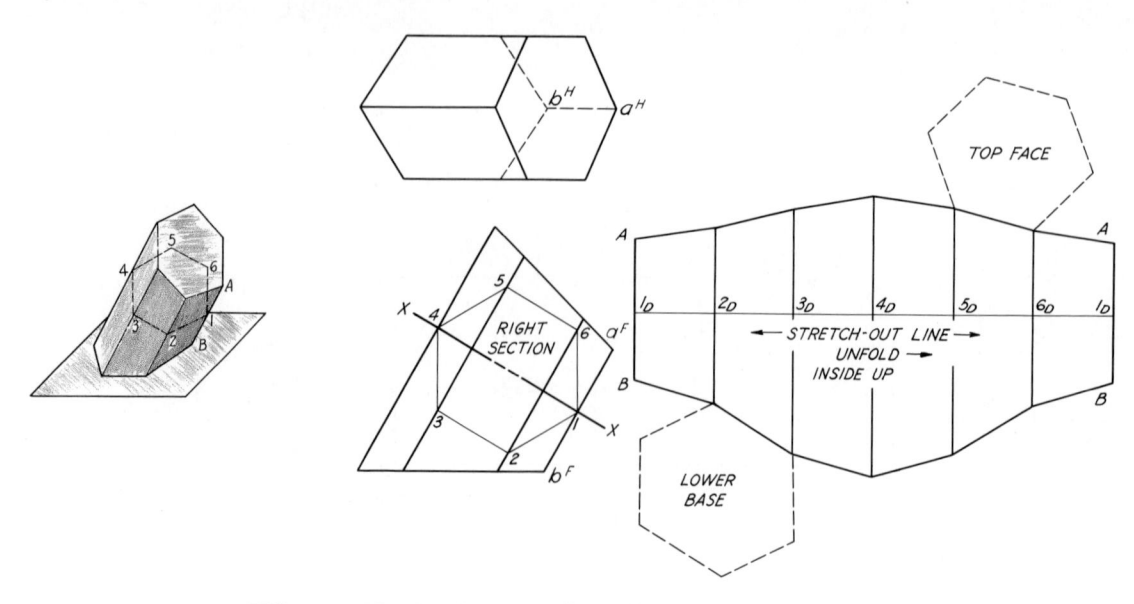

FIG. 11.6. The development of an oblique prism.

out on a plane, the base develops into a straight line (Fig. 11.7). The length of this line, which is equal to the circumference of a right section ($\pi \times$ diam), may be calculated and laid off as the stretch-out line $1_D 1_D$.

Since the cylinder can be thought of as being a many-sided prism, the develop-

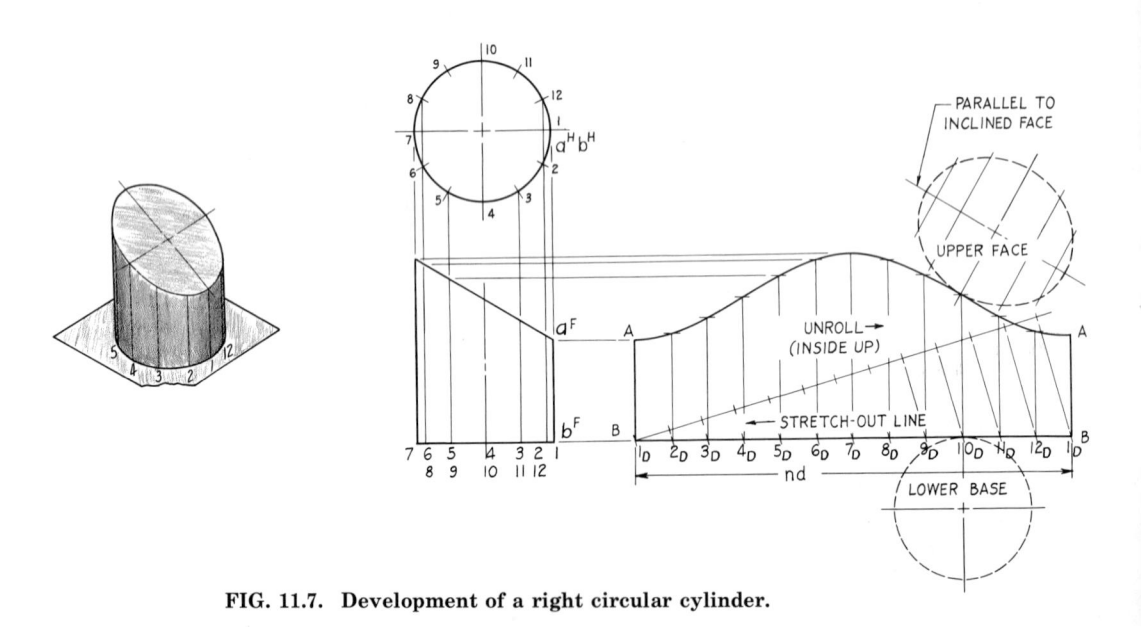

FIG. 11.7. Development of a right circular cylinder.

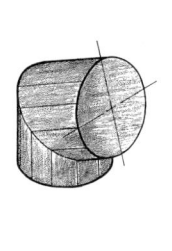

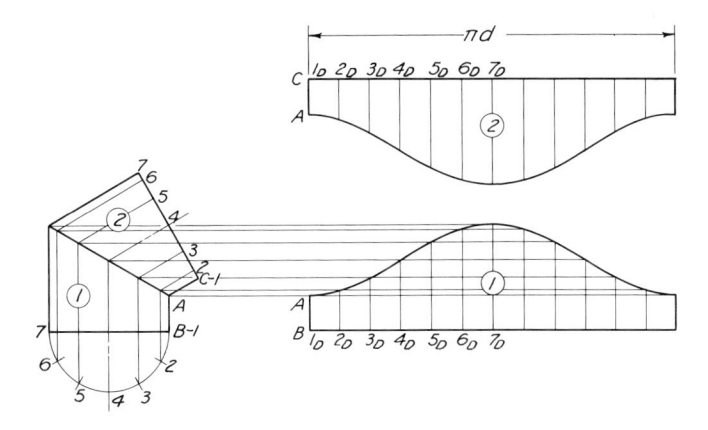

FIG. 11.8. Two-piece elbow.

ment may be constructed in a manner similar to the method illustrated in Fig. 11.5. The elements drawn on the surface of the cylinder serve as edges of the many-sided prism. Twelve or twenty-four of these elements ordinarily are used, the number depending on the size of the cylinder. Usually they are spaced by dividing the circumference of the base, as shown by the circle in the top view, into an equal number of parts. The stretch-out line is divided into the same number of equal parts, and perpendicular elements are drawn through each division point. Then the true length of each element is projected to its respective representation on the development, and the development is completed by joining the points with a smooth curve. In joining the points, it is advisable to sketch the curve in lightly, freehand, before using the French curve. Since the surface of the finished cylindrical piece forms a continuous curve, the elements on the development are not heavied. When the development is symmetrical, as in this case, only one-half need be drawn.

A piece of this type might form a part of a two-piece, three-piece, or four-piece elbow. The pieces are usually developed as illustrated in Fig. 11.8. The stretch-out line of each section is equal in length to the computed perimeter of a right section.

11.9
To Develop an Oblique Cylinder. Since an oblique cylinder theoretically may be thought of as enclosing a regular oblique prism having an infinite number of sides, the development of the lateral surface of the cylinder shown in Fig. 11.9 may be constructed by using a method similar to the method illustrated in Fig. 11.6. The circumference of the right section becomes stretch-out line $1_D 1_D$ for the development.

11.10
To Determine the True Length of a Line. In order to construct the development of the lateral surface of some objects, it frequently is necessary to determine the true lengths of oblique lines that represent the edges. The general method for determining the true lengths of lines inclined to all of the coordinate planes of projection has been explained in detail in Sec. 6.29. This article should be reviewed before reading the discussion that follows.

If a line is oblique to each of the three planes of projection, none of its principal projections will show its true length. Note

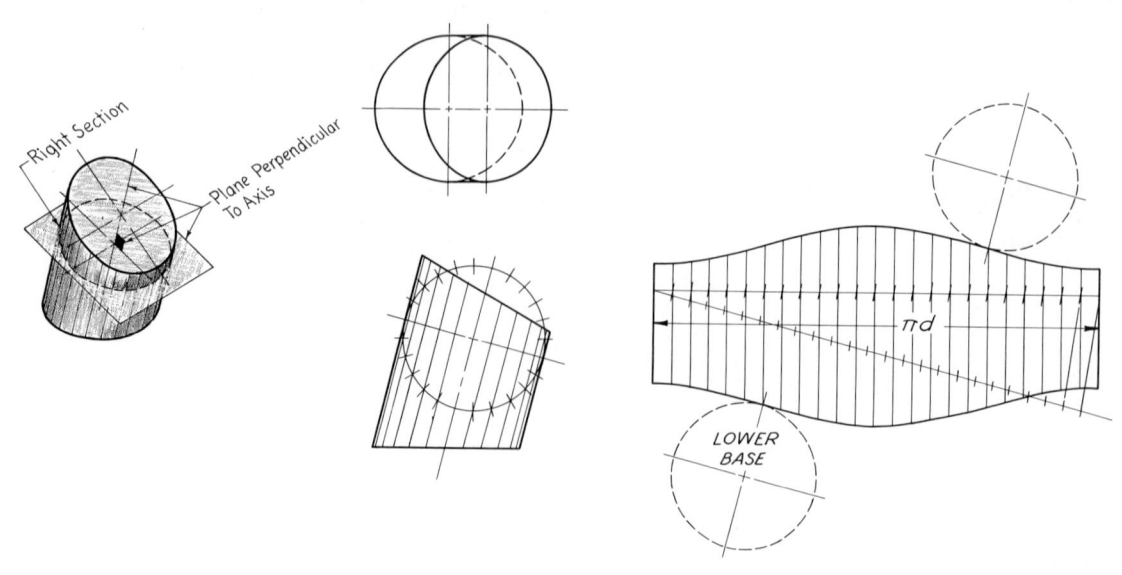

FIG. 11.9. Development of an oblique cylinder.

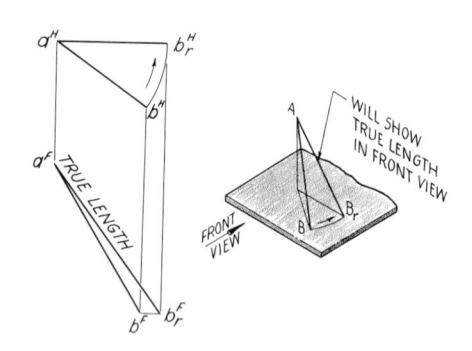

FIG. 11.10. Revolution to position parallel to frontal plane.

in Fig. 11.10 that the principal projections of the line AB are inclined. To determine the true length of AB, it may be revolved into a position parallel to either the F, H, or P coordinate planes, as shown in Figs. 11.10, 11.11, and 11.12. In Fig. 11.10, AB has been revolved into a position parallel to the F (frontal) plane. The view of AB revolved, $a^F b^F r$, shows the true length. In Fig. 11.11, AB was revolved parallel to the H (top) plane, and $a^H b^H r$ shows the true length. In Fig. 11.12, the line is shown revolved parallel to the P (profile) coordinate plane.

11.11
True-length Diagrams. When it is necessary in developing a surface to find the true lengths of a number of edges or elements, some confusion may be avoided by constructing a true-length diagram adjacent to the orthographic view, as shown

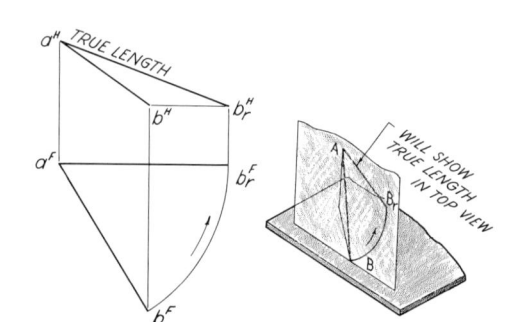

FIG. 11.11. Revolution to position parallel to horizontal plane.

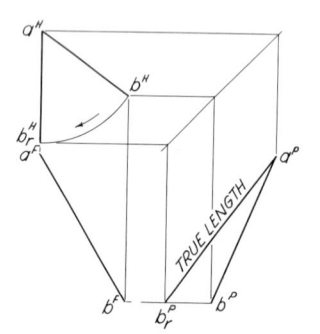

FIG. 11.12. Revolution to position parallel to profile plane.

in Fig. 11.13. The elements were revolved into a position parallel to the F (frontal) plane so that their true lengths show in the diagram. This practice prevents the front view in the illustration from being cluttered with lines, some of which would represent elements and others their true lengths.

Figure 11.15 shows a diagram that gives the true lengths of the edges of the pyramid. Each line representing the true length of an edge is the hypotenuse of a right triangle whose altitude is the altitude of the edge in the front view and whose base is equal to the length of the projection of the edge in the top view. The lengths of the top projections of the edges of the pyramid are laid off horizontally from the vertical line, which could have been drawn at any distance from the front view. Since all the edges have the same altitude, this line is a common vertical leg for all the right triangles in the diagram. The true-length diagram shown in Fig. 11.13 could very well have been constructed by this method.

11.12
To Develop a Right Pyramid. To develop (unfold) the lateral surface of a right pyramid, it is first necessary to determine the true lengths of the edges and the true size of the base. With this information, the development can be constructed by laying out the faces in successive order with their common edges joined. If the surface is imagined to be unfolded by turning the pyramid, as shown in Fig. 11.2, each triangular face is revolved into the plane of the paper about the edge that is common to it and the preceding face.

Since the edges of the pyramid shown in Fig. 11.14 are all equal in length, it is necessary only to find the length of the one edge $A1$ by revolving it into the position $a^F 1r$. The edges of the base, 1–2, 2–3, and so on, are parallel to the horizontal plane of projection and conse-

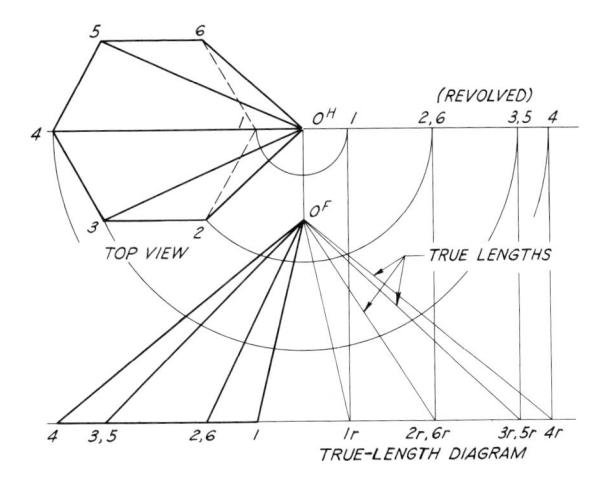

FIG. 11.13. A true-length diagram (the revolution method).

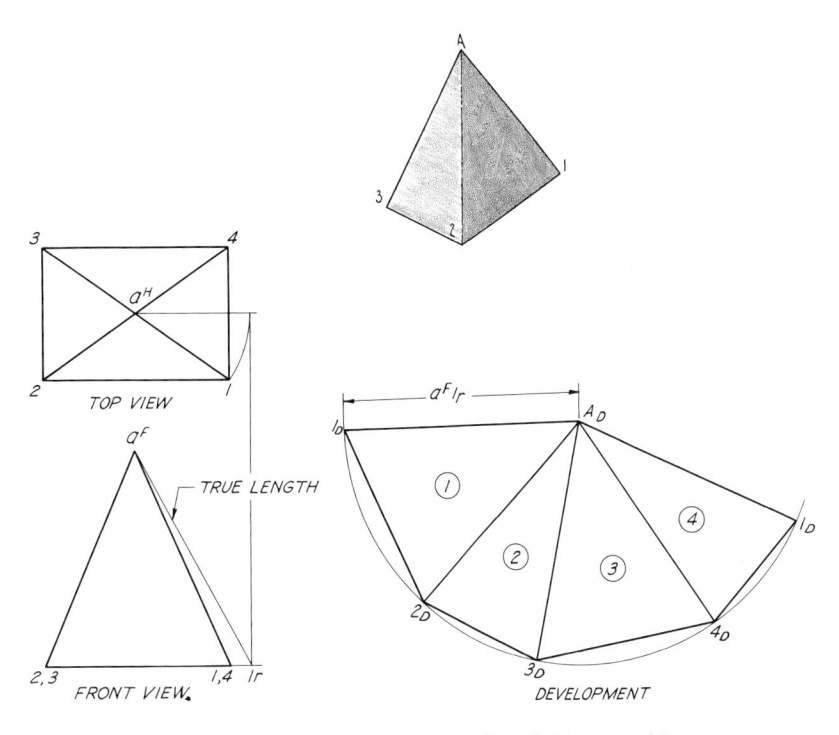

FIG. 11.14. The development of a rectangular right pyramid.

quently show in their true length in the top view. With this information, the development is easily completed by constructing the four triangular surfaces.

11.13
To Develop the Surface of a Frustum of a Pyramid. To develop the lateral surface of the frustum of a pyramid (Fig. 11.15), it is necessary to determine the true lengths of edges of the complete pyramid as well as the true lengths of edges of the frustum. The desired development is obtained by first constructing the development of the complete pyramid and then laying off the true lengths of the edges of the frustum on the corresponding lines of the development.

It may be noted with interest that the true length of the edge $B3$ is equal to the length $b'3'$ on the true-length line a^F3' and that the location of point b' can be established by the shortcut method of projecting horizontally from point b^F. Point b' on a^F3' is the true revolved position of point B, because the path of point B is in a horizontal plane that projects as a line in the front view.

11.14
To Develop a Right Cone. As previously explained in Sec. 11.4, the development of a regular right circular cone is a sector of a circle. The development will have a radius equal to the slant height of the cone and an included angle at the center equal to $(r/s) \times 360°$ (Fig. 11.16). In this equation, r is the radius of the base and s is the slant height.

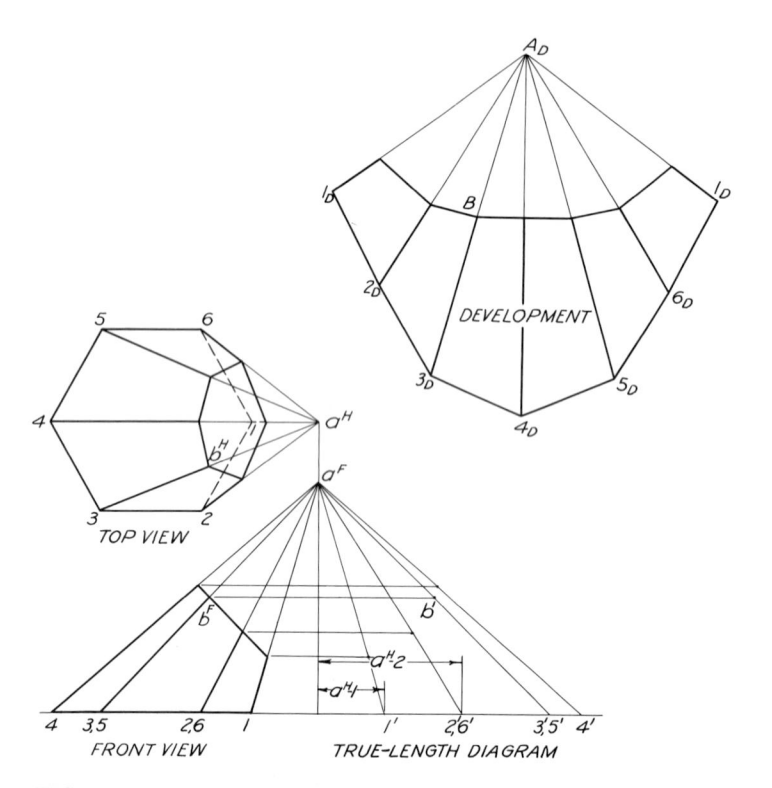

FIG. 11.15. Development of the frustum of a pyramid.

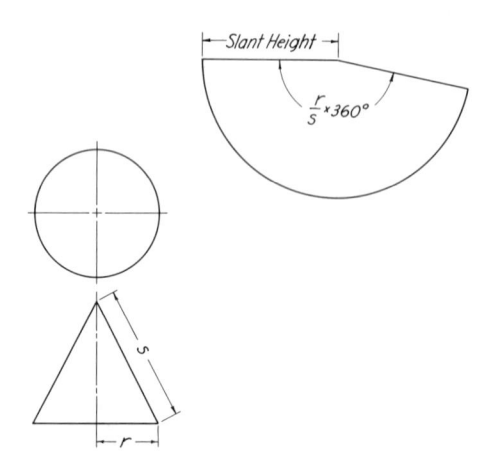

FIG. 11.16. Development of a right cone.

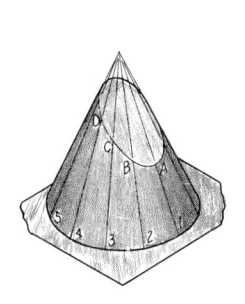

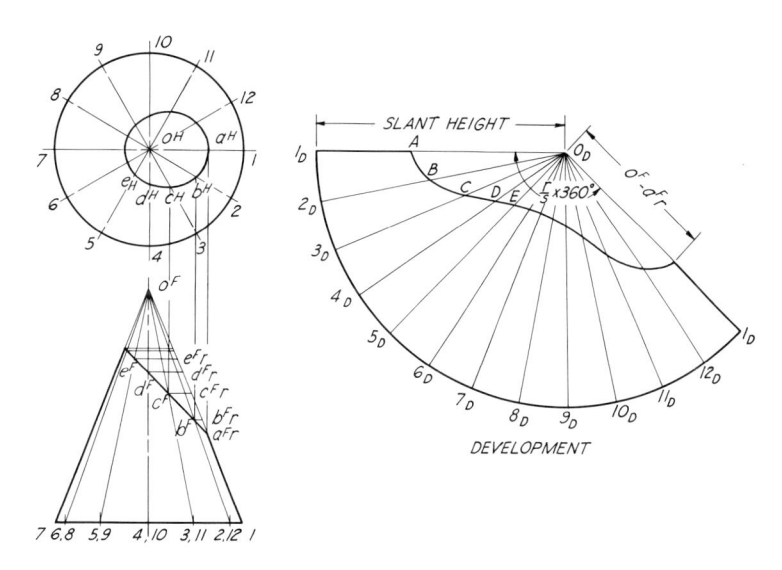

FIG. 11.17. Development of a truncated cone.

11.15
To Develop a Right Truncated Cone. The development of a right truncated cone must be constructed by a modified method of triangulation, in order to develop the outline of the elliptical inclined surface. This commonly used method is based on the theoretical assumption that a cone is a pyramid having an infinite number of sides. The development of the incomplete right cone shown in Fig. 11.17 is constructed on a layout of the whole cone by a method similar to the standard method illustrated for the frustum of a pyramid in Fig. 11.15.

Elements are drawn on the surface of the cone to serve as edges of the many-sided pyramid. Either 12 or 24 are used, depending on the size of the cone. Their location is established on the developed sector by dividing the arc representing the unrolled base into the same number of equal divisions, into which the top view of the base has been divided. At this point in the procedure, it is necessary to determine the true lengths of the elements of the frustum in the same manner that the true lengths of the edges of the frustum of a pyramid were obtained in Fig. 11.15. With this information, the desired development can be completed by setting off the true lengths on the corresponding lines of the development and joining the points thus obtained with a smooth curve.

11.16
The Triangulation Method of Developing Approximately Developable Surfaces. A nondevelopable surface may be developed approximately if the surface is assumed to be composed of a number of small developable surfaces (Fig. 11.18). The particular method ordinarily used for warped surfaces and the surfaces of oblique cones is known as the *triangulation method*. The procedure consists of completely covering the lateral surface with numerous small triangles that will lie approximately on the surface (Fig. 11.19). These triangles, when laid out in their true size with their common edges joined, produce an approximate development that is

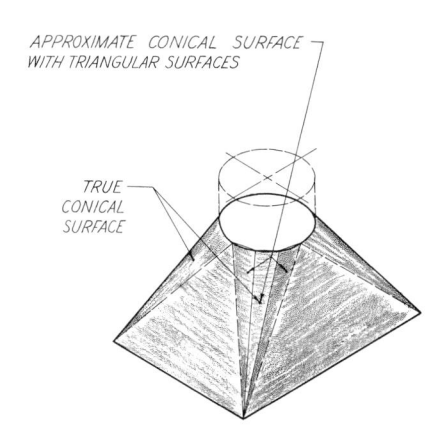

FIG. 11.18. Triangulation of a surface.

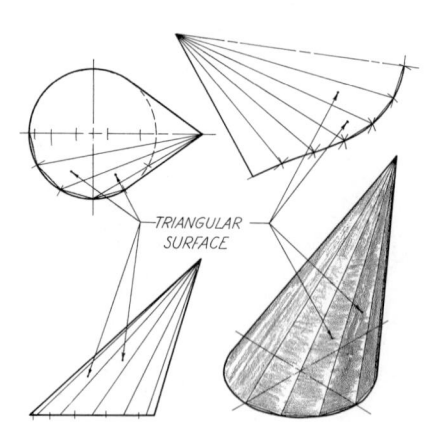

FIG. 11.19. Triangulation of an oblique cone.

accurate enough for most practical purposes.

Although this method of triangulation is sometimes used to develop the lateral surface of a right circular cone, it is not recommended for such a purpose. The resulting development is not as accurate as it would be if constructed by one of the standard methods (Secs. 11.14 and 11.15).

11.17
To Develop an Oblique Cone Using the Triangulation Method. A development of the lateral surface of an oblique cone is constructed by a method similar to that used for an oblique pyramid. The surface is divided into a number of unequal triangles having sides that are elements on the cone and bases that are the chords of short arcs of the base.

The first step in developing an oblique cone (Fig. 11.20) is to divide the circle representing the base into a convenient number of equal parts and draw elements on the surface of the cone through the division points (1, 2, 3, 4, 5, and so on). To construct the triangles forming the development, it is necessary to know the true lengths of the elements (sides of the triangles) and chords. In the illustration, all the chords are equal. Their true lengths are shown in the top view. The true lengths of the oblique elements may be determined by one of the standard methods explained in Sec. 11.11.

Since the seam should be made along the shortest element, $A1$ will lie on the selected starting line for the development and $A7$ will be on the center line. To obtain the development, the triangles are constructed in order, starting with the triangle A-1-2 and proceeding around the cone in a clockwise direction (as shown by the arrow in the top view). The first step in constructing triangle A-1-2 is to set off the true length a^F1' along the starting line. With point A_D of the development as a center, and with a radius equal to a^F2', strike an arc; then, with point 1_D as a center, and with a radius equal to the chord 1-2, strike an arc across the first arc to locate point 2_D. The triangle $A_D2_D3_D$ and the remaining triangles are formed in exactly the same manner. When all the triangles have been laid out, the development of the whole conical surface is completed by drawing a smooth curve through the end points of the elements.

11.18
Transition Pieces. A few of the many types of transition pieces used for connecting pipes and openings of different shapes and sizes are illustrated pictorially in Fig. 11.21.

11.19
To Develop a Transition Piece Connecting Rectangular Pipes. The transition piece shown in Fig. 11.22 is designed to connect two rectangular pipes of different sizes on

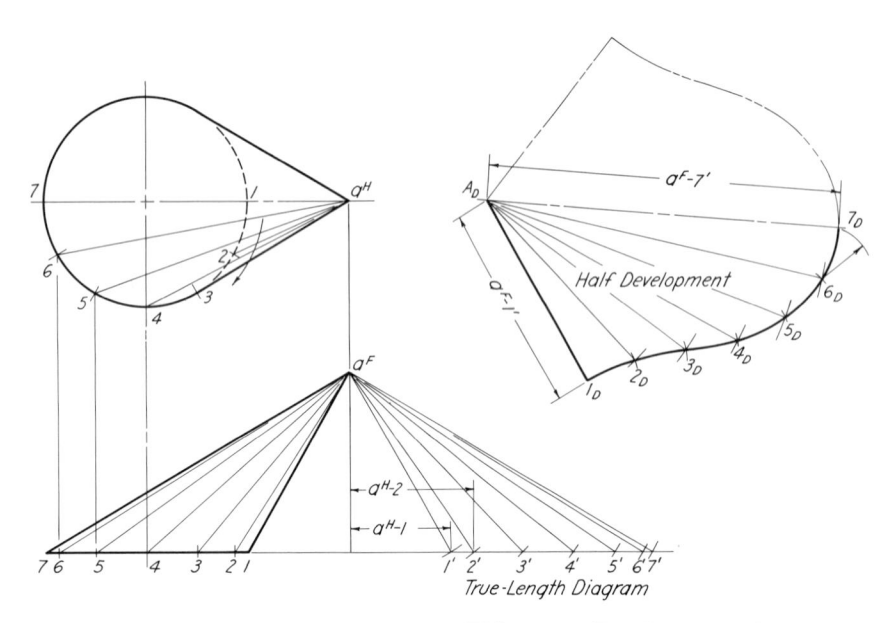

FIG. 11.20. Development of an oblique cone.

CHAP. 11 / DEVELOPMENTS AND INTERSECTIONS **225**

different axes. Since the piece is a frustum of a pyramid, it can be accurately developed by the method explained in Sec. 11.13.

11.20
To Develop a Transition Piece Connecting Two Circular Pipes. The transition piece shown in Fig. 11.23 connects two circular pipes on different axes. Since the piece is a frustum of an oblique cone, the surface must be triangulated, as explained in Sec. 11.17, and the development must be constructed by laying out the triangles in their true size in regular order. The general procedure is the same as that illustrated in Fig. 11.20. In this case, however, since the true size of the base is not shown in the top view, it is necessary to construct a partial auxiliary view to find the true

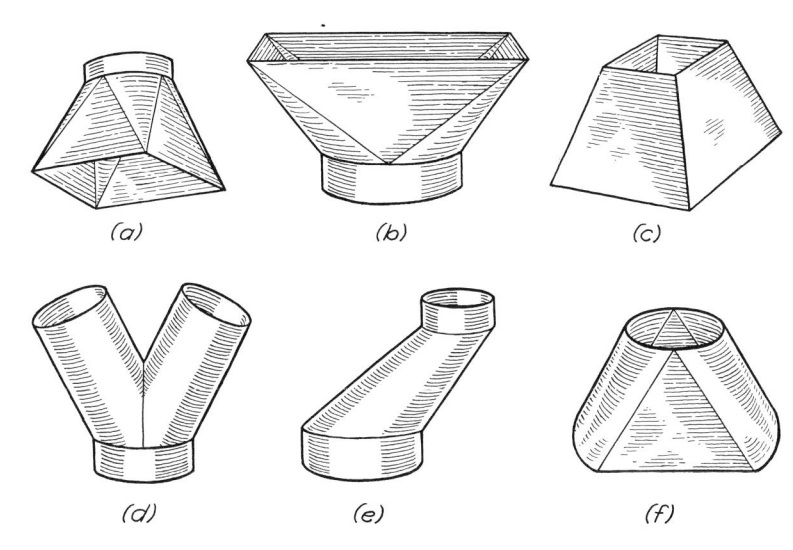

FIG. 11.21. Transition pieces.

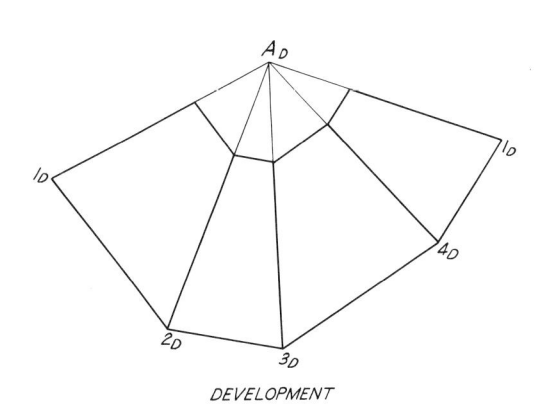

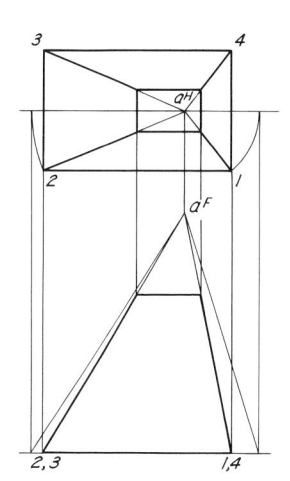

FIG. 11.22. Transition piece.

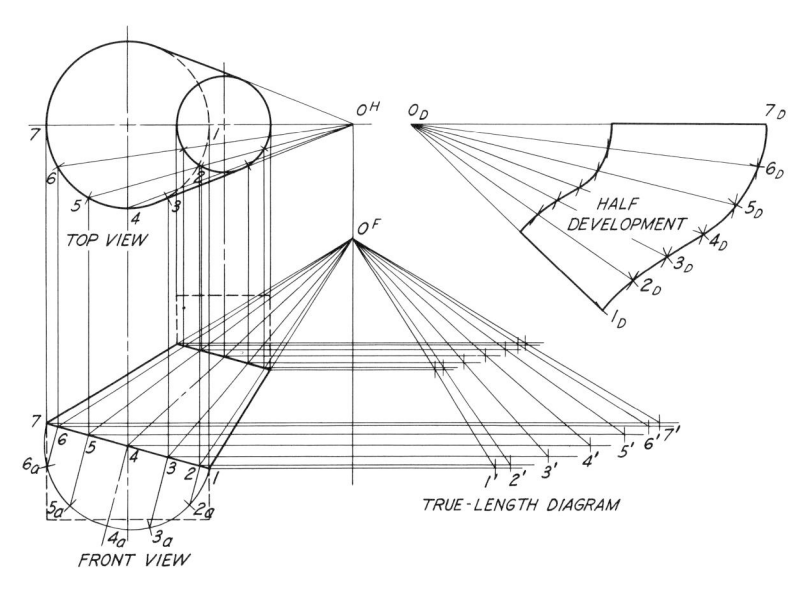

FIG. 11.23. Transition piece connecting two pipes.

lengths of chords between the end points of the elements.

11.21
To Develop a Transition Piece Connecting a Circular and a Square Pipe. A detailed analysis of the transition piece shown in Fig. 11.24 reveals that it is composed of four isosceles triangles whose bases form the square base of the piece and four conical surfaces that are parts of oblique cones. It is not difficult to develop this type of transition piece because, since the whole surface may be "broken up" into component surfaces, the development may be constructed by developing the first and then each succeeding component surface separately (Fig. 11.18). The surfaces are developed around the piece in a clockwise direction, in such a manner that each successive surface is joined to the preceding surface at their common element. In the illustration, the triangles 1LO, 4LM, 7MN, and 10NO are clearly shown in top view. Two of these, 1LO and 10NO, are visible on the pictorial drawing. The apexes of the conical surfaces are located at the corners of the base.

Before starting the development, it is necessary to determine the true lengths of the elements by constructing a true-length diagram, as explained in Sec. 11.11. The true lengths of the edges of the lower base (LM, MN, NO, and OL) and the true lengths of the chords (1-2, 2-3, 3-4, and so on) of the short arcs of the upper base are shown in the top view. The development is constructed in the following manner: First, the triangle $1_D PL$ is constructed, using the length $p^H l^H$ taken from the top view and true lengths from the diagram. Next, using the method explained in Sec. 11.17, the conical surface, whose apex is at L, is developed in an attached position. Triangle $4_D LM$ is then added, and so on, until all component surfaces have been drawn.

11.22
To Develop a Transition Piece Having an Approximately Developable Surface by the Triangulation Method. Figure 11.25 shows a half development of a transition piece that has a warped surface instead of a partially conical one, such as that discussed in Sec. 11.21. The method of

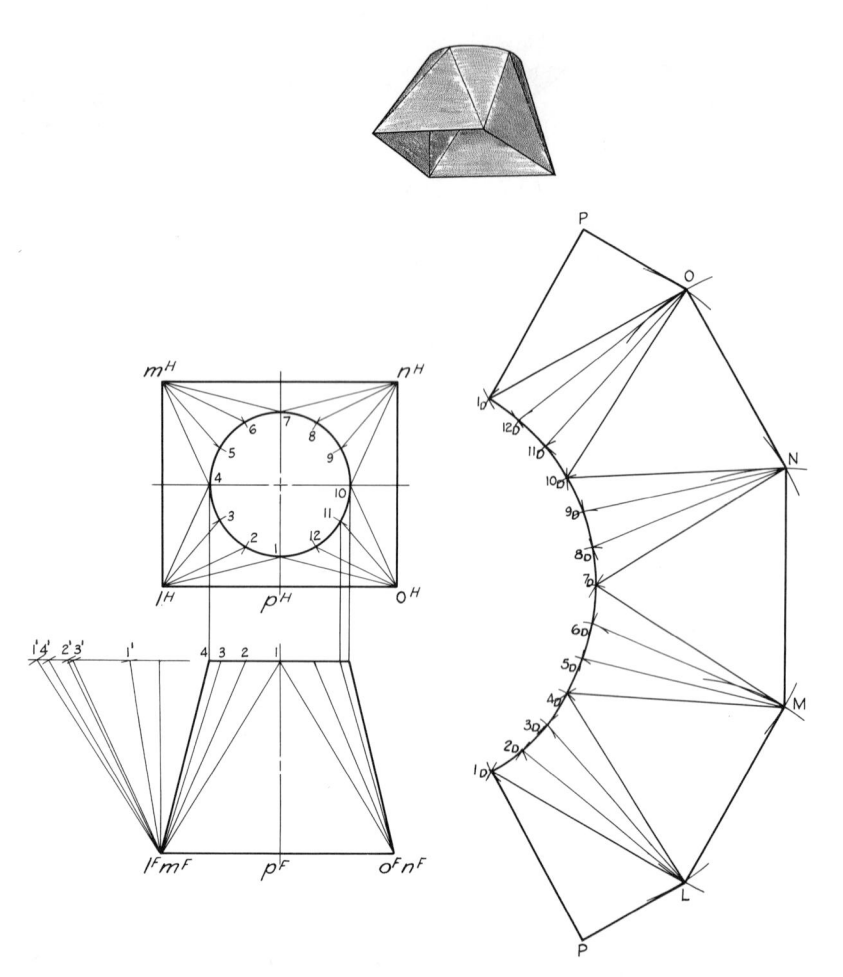

FIG. 11.24. Transition piece connecting a circular and square pipe.

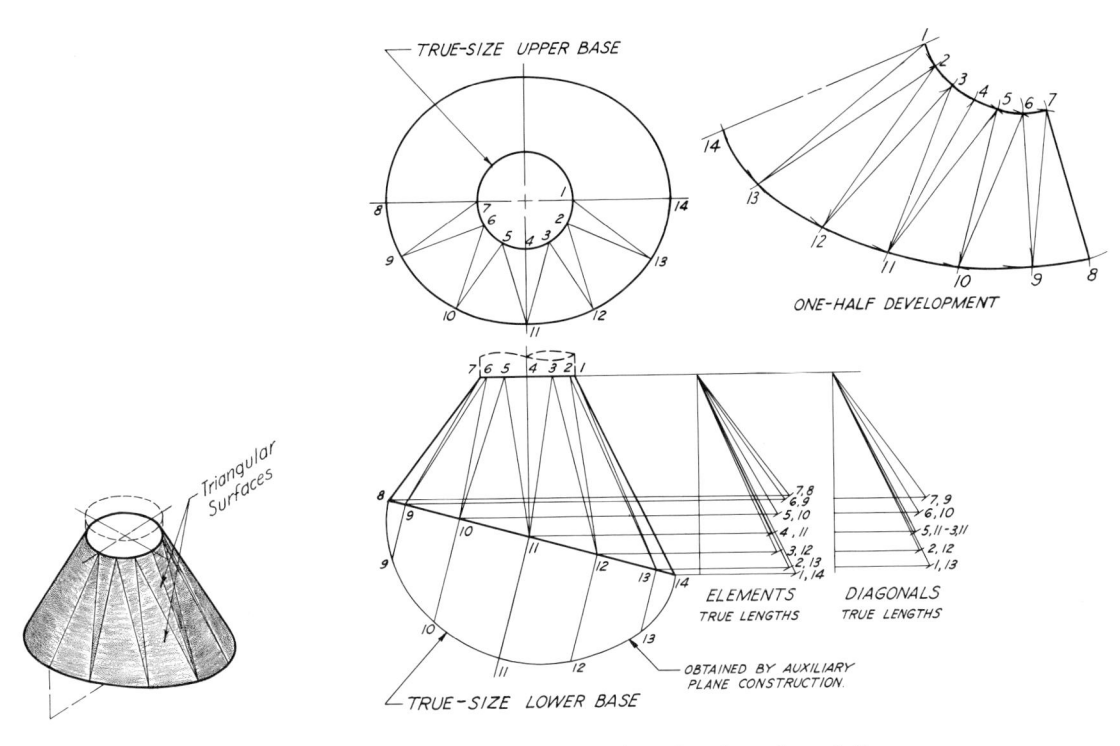

FIG. 11.25. Development of transition piece by triangulation.

constructing the development is somewhat similar, however, in that it is formed by laying out, in true size, a number of small triangles that approximate the surface. The true size of the circular intersection is shown in the top view, and the true size of the elliptical intersection is shown in the auxiliary view, which was constructed for that purpose.

The front half of the circle in the top view should be divided into the same number of equal parts as the half-auxiliary view. By joining the division points, the lateral surface may be initially divided into narrow quadrilaterals. These in turn may be subdivided into triangles by drawing diagonals, which, though theoretically curved lines, are assumed to be straight. The true lengths of the elements and the diagonals are found by constructing two separate true-length diagrams by the method illustrated in Fig. 11.15.

11.23

To Develop a Sphere. The surface of a sphere is a double-curved surface that can be developed only by some approximate method. The standard methods commonly used are illustrated in Fig. 11.26.

In (a) the surface is divided into a number of equal meridian sections of cylinders. The developed surfaces of these form an approximate development of the sphere. In drawing the development it is necessary to develop the surface of only one section, for this can be used as a pattern for the developed surface of each of the others.

In (b) the sphere is cut by parallel planes, which divide it into a number of

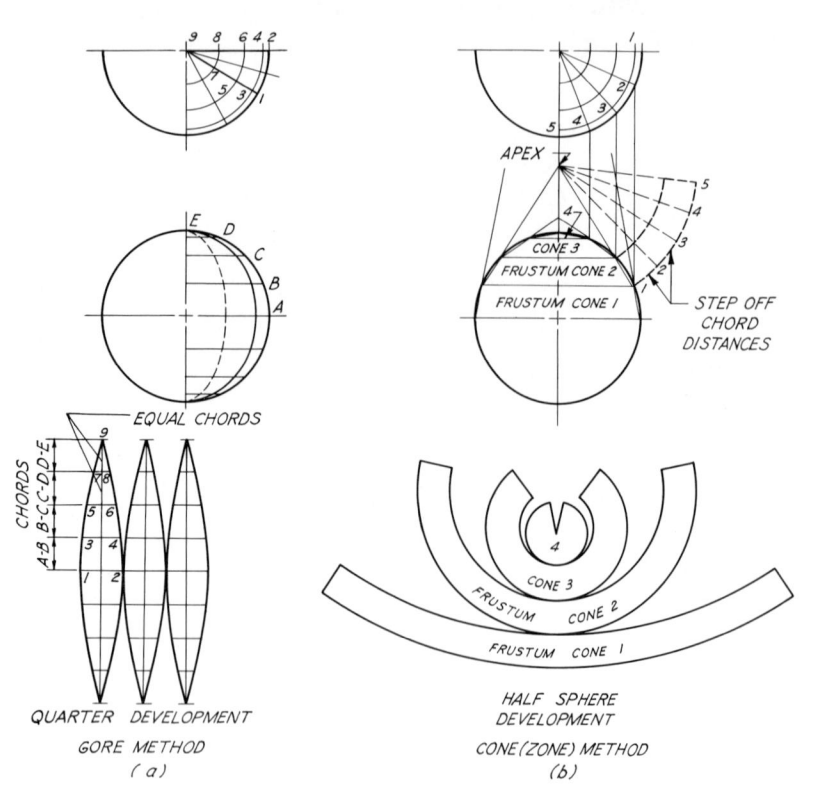

FIG. 11.26. The approximate development of a sphere.

horizontal sections, the surfaces of which approximate the surface of the sphere. Each of these sections may be considered the frustum of a right cone whose apex is located at the intersection of the chords extended.

B: INTERSECTIONS

11.24
Lines of Intersection of Geometric Surfaces. The line of intersection of two surfaces is a line that is common to both. It may be considered the line that would contain the points in which the elements of one surface would pierce the other.

Almost every line on a practical orthographic representation is a line of intersection; therefore, the following discussion may be deemed an extended study of the same subject. The methods presented in this chapter are the recognized easy procedures for finding the more complicated lines of intersection created by intersecting geometric surfaces.

In order to complete a view of a working drawing or a view necessary for developing the surfaces of intersecting geometric shapes, one frequently must find the line of intersection between surfaces. On an ordinary working drawing the line of intersection may be "faked in" through a few critical points. On a sheet-metal drawing, however, a sufficient number of points must be located to obtain an accurate line of intersection and an ultimately accurate development.

The line of intersection of two surfaces is found by determining a number of points common to both surfaces and drawing a line or lines through these points in correct order. The resulting line of intersection may be straight, curved, or straight and curved. The problem of finding such a line may be solved by one of two general methods, depending on the type of surfaces involved.

For the purpose of simplifying this discussion of intersections, it should be assumed that all problems are divided into these two general groups:

Group I. Problems involving two geometric figures, both of which are composed of plane surfaces.

Group II. Problems involving geometric figures which have either single-curved or double-curved surfaces.

For instance, the procedure for finding the line of intersection of two prisms is the same as that for finding the line of intersection of a prism and a pyramid; hence, both problems belong in the same group (Group I). Since the problem of finding the line of intersection of two cylinders and the problem of finding the line of intersection of a cylinder and a cone both involve single-curved surfaces, these two also belong in the same group (Group II).

Problems of the first group are solved by locating the points through which the edges of each of two geometric shapes pierce the other. These points are vertices of the line of intersection. Whenever one of two intersecting plane surfaces appears as a line in one view, the points through which the lines of the other surfaces penetrate it usually may be found by inspecting that view.

Problems of the second group may be solved by drawing elements on the lateral surface of one geometric shape in the region of the line of intersection. The points at which these elements intersect the surface of the other geometric shape are points that are common to both surfaces and consequently lie on their line of intersection. A curve, traced through these points with the aid of a French curve, will be a representation of the required intersection. To obtain accurate results, some of the elements must be drawn through certain critical points at which the curve changes sharply in direction. These points usually are located on contour elements. Hence, the usual practice is to space the elements equally around the surface, starting with a contour element.

11.25
Determination of a Piercing Point by Inspection (Fig. 11.27). It is easy to determine where a given line pierces a surface when the surface appears as an edge view (line) in one of the given views. For example, when the given line AB is extended as shown in (a), the F-view of the piercing point C is observed to be at c^F, where the frontal view of the line AB extended intersects the line view of the surface. With the position of c^F known, the H-view of point C can be quickly found by projecting upward to the H-view of AB extended.

In (b) the H-view (f^H) of the piercing point F is found first by extending $d^H e^H$ to intersect the edge view of the surface pierced by the line. By projecting downward, f^F is located on $d^F e^F$ extended.

In (c) the views of the piercing point K are found in the same manner as in (b), the only difference being that the edge view of the surface pierced by the line appears as a circle arc in the H-view instead of a straight line. It should be noted that a part of the line is invisible in the F-view because the piercing point is on the rear side of the cylinder.

The F- and H-views of the piercing point R in (d) may be found easily by projection after the P-view (r^P) of R has been once established by extending $p^P q^P$ to intersect the line view of the surface.

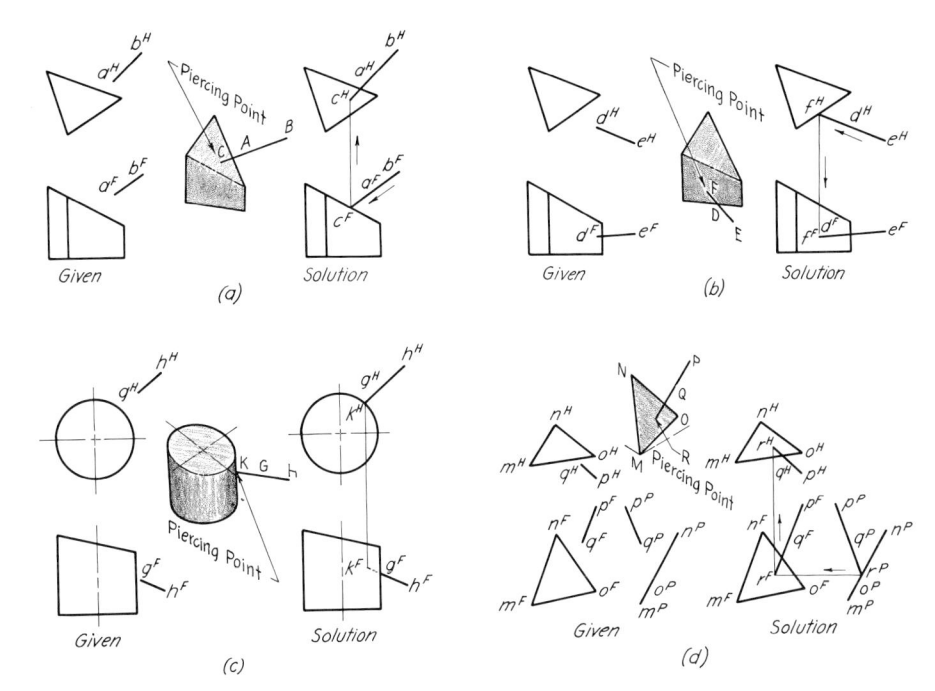

FIG. 11.27. Determination of a piercing point by inspection.

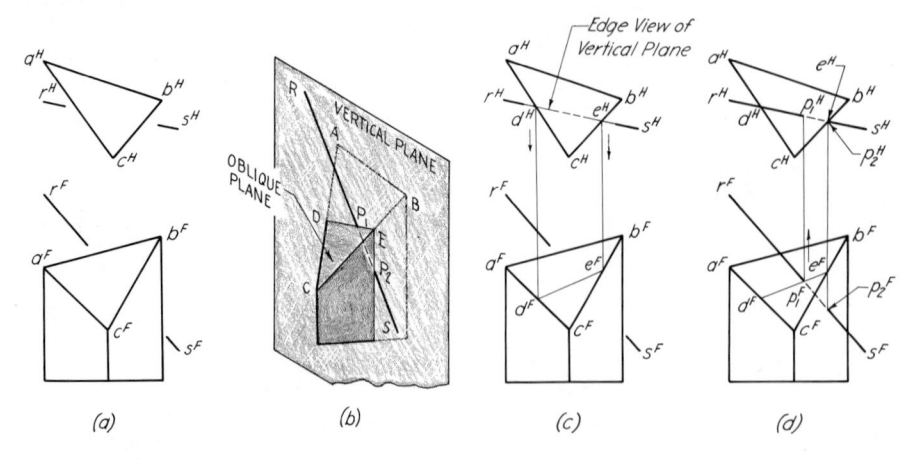

230 PART II / SPATIAL GRAPHICS: SHAPE DESCRIPTION AND SPATIAL RELATIONSHIPS

FIG. 11.28. Use of a line-projecting plane.

projecting plane (cutting plane) may be used to establish a line of intersection that will contain the piercing point. In the illustration, a vertical projecting plane was selected that would contain the given line RS and intersect the given plane ABC along line DE, as illustrated by the pictorial drawing.

SOLUTION: Draw the H-view of the projecting plane through $r^H s^H$ to establish $d^H e^H$, as shown in the H-view in (c). Locate $d^F e^F$ and draw the F-view of the line of intersection. Then, complete the line view $r^F s^F$ to establish p_1^F at the point of intersection of $r^F s^F$ and $d^F e^F$. Finally, locate p_1^H on $r^H s^H$ by projecting upward from p_1^F, as shown in (d).

11.26
Determination of a Piercing Point Using a Line-projecting Plane. When a line pierces a given oblique plane and an edge view is not given, as in Fig. 11.28, a line-

11.27
To Find Where a Line Pierces a Geometric Solid-cylinder-cone-sphere Using Projecting Planes (Fig. 11.29). The points where a line pierces a cylinder, cone, or sphere may be found easily through the use of a projecting plane (cutting plane) that contains the given line, as illustrated in (a), (b), and (c).

In (a) the intersections of the projecting plane and the cylinder are straight-line elements because the projecting plane used is parallel to the axis of the cylinder. The use of planes parallel to the axis permits the rapid solution of this type of problem. As shown by the pictorial drawing, the vertical projecting plane cuts elements on both the right and left sides of the cylinder. The line AB intersects the element RS at C and the other element at D. Points C and D are the piercing points.

The piercing points of a line and a cone are the points of intersection of the line and the two specific elements of the cone that lie in the projecting plane containing the line as shown in (b). The vertex of the cone and the given line fix the position of the projecting plane, the plane of the

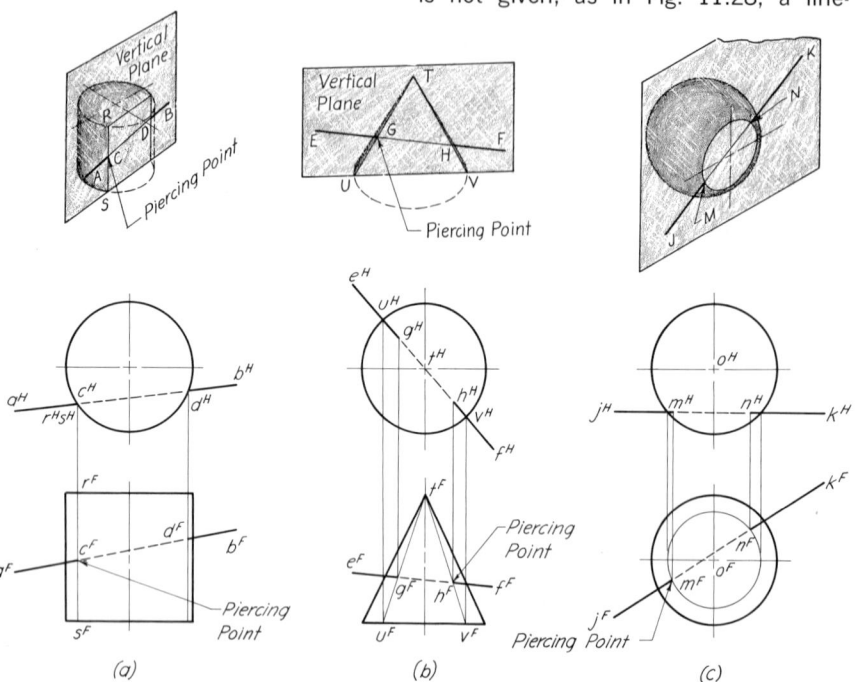

FIG. 11.29. To determine where a line pierces a geometric solid.

elements. In the illustration, the vertical projecting plane, taken through the line EF and the vertex of the cone T, cuts the base of the cone at U and V, the points needed to establish the F-views of the elements lying in the plane. The points of intersection of the given line EF and these elements are points G and H, the points where the line pierces the cone. If the given line had not been in a position to intersect the axis of the cone, it would have been necessary to use an oblique cutting plane through the apex.

A projecting plane that contains a line piercing a sphere will cut a circle on the surface of the sphere; therefore, points where the given line intersects the circle will be points where the line pierces the sphere. [See the pictorial drawing in (c).] In the illustrations, a vertical projecting plane was used containing the given line JK. The F-views of the piercing points M and N ($m^F n^F$) were found first at the points of intersection of the line and the circle. The H-views ($m^H n^H$) of the piercing points were found by projecting upward from m^F and n^F in the F-view.

11.28
To Determine the Points Where a Line Pierces a Cone, General Case. In Sec. 11.27, the statement was made that the piercing points of a line and a cone are the points of intersection of the line and the two specific elements of the cone that lie in the projecting plane containing the line and the apex of the cone [Fig. 11.29(b)]. This pertained to a special condition for which a line-projecting plane could be used. For other cases, the following general statement applies: The piercing points of a line and any surface must lie on the lines of intersection of the given surface and a cutting plane that contains the line. Obviously, an infinite number of cutting planes could have been assumed that would have contained the line AB in Fig. 11.30, but all would have

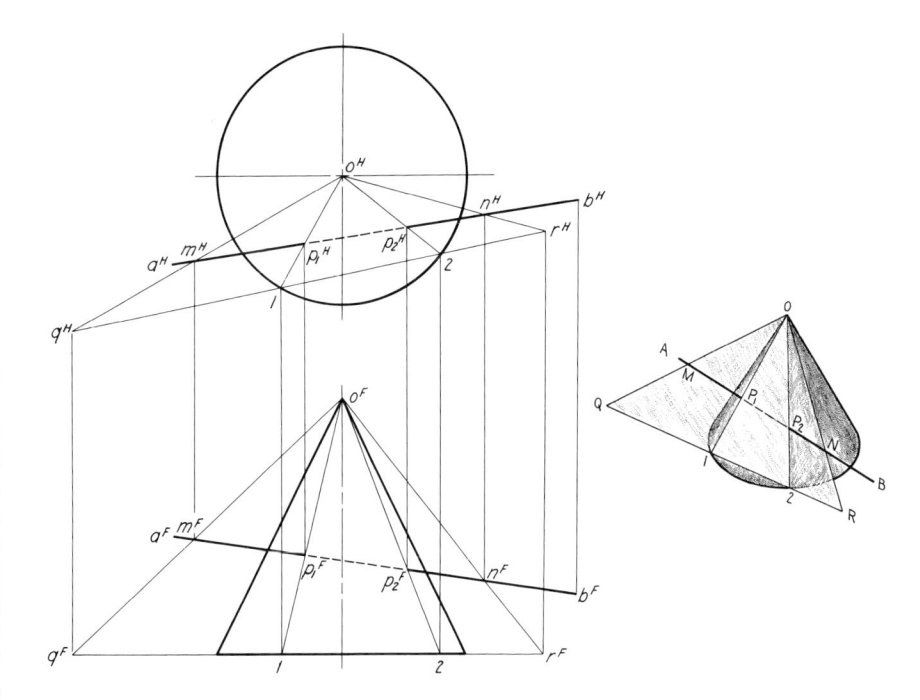

FIG. 11.30. To determine the points where a line pierces a cone—general case.

resulted in curved lines of intersection, except in the case of the one plane that was selected to pass through the apex O of the cone. As can be noted by observing the pictorial drawing, this choice gives a plane that intersects the cone along two straight-line elements.

SOLUTION: (1) Form a cutting plane containing the line AB and the apex O by drawing a line from O to an assumed point M on line AB. Lines AB and OM define the cutting plane. (2) Extend the cutting plane until it intersects the plane of the base of the cone. In the pictorial illustration it should be noted that OM and ON extended establish the line of intersection QR between the cutting plane and the plane of the base of the cone. Line ON, drawn from O to an assumed point N, is an additional line in the plane. (3)

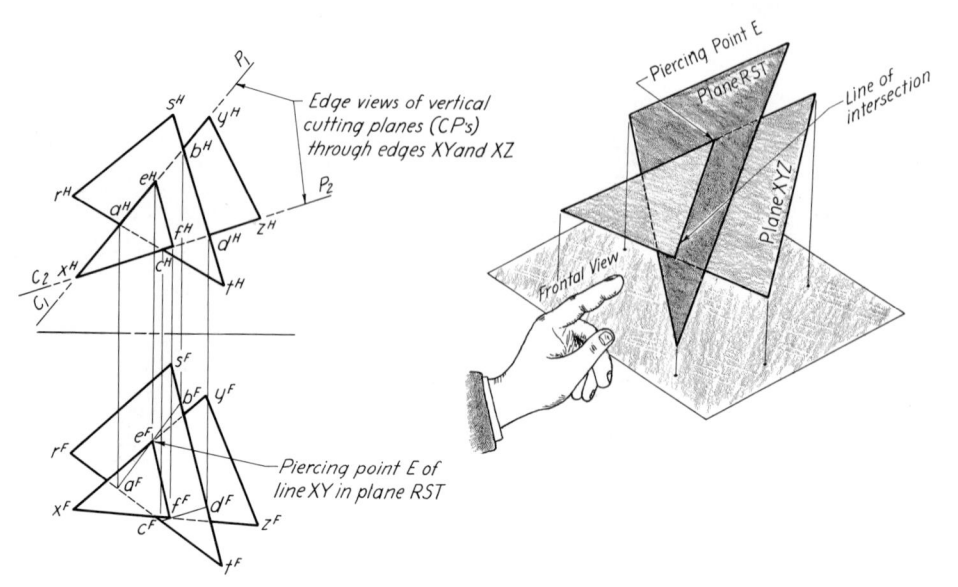

FIG. 11.31. To find the intersection line of two planes.

Project points 1 and 2, where the line $q^H r^H$ intersects the curve of the base of the cone in the H-view, to the F-view, and draw the views of the elements of intersection $O^F 1$ and $O^F 2$ in the F-view. Points $p_1{}^F$ and $p_2{}^F$, where the F-views of these elements intersect $a^F b^F$, are the F-views of the piercing points of the line AB and the given cone. (4) Project the F-views of the piercing points to the H-view to locate $p_1{}^H$ and $p_2{}^H$.

When the line and cone are both oblique an added view (auxiliary view), showing the base as an edge, may be needed to obtain a quick and accurate solution employing the steps illustrated in Fig. 11.30.

11.29
To Find the Intersection of Two Planes, Line-projecting Plane Method. The intersection of two oblique planes may be determined by finding where two of the lines of one plane pierce the other plane, as illustrated by the pictorial drawing in Fig. 11.31. The procedure that is illustrated employs line-projecting planes to find the piercing points of the lines XY and XZ and the oblique plane RST. Therefore, it might be said that the solution requires the determination of the piercing point of a line and an oblique plane, as explained in Sec. 11.26.

GIVEN: The oblique planes RST and XYZ.

SOLUTION: Since the (vertical) line-projecting plane $C_1 P_1$ is to contain the line XY of the plane XYZ, draw the line-view representation of this projecting plane to coincide with $x^H y^H$. Next, project the line of intersection AB between the line-projecting plane $C_1 P_1$ and plane RST from the top view, where it appears as $a^H b^H$ in the edge-view representation of $C_1 P_1$ to the front view. Then, since it is evident that the line AB is not parallel to XY, which lies in the projecting plane (see F-view), the line XY intersects AB. The location of this intersection at E is established first in the F-view, where the line $x^F y^F$ intersects $a^F b^F$ at e^F. The H-view of E, that is, e^H, is found by projecting upward from e^F in the F-view to the line view $x^H y^H$. The other end of the line of intersection between the two given planes at F is found by using the line-projecting plane $C_2 P_2$ and following the same procedure as for determining the location of point E.

11.30
To Find the Intersection of a Cylinder and an Oblique Plane. There are two distinct and separate methods shown in Fig. 11.32 for finding the line of intersection of an oblique plane and a cylinder. Both methods appear together on the drawing at the left. The selected line method is illustrated pictorially in (b), while the cutting-plane method is shown in (c).

In the application of the selected line

method, any line of the given plane, such as line BR, is drawn in the F- and H-views (a). It can be noted by observing, in the pictorial drawing in (b), that this particular line pierces the cylinder at points P_1 and P_2 to give two points on the line of intersection. On the multiview drawing, the locations of the H-views of points P_1 and P_2 can readily be recognized as being at the points labeled p_1^H and p_2^H, where the line view $b^H r^H$ intersects the edge view of the surface of the cylinder. The F-views (p_1^F and p_2^F) of points P_1 and P_2 were found by projecting downward from p_1^H and P_2^H to the line view $b^F r^F$. Additional points along the line of intersection, as needed, can be obtained by using other lines of the plane.

The line of intersection of this same plane and cylinder could have been almost as easily determined through the use of a series of line-projecting (cutting) planes passed parallel to the axis of the cylinder, as illustrated in (c). It should be noted that the vertical cutting plane shown cuts elements on the cylinder that intersect XY, the line of intersection of the cutting plane and the given plane, at points P_3 and P_4. Points P_3 [not visible in (c)] and P_4 are two points on the line of intersection, for they lie in both the cutting plane and the given plane and are on the surface of the cylinder. After the position of the cutting plane has been established in (a) by drawing the line representation in the H-view, x^H and y^H must be projected downward to the corresponding lines of the plane in the F-view. Line $x^F y^F$ as then drawn is the F-view of the line of intersection of the cutting plane and given plane. Finally, as the last step, the intersection elements that appear as points in the H-view at p_3^H and p_4^H must be drawn in the F-view. The F-views of points P_3 and P_4 (p_3^F and p_4^F) are at the intersection of the F-views of the elements and the line $x^F y^F$.

A series of selected planes will give the

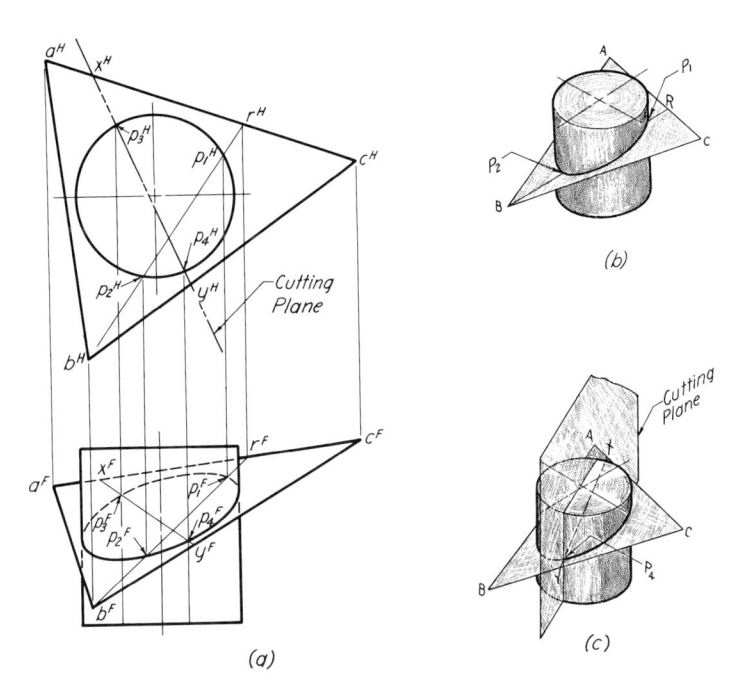

FIG. 11.32. To find the intersection of a cylinder and a plane.

points needed to complete the F-view of the intersection.

11.31
To Find the Intersection of a Cone and an Oblique Plane. When the intersecting plane is oblique, as is true in Fig. 11.33, it is usually desirable to employ the cutting-plane method shown in (a) rather than to resort to the use of an additional view, as in (b). Since the given cone is a right cone, any one vertical cutting plane, passing through the apex O, will simultaneously cut straight lines on the conical surface and across the given oblique plane. The pictorial illustration shows that the cutting plane X-Y intersects the cone along the two straight-line elements O-2 and O-8 and the plane along the line RS. Points G and H, where the elements intersect the line RS, are

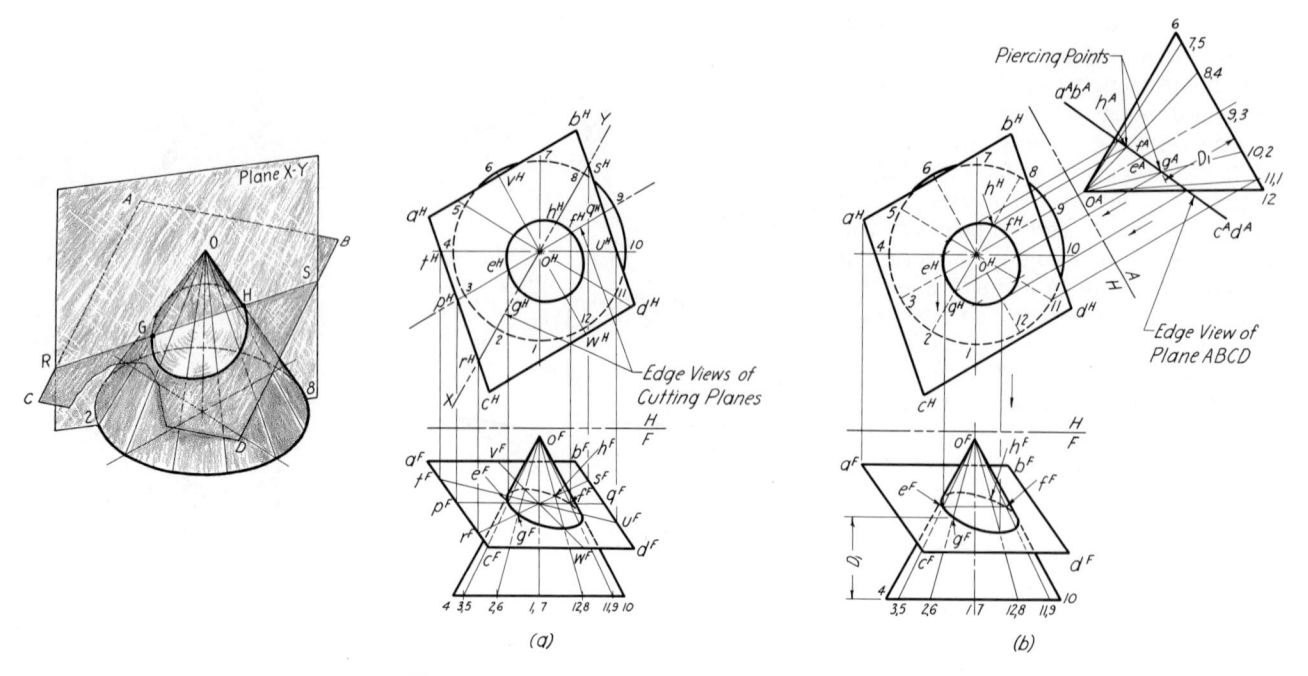

FIG. 11.33. To find the intersection of a cone and a plane.

points along the required line of intersection because both points lie in the given plane $ABCD$ and are on the surface of the cone. In (a), the line representation of the cutting plane XY in the H-view establishes the position of the H-view ($r^H s^H$) of the line RS. The H-views of elements O-2 and O-8 also lie in the edge view of the cutting plane XY. With this much known, the F-views of the two elements and line RS may be drawn. Points g^F and h^F are at the intersection of $r^F s^F$ and o^F-2 and o^F-8, respectively. A series of cutting planes passed similarly furnishes the points needed to complete the solution.

At times one might prefer to determine the line of intersection through the use of a constructed auxiliary view that shows the given plane as an edge. In this case, when selected elements may be seen to intersect the line view of the plane in the auxiliary view, the solution becomes quite simple, because all that is required is to project the point of intersection of an element and the line view of the plane to the F- and H-views of the same element. For example, the A-view (o^A-8) of the element O-8 can be seen to intersect the edge line $a^A b^A c^A d^A$ at h^A, the A-view of point H. By projecting to line o^H-8, the H-view of H (h^H) may be easily established. The F-view of H (h^F) lies directly below h^H on o^F-8. Through the projected views of other points, located similarly, smooth curves may be drawn to form the F- and H-view representations, as shown.

11.32
To Find the Intersection of a Sphere and an Oblique Plane. Horizontal cutting planes have been used to find the line of intersection of the sphere and oblique plane shown in Fig. 11.34. Two ap-

CHAP. 11 / DEVELOPMENTS AND INTERSECTIONS 235

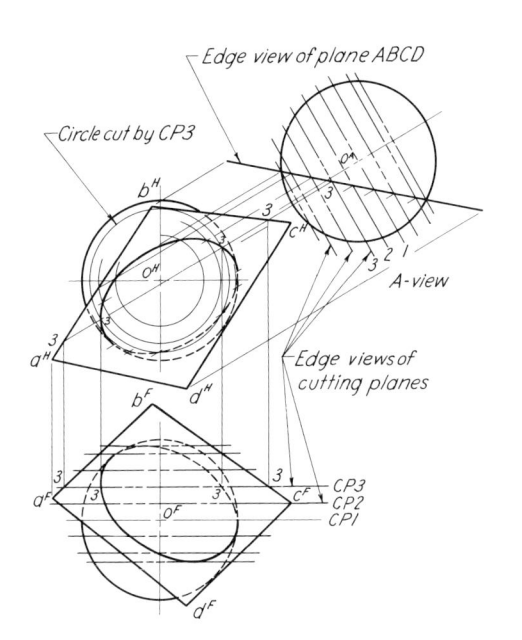

FIG. 11.34. To find the intersection of a sphere and an oblique plane.

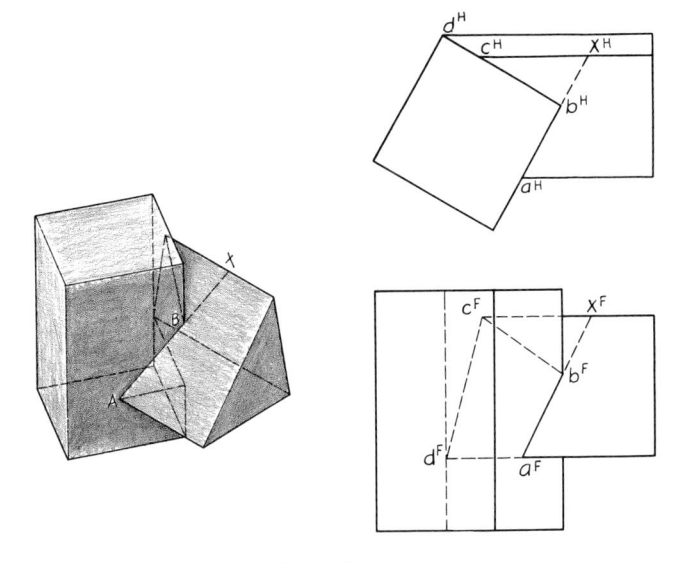

FIG. 11.35. Intersecting prisms.

proaches to the solution have been given on the line drawing. The horizontal cutting planes, as selected, cut circles from the sphere and straight lines from the given oblique plane. For example, the cutting plane CP_3 in the F-view cuts the horizontal line 3–3 from plane $ABCD$ and a circle from the sphere. This circle appears as an edge in the F-view and shows in its true diameter. In the H-view it will show in true shape. The line and circle intersect at two points that also have been identified by the number 3, the number assigned to the cutting plane in which these two points lie. These points now located in the H-view are projected to the CP_3 line in the F-view. The curved line through points, that have been determined by a series of planes, is a line common to both surfaces and is therefore the line of intersection.

This problem could also have been solved by using an auxiliary view showing the plane $ABCD$ as an edge. As before, the horizontal cutting planes will cut circles from the sphere and lines from the plane. However, in this case both the lines and the intersections show as points in the A-view. For each CP, these points must be projected from the auxiliary view to the corresponding circle in the H-view. The F-views of these points on the line of intersection may be found by projection and by using measurements taken from the A-view.

11.33
To Find the Intersection of Two Prisms. In Fig. 11.35, points A, C, and D, through which the edges of the horizontal prism pierce the vertical prism, are first found in the top view (a^H, c^H, and d^H) and are then projected downward to the corresponding edges in the front view. Point B, through which the edge of the vertical prism pierces the near face of the triangu-

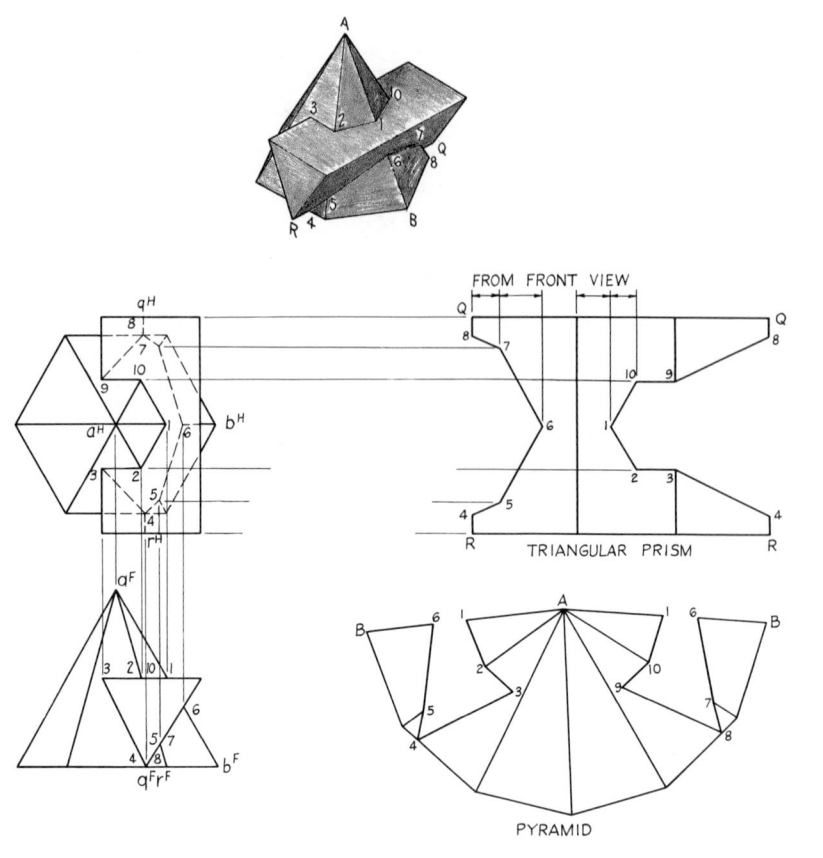

FIG. 11.36. Intersecting pyramid and prism.

tween the points a^F and x^F. Since point B is located on line AX (see pictorial) at the point where the edge of the prism pierces the line, its location in the front view is at point b^F where the edge cuts the line $a^F x^F$.

11.34

To Find the Intersection of a Pyramid and a Prism (Fig. 11.36). The intersection of a right pyramid and a prism may be found by the same general method used for finding the intersection of two prisms (Sec. 11.33).

11.35

To Determine the Intersection of a Prism and a Pyramid Using Line-Projecting Planes. Frequently, it becomes necessary to draw the line of intersection between two geometric shapes so positioned that the piercing points of edges cannot be found by inspection if only the principal views are to be used. In this case, one must resort to the method discussed in Sec. 11.26 to determine where a line, such as the edge line GD of the prism shown in Fig. 11.37, pierces a surface. As illustrated by the pictorial drawing, a vertical plane passed through the edge DG of the prism, intersects the surface ABC of the pyramid along line MN that contains point D, the piercing point of DG. In (a), the H-view ($m^H n^H$) of the line MN lies along $d^H g^H$ extended to m^H on the edge of the pyramid, because the H-view of the cutting plane appears as an edge that coincides with $d^H g^H$. With the F-view of MN established by projecting downward from $m^H n^H$ in the H-view, the frontal view of the piercing point D is at d^F where the view of the edge line DG of the prism intersects $m^F n^F$. The H-view of D is found by projecting upward from d^F. The two other piercing points, at E and F, are found in the same manner using two other line-projecting planes.

lar prism, cannot be found in this manner because the side view from which it could be projected to the front view is not shown. Its location, however, can be established in the front view without even drawing a partial side view, if some scheme like the one illustrated in the pictorial drawing is used. In this scheme, the intersection line AB, whose direction is shown in the top view as line $a^H b^H$, is extended on the triangular face to point X on the top edge. Point x^H is projected to the corresponding edge in the front view and a light construction line is drawn be-

CHAP. 11 / DEVELOPMENTS AND INTERSECTIONS   **237**

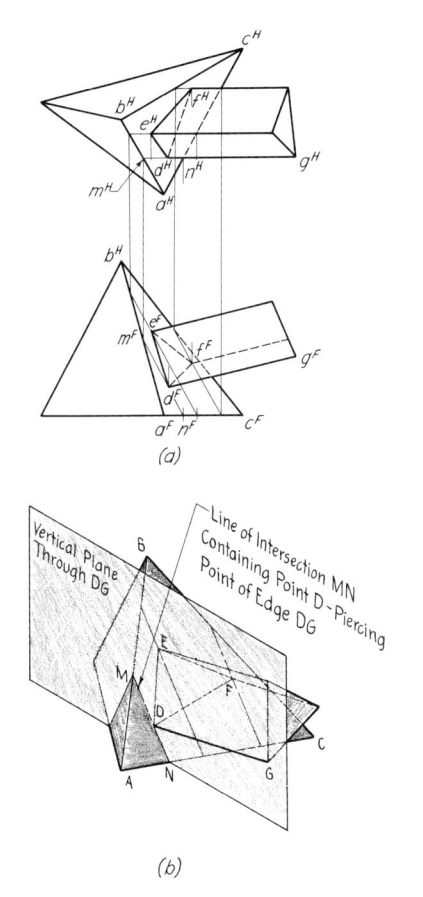

FIG. 11.37. Intersecting pyramid and prism.

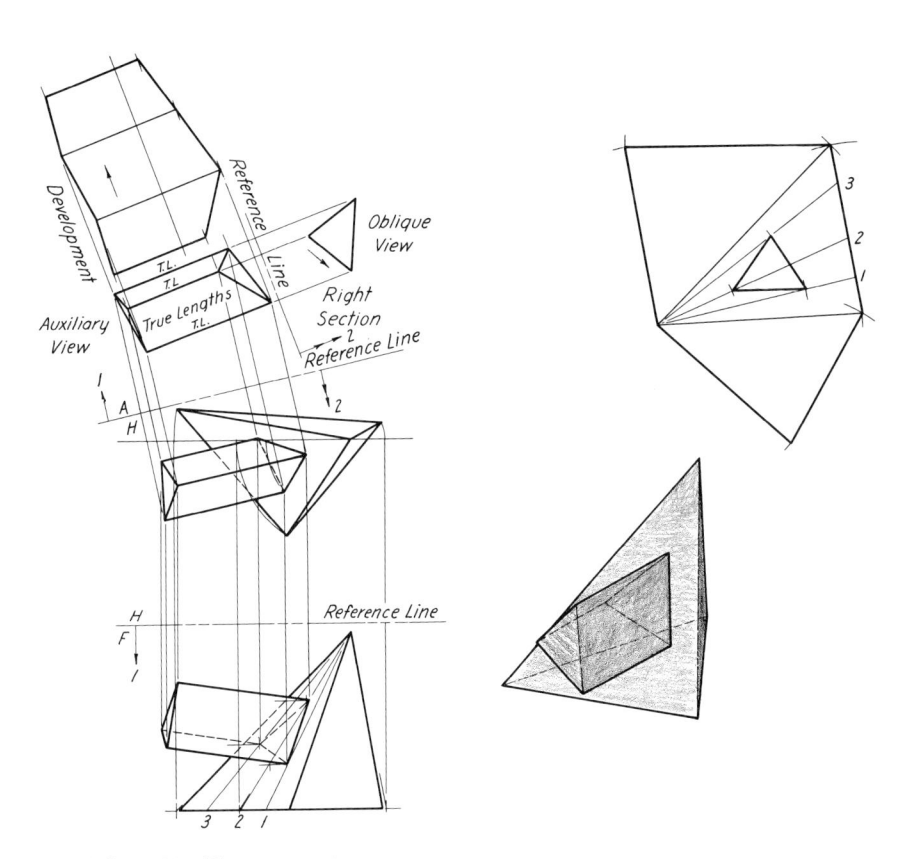

FIG. 11.38. To construct a development using auxiliary views.

11.36
To Construct a Development Using Auxiliary Views. When one of the components is oblique to the principal planes of projection, as is the prism in Fig. 11.38, the construction work needed for the development can be simplified somewhat through the use of an auxiliary view to find the true lengths of the edges and an oblique (secondary auxiliary) view to show a right section. Since the plane on which the auxiliary view is projected is a vertical one that is parallel to the edges of the prism, the distances perpendicular to the AH reference line are height distances. In making the construction, distances are taken from the F-view in the direction of the single-headed arrow for use in the auxiliary view in the direction indicated by a similar arrow. For the oblique view, projected on an O-plane that is perpendicular to both the A-plane and the edges of the prism, distances are taken from the AH reference line in the direction of the arrow numbered 2 to be laid out from the reference line for the O-view. Since this is the

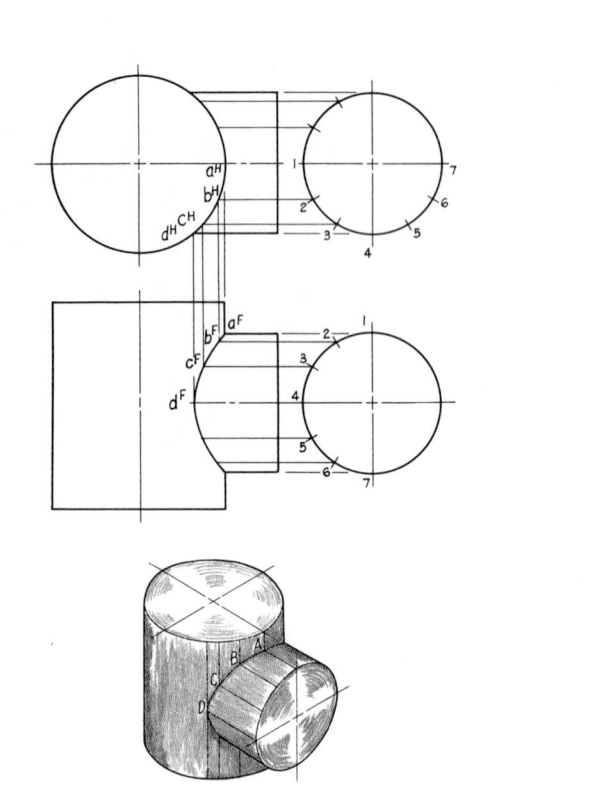

FIG. 11.39. Intersecting cylinders.

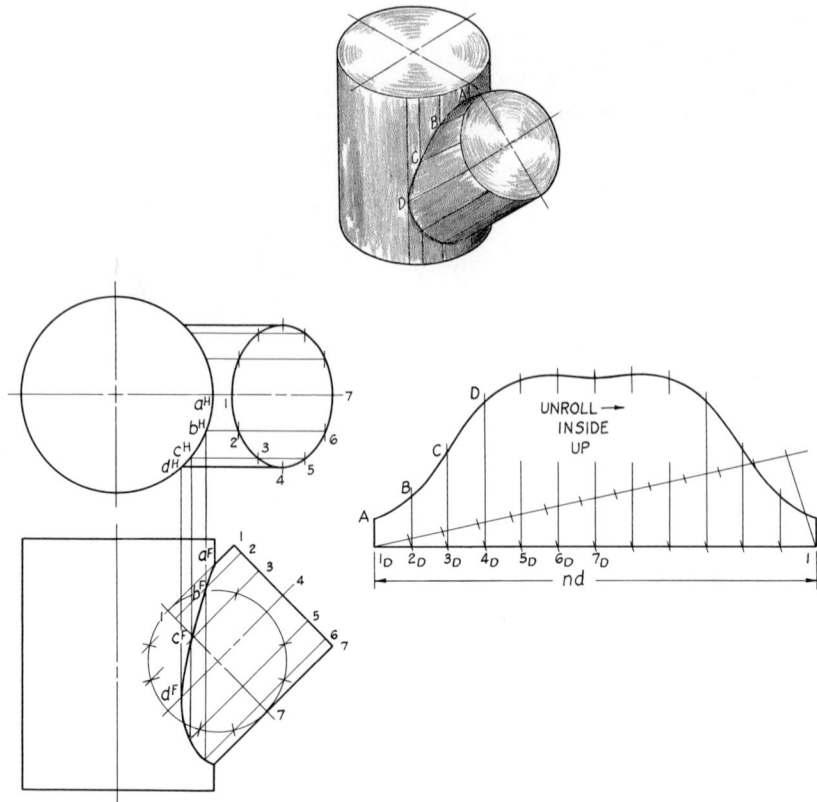

FIG. 11.40. Intersecting cylinders.

second auxiliary, the arrows indicating the direction for equal distances have been given two heads.

If there is sufficient space available, the true-length measurements for the edges in the development may be projected directly from the auxiliary view showing the true lengths. The true distances between these edges, taken from the right section in the direction of the arrow, are laid off along the stretch-out line. The arrow on the development indicates the direction in which the successive faces are laid down when the prism is turned to unroll the lateral surface inside-up.

11.37
To Find the Intersection of Two Cylinders.
If a series of elements are drawn on the surface of the small horizontal cylinder, as in Fig. 11.39, the points A, B, C, and D in which they intersect the vertical cylinder will be points on the line of intersection (see pictorial). These points, which are shown as a^H, b^H, c^H, and d^H in the top view, may be located in the front view by projecting them downward to the corresponding elements in the front view, where they are shown as points a^F, b^F, c^F, and d^F. The desired intersection is represented by a smooth curve drawn through these points.

11.38
To Find the Intersection of Two Cylinders Oblique to Each Other. The first step in finding the line of intersection of two cylinders that are oblique to each other (Fig. 11.40) is to draw a revolved right section of the oblique cylinder directly on the front view of that cylinder. If the circumference of the right section is then divided into a number of equal divisions and elements are drawn through the division points, the points A, B, C, and D in which the elements intersect the surface of the vertical cylinder will be points on the line of intersection (see pictorial). In the case of the illustration shown, these points are found first in the top view and then are projected downward to the corresponding elements in the front view. The line of intersection in the front view is represented by a smooth curve drawn through these points.

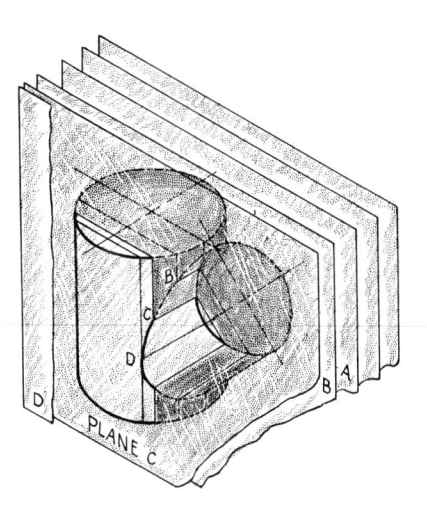

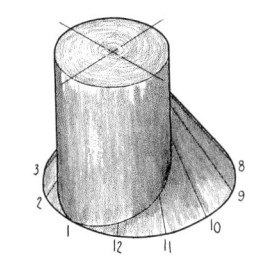

11.39
To Find the Intersection of Two Cylinders Using Line-Projecting (Cutting) Planes. The line of intersection of the two cylinders shown in Fig. 11.40 could have been determined through the use of a series of parallel line-projecting (cutting) planes passed parallel to their axes (Fig. 11.41). The related straight-line elements cut on the cylinders by any one cutting plane, such as C, intersect on the line of intersection of the cylinders. As many line-projecting planes as are needed to obtain a smooth curve should be used and they should be placed rather close together where a curve changes sharply.

11.40
To Find the Intersection of a Cylinder and a Cone. The intersection of a cylinder and a cone may be found by assuming a number of elements on the surface of the cone. The points at which these elements cut the cylinder are on the line of intersection (see Figs. 11.42 and 11.43). In selecting the elements, it is the usual practice to divide the circumference of the base into a number of equal parts and draw elements through the division points. To obtain needed points at locations where the intersection line will change suddenly in curvature, however, there should be additional elements.

In Fig. 11.42, the points at which the elements pierce the cylinder are first found in the top view and are then projected to

FIG. 11.41. To find the intersection of two cylinders using line-projecting planes.

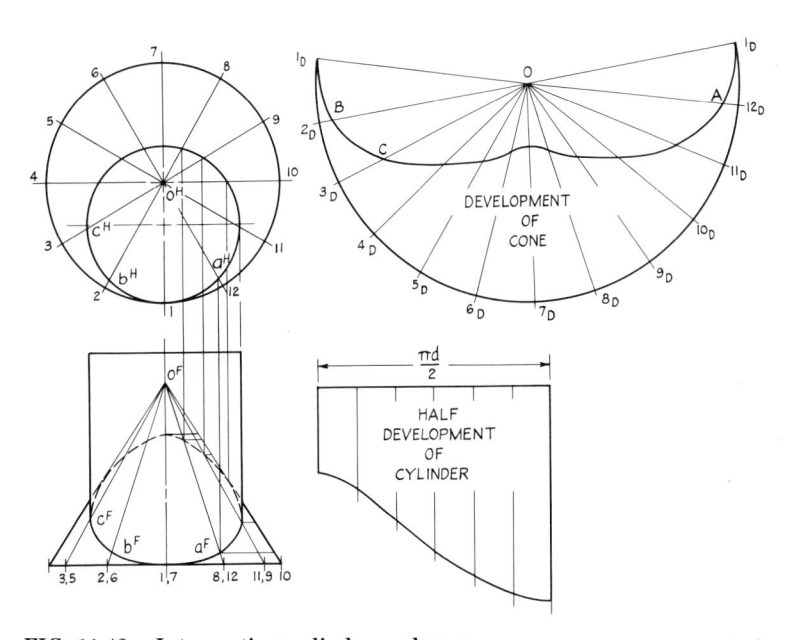

FIG. 11.42. Intersecting cylinder and cone.

the corresponding elements in the front view. A smooth curve through these points forms the figure of the intersection.

To find the intersection of the cone and cylinder combination shown in Fig. 11.43, line-projecting cutting planes were passed through the vertex O parallel to the axis of the cylinder to cut intersecting elements on both geometric forms. The partial auxiliary is needed to establish these planes, because it is only in a view showing the axis of the cylinder as a point that these planes and the surface of the cylinder will show as edge views. Each cutting plane cuts one needed straight-line element from the conical surface and two straight-line elements from the cylindrical surface. Cutting plane 5, for example, cuts one element (numbered 5) from the near side of the cone and an upper and lower element from the surface of the cylinder. The intersection of these three elements, all numbered 5, establish the location of points A and B on the line of intersection.

An alternate method for finding the line of intersection of a cylinder and a right cone is illustrated in Fig. 11.44. Here horizontal cutting planes are passed through both geometric shapes in the region of their line of intersection. In each cutting plane, the circle cut on the surface of the cone will intersect elements cut on the cylinder at two points common to both surfaces (see pictorial). A curved line traced through a number of such points in different planes is a line common to both surfaces and is therefore the line of intersection.

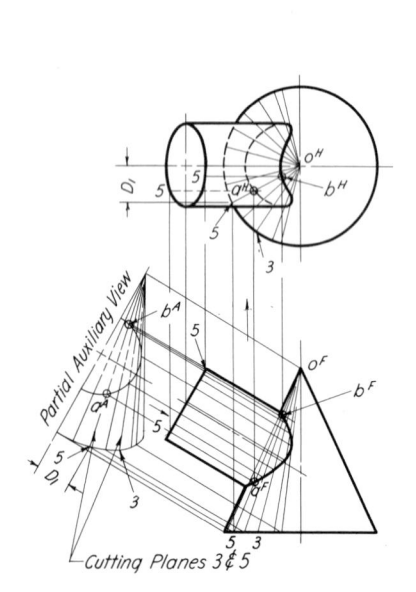

FIG. 11.43. To find the intersection of a cone and a cylinder.

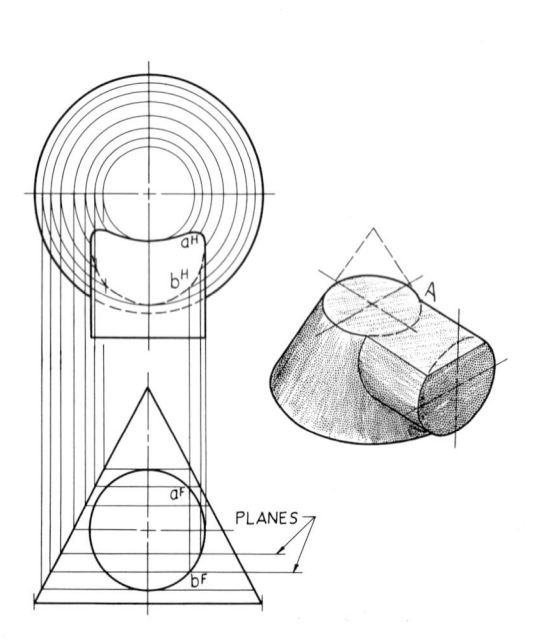

FIG. 11.44. Intersecting cylinder and cone.

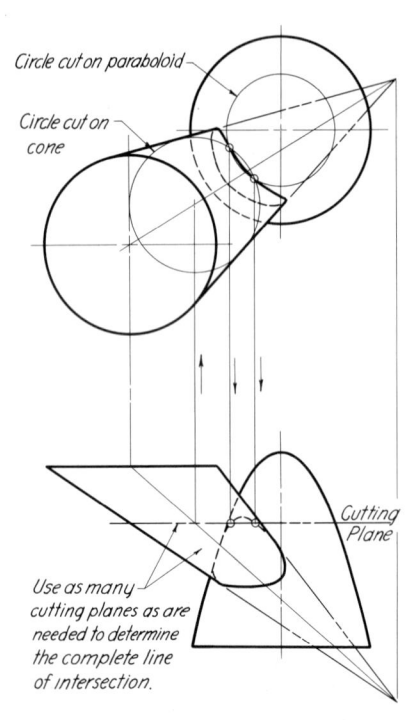

FIG. 11.45. Intersection of a cone and a paraboloid.

11.41
To Find the Intersection of an Oblique Cone and a Paraboloid. The method that is illustrated in Fig. 11.45 for finding the line of intersection of a cone and a paraboloid may be used effectively for the solution of many other intersection problems involving different geometric forms, such as two cones or a cone and a cylinder having parallel bases. For the arrangement as shown, a horizontal cutting plane will intersect each geometric form in a circle. When a number of horizontal cutting planes are passed through both geometric shapes in the region of their line of intersection, each plane cuts a circle on the cone that intersects a circle cut on the paraboloid at two points common to both surfaces. The curved line traced through the points that have been determined by the several planes is a line common to both surfaces and is therefore the line of intersection.

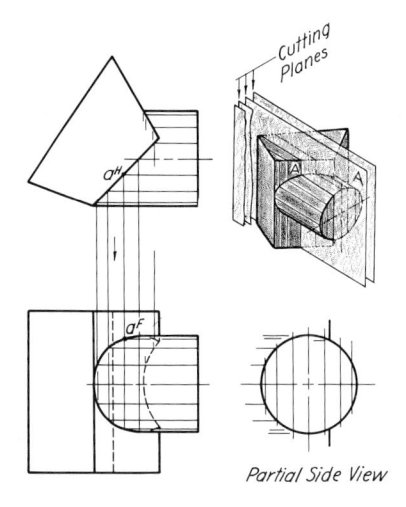

11.42
To Find the Intersection of a Prism and a Cylinder. In Fig. 11.46 it is required to find the intersection between the cylinder and two of the plane surfaces of the prism so that a pattern for the hole can be cut in the prism to match the cylinder. Although the intersection could have been secured merely by determining, through inspection, the piercing points of elements drawn arbitrarily on the cylinder, vertical line-projecting planes were used to illustrate an approach to this type of problem that is used by many people. The cutting planes are located in the view showing the right section of the cylinder. From this first step, the positions for the lines and elements cut on the prism and cylinder, respectively, can be determined by projection. Each line-projecting (cutting) plane cuts a line on a plane surface of the prism and related elements on the cylinder that intersect on the line of intersection. A sufficient number of line-projecting planes should be used to enable one to draw a smooth curved-line representation of the intersection. If more points are desired, at a location where a curve changes sharply, additional cutting planes may be added.

11.43
To Find the Intersection of a Prism and a Cone. The complete line of intersection may be found by drawing elements on the surface of the cone (Fig. 11.47) to locate points on the intersection as explained in Sec. 11.40. To obtain an accurate curve, however, some thought must be given to the placing of these elements. For instance, although most of the elements may be equally spaced on the cone to facilitate the construction of its development, additional ones should be drawn through the critical points and in regions where the line of intersection changes sharply in curvature. The elements are drawn on the view that will reveal points on the intersection, then the determined points are projected to the corresponding elements in the other view or views. In

FIG. 11.46. To find the intersection of a prism and a cylinder.

FIG. 11.47. Intersecting cone and prism.

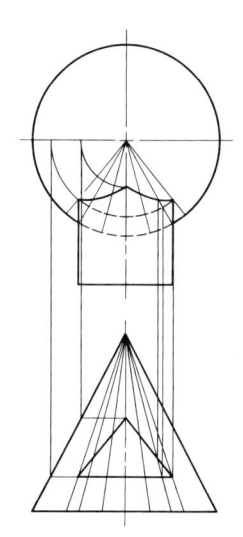

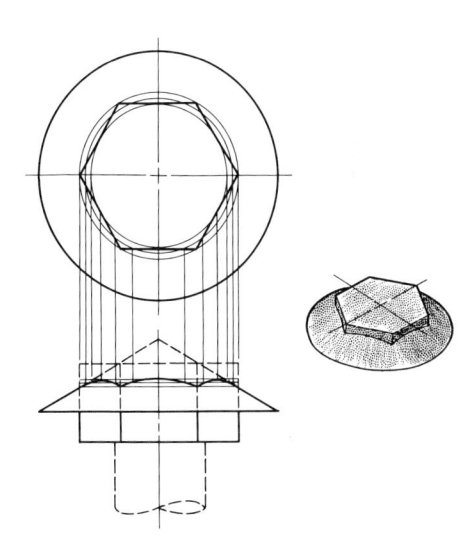

FIG. 11.48. Cone and hexagonal prism.

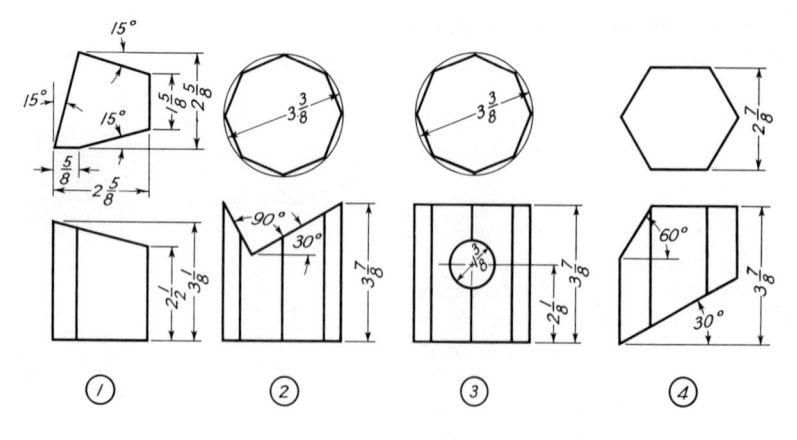

FIG. 11.49. Prisms.

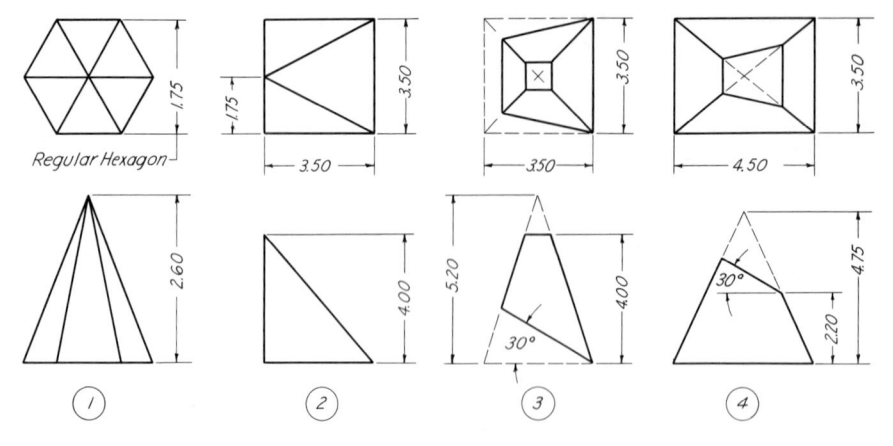

FIG. 11.50. Pyramids.

are points common to the lateral surfaces of both shapes and are therefore points on the required line of intersection. It should be noted that the resulting solution represents a chamfered bolthead.

PROBLEMS

1. (Fig. 11.49). Develop the lateral surface of one or more of the prisms as assigned.

2. (Fig. 11.50). Develop the lateral surface of one or more of the pyramids as assigned. Make construction lines light. Show construction for finding the true lengths of the lines.

3. (Fig. 11.51). Develop the lateral surface of one or more of the cylinders as assigned. Use a hard pencil for construction lines and make them light.

4. (Fig. 11.52). Develop the lateral surface of one or more of the cones as assigned. Show all construction. Use a hard pencil for construction lines and make them light. In each case start with the shortest element and unroll, inside-up. It is suggested that 12 elements be used, in order to secure a reasonably accurate development.

5. (Fig. 11.53). Develop the lateral surface of one or more of the transition pieces as assigned. Show all construction lines in light, sharp pencil lines. Use a sufficient number of elements on the curved surfaces to ensure an accurate development.

6. (Fig. 11.54). Develop the sheet-metal connections. On pieces 3 and 4, use a sufficient number of elements to obtain a smooth curve and an accurate development.

7–8. (Figs. 11.55 and 11.56). Draw the line of intersection of the intersecting geometric shapes as assigned. Show the invisible portions of the lines of intersection as well as the visible. Consider that the interior is open.

9–10. (Figs. 11.57 and 11.58). Draw the line of intersection of the intersecting geometric shapes as assigned. It is suggested that the elements used to find points along the intersection be spaced 15° apart. Do not erase the construction lines. One shape does not pass through the other.

this particular illustration a part of the line of intersection in the top view is a portion of the arc of a circle that would be cut by a horizontal plane containing the bottom surface of the prism.

If the surfaces of the prism are parallel to the axis of the cone, as in Fig. 11.48, the line of intersection will be made up of the tips of a series of hyperbolas. The intersection may be found by passing planes that will cut circles on the surface of the cone. The points at which these cutting circles pierce the faces of the prism

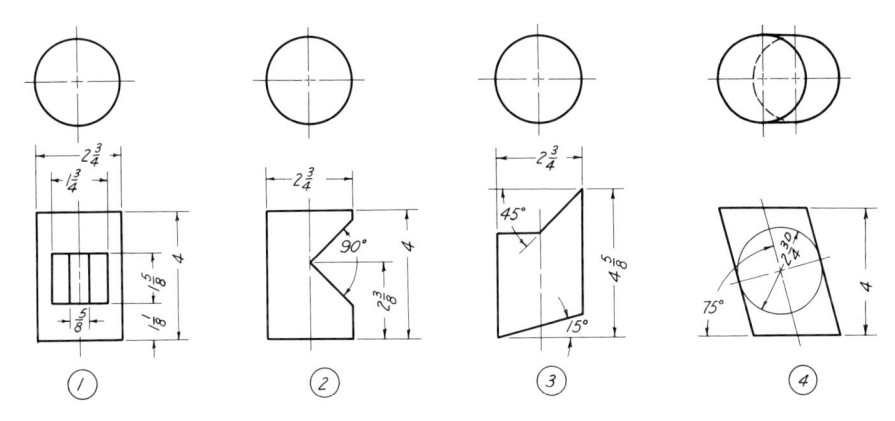

FIG. 11.51. Cylinders.

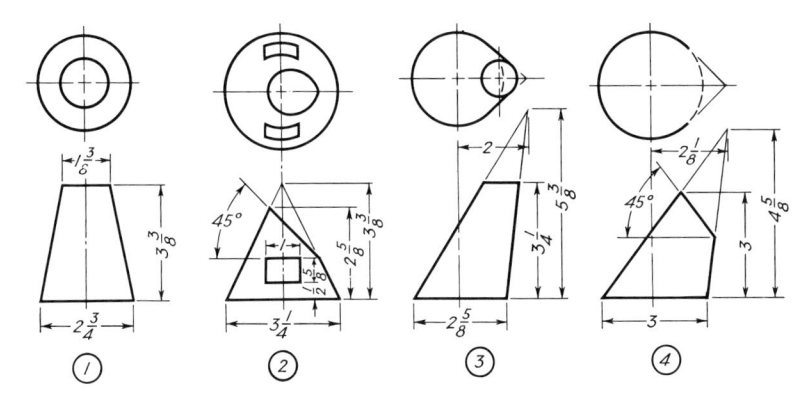

FIG. 11.52. Cones.

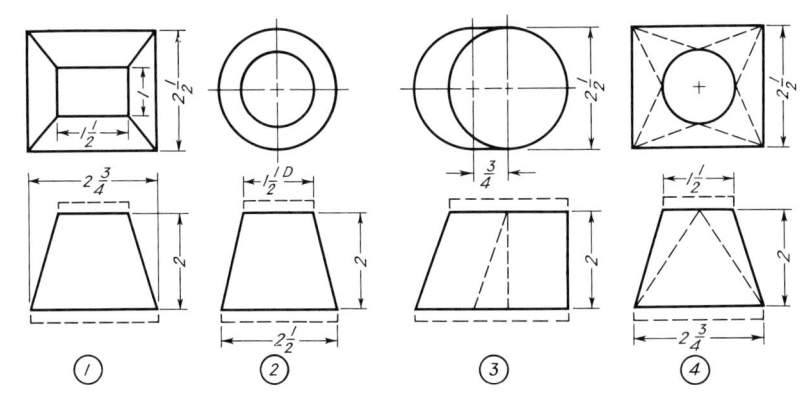

FIG. 11.53. Transition pieces.

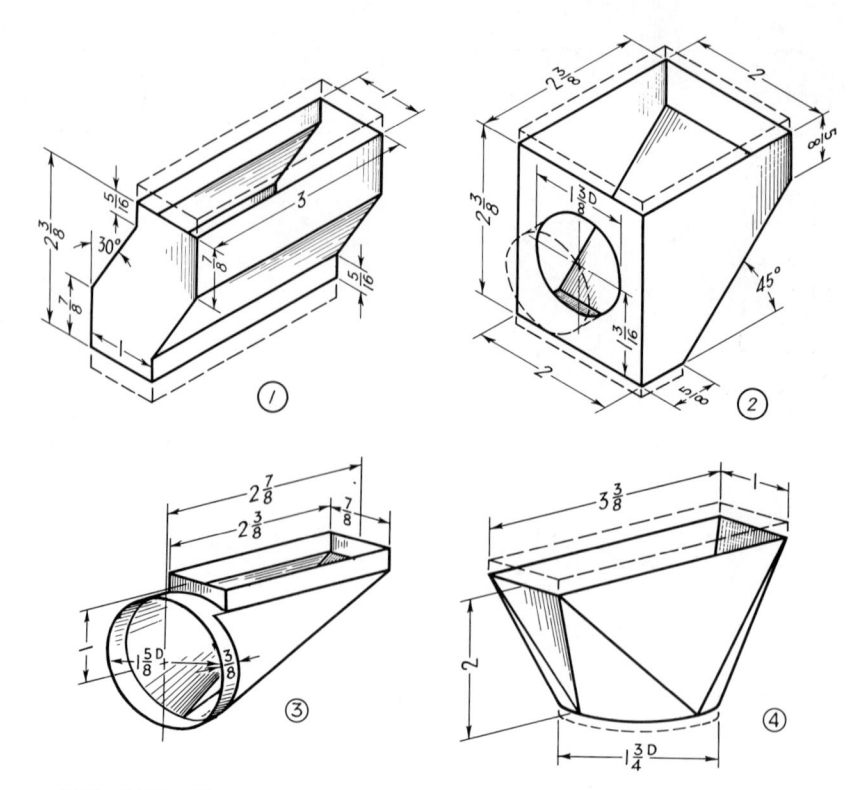

FIG. 11.54. Sheet-metal connections (transitions).

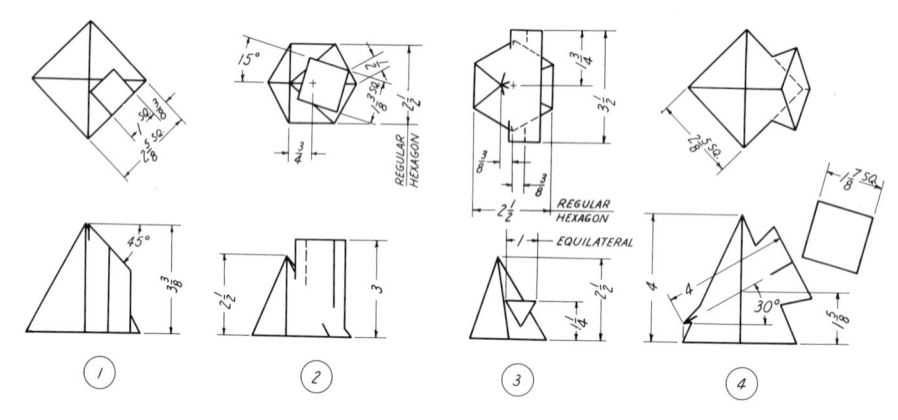

FIG. 11.55. Intersecting surfaces.

CHAP. 11 / DEVELOPMENTS AND INTERSECTIONS   **245**

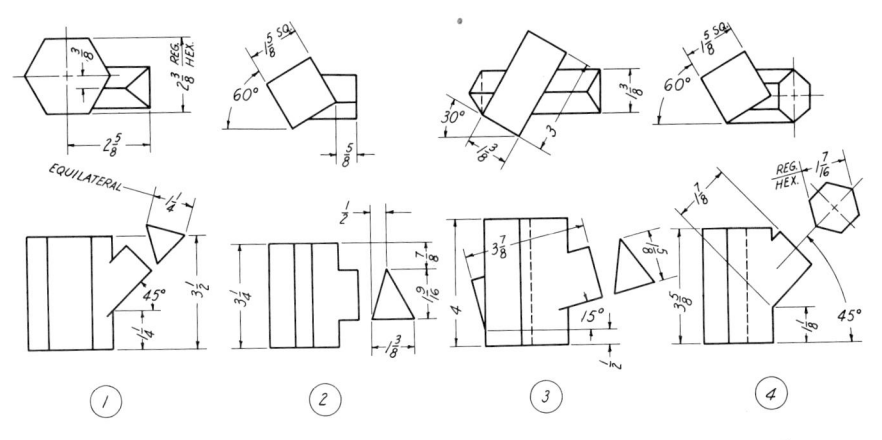

FIG. 11.56. Intersecting surfaces.

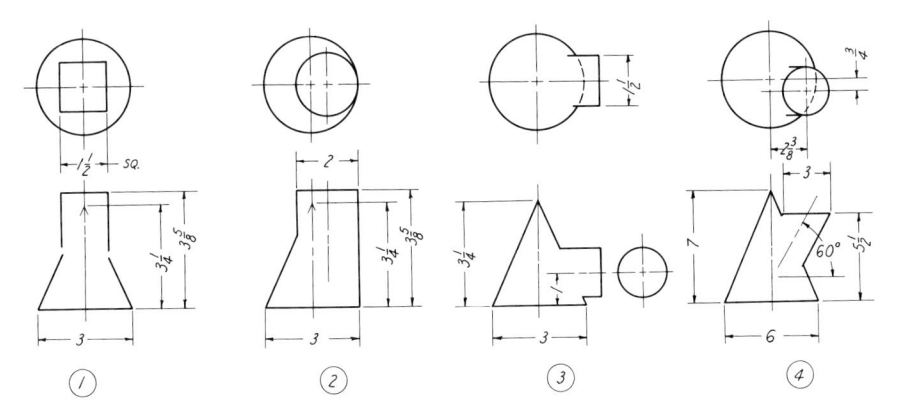

FIG. 11.57. Intersecting surfaces.

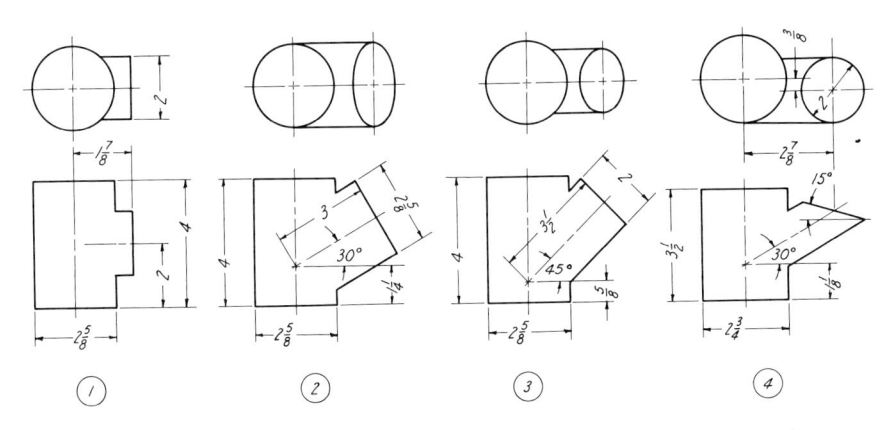

FIG. 11.58. Intersecting surfaces.

11. (Fig. 11.59). Draw the line of intersection of the intersecting geometric shapes as assigned. Show the invisible portions of the line of intersection as well as the visible. The interior of the combination is hollow. One shape does not pass through the other. Show construction with light, sharp lines drawn with a hard pencil.

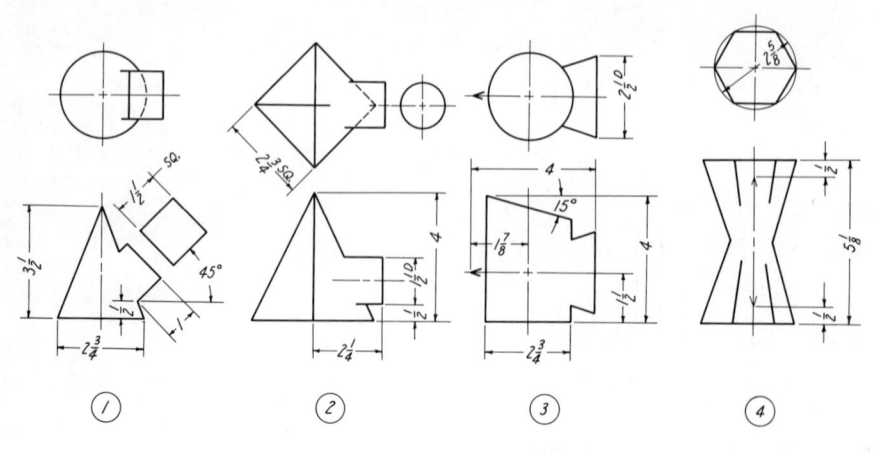

FIG. 11.59. Intersecting surfaces.

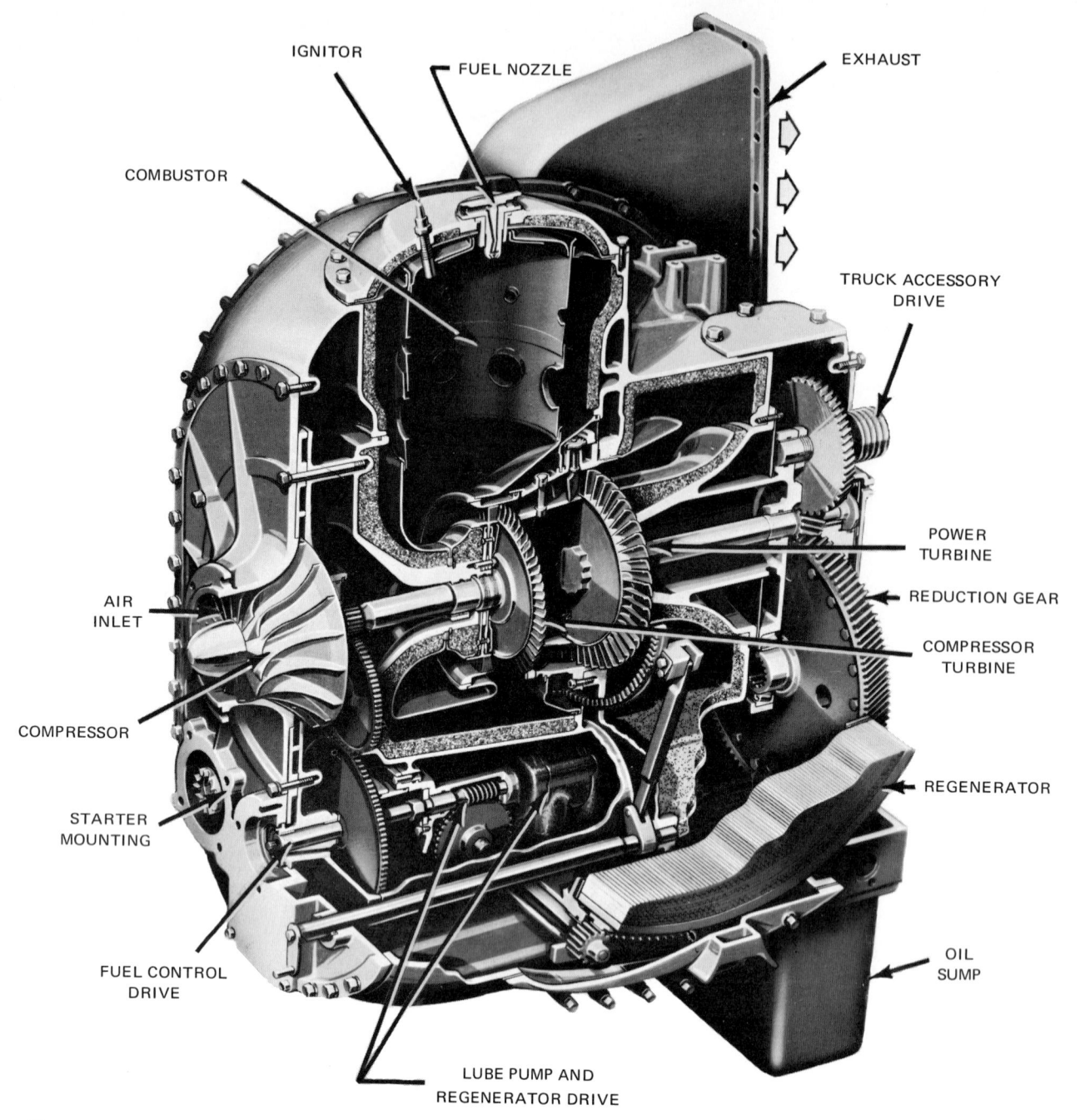

The new research prototype gas turbine engine shown is a low pressure, regenerative power plant. The compressor in the 375-horsepower engine turns at 37,500 revolutions per minute, the output shaft at only 3000 RPM. It weighs 1700 pounds installed, with a length of 40 inches and a height of 39 inches. The pictorial representation of this engine is an excellent example of an industrial illustration. (*Courtesy Ford Motor Company.*)

Pictorial Presentation

12.1

Introduction. An orthographic drawing of two or more views describes an object accurately in form and size, but, since each of the views shows only two dimensions without any suggestion of depth, such a drawing can convey information only to those who are familiar with graphic representation. For this reason, multiview drawings are used mainly by engineers, draftsmen, contractors, and shopmen.

Frequently, however, engineers and draftsmen find they must use conventional picture drawings to convey specific information to persons who do not possess the trained imagination necessary to construct mentally an object from views. To make such drawings, several special schemes of one-plane pictorial drawing have been devised that combine the pictorial effect of perspective with the advantage of having the principal dimensions to scale. But pictorial drawings, in spite of certain advantages, have disadvantages that limit their use. A few of these are as follows:

1. Some drawings frequently have a distorted, unreal appearance that is disagreeable.

2. The time required for execution is, in many cases, greater than for an orthographic drawing.

3. They are difficult to dimension.

4. Some of the lines cannot be measured.

Even with these limitations, pictorial drawings are used extensively for technical publications, Patent Office records, piping diagrams, and furniture designs (Fig. 12.1). Occasionally they are used, in one form or another, to supplement and clarify machine and structural details that would be difficult to visualize (Fig. 12.2).

12.2

Divisions of Pictorial Drawing. Single-plane pictorial drawings are classified in three general divisions: (1) axonometric projection, (2) oblique projection, and (3) perspective projection (Fig. 12.3).

Perspective methods produce the most realistic drawings, but the necessary construction is more difficult and tedious than the construction required for the conventional methods classified under the other two divisions. For this reason, engineers customarily use some form of either axonometric or oblique projection. Modified methods, which are not theoretically correct, are often used to produce desired effects.

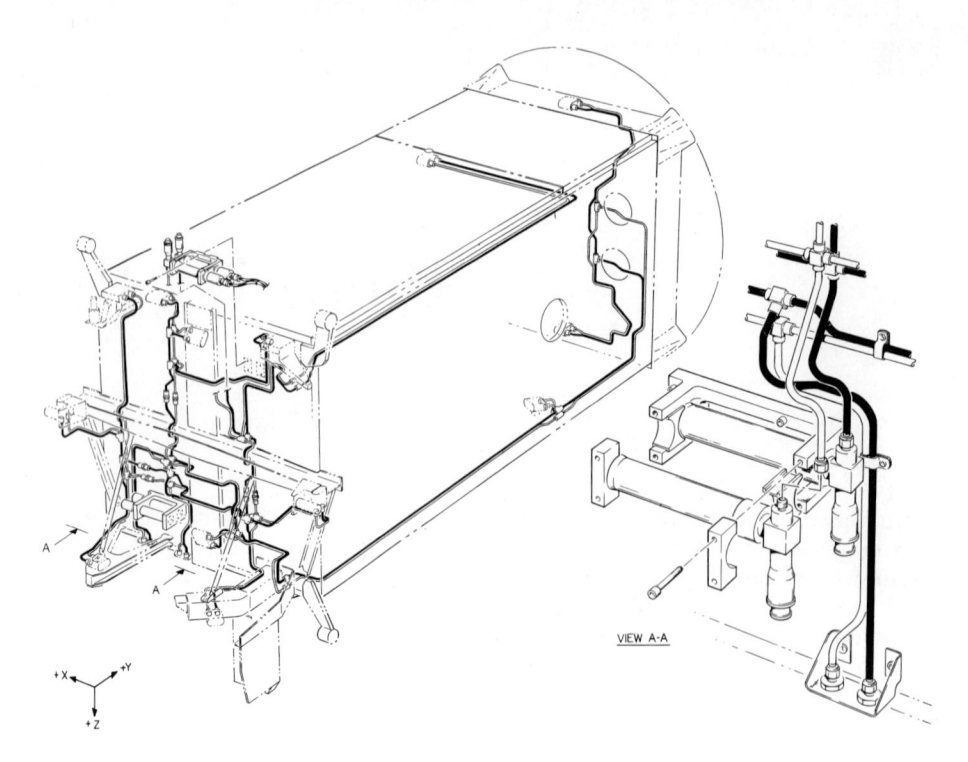

FIG. 12.1. Pictorial illustrations of assembled units are used extensively in instruction manuals. This drawing, showing a release system assembly, appeared in a manual covering the mechanical units of an orbiting geophysical observatory. (*Courtesy TRW Systems Group-Space Technology Laboratories*)

A: AXONOMETRIC PROJECTION

12.3
Divisions of Axonometric Projection. Theoretically, axonometric projection is a form of orthographic projection. The distinguishing difference is that only one plane is used instead of two or more, and the object is turned from its customary position so that three faces are displayed (Fig. 12.4). Since an object may be placed in a countless number of positions relative to the picture plane, an infinite number of views may be drawn, which will vary in general proportions, lengths of edges, and sizes of angles. For practical reasons, a few of these possible positions have been classified in such a manner as to give the recognized divisions of axonometric projection: (1) isometric, (2) dimetric, and (3) trimetric.

Isometric projection is the simplest of these, because the principal axes make equal angles with the plane of projection

CHAP. 12 / PICTORIAL PRESENTATION   251

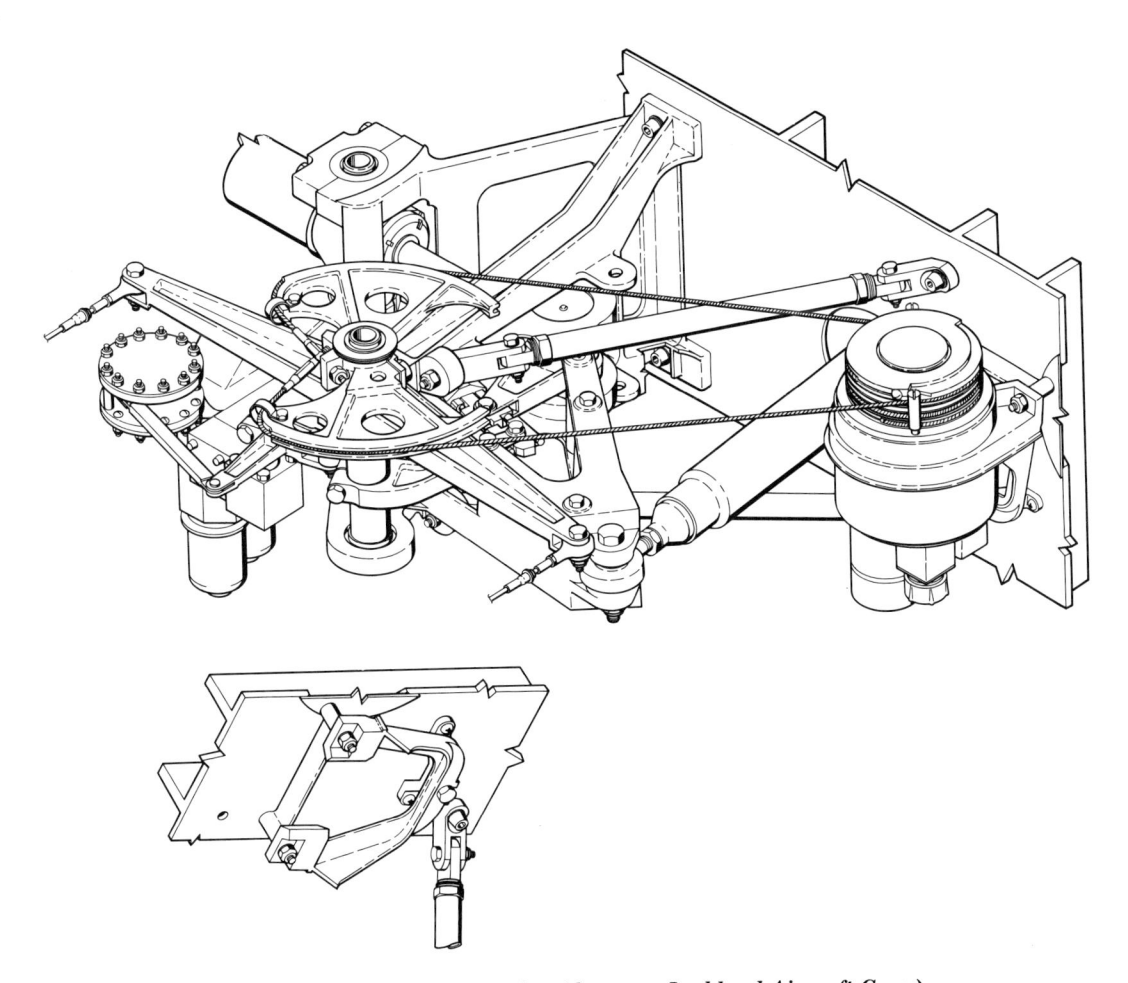

FIG. 12.2. A pictorial illustration (*Courtesy Lockheed Aircraft Corp.*).

AXONOMETRIC   OBLIQUE   PERSPECTIVE

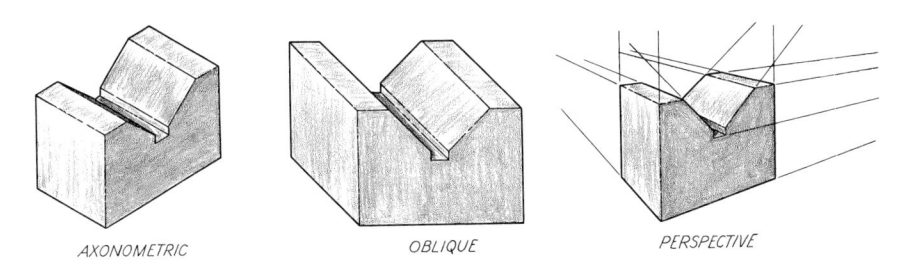

FIG. 12.3. Axonometric, oblique, and perspective projection.

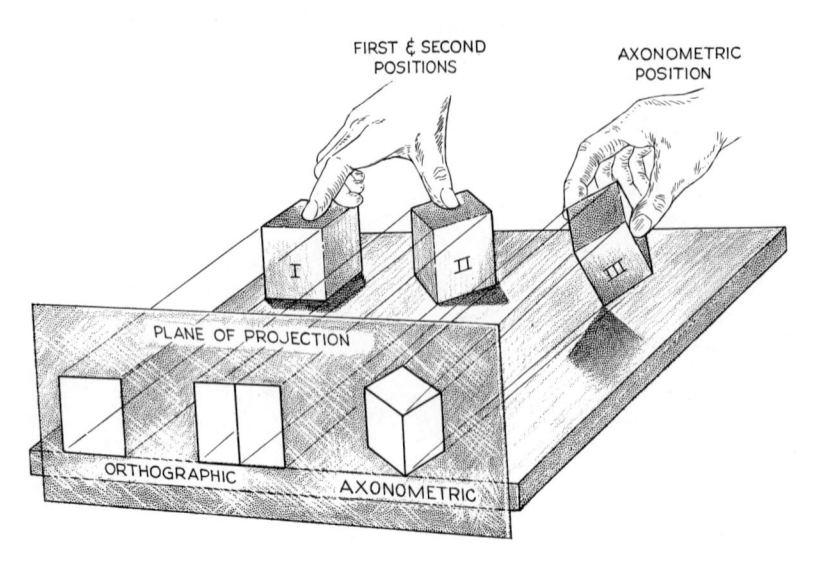

FIG. 12.4. Theory of axonometric projection.

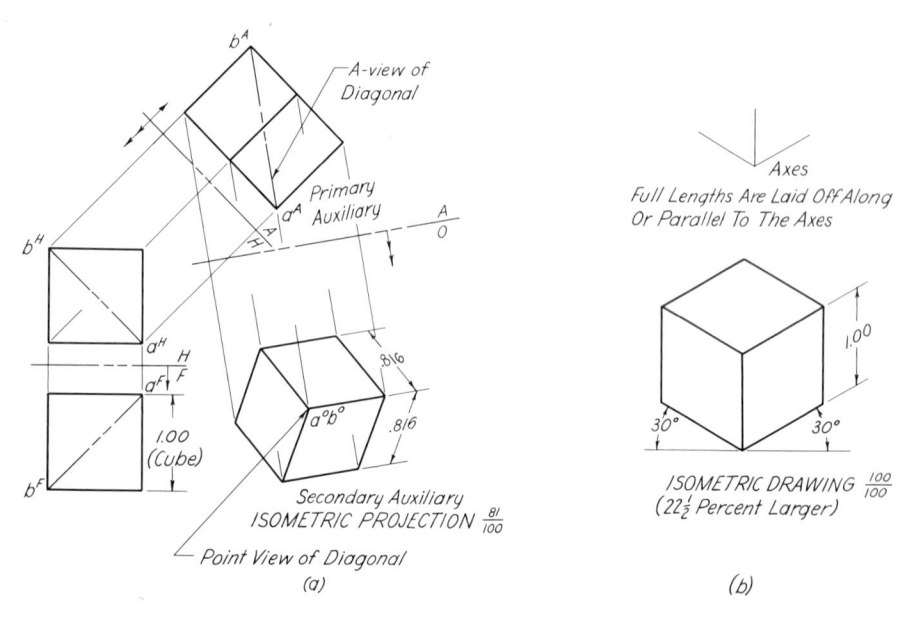

FIG. 12.5. Comparison of isometric projection and isometric drawing.

and the edges are therefore foreshortened equally.

12.4

Isometric Projection. If the cube in Fig. 12.4 is revolved through an angle of 45° about an imaginary vertical axis, as shown in II, and then tilted forward until its body diagonal is perpendicular to the vertical plane, the edges will be foreshortened equally and the cube will be in the correct position to produce an isometric projection.

The three front edges, called isometric axes, make angles of approximately 35° 16' with the vertical plane of projection, or picture plane. In this form of pictorial, the angles between the projections of these axes are 120°, and the projected lengths of the edges of an object, along and parallel to these axes, are approximately 81% of their true lengths. It should be observed that the 90° angles of the cube appear in the isometric projection as either 120° or 60°.

Now, if instead of turning and tilting the object in relation to a principal plane of projection, an auxiliary plane is used that will be perpendicular to the body diagonal, the view projected on the plane will be an axonometric projection. Since the auxiliary plane will be inclined to the principal planes on which the front, top, and side views would be projected, the auxiliary view, taken in a position perpendicular to the body diagonal, will be a secondary auxiliary view, as shown in Fig. 12.5.

12.5

Isometric Scale. An isometric scale (proportional scale) for laying off distances parallel to isometric axes may be made by the simple graphical method shown in Fig. 12.6. Usually, the scale is drawn along the edge of a strip of paper or cardboard. Its use is illustrated in Fig. 12.7.

12.6

Isometric Drawing. Objects seldom are drawn in true isometric projection, the use of an isometric scale being inconvenient and impractical. Instead, a conventional method is used in which all foreshortening is ignored, and actual true lengths are laid off along isometric axes and isometric lines. To avoid confusion and to set this method apart from true isometric projection, it is called isometric drawing.

The isometric drawing of a figure is slightly larger (approximately 22½%) than the isometric projection, but, since the proportions are the same, the increased size does not affect the pictorial value of the representation (see Fig. 12.5). The use of a regular scale makes it possible for a draftsman to produce a satisfactory drawing with a minimum expenditure of time and effort.

In isometric drawing, lines that are parallel to the isometric axes are called *isometric lines*.

12.7

To Make an Isometric Drawing of a Rectangular Object. The procedure followed in making an isometric drawing of a rectangular block is illustrated in Fig. 12.8. The three axes that establish the front edges, as shown in (b), should be drawn through point A so that one extends vertically downward and the other two upward to the right and left at an angle of 30° from the horizontal. Then the actual lengths of the edges may be set off, as shown in (c) and (d), and the remainder of the view completed by drawing lines parallel to the axes through the corners thus located, as in (e) and (f).

Hidden lines, unless absolutely necessary for clearness, always should be omitted on a pictorial representation.

12.8

Nonisometric Lines. Those lines that are inclined and are not parallel to the iso-

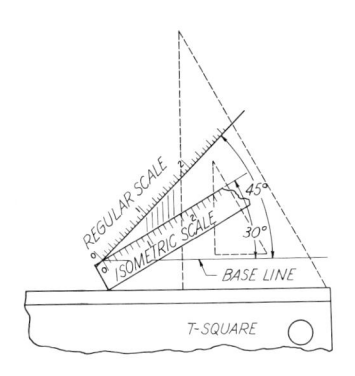

FIG. 12.6. Isometric scale.

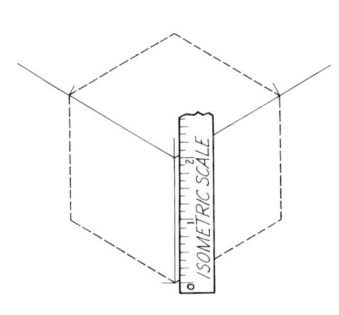

FIG. 12.7. Use of an isometric scale.

metric axes are called *nonisometric lines*. Since a line of this type does not appear in its true length and cannot be measured directly, its position and projected length must be established by locating its extremities. In Fig. 12.9, AB and CD, which represent the edges of the block, are nonisometric lines. The location of AB is established in the pictorial view by locating points A and B. Point A is on the top

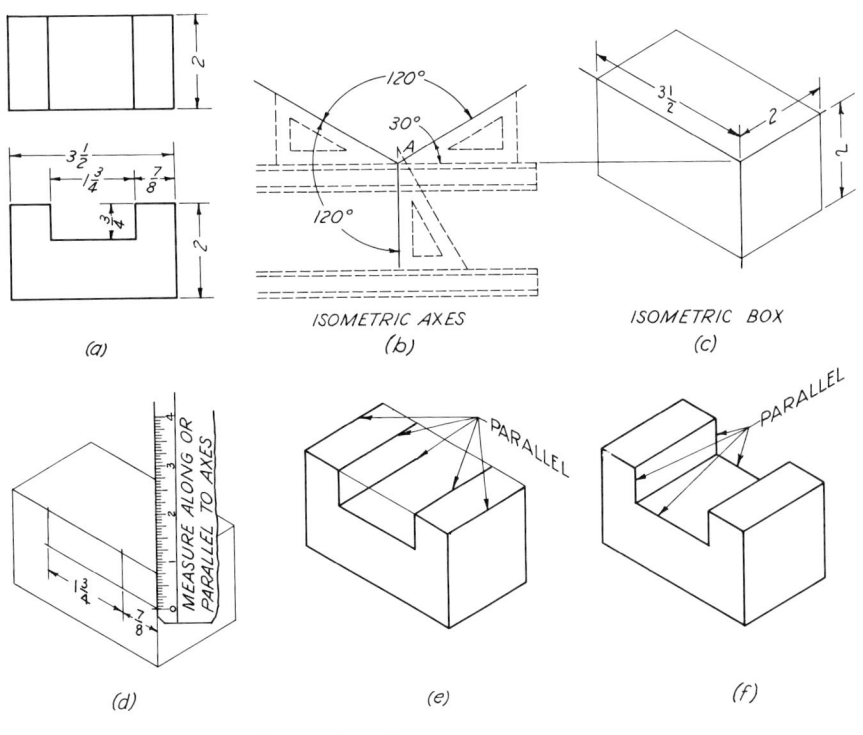

FIG. 12.8. Procedure for constructing an isometric drawing.

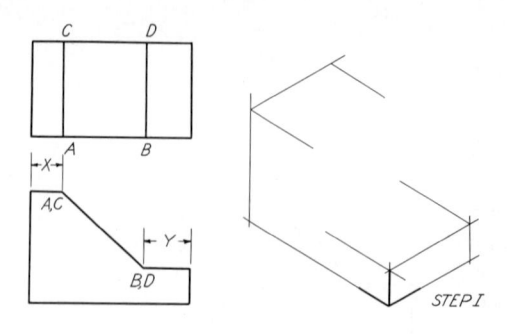

FIG. 12.9. Nonisometric lines.

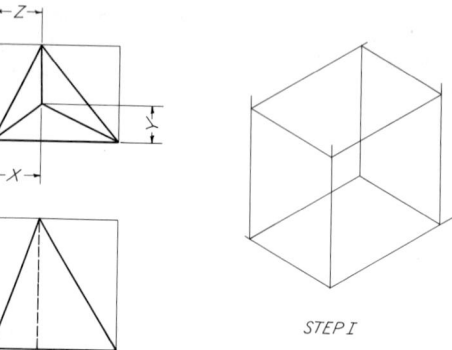

FIG. 12.10. Box construction.

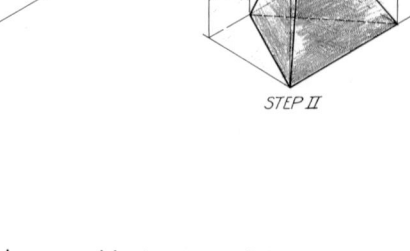

edge, X distance from the left-side surface. Point B is on the upper edge of the base, Y distance from the right-side surface. All other lines coincide with or are parallel to the axes and, therefore, may be measured off with the scale.

The pictorial representation of an irregular solid containing a number of nonisometric lines may be conveniently constructed by the box method; that is, the object may be enclosed in a rectangular box so that both isometric and nonisometric lines may be located by points of contact with its surfaces and edges (see Fig. 12.10).

A study of Figs. 12.9 and 12.10 reveals the important fact that lines that are parallel on an object are parallel in the pictorial view, and, conversely, lines that are not parallel on the object are not parallel on the view. It is often possible to eliminate much tedious construction work by the practical application of the principle of parallel lines.

12.9

Coordinate Construction Method. When an object contains a number of inclined surfaces, such as the one shown in Fig. 12.11, the use of the coordinate construction method is desirable. In this method, the end points of the edges are located in relation to an assumed isometric base line located on an isometric reference plane. For example, the line RL is used as a base line from which measurements are made along isometric lines, as shown. The distances required to locate point A are taken directly from the orthographic views.

Irregular curved edges are most easily drawn in isometric by the offset method, which is a modification of the coordinate construction method (Fig. 12.12). The position of the curve can be readily established by plotted points located by measuring along isometric lines.

12.10
Angles in Isometric Drawing. Since angles specified in degrees do not appear in true size on an isometric drawing, angular measurements must be converted in some manner to linear measurements that can be laid off along isometric lines. Usually, one or two measurements taken from an orthographic view may be laid off along isometric lines on the pictorial drawing to locate an inclined edge that has been specified by an angular dimension. The scale used for the orthographic view must be the same as the one being used in preparing the pictorial drawing.

In Fig. 12.13(a), the position of the inclined line AB was established on the isometric drawing by using the distance X taken from the front view of the orthographic drawing. When an orthographic drawing has already been prepared to a different scale than the scale being used for the pictorial representation, one can draw a partial orthographic view and take off the needed dimensions. A practical application of this idea is shown in (b). By making the construction of a partial view at the place where the angle is to appear on the isometric drawing, the position of the required line can be obtained graphically.

If desired, the tangent method, as explained in Sec. 4.11, may be used, as shown in (c). In using this method, a length equal to 10 units (any scale) is laid off along an isometric line that is to form one side of the angle. Then, a distance equal to 10 times the tangent of the angle is set off along a second isometric line that represents the second leg of the right triangle in pictorial. A line drawn through the end points of these lines will be the required line at the specified angle.

12.11
Circle and Circle Arcs in Isometric Drawing. In isometric drawing, a circle appears as an ellipse. The tedious construction

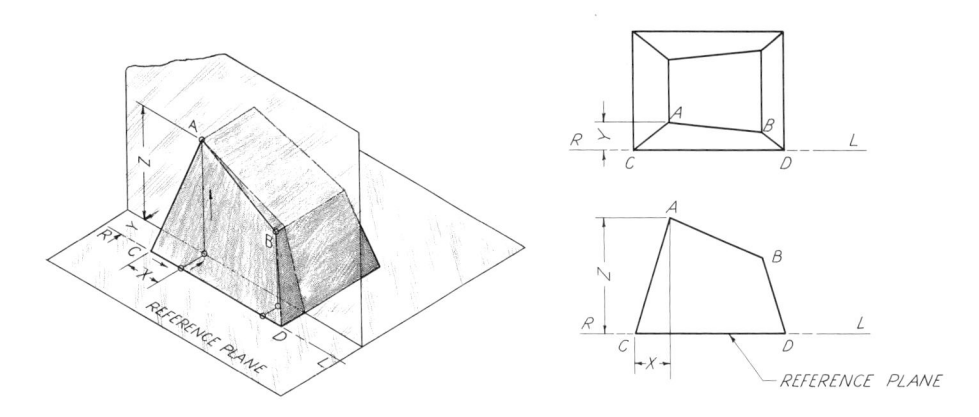

FIG. 12.11. Co-ordinate construction.

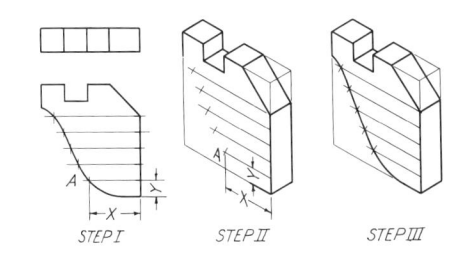

FIG. 12.12. Offset construction.

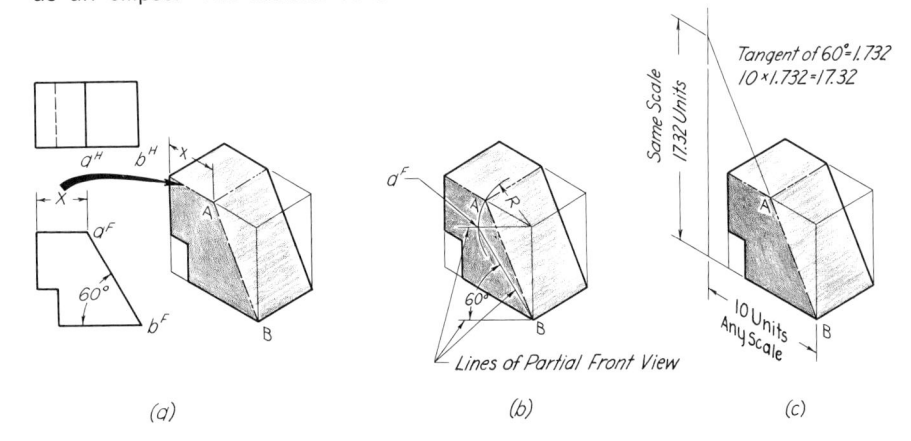

FIG. 12.13. Angles in isometric.

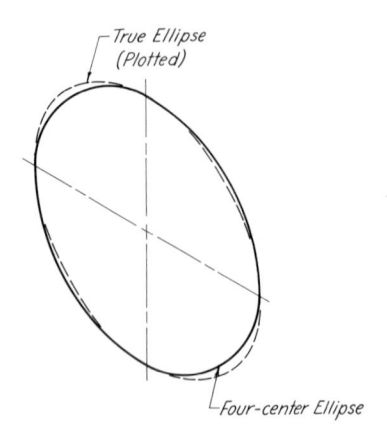

FIG. 12.14. Pictorial ellipses.

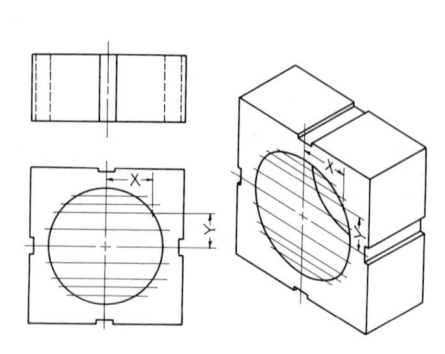

FIG. 12.15. To plot an isometric circle.

required for plotting an ellipse accurately (Figs. 12.14 and 12.15) often is avoided by using some approximate method of drawing. The representation thus obtained is accurate enough for most work, although the true ellipse, which is slightly narrower and longer, is more pleasing in shape (Fig. 12.14). For an approximate construction, a four-center method is generally used.

To draw an ellipse representing a pictorial circle, a square is conceived to be circumscribed about the circle in the orthographic projection. When transferred to the isometric plane in the pictorial view, the square becomes a rhombus (isometric square) and the circle an ellipse tangent to the rhombus at the midpoints of its sides. If the ellipse is to be drawn by the four-center method (Fig. 12.16), the points of intersection of the perpendicular bisectors of the sides of the rhombus will be centers for the four arcs forming the approximate ellipse. The two intersections that lie on the corners of the rhombus are centers for the two large arcs, while the remaining intersections are centers for the two small arcs. Furthermore, the length along the perpendicular from the center of each arc to the point at which the arc is tangent to the rhombus (midpoint) will be the radius. All construction lines required by this method may be made with a T-square and a 30° × 60° triangle.

The amount of work may be still further shortened and the accuracy of the construction improved by following the procedure shown in Fig. 12.17. The steps in this method are as follows:

Step I. Draw the isometric center lines of the required circle.

Step II. Using a radius equal to the radius of the circle, strike arcs across the isometric center lines.

Step III–IV. Through each of these

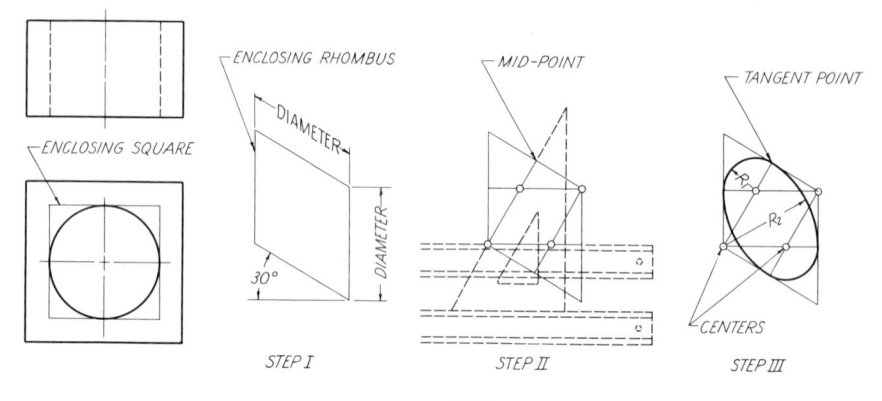

FIG. 12.16. Four-center approximation.

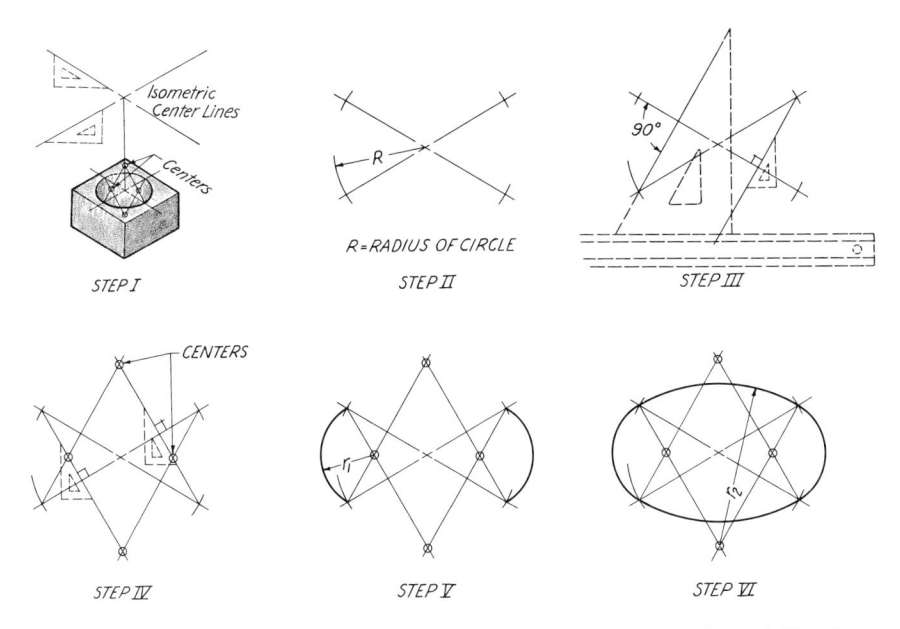

FIG. 12.17. Steps in drawing a four-center isometric circle (ellipse).

points of intersection erect a perpendicular to the other isometric center line.

Steps V–VI. Using the intersection points of the perpendiculars as centers and lengths along the perpendiculars as radii, draw the four arcs that form the ellipse (Fig. 12.18).

A circle arc will appear in pictorial representation as a segment of an ellipse. Therefore, it may be drawn by using as much of the four-center method as is required to locate the needed centers (Fig. 12.19). For example, to draw a quarter circle, it is only necessary to lay off the true radius of the arc along isometric lines drawn through the center and to draw intersecting perpendiculars through these points.

To draw isometric concentric circles by the four-center method, a set of centers must be located for each circle (Fig. 12.20).

When several circles of the same diameter occur in parallel planes, the construction may be simplified. Figure 12.21 shows two views of an object and its cor-

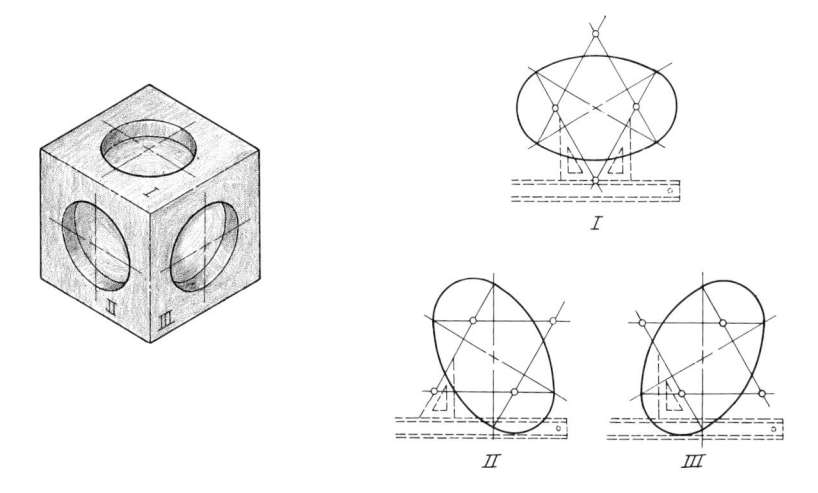

FIG. 12.18. Isometric circles.

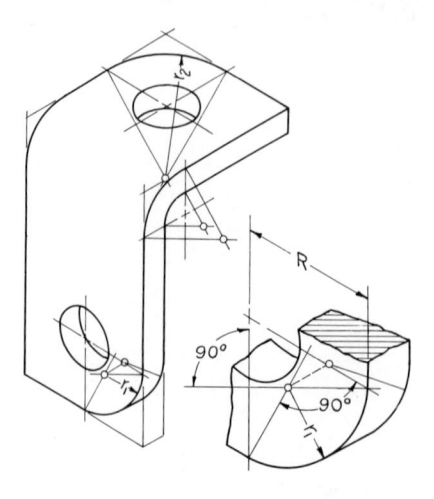

FIG. 12.19. Isometric circle arcs.

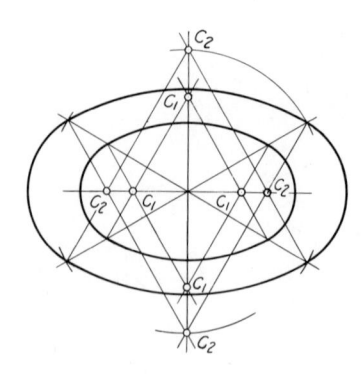

FIG. 12.20. Isometric concentric circles.

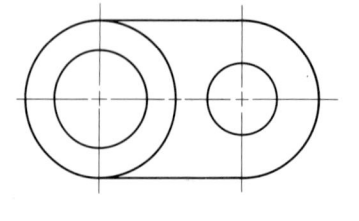

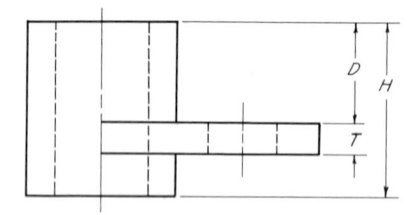

Vertically below center in top surface (H distance equals the over-all height of the cylinder)

Drop center a distance equal to the thickness (T) to obtain the needed curve on the lower surface.

FIG. 12.21. Isometric parallel circles.

responding isometric drawing. In Fig. 12.21, the centers for the ellipse representing the upper base of the large cylinder are found in the usual way, while the centers for the lower base are located by moving the centers for the upper base downward a distance equal to the height of the cylinder. By observing that portion of the object projecting to the right, it can be noted that corresponding centers lie along an isometric line parallel to the axis of the cylinder.

Circles and circle arcs in nonisometric planes may be plotted by using the offset or coordinate method. Sufficient points for establishing a curve must be located by transferring measurements from the orthographic views to isometric lines in the

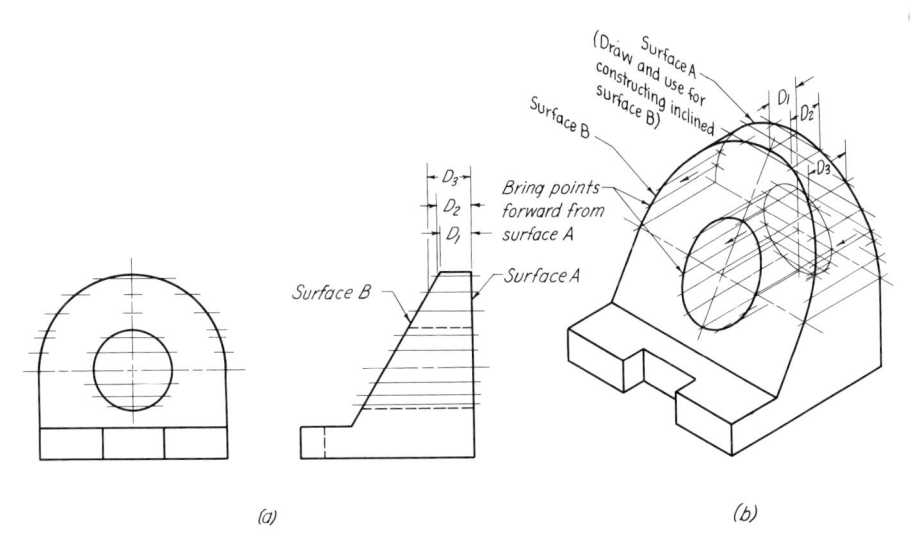

FIG. 12.22. Circles in nonisometric planes.

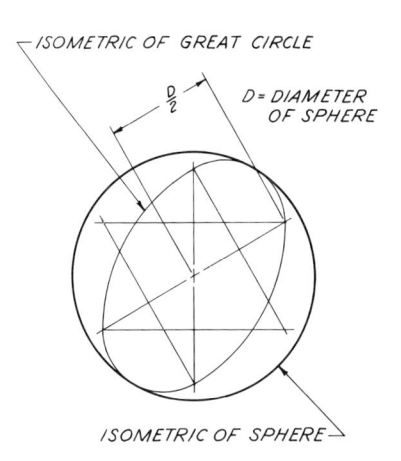

FIG. 12.23. Isometric drawing of a sphere.

pictorial view. There is a rapid and easy way for drawing the cylindrical portion of the object shown in Fig. 12.22. The semicircular arc must be plotted on the rear surface as the first step. Then, after this has been done, each point is brought forward to the inclined face. The offset distances (D_1, D_2, D_3, etc.) at each level are taken from the side view in (a).

The pictorial representation of a sphere is the envelope of all of the great circles that could be drawn on the surface. In isometric drawing, the great circles appear as ellipses and a circle is their envelope. In practice it is necessary to draw only one ellipse, using the true radius of the sphere and the four-center method of construction. The diameter of the circle is the long diameter of the ellipse (Fig. 12.23).

12.12
Positions of Isometric Axes. It is sometimes desirable to place the principal isometric axes so that an object will be in position to reveal certain faces to a better advantage (Fig. 12.24).

The difference in direction should cause no confusion, since the angle between the axes and the procedure followed in constructing the view are the same for any position. The choice of the direction may depend on the construction of the object, but usually this is determined by the position from which the object is ordinarily viewed.

Reversed axes (b) are used in architectural work to show a feature as it would be seen from a natural position below.

Sometimes long objects are drawn with the long axis horizontal, as shown in Fig. 12.25.

12.13
Isometric Sectional Views (Fig. 12.26). Generally, an isometric sectional view is

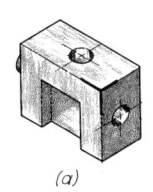

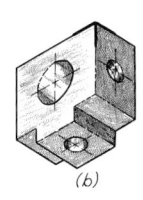

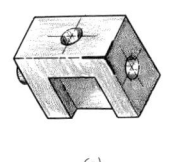

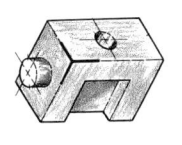

FIG. 12.24. Convenient positions of axes.

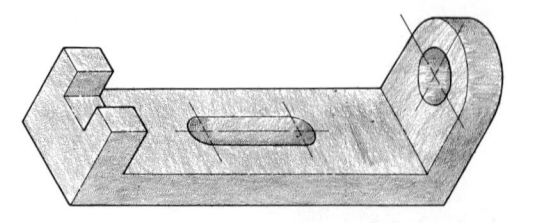

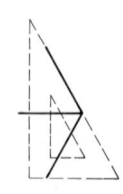

FIG. 12.25. Main axis horizontal—long objects.

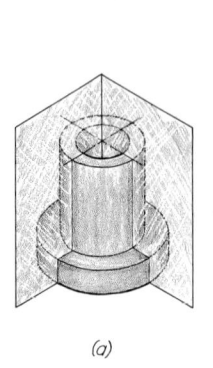

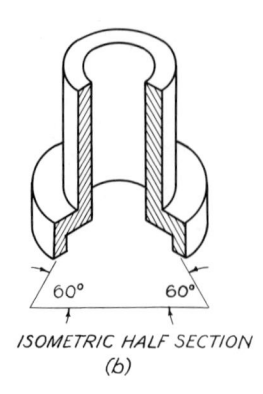

FIG. 12.26. Isometric half section.

used for showing the inner construction of an object when there is a complicated interior to be explained or when it is desirable to emphasize features that would not appear in a usual outside view. Sectioning in isometric drawing is based on the same principles as sectioning in orthographic drawing. Isometric planes are used for cutting an object, and the general procedure followed in constructing the representation is the same as for an exterior view.

Figure 12.26 shows an isometric half section. It is easier, in this case, to outline the outside view of the object in full and then remove a front quarter with isometric planes.

Figure 12.27 illustrates a full section in isometric. The accepted procedure for constructing this form of sectional view is to draw the cut face and then add the portion that lies behind.

Section lines should be sloped at an angle that produces the best effect, but they should never be drawn parallel to object lines. In Fig. 12.28, (*a*) illustrates the slope that is correct for most drawings, while (*b*), (*c*), and (*d*) show the poor effect produced when this phase of section lining is ignored. Ordinarily, isometric section lines are drawn at 60°.

12.14

Dimetric Projection. The view of an object that has been so placed that two of its axes make equal angles with the plane of projection is called a *dimetric projection*. The third axis may make either a smaller or larger angle. All of the edges along or parallel to the first two axes are foreshortened equally, while those parallel to the third axis are foreshortened a different amount. It might be said that dimetric

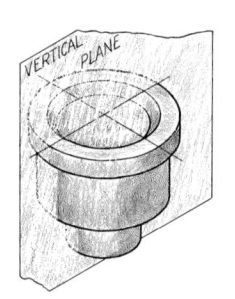

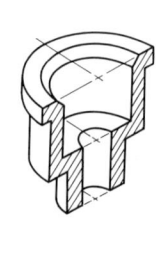

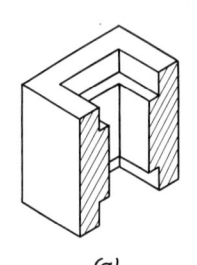

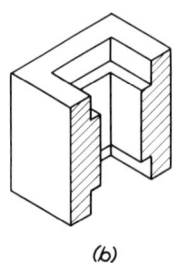

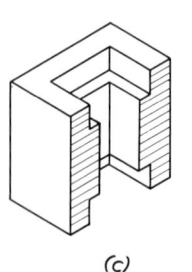

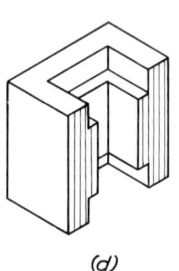

FIG. 12.27. Isometric full section.   **FIG. 12.28.** Section lining.

projection, a division of axonometric projection, is like isometric projection in that the object must be placed to satisfy specific conditions. Similarly, a dimetric projection may be drawn by using the auxiliary view method. The secondary auxiliary view is the dimetric projection. The procedure is the same as for an isometric projection (Fig. 12.5), except that the line of sight is taken in the direction necessary to obtain the desired dimetric projection. Obviously, an infinite number of dimetric projections is possible.

In practical application, dimetric projection is sometimes modified so that regular scales can be used to lay off measurements to assumed ratios. This is called *dimetric drawing*. [Fig. 12.29(a)].

The angles and scales may be worked out* for any ratios, such as $1:1:\frac{1}{2}$ (full size:full size:half size); $1:1:\frac{3}{4}$ (full size:full size:three-fourths size). For example, the angles for the ratios $1:1:\frac{1}{2}$ are 7° 11′ and 41° 25′. After the scales have been assumed and the angles computed, an enclosing box may be drawn in conformity to the angles and the view completed by following the general procedure used in isometric drawing, except that two scales must be used. The positions commonly used, along with the scale ratios and corresponding angles, are shown in Fig. 12.29(b). The first scale given in each ratio is for the vertical axis. Since two of the axes are foreshortened equally, while the third is foreshortened in different ratio, obviously two scales must be used. This is an effective method of representation.

12.15
Trimetric Projection (Fig. 12.31). A trimetric projection of an object is the view obtained when each of the three axes makes a different angle with the plane of projection. As might be expected, a trimetric projection may be constructed by drawing successive auxiliary views. However, since there are an unlimited number of possible lines of sight that will produce unequal foreshortening in the directions of the three axes, considerable thought must be given to the selection of a position that will show the object pictorially to the best advantage in the second auxiliary view. Making this decision is not easy. This form of pictorial representation has been used to some extent by certain aircraft companies for the preparation of production illustrations.

12.16
To Construct an Axonometric Projection (Isometric, Dimetric, or Trimetric) Directly From the Orthographic Views. A true axonometric projection can be prepared by projecting directly from two or more of the orthographic views of an object. The method, commonly called the method of intersections, was developed some years prior to 1937, the year that it was first published by Professor L. Eckhart of the Vienna College of Engineering. Since then it has been rather widely used in the United States by those whose principal task is the preparation of pictorial drawings of complicated parts for which the orthographic views may be available. The underlying principles and basic procedure for the preparation of an isometric projection have been illustrated in Fig. 12.30.

In (a) the relationship of the axonometric plane to the three principal planes has been shown pictorially, and it must be understood at this point in the discussion that, since the picture plane and the axonometric plane are coincident, the axonometric triangle will be in true size. Also two other facts must be noted. First, since axonometric projection is true orthographic projection, the projection lines are perpendicular to the plane of projec-

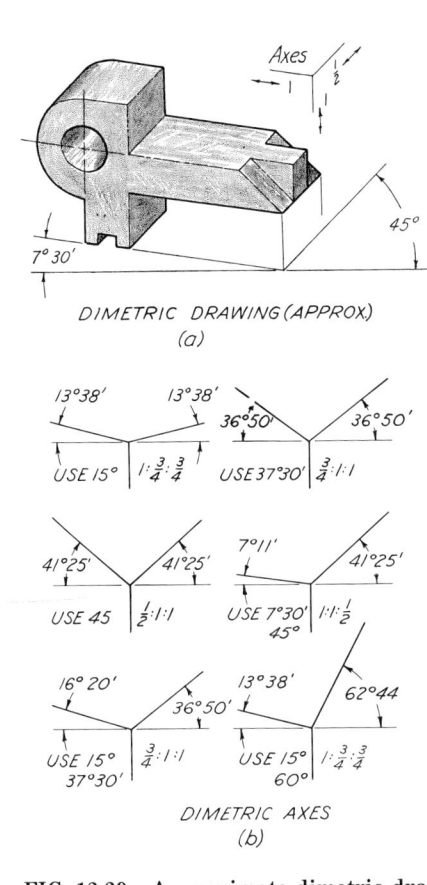

FIG. 12.29. Approximate dimetric drawing.

---

*Formula: $\cos \alpha = -\sqrt{2s_1^2 s_2^2 - s_2^4}/2s_1 s_2$. In this formula, α is one of the equal angles, s_1 is one of the equal scales, and s_2 is the third scale.

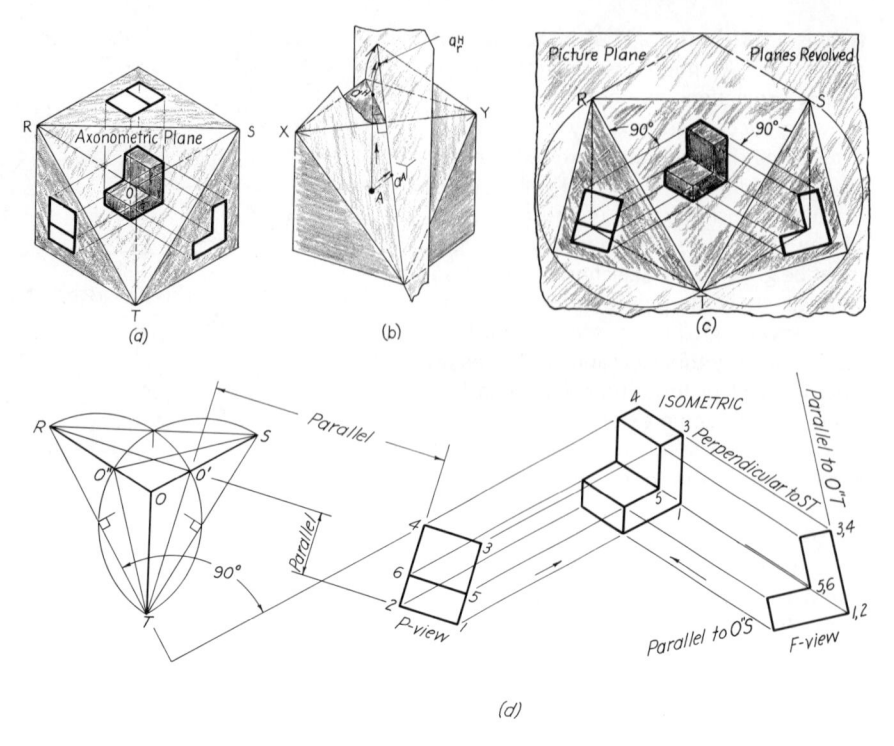

262   PART II / SPATIAL GRAPHICS: SHAPE DESCRIPTION AND SPATIAL RELATIONSHIPS

FIG. 12.30. To construct an axonometric projection from the orthographic views.

To start the graphical diagram in (*d*) three mutually perpendicular lines were drawn to represent the three intersecting edges *OR*, *OS*, and *OT* of the cube (see *a*). By geometry, *OR* will be perpendicular to *ST*, *OS* will be perpendicular to *RT*, and *OT* will be perpendicular to *RS*. With this diagram as now laid out, the right triangle *OST* may readily be revolved into the axonometric plane *RST*. One of the advantages of starting the diagram with the axes, as was done in the illustration, is that the forward triangle may then be revolved into the axonometric plane to determine the position of the orthographic views, instead of the rear triangle as in (*c*), which would require the construction of the entire box. In revolving the right triangle *OST*, which must show in true size as *O″ST* in the axonometric plane, it is necessary to apply the geometric principle that any two lines will form a right angle that are drawn from a point on the circumference of a circle to the end points of its diameter. Hence, point *O* moves along *OR*, which is perpendicular to *ST*, to a position on the semicircle that has been constructed on *ST* as a diameter. Similarly, *O* moves to *O′* on *OS* when the right triangle *ORT* has been revolved into the axonometric plane.

With the diagram constructed as explained, the step-by-step procedure for preparing the axonometric drawing shown is as follows:

1. Draw the *F*-view in some convenient location with the principal edges of the view parallel to the revolved positions of the two axes for the view, that is, with the base edge parallel to *O″S* and the edge that is perpendicular to the base parallel to *O″T*.

2. Draw the *P*-view at another location with the edges of the view parallel to the revolved position of the axes for the *P*-view.

tion. Second, when a point is projected on adjacent planes (see *b*) and one of the planes is revolved into the plane of the other, the two views of the point will lie on a single line that is perpendicular to the fold line—that is, the line of intersection *XY* of the two planes.

In (*c*) the principal planes have been shown revolved into the plane of the axonometric triangle, and it should now become evident to the reader how orthographic views might be used to obtain an axonometric projection once their revolved positions have been determined. By observing the drawing in (*c*) one can see that the projecting lines are perpendicular to the axis of rotation and that the principal edges of each view are parallel to the corresponding edges of the revolved plane.

3. From the corners of the *F*-view draw projecting lines perpendicular to *ST* and parallel to *OR*.

4. From the corners of the *P*-view draw projecting lines perpendicular to *RT* and parallel to *OS*.

The intersection of these projecting lines with those from the *F*-view establishes the desired isometric projection.

When none of the angles formed by the coordinate axes of the diagram are equal, the resulting pictorial representation will be a trimetric projection. When two of the angles are equal a dimetric projection is obtained. In Fig. 12.30(*d*) all three of the angles were made equal because an isometric projection was deemed desirable (since engineers and draftsmen are accustomed to seeing isometric drawings and sketches in their daily work).

In preparing the trimetric projection shown in Fig. 12.31, a preliminary pictorial sketch was made to show the general appearance desired for the finished pictorial. Then the axes in the diagram were drawn very nearly parallel to the principal lines of the sketch. Otherwise, the procedure followed in constructing the pictorial representation was the same as has been explained for an isometric projection. To draw the elliptical projection of the circular arc, two points, numbered 1 and 2 in both orthographic views, were assumed along the arc. More points may be used when needed.

B: OBLIQUE PROJECTION

12.17
Oblique Projection. In oblique projection, the view is produced by using parallel projectors that make some angle other than 90° with the plane of projection. Generally, one face is placed parallel to the picture plane and the projection lines are

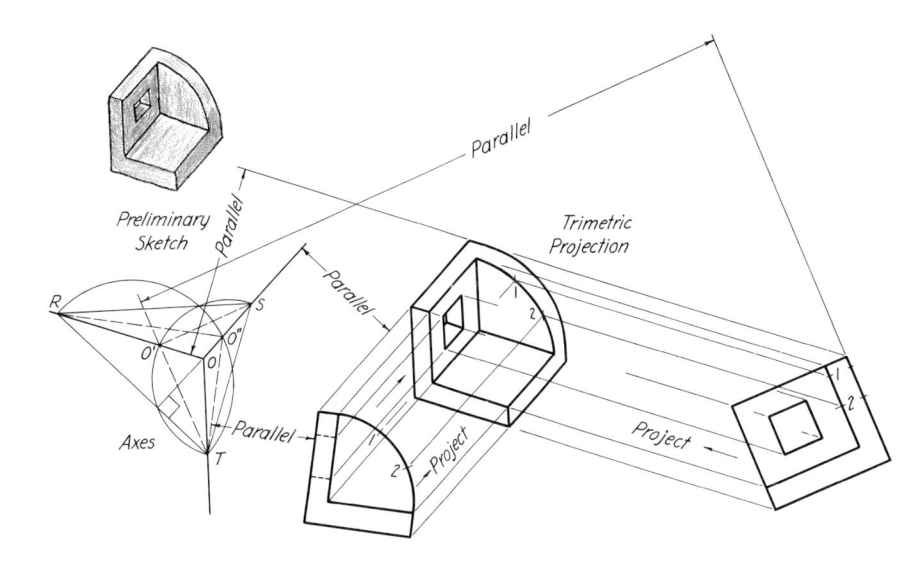

FIG. 12.31. To construct a trimetric projection.

taken at 45°. This gives a view that is pictorial in appearance, as it shows the front and one or more additional faces of an object. In Fig. 12.32, the orthographic and oblique projections of a cube are shown. When the angle is 45°, as in this illustration, the representation is sometimes called *cavalier projection*. It is generally known, however, as an *oblique projection* or an *oblique drawing*.

12.18
Principle of Oblique Projection. The theory of oblique projection can be explained by imagining a vertical plane of projection in front of a cube parallel to one of its faces (Fig. 12.32). When the projectors make an angle of 45° in any direction with the picture plane, the length of any oblique projection $A'B'$ of the edge AB is equal to the true length of AB. Note that the projectors could be parallel to any element of a 45° cone having its base in the plane of projection. With projectors at this particular angle (45°), the face parallel to the plane is projected in its true size and shape and the edges perpendicular to the

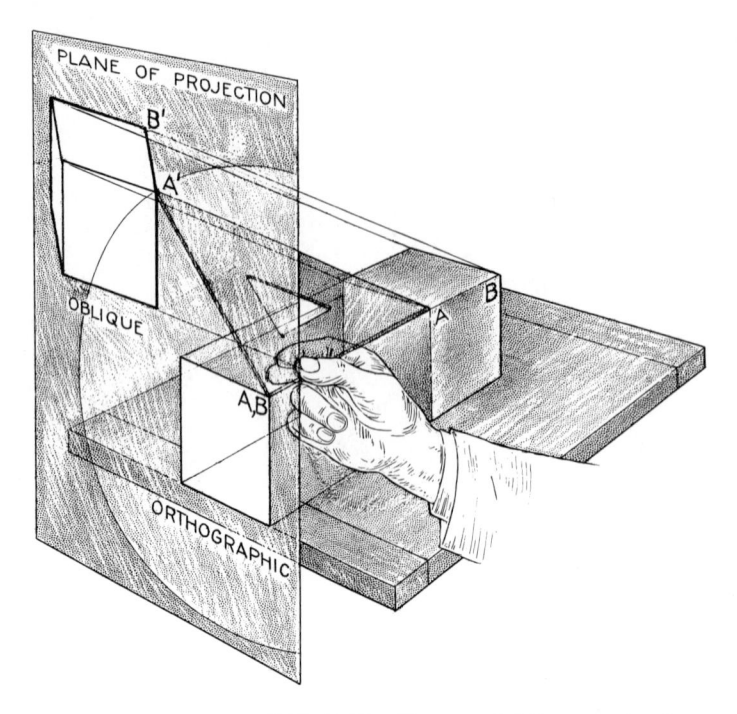

FIG. 12.32. Theory of oblique projection.

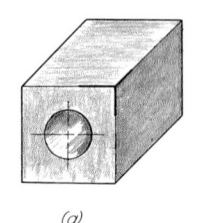

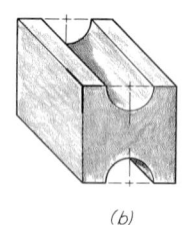

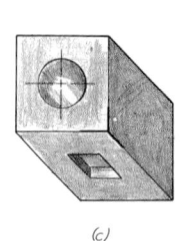

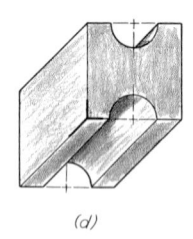

FIG. 12.33. Various positions of the receding axis.

picture plane are projected in their true length. If the projectors make a greater angle, the oblique projection will be shorter, while if the angle is less, the projection will be longer.

12.19
Oblique Drawing. This form of drawing is based on three mutually perpendicular axes along which, or parallel to which, the necessary measurements are made for constructing the representation. Oblique drawing differs from isometric drawing principally in that two axes are always perpendicular to each other, while the third (receding axis) is at some convenient angle, such as 30°, 45°, or 60° with the horizontal (Fig. 12.34). It is somewhat more flexible and has the following advantages over isometric drawing: (1) circular or irregular outlines on the front face show in their true shape; (2) distortion can be reduced by foreshortening along the receding axis; and (3) a greater choice is permitted in the selection of the positions of the axes. A few of the various views that can be obtained by varying the inclination of the receding axis are illustrated in Fig. 12.33. Usually, the selection of the position is governed by the character of the object.

12.20
To Make an Oblique Drawing. The procedure to be followed in constructing an oblique drawing of an adjustable guide is illustrated in Fig. 12.34. The three axes that establish the perpendicular edges in (*b*) are drawn through point *O* representing the front corner. *OA* and *OB* are perpendicular to each other and *OC* is at any desired angle (say, 30°) with the horizontal. After the width, height, and depth have been set off, the front face may be laid out in its true size and shape, as in (*c*), and the view can be completed by drawing lines parallel to the receding axis through the established corners. The circle and semicircle are shown parallel to the picture plane in order to avoid distortion and because, from the draftsman's standpoint, it is easier to draw a circle than to construct an ellipse.

In general, the procedure for constructing an oblique drawing is the same as for an isometric drawing.

12.21
Use of a Basic Plane. If the front face of an object is in one plane, it will appear

CHAP. 12 / PICTORIAL PRESENTATION **265**

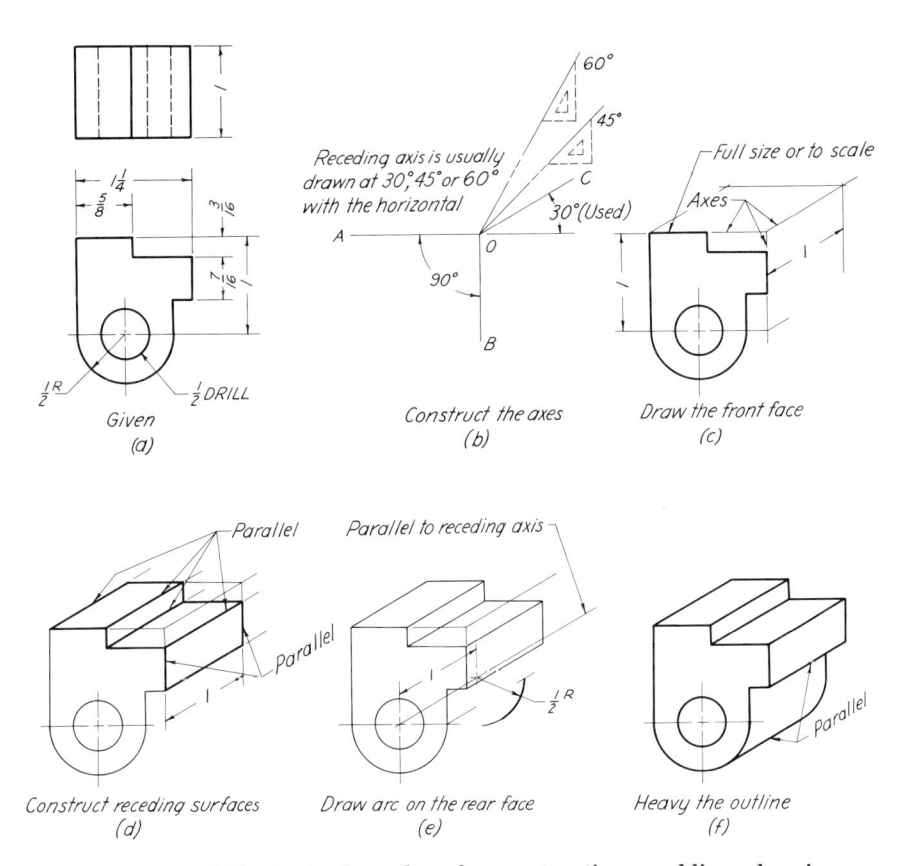

FIG. 12.34. Procedure for constructing an oblique drawing.

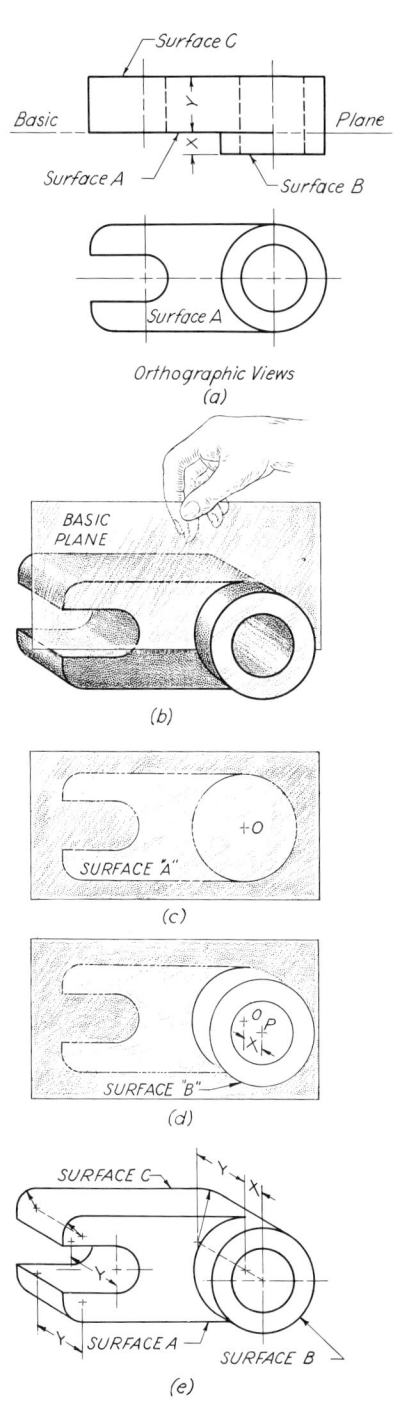

FIG. 12.35. Basic plane theory of construction.

in the oblique drawing exactly the same as in orthographic drawing. Note this fact in Fig. 12.34. But the front of many objects is composed of two or more parallel planes whose relationship must be carefully established. The convenient way to accomplish this is to use one of the planes as a basic (starting) plane and work from it in the direction of the receding axis, as illustrated in Fig. 12.35. Since the front surface A presents the contour shape, it should be selected as the basic plane and drawn first as the front of the oblique projection, as shown in (c). The center P of the circles for surface B may be located easily by measuring along the axis of the hole from O, in plane A, a distance X equal to the distance between the planes. The measurement must be made forward along the axis from O, because surface B is in front of A. The centers of the arcs on the surface C are located in a similar manner, except that the direction of making the measurements is from the basic plane toward the back.

When an object has one or more inclined surfaces with a curved outline, it may be drawn by constructing a right section and making offset measurements, as shown in Fig. 12.39.

12.22

Rules for Placing an Object. Generally, the most irregular face, or the one containing

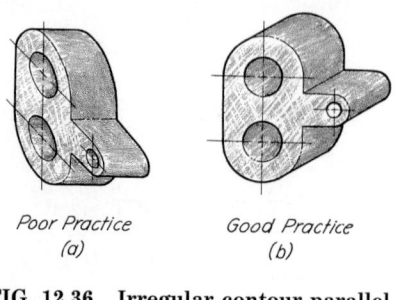

266 PART II / SPATIAL GRAPHICS: SHAPE DESCRIPTION AND SPATIAL RELATIONSHIPS

Poor Practice
(a)

Good Practice
(b)

FIG. 12.36. Irregular contour parallel to picture plane.

(a)

(b)

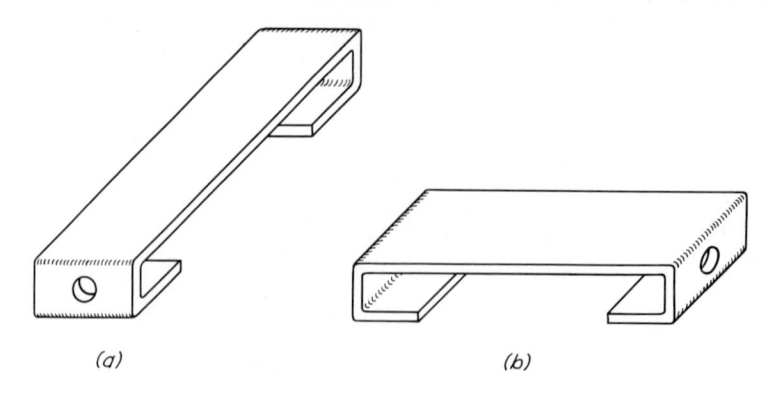

FIG. 12.37. Long axis parallel to picture plane.

the most circular outlines, should be placed parallel to the picture plane, in order to minimize distortion and simplify construction. By following this practice, all or most of the circles and circle arcs can be drawn with a compass, and the tedious construction that would be required to draw their elliptical representations in a receding plane is eliminated. In selecting the position of an object, two rules should be followed. The first is to place the face having the most irregular contour, or the most circular outlines, parallel to the picture plane. Note in Fig. 12.36 the advantage of following this rule.

When the longest face of an object is used as the front face, the pictorial view will be distorted to a lesser degree and, therefore, will have a more realistic and pleasing appearance. Hence, the second rule is to place the longest face parallel to the picture plane. Compare the views shown in Fig. 12.37 and note the greater distortion in (a) over (b).

If these two rules clash, the first should govern. It is more desirable to have the irregular face show its true shape than it is to lessen the distortion in the direction of the receding axis.

12.23
Angles, Circles, and Circle Arcs in Oblique. As previously stated, angles, circles, and irregular outlines on surfaces parallel to the plane of projection show in true size and shape. When located on receding faces, the construction methods used in isometric drawing may usually be applied. Figure 12.38 shows the method of drawing the elliptical representation of a circle on an oblique face. Note that the method is identical with that used for constructing isometric circles, except for the slight change in the position of the axes.

Circle arcs and circles on inclined planes must be plotted by using the offset or coordinate method (Fig. 12.39).

(a)   (b)   (c)

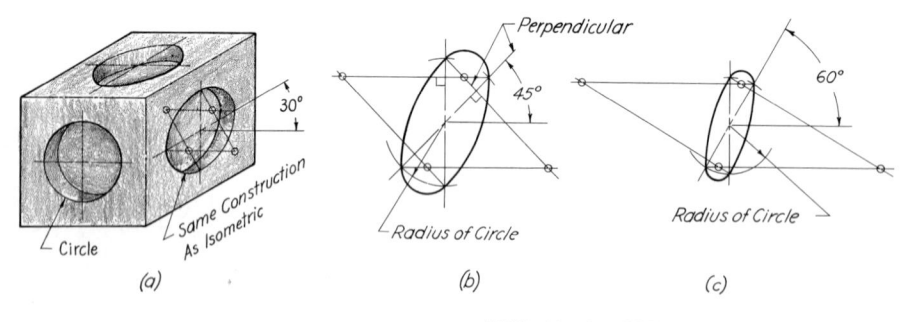

FIG. 12.38. Oblique circles.

12.24
Reduction of Measurements in the Direction of the Receding Axis. An oblique drawing often presents a distorted appearance that is unnatural and disagreeable to the eye. In some cases the view constructed by this scheme is so misleading in appearance that it is unsatisfactory for any practical purpose. As a matter of interest, the effect of distortion is due to the fact that the receding lines are parallel and do not appear to converge as the eye is accustomed to anticipating (Fig. 12.40).

The appearance of excessive thickness can be overcome somewhat by reducing the length of the receding lines. For practical purposes, measurements usually are reduced one-half, but any scale of reduction may be arbitrarily adopted if the view obtained will be more realistic in appearance. When the receding lines are drawn one-half their actual length, the resulting pictorial view is called a *cabinet drawing*. Figure 12.41 shows an oblique drawing (a) and a cabinet drawing (c) of the same object, for the purpose of comparison.

12.25
Oblique Sectional Views. Oblique sectional views are drawn to show the interior construction of objects. The construction procedure is the same as for an isometric sectional view, except that oblique planes are used for cutting the object. An oblique half section is illustrated in Fig. 12.42.

12.26
Pictorial Dimensioning. The dimensioning of isometric and other forms of pictorial working drawings is done in accordance with the following rules:

1. Draw extension and dimension lines (except those dimension lines applying to cylindrical features) parallel to the pictorial axes in the plane of the surface to which they apply (Fig. 12.43).

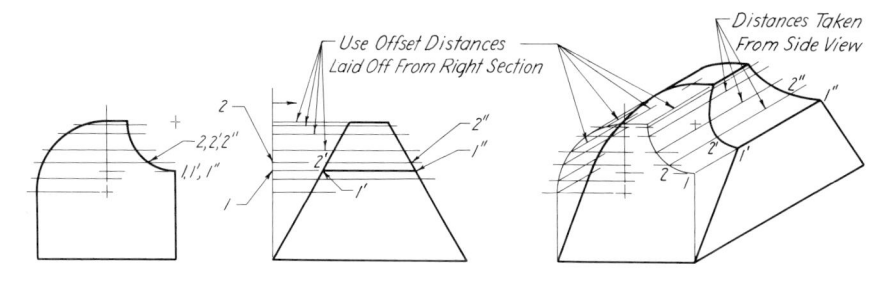

FIG. 12.39. Curved outlines on an inclined plane.

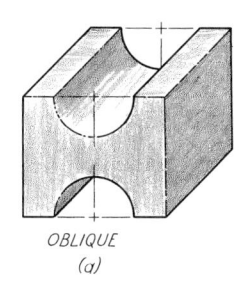

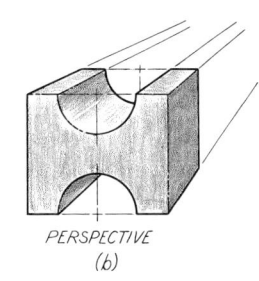

FIG. 12.40. Comparison of oblique and perspective.

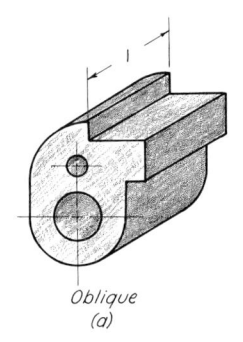

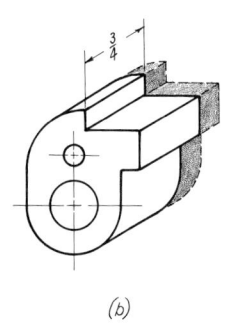

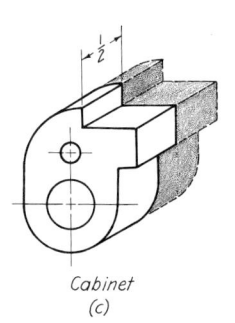

FIG. 12.41. Foreshortening in the direction of the receding axis.

2. If possible, apply dimensions to visible surfaces.

3. Place dimensions on the object, if, by so doing, better appearance, added clearness, and easy readings result.

4. Notes may be lettered either in pic-

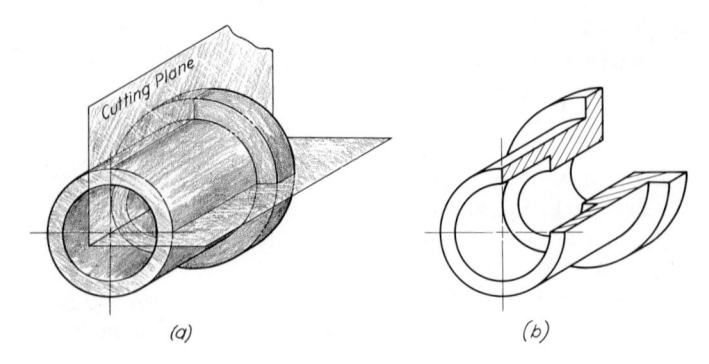

FIG. 12.42. Oblique half section.

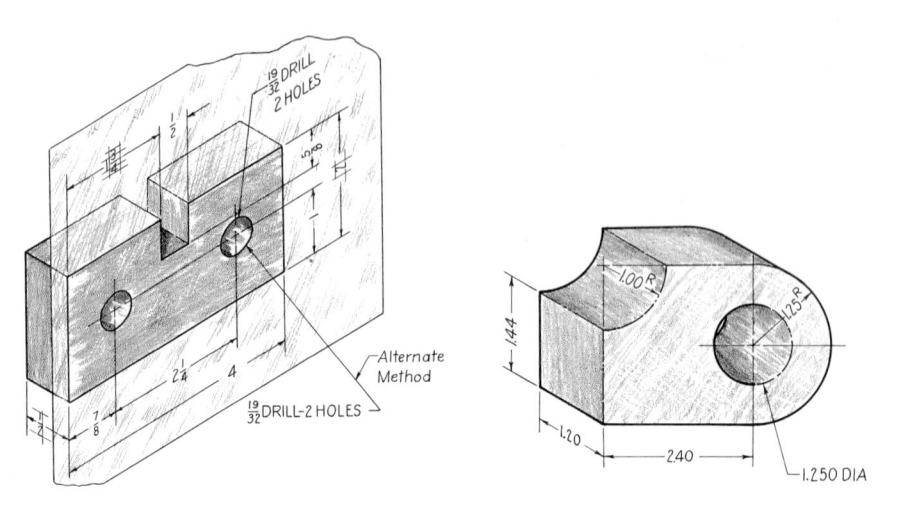

FIG. 12.43. Extension and dimension lines in isometric (left); numerals, fractions, and notes in oblique (right).

torial or as on ordinary drawings. When lettered as on ordinary drawings the difficulties encountered in forming pictorial letters are avoided (Fig. 12.43).

5. Make the figures of a dimension appear to be lying in the plane of the surface whose dimension it indicates, by using vertical figures drawn in pictorial (Fig. 12.43). (Note: Guide lines and slope lines are drawn parallel to the pictorial axes.)

12.27
Conventional Treatment of Pictorial Drawings. When it is desirable for an isometric or an oblique drawing of a casting to present a somewhat more or less realistic appearance, it becomes necessary to represent the fillets and rounds on the unfinished surfaces. One method commonly used by draftsmen is shown in Figure 12.44(*a*). On the drawing in (*b*) all of the edges have been treated as if they were

sharp. The conventional treatment for threads in pictorial is illustrated in (b) and (c).

C: PERSPECTIVE PROJECTION

12.28
Perspective. In perspective projection an object is shown much as the human eye or camera would see it at a particular point. Actually, it is a geometric method by which a picture can be projected on a picture plane in much the same way as in photography. Perspective drawing differs from the methods previously discussed in that the projectors or visual rays intersect at a common point known as the *station point* (Fig. 12.47).

Since the perspective shows an object as it appears instead of showing its true shape and size, it is rarely used by engineers. It is more extensively employed by architects to show the appearance of proposed buildings, by artist-draftsmen for production illustrations, and by illustrators in preparing advertising drawings.

Figure 12.2 shows a type of production illustration that has been widely used in assembly departments as an aid to those persons who find it difficult to read an orthographic assembly. This form of presentation, which may show a mechanism both exploded and assembled, has made it possible for industrial concerns to employ semitrained personnel. Figure 12.59 shows a type of industrial drawing made in perspective that has proved useful in aircraft plants. Because of the growing importance of this type of drawing, and also because engineers frequently will find perspective desirable for other purposes, its elementary principles should be discussed logically in this text. Other books on the subject, some of which are listed in the bibliography, should be studied by architectural students and those inter-

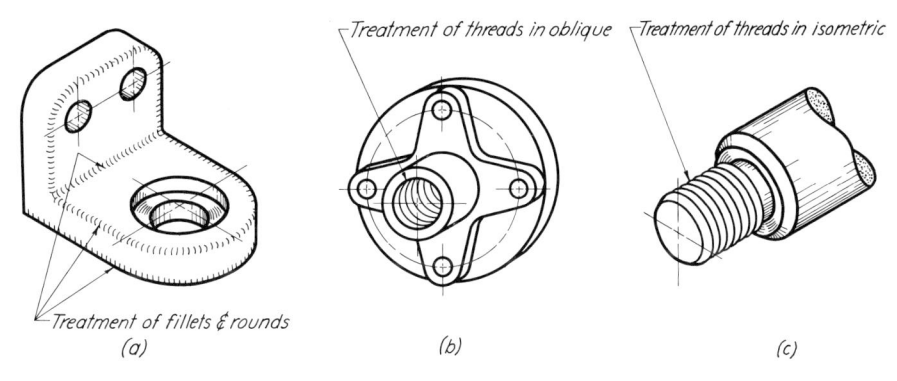

FIG. 12.44. Conventional treatment of fillets, rounds, and threads in pictorial.

ested in a more thorough discussion of the various methods.

The fundamental concepts of perspective can be explained best if the reader will imagine himself looking through a picture plane at a formal garden with a small pool flanked by lampposts, as shown in Fig. 12.45. The point of observation, at which the rays from the eye to the objects in the scene meet, is called the *station point*, and the plane on which the view is formed by the piercing points of the visual rays is known as the *picture plane* (*PP*). The piercing points reproduce the scene, the size which depends on the location of the picture plane.

It should be noted that objects of the same height intercept a greater distance on the picture plane when close to it than when farther away. For example, rays from the lamppost at 2 intercept a distance 1-2 on the picture plane, while the rays from the pole at 4, which actually is the same height, intercept the lesser distance 3-4. From this fact it should be observed that the farther away an object is, the smaller it will appear, until a point is reached at which there will be no distance intercepted at all. This happens at the horizon.

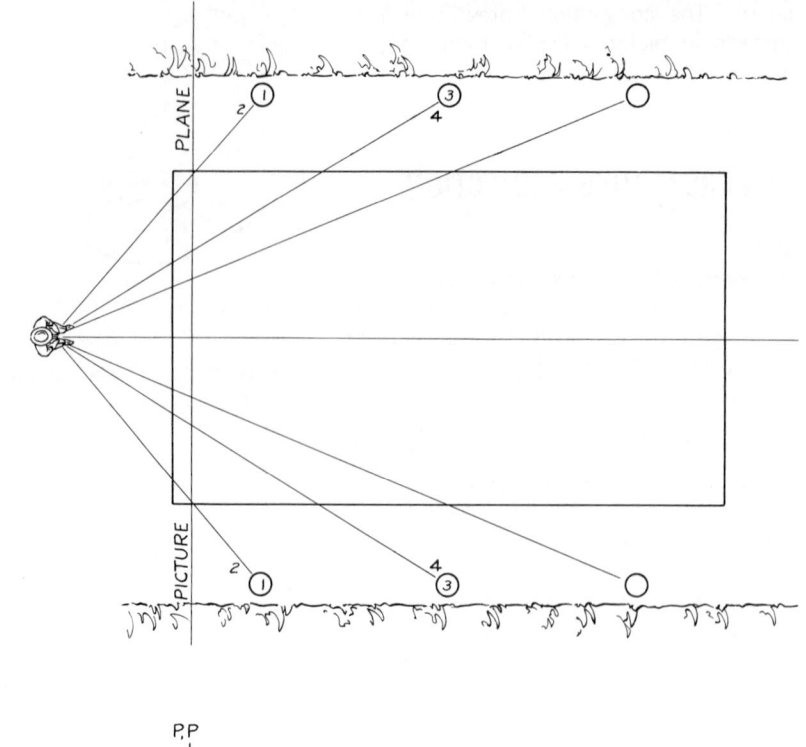

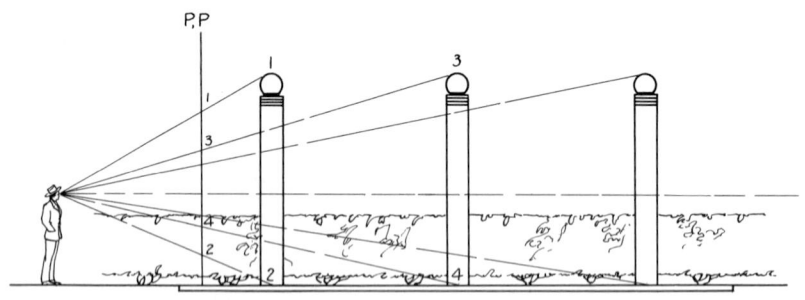

FIG. 12.45. The picture plane.

Figure 12.46 shows the scene observed by the man in Fig. 12.45 as it would be formed on the picture plane. The posts farther from the picture plane diminish in height, as each one has a height on the picture plane equal to the distance it intercepts, (Fig. 12.45). The lines of the pool and hedge converge to the center of vision or vanishing point, which is located directly in front of the observer on the horizon.

12.29
Perspective Nomenclature. Figure 12.47 illustrates pictorially the accepted nomenclature of perspective drawing. The *horizon line* is the line of intersection of the horizontal plane through the observation point (eye of the observer) and the picture plane. The horizontal plane is known as the *plane of the horizon*. The *ground line* is the line of intersection of the ground

plane and the picture plane. The *CV point* is the center of vision of the observer. It is located directly in front of the eye in the plane of the horizon on the horizon line.

12.30
Location of Picture Plane. The picture plane is usually placed between the object and the *SP* (station point). In parallel perspective (Sec. 12.36) it may be passed through a face of the object in order to show the true size and shape of the face.

12.31
Location of the Station Point. Care must be exercised in selecting the location for the station point, for its position has much to do with the appearance of the finished perspective drawing. A poor choice of position may result in a distorted perspective that will be decidedly displeasing to the eye.

In general, the station point should be offset slightly to one side and should be located above or below the exact center of the object. However, it must be remembered that the center of vision must be near the center of interest for the viewer.

One should always think of the station point as the viewing point, and its location should be where the object can be viewed to the best advantage. It is desirable that it be at a distance from the picture plane equal to at least twice the maximum dimension (width, height, or depth) of the object, for at such a distance, or greater, the entire object can be viewed naturally, as a whole, without turning the head.

A wide angle of view is to be avoided in the interest of good picturization. It has been determined that best results are obtained when the visual rays from the station point (*SP*) to the object are kept within a cone having an angle of not more than 30° between diametrically opposing elements (see Fig. 12.48).

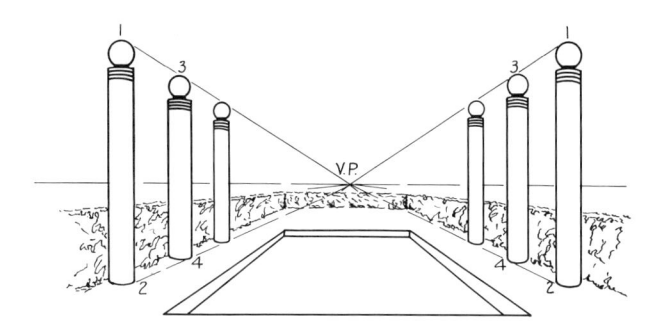

FIG. 12.46. The picture (perspective).

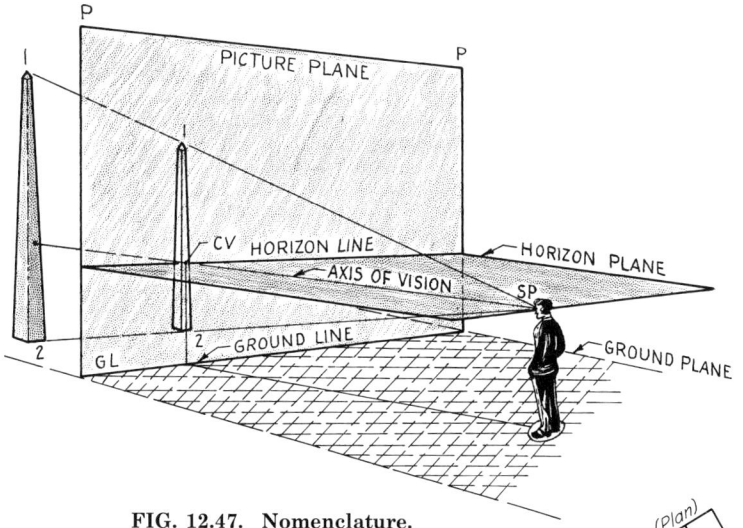

FIG. 12.47. Nomenclature.

In locating an object in relation to the picture plane, it is advisable to place it so that both of the side faces do not make the same angle with the picture plane and thus will not be equally visible. It is common practice to choose angles of 30° and 60° for rectangular objects.

12.32
Position of the Object in Relation to the Horizon. When making a perspective of a tall object, such as a building, the horizon usually is assumed to be at a height

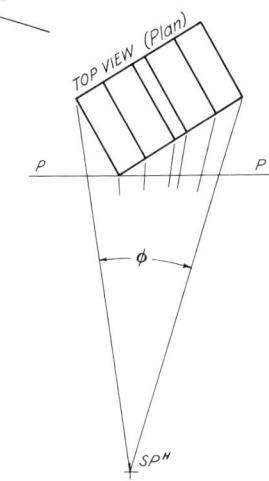

FIG. 12.48. Angle of vision.

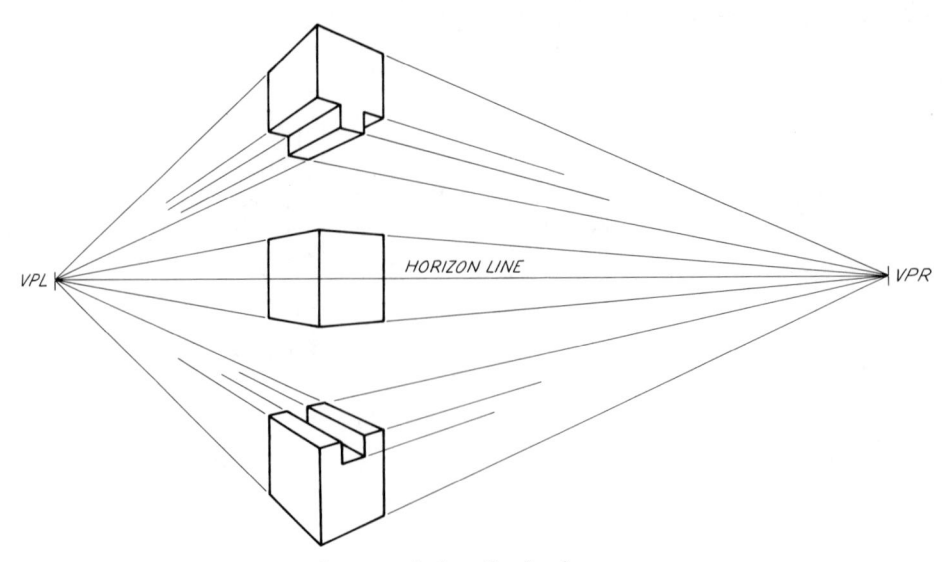

FIG. 12.49. Objects on, above, or below the horizon.

above the ground plane equal to the standing height of a man's eye, normally about 5 ft 6 in.

A small object may be placed either above or below the horizon (eye level), depending on the view desired. If an object is above the horizon, it will be seen looking up from below, as shown in Fig. 12.49. Should the object be below the horizon line, it will be seen from above.

12.33
Lines. The following facts should be recognized concerning the perspective of lines:

1. Parallel horizontal lines vanish at a single VP (vanishing point). Usually the VP is at the point where a line parallel to the system through the SP pierces the PP (picture plane).

2. A system of horizontal lines has its VP on the horizon.

3. Vertical lines, since they pierce the picture plane at infinity, will appear vertical in perspective.

4. When a line lies in the picture plane, it will show its true length because it will be its own perspective.

5. When a line lies behind the picture plane, its perspective will be shorter than the line.

12.34
Perspective by Multiview Projection. Adhering to theory that a perspective drawing is formed on a picture plane by visual rays from the eye to the object, as illustrated in Fig. 12.45, a perspective can be drawn by using multiview projection (see Fig. 12.50). The multiview method may be the easiest for a student to understand but it is not often used by an experienced person because considerably more line work is required if the scene or object to be represented is at all complicated. The top and side views are drawn in multiview projection and the picture plane (as an

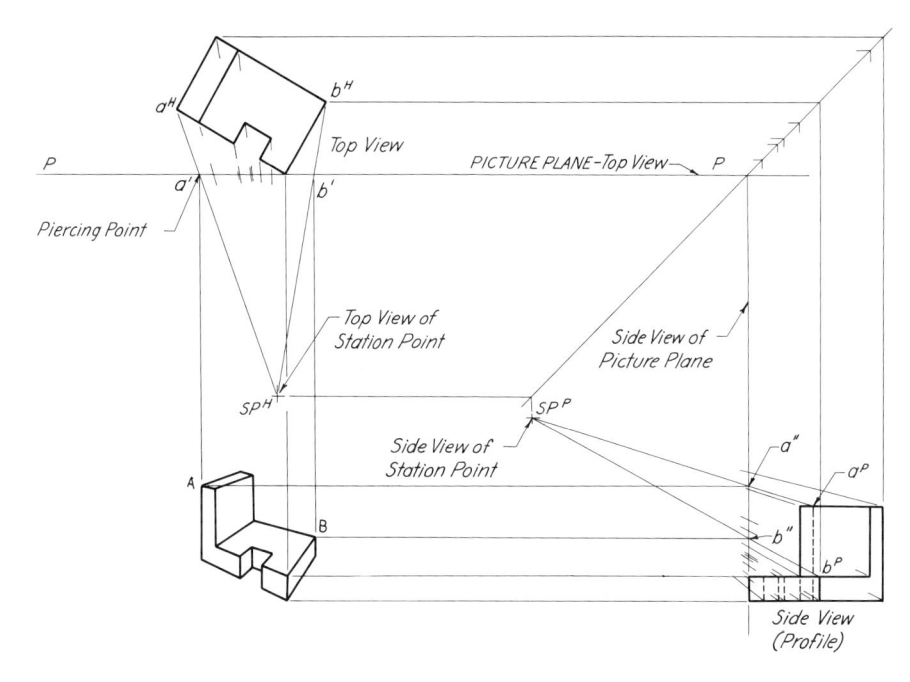

FIG. 12.50. Perspective drawing—orthographic method.

edge view) and the station point are shown in each case. SP^H and its related views of the rays are in the top view, while SP^P and its projections of the rays belong to the side view. The front view of the picture plane is in the plane of the paper.

After the preliminary layout has been completed point A may be located in the perspective by the following procedure:

Step I. Draw the top view ($SP^H a^H$) and the side view ($SP^P a^P$) of the visual ray from the eye to point A.

Step II. From a' (the top view of the piercing point of the ray) draw a projection line downward.

Step III. From a'' (the side view of the piercing point) draw a horizontal projection line to intersect the one drawn from a'.

Point A of the perspective is at this intersection.

Point B and the other points that are needed for the perspective representation are found in the same manner as point A.

12.35
Types of Perspective. In general, there are two types of perspective: *parallel perspective* and *angular perspective*. In parallel perspective, one of the principal faces is parallel to the picture plane and is its own perspective. All vertical lines are vertical, and the receding horizontal lines converge to a single vanishing point. In angular perspective, the object is placed so that the principal faces are at an angle with the picture plane. The horizontal lines converge at two vanishing points.

12.36
Parallel Perspective. Figure 12.51 shows the parallel perspective of a rectangular block. The *PP* line is the top view of the

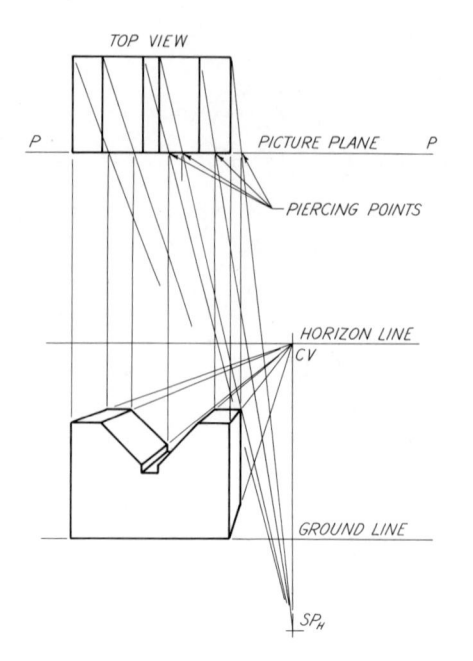

FIG. 12.51. Parallel perspective.

FIG. 12.52. Circles in parallel perspective.

picture plane, SP_H is the top view of the station point, and CV is the center of vision. The receding horizontal lines vanish at CV. The front face, since it lies in the picture plane, is its own perspective and shows in its true size. The lines representing the edges back of the picture plane are found by projecting downward from the points at which the visual rays pierce the picture plane, as shown by the top views of the rays. Figure 12.52 shows a parallel perspective of a cylindrical machine part.

12.37
Angular Perspective. Figure 12.53 shows pictorially the graphical method for the preparation of a two-point perspective drawing of a cube. To visualize the true layout on the surface of a sheet of drawing paper, it is necessary to revolve mentally the horizontal plane downward into the vertical or picture plane. On completion of Sec. 12.37, it is suggested that the reader turn back and endeavor to associate the development of the perspective in Fig. 12.54 with the pictorial presentation in Fig. 12.53. For a full understanding of the construction in Fig. 12.54, it is necessary to differentiate between the lines that belong to the horizontal plane and those that are on the vertical or picture plane. In addition, it must be fully realized that there is a top view for the perspective that is a line and that in this line view lie the points that must be projected downward to the perspective representation (front view).

Figure 12.54 shows an angular perspective of a block. The block has been placed so that one vertical edge lies in the picture plane. The other vertical edges are parallel to the plane, while all of the horizontal lines are inclined to it so that they vanish

275

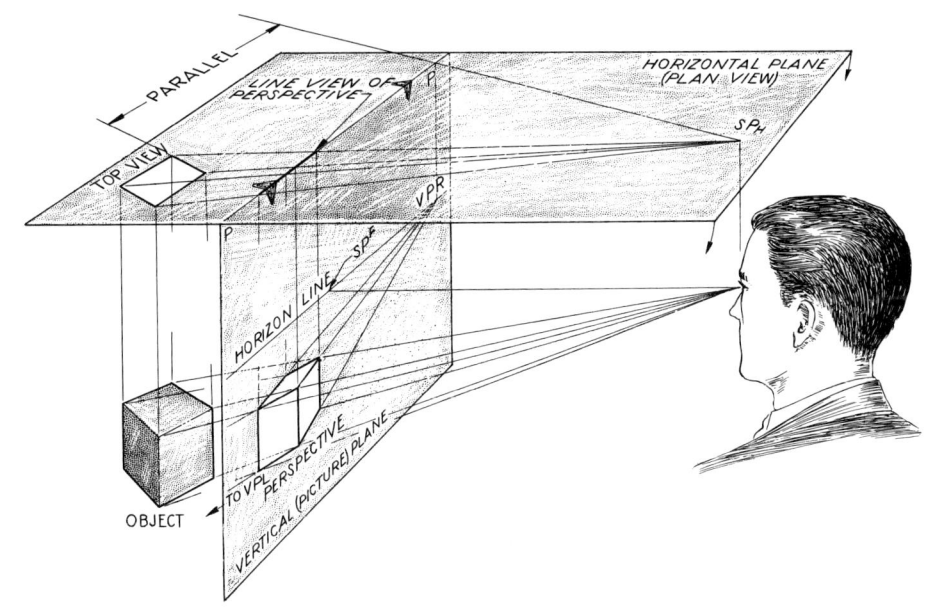

FIG. 12.53. Angular perspective.

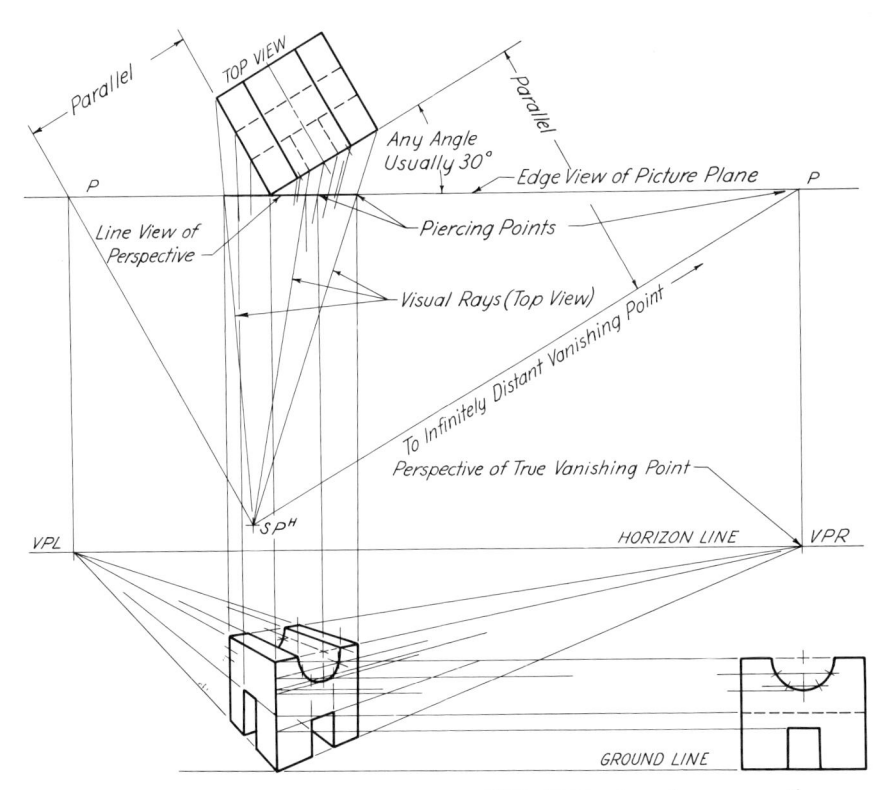

FIG. 12.54. Angular perspective.

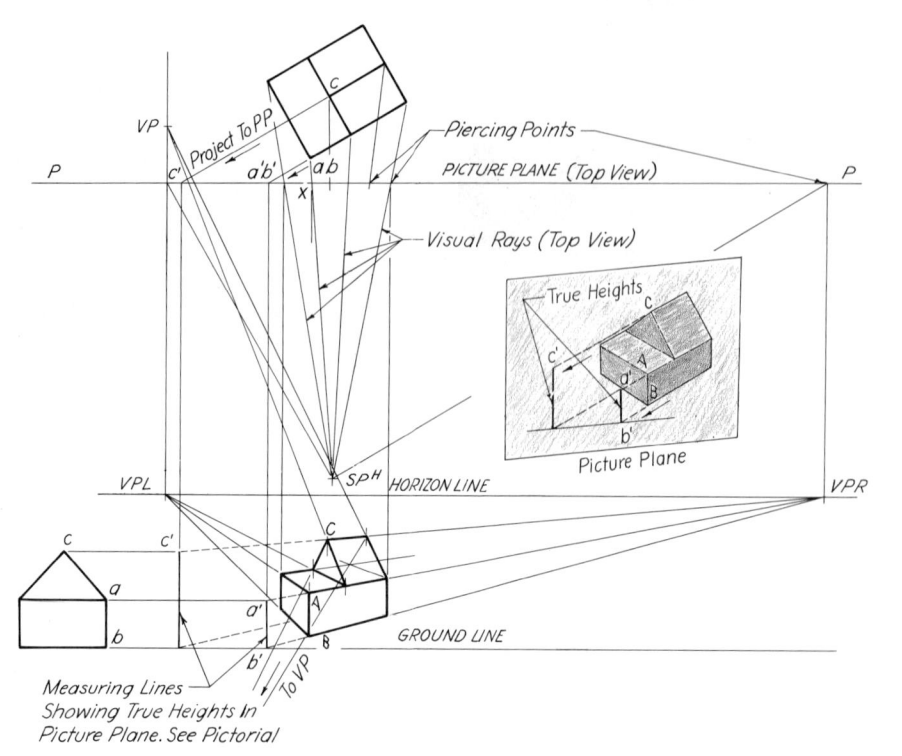

FIG. 12.55. Use of measuring lines.

measurements from the orthographic front view. The lines shown from these division points along this line to the vanishing points (*VPL–VPR*) established the direction of the receding horizontal edge lines in the perspective. The positions of the back edges were determined by projecting downward from the points at which the projectors from the station point (*SP*) to the corners of the object pierced the picture plane, as shown by the top view of the object and projectors.

12.38
Use of Measuring Lines. Whenever the vertical front edge of an object lies in the picture plane, it can be laid off full length in the perspective, because theoretically, it will be in true length in the picture formed on the plane by the visual rays (see Fig. 12.54). Should the near vertical edge lie behind the picture plane, as is the case with the edge line *AB* in Fig. 12.55, the use of a measuring line becomes desirable. The measuring line $a'b'$ is the vertical edge *AB* moved forward to the picture plane, where it will appear in its true height. Some prefer to think of the vertical side as being extended to the picture plane so that the true height of the side is revealed. The length and position of *AB* is established in the perspective picture by first drawing vanishing lines from a' and b' to *VPR*; then the top view of the edge in the picture plane (point *X*) is projected downward to the front-view picturization. Points *A* and *B* must fall on the vanishing lines from a' and b' to *VPR* respectively.

A measuring line may be used to establish the "picture height" of any feature of an object. For example, in Fig. 12.55, the vertical measuring line through c' was used as needed to locate point *C* and the top line of the object in the perspective.

12.39
Vanishing Points for Inclined Lines. In general, the perspective of any inclined

at the two vanishing points, *VPL* and *VPR*, respectively.

In constructing the perspective shown in this illustration, an orthographic top view was drawn in such a position that the visible vertical faces made angles of 30° and 60° with the picture plane. Next, the location of the observer was assumed and the horizon line was established. The vanishing points *VPL* and *VPR* were found by drawing a 30° line and a 60° line through the *SP*. Since these lines are parallel to the two systems of receding horizontal lines, each will establish a required vanishing point at its intersection with the picture plane. The vertical line located in the picture plane, which is its own perspective, was selected as a measuring line on which to project vertical

straight line can be found by locating the end points of the line perspectively. By this method, an end point may be located by drawing the perspective representations of any two horizontal lines intersecting at the endpoint. Where several parallel inclined lines vanish to the same vanishing point, it may prove to be worth while to locate the *VP* for the system in order to conserve time and achieve a higher degree of accuracy.

Just as in the case of other lines, the vanishing point for any inclined line may be established by finding the piercing point in the picture plane (*PP*) of a line through *SP* parallel to the given inclined line.

In Fig. 12.56 the inclined lines are *AB* and *CD*. If one is to understand the construction shown for locating vanishing point *VPI*, he must recognize that vertical planes vanish in vertical lines and that a line in a vertical plane will vanish at a point on the vanishing line of the plane. The preceding statements being true, the vanishing point *VPI* for line *CD* must lie at some point on a vertical line through *VPR*, since *CD* and *CE* lie in the same vertical plane. *VPI* is the point at which a line drawn parallel (in space) to *CD* through *SP* pierces the picture plane.

On the drawing, the distance *D* that *VPI* is above *VPR* may be found easily through the construction of a right triangle with *SPQ* as a base. Angle β is the slope angle for line *CD* (see side view). The needed distance *D* is the line *QR*, or the short leg of the triangle.

12.40

Use of Measuring Points. Frequently, it is desirable to use measuring points in preparing a perspective drawing, because their use permits the laying off of a series of direct measurements that can be transferred quickly and accurately to the perspective. Measuring points are, in reality, special vanishing points that are

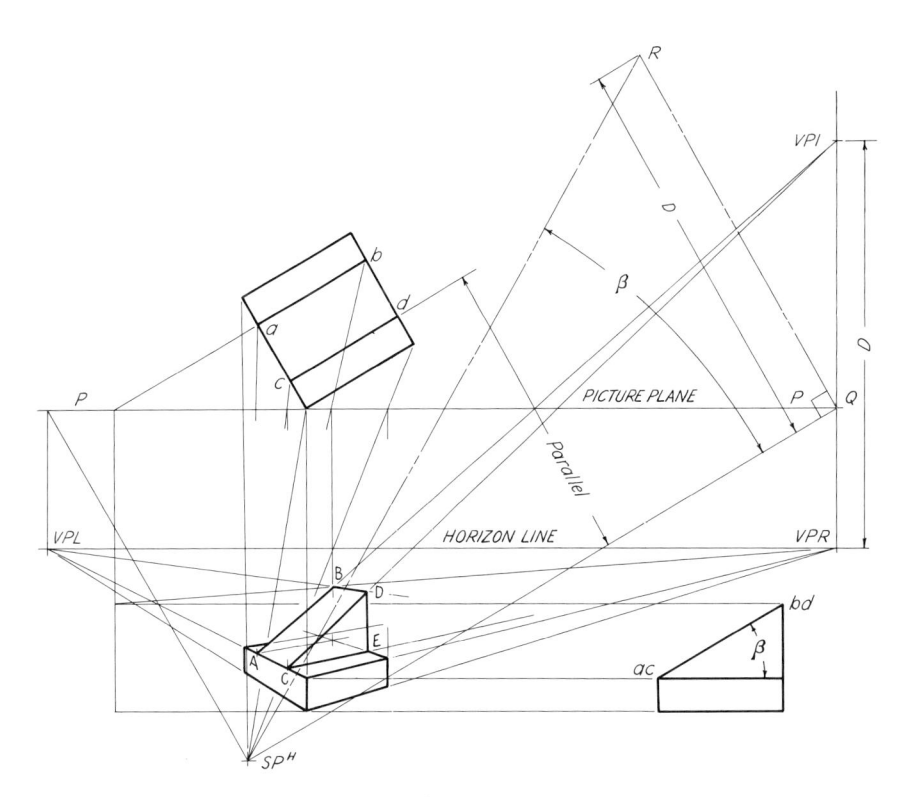

FIG. 12.56. Vanishing point for inclined lines.

used to establish distances in perspective along perspective lines.

To understand the measuring point method, one must realize that, in theory, a vertical face is rotated into the picture plane so that direct measurements may be made along the horizontal ground line to the same scale as the top view. In Fig. 12.57 the vertical face containing line *AB* was revolved into the picture plane to position ab_r. The vanishing point of the line bb_r is *MPR*. The position of *MPR* was established by first drawing a line from *SP* parallel to bb_r to a piercing point in the picture plane and then projecting to the horizon line.

Another method for determining the location of measuring points is included

278 PART II / SPATIAL GRAPHICS: SHAPE DESCRIPTION AND SPATIAL RELATIONSHIPS

established the desired lengths along the line AB, which represents the perspective of the lower edge of the object. Height distances were laid off along the measuring line through the vertical edge lying in the picture plane at a. With width, height, and depth distances established, the perspective drawing was completed by following the procedure given in Sec. 12.37.

12.41
Circles in Perspective. If a circle is on a surface that is inclined to the picture plane (PP), its perspective will resemble an ellipse. It is the usual practice to construct the representation within an enclosing square by finding selected points along the curve in the perspective, as shown in Fig. 12.58(a). Any points might be used, but it is recommended that points be located on 30° and 60° lines.

In (a), the perspective representation of the circle was found by using visual rays and parallel horizontal lines in combination. In starting the construction, the positions of several selected points, located on the circumference and lying on horizontal lines in the plane of the circle, were established in both views. After these lines had been drawn in the perspective in the usual manner, the locations of the points along them were determined through the use of visual rays, as shown. Specifically, the position of a point in the perspective was found by projecting downward from the piercing point of the ray from the point and the picture plane (see line view) to the perspective view of the line on which the point must lie. In (b), the same method was applied to construct the perspective view of a circle in a horizontal plane. It should be noted in this case that the horizontal lines, as established in the top view, were extended to cut the picture plane so that the true height of these lines at the plane could

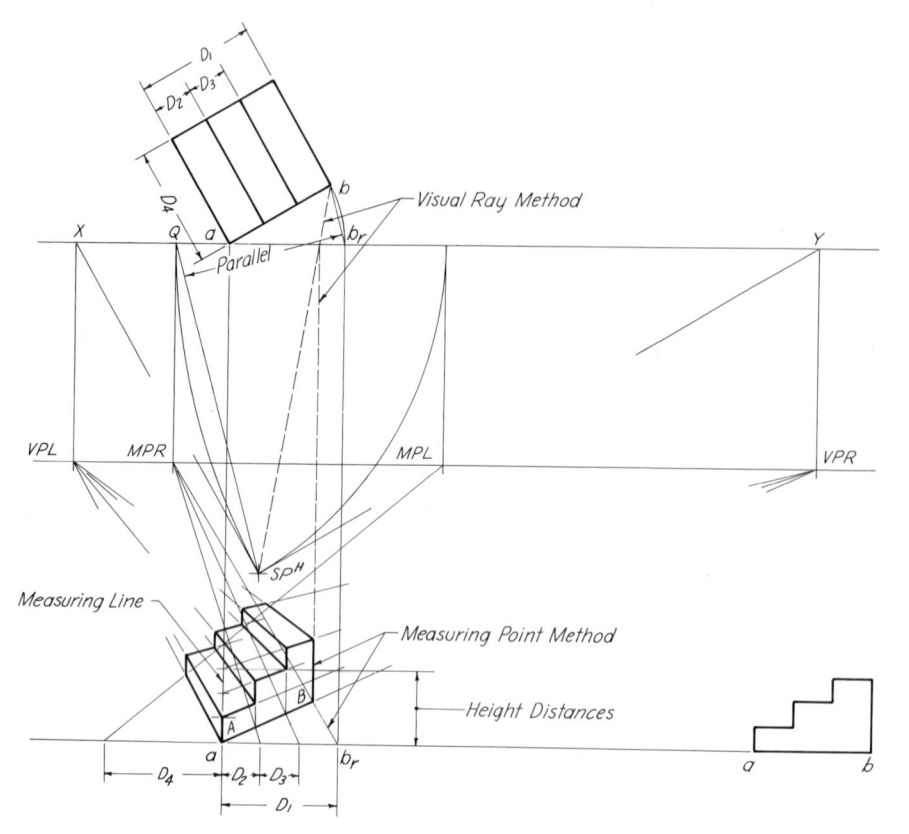

FIG. 12.57. Use of measuring points.

in this same illustration. By this second method, the location of a measuring point can be readily found by swinging an arc with the plan view of the vanishing point as a center and using a radius equal to the distance from this center to the SP. For example, the location of MPR on the horizon was determined by swinging an arc from Y using the distance from Y to SP as a radius. The point of intersection of this arc and picture plane (in plan) projected to the horizon established the position of MPR for use in preparing the perspective drawing shown. MPL was similarly located.

The scaled lengths (D_1, D_2, and D_3) laid off along ab_r, when vanished to MPR,

CHAP. 12 / PICTORIAL PRESENTATION **279**

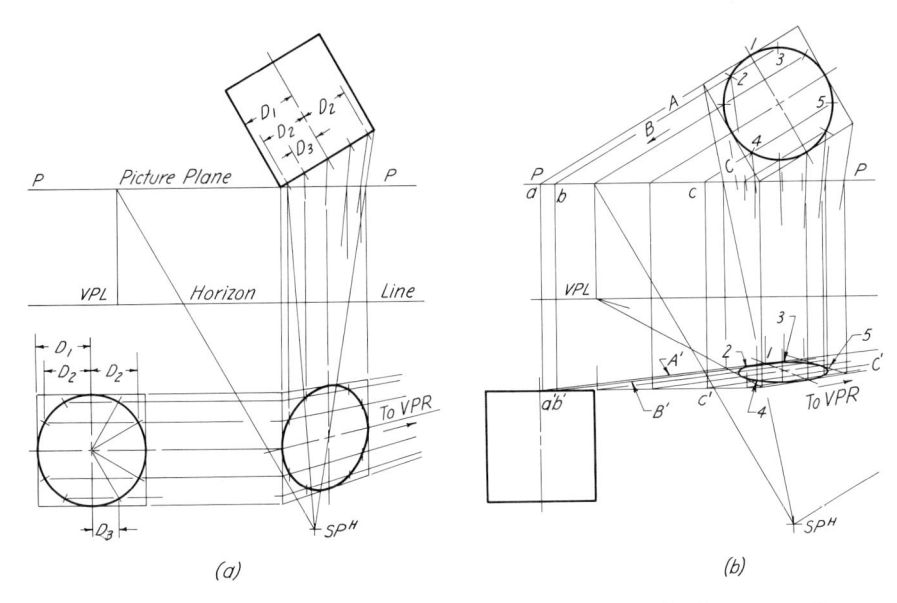

(a) *(b)*

FIG. 12.58. Circles in perspective.

be used in the perspective view for locating the end points of the perspective representations (at the left).

D: INDUSTRIAL ILLUSTRATIONS

12.42

Technical Illustration Drawings. The design and manufacturing procedures of present-day mass production require various types of pictorial illustrations to communicate ideas and concepts to large numbers of persons who are all working towards a common objective. These illustration drawings are of value at all stages of a project from the design phase, where they may be only pencil-shaded freehand sketches, through all of the stages of production that we may consider to include not only the assembly but final installation of the systems as well. They are used in operation and maintenance manuals to make complex and difficult tasks understandable to those persons who may be unable to interpret conventional drawings (Fig. 12.59). Pictorial illustrations range from simple types of line drawings (Fig. 12.60) that have already been discussed to artists' renderings that have the realism of photographs. An artist's rendering, such as the one shown in Fig. 12.61, is usually prepared to reinforce an oral or written report that is to be presented before a decision-making group that consists to some extent of persons who would otherwise be unable to understand construction details. Drawings of this type are depended on to sell a project.

Illustration drawings are used for many purposes in every field of engineering technology. They appear in advertising literature, operation and service manuals (Fig. 12.62), patent applications (Fig. 12.65) and textbooks (Fig. 12.72). Illustration drawings may be working drawings, assembly drawings, piping and wiring dia-

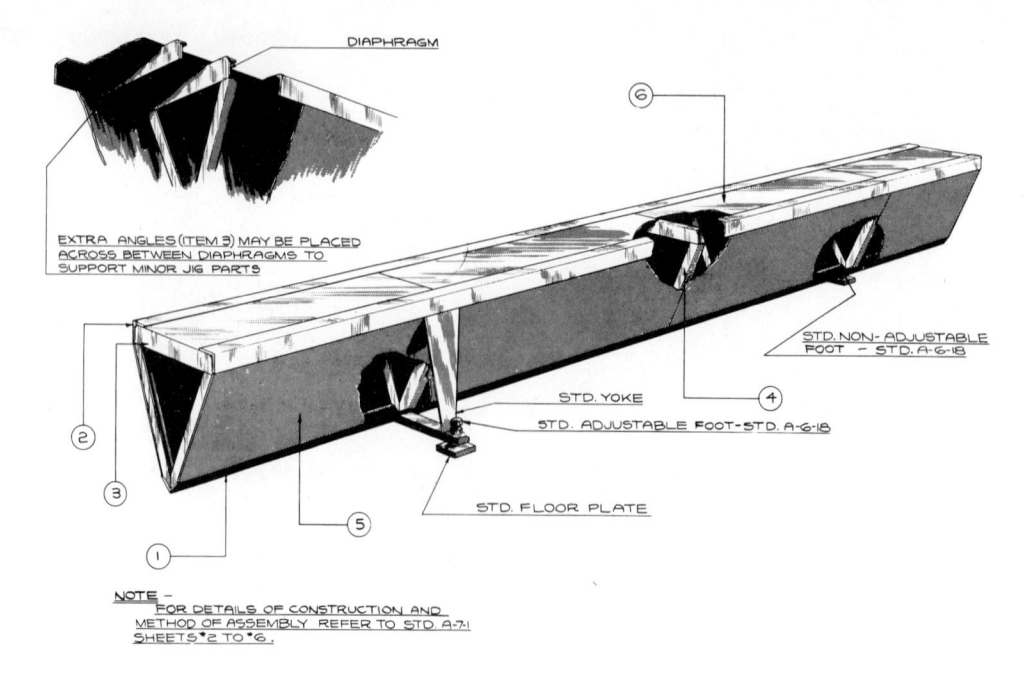

FIG. 12.59. A production illustration prepared in perspective. (*Courtesy Craftint Mfg. Co.*)

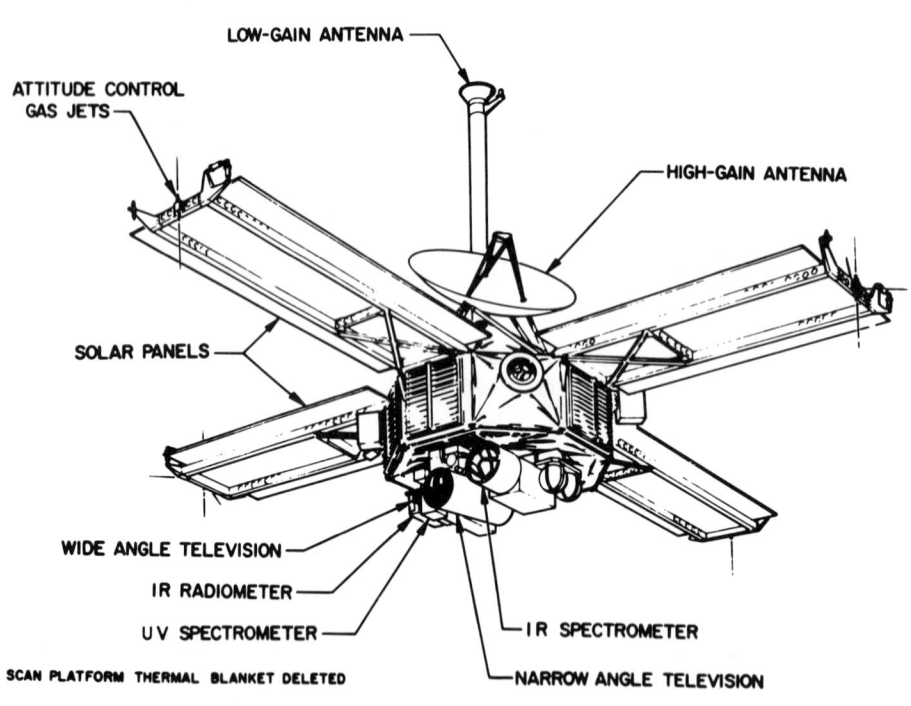

FIG. 12.60. A pictorial representation of the Mariner 3. This Spacecraft was instrumented to provide data basic to the physical characteristics of the planet Mars. (*Courtesy of NASA*)

CHAP. 12 / PICTORIAL PRESENTATION 281

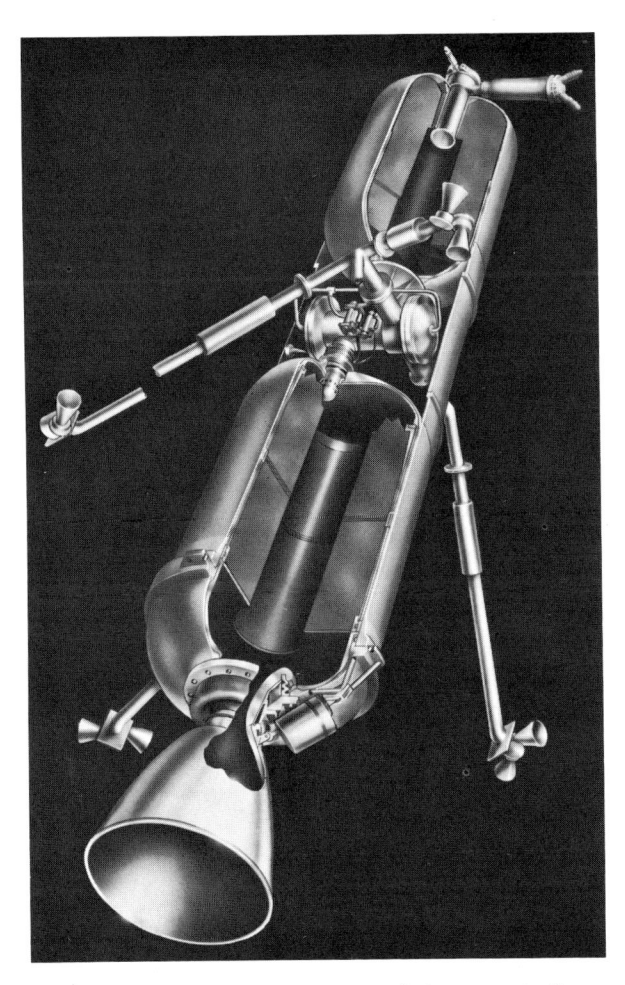

FIG. 12.61. An artist's concept of a rocket control system. (*Courtesy Aeronutronic Division, Philco-Ford*)

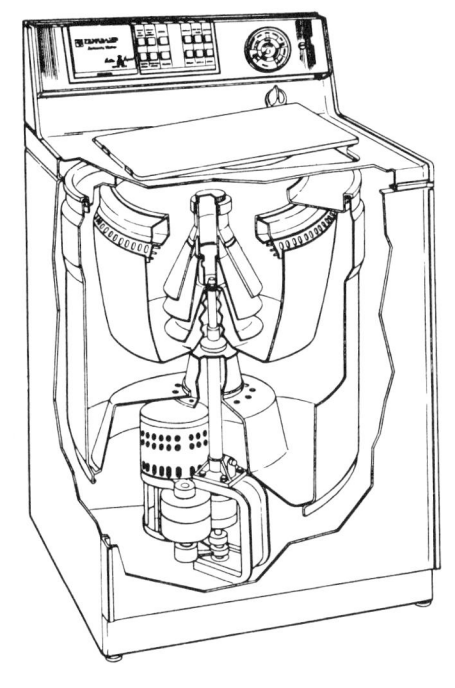

FIG. 12.62. A manufacturing illustration. Drawings of this type are used in service manuals and for original manufacture. Such drawings have also proved to be invaluable in the finalization of a design. (*Courtesy General Motors Corp.*)

grams, and architectural and engineering renderings that are almost true-to-life. Typical examples of pictorial drawings that were prepared to facilitate assembly are shown in Figs. 12.2 and 17.13. Figure 24.1 shows an electronic diagram that appeared in a service manual.

12.43
Design Illustrations. Design illustrations are prepared to clarify conventional engineering design and production drawings and written specifications. These are used for the communication of ideas and concepts concerning the details of complicated designs. Properly prepared, drawings of this type reveal the relationship of the components of a system so clearly that the principles of operation of a unit can be understood by almost everyone, even by persons who may be relatively unfamiliar with graphic methods. It is com-

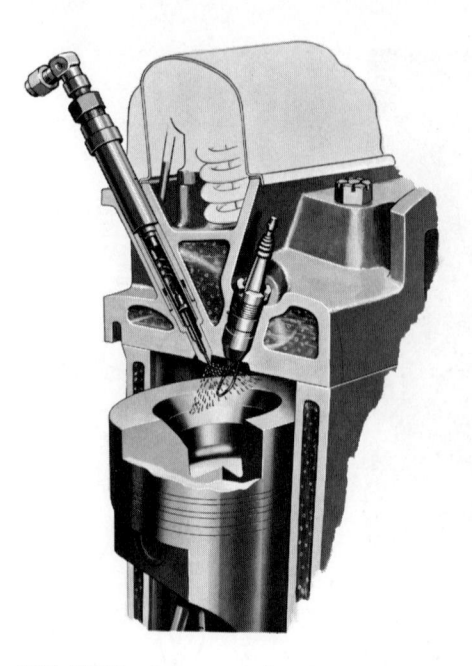

FIG. 12.63. A new combustion process developed by the Ford Motor Company is shown here in a cutaway view. (*Courtesy Ford Motor Company*)

mon practice to prepare a series of such drawings to clarify complex details of construction, to indicate the function of closely related parts, and reveal structural features. A pictorial of this type is shown in Fig. 12.63. It was used to supplement a technical paper presented at a recent Society of Automotive Engineers Congress held in Detroit.

12.44
Shading Methods. A pictorial illustration can be improved and given a more realistic appearance by shading to produce the effect of surface texture. To this shades and shadows may be added to give additional realism. The use of pencil shading is most common. Ink shading (see Fig. 12.72) produces clean illustrations of high quality that are well suited for reproductions in texts and brochures. The techniques of surface shading by means of ink lines will be discussed in Sec. 12.45.

Some of the other more basic methods of representing surface textures under light and shade involve the use of Rossboard, Craftint paper, Zip-a-tone overlay film, and the airbrush.

Most of the shaded pictorial drawings in this text were drawn on Rossboard. This popular drawing paper, with its rough plaster-type surface, is available in many textured patterns. Surface shading is done with a very soft pencil.

Craftint papers, single-tone or double-tone, have the pattern in the paper. Drawings are prepared on these papers in the usual manner and regular black waterproof drawing ink is used for the finished lines. Solid black areas are filled in with ink before the areas where shading is desired are brushed with a developer that brings out the surface pattern. These papers are available in many shading patterns. The drawing shown in Fig. 12.59 was prepared on Craftint paper.

Zip-a-tone clear cellulose overlay screens with printed shading patterns of dots and lines provide an easy method of surface shading suitable for high-quality printed reproductions (Fig. 12.64). The screen, backed with a clear adhesive, is applied as a sheet or partial sheet to the areas to be shaded. Unwanted portions are removed with a special cutting needle or razor blade, before the screen is rubbed down firmly to complete the bond between screen and paper.

A high degree of realism can be achieved using a small spray gun that in the language of the artist is known as an *airbrush*. This delicate instrument sprays a fine mist of diluted ink over the surface of the drawing to produce variations of tone. A capable artist can produce a representation that has the realism of a photograph. The pictorial illustration in Fig. 12.61 is an excellent example of airbrush rendering by a commercial illustrator. The

CHAP. 12 / PICTORIAL PRESENTATION 283

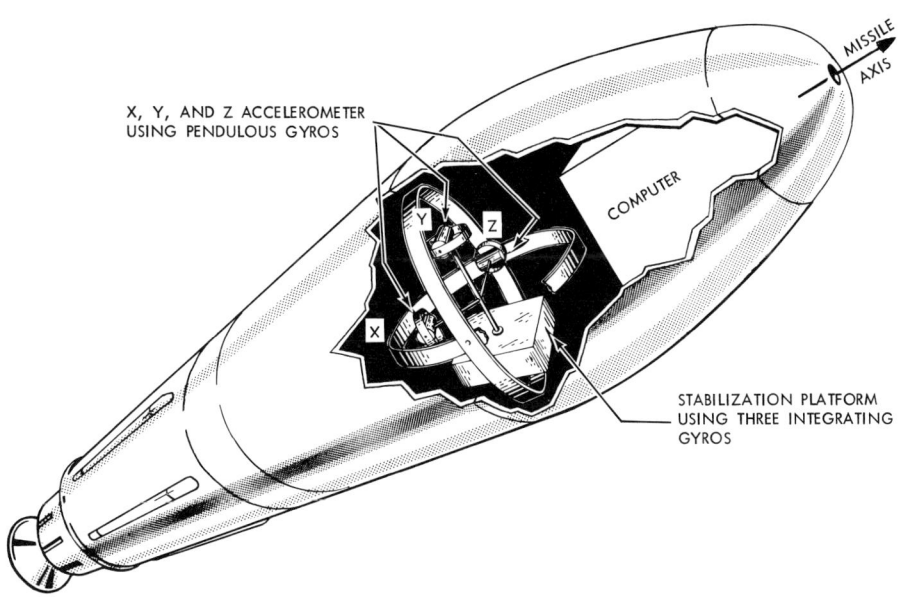

FIG. 12.64 This pictorial representation shows the principle elements of the inertial guidance system in a missile vehicle. (*Courtesy General Motors Corp*)

airbrush is sometimes used to retouch photographs to improve their appearance for reproduction.

12.45
Surface Shading by Means of Lines (Fig. 12.65). Line shading is a conventional method of representing, by ruled lines, the varying degrees of illumination on the surfaces of an object. It is a means of giving clearer definition to the shapes of objects and a finished appearance to certain types of drawings. In practice, line shading is used on Patent Office drawings, display drawings, and on some illustrations prepared for publications. It is never used on ordinary drawings, and for this reason few draftsmen ever gain the experience necessary to enable them to employ it effectively.

In shading surfaces, the bright areas are left white and the dark areas are represented by parallel shade lines (Figs. 12.66

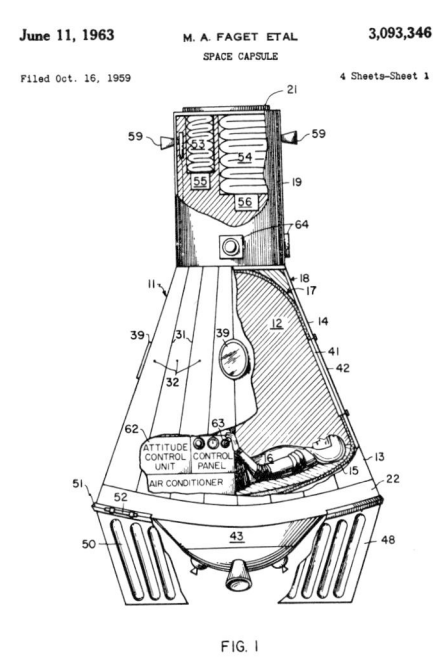

FIG. 12.65. A patent drawing with surface shading.

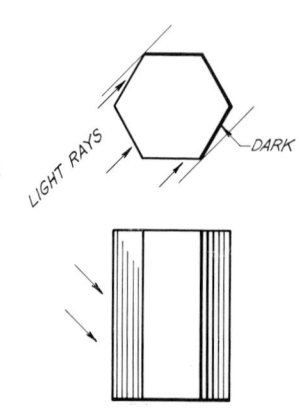

FIG. 12.66. Surface shading on a prism.

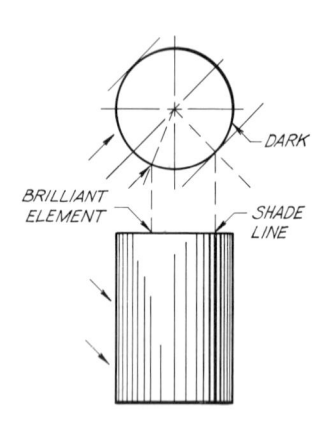

FIG. 12.67. Surface shading on a cylinder.

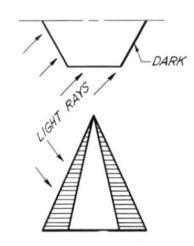

FIG. 12.68. Pyramid.

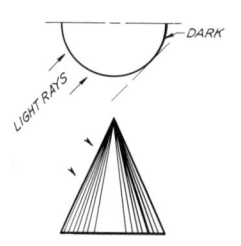

FIG. 12.69. Cone.

and 12.67). Varying degrees of shade may be represented in one of the following ways:

1. By varying the weight of the lines while keeping the spacing uniform, as in Fig. 12.66.

2. By using uniform straight lines and varying the spacing.

3. By varying both the weight of the lines and the spacing, as in Fig. 12.67.

The rays of light are assumed to be parallel and coming from the left, over the shoulder of the draftsman (Fig. 12.66). In accordance with this, two of the visible faces of the hexagonal prism, shown in Fig. 12.66, would be illuminated, while the remaining visible inclined face would be dark. It should be noted that the general principle of shading is modified in the case of flat inclined surfaces, which, theoretically, would be uniformly lighted. Such surfaces are shaded in accordance with a conventional scheme, the governing rule of which may be stated as follows: *The portion of an illuminated inclined surface nearest the eye is the lightest, while the portion of a shaded inclined surface nearest the eye is the darkest.* In the application of this rule, the shading on an inclined illuminated face will increase in density as the face recedes, while on an unilluminated inclined surface it will decrease in density as the face recedes, as shown in Fig. 12.66.

A cylinder would be shaded as shown in Fig. 12.67. The lightest area on the surface is at the *brilliant line*, where light strikes it and is reflected directly to the eye; the darkest is along the *shade line*, where the light rays are tangent to the surface. The brilliant line passes through the point at which the bisector for the angle formed by a light ray to the center and the visual ray from the center line to the eye would pierce the external surface. In shading a cylinder, the density of the shading is increased in both directions, from the bright area along the brilliant line to the contour element on the left and the shade line on the right. The density of the shading is slightly decreased on the shaded portion beyond the shade line. Since one would expect this area to be even darker, some draftsmen extend the dark portion to the contour element. On very small cylinders, the bright side (left side) usually is not shaded.

A pyramid may be shaded as shown in Fig. 12.68.

The surface of a cone will be the darkest at the element where the light rays are tangent to the surface (Fig. 12.69).

A sphere is shaded by drawing concentric circles having either the geometric center of the view or the "brilliant point" as a center (Fig. 12.70). The darkest portion of the surface is along the shade line, where the parallel rays of light are tangent to the sphere and the lightest portion is around the *brilliant point*. The *brilliant point* is where the bisector of the angle between a light ray to the center and the visual ray from the center to the eye pierces the external surface. The construction necessary to determine the dark line and the brilliant point is shown in Fig. 12.70(*b*).

Although good line shading requires much practice and some artistic sense, a skillful draftsman should not avoid shad-

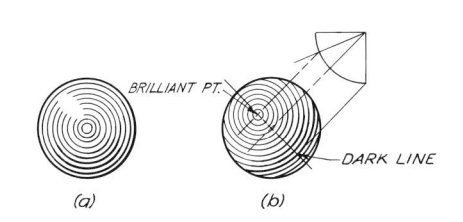

FIG. 12.70. Surface shading on a sphere.

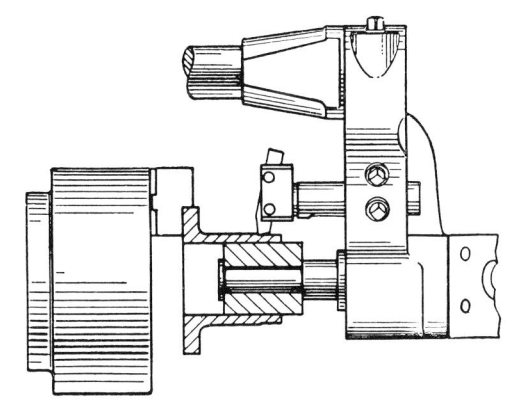

FIG. 12.71. A line-shaded drawing (*From Doyle,* Tool Engineering, *Prentice-Hall, Inc.*).

FIG. 12.72. A line-shaded pictorial drawing (*Courtesy Socony-Vacuum Oil Co.*).

ing the surfaces of an object simply because he never before has attempted to do so. After careful study, he should be able to produce fairly satisfactory results. Often the shading of a view makes it possible to eliminate another view that otherwise would be necessary.

Figures 12.71 and 12.72 show applications of line shading on technical illustrations.

PROBLEMS

The student will find that a preliminary sketch will facilitate the preparation of isometric and oblique drawings of the problems of this chapter. On such a sketch he may plan the procedure of construction. Since many technologists and designers frequently find it necessary to prepare pictorial sketches during discussions with untrained persons who cannot read orthographic views, it is recommended that some problems be sketched freehand on either plain or pictorial grid paper (see Fig. 13.21). Additional problems may be found at the end of Chapters 7 and 13.

1–9. (Figs. 12.73–12.81). Prepare instrumental isometric drawings or freehand sketches of the objects as assigned.

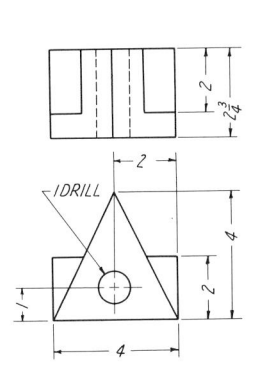

FIG. 12.73.

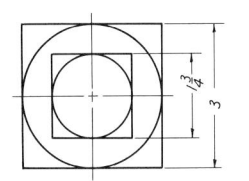

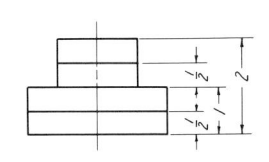

FIG. 12.74.

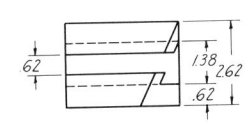

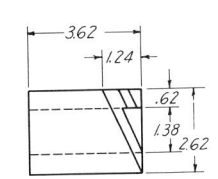

FIG. 12.75.

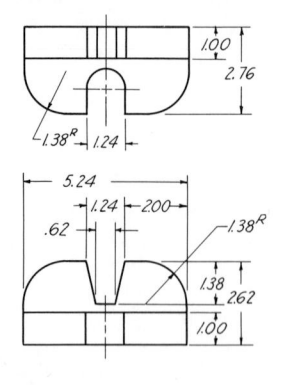

FIG. 12.76.

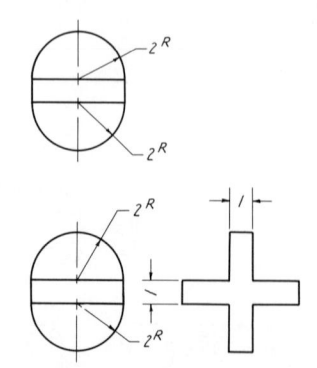

FIG. 12.77.

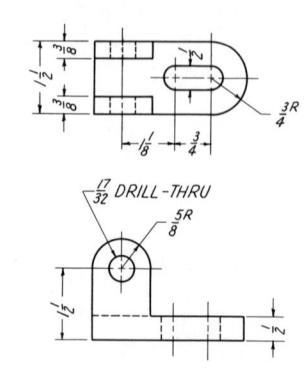

FIG. 12.78.

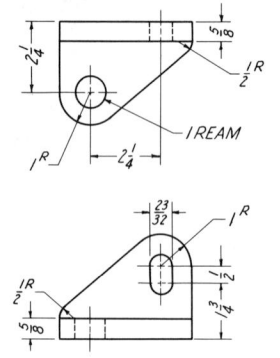

FIG. 12.79.

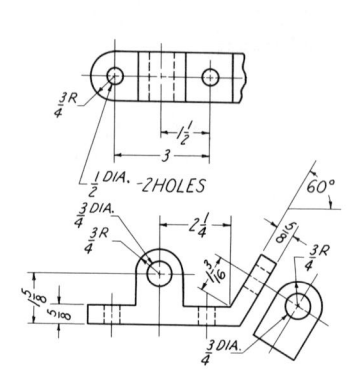

FIG. 12.80.

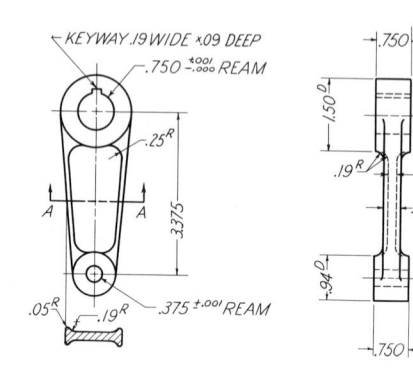

FIG. 12.81.

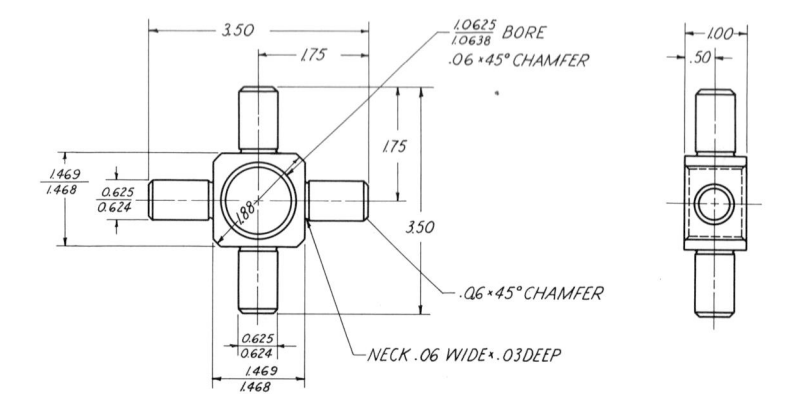

FIG. 12.82. Differential spider.

10–14. (Figs. 12.77–12.81). Prepare instrumental oblique drawings or freehand sketches of the objects as assigned.

15. (Fig. 12.82.) Make an isometric drawing of the differential spider.

16. (Fig. 12.83). Make an isometric drawing of the stepladder. Select a suitable scale.

17. (Fig. 12.84). Make an isometric drawing of the sawhorse. Select a suitable scale.

18. (Fig. 12.85). Make an oblique drawing of the locomotive driver nut.

19. (Fig. 12.86). Make an oblique drawing of the adjustment cone.

CHAP. 12 / PICTORIAL PRESENTATION **287**

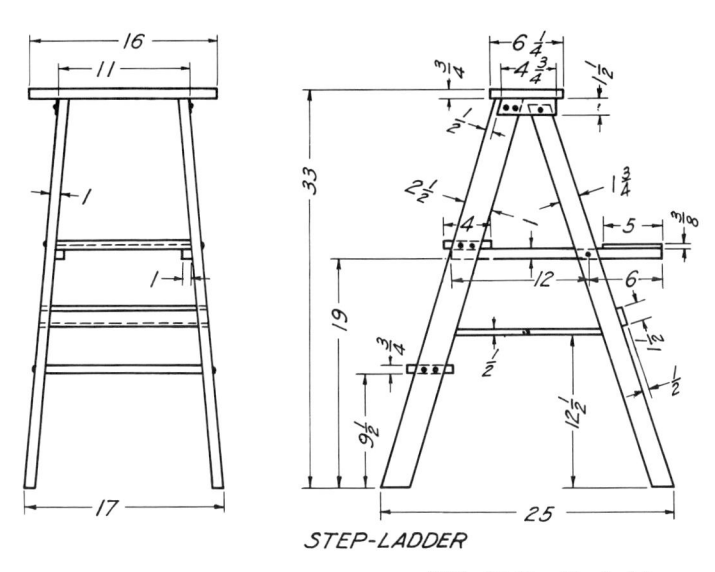

FIG. 12.83. Stepladder.

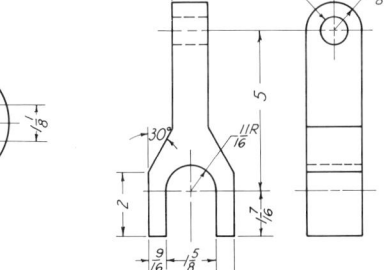

FIG. 12.84. Sawhorse.

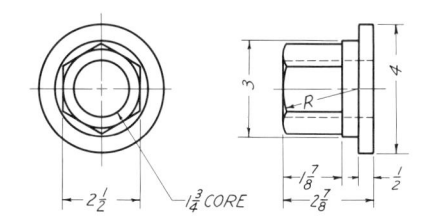

FIG. 12.85. Locomotive driver nut.

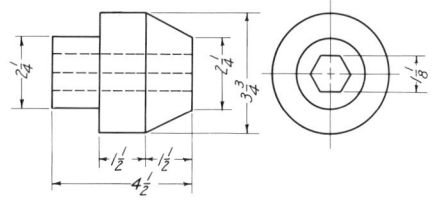

FIG. 12.86. Adjustment cone.

FIG. 12.87. Fork.

20. (Fig. 12.87). Make an oblique drawing of the fork.

21. (Fig. 12.88). Make an oblique drawing of the feeder guide.

22. (Fig. 12.89). Make an isometric drawing of the hinge bracket.

23. (Fig. 12.90). Make an isometric drawing of the alignment bracket.

24. (Fig. 12.91). Make an isometric drawing of the stop block.

25. (Figs. 12.86–12.88). Make a parallel perspective drawing as assigned.

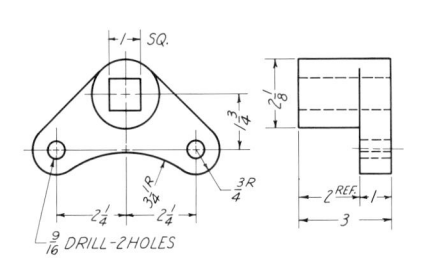

FIG. 12.88. Feeder guide.

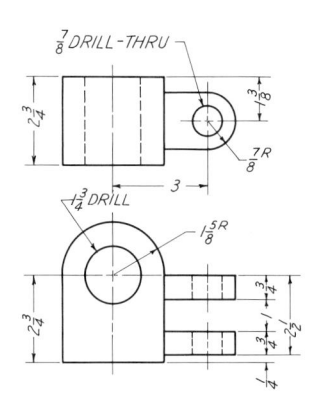

FIG. 12.89. Hinge bracket.

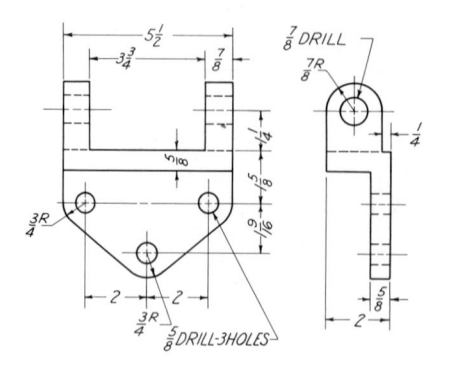

FIG. 12.90. Alignment bracket.

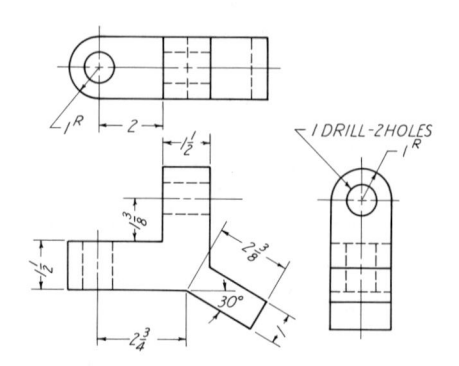

FIG. 12.91. Stop block.

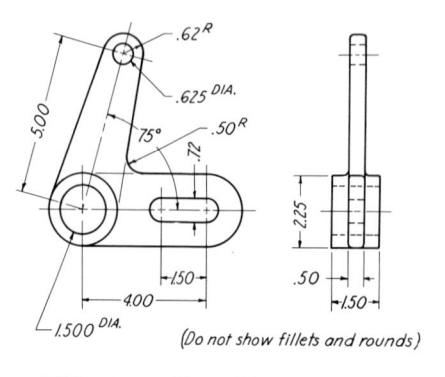

FIG. 12.92. Slotted bell crank.

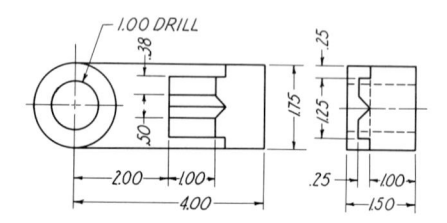

(Do not show fillets and rounds)

FIG. 12.93. Control guide.

26. (Figs. 12.89–12.91). Make an angular perspective drawing as assigned.

27. (Fig. 12.92). Make a pictorial drawing (oblique, isometric, or perspective) of the slotted bell crank.

28. (Fig. 12.93). Make a pictorial drawing (oblique, isometric, or perspective) of the control guide.

GRAPHICS FOR DESIGN AND COMMUNICATION

III

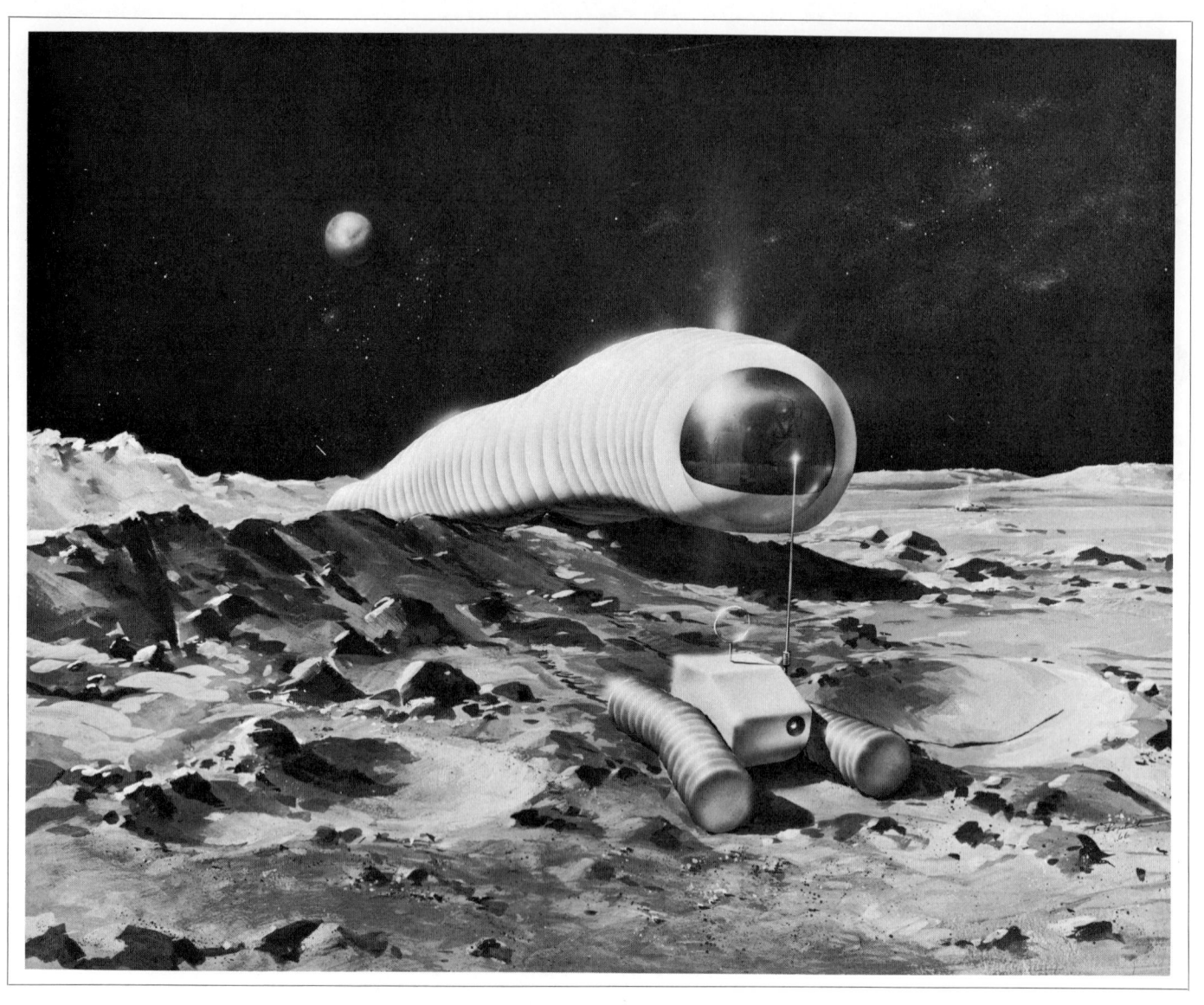

An Artist Concept of a Lunar Surface Vehicle (Moon Crawler). The representation shown suggests a type of vehicle that might be used for travel across the rough terrain of the moon. Artist renderings of this type are needed for an evaluation of a conceptual design when many of the persons involved in the decision making may be government officials and others who do not have a strong scientific and technical background.
(*Courtesy Philco-Ford Corp., Aeronutronic Division.*)

Introduction to Design: Sketching and Creative Thinking

13

13.1
Introduction. From the earliest times pictorial representations have been the means of conveying the ideas of one person to another person and of one group to another group (Fig. 13.2). There is little doubt that our ancestors traced out in the dust on the cave floor many crude pictures to supplement their gutteral utterances. On their cave walls these same primitive men and women drew pictures, which today convey to others the stories of their lives. They used the only permanent means they were aware of at that time.

At present, we have at our command the spoken languages, which no doubt developed from limited semiintelligent throat sounds, and the written languages, graphical and symbolic in form. The descriptive powers of the various forms of presentation may be compared in Fig. 13.1. The use of sign language representation (a) is rather easy to learn and may be quickly executed but interpretation is restricted to persons who understand the particular language in which it is presented. The multiview representation, shown in (b), may be understood universally by persons who have been trained in its use. However, the given views will prove to be almost meaningless to the many who have not had the advantage of needed training. What then is the one form of representation that can be understood and may be used by all? It is the pictorial form shown in (c).

It is necessary that a designer be capable of executing well-proportioned and understandable freehand pictorial sketches, for it is one of the most important modes of expression that he has

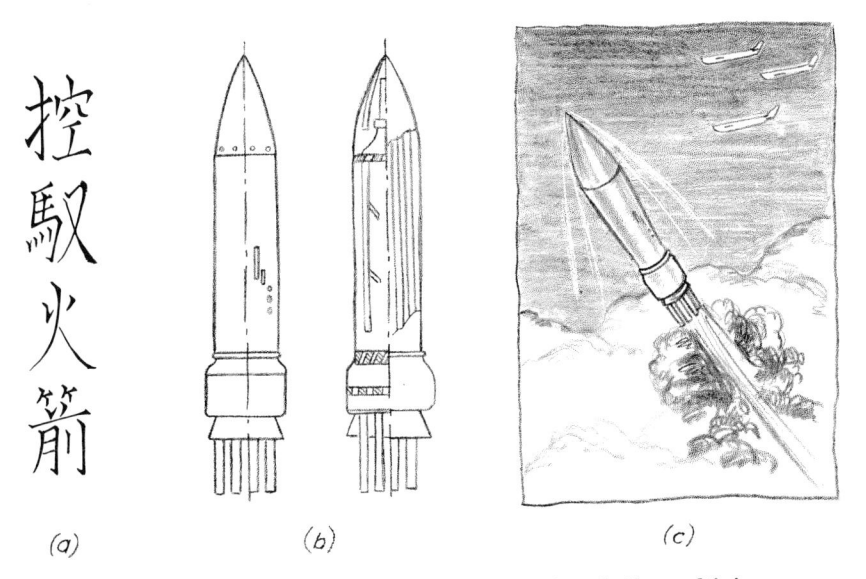

FIG. 13.1. Graphic methods for presenting ideas (symbolic, multiview, and pictorial).

291

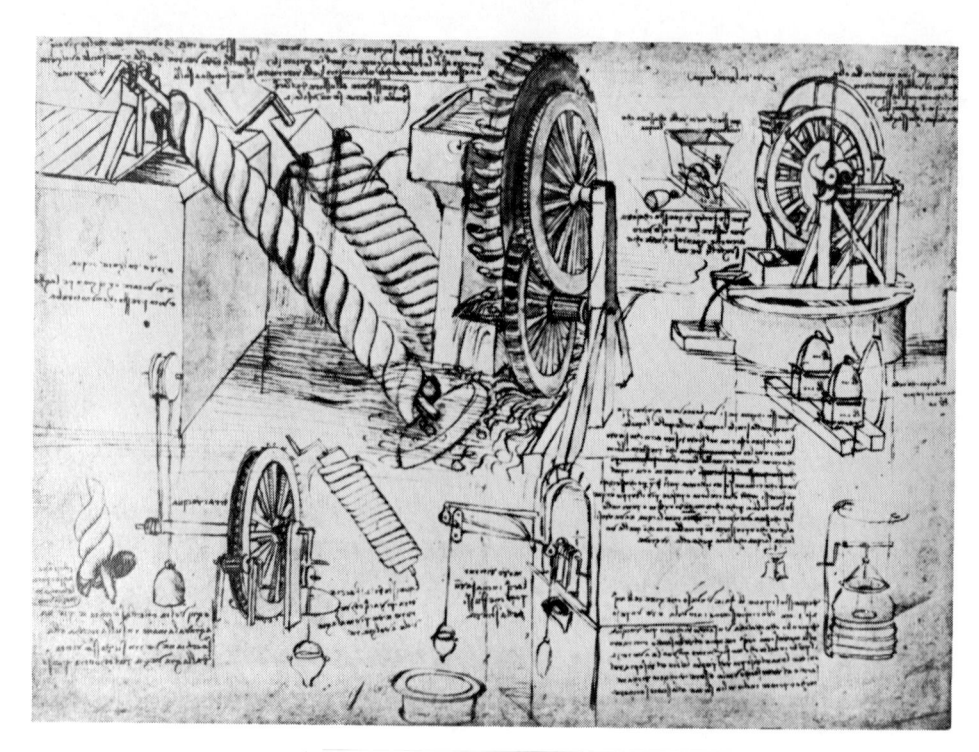

FIG. 13.2. Sketch showing Archimedean screw and wheel by Leonardo da Vinci (1452–1519), engineer, scientist, and painter. (*From Collections of Fine Arts Department, International Business Machines Corporation*)

available for use. Like other means for conveying ideas, when depended on alone, it will usually prove to be inadequate. However, when used in combination with the written or spoken language and related graphical representations, it makes a full understanding by others become sure and not just possible (Fig. 13.2). Each method of expression is at hand to supplement another to convey the intended idea.

The designer should be capable of speaking his own language and possibly one foreign language fluently; he should be able to write to present his ideas clearly and accurately; he should be familiar with the graphical method of presenting shape through the use of multiviews; and finally, he should be competent to execute well-proportioned and understandable pictorial sketches, which are needed to clarify and insure complete transfer of his ideas to others (Fig. 13.3).

The designer is a creative person living in a world where all that he creates must exist in space. He must visualize space conditions, space distances, and movement in space. In addition he must be able to retain as well as alter the image of his idea, which will at the very start exist only in his mind.

As his idea forms the designer nearly always resorts to sketching to organize his

FIG. 13.3. Heli-lifted classrooms may be transported to every part of the earth by 1985. The lessons would be projected in 3-D. Transmittal would be carried by laser beams, relayed by satellite. (*Courtesy Raymond Loewy/William Smith, Inc. and Charles Bruning Company*)

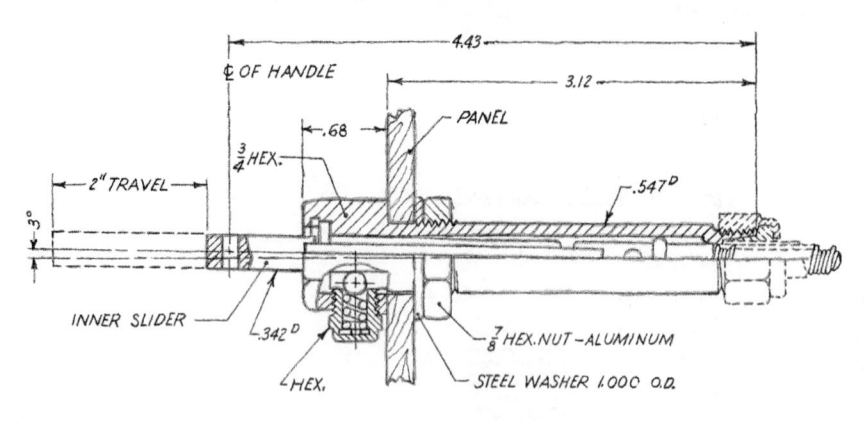

FIG. 13.4. A design sketch for a connector of a remote control unit. (*Courtesy Teleflex, Inc.*)

thoughts quickly and more clearly visualize the problems that appear. The first ideas may be sketched in pictorial form as they are visualized. Later, in making a preliminary study, a combination of orthographic design sketches and pictorial sketches may quickly pile up on his desk as problems are recognized and possible solutions are recorded for reference and for conferences with others.

The designer's use of sketches, both pictorial and orthographic (Fig. 13.4), continues throughout the preliminary design stages and into the development and detailing stages. This comes about because he is usually called on to serve as both planner and director. Throughout all stages in the development of a structure, he must solve problems and calrify instructions. Very often a pictorial sketch of some detail of construction will prove to be more intelligible and will convey the idea much better than an orthographic sketch, even when dealing with an experienced draftsman or detailer (Fig. 13.7).

Design sketches may be done in the quiet of the designer's office or amid the confusion of the conference table. To meet the requirement of speed of preparation, one must resist all temptation to use instruments of any type and rely on the pencil alone, for the true measure of the quality of a finished sketch is neatness and good proportion rather than the straightness of the lines. A pictorial sketch need not be an artistic masterpiece to be useful.

Students may employ pictorial sketches to advantage as an aid in visualizing and organizing problems. Sales engineers may frequently include pictorial sketches with orthographic sketches when preparing field reports on the needs and suggestions of the firm's customers.

With some training anyone can prepare pictorial sketches that will be satisfactory for all practical purposes. Artistic ability is not needed. This fact is important, for many persons lack only the necessary confidence to start making pictorial sketches.

Training for making pictorial sketches must include the presentation of basic fundamentals, as is done with other how-to-do-it subjects. As learning the mechanics of English does not make one a creative writer, so training in sketching will not make one a creative engineer. However, sketching is the means of recording creative thoughts.

Some design sketches, drawn by an electrical engineer, are shown in Fig. 13.5. These sketches were prepared in making a study of the wiring to the electronic control panel for an automatic machine.

13.2

Thinking with a Pencil. As an attempt is made to bring actuality to a plan, sketches undergo constant change as different ideas develop. An eraser may be in constant use or new starts may be made repeatedly, even though one should think much and sketch only when it would appear to be worthwhile. Sketching should be done as easily and freely as writing, so that the mind is always centered on the idea and not on the technique of sketching. To reach the point where one can

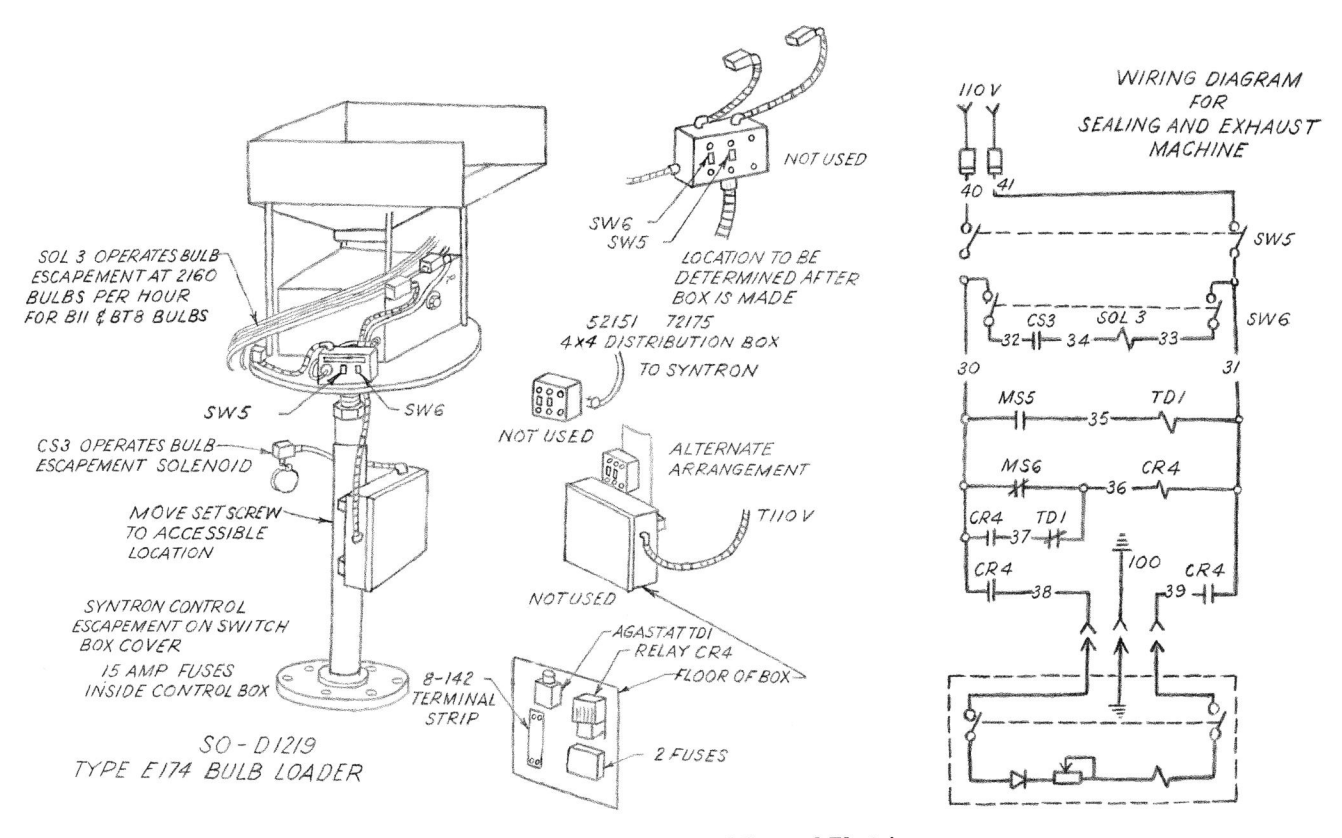

CHAP. 13 / INTRODUCTION TO DESIGN: SKETCHING AND CREATIVE THINKING 295

FIG. 13.5. A portion of a design sketch. (*Courtesy of General Electric Company.*)

"think with the pencil" is not easy. Continued practice is necessary until one can sketch with as little thought about how it is done as he gives to how he uses a knife and fork at the dinner table.

Two idea sketches for the dashboard panel of an automobile are shown in Fig. 13.6. Persons who prepare sketches for the styling division of a company must have a feeling for beauty as well as an understanding of engineering design. The engineer and technologist of the future must be style conscious if their products are to enjoy a sales advantage over that of a competitor.

It has been assumed that the student has read Chapter 7 covering "Freehand

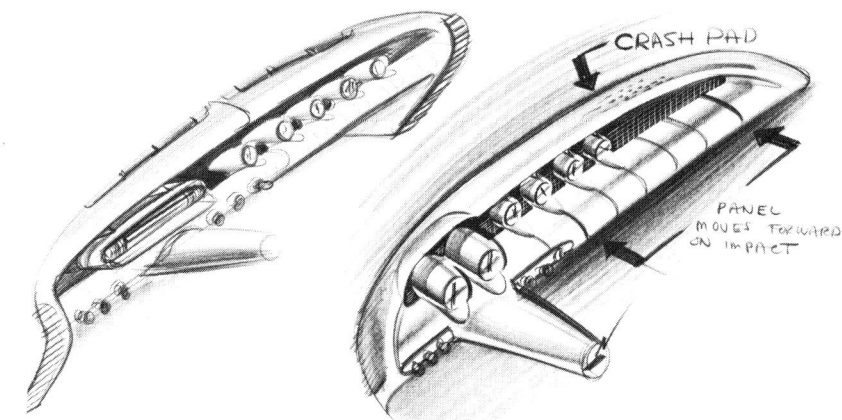

FIG. 13.6. Design sketches for a dashboard panel. (*Courtesy General Motors Corp.*)

FIG. 13.7. An idea sketch in isometric.

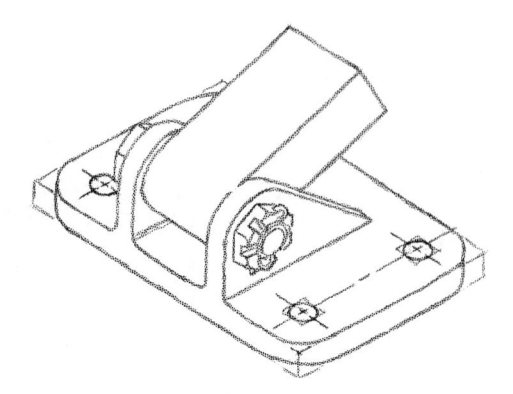

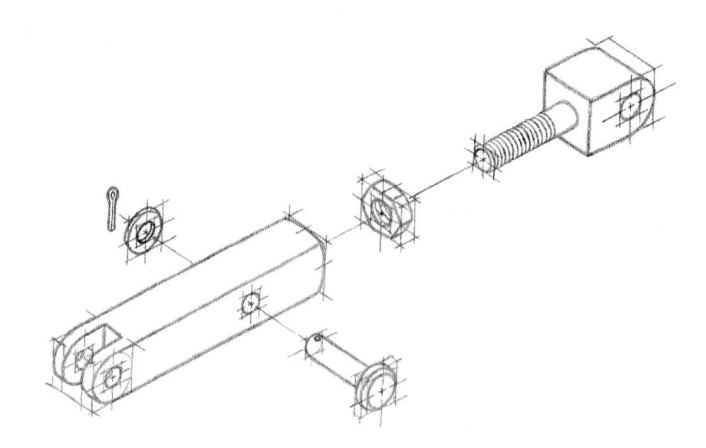

FIG. 13.8. A sketch of a simple mechanism.

Drawing," for the techniques discussed there apply to all forms of technical sketching.

The practices presented in Chapter 12 for the mechanical methods, axonometric, oblique, and perspective, are followed generally in pictorial sketching, except that angles are assumed and lengths are estimated.

13.3
Sketches in Isometric. In making a sketch in isometric, an experienced person frequently foreshortens receding distances until the proportions satisfy the eye. In addition, some who are a little more confident will make the receding lines converge slightly. A pictorial sketch treated in this manner is said to be in pseudoperspective. The procedures to be followed in preparing isometric sketches have been presented in detail in Sec. 7.16.

An idea sketch is shown in Fig. 13.7. A sketch giving the parts of a simple mechanism arranged for assembly is shown in Fig. 13.8.

13.4
Sketches in Oblique. The preparation of sketches in oblique has been explained in Sec. 7.18.

13.5
Perspective Sketching. A sketch that has been prepared in accordance with the concepts of perspective will present a somewhat more pleasing and realistic effect than one in oblique or isometric. A perspective sketch actually presents an object as it would appear when observed from a particular point. The recognition of this fact, along with an understanding of the concepts that an object will appear smaller at a distance than when it is close and that horizontal lines converge as they recede until they meet at a vanishing point, should enable one to produce sketches having a perspective appearance. In sketching an actual object, a position should be selected that will show it to the best advantage. When the object exists only in one's mind or on paper in orthographic form, then the object must be visualized and the viewing position assumed.

At the start, the principal lines should be sketched in lightly, extending each line for some length toward its vanishing point. After this has been accomplished, the enclosing perspective squares for circles should be blocked in and the outline for minor details added. When the object lines have been darkened, the construction lines extending beyond the figure may be erased.

Figure 13.9 shows a parallel or one-point perspective that bears some resemblance to an oblique sketch. All faces in planes parallel to the front show their true shape. All receding lines should meet at a single vanishing point. Figure 13.10 is an angular or two-point perspective.

As stated previously, a two-point perspective sketch shows an object as it would appear to the human eye at a fixed point in space and not as it actually exists. All parallel receding lines converge (Fig. 13.12). Should these receding lines be horizontal, they will converge at a vanishing point on the eyeline. Those lines extending toward the right converge to a vanishing point to the right (VP_R), and those to the left converge to the left (VP_L). These vanishing points are at the level of the observer's eye (Fig. 13.12). A system of lines that is neither perpendicular nor horizontal will converge to a VP for inclined lines.

In one-point perspective one of the principal faces is parallel to the picture plane. All of the vertical lines will appear as vertical, and the receding horizontal lines will converge to a single vanishing point (Fig. 13.13).

Those interested in a complete discussion of the geometry of perspective drawing should read Secs. 12.28-12.41. The beginner should make two or three mechanically drawn perspectives at the start to fix the fundamentals of the methods of perspective projection in his mind, even though there is some difference between sketching what one sees or imagines and true geometrical perspective.

In making a sketch in artist's perspective, several fundamental concepts must be recognized.

First, a circle sketched in perspective will resemble an ellipse (Fig. 13.12). The long diameter of the representation of a circle on a horizontal plane is always in a horizontal direction (Fig. 13.14).

Second, if an object or a component part of an object is above the eyeline, it will be seen from below. Should the object be below the eyeline, it will be seen from above (Fig. 13.12). The farther the object is removed below or above the eyeline, the more one can see of the top or the bottom surface.

Third, the nearest vertical edge of an object will be the longest vertical line of the view, as shown in Fig. 13.12. When two or more objects of the same actual height appear in a perspective sketch, their represented heights will decrease in the view as they near the vanishing point.

13.6

Determining Proportions. When an object exists only as an image in one's mind, all proportions can be assumed. However, when sketching by eye an object that already exists, it becomes necessary to be able to compare the relationship between the width, height, and depth dimensions as they are seen. That is, some sort of a measuring stick is needed to compare these lengths in the proportions that they are being seen, at the fixed position of the observer, who is at some distance from the object itself. To satisfy this need most sketchers use the most convenient thing that is available—their sketching pencils. Apparent lengths can be determined along the body of the pencil held at arm's length in a plane perpendicular to the line of sight, as shown in Fig. 13.11. One marks with the tip of the thumbnail the length on the object that is covered from the top of the pencil downward. With this basic distance established, the arm is rotated until the pencil coincides with another edge of the object and then an estimate is made about whether the second line is to be made one-fifth, one-fourth, one-half, or three-fourths as long as the first. To make an estimate of a proportion in terms closer than fifths is impractical and unnecessary.

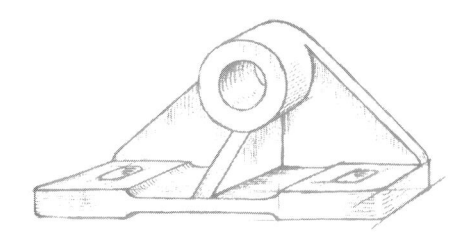

FIG. 13.9. A sketch in parallel perspective.

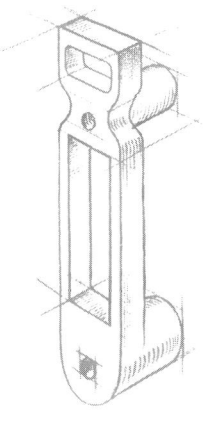

FIG. 13.10. A sketch in angular perspective.

FIG. 13.11. Obtaining proportions by means of a pencil.

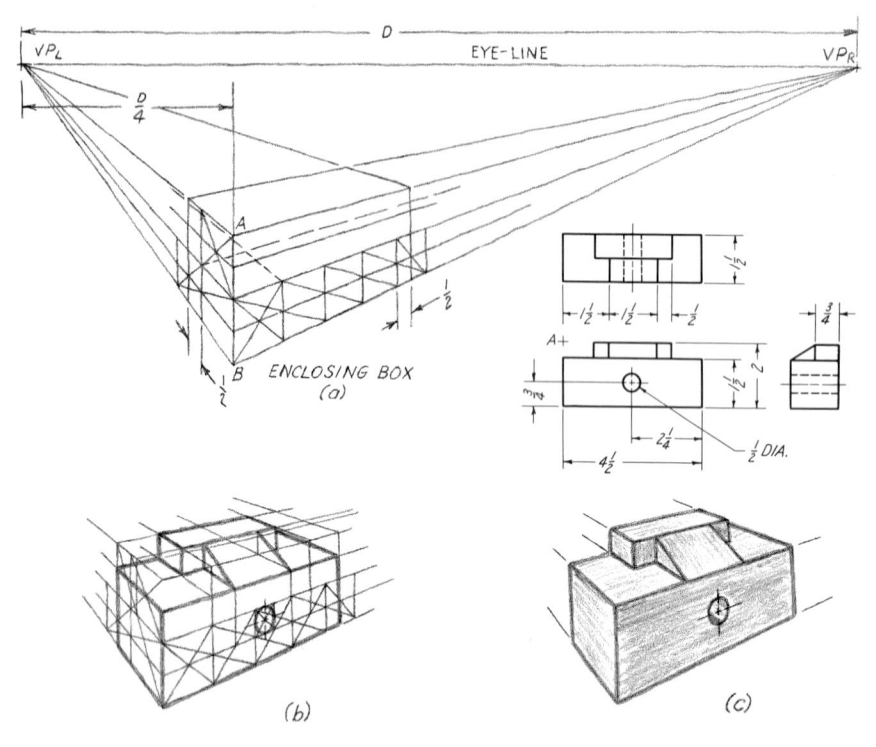

FIG. 13.12. Preparing a perspective sketch.

13.7

To Make a Perspective Sketch. The application of proportioning methods to the construction and division of an enclosing box is shown in Fig. 13.12. Read Secs. 7.10 and 7.17. The construction of a required perspective by steps is as follows:

Step I. Sketch the eyeline. This line should be well toward the top of the sheet of sketch paper.

Step II. Locate VP_L and VP_R on the eyeline. These vanishing points should be placed as far apart as possible.

Step III. Assume the position and length for the near front edge AB. The length of this line, along with the spacing of the vanishing points, establishes the size of the finished sketch. The position of AB determines how the visible surfaces are to appear. For instance, if the line AB had been moved downward from the position shown in (*a*), much more of the top surface would be seen in (*b*) and (*c*). Should AB have been moved to the right from its position shown in (*a*), the left side would have become more prominent. If AB were placed midway between the two vanishing points, then both the front and left-side surfaces would be at 45° with the picture plane for the perspective. As it has been placed in (*a*), the side face is at 60° to the picture plane, while the front face is at 30°. Before establishing the position for the near front edge, one must decide which surfaces are the most important surfaces and how they may best be displayed in the sketch.

Step IV. Sketch light construction lines from points A and B to each vanishing point.

Step V. Determine the proportions for the enclosing box, in this case $4\frac{1}{2}$, 2, and $1\frac{1}{2}$, and mark off two equal units along AB.

Step VI. Sketch perspective squares, representing the faces of 1-unit cubes, starting at *AB* and working toward each vanishing point. In cases where an overall length must be completed with a partial unit, a full-perspective square must be sketched at the end.

Step VII. Subdivide any of the end squares if necessary and sketch in the enclosing box (*a*).

Step VIII. Locate and block in the details, subdividing the perspective squares as required to establish the location of any detail. When circles are to be sketched in perspective by a beginner, it is advisable to sketch the enclosing box first using light lines (*b*).

Step IX. Darken the object lines of the sketch. Construction lines may be removed and some shading added to the surfaces as shown in (*c*), if desired.

A sketch in one-point perspective might be made as shown in Fig. 13.13. For this particular sketch the enclosing box was made to the assumed overall proportions for the part. Then the location of the details was established by subdividing the regular rectangle of the front face of the enclosing box and the perspective rectangle of the right side.

13.8
Pencil Shading. The addition of some shading to the surfaces of a part will force its form to stand out against the white surface of the sketching paper and will increase the effect of depth in a view that might otherwise appear to be somewhat flat.

Seldom are technologists and engineers able to do creditable work in artistic shading with cast shadows included as they could many years ago when training in art was part of an engineer's education. It is unfortunate that they lack this training at the present time, for art and design go

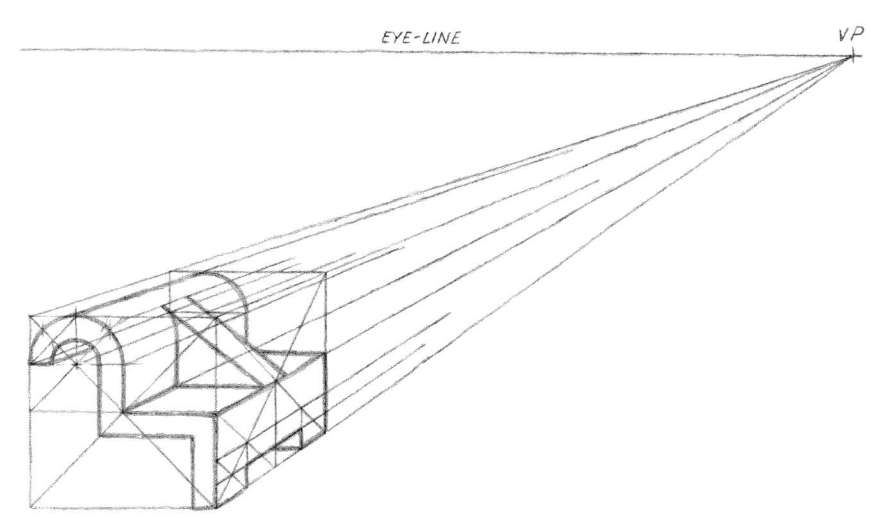

FIG. 13.13. A sketch made in one-point perspective.

hand in hand. This is especially true today, for a pleasing and appealing styling sells more products than good mechanical design (Fig. 13.6).

Within the scope of this chapter, written for beginning students, it will only be possible to present a few simple rules as a guide for those making a first attempt at surface shading. However, continued practice and some thought should lead one to the point where he can do a creditable job of shading and definitely improve a pictorial sketch.

When shading an imaginary part, a designer may consider the source of the light to be located in a position to the left, above, and in front of the object. Of course, if the part actually exists and is being sketched by viewing it, then the sketcher should attempt to duplicate the degrees of shade and shadows as they are observed.

With the light source considered to be to the left, above, and in front of the object, a rectangular part would be shaded as shown in Fig. 13.14(*a*). The use of gradation of tone on the surfaces gives

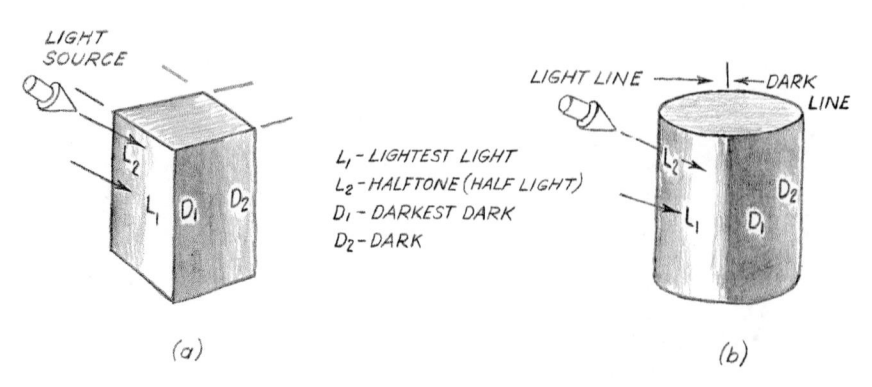

FIG. 13.14. Shading rectangular and cylindrical parts.

L_1 - LIGHTEST LIGHT
L_2 - HALFTONE (HALF LIGHT)
D_1 - DARKEST DARK
D_2 - DARK

additional emphasis to the depth. To secure this added effect by shading, the darkest tone on the surface that is away from the light must be closest to the eye. As the surface recedes the tone must be made lighter in value with a faint trace of reflected light showing along the entire length of the back edge. On the lighted side, the lightest area must be closest to the eye, as indicated by the letter L_1 in (a). To make this lighted face appear to go into the distance, it is made darker as it recedes, but it should never be made as dark as the lightest of the dark tones on the dark surface.

Shading a cylindrical part is not as easy to do as shading a rectangular part but, if it is realized that practically half of the cylinder is in the light and half in the dark and that the lightest light and the darkest dark fall along the elements at the quarter-points of each half, then one should not find the task too difficult (b). The two extremes are separated by lighter values of shade. The first quarter on the lighted side must be made lighter than the last quarter on the dark side. In starting at the left and going counterclockwise there is a dark shade of light blending into the full light at the first quarter-point. From this point and passing the center to the dark line, the tone should become gradually darker. If vertical lines are used for shading, they should be spaced closer and closer together as they approach the dark line. The extreme-right-hand quarter should show the tones of reflected light.

There are two ways that pencil shading may be applied. If the paper has a medium-rough surface, solid tone shading may be used with one shade blending into the other. For the best results, the light tones are put on first over all areas to be shaded. The darker tones are then added by building up lighter tones to the desired intensity for a particular area. For this form of shading, a pencil with flattened point is used.

The other form of shading, and the one that is best suited for quick sketches, is produced with lines of varied spacing and weight. Light lines with wide spacing are used on the light areas and heavy lines that are closely spaced give the tone for the darkest areas. No lines are needed for the lightest of the light areas.

13.9
Conventional Treatment of Fillets, Rounds, and Screw Threads. Sketches that are not given full pencil shading may be given a more or less realistic appearance by representing the fillets and rounds of the unfinished surfaces as shown in Fig. 12.44 in the preceding chapter. The conventional treatment for screw threads is shown in (b) and (c) of the same illustration.

13.10
Use of an Overlay Sheet. In preparing a design sketch, an overlay sheet may be used to advantage in making a sketch that is complicated by many details (Fig. 13.15). In this case, a quick sketch showing the general outline of the principal parts is made first in a rather rough form. Then an overlay sheet is placed over this outline sketch and the lines are retraced.

USE OF AN OVERLAY SHEET

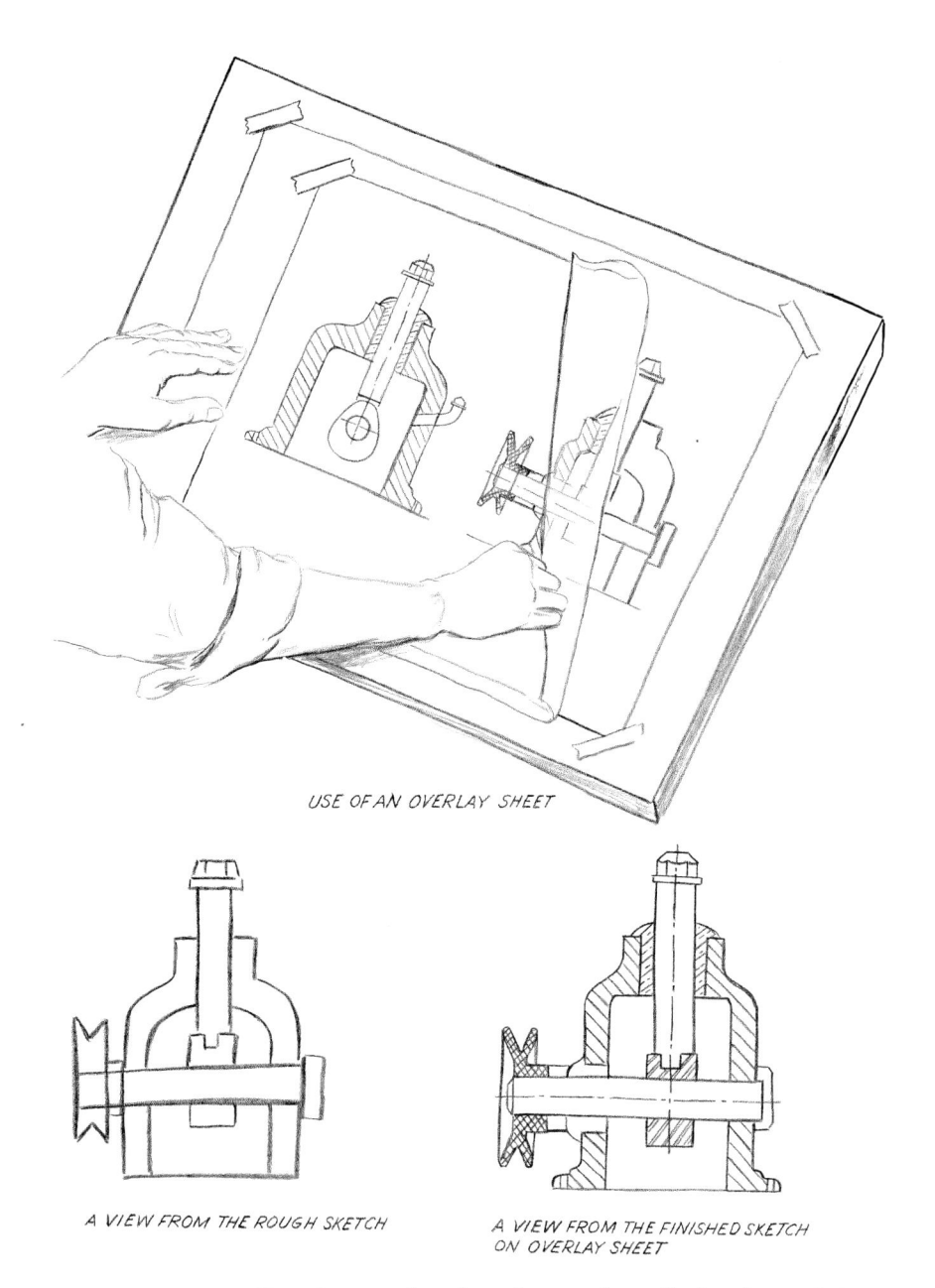

A VIEW FROM THE ROUGH SKETCH

A VIEW FROM THE FINISHED SKETCH ON OVERLAY SHEET

FIG. 13.15. Use of an overlay sheet for creating a final and complete sketch of a mechanism.

302

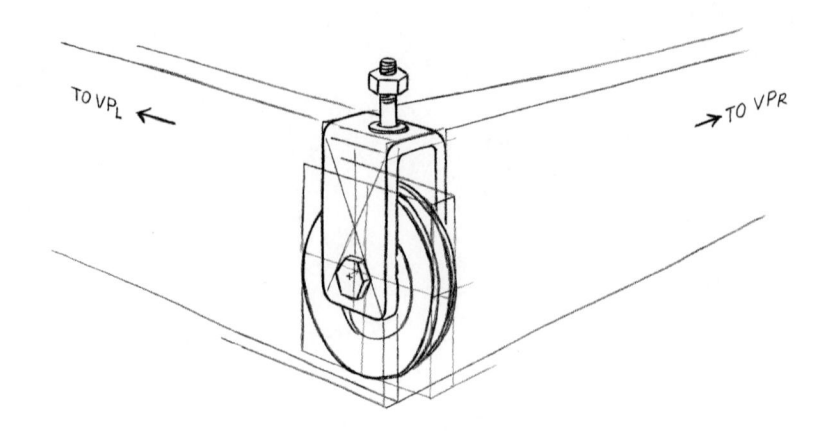

Horizon Line

← TO VP_L   TO VP_R →

TO VP_L ←   → TO VP_R

Block-in assembly in outline

OVERLAY SHEET

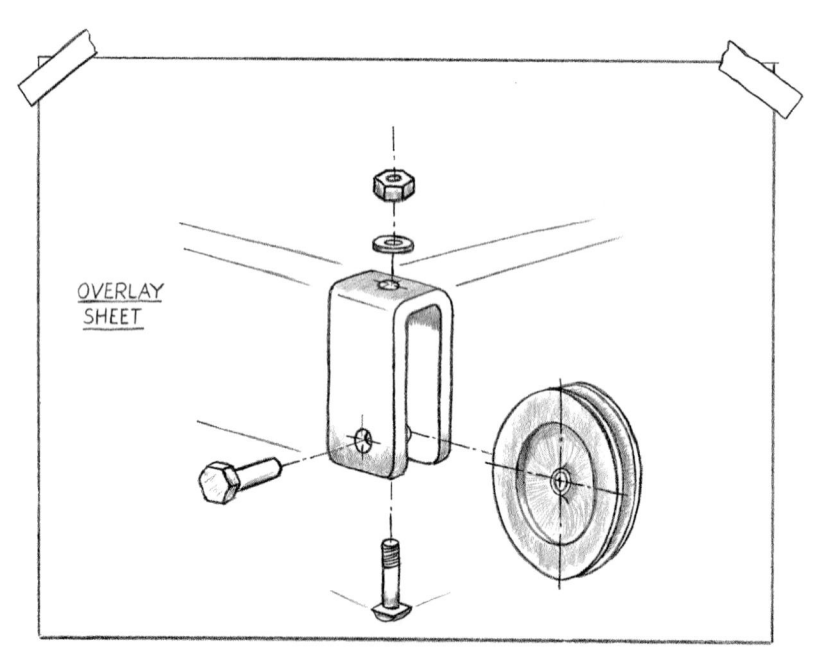

FIG. 13.16. A sketch showing the parts of a mechanism in exploded positions.

Retrace parts on overlay sheet in exploded positions from assembly sketch

In doing so, slight corrections can be made for any errors existing in the proportions of the parts or in the position of any of the lines of the original rough sketch. When this has been done, the representation of the related minor parts are added. If at any time one becomes discouraged with a sketch (multiview or pictorial) that he is making and feels that he should make a new start, he should use an overlay sheet, for there are usually many features on his existing sketch that may be retraced with a great saving of time.

13.11

Illustration Sketches Showing Mechanisms Exploded. A sketch of a mechanism showing the parts in exploded positions along the principal axes is shown in Fig. 13.16. Through the use of such sketches those who have not been trained to read multiview drawings may readily understand how a mechanism should be assembled, for both the shapes of the parts and their order of assembly, as denoted by their space relationship, is shown in pictorial form.

Illustration sketches may be made for discussions dealing with ideas for a design, but more frequently they are prepared for explanatory purposes to clarify instructions for preparing illustration drawings in a more finished form as assembly illustrations, advertising illustrations, catalogue illustrations, and illustrations for service and repair charts.

Many persons find that it is desirable, when preparing sketches of exploded mechanisms, to first block in the complete mechanism with all of the parts in position. At this initial stage of construction, the parts are sketched in perspective in rough outline and the principal axes and object lines are extended partway toward their vanishing points.

When the rough layout has been completed to the satisfaction of the person preparing the sketch, an overlay sheet is placed over the original sketch and the parts are traced directly from the sketch beneath in exploded positions along the principal axes and along the axes of holes. Frequently some beginners make a traced sketch of each individual part and place the sketches in exploded positions before preparing the finished sketch. Others with more experience accomplish the same results by first tracing the major part along with the principal axes and then moving the overlay sheet as required to trace off the remaining parts in their correct positions along the axes.

It should be recognized that in preparing sketches of exploded mechanisms in this manner the parts are not shown perspectively reduced although they are removed from their original place in the pictorial assembly outward and toward the vanishing points. To prepare a sketch of this type with all of the parts shown in true geometrical perspective would result in a general picture that would be misleading and one that would be apt to confuse the nontechnical person because some parts would appear much too large or too small to be mating parts.

13.12

Idea Sketches. A pictorial sketch may be used to advantage in studying an idea for a complete unit, as was done for the quick-acting clamp shown in Fig. 13.17. Another example is given in Fig. 13.18, where a suggested arrangement for a remote control system is shown. Only a minimum number of lines were used to suggest the outline of the boat, for using unnecessary lines on a sketch is undesirable since they make the sketch more difficult to understand.

In Fig. 13.19 the results of some progressive thinking on a particular problem are shown. The changes that an original design may undergo result from the minor problems that usually develop and from

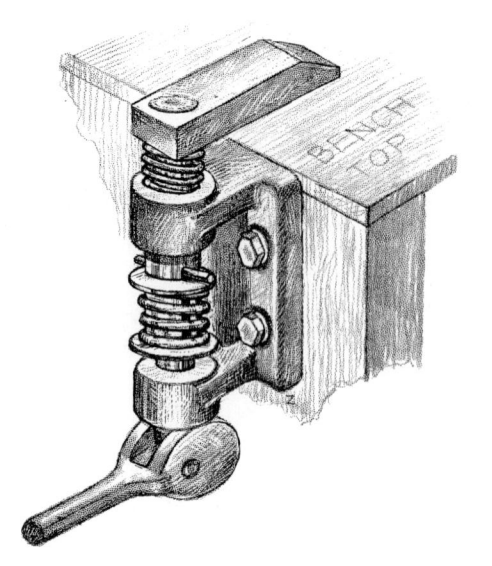

FIG. 13.17. Idea sketch for a quick acting machine clamp.

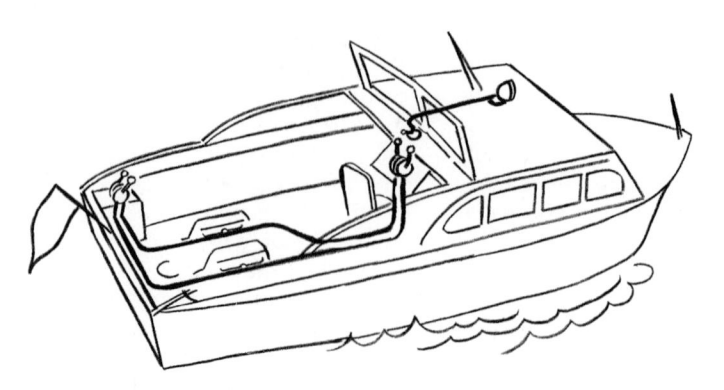

FIG. 13.18. Idea sketch showing remote control system for a motor boat. (*Courtesy Teleflex, Inc.*)

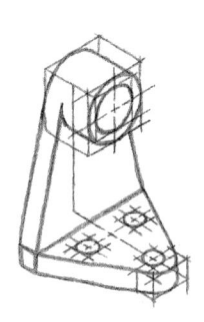

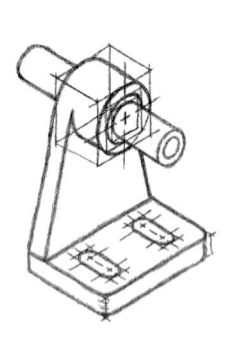

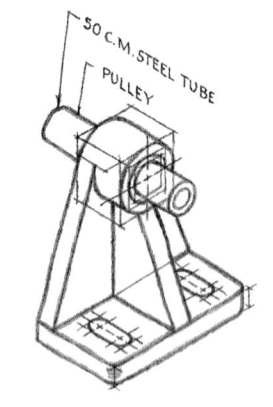

FIG. 13.19. Successive idea sketches made to determine the form for a control rod bracket.

new ideas that seem to improve it. Frequently these new ideas come as casual thoughts of one's colleagues, or they may arise in a formal way around a conference table when those who represent the design and production departments of a firm meet with the representatives of management and prospective customers. Each new idea that is presented must be thoroughly explored before being discarded as unnecessary or undesirable.

At such conferences, the representation of an idea in some pictorial form assures one that there will be a complete understanding of an idea by all of those who are present, be they engineers, technologists, or businessmen.

After a rather complete pictorial representation has once been prepared for showing a suggested change for an existing mechanism or an entirely new idea for a nonexistent structure, subsequent alterations may be represented on transparent overlay sheets (see Sec. 13.10). The sketch on the overlay is made by tracing as much of the original sketch as needed. Sometimes it will be desirable to make the sketch on the overlay nearly complete, while at other times all that will be needed is a complete sketch of a particular detail along with a few additional lines that will suggest the outline of the main structure or mechanism.

Idea sketches of single parts are made frequently when deciding on the form that the part must take if it is to fulfill its function. In making such sketches, it is a rare occasion when the first sketch made by the designer or draftsman proves to be satisfactory (Fig. 13.19). Usually several ideas must be considered and discarded before one is found that will satisfy all concerned with the design or alteration that is being developed.

13.13
Creative Sketching—Beginning Student. The spark that sets one off on a project is not the touch of genius, but rather an open-minded recognition of the urgent need and the economic possibilities afforded. Very little is known about why some possess the inherent drive that is behind all forms of creativity, while others do not, but the opportunity to exercise some creativeness and thoughtful judgment will aid and strengthen one's confidence. For this reason a few of the problems offered are presented to require the beginning student to create new products that will satisfy some particular requirements. In preparing the sketches for these problems, emphasis must necessarily be placed on the form of the unit and on the technique of sketching. Finished sketches can be evaluated only on quality, originality, and how well the idea as represented will fulfill the need. Structural strength and correctness of design, although important, must be overlooked.

One often becomes discouraged with his efforts toward creating even simple items, when he becomes aware of the amount of time that he is taking in making repeated attempts to satisfy conditions and requirements. The student, however, should remember that creative work must necessarily be time consuming, for step-by-step guidance is not at hand. Furthermore, the value of creative work can never be measured in terms of time or money. For instance, would it be reasonable to evaluate a creation of our great Thomas A. Edison in terms of the number of hours that he worked on that particular project?

When the mind seems to be stalled on dead center, it will often be helpful to start a sketch of just anything that might meet the requirements, for as one's mind and pencil work together, new ideas may make an appearance.

13.14
Design. In the dictionary, design is defined as follows: (1) to form or conceive in the mind, (2) to contrive a plan, (3) to plan and fashion the form of a system (structure), and (4) to prepare the preliminary sketches and/or plans for a system that is to be produced. Engineering design is a decision-making process used for the development of engineering systems for which there is human need. To design is to conceive, to innovate, to create. One may design an entirely new system, or modify and rearrange existing things in a new way for improved usefulness or performance. Engineering design begins with the recognition of a social or economic need. The need, as identified, must first be translated into an apparently acceptable idea by conceptulization and decision making. Then, the idea must in turn be tested against the physical laws of nature before one can be certain that it is workable. This requires that the designer have a full knowledge of the fundamental physical laws of the basic sciences, a working knowledge of the so-called engineering sciences, and the ability to communicate ideas both graphically (Fig. 13.2) and orally. He should be well grounded in economics and be familiar with manufacturing methods. Some knowledge of both sales and advertising will prove worthwhile, since usually what is produced must be distributed at a profit. Proficiency in designing can be attained only through total involvement—that is, through prac-

tice to acquire the art of continually providing new and novel ideas. In developing the design, the engineer or technologist must apply his knowledge of the engineering and material sciences. He must also take into account related human factors, reliability, marketability, and oftentimes much more. It may therefore be said that the ability to design is both an art and a science. It is the art of the practice of designing that marks the designer and the engineer as being professional.

A truly creative person will almost never follow a set pattern of action in developing an idea. To do so would tend to structure his thinking and might limit the creation of possible solutions. The design process calls for unrestrained creative ingenuity and continual decision making by a free-wheeling mind. However, the total development of an idea, from the recognition of a need to the final product, does appear to proceed loosely in stages (steps) that are recognized by authors and educators. These steps given in a sequential order are:

FIG. 13.20. Creative thinking produces new ways of life for man. The Minigap System shown above links cars together into a caravan that is lead by a specially built leader vehicle. Computers inside the cars take over control of brakes, accelerator, and steering to free the motorist from the task of driving as long as he remains hooked-up. Caravans can mix in the traffic flow with other vehicles. (*Courtesy Ford Motor Company*)

1. *Task definition* (goal). An expression of a commitment to produce a system that will satisfy the need as already identified.

2. *Task specifications.* A listing of parameters and data that will serve to control the design. This stage may be preceded by some preliminary research to collect present available information related to the goal.

3. *Ideation.* Formulation of ideas (brainstorming).

4. *Conceptualization.* The creation of possible solutions. This stage usually requires the preparation of many freehand sketches.

5. *Analysis.* Testing several choice solutions against physical laws, human factors, marketability, production costs, and so forth. This is a decision-making stage.

6. *Experimental testing.* Constructing and testing an experimental prototype to prove workability, durability, serviceability, and so forth.

7. *Design* (solution) *description.* The complete description consists of a design report, necessary drawings, parts list, specifications, cost analysis, and so forth (Fig. 13.20).

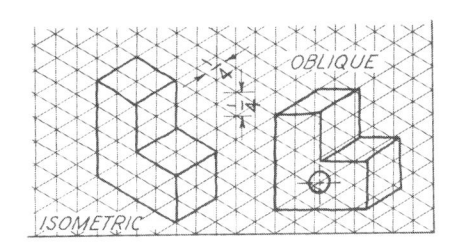

CHAP. 13 / INTRODUCTION TO DESIGN: SKETCHING AND CREATIVE THINKING   **307**

FIG. 13.21. Sketches on isometric paper.

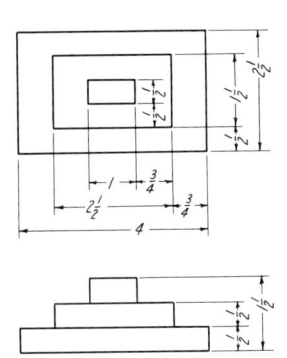

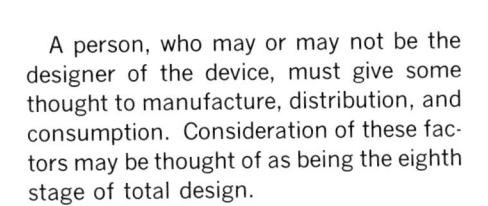

FIG. 13.22.

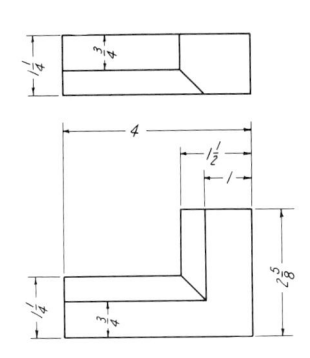

FIG. 13.23.

A person, who may or may not be the designer of the device, must give some thought to manufacture, distribution, and consumption. Consideration of these factors may be thought of as being the eighth stage of total design.

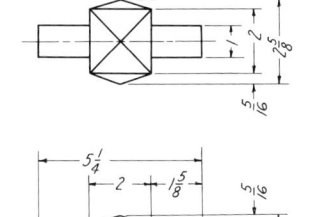

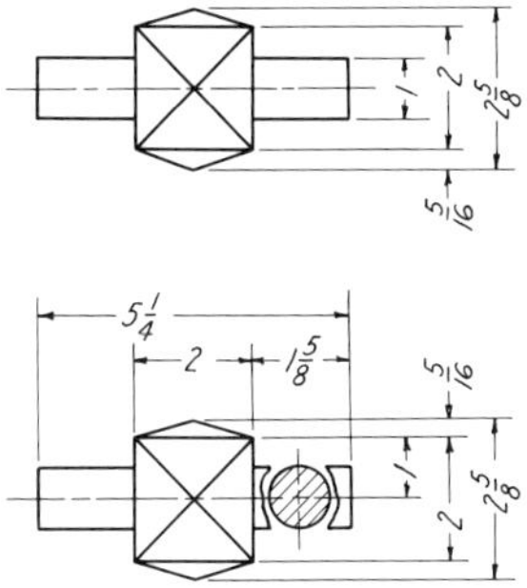

13.15
Materials—Technique. For pictorial sketching, the materials needed are an HB or F pencil, a soft eraser, and some paper. Although one should become proficient in sketching on plain white bond paper, a specially ruled paper, shown in Fig. 13.21, can be used by those who need the help of guidelines.

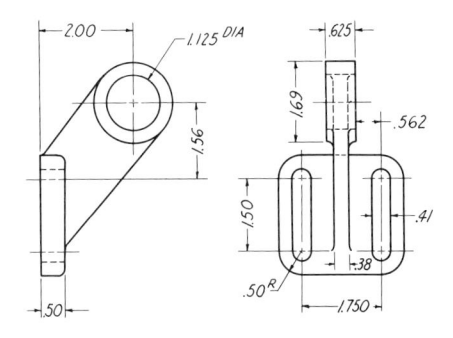

FIG. 13.24.

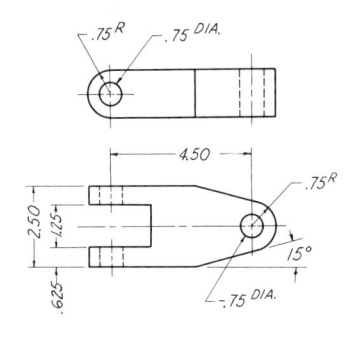

FIG. 13.25.

PROBLEMS

The problems presented in this chapter were selected to give practice in preparing sketches—multiview, axonometric, oblique, or perspective. In addition to developing proficiency in sketching, these problems offer the student further opportunity to gain experience in reading drawings. Additional problems that are suitable for sketching may be found in Chapters 7 and 12.

1-6. (Figs. 13.22–13.27). Make freehand perspective sketches of the objects as assigned.

The following problems are offered as suggestions to stimulate creativity and give some

(Do not show fillets and rounds)

FIG. 13.26.

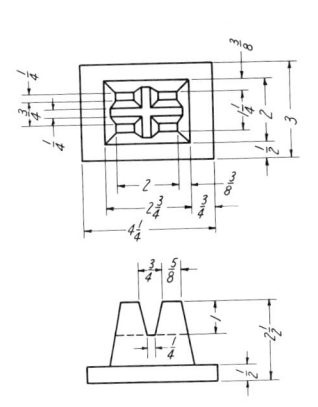

additional experience in both pictorial and multiview sketching. Students who have an inclination to design useful mechanisms should be encouraged to select a problem for themselves, for the creative mind works best when directed

FIG. 13.27.

to a task in which it already has some interest. However, the young beginner should confine his activities to ideas for simple mechanisms that do not require extensive training in machine design and the engineering sciences.

7. Prepare design sketches (both pictorial and multiview) for an open-end wrench to fit the head of a bolt (regular series) having a body diameter of 1 in. Give dimensions on the multiview sketch and specify the material.

8. Prepare design sketches (both pictorial and multiview) for a wrench having a head with four or more fixed openings to fit the heads of bolts having nominal diameters of $\frac{5}{8}$, $\frac{3}{4}$, $\frac{7}{8}$, and 1 in. Dimension the multiview sketch and specify the material.

9. Prepare a series of design sketches for a bumper hitch (curved bumper) for attaching a light two-wheel trailer to a passenger automobile. Weight of trailer is 295 lb.

10. Prepare sketches for a hanger bracket to support a $\frac{1}{2}$-in. control rod. The bracket must be attached to a vertical surface to which the control rod is parallel. The distance between the vertical surface and the center line of the control rod is 4 in.

11. Prepare sketches for a mechanism to be attached to a two-wheel hand truck to make it easy to move the truck up and down stairs with a heavy load.

12. Prepare sketches for a quick-acting clamp that can be used to hold steel plates in position for making a lap weld.

13. Prepare a pictorial sketch of a bracket that will support an instrument panel at an angle of 45° with a vertical bulkhead to which the bracket will be attached. The bracket should be designed to permit the panel to be raised or lowered a height distance of 4 in. as desired.

14. Prepare sketches for an adjustable pipe support for a $1\frac{1}{2}$-in. pipe that is to carry a chemical mixture in a factory manufacturing paint. The pipe is overhead and is to be supported at 10-ft intervals where the adjustable supports can be attached to the lower chords of the roof trusses. The lower chord of a roof truss is formed by two angles $2\frac{1}{2} \times 2\frac{1}{2} \times \frac{5}{16}$ that are separated by $\frac{3}{8}$-in.-thick washers.

15. Prepare sketches and working drawings for an easy-to-operate fast-release glider hitch. It is suggested that the student talk with several members of a local glider club to determine the requirements for the hitch and what improvements can be made for the hitch that is being used. Follow the stages of design listed in Sec. 13.14.

16. Prepare design sketches for a camera mounting that may be quickly attached and removed from any selected surface on an automobile, boat, or other type of moving vehicle. The device is to sell for not more than $9.95. Standard parts are to be used if possible. Follow through the several stages of design listed in Sec. 13.14 as required by the instructor. Make either a complete set of working drawings or drawings of selected parts.

17. *Class Projects.* Each student in the class is to prepare a description (on a single sheet of paper) of an innovational idea of a needed design that he deems to be suitable for a group project. From among the ideas collected several of the most worthy will be assigned to the class for development, one idea to each group. Each group of students is to be considered as a project group and shall be headed by one student member who may be thought of as being the project engineer. The instructor will assume the role of coach for all of the groups. About midway in the total time period assigned for the development of the design, each group is to submit a written preliminary design report that shall be accompanied by sketches. A final design report (read Sec. 13.14) will be due when the project has been completed. Each report will be judged on the following: (1) evidence of good group organization, (2) quality of technical work, (3) function and appearance, (4) economic analysis, (5) manufacturing methods and requirements, and (6) over-all effectiveness of communication (written and/or oral). NOTE: The instructor will decide whether or not finished shop drawings are to be made for all of the parts. Information needed for the preparation of finished drawings may be found in Part III of this text.

18. Make a freehand exploded pictorial representation of the ladder shoe shown in Fig. 13.28. Show the parts as if all intersecting surfaces were sharp, thus eliminating any consideration of representing fillets and rounds.

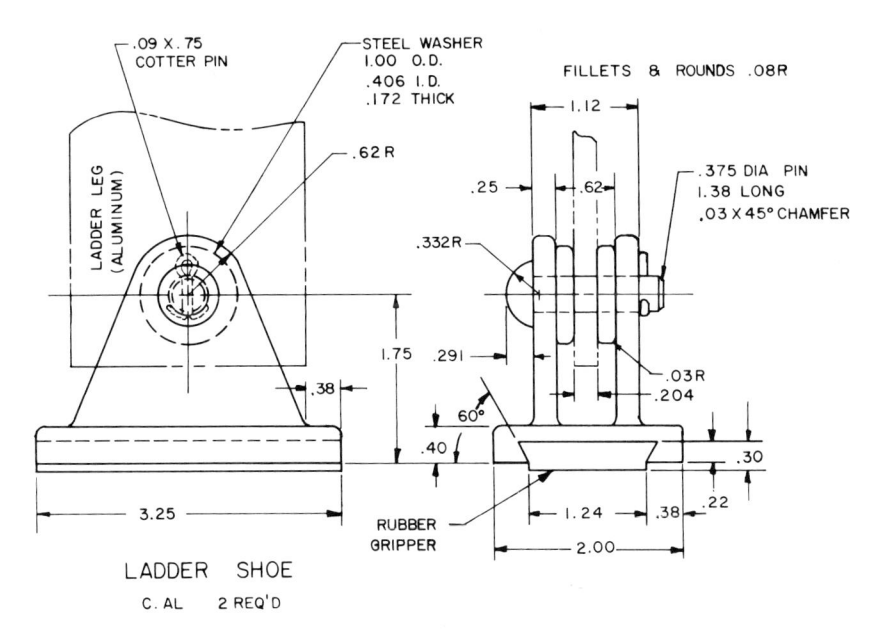

FIG. 13.28. Ladder shoe.

Detail (working) drawings, as discussed in Chapter 17, provide the complete instructions needed for the production of the parts of an assembled unit, such as the jet engine shown above. Since every part, no matter how small, must be produced in the shops of some company; it is necessary for a detailer who is responsible for the drawing to have a general knowledge of the production methods. This means that he must be familiar with the capabilities as well as the limitations of the general purpose machine tools. Even a limited knowledge of the machine tools presented in this chapter will be found to be helpful in understanding automatic mass-production machines and our so-called numerically controlled machine tools since these operate on the same principles as the general purpose machines. Numerically controlled machine tools, their programming and operation, have been discussed in Chapter 19.
(*Courtesy of Pratt & Whitney Aircraft-Division of United Aircraft Corp.*)

Shop Processes and Shop Terms

14.1
Shop Processes. An engineering draftsman must be thoroughly familiar with the fundamental shop processes before he is qualified to prepare drawings that will fulfill the requirements of the production shops. In preparing working drawings, he must consider each and every individual process involved in the production of a piece and then specify the processes in terms that the shopman will understand. See Figs. 14.22 and 14.23. All too frequently, drawings that specify impractical methods and impossible operations are sent to the shops. Most of these impractical specifications are the result of a lack of knowledge, on the draftsman's part, of what can or cannot be done by skilled craftsmen using modern machines and tools.

Although an accurate knowledge of the shop processes can be acquired only through actual experience in the various shops, it is possible for an apprentice draftsman to obtain a working knowledge of the fundamental operations through study and observation. This chapter presents and explains the principal operations in the pattern shop, foundry, forge shop, and machine shop.

14.2
Castings. Castings are formed by pouring molten metal into a mold or cavity. In sand molding, the molten metal assumes the shape of the cavity that has been formed in a sand mold by ramming a prepared moist sand around a pattern and then removing the pattern. Although a casting shrinks somewhat in cooling, the metal hardens in the exact shape of the pattern used (Fig. 14.1).

A sand mold consists of at least two sections. The upper section, called the *cope*, and the lower section, called the *drag*, together form a box-shaped structure called a *flask*.

When large holes ($\frac{3}{4}$ in. and over) or interior passageways and openings are needed in a casting, dry sand cores are placed in the cavity. Cores exclude the metal from the space they occupy and thus form desired openings. Large holes are cored in order to avoid an unnecessary boring operation. A dry sand core is formed by ramming a mixture of sand and a binding material into a core box that has been made in the pattern shop. To make a finished core rigid, the coremaker places it in a core oven, where it is baked until it is hard.

The molder when making a mold inserts in the sand a sprue stick that he removes after the cope has been rammed. This resulting hole, known as the *sprue*, conducts the molten metal to the *gate,* which is a passageway cut to the cavity. The

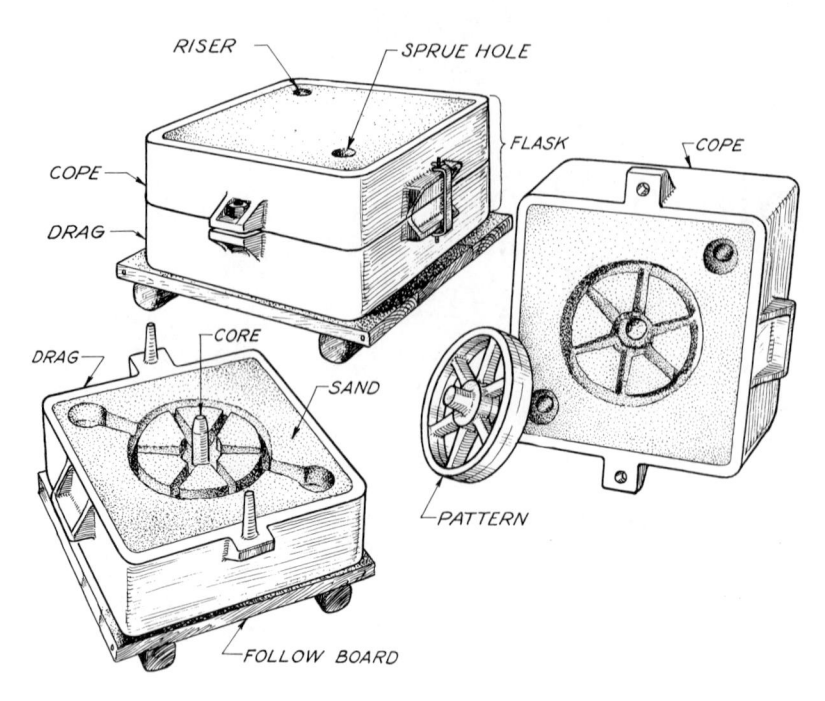

FIG. 14.1. Sand mold.

adjacent hole, called the *riser*, provides an outlet for excess metal.

14.3
The Pattern Shop. The pattern shop prepares patterns of all pieces that the foundry is to cast. Although special pattern drawings are frequently submitted, the patternmaker ordinarily uses a drawing of the finished piece that the draftsman has prepared for both the pattern shop and the machine shop (Fig. 14.22). The finish marks on such a drawing are just as important to him as to the machinist, for he must allow, on each surface to be finished, extra metal, the amount of which depends on the method of machining and the size of the casting. In general, this amount varies from $\frac{1}{16}$ in., on very small castings, to as much as $\frac{3}{4}$ in., on large castings.

It is not necessary for the draftsman to specify on his drawing the amount to be allowed for shrinkage, for the patternmaker has available a "shrink rule," which is sufficiently oversize (approximately $\frac{1}{8}$ in. per ft) to take care of the shrinkage.

A pattern usually is first constructed of light, strong wood, such as white pine or mahogany, which, if only a few castings are required, may be used in making sand molds. In quantity production, however, where a pattern must be used repeatedly, the wooden one will not hold up, so a metal pattern (aluminum, brass, and so on) is made from it and is used in its place.

Every pattern must be constructed in such a way that it can be withdrawn from each section of the sand mold. If the pattern consists of two halves (split), the plane of separation should be so located that it will coincide with the plane of separation of the cope and the drag (Fig. 14.1). Each portion of the pattern must be slightly tapered, so that it can be withdrawn without leaving a damaged cavity. The line of intersection, where the dividing plane cuts the pattern, is called the *parting line*. Although this line is rarely shown on a drawing, the draftsman should make certain that his design will allow the patternmaker to establish it. Ordinarily, it is not necessary to specify the slight taper, known as *draft*, on each side of the parting line, for the patternmaker assumes such responsibility when constructing the pattern.

A "filled-in" interior angle on a casting is called a *fillet*, to distinguish it from a rounded exterior angle, which is known as a *round* (Fig. 6.50). Sharp interior angles are avoided for two reasons: They are difficult to cast; and they are likely to be potential points of failure because the crystals of the cooling metal arrange themselves at a sharp corner in a weak pattern. Fillets are formed by nailing quarter rounds of wood or strips of leather into the sharp angles or by filling the angles with wax.

14.4

The Foundry. Although a draftsman is not directly concerned with the foundry, since the patternmaker takes his drawing and prepares the pattern and core boxes for the molder, it is most important that he be familiar with the operations in making a sand mold and a casting. Otherwise, he will find it difficult to prepare an economical design, the cost of which depends on how simple it is to mold and cast.

14.5

Die Casting. Die casting is an inexpensive method for producing certain types of machine parts, particularly those needing no great strength, in mass production. The castings are made by forcing molten metal or molten alloy into a cavity between metal dies in a die-casting machine. Parts thus produced usually require little or no finishing.

14.6

The Forge Shop. Many machine parts, especially those that must have strength and yet be light, are forged into shape, the heated metal being forced into dies with a drop hammer. Drop forging, since heated metal is made to conform to the shape of a cavity, might be considered a form of casting. However, because dies are difficult to make and are expensive, this method of production is used principally to make parts having an irregular shape that would be costly to machine and could not be made from casting material. Forgings are made of a high-grade steel. Dies are made by expert craftsmen who are known simply as diemakers.

Generally, special drawings, giving only the dimensions needed, are made for the forge shop (Fig. 14.2).

14.7

Standard Stock Forms. Many types of metal shapes, along with other materials

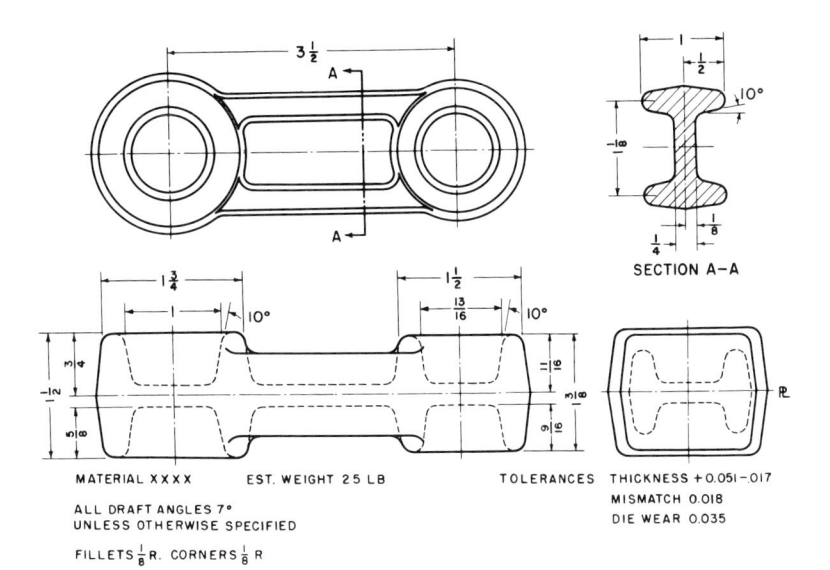

FIG. 14.2. A forging drawing.*

that are used in the shops for making parts for structures, are purchased from manufacturers in stock sizes. They are made available from the stock department, where rough stock, such as rods, bars, plates, sheet metal, and so on, is cut into sizes desired by the machine shop.

14.8

The Machine Shop. In general, the draftsman is more concerned with machine-shop processes than with the processes in other shops, for all castings and forgings that have been prepared in accordance with his drawings must receive their final machining in the machine shop (Fig. 14.22). Since all machining operations must be considered in the design and then properly specified, a draftsman must be thoroughly familiar with the limitations as well as the possibilities of such common machines as the lathe, drill press, boring machine, shaper, planer, milling machine, and grinder. An explanation of the operation and capabilities of each machine will be given in the following sections.

---

*ANS Y14.9–1958.

FIG. 14.3. Lathe operation—turning.

FIG. 14.4. Boring on a lathe.

14.9
The Lathe. Many common operations, such as turning, facing, boring, reaming, knurling, threading, and so on, may be performed with this widely used machine. In general, however, it is used principally for machining (roughing-out) cylindrical surfaces to be finished on a grinding machine. Removing metal from the exterior surfaces of cylindrical objects is known as *turning* and is accomplished by a sharp cutting tool that removes a thin layer of metal each time it travels the length of a cylindrical surface on the revolving work (Fig. 14.3). The piece, which is supported in the machine between two aligned centers, known as the *dead center* and the *live center,* is caused to rotate about an axis by power transmitted through a lathe dog, chuck, or faceplate. The work revolves against the cutting tool, held in a tool post, as the tool moves parallel to the longitudinal axis of the piece being turned. Cutting an interior surface is known as *boring* (Fig. 14.4). A note is not necessary on a drawing to indicate that a surface is to be turned on a lathe.

When a hole is reamed, it is finished very accurately with a fluted reamer of the exact required diameter. If the operation is performed on a lathe, the work revolves as the nonrotating reamer is fed into the hole by turning the handwheel on the tail stock (see Fig. 14.5).

Screw threads may be cut on a lathe by a cutting tool that has been ground to the shape required for the desired thread. The thread is cut as the tool travels parallel to the axis of the revolving work at a fixed speed (Fig. 14.6).

Knurling is the process of roughening or embossing a cylindrical surface. This

FIG. 14.5. Reaming on a lathe.

CHAP. 14 / SHOP PROCESSES AND SHOP TERMS   **315**

FIG. 14.6. Cutting on a lathe.

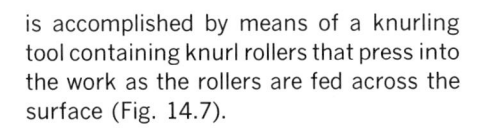

FIG. 14.7. Knurling.

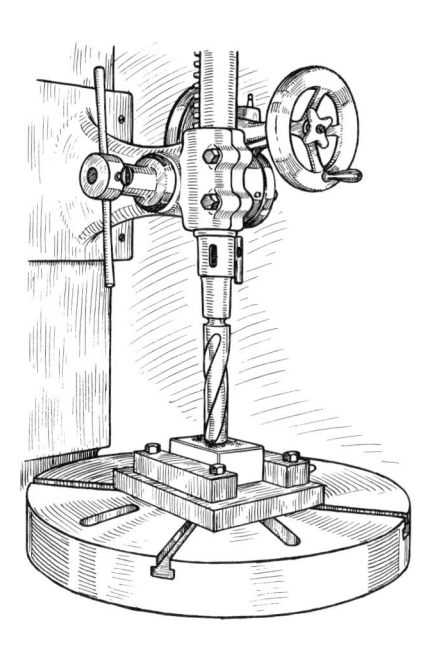

FIG. 14.8. A drill press.

is accomplished by means of a knurling tool containing knurl rollers that press into the work as the rollers are fed across the surface (Fig. 14.7).

14.10
The Drill Press. A drill press is a necessary piece of equipment in any shop because, although it is used principally for drilling, as the name implies (Fig. 14.8), other operations, such as reaming, counterboring, countersinking, and so on, may be performed on it by merely using the proper type of cutting tool. The cutting tool is held in position in a chuck at the end of a vertical spindle that is made to revolve, through power from a motor, at a particular speed suitable for the type of metal being drilled. The most flexible drill press, especially for large work, is the radial type, which is so designed that the spindle is mounted on a movable arm that can be revolved into any desired position for drilling. With this machine, holes may be drilled at various angles and locations without shifting the work, which may be either clamped to the horizontal table or held in a drill vise or drill jig. The ordinary type of drill press without a movable arm is usually found in most shops along with the radial type. A multispindle drill is used for drilling a number of holes at the same time.

Figure 14.9 shows a setup on a drill press for performing the operation of counterboring. A counterbore is used to enlarge a hole to a depth that will allow the head of a fastener, such as a fillister-head cap screw, to be brought to the level of the surface of the piece through which it passes. A counterbore has a piloted end having approximately the same diameter as the drilled hole.

Figure 14.10 shows a setup for the operation of countersinking. A countersink is used to form a tapering depression that will fit the head of a flathead machine screw or cap screw and allow it to be brought to the level of the surface of the piece through which it passes.

A plug tap is used to cut threads in a drilled hole (Fig. 14.11).

A spotfacer is used to finish a round spot that will provide a good seat for the head of a screw or bolt on the unfinished surface of a casting. Figure 14.12 shows

FIG. 14.9. Counterboring on a drill press.

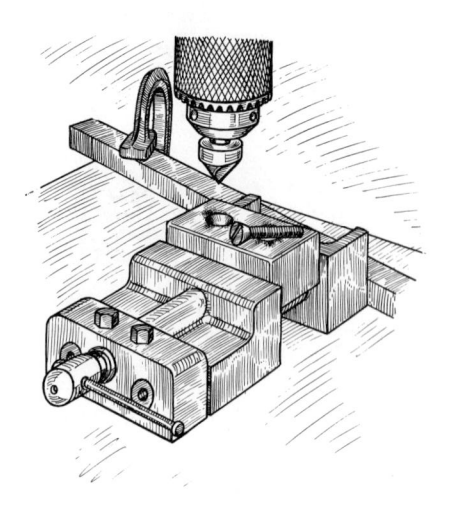

FIG. 14.10. Countersinking on a drill press.

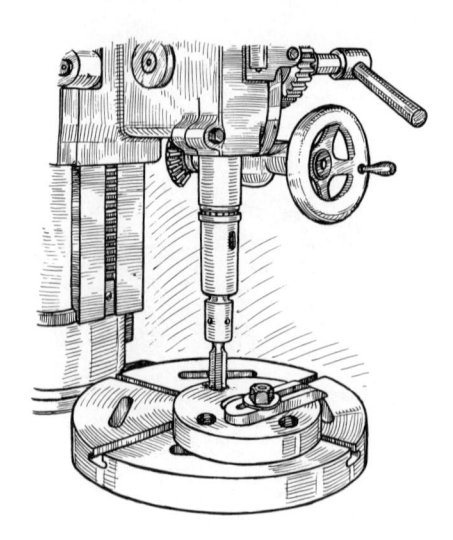

FIG. 14.11. Tapping on a drill press.

PLUG TAP

BOTTOMING TAP

STRAIGHT REAMER

TAPER REAMER

COUNTERSINK   COUNTERSINK

COUNTERBORE

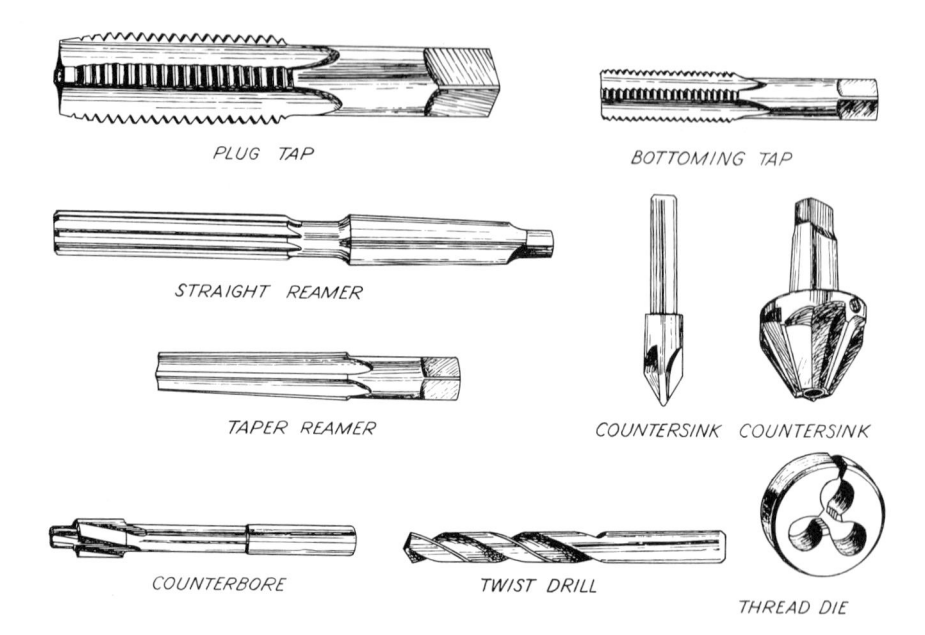

TWIST DRILL

THREAD DIE

FIG. 14.12. Various cutting tools.

various cutting tools commonly used for forming holes and cutting threads.

14.11
Hand Reaming. A hole may be finished to an accurate size by hand reaming, as shown in Fig. 14.13. The reamer in this illustration is of a special type known as a *line reamer*.

14.12
Boring (Fig. 14.14). Boring is the operation of enlarging a circular hole for accuracy in roundness or straightness and may be accomplished on a lathe, drill press, milling machine, or boring mill. When the hole is small and of considerable length, the operation may be performed on a lathe. If the hole is large, the work is usually done on a boring mill, of which there are two types—the vertical and the horizontal. On a vertical boring machine, the work is fastened on a horizontal revolving table, and the cutting tool or tools, which are stationary, advance vertically into it as the table revolves. On a horizontal boring machine, the tool revolves and the work is stationary.

14.13
The Milling Machine. A milling machine is used for finishing plane surfaces and for milling gear teeth, slots, keyways, and so on. In finishing a plane surface, a rotating circular cutter removes the metal for a desired cut as the work, fastened to a moving horizontal bed, is automatically fed against it. Several types of milling cutters are shown in Fig. 14.16.

Figure 14.15 shows a setup for milling gear teeth in a gear blank. Note the form of this particular type of cutter.

CHAP. 14 / SHOP PROCESSES AND SHOP TERMS **317**

FIG. 14.13. Hand reaming.

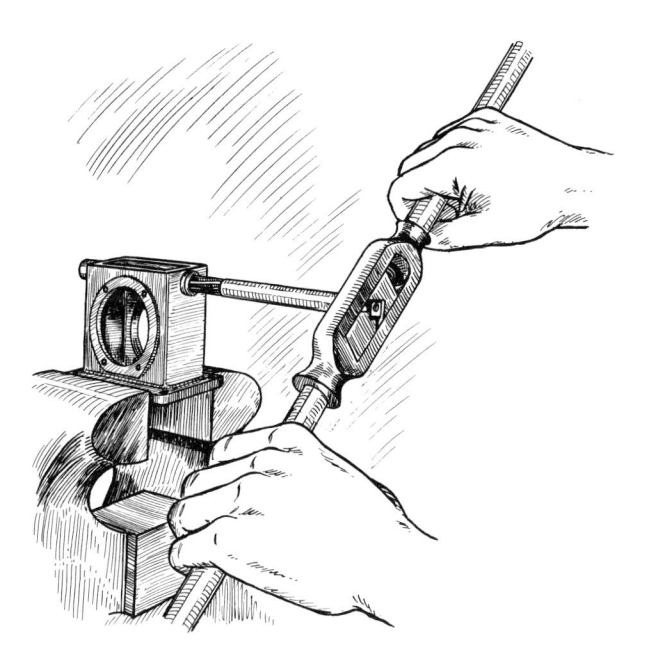

FIG. 14.15. Cutting gear teeth on a milling machine.

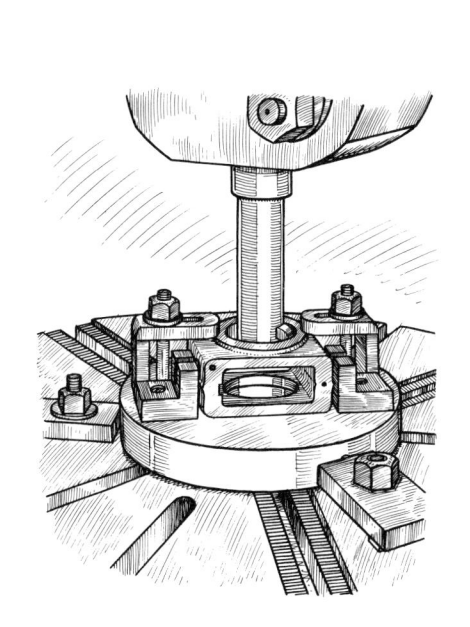

FIG. 14.14. Boring on a boring mill.

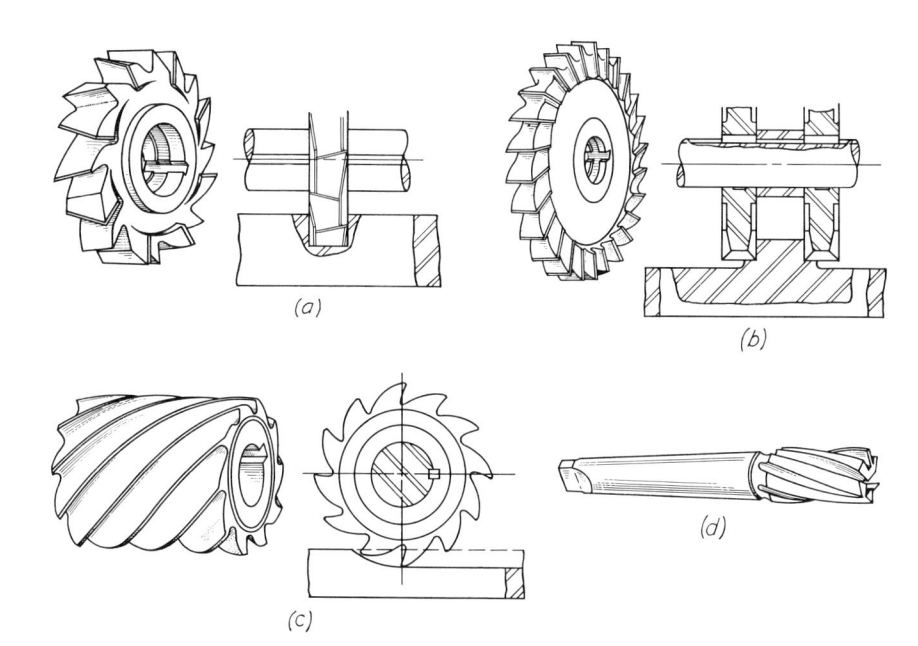

FIG. 14.16. Milling cutters and operations.

14.14
The Shaper (Fig. 14.17). A shaper is used for finishing small plane surfaces and for cutting slots and grooves. In action, a fast-moving reciprocating ram carries a tool across the surface of the work, which is fastened to an adjustable horizontal table. The tool cuts only on the forward stroke.

14.15
The Planer. The planer is a machine particularly designed for cutting down and finishing large flat surfaces. The work is fastened to a long horizontal table that moves back and forth under the cutting tool. In action, the tool cuts as the table moves the surface against it. Unlike the cutter on the shaper, it is stationary except for a slight movement laterally for successive cuts.

14.16
The Grinding Machine. A grinding machine has a rotating grinding wheel that, ordinarily, is either an emery wheel (fine or coarse) or some type of high-speed wheel made of carborundum (Fig. 14.18). Grinding consists of bringing the surface

FIG. 14.17. Shaper.

Grinding a Flat Surface
(a)

Internal Grinding
(b)

Grinding a Curved Outline
(c)

Principle of Cylindrical Grinding
(d)

Principle of Centerless Grinding
(e)

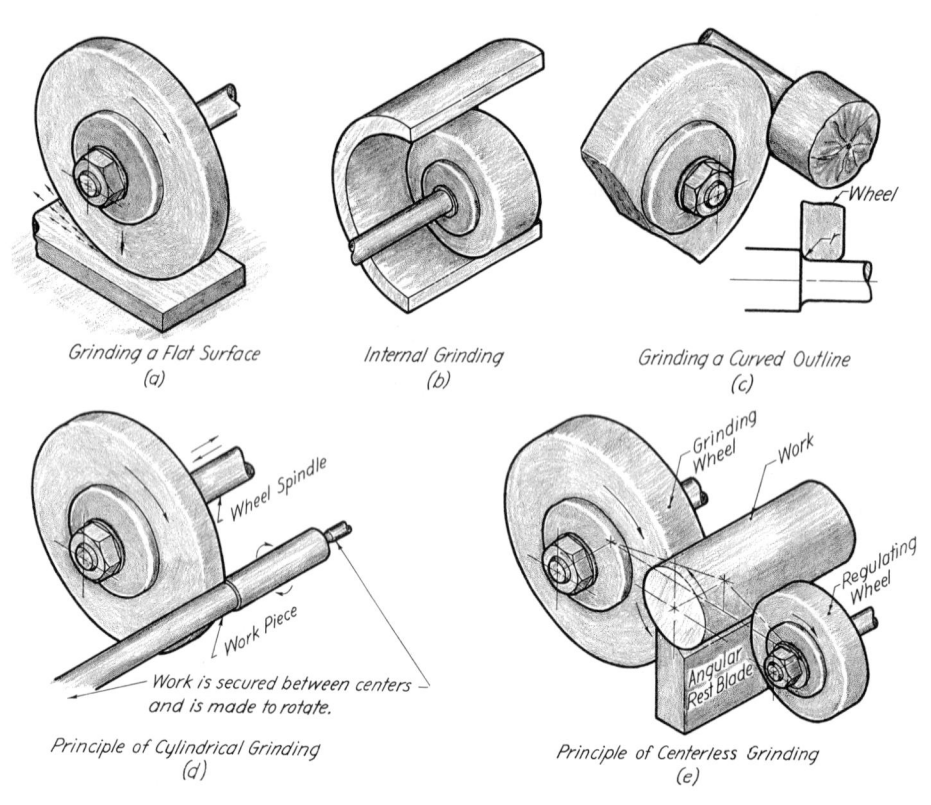

FIG. 14.18. Grinding surfaces.

to be ground into contact with the wheel. Although grinding machines are often used for "roughing" and for grinding down projections and surfaces on castings, their principal use, as far as a draftsman is concerned, is for the final finishing operation that will bring the cylindrical surface of a piece of work down to accurate dimensions. Very fine surface finishes with tolerances as close as 1 or 2 microinches may be obtained by grinding. Grinding wheels of special form are used for grinding threads when close fits are desired and for forming other shapes.

When a flat surface is to be brought to a super finish, a surface grinder is used. The work, clamped to either a reciprocating or rotating worktable, passes under a rapidly rotating abrasive wheel, as illustrated in Fig. 14.18(*a*).

In grinding the external surface of a shaft, as illustrated in (*d*), the work, mounted between centers, rotates slowly while in contact with the rapidly rotating grinding wheel moving along the work as indicated by the arrows. The grinding wheel is mounted so that it may be moved up to the work or away from it. Normally, the depth of cut is about 0.002 in. per pass. However, finishing cuts may be made as fine as 0.0001 in. per pass to bring the finished size within the dimensional limits given on a detail drawing.

As might be expected with centerless grinding the work is not held between centers, as in the case of cylindrical grinding. Rather, it may be said to be fed along against the grinding wheel by a regulating wheel while being supported on a rest blade. See Fig. 14.18(*e*). It should be noted that, with both the grinding wheel and regulating wheel rotating in a clockwise direction, the work is forced to rotate counterclockwise. Pressure from the grinding wheel forces the work against both the work rest and the regulating wheel. A centerless grinder produces work that is round and of constant diameter.

Internal grinding for fine finish and close tolerances is illustrated in (*b*). Form grinding is shown in (*c*).

14.17
Broaching. A broach is a tool used to cut keyways and to form square, rectangular, hexagonal, or irregular-shaped holes. It is a hard, tempered cutting tool with serrated cutting edges that enlarge a drilled, punched, or cored hole to a required shape. In operation, each tooth removes a chip of material from the surface except the last few teeth, which are to size (Fig. 14.19). A broach produces a fine finish with the work accurately sized. This is accomplished with a single pass. Broaches, whether used to finish an internal (hole) or an external surface, are either pushed or pulled. A special broaching machine is used for pulling broaches. Some form of press, hydraulic or otherwise, is required for push broaches.

The cutting of a keyway using a slotter (broach) is illustrated in Fig. 14.20. A guide bushing has been inserted in the

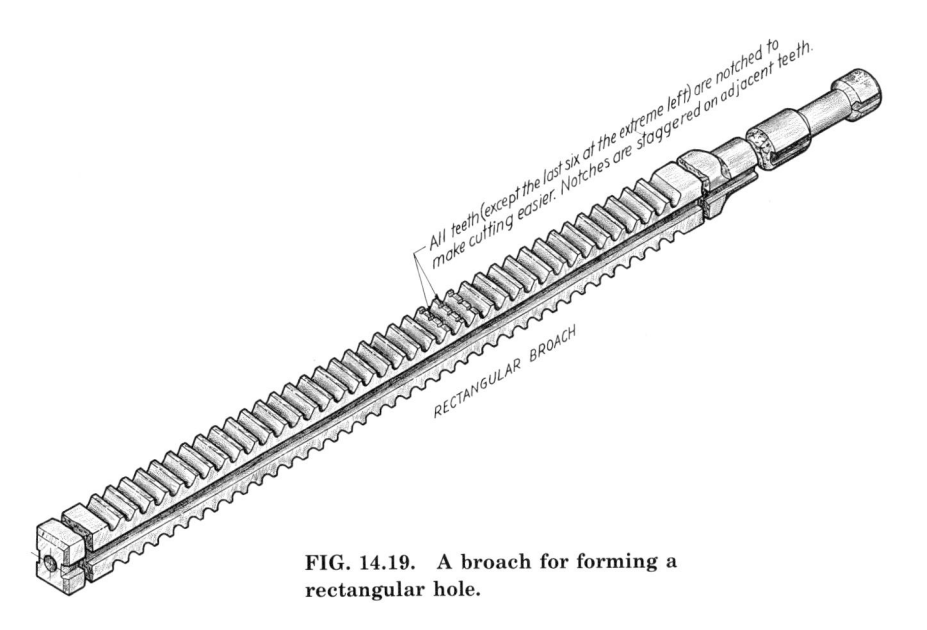

FIG. 14.19. A broach for forming a rectangular hole.

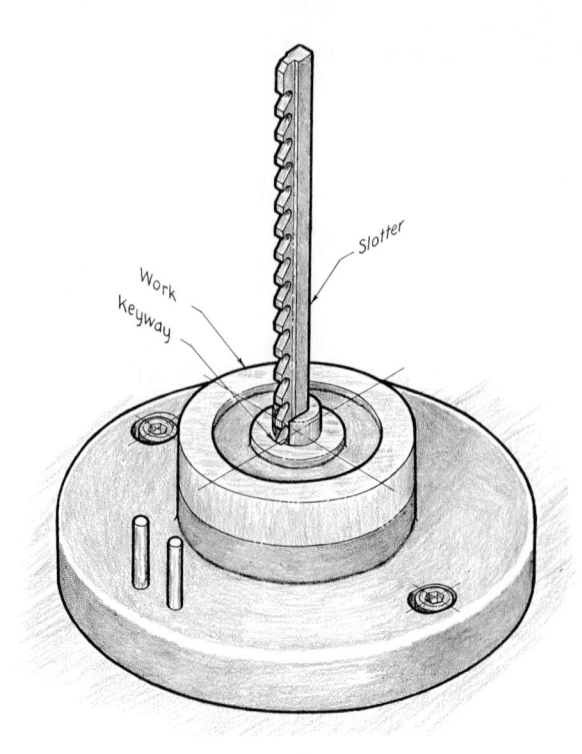

FIG. 14.20. Cutting a keyway.

Heavy lines indicate broached surfaces.

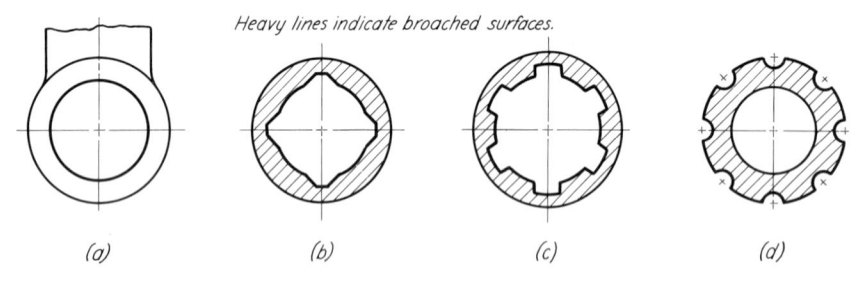

(a)   (b)   (c)   (d)

FIG. 14.21. Some typical broached contours.

hole in the piece to hold the tool in position.

Some typical broached contours are shown in Fig. 14.21.

14.18
Superfinishing: Polishing, Honing, and Lapping. Polishing consists of bringing a ground surface into contact with a revolving disc of leather or cloth, thus producing a lustrous smoothness that would be impossible to obtain by using even the finest grinding wheel. The operation is specified on a drawing by a note: "polish" or "grind and polish."

Honing and lapping are methods of producing superfinishes, after grinding, through the use of abrasives. For honing cylindrical bores, fine-grained abrasive sticks, which are available in many styles and grades, are used to minimize scratches and to finish the bore to precision limits.

Lapping is a final stock-removing operation that is performed by rubbing the surfaces of parts to be lapped over a lap of soft metal to which has been applied a powdered abrasive mixed with a lubricant.

14.19
Jigs and Fixtures. Often, when an operation must be performed many times in making a part in quantities on a general machine, one of two devices, a *jig* or a *fixture,* may be used to facilitate production and ensure accuracy without making repeated measurements. The design and construction of jigs and fixtures is discussed in Chapter 23.

14.20
Special Production Machines. In large industrial concerns, most mechanical parts are made on either semiautomatic or fully automatic machines by semiskilled operators. A discussion of even a few of these, however, is beyond the scope of a general drawing text in which each subject is limited to a few pages. Since most specialized mass-production machines, having mechanisms that control the movement of cutting tools, operate on the same general principles as the general-purpose machines, a young engineering draftsman should be able to determine

their limitations and capabilities through observation, if he has a general knowledge of such machines as the lathe, shaper, drill press, milling machine, and so on. No prospective designer or draftsman should ever forgo an opportunity to observe special production machines for he must have a thorough understanding of all shop machines and methods, if his drawings are to be satisfactory for the shops.

In use at the present time are production machines that follow directions given on punched tapes and gages that measure electrically to millionths of an inch. The use of tapes and computers by industry does not mean that the draftsmen and engineers will have less work to do and that there will be fewer of them. It does mean, however, that the men assigned to both areas must keep themselves informed and up-to-date on late developments. The draftsman should learn how to dimension the drawing of a part to meet the requirement for programming the machine or machines that will perform the shop operations. He must have a more thorough understanding of basic fundamentals than in the past and at the same time be willing to accept change. Numerically controlled machine tools are discussed in Chapter 19.

The fact must be recognized that automation is here and the only question the technically trained man of today can ask himself is whether or not he, as an individual, can adjust to new knowledge and different requirements.

14.21
Manufacturing Processes and the Detail Drawing. In preparing the detail drawing that is needed for the production of a part, the draftsman must give considerable thought to the manufacturing processes that will be required to make the conception a reality. Machined surfaces must be indicated and the dimensions selected and placed with the manufacturing methods in mind. Shop notes, as they may be needed, must be prepared in accordance with the recommendations given in the appropriate ANSI standards.

The detail working drawing of the inlet cover shown in Fig. 14.22 has been prepared for use by both the pattern shop and the machine shop since these two shops will be involved in the production of the part. It should and does contain all of the dimensions and notes needed, first, to make the pattern for the casting and,

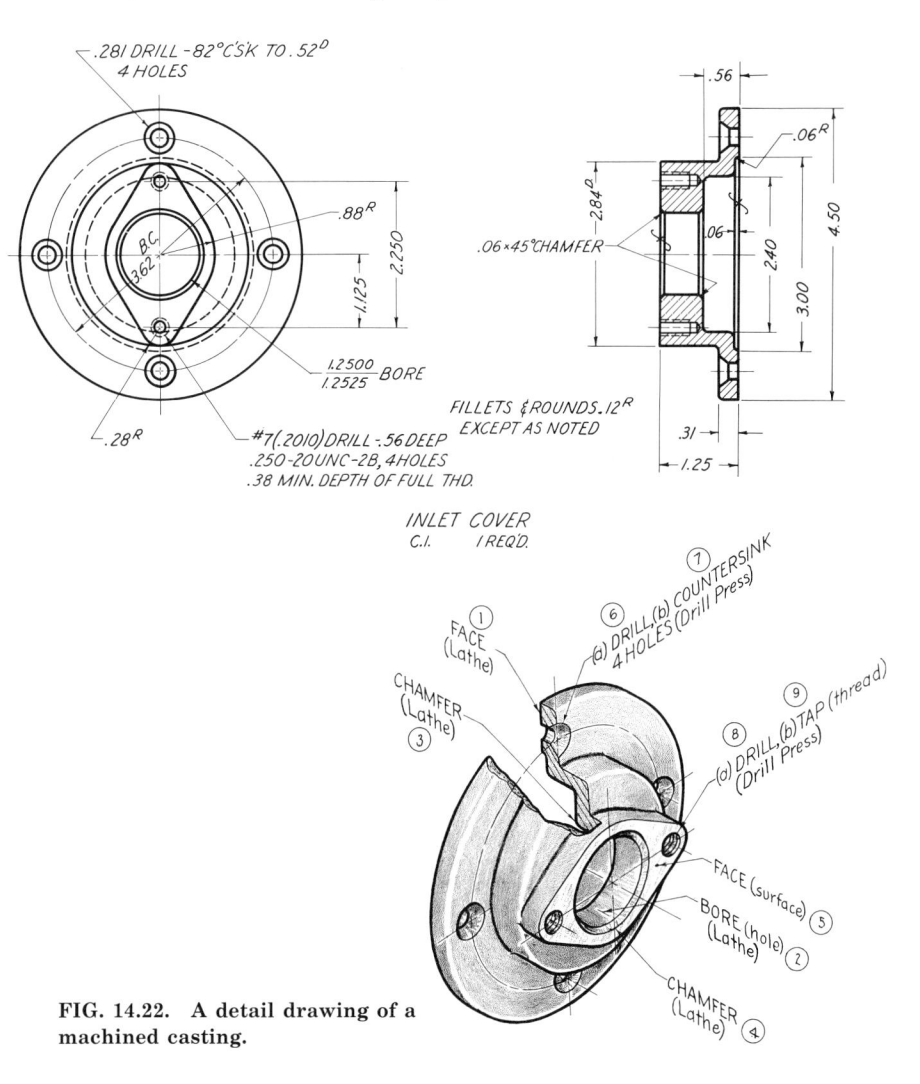

FIG. 14.22. A detail drawing of a machined casting.

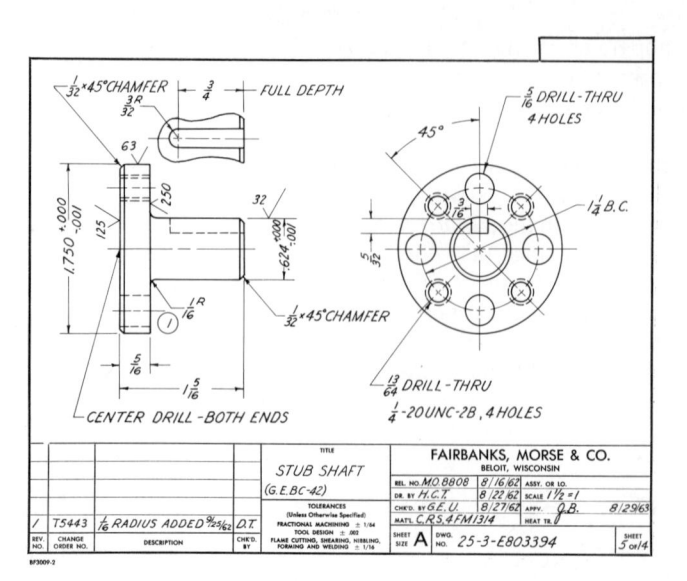

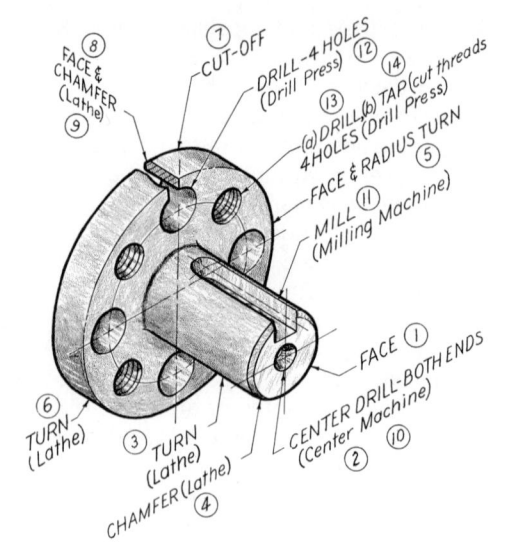

FIG. 14.23. A detail drawing of a part to be machined from cold rolled stock. (*Courtesy Fairbanks, Morse & Co.*)

second, to machine the cast part to obtain the finished inlet cover ready for use.

The pictorial drawing gives an interpretation, in shop terms, of the machining operations required by the detail drawing. The sequence of these operations is indicated by the numbers enclosed within circles.

By looking in the record strip of the drawing shown in Fig. 14.23, one finds that the material specified for the stub shaft is cold-rolled steel. As in the case of all such parts that are machined from standard stock most of the surfaces must be machined. Where an existing surface on the raw stock is accurate enough, it may be left untouched. Sharp corners are either chamfered, as indicated by the note, or are broken (see Fig. 16.55). Both external and internal corners may be rounded when necessary. For example, a $1/16R$ has been specified for the interior corner on the stub shaft.

The pictorial drawing gives an interpretation of the machining operations required to produce the shaft.

14.22

Measuring Tools. Figures 14.24, 14.25, and 14.26 show a few of the measuring tools commonly available in shops. When great accuracy is not required, calipers are used (Fig. 14.25). The outside calipers are suited for taking external measurements,

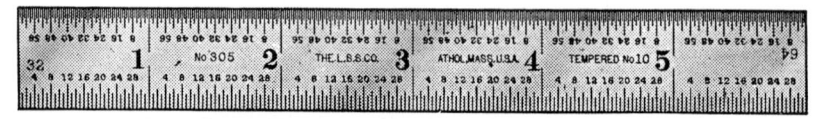

FIG. 14.24. The steel rule.

as, for example, from a shaft. They are adjusted to fit the piece, and then the setting is applied to a rule to make a reading. The inside calipers have out-turned toes, which fit them for taking internal measurements, as, for example, in measuring either a cylindrical or a rectangular hole. When extreme accuracy is required, some form of micrometer calipers may be used (Fig. 14.26).

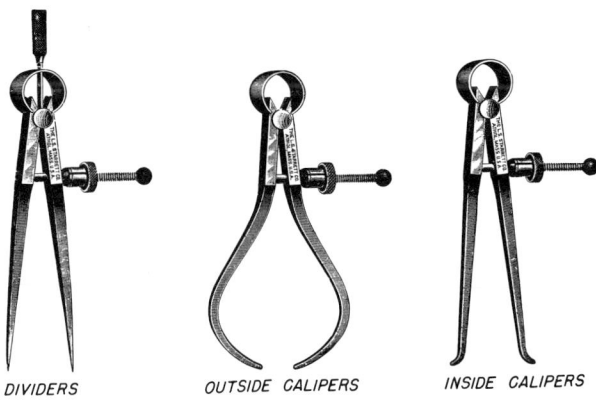

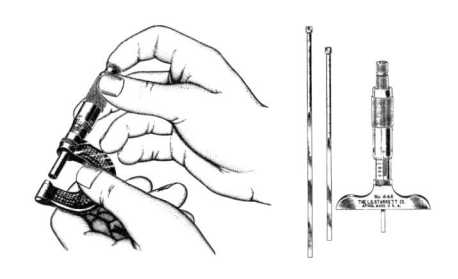

FIG. 14.25. Calipers.

FIG. 14.26. Micrometers.

GLOSSARY OF COMMON SHOP TERMS

Anneal (*v*). To heat a piece of metal to a particular temperature and then allow it to cool slowly for the purpose of removing internal stresses.

Bore (*v*). To enlarge a hole using a boring bar in order to make it smooth, round, and coaxial. Boring is usually done on a lathe or boring mill.

Boss (*n*). A circular projection, which is raised above a principal surface of a casting or forging.

Braze (*v*). To join two pieces of metal by the use of hard solder. The solder is usually a copper-zinc alloy.

Broach (*v*). To machine a hole to a desired shape, usually other than round. The cutting tool, known as a broach, is pushed or pulled through the rough-finished hole. It has transverse cutting edges.

Burnish (*v*). To smooth or apply a brilliant finish.

Bushing (*n*). A removable cylindrical sleeve, which is used to provide a bearing surface.

Carburize (*v*). To harden the surface of a piece of low-grade steel by heating in a carbonizing material to increase the carbon content and then quenching.

Case-harden (*v*). To harden a surface as described above or through the use of potassium cyanide.

Chamfer (*v*). To bevel an external edge or corner.

Chase (*v*). To cut screw threads on a lathe using a chaser, a tool shaped to the profile of a thread.

Chill (*v*). To cool the surface of a casting suddenly so that the surface will be white and hard.

Chip (*v*). To cut away or remove surface defects with a chisel.

Collar (*n*). A cylindrical part fitted on a shaft to prevent a sliding movement.

Color-harden (*v*). (See Case-harden.) A piece is color-hardened mainly for the sake of appearance.

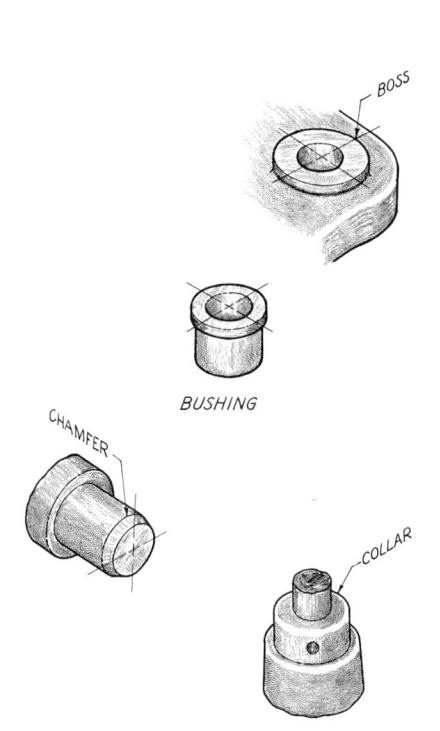

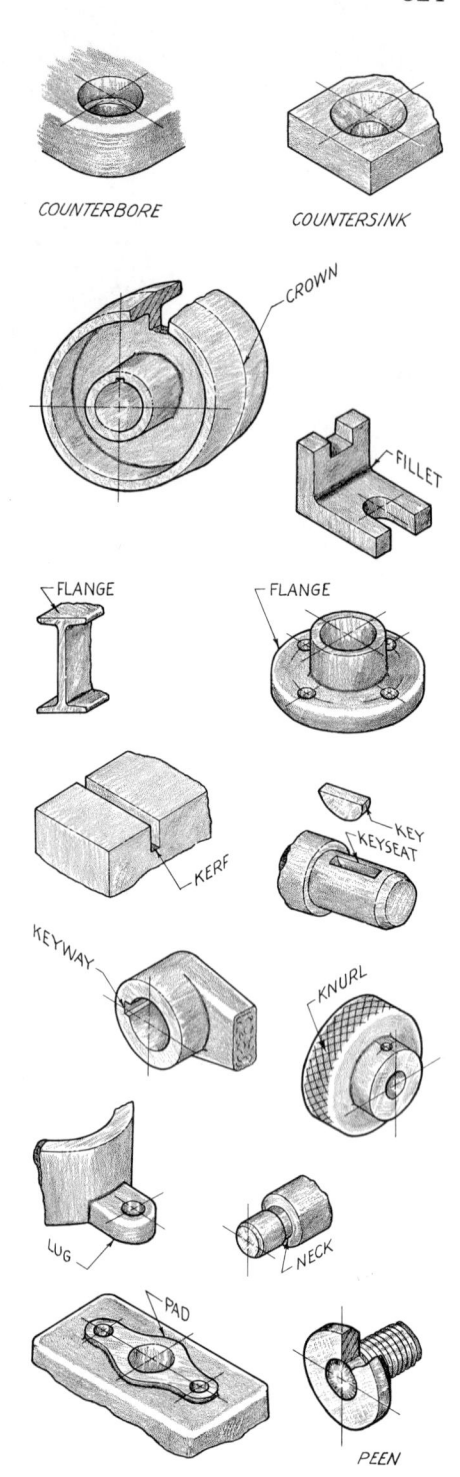

Core (v). To form a hole or hollow cavity in a casting through the use of a core.

Counterbore (v). To enlarge the end of a cylindrical hole to a certain depth, as is often done to accommodate the head of a fillister-head screw. (n) The name of the tool used to produce the enlargement.

Countersink (v). To form a conical enlargement at the end of a cylindrical hole to accommodate the head of a screw or rivet. (n) The name of the tool used to form a conical-shaped enlargement.

Crown (n). The angular or curved contour of the outer surface of a part, such as on a pulley.

Die (n). A metal block used for forming or stamping operations. A thread-cutting tool for producing external threads.

Die Casting (n). A casting that has been produced by forcing a molten alloy having an aluminum, copper, zinc, tin, or lead base into a metal mold composed of two halves.

Die Stamping (n). A piece that has been cut or formed from sheet metal through the use of a die.

Draw (v). To form metal, which may be either cold or hot, by a distorting or stretching process. To temper steel by gradual or intermittent quenching.

Drill (v). To form a cylindrical hole in metal. (n) A revolving cutting tool designed for cutting at the point.

Drop Forging (n). A piece formed while hot between two dies under a drop hammer.

Face (v). To machine on a lathe a flat face, which is perpendicular to the axis of rotation of the piece.

Feather (n). A rectangular sliding key, which permits a pulley to move along the shaft parallel to its axis.

File (v). To shape, finish, or trim with a fine-toothed metal cutting tool, which is used with the hands.

Fillet (n). A rounded filling, which increases the strength at the junction of two surfaces that form an internal angle.

Fit (n). The tightness of adjustment between the contacting surfaces of mating parts.

Flange (n). The top and bottom member of a beam. A projecting rim added on the end of a pipe or fitting for making a connection.

Forge (v). To shape hot metals by hammering, using a hand-hammer or machine.

Galvanize (v). To coat steel or iron by immersion in a bath of zinc.

Graduate (v). To mark off or divide a scale into intervals.

Grind (v). To finish a surface through the action of a revolving abrasive wheel.

Kerf (n). A groove or channel cut by a saw or some other tool.

Key (n). A piece used between a shaft and a hub to prevent the movement of one relative to the other.

Keyway or Keyseat (n). A longitudinal groove cut in a shaft or a hub to receive a key. A key rests in a keyseat and slides in a keyway.

Knurl (v). To roughen a cylindrical surface to produce a better grip for the fingers.

Lap (v). To finish or polish with a piece of soft metal, wood, or leather impregnated with an abrasive.

Lug (n). A projection or ear, which has been cast or forged as a portion of a piece to provide a support or to allow the attachment of another part.

Malleable Casting (n). A casting that has been annealed to toughen it.

Mill (v). To machine a piece on a milling machine by means of a rotating toothed cutter.

Neck (v). To cut a circumferential groove around a shaft.

Pack-harden (v). To case-carburize and harden.

Pad (n). A low, projecting surface, usually rectangular.

Peen (v). To stretch or bend over metal using the peen end (ball end) of a hammer.

Pickle (v). To remove scale and rust from a casting or forging by immersing it in an acid bath.

Plane (v). To machine a flat surface on a planer, a machine having a fixed tool and a reciprocating bed.

Polish (v). To make a surface smooth and lustrous through the use of a fine abrasive.

Punch (v). To perforate a thin piece of metal by shearing out a circular wad with a non-rotating tool under pressure.

Ream (v). To finish a hole to an exact size using a rotating fluted cutting tool known as a reamer.

Rib (n). A thin component of a part that acts as a brace or support.

Rivet (n). A headed shank, which more or less permanently unites two pieces. (v) To fasten steel plates with rivets.

Round (n). A rounded external corner on a casting.

Sandblast (v). To clean the surface of castings or forgings by means of sand forced from a nozzle at a high velocity.

Shear (v). To cut off sheet or bar metal through the shearing action of two blades.

Shim (n). A thin metal plate, which is inserted between two surfaces for the purpose of adjustment.

Spline (n). A keyway, usually for a feather key. (See Feather.)

Spotface (v). To finish a round spot on the rough surface of a casting at a drilled hole for the purpose of providing a smooth seat for a bolt or screw head.

Spot Weld (v). To weld two overlapping metal sheets in spots by means of the heat of resistance to an electric current between a pair of electrodes.

Steel Casting (n). A casting made of cast iron to which scrap steel has been added.

Swage (v). To form metal with a "swage block," a tool so constructed that through hammering or pressure the work may be made to take a desired shape.

Sweat (v). To solder together by clamping the pieces in contact with soft solder between and then heating.

Tack Weld (n). A weld of short intermittent sections.

Tap (v). To cut an internal thread, by hand or with power, by screwing into the hole a fluted tapered tool having thread-cutting edges.

Taper (v). To make gradually smaller toward one end. (n) Gradual diminution of diameter or thickness of an elongated object.

Taper Pin (n). A tapered pin used for fastening hubs or collars to shafts.

Temper (v). To reduce the hardness of a piece of hardened steel through reheating and sudden quenching.

Template (n). A pattern cut to a desired shape, which is used in layout work to establish shearing lines, to locate holes, etc.

Tumble (v). To clean and smooth castings and forgings through contact in a revolving barrel. To further the results, small pieces of scrap are added.

Turn (v). To turn-down or machine a cylindrical surface on a lathe.

Undercut (n). A recessed cut.

Upset (v). To increase the diameter or form a shoulder on a piece during forging.

Weld (v). To join two pieces of metal by pressure or hammering after heating to the fusion point.

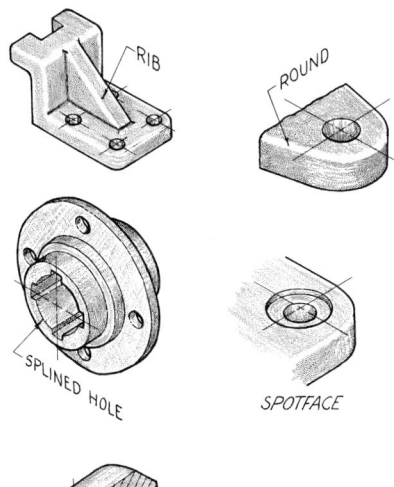

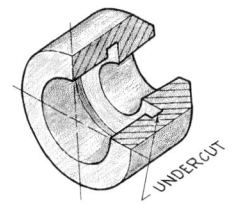

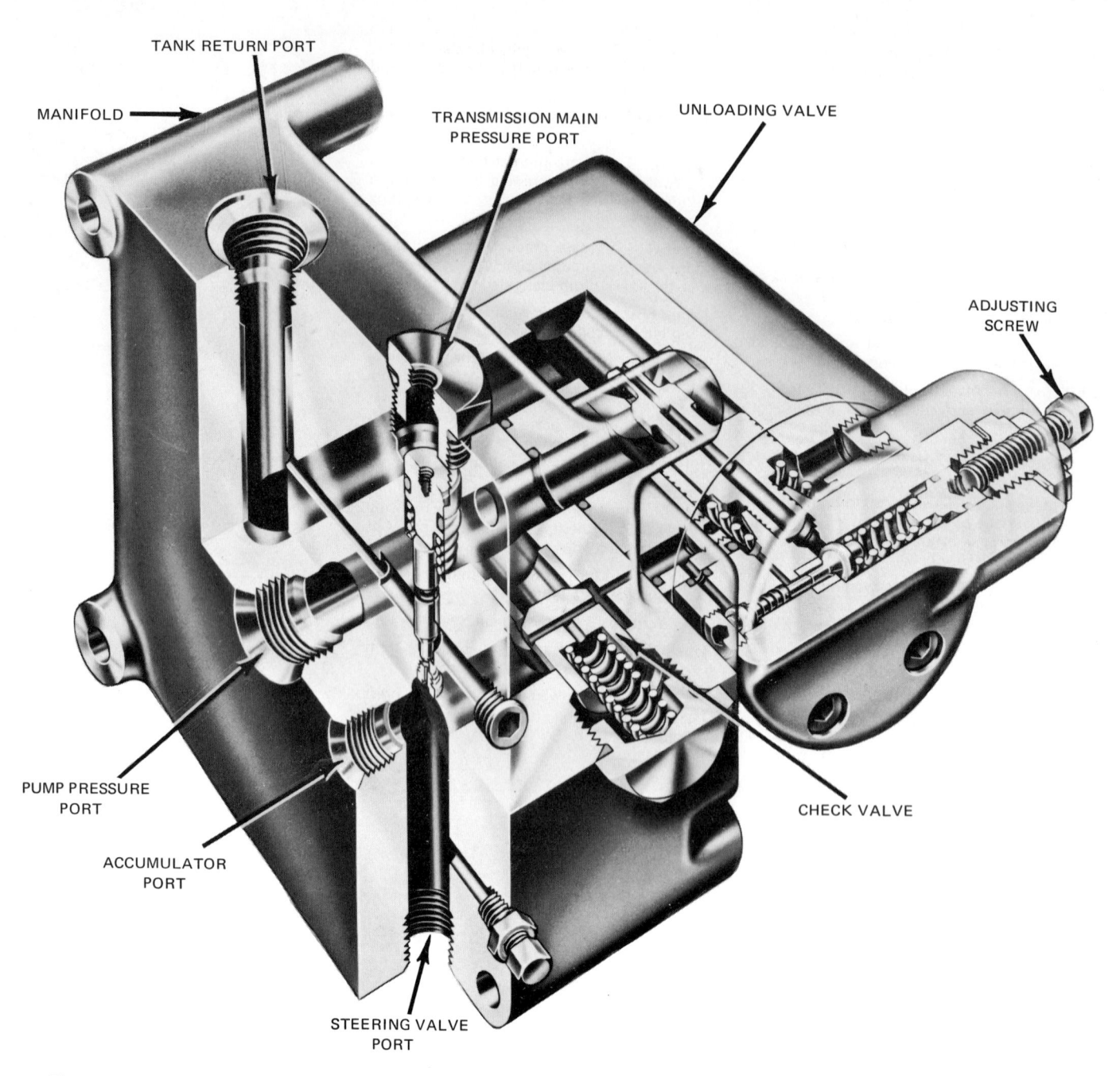

The manifold and unloading control valve shown is part of the hydraulic steering and braking circuits. It maintains the hydraulic system at a constant pressure. Units of this type require the use of springs and fasteners.
(*Courtesy General Motors Corporation*)

Representation and Specification of Threads, Fasteners, and Springs

15

A: SCREW THREADS

15.1
Introduction. In the commercial field, where the practical application of engineering drawing takes the form of working drawings, knowledge of screw threads and fasteners is important. There is always the necessity for assembling parts either with permanent fastenings such as rivets, or with bolts, screws, and so forth, which may be removed easily.

Engineers, detailers, and draftsmen must be completely familiar with the common types of threads and fastenings, as well as with their use and the correct methods of representation, because of the frequency of their occurrence in structures and machines. Information concerning special types of fasteners may be obtained from manufacturers' catalogues.

A young technologist in training should study Fig. 15.1 to acquaint himself with the terms commonly associated with screw threads.

15.2
Threads. The principal uses of threads are (1) for fastening, (2) for adjusting, and (3) for transmitting power. To satisfy most of the requirements of the engineering profession, the different forms of threads shown in Fig. 15.2 are used.

The (ANS) Unified thread form (Figs. 15.2 and 15.3), now recognized as the standard thread form in the United States, Great Britain and Canada, is a modification of the American National (N) thread form in use by American industry since 1935 (still in use to a limited extent). Since the thread forms are essentially the same, the new *Unified* thread form has found ready acceptance and it can be said to have superseded the old (N) form

The sharp V is used to some extent where adjustment and holding power are essential.

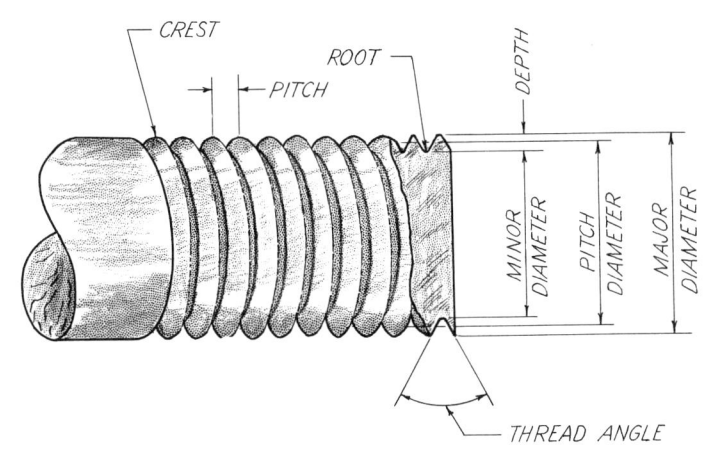

FIG. 15.1. Screw thread nomenclature.

327

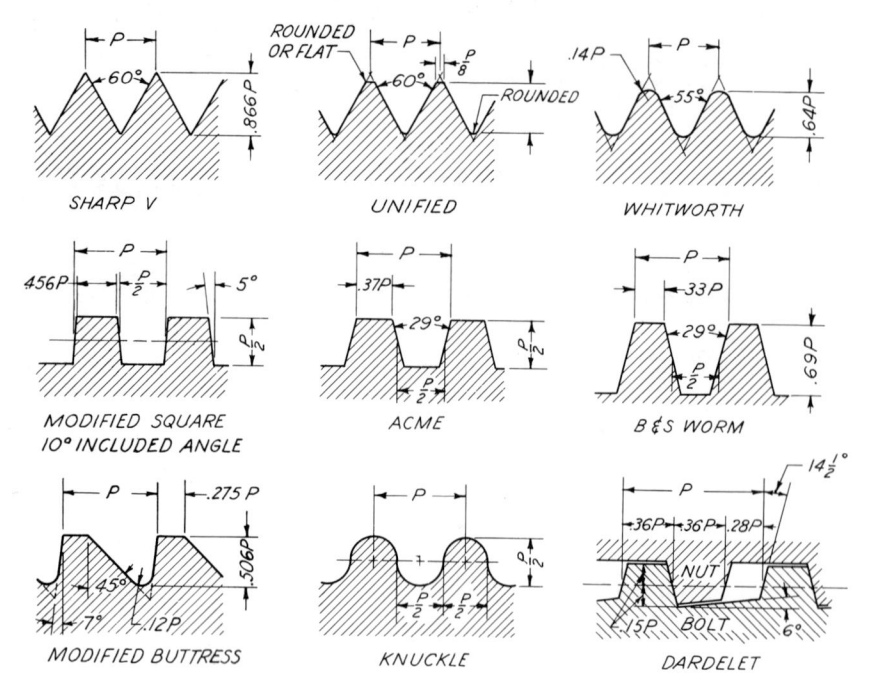

FIG. 15.2. Screw threads.

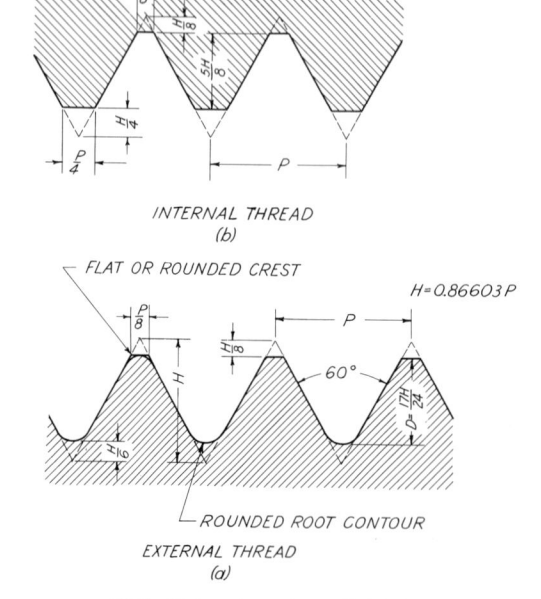

FIG. 15.3. American-British unified thread.

For the transmission of power and motion, the modified square, Acme, and Brown and Sharpe worm threads have been adopted. The modified square thread, which is now rarely used, transmits power parallel to its axis. A still further modification of the square thread is the stronger Acme, which is easier to cut and more readily disengages split nuts (as lead screws on lathes). The Brown and Sharpe worm thread, with similar proportions but with longer teeth, is used for transmitting power to a worm wheel.

The knuckle thread, commonly found on incandescent lamps, plugs, and so on, can be cast or rolled.

The Whitworth and buttress threads are not often encountered by the average engineer. The former, which fulfills the same purpose as the American Standard thread, is used in England but is also frequently found in this country. The buttress or breech-block thread, which is designed to take pressure in one direction, is used for breech mechanisms of large guns and for airplane propeller hubs. The thread form has not been standardized and appears in different modified forms.

The Dardelet thread is self-locking in assembly.

15.3

American–British Unified Thread. The Unified Thread Standard came into existence after the representatives of the United States, Great Britain, and Canada signed a unification agreement on Nov. 18, 1948 in Washington, D.C. This accord, which made possible the interchangeability of threads for these countries, created a new thread form (Fig. 15.3) that is a compromise between our own American National Standard design and the British Whitworth. The external thread of the new form has a rounded root and may have either a flat or rounded crest. The Unified thread is a general-purpose thread for screws, bolts, nuts, and other threaded parts (ANS B1.1–1960).

15.4
Multiple-start Threads. Whenever a quick advance is desired, as on fountain pens, valves, and so on, two or more threads are cut side by side. Two threads form a double (2-START) thread; three, a triple (3-START) thread; and so on. A thread that is not otherwise designated is understood to be a single-start thread. All threads included in ANS B1.1–1960 are single-start unless specifically identified as being multiple-start.

Fig. 15.4 shows heavy strings wound around a rod for the purpose of demonstrating single-start and double (2-START) threads. The center line of the single string, representing the single thread, assumes the form of a helix. In the case of the double (2-START) thread, it should be noted that there are two strings side by side that are shaded differently for clarity. On a double (2-START) thread, each thread starts diametrically opposite the other one.

In drawing a single or an odd-number multiple-start thread, a crest is always diametrically opposite a root; in a double or other even-number multiple-start thread, a crest is opposite a crest and a root opposite a root.

15.5
Right-hand and Left-hand Threads. A right-hand thread advances into a threaded hole when turned clockwise; a left-hand thread advances when turned counterclockwise. They can be easily distinguished by the thread slant. A right-hand thread on a horizontal shank always slants upward to the left (\) and a left-hand, upward to the right (/). A thread is always considered to be right-hand if it is not otherwise specified. A left-hand thread is always marked LH on a drawing.

15.6
Pitch. The pitch of a thread is the distance from any point on a thread to the corresponding point on the adjacent thread, measured parallel to the axis, as shown in Fig. 15.1

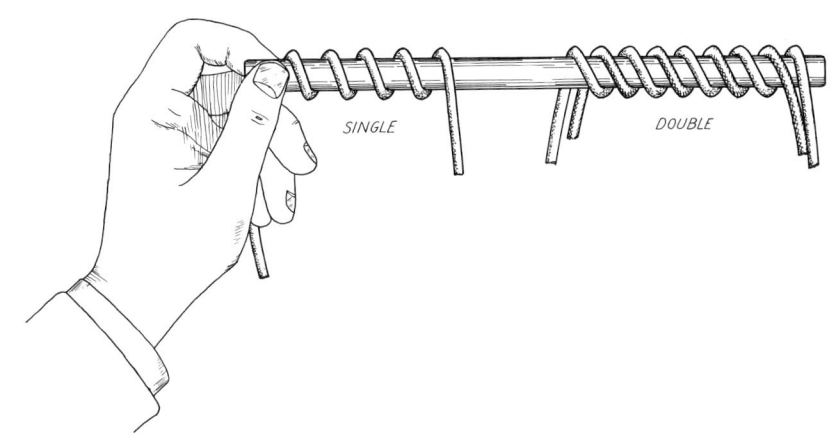

FIG. 15.4. Demonstration of a helix as related to a single-start and double (2-START) screw thread.

15.7
Lead. The lead of a screw may be defined as the distance advanced parallel to the axis when the screw is turned one revolution (Fig. 15.5). For a single thread, the lead is equal to the pitch; for a double (2-START) thread, the lead is twice the pitch; for a triple (3-START) thread, the lead is three times the pitch, and so on.

15.8
Detailed Screw-Thread Representation. The true representation of screw threads

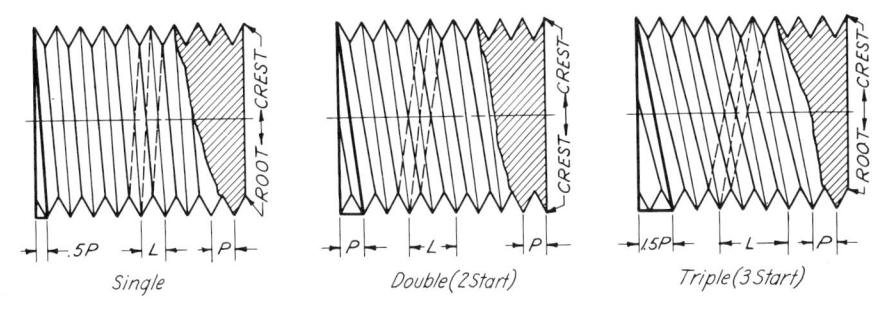

FIG. 15.5. Single-start and multiple-start threads.

330 PART III / GRAPHICS FOR DESIGN AND COMMUNICATION

(a)

(b)

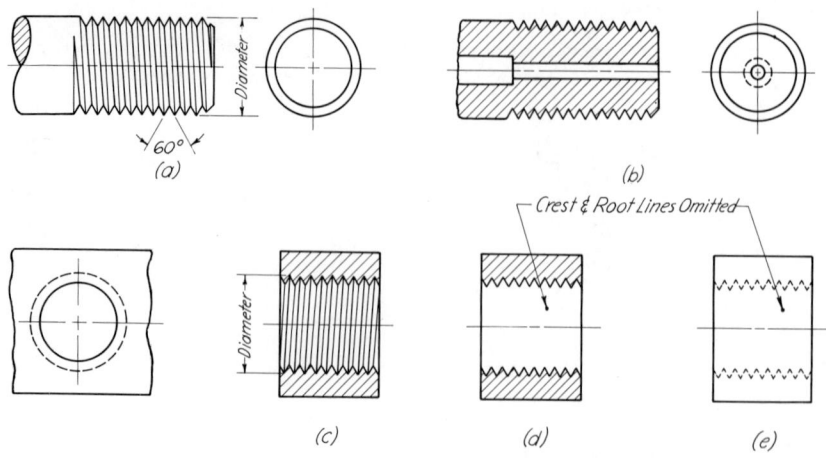

Crest & Root Lines Omitted

(c) (d) (e)

FIG. 15.6. Detailed representation.

by helical curves, requiring unnecessary time and laborious drafting, is rarely used. The detailed representation, closely approximating the actual appearance, is preferred in commercial practice, for it is much easier to represent the helices with slanting lines and the truncated roots and crests with sharp "V's" (Fig. 15.6). Since detailed rendering is also time consuming, its use is justified only in those few cases where appearance and permanency are important factors and when it is necessary to avoid the possibility that confusion might result from the use of one of the symbolic methods. The preparation of a detailed representation is a task that belongs primarily to a draftsman, the engineer being concerned only with specifying that this form be used.

The steps in drawing a Unified thread are shown in Figs. 15.7 and 15.8.

$P = \dfrac{1}{\text{NUMBER OF THREADS PER INCH}}$

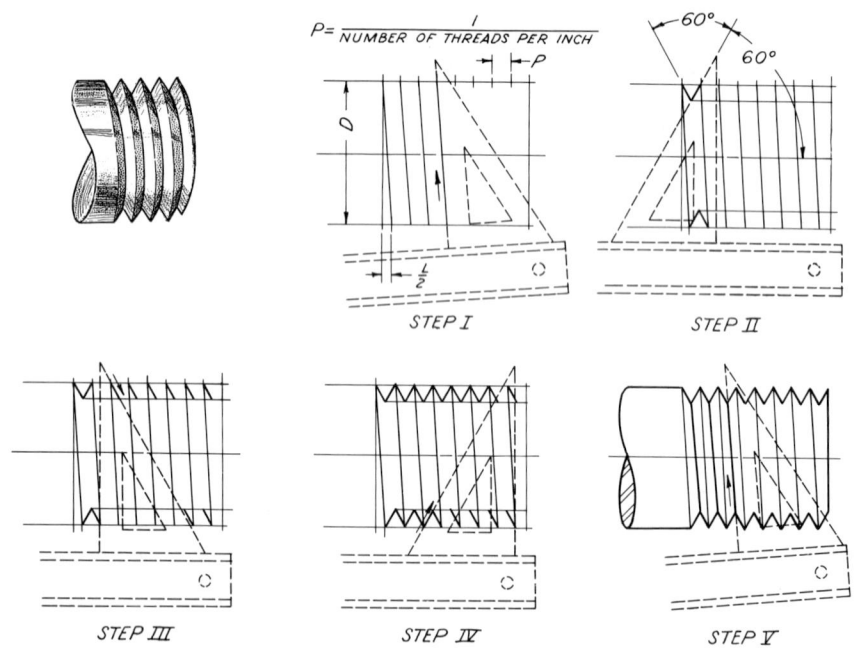

STEP I STEP II

STEP III STEP IV STEP V

FIG. 15.7. Detailed representation of Unified and American and sharp V-threads (external).

CHAP. 15 / REPRESENTATION AND SPECIFICATION OF THREADS, FASTENERS, AND SPRINGS 331

The stages in drawing the detailed representation of modified square and Acme threads are shown in Figs. 15.9, 15.10, and 15.11. All lines of the finished square thread are made the same weight. The root lines of the Acme thread may be made heavier than the other lines.

15.9
American National Standard Conventional Thread Symbols (Fig. 15.12). To save valuable time and expense in the preparation of drawings, the American National Standards Institute has adopted the "schematic" and "simplified" series of thread symbols to represent threads having a diameter of 1 in. or less.

The root of the thread for the simplified representation of an external thread is

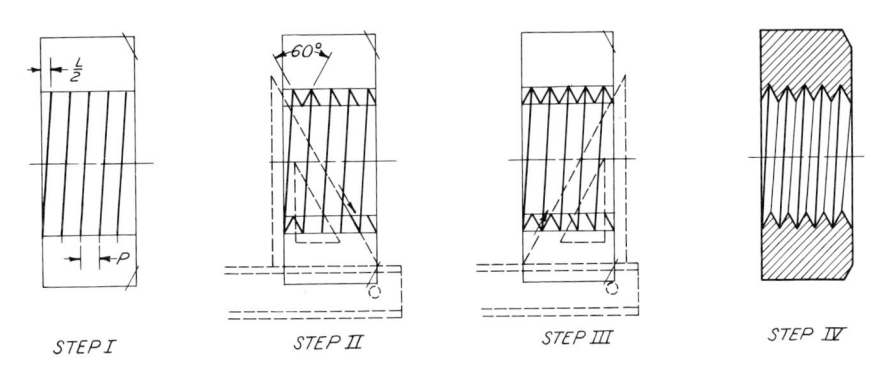

FIG. 15.8. Detailed representation of Unified and American and sharp V-threads (internal).

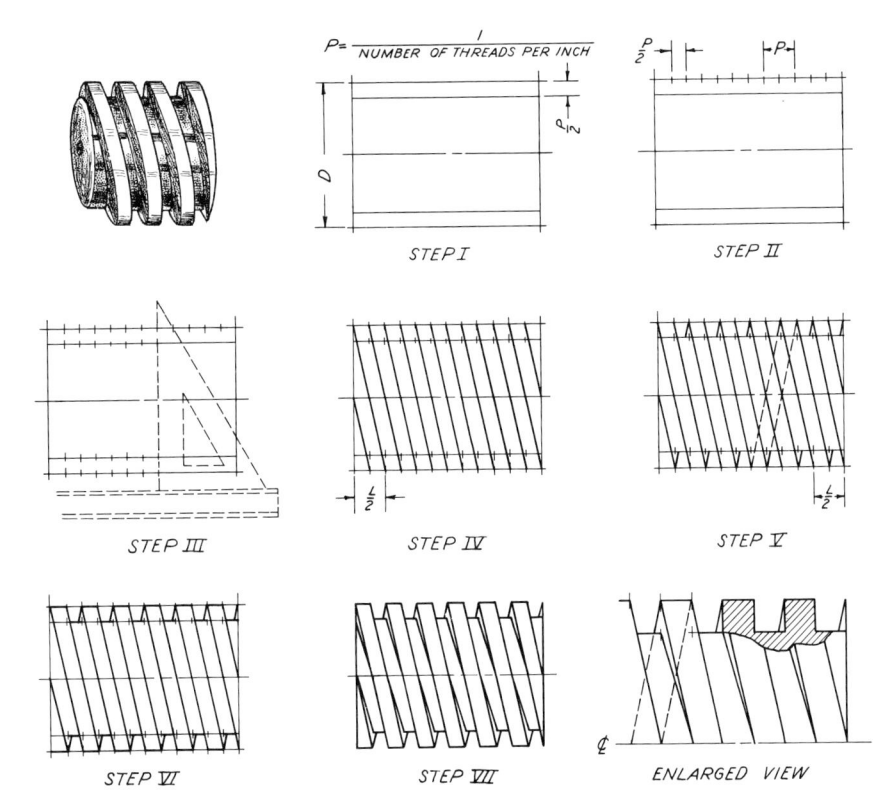

FIG. 15.9. Detailed representation of square threads (modified).

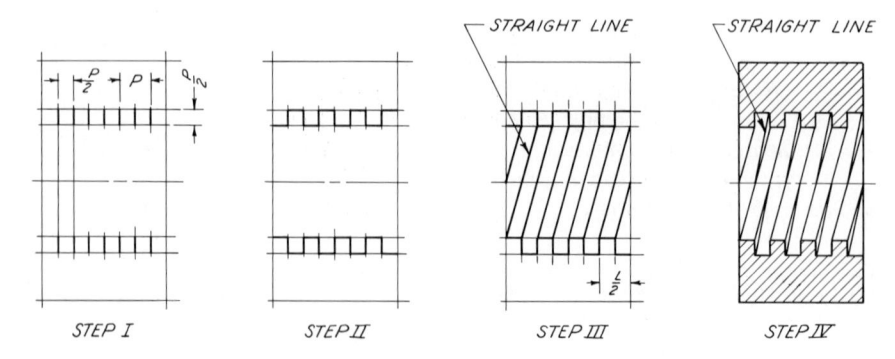

FIG. 15.10. Detailed representation of square threads (internal).

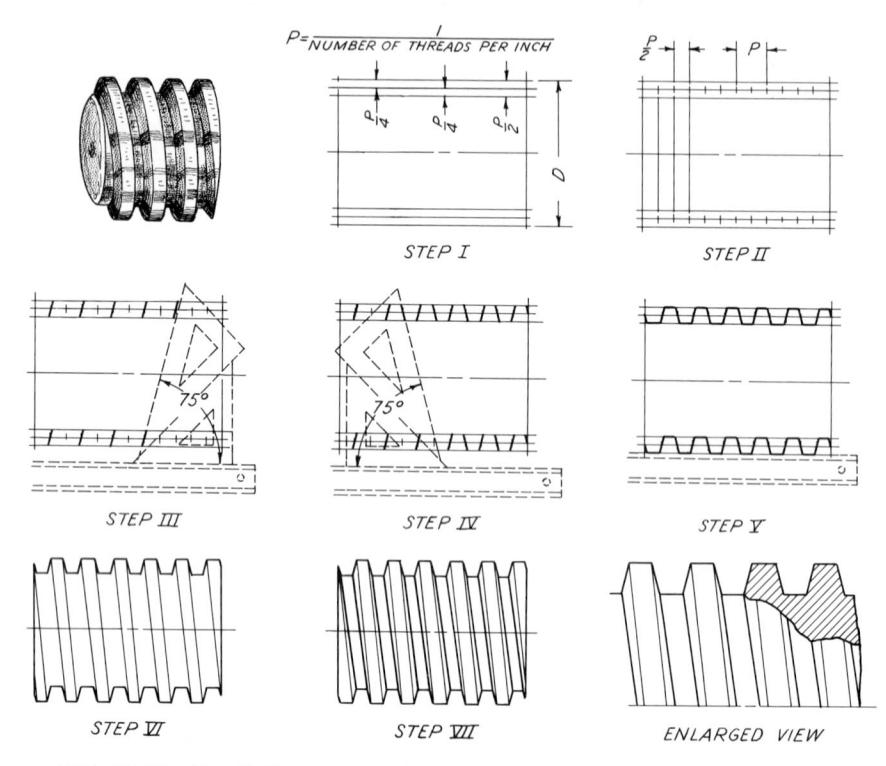

FIG. 15.11. Detailed representation of Acme thread.

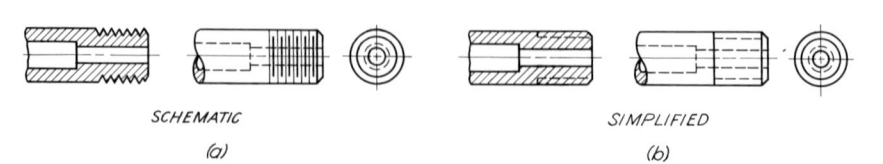

FIG. 15.12. External thread representation.

CHAP. 15 / REPRESENTATION AND SPECIFICATION OF THREADS, FASTENERS, AND SPRINGS   333

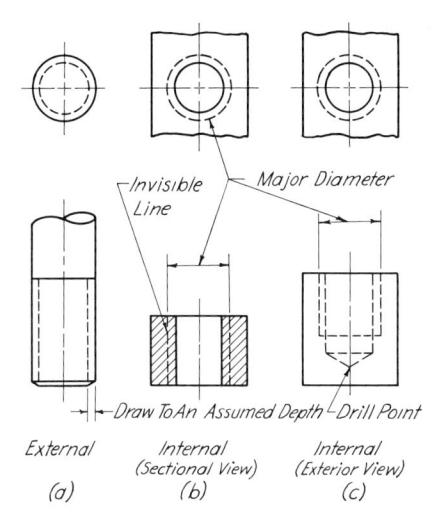

FIG. 15.13. Simplified representation.

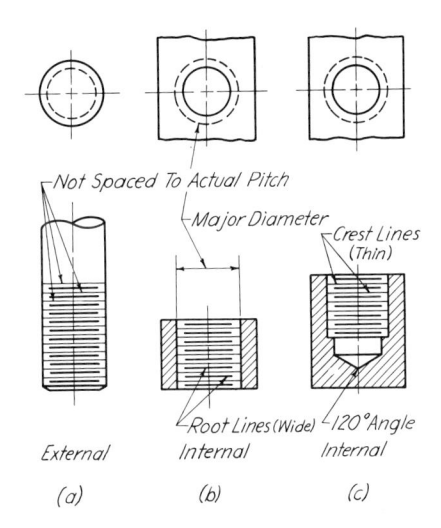

FIG. 15.14. Schematic representation.

shown by invisible lines drawn parallel to the axis [Fig. 15.13(a)].

The schematic representation consists of alternate long and short lines perpendicular to the axis. Although these lines, representing the crests and roots of the thread, are not spaced to actual pitch, their spacing should indicate noticeable differences in the number of threads per inch of different threads on the same working drawing or group of drawings (Fig. 15.14). The root lines are made heavier than the crest lines (Fig. 15.15).

Before a hole can be tapped (threaded), it must be drilled to permit the tap to enter. See Table 2 in the Appendix for tap drill sizes for standard threads. Since the last of the thread cut is not well formed or usable, the hole must be shown drilled and tapped deeper than the screw will enter [Fig. 15.16(d), (e), and (f)]. To show the threaded portion extending to the bottom of the drilled hole indicates the use of a bottoming tap to cut full threads at the bottom. This is an extra and expensive operation not justified except in cases where the depth of the hole and the distance the screw must enter are limited [see Fig. 15.16(g), (h), and (i)].

Figure 15.17 shows a simplified method of representation for square threads.

15.10

Threads in Section. The detailed representation of threads in section, which is used for large diameters only, is shown in Fig. 15.8. Since the far side of an internal thread in section is visible, the crest and root lines incline in the opposite direction to those of an external thread having the same specifications.

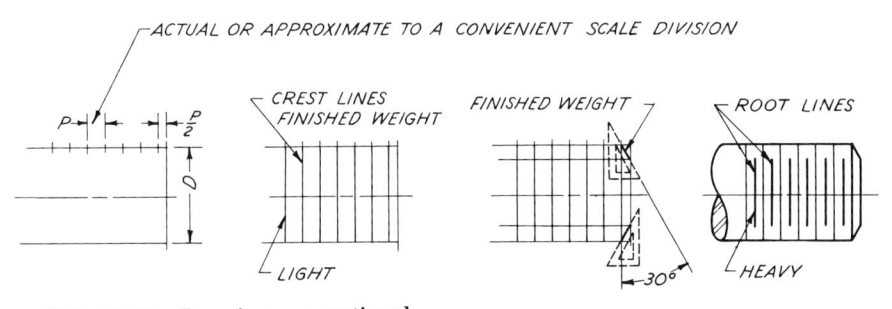

FIG. 15.15. Drawing conventional threads—schematic representation.

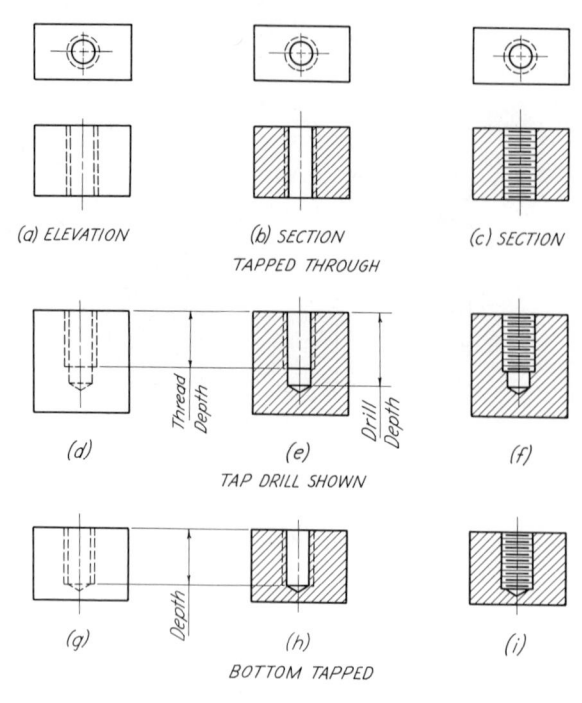

334 PART III / GRAPHICS FOR DESIGN AND COMMUNICATION

FIG. 15.16. Representation of internal threads.

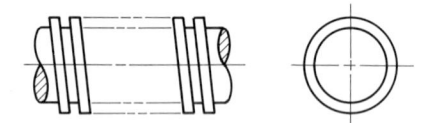

FIG. 15.17. Simplified representation of a square thread.

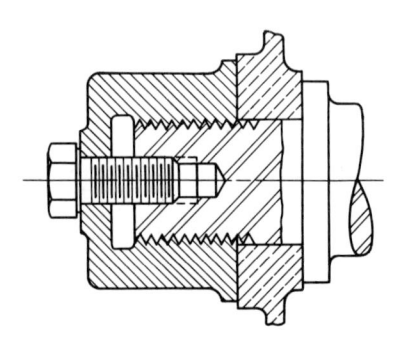

FIG. 15.18. Threads in section.*

The schematic and simplified representations for threads of small diameter are shown in Figs. 15.12 and 15.16.

A sectioned assembly drawing is shown in Fig. 15.18. When assembled pieces are both sectioned, the detailed representation is used, and the thread form is drawn. Simplified representation could have been used for the thread on the cap screw instead of the schematic representation shown (Fig. 16.96).

15.11
Unified and American Screw-thread Series. The Unified and American screw thread series, as given in ANS(ASA) B1.1–1960 consists of six series and a selection of special threads that cover

ANS(ASA)Y14.6–1957.

special combinations of diameter and pitch. Each series differs from the other by the number of threads per inch for a specific diameter (see Tables 2 and 3 in the Appendix).

The coarse-thread series (UNC and NC) is designated UNC for sizes above $\frac{1}{4}$ in. in diameter. This series is recommended for general industrial use.

The fine-thread series (UNF and NF), designated UNF for sizes above $\frac{1}{4}$ in., was prepared for use when a fine thread is required and for general use in the automotive and aircraft fields.

The extra-fine-thread series (UNEF and NEF) is used for automotive and aircraft work when a maximum number of threads is required for a given length.

The 8 thread series (8N) is a uniform pitch series for large diameters. It is sometimes used in place of the coarse-thread series for diameters greater than 1 in. This series was originally intended for high-pressure joints.

The 12 thread series (12UN or 12N) is a uniform pitch series intended for use with large diameters requiring threads of medium-fine pitch. This series is used as a continuation of the fine-thread series for diameters greater than $1\frac{1}{2}$ in.

The 16 thread series (16UN or 16N) is a uniform pitch series for large diameters requiring a fine-pitch thread. This series is used as a continuation of the extra-fine-thread series for diameters greater than 2 in.

15.12
Unified and American Screw-thread Classes. Classes of thread are determined by the amounts of tolerance and allowance specified. Under the new unified system, classes 1A, 2A, and 3A apply only to external threads; classes 1B, 2B, and 3B apply to internal threads. Classes 2 and 3 from the former American Standard (ASA) have been retained without change in the new Unified and American Thread

Standard for use in the United States only, but they are not among the unified classes even though the thread forms are identical. These classes are used with the American thread series (NC, NF, and N series), which covers sizes from size 0 (.060) to 6 in.

Class 1A and class 1B replace class 1 of the old American Standard.

Class 2A and class 2B were adopted as the recognized standards for screws, bolts, and nuts.

Class 3A and class 3B invoke new classes of tolerance. These classes along with class 2A and class 2B should eventually replace class 2 and class 3 now retained from the American (National) Standard. Class 2 and class 3 are defined in the former standard ANS(ASA) B1.1–1935 as follows:

Class 2 fit. Represents a high quality of commercial thread product and is recommended for the great bulk of interchangeable screw-thread work.

Class 3 fit. Represents an exceptionally high quality of commercially threaded product and is recommended only in cases where the high cost of precision tools and continual checking is warranted.

15.13
Identification Symbols for Unified Screw Threads. Threads are specified under the new unified system by giving the diameter, number of threads per inch, initial letters (UNC, UNF, etc.), and class of thread (1A, 2A, and 3A; or 1B, 2B, and 3B) (see Fig. 15.19).

Unified and American National threads are specified on drawings, in specifications, and in stock lists by thread information given as shown in Fig. 15.20. A multiple-start thread is designated by specifying in sequence the nominal size, pitch, and lead.

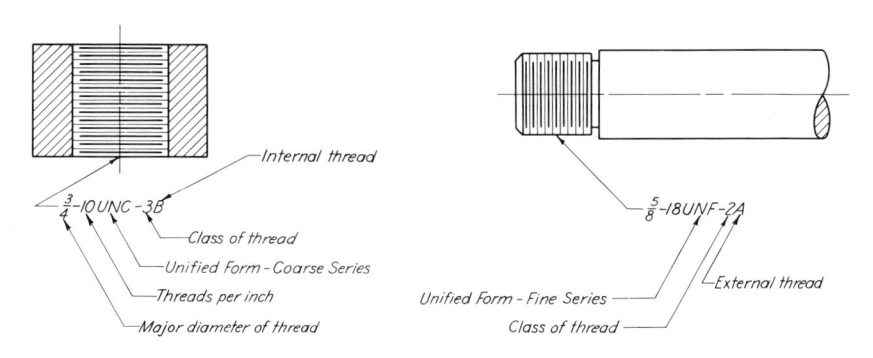

FIG. 15.19. Unified thread identification symbols.

15.14
Thread Dimensioning. In general, the thread length dimension shown on a drawing should be the length of the complete (full-form) threads. The incomplete threads should be beyond this dimensioned length. It should be noted in Fig. 15.21 that the chamfer at the start of the

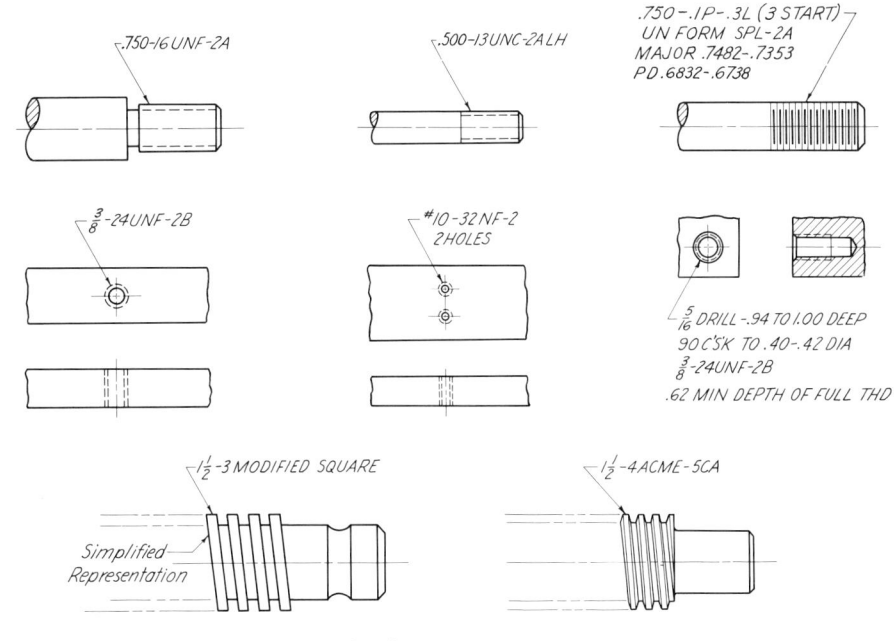

FIG. 15.20. Thread identification symbols.

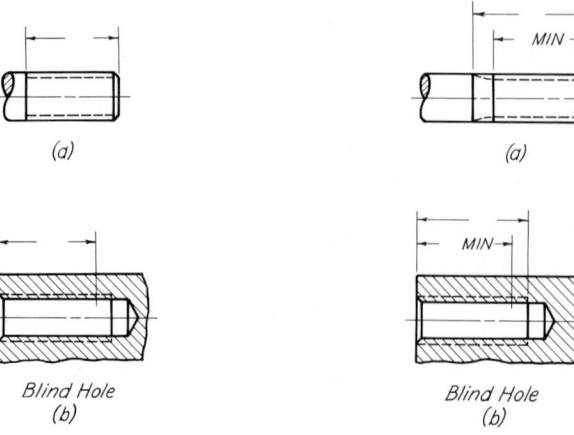

336 PART III / GRAPHICS FOR DESIGN AND COMMUNICATION

FIG. 15.21. Dimensioning full-form thread lengths.

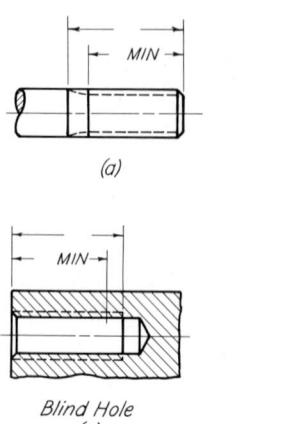

FIG. 15.22. Dimensioning to indicate incomplete thread length.

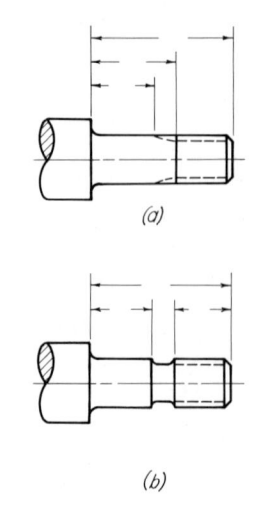

FIG. 15.23. Dimensioning of unthreaded lengths.

thread (not exceeding two pitches in length) is included in the dimensioned length of the complete threads. Should it be necessary to control the number of incomplete threads, the overall thread length, including the incomplete threads, should be given in addition to the dimension for the full thread length, as shown in Fig. 15.22. To indicate complete threads as near the head (or shoulder) as practicable on short bolts, screws, and so forth, it is recommended that the maximum permissible distance be given from the head (or shoulder) to the nearest complete thread.

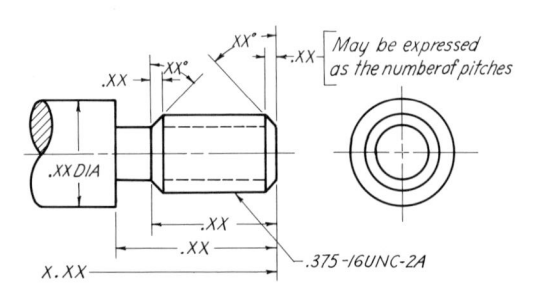

FIG. 15.24. Dimensioning of chamfers and external reliefs.

When it is a functional requirement to maintain a definite length of unthreaded and unscored body on a threaded part, the unthreaded length should be dimensioned as shown in Fig. 15.23.

When an external thread is relieved, the thread is complete (full-form) for the entire length. The thread relief table given in ANS Y14.6 should be consulted in determining the maximum diameter of the relief, which must be less than the minor diameter of the thread. Chamfers and external reliefs should be dimensioned as shown in Fig. 15.24.

When a blind hole is relieved, the minimum diameter of the relief should be greater than the major diameter of the thread. Countersunk holes and internal reliefs may be dimensioned as shown in Fig. 15.25. The included angle of the countersunk hole is usually 90° ± 5°.

15.15

Square Threads. Square threads can be completely specified by a note. The nominal diameter is given first, followed by the number of threads per inch and the type of thread (see Fig. 15.20).

15.16
Acme and Stubb Acme Threads. Acme threads have been standardized in a preferred (single) series of diameter-pitch combinations by the American National Standards Institute (B 1.5-1952). The standard provides two types of Acme threads, the general-purpose and centralizing. The three classes of general-purpose threads (2G, 3G, and 4G) have clearances on all diameters for free movement. The five classes of centralizing threads (2C, 3C, 4C, 5C, and 6C) have a limited clearance at the major diameters of the external and internal threads to ensure alignment of mating parts and to prevent wedging on the flanks of the thread.

Acme threads are specified by giving the diameter, number of threads per inch, type of thread, and class (Fig. 15.20). The letter A or B is added to indicate an external or an internal thread.

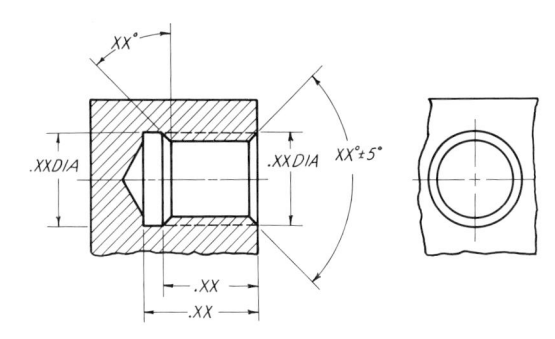

FIG. 15.25. Dimensioning countersunk holes and internal reliefs.

Examples

1 3/8-4 ACME-2GA or 1.375-4 ACME—2GA

1 3/4-4 ACME-2GB-LH

3/4-6 ACME-4CB or .750-6 ACME-4CB

2 3/4-3 ACME-3GA-2-START (2-START indicates a double thread)

15.17
Buttress Threads. The buttress thread is designed for exceptionally high stress along the axis of the thread in one direction only. No pitch-diameter series has been recommended due to the need for special design of most components. The ANS(ASA) B1.9-1953 standard covers three classes of buttress threads. These are 1A, 2A, and 3A for external threads and 1B, 2B, and 3B for internal threads.

Buttress threads are specified by giving, in order, the diameter, threads per inch, type of thread (National Buttress), and class.

Examples

5/8-20 BUTTRESS-2A

10-10 BUTTRESS-3B (2-START) (Optionally, these threads may be designated by giving the pitch followed by the letter P instead of the number of threads per inch.)

.625-.05P BUTTRESS-2A

B: FASTENERS

15.18
American National Standard Bolts and Nuts (Fig. 15.26). Commercial producers of bolts and fasteners manufacture their products in accordance with the standard specifications given in the American National Standard entitled *Square and Hexagon Bolts and Nuts* (Revised 1965).* See Table 6 in the Appendix.

The ANSI(ASA) has approved the specifications for three series of bolts and nuts:

1. *Regular series.* The regular series was adopted for general use.

2. *Heavy series.* Heavy boltheads and nuts are designed to satisfy the special commercial need for greater bearing surface.

*ANS (ASA)B18.2-1965.

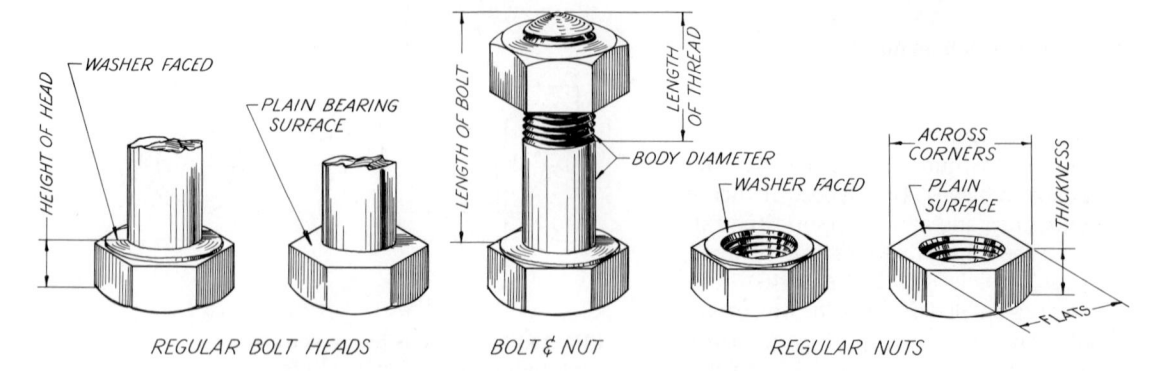

FIG. 15.26. American Standard bolts and nuts.

3. *Light-series nuts.* Light nuts are used under conditions requiring a substantial savings in weight and material. They are usually supplied with a fine thread.

The amount of machining is the basis for further classification of hexagonal bolts and nuts in both the regular and heavy series as unfinished and semifinished.

Square-head bolts and nuts are standardized as unfinished only.

Unfinished heads and nuts are not washer-faced, nor are they machined on any surface.

Semifinished boltheads and nuts are machined or treated on the bearing surface to provide a washer face for boltheads and either a washer face or a circular bearing surface for nuts. Nuts, not washer-faced, have the circular bearing surface formed by chamfering the edges.

Bolts and nuts are *always* drawn across corners in all views. This recognized commercial practice, which violates the principles of true projection, prevents confusion of square and hexagonal forms on drawings.

The chamfer angle on the tops of heads and nuts is 30° on hexagons and 25° on squares, but both are drawn at 30° on bolts greater than 1 in. in diameter.

Bolts are specified in parts lists and elsewhere by giving the diameter, number of threads per inch, series, class of thread, length, finish, and type of head.

Example

$\frac{1}{2}$-13 UNC-2A $\times$ 1$\frac{3}{4}$ SEMIFIN HEX HD BOLT

Frequently it is advantageous and practical to abbreviate the specification thus:

Example

$\frac{1}{2} \times$ 1$\frac{3}{4}$ UNC SEMIFIN HEX HD BOLT

Although bolt lengths have not been standardized in construction practice, because of the varied requirements in engineering design, length increments for length under the head to the end of a hexagonal bolt can be considered as $\frac{1}{8}$ in. for bolts $\frac{1}{4}$-$\frac{3}{4}$ in. in length, $\frac{1}{4}$ in. for bolts $\frac{3}{4}$-3 in. in length, and $\frac{1}{2}$ in. for bolts 3-6 in. in length. Length increments for square-head bolts are $\frac{1}{8}$ in. for bolts $\frac{1}{4}$-$\frac{3}{4}$ in. in length, and $\frac{1}{4}$ in. for bolts $\frac{3}{4}$-4$\frac{3}{4}$ in. in length.

The minimum thread length for bolts up to and including 6 in. in length will be twice the diameter plus $\frac{1}{4}$ in. For lengths over 6 in. the minimum thread length will be twice the diameter of the bolt plus $\frac{1}{2}$ in. [ANS(ASA)B18.2-1965].

15.19
To Draw Boltheads and Nuts. Using the dimension taken from the tables, draw the lines representing the top and contact surfaces of the head or nut and the diameter of the bolt. Lay out a hexagon about an inscribed chamfer circle having a diameter equal to the distance across the flats (Fig. 15.27) and project the necessary lines to block in the view. Draw in the arcs after finding the centers, as shown in Fig. 15.27.

A square-head bolt or nut may be drawn by following the steps indicated in Fig. 15.28.

The engineer and experienced draftsman wisely resort to some form of template for drawing the views of a bolthead or nut (see Fig. 3.14). To draw the views as shown in Figs. 15.27 and 15.28 consumes valuable time needlessly.

15.20
Studs. Studs, or stud bolts, which are threaded on both ends, as shown in Fig. 15.29, are used where bolts would be impractical and for parts that must be removed frequently (cylinder heads, steam chest covers, pumps, and so on). They are first screwed permanently into the tapped holes in one part before the removable member with its corresponding clearance holes is placed in position. Nuts are used on the projecting ends to hold the parts together.

Since studs are not standard they must be produced from specifications given on a detail drawing. In dimensioning a stud, the length of thread must be given for both the stud end and nut end along with an overall dimension. The thread information is given by note.

In a bill of material, studs may be specified as follows:

Example

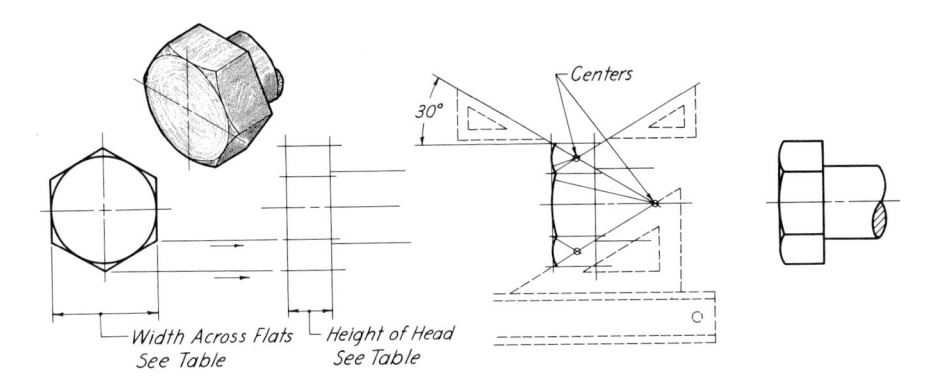

$\frac{1}{2}$–13 UNC–2A × $2\frac{3}{4}$ STUD

FIG. 15.27. Steps in drawing a hexagonal bolt head.

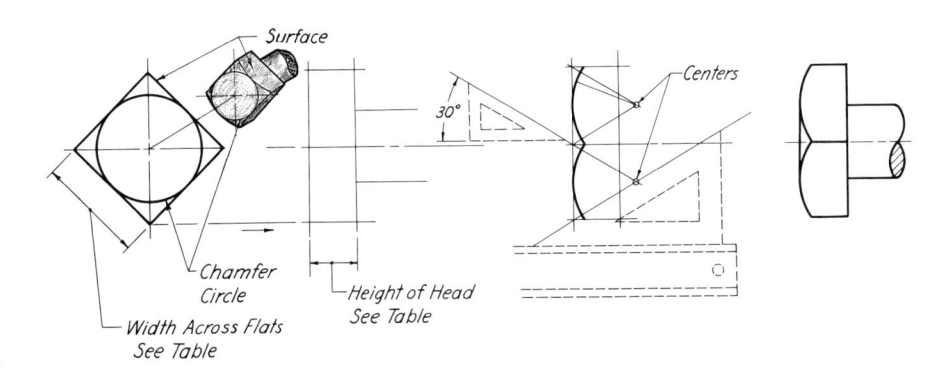

FIG. 15.28. Steps in drawing a square bolt head.

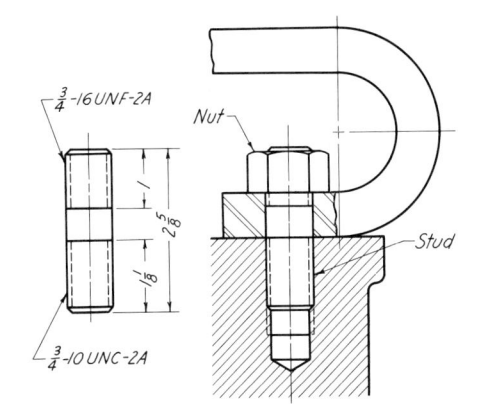

FIG. 15.29. Stud bolt.

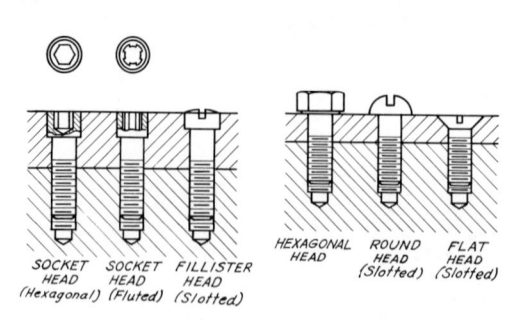

FIG. 15.30. Cap screws.

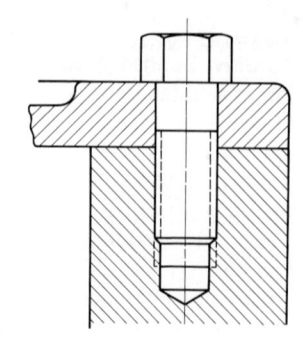

FIG. 15.31. Hexagonal-head cap screw.

It is good practice to abbreviate the specification thus:

Example

$\frac{1}{2} \times 2\frac{3}{4}$ STUD

15.21
Cap Screws (Fig. 15.30). Cap screws are similar to machine screws. They are available in four standard heads, usually in finished form. When parts are assembled, the cap screws pass through clear holes in one member and screw into threaded holes in the other (Fig. 15.31). Hexagonal cap screws have a washer face $\frac{1}{64}$ in. thick with a diameter equal to the distance across flats. All cap screws 1 in. or less in length are threaded very nearly to the head.

Cap screws are specified by giving the diameter, number of threads per inch, series, class of thread, length, and type of head.

Example

$\frac{5}{8}$-11 UNC-2A $\times$ 2 FIL HD CAP SC

It is good practice to abbreviate the specification thus:

Example

$\frac{5}{8} \times 2$ UNC FIL HD CAP SC

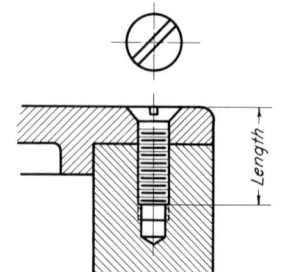

FIG. 15.32. Use of a machine screw.

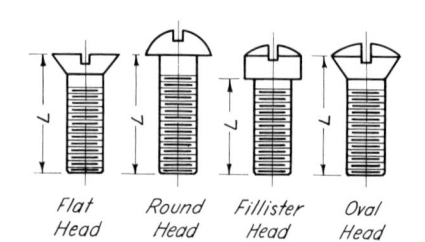

FIG. 15.33. Types of machine screws.

15.22
Machine Screws. Machine screws, which fulfill the same purpose as cap screws, are used chiefly for small work having thin sections (Fig. 15.32). Under the approved American National Standard they range from No. 0 (.060 in. diam.) to $\frac{3}{4}$ in. (.750 in. diam.) and are available in either the American Standard Coarse or Fine-Threaded Series. The four forms of heads shown in Fig. 15.33 have been standardized.

To specify machine screws, give the diameter, threads per inch, thread series, class of thread, length, and type of head.

Example

No. 12-24 NC-3 $\times$ $\frac{3}{4}$ FIL HD MACH SC

It is good practice to abbreviate by omitting the thread series and class of fit.

Example

No. 12-24 $\times$ $\frac{3}{4}$ FIL HD MACH SC

15.23
Commercial Lengths: Studs, Cap Screws, Machine Screws. Unless a fastening of any of these types carries a constant and appreciable fatigue stress, the usual practice is to have it enter a distance related to its nominal diameter (Fig. 15.34). If the

CHAP. 15 / REPRESENTATION AND SPECIFICATION OF THREADS, FASTENERS, AND SPRINGS **341**

depth of the hole is not limited, it should be drilled to a depth of 1 diameter beyond the end of the fastener to permit tapping to a distance of ½ diameter below the fastener.

The length of the fastening should be determined to the nearest commercial length that will allow it to fulfill minimum conditions. In the case of a stud, care should be taken that the length allows for a full engagement of the nut. Commercial lengths for fasteners increase by the following increments:

Standard length increments
For fastener lengths ¼–1 in. = ⅛ in.
For fastener lengths 1–4 in. = ¼ in.

For fastenings and other general-purpose applications, the engagement length should be equal to the nominal diameter (*D*) of the thread when both components are of steel. For steel external threads in cast iron, brass, or bronze, the engagement length should be 1½*D*. When assembled into aluminum, zinc, or plastic the engagement should be 2*D*.

15.24
Set Screws. Set screws are used principally to prevent rotary motion between two parts, such as that which tends to occur in the case of a rotating member mounted on a shaft. A set screw is screwed through one part until the point presses firmly against the other part (Fig. 15.35).

The several forms of safety heads shown in Fig. 15.36 are available in combination with any of the points. Headless set screws comply with safety codes and should be used on all revolving parts. The many serious injuries that have been caused by the projecting heads of square-head set screws have led to legislation prohibiting their use in some states [Fig. 15.35(c)].

Set screws are specified by giving the

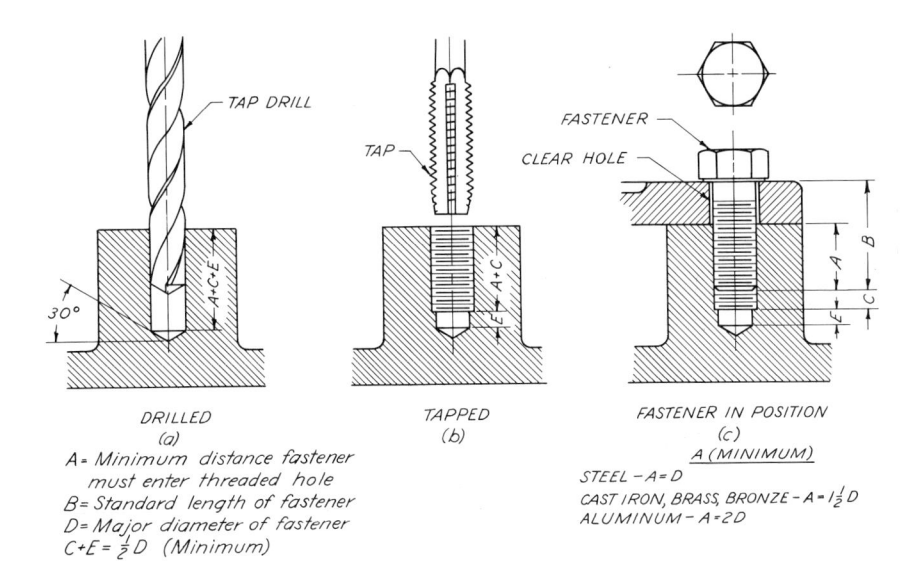

DRILLED
(a)
A = Minimum distance fastener must enter threaded hole
B = Standard length of fastener
D = Major diameter of fastener
C + E = ½ D (Minimum)

TAPPED
(b)

FASTENER IN POSITION
(c)
A (MINIMUM)
STEEL — A = D
CAST IRON, BRASS, BRONZE — A = 1½D
ALUMINUM — A = 2D

FIG. 15.34. Threaded hole and fastener.

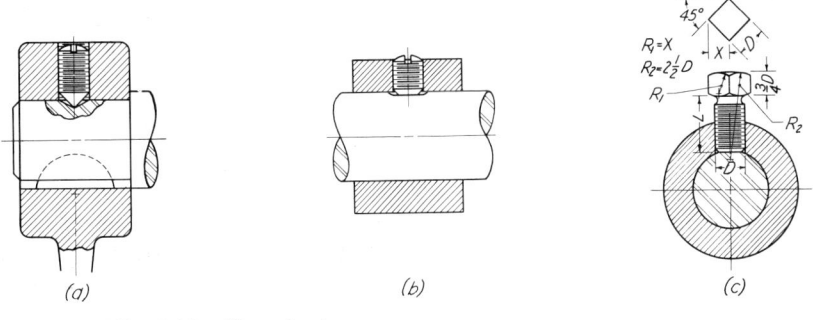

FIG. 15.35. Use of set screws.

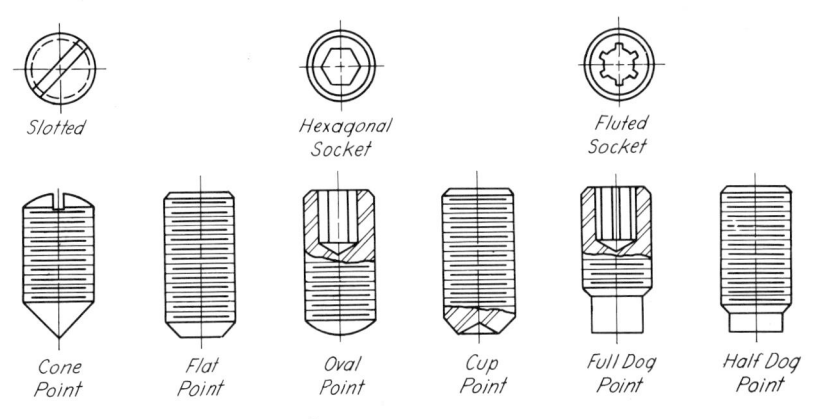

Slotted   Hexagonal Socket   Fluted Socket

Cone Point   Flat Point   Oval Point   Cup Point   Full Dog Point   Half Dog Point

FIG. 15.36. Set screws.

diameter, number of threads per inch, series, class of thread, length, type of head, and type of point.

Example

¼–20 UNC–2A × ½ SLOTTED CONE PT SET SC

The preferred abbreviated form gives the diameter, number of threads per inch, length, type of head, and type of point.

Example

¼–20 × ½ HEX SOCKET CONE PT SET SC

15.25
Keys. Keys are used in the assembling of machine parts to secure them against relative motion, generally rotary, as is the case between shafts, cranks, wheels, and so on. When the relative forces are not great, a round key, saddle key, or flat key is used (Fig. 15.37). For heavier duty, rectangular keys are more suitable (Fig. 15.38).

The square key (Fig. 15.39) and the Pratt and Whitney key (Fig. 15.40) are the two keys most frequently used in machine design. A plain milling cutter is used to cut the keyway for the square key, and an end mill is used for the Pratt and Whitney keyway. Both keys fit tightly in the shaft and in the part mounted on it.

The gib-head key (Fig. 15.41) is designed so that the head remains far enough from the hub to allow a drift pin to be driven to remove the key. The hub side of the key is tapered ⅛ in. per ft to ensure a fit tight enough to prevent both axial and rotary motion. For this type of key, the keyway must be cut to one end of the shaft.

15.26
Woodruff Keys. A Woodruff key is a flat segmental disc with either a flat or a round bottom (Fig. 15.42). It is always specified by a number, the last two digits of which indicate the nominal diameter in eighths of an inch, while the digits preceding the last two give the nominal width in thirty-seconds of an inch.

A practical rule for selecting a Woodruff key for a given shaft is as follows: Choose a standard key that has a width approximately equal to one-fourth of the diameter of the shaft and a radius nearly equal (plus or minus) to the radius of the shaft. Table 18 in the Appendix gives the dimensions for American Standard Woodruff keys.

When Woodruff keys are drawn, it should be remembered that the center of

FIG. 15.37. Light duty keys.

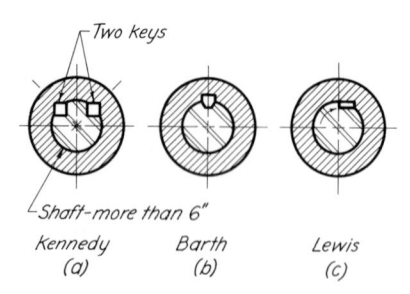

FIG. 15.38. Heavy duty keys.

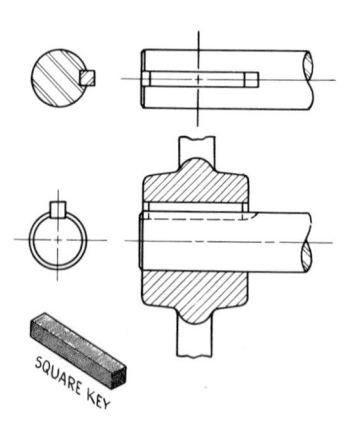

FIG. 15.39. A square key.

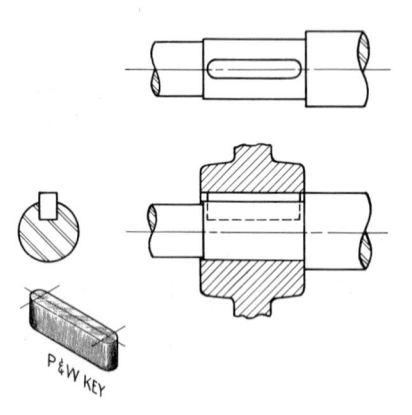

FIG. 15.40. A Pratt and Whitney key.

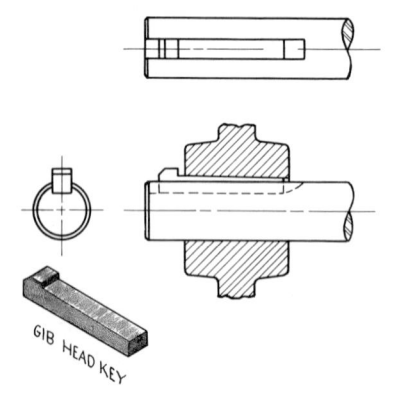

FIG. 15.41. A gib-head key.

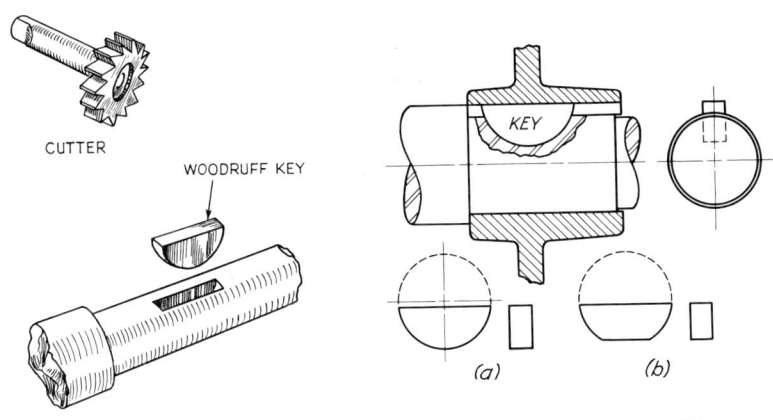

CHAP. 15 / REPRESENTATION AND SPECIFICATION OF THREADS, FASTENERS, AND SPRINGS   **343**

FIG. 15.42. A Woodruff key.

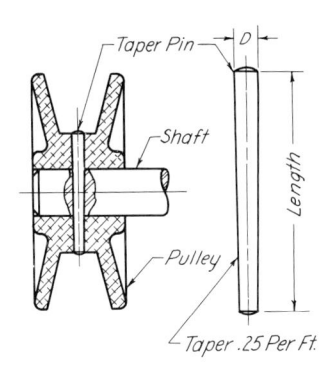

FIG. 15.43. Use of a taper pin.

the arc is placed above the top of the key at a distance shown in column E in the table.

15.27
Taper Pins. A taper pin is commonly used for fastening collars and pulleys to shafts, as illustrated in Fig. 15.43. The hole for the pin is drilled and reamed with the parts assembled. When a taper pin is to be used, the drawing callout should read as follows:

#3 (.213) DRILL AND REAM FOR #4 TAPER PIN WITH PC #6 IN POSITION

Drill sizes and exact dimensions for taper pins are given in Table 20 in the Appendix.

15.28
Locking Devices. A few of the many types of locking devices that prevent nuts from becoming loose under vibration are shown in Figs. 15.44 and 15.45.

Figure 15.44 shows six forms of patented spring washers. The ones shown in (D), (E), and (F) have internal and external teeth.

In common use is the castellated nut with a spring cotter pin that passes

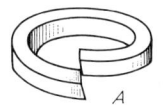

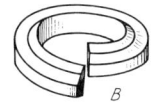

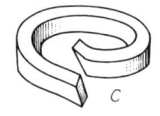

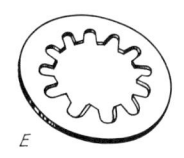

FIG. 15.44. Special lock washers.

through the shaft and the slots in the top [Fig. 15.45(a)]. This type is used extensively in automotive and aeronautical work.

Figure 15.45(b) shows a regular nut that is prevented from loosening by an American National Standard jam nut.

In Fig. 15.45(c) the use of two jam nuts is illustrated.

A regular nut with a spring-lock washer is shown in Fig. 15.45(d). The reaction provided by the lock washer tends to prevent the nut from turning.

A regular nut with a spring cotter pin through the shaft, to prevent the nut from backing off, is shown in Fig. 15.45(e).

(a)   (b)   (c)   (d)

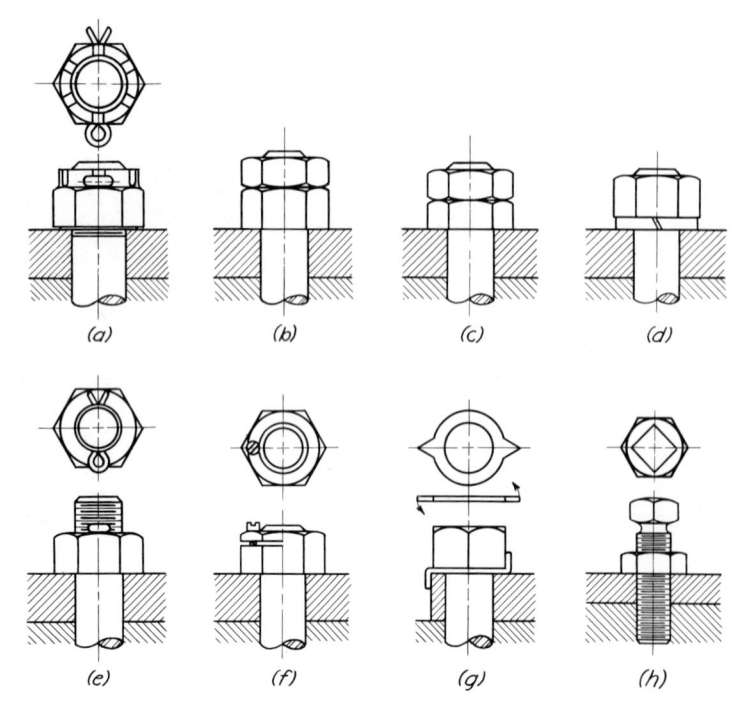

(e)   (f)   (g)   (h)

FIG. 15.45. Locking schemes.

Special devices for locking nuts are illustrated in Fig. 15.45 (*f*) and (*g*). A set screw may be held in position with a jam nut, as in (*h*).

15.29
Areo Thread. The Areo-thread screw-thread system allows the use of high-strength cap screws and studs in light soft metals, such as aluminum and magnesium, through the use of a phosphor bronze or stainless steel coilspring lining in the tapped hole, as shown in Fig. 15.46. This coil (screw bushing) is formed to fit a modified American Standard thread. Special tools are needed for inserting the coil in the tapped hole.

15.30
Miscellaneous Bolts, Screws, and Nuts. Other types of bolts and screws that have been adopted for commercial use are illustrated in Fig. 15.47.

Wood screws have threads proportioned for the holding strength of wood. They are available with different forms of heads (flat, round, and oval).

Some of the fastenings shown in Fig. 15.47 have been standardized by the American National Standards Institute.

15.31
Phillips Head. The Phillips head, shown in Fig. 15.48 for a wood screw, is one of various types of recessed heads. Although special drivers are usually employed for installation, an ordinary screwdriver can be used. Machine screws, cap screws, and many special types of fasteners are available with Phillips heads.

15.32
Rivets. Rivets are permanent fasteners used chiefly for connecting members in such structures as buildings and bridges and for assembling steel sheets and plates for tanks, boilers, and ships. They are cylindrical rods of wrought iron or soft steel, with one head formed when manufactured. A head is formed on the other end after the rivet has been put in place through the drilled or punched holes of the mating parts. A hole for a rivet is generally drilled, punched, or punched and reamed $1/16$ in. larger than the diameter of the shank of the rivet [Fig. 15.49(*a*)]. Figure 15.49(*b*) illustrates a rivet in position. Small rivets, less than $1/2$ in. in diameter, may be driven cold, but the larger sizes are driven hot. For specialized types of engineering work, rivets are manufactured of chrome–iron, aluminum, brass, copper, and so on. Standard dimensions for small rivets are given in Table 15 in the Appendix.

The type of rivets and their treatment are indicated on drawings by the American National Standard conventional symbols shown in Fig. 25.6.

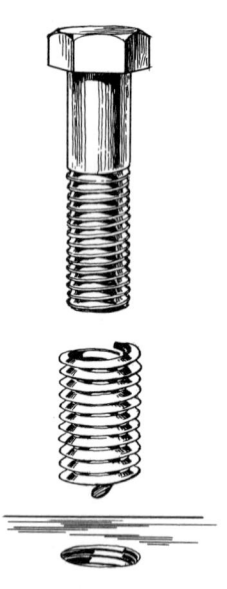

FIG. 15.46. Areo thread.

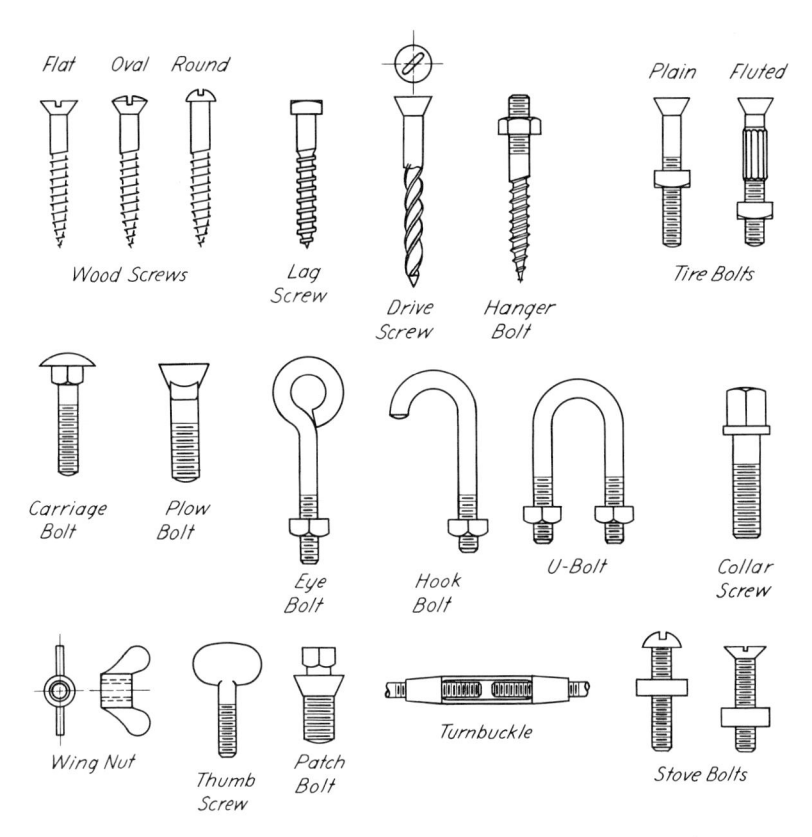

CHAP. 15 / REPRESENTATION AND SPECIFICATION OF THREADS, FASTENERS, AND SPRINGS   345

FIG. 15.47. Miscellaneous bolts, screws, and nuts.

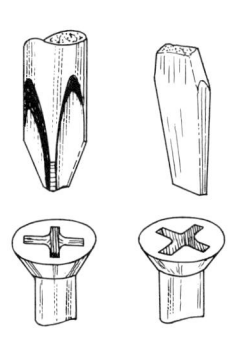

FIG. 15.48. Phillips head screw.

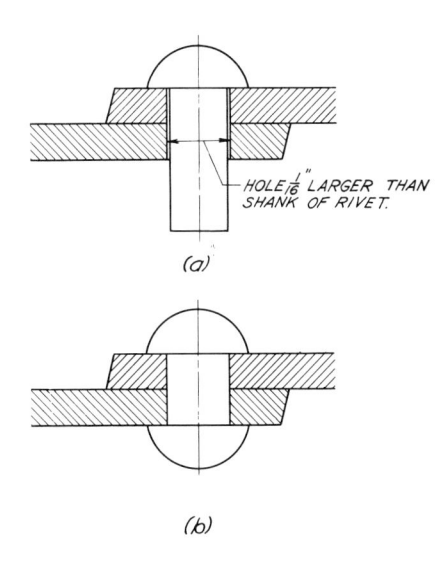

FIG. 15.49. Riveting procedure.

15.33
Riveted Joints. Joints on boilers, tanks, and so on, are classified as either lap joints or butt joints (Fig. 15.50). Lap joints are generally used for seams around the circumference. Butt joints are used for longitudinal seams, except on small tanks where the pressure is to be less than 100 lb per sq in.

C: SPRINGS

15.34
Springs. In production work, a spring is largely a matter of mathematical calculation rather than drawing, and it is usually purchased from a spring manufacturer, with the understanding that it will fulfill specified conditions. For experimental work, and when only one is needed, it may be formed by winding oil-tempered spring wire or music wire around a cylindrical bar. As it is wound, the wire follows the helical path of the screw thread. For this reason the steps in the layout of the representation for a spring are similar to the screw thread. Pitch distances are marked off, and the coils are given a slope of one-half of the pitch. Figure 15.51(a) shows a partial layout of a tension spring. Other types of ends are shown in (b). A compression spring layout, with various types of ends, is illustrated in Fig. 15.52.

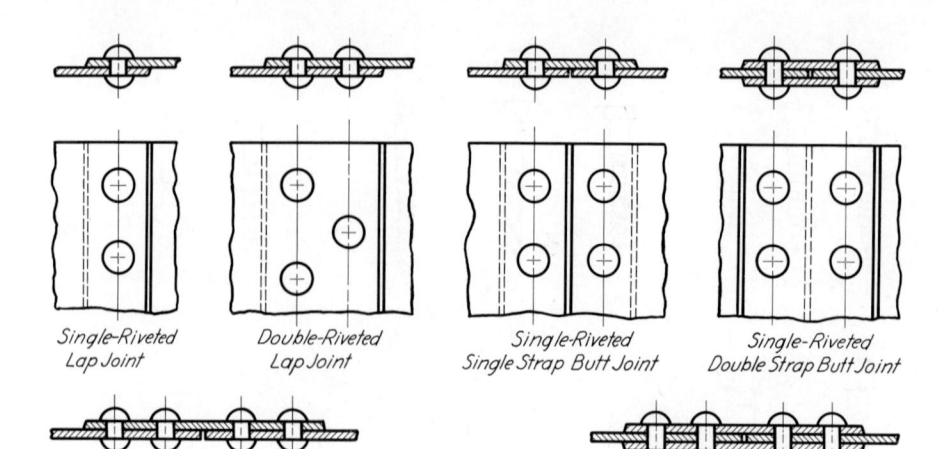

FIG. 15.50. Forms of riveted joints.

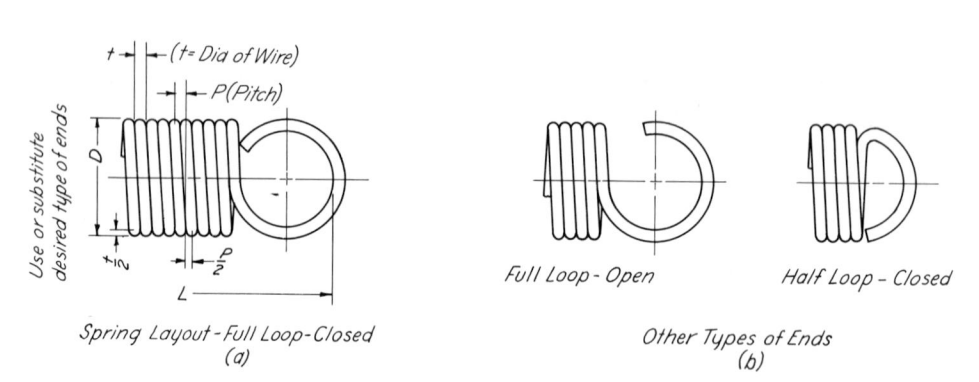

FIG. 15.51. Tension springs.

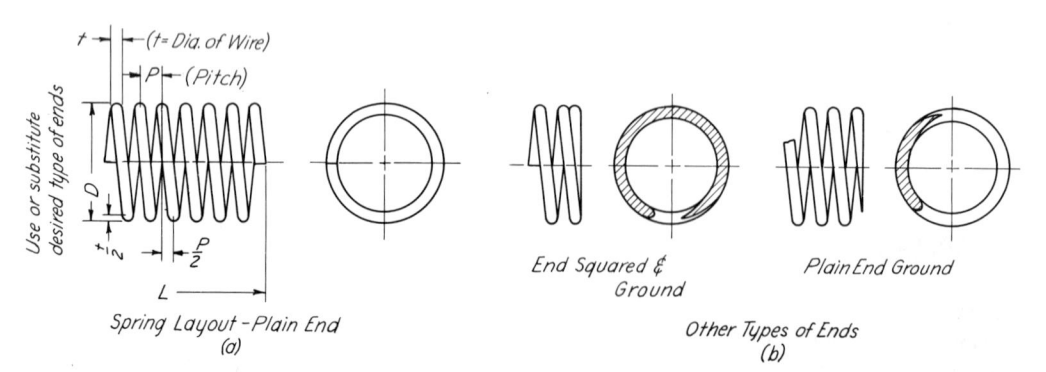

FIG. 15.52. Compression springs.

CHAP. 15 / REPRESENTATION AND SPECIFICATION OF THREADS, FASTENERS, AND SPRINGS **347**

Single-line symbols for the representation of springs are shown in Fig. 15.53.

When making a detail working drawing of a spring, it should be shown to its free length. On either an assembly or detail drawing, a fairly accurate representation, neatly drawn, will satisfy all requirements.

It is common practice in industry to rely on a printed spring drawing, accompanied by a filled-in printed form, to convey the necessary information for the production of a needed spring by a reliable manufacturer. The best procedure is to give the spring characteristics along with a list of necessary dimensions and then depend on an experienced spring designer, at the plant where the spring will be produced, to finalize the design.

The method of representing and dimensioning a compression spring is shown in Fig. 15.54. The spring is represented by a rectangle with diagonals (printed or drawn). Pertinent information is added as dimensions and notes. Either an ID (inside diameter) or an OD (outside diameter) dimension is given, depending on how the spring is to be used.

A method of representing and dimensioning an extension spring is shown in Fig. 15.55. Although drawings of this type may be printed forms, it is often necessary to prepare a drawing showing the ends and a few coils, since extension springs may have any one of a wide variety of types of ends. Needed information is presented in tabular form, as shown, with or without a complete spring design. When no printed form is available, a drawing similar to the one shown in Fig. 15.55 must be prepared.

A torsion spring offers resistance to a torque load. The extended ends form the torque arms, which are rotated about the axis of the spring. One method of representing and dimensioning torsion springs is shown in Fig. 15.56. A printed form

*ANS(ASA)Z14.1–1946.

FIG. 15.53. Single line representation of springs.*

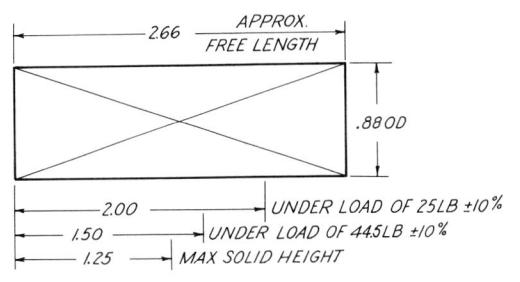

Compression Spring (a)
Torsion Spring (b)
Tension Spring — Ends shaped as required (c)

FIG. 15.54. Drawing showing a compression spring.

2.66 APPROX. FREE LENGTH
.88 OD
2.00 — UNDER LOAD OF 25 LB ±10%
1.50 — UNDER LOAD OF 44.5 LB ±10%
1.25 — MAX SOLID HEIGHT
MATERIAL: .105 HARD DRAWN SPRING STEEL WIRE
12 COILS   10 ACTIVE
CLOSED ENDS GROUND
FINISH: PLAIN

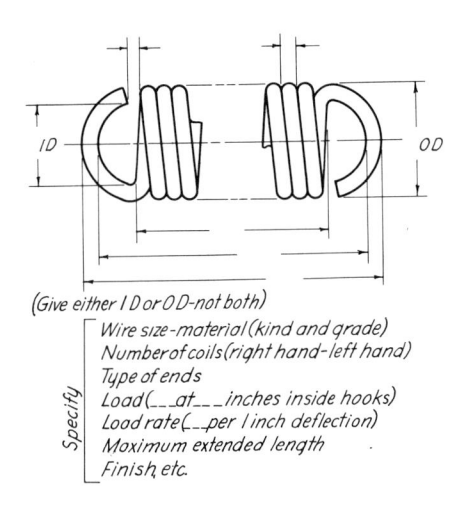

FIG. 15.55. Extension spring drawing.

(Give either ID or OD—not both)

Specify:
- Wire size–material (kind and grade)
- Number of coils (right hand–left hand)
- Type of ends
- Load (___ at ___ inches inside hooks)
- Load rate (___ per 1 inch deflection)
- Maximum extended length
- Finish, etc.

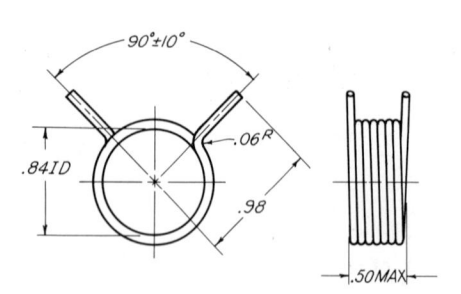

FIG. 15.56. The representation and dimensioning of a torsion spring.

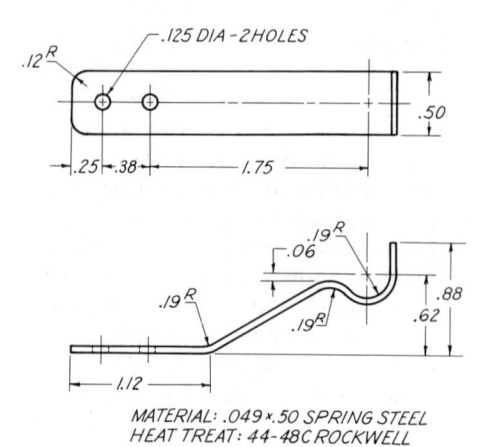

FIG. 15.57. A drawing showing a flat spring.

may be used when there is sufficient uniformity in product requirements to warrant the preparation of a printed form or several printed forms. When a printed form is not available, a drawing similar to the one shown must be prepared.

The term *flat spring* includes all springs made of a strip material. One method of representing and dimensioning flat springs is shown in Fig. 15.57.

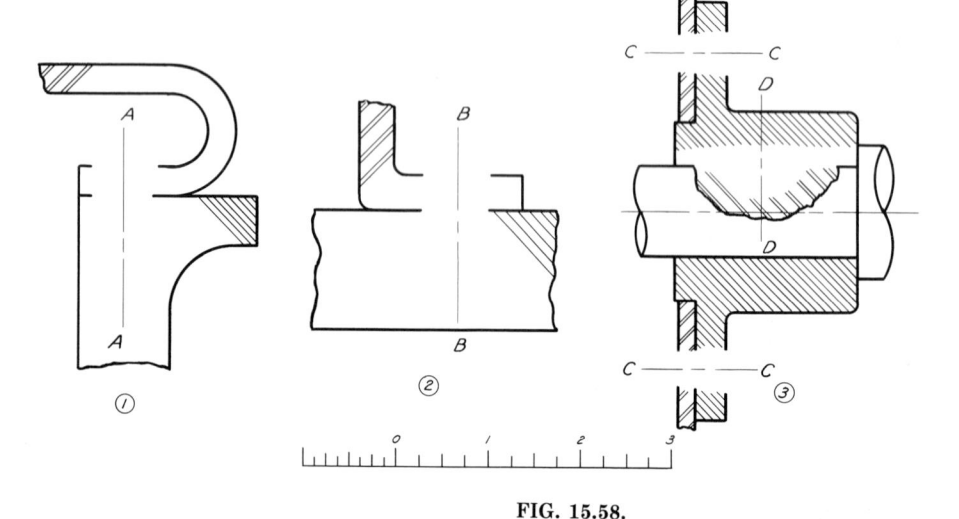

FIG. 15.58.

PROBLEMS

Excellent practice in drawing (or sketching) the representations of threads, threaded fasteners, keys, and rivets is provided by the problems of this chapter.

1. Draw or sketch the three layouts shown in Fig. 15.58 to full size, using the given scale to determine the measurements. On layout ① complete the drawing to show a suitable fastener on center line *AA*. On layout ② show a ½-in. hexagonal-head cap screw on center line *BB*. On layout ③ show a ⅜-in. button-head rivet on center lines *CC* and a No. 608 Woodruff key on center line (CL) *DD*. Use the schematic symbol for the representation of threads.

2. (Fig. 15.59). Reproduce the views of the assembly of the alignment bearing. On CL's *A* show ¼-in. button-head rivets (four required).

CHAP. 15 / REPRESENTATION AND SPECIFICATION OF THREADS, FASTENERS, AND SPRINGS   **349**

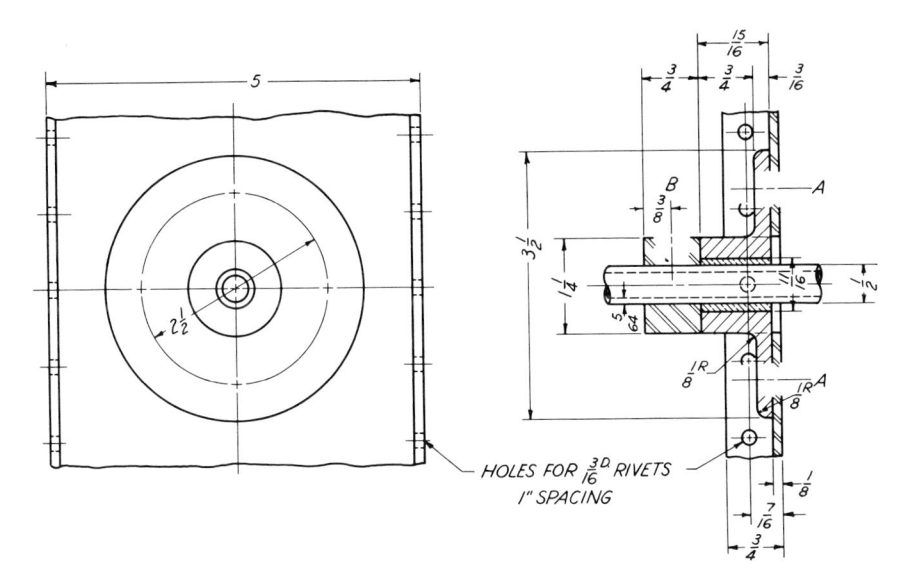

FIG. 15.59.   Alignment bearing.

On CL *B* show a $\frac{5}{16} \times \frac{1}{2}$ American Standard square-head set screw. Do not dimension the views.

3. (Fig. 15.60). Reproduce the views of the assembly of the impeller drive. On CL's *A* show $\frac{1}{4}$-20 UNC × $\frac{1}{2}$ round-head machine screws and regular lock washers. On CL *B* show a No. 406 Woodruff key. On CL *C* show a standard No. 2 × $1\frac{1}{2}$ taper pin.

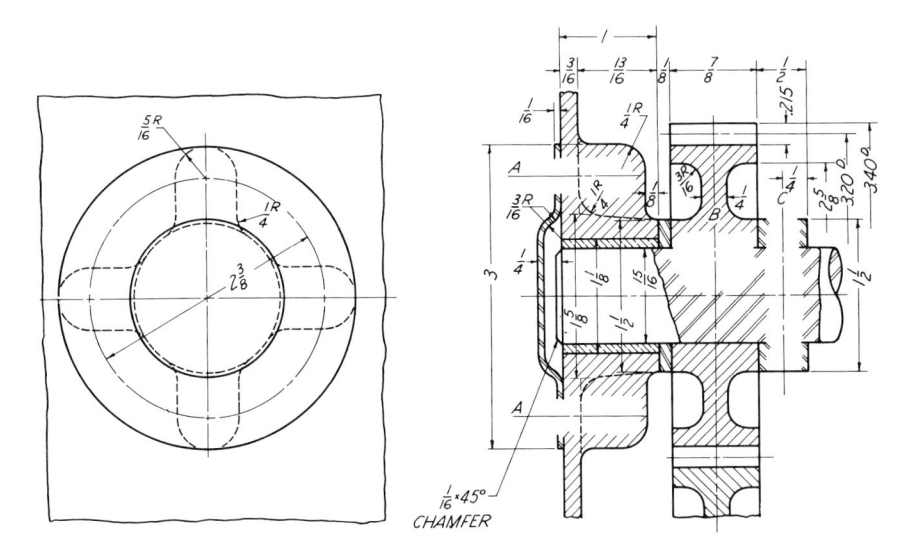

FIG. 15.60.   Impeller drive.

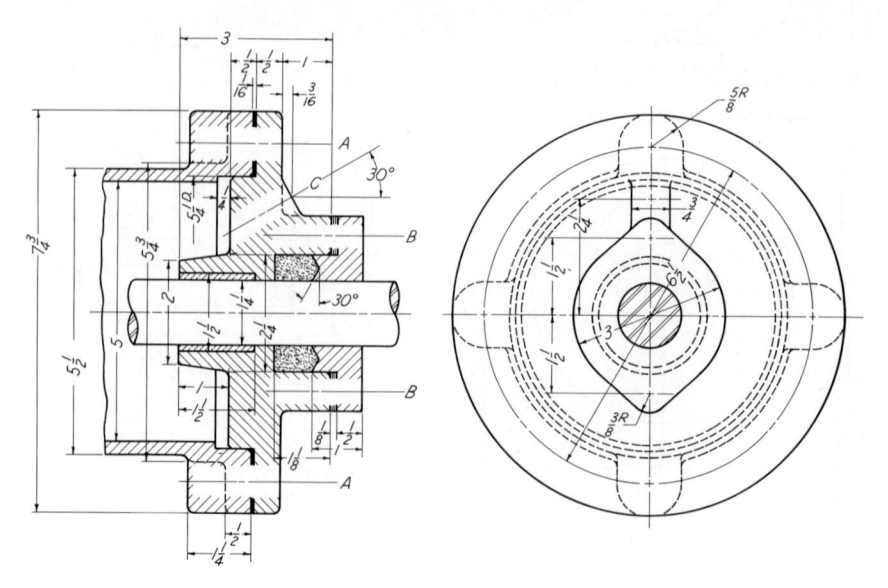

FIG. 15.61. Bearing head.

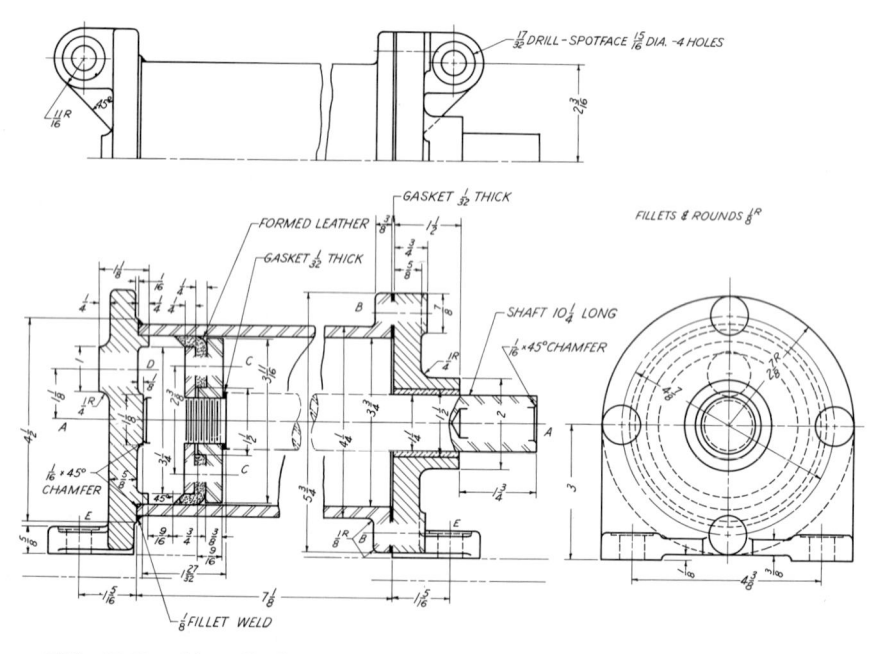

FIG. 15.62. Air cylinder.

4. (Fig. 15.61). Reproduce the views of the assembly of the bearing head. On CL's A show $\frac{1}{2}$-UNC studs with regular lock washers and regular semifinished hexagonal nuts (four required). On CL's B show $\frac{3}{8}$-UNC $\times$ $1\frac{1}{4}$ hexagonal-head cap screws (two required. On CL C drill through and tap $\frac{1}{8}$-in. pipe thread.

5. (Fig. 15.62). Reproduce the views of the assembly of the air cylinder. On CL AA at the left end of the shaft show a 1-UNF semifinished hexagonal nut. At the right end show a hole tapped $\frac{3}{4}$-UNF $\times$ $1\frac{1}{2}$ deep. Between the piston and the (right) end plate draw a spring 3 in. OD, five full coils, $\frac{1}{4}$-in. wire. On CL's B show $\frac{3}{8}$-UNC $\times$ $1\frac{1}{4}$ hexagonal-head cap screws. On CL's C draw $\frac{1}{4}$-UNC $\times$ $\frac{3}{4}$ flathead cap screws with heads to the left. On CL D show a $\frac{1}{4}$-in. standard pipe thread. On CL's E show $\frac{1}{2}$-UNC $\times$ $1\frac{3}{4}$ semifinished hexagonal-head bolts. Use semifinished hexagonal nuts. Show visible fasteners on the end view.

VELA LV- Nuclear Detection Satellite in assembly stage before solar panels are applied. Innumerable dimensioned drawings are required for the production of finished products such as the satellite shown above. The specification of size added to the shape description provided by the views supplies the information needed to produce the component parts of the complete system.
(*Courtesy TRW Systems Group***)**

Size Description: Dimensions and Specifications

A: FUNDAMENTALS AND TECHNIQUES

16.1
Introduction. A detail drawing, in addition to giving the shape of a part, must furnish information such as the distances between surfaces, locations of holes, kind of finish, type of material, number required, and so forth. The expression of this information on a drawing by the use of lines, symbols, figures, and notes is known as *dimensioning*.

Intelligent dimensioning requires engineering judgment and a thorough knowledge of the practices of patternmaking, forging, and machining.

16.2
Theory of Dimensioning. Any part may be dimensioned easily and systematically by dividing it into simple geometric solids. Even complicated parts, when analyzed, usually are found to be composed principally of cylinders and prisms and, frequently, frustums of pyramids and cones. The dimensioning of an object may be accomplished by dimensioning each elemental form to indicate its size and relative location from a center line, base line, or finished surface. A machine drawing requires two types of dimensions: *size dimensions* and *location dimensions*.

16.3
Size Dimensions (Fig. 16.2). Size dimensions give the size of a piece, component part, hole, or slot.

Figure 16.1 should be carefully analyzed, as the placement of dimensions shown is applicable to the elemental parts of almost every piece.

The rule for placing the three principal dimensions (width, height, and depth) on the drawing of a prism or modification of a prism is as follows: *Give two dimensions on the principal view and one dimension on one of the other views.*

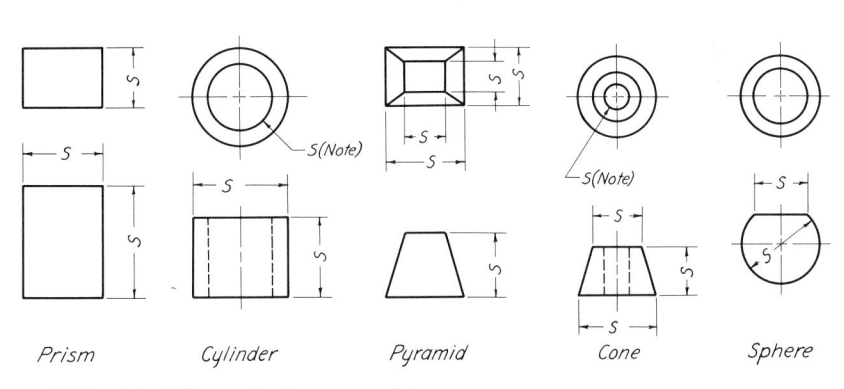

FIG. 16.1. Dimensioning geometric shapes.

353

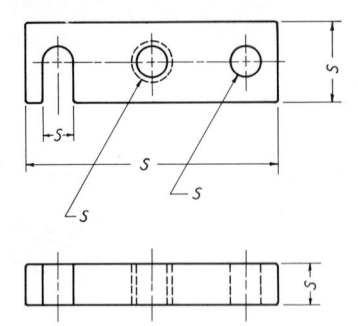

FIG. 16.2. Size dimensions.

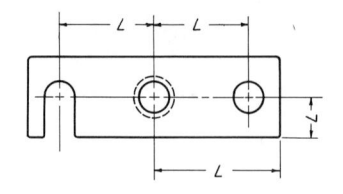

FIG. 16.3. Location dimensions.

The circular cylinder, which appears as a boss or shaft, requires only *the diameter and length, both of which are shown preferably on the rectangular view.* It is better practice to dimension a hole (negative cylinder) by giving the diameter and operation as a note on the contour view with a leader to the circle (Figs. 16.1 and 16.55).

Cones are dimensioned by giving *the diameter of the base and the altitude on the same view.* A taper is one example of a conical shape found on machine parts (Fig. 16.50).

Pyramids, which frequently form a part of a structure, are dimensioned by giving *two dimensions on the view showing the shape of the base.*

A sphere requires only the diameter.

16.4

Location Dimensions. Location dimensions fix the relationship of the component parts (projections, holes, slots, and other significant forms) of a piece or structure (Fig. 16.3). Particular care must be exercised in the selection and placing of location dimensions because on them depends the accuracy of the operations in making a piece and the proper mating of the piece with other parts. To select location dimensions intelligently, one must first determine the contact surfaces, finished surfaces, and center lines of the elementary geometric forms and, with the accuracy demanded and the method of production in mind, decide from what other surface or center line each should be located. Mating location dimensions must be given from the same center line or finished surface on both pieces.

Location dimensions may be from center to center, surface to center, or surface to surface (Fig. 16.4).

16.5

Procedure in Dimensioning. The theory of dimensioning may be applied in six steps, as follows:

1. Mentally divide the object into its component geometrical shapes.

2. Place the size dimensions on each form.

3. Select the locating center lines and surfaces after giving careful consideration to mating parts and to the processes of manufacture.

4. Place the location dimensions so that each geometrical form is located from a center line or finished surface.

5. Add the overall dimensions.

6. Complete the dimensioning by adding the necessary notes.

16.6

Placing Dimensions. Dimensions must be placed where they will be most easily understood—in the locations where the reader will expect to find them. They generally are attached to the view that shows the contour of the features to which they apply, and a majority of them usually will appear on the principal view (Fig. 16.14). Except in cases where special convenience and ease in reading are desired, or when a dimension would be so far from the form to which it referred that it might be misinterpreted, dimensions should be placed outside a view. They should appear directly on a view only when clarity demands.

L_1 – Center to Center
L_2 – Surface to Center
L_3 – Surface to Surface

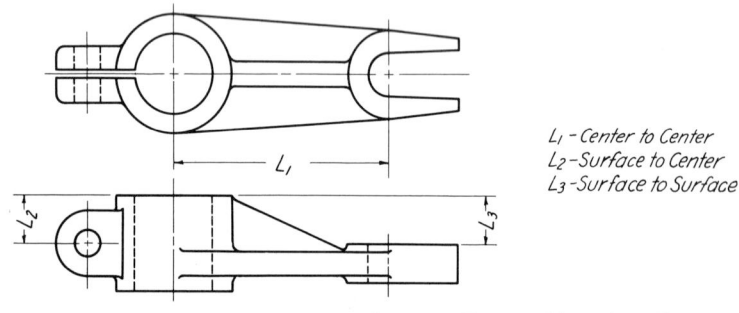

FIG. 16.4. Types of location dimensions.

All extension and dimension lines should be drawn before the arrowheads have been filled in or the dimensions, notes, and titles have been lettered. Placing dimension lines not less than ½ in. from the view and at least ⅜ in. from each other will provide spacing ample to satisfy the one rule to which there is no exception: *Never crowd dimensions*. If the location of a dimension forces a poor location on other dimensions, its shifting may allow all to be placed more advantageously without sacrificing clarity. Important location dimensions should be given where they will be conspicuous, even if a size dimension must be moved.

16.7

Dimensioning Practices. A generally recognized system of lines, symbols, figures, and notes is used to indicate size and location. Figure 16.5 illustrates dimensioning terms and notation.

A *dimension line* is a lightweight line that is terminated at each end by an arrowhead. A numerical value, given along the dimension line, specifies the number of units for the measurement that is indicated (Fig. 16.6). When the numerals are in a single line, the dimension line is broken near the center, as shown in (a) and (b). Under no circumstances should the line pass through the numerals. When the numerals are in two lines the dimension line may be drawn without a break and one line of numerals may be placed above the dimension line and the other below, as in (c).

Extension lines are light, continuous lines extending from a view to indicate the extent of a measurement given by a dimension line that is located outside a view. They start 1/16 in. from the view and extend ⅛ in. beyond the dimension line (Fig. 16.5).

Arrowheads are drawn for each dimension line, before the figures are lettered. They are made with the same pen or pencil used for the lettering. The size of an arrowhead, although it may vary with the size of a drawing, should be uniform on any one drawing. To have the proper proportions, the length of an arrowhead must be approximately three times its spread (AN Standard). This length for average work is usually ⅛ in. Figure 16.7 shows enlarged drawings of arrowheads of correct proportions. Although many draftsmen draw an arrowhead with one stroke, the beginner will get better results by using two slightly concave strokes drawn toward the point (a) or, as shown in (b), one stroke drawn to the point and one away from it.

A *leader* or *pointer* is a light, continuous line (terminated by an arrowhead) that extends from a note to the feature of a piece to which the note applies (Fig. 16.5). It should be made with a straightedge and should not be curved or made freehand.

A leader pointing to a curve should be radial, and the first ⅛ in. of it should be in a line with the note (Fig. 16.5).

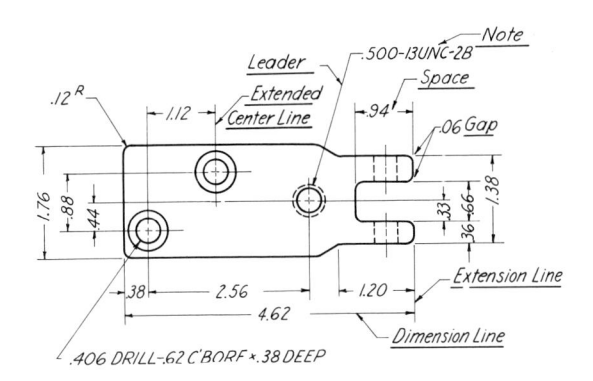

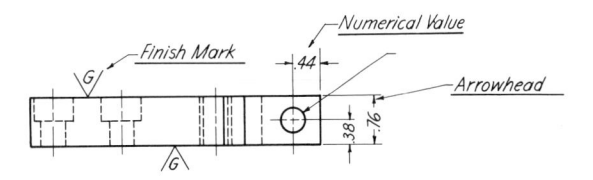

FIG. 16.5. Terms and dimensioning notation.

Break line for numeral and fraction
(a) Fractional Dimension

Break dimension lines for values
(b) Decimal Dimensions

Numerals in two lines may be given without a break in the dimension line
(c) Decimal Dimensions – Alternate Treatment

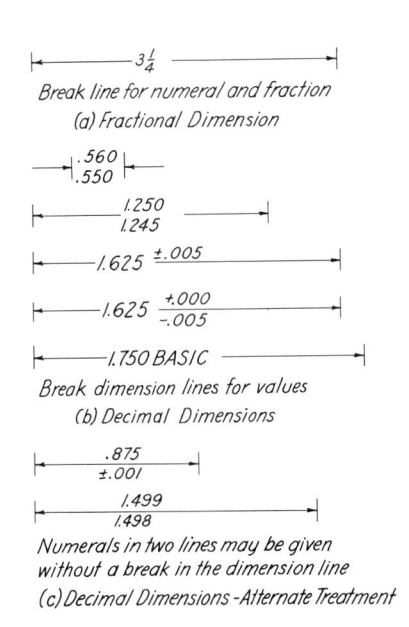

FIG. 16.6. A dimension line.

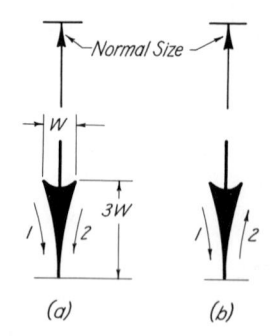

FIG. 16.7. Formation of arrowheads.

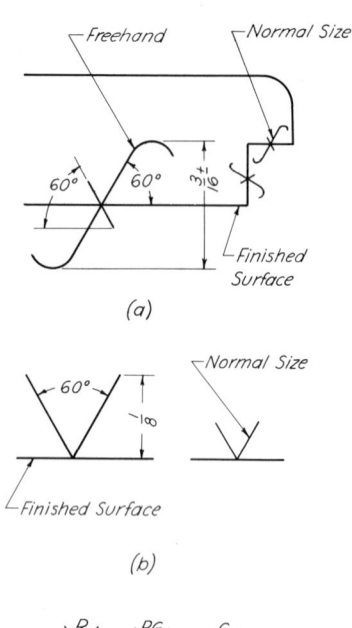

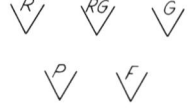

FIG. 16.8. Finish marks.

R = Rough Finish
RG = Rough Grind
G = Grind
P = Polish
F = File

Finish marks indicate the particular surfaces of a rough casting or forging that are to be machined or "finished." They are placed in all views, across the visible or invisible lines that are the edge views of surfaces to be machined (Fig. 16.8).

The modified italic *f*, shown in Fig. 16.8(*a*), is the form of finish mark that is preferred for general use. The student will find that careful adherence to the dimensions shown will improve the appearance of the *f* marks on his drawing.

Figure 16.8(*b*) shows the 60° V-style of mark with its point touching the line view of the surface to be machined. In commercial practice a code letter oftentimes is used to indicate the type of machining required. The code letter or letters are placed in the V, as shown in (*c*).

It is not necessary to show finish marks on holes. They are also omitted, and a title note, "finish all over," is substituted, if the piece is to be completely machined. Finish marks are not required when limit dimensions are used.

Dimension figures should be lettered either horizontally or vertically with the whole numbers equal in height to the capital letters in the notes and guidelines and slope lines must be used. The numerals must be legible; otherwise, they might be misinterpreted in the shop and cause errors, which would be embarrassing to the draftsman.

16.8
Fractional Dimensioning. For ordinary work, where accuracy is relatively unimportant, shopmen work to nominal dimensions given as common fractions of an inch, such as $\frac{1}{2}$, $\frac{1}{4}$, $\frac{1}{8}$, $\frac{1}{16}$, $\frac{1}{32}$, and $\frac{1}{64}$. When dimensions are given in this way, many large corporations specify the required accuracy through a note on the drawing that reads as follows: *Permissible variations on common fraction dimensions to machined surfaces to be ±.010 unless otherwise specified.* It should be understood that the allowable variations will differ among manufacturing concerns because of the varying degree of accuracy required for different types of work.

16.9
Decimal System. Since the use of the decimal system for expressing dimensional values has made rapid gains in American industry and is now accepted in the aircraft and automotive fields, many of the examples in this chapter will show decimal dimensions (Sec. 3.19). At present, the fractional system, which dominated the whole of American industry until the Ford Motor Company adopted the decimal-inch some 40 years ago, is still used widely in those fields that are not under the direct influence of the automotive and aircraft companies. How long the present coexistence of the two systems will last cannot be foretold. It could be only a few years or it could be many years before the decimal system completely replaces the fractional system.

However, this need not be of great concern to the student, for he should be primarily interested in the selection and placement of dimensions. At a later time he will find it easy to use either the fractional or decimal systems as required in his field of employment. To assist one to use either system, a Standard Conversion Table has been provided in the Appendix (Table 1).

In Fig. 16.9 a drawing is shown that illustrates decimal dimensioning.

The recommendation for decimal dimensioning, as given in ANS Y14.5–1966, reads as follows:

> Optionally, decimals may be used to replace common fractions altogether. The elimination of common fractions simplifies computations; decimals can be added, subtracted, multiplied or divided more easily than fractions.... The following conventions are generally observed by those who have adopted the

decimal system. However, the advantages of using decimals can be gained, whether or not all of these rules are followed.

(*a*) Two-place decimals are used for dimensions where tolerance limits of ±.01 or more can be allowed (Fig. 16.9).

(*b*) Decimals to three or more places must be used for tolerance limits less than ±.010 [see Fig. 16.6(*b*) and (*c*)].

(*c*) The second decimal place in a two-place decimal should preferably be an even digit (.02, .04, .06 are preferred to .01, .03, .05, etc.), so that when divided by two, as in obtaining a radius from a diameter, the result will remain a two-place decimal. Odd two-place decimals are used where necessary for design reasons; as, to provide clearance, strength, smooth curves, etc.

(*d*) Common fractions may be used to indicate standard nominal sizes of materials, punched holes, drilled holes, threads, keyways and other features produced by tools that are so designated.

Examples:

¼-20 UNC-2A; ⁵⁄₁₆ Drill; Stock ⅝ × ⅞.

(*e*) Where it is desired to use decimals exclusively, nominal sizes of materials, threads and other features produced by commercial tools may be expressed in decimal equivalents of commercial sizes; as, .625 HEX.

16.10
Use of the Metric System. Since the metric system has worldwide acceptance and has been legalized for use in this country (approved by act of Congress in 1866), engineers and draftsmen in the United States will find it advantageous to be able to interpret and quite possibly prepare detail drawings using metric dimensioning. At present, there are persons who argue strongly that American industry must change over to this system if the United States is to retain leadership in world trade. In any case, metric dimensioning is appearing more frequently

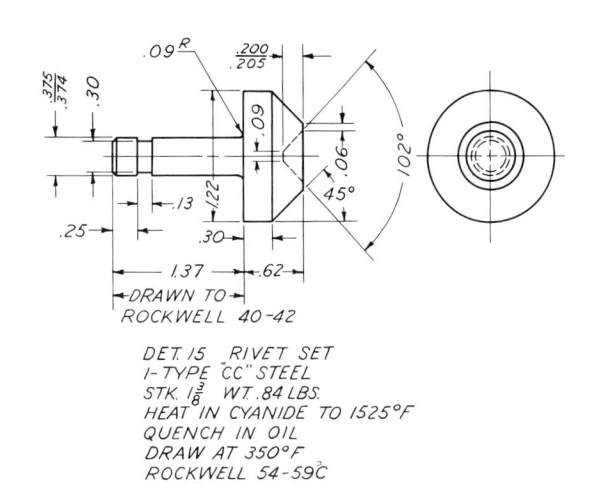

FIG. 16.9. Decimal dimensioning. (*Courtesy Ford Motor Co.*)

than in the past on drawings made in the United States (an example has been shown in Fig. 16.10). The unit of measurement is the millimeter (mm) and, since this fact is generally known by all persons using the system, no indicating marks are needed.

Under the metric system, drawings are prepared to scales based on divisions of 10, such as 1 to 2, 1 to 5, 1 to 10, and so forth. A millimeter is one-thousandth part of a meter, which our government has established as being 39.37 in. in length.

B: GENERAL DIMENSIONING PRACTICES

16.11
Selection and Placement of Dimensions and Notes. The reasonable application of the selected dimensioning practices that follow should enable a student to dimension acceptably. The practices in boldface type should never be violated. In fact, these have been so definitely established by practice that they might be called rules.

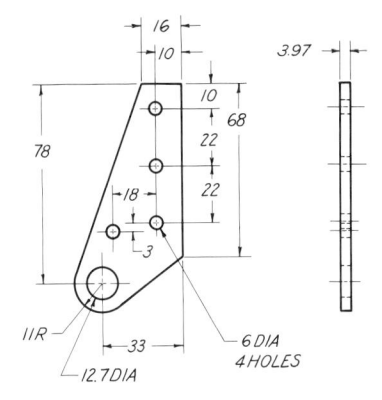

FIG. 16.10. Metric dimensioning (dimensions are in millimeters).

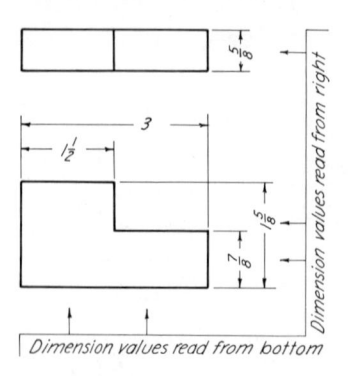

FIG. 16.11. Reading dimensions aligned.

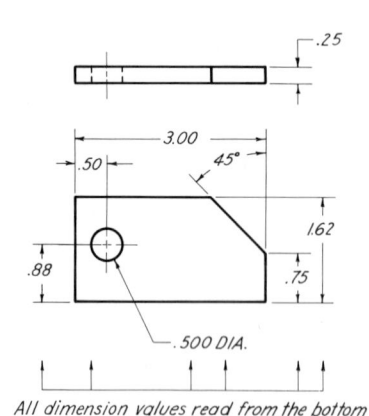

FIG. 16.12. Reading dimensions—unidirectional.

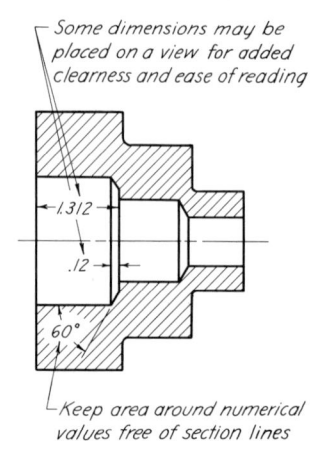

FIG. 16.13. Dimensions on the view.

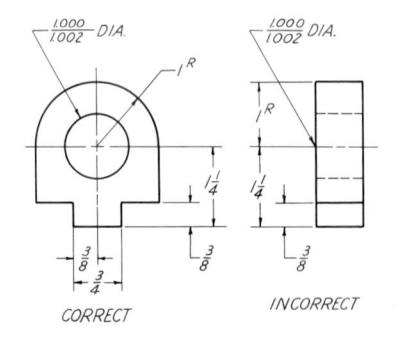

FIG. 16.14. Contour principle of dimensioning.

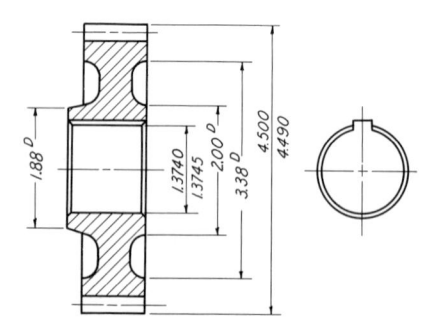

FIG. 16.15. Parallel dimensions.

1. Place dimensions using either of two recognized methods—aligned or unidirectional.

a. *Aligned method.* Place the numerals for the dimension values so that they are readable from the bottom and right side of the drawing. An aligned expression is placed along and in the direction of the dimension line (Fig. 16.11). Make the values for oblique dimensions readable from the directions shown in Fig. 16.31.

b. *Unidirectional method.* Place the numerals for the dimension values so that they can be read from the bottom of the drawing (see Fig. 16.12). The fraction bar for a common fraction should be parallel to the bottom of the drawing (Fig. 16.14).

2. Place dimensions outside a view, unless they will be more easily and quickly understood if shown on the view (Figs. 16.12 and 16.13).

3. Place dimensions between views unless the rules, such as the contour rule, the rule against crowding, and so forth, prevent their being so placed.

4. Do not use an object line or a center line as a dimension line.

5. Locate dimension lines so that they will not cross extension lines.

6. If possible, avoid crossing two dimension lines.

7. A center line may be extended to serve as an extension line (Fig. 16.14).

8. Keep parallel dimensions equally spaced (usually ⅜ in. apart) and the figures staggered (Fig. 16.15).

9. Always give locating dimensions to the centers of circles that represent holes, cylindrical projections, or bosses (Figs. 16.5 and 16.14).

10. If possible, attach the location dimensions for holes to the view on which they appear as circles (Fig. 16.16).

11. Group related dimensions on the

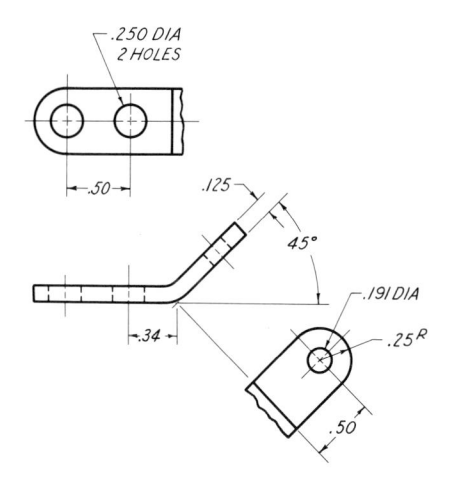

CHAP. 16 / SIZE DESCRIPTION: DIMENSIONS AND SPECIFICATIONS 359

FIG. 16.16. Dimensioning an angle bracket.

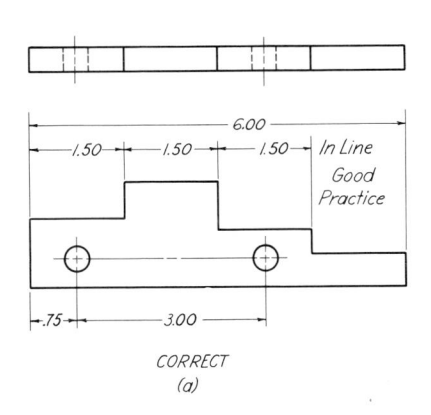

FIG. 16.17. Consecutive dimensions.

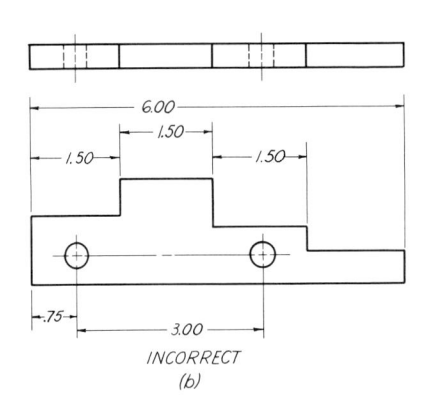

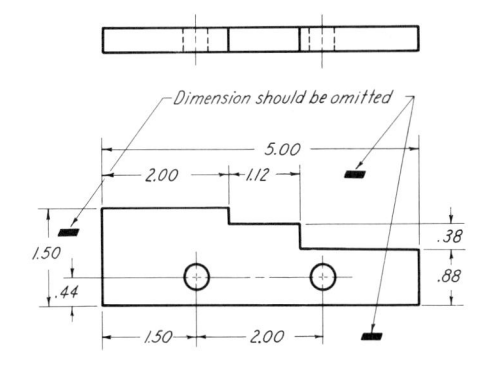

FIG. 16.18. Omit unnecessary dimensions.

view showing the contour of a feature (Fig. 16.14).

12. Arrange a series of dimensions in a continuous line (Fig. 16.17).

13. Dimension from a finished surface, center line, or base line that can be readily established (Figs. 16.38 and 16.51).

14. Stagger the figures in a series of parallel dimension lines to allow sufficient space for the figures and to prevent confusion (Fig. 16.15).

15. Place longer dimensions outside shorter ones so that extension lines will not cross dimension lines.

16. Give three overall dimensions located outside any other dimensions (unless the piece has cylindrical ends—see 42 and Fig. 16.42).

17. When an overall is given, one intermediate distance should be omitted unless noted (REF) as being given for reference (Figs. 16.18 and 16.19).

18. Do not repeat a dimension. One of the duplicated dimensions may be missed if a change is made. Give only those dimensions that are necessary to produce or inspect the part.

19. Make decimal points of a sufficient size so that dimensions cannot be misread.

20. **When dimension figures appear on a sectional view, show them in a small uncrosshatched portion so that they may be easily read.** This may be accomplished by doing the section lining after the dimensioning has been completed (Fig. 16.20).

21. When an arc is used as a dimension

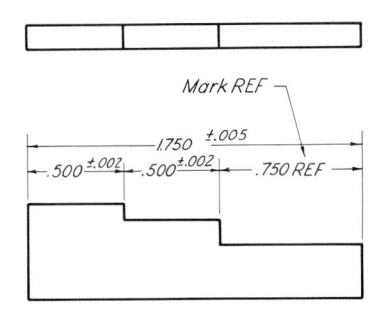

FIG. 16.19. Mark dimensions REF, if given for reference.

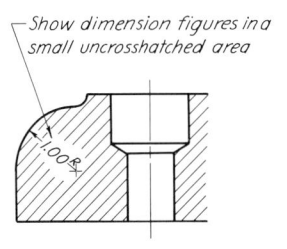

FIG. 16.20. Dimension figures on a section view.

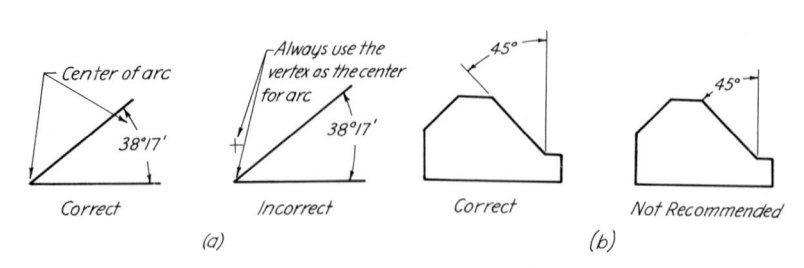

FIG. 16.21. To dimension an angle.

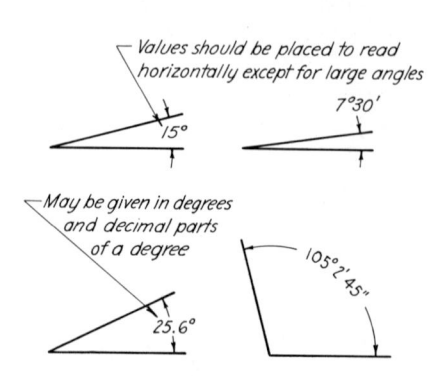

FIG. 16.22. Angular dimensions.

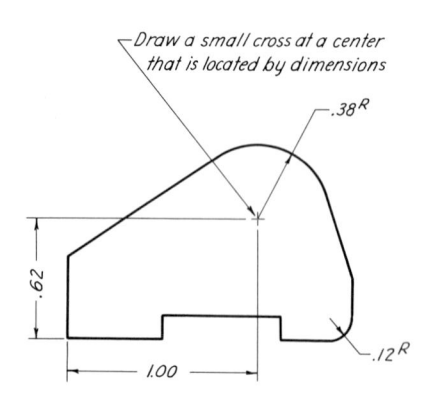

FIG. 16.23. Dimensioning a circular arc.

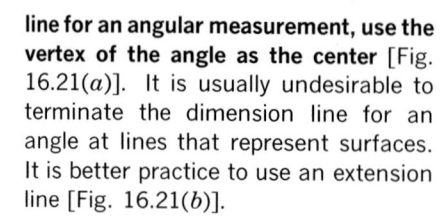

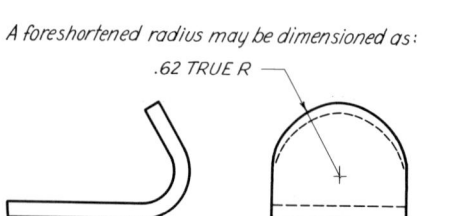

FIG. 16.24. To dimension a circular arc—true R.*

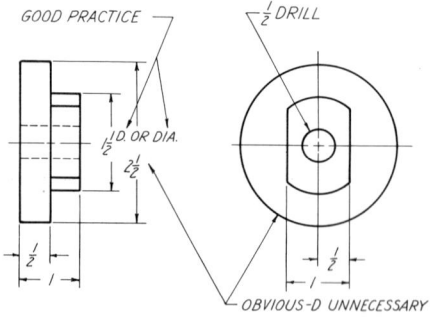

FIG. 16.25. Dimensioning a cylindrical piece.

line for an angular measurement, use the vertex of the angle as the center [Fig. 16.21(a)]. It is usually undesirable to terminate the dimension line for an angle at lines that represent surfaces. It is better practice to use an extension line [Fig. 16.21(b)].

22. Place the figures of angular dimensions so they will read from the bottom of a drawing, except in the case of large angles (Fig. 16.22).

23. Dimension an arc by giving its radius followed by the abbreviation R, and indicate the center with a small cross. [Locate the center by dimensions. (Fig. 16.23).]

24. TRUE R is added after the radius value, where the radius is dimensioned in a view that does not show the true shape of the arc (Fig. 16.24).

25. **Show the diameter of a circle, never the radius.** If it is not clear that the dimension is a diameter, the figures should be followed by the abbreviation D or DIA (Figs. 16.25 and 16.26). Often this will allow the elimination of one view.

26. When dimensioning a portion of a sphere with a radius the term SPHER R is added (Fig. 16.27).

27. Letter all notes horizontally (Fig. 16.51).

28. **Make dimensioning complete, so that it will not be necessary for a workman to add or subtract to obtain a desired dimension or to scale the drawing.**

29. Give the diameter of a circular hole, never the radius, because all hole-forming tools are specified by diameter. If the hole does not go through the piece, the depth may be given as a note (Fig. 16.28).

30. Never crowd dimensions into small spaces. Use the practical methods suggested in Fig. 16.29.

*ANS(USAS) Y14.5–1966.

CHAP. 16 / SIZE DESCRIPTION: DIMENSIONS AND SPECIFICATIONS   **361**

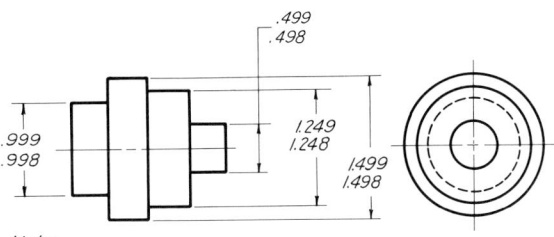

FIG. 16.26. Dimensioning machined cylinders.*

Note: Although it is better practice to use a minimum of two views, a cylindrical part may be completely described in one view (no end view) by using the abbreviation DIA with the dimension.

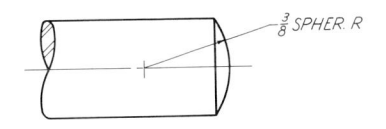

FIG. 16.27. Dimensioning a piece with a spherical end.

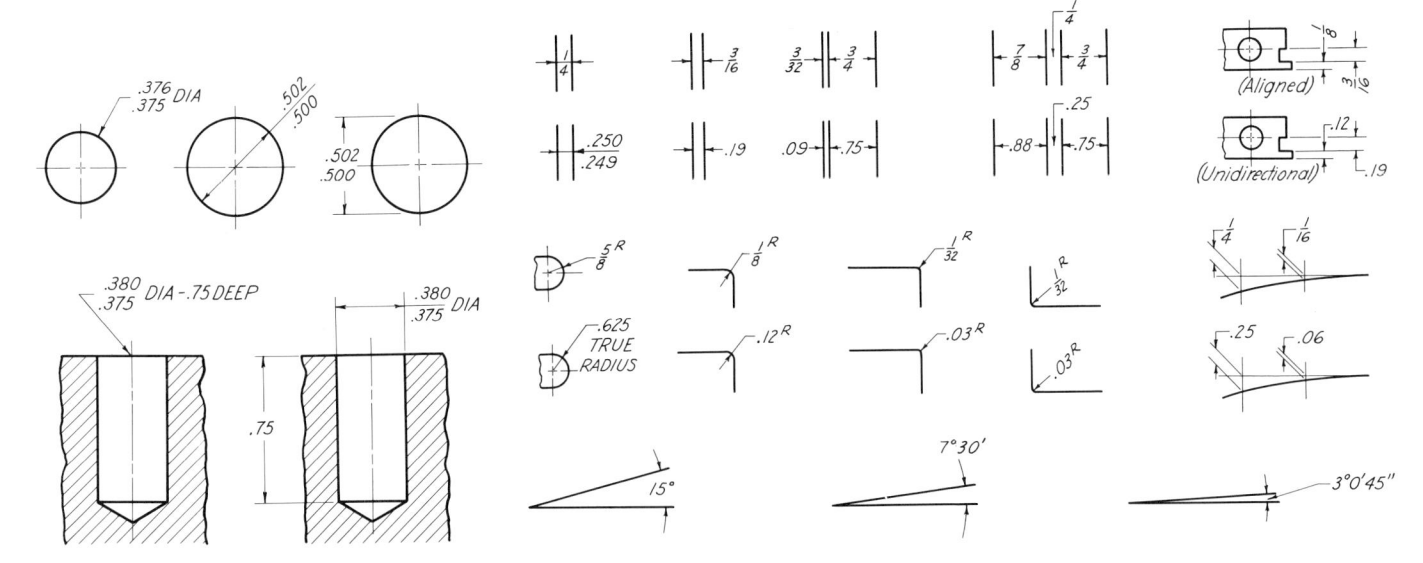

FIG. 16.28. Dimensioning holes.*

FIG. 16.29. Dimensioning in limited spaces.

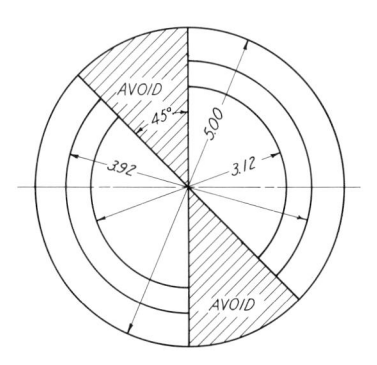

FIG. 16.30. Areas to avoid.

31. Avoid placing inclined dimensions in the shaded areas shown in Fig. 16.30. Place them so that they may be conveniently read from the right side of the drawing. If this is not desirable, make the figures read from the left in the direction of the dimension line [Fig. 16.31(a)]. The unidirectional method is shown in (b).

32. Omit superfluous dimensions. Do not supply dimensional information for the same feature in two different ways.

33. Give dimensions up to 72 in. in inches, except on structural and architectural drawings (Fig. 16.32). Omit the inch marks when all dimensions are in inches.

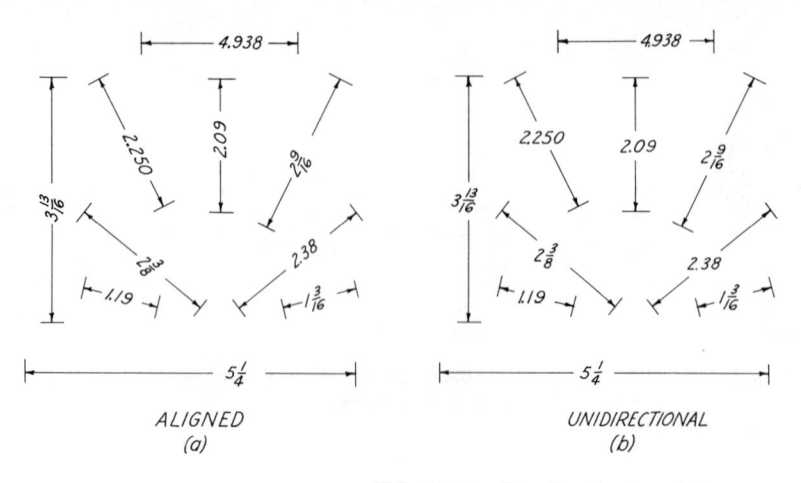

FIG. 16.31. Reading horizontal, vertical, and oblique dimensions.

ALIGNED (a)

UNIDIRECTIONAL (b)

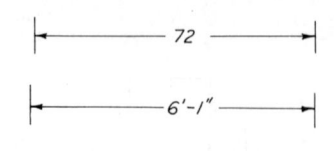

FIG. 16.32. Dimension values.

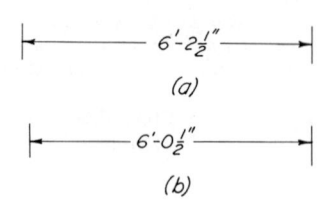

FIG. 16.33. Feet and inches.

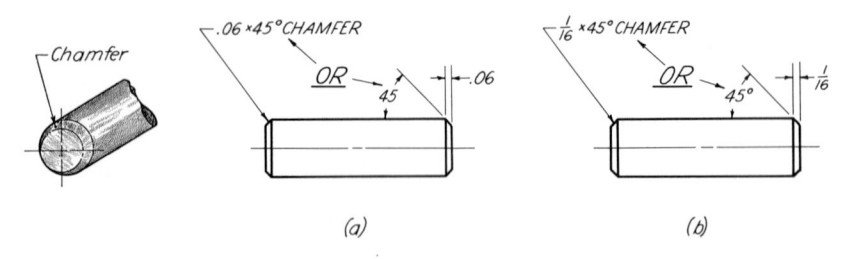

FIG. 16.34. Dimensioning a chamfer.

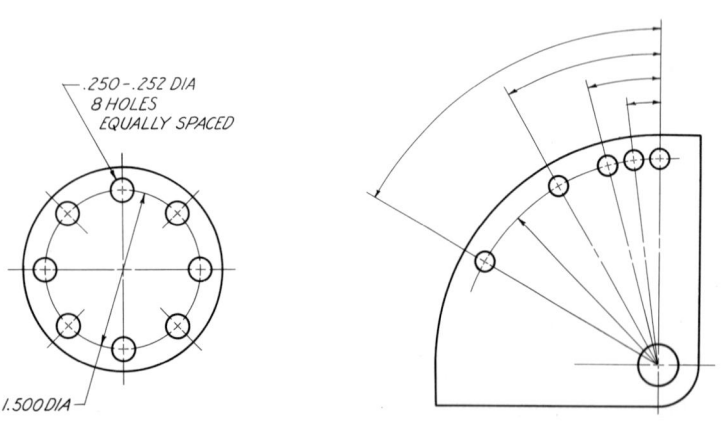

FIG. 16.35. Equally spaced holes.*

FIG. 16.36. Locating holes on a circle by polar coordinates.*

34. Show dimensions in feet and inches as illustrated in Fig. 16.33. Note that the use of the hyphen in (a) and (b) and the cipher in (b) eliminates any chance of uncertainty and misinterpretation.

35. If feasible, design a piece and its elemental parts to such dimensions as ⅜, ½, ⅝, or .40 and .50 in. Avoid such fractions as $^{17}/_{32}$ and $^{19}/_{64}$ and such decimals as .19 and .53.

36. Dimension a chamfer by giving the angle and length as shown in Fig. 16.34. For a 45° angle only, it is permissible to give the needed information as a note. The word chamfer may be omitted in the note form.

37. Equally spaced holes in a circular flange may be dimensioned by giving the diameter of the bolt circle, across the circular center line, and the size and number of holes, in a note (Fig. 16.35).

38. When holes are unequally spaced on a circular center line, give the angles as illustrated in Fig. 16.36.

*ANS(USAS) Y14.5-1966.

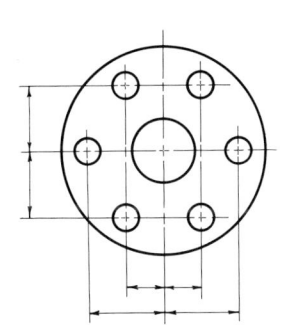

FIG. 16.37. Accurate location dimensioning of holes.*

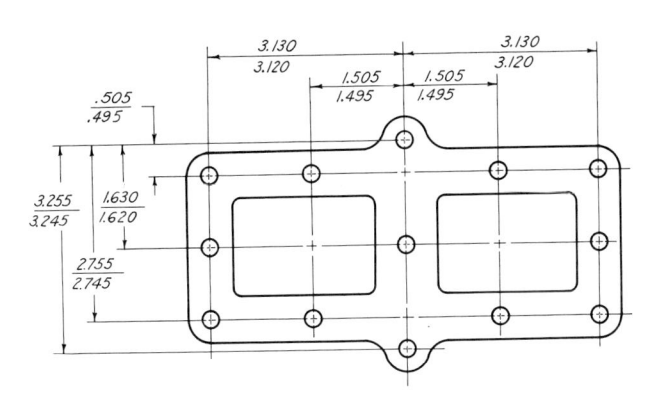

FIG. 16.38. Location dimensioning of holes.

39. Holes that must be accurately located should have their location established by the coordinate method. Holes arranged in a circle may be located as shown in Fig. 16.37 rather than through the use of angular measurements. Figure 16.38 shows the application of the coordinate method to the location of holes arranged in a general rectangular form. The method with all dimensions referred to datum lines is sometimes called *base-line dimensioning*.

40. Dimension a curved line by giving offsets or radii.
a. A noncircular curve may be dimensioned by the coordinate method illustrated in Fig. 16.39. Offset measurements are given from datum lines.
b. A curved line, which is composed of circular arcs, should be dimensioned by giving the radii and locations of either the centers or points of tangency (Figs. 16.40 and 16.41).

41. Show an offset dimension line for an arc having an inaccessible center (Fig. 16.41). Locate with true dimensions the point placed in a convenient location that represents the true center.

*ANS(USAS) Y14.5-1966.

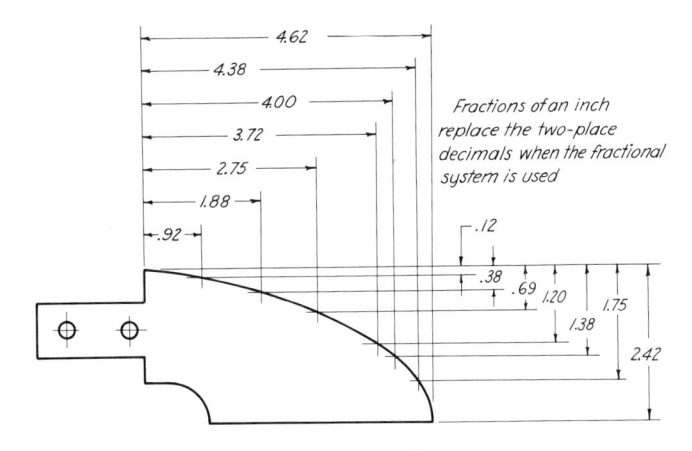

FIG. 16.39. Dimensioning curves by offsets.

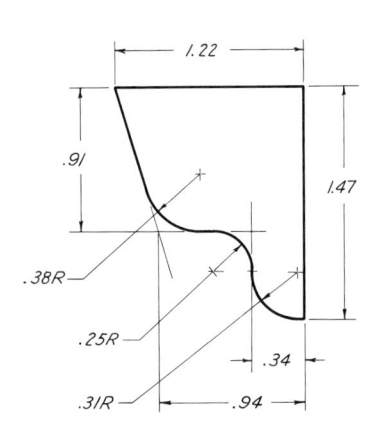

FIG. 16.40. Dimensioning curves consisting of circular arcs.*

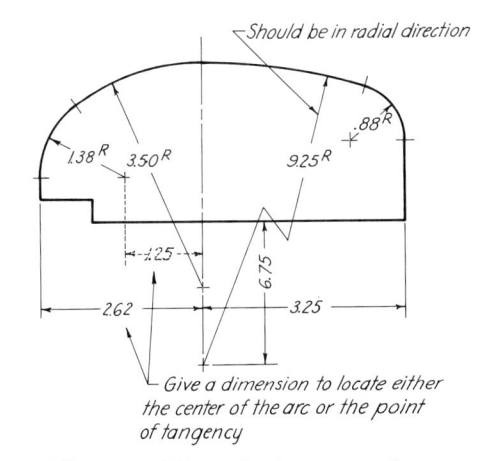

FIG. 16.41. Dimensioning curves by radii.

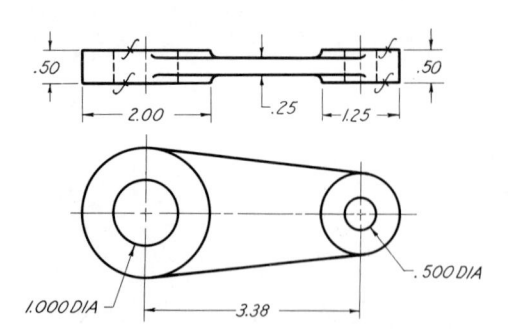

FIG. 16.42. Dimensioning a part with cylindrical ends—link.

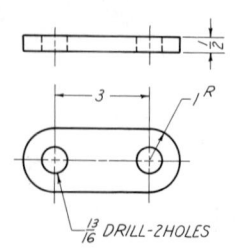

FIG. 16.43. Link with rounded ends.

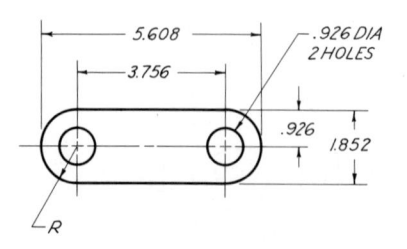

FIG. 16.44. Dimensioning a part with rounded ends.*

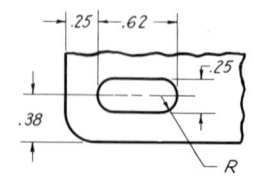

FIG. 16.45. Dimensioning a slot.

42. Dimension, as required by the method of production, a piece with cylindrical ends. Give the diameters and center-to-center distance (Fig. 16.42). No overall is required.

43. The method to be used for dimensioning a piece with rounded ends is determined by the degree of accuracy required and the method of production (Figs. 16.43–16.45).

a. It has been customary to give the radii and center-to-center distance for parts and contours that would be laid out and/or machined using centers and radii. A link (Fig. 16.43) or a pad with a slot is dimensioned in this manner to satisfy the requirements of the patternmaker and machinist. An overall dimension is not needed.

b. Overall dimensions are recommended for parts having rounded ends when considerable accuracy is required.

The radius is indicated but is not dimensioned when the ends are fully rounded. In Fig. 16.44, the center-to-center hole distance has been given because the hole location is critical.

c. Slots are dimensioned by giving length and width dimensions. They are located by dimensions given to their longitudinal center line and to either one end or a center line (Fig. 16.45).

d. When the location of a hole is more critical than the location of a radius from the same center, the radius and the hole should be dimensioned separately (Fig. 16.46).

44. A keyway on a shaft or hub should be dimensioned as shown in Fig. 16.47. Woodruff keyslots are dimensioned as shown in (b).

* ANS(ASA) Y14.5–1957.
** ANS(USAS) Y14.5–1966.

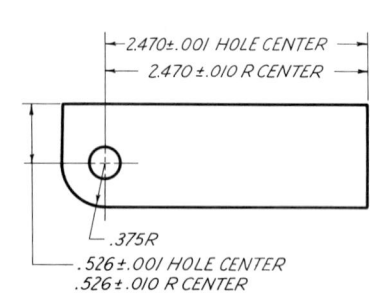

FIG. 16.46. Dimensioning a piece with a hole and rounded end.**

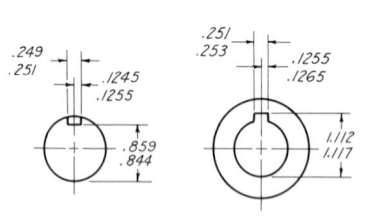

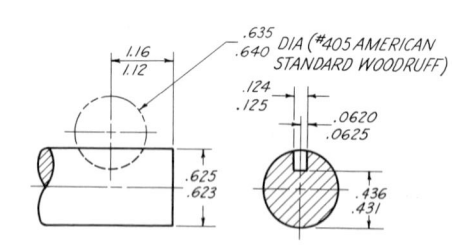

FIG. 16.47. Dimensioning keyways and keyslots.**

(a) Keyways For Stock Keys

(b) Woodruff Keyslots

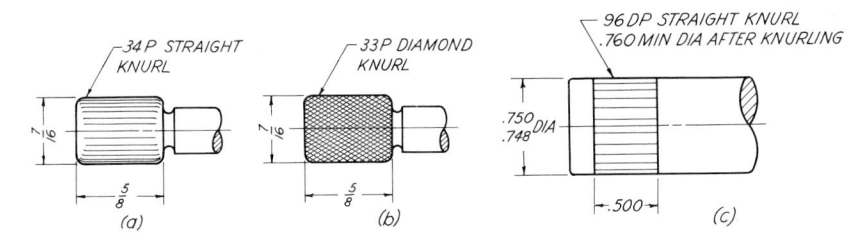

FIG. 16.48. Dimensioning knurls.

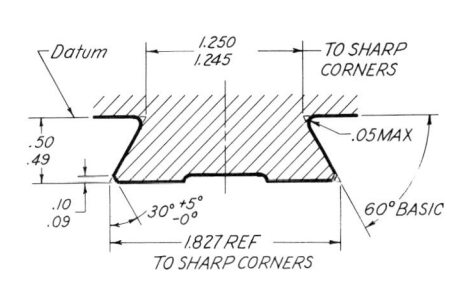

45. When knurls are to provide a rough surface for better grip, it is necessary to specify the pitch and kind of knurl, as shown in Fig. 16.48(a) and (b). When specifying knurling for a press fit, it is best practice to give the diameter before knurling with a tolerance and include the minimum diameter after knurling in the note that gives the pitch and type of knurl, as shown in (c).

46. Snug-fitting dovetailed parts should be dimensioned with tolerances as shown in Fig. 16.49. Dimensions are given to sharp corners. Flats may be substituted for rounded corners if desired.

47. Dimension standard and special tapers as illustrated in Fig. 16.50. Standard tapers require one diameter, the length, and a note specifying the taper by number. The usual practice is to give the diameter at the large end.

Special conical tapers may be dimensioned in different ways, as illustrated in (b), (c), and (d). The recommendation given in ANS (ASA) Y14.5–1957 reads as follows:

Conical tapers. The following dimensions may be given in different combinations, to specify the size and form of tapered conical surfaces:
(a) the diameter at each end of the taper;
(b) the length of the taper;
(c) the diameter at a selected cross-sectional plane; this plane may or may not be within the length of the tapered piece;
(d) the distance locating a cross-sectional plane at which a diameter is specified;
(e) the rate of taper;
(f) the included angle.

The dimensioning of noncritical tapers is shown in Fig. 16.50(b) and (c).

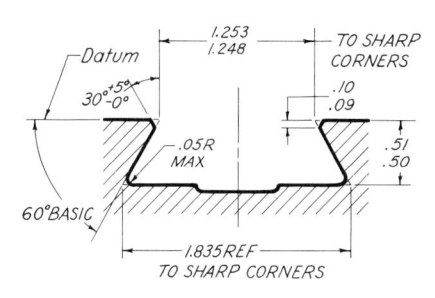

FIG. 16.49. Dimensioning a dovetail slot and tongue.*

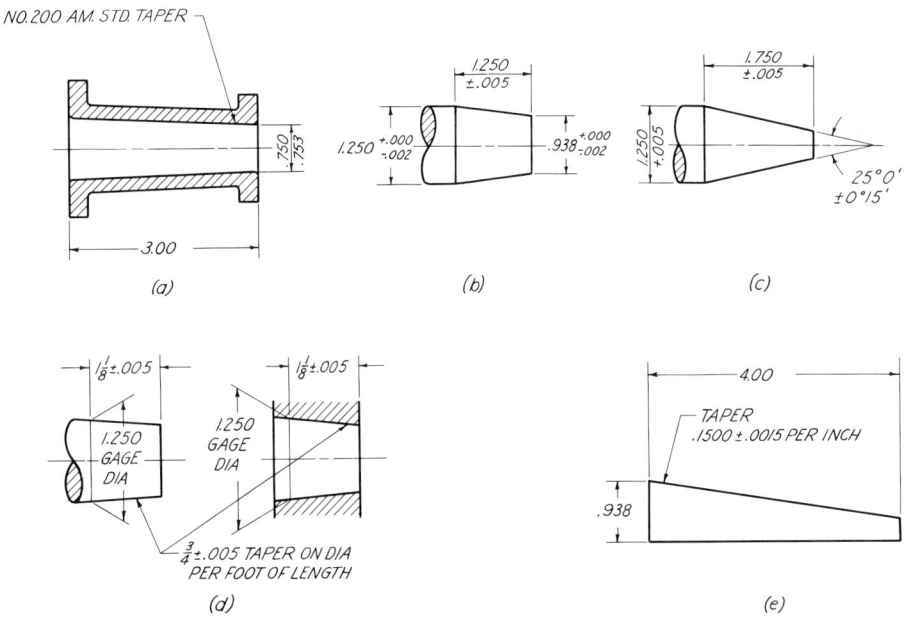

FIG. 16.50. Dimensioning tapers.

*ANS(ASA) Y14.5–1957.

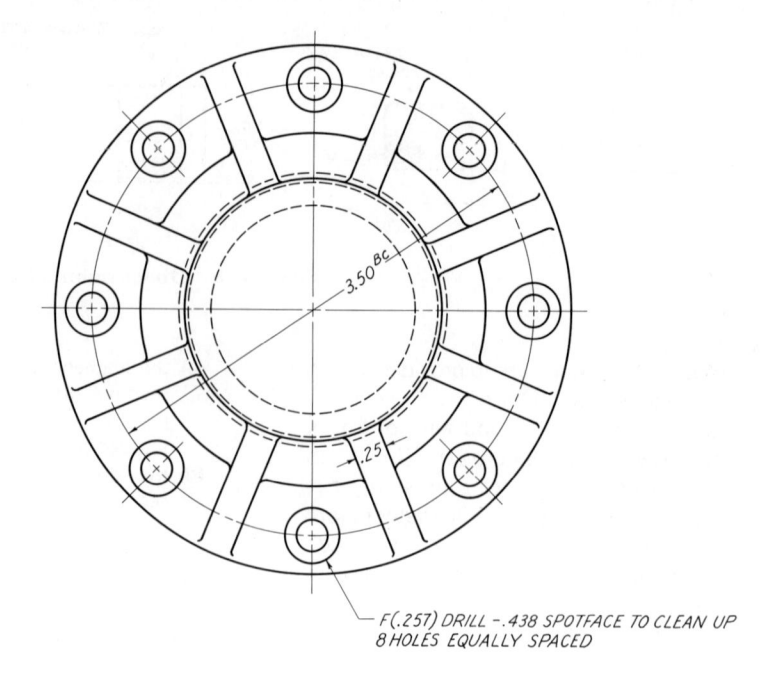

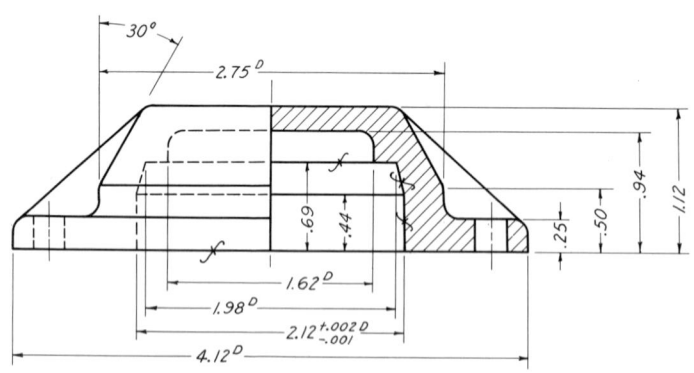

FIG. 16.51. Dimensioning a half section.

The dimensions and notes given in (d) are considered adequate for tapers that engage one another permanently or intermittently.

Flat tapers may be dimensioned as shown in (e).

When given in a note, taper may be specified either in inches per foot or inches per inch [(d) and (e)].

48. A half section may be dimensioned through the use of hidden lines on the external portion of the view (Fig. 16.51).

49. The fact that a dimension is out of scale may be indicated by a wavy line placed underneath the dimension value (Fig. 16.52).

50. In sheet-metal work, mold lines are used in dimensioning instead of the centers of the arcs (see Fig. 16.53). A mold line (construction line) is the line at the intersection of the plane surfaces adjoining a bend.

16.12
Dimensions from Datum. When it is necessary to locate the holes and surfaces of a part with a considerable degree of accuracy, it is the usual practice to specify their position by dimensions given from a datum (Fig. 16.54) in order to avoid cumulative tolerances. By this method the different features of a part are located with respect to carefully selected datums and not with respect to each other (Fig. 16.38). Lines and surfaces that are selected to serve as datums must be easily recognizable and accessible during production. Corresponding datum points, lines, or surfaces must be used as datums on mating parts.

16.13
Notes (Fig. 16.55). The use of properly composed notes often adds clarity to the presentation of dimensional information involving specific operations. Notes also are used to convey supplementary instructions about the kind of material, kind of fit, degree of finish, and so forth. Brevity in form is desirable for notes of general information or specific instruction. In the case of threaded parts one should use the terminology recommended by ANSI for the American–British Unified thread. See Chapter 15.

*ANS(ASA) Y14.5–1957.

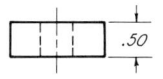

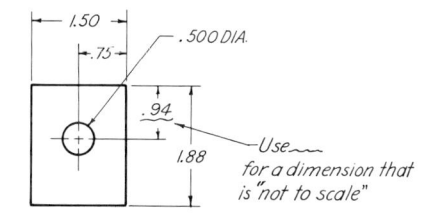

FIG. 16.52. Dimension out of scale.

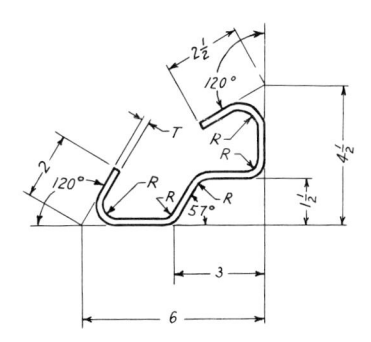

FIG. 16.53. Profile dimensioning.

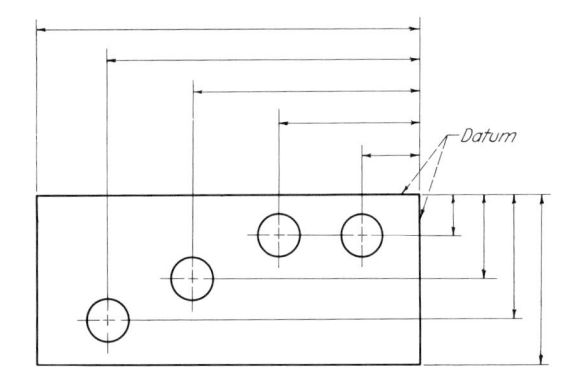

FIG. 16.54. Dimensions from datum lines.*

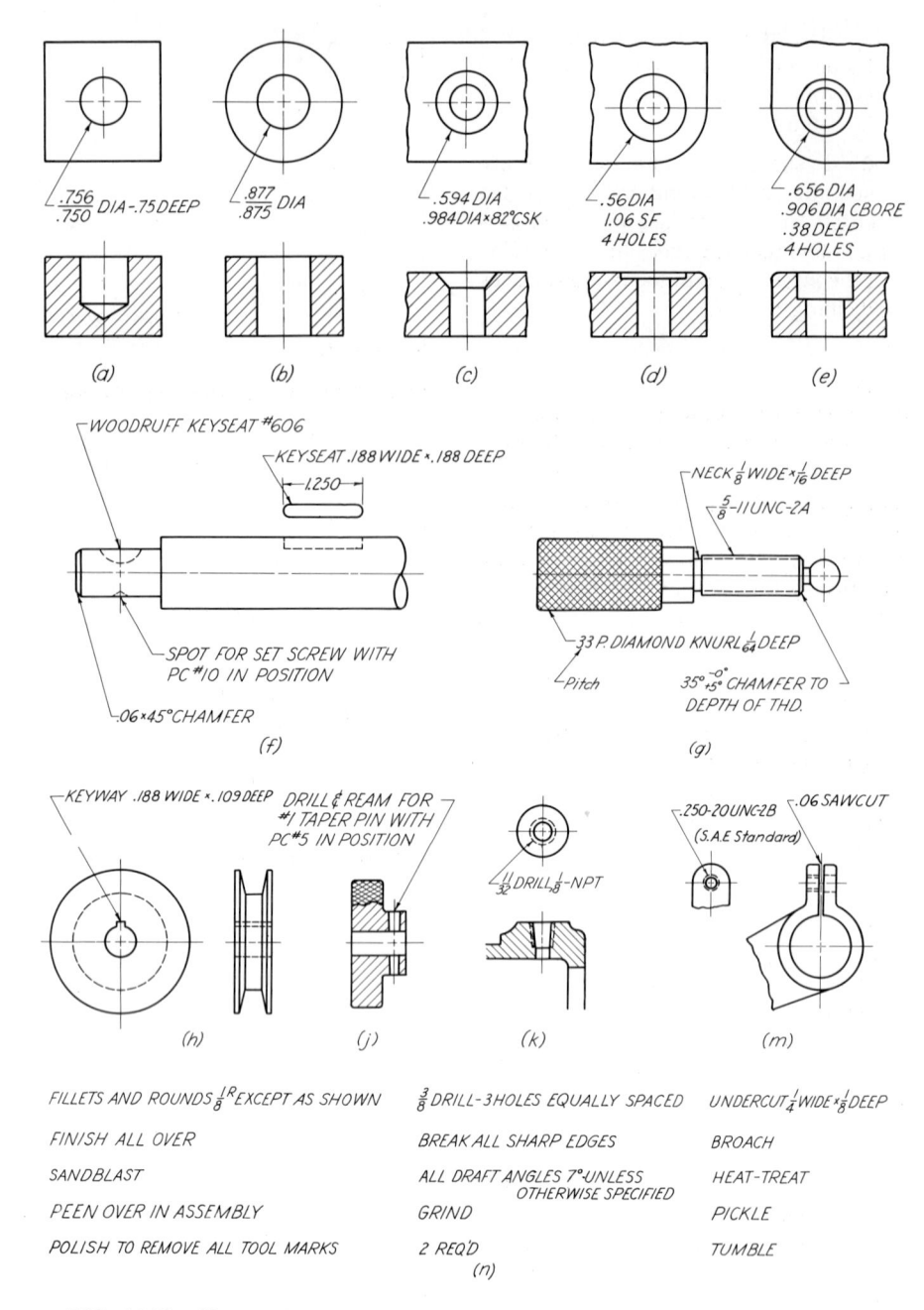

FIG. 16.55. Shop notes.

C: LIMIT DIMENSIONING AND GEOMETRIC TOLERANCING

16.14

Limit Dimensions. Present-day competitive manufacturing requires quantity production and interchangeability for many closely mating parts. The production of each of these mating parts to an exact decimal dimension, although theoretically possible, is economically unfeasible, since the cost of a part rapidly increases as an absolute correct size is approached. For this reason, the commercial draftsman specifies an allowable error (tolerance) between decimal limits (Fig. 16.56). The determination of these limits depends on the accuracy and clearance required for the moving parts to function satisfactorily in the machine. Although manufacturing experience is often used to determine the proper limits for the parts of a mechanism, it is better and safer practice to adhere to the fits recommended by the American National Standards Institute in ANS(USAS) B4.1-1967. This standard applies to fits between plain cylindrical parts. Recommendations are made for preferred sizes, allowances, tolerances, and fits for use where applicable. Up to a diameter of 20 in. the standard is in accordance with ABC (American-British-Canadian) conference agreements.

There are many factors that a designer must take into consideration when selecting fits for a particular application. These factors might be the bearing load, speed, lubrication, materials, and length of engagement. Frequently temperature and humidity must be taken into account. Considerable practical experience is necessary to make a selection of fits or to make the subsequent adjustments that might be needed to satisfy critical functional requirements. In addition, manufacturing economy must never be overlooked.

Those interested in the selection of fits should consult texts on machine design and technical publications, for coverage of this phase of the dimensioning of cylindrical parts is not within the scope of this book. However, since it is desirable to be able to determine limits of size following the selection of a fit, attention in this section will be directed to the use of Table 26 (Appendix). Whenever the fit to be used for a particular application has not been specified in the instructions for a problem or has not been given on the drawing, the student should consult his instructor after a tentative choice has been made based on the brief descriptions of fits as given in this section.

To compute limit dimensions it is necessary to understand the following associated terms.*

Nominal size. The nominal size is the designation which is used for the purpose of general identification.

---

*Extracted from *American National Standard Preferred Limits and Fits for Cylindrical Parts* [ANS(USAS) B4.1-1967] with permission of the publisher, The American Society of Mechanical Engineers, 345 East 47th St., New York, N.Y. 10017.

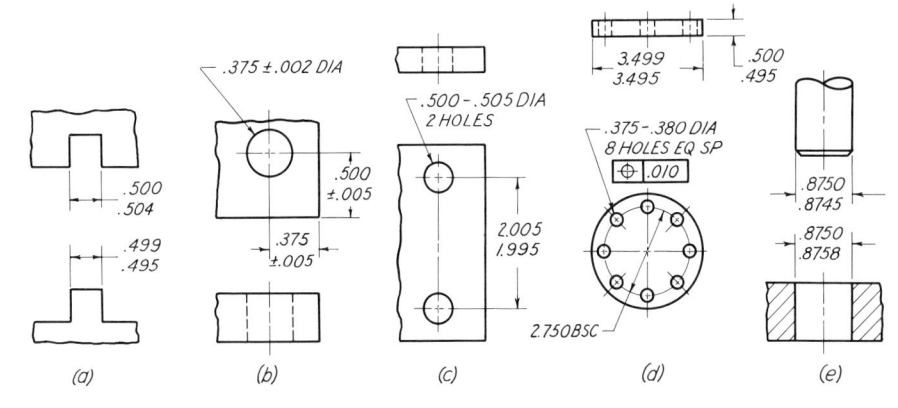

FIG. 16.56. Limit dimensioning for the production of interchangeable parts.

Basic size. The basic size is that size from which the limits of size are derived by the application of allowances and tolerances.

Allowance. An allowance is a prescribed difference between the maximum material limits of mating parts. It is a minimum clearance (positive allowance) or maximum interference (negative allowance) between such parts.

Tolerance. A tolerance is the total permissible variation of a size. The tolerance is the difference between the limits of size.

Limits of size. The limits of size are the applicable maximum and minimum sizes.

Fit. Fit is the general term used to signify the range of tightness or looseness which may result from the application of a specific combination of allowances and tolerances in the design of mating parts.

Clearance fit. A clearance fit is one having limits of size so prescribed that a clearance always results when mating parts are assembled.

Interference fit. An interference fit is one having limits of size so prescribed that an interference always results when mating parts are assembled.

Transition fit. A transition fit is one having limits of size so prescribed that either a clearance or an interference may result when mating parts are assembled.

Basic hole system. A basic hole system is a system of fits in which the design size of the hole is the basic size and the allowance, if any, is applied to the shaft.

Basic shaft system. A basic shaft system is a system of fits in which the design size of the shaft is the basic size and the allowance, if any, is applied to the hole.

Tables 26A, B, C, D, and E in the Appendix cover three general types of fits: running fits, locational fits, and force fits. For educational purposes standard fits may be designated by means of letter symbols, as follows:

RC—Running or Sliding Clearance Fit
LC—Locational Clearance Fit
LT—Transition Clearance or Interference Fit
LN—Locational Interference Fit
FN—Force or Shrink Fit

It should be understood that these letters are not to appear on working drawings. Only the limits for sizes are shown.

When a number is added to these letter symbols a complete fit is represented. For example, FN4 specifies, symbolically, a class 4 force fit for which the limits of size for mating parts may be determined from use of Table 26E. The minimum and maximum limits of clearance or interference for a particular application may be read directly from this table.

Classes of fits as given in these tables are as follows:

Running and Sliding Fits—Classes RC1–RC9
Locational Clearance Fits—Classes LC1–LC11
Locational Transition Fits—Classes LT1–LT6
Locational Interference Fits—Classes LN1–LN3
Force and Shrink Fits—Classes FN1–FN5

*Running and Sliding fits.** Running and Sliding fits are intended to provide a similar running performance, with suitable lubrication allowance, throughout the range of sizes. The clearances for the first two classes, used chiefly as

---

*Extracted from *American Standard Preferred Limits and Fits for Cylindrical Parts* [ANS(USAS) B4.1–1967].

slide fits, increase more slowly with diameter than the other classes, so that accurate location is maintained even at the expense of free relative motion.

A brief description of the fits is given here. For a more complete understanding one should read and study the standard.

RC1 Close sliding fits are intended for accurate location of parts which must assemble without perceptible play.

RC2 Sliding fits are intended for accurate location but with greater maximum clearance than Class RC1.

RC3 Precision running fits are about the closest fits which can be expected to run freely and are intended for precision work at slow speeds and light journal pressures, ...

RC4 Close running fits are intended chiefly for running fits on accurate machinery with moderate surface speeds and journal pressures, ...

RC5⎱
RC6⎰ Medium running fits are intended for higher running speeds, or heavy journal pressures, or both.

RC7 Free running fits are intended for use where accuracy is not essential or where large temperature variations are likely to be encountered, ...

RC8⎱
RC9⎰ Loose running fits are intended for use where wide commercial tolerances may be necessary, together with an allowance, on the external member.

*Locational fits.** Locational fits are divided into three groups: clearance fits (LC), transition fits (LT), and interference fits (LN).

L C. Locational clearance fits are intended for parts which are normally stationary, but which can be freely assembled or disassembled. They run from snug fits for parts requiring accuracy of location, through the medium clearance fits for parts such as ball, race and housing, to the looser fastener fits where freedom of assembly is of prime importance.

LT. Locational transition fits are a compromise between clearance and interference fits, for application where accuracy of location is important, but either a small amount of clearance or interference is permissible.

LN. Locational interference fits are used where accuracy of location is of prime importance, and for parts requiring rigidity and alignment with no special requirements for bore pressure.

*Force fits.** Force or shrink fits constitute a special type of interference fit, normally characterized by maintenance of constant bore pressures throughout the range of sizes.

FN1 Light drive fits are those requiring light assembly pressures, and produce more or less permanent assemblies.

FN2 Medium drive fits are suitable for ordinary steel parts, or for shrink fits on light sections.

FN3 Heavy drive fits are suitable for heavier steel parts, or for shrink fits in medium sections.

FN4⎱
FN5⎰ Force fits are suitable for parts which can be highly stressed, or for shrink fits where the heavy pressing forces required are impractical.

16.15
Computation of Limits of Size for Cylindrical Parts. To obtain the correct fit between two engaging parts, compute limit dimensions that modify the nominal size of both. Numerical values of the modifications necessary to obtain the proper

allowance and tolerances for various diameters for all fits mentioned previously are given in Tables 26A, B, C, D, and E in the Appendix.

The two systems in common use for computing limit dimensions are (1) the basic hole system, and (2) the basic shaft system. The same ANSI (USASI) tables may be used conveniently for both systems.

16.16
Basic Hole System. Because most limit dimensions are computed on the basic hole system, the illustrated example shown in Fig. 16.57 involves the use of this system. If, as is the usual case, the nominal size is known, all that is necessary to determine the limits is to convert the nominal size to the basic hole size and apply the figures given under "standard limits,"

adding or subtracting (according to their signs) to or from the basic size to obtain the limits for both the hole and the shaft.

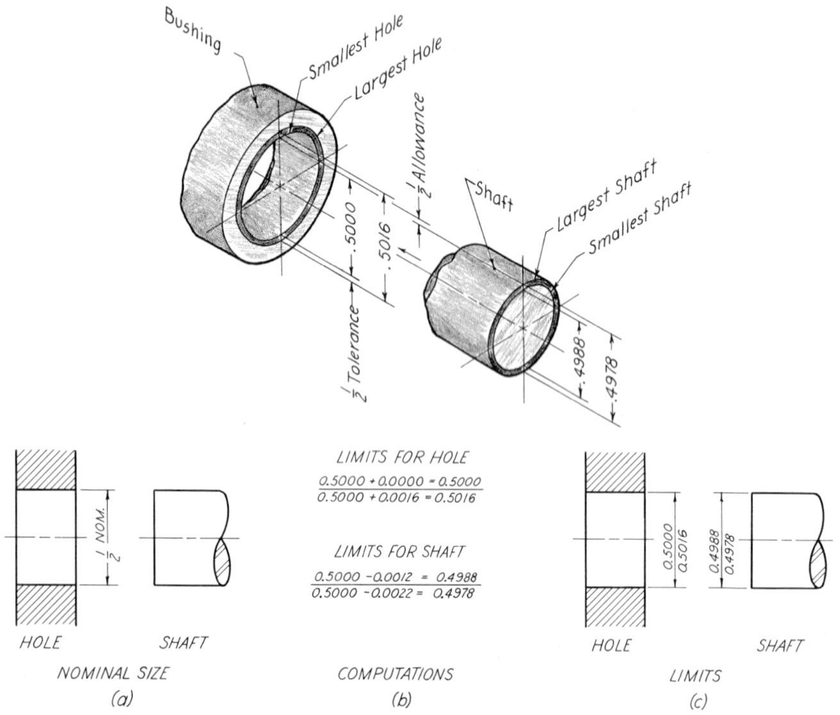

Example

Suppose that a $\frac{1}{2}$-in. shaft is to have a class RC6 fit in a $\frac{1}{2}$-in. hole [Fig. 16.57(a)]. The nominal size of the hole is $\frac{1}{2}$ in. The basic hole size is the exact theoretical size .5000.

From Table 26A it is found that the hole may vary between +.0000 and +.0016, and the shaft between −.0012 and −.0022. As can be readily observed, these values result in a variation (tolerance) of .0016 between the upper and lower limits of the hole, while the variation (tolerance) for the shaft will be .0010. The allowance (minimum clearance) is .0012, as given in the table.

The limits of the hole are

$$\frac{(.5000 + .0000)}{(.5000 + .0016)} = \frac{.5000}{.5016}$$

The limits on the shaft are

$$\frac{(.5000 - .0012)}{(.5000 - .0022)} = \frac{.4988}{.4978}$$

In the past limits have been placed in the order in which they will be approached when the part is machined [Fig. 16.57(c)]. This practice leads to the minimum limit being placed above for an internal dimension and the maximum limit above for an external dimension. However, a recent proposal requires that the maximum limit always be placed directly above the minimum limit where dimensions are associated with dimension lines (ANS Y14.5–1966). However, when both limits are given in a horizontal line in association with a leader or note, the minimum limit is to be given first [Fig. 16.56(d)].

16.17
Basic Shaft System. When a number of parts requiring different fits but having the same nominal size must be mounted on a shaft, the basic shaft system is used because it is much easier to adjust the limits for the holes than to machine a

FIG. 16.57. Computation of limits (basic hole system).

shaft of one nominal diameter to a number of different sets of limits required by different fits.

For basic shaft fits the maximum size of the shaft is basic. The limits of clearance or interference are the same as those shown in Tables 26A, B, C, D, and E for the corresponding fits. The symbols for basic shaft fits are identical with those used for the standard fits with a letter S added. For example, LC4S specifies a locational clearance fit, class 4, as determined on a basic shaft basis.

Basic Shaft System—Clearance Fits. To determine the needed limits, increase each of the limits obtained, using the basic hole system, by the value given for the upper shaft limit. For example, if the same supposition (nominal size and fit requirement) is made as for the preceding illustration, the limits shown in Fig. 16.58 can be most easily obtained by adding .0012 to each of the limits shown for the hole and shaft in Fig. 16.57.

Basic Shaft System—Interference and Transition Fits. To determine the needed limits, subtract the value shown for the upper shaft limit from the basic hole limits.

Example

The basic shaft limits are to be determined using an FN2 fit and the same nominal diameter as for the two previous illustrations.

$$\text{Hole } \frac{.5000 - .0016}{.5007 - .0016} = \frac{.4984}{.4991}$$

$$\text{Shaft } \frac{.5016 - .0016}{.0512 - .0016} = \frac{.5000 \text{ (basic size)}}{.4996}$$

In brief, it can be stated that the limits for hole and shaft, as given in Tables 26A–E, are increased for clearance fits or decreased for transition or interference fits by the value shown for the upper shaft limit, which is the amount required to change the maximum shaft to basic size.

16.18
Tolerances. Necessary tolerances may be expressed by general notes printed on a drawing form or they may be given with definite values for specific dimensions (Fig. 16.64). When expressed in the form of a printed note, the wording might be as follows: ALLOWABLE VARIATION ON ALL FRACTIONAL DIMENSIONS IS ±.010 UNLESS OTHERWISE SPECIFIED. A general note for tolerance on decimal dimensions might read: ALLOWABLE VARIATION ON DECIMAL DIMENSIONS IS ±.001. This general note would apply to all decimal dimensions where limits were not given.

The general notes on tolerances should be allowed to apply to all dimensions where it is not necessary to use specific tolerances.

16.19
Unilateral Tolerances. Unilateral tolerances may be expressed in any one of several ways, as shown in Fig. 16.59.

Two limits may be given, as in (*a*), or the basic size can be shown to the required number of decimal places, followed by a plus tolerance above a minus tolerance, as in (*b*). Another method illustrated in (*c*) gives the preferred dimension with a tolerance that may be plus or minus but not both. When the dimension is given as a fraction the zero tolerance is expressed by a 0 (cipher).

16.20
Bilateral Tolerances. Bilateral tolerances are expressed with a divided tolerance (Fig. 16.60). Whenever the plus and minus values are unequal, as in (*c*), the plus value is placed above the dimension line.

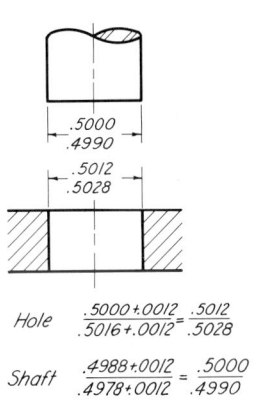

FIG. 16.58. Computation of limits (basic shaft system).

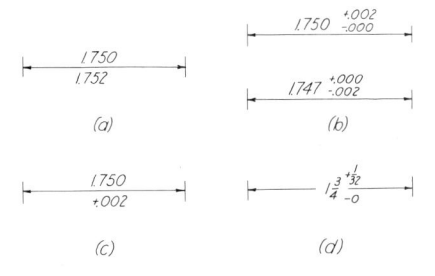

FIG. 16.59. Unilateral tolerances.

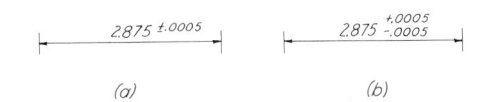

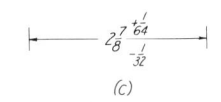

FIG. 16.60. Bilateral tolerances.

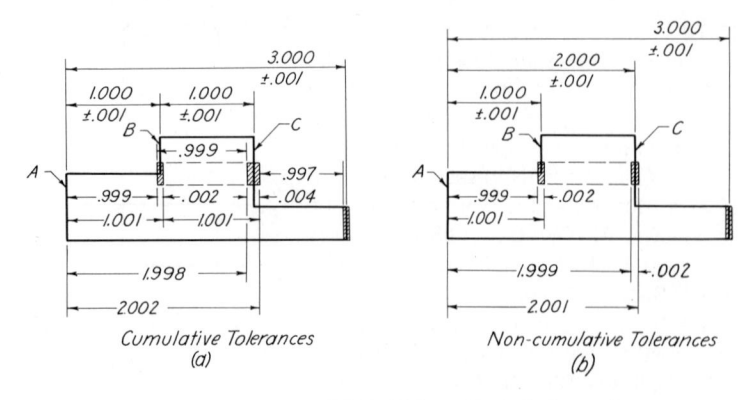

FIG. 16.61. Cumulative tolerances.

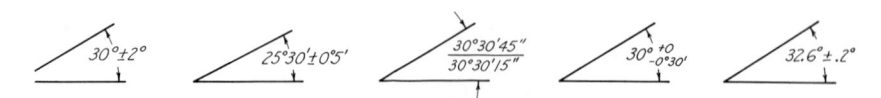

FIG. 16.62. Angular tolerances.

FIG. 16.63. Geometric characteristic symbols.*

The use of a datum plane makes it possible to take full advantage of permissible variations in size and still satisfy all requirements for the proper functioning of the part.

16.22
Specification of Angular Tolerances. Angular tolerances may be expressed in degrees, minutes, or seconds (see Fig. 16.62). If desired, an angle may be given in degrees and decimal parts of a degree with the tolerance in decimal parts of a degree.

16.23
Geometric Tolerancing. Geometric tolerances specify the maximum variation that can be allowed in form or position from true geometry. Actually, a geometrical tolerance is either the width or diameter of a tolerance zone within which a surface or axis of a hole or cylinder can lie with the resulting part satisfying the necessary standards of accuracy for proper functioning and interchangeability. Whenever tolerances of form are not specified on a drawing for a part, it is understood that the part as produced will be acceptable regardless of form variations. Expressions of tolerances of form control straightness, flatness, parallelism, squareness, concentricity, roundness, angular displacement, and so forth.

16.21
Cumulative Tolerances. An undesirable condition may result when either the location of a surface or an overall dimension is affected by more than one tolerance dimension. When this condition exists, as illustrated in Fig. 16.61(a), the tolerances are said to be cumulative. In (a) surface B is located from surface A and surface C is related in turn to surface B. With the tolerances being additive, the tolerance on C is the sum of the separate tolerances (±.002). In respect to A, the position of C may vary from 1.998 to 2.002. This tolerance, as illustrated by the shaded rectangle, is .004 in. When consecutive dimensioning is used, one dimension should always be omitted to avoid serious inconsistency. The distance omitted should be the one requiring the least accuracy. To avoid the inconsistency of cumulative tolerances it is the preferred practice to locate the surfaces from a datum plane, as shown in (b), so that each surface is affected by only one dimension.

16.24
Symbols for Tolerances of Position and Form. The characteristic symbols shown in Fig. 16.63 have been suggested for use in lieu of, or in conjunction with, notes to express positional and form tolerances. In general, these symbols are the same as those given in Mil. Std. 8C-1962 for use by the armed services. Figure 16.64 shows typical feature control symbols ap-

*Compiled from ANS(USAS) Y14.5–1966.

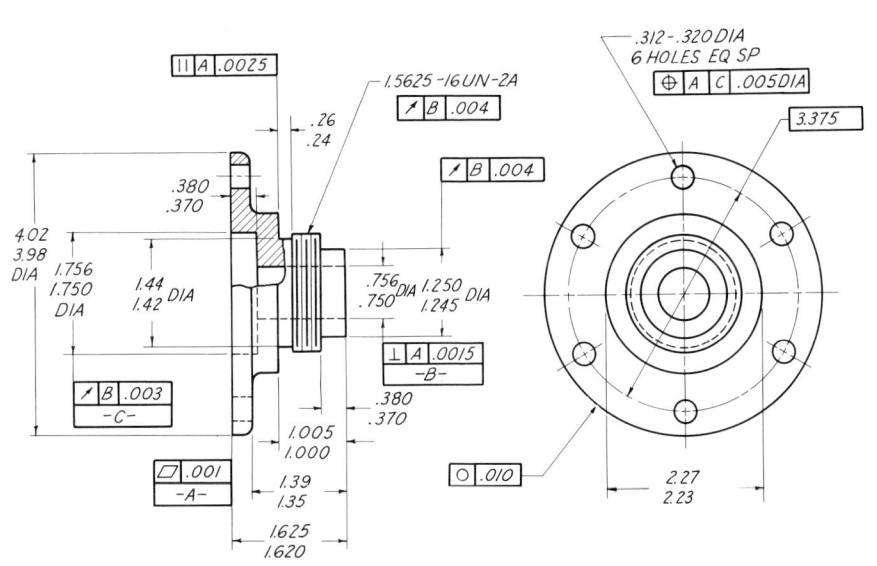

CHAP. 16 / SIZE DESCRIPTION: DIMENSIONS AND SPECIFICATIONS 375

FIG. 16.64. Use of symbols in specifying positional and form tolerances.*

*ANS(USAS) Y14.5–1966.

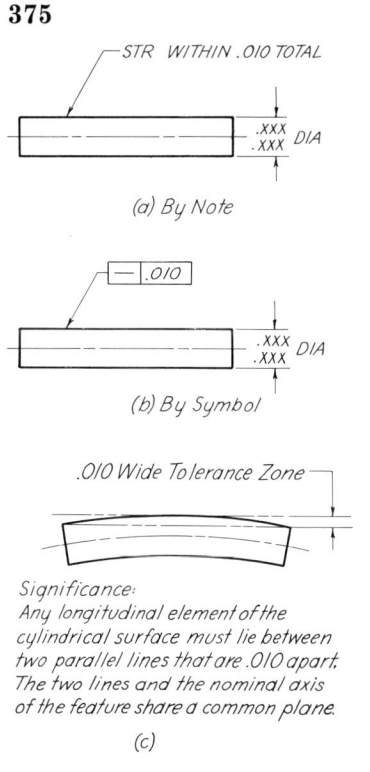

FIG. 16.65. Specification for straightness.

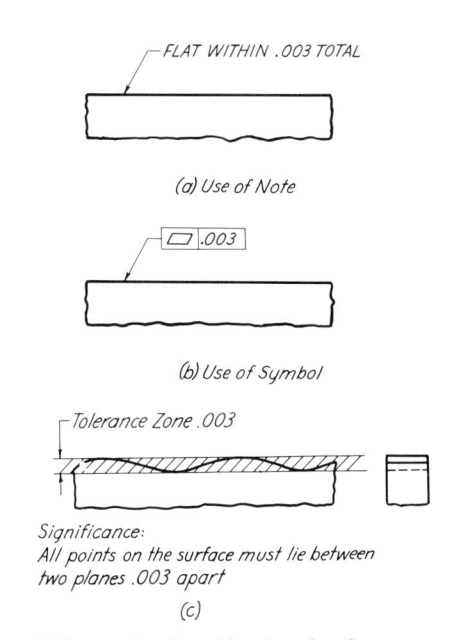

FIG. 16.66. Specification for flatness.

plied to a drawing. After making a careful study of this drawing, the reader is urged to relate and compare the notes and symbolic callouts used with callouts and their illustrated significance as given in Figs. 16.65–16.72 inclusive.

When a positional or form tolerance must be related to a datum, this relationship shall be indicated in the feature control symbol by placing the datum reference letter(s) between the geometric characteristic symbol and the tolerance, as shown by the example below and at the right in Fig. 16.63. It should be noted that vertical lines are used to separate the entries. Suggested dimensions for a short frame are given with the example at the left. For additional entries the frame is increased in length as may be necessary to avoid crowding. Feature control symbols may be associated with the feature(s) being toleranced by any one of the several methods shown in Fig. 16.64.

16.25
Tolerance Specifications for Straightness. Straightness is specified either by a note that is lettered on the drawing in the form shown in Fig. 16.65(a) or by symbol, as illustrated in (b). The significance of the call out has been explained in (c).

16.26
Tolerance Specification for Flatness. The call out used to control flatness requires that all points of the actual surface must lie between two parallel planes that are a distance apart equal to the specified tolerance (see Fig. 16.66). The expressions MUST NOT BE CONCAVE or MUST NOT BE CONVEX may be added to the specification note if desired.

16.27
Tolerance Specification for Perpendicularity. Examples of callouts used to gov-

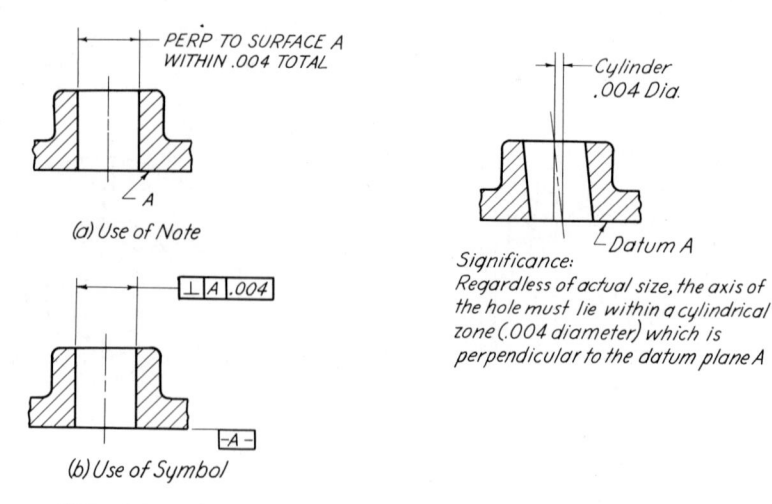

FIG. 16.67. Specification for perpendicularity (RFS).

ern perpendicularity and their significance are shown in Figs. 16.67 and 16.68. It should be noted that for the condition illustrated in Fig. 16.67, the tolerance zone is cylindrical.

FIG. 16.68. Specification for perpendicularity.

16.28
Tolerance Specification for Parallelism. An example of a callout to be used to control parallelism is shown in Fig. 16.69. In using this method, the datum is considered as a plane established by the high points of surface A. All points of the other surface must lie between two planes that are parallel to the datum.

16.29
Tolerance Specification for Concentricity (Fig. 16.70). When the cylindrical or conical features of a part must be basically concentric, it is the usual practice to specify the permissible eccentricity in terms of the maximum permissible deviation from concentricity.

16.30
Tolerance Specification for Angularity. The drawing callout that is commonly used to specify the tolerance for control of angularity is shown in Fig. 16.71 in its two forms. The term *angularity* is used to define the relation of such features as surfaces, axes, and so forth, to one another when they are not perpendicular.

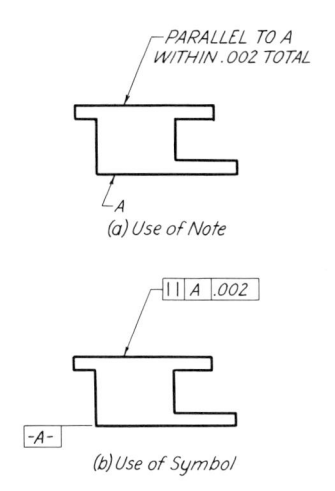

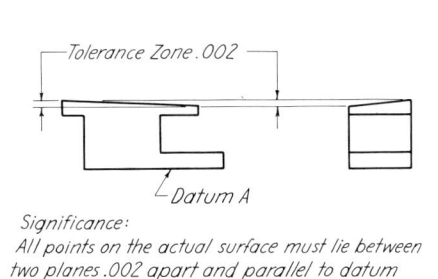

FIG. 16.69. Specification for parallelism.

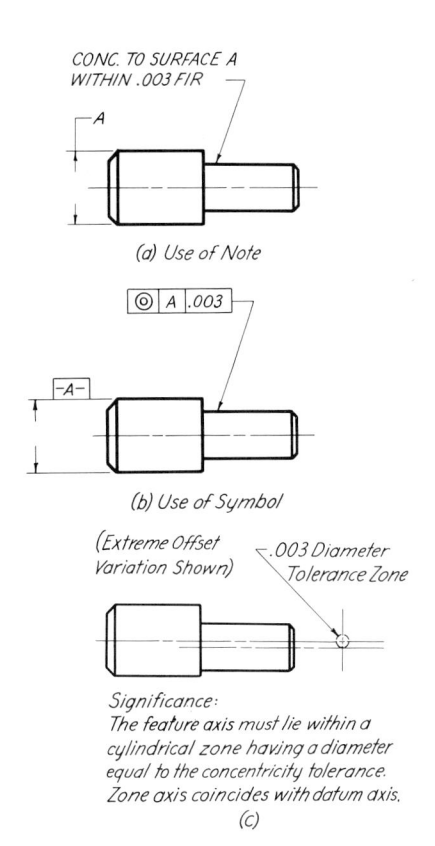

FIG. 16.70. Specification for concentricity.

16.31
Profile Tolerancing. Where a uniform amount of variation may be permitted along a profile, a zone tolerance may be specified. The zone is indicated at a conspicuous location by two phantom lines drawn parallel to the profile when the zone is bilateral, that is, symmetrical about the contour line, as shown in Fig. 16.72. Only one phantom line is needed for a unilateral zone that may lie on either side of the true profile. As can be observed from the illustration, the finished surface must lie within the specified tolerance zone. The variation to be permitted and the extent of the tolerance zone may be specified by dimensions and a note. On the drawing, the note or applicable control symbol (see author's note on illustration) should appear with the view where the surface is represented in profile.

*ANS(USAS) Y14.5-1966.

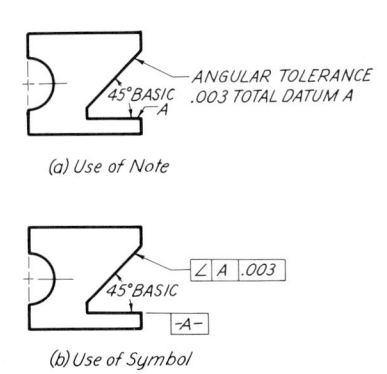

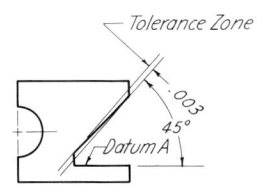

FIG. 16.71. Specification for angularity.

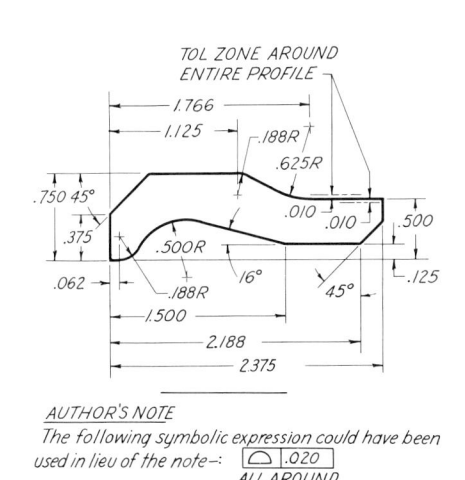

FIG. 16.72. Profile (zone) tolerancing.*

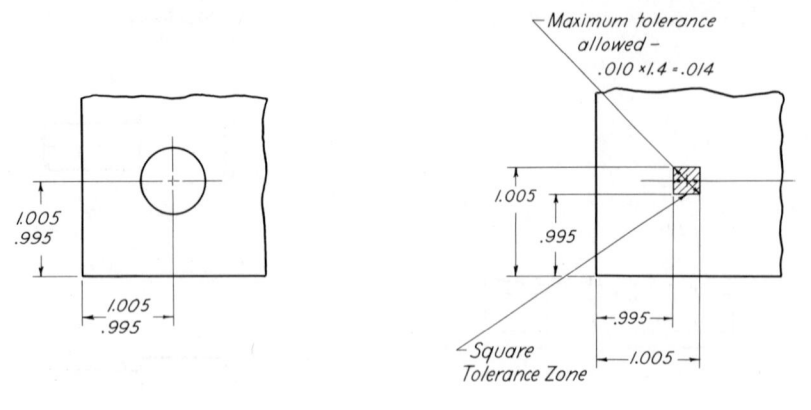

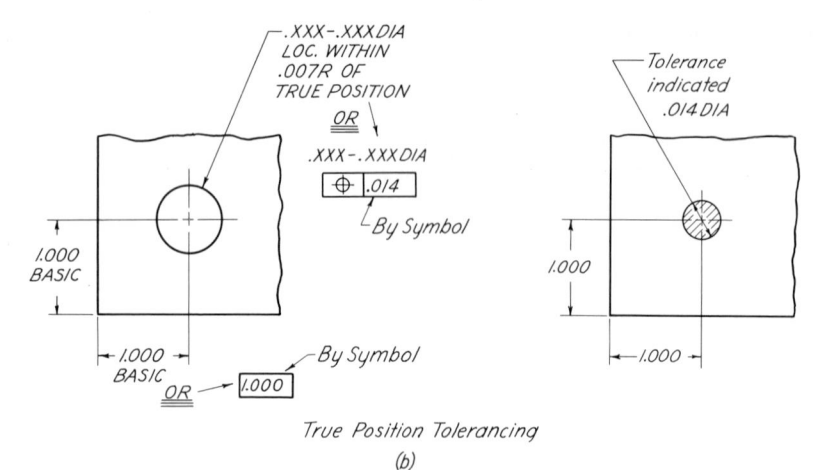

FIG. 16.73. Comparison between coordinate tolerancing and true position tolerancing.

16.32
True-Position Dimensioning. In the past, it has been the usual practice to locate points by means of rectangular dimensions given with tolerances. A point located in this manner will lie within a square tolerance zone when the positioning dimensions are at right angles to each other, as in Fig. 16.73(a). Where features are located by radial and angular dimensions with tolerances, wedge-shaped tolerance zones result, as illustrated in Fig. 16.74.

In making a comparison of coordinate tolerancing and true-position tolerancing of circular features, it can be noted in the case of coordinate tolerancing, as illustrated in Fig. 16.73(a), that the actual position of the feature can be anywhere within the .010 square and that the maximum allowable variation from the desired position occurs along the diagonal of the square. With this allowable variation along the diagonal being 1.4 times the specified tolerance, the diameter of the cylinder for true-position tolerancing of the same feature [see (b)] could be 1.4 times the tolerance that would be used in coordinate tolerancing without any increase in the maximum allowable variation. True-position tolerancing increases the permissible tolerance in all directions, without detrimental effect on the location of the feature. True-position dimensioning takes into full account the relations that must be maintained for the interchangeable assembly of mating parts and it permits the design intent to be expressed more simply and precisely. Furthermore, the true-position approach to dimensioning corresponds to the control furnished by position and receiver gages with round pins. Such gages are commonly used for the inspection of patterns of holes in parts that are being mass produced. A full discussion of the advantages of true-position tolerancing may be found in Appendix B of ANS(USAS) Y14.5-1966.

Positional tolerancing can be used for specific features of a machine part. When the part contains a number of features arranged in groups, positional tolerances can be used to relate each of the groups to one another as necessary and to tolerance the position of the features within a group independently of the features of the other groups.

The term "true position" denotes the theoretically exact position for a feature.

CHAP. 16 / SIZE DESCRIPTION: DIMENSIONS AND SPECIFICATIONS 379

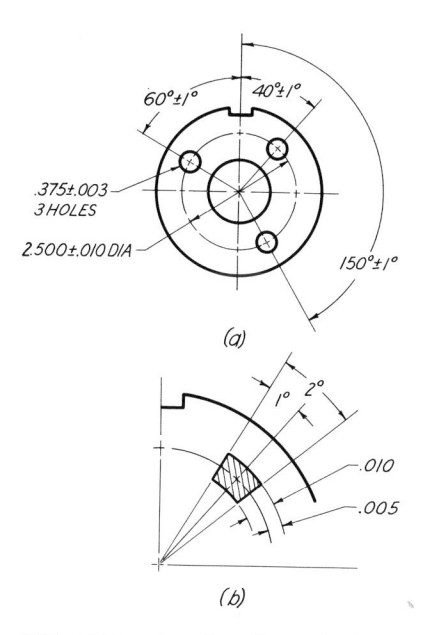

FIG. 16.74. Angular dimensioning.*

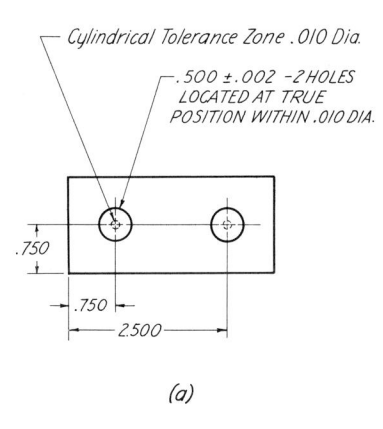

FIG. 16.75. True position dimensioning.

In practice, the basic (exact) location is given with untoleranced dimensions and a positional tolerance is added to the note specifying the size and number of features (Fig. 16.75).

Basic (untoleranced) location dimensions must be excluded from the general tolerances, usually specified near the title block. This may be done in any one of several ways, as follows: (a) by a general note—UNTOLERANCED DIMENSIONS LOCATING TRUE POSITION ARE BASIC; (b) by adding the word Basic (or BSC) to each of the locating dimensions; (c) by enclosing each of the true-position-locating dimensions in a rectangular box; or (d) by reference to a separate specification document. See Fig. 16.73(b).

For true-position tolerancing characteristic phrases or symbols are included in the hole (or feature) callout (Fig. 16.73). Either the diameter method or the radius method may be used for specifying the true-position tolerance. However, it must be realized that the radius represents deviation from true position and that the tolerance is twice the radius. Since both methods achieve the same dimensional control, the expression to be included with the hole call out may be given in either of two ways:

1. LOCATED AT TRUE POSITION WITHIN .010 DIA

2. LOCATED WITHIN .005R OF TRUE POSITION

When the alignment between mating parts depends on some functional surface, this surface is selected as a datum for dimensioning, and the datum is identified in the note. Such a note for a cylindrical part might read: .XXX—.XXX DIA 6 HOLES LOC AT TRUE POS WITHIN .006 DIA IN RELATION TO SURF A.

The requirement of true-position dimensioning for a cylindrical feature is illustrated in Fig. 16.76(a). It must be understood that the axis of the hole at all points must lie within the specified cylindrical tolerance zone having its center located at true position. This cylindrical tolerance

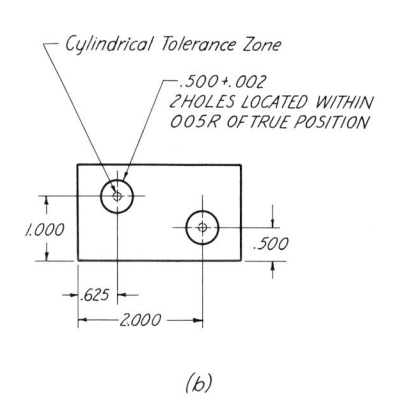

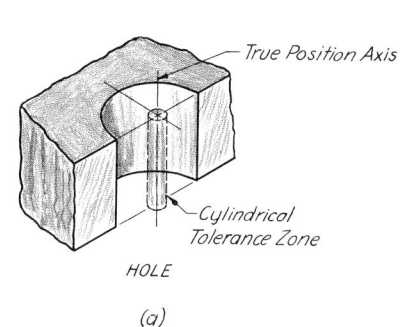

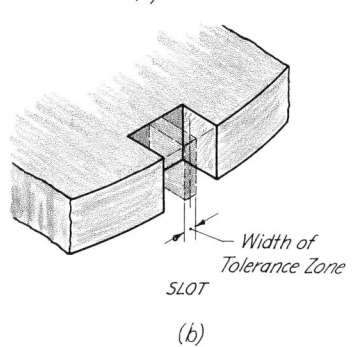

FIG. 16.76. Meaning of true position dimensioning.

*ANS(ASA) Y14.5–1957.

zone also defines the limits within which variations in the squareness of the axis of the hole in relation to the flat surface must be confined.

For noncircular features, such as slots and tabs, the positional tolerance is usually applied only to surfaces related to the center plane of the feature. In applying true-position dimensioning to such features, it will be found that the principal difference is in the geometric form of the tolerance zone within which the center plane of the feature must be contained. See Fig. 16.76(*b*). The center plane of the tolerance zone must be located at true position. It should be noted that this tolerance zone also defines the limits within which variations in the squareness of the center plane of the slot must be contained. Notes specifying slots might read:

1. 6 SLOTS EQ SP AND LOC WITHIN .005 EACH SIDE OF TRUE POS

2. .XXX–.XXX 2 SLOTS LOC AT TRUE POS WITHIN .008 TOTAL IN RELATION TO SURFACES *A* and *B*.

Fig. 16.77 shows the application of true-position dimensioning to both holes and tabs. It should be noted that the tolerance zone has been specified by radius.

See Fig. 16.64 for the use of symbols in lieu of notes in specifying positional tolerances.

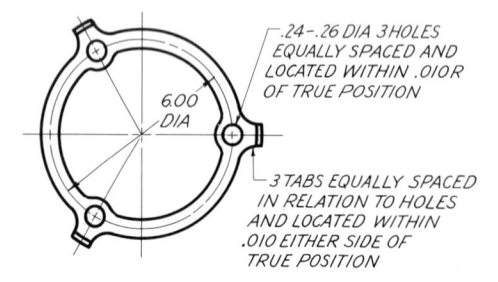

The illustrations used with this much simplified discussion have been presented with the sole idea of showing as briefly as possible what is meant by true-position dimensioning. They are not to be thought of as being practical examples. Dotted circles have been added to the illustrations in Fig. 16.75 only to call attention to the imaginary tolerance zones. Those who may have the need for the use of this method of tolerancing should consult ANS(USAS) Y14.5-1966 to acquire a full understanding of true-position dimensioning.

16.33

True-Position Dimensioning—Application of the MMC Principle. The least desirable situation exists for the assembly of mating parts when both parts are at their maximum metal condition (designated MMC). The expression *maximum metal condition* by itself, as applied to an internal feature of a finished part, means that the internal feature (hole, slot, etc.) is at its minimum allowable size. In the case of external features (shafts, lugs, tabs, etc.), a maximum material condition exists when these features are at their maximum allowable sizes. MMC occurs for mating parts, say, for a hole and a shaft, when the shaft is at its maximum size and the hole is at its smallest size. Thus, at MMC, there is least clearance between these parts. In general, tolerance of position and the MMC of mating features are considered together in relationship to each other. This leads to the situation where the specified limits of location frequently may be exceeded and acceptable parts produced when the mating features are away from their maximum material limits of size. With this latter condition permissible, it becomes desirable to indicate the fact that specified limits of location need be observed only under MMC. If this is not stated in a

FIG. 16.77. True position dimensioning—holes and tabs.*

*ANS(ASA) Y14.5-1957.

general note or a specification, the abbreviation MMC should be added to the true-position note on the drawing, as shown in Fig. 16.78.

True-position tolerancing on the MMC basis is both practical and economical for the mass production of interchangeable parts. However, the MMC basis should not be applied where it would be inconsistent with functional requirements.

In those relatively few cases where the more economical MMC basis is not applicable and the positional tolerance must be stated without reference to MMC, the more restrictive "regardless of feature size" (RFS) basis is specified (Fig. 16.78). This is accomplished by adding the abbreviation RFS (or S, its symbolic equivalent, as shown in Fig. 16.63) to the true-position callout.

Additional information concerning the meaning of MMC as related to positional tolerances may be found in ANS(USAS) Y14.5-1966.

16.34
Surface Quality. The improvement in machining methods within recent years coupled with a strong demand for increased life for machined parts has caused engineers to give more attention to the quality of the surface finish. Not only the service life but also the proper functioning of the part as well may depend on obtaining the needed smoothness quality for contact surfaces.

On an engineering drawing a surface may be represented by line if shown in profile or it may appear as a bounded area in a related view. Machined and ground surfaces, however, do not have the perfect smoothness represented on a drawing. Actually a surface has three dimensions, namely, length, breadth, and curvature (waviness), as illustrated in Fig. 16.79(a). In addition there will be innumerable

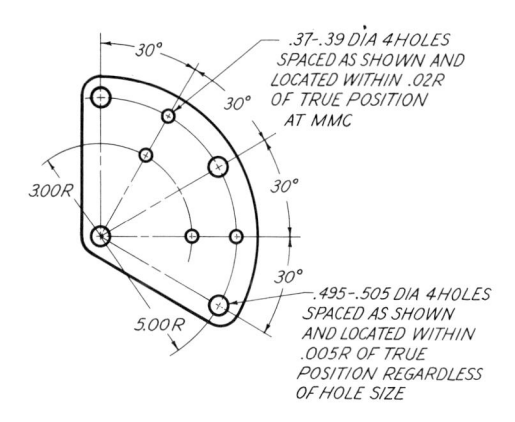

FIG. 16.78. True position tolerancing—MMC and RFS.*

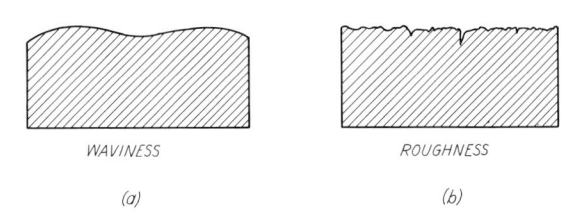

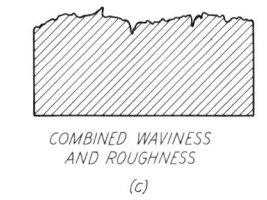

FIG. 16.79. Surface definitions illustrated.

peaks and valleys of differing lengths, widths, and heights. An exaggerated profile of surface roughness is shown in (b). Combined waviness and roughness is illustrated in (c).

The following terms must be understood before the surface symbol shown in Fig. 16.81 can be properly applied:

Surface texture. This term refers to repetitive or random deviations from the nominal surface, which form the pattern of the surface. Included are roughness, waviness, lay, and flaws (Fig. 16.80).

Roughness. Roughness is the relatively

*ANS(ASA) Y14.5-1957.

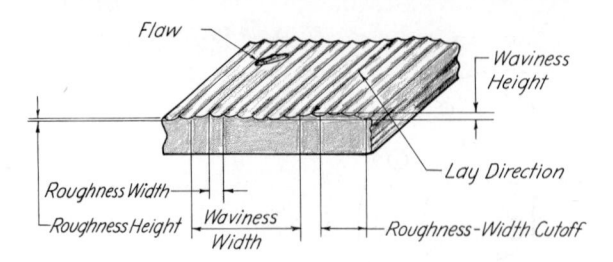

FIG. 16.80. Surface texture definitions.*

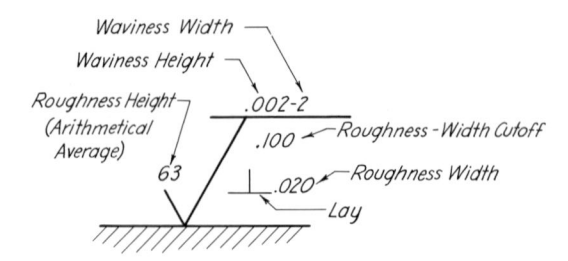

FIG. 16.81. Surface texture symbol.

tive surface irregularities to be included in the measurement of average roughness height. It is measured in inches (Fig. 16.80).

Waviness. Waviness is the surface undulations that are of much greater magnitude than the roughness irregularities. Waviness may result from machine or work deflections, vibrations, warping, strains, or similar causes.

Waviness height. Waviness height is the peak-to-valley distance (Fig. 16.80). It is rated in inches.

Waviness width. Waviness width (rated in inches) is the spacing of successive wave valleys or wave peaks (Fig. 16.80).

Flaws. Flaws are irregularities, such as cracks, checks, blowholes, scratches, and so forth, that occur at one place or at relatively infrequent or widely varying intervals on the surface (Fig. 16.80).

Lay. Lay is the predominant direction of the tool marks of the surface pattern (Fig. 16.84).

Microinch. A Microinch is one-millionth (.000001) of an inch.

16.35
Designation of Surface Characteristics (Fig. 16.81). A surface whose finish is to be specified should be marked with the finish mark having the general form of a check mark ($\sqrt{}$) so that the point of the symbol shall be on the line representing the surface, on the extension line, or on a leader pointing to the surface. Good practice dictates that the long leg and the extension shall be to the right as the drawing is read. See Fig. 16.82. Figure 16.83 illustrates the specification of roughness, waviness, and lay by listing rating values on the symbol.

Where it is desired to specify only the surface-roughness height, and the width

finely spaced surface irregularities that are produced by the cutting action of tool edges and abrasive grains on surfaces that are machined.

Roughness height. Roughness height is the average (arithmetical) deviation from the mean line of the profile. It is expressed in microinches (Fig. 16.80).

Roughness width. Roughness width is the distance between successive peaks or ridges, which constitute the predominant pattern of roughness. Roughness width is measured in microinches (Fig. 16.80).

Roughness width cutoff. This term indicates the greatest spacing of repeti-

*ANS(ASA) B46.1–1962.

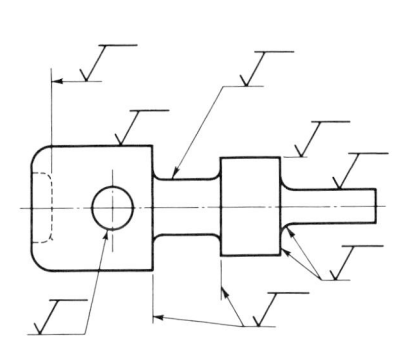

CHAP. 16 / SIZE DESCRIPTION: DIMENSIONS AND SPECIFICATIONS   **383**

FIG. 16.82. Application of surface texture symbols to a drawing of a machine part.*

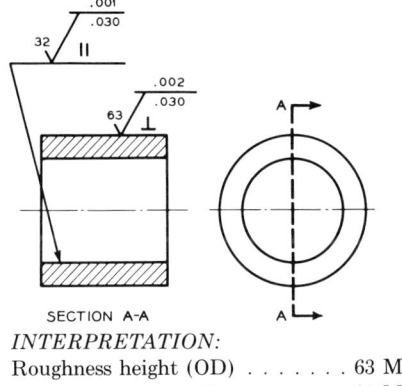

INTERPRETATION:
Roughness height (OD) . . . . 63 Mu in.
Roughness height (ID) . . . . 32 Mu in.
Roughness-width cutoff 030
Waviness height (OD) 002
Waviness height (ID) 001
Lay (OD) . . . . Circumferential
Lay (ID) . . . . Axial

FIG. 16.83. Application of the symbol with significance explanations.*

of roughness or direction of tool marks is not important, the simplest form of the symbol may be used. The numerical value is placed in the √, as shown in Fig. 16.81.

Where it is desired to specify waviness height in addition to roughness height, a straight horizontal line must be added to the top of the simple symbol (Fig. 16.81). The numerical value of height waviness would be shown above this line.

If the nature of the preferred lay is to be shown in addition to these two characteristics, it will be indicated by the addition of a combination of lines, as shown in Fig. 16.81. Parallel or perpendicular lines indicate that the dominant lines on the surface are parallel or perpendicular to the boundary line of the surface in contact with the symbol (Fig. 16.84).

Roughness width is placed to the right of the lay symbol, as shown in Fig. 16.81.

The use of only one number to specify the height or width of roughness or waviness will indicate the arithmetical average.

The chart in Fig. 16.85 shows the expected surface roughness in microinches for surfaces produced by common production methods.

*ANS(ASA) B46.1-1962.

The surface-quality symbol, which is used only when it is desirable to specify surface smoothness, should not be confused with a finish mark, which indicates the removal of material. A surface-quality symbol might be used for a surface on a die casting, forging, or extruded shape where the surface is to have a natural finish and no material is to be removed.

Surface finish should be specified only by experienced persons because the function of many parts does not depend on the smoothness quality of a surface or surfaces. In addition, surface quality need not be necessarily indicated for many parts that are produced to close dimensional tolerances because a satisfactory surface finish may result from the required machining processes. It should be remembered that the cost of producing a part will generally become progressively greater as the specification of surface finish becomes more exacting.

\multicolumn{3}{c	}{LAY SYMBOLS}
SYMBOL	DESIGNATION	EXAMPLE
$\parallel$	Lay parallel to the line representing the surface to which the symbol is applied.	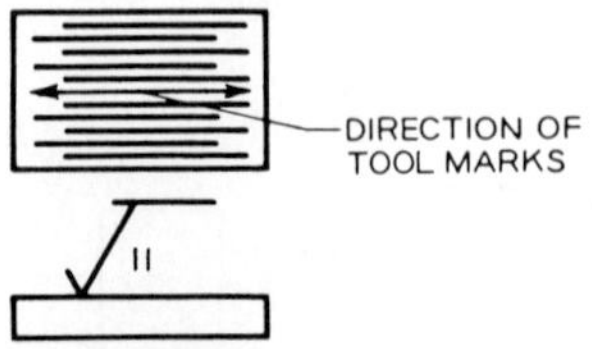 DIRECTION OF TOOL MARKS
$\perp$	Lay perpendicular to the line representing the surface to which the symbol is applied.	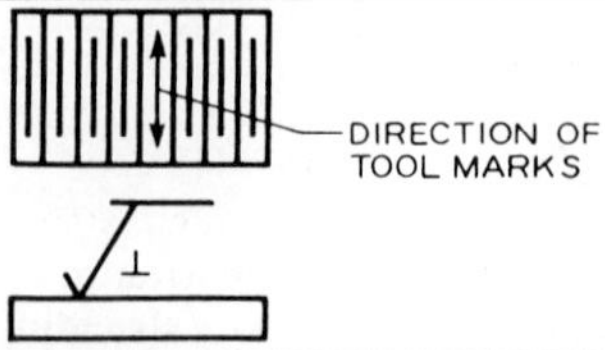 DIRECTION OF TOOL MARKS
X	Lay angular in both directions to line representing the surface to which symbol is applied.	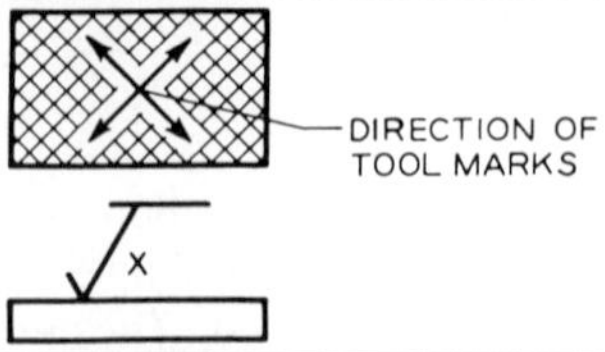 DIRECTION OF TOOL MARKS
M	Lay multidirectional	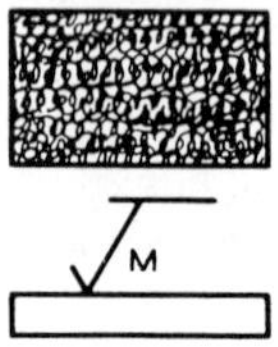
C	Lay approximately circular relative to the center of the surface to which the symbol is applied.	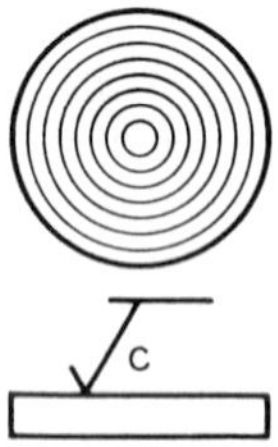
R	Lay approximately radial relative to the center of the surface to which the symbol is applied.	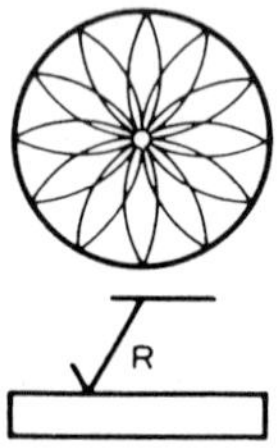

FIG. 16.84. Lay notations.*

*ANS(ASA) B46.1–1962.

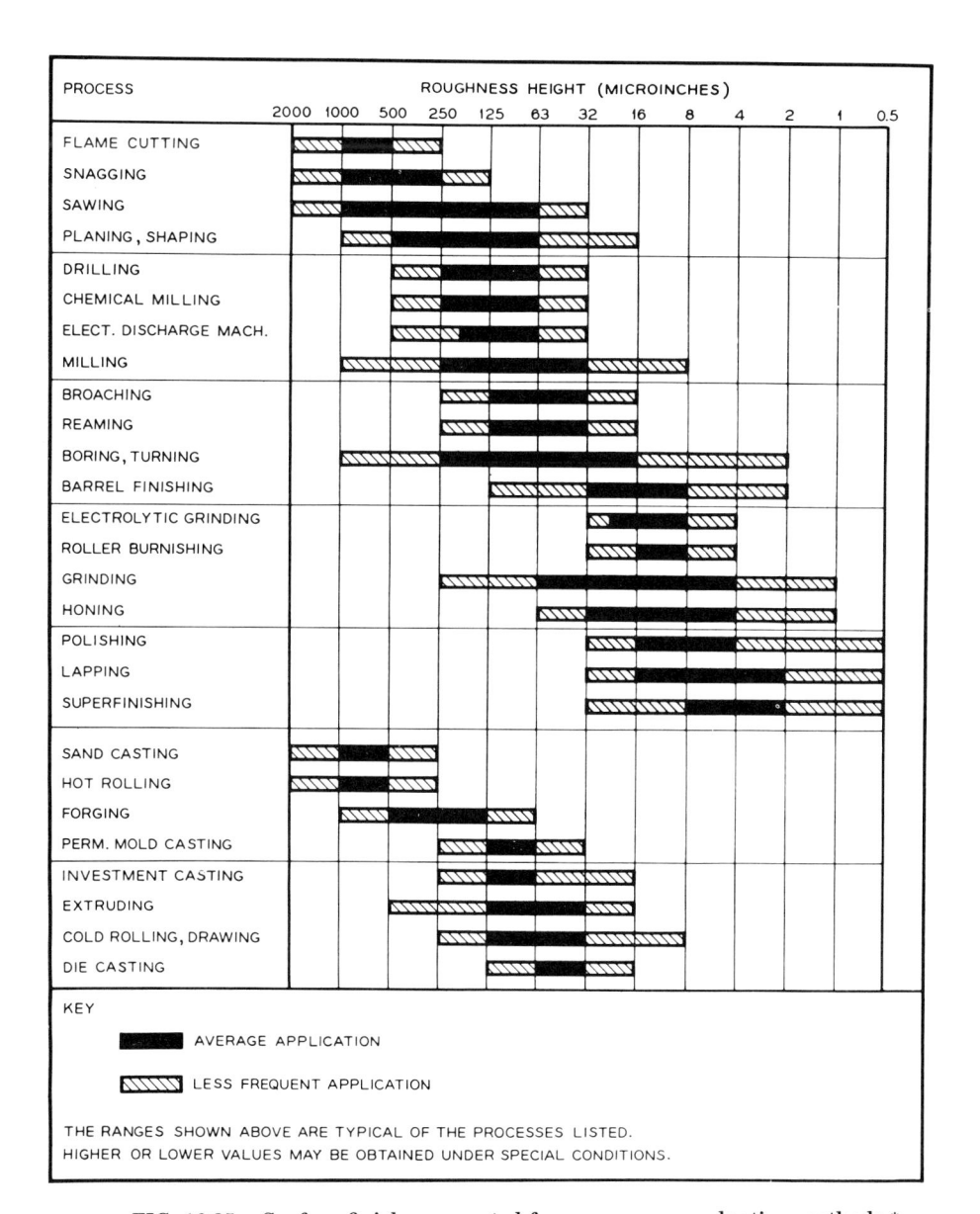

CHAP. 16 / SIZE DESCRIPTION: DIMENSIONS AND SPECIFICATIONS **385**

PROCESS	ROUGHNESS HEIGHT (MICROINCHES) 2000 1000 500 250 125 63 32 16 8 4 2 1 0.5
FLAME CUTTING	
SNAGGING	
SAWING	
PLANING, SHAPING	
DRILLING	
CHEMICAL MILLING	
ELECT. DISCHARGE MACH.	
MILLING	
BROACHING	
REAMING	
BORING, TURNING	
BARREL FINISHING	
ELECTROLYTIC GRINDING	
ROLLER BURNISHING	
GRINDING	
HONING	
POLISHING	
LAPPING	
SUPERFINISHING	
SAND CASTING	
HOT ROLLING	
FORGING	
PERM. MOLD CASTING	
INVESTMENT CASTING	
EXTRUDING	
COLD ROLLING, DRAWING	
DIE CASTING	

KEY
■ AVERAGE APPLICATION
▧ LESS FREQUENT APPLICATION

THE RANGES SHOWN ABOVE ARE TYPICAL OF THE PROCESSES LISTED. HIGHER OR LOWER VALUES MAY BE OBTAINED UNDER SPECIAL CONDITIONS.

FIG. 16.85. Surface finishes expected from common production methods.*

*ANS(ASA) B46.1–1962.

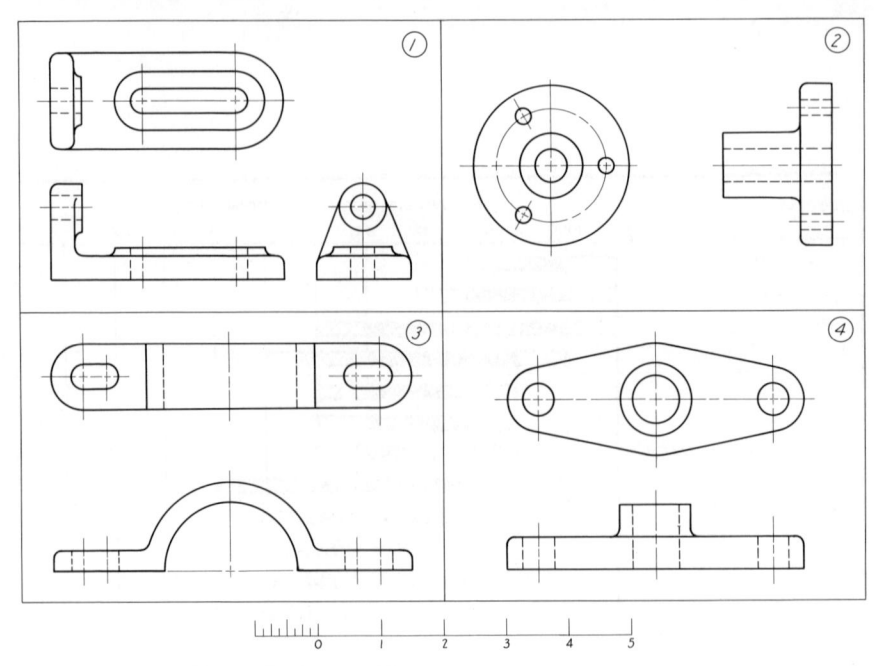

FIG. 16.86. Dimensioning problems.

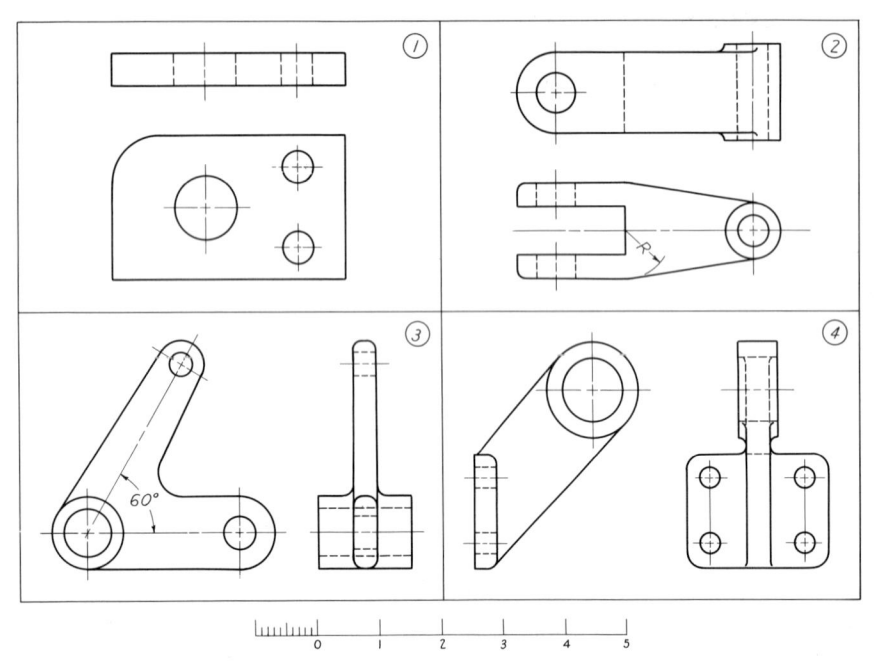

FIG. 16.87. Dimensioning problems.

PROBLEMS

The following problems offer the student the opportunity to apply the rules of dimensioning given in this chapter. If it is desirable, decimals of an inch may be used in place of fractions. Use Table 1 in the Appendix.

1-2. (Figs. 16.86–16.87). Reproduce the given views of an assigned part. Determine the dimensions by transferring them from the drawing to the open-divided scale by means of the dividers. Decimal-inch dimensioning is to be used for the parts given in Fig. 16.87.

3-9. (Figs. 16.88–16.94). Make a fully dimensioned multiview sketch or drawing of an assigned part. Draw all necessary views. Give a detail title with suitable notes concerning material, number required, etc. These parts have been selected from different fields of industry—automotive, aeronautical, chemical, electrical, etc.

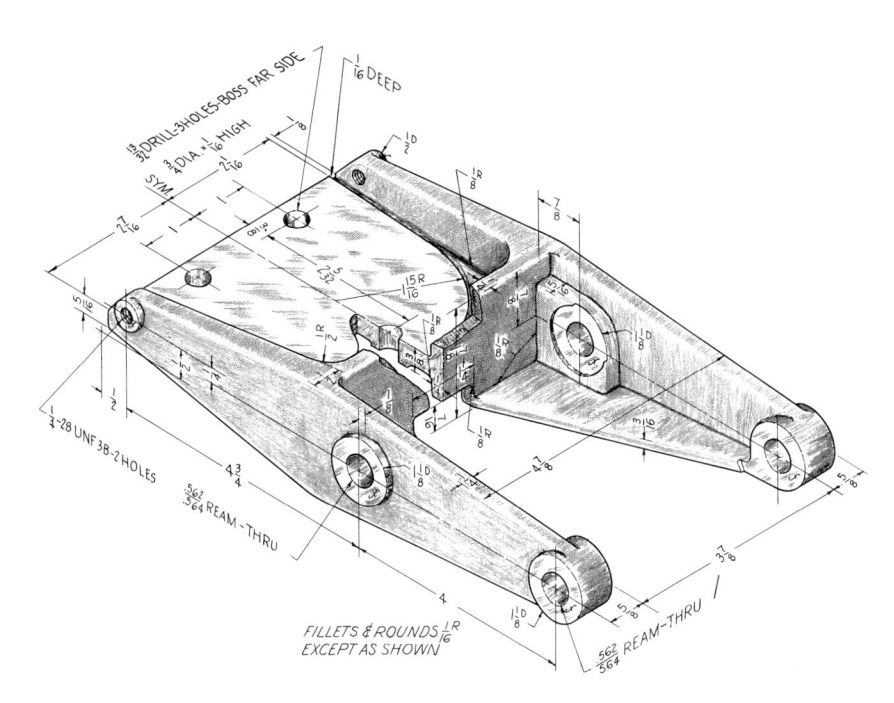

CHAP. 16 / SIZE DESCRIPTION: DIMENSIONS AND SPECIFICATIONS   **387**

FIG. 16.88.   Control pedal—airplane control system.

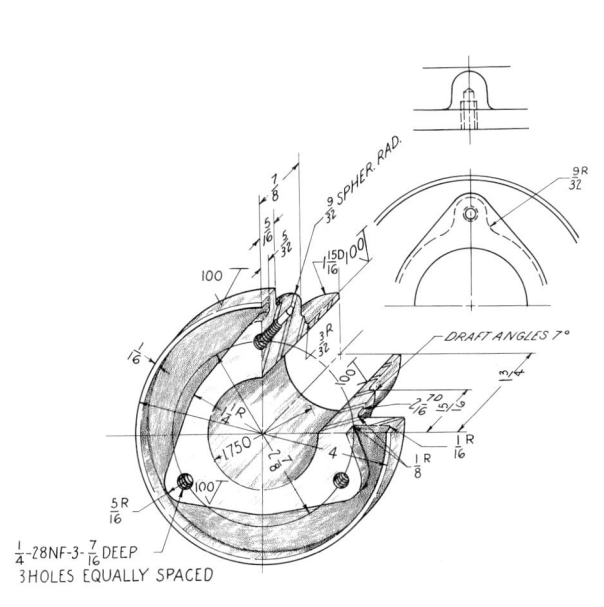

FIG. 16.89.   Inlet flange—airplane cooling system.

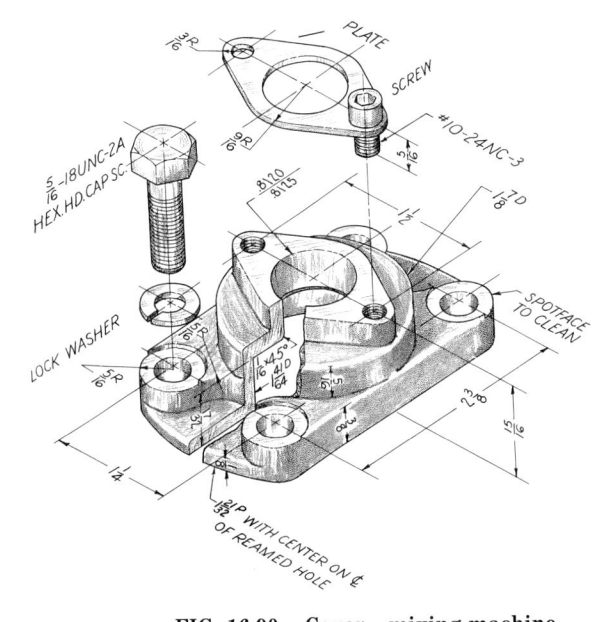

FIG. 16.90.   Cover—mixing machine.

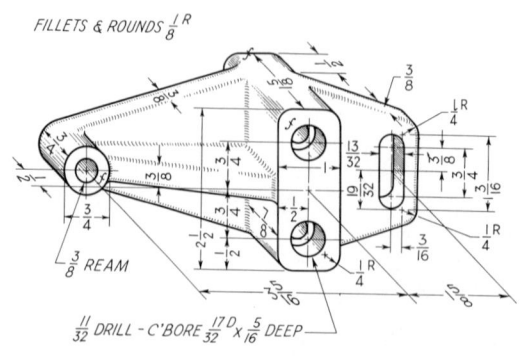

FIG. 16.91. Elevator bracket.

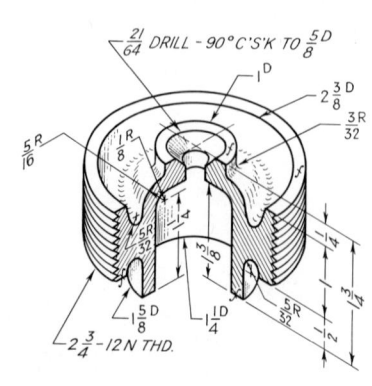

FIG. 16.92. Valve seat.

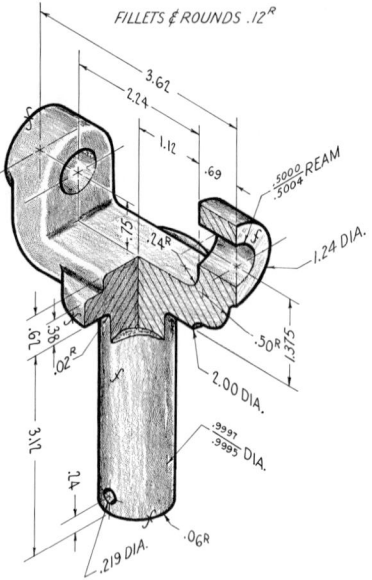

FIG. 16.93. Yoke.

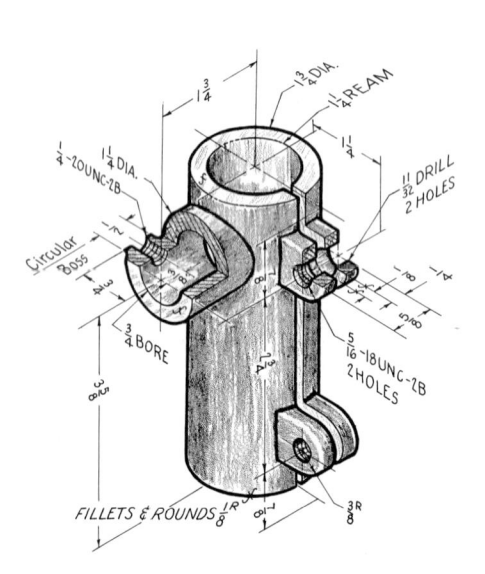

FIG. 16.94. Torch holder—welding.

10. (Fig. 16.95). Make a fully dimensioned multiview sketch or drawing of the rocker arm. Show a detail section taken through the ribs. *Supplementary information:* (1) The distance from the center of the shaft to the center of the hole for the pin in 4.00 in. The distance from the shaft to the threaded hole is 4.50 in. (2) The nominal diameter of the hole for the shaft is 1.875 in. The hole in the rocker arm is to be reamed for a definite fit. Consult your instructor. The diameter of the pin is .969 in. (3) The diameter of the threaded boss is 2.00 in. (4) The diameter of the roller is 2.25 in., and its length is 1.46 in. Total clearance between the roller and finished faces is to be .03 in. (5) The inside faces of the arms are to be milled in towards the hub far enough to accommodate the roller. (6) The rib is .62 in. thick. (7) The lock nut has 1¼–12 UNF thread. (8) Fillets and rounds .12 in. R except where otherwise noted.

11. (Fig. 16.96). Make a fully dimensioned drawing of an assigned part of the shaft support.

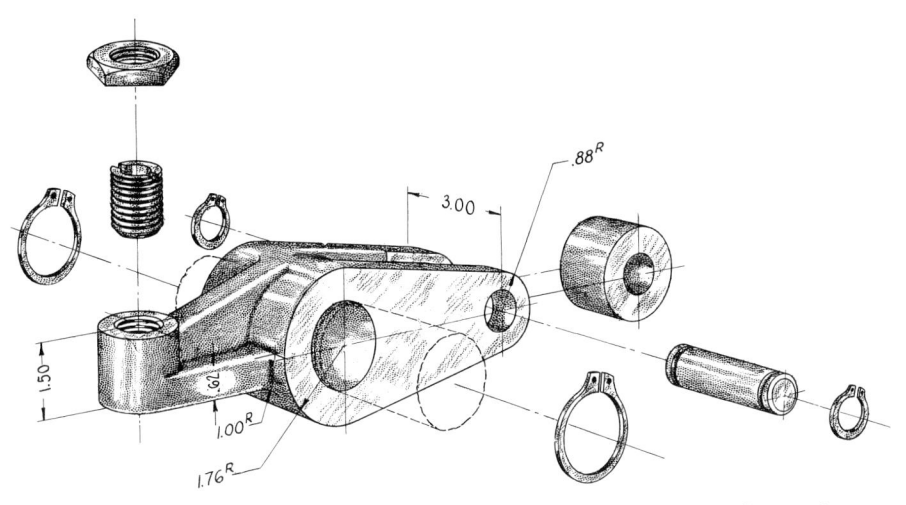

FIG. 16.95. Rocker arm—marine engine.

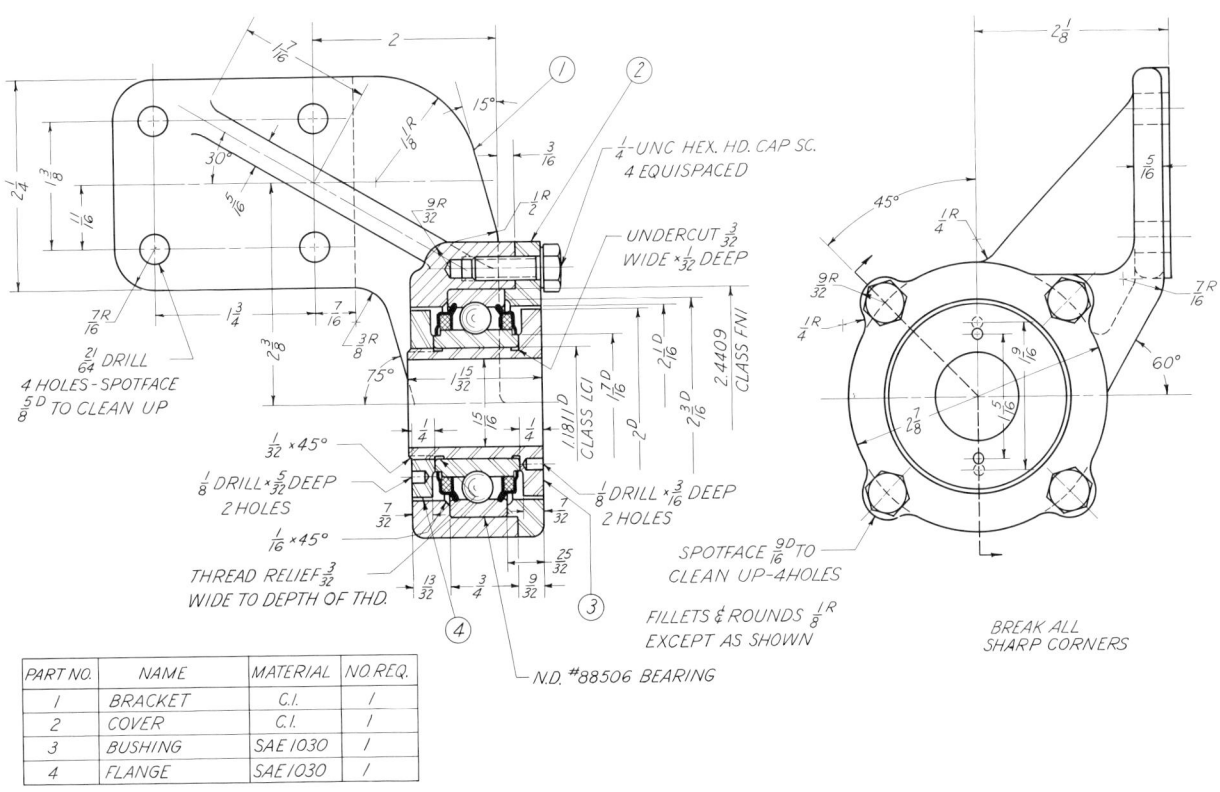

FIG. 16.96. Shaft support.

ORSIII OV5-8 Satellite-friction experiment. Working drawings prepared in the drafting room convey the ideas of the designer to the men who must fabricate the parts and assemble the system. Many drawings were needed for the satellite shown above. Communication drawings, both detail and assembly, are discussed in the chapter that follows.
(*Courtesy of TRW Systems Group*)

Design and Communication Drawings

17.1
Communication Drawings. These varied types of engineering drawings, ranging from design drawings to exploded pictorial drawings, have one thing in common, and that is that they are prepared to convey needed ideas and facts to others. Since all serve the same purpose, they may be classed together as "communication drawings," this term being almost all-inclusive.

In this chapter we will be concerned mainly with the types of drawings that are prepared by draftsmen under an engineer's supervision and that are to serve as communications to others beyond the engineering department. The preparation of idea sketches, both multiview and pictorial, has been discussed in detail in Chapters 7 and 13. Charts and graphs, which may also be thought of as communication drawings, are presented in Chapter 28. Charts and graphs are used by engineers to supplement written reports and technical papers.

17.2
Sketches and Design Drawings. The first stage in the development of an idea for a structure or machine is to prepare freehand sketches and to make the calculations required to determine the feasibility of the design. From these sketches the designer prepares a layout, on which an accurate analysis of the design is worked out. It is usually drawn full-size and is executed with instruments in pencil (Fig. 17.1). The layout should be complete enough to allow a survey of the location of parts (to avoid interference), the accessibility for maintenance, the requirements for lubrication, and the method of assembly.

Usually, only center distances and certain fixed dimensions are given. The general dimensioning, as well as the determination of material and degree of finish of individual parts, is left for the draftsman who makes the detail drawings while using the layout drawing as a guide.

Design layouts require both empirical and scientific design. Empirical design involves the use of charts, formulas, tables, and so forth, which have been derived from experimental studies and scientific computations. Scientific design, which requires a broad knowledge of the allied fields, such as mechanics, metallurgy, and mathematics, is used when a new machine is designed to operate under special specified conditions for which data are not available in any handbook.

17.3
Classes of Machine Drawings. There are

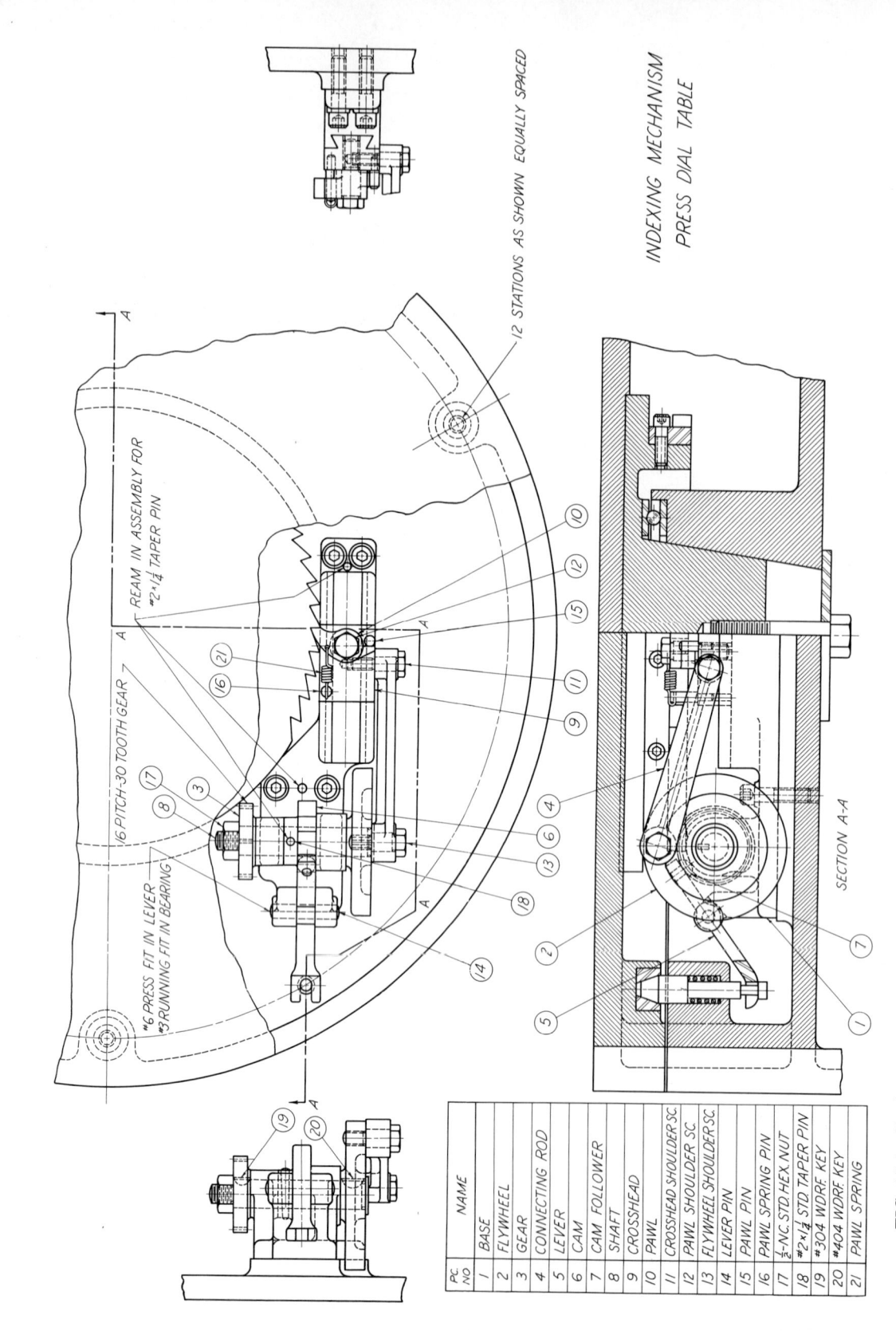

FIG. 17.1. Design assembly drawing.

two recognized classes of machine drawings: detail drawings and assembly drawings.

17.4
Set of Working Drawings. A complete set of working drawings for a machine consists of detail sheets giving all necessary shop information for the production of individual pieces and an assembly drawing showing the location of each piece in the finished machine. In addition, the set may include drawings showing a foundation plan, piping diagram, oiling diagram, and so on.

17.5
Detail Drawing. A detail drawing should give complete information for the manufacture of a part, describing with adequate dimensions the part's size. Finished surfaces should be indicated and all necessary shop operations shown. The title should give the material of which the part is to be made and should state the number of the parts that are required for the production of an assembled unit of which the part is a member. Commercial examples of detail drawings are shown in Figs. 17.2, 17.3, 17.4 and 17.6.

Since a machinist will ordinarily make one part at a time, it is advisable to detail each piece, regardless of its size, on a separate individual sheet. In some shops, however, custom dictates that related parts be grouped on the same sheet, particularly when the parts form a unit in themselves. Other concerns sometimes group small parts of the same material together thus: castings on one sheet, forgings on another, special fasteners on still another, and so on.

17.6
Making a Detail Drawing. With a design layout or original sketches as a guide, the procedure for making a detail drawing is as follows:

1. Select the views, remembering that, aside from the view showing the characteristic shape of the object, there should be as many additional views as are necessary to complete the shape description. These may be sectional views that reveal a complicated interior construction, or auxiliary views of surfaces not fully described in any of the principal views.

2. Decide on a scale that will allow, without crowding, a balanced arrangement of all necessary views and the location of dimensions and notes. Although very small parts should be drawn double-size or larger, to show detail and to allow for dimensions, a full-size scale should be used when possible. In general, the same scale should be used for pieces of the same size.

3. Draw the main center lines and block in the general outline of the views with light, sharp 6H pencil lines.

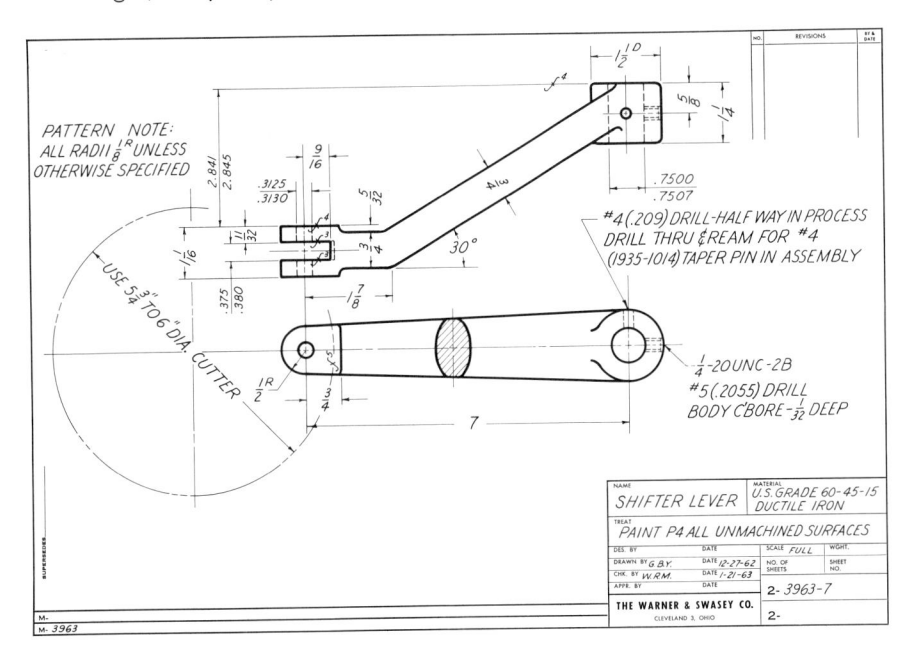

FIG. 17.2. A detail drawing (*Courtesy Warner & Swasey Co.*).

17.7
One-view Drawings. Many parts, such as shafts, bolts, studs, and washers, may require only one properly dimensioned view. In the case of each of these parts, a note can imply the complete shape of the piece without sacrificing clearness. Most engineering departments, however, deem it better practice to show two views.

17.8
Detail Titles. Every detail drawing must give information not conveyed by the notes and dimensions, such as the name of the part, part number, material, number required, and so on. The method of recording and the location of this information on the drawing varies somewhat in different drafting rooms. It may be lettered either in the record strip or directly below the views (Figs. 17.3 and 17.4).

If all surfaces on a part are machined, finish marks are omitted and a title note, "FINISH ALL OVER," is added to the detail title.

17.9
Title Blocks and Record Strips. The purpose of a title or record strip is to present in an orderly manner the name of the machine, name of the manufacturer, date, scale, drawing number, and other drafting-room information.

Every commercial drafting room has developed its own standard title forms, whose features depend on the processes of manufacture, the peculiarities of the plant organization, and the established customs of particular types of manufacturing. In large organizations, the blank form, along with the borderline, is printed on standard sizes of drawing or tracing paper.

A record strip is a form of title extending almost the entire distance across the bottom of the sheet. In addition to the usual title information, it may contain a section for recording revisions, changes,

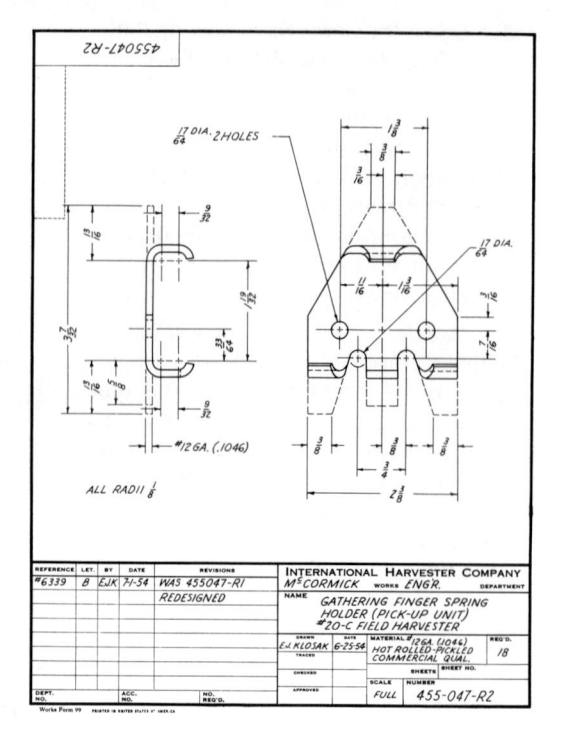

FIG. 17.3. A detail drawing (*Courtesy International Harvester Co.*).

4. Draw main circles and arcs in finished weight.

5. Starting with the characteristic view, work back and forth from view to view until the shape of the object is completed. Lines whose definite location and length are known may be drawn in their finished weight.

6. Put in fillets and rounds.

7. Complete the views by darkening the object lines.

8. Draw extension and dimension lines.

9. Add arrowheads, dimensions, and notes.

10. Complete the title.

11. Check the entire drawing carefully.

and so on, with the dates on which they were adopted (Fig. 17.5).

17.10
Contents of the Title (Figs. 17.3 and 17.8). The title on a machine drawing generally contains the following information:

1. Name of the part.

2. Name of the machine or structure. (This is given in the main title and is usually followed by one of two words: *details* or *assembly*.)

3. Name and location of the manufacturing firm.

4. Name and address of the purchasing firm, if the structure has been designed for a particular company.

5. Scale.

6. Date. (Often spaces are provided for the date of completion of each operation in the preparation of the drawing. If only one date is given, it is usually the date of completion of the drawing.)

7. Initials or name of the draftsman who made the pencil drawing.

8. Initials of the checker.

9. Initials or signature of the chief draftsman, chief engineer, or another in authority who approved the drawing.

10. Initials of the tracer (if drawing has been traced).

11. Drawing number. This generally serves as a filing number and may furnish information in code form. Letters and numbers may be so combined to indicate departments, plants, model, type, order number, filing number, and so on. The drawing number is sometimes repeated in the upper-left-hand corner (in an upside-down position), so that the drawing may be quickly identified if it should become reversed in the file.

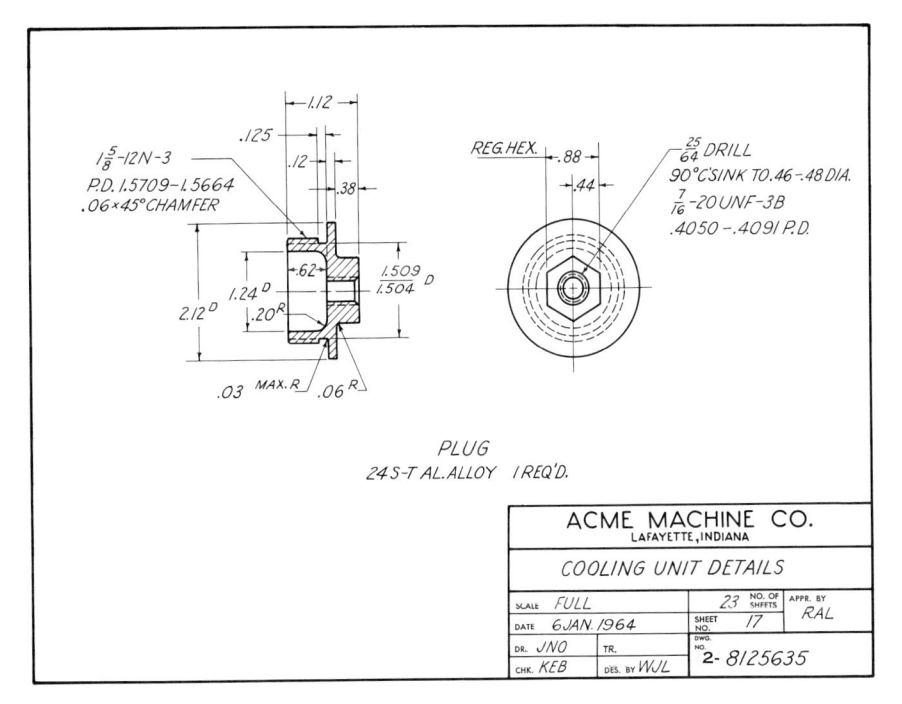

FIG. 17.4. A working drawing (decimal dimensioning).

Some titles furnish information such as material, part number, pattern number, finish, treatment, estimated weight, superseded drawing number, and so on.

17.11
Corrections and Alterations. Alterations on working drawings are made either by

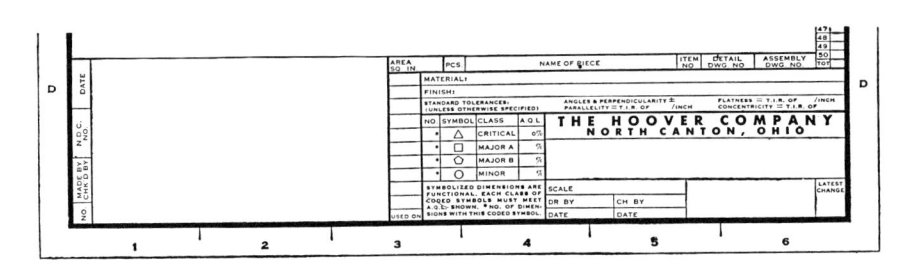

FIG. 17.5. A record strip (*Courtesy The Hoover Co.*).

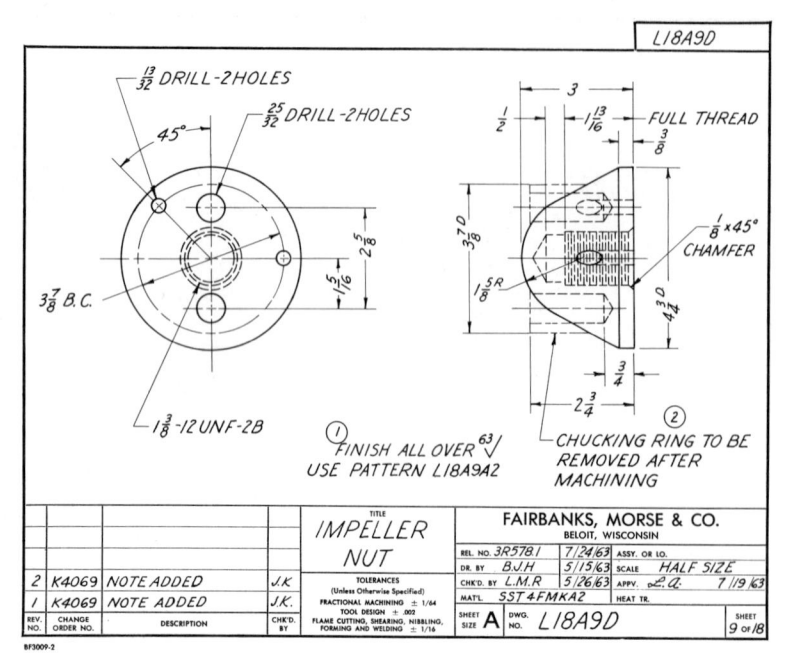

FIG. 17.6. Alterations. (*Courtesy Fairbanks, Morse & Co.*).

cancellation or by erasure. Cancellations are indicated by parallel inclined lines drawn through the views, lines, notes, or dimensions to be changed.

Superseding dimensions should be placed above or near the original ones. If alterations are made by erasure, the changed dimensions are often underlined.

All changes on a completed or approved drawing should be recorded in a revision record that may be located either adjacent to the title block (Fig. 17.6) or at one corner of the drawing (Fig. 17.8). This note should contain the identification symbol, date, authorization number, character of the revision, and the initials of the draftsman and checker who made the change. The identification symbol is a numeral or letter placed in a small circle near the alteration on the body of the drawing (Fig. 17.6).

If changes are made by complete erasure, record prints should be made for the file before the original is altered. Many companies make record prints whenever changes are extensive.

Since revisions on completed drawings are usually necessitated by unsatisfactory methods of production or by a customer's request, they should never be made by a draftsman unless an order has been issued with the approval of the chief engineer's office.

17.12
Pattern-shop Drawings. Sometimes special pattern-shop drawings, giving information needed for making a pattern, are required for large and complicated castings. If the patternmaker receives a drawing that shows finished dimensions, he provides for the draft necessary to draw the pattern and for the extra metal for machining. He allows for shrinkage by making the pattern oversize. When, however, the draft and allowances for finish are determined by the engineering department, no finish marks appear on the drawing. The allowances are included in the dimensions.

17.13
Forge-shop Drawings. If a forging is to be machined, separate detail drawings usually are made for the forge and machine shops. A forging drawing gives all the nominal dimensions required by the forge shop for a completed rough forging. See Fig. 14.2.

17.14
Machine-shop Drawings. Rough castings and forgings are sent to the machine shop to be finished. See Fig. 14.22. Since the machinist is not interested in the dimensions and information for the previous stages, a machine-shop drawing fre-

quently gives only the information necessary for machining.

17.15
Assembly Drawings. A drawing that shows the parts of a machine or machine unit assembled in their relative working positions is an assembly drawing. There are several types of such drawings: design assembly drawings, working assembly drawings, unit assembly drawings, installation diagrams, and so on, each of which will be described separately (Figs. 17.7–17.9 and 17.12–17.14).

17.16
Working Assembly Drawings. A working assembly drawing, showing each piece completely dimensioned, is sometimes made for a simple mechanism or unit of related parts. No additional detail drawings of parts are required.

17.17
Subassembly (Unit) Drawings. A unit assembly is an assembly drawing of a group of related parts that form a unit in a more complicated machine. Such a drawing would be made for the tail stock of a lathe, the clutch of an automobile, or the carburetor of an airplane. A set of assembly drawings thus takes the place of a complete assembly of a complex machine (Fig. 17.8).

17.18
Bill of Material or Parts List. A bill of material is a list of parts placed on an assembly drawing just above the title block, or, in the case of quantity production, on a separate sheet. The bill contains the part (item or key) number, descriptive name, material, quantity (number) required, and so on, of each piece. Additional information, such as stock size, pattern number (castings), and so forth, is sometimes listed.

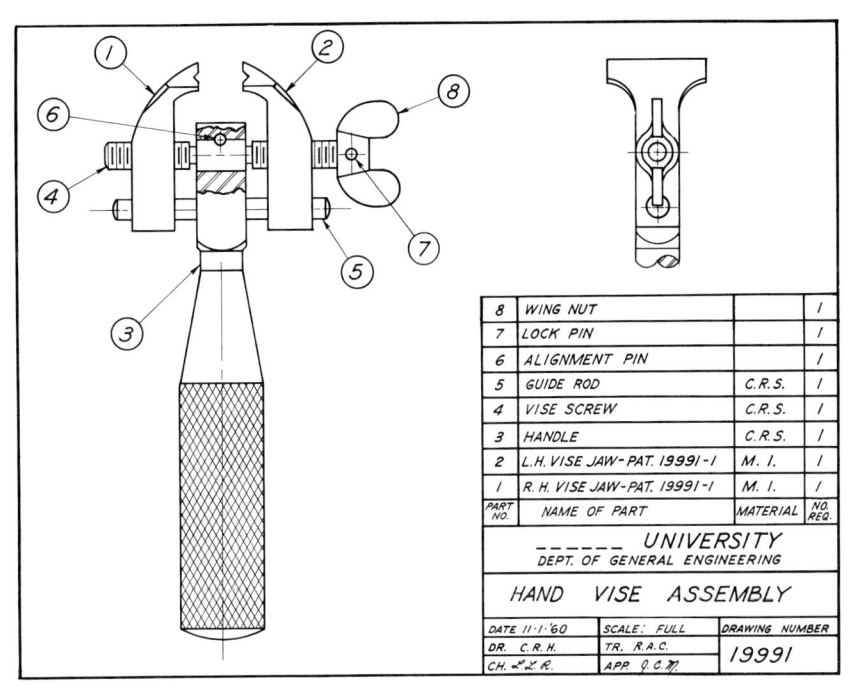

FIG. 17.7. An assembly drawing.

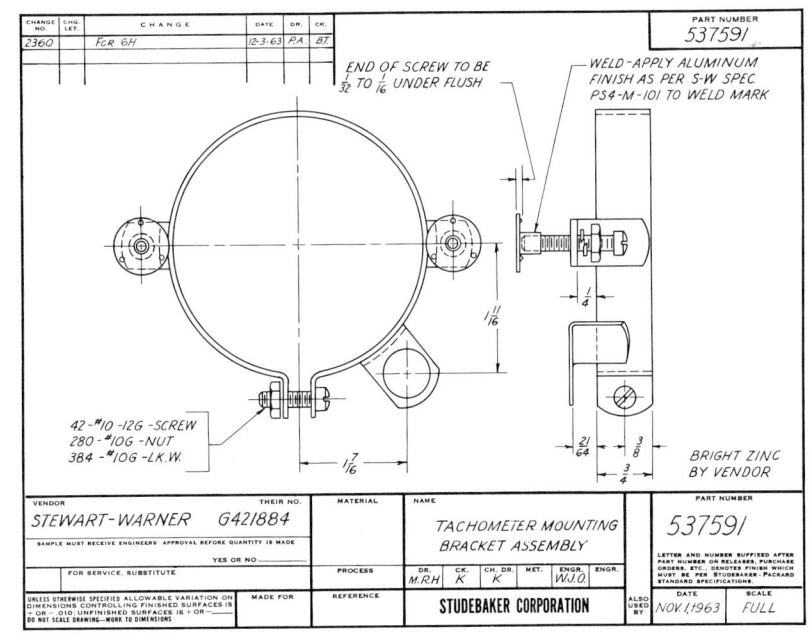

FIG. 17.8. A unit assembly drawing (*Courtesy Studebaker Corp.*).

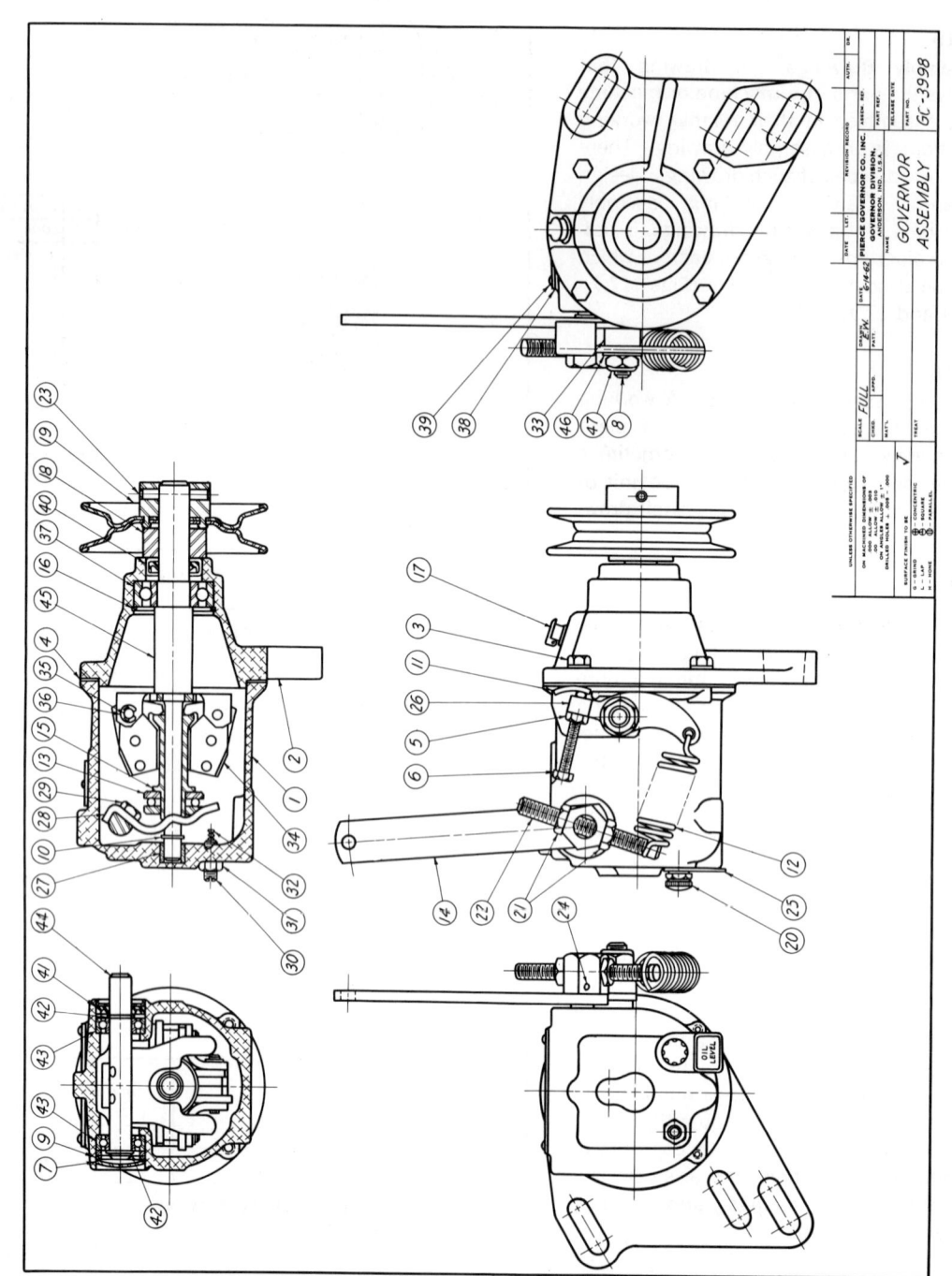

398 PART III / GRAPHICS FOR DESIGN AND COMMUNICATION

FIG. 17.9. An assembly drawing (*Courtesy Pierce Governor Co., Inc.*).

PIERCE GOVERNOR ASSEMBLY GC-3998
PARTS LIST

Key No.	Part Name	Part No.	Quantity
1	Governor Body	G-9042-16	1
2	Governor Flange	G-9138-3	1
3	Sems Fastener	X-1784	4
4	Gasket	X-1425	1
5	Hex. Nut	X-977	1
6	Hex. Head Screw	X-890-4	1
7	Welch Plug	X-2019	1
8	Shoulder Stud	G-9799	1
9	Washer	X-2307	2
10	Snap Ring	X-1923	1
11	Stop Bracket	G-9556	1
12	Governor Spring	SN-1304	1
13	Thrust Bearing	X-1336-A	1
14	Throttle Lever Assembly	A-6325	1
15	Thrust Sleeve	G-10813	1
16	Snap Ring—Internal	X-1921	1
17	Oil Cup	X-2053	1
18	Spacer	G-12614-1	1
19	Governor Pulley	G-10908-1	1
20	Oil Lever Check	X-2054	1
21	Hex. Nut	X-1011-1	2
22	Adj. Screw Eye	G-12306	1
23	Roll Pin	X-2620	1
24	Roll Pin	X-2602	1
25	Oil Lever Tag	X-1945	1
26	Spring Adj. Lever	G-5715	1
27	Bushing	X-2721	1
28	Yoke	G-9838	1
29	Sems Fastener	X-1687	2
30	Bumper Screw	G-5113-1	1
31	Hex. Nut	X-246-4	1
32	Bumper Spring	SN-1481	1
33	Spacer	G-11886-1	1
34	Laminated Weight Assembly	A-2446	4
35	Weight Pin	G-14007	4
36	"E" Retaining Ring	X-2996	4
37	Ball Bearing	X-310	1
38	Name Plate	X-581	1
39	Escutcheon Pin	X-455	2
40	Oil Seal	X-652	1
41	Rocker Shaft Oil Seal	A-6118	1
42	External Snap Ring	X-1904	2
43	Ball Bearing	X-328	2
44	Rocker Shaft	G-11698	1
45	Spider and Shaft Assembly	A-6637	1
46	Washer	X-2026-4	1
47	Elastic Stop Nut	X-1845	1

FIG. 17.10. Parts list-Governor Assembly (Fig. 17.9).

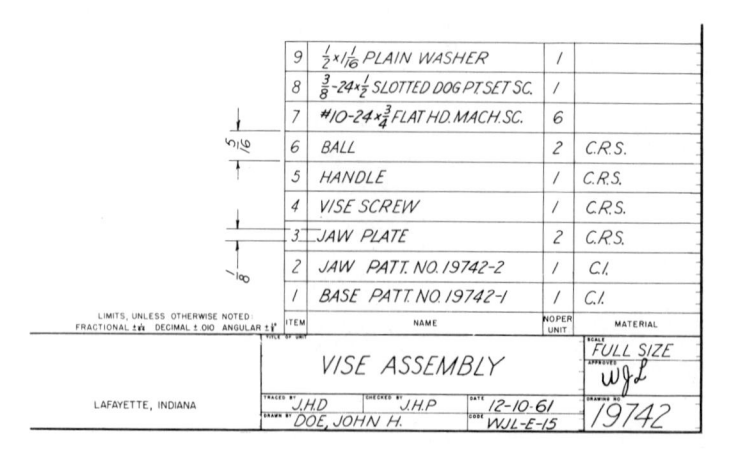

9	1/2 x 1/16 PLAIN WASHER	1	
8	3/8-24 x 1/2 SLOTTED DOG PT. SET SC.	1	
7	#10-24 x 3/4 FLAT HD. MACH. SC.	6	
6	BALL	2	C.R.S.
5	HANDLE	1	C.R.S.
4	VISE SCREW	1	C.R.S.
3	JAW PLATE	2	C.R.S.
2	JAW PATT. NO. 19742-2	1	C.I.
1	BASE PATT. NO. 19742-1	1	C.I.
ITEM	NAME	NO PER UNIT	MATERIAL

VISE ASSEMBLY — FULL SIZE — WJL
LAFAYETTE, INDIANA — TRACED BY J.H.D — CHECKED BY J.H.P — DATE 12-10-61 — DRAWING NO. 19742
DRAWN BY DOE, JOHN H. — CODE WJL-E-15

FIG. 17.11. A bill of material.

Suggested dimensions for ruling are shown in Fig. 17.11. For $\frac{1}{8}$-in. letters, the lines should never be spaced closer than $\frac{5}{16}$ in. Fractions are made slightly less than full height and are centered between the lines.

When listing standard parts in a bill of material, the general practice is to omit the name of the materials and to use abbreviated descriptive titles. A pattern number may be composed of the commercial job number followed by the assigned number one, two, three, and so on. It is suggested that parts be listed in the following order: (1) castings, (2) forgings, (3) parts made from bar stock, and (4) standard parts.

Sometimes bills of material are first typed on thin paper and then blueprinted. The form may be ruled or printed (Fig. 17.10).

17.19

Title. The title strip on an assembly drawing usually is the same as that used on a detail drawing. It will be noted, when lettering in the block, that the title of the drawing is generally composed of the name of the machine followed by the word *assembly* (Figs. 17.7 and 17.9).

17.20

Making the Assembly Drawing. The final assembly may be traced from the design assembly drawing, but more often it is redrawn to a smaller scale on a separate sheet. Since the redrawing, being done from both the design and detail drawings, furnishes a check that frequently reveals errors, the assembly always should be drawn before the details are accepted as finished and the blueprints are made. The assembly of a simple machine or unit is sometimes shown on the same sheet with the details.

Accepted practices to be observed on assemblies are as follows:

1. *Sectioning.* Parts should be sectioned using the American Standard symbols shown in Fig. 8.33. The practices of sectioning apply to assemblies.

2. *Views.* The main view, which is usually in full section, should show to the best advantage nearly all the individual parts and their locations. Additional views are shown only when they add necessary information that should be conveyed by the drawing.

3. *Hidden lines.* Hidden lines should be omitted from an assembly drawing, for they tend merely to overload it and create confusion. Complete shape description is unnecessary, since parts are either standard or are shown on detail drawings.

4. *Dimensions.* Overall dimensions and center-to-center distances indicating the relationship of parts in the machine as a whole are sometimes given. Detail dimensions are omitted, except on working-assembly drawings.

5. *Identification of parts.* Parts in a machine or structure are identified on the assembly drawing by numbers that are used on the details and in the bill of material (Fig. 17.7). These should be made at least $3/16$ in. high and enclosed in a $3/8$-in. circle. The centers of the circles are located not less than $3/4$ in. from the nearest line of the drawing. Leaders, terminated by arrowheads touching the parts, are drawn radial with a straightedge. The numbers, in order to be centered in the circles, should be made first and the circles drawn around them. An alternative method used in commercial practice is to letter the name and descriptive information for each part and draw a leader pointing to it in the main view.

17.21
Checking Drawings. Checking, the final assurance that the machine is correctly designed, should be done by a person (checker or squad foreman) who has not prepared the drawings but who is thoroughly familiar with the principles of the design. He must have a broad knowledge of shop practices and assembly methods. In commercial drafting rooms, the most experienced men are assigned to this type of work. The assembly drawing is checked against the detail drawings and corrections are indicated with either a soft or colored pencil. The checker should:

1. Survey the machine as a whole from the standpoint of operation, ease of assembly, and accessibility for repair work. He should consider the type, strength, and suitability of the materials.

2. Check each part with the parts adjacent to it, to make certain that proper clearances are maintained. (To determine whether or not all positions are free of interference, it may be necessary to lay out the extreme travel of moving parts to an enlarged scale.)

3. Study all drawings to see that each piece has been illustrated correctly and that all necessary views, types of views, treatments of views, and scales have been shown.

4. Check dimensions by scaling; calculate and check size and location dimensions that affect mating parts; determine the suitability of dimensions from the standpoint of the various departments' needs, such as pattern, forge, machine, assembly shop, and so on; examine views for proper dimensioning and mark unnecessary, repeated, or omitted dimensions.

5. Check tolerances, making sure the computations are correct and that proper fits have been used, so that there will be no unnecessary production costs.

6. See that finishes and such operations as drilling, reaming, boring, tapping, and grinding are properly specified.

7. Check specifications for material.

8. Examine notes for correctness and location.

9. See that stock sizes have been used for standard parts, such as bolts, screws, keys, and so on. (Stock sizes may be determined from catalogs.)

10. Add any additional explanatory notes that should supply necessary information.

11. Check the bill of material to see that each part is completely and correctly specified.

12. Check items in the title block.

13. Make a final survey of the drawing in its entirety, making certain there is either a check or correction for each dimension, note, and specification.

17.22
Installation Assembly Drawings. An installation drawing gives useful information for putting a machine or structure together. The names of parts, order of as-

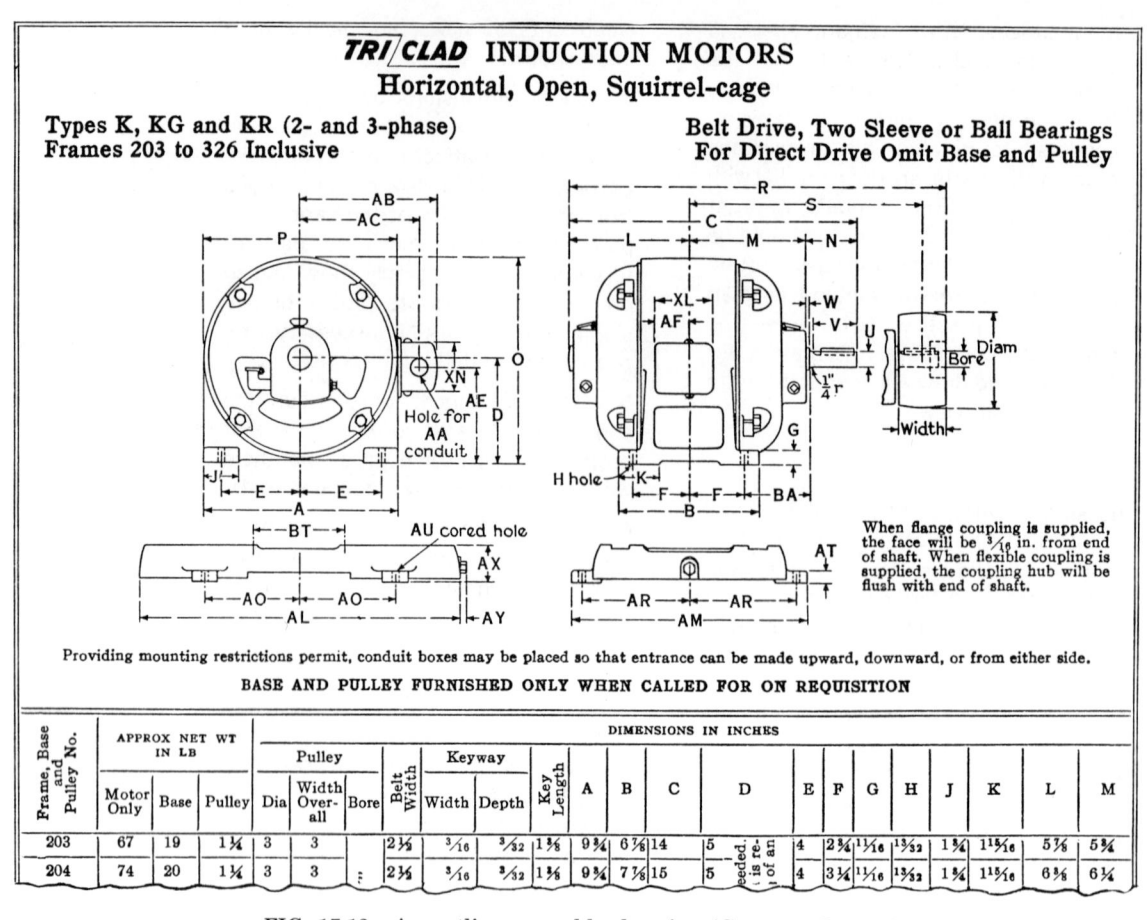

TRI/CLAD INDUCTION MOTORS
Horizontal, Open, Squirrel-cage

Types K, KG and KR (2- and 3-phase)
Frames 203 to 326 Inclusive

Belt Drive, Two Sleeve or Ball Bearings
For Direct Drive Omit Base and Pulley

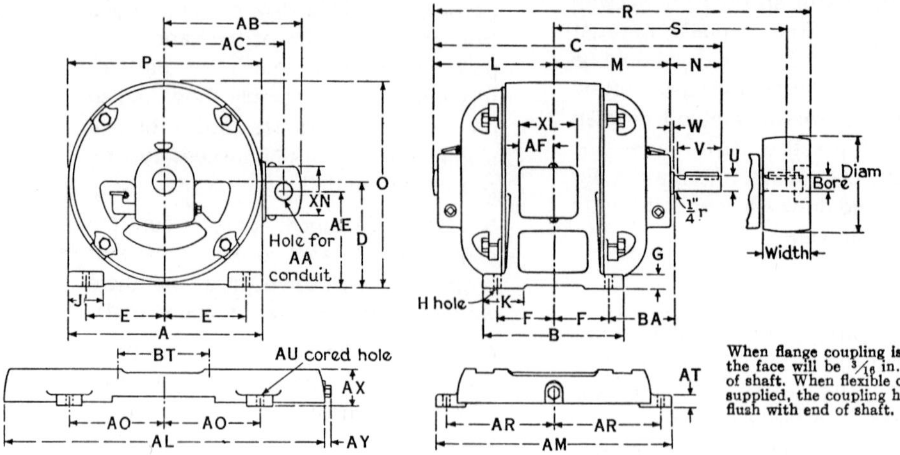

When flange coupling is supplied, the face will be 3/16 in. from end of shaft. When flexible coupling is supplied, the coupling hub will be flush with end of shaft.

Providing mounting restrictions permit, conduit boxes may be placed so that entrance can be made upward, downward, or from either side.

BASE AND PULLEY FURNISHED ONLY WHEN CALLED FOR ON REQUISITION

Frame, Base and Pulley No.	APPROX NET WT IN LB			DIMENSIONS IN INCHES																			
				Pulley				Keyway															
	Motor Only	Base	Pulley	Dia	Width Over-all	Bore	Belt Width	Width	Depth	Key Length	A	B	C	D	E	F	G	H	J	K	L	M
203	67	19	1¼	3	3		2½	3/16	3/32	1⅜	9¾	6⅞	14	5 eeded. is re- of an	4	2¾	11/16	13/32	1¾	1 15/16	5⅞	5¾
204	74	20	1¼	3	3	:	2½	3/16	3/32	1⅜	9¾	7⅞	15	5	4	3¼	11/16	13/32	1¾	1 15/16	6⅜	6¼

FIG. 17.12. An outline assembly drawing (*Courtesy General Electric Co.*).

sembling parts, location dimensions, and special instructions for operating may also be shown.

17.23
Outline Assembly Drawings. Outline assembly drawings are most frequently made for illustrative purposes in catalogs. Usually they show merely overall and principal dimensions (Fig. 17.12). Their appearance may be improved by the use of line shading.

17.24
Exploded Pictorial Assembly Drawings for Parts Lists and Instruction Manuals. Exploded pictorial assembly drawings are used frequently in the parts lists sections of company catalogs and in instruction manuals. Drawings of this type are easily understood by those with very little experience in reading multiview drawings. Figure 17.13 shows a commercial example of an exploded pictorial assembly drawing.

17.25
Diagram Assembly Drawings. Diagram drawings may be grouped into two general classes: (1) those composed of single lines and conventional symbols, such as piping

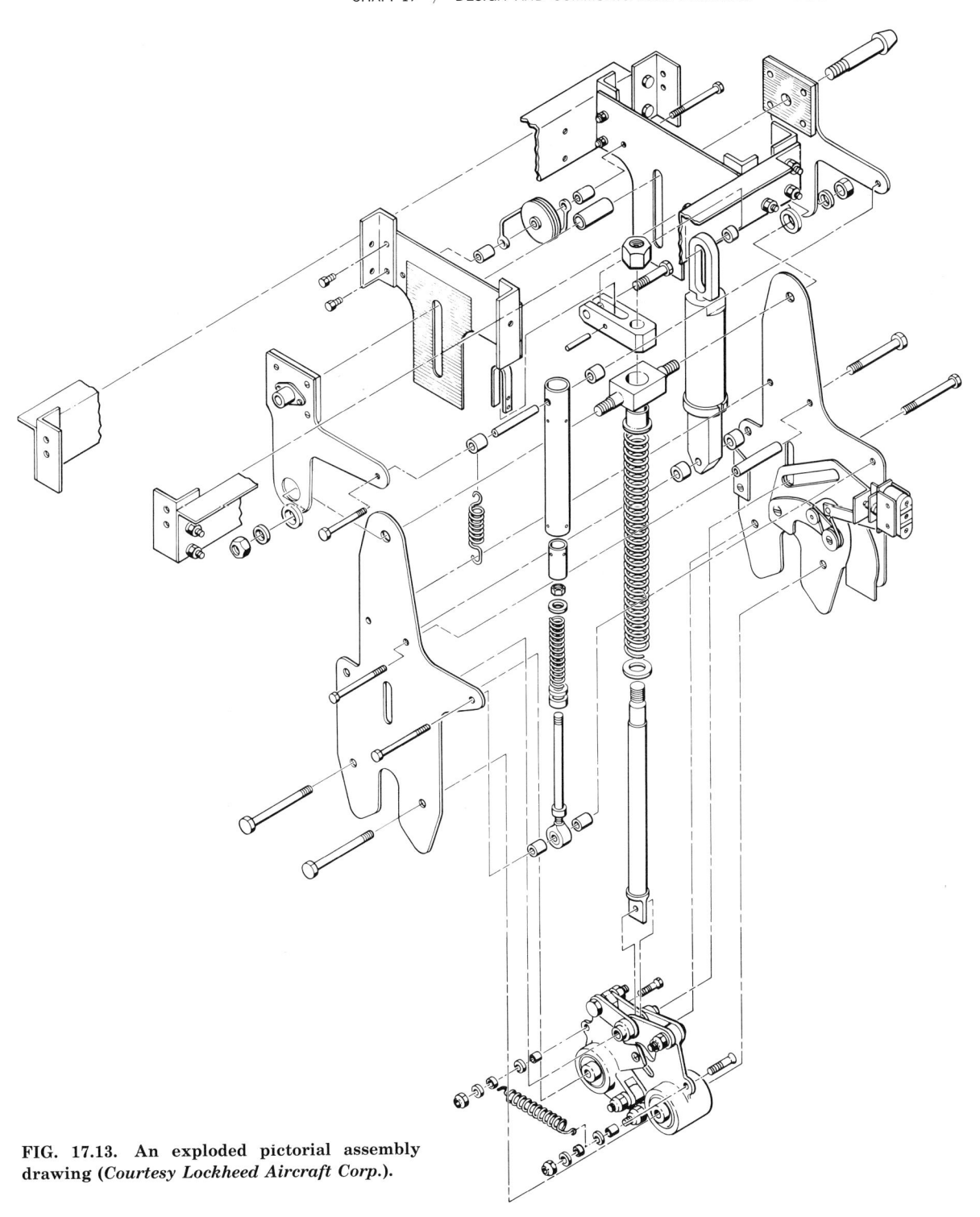

FIG. 17.13. An exploded pictorial assembly drawing (*Courtesy Lockheed Aircraft Corp.*).

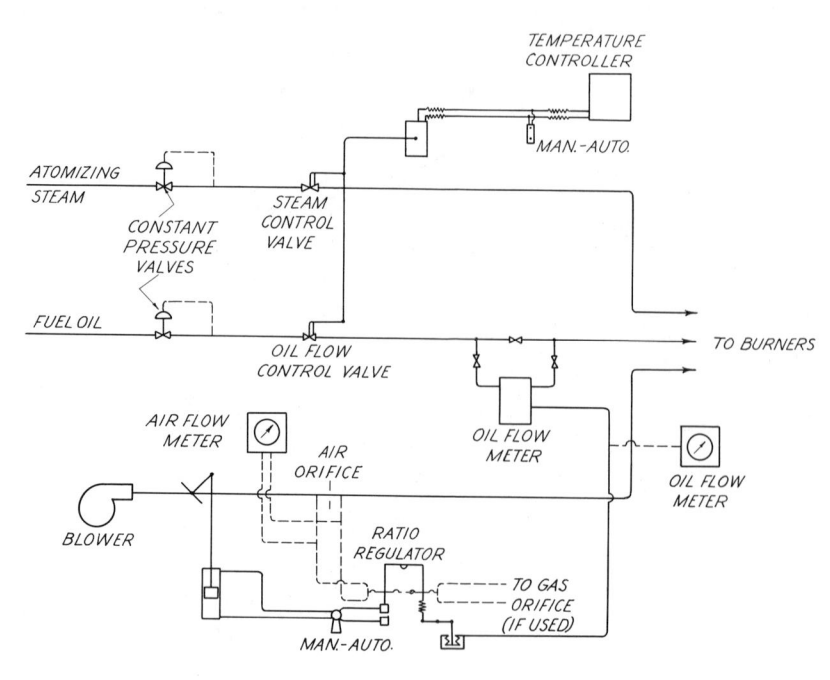

FIG. 17.14. A diagram assembly drawing (*Courtesy "Instruments Magazine"*).

diagrams, wiring diagrams, and so on (Fig. 17.14); and (2) those drawn in regular projection, such as an erection drawing, which may be shown in either orthographic or pictorial projection.

Piping diagrams give the size of pipe, location of fittings, and so on. To draw an assembly of a piping system in true orthographic projection would add no information and merely entail needless work.

A large portion of electrical drawing is composed of diagrammatic sketches using conventional electrical symbols (Fig. 17.15). Electrical engineers therefore need to know the American National (ASA) Standard wiring symbols given in the Appendix.

17.26
Chemical Engineering Drawings. In general, the chemical engineer is concerned with plant layouts and equipment design. He must be well informed on the types of machinery used in grinding, drying, mixing, evaporation, sedimentation, and distillation, and must be able to design or select conveying machinery.

It is obvious that the determining of the sequence of operations, selecting of machinery, arranging of piping, and so on, must be done by a trained chemical engineer who can speak the basic language of the mechanical, electrical, or civil engineer with whom he must cooperate. To be able to do this, he must have a thorough knowledge of the principles of engineering drawing.

Plant layout drawings, the satisfactory development of which requires numerous preliminary sketches (layouts, scale diagrams, flow sheets, and so on), show the location of machines, equipment, and the like. Often, if the machinery and apparatus are used in the manufacturing of chemicals and are of a specialized nature, a chemical engineer is called on to do the designing. It even may be necessary for him to build experimental apparatus.

17.27
Electrical Engineering Drawings. Electrical engineering drawings are of two types: machine drawings and diagrammatic assemblies (Fig. 17.15). Working drawings, which are made for electrical machinery, involve all of the principles and conventions of the working drawings of the mechanical engineer. Diagrammatic drawings have been discussed in Sec. 17.25. The practices to be followed in preparing drawings of electrical systems are presented in Chapter 24.

17.28
Civil Engineering Drawings. The civil engineer is concerned with a broad field of construction and with civic planning. The drawings prepared for civil engineers may

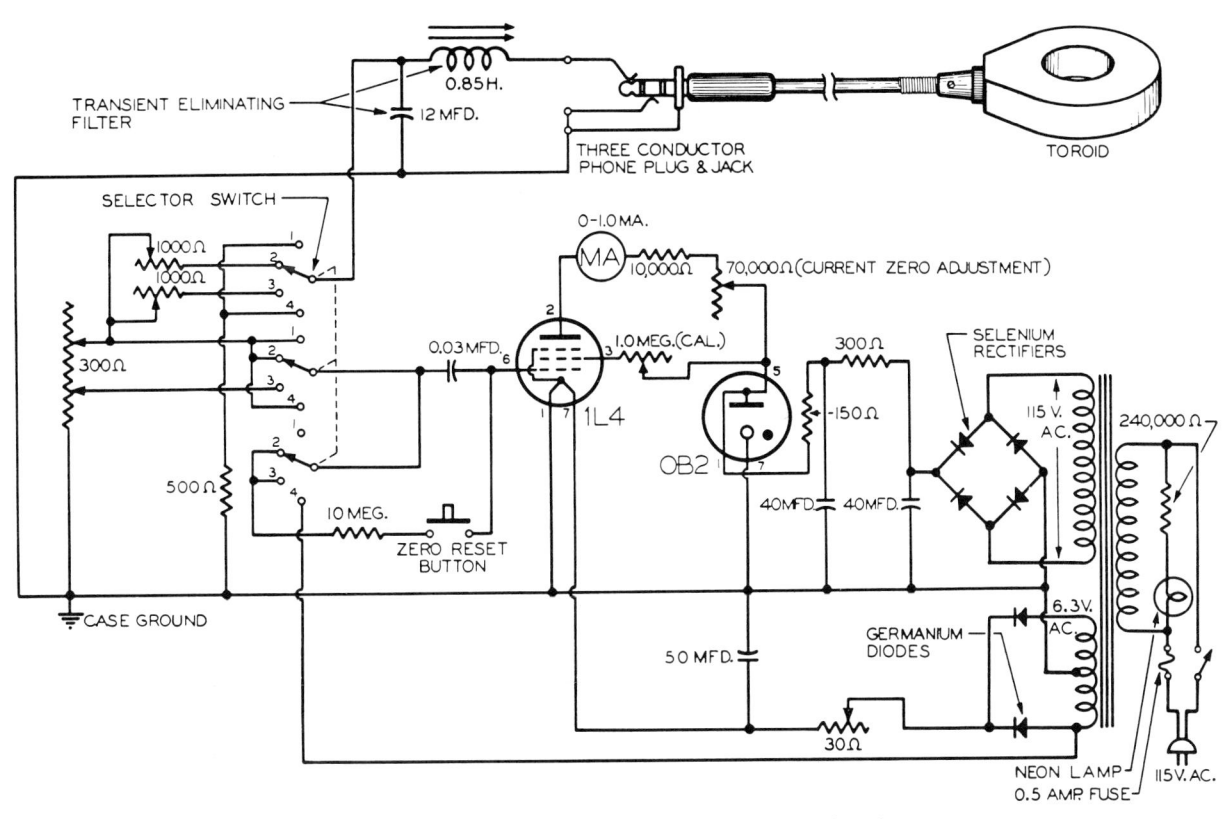

FIG. 17.15. A schematic drawing *(Courtesy General Motors Corp.)*.

PROBLEMS

The four general types of problems presented in this chapter have been designed to furnish practice in the preparation of working drawings or sketches. The first type is composed of dimensioned pictorial drawings of individual pieces taken from a variety of mechanisms. The student should prepare complete working detail drawings of these pieces as they may be assigned by his instructor. It should be recognized

be in the nature of maps for city, state, and nationwide planning for streets, water systems, sewerage systems, airports, highways, railroads, harbor and waterways or they may be design, fabrication, and erection drawings for concrete and steel structures, as in the case of buildings and bridges. Information needed for the preparation of drawings of these types may be found in Chapters 25 and 27.

that dimensions are not necessarily placed the same on orthographic views as they are on pictorial drawings. To make it possible for the student to apply the principles presented in Chapter 16, no special effort has been made to place dimensions in accordance with the rules of good practice.

The second type of problem is that which shows in pictorial all the parts of a unit mecha-

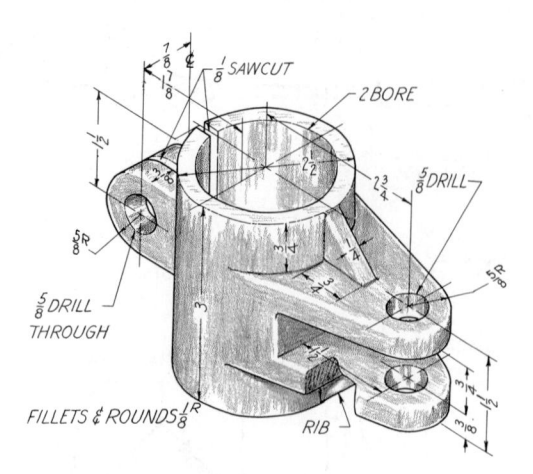

FIG. 17.16. Guide bracket.

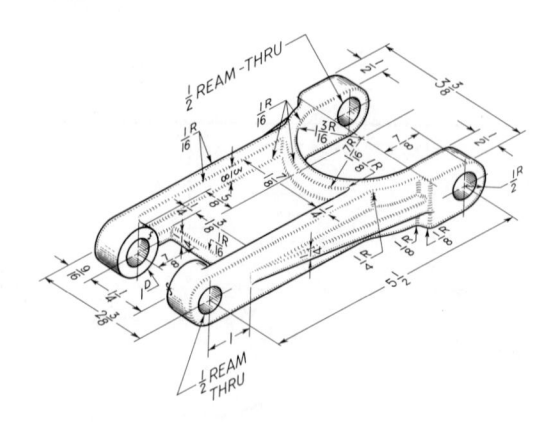

FIG. 17.17. Link.

nism. This gives the student an opportunity to prepare a complete set of working drawings of a simple unit. It is suggested that the detail drawings be prepared before the assembly is drawn.

The third and fourth types provide practice in both reading and preparing drawings, the third requiring the preparation of detail drawings from given assembly drawings, the fourth requiring the making of assembly drawings from the details.

1–13. (Figs. 17.16–17.28). Make a detail drawing of an assigned machine part. Draw all necessary views. Give a detail title with suitable notes concerning material, number required, etc.

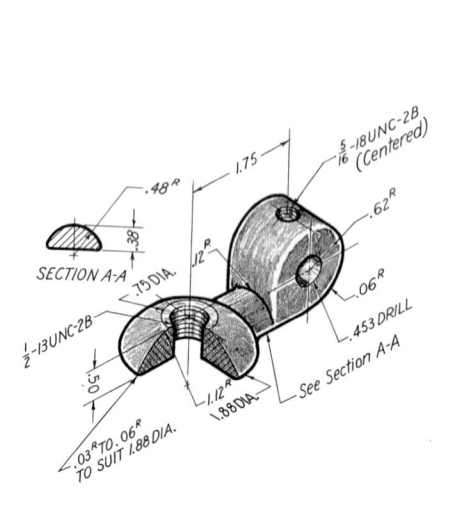

FIG. 17.18. Handle block.

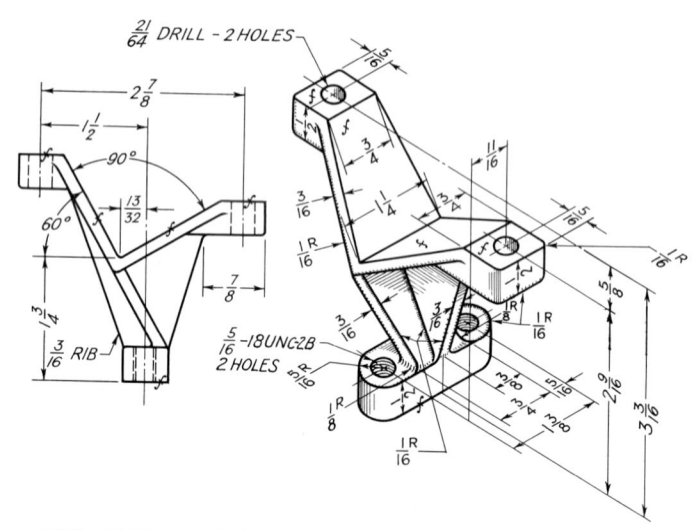

FIG. 17.19. Angle bracket.

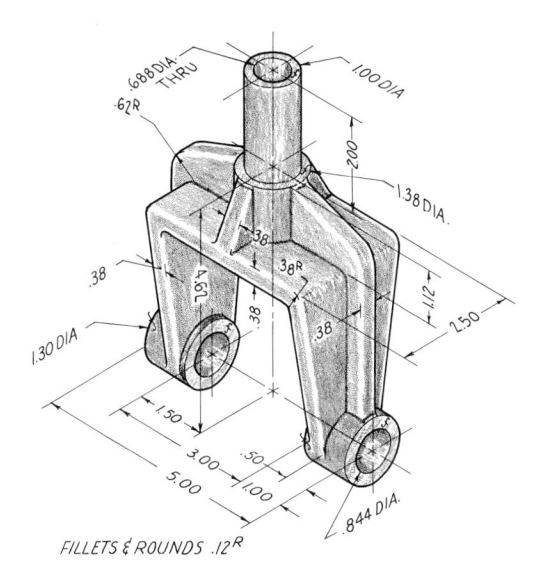

FIG. 17.20. Caster frame.

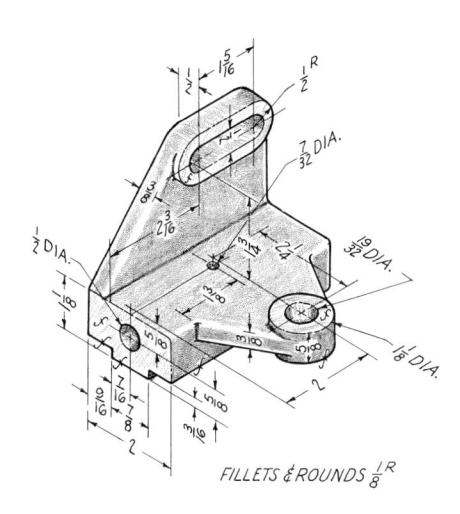

FIG. 17.21. Slide bracket.

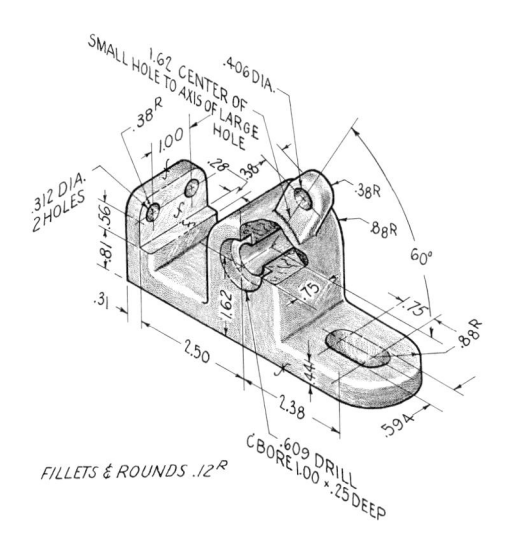

FIG. 17.22. Stabilizer bracket.

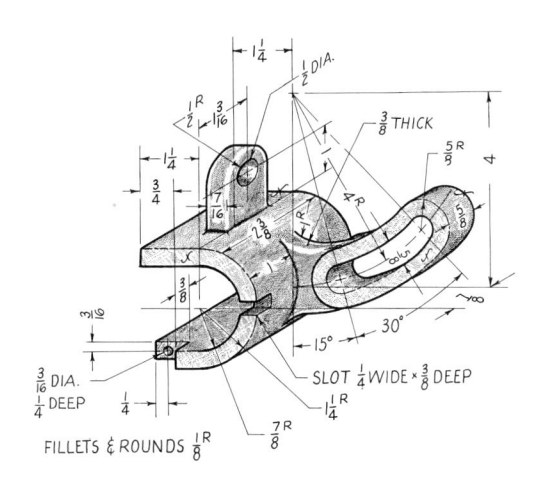

FIG. 17.23. Gear-shifter link.

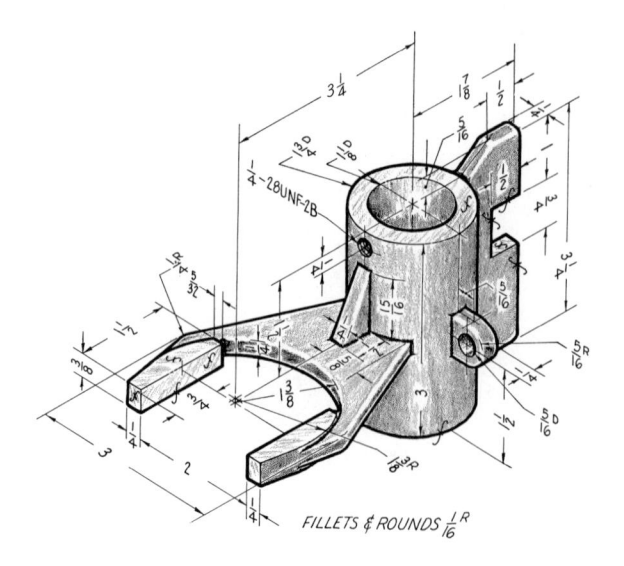

FIG. 17.24. Gear shifting fork.

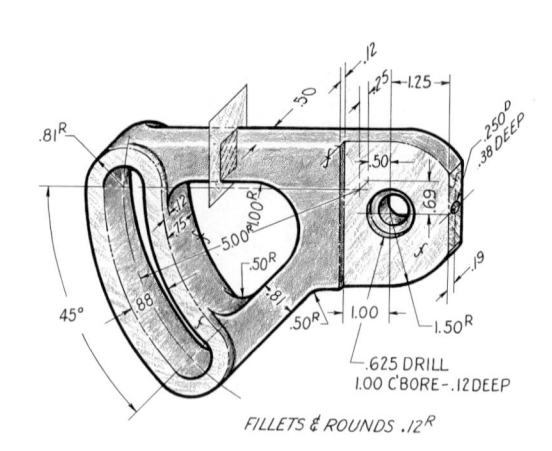

FIG. 17.25. Shifter guide.

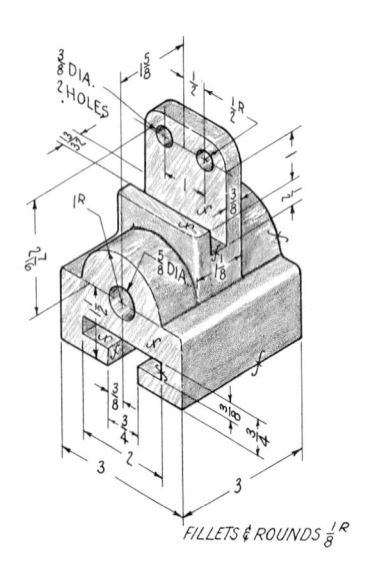

FIG. 17.26. Slide block.

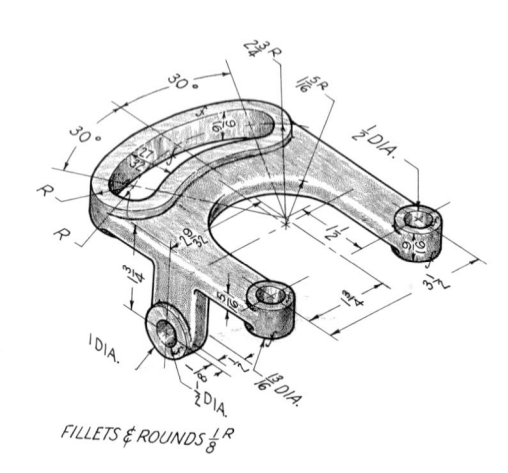

FIG. 17.27. Shifter arm.

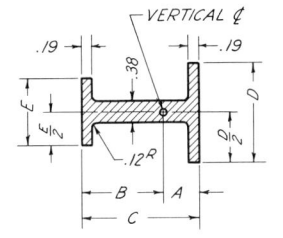

FIG. 17.28. Shaft hanger.

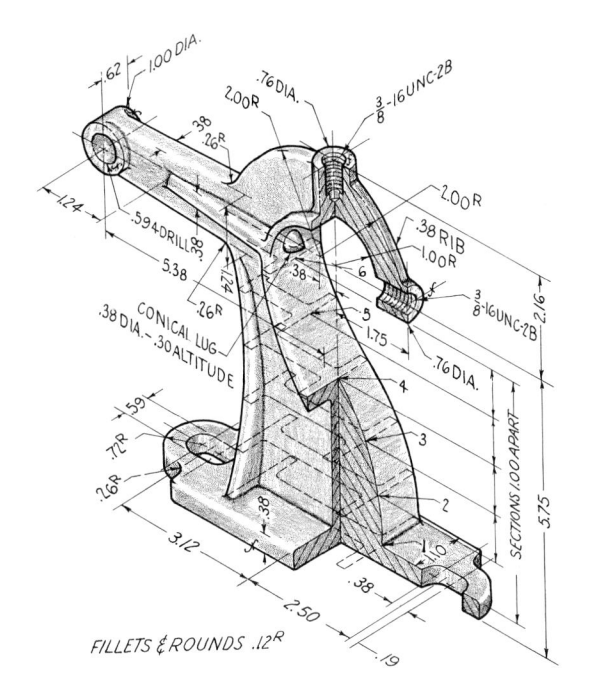

SECTION NUMBER	A	B	C	D	E
1	1.00	2.00	3.00	1.88	1.62
2	.94	1.88	2.82	1.75	1.38
3	.62	1.82	2.44	1.62	1.12
4	0.00	1.88	1.88	1.50	.88
5	.68	2.12	1.44	1.38	.62
6	1.00	–	–	1.25	–

14. (Fig. 17.29). Make a two-view freehand detail sketch of the fan spindle. Determine dimensions by transferring them from the drawing to the open-divided scale, by means of the dividers. The material is SAE 1045, CRS. Shaft limits for the bearings are

$$\frac{.7874}{.7867} \quad \text{and} \quad \frac{.9840}{.9836}.$$

Use an RC7 fit between spindle and felt retainer, spindle and felt-retaining washer, and spindle and cone-clamp washer.

15. (Fig. 17.29). Make a complete two-view detail drawing of the fan pulley. It is suggested that a half-circular view and a full-sectional view be shown. Determine the dimensions as suggested in Problem 14. Housing limits for the given bearings are

$$\frac{1.8497}{1.8503} \quad \text{and} \quad \frac{2.4401}{2.4409}.$$

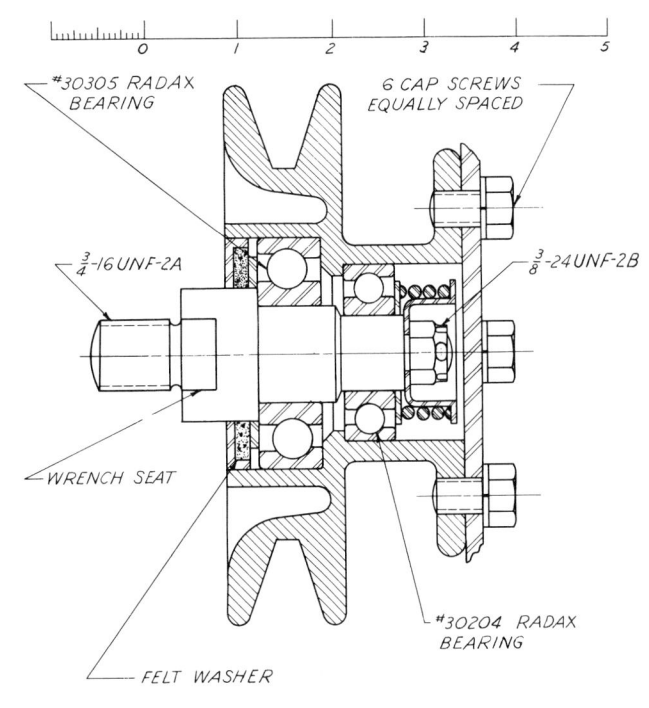

FIG. 17.29. Fan assembly.

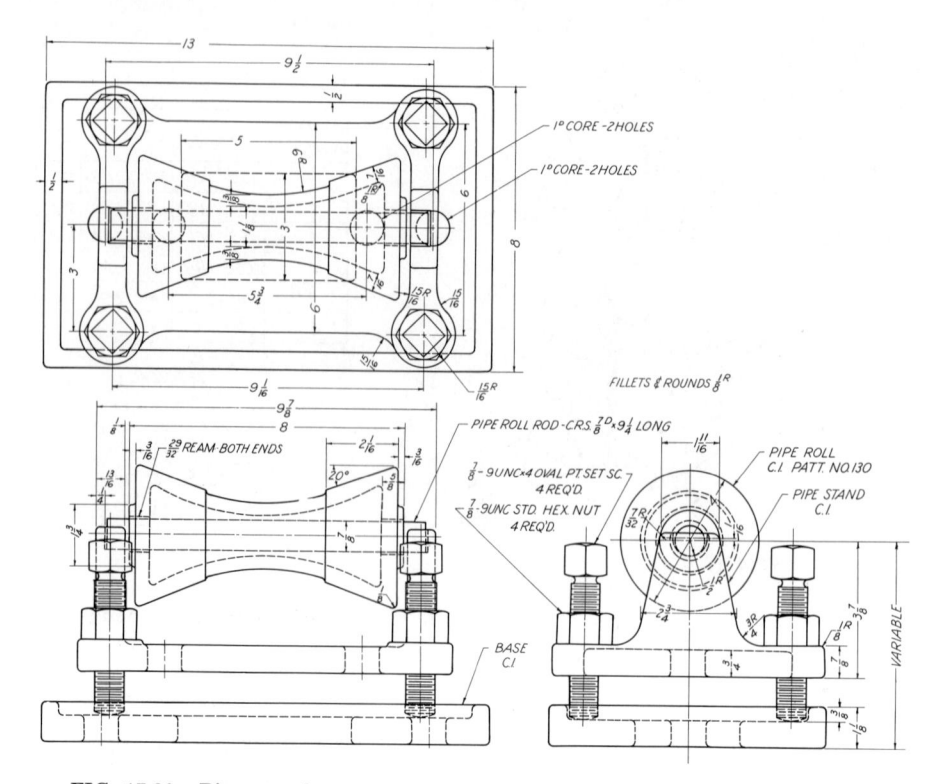

FIG. 17.30. Pipe stand.

16. (Fig. 17.30). Make a detail drawing of an assigned part of the pipe stand.

CHAP. 17 / DESIGN AND COMMUNICATION DRAWINGS   411

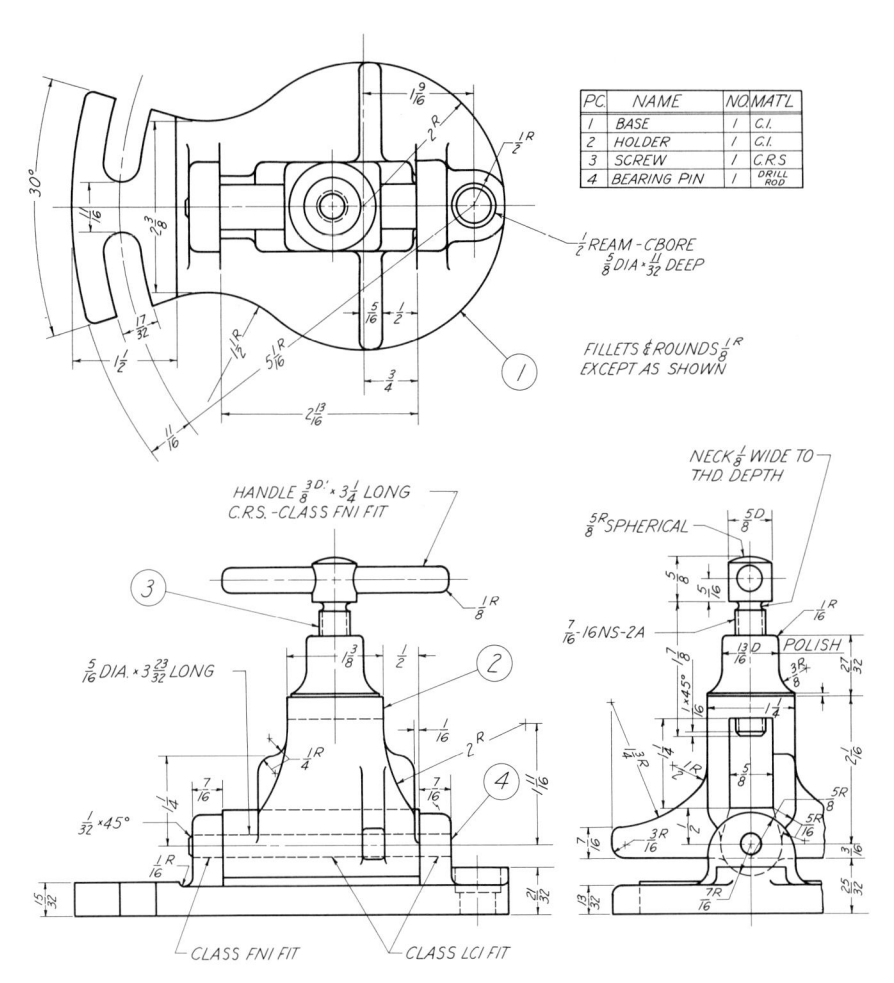

FIG. 17.31. Tool holder.

17. (Fig. 17.31). Make a fully dimensioned drawing of an assigned part of the tool holder.

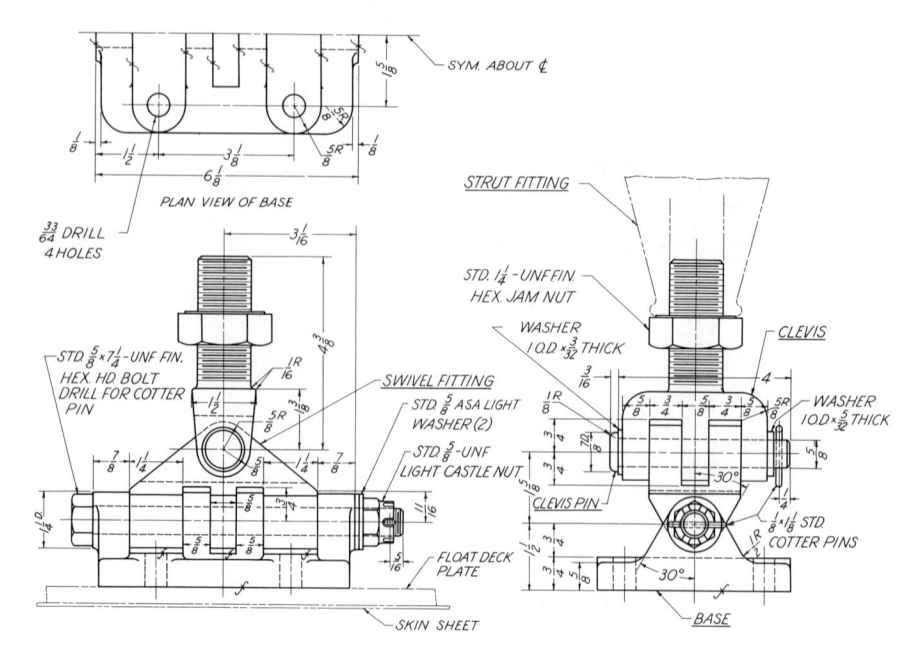

FIG. 17.32. Flexible joint.

18. (Fig. 17.32). Make a detail working drawing of an assigned part of the flexible joint. Compose a suitable title, giving the name of the part, the material, etc.

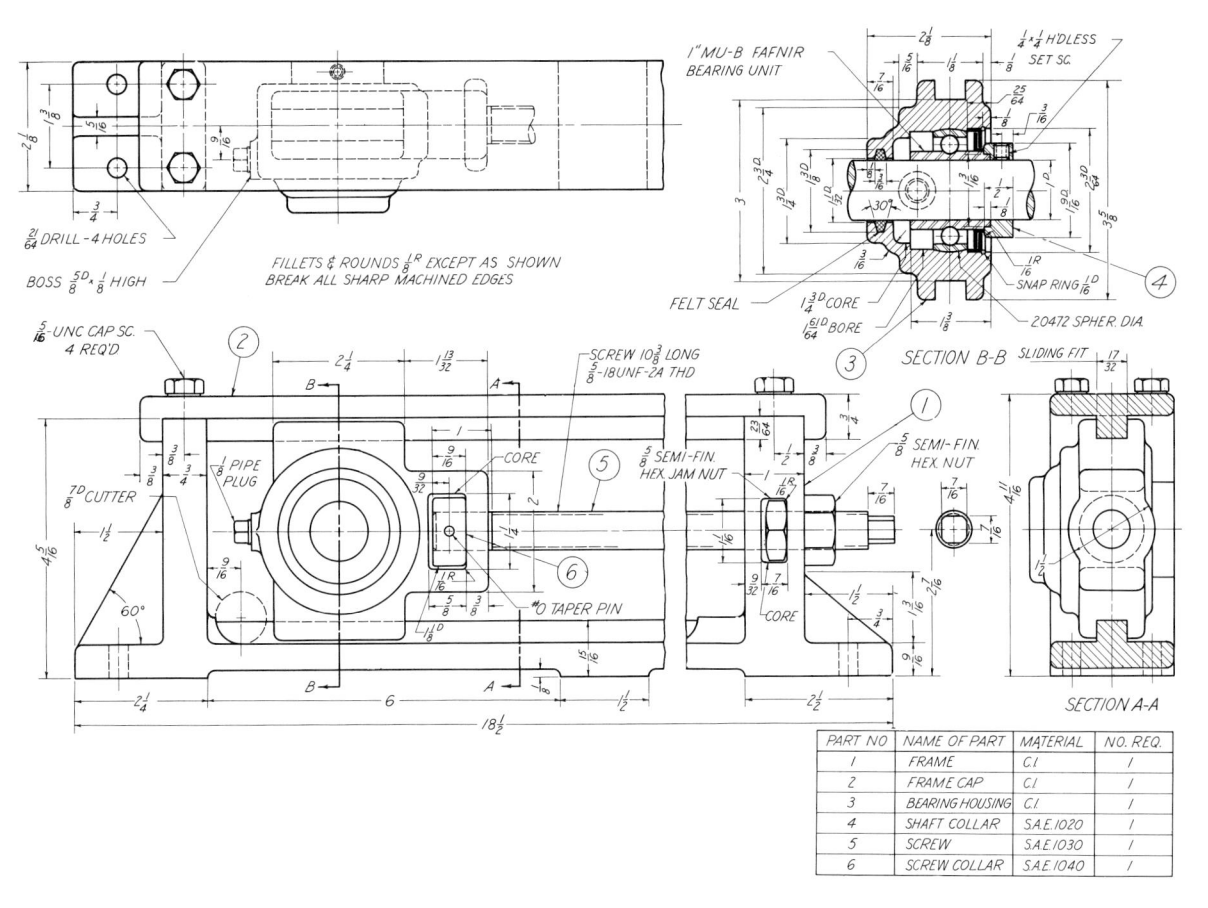

FIG. 17.33. Conveyor take-up unit.

19. (Fig. 17.33). Make a detail drawing of an assigned part of the conveyor take-up unit.

PC.NO.	NAME	QUAN.	MATERIAL	PC.NO.	NAME	QUAN.	MATERIAL
1	STANDARD	1	MALL. IRON	5	GROOVE PIN	3	7/32 D × 5/8 STEEL ROD
2	SCREW	1	S.A.E. 1120 FORGING	6	LEVER BAR	1	REROLLED RAIL STK.
3	CAP	1	S.A.E. 1045 FORGING	7	7/8 DIA. BALL BEARING	1	STD.
4	THRUST WASHER	1	S.A.E. 2315				

20. (Fig. 17.34). Make a detail drawing of an assigned part of the Simplex ball-bearing screw jack.

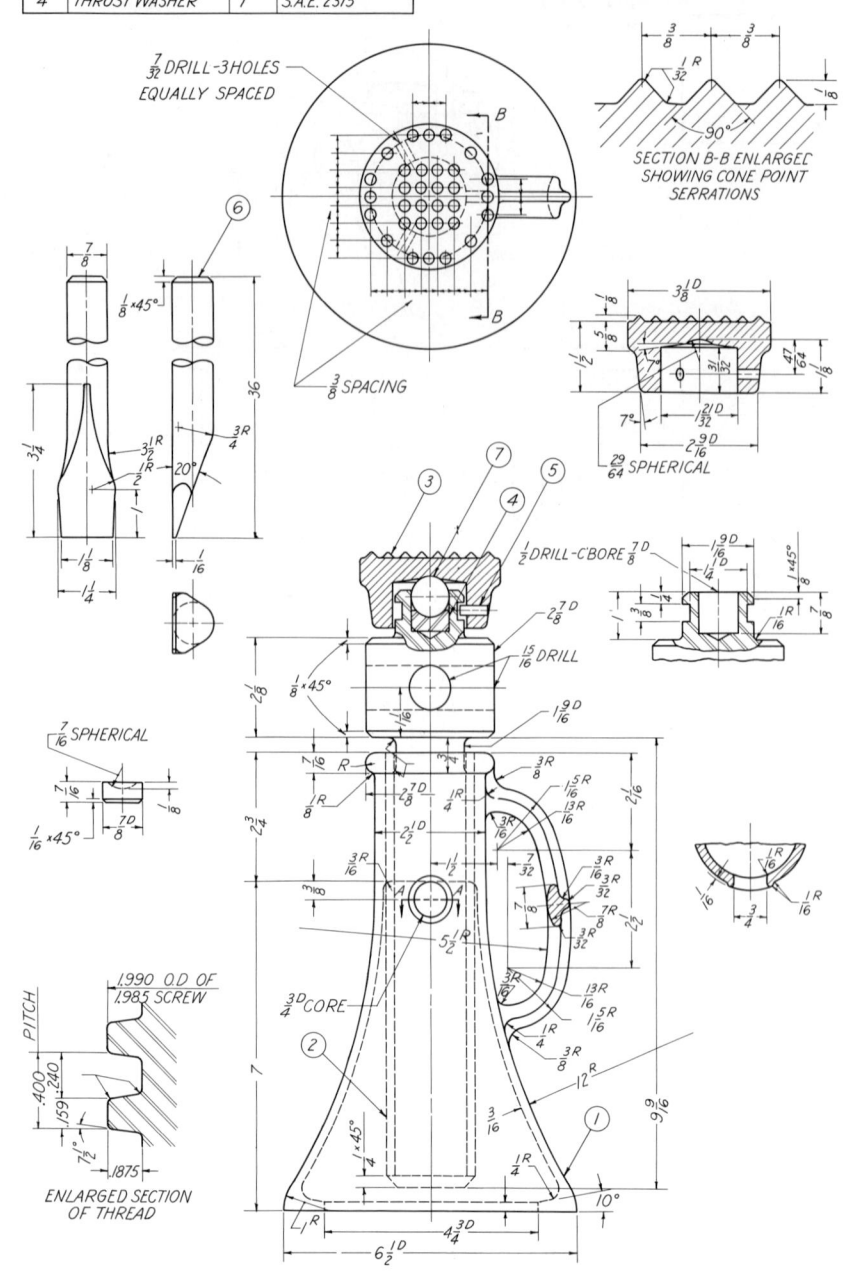

FIG. 17.34. Simplex ball-bearing screw jack (*Courtesy Templeton, Kenly & Co.*).

21. (Fig. 17.35). Make a detail drawing of an assigned part of the bench arbor press.

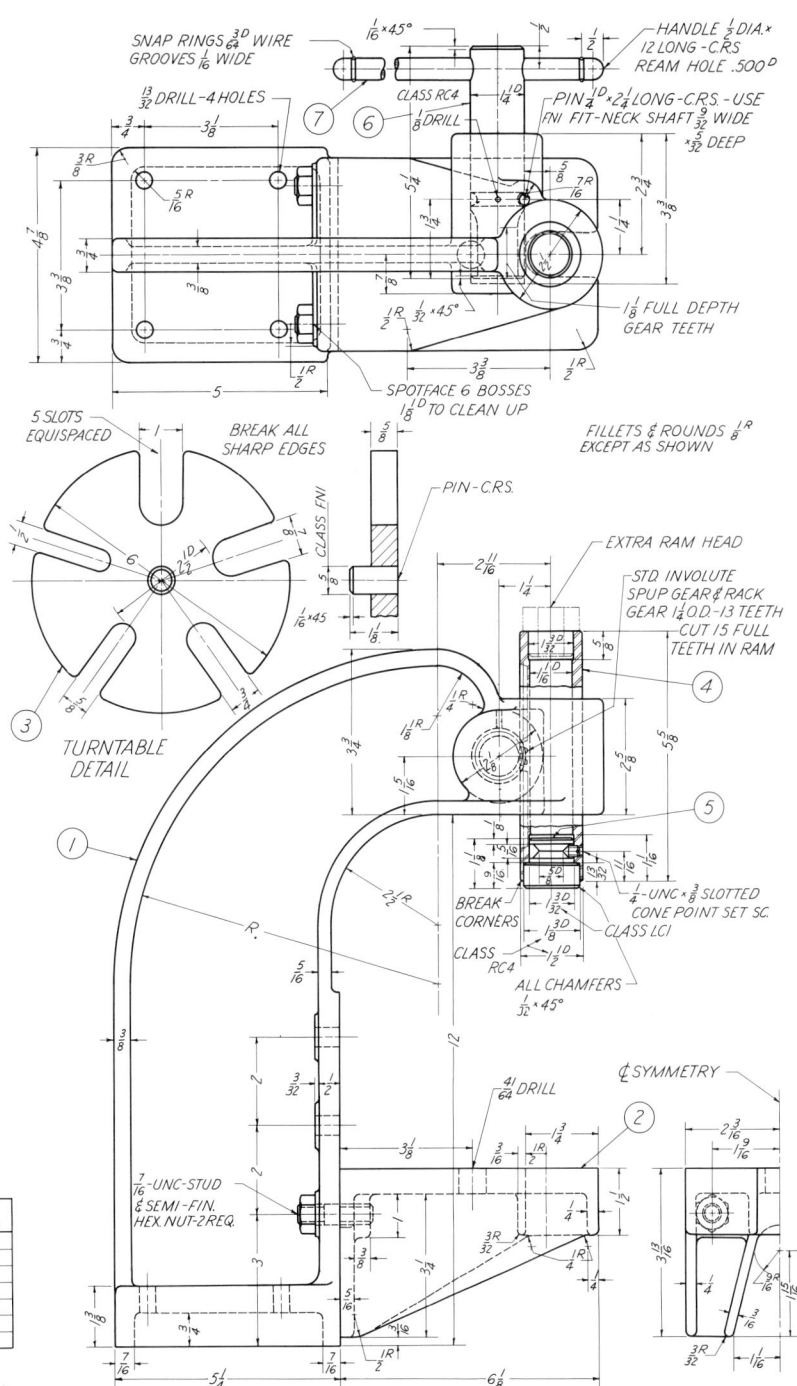

FIG. 17.35. Bench arbor press.

PART NO.	NAME	MATERIAL	NO. REQ.
1	BASE	C.I.	1
2	TABLE	C.I.	1
3	TURNTABLE	C.I.	1
4	RAM	S.A.E. 1045	1
5	RAM HEAD	S.A.E. 1040	1
6	SPINDLE	S.A.E. 1045	1
7	HANDLE	C.R.S.	1

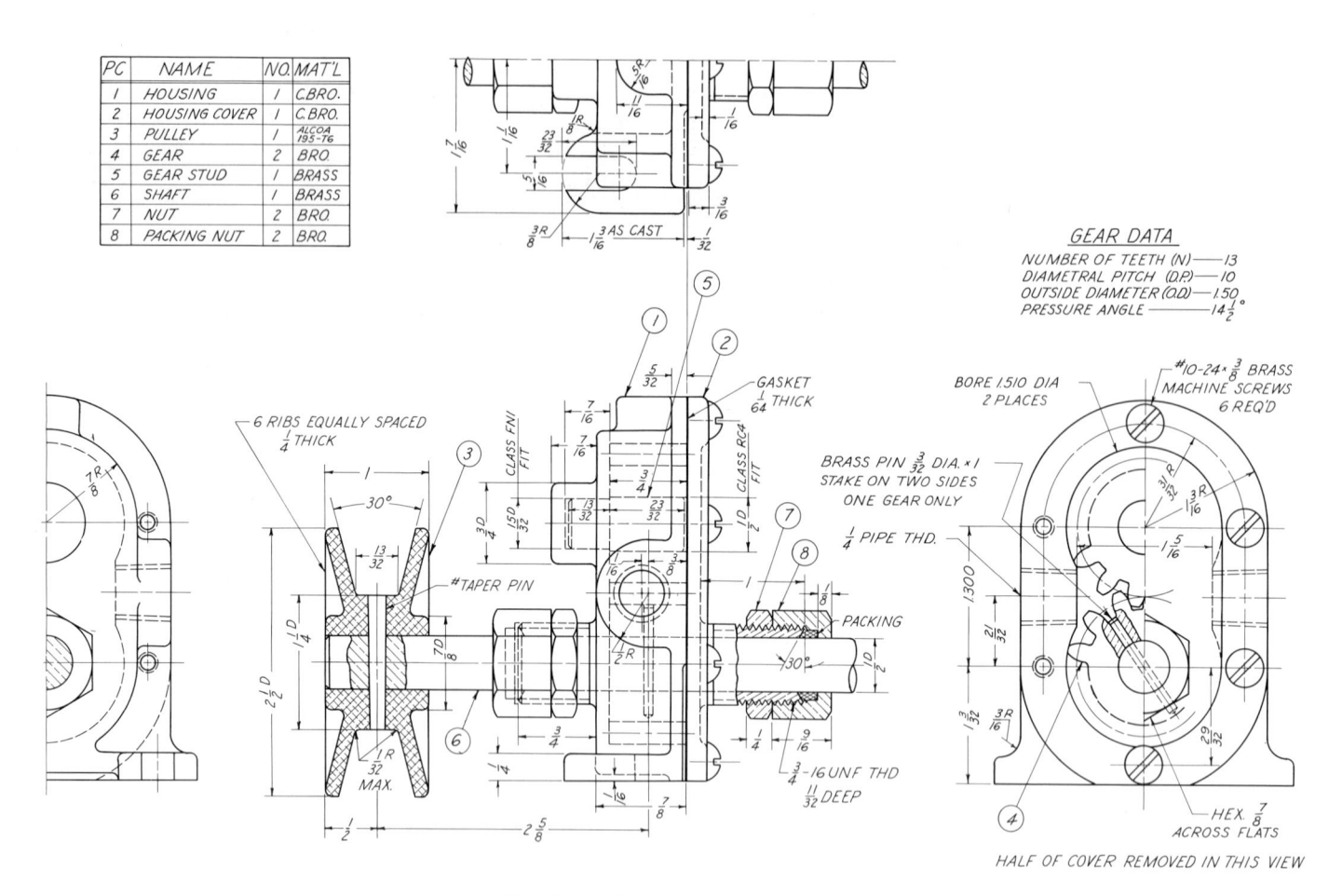

FIG. 17.36. Gear pump.

22. (Fig. 17.36). Make a detail drawing of an assigned part of the gear pump.

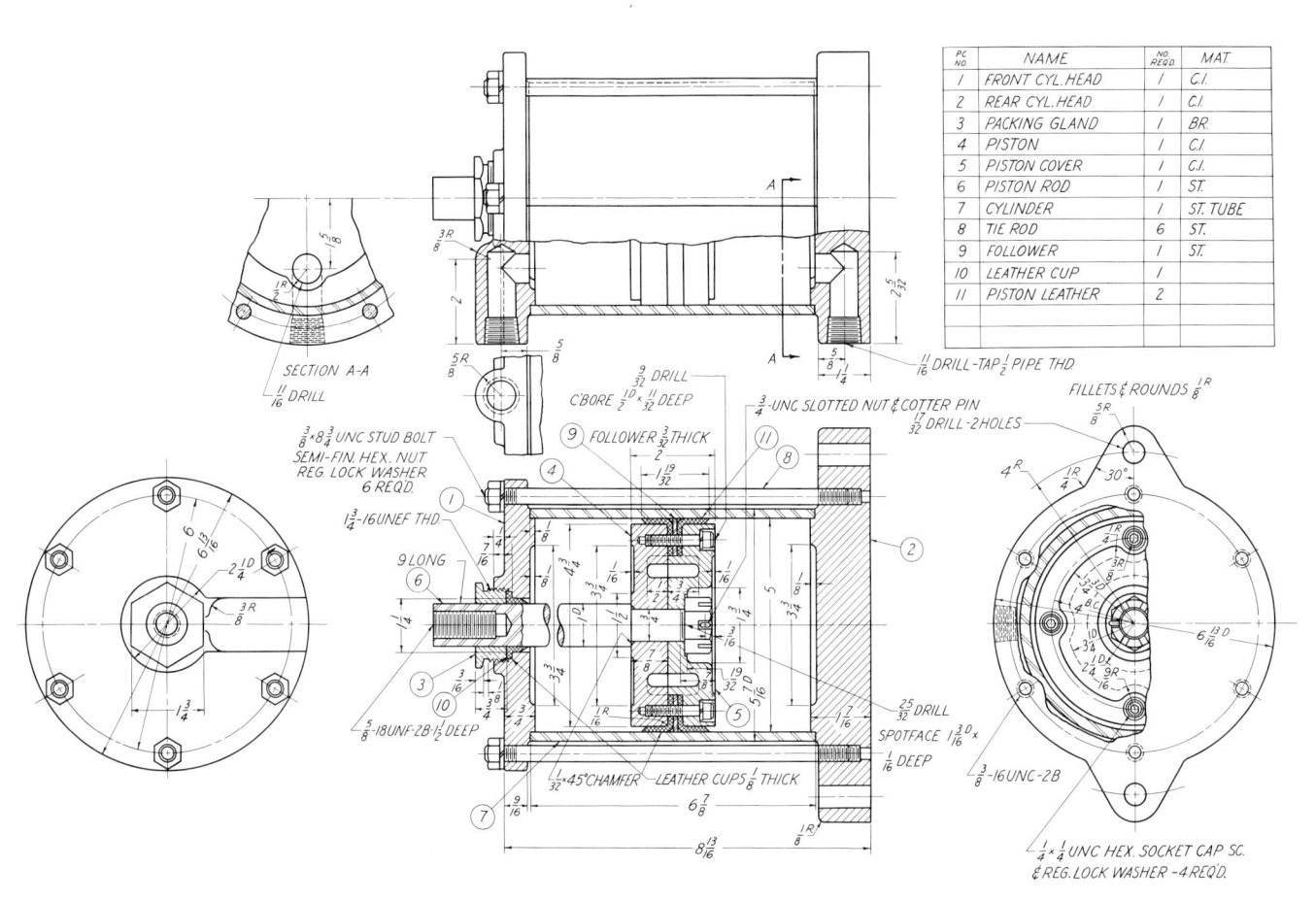

FIG. 17.37. Air cylinder.

23. (Fig. 17.37). Make a detail drawing of an assigned part of the air cylinder.

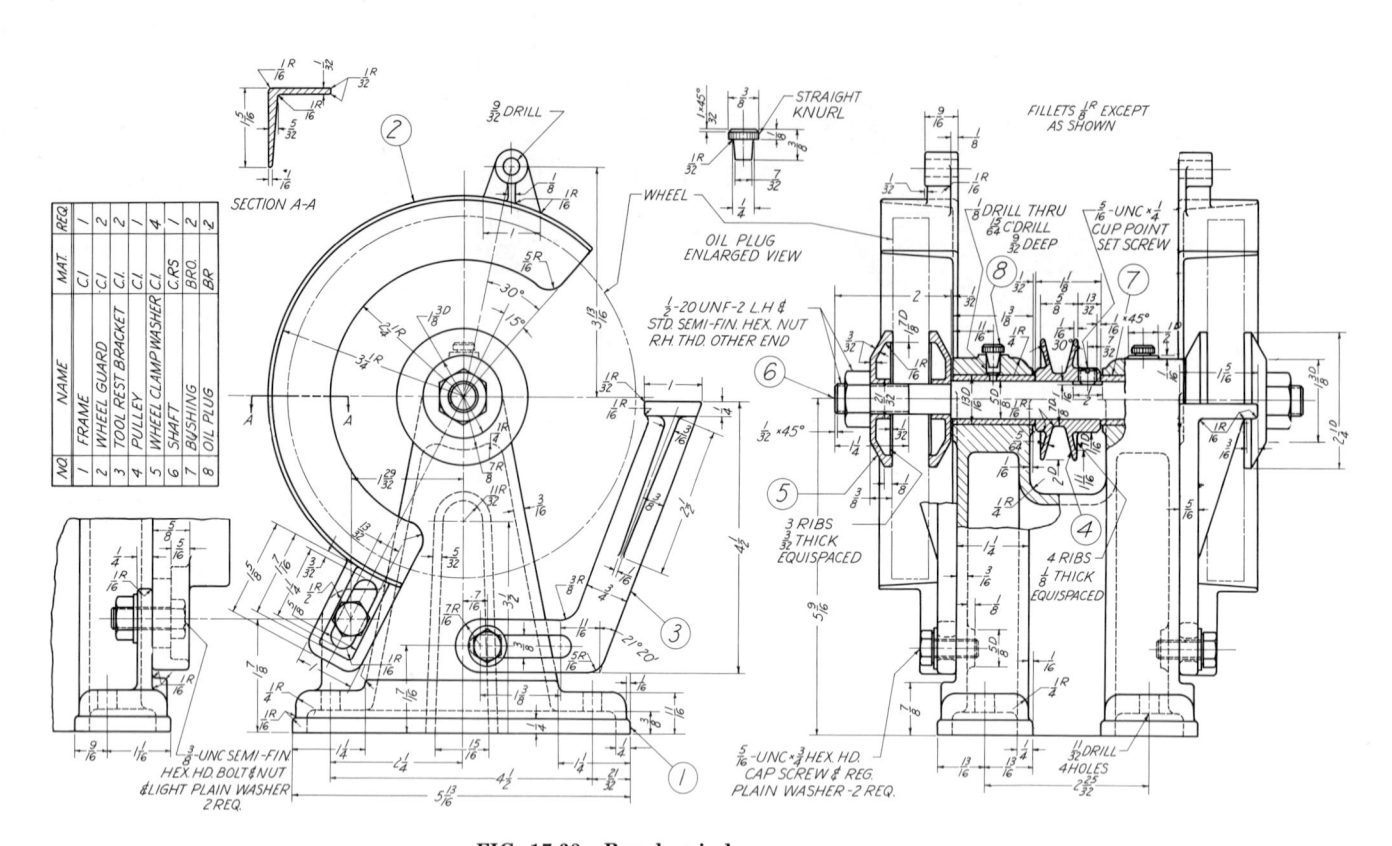

FIG. 17.38. Bench grinder.

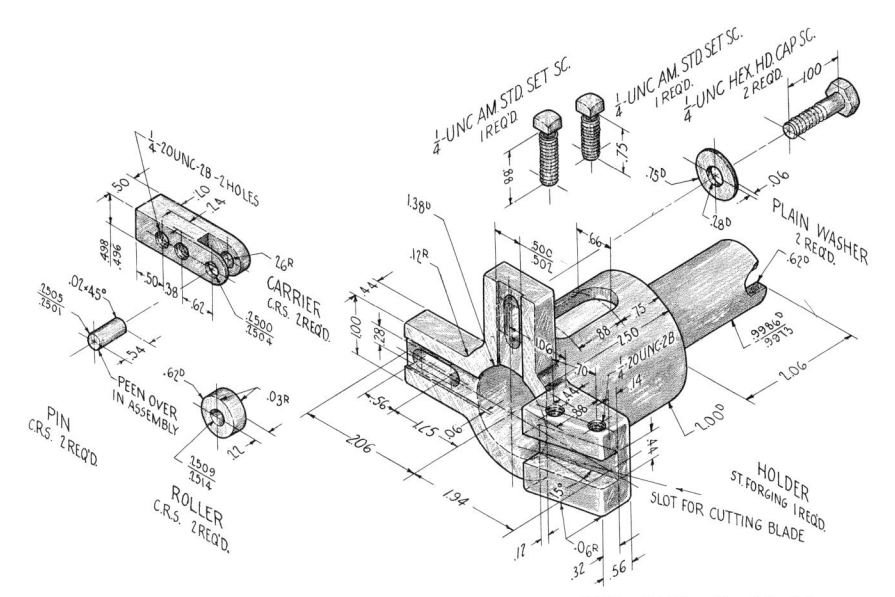

FIG. 17.39. Tool holder.

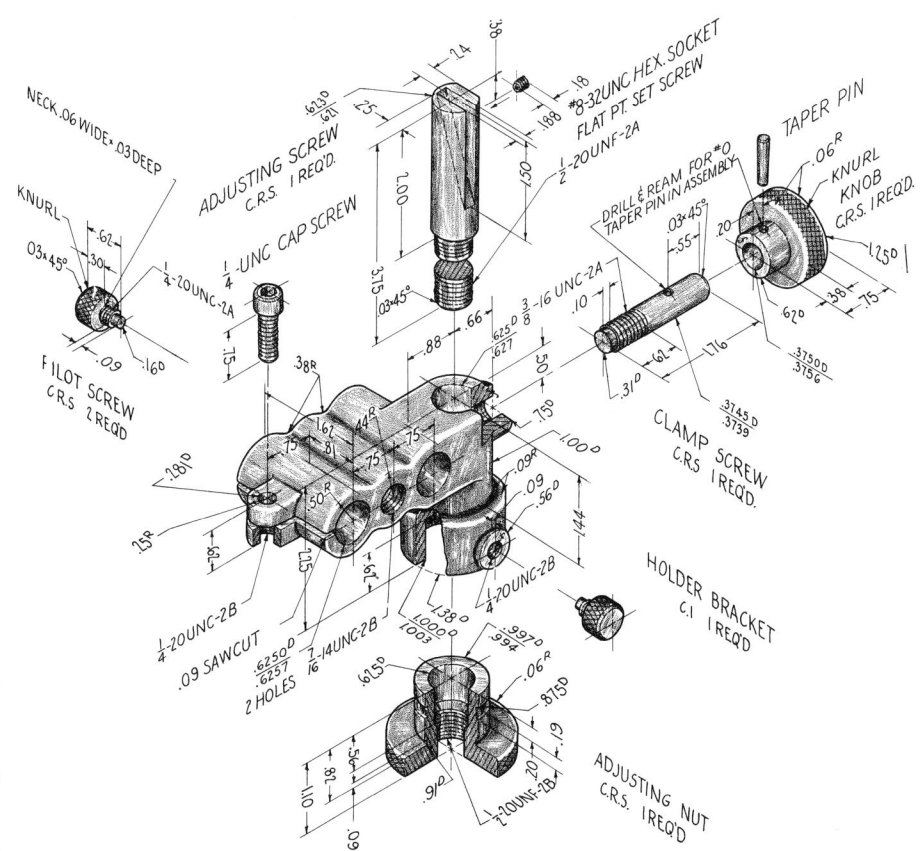

24. (Fig. 17.38). Make a detail drawing of an assigned part of the bench grinder.

25. (Fig. 17.39). Make detail drawings of the carrier and the holder. Make an assembly drawing showing all of the parts in their relative positions.

26. (Fig. 17.40). Make a complete set of working drawings of the adjustable attachment. The complete set should consist of detail drawings of the individual parts and an assembly drawing complete with a bill of material.

FIG. 17.40. Adjustable attachment.

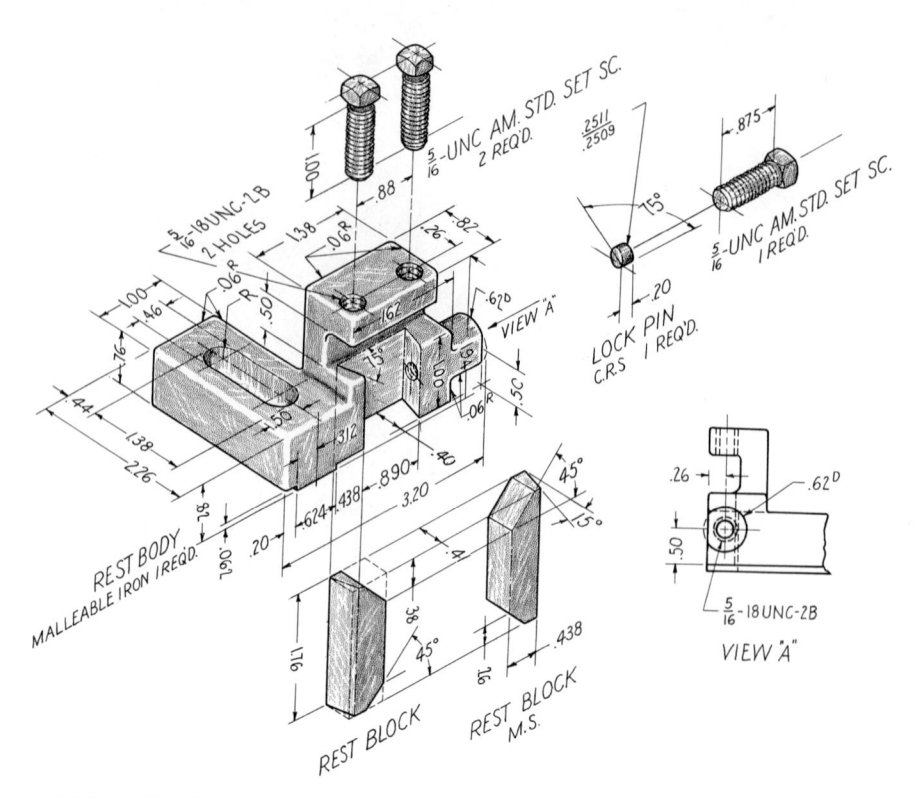

FIG. 17.41. Stock rest.

27. (Fig. 17.41). Make detail drawings of the rest body and the rest block. Make an assembly drawing showing the parts of the stock rest assembled in their relative positions.

28. (Fig. 17.42). Make a two-view assembly drawing of the cup center, using the given details. Use the schematic symbol for screw threads. Study the pictorial drawing carefully before starting the views.

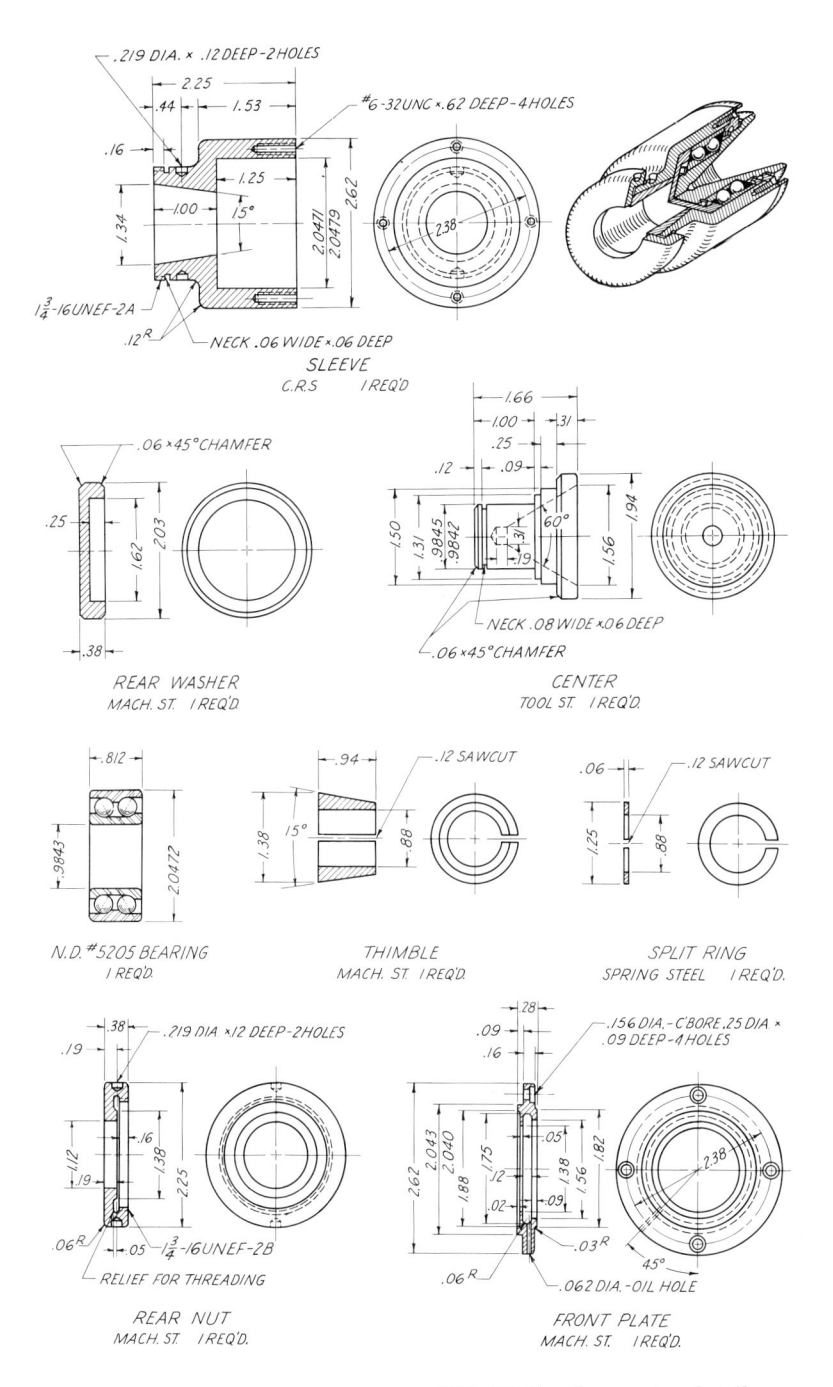

FIG. 17.42. Cup center details.

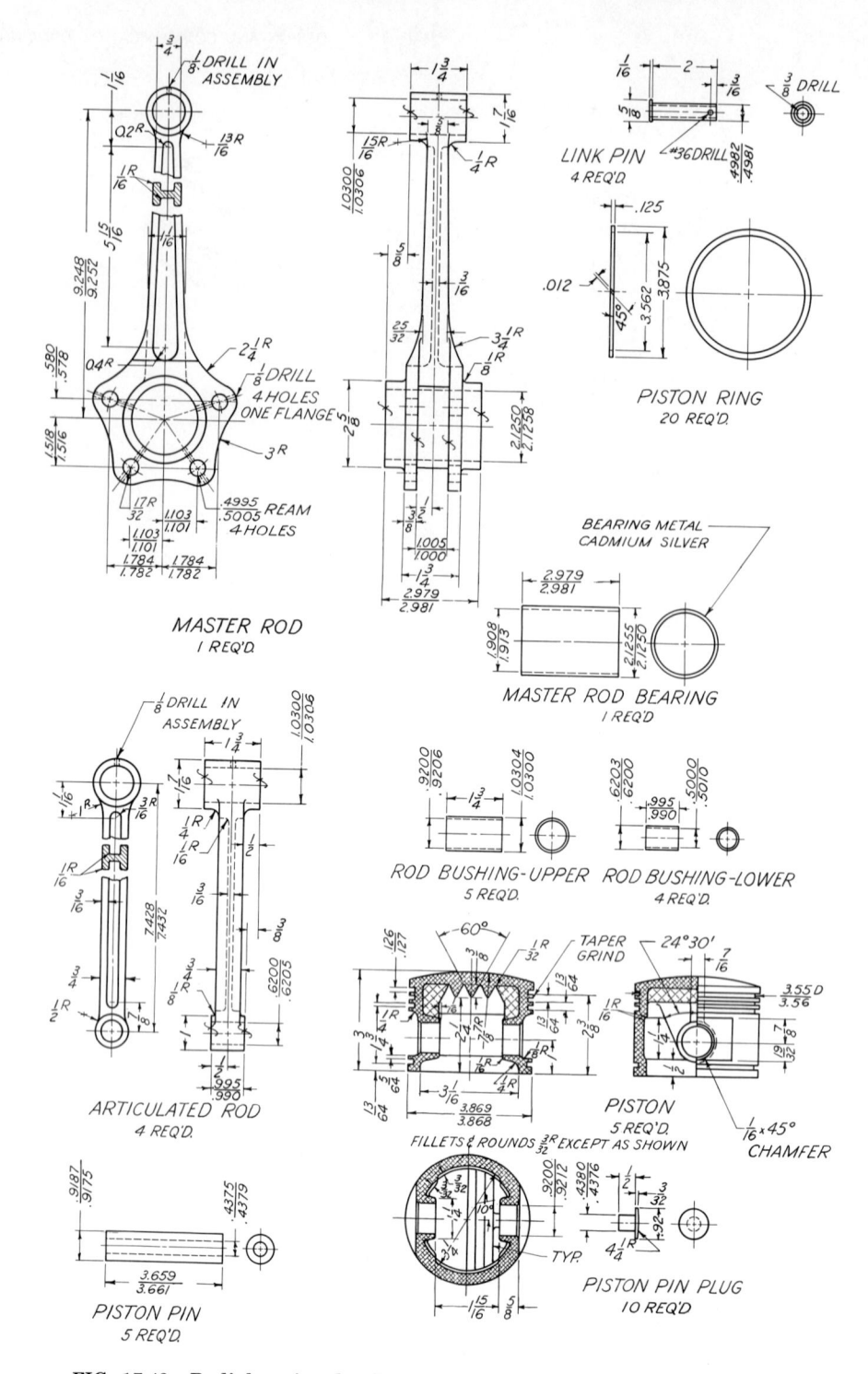

FIG. 17.43. Radial engine details.

CHAP. 17 / DESIGN AND COMMUNICATION DRAWINGS   423

29. (Fig. 17.43). Make an assembly drawing of the radial engine unit, using the given details. It is suggested that one piston be shown in full section so that the relative positions of the parts will be revealed.

30. (Figs. 17.44–17.46). Make an assembly drawing of the hand-clamp vise, using the given details. Use the schematic symbol for screw threads.

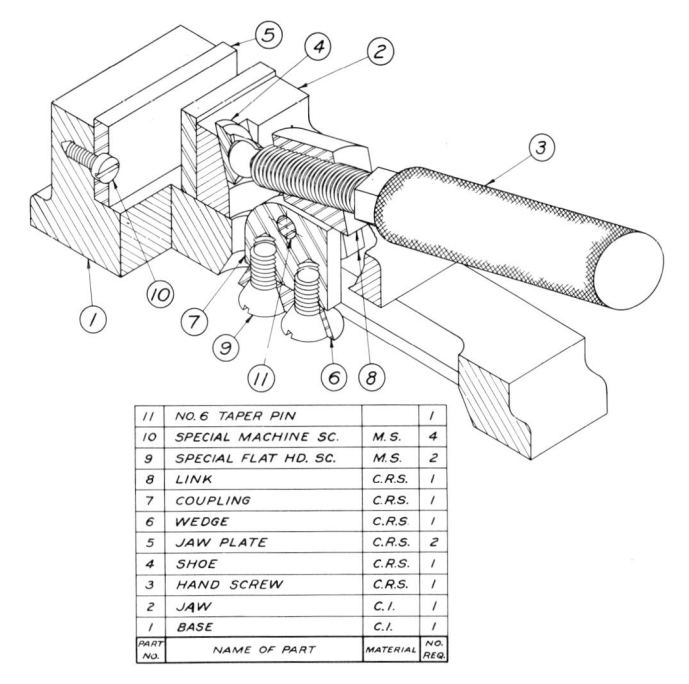

PART NO.	NAME OF PART	MATERIAL	NO. REQ.
11	NO. 6 TAPER PIN		1
10	SPECIAL MACHINE SC.	M.S.	4
9	SPECIAL FLAT HD. SC.	M.S.	2
8	LINK	C.R.S.	1
7	COUPLING	C.R.S.	1
6	WEDGE	C.R.S.	1
5	JAW PLATE	C.R.S.	2
4	SHOE	C.R.S.	1
3	HAND SCREW	C.R.S.	1
2	JAW	C.I.	1
1	BASE	C.I.	1

FIG. 17.44. Hand clamp vise.

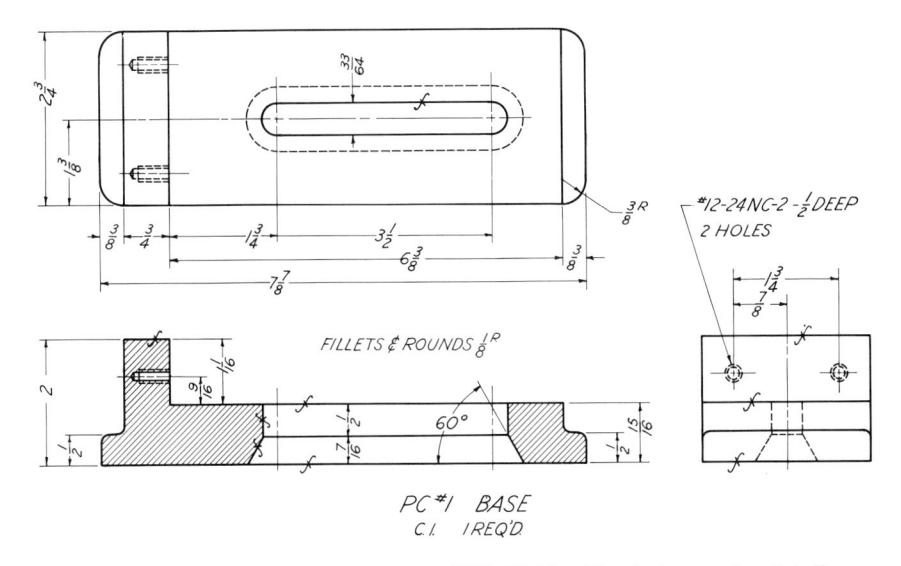

FIG. 17.45. Hand clamp vise details.

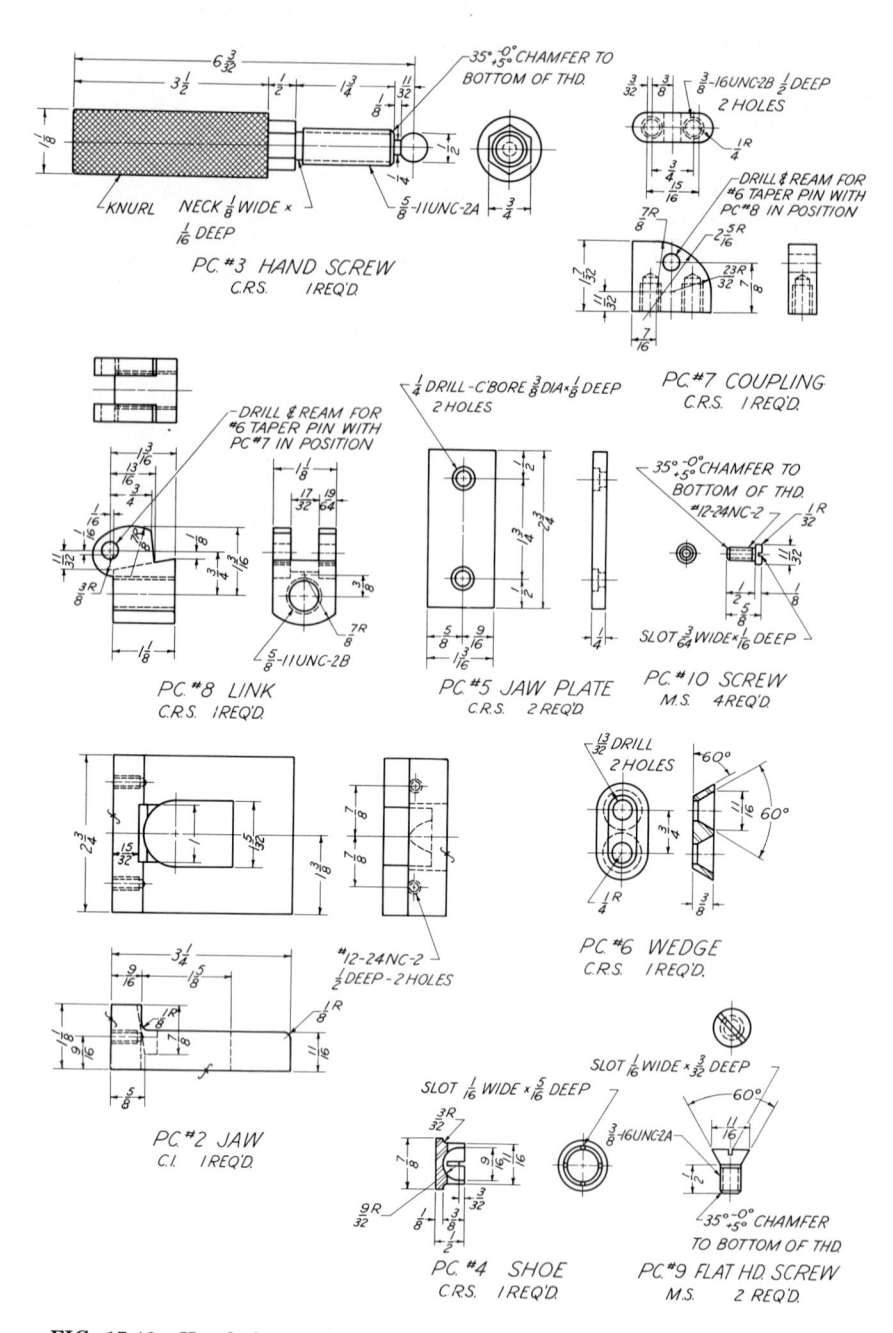

FIG. 17.46. Hand clamp vise details.

CHAP. 17 / DESIGN AND COMMUNICATION DRAWINGS   **425**

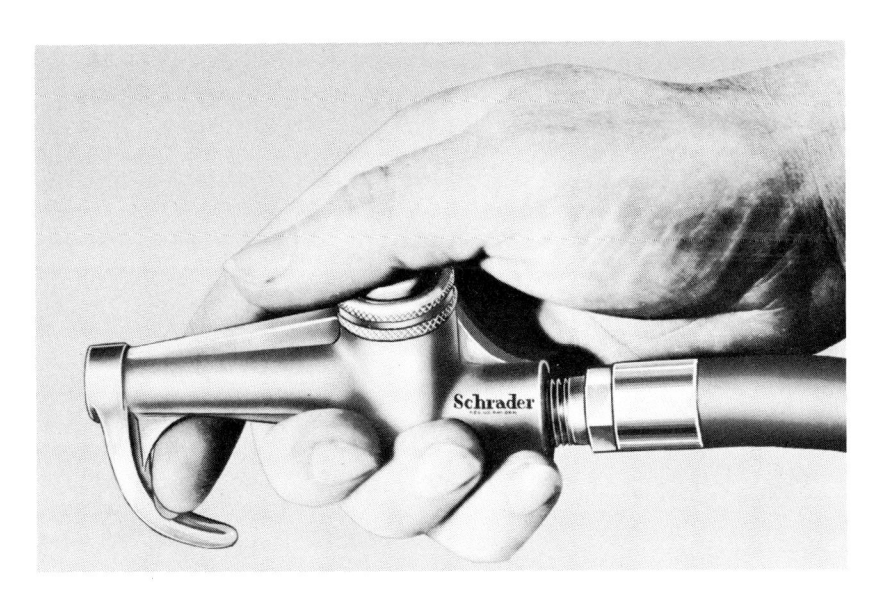

FIG. 17.47. Blow gun *(Courtesy A. Schrader's Son Mfg. Co.).*

31. (Figs. 17.47–17.49). Make an assembly drawing of the blowgun.

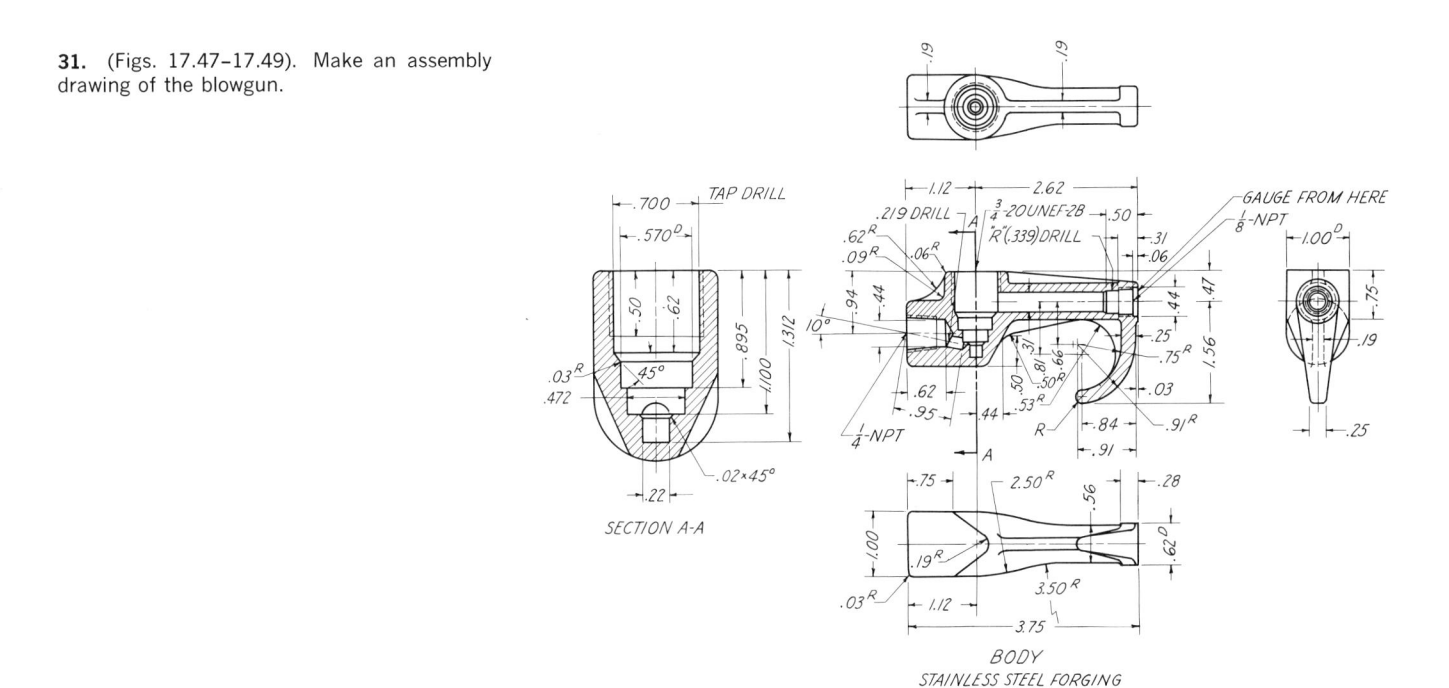

FIG. 17.48. Blow gun details.

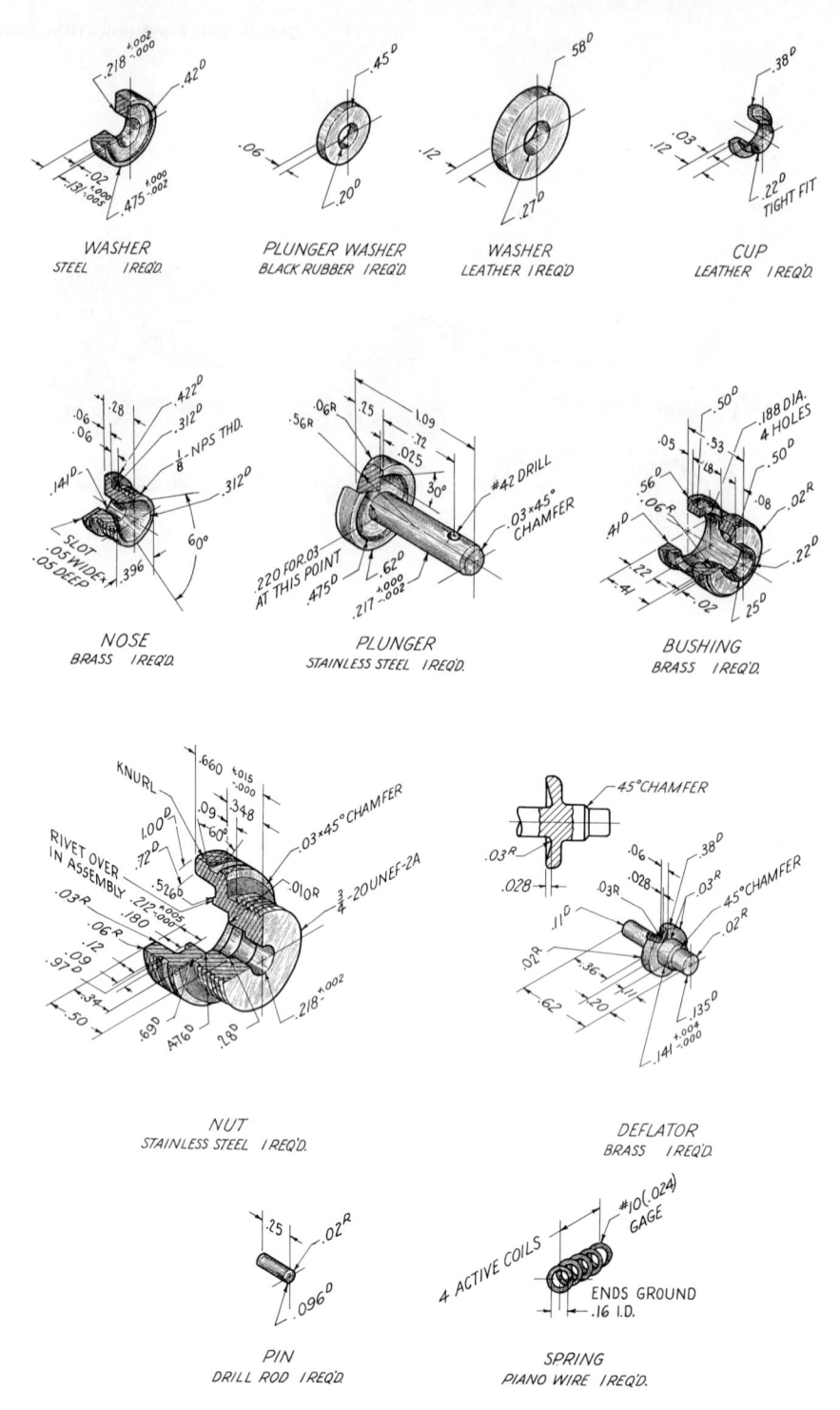

FIG. 17.49. Blow gun.

32. (Figs. 17.50–17.52). Make an assembly drawing of the hand grinder.

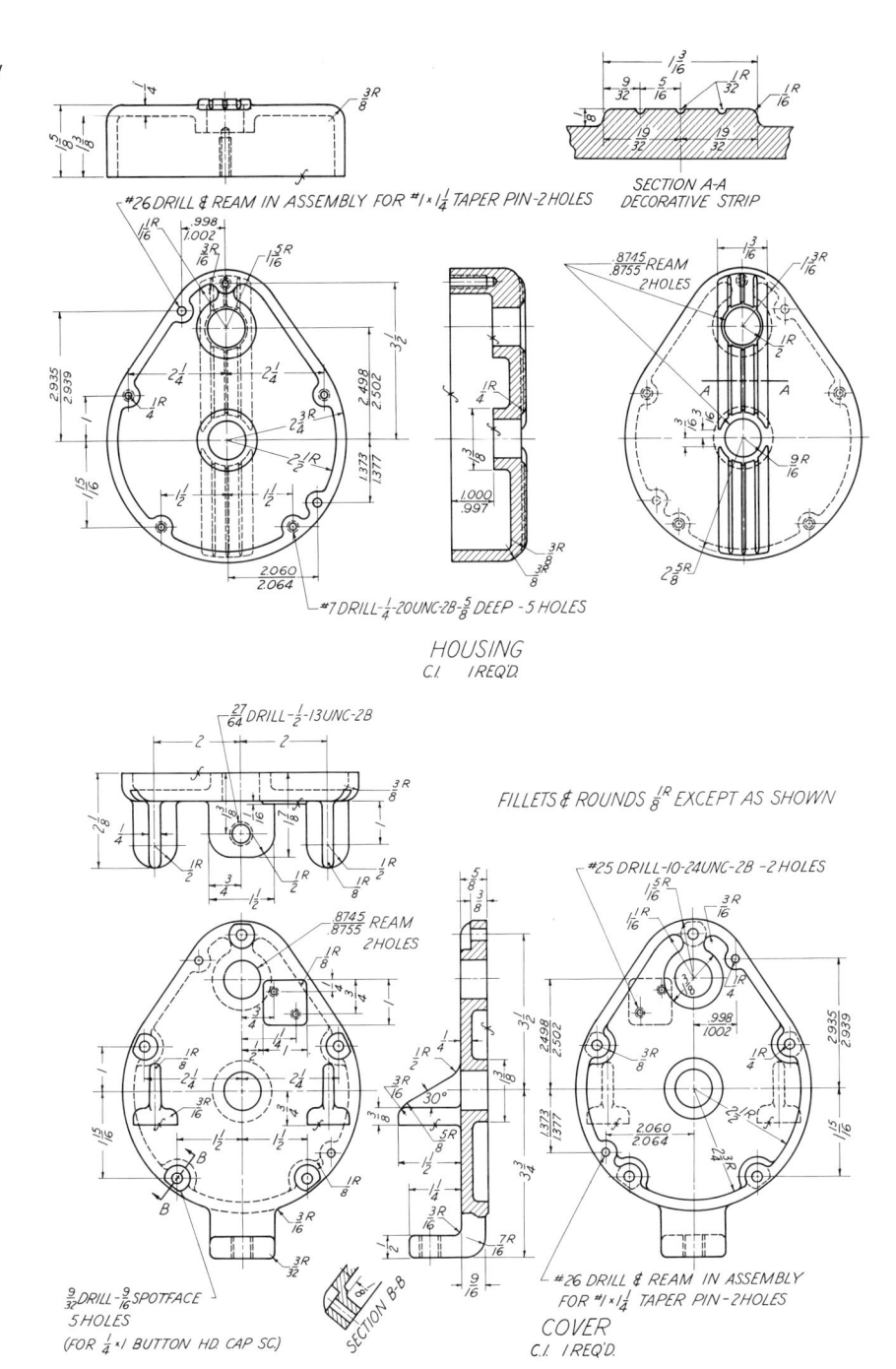

FIG. 17.50. Hand grinder details. (See Fig. 17.52)

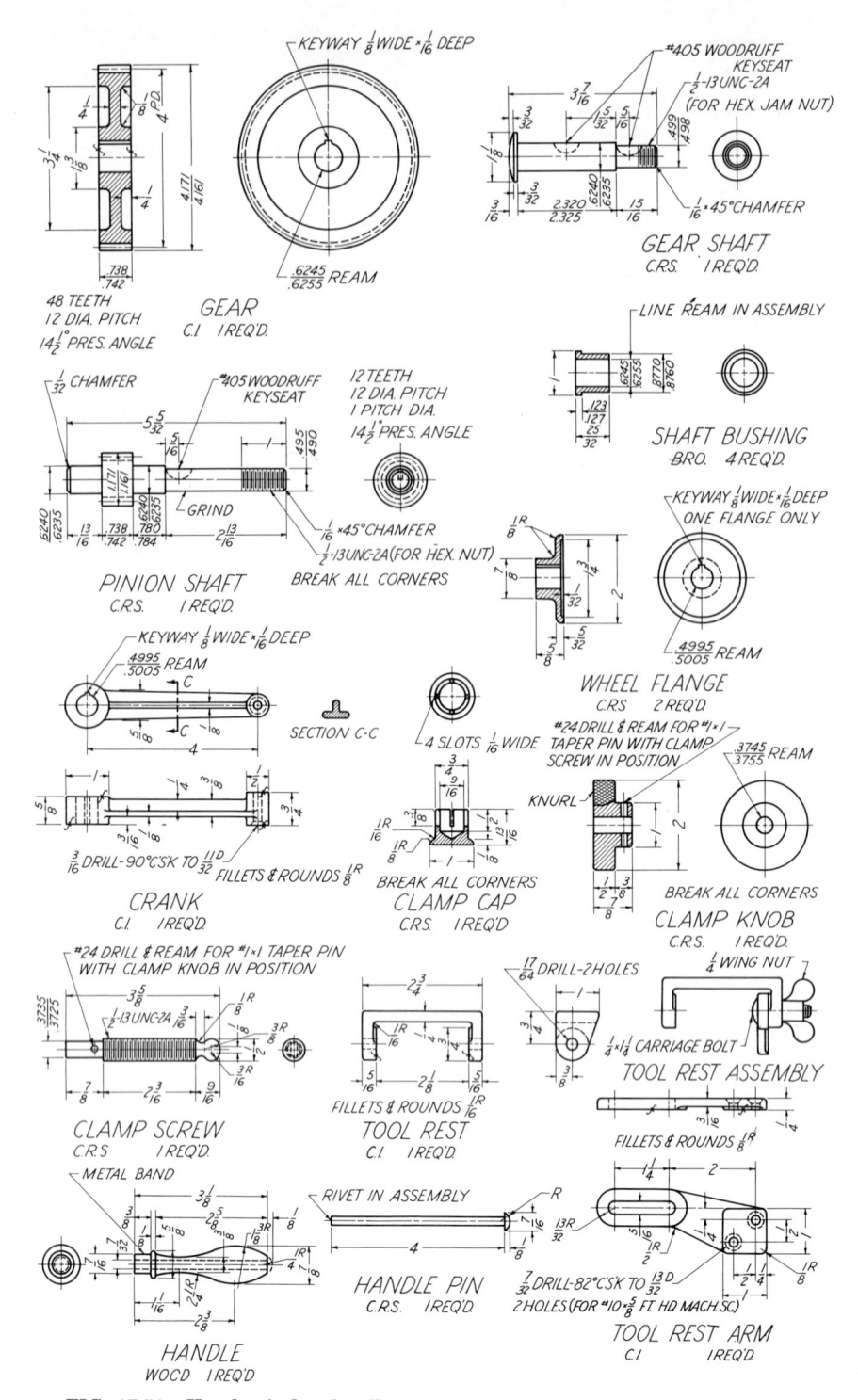

FIG. 17.51. Hand grinder details.

CHAP. 17 / DESIGN AND COMMUNICATION DRAWINGS 429

FIG. 17.52. Hand grinder.

33. (Figs. 17.53–17.55). Make an assembly drawing of the right-angle head, using the given details.

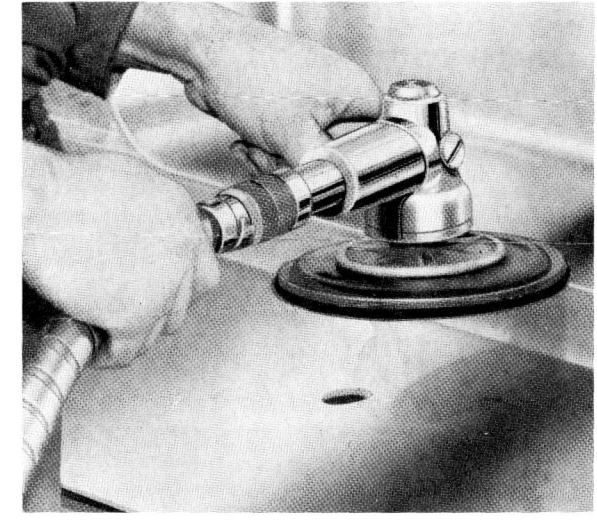

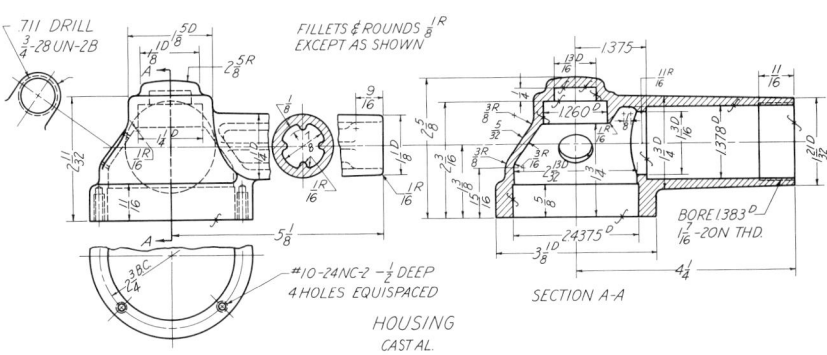

FIG. 17.53. Right-angle head details (*Courtesy R. C. Haskins Co.*).

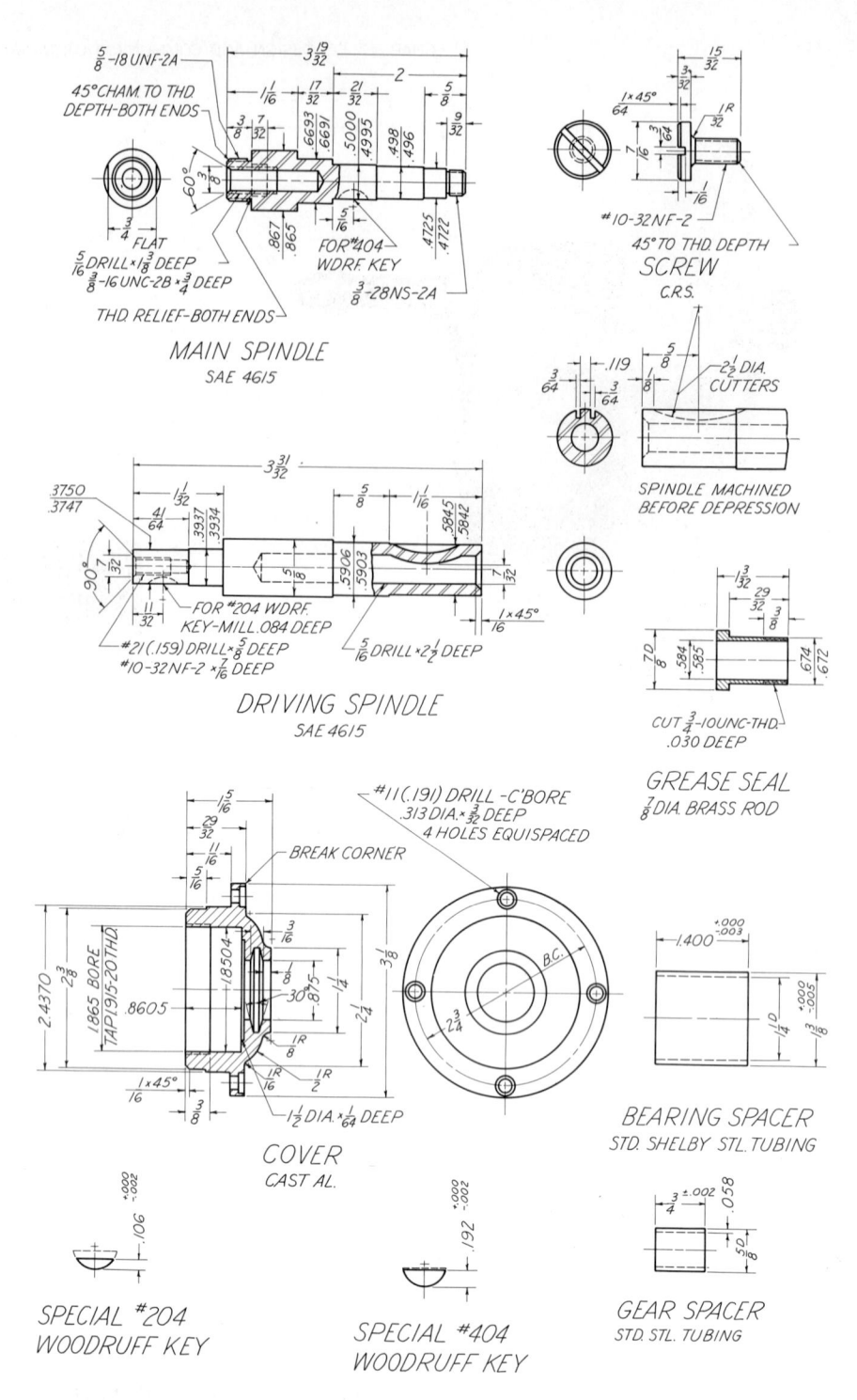

FIG. 17.54. Right-angle head details.

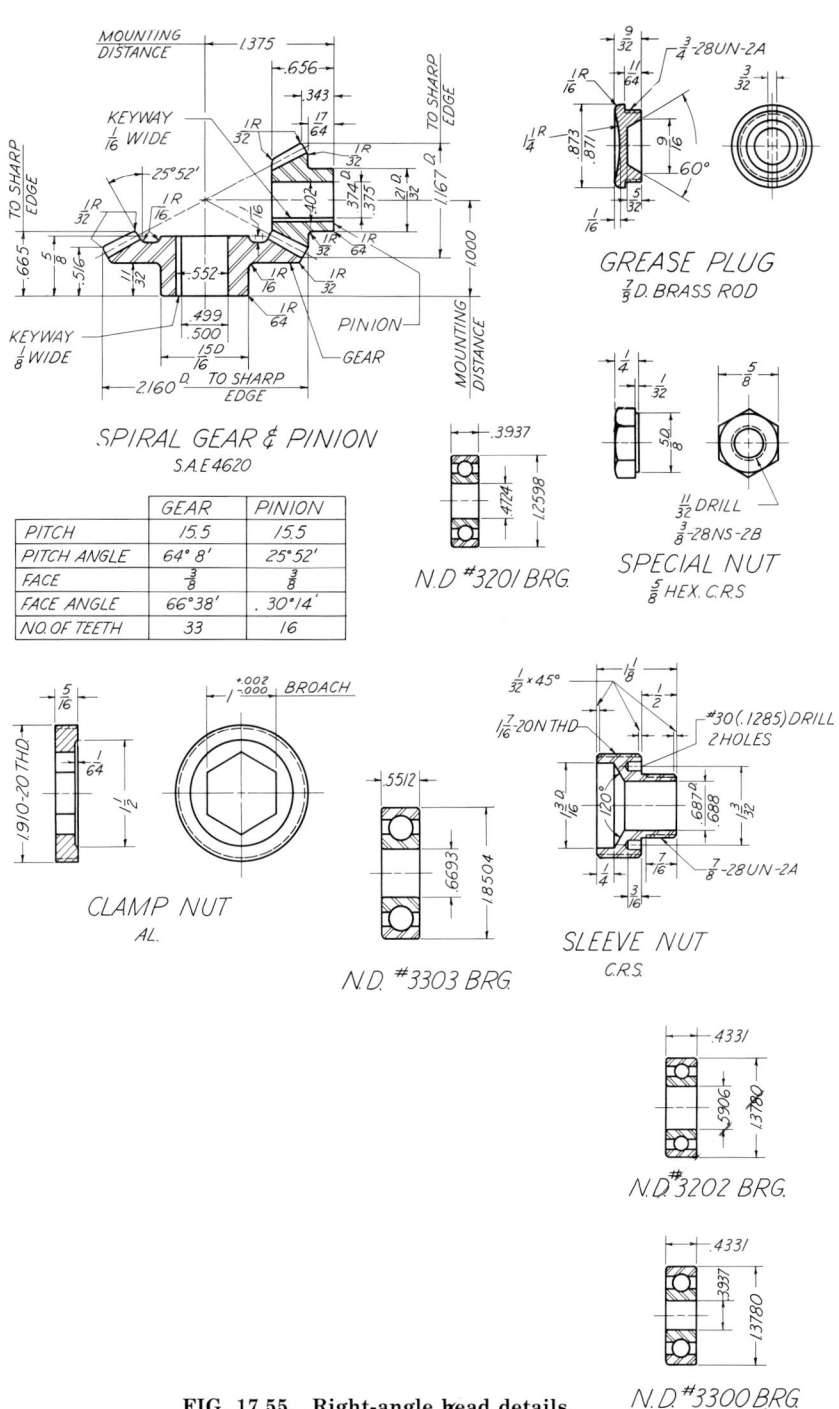

FIG. 17.55. Right-angle head details.

COMPUTER GRAPHICS AND NUMERICAL CONTROL

IV

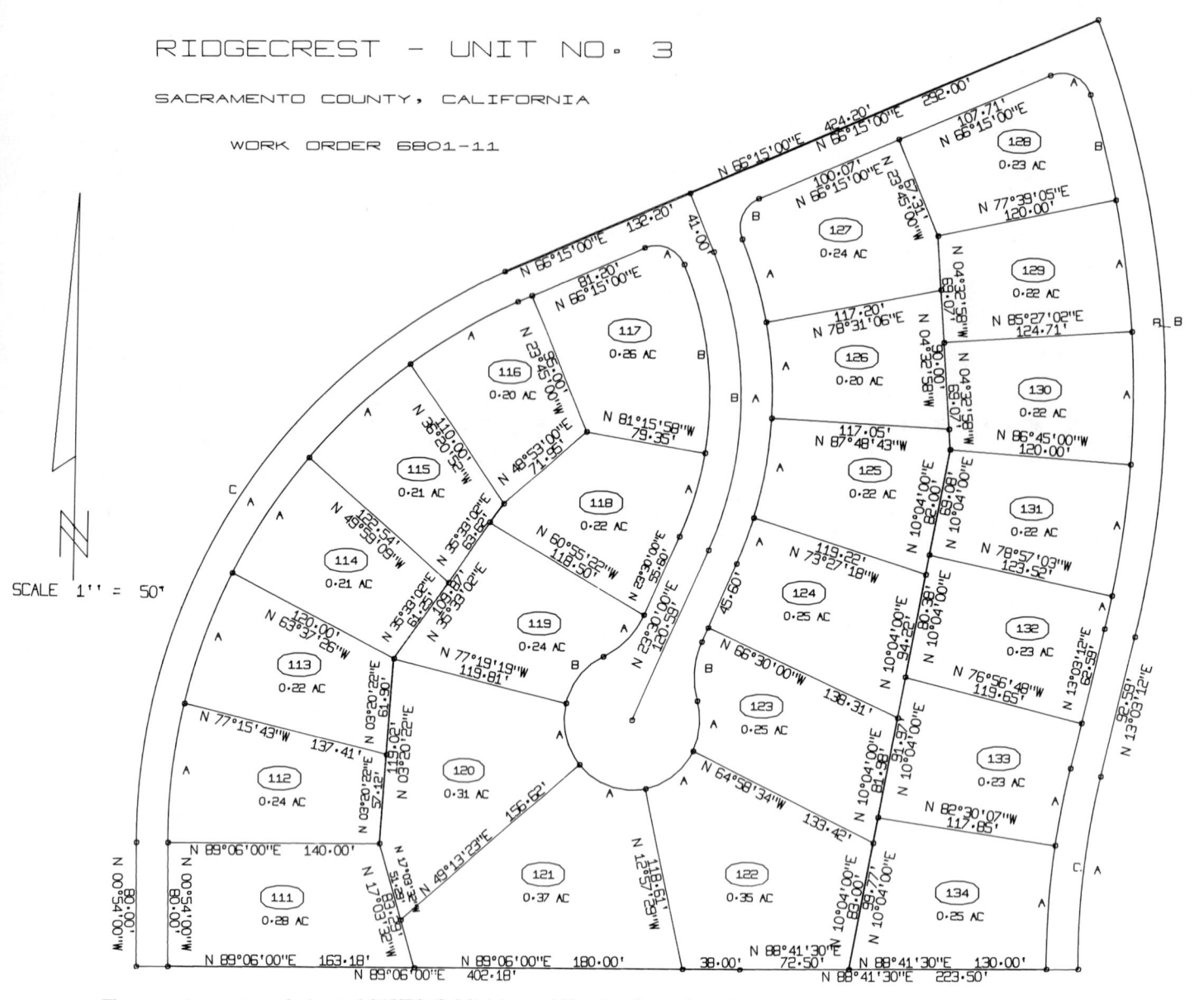

The computer program designated SAMPS (Subdivision and Mapping System) plots a complete subdivision map with bearings, distances, and other information ordinarily given on a map of this type (see Fig. 27.4). As developed by PMT Associates of Sacramento, California, the program can also be used for plotting control networks, for surveying jobs and for primary control of aerial photographs. The program provides for choice of plotting scale, rotation of plotting axes, plotting of lines and points, plotting of a north arrow, and annotation of distances and bearings. The subdivision plot shown above was drawn on a CalComp Model 702 flatbed plotter operating on-line with an IBM 1130 computer.
(Courtesy of PMT Associates-Engineers, Land Surveyors, Planners)

Computer-aided Design and Automated Drafting

A: COMPUTER-AIDED DESIGN

18.1
The Computer. A computer is not an electronic brain, as many would have us believe. Rather, it is an electronic calculating machine working in a manner that would be considered stupid on the part of a human being, since essentially the machine only adds and subtracts. And yet, by doing what it has been directed to do, with greater than human speed, the computer is capable of masterful performances that are carried out with technical precision. At times, it seems almost to perform miracles—but only almost.

A computer differs from what one ordinarily considers a calculator in that it has components for an internal memory storage system for instructions. It can be said that a computer can calculate, store, compare, correct itself, and then calculate some more *as programmed*.

18.2
Use of the Computer (Fig. 18.1). Computers must be instructed in considerable detail. However, the computer program represents more than just detailed instructions. It includes the problem definition, analysis, and flow charting that are a part of the initial preparation. When the program is written in actual machine coding, the programmer must first analyze the problem in terms of operations that the computer can perform and then write the program supplying tables, formulas, codes, and so forth, as needed for the specific application. To do this, the programmer must understand the computer in detail. Since this method of programming is often difficult, even for a qualified person, and at times is found to be impractical, several recognized programming languages have been developed that permit the programmer to give instructions to the computer by using statements and symbols, each statement representing many machine language instructions. Use of these high-level languages, such as FORTRAN (FORmula TRANslation), eliminates much of the painstaking detail of computer programming. Furthermore, since FORTRAN statements closely resemble mathematical terminology, a working knowledge of the language can be acquired with about a week of instruction. With a program called a compiler, the computer translates FORTRAN programs into more detailed instructions for its own operation. Other programming languages are COBOL (COmmon Business Oriented Language), and ALGOL (ALGOrithmic Language).

Instructions, fed to the computer by

FIG. 18.1. A computer system. (*Courtesy International Business Machines Corp.*) Key components: Center-rear: processing unit and main storage, console and typewriter. Left-rear: magnetic tape units. Left-center: card read punch. Right-center: printer. Foreground: magnetic disk drives.

punched cards, paper tape, or magnetic tape (Fig. 18.2), constitute the so-called program.

18.3
Language of the Computer (Input). Punched cards, punched tapes, and magnetic tapes (Fig. 18.2) with information recorded as magnetized spots (called *bits*) are the conventional means for making contact with an electronic computer in the only language that the computer recognizes, the language of electrical impulses. The information supplied by these patterns of holes or magnetic spots are translated by a "sensing element" or

"feeler" into the on–off binary language of the computer. Up-to-date punched-tape and punched-card sensing elements use photoelectric cells that transmit current when light reaches them. Paper tapes are punched by an input tape-punching device.

On magnetic tape, data are recorded in continuous parallel tracks. Usually, there are either six or eight data tracks and one checking track, depending on the format. Clocking mechanisms and changes in magnetic polarity indicate separate bits in the tracks. (A bit is a binary digit, either 0 or 1.) In the tape drive, a magnetic read–write head simultaneously reads a bit at a time from each of the tracks. The six or eight bits read represent a complete character. (Eight bits, called a *byte,* can represent two decimal digits or one character.) Using binary-coded decimal coding, the letters of the alphabet as well as decimal numbers may be recorded on magnetic tape. The BCD format also provides for punctuation marks and permits the use of special characters.

Punched cards, such as the one shown in Fig. 18.2, are stacked into a "card reader," which senses the cards and translates the information furnished by the perforations into the pulse language of the computer.

To permit more efficient use of a computer, the pulses punched into the paper may be transferred first to a magnetic tape and then from it to the computer. Magnetic tapes can deliver magnetized pulses at the rate of 180,000 characters (or 360,000 decimal digits) per second, a stretch of time in which a human can say only "one and two" at the usual word rate of a speaking voice.

18.4

Computer Storages. Every computer must have a memory system; that is, it must have repositories for the storage of information. Input and output storages receive

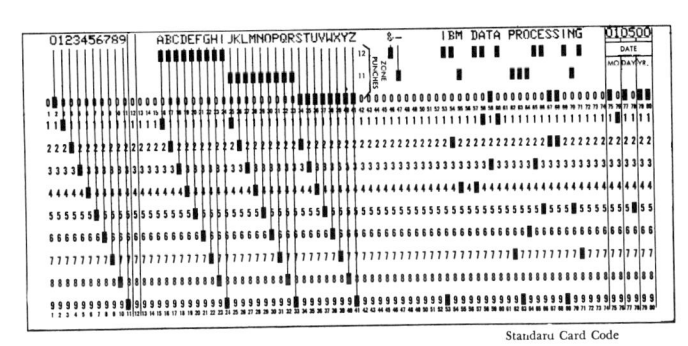

(a) Punched Card

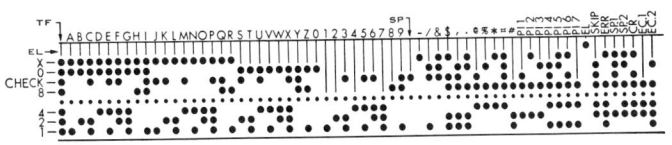

(b) Paper Tape—eight channel code

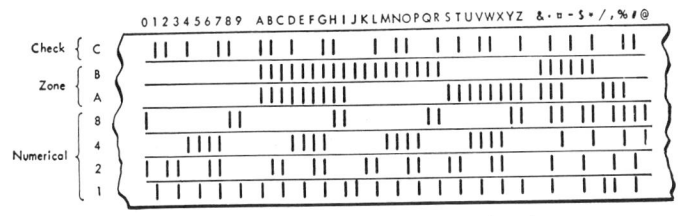

(c) Magnetic Tape—seven-bit alphanumeric code

FIG. 18.2. Data recording media-punched card, papertape, and seven-track magnetic tape. (*Courtesy International Business Machines Corp.*)

data needed for calculation and note the results before these results are typed out by the high-speed printer. There are also intermediate (short) storages, in addition to these, that receive results that the computer will need for continued calculation. A special component for intermediate storage, the accumulator, receives totals to be returned immediately to the matrix.

The three categories of computer storage are (1) the main memory; (2) auxiliary storage, which includes direct-access devices such as magnetic disc units and magnetic drums; and (3) bulk storage, involving the use of punched cards and magnetic tape. See Fig. 18.1

18.5
Computer Output. Up to this point, we have focused our attention on how information is fed into electronic computers by means of an input unit and to some extent on how the computer digests data and makes the necessary calculations. All of this action would quite naturally be useless, however, if the computer could not express the results of the calculations. The apparatus needed for this purpose is called an *output unit*. Several types of units are available to satisfy different requirements.

One such unit is the tape punch having perforating pins that are actuated by the electrical impulses of the computer. A tape-punch unit is capable of punching 50 or more characters per second in the paper tape. Punched tapes are deciphered by a printer that converts every character into either a letter or a number. Output card punches are also available. Punched-card information may be converted to printed copy through the computer or by using special auxiliary equipment.

When the results obtained represent an intermediate step and there is no need to read the results at the time, the pulses issued by the computer are picked up on magnetic tape to be held in reserve, say, for use a month later. When it becomes necessary to learn what is on a magnetic tape, it may be run through a complicated electronic device that sends the magnetic impulses to a high-speed output printer. This high-speed printing device is almost a miracle in itself because it can print a full line at a time (up to 132 characters) at a rate of 1,100 lines a minute.

Information may be transferred, without changing the code, from magnetic tapes to punched tapes or cards and, as also might be expected, from punched cards to magnetic tapes. This is accomplished by devices known as *converters*.

18.6
Communicating With a Computer. Improvement in programming is gradually eliminating the formidable barrier that has existed between the computer and its prospective users. In the years ahead computers will become commonplace and they will have capabilities that will make it possible for them to be used by almost anyone. The day when each of us can consult with his own computer lies just ahead. With this thought in mind, it will be shown how man and computer can work together as partners with man in control of the creative aspect of the design process. To instruct the computer as he would a menial, the user needs little more than a working knowledge of basic graphics, since the programming barrier is fading away to a great extent in this area.

18.7
Computer Graphics. In addition to making extensive use of conventional computer techniques for engineering and scientific analysis, the engineering team can, with the aid of one of several graphic data processing systems, bring a large-scale digital computer to bear on those problems that can best be analyzed and finally formalized by using and modifying graphical representation. This great step forward in automated graphics makes it possible for an engineer or designer to do at least a part of his creative work on a graphic input–output cathode-ray console that is connected directly to the computer (see Fig. 18.3). The means for man–machine communication is not in the future; it is available now and several practical systems are in daily use for design and production work in the aerospace and automotive fields.

The direct man–computer interaction that this system affords leads to quick answers for even small problems and permits concepts to be evaluated and tested and then accepted or rejected. This relationship in which the computer has become man's immediate partner in creative design became possible only when a way was found to make the computer correctly interpret drawings and, if desired, make a drawing after the intentions of its human partner had been made known. Properly used, these systems can relieve both the engineer and the man at the drawing board of endless calculations and of much of the tedious work connected with making layout and detail drawings. Such systems bring together the talents and creativity of the user and the power and speed of the digital computer in conjunction with digitized plotters or CRT consoles with appropriate supporting equipment.

In general, the term computer-aided design implies that the computer assists the designer in analyzing and modifying previously created design within new design parameters that he, the designer, has established. Almost any designer or draftsman can use graphic data processing effectively and can analyze, modify, and distribute design information even though he may have only a limited knowledge of computer programming. This is true because the designer at the console and the computer are in two-way communication while using the designer's own graphic language of lines, symbols, pictures, and words.

The computer system described thus does not replace the man, nor does it eliminate the requirement that a designer have a working knowledge of engineering graphics.

In predicting the future of the graphic science, one should expect that the designer and draftsman will both find it necessary to have a deeper knowledge of descriptive geometry and to know more about the preparation of communication drawings for production than in the past.

FIG. 18.3. Man-machine communication. "At the General Motors Research Laboratories, using the new GM DAC-I system (Design Augmented by Computers), a research engineer checks out a computer program that allows him to modify a design "drawing." A touch of the electric "pencil" to the tube face signals the computer to begin an assigned task, in this case, "Line Deletion," where indicated. The man may also instruct the computer using the keyboard at right, the card reader below the keyboard, or the program control buttons below the screen. Hundreds of special computer programs, written by GM computer research programmers, are needed to carry out these studies in man-machine communications."

The graphic language, so fundamental to the design process, has now become a computer language. As such, it has proved to be a reliable means for a conversational type of man–machine communication.

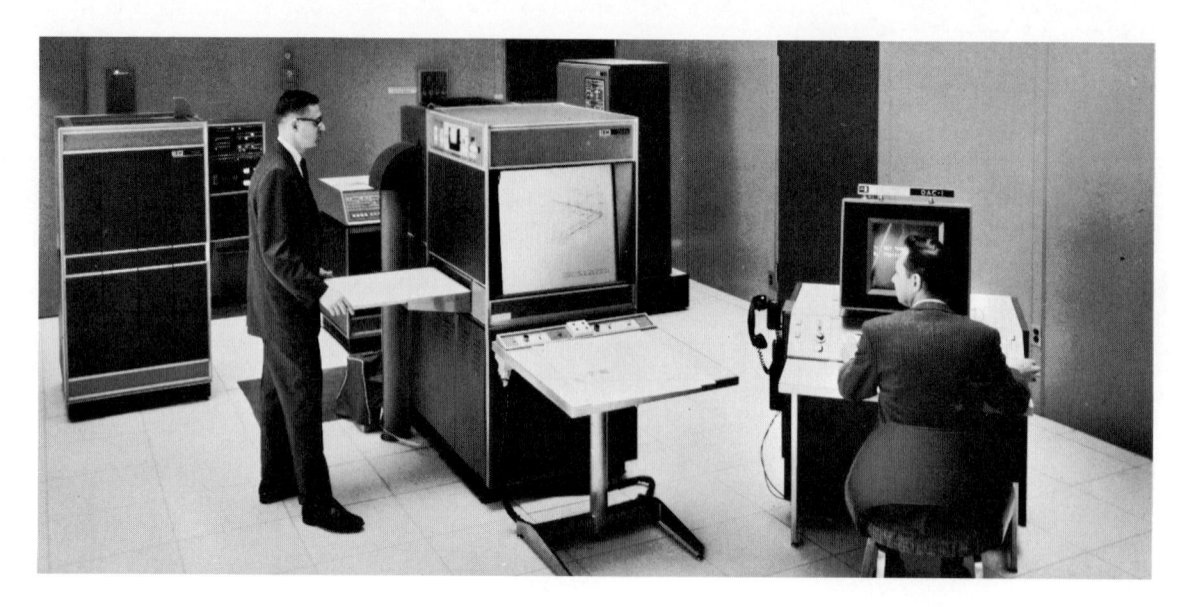

FIG. 18.4. GM-DAC-1 graphic processing components. (*Courtesy of General Motors Corporation*)

18.8
The Main Elements of the DAC–1 Digital Graphic Input–Output System. The main elements of the GM graphic data processing system shown in Fig. 18.4 are as follows:

1. A large-scale digital computer system (with supporting software) that is capable of storing vast amounts of information and retrieving specifically desired information rapidly.

2. One or more graphic consoles with viewing screens.

3. A film recorder (35mm) for "hard copy" of graphic information that has been computer generated.

4. A 35mm film scanner for the input of data in graphical form. This unit of the system converts images recorded on microfilm to digital form for further processing.

18.9
The DAC–1 Display Console. It is at the display console that the man–machine conversation takes place. The principal feature of the console is the cathode-ray-tube (CRT) screen on which the computer-programmed graphic and alphanumeric information is displayed (Fig. 18.3). Close at hand on the console are the keyboards and the light pencil that provide convenient means of entering and modifying rapidly displayed computer-programmed graphic and alphanumeric information. At the console unit the user has direct access to data (previously stored in the system's main or auxiliary storage units in digital form) that he may study and then modify and redisplay.

18.10
GM DAC–1 Image Processing Unit. The DAC–1 computerized design and drafting

system provides for both the input and output of data in a graphical form. A direct output for engineering and manufacturing use can be in the form of hard copy, a drawing prepared by an on-line plotter, or a programmed tape that can be used to actuate an automated production machine. At this point in our discussion our attention will be directed to the special image processor that enables the computer to read and generate drawings (Fig. 18.5). The use of tapes with plotters adaptable for off-line operation will be discussed later in this chapter. Information on tape-controlled production machines has been given in Chapter 19.

The image processing unit provides means for the input and output of data in graphical form. Primarily, this component contains a CRT photo-recorder, projectors, CRT photo-scanner, an input camera, and the rapid film processing equipment needed to develop 35mm film. When the film is developed within the recorder, the image can be viewed on a rear projection screen that is located for easy viewing by the user (Fig. 18.4).

After an input copy has been inserted into the image processor on a tray and then photographed and developed, the 35mm negative is positioned so that the CRT photo-scanner can "read it." The film scanner converts the image furnished by the 35mm negative (light lines on dark background) directly to digital data that is sent either to the computer or to memory storage. Basically, the near miracle is accomplished via an electronic beam that, when it determines whether each of many addressable points is above or below a set level of light intensity, notes the result in computer (digital) language. The digital information thus developed may now be either modified or stored permanently.

From the high-speed recorder of the image processor, on 35mm film, come the permanent records of drawings, charts,

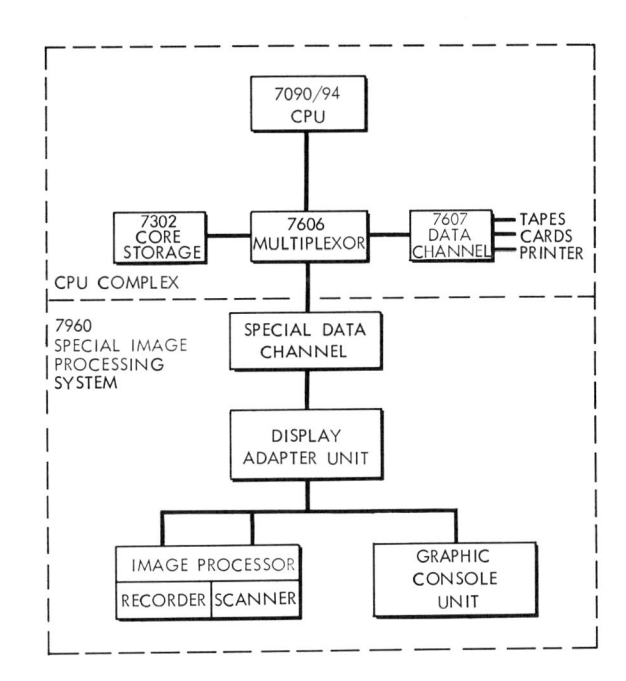

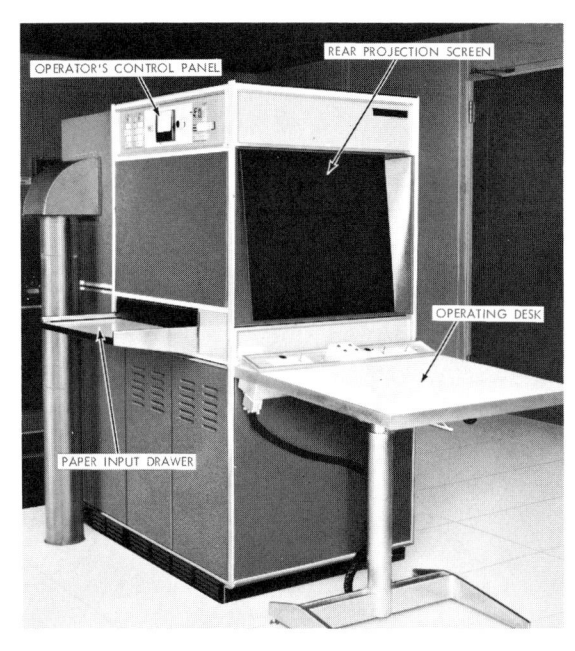

FIG. 18.5. The DAC-1 image processing unit. (*Courtesy General Motors Corp.*)

and parts lists that are needed by designers and draftsmen. The film, exposed to a high-resolution CRT and developed within the recorder, can be viewed at development on a rear projection screen, as stated previously. Finally, conventional working copies (on paper) may be readily obtained using modern viewer–copier equipment and recorder-produced exposures mounted in aperture cards. It was the development of image processing units, such as the DAC–1 described, that extended the capability of computers to the point where they can accept, interpret, analyze, relate, and finally produce needed output in graphic form.

18.11
The IBM 2250 Display Unit (Fig. 18.6). Images are generated on the CRT at the console by computer-programmed positioning and deflection of the CRT's electronic beam to the more than one-million possible points (grid format of 1024 by 1024 addressable points) of the 12 in. $\times$ 12 in. effective display area. The beam is deflected to each point on the screen that is addressed by the program, either intensifying it or not intensifying it, as directed. The image as we see it on the face of the CRT (screen) is produced by the beam hitting a phosphor coating causing the coating to glow for just an instant. Operating under this condition, the information normally displayed fades rapidly (within a fraction of a second); therefore, the display must be regenerated approximately 30–40 times every second for a flicker-free representation of high resolution. A buffer is used to regenerate the display independently of the computer.

Alphanumeric symbols may be formed by synthesizing the characters from a series of individually programmed dots or line segments, either horizontal or vertical. To improve computer efficiency, an optional character generator can be used for computer independent formation of all alphanumeric symbols.

The position-indicating light pencil, when used in conjunction with the keyboards and programs in storage, provides the means whereby the image displayed can be altered (Fig. 18.3). It may be used at will to create, remove (erase), enlarge, or rearrange any part of a displayed image that, as a whole, may consist of points, line segments of any length and orientation, simple and complex geometric shapes, and appropriate graphical symbols and statements. The light pencil (receiving device), having a photocell element that senses a spot of light directly under its point, signals the system. In turn, based on where the cathode-ray beam was scanning at that instant, the system sets a register, which indicates the position of the light pencil on the face of the display. When the control system feeds this positional information to the computer, the

FIG. 18.6. Example of a display (note programmed function and alphanumeric keyboards). (*Courtesy International Business Machines Corp.*)

computer in turn relates the identified portion of the image to the equivalent digital representation stored in memory.

After a picture has once been generated, either the man with his light pencil or the computer may direct the other to reconsider a portion of the image. The computer may react, as programmed, to any portion of the display by placing an X at the point in the display that the man should consider. Thus, the machine suggests while the man directs. Each reacts to the other.

The programmed function keyboard (Fig. 18.6, bottom right) consists of program control keys, status indicator lights and sensing switches for use with interchangeable (plastic) descriptive overlays. An overlay identifies a series of program functions contained in the computer memory system. When a key is depressed, the computer receives a signal to act on the image as directed by the program subroutine associated with the key selected. For example, the signal given might direct the computer to either enlarge, reduce, or delete a portion of the programmed image displayed. Any of these actions can be performed by the computer in a fraction of a second. To complete the same task manually might take minutes or even hours.

With the alphanumeric typewriter-type keyboard shown in Fig. 18.6, the user can compose statements consisting of letters, numbers, or symbols and can perform editing functions. The message, as composed, is displayed on the screen for verification. It may then be transferred on demand to the computer's main memory. The statement or message composed could be a parts list, a dimension value, an electrical value for a circuit component, a descriptive note, or a drawing title.

Through the use of graphic data processing as described, the designer can create a complete digital description of a design within the system.

18.12
Design Programs. It has been stated in Section 18.7 that the designer can use a computer-aided design system even though he may know little about computer programming. This statement can be true only if it is possible for him to select from a library of previously created design programs those programs suitable for the design functions required for the specific job that faces him. Since it is not to be expected that he will be able to do this on all occasions, the designer or draftsman is fortunate if he has at least a basic understanding of how programs are prepared.

Programs and related design data are stored on tapes or disc files as digital descriptions and operational routines. Sets of words and numbers may represent standard graphic items, such as dimensions, part descriptions, and even formulas. In time, when graphic data processing systems have wider use and have been improved, more standard computer programs will become available and the tedious task of writing and developing programs may, to a great extent, be relegated to the past.

18.13
How a Graphic Data Processing System is Used. At present, how do we use an existing graphic data processing system, say DAC-1 (Fig. 18.3), under special program control?

First, the designer writes out the statements that give a short description of his problem. In the case of auto-body design, the problem is very often a descriptive geometry problem requiring drawings and sketches as guides. These statements are then keypunched on cards and entered into the computer memory. With this much accomplished, the designer, at the display console, is ready to command the computer to perform the functions requested. In executing the program, the computer checks each statement and displays an error comment if an error is detected. When and if this happens, the designer inspects the statement, makes the needed corrections, and instructs the computer to proceed.

Once the program has been executed, the computer should respond by displaying a simple line drawing, as shown in Fig. 18.3. In inspecting the solution to determine whether or not it is acceptable, the engineer using DAC-1 may enlarge any portion and view it from any angle. If not satisfied, he may then modify the design by entering other statements, by changing statement parameters, or by simply adding or deleting lines. When he is satisfied, he can, as has been explained in Sec. 18.10, direct the computer to produce either permanent copy or control tapes for automatic drafting machines or machine tools. Since the program is general, it may now be placed in the library of design programs for use at a later time for a specific job.

18.14
Design of Electronic Circuits. Using a graphic data processing system, a designer has almost unlimited flexibility in designing an electronic circuit because so little time is needed to rearrange and analyze components. For example, if a designer should wish to see what would happen if a component were changed (or eliminated) in an electronic circuit that has been displayed on the screen along with the waveform that circuit would produce, he can get an immediate answer. By entering the new value and working with his light pencil and the program in storage, he can see on the screen almost immediately the new waveform that would result from the change. At the same time, the old circuit has been stored in the computer's memory and may be recalled if needed.

18.15
Achievements of Graphic Input–Output Systems. Computers with graphic input-output systems are capable of performing marvelous feats. For example, either a single feature or a related group of features in a design display may be rotated, repositioned, enlarged, or reduced in size at will. When special attention must be given to an individual feature requiring development, that feature may be shown enlarged. This may be done with the rest of the graphic image out of view, that is, not showing on the screen. If need be, a standard element, such as a rivet or a cap screw that has been drawn and stored away in computer memory, may be added by pushing an appropriate button. Once the task of adding necessary details has been completed, the feature can again be brought back to scale and the complete image shown as before.

The first program to provide a graphical link with the computer was developed at Massachusetts Institute of Technology's Lincoln Laboratory some years ago. The first program, known as SKETCHPAD, proved beyond any doubt that a computer system could be developed that would interact with a creative designer.

SKETCHPAD impresses the casual observer. To attract attention it can be programmed to display an animated movie of a small automobile moving along a winding road. With this capability put to a better use, it can animate drawings to show parts in motion, which, for example, makes it possible to study linkages in action. Straight lines, circles, and curves can be sketched on the screen and as each line or shape is drawn all freehand irregularities can be removed. SKETCHPAD is an excellent draftsman.

Programs exist for the creation of exotic shapes (airfoils, hydrofoils, etc.). A program, prepared at MIT under the supervision of Professor Coons, shows that by varying chords a shape can be changed accordingly and then reevaluated. In a motion picture showing actual use of this program, the shape displayed was rotated in alternate directions and tilted at different angles to permit the operator to view it from several directions, even from the rear.

In computer-aided design, new developments occur with increasing frequency and the "state of the art" advances steadily despite the fact that new achievements come only at great expense. As of today, we are moving away to some extent from gibberish geometric languages and English-like statements in using sketches to talk to the computer. In the near future, voice control may be added to the SKETCHPAD concept, and drawings and rough sketches coupled with the voice will be accepted methods for input. When this point has been reached, automated drafting and design will be an actuality and a computer-graphic system will not be as inconvenient to use as it is now.

B: AUTOMATED DRAFTING

18.16

Digital Drafting Systems. Present models of automated drafting systems now on the market are digitally controlled. That is, the input (instructions) to the control system of the drafting machine is entered in digital form on punch cards, punch tape, or magnetic tape. The information supplied may be in either straight binary or binary-coded decimal form, the latter format being the most widely accepted.

A few of the many fine automated drafting machines in use today are The CI Digital Drafting System, (Computer Industries, Inc.), The Gerber Plotting System, The Orthomat (Universal Drafting Machine Corp.), The Coradomat, The Calcomp System (California Computer Products), and The IBM 1620 Drafting System with the 1627 Plotter.

The all-digital design approach of high-speed $X-Y$ plotting and drafting machines provides for flexible internal programming so that the plotter will execute on command a circle, a dashed line, a center line, and so forth. The Gerber Plotting System produces high-quality displays of computer-generated digital information. The Orthomat can automatically translate complex formulas into reliable line drawings.

The Gerber Series 2000, Universal Drafting Machine Orthomat, and the Computer Industries Digital Drafting System are sophisticated drafting systems having the following capabilities:

Accuracy: $\pm.002$ in.

Speed: At least 500 in. per min.

Table size: 5 ft. in (Y) and up to 20 ft. in (X)

Control unit-data processor for controlling the drafting system and providing computing logic.

California Computer Products 500 Series Incremental Plotters (Fig. 18.7), the IBM 1627, and the Computer Industries Delta Incrementals are less sophisticated plotting systems that operate on a stepping principle and do not provide as high-quality output as the more sophisticated drafting systems.

The IBM 1627 Plotter and the Computer Industries Digitizing System (partly manual and the opposite of automated drafting) will be discussed later in detail.

Automated drafting may be defined as being the drawing of lines (ink or pencil) or the formation of scribe (groove) marks on a working surface with little or no human intervention (see Fig. 18.8). The medium used for the drawing may be either paper, plastic, film, metal, or any material with a scribe coat.

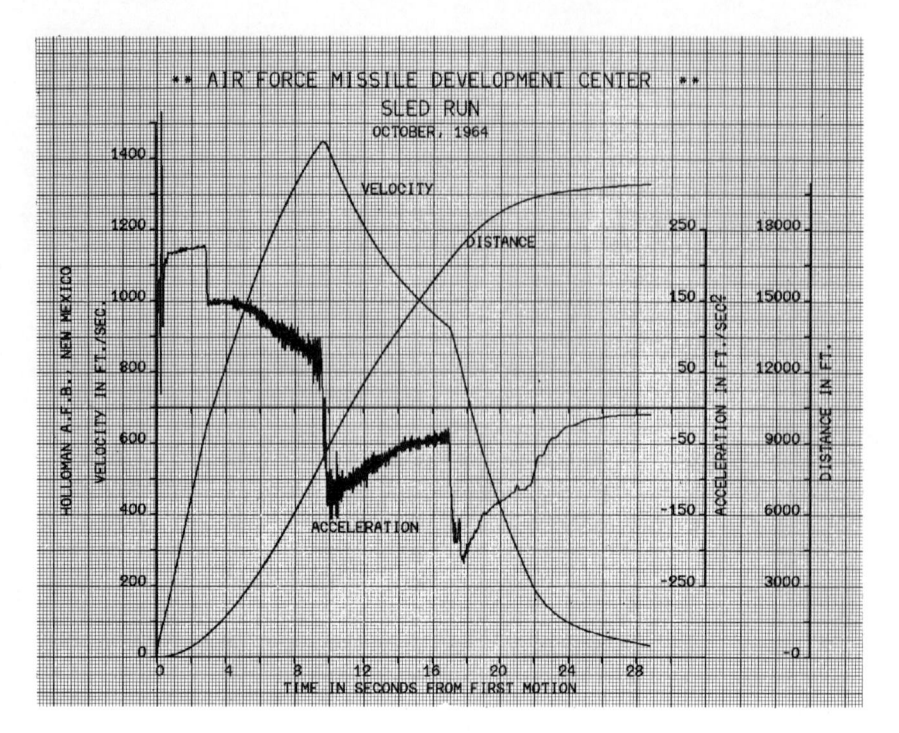

FIG. 18.7. An example of computer-plotter output. *Plotters make rough sledding easier at Holloman.* Shown above is the plot of dynamic time history for a rocket sled run at Holloman Air Force Base high speed track. To cope with growing volume of computed data, the Air Force Missile Development Center at Holloman turns out a large percentage of its scientific and test data in this form. A general plot program and two Cal-Comp Model 565 plotters are used to produce fully annotated linear or logarithmic charts, ready for direct reproduction. The pair of 565's is operated on-line with a CDC 3600/160A computer system. A time share program is used for simultaneous full-speed operation of the plotters, three line printers, a card reader, a card punch, and a data link. (*Courtesy California Computer Products, Inc.*)

Of most interest to the user of an all-digital electronic plotter are the control system and the drafting equipment itself. Basically, the control system consists of a punch card or tape reader (punch or magnetic) and a translator. The translator converts input information received from the reader into a series of command signals to the servomotors of the drawing head. The drawing head responds as directed, checks its position, and then indicates that the command, as given, has been performed. Informing the control system when a command has been accomplished is made possible by a so-called feedback device, a mechanical–electrical system designed to provide mechanical error correction.

Depending on the model, a drafting machine can have either a horizontal, vertical, or tilting table. Although the horizontal table requires more floor space than a vertical table and cannot be viewed as readily, there are other advantages to its use that causes it to be favored for very accurate work. A tilting table can be positioned horizontally or it can be adjusted to be almost vertical.

A drawing head has a turret (revolving) mechanism that may have four, six, or eight stations, depending again on the model. The stations accommodate the pens, pencils, or scribes that can be selected and used under program control. Ordinarily Rapidograph-type pens are used; however, ball-point-type pens serve better for drawing at high speed. For wide lines felt marker pens have been used and found to be satisfactory.

A rotary scriber is primarily used for printed circuitry. The turret has the same basic station arrangement as the turret for the normal drafting machine. However, instead of pens at each of the positions there are small end-mill-type tools that cover a range of sizes.

The two types of control systems are the incremental system and the absolute sys-

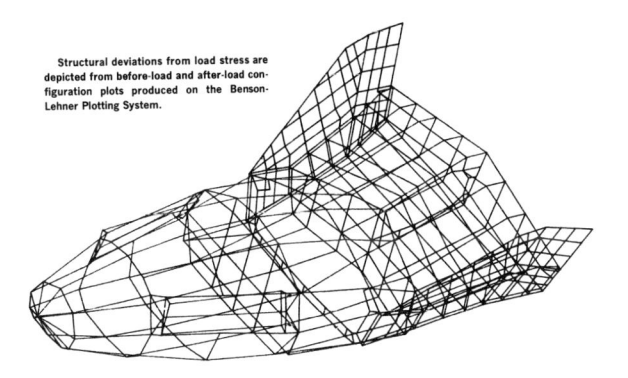

CHAP. 18 / COMPUTER-AIDED DESIGN AND AUTOMATED DRAFTING   447

Structural deviations from load stress are depicted from before-load and after-load configuration plots produced on the Benson-Lehner Plotting System.

FIG. 18.8. Analysis load configuration of the prime maneuverable re-entry vehicle. (*Courtesy Martin Marietta Corporation*) The data processing center of this company is presently utilizing a Computer Industries Magnetic Tape STE Plotting System to study load configurations on the prime maneuverable re-entry vehicle. A mathematical structure is shown being plotted on the STE in what is considered an unloaded configuration (see plot above). Then, theoretical load configurations are applied through the computer to different parts of the structure. New plotting tapes are generated and replots are made of the new load structure. By visually comparing before- and after-load plots, company engineers are able to determine deviation and stress of the structure due to loading.

tem. At the present time, the incremental with its delta motion is the most widely used. This system requires the ΔX and ΔY values for the distance from the "where-now" location to the next position ahead where it is going. The somewhat different approach provided by the absolute system requires that the X and Y coordinates of the next point be related to the very first, that is, the starting point (set point or zero point).

In addition to the X-Y coordinate information that is needed to meet position requirements, there are control commands associated with the drawing of a line segment, such as: move to origin, move and plot, pen up and move, pen down and move, rotate turret, draw dotted line, pause and change pen, and so forth.

Circles and curves must be approximated with straight lines. For these to be drawn accurately, acceleration and deceleration blocks and feed numbers must be calculated. These data can best be calculated by a computer.

The Computer Industries drafting machine (plotter) shown in Fig. 18.8 is suitable for a wide range of applications from contour map generation to automatic drafting and graphical verification of machine-tool tapes. A four-station drawing head is provided, with each station accommodating a standard holder for either an inking or a scribing device. The carriages are positioned by means of digital servo systems. For the model shown, the effective working area is 60 in. on both the X and Y axes for all styli (marking devices).

All control functions, operator functions and input–output devices are contained in the separate control unit, which includes a general-purpose computer. The computer includes a 4 K core memory and high-speed arithmetic unit.

The computer continuously monitors the position of the stylus carriage (marking device carrier) and controls the drive system as required by operator control and input–output devices. The standard input–output device is an ASR-33 Teletypewriter with paper tape reader and punch (magnetic tape input optional). Additional controls have been provided for manual entry as part of the computer. The digital servo control signals from the computer are processed within the control unit to form suitable outputs to the servomotors.

Performance Capabilities. Straight-line interpolation is performed digitally for lines up to 8 in. of projected length. The format may be either coordinate, delta, or incremental.

Stored in prime form in core memory are 64 alphanumeric characters and symbols. These characters, having a prime height of .064 in., may be drawn by any of the styli, scaled up to 1.024 in., and rotated to eight angular orientations. With the X and Y coordinates of the first character of a line specified, subsequent characters are spaced to the right to form lines of up to 120 characters per line.

The usable speed is 12 in. per sec. for all modes of operation.

Accuracy relative to reference point is .002 in. over the entire working area for both static and dynamic operation; repeatability is .001 in. The encoder resolution is .00025 in. for the X-axis and .000375 in. for the Y-axis.

A few of the optional features available to users are (1) additional characters and symbols, up to 255 in number; (2) interpolation of circular, elliptical, or other conic sections; (3) routing head in lieu of a stylus carriage; (4) photographic head suitable for generation of printed-circuit work in lieu of stylus carriage; (5) digitizing head for operation with CRT monitor in lieu of stylus carriage (see Sec. 18.18); and (6) a drive system for paper advance.

At the present time, there are several recognized computer programming systems in general use. Although all of them no doubt meet the needs for which they were created, only four will be mentioned here. They are APT (Automatically Programmed Tools), which is particularly suited for use in engineering education; Autoprompt, developed by IBM; Alladin, developed by the Allison Division of General Motors; and Autodraft, which represents the joint efforts of IBM and North American Aviation, Inc. Both APT and Autoprompt were developed primarily for N/C (numerically controlled) machine tools. Alladin and Autodraft are drafting language systems.

In preparing a program, it is necessary for the draftsman to describe the shapes that are to be drawn. A description may be either in digital form or an equation given in the vocabulary of the system being used. The program that he prepares using these descriptions becomes, as one might expect, a complete sequence of coded instructions that must be followed by the drafting machine. This encoded information is then keypunched and fed to the computer. The computer in turn performs the calculations necessary to digitize it for either punched-tape or magnetic tape output.

18.17
IBM Drafting System. The IBM 1620 Drafting System is a series of programs using the IBM 1620 Data Processing System to produce detail (working) drawings on the IBM 1627 plotter (Fig. 18.9). This drafting system accepts one simple input language with the power and versatility of doing almost everything one would expect it to do. IBM disc files are used to store data and programs for rapid processing, and it is possible for the user to store subdrawings on file to be used as needed to meet his particular requirements.

Only those who have full knowledge of the principles of projection and who are acquainted with the idioms and practices

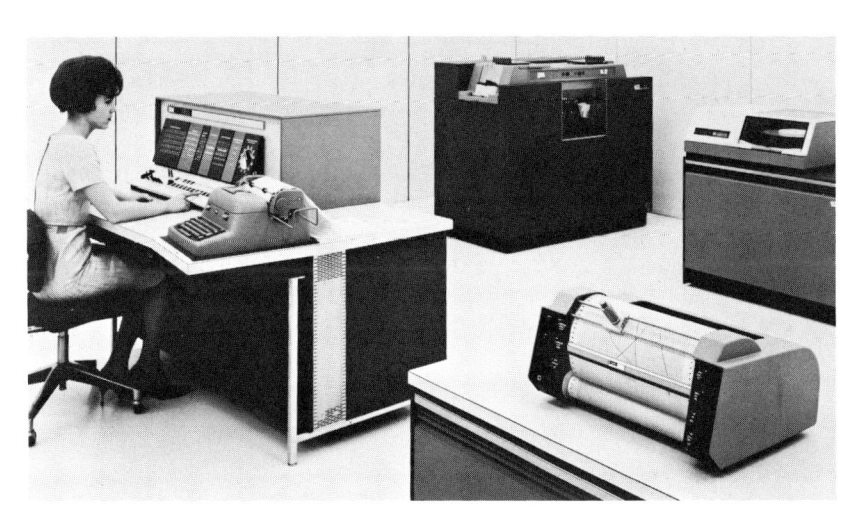

FIG. 18.9. The IBM 1620 Drafting System. (*Courtesy International Business Machines Corp.*)

of industrial drawing as well can use the 1620 Drafting System. This all-important fact is made clear in the general-flow diagram shown in Fig. 18.10, where the first block indicates that a layout and/or sketch is required as a first step. With the layout or sketch as a guide and using an English-like vocabulary, the designer or draftsman prepares a series of statements to describe the drawing to be produced. The easy-to-write input language that he must use consists of geometric, arithmetic, dimensional, and control and annotative statements. Several examples of typical statements will be given with the discussions that follow.

The reader should turn again to the flow diagram shown in Fig. 18.10 and follow it through from the preliminary sketch to the final engineering drawing. In doing so, it should be noted that the punch cards containing the statements prepared by the draftsman are read by the IBM 1620, which converts these statements into commands that direct the plotter producing the drawing. A drawing that has been

```
          Engineering  ──▶  Drafting
          Sketch or         Statements
          Layout
                                │
                                ▼
                          Statement
                          Cards
                                │
                                ▼
          1622            1620              1311
          Card Read ───   System   ───      Disk Storage
          Punch                             Drive
                           │
                           ▼
                        IBM 1627
                        Plotter
                           │
                           ▼
                        [drawing]            Engineering Drawing
```

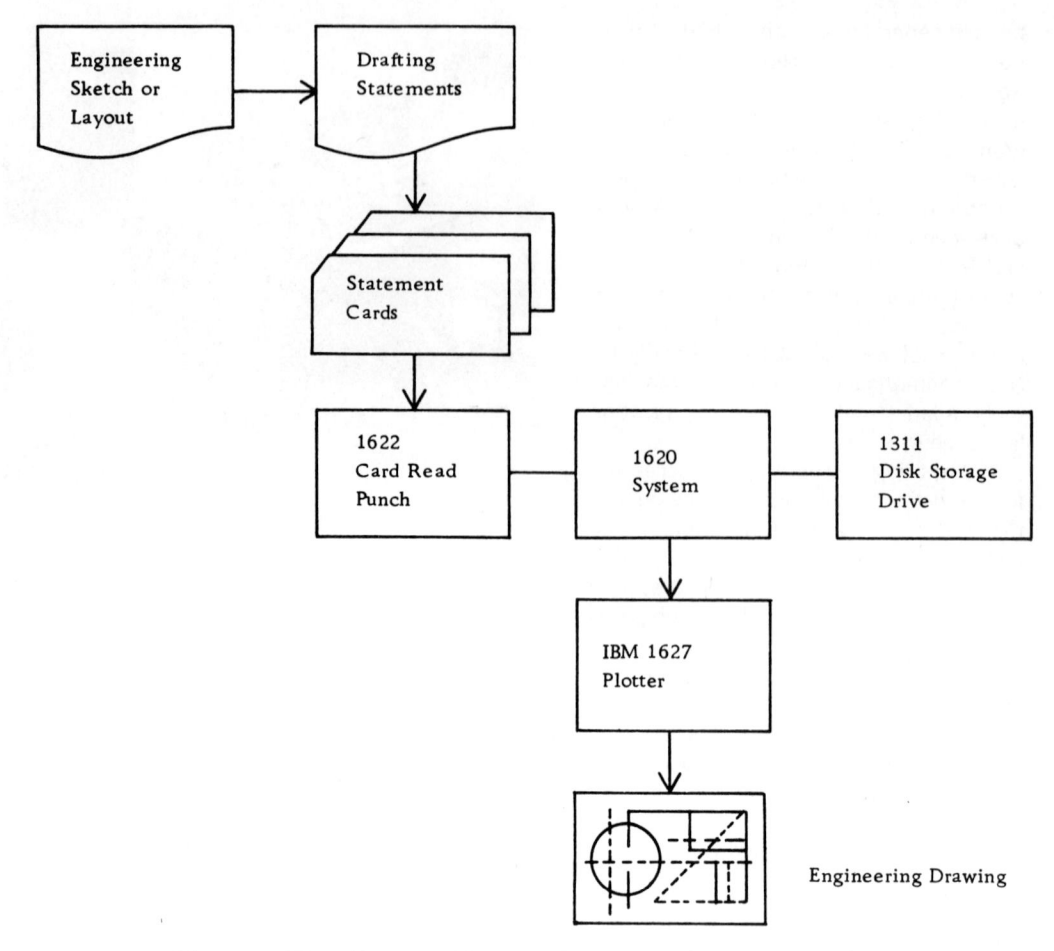

FIG. 18.10. Flow diagram. (*Courtesy International Business Machines Corp.*)

produced using the IBM Drafting System is shown in Fig. 18.11. Those who take time to study the line drawing and the alphanumeric characters (using a reading glass, if available) will note that there are no curved lines as such on the drawing. Circles and circle arcs are formed by very short straight lines, as are the inclined zig-zag lines for the leaders, shown without arrowheads. Horizontal and vertical lines are continuous. This type of execution is typical of *X-Y* plotters.

Examples of the four families of statements that constitute the input language will be given in the following order: geometric, arithmetic, annotative, and control.

Geometric Statements. Geometric statements define the geometry of the part. The definitions may be written either in terms of absolute coordinates, relative coordinates, or as functions of other geometric elements.

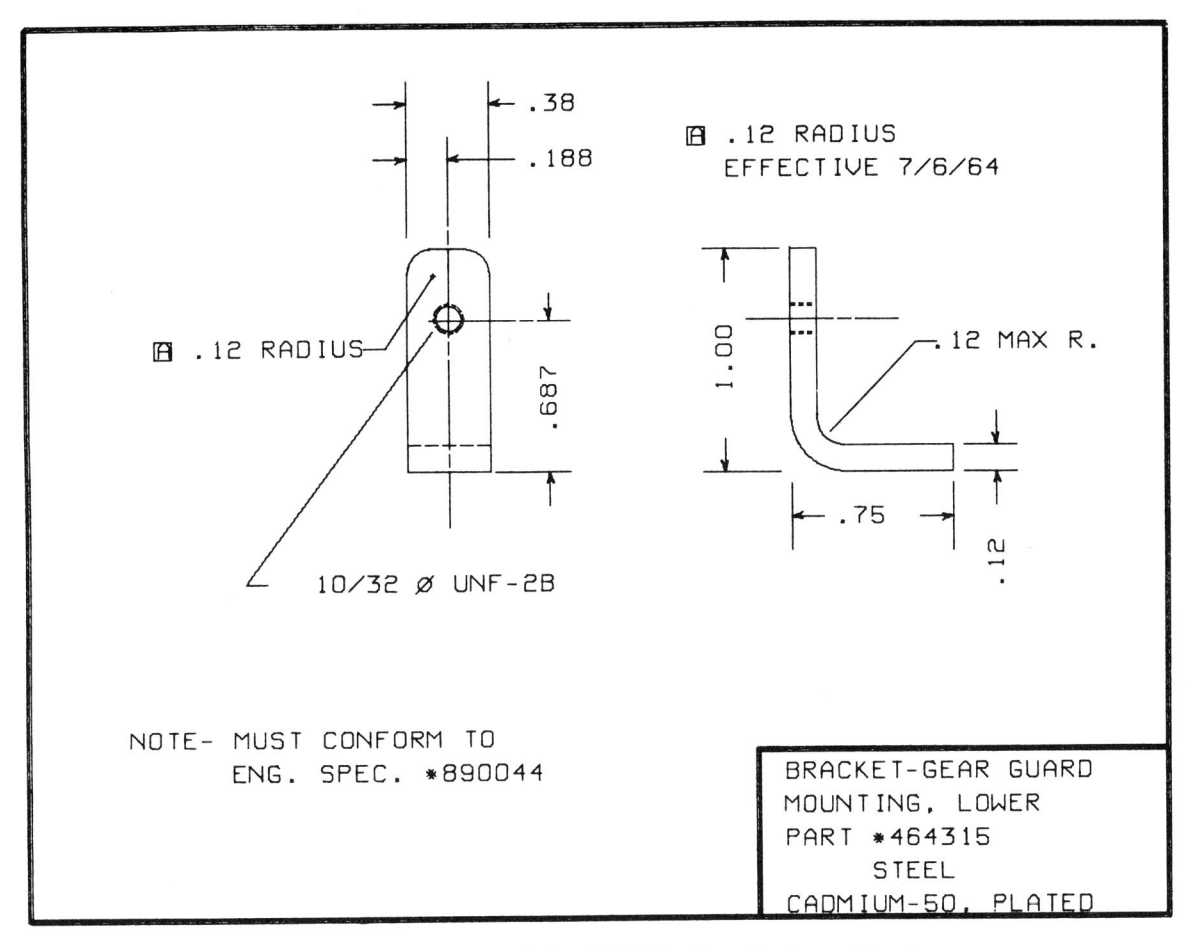

FIG. 18.11. A drawing produced by IBM Drafting System. (*Courtesy International Business Machines Corp.*)

A point may be defined by the following statement:

P1 = POINT/1, 2

where P1 is an arbitrary form of identification (name) assigned to the point, POINT indicates that a point is being defined, and the two digits (1 and 2) are the coordinates of the desired point (Fig. 18.12).

The statement for the line shown in Fig. 18.12 might read as follows:

L1 = LINE/ − 1.04, 4.50, 3.06, 4.50

In this statement, the word LINE indicates that a line, identified as L1, is being defined. The values given are the coordinates of the end points.

A statement defining the large circle shown in Fig. 18.12 could be expressed as follows:

C1 = CIRCLE/2, 3.06, 1

where *C*1 is an arbitrary symbol for iden-

```
              Point 1
              P1 = POINT/1, 2

              Line 1
              L1 = LINE/-1.04, 4.50, 3.06, 4.50

              Large Hole
              C1 = CIRCLE/2, 3.06, 1

              Small Hole (Left)
              C2 = CIRCLE/-1.50, 3.125, HOLE
```

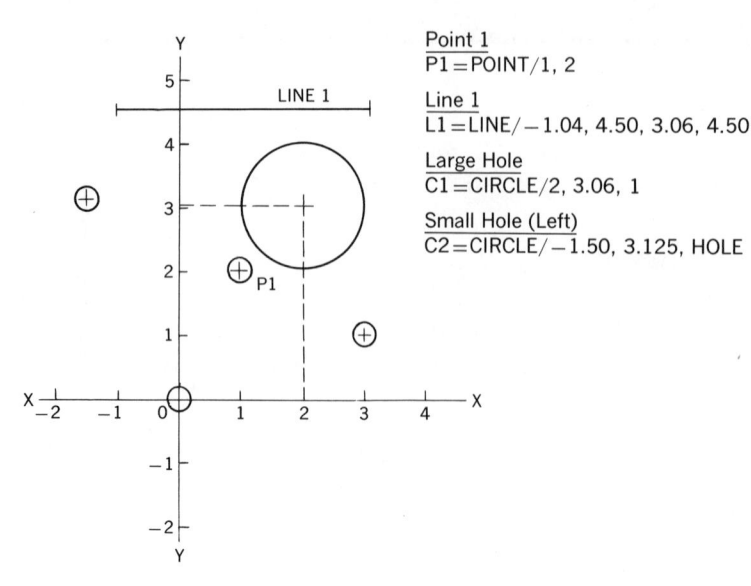

FIG. 18.12. Definition of a point, line, and circle.

tifying the circle, CIRCLE indicates the type of statement as circle definition, and the three values (2, 3.06, and 1) represent the X and Y coordinates and the radius of the circle in inches, respectively.

Continuing, a statement that would define the center point of the circle could be expressed as follows:

$$P1 = POINT/2, 3.06$$

Now, with the symbol P1 defined by actual X and Y coordinates, the statement defining the circle may be written as follows:

$$C1 = CIRCLE/P1, 1$$

The statements for the small hole at the upper-left might read as follows:

$$HOLE = .375/2$$
$$C2 = CIRCLE/ - 1.50, 3.125, HOLE$$

The statement defining the size of the several circles representing the small holes need not be repeated for other holes of the same size.

Arithmetic Statements. These statements are for definitions of data that are not readily available. An arithmetic statement may either appear by itself, as

$$A = B + C/3.4$$

or in a nested statement expressed as follows:

$$CIRCLE/P1, 1.875/2$$

Annotative Statements—Notes. The information needed to present a note is as follows:

1. The "from" point, that is, the point on the line drawing to which the arrow points.

2. The "to" point, that is, the point where the "callout" (textual) information is placed.

3. With only one point being given, the point describes the beginning of the text matter.

4. The text itself. This is a line of textual material (note) written as it is to appear on the drawing with the symbol @ given at the beginning and end of the text, as shown in Fig. 18.13.

The statement for the note in Fig. 18.13 could be expressed as follows:

$$NOTE/P1, 1, 1, @ CHAMFER .05 @$$

Dimensions. In general, the statement given to the right of the dimension in Fig. 18.14 will generate two extension lines to the labeled points, a dimension line with an arrowhead at each end and will automatically compute the dimension. In Fig. 18.15, the statement relates the dimension to a reference line through the origin (ORG).

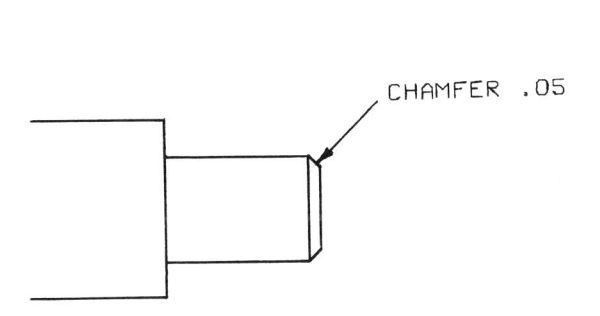

FIG. 18.13. A note on a drawing.

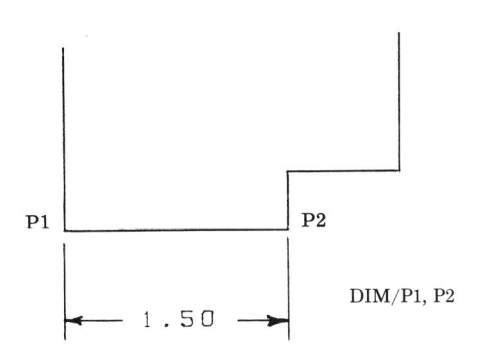

FIG. 18.14. A dimension.

FIG. 18.15. A dimension.

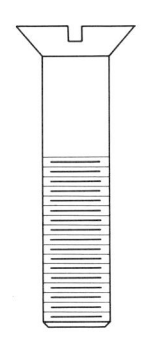

FIG. 18.16. Example of a macro (subdrawing).

Control Statements. There are control statements available to control logic ability, macros, program loops, and line class capabilities.

Macro Subdrawings. Predefined subdrawings stored permanently in disk storage may be recalled as required by a single language statement that lists appropriate dimensions. Generally, these are subdrawings of elements that may be used repeatedly, such as the representations for keyways, bolts, rivets, gear teeth, and so forth. In special cases, it is possible for a whole drawing to be a macro or subpicture. An example of a macro that has been stored on the disc pack and has been called for by its assigned name and parameter list has been shown in Fig. 18.16. The statement needed would be expressed as follows:

CALL/CAPSCR, A = 2, B = .210,
           C = 7/16, D = 13/16

where A is length,
      B is height of head,
      C is nominal diameter, and
      D is diameter of head.

Plotters other than the IBM 1627 may be used with the IBM 1620. Some of these may be equipped with an interface unit for on-line operation from an IBM 1620 computer. All necessary electronic packages are provided to be added to the IBM 1620 for an efficient data transfer rate.

In presenting this more or less lengthy description of the IBM Drafting System, the intention has not been to laud a particular system. Rather, it has been the thought of the author that, by discussing the programming language of this system, the reader would gain some idea of how one instructs a computer control system that will in turn direct a plotter serving as his draftsman. However, one must realize that only an introduction to programming has been presented here and that a designer or draftsman will need more instruction and considerable experience before he will be able to use this versatile drafting tool to the limits of its capabilities.

Computerized drafting does accomplish what is expected of it but at the present stage of development its use is admittedly costly for the preparation of ordinary detail drawings. A detail drawing produced on a plotter is shown in Fig. 18.17.

18.18
Use of the Computer in Automobile-Body Design. The Ford Motor Company has recently adopted a numerically controlled die-making process that eliminates much of the time-consuming drafting work that lies between the stylist's clay model and

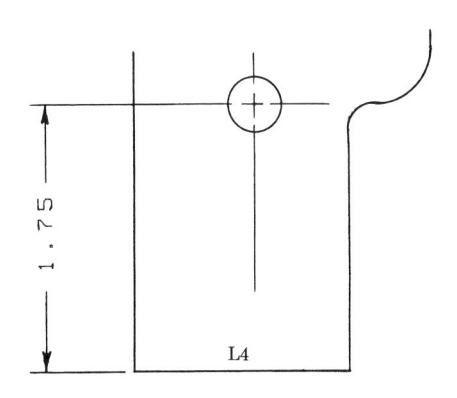

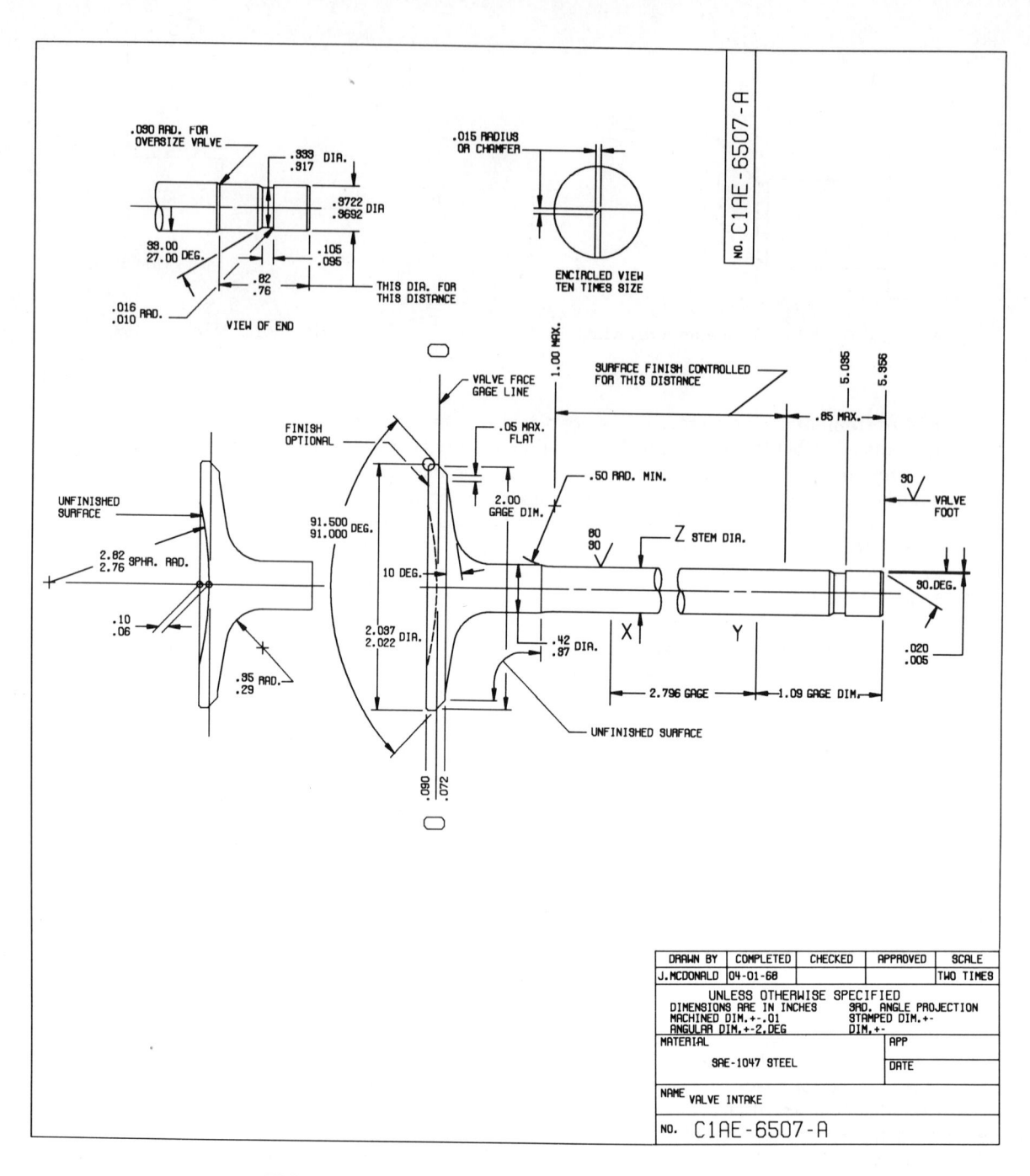

FIG. 18.17. A detail drawing produced by a plotter. (*Courtesy Ford Motor Company*)

CHAP. 18 / COMPUTER-AIDED DESIGN AND AUTOMATED DRAFTING **455**

FIG. 18.18. Contour Data Reader. (*Courtesy Ford Motor Company*)

the body dies needed for a new car. Traditionally, many man-hours were spent preparing drawings from the clay model, making templates from these drawings, and finally producing "tracer masters" from a carved-wood model. It was from these masters that a set of body dies were cut by large milling machines. The new system bypasses much of the drafting work and nearly all of the handwork by body craftsmen.

For this numerically controlled die-making process the Computer Industries Contour Digitizing System is used, which includes a Coordinatograph with magnetic reading heads, a television camera, and a lens system mounted on the reading arm. The image displayed on the screen at the operator's console is magnified 15 times for increased optical accuracy. See Fig. 18.18.

Basically, the system translates drawings of body contours into computer language. To accomplish this the operator takes "read-outs" at predetermined layout points. With television camera positioned at a point, the operator pushes the read-out button and the coordinates of the point, shown on the screen, are punched on a card. These subject data on punched cards (converted to magnetic tape) are then incorporated into the Ford Computer

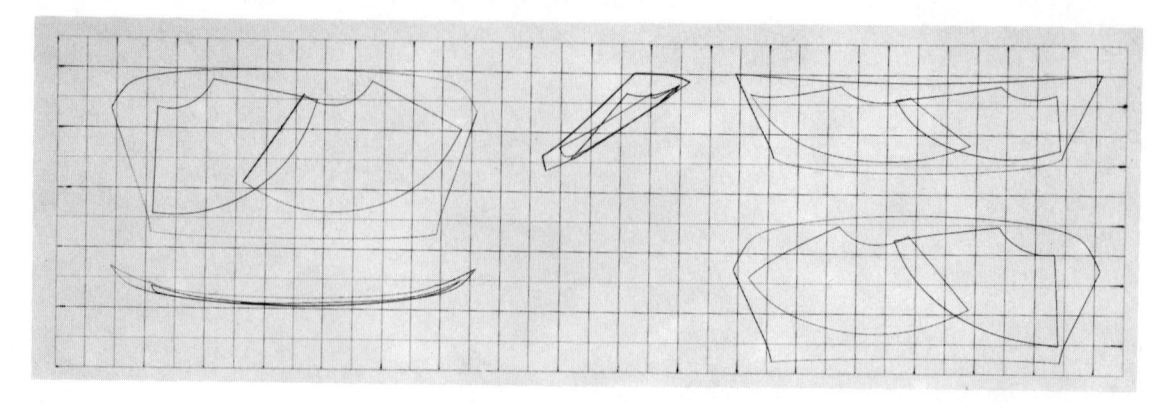

FIG. 18.19. Contour digitizer computer generated drawings. (*Courtesy Ford Motor Company*)

Program and output tapes are generated for verification and for numerically controlled drafting (Fig. 18.19). Orthographic and perspective drawings are prepared as required for verification and checks are made on the computer-generated cutter path. On completion of these steps, the data are transferred to punched paper tape. This final tape is prepared for a numerically controlled, multiaxis machine that cuts the needed body dies automatically.

18.19
CRT Plotting Systems. The CRT microfilm printer–plotter has undergone gradual improvement since the first system was placed in use in 1960. During the first years, the cost of CRT plotters was so high that they could be found only at aerospace and government research centers. However, extensive research and development work has led to the recent announcement of several economical systems with the flexibility needed for high-speed computer output, data analysis, automatic drafting and circuit board design. Use of CRT printer–plotters, such as the DD 80 (Data Display Inc.) and the CI 120 (Computer Industries, Inc.), is expected to rise rapidly. CRT plotters should soon be appearing in increasing numbers at medium-size computer centers and in the design rooms of the larger industrial organizations.

The economical CI 120 shown in Fig. 18.20 is an expandable modular system, completely solid state, that features high-reliability, silicon logic circuits. The design is such that the system can be either an off-line CRT plotter (operating from magnetic tape input) or an on-line system operating with a digital computer. Operating on-line, the CI 120 produces copy of drawings, graphs, and records in somewhat the same manner as does the microfilm recorder of the DAC–1 image processing system. In fact, a CRT microfilm printer–plotter could be used as a unit of any computer-aided design system, not representing a special development. The DAC–1 image processing system, with film scanning capabilities for direct graphic input, must be recognized as being a unique one-of-a-kind system that represents the joint research efforts of General Motors and IBM. A system having the complete capabilities of the DAC–1 image processing system is not available at this time.

CRT microfilm printer–plotters have been discussed under automated drafting

CHAP. 18 / COMPUTER-AIDED DESIGN AND AUTOMATED DRAFTING   457

as such because they can be operated off-line. CRT plotters could have been included just as well with that portion of this chapter covering computer-aided design.

Input data, decoded and displayed on a high-resolution cathode-ray tube, is photographed using a high-speed 35mm magazine camera. This film is fed from a continuous roll that may be up to 400 ft. in length.

Long continuous charts can be produced using program-controlled precision film advance that permits the butting of consecutive data frames. The so-called "thru-put" is 120 full printing format frames per minute.

The average plotting time for a typical plot is less than 1 sec. Should a "quick-look" hard copy be needed, the auxiliary hard copy camera can be used to obtain copy directly on 9-in. paper within 4 sec. This is accomplished by an integrally mounted processor that is relatively inexpensive.

When output is to have a repetitive format, it is possible to superimpose a form on the CRT display. To do this saves the computer time needed to generate the form each time.

18.20
The Illustromat. The Illustromat 1100 shown in Fig. 18.21 is a computer-directed drafting machine that is capable of producing either perspective or axonometric views or three-dimensional stereodrawings that are mathematically and visually accurate. A finished view can have any tilt and be drawn to a desired size. In addition, this versatile drafting machine can draw scaled pantographs (enlargements or reductions) or draw a third view from a blueprint showing only two views. The Illustromat can perform all of these tasks nearly 5 times faster than an experienced draftsman or illustrator. This alone justifies its cost in dollars.

FIG. 18.20. The CI 120 CRT microfilm printer/plotter. (*Courtesy Computer Industries, Inc.*)

The three primary components of the Illustromat are as follows:

1. A horizontal tracing assembly with two tracing styli, supported by a movable gantry;

2. The control panel that operates the solid-state analog computer; and

3. The vertical X–Y plotting board with a motorized pen. The drawing area of the plotter is approximately 36 × 43 in.

To prepare the machine for use, the operator places the drawing showing the orthographic views of the object on the horizontal board and attaches a sheet of paper of proper size for the three-dimensional view to the vertical board.

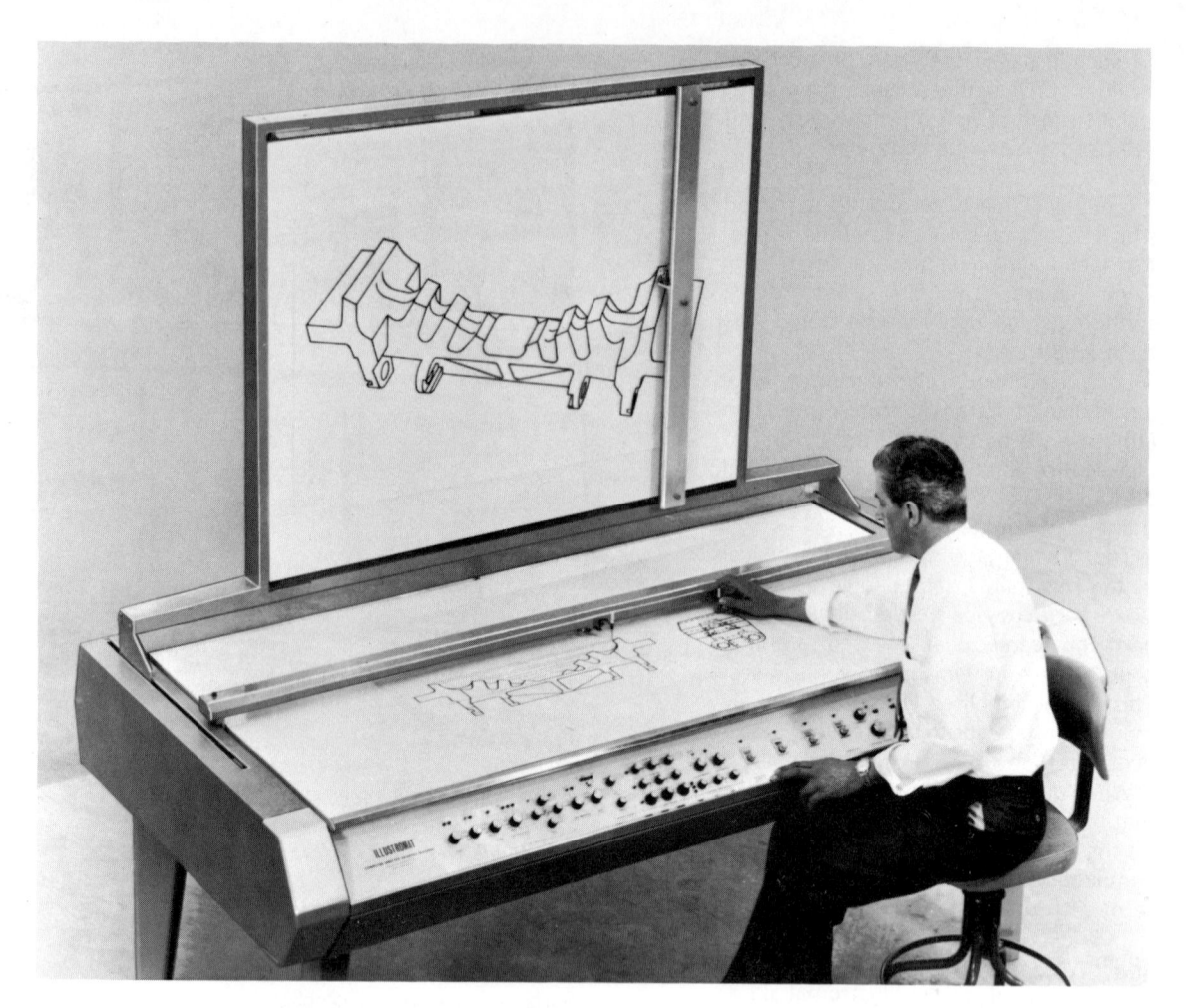

FIG. 18.21. The Illustromat 1100 computer-directed drafting machine. Shown here is a perspective illustration of a casting, drawn from a print. (*Courtesy Perspective, Inc.*)

Then, after initial balance has been established, he adjusts the controls for station point, rotation, tilt, and scale, as needed.

To obtain the three-dimensional view, the operator, using the styli ganged to the gantry above the horizontal board, traces the orthographic views in the manner shown in Fig. 18.21. Line information from these views enters into the analog computer. The computer in turn converts these two-dimensional data into three dimensional data and directs the pen on the X–Y plotting board. Thus, by the simple process of tracing from two views, input information can be given to the computer.

18.21
Applications of Plotting and Digitizing Systems. Computer-operated drafting machines are widely used for the preparation of perspective and axonometric drawings and integrated-circuit-board layouts. They

do mapping, perform lofting, and plot impeller, airscrew, and wing sections. By utilizing their now recognized capabilities, drafting systems can prepare a perspective of an aerodynamic configuration composed of station lines or plot a series of compound surfaces and almost immediately present a perspective of these same surfaces for inspection and evaluation. This has been demonstrated using Autoprompt as a drafting language.

To recrate the maneuvers of aircraft, animated motion pictures have been made with the cockpit and terrain features both included to provide orientation and to relate most of what a pilot would see from his position in the plane. Of course, a higher degree of realism could have been obtained by making a motion picture from the plane doing the maneuver, but only at a much higher cost. The automated drawing was done by a Mosely plotter and a little final rendering was added to bring about some realism. The creation of these highly complex three-dimensional scenes for a rough movie-type sequence has been largely the work of several outstanding engineering "graphicians" at The Boeing Company. The results of their work appear in a book entitled *Computer Graphics in Communication.** The author is William A. Fetter, who was a member of a small group of persons assigned to the project. Some of the work of these men included maneuver simulation of a bank and turn and then a dive and pullout, pilot views of landing on a CVA–19 under simulated heavy seas, and pilot views of landing at an airport.

Three-dimensional graphs with scales and rotated perspective views have been prepared using an Orthomat plotter. Properly programmed, other plotters can perform the same tasks.

Now coming to the attention of people in industry is the application of plotting systems to the graphic interpretation of machining routines that have been programmed by a computer. The graphic interpretation provides a quick check and eliminates the need for running tests of routines on a numerically controlled machine tool. As stated elsewhere in this chapter, drafting machines can also produce drawings to verify cutter-tool paths specified by machine control tapes. For quality control, a drafting machine can be used as an aid in establishing checkpoints on inspection tapes and in making scribed optical comparator charts and boards.

The solid-state CI LARR V with the Telecordex electronic system offers unequalled digitizing flexibility. It can be customized for a particular application. In Fig. 18.22, the LARR V is being utilized to digitize a printed circuit. As can be observed in this case, the output will be on magnetic tape.

A plot of acceleration, velocity, and distance curves is shown in Fig. 18.23.

---

*William A. Fetter, *Computer Graphics in Communication,* New York: McGraw-Hill, Inc., 1966.

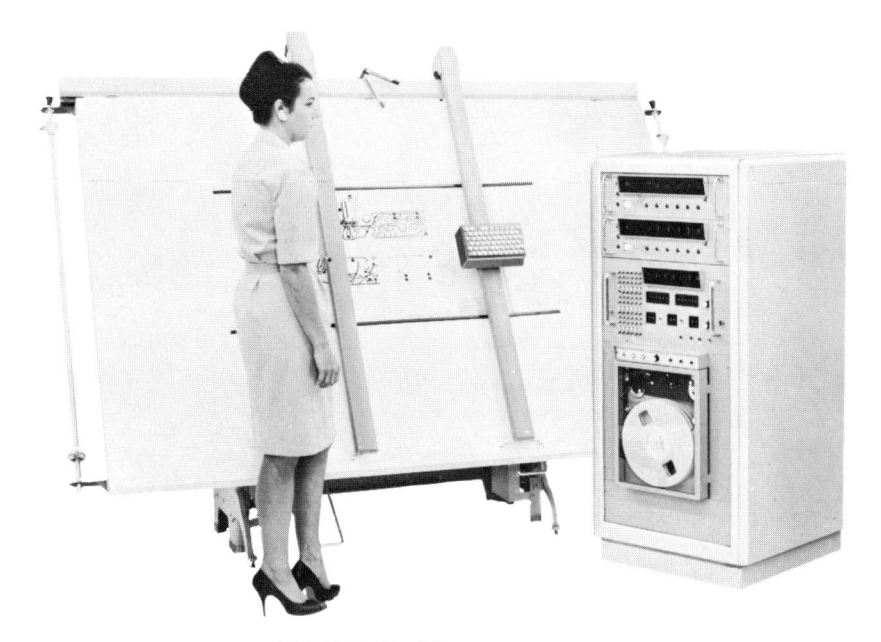

FIG. 18.22. The CI LARR V with magnetic tape output. (*Courtesy Computer Industries, Inc.*)

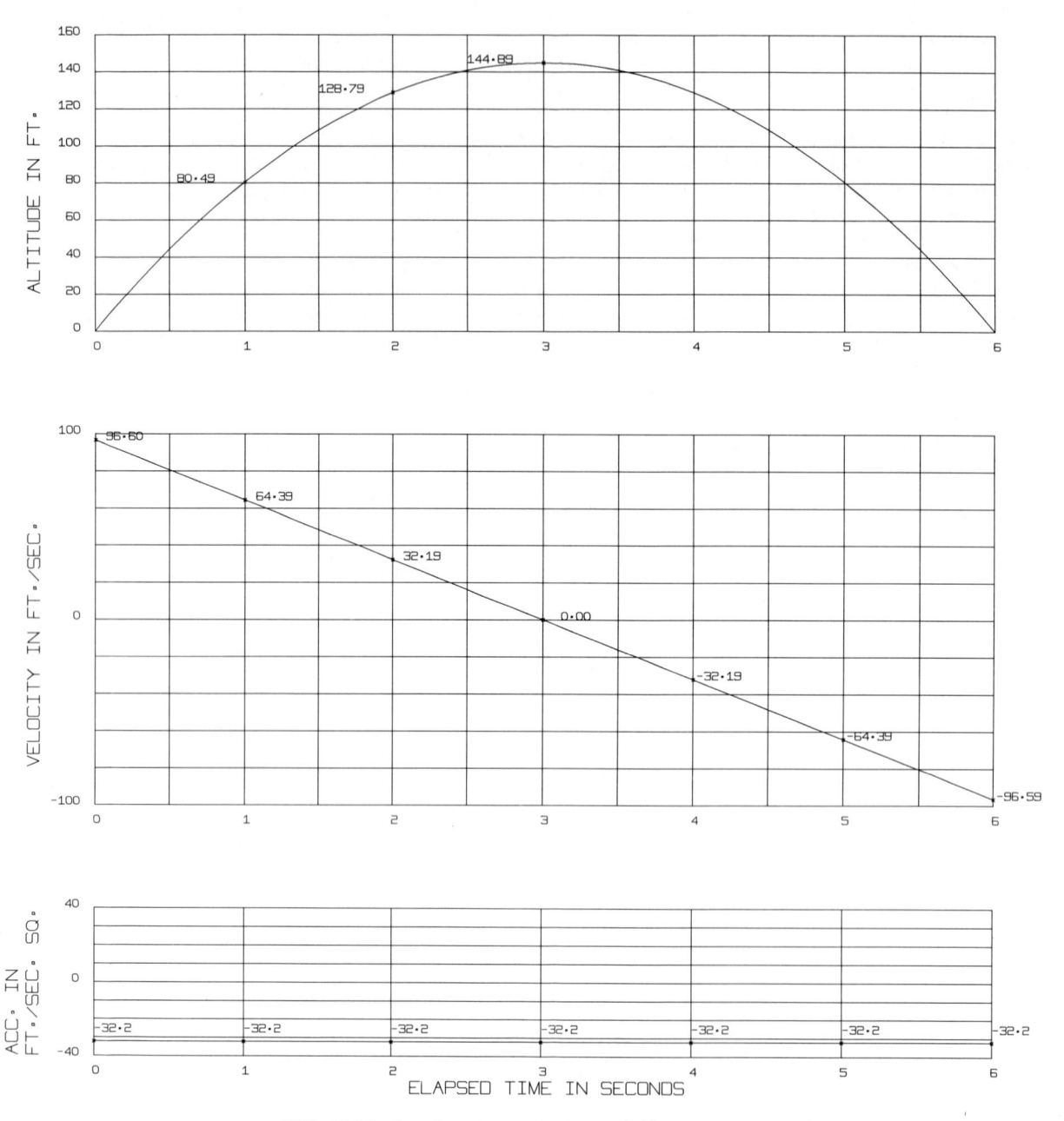

FIG. 18.23 Acceleration, velocity and distance curves. These plots were done on a CI 305 Digital Incremental Plotter connected on-line with an IBM 1130 Computer. (*Courtesy Computer Industries, Inc.*)

C: AUTOMATED PHOTODRAFT SYSTEMS

18.22
Keuffel & Esser Photomechanical System.
The K & E Photodraft system is one of several automated systems now coming into general use for preparing schematics and other similar types of drawings directly on film. This system uses a coded punch tape, a negative master symbol disc, a beam of light, and a roll of photosensitive material to produce a translucent original. The line quality is such that the schematic can be reduced to microfilm and then blown up to full size at a later time. The use of this system reduces both material and labor costs, as should be expected, and at the same time relieves designers and skilled draftsmen from routine production drafting that can only be boring to them.

Basically, the photodraft system consists of a keyboard unit, a photographic unit with a negative master symbol disc, and a processor. See Fig. 18.24. The symbol disc may contain up to 168 symbols, numbers, and letters, as may be needed to meet requirements. The purchaser has his choice of symbols.

In using this system, the designer's work is finished when he has made a rough sketch of his design on graph paper having squares synchronized to movement of the keyboard unit [Fig. 18.25(a)]. His sketch may be done entirely freehand, but he should include all of the symbols, letters, and numbers that are required since the final drawing may be produced by an operator with minimal training. From this point on, the responsibility for the pro-

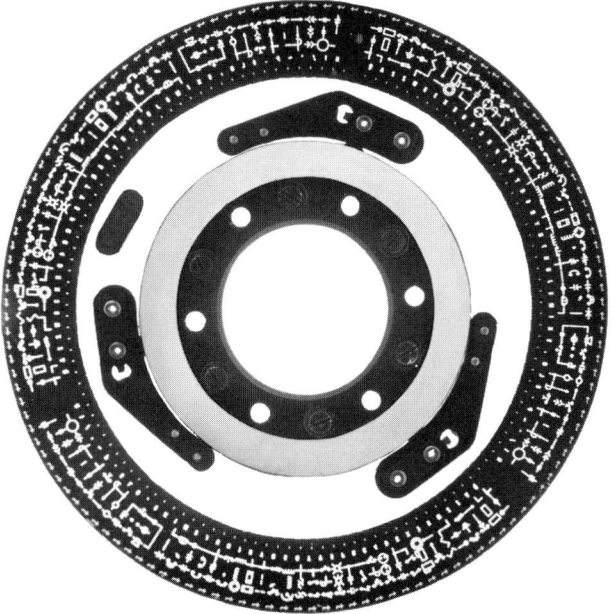

FIG. 18.24. K & E Photo-draft system, keyboard and photographic units. (*Courtesy of Keuffel & Esser Co.*)

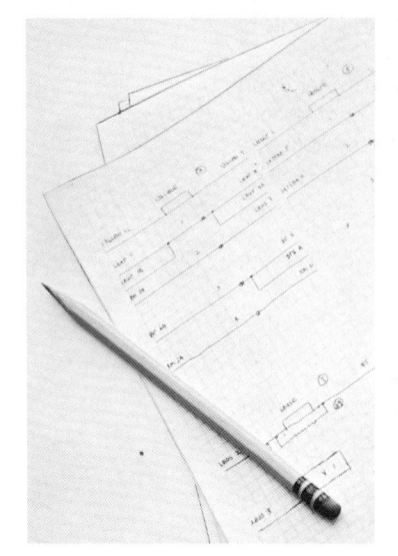

(a) Engineer's sketch.

(b) Operator types over engineer's rough outlines.

(c) Operator checks symbols and positions. Corrects tape if required.

(d) With tape inserted, photographic unit is ready to work.

(e) Magazine removed. Exposed material ready to be inserted in processor.

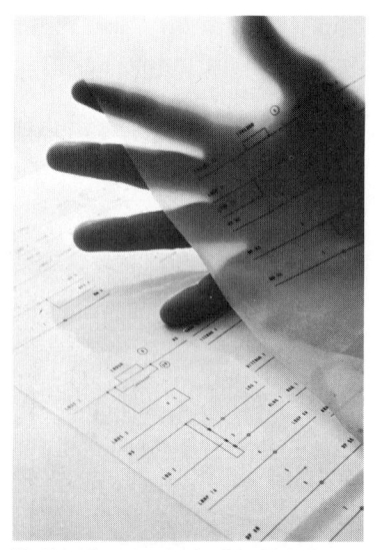

(f) Translucent reproducible original ready for making copies.

FIG. 18.25. The photo-draft system in use. (*Courtesy Keuffel & Esser Co.*)

duction of the needed translucency rests with the operator.

To produce the coded tape [see (c)] that directs the photographic unit, the operator inserts a diazo of the engineer's rough sketch into the keyboard unit and types directly over the rough outline, being careful to incorporate all of the lines, symbols, numbers, and letters as indicated [see b)]. To correct errors, the operator presses two buttons. These will nullify a symbol, a series of symbols, or even complete lines. When copying has been finished, checking is easy since the unit produced its own proof copy at the same time it punched the tape. The operator need only compare symbols and positions and, if no corrections are needed, the tape is ready for use with the photographic unit (Fig. 18.24).

With the tape inserted, the photographic unit is ready to operate. In use, as it automatically performs its task, each code on the tape positions the master symbol disc [see (d)]. With the correct symbol in place, a beam of light passes through the symbol and exposes it in exact position on the photosensitive material lodged in the unit. The unit operates at a rate of about 200 exposures per minute.

The last step between the rough sketch and the translucent original is the processing of the exposed material [see (e)]. Within approximately 1 min. after the magazine has been removed from the photographic unit and the exposed material inserted in the processor, an original is available either for reproduction of full-size copies or for microfilming and enlarging.

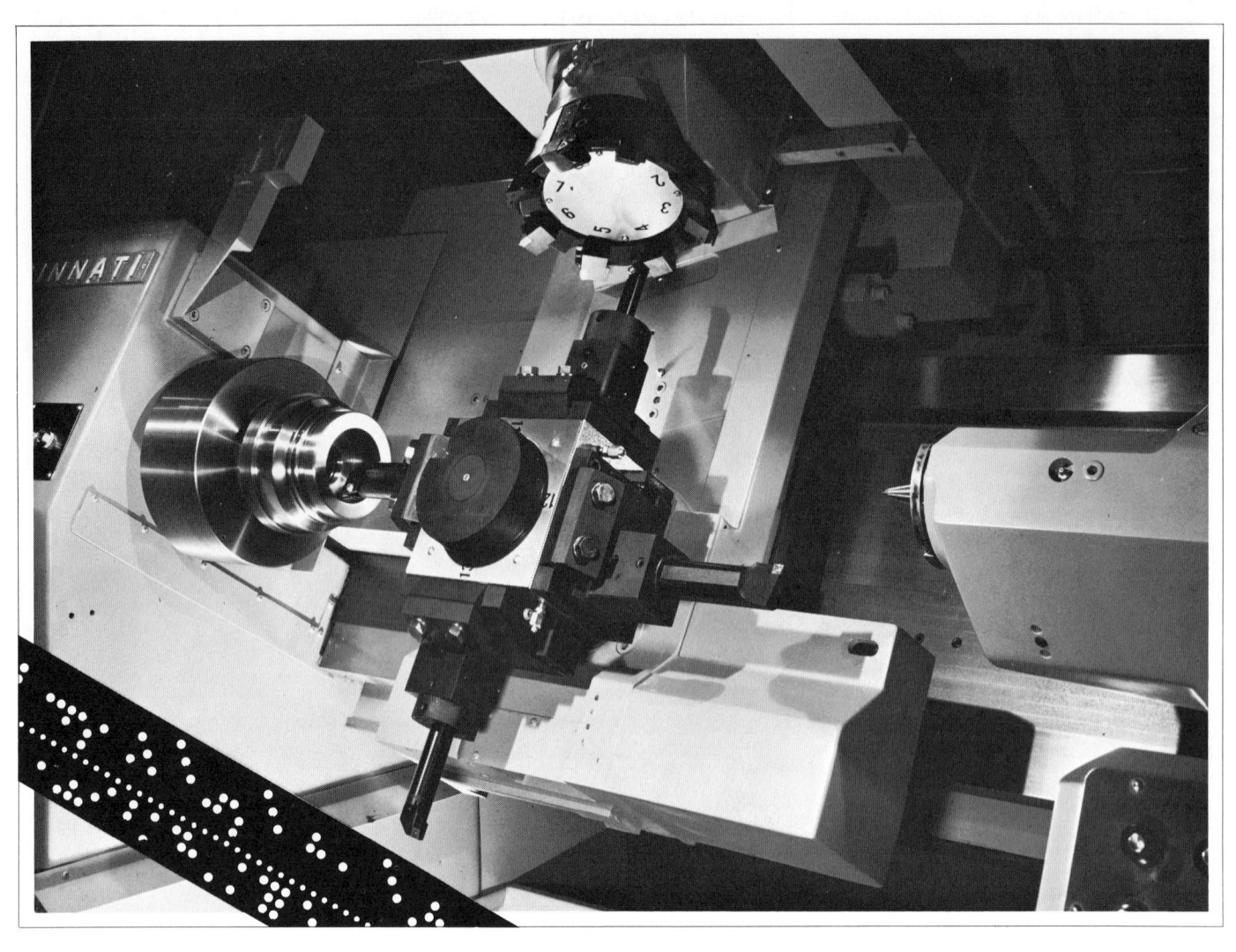

With the coming of numerical control (NC) American industry stands at the threshold of a new era. In some industries, numerical control now starts at the product design level where engineers and technologists utilize the computer for creating mathematical models that may ultimately become line drawings prepared on a plotter (see Chapter 18). Under a total system concept, now a practical reality, numerical control will be utilized from the very early stages of the design through drafting, manufacturing, and quality control. We are entering the electronic age—an age that may be identified in history as the "second industrial revolution." Graphic methods have now assumed new importance and the graphic language has become a means for communication with a computer.
(*Courtesy Cincinnati Milling Machine Co.*)

Numerically Controlled Machine Tools

19

19.1
N/C Machine Tools. In use at the present time are production machines that follow directions given on punched tapes and gages that measure electrically to millionths of an inch. The use of tapes and computers by industry does not mean that the draftsmen and engineers will have less work to do and that there will be fewer of them. It does mean, however, that the men assigned to both areas must keep themselves informed and up-to-date on late developments. The draftsman should learn how to dimension the drawing of a part to meet the requirements for programming the machine or machines that will perform the shop operations (Fig. 19.8). He must have a more thorough understanding of basic fundamentals than in the past and at the same time be willing to accept change.

The fact must be recognized that automation is here and the only question the technically trained man of today can ask himself is whether or not he, as an individual, can adjust to new knowledge and different requirements.

19.2
Numerically Controlled Equipment. The term *numerical control* (N/C), as applied to automated production machines, denotes a method of electronically controlling the operation and motions of a machine tool. This method may be considered relatively new since the first of these machines was placed in operation only a little more than a decade ago. Early machine tools with built-in intelligence were numerically controlled milling and profiling machines that provided faster and less expensive means for producing aircraft parts. Now, numerical control has been applied to other machine tools. such as lathes, drilling and boring machines, welding and flame cutting machines, punching machines, and inspection devices. The day may be near when the designer, with sketches as a guide, will reduce his ideas to APT (Automatically Programmed Tools) language and then have a computer complete his design and prepare the instruction tape needed for machining (read Chapter 18).

There are two basic types of numerical control: (1) contouring or continuous path and (2) positioning or point-to-point. In the case of the contouring system, generally applied to milling machines, the path is continuously controlled. Normally, the path consists of very short straight-line segments, which approximate specified circular or curved lines. This system is used for machining items such as dies, gears, cams, and pieces having contoured

465

surfaces. For most types of contour machining, the computer is used for instruction calculations.

The cutting tool is controlled mainly with respect to its final position for the point-to-point system as it is primarily applied to drilling and boring operations (Fig. 19.8). The path that a tool may take when directed from one point to another when drilling is relatively unimportant since the tool is not in contact with the workpiece during the movement. When the operations are not complex, the instruction tape may be prepared without the aid of a computer.

Numerically controlled equipment has either a two-axis or a "three-and-more-axis" system. As one might expect, the two-axis system is for two-dimensional machining, while the three-and-more-axis system makes three-dimensional machining possible.

A numerically controlled machine tool must have complete instructions to perform an operation at a specified location. This is accomplished by the machine control unit that contains the data processing equipment needed to translate programmed information into operating commands (electrical pulses) for the machine-tool system with its servomechanism drives and related feedback and measuring devices. Basically, the control unit consists of an input section, an interpolating or command-generating section, and a servoloop (drive) section. The input section, with tape reader and temporary storage capabilities, decodes and processes the programmed information for eventual transfer to the interpolating section (Fig. 19.1). The instructions, presented as a series of holes punched in tape (either paper or aluminum–mylar), are read by a tape reader that may be either photoelectric or mechanical. Provided with both temporary and active storage areas, the complete control unit can receive new information from tape for temporary storage while using information in active storage. The information transferred into the interpolating section (active storage) is processed by logic circuitry that periodically sends signals (pulses) to the servoloop section. The digital or pulse information received by the servoloop section is, in turn, converted to an analog form and directed to the servomechanisms of the machine tool. Each command pulse (converted to an analog voltage) will create a definite movement of a slide, the actual movement itself being accomplished by some form of auxiliary equipment, such as a hydraulic motor, a hydraulic cylinder, or an electric motor (ac or dc) attached to the machine tool itself.

As stated before, the information on the control tape must provide complete instructions in a logical sequence. With a print or a sketch at hand, the parts programmer prepares a process (program) sheet (Fig. 19.4). On this sheet he lists the movements and operations necessary to machine the piece to the dimensions specified. This information, in order, is then punched on the control tape by a machine (tape punch) that resembles an electric typewriter. As the operator types the digits, symbols, or letters, the device translates the information into a binary-coded-decimal form and at the same time punches the tape (see Fig. 18.2). Manually programming a machine tool to machine a part is not always an easy task. It may be both frustrating and time consuming, for records show that it may require as many as 250–400 hr to prepare a program for a particularly complicated piece.

Numerical control may be the most important metalworking development of the Twentieth Century. It will grow rapidly in use, and as metalworking assumes a new aspect, new job patterns will result that will require higher skills and considerably more technical training for the individual. It has been predicted that by 1980, N/C machines may do up to 80% of the work

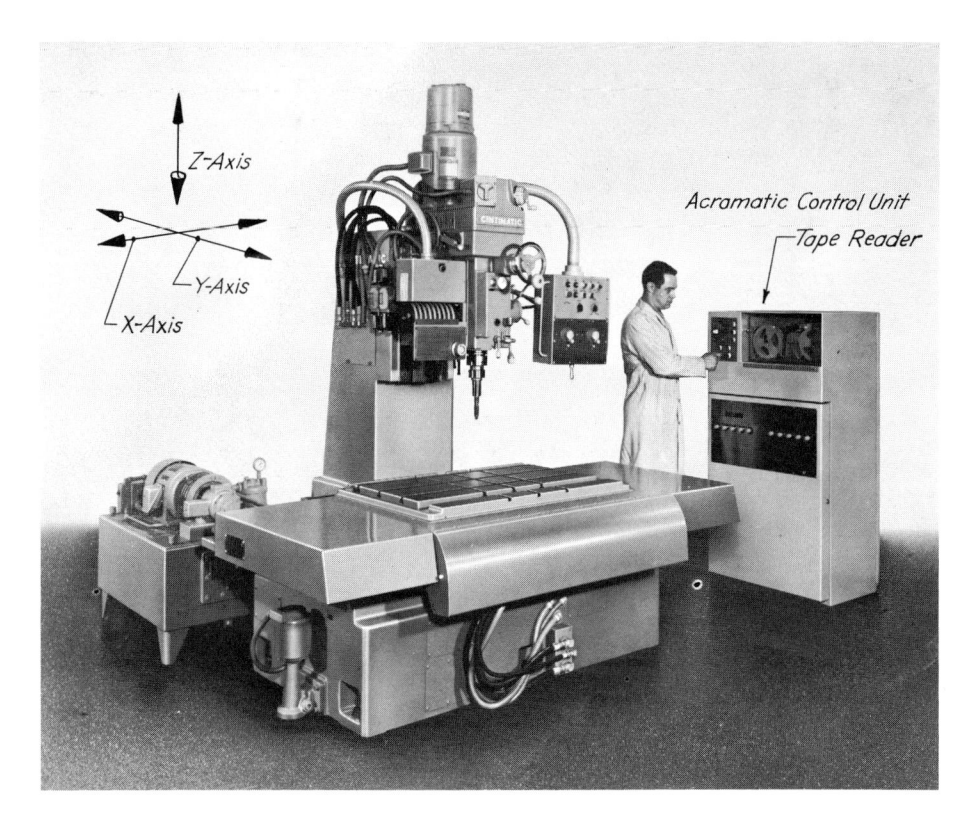

FIG. 19.1. The Cintimatic Vertical Machining Center shown above automatically drills, taps, mills, and bores in one setting. Work table positioning accuracy is ±.001 in 24 inches and its repeatability is ±.0005″. (*Courtesy Cincinnati Milling Machine Co.*)

now done by general-purpose machines (Fig. 19.2). Numerical control may well revolutionize our national economy and ultimately bring about great changes in our social structure. These changes must be faced knowing that there is no turning back from our plunge into the electronic age.

19.3
Use of Cartesian Coordinates (Fig. 19.3).
The standard Cartesian coordinate system is used to designate machine-tool axes and is the basis for all programming for numerical control. Most numerical-control systems use only the first quadrant for dimensioning purposes in accordance with the recommendation given in the EIA (Electronics Industry Association) standards. This practice of considering the workpiece to be positioned in a right-handed Cartesian system provides an accepted frame of reference that enables a programmer to relate a workpiece to almost any numerically controlled machine tool in general use. The geometry of the workpiece is described within the framework of X, Y, and Z axes by relating all critical points of the part to the origin. The position of a point is established by giving its

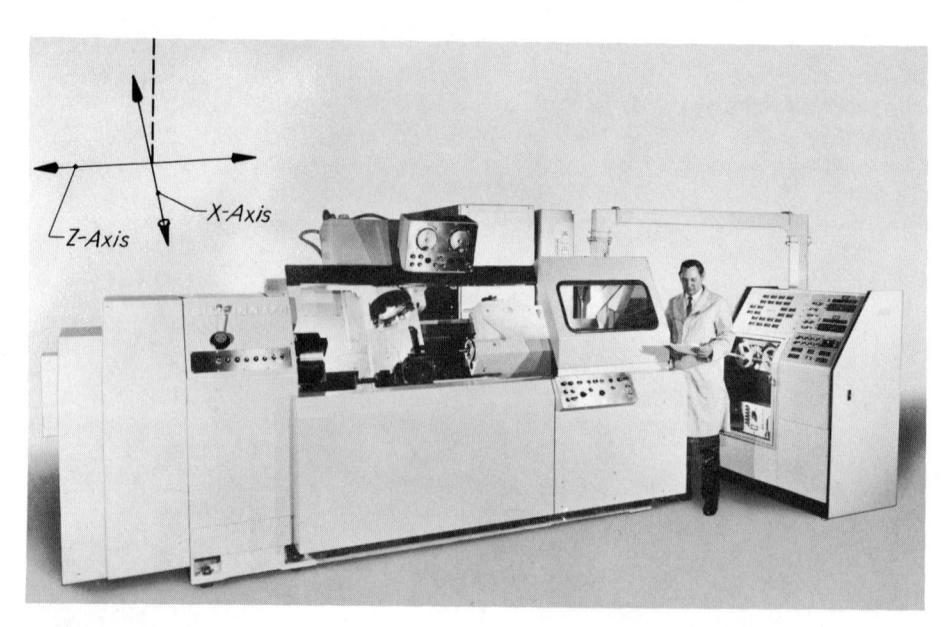

FIG. 19.2. Tape (N/C) controlled turning machine that automatically performs all turning operations including facing, grooving, contouring, threading, boring, drilling, and reaming. The Acramatic control for the lathe shown above features: (1) complete integrated circuit electronics; (2) four digit, feed rate coding in inches per minute; (3) Automatic acceleration and deceleration without special coding; (4) Incremental programming; (5) 300-row-per-second tape reader; (6) buffer storage; (7) manual data imput; (8) Linear interpolation; (9) Circular interpolation; (10) threading. The last two features are optional. (*Courtesy Cincinnati Milling Machine Co.*)

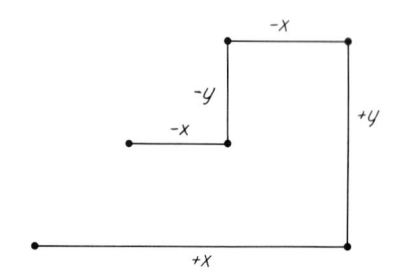

FIG. 19.3. Cartesian—coordinate system.

distances from the origin, measured parallel to the mutually perpendicular axes.

Although the angular orientation and the location of the origin is not the same for all machines (see Figs. 19.1 and 19.2), the X and Y axes usually lie in a horizontal plane. In the plane of the X and Y axes, measurements taken along the X axis to the right are plus ($+$), while those taken to the left in the opposite direction are considered to be minus ($-$). The Z axis, perpendicular to both the X and Y axes, is always parallel to the axis of the cutting tool. Finally, the longest motion of which a machine is capable is usually in the direction of the X axis. See Fig. 19.1.

In preparing programs one must always remember that the machine axis designation is always based on a coordinate system associated with that particular machine. A study of Fig. 19.9 reveals the fact that the cycle file (see copy 1) was prepared relating all measurements to the initial point O (origin) at the center of the bolt circle (Fig. 19.8). However, the part program shows the location of the zero position of the machine tool being used to be -20.000, -20.000 with respect to the initial point O on the workpiece.

19.4
The Programming Process and Manual Tape Preparation (Fig. 19.4). It is essen-

tial for those who are concerned with numerical control, as it applies to design, drafting, and production, to have a thorough understanding of the programming of numerically controlled equipment. The programming process is known as *part programming*. Part programming, however, may involve the use of million-dollar computers and computer programs in the process of producing needed numerical-control tapes.

The usual steps in the programming process are as follows:

1. Make an analysis of the part and consider its relation to the machine tool.

2. Consider the tooling required to produce the workpiece. That is, determine the type of holding device, the style and size of cutters, and so forth.

3. Determine the operations required and the sequence in which they must be performed.

Some parts may be programmed exceedingly fast because of their simplicity. This may be done with the aid of a desk calculator and trigonometry tables. In the case of the simplest NC machine tools, which have only the X and Y distances controlled by perforated tape, parts of the total operation may be performed by the machinist manually in accordance with instructions that are included in the program manuscript. After deciding on the machining sequence, the programmer must list on the program sheet (see Fig. 19.4) all tool movements, operations, tool selections, speeds, feeds, coolant control, and tool changes. He must remember as he prepares the program sheet that he alone controls every phase of the manufacturing process.

A portion of the programming for the workpiece shown in Fig. 19.4 is given for sequences numbered H046–N056 (see column 1). The sequence numbers show the order in which the machining operations are to be performed. Column 2 (from the left), preparatory function, is for programming the operating mode, such as drill, tap, mill, or bore. The function code G81 calls for the machine to drill.

The X and Y columns are for listing the hole locations. These are programmed in positive numbers in the first quadrant. The 0 position for the X and Y axes corresponds to the left-front corner of the table. It should be noted that, aside from calling for a drilling cycle, the sequence number H046 also calls for the table to move to the hole position 16.500 in. along the X axis and 6.000 in. along the Y axis.

Entries in the column headed "Miscellaneous Function" are for such items as specifying what depth of collar to use. The code M57 calls for the use of depth stop No. 7.

The sequence numbers that follow through N054 call for the table to move to the hole positions called for in the drilling cycle. At sequence number N054, the code M06 (see column 5) stops the automatic drilling cycle. At this point the tool, feed, or speeds are changed as called for in the manuscript instructions. In looking ahead to sequence number H055, we see that preparatory function G84 has been specified. This command cycle code calls for a tapping sequence that instructs the machine to move rapidly to gage height, feed to depth, reverse spindle, feed out, and then move to upper limit. No other instructions are needed to perform this operation.

Sequence number N056 calls for a move to a new hole position in the same tapping sequence.

By following the solid black arrows in Fig. 19.5, it can be noted that the next step is punching the information given on the program form (process sheet) into the tape. Before this is done, however, it is wise to have the completed draft checked by a second programmer. If no errors are

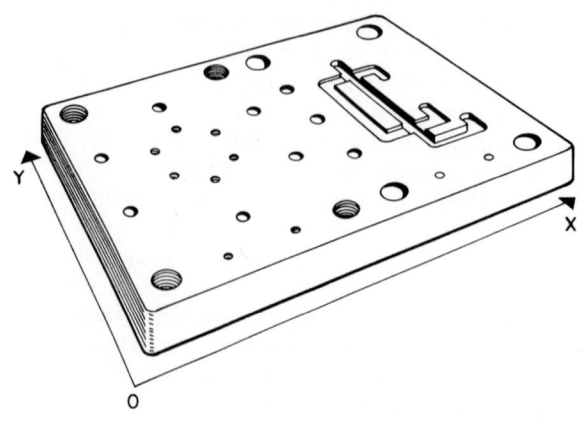

SEQ. NO.	PREP. FUNCT.	X POSITION	Y POSITION	MISC. FUNCT.	POS. NO.	FEED IN./REV.	SPEED RPM	DEPTH OF CUT	TOOL REMARKS
H046	G81	X16 500	Y06 000	M57	30	.005	1060	1.375	21/32 DRILL—5 IPM
N047			Y14 000		31				
N048		X11 000			32				
N049		X09 000			33				
N050		X03 500			34				
N051			Y06 000		35				
N052		X09 000			36				
N053		X11 000			37				
N054		X06 250	Y10 000	M06	38				
H055	G84	X06 250	Y10 000	M58	20	.047	490	.750	1/4-20 N.C. TAP 23 IPM
N056		X11 000	Y06 000		21				

FIG. 19.4. A program sheet showing a portion of the programming for the workpiece shown. (*Courtesy Cincinnati Milling Machine Co.*)

found, the manuscript is turned over to a typist, who enters the programmed numerical commands on a Friden Flexowriter or similar machine having a keyboard much like that of an electric typewriter. As the operator types, two outputs result. One is in the form of a master document that is called a print-out. This is an exact copy of the manuscript that was typed. The other output, made simultaneously, is a control tape with a series of perforations. See Fig. 19.9. A second tape may then be made using the data tape verification unit and the first tape. The automatic retyping of the process sheet produces a second tape. Mechanical proofreading is thus provided since the second tape will not punchout if it differs in any way from the first tape.

The tape used is standard 1-in. wide paper or mylar-coated tape. Using a word address format, this eight-track tape is perforated in accordance with EIA Standard RS–273 (Fig. 19.6). Tab and delete codes are permitted. The code perforations are punched across the 1-in. width of the tape. The eight positions that are available for code holes are called *chan-*

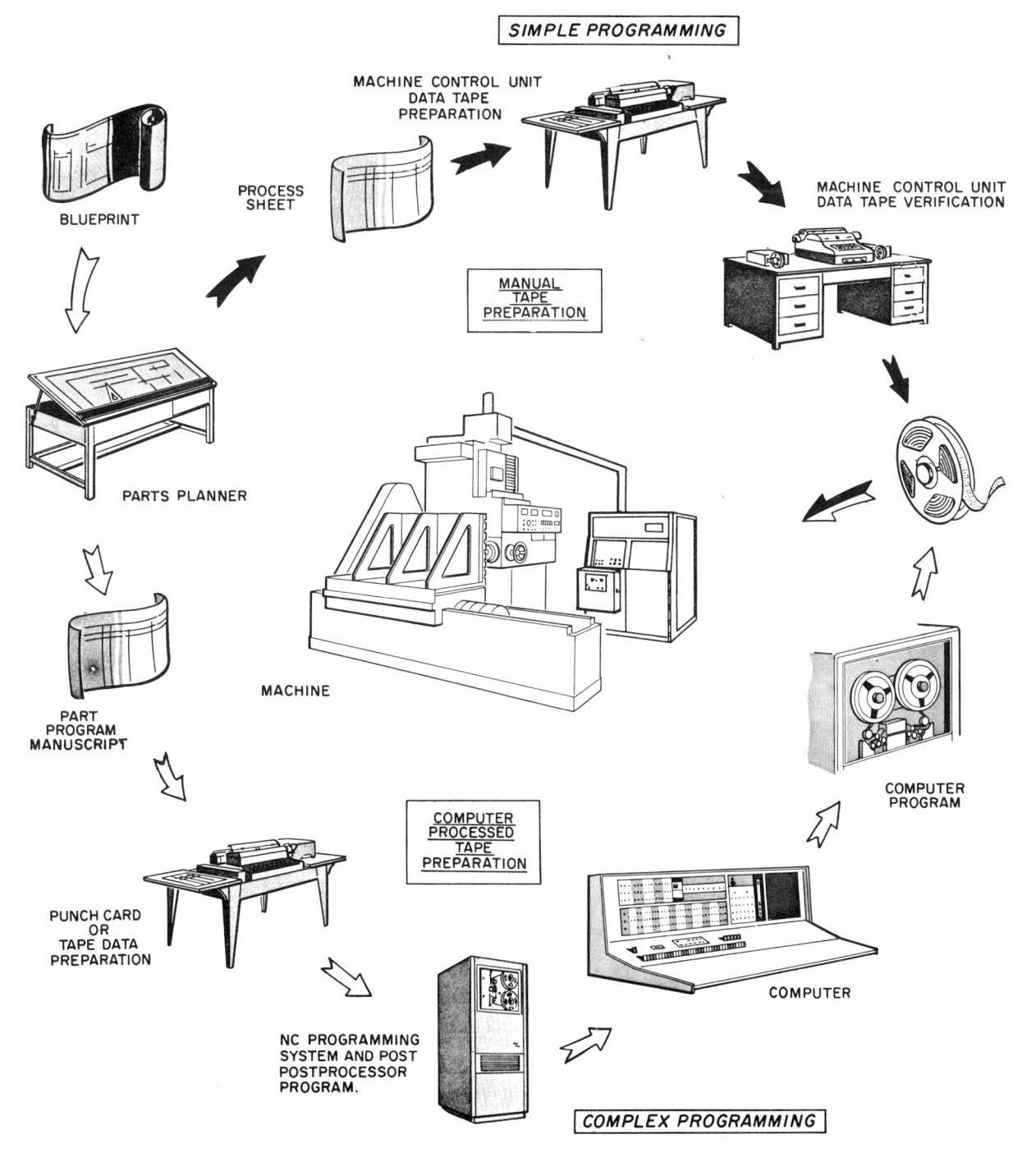

FIG. 19.5. Simple and complex programming. (*Courtesy Bendix Corporation*)

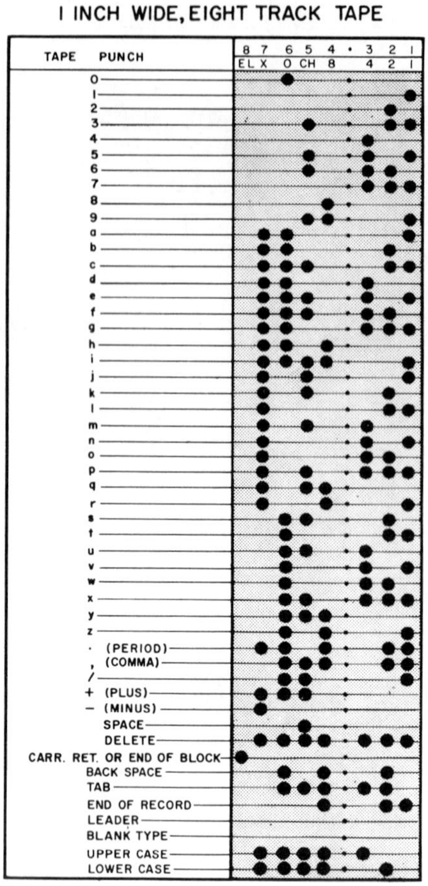

FIG. 19.6. EIA standard coding.

nels (Fig. 19.6). Tape feed holes, located between the third and fourth channels, ensure the proper positioning of the tape in the tape punch as well as in the tape reader. The upper portion of the tape shown in Fig. 19.7 shows a block containing X and Y commands.

19.5
Computer-assisted Programming. Computer programs, requiring only minimal input using a problem-oriented language, offer the most reasonable approach to contour machining (Fig. 19.11). The work of the part programmer in this case is considerably simplified since the computer assumes the tedious task of making the necessary computations as well as the logical decisions. It is not even necessary for him to have intimate knowledge of the specific codes required for a particular control unit. With accurate postprocessing, all control units can be programmed by using the same problem-oriented language (APT–ADAPT–REMAPT) for the part program input to a computer. However, since both APT and ADAPT are basically computer programs, the part programmer and computer programmer will find it necessary to work closely together. This is true because the part programmer, using the standard Cartesian system, defines his part geometrically as being made up of planes, circles, conicals, and so forth.

19.6
Time-shared Computer Services. Even in very small industrial plants a parts programmer can now take advantage of a million-dollar computer to prepare control tapes for N/C machine tools in a few minutes. This has been made possible through a time-sharing concept now in operation all over the country. A teletypewriter unit that can be installed on the programmer's desk gives him access to his own personal large computer. The computer is linked to the teletypewriter by public telephone lines. In some cities, it is possible for users to dial local telephone numbers to gain access to remote computers. This can be done without incurring long-distance charges. The programmer, at the keyboard of his teletypewriter, can use library programs stored in the computer to describe and analyze part geometry, calculate X and Y coordinates, generate data for machine-tool controllers, and receive as computer output punched EIA coded tape at his terminal. It is possible

CHAP. 19 / NUMERICALLY CONTROLLED MACHINE TOOLS   473

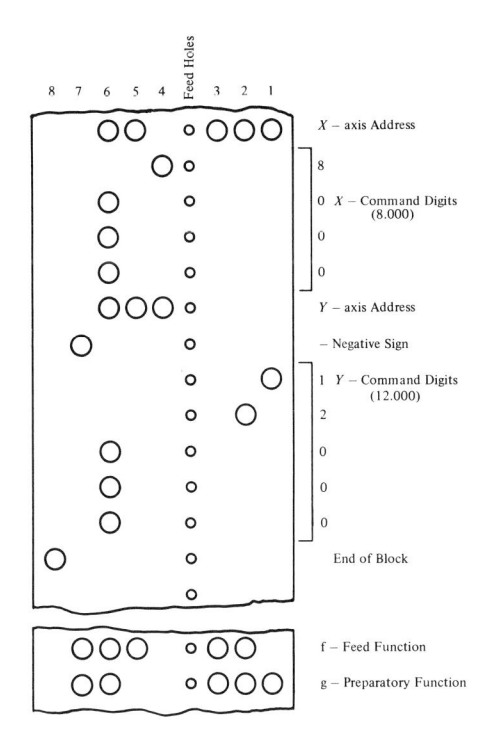

FIG. 19.7. Two portions of a tape illustrating format. Upper portion shows block containing X and Y commands.

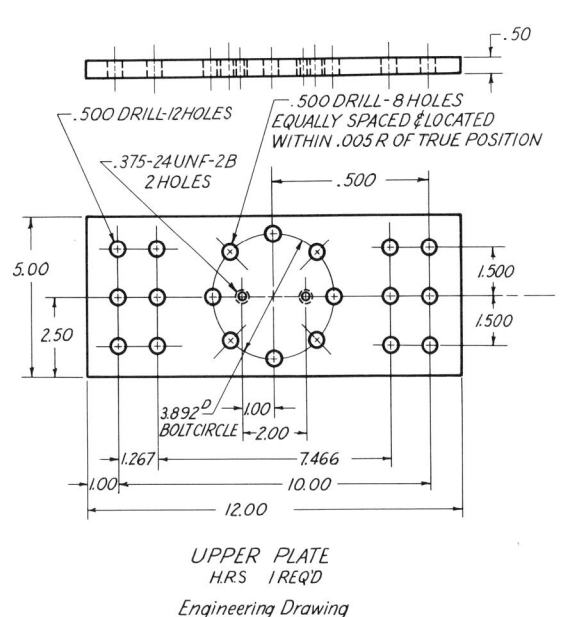

FIG. 19.8. Positional dimensioning using x and y coordinates. This plate was drilled and tapped on the N/C machine shown in Fig. 19.1.

at the present time to prepare N/C tape for two- and three-axis machine tools. The programs available can also be used to prepare control tapes for contouring operations.

The part programs needed to produce the workpieces shown in Figs. 19.8 and 19.10 were prepared using the time-sharing services offered by General Electric.* This system utilizes the REMAPT (program) language. In the case of the program for the upper plate (see Fig. 19.9) explanations have been given for many of the statements. Each statement of the sequence contains a unit of information that is complete in itself as an instruction related to a particular machine operation.

The cycle file of the program for the upper plate (Fig. 19.9) shows that the programmer selected point O, the center of the bolt circle, as his starting point ($x = 0$; $y = 0$). See sequence 10. All other center points for the holes were located from O.

Contouring control, used for milling, turning, and similar operations, is much more complex than point-to-point control. This is so because the workpiece must be completely described and the path of the cutting tool rigidly controlled along a tight course.

---

*These parts were selected and the programs were prepared by Thomas J. Heeg, Sales Engineer, Major Tool & Machine, Inc., Indianapolis, Indiana.

PART IV / COMPUTER GRAPHICS AND NUMERICAL CONTROL

```
Program Input
  10 PARTNØ UPPER PLATE
  20 SEQNØ 1,1  start with sequence 001 and increase by increments of 1
  30 ØRIGIN -20.000,-20.000,0  Zero position of machine with respect to center of part (point 0)
  40 PPRINT CENTER DRILL ALL HØLES
  50 HBLØCK DRILL DEPTH 51  Cam number for depth control
  60 CØPY 1  Copy 1 of cycle file
  70 CØPY 2
  80 CANCEL TLCHG BLØCK  Fixed-cycle cancel; TLCHG = Tool change (MO6 code)
  90 PPRINT DRILL 1/2 DIA HØLES
 100 HBLØCK DRILL DEPTH 52  Drill-preparatory function g81 (drilling sequence)
 110 CØPY 1
 120 CANCEL TLCHG BLØCK
 130 PPRINT TAP DRILL 3/8-24 HØLES
 140 HBLØCK DRILL DEPTH 53  Cam number
 150 CØPY 2  Copy 2 of cycle file
 160 CANCEL TLCHG BLØCK                                    Cam 54 for tap drilling
 170 PPRINT CHAMFER HØLES CAM 54 FØR 3/8-24 &55 FØR 1/2    holes for 3/8-24 thread
 180 HBLØCK DRILL DEPTH 54
 190 CØPY 2                         HBLOCK code statement makes it possible to search back
 200 HBLØCK DRILL DEPTH 55  and pick up the sequence at a particular location.
 210 CØPY 1
 220 CANCEL TLCHG BLØCK
 230 PPRINT TAP 3/8-24 HØLES  A PPRINT statement is followed by operator information
 240 HBLØCK TAP DEPTH 56
 250 CØPY 2
 260 CANCEL GØTØ 20,10
 270 ENDIT  Output MO2, end of tape and rewind statement
 280 20*FINI  For computer, indicates end of program

KEY
READY
SAVE
READY
NEW CØPY1&2
READY
TAPE
READY
  10 GØCIRC 0,0,1.946,0,315,8   Geometry of circle at 0 and
  20 GØTØ 5,-1.5  Go incrementally from present position to 5, -1.5
                                 angle at first and last hole
  30 GØDLTA 0,1.5
  40 GØDLTA 0,1.5
  50 GØDLTA -1.267,0
  60 GØDLTA 0,-1.5                                         Cycle
  70 GØDLTA 0,-1.5                                         File
  80 GØDLTA 10,0  Copy 1 - cycle file                      Copy 1
  90 GØDLTA 0,1.5
 100 GØDLTA 0,1.5                                          Copy 2
 110 GØDLTA -1.267,0
 120 GØDLTA 0,-1.5
 130 GØDLTA 0,-1.5 END
 140 GØTØ -1.0
 150 GØDLTA 2,0 END  Copy 2 - cycle file
KEY
READY
SAVE
READY
ØLD
ENTER FILE NAME-NCPPX$***  A General Electric Computer Software program
READY                       for numerical control
RUN

NCPPX$        17:19      01/06/70

VERSIØN ØF 10/20/69                        MTDF-Identifies the machine
PART,MTDF,CYCLES,PTS?PLATE,MACH1,CØPY,0    that is to be used.

0=LIST,1=TAPE,2=ERRØR SEARCH,3=FILE,4=FILE&TAPE,5=FILE TØ TAPE?0
```

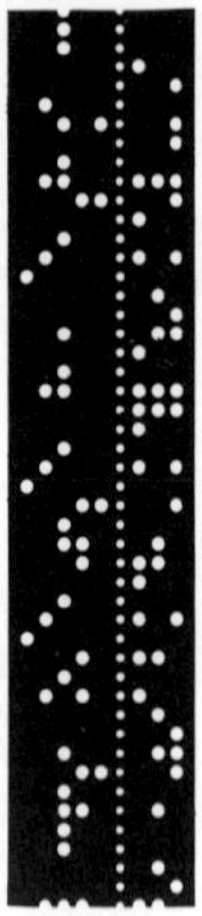

FIG. 19.9. Computer print-out of input data used to prepare the tape needed to drill and tap the upper plate shown in Fig. 19.8. (*Courtesy Major Tool and Machine, Inc.*)*

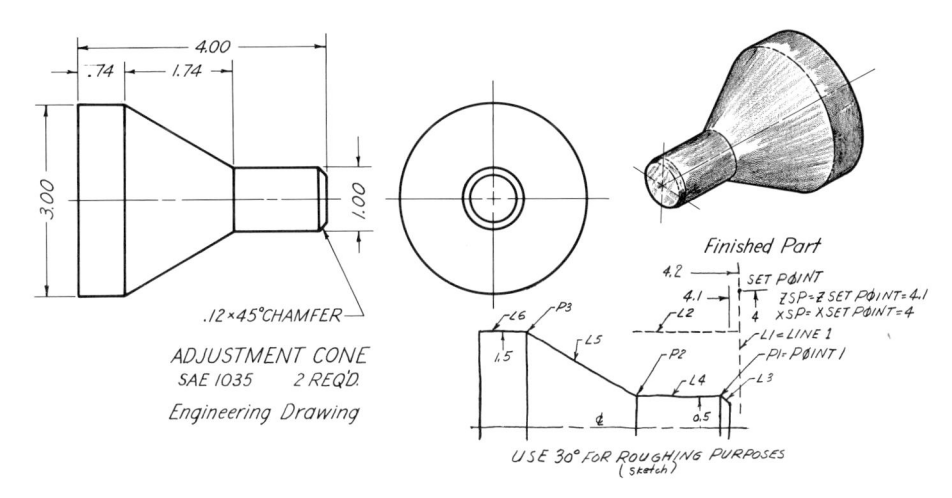

FIG. 19.10. Engineering drawing and programming sketch of adjustment cone.

The adjustment cone shown in Fig. 19.10 was produced from a solid 3.00-in. bar on the turning machine shown in Fig. 19.2. The program statements for preparing the control tape are given in Fig. 19.11.

The step-by-step explanation of the programming process is as follows:

1. Label and dimension all lines on a pencil sketch (Fig. 19.10).

2. Programmer prepares program statements for adjustment cone (lines 10–760).

3. Lines 410–435 (see Fig. 9.11) are a roughing program that has been prepared and is inserted in programs as needed. It is retained on punched tape.

4. Lines 10–760 are put on punched tape.

5. The two tapes are fed into the computer via teletype and saved. Next, the program is listed out as the computer received it. This print-out must be checked for programming, typing, and transmission errors. This print-out has not been shown because of its length (66 lines).

6. Then the program (as corrected) is run into the computer. Received from this run are the following:
a. Cutter location listing—CLL (not shown—144 lines)
b. Postprocessor listing—PPL (not shown—38 lines of calculations)
c. Punch tape listing PCT (not shown—39 lines)

7. Finally, tape is punched (Punch/0)

```
:MAJOR/TOOL:

GE MARK II  T/S FROM BROOK PARK  N#1
TERMINAL 036 ON AT 10:17  01/09/70
USER NUMBER--NAA03000,1458
SYSTEM--REM
NEW OR OLD--NEW CONE
READY
TAPE
READY

10PARTNO ADJUSTMENT CONE
20SEQNO/001
30MACHIN/GLATHE,.06,OPTAB,38,14
40CLPRNT
50ZSP=4.2
60XSP=4.0
70SETPT=POINT/4.2,4.0
80ORIGIN/ZSP,XSP,0
90L1=LINE/XCOORD,4.2
100L2=LINE/XCOORD,4.1
110P1=POINT/(4.1-.12),.5
120L3=LINE/P1,ATANGL,-45
130L4=LINE/YCOORD,.5
140P2=POINT/2.58,.5
150P3=POINT/.84,1.5
160L5=LINE/2.58,.5,.84,1.5
170L6=LINE/YCOORD,1.5
600FROM/SETPT
610CUTTER/.0625
620TURSET/4,1,TLSET,.03125,.03125
630SPINDL/825,RPM,CLW
640FEDRAT/.015,IPR
650CALL/ANGRGH,ANG=30,RAD=.03125,DEPCUT=.250,YTOP=1.5,$
660  YBOT=0.5,ZLEFT=.84,ZRIGHT=4.2
670TURRET/5,1,TLSET,.03125,.03125
680RAPID
690INDIRV/0,-1,0
700GO/L3
710TLRGT,GORGT/L3,PAST,L4
720GOLFT/L4,TO,L5
730GORGT/L5,PAST,L6
740GOTO/(ZSP+.03125),(XSP+.03125),0
750END
760FINI
410ANGRGH=MACRO/ANG,RAD,DEPCUT,YTOP,YBOT,ZLEFT,ZRIGHT
411LOWER=DEPCUT
412LAST=0
413YCUR=YTOP
414 1) INDIRV/0,-1,0
415GO/TO,(LINE/PARLEL,(LINE/PARLEL,(LINE/YCOORD,YTOP),$
416  YLARGE,DEPCUT),YSMALL,LOWER)
417TLRGT,GORGT/(LINE/PARLEL,(LINE/PARLEL,(LINE/YCOORD,YTOP),$
418  YLARGE,DEPCUT),YSMALL,LOWER),TO,(LINE/(POINT/ZLEFT,YTOP),$
419  ATANGL,ANG)
420RAPID
421DNTCUT
422GORGT/(LINE/(POINT/ZLEFT,YTOP),ATANGL,ANG),ON,$
423  (LINE/PARLEL,(LINE/YCOORD,YTOP),YLARGE,DEPCUT)
424GORGT/(LINE/PARLEL,(LINE/YCOORD,YTOP),YLARGE,$
425  DEPCUT),ON,(LINE/XCOORD,ZRIGHT)
426CUT
427LOWER=LOWER+DEPCUT
428YCUR=YCUR-DEPCUT
429 IF(LAST)4,4,3
430 4)IF(YCUR-.030-RAD-YBOT)2,2,1
431 2)LOWER=DEPCUT+YTOP-YBOT-.030-RAD
432LAST=1
433JUMPTO/1
434 3)LOOPND
435TERMAC
KEY
READY
SAVE
```

FIG. 19.11 Print-out of statements used to prepare the control tape for production of the adjustment cone. Contour control has been utilized here. (*Courtesy Major Tool and Machine, Inc.*)

DESIGN AND COMMUNICATION DRAWING IN SPECIALIZED FIELDS

V

The Westinghouse Electric Corporation uses a CalComp plotter on-line with an IBM 360 computer to aid in the design of special purpose cams. The layout drawing shown below was prepared using a computer program developed at the Lamp Division of this company. It is reported that the typical cam design now requires approximately five minutes card punching time, two minutes computer time, and five minutes or less plotting time for a total of twelve minutes. Manual methods for the same task usually required twenty-five to thirty hours. (*Courtesy Westinghouse Electric Corporation*)

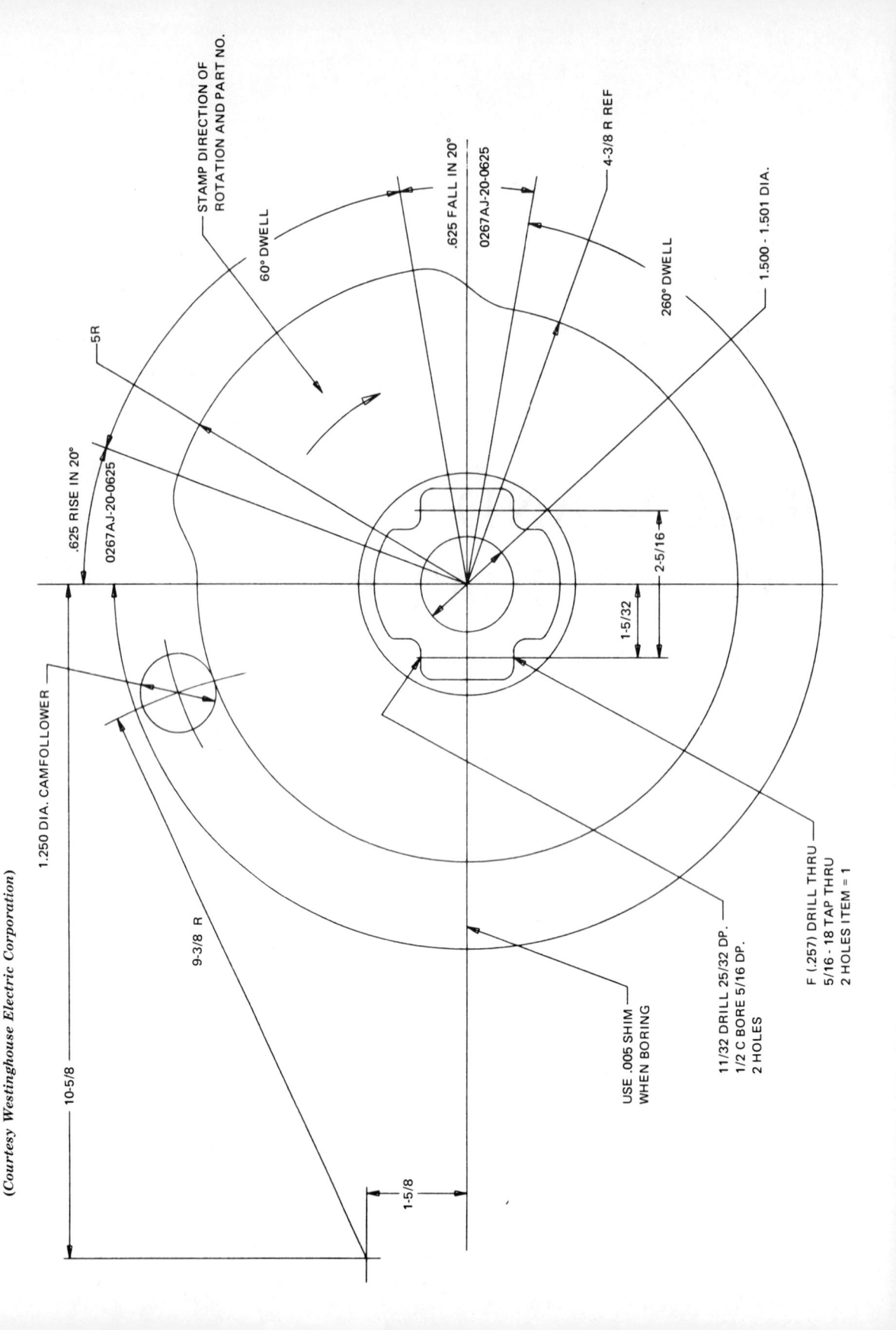

Machine Elements

20.1

Gears. The draftsman frequently is called on to make representations of gears and gear teeth. It is therefore important for him to know the general proportions and nomenclature pertaining to gearing. In Fig. 20.1 the nomenclature for bevel gears is shown. It will be noted that, in general, the definitions pertaining to gear-tooth parts can be represented in a right section of the gear.

The theory of gears is a part of the study of mechanisms. In working drawings of gears and toothed wheels it is necessary to draw at least one tooth of each gear. Some of the terms used in defining gear teeth are shown in Fig. 20.2

Two systems of generating tooth curves are in general use, the *involute system* and the *cycloidal system*. The curve most commonly used for gear-tooth profiles is the involute of a circle.

An involute is the curve generated by a point on a straightedge as the straightedge is rolled on a cylinder. It also may be defined as the curve generated by a point on a taut string as the string is unwrapped from a cylinder. The circle from which the involute is developed is called the *base circle*.

A method of constructing an involute curve is shown in Fig. 20.3. Starting with point 0, on the base circle, divide the base circle into a convenient number of equal arcs of length 0–1, 1–2, 2–3, and so forth. (Where the lengths of the divisions on the base circle are not too great, the chord can be taken as the length of the arc.) Draw a tangent to the base circle at point 0, and divide this line to the left of 0 into equal parts of the same lengths as the arcs. Next, draw tangents to the circle from points 1, 2, 3, and so on. With the

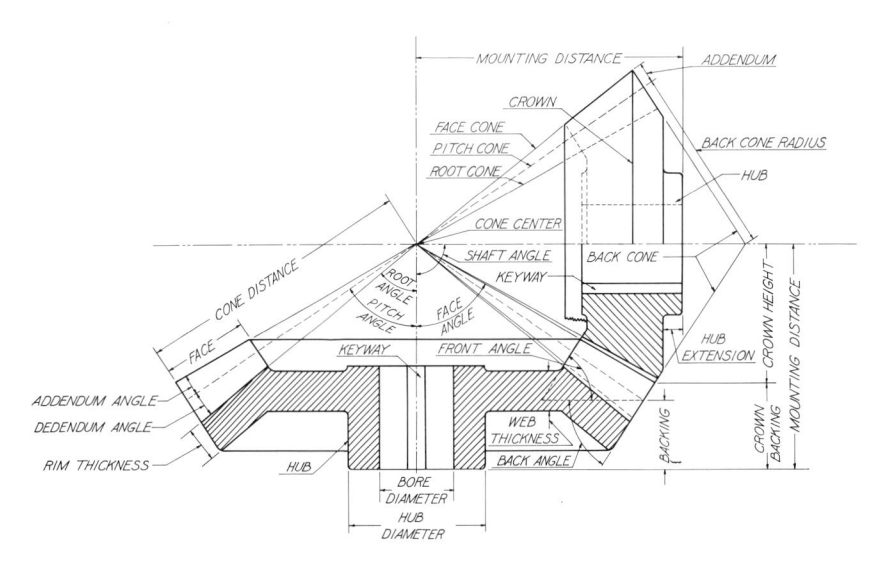

FIG. 20.1. Bevel-gear nomenclature.

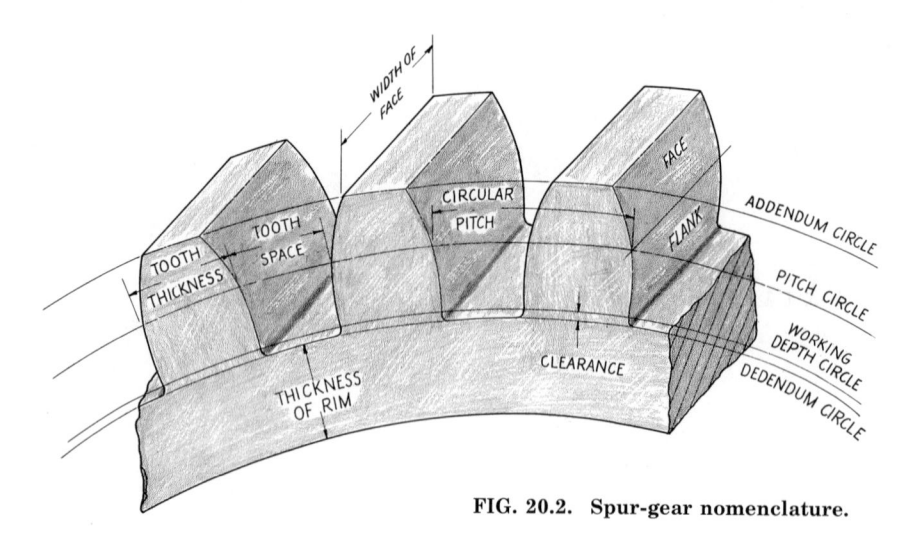

center of the base circle "O" as a pivot, draw concentric arcs from 1', 2', 3', and so forth, until they intersect the tangent lines drawn from 1, 2, 3, and so forth. The intersection of the arcs and the tangents are points on the required involute curve, such as 1'', 2'', 3'', and so forth. The illustration in Fig. 20.3 shows the portion XY of the tooth outline as part of the involute curve.

The cycloidal system, as the name implies, has tooth curves of cycloidal form. A *cycloid* is the curve generated by a point on the circumference of a circle as the circle rolls on a straight line. If the circle rolls on the outside of another circle, the curve generated is called an *epicycloid;* if it rolls on the inside of another circle, the curve generated is called a *hypocycloid*. In Fig. 20.4, let R be the radius of the fixed

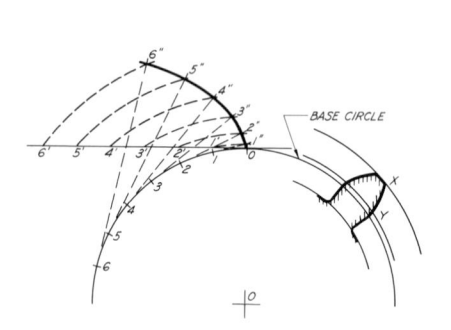

FIG. 20.2. **Spur-gear nomenclature.**

FIG. 20.3. **Involute tooth.**

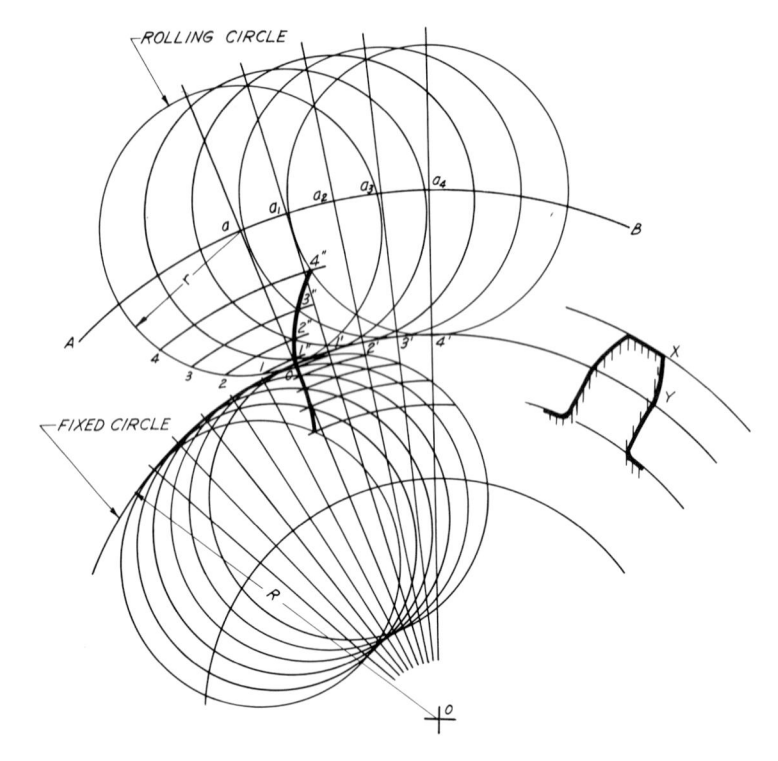

FIG. 20.4. **Tooth curves—cycloidal form.**

circle and r be the radius of the rolling circle. Draw through a a circle arc, AB, concentric with the fixed circle. Lay off on the rolling circle a convenient number of divisions, such as 0-1, 1-2, 2-3, and so forth; then divide the fixed-circle circumference into divisions of the same length, such as 0-1', 1'-2', 2'-3', and so on. Through these points on the fixed circle, draw radii and extend them to intersect the arc AB, thus producing points a_1, a_2, a_3, and so on. These points will be the centers of the successive positions of the rolling circle. Draw the positions of the rolling circle, using the centers a_1, a_2, a_3, and so forth. Next draw, on the rolling circle with the center "O" of the fixed circle as the pivot point, concentric arcs through points 1, 2, 3, and so forth. The intersection of these arcs with the rolling circles about a_1, a_2, a_3, and so forth, determine points, such as $1''$, $2''$, $3''$, and so forth, on the epicyclic curve. The illustration in Fig. 20.4 shows XY of the tooth outline as part of the epicyclic curve.

The hypocyclic curve construction is the same as that for the epicyclic curve. In the construction of the hypocyclic curve, if the rolling circle has a diameter equal to one-half of the diameter of the fixed circle, the hypocyclic curve thus generated will be a radial line of the fixed circle.

Gear Terms

1. The addendum circle is drawn with its center at the center of the gear and bounds the ends of the teeth. See Fig. 20.2.

2. The dedendum circle, or root circle, is drawn with its center at the center of the gear and bounds the bottoms of the teeth. See Fig. 20.2.

3. The pitch circle is a right section of the equivalent cylinder the toothed gear may be considered to replace.

4. Pitch diameter is the diameter of the pitch circle.

5. The addendum is the radial distance from the pitch circle to the outer end of the tooth.

6. The dedendum is the radial distance from the pitch circle to the bottom of the tooth.

7. The clearance is the difference between the dedendum of one gear and the addendum of the mating gear.

8. The face of a tooth is that portion of the tooth surface lying outside the pitch circle.

9. The flank of a tooth is that portion of the tooth surface lying inside the pitch circle.

10. The thickness of a tooth is measured on the arc of the pitch circle. It is the length of an arc and not the length of a straight line.

11. The tooth space is the space between the teeth measured on the pitch circle.

12. Backlash is the difference between the tooth thickness of one gear and the tooth space on the mating gear, measured on the pitch circles.

13. The circular pitch of a gear is the distance between a point on one tooth and the corresponding point on the adjacent tooth, measured along the arc of the pitch circle. The circular pitches of two gears in mesh are equal.

14. The diametral pitch is the number of teeth per inch of pitch diameter. It is obtained by dividing the number of teeth by the pitch diameter.

15. The face of a gear is the width of its rim measured parallel to the axis. It should not be confused with the face of a tooth, for the two are entirely different.

16. The pitch point is on the line joining the centers of the two gears where the pitch circles touch.

17. The common tangent is the line tangent to the pitch circles at the pitch point.

18. The pressure angle is the angle between the line of action and the common tangent.

19. The line of action is a line drawn through the pitch point at an angle (equal to the pressure angle) to the common tangent.

20. The base circle is used in involute gearing to generate the involutes that form the tooth outlines. It is drawn from the center of each pair of mating gears tangent to the line of action.

21. When two gears mesh with each other, the larger is called the *gear* and the smaller the *pinion*.

It should be noted that *circular pitch* is a linear dimension expressed in inches, whereas *diametral pitch* is a ratio. There must be a whole number of teeth on the circumference of a gear. Thus it is necessary that the circumference of the pitch circle, divided by the circular pitch, be a whole number.

For circular pitch, let P' = circular pitch in inches, D = pitch diameter, and T = number of teeth. Then

$$TP' = \pi D, \quad T = \frac{\pi D}{P'}, \quad P' = \frac{\pi D}{T},$$

and

$$D = \frac{TP'}{\pi}$$

For diametral pitch, let P = diametral pitch, D = pitch diameter, and T = number of teeth. Then

$$T = PD, \quad D = \frac{T}{P}, \quad \text{and} \quad P = \frac{T}{D}$$

The Brown and Sharpe $14\frac{1}{2}$-degree involute system has been adopted as one of the American standards and is commonly known as the $14\frac{1}{2}$-degree composite system. The tooth proportions of this system are given in terms of the diametral pitch P and circular pitch P'.

Pressure angle = $14\frac{1}{2}°$.

Addendum (inches) = 1/diametral pitch = $1/P$.

Dedendum (inches) = addendum plus clearance = $(1/P) + 0.05P'$.

Clearance = $0.05 \times$ circular pitch = $0.05P'$.

Whole depth of tooth = $2 \times$ addendum + clearance = $2 \times (1/P) + 0.05P'$.

Working depth of tooth = $2 \times$ addendum = $2 \times (1/P)$.

Thickness of tooth = circular pitch/2 = $P'/2$.

Width of tooth space = circular pitch/2 = $P'/2$.

Minimum radius of fillet = clearance = $0.05P'$.

In the above calculations the backlash is zero. Actually, however, it is common practice to provide backlash, and this is accomplished by using standard cutters and cutting the teeth slightly deeper than for standard teeth.

20.2

To Lay Out a Pair of Standard Involute Spur Gears. The following facts are known regarding the laying out of a pair of standard spur gears: (1) number of teeth on each gear—large gear 24, small gear 16; (2) diametral pitch = 2; (3) pressure angle = $14\frac{1}{2}°$.

To draw a pair of spur gears, determine the pitch diameters thusly:

$$D = \frac{T}{P} = \frac{24}{2} = 12 \text{ in.} \quad \text{(for large gear)}$$

$$D = \frac{T}{P} = \frac{16}{2} = 8 \text{ in.} \quad \text{(for small gear)}$$

In Fig. 20.5, with radii O_1P and O_2P equal to 6 and 4 in., respectively, draw the pitch circles and, through P, draw the common tangent. Draw the line of action

XY at an angle of $14\frac{1}{2}°$ to the common tangent. Drop perpendiculars from the centers O_1 and O_2, cutting the line of action at A and B, respectively. O_1A and O_2B are the radii of the base circles that can now be drawn.

From Sec. 20.1, determine the addendum and dedendum of the teeth, and draw in the respective addendum and dedendum circles.

Divide the pitch circle of the smaller gear into 16 equal parts and the pitch circle of the larger gear into 24 equal parts, which will give the circular pitch. Assuming that no allowance is made for backlash, bisect the circular pitch on each of the gears, which will give 32 equal divisions on the small gear and 48 equal divisions on the large gear.

At any point on the base circle of each gear, develop an involute (see Fig. 20.3) and draw in the curves between the base and addendum circles through alternate points on the pitch circles. This produces one side of all the teeth in each gear. The curve for the other side of the tooth is the reverse of the side just drawn. The part of the tooth between the base and dedendum circles is part of a radial line drawn from the base circles to the centers of the gears. The tooth is finished by putting in a small fillet between the working depth and dedendum circles.

20.3

Dimensioning Gears. On a detail drawing, a gear may be represented by a one-view section, except for the larger sizes, where it is necessary to show spokes, and for the small sizes, when a full description of some feature would not be given. A second view was drawn in Fig. 20.6 to reveal the shape of the keyway. In dimensioning, it is recommended that the dimensions be given on the view or views, as shown in Figs. 20.6 and 20.7 and that the cutting data be incorporated in an accompanying table.

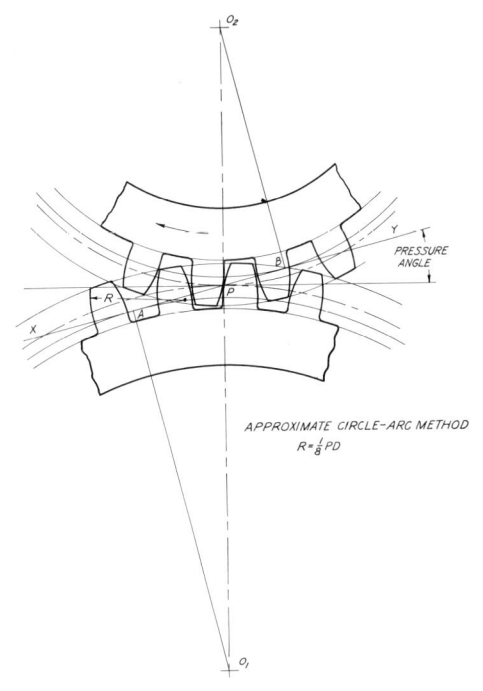

FIG. 20.5. To draw a pair of spur gears.

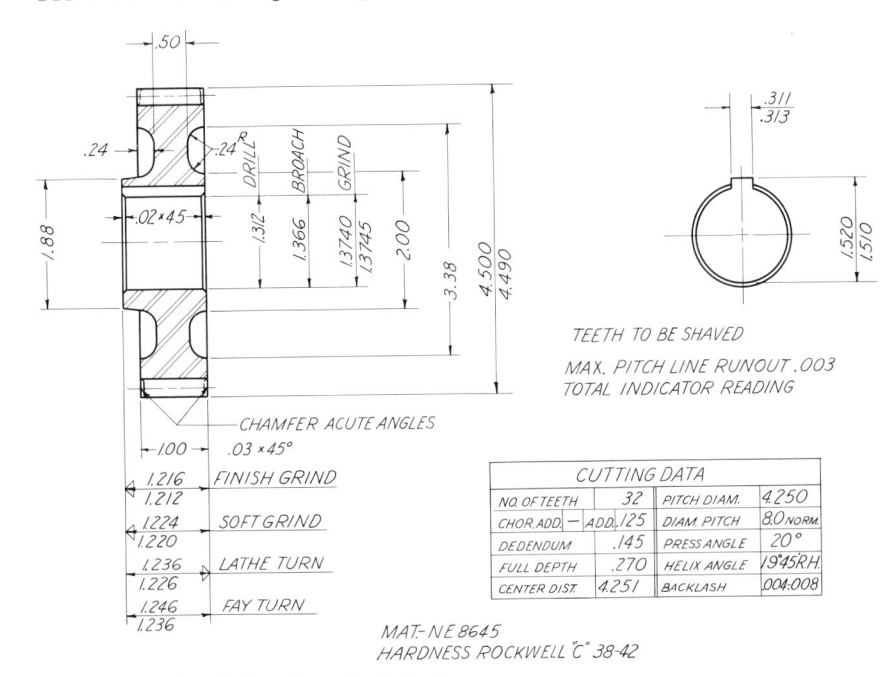

FIG. 20.6. Detail drawing of a helical gear (*Courtesy Fairfield Mfg. Co.*).

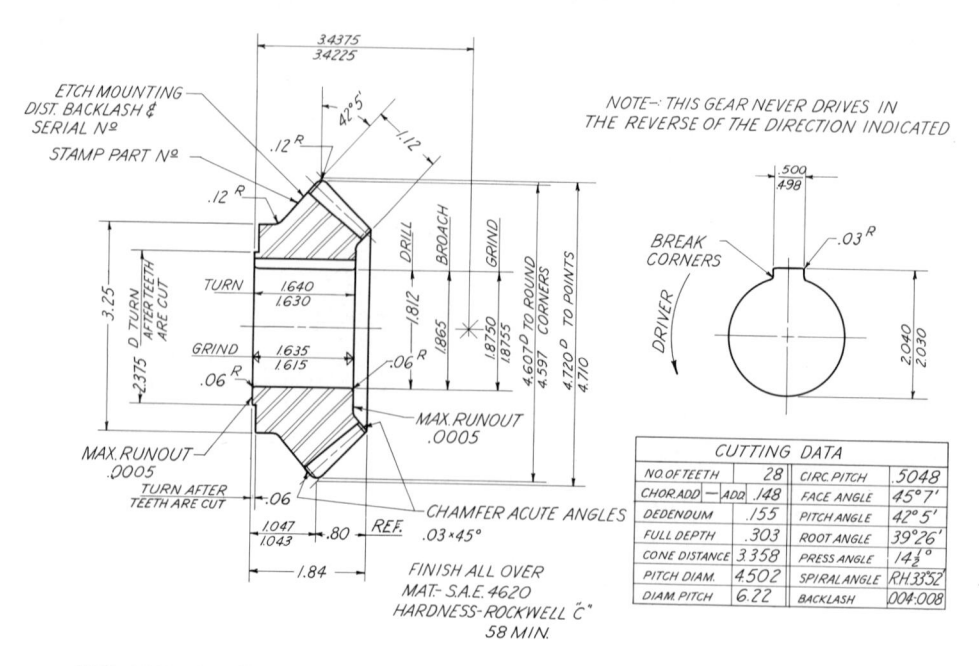

FIG. 20.7. Detail drawing of a spiral bevel gear (*Courtesy Fairfield Mfg. Co.*).

20.4
Working Drawings of Gears. Figure 20.6 shows a working drawing of a helical gear. In practice it is customary to show one view in section and just enough of the circular view to supply needed information for the shop. Individual teeth are never shown on the circular view unless the drawing is to be used for display purposes. In some drafting rooms where practice requires a full circular view, the addendum and root circles are drawn, using a phantom line and the pitch circle is given as a center line.

It should be noted that the dimensions for the gear blank are given on the sectioned view, while the necessary data for cutting the teeth are given in a table. This is in accordance with the practice recommended in Sec. 20.3.

A working drawing of a spiral bevel gear is shown in Fig. 20.7. The same practices apply for spur gears. Before starting to prepare a working drawing of a bevel gear one should study Fig. 20.1, which illustrates bevel-gear nomenclature.

Figure 20.8 shows a working drawing of a worm.

20.5
Cams. A cam is a plate, cylinder, or any solid having a curved outline or curved groove that, by its oscillating or rotating motion, gives a predetermined motion to another piece, called the follower, in contact with it. The cam plays a very important part in the operation of many classes of machines. Cam mechanisms are commonly used to operate valves in automobiles and stationary and marine internal combustion engines. They also are used in automatic screw machines, clocks, locks, printing machinery, and in nearly all kinds of machinery that we generally

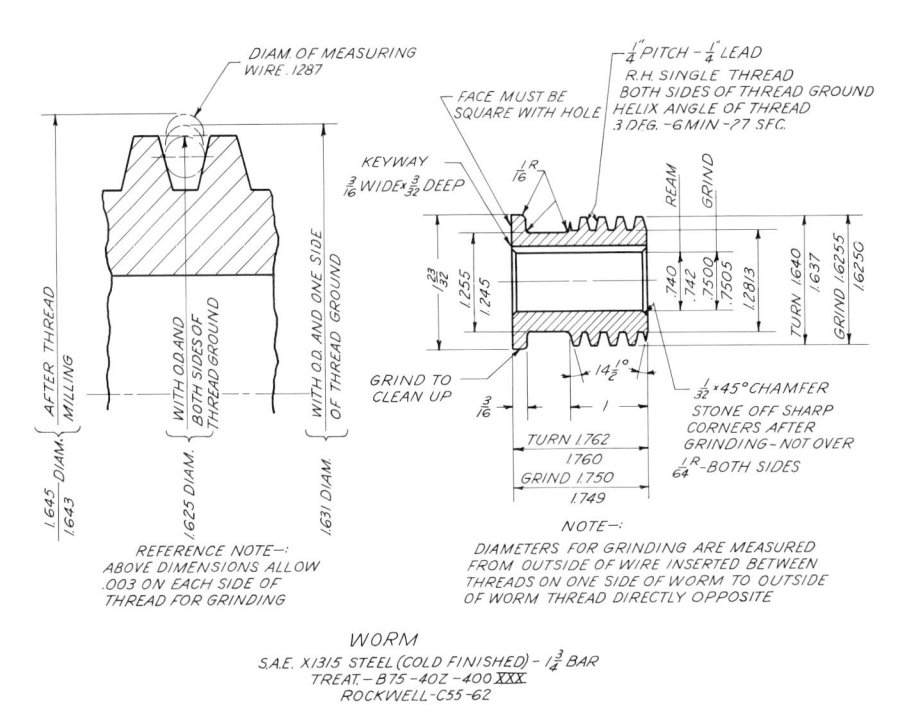

FIG. 20.8. Detail drawing of a worm (*Courtesy Warner & Swasey Co.*).

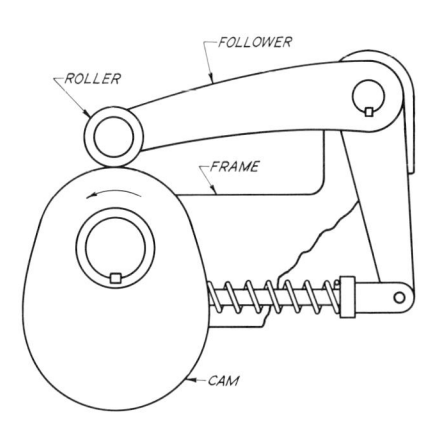

FIG. 20.9. Disc cam and follower.

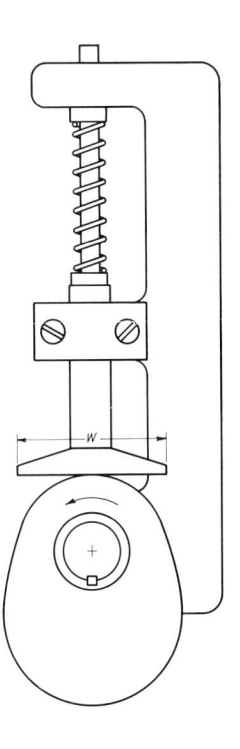

FIG. 20.10. Disc cam and follower.

regard as "automatic machines." The applications of cams are practically unlimited, and their shapes or outlines are found in wide variety.

All cam mechanisms consist of at least three parts: (1) the cam, which has a contact surface either curved or straight; (2) the follower, whose motion is produced by contact with the cam surface; and (3) the frame, which supports the cam and guides the follower.

The most common type of cam is the disc or plate cam. Here the cam takes the form of a revolving disc or plate, the circumference of the disc or plate forming the profile with which the follower makes contact. In Figs. 20.9 and 20.10, two simple examples of a disc cam and follower are shown. In Fig. 20.9, the cam is given a motion of rotation, thus causing the follower to rise and then return again to its initial position. In cams of this type it is necessary to use some external force, such as the spring, to keep the follower in contact with the cam at all times. Contact between the follower and the cam is made through a roller, which serves to reduce friction. It is sometimes necessary to use a flat-faced follower, instead of the roller type, an example of which is shown in Fig. 20.10. The follower face that comes in contact with the cam is usually provided with a hardened surface, to prevent excessive wear.

Another type of cam is one in which the follower is constrained to move in a definite path without the application of external forces. See Fig. 20.11. In this type, two contact surfaces of the follower bear on the cam at the same time, thus controlling the motion of the follower in two directions.

20.6
Design of a Cam. The design of a cam outline is governed by the requirements with respect to the motion of the follower. In the layout of a cam, the initial position, displacement, and character of the motion of the follower are generally known. It is convenient to make first a graphical representation of the follower movement, a procedure that is called *making a displacement diagram.* This is a linear curve in which the length of the diagram represents the time for one revolution of the cam. The height of the diagram represents the total displacement of the follower; the length is made to any convenient length and is divided into equal time intervals, the total representing one rotation of the cam.

In Fig. 20.12 is shown a displacement diagram in which the follower rises 2 in. during 180° of rotation of the cam, then rests for 30° and returns to its initial position for the remainder of the cam revolution. Cam outlines should be designed to avoid sudden changes of motion at the beginning and end of the follower stroke. This can be accomplished by having a uniformly accelerated and decelerated motion at the beginning and end of the constant-velocity curve. The construction for uniformly accelerated motion is shown in Fig. 20.12. On a line, OX, making any convenient angle with OA, mark off any unit of length in this figure equal to Oa. The next point, b, is found by marking off, from O, 4 units of length. Point c is found by marking off 9 units of length. Next, project the intersection (point s) of time-unit 3 and the constant-velocity line over to the line OA, thus locating point t. Connect points c and t with a straight line and draw parallel lines from a and b intersecting the line OA. From these intersections draw lines parallel to ts, intersecting the time-unit lines 1 and 2, respectively. These intersections are points on the displacement curve. With uniformly decelerated motion, the series of points are laid off in the reverse order, such as 9-4-1. It will be noted that the units are laid off according to the square of the time unit. Thus, if there were 4 time units, the acceleration curve would be laid off according to the ratio of 1, 4, 9, 16, and the deceleration, 16, 9, 4, 1.

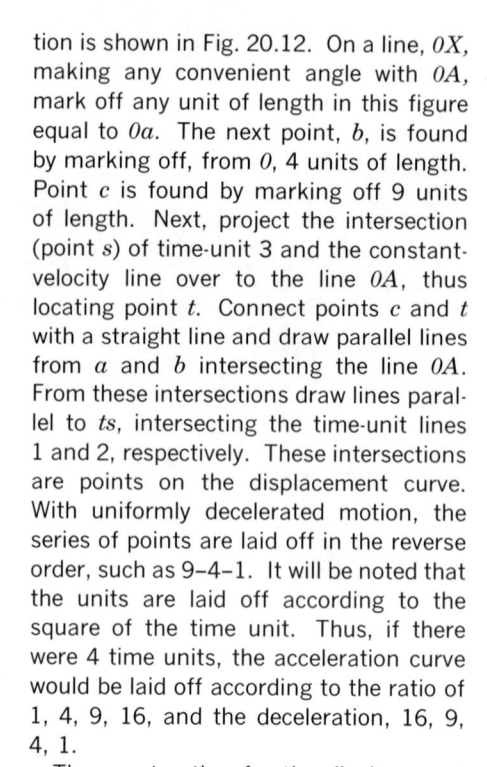

The construction for the displacement diagram for simple harmonic motion is shown in the same figure. A semicircle is drawn as shown, the follower displacement being used as a diameter, and is then divided into a convenient number of parts equal to the number of cam displacement units. Horizontal projection lines are drawn from the semicircle, and the intersections of these lines with the cam displacement lines are points on the displacement curve. Thus, the projection of point 15 on the semicircle to time-unit line 15 locates one point on the displacement curve for simple harmonic motion.

The next step is that of finding the cam profile necessary to produce these movements. The construction is shown in Fig. 20.13. Select a base circle of convenient size, and on it lay off radial lines according to the number of time units of cam displacement. Draw line OB extended to W, and on it lay off the distances y_1, y_2, y_3,

FIG. 20.11. Cam and follower.

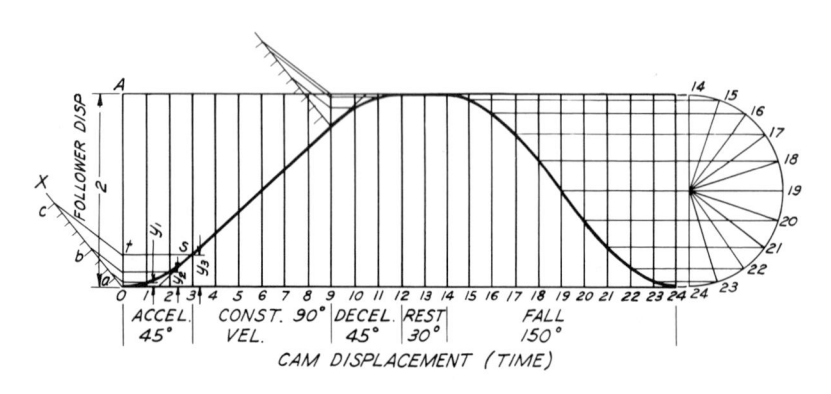

FIG. 20.12. A displacement diagram.

and so forth, obtained from the displacement diagram, from the center of the roller shown in the starting position, thus locating points B_1, B_2, B_3, and so forth. With O as a center, draw arcs B_1-B_1', B_2-B_2', B_3-B_3', and so forth, and at B_1', B_2', B_3', and so forth, draw in the circles representing the diameter of the roller. To complete the cam outline, draw a smooth curve tangent to the positions of the roller.

20.7
Bearings. A draftsman ordinarily is never called on to make a detail drawing of a ball or roller bearing, because bearings of these two types are precision-made units that are purchased from reliable manufacturers. All draftsmen working on machine drawings, however, should be familiar with the various types commonly used and should be able to represent them correctly on an assembly drawing. An engineer will find it necessary to determine shaft-mounting fits and housing-mounting fits from a manufacturer's handbook, in order to place the correct limits on shafts and housings. Figure 20.14 shows two types of ball bearings. A roller bearing is shown in Fig. 20.15.

Ball bearings may be designed for loads either perpendicular or parallel to the shaft. In the former, they are known as radial bearings and in the latter, as thrust bearings. Other types, designated by various names, are made to take both radial and thrust loads, either light or heavy. In most designs, bearings are forced to take both radial and thrust loads. Ball bearings are designated by a letter and code number, the last number of which represents the bearing bore. They may be extra light, light, medium, or heavy and still have the same bore number. That is, bearings of different capacities and different outer diameters can fit shafts having the same nominal size. Tables 27 and 28 in the Appendix give all the necessary

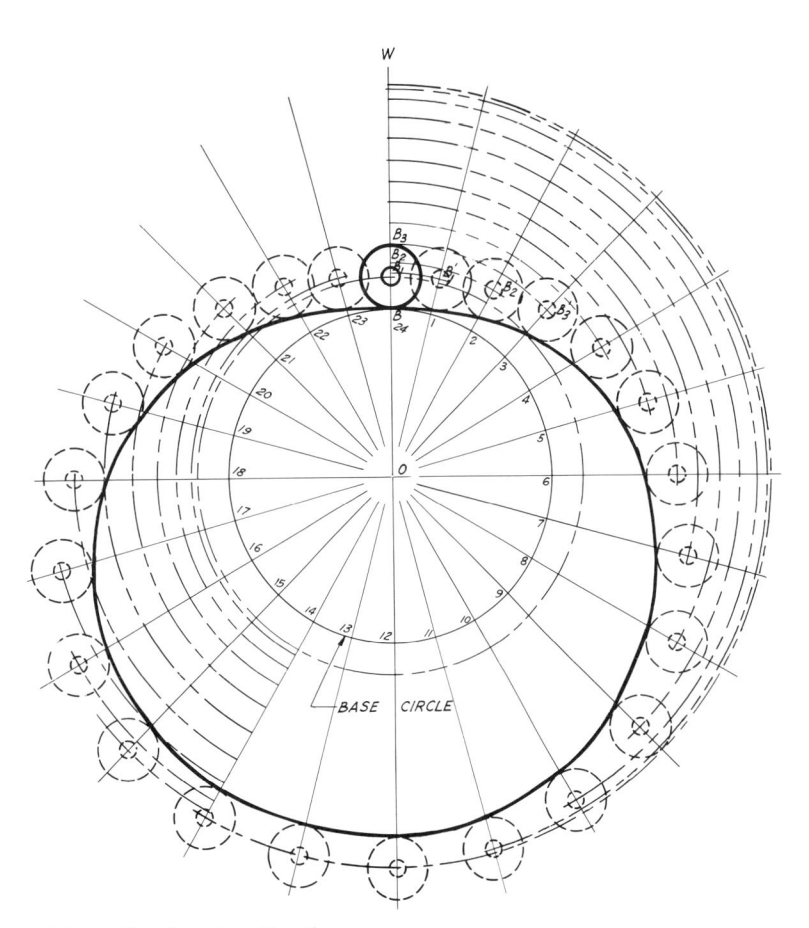

FIG. 20.13. Construction for cam profile.

FIG. 20.14. Ball bearings.

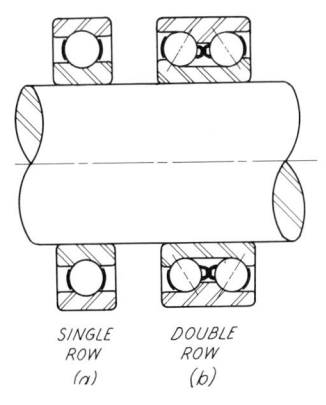

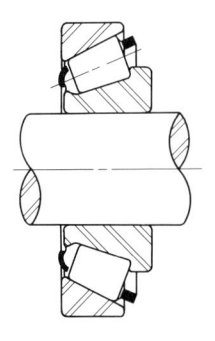

FIG. 20.15. Roller bearing.

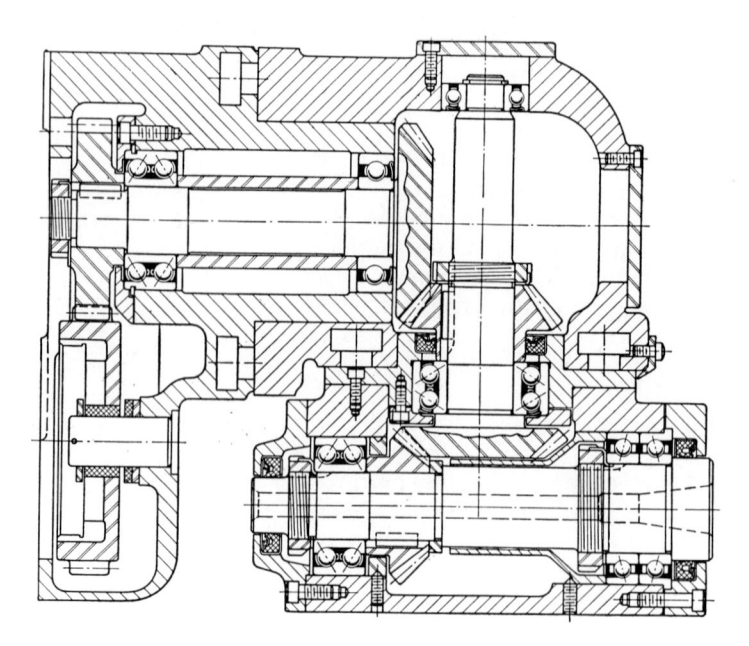

FIG. 20.16. Ball bearings (*Courtesy New Departure Bearing Co.*).

information concerning the bearings used in the problems of this text. Figure 20.16 shows typical mountings in a single mechanism.

Roller bearings are designed for both radial and thrust loads. The bearing consists of tapered rollers that roll between an inner and an outer race. The rollers are enclosed in a retainer (cage) that keeps them properly spaced.

PROBLEMS: Gears and Cams

Gear Problems

1–6. Following the method shown in Sec. 20.2, lay out a pair of standard involute spur gears as assigned from the given table. The pinion is the driver.

PROB. NO.	GEAR CIRCULAR PITCH (INCHES)	GEAR DIAMETRAL PITCH	GEAR PITCH DIA.	GEAR NO. OF TEETH	PINION CIRCULAR PITCH (INCHES)	PINION DIAMETRAL PITCH	PINION PITCH DIA.	PINION NO. OF TEETH	PRESSURE ANGLE
1	1.31			24	1.31			16	14½°
2		2		20		2		14	14½°
3		2.5	10			2.5	8		14½°
4	1.0			30	1.0			20	14½°
5	2.0			18	2.0			12	14½°
6		3	8			3	6		14½°

Cam Problems

Cam Data

Diameter of cam shaft. . . . $1\frac{1}{4}$ in.
Diameter of cam hub . . . . $2\frac{1}{4}$ in.
Diameter of roller . . . . 1 in.
Keyway . . . . $\frac{1}{4} \times \frac{1}{8}$ in.
Diameter of base circle . . . $2\frac{3}{4}$ in.
Follower displacement . . . . 2 in.
Scale: full-size
Cam rotation: as noted

Determine points on the cam profiles at intervals of 15°.

7. Using the above data, design a plate cam to satisfy the following conditions: (a) a rise of 2 in. in 180°, with constant velocity, except for uniform acceleration for the first 30° and uniform deceleration for the last 45°; (b) rest 30°; and (c) return with simple harmonic motion. Use clockwise cam rotation.

8. Same as problem 7, except that the follower is of the flat-face type and is $2\frac{1}{2}$ in. wide.

9. Using the data for Problem 7, design a plate cam to satisfy the following conditions: (a) rise of 2 in. during 180°, the first 45° of which is uniformly accelerated motion, the next 60° being constant velocity, and the last 75° of rise being uniformly decelerated motion; (b) rest 15°; and (c) return to starting position with simple harmonic motion. Use counterclockwise cam rotation.

10. Same as Problem 9, except that the follower is of the flat-face type and is $2\frac{1}{2}$ in. wide.

11. Using the data for Problem 7, design a plate cam to satisfy the following conditions: (a) rise to 2 in. during 150°, by simple harmonic motion; (b) rest 30°; and (c) return to starting position during remainder of the revolution, with uniformly accelerated and decelerated motion, the value of the deceleration being twice that of the acceleration. Use clockwise cam rotation.

12. Using the data for Problem 7, except that the follower is to be of the flat-face type, $2\frac{1}{2}$ in. wide, design a plate cam to satisfy the following conditions: (a) rise of 2 in, with simple harmonic motion, in 120°; (b) rest 30°; (c) return in 150°, with constant velocity, except for uniform acceleration for the first 45° and uniform deceleration for the last 30° of fall; and (d) rest the balance of the revolution. Use counterclockwise cam rotation.

Part of piping arrangement at a Du Pont petroleum chemicals plant.
(*Courtesy E. I. du Pont de Nemours & Company*)

Piping Drawings and Models

A: PIPING DRAWINGS

21.1

Since piping is used in all types of construction for conveying fluids and gases such as oil, water, steam, and chemicals, some knowledge of it is essential not only for the draftsman making drawings but for the engineer who must select and use pipe in the design of machines, power plants, water systems, and so on. There are so many types of fittings and materials used for various purposes that only the most common can be discussed briefly in this chapter. Additional information may be obtained from publications of research associations and from the catalogs of manufacturers.

21.2

Pipe Materials. Cast-iron pipe is suitable for underground gas and water mains, plumbing lines, and low-pressure steam systems.

Steel pipe is used chiefly where high temperatures and high pressures are encountered. The addition of such alloys as nickel, chromium, and the like makes the steel pipe more resistant to corrosion at high temperatures.

Seamless brass pipe is the most satisfactory type for hot-water lines, condenser tubes, and so on, but it is expensive and, therefore, is used only when conditions justify the extra cost.

For lines having turns and bends in inaccessible locations, copper tubing is frequently used. But copper pipe, even though it is flexible and can resist the corrosive action of chemicals, is not always practical. It cannot be used in any system subject to high temperatures and repeated stress.

Lead and lead-lined pipe is widely used for chemical work, particularly where piping is subject to the action of acids.

Galvanized pipe (ordinary iron pipe that has been dipped in molten zinc to prevent rust) is suitable for lines conveying drinking water.

21.3

Special Pipe and Tubing. Special-purpose pipe and tubing, made from a variety of materials, such as stainless steel, brass, bronze, aluminum, and plastics, are now being manufactured. Plastic pipe and plastic-lined pipe are being used extensively in the chemical industry in place of metal pipe because plastic does not corrode and has high resistance to a wide range of chemicals. Plastic pipe is easily bent and resists weathering. In the heavy

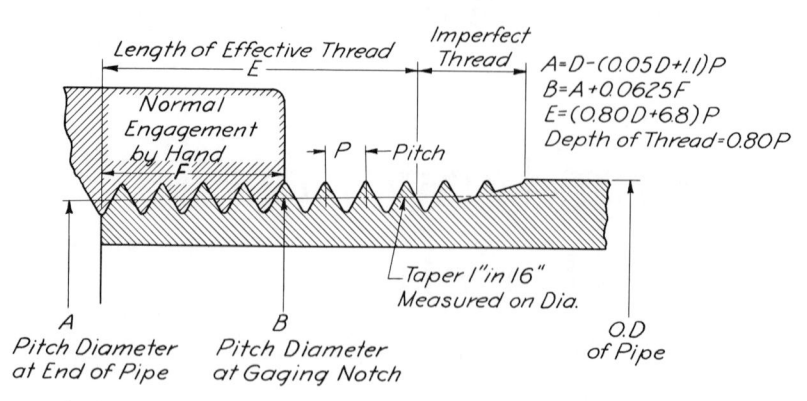

$A = D - (0.05D + 1.1)P$
$B = A + 0.0625F$
$E = (0.80D + 6.8)P$
Depth of Thread = 0.80P

FIG. 21.1. American National taper pipe thread.

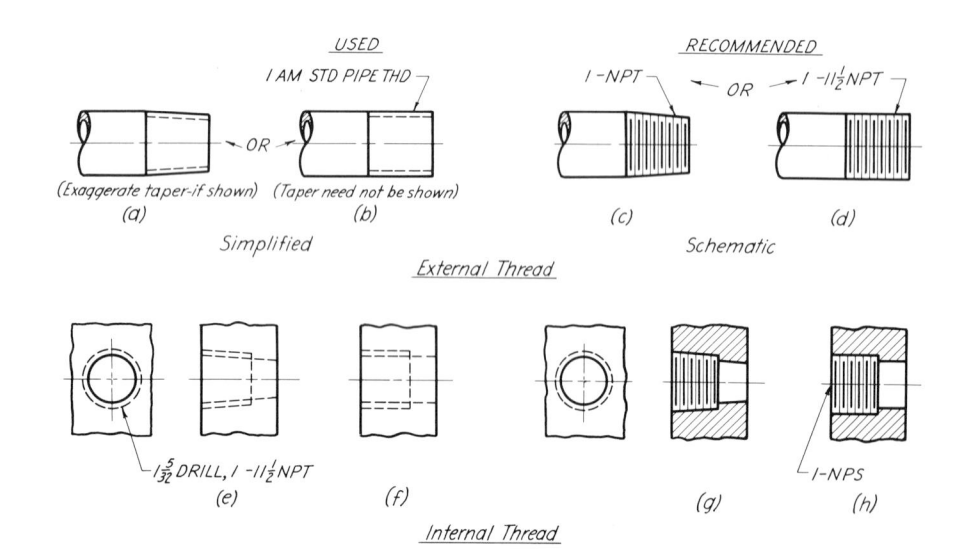

FIG. 21.2. Representation and specification of pipe threads.

weights it may be threaded. The principal disadvantages are its higher cost and temperature–pressure limitations. Where strength is needed, a metal pipe lined with plastic may be used.

21.4

American National Standard Pipe Thread (NPT) for General Use. The American National Standard pipe taper thread, illustrated in Fig. 21.1, is similar to the ordinary American National Standard thread and has the same thread angle; but it is tapered $\frac{1}{16}$ in. per in., to ensure a tight joint at a fitting. The crest is flattened and the root is filled in so that the depth of the thread is 0.80P. The number of threads per inch for any given nominal diameter can be obtained from Table 21 in the Appendix.

The distance a pipe enters a fitting is fixed for any nominal diameter. Numerical values for this distance may be determined from Table 21.

An American National Standard straight pipe thread, having the same number of threads per inch as the taper thread, is in use for pressure-tight joints for couplings, for pressure-tight joints for grease and oil fittings, and for hose couplings and nipples. This thread may also be used for free-fitting mechanical joints. Usually a taper external thread is used with a straight internal thread, for pipe material is sufficiently ductile for an adjustment of the threads.

The NPT threads are for general use. When taper pipe threads are used and the joints are made up wrench-tight with a lubricant or sealer, they will be pressure tight.

21.5

Specification of Threads. In specifying pipe threads, the ANSI recommends that the note be formulated using symbolic letters as illustrated in Fig. 21.2. For example, the specification for a 1-in. standard taper pipe thread should read:

$$1-\text{NPT}$$

The letters NPT, following the nominal diameter, indicate that the thread is

American National Standard (N), pipe (P), taper (T) thread.

Continuing with the same scheme of using letters, the specification for a 1-in. straight pipe thread would read

1-NPS[American National Standard (N)-pipe (P)-Straight (S)]

The form of note given in Fig. 21.2(*b*) reading 1 AM STD PIPE THD, is quite commonly used in practice.

The letter symbols that have been adopted by the ANSI have the following significance:

N—American National Standard
P—Pipe
T—Taper
S—Straight
C—Coupling
H—Hose coupling
L—Lock nut
M—Mechanical joints
R—Railing
F—Fuel and oil
I—Intermediate
SPL—Special

21.6

Threads for Joints and Couplings. Pipe threads are used for several types of joints. The significance of the letters designating the threads for these joints is given in Sec. 21.5. Where the letter S appears in the designation, a straight thread is indicated.

NPTR—Taper pipe thread for rail fittings. These threads are the same as the NPT threads except the external thread is shortened in order to permit use of the larger end of the pipe thread.

NPSC—Internal straight pipe threads in pipe fittings. These threads are straight threads of the same thread form as the NPT thread shown in Fig. 21.1. NPSC threads form a pressure-tight joint when assembled with an external taper (NPT) pipe thread using a lubricant or sealer.

NPSH—Straight pipe thread for loose-fitting mechanical joints for hose couplings. Ordinarily, straight internal and external threads are used for hose-coupling joints. One of several standards for hose threads is based on the American National Standard pipe thread.

NPSL—Straight pipe threads for loose-fitting mechanical joints with lock nuts. These threads are straight threads of the same form as the NPT thread. The external NPSL thread has the largest diameter that can be cut on standard pipe. Usually, straight internal threads are used with these straight external threads.

NPSM—Straight pipe threads for free-fitting mechanical joints for fixtures.

21.7

Dryseal (American National Standard) Pipe Threads (NPTF, NPSF, and NPSI). With these threads, truncation at the crest and root is controlled to ensure metal-to-metal contact coincident with, or prior to, flank contact. This contact at root and crest makes a pressure-tight joint to prevent spiral leakage. Although a lubricant or sealer is not required, the use of a lubricant to minimize galling is not objectionable.

NPTF—Taper pipe thread. This series of threads covers both external and internal threads. These threads are suitable for pipe joints in practically every type of service.

PTF-SAE SHORT—This series conforms to the NPTF series except that (1) the full thread length of the external thread is shortened by one thread at the small end, and (2) the full thread length of the internal thread is shortened by eliminating one thread at the large end.

NPSF—Straight pipe thread (internal only) for fuel and oil. This series of threads is generally used for soft and ductile materials, which will adjust to the taper of external threads in assembly.

NPSI—Intermediate straight pipe thread (internal only). This series of threads is suited for hard or brittle materials where the section is heavy and where there will be little expansion with the external taper threads in assembly.

Dryseal threads are specified as follows:

$\frac{1}{4}$—18 DRYSEAL NPTF
$\frac{1}{8}$—27 DRYSEAL NPSI

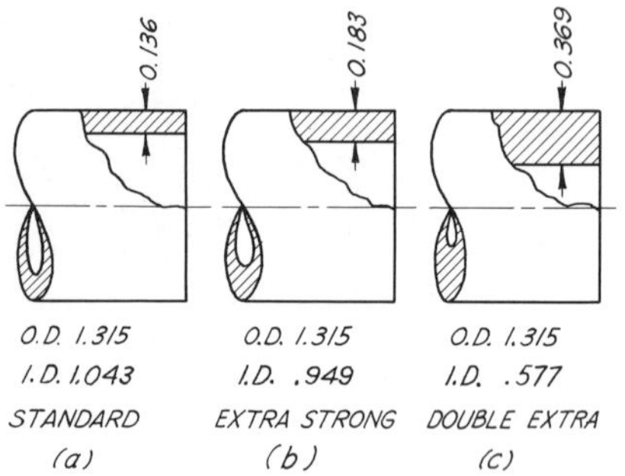

21.8
Drawing Pipe Threads. The taper on a pipe thread is so slight that it will not attract attention on a drawing unless it is exaggerated. If it is shown at all, it is usually magnified to $\frac{1}{8}$ in. per in.

Pipe threads are generally represented by the same conventional symbols used for ordinary American National Standard thread. See Fig. 21.2.

21.9
Specification of Wrought-iron and Steel Pipe. The standardized weights commonly used are the standard, extra-strong, and double-extra-strong. All are specified by the nominal inside diameter.

The nominal inside diameter of standard pipe is less than the actual diameter, because early manufacturers made the wall thickness greater than necessary and, in correcting, took all of the excess from the inside to avoid altering the size of openings in fittings. Metal was added to the inside to increase wall thicknesses for the extra-strong and double-extra-strong. As a result, all three weights of pipe for any given nominal diameter have the same outside diameter and can be used with the same fittings.

Wrought-iron or steel pipe greater than 12 in. in diameter is specified by giving the outside diameter and the thickness of the wall.

Fig. 21.3 illustrates the relative wall thickness of 1-in. standard, extra-strong, and double-extra-strong pipe.

21.10
Sizes of Wrought-iron, Steel, and Cast-iron Pipe. The standard-weight pipe is used for normal pressures. It may be purchased in sizes ranging from $\frac{1}{8}$ to 12 in. (nominal diameter). Pipe is received threaded on both ends with a plain coupling attached.

Extra-strong pipe, designed for steam and hydraulic pressures over 125 lb per sq in., also is manufactured in sizes $\frac{1}{8}$–12 in.

Double-extra-strong pipe, designed for extremely high pressures, is furnished in nominal diameters from $\frac{1}{2}$ to 8 in. in the same lengths as the extra-strong.

Cast-iron pipe, in sizes ranging up to 48

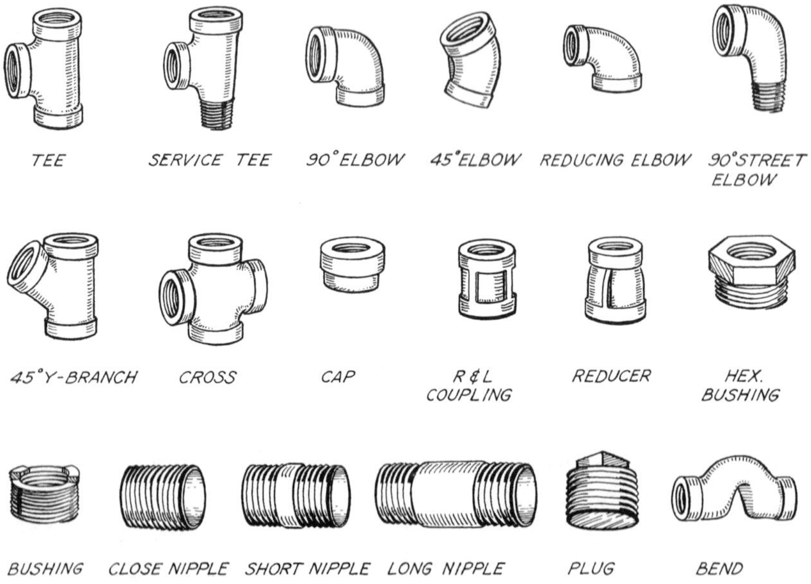

FIG. 21.3. Comparison of different weights of 1 in. wrought-iron pipe.

FIG. 21.4. Screwed fittings.

in., can be used for pressures up to 350 lb per sq in.

21.11
Pipe Fittings. Fittings are parts, such as elbows, tees, crosses, couplings, nipples, flanges, and so on, that are used to make turns and connections. They fall into three general classes: screwed, welded, and flanged. See Figs. 21.4–21.6.

In small piping systems and for house plumbing, screwed fittings are generally used.

Welded fittings are used where connections are to be permanent. They are manufactured of forged seamless steel having the same thickness as the pipe. In this type of construction, the weld is depended on to seal the joint and to carry the pipeline stresses. Many miles of line having welded fittings are giving satisfactory service to pipeline corporations.

Flanged fittings are used in large piping systems where pressures are high and the connection must be strong enough to carry the weight of large pipes. Table 25 in the Appendix gives the dimensions for American National Standard 125-lb cast-iron flange fittings. Several types of flanges and flanged joints are shown in Figs. 21.7 and 21.8.

21.12
Screwed Fittings (Fig. 21.4). Straight sections of pipe are connected by a short cylindrical fitting (threaded on the inside), which is known as a *coupling*. A *right and left coupling*, which can be recognized by the ribs on the outside, is often used to close a system. A *union* is preferable, however, where pipe must be frequently disconnected.

A *cap* is screwed on the end of a pipe to close it.

A *plug* is used to close an opening in a fitting.

A *nipple* is a short piece of pipe that has been threaded on both ends. If it is threaded the entire length, it is called a *close nipple;* if not, it is called a *short* or *long nipple*. Extra-long nipples may be purchased.

A *bushing* is used to reduce the size of an opening in a fitting when it would be inconvenient to use a reducing fitting.

Tees, crosses, and *laterals* form the connections for lines and branches in a piping system.

By standardizing the screwed fittings, the American National Standards Institute has eliminated many difficulties that would arise if each manufacturer produced the varied sizes of elbows, tees, laterals, and so on, according to his own specifications. The adopted dimensions, now recognized by all manufacturers, will be found in Tables 22, 23, and 24 in the Appendix. See Fig. 21.13.

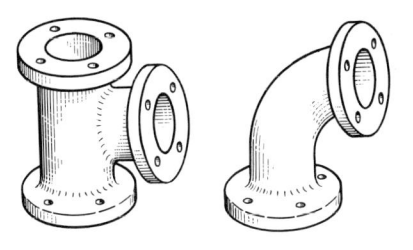

FIG. 21.5. Flanged fittings.

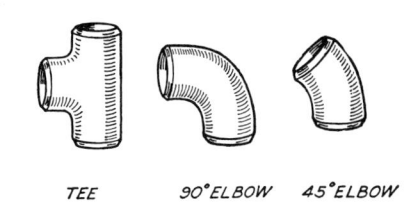

TEE   90° ELBOW   45° ELBOW

FIG. 21.6. Welded fittings.

(a)   (b)   (c)

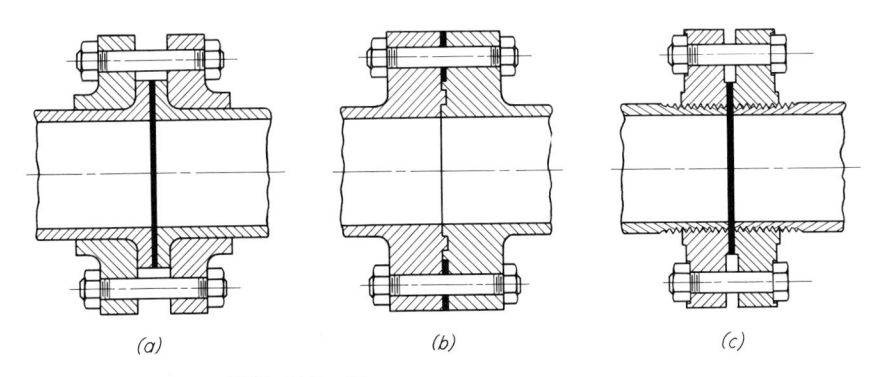

FIG. 21.7. Flanges.

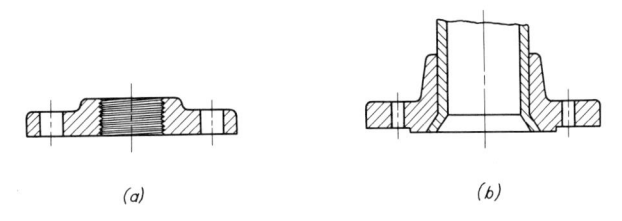

(a)   (b)

FIG. 21.8. Flanges.

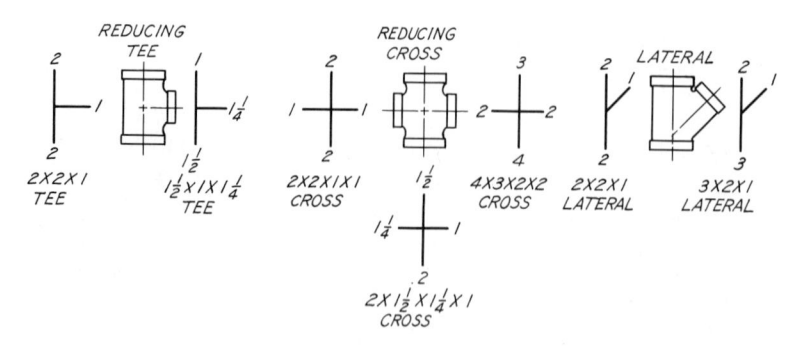

FIG. 21.9. Specification of fittings.

21.13
Specification of Fittings. A fitting is specified by giving the nominal inside diameter of the pipe for which the openings are threaded, the type of fitting, and the material. If it connects more than one size of pipe, it is called a reducing fitting, and the largest opening of the through run is given first, followed in order by the opposite end and the outlet. Figure 21.9 illustrates the order of specifying reducing fittings. If all of the openings are for the same size of pipe, the fitting is known as a straight tee, cross, and so on. A straight fitting is specified by the size of the openings followed by the name of the fitting (2-in. tee, 4-in. cross, etc.).

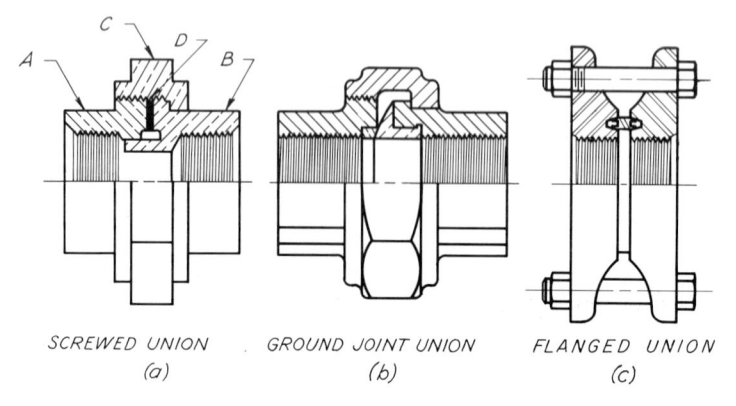

FIG. 21.10. Unions.

21.14
Unions. Screwed or flanged unions connect pipes that must be frequently disconnected for the purpose of making repairs. In many cases, screwed unions are used for making the final closing connection in a line. The union illustrated in Fig. 21.10(a) is made up of three separate pieces. The mating parts, A and B, are screwed on the ends of the two pipes. The third part, the nut, draws them together so that A and B will be against the gasket, D, to ensure a tight joint. In systems having pipes more than 2 in. in diameter, screwed unions are not generally used, because the stronger and more substantial flange unions, such as the one shown at (c), become desirable. A screwed union with a ground metal seat is shown at (b).

21.15
Valves. Valves are used in piping systems to stop or control the movement of fluids and gases. A few of the many forms are illustrated in Fig. 21.11. Of these, the globe valve and gate valve are the two types most frequently used.

Globe valves are used for throttling steam, in both high- and low-pressure steam lines, and to regulate the passage of other fluids. Their design, however, creates a slight retardation to the flow, because the fluid is forced to make a double turn and pass through the opening at 90° to the axis of the pipe. The valve disc is raised or lowered to stop or regulate the flow through a circular opening.

A gate valve allows a straight-line movement of a fluid and offers only slight resistance to the flow. Since the disc moves completely out of the passage and leaves a full opening, this type of valve is particularly suitable for water lines, oil lines, and the like.

A swing-type check valve permits movement in one direction only and prevents any back flow. It will be noted from a study of this valve that the design makes

CHAP. 21 / PIPING DRAWINGS AND MODELS   **497**

GLOBE VALVE   SWING CHECK VALVE   GATE VALVE

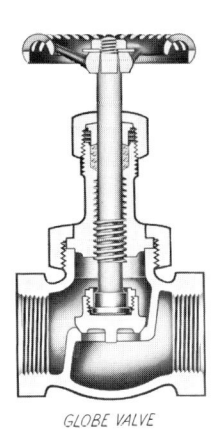

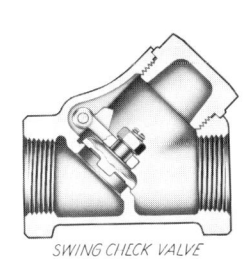

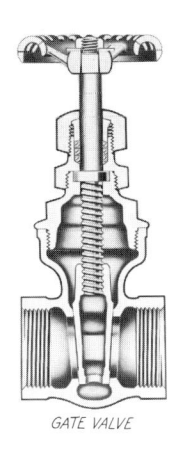

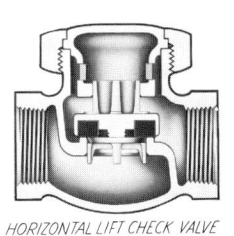

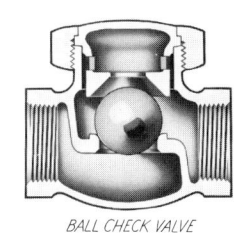

HORIZONTAL LIFT CHECK VALVE   BALL CHECK VALVE   FOUR-WAY STEAM COCK

FIG. 21.11. Valves (*Courtesy Crane Co.*).

the action automatic. Such valves are used in feedwater lines to boilers. The ball-check valve is preferred for heavy liquids.

The dimensions of the valves given in Fig. 21.11, as well as those for many special types, may be found in the catalogs of manufacturers.

21.16
Piping Drawings. Since standard pipe and fittings can be purchased for almost any purpose, a piping drawing usually shows only the arrangement of a system in some conventional form and gives the size and location of fittings. The drawing may be a freehand sketch, single-line diagram, double-line diagram, or pictorial diagram.

Occasionally, when conditions necessitate the design of special valves or the redesign of an existing type, complete working drawings are made.

Single-line drawings or sketches are made in orthographic projection or are drawn as though the entire system were swung into one plane (Fig. 21.12). On these drawings, single lines represent the runs of pipe, regardless of variations in diameters; conventional symbols are used for the fittings. A developed single-line sketch is frequently used for repair work, small jobs, and for making studies and calculations. For more complicated small-scale layouts, a single-line diagram drawn in orthographic projection is more suitable.

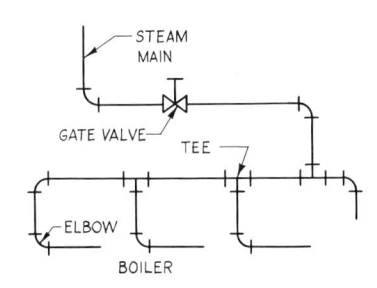

FIG. 21.12. Single-line drawing.

498   PART V / DESIGN AND COMMUNICATION DRAWING IN SPECIALIZED FIELDS

Double-line diagrams are drawn when many similar installations are to be made at the plants of various purchasers of pumps, manufacturing equipment, heating equipment, and so on (Fig. 21.13).

A diagrammatic isometric layout (Fig. 21.14) showing a piping system in space reveals the changes in direction and the difference in levels more clearly than does any other type of line diagram. Pictorial diagrams are often used for preliminary layouts.

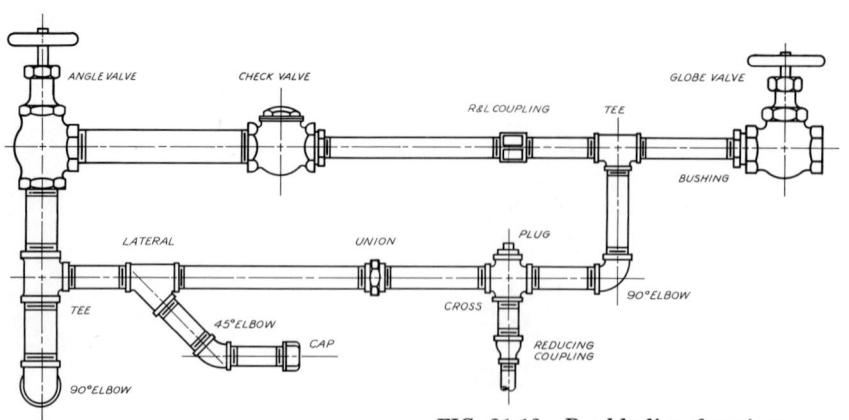

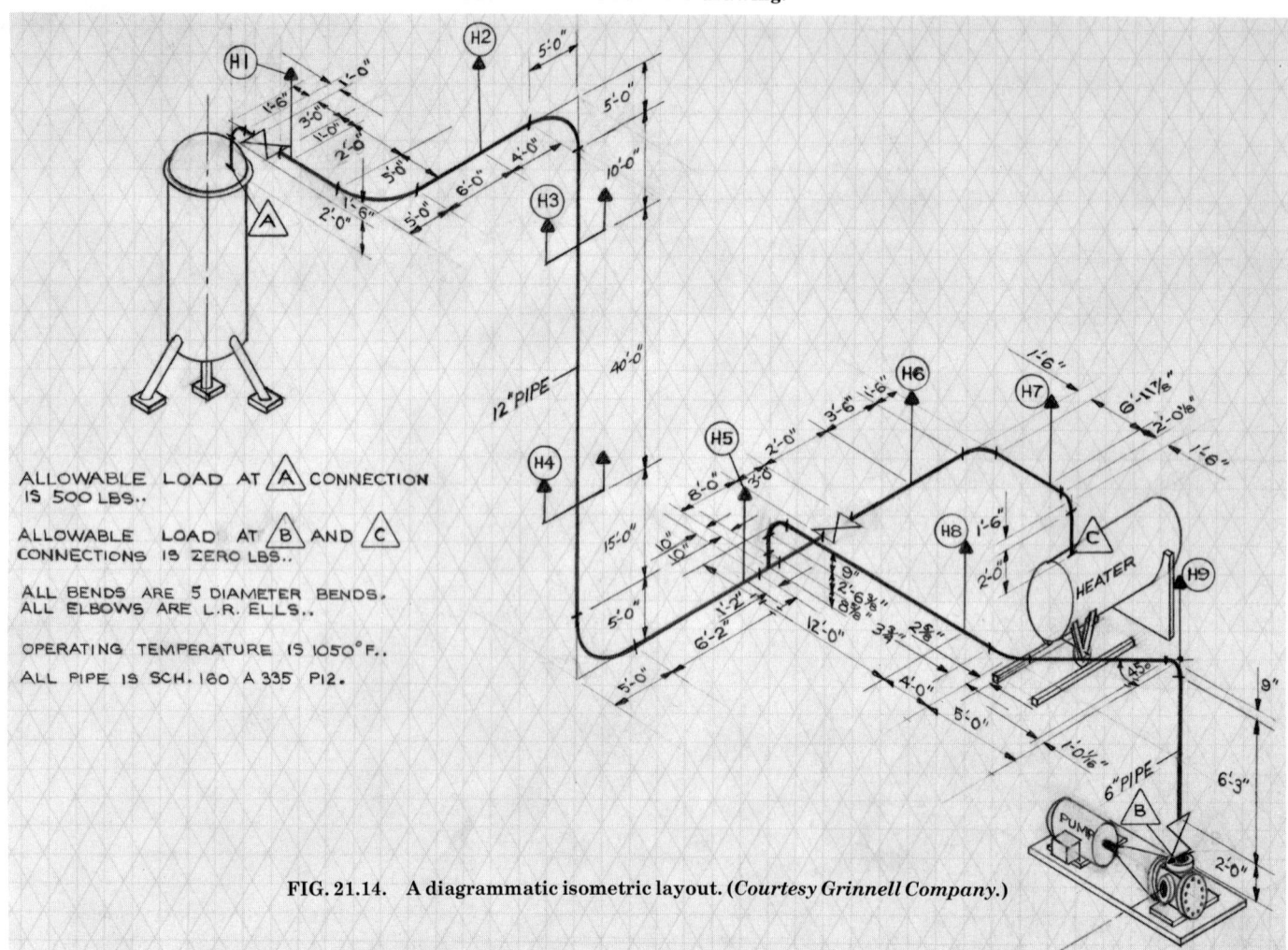

FIG. 21.13. Double-line drawing.

FIG. 21.14.   A diagrammatic isometric layout. (*Courtesy Grinnell Company.*)

21.17

Dimensions on Piping Drawings. The rules for dimensioning working drawings apply to piping drawings. Fittings and pipes are always located by giving center-to-center distances, because the determination of pipe lengths is generally left to the pipefitter. Notes should be used to specify the nominal size and type of each fitting and the nominal size of the pipe in each run. In addition, it is good practice to indicate, on a flanged valve, the diameter of the handwheel and its distance above the center of the fitting when wide open. It may be necessary to give overall dimensions for other apparatus, if the maximum space to be allowed is important.

The date and a descriptive title should be given on all piping sketches and drawings.

21.18

Conventional Symbols. Figure 21.15 shows a few of the conventional symbols for fittings that have been approved by the American National Standards Institute.

B: PROCESS MODELS

21.19

Piping Models (Fig. 21.16). Plant models with extensive piping installations usually portray complete process systems. The use of piping models varies widely from company to company. At times, some companies build models only after complete sets of design drawings, including piping assembly drawings, have been prepared. These conventional drawings show the piping along with related mechanical equipment, structural steel components, electrical conduit, and so forth. This usage makes the model an instrument that provides the means for review and complete checking of the entire system before final confirmation of the total de-

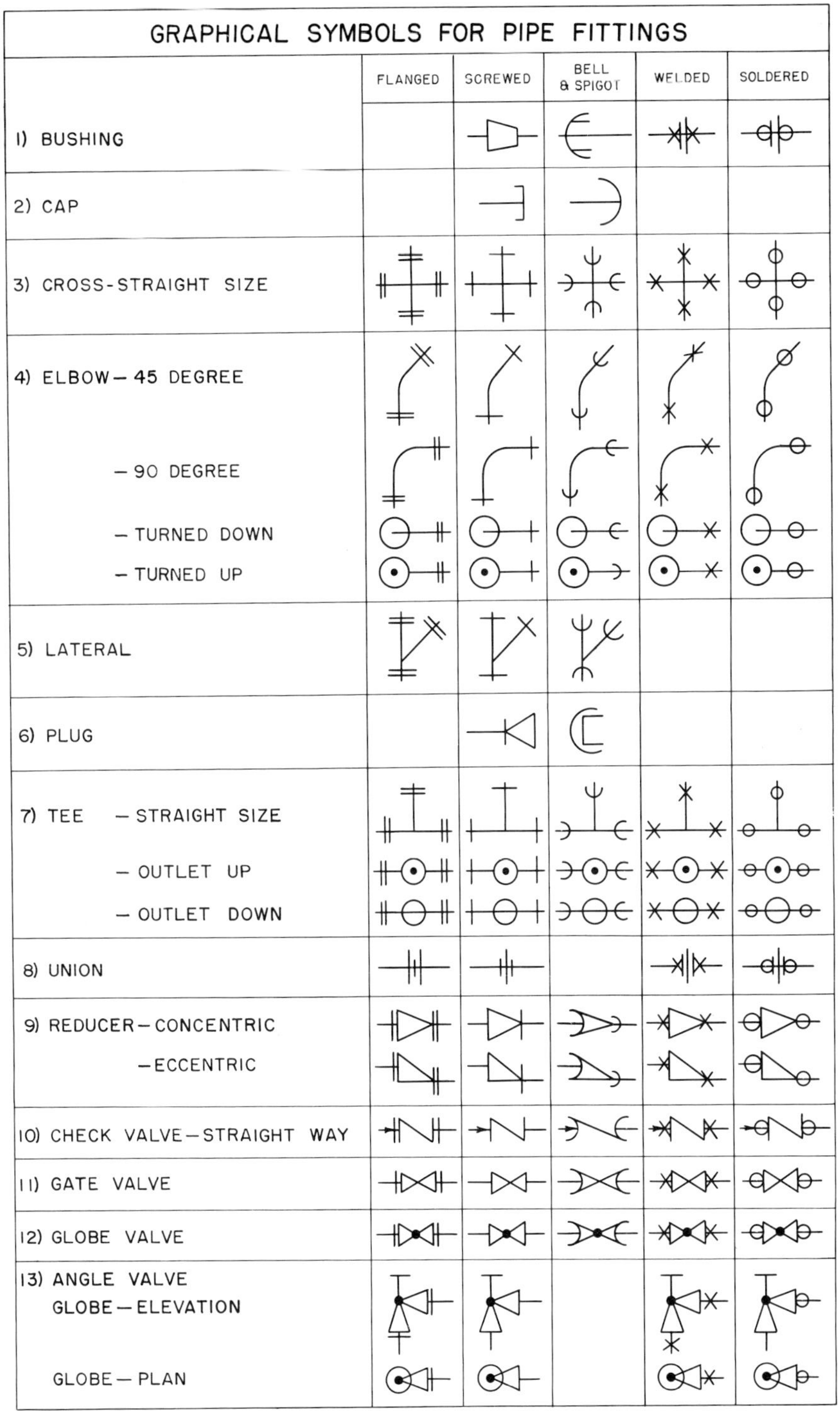

*ANS (ASA) Z.32.2.3–1949 (R1953)

GRAPHICAL SYMBOLS FOR PIPE FITTINGS	FLANGED	SCREWED	BELL & SPIGOT	WELDED	SOLDERED
1) BUSHING					
2) CAP					
3) CROSS—STRAIGHT SIZE					
4) ELBOW— 45 DEGREE					
— 90 DEGREE					
— TURNED DOWN					
— TURNED UP					
5) LATERAL					
6) PLUG					
7) TEE — STRAIGHT SIZE					
— OUTLET UP					
— OUTLET DOWN					
8) UNION					
9) REDUCER— CONCENTRIC					
— ECCENTRIC					
10) CHECK VALVE—STRAIGHT WAY					
11) GATE VALVE					
12) GLOBE VALVE					
13) ANGLE VALVE GLOBE—ELEVATION					
GLOBE — PLAN					

FIG. 21.15. Conventional symbols for fittings.*

sign. However, due to somewhat different design and construction habits, other companies build models without first preparing assembly piping drawings. In this case, the piping system is designed directly on the model with the aid of flow diagrams. When this practice is followed every pipeline and all piping accessories, such as metering instruments, valves, traps, strainers, and so forth, must be placed in proper location. When almost all design work has been done directly on the model and only a few drawings, flow charts, and sketches have been prepared, the model with all related systems shown ultimately becomes the means for communicating design information to the construction crews in the field (Fig. 21.17).

Since in most cases it is difficult to coordinate an entire processing system that involves complicated piping, all phases of the total system should be shown on the model along with the necessary piping. If all of the related mechanical and electrical equipment, along with minor structural components, platforms, ladders, and supports, are properly positioned with related items such as ducts, chutes, instruments, electrical conduits, and lights, and each pipe is traced out and checked to see that requirements are met, it is most likely that all phases of the total system will fit together at the construction site.

When the model is nearing completion, the design should be examined critically for inaccuracies and faulty representation. In reviewing the model at this stage those responsible for the project should determine whether the proposal fulfills the requirements of the process and the most economical design has been adopted.

Piping models are built to scales that vary from $\frac{1}{4}$ in. to the foot to 1 in. to the foot. When conventional design and working drawings have been prepared and accuracy of the model is not important, a small-size model prepared to a scale of

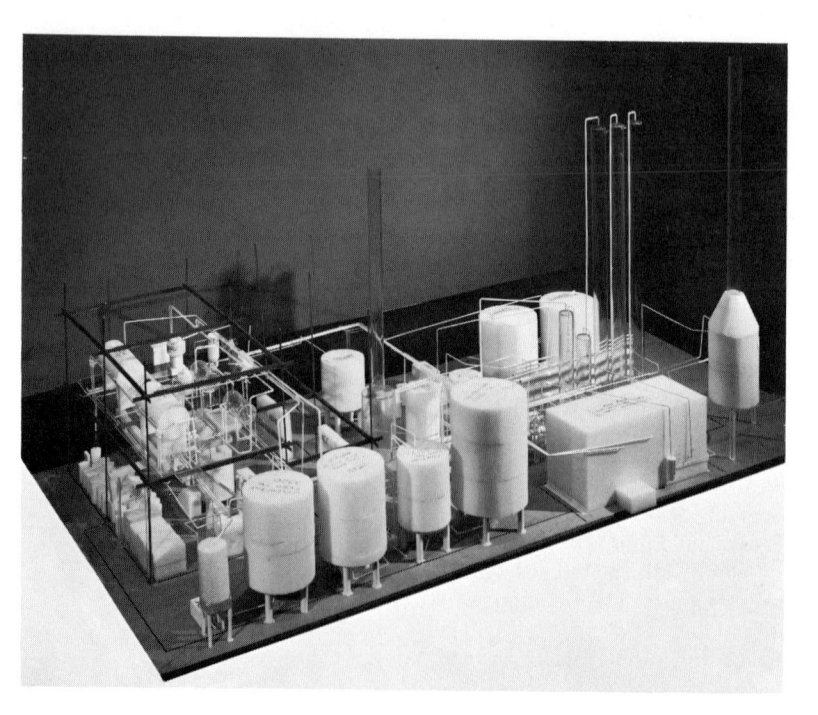

FIG. 21.16. A typical equipment layout model showing processing. (*Courtesy Procter and Gamble*)

either ¼ or ⅜ in. to the foot proves to be satisfactory. However, if the design is to be worked out on the model, the scale should be at least ¾ in. to the foot.

When the representation of each piece of equipment has been mounted in its proper location on the basic model, consisting essentially of a baseboard and a replica of the structural design, the piping can be installed through and around the formed background (Fig. 21.16). The two techniques that are commonly employed for the piping are known as (1) the "fine-wire" method and (2) the "true-scale" technique. When the fine-wire method is used, a fine wire with fibre discs or rubber sleeves mounted along its length is used to represent the pipe. The wire, normally $\frac{1}{16}$ in. in diameter, represents the center line of the pipe, while the outside diameter of the discs or sleeves indicates the outside diameter of the pipe.

Because fine-wire models sometimes prove unsatisfactory due to built-in inaccuracies and poor representation, many companies are now using the true-scale technique for building so-called true-scale models (Fig. 21.17). In building these models, plastic rod or plastic tubing, having outside diameters equal to the scaled diameters of the various sizes of standard pipe, are used for the piping. A full line of true-scale piping and piping components of plastic may be purchased ready for use. Plastic, as a model material, is easy to work, light in weight, and may be readily joined using solvent cements. It is for these reasons that it is so widely used for models.

After a model has been reviewed and approved it is color-coded, tagged, and made ready for shipment to the plant construction site. On models that have been prepared primarily for confirmation and approval, pipelines are coded to indicate particular systems to which the lines belong. That is, water lines might be shown in blue, while lines carrying a speci-

FIG. 21.17. A complete true scale production engineering model ready for use at the construction site. (*Courtesy Procter and Gamble*)

fied chemical might be presented in green. In the case of models for which there are few, if any, conventional drawings, pipelines are coded to indicate their construction specification.

Three-dimensional models enable designers to discover errors, detect interferences, and determine the most economical design more readily than would be possible from drawings alone. In addition, models prove invaluable to those directing construction work in the field. However, drawings will always be needed since not all details can be incorporated and indicated on a model.

PROBLEMS

1. Make a freehand sketch (on $\frac{1}{8}$-in. grid paper, if it is available) of a 1-in. nipple connecting, a 1-in. cast-iron elbow, and a $2 \times 2 \times 1$-in. malleable-iron tee. The distance between centers of fittings is to be 6 in. Enter neatly, in draftsman's style, the length of the nipple to the nearest $\frac{1}{8}$ in.

2. Make a freehand sketch (on $\frac{1}{8}$-in. grid paper) of a $1 \times 1 \times 1$-in. malleable-iron tee and a 1-in. cast-iron elbow joined by a length of pipe. The distance between centers of fittings is 4 in. Enter the length of the connecting pipe to the nearest $\frac{1}{8}$ in.

3. Make a single-line multiview sketch of the portion of a piping system shown in Fig. 21.18.

4. Make a double-line developed drawing of the portion of a piping system shown in Fig. 21.18. Use 2-in. pipe and screwed fittings. Select a suitable scale. Determine the measurements by transferring distances from the drawing to the open-divided scale in the figure.

5. Dimension the drawing of Problem 4.

6. Make a detail (working) drawing of an assigned part of the air cleaner shown in Fig. 21.19. Determine the dimensions by transferring them from the drawing to the accompanying scale by means of the dividers (study the pictorial representation).

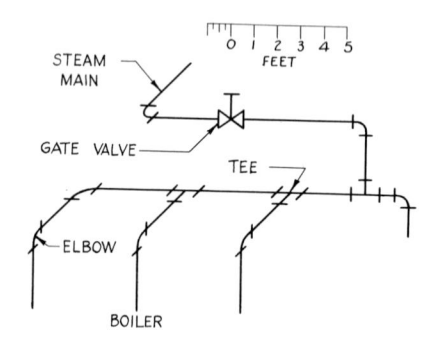

FIG. 21.18. Pictorial line diagram.

CHAP. 21 / PIPING DRAWINGS AND MODELS 503

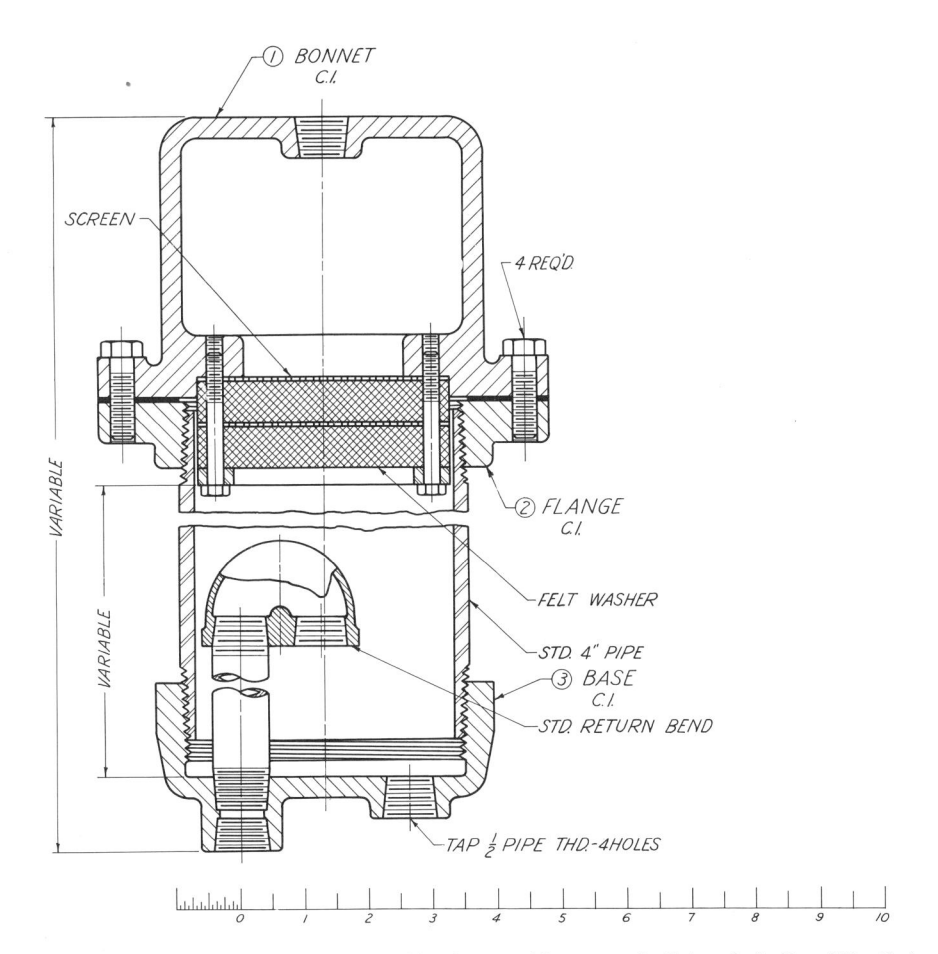

FIG. 21.19. Air cleaner (*Courtesy A. Schrader's Son Mfg. Co.*).

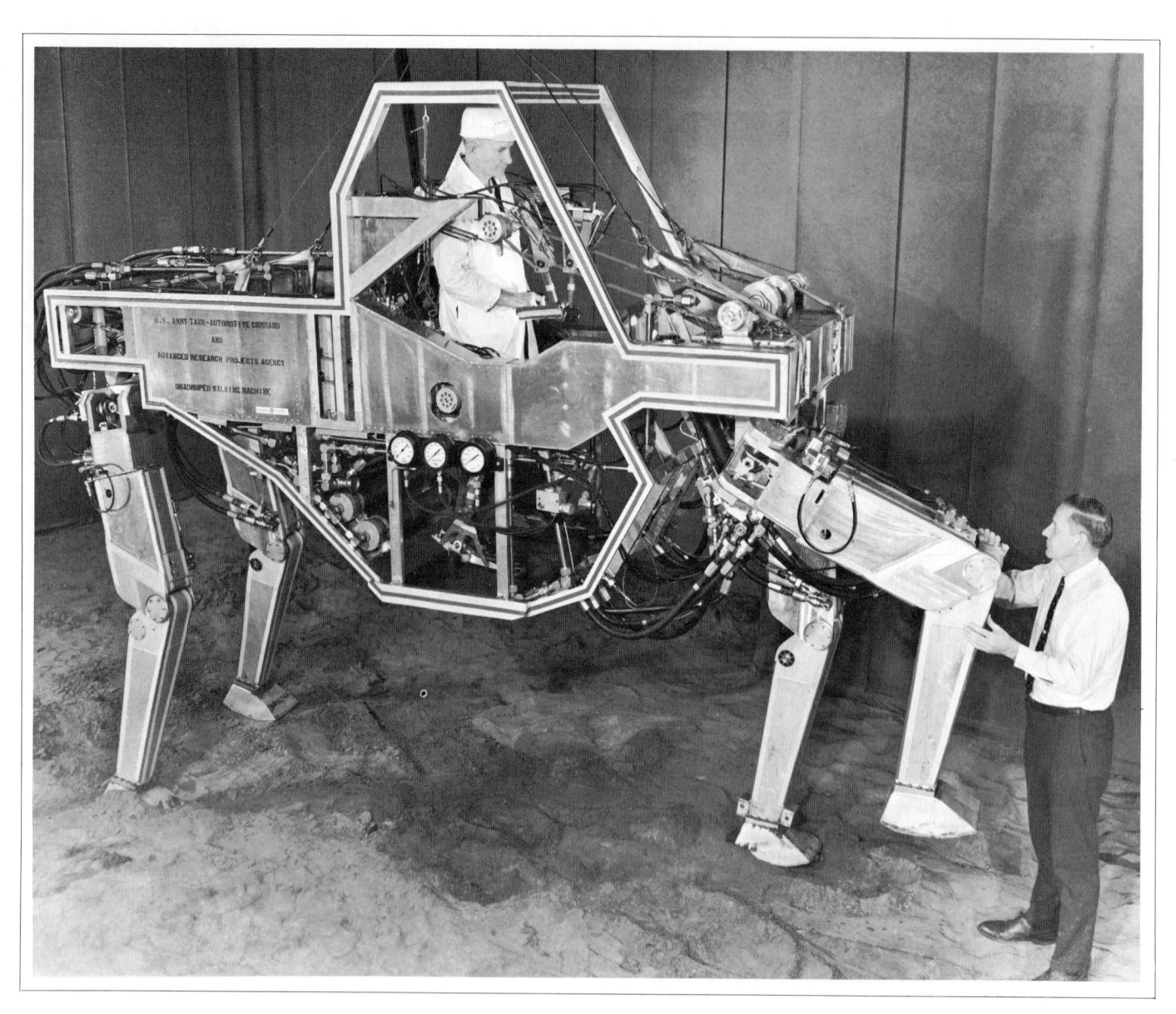

Research prototype of a quadruped machine, fabricated by General Electric Company engineers. It was developed for materials-handling under the most severe conditions. By means of an advanced control system, the machine mimics and amplifies the linear movements of the operator. The right front leg of the unit is controlled by the operator's right arm, its left front leg by his left arm, its right rear leg by his right leg, and its left rear leg by his left leg.

Units of this type require considerable welding.

(*Courtesy General Electric Company*)

Welding Drawings

22

22.1
Welding Processes. For convenience, the various welding processes used in commercial production may be classified into three types: pressure processes, nonpressure processes, and casting processes. The nonpressure processes are arc welding and gas welding. Metallic arc welding is the joining of two pieces of metal through the use of a sustained arc formed between the work and a metal rod held in a holder (Fig. 22.1). The intense heat melts the metal of the work and at the same time heats the end of the electrode, causing small globules to form and cross the arc to the weld. In gas welding, the heat is produced by a burning mixture of two gases, which ordinarily are oxygen and acetylene. The weld is formed by melting a filler rod with the torch flame, along the line of contact, after the metal of the work has been preheated to a molten state. This method is essentially a puddling process, in that the weld is produced by a small moving molten pool that is maintained by the flame constantly directed on it. Resistance welding is a pressure process, the fusion being made through heat and mechanical pressure. The work is heated by a strong electrical current that passes through it until fusion temperature is reached; then pressure is applied to create the weld.

The forms of resistance welding are projection welding, seam welding, spot welding, and flash welding. In spot welding, the parts are overlapped and welds are made at successive single spots. A seam weld is similar to a spot weld, except that a continuous weld is produced. In

FIG. 22.1. Arc welding. (*Courtesy Lincoln Electric Company*)

505

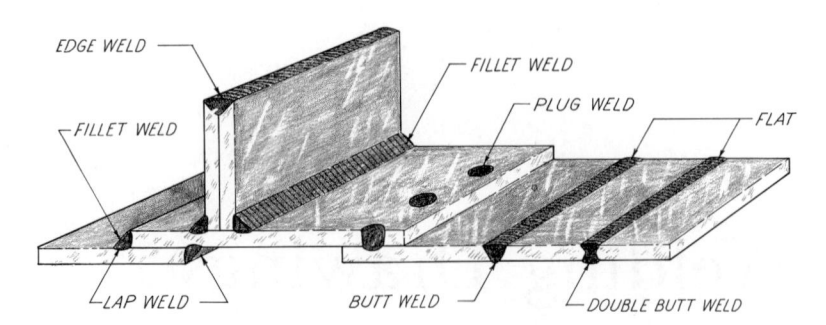

FIG. 22.2. Types of welds.

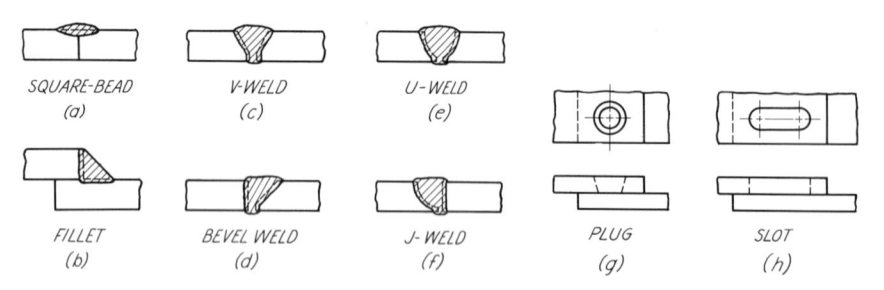

FIG. 22.3. Types of welds.

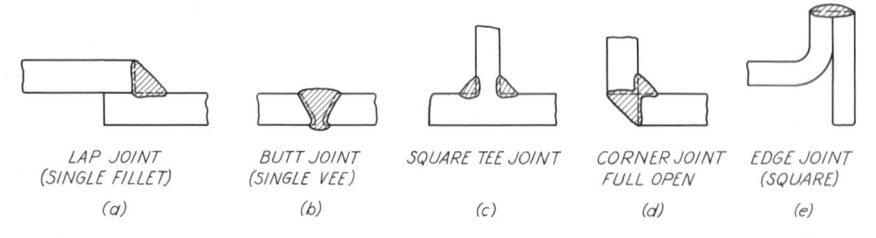

FIG. 22.4. Types of welded joints.

power is shut off and the two ends are forced together to cool in a fused position.

Thermit welding can be considered a casting process, in that molten iron is run into a mold built around the parts at the point at which they are to be connected. The liquid metal is obtained from a mixture of finely divided iron oxide and aluminum, which is ignited in a crucible. In the chemical reaction that takes place, the oxygen passes from the iron oxide to the aluminum, leaving free molten iron that flows into the mold around the preheated parts forming the joint. The metal of the members being welded fuses with the liquid metal and forms a weld when the joint is cool.

22.2

Types of Welds. Figure 22.2 illustrates in pictorial some of the various types of welds. Cross-sectional views of the fundamental welds that are commonly encountered are shown in Fig. 22.3.

22.3

Classification of Weld Joints. Welded joints are classified in accordance with the method of assembly of the parts at a joint. See Figure 22.4.

22.4

Working Drawings of Welded Parts. Figure 22.5 shows a part that is to be constructed by welding rolled shapes. It should be noted that each joint is completely specified through the use of a welding symbol. A careful study will show that the drawing, except for the absence of fillets and rounds and the fact that properly composed welding symbols are directed to the necessary joints, is very much like a casting drawing.

A satisfactory welding design may be produced by a competent designer who possesses a fair amount of ingenuity, and the necessary drawing can be made by any draftsman who has a thorough under-

projection welding, one part is embossed and welds are made at the successive projections. In making a flash weld, the two pieces to be joined are held end to end in jaws and act as electrodes. At the right instant, after the facing metal has been heated by the arc across the gap, the

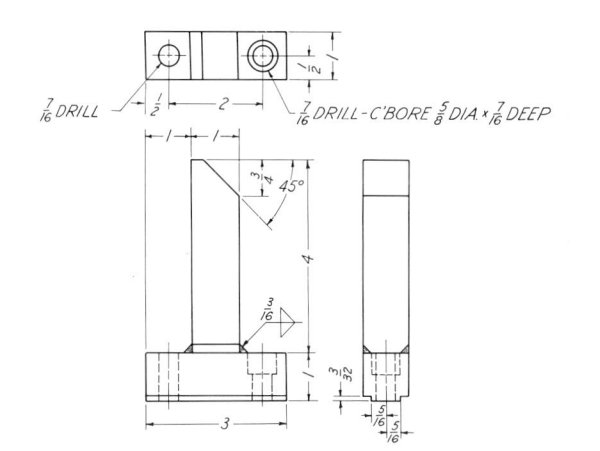

FIG. 22.5. A welding drawing.

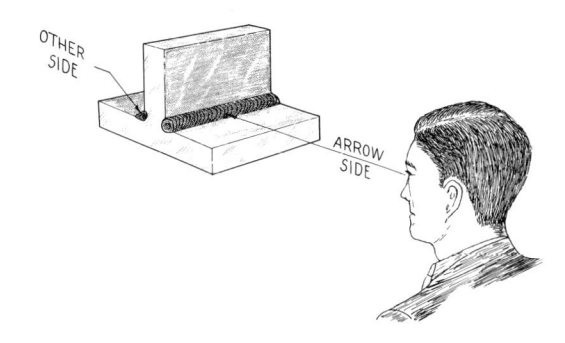

FIG. 22.6. Arrow-side and other-side welds.

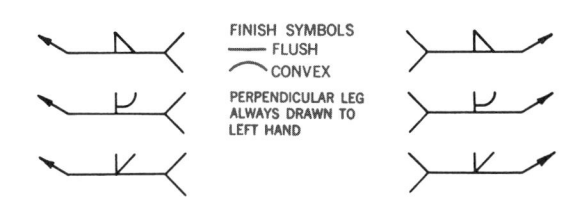

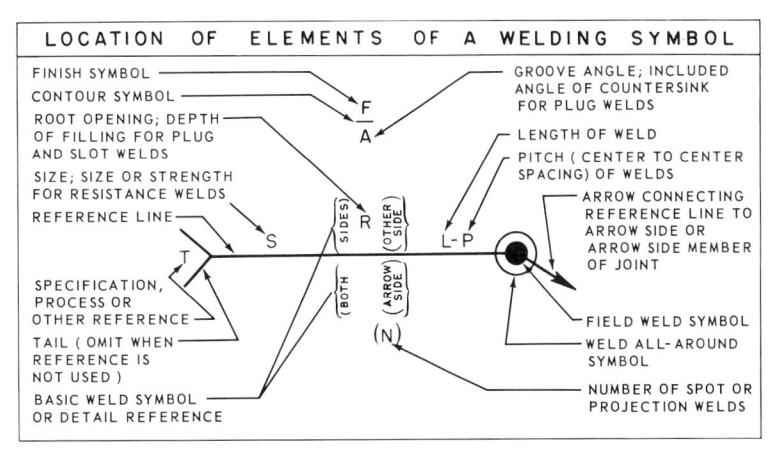

FIG. 22.7. The basic welding symbol.†

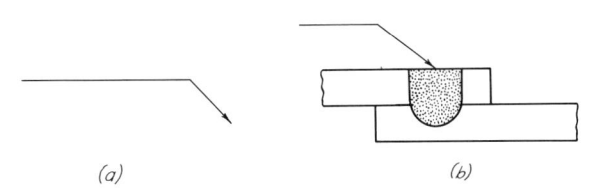

FIG. 22.8. Welding arrow.

standing of the use of the symbols recommended in ANS Y32.3-1959.

22.5
Arrow-side and Other-side Welds (Fig. 22.6). "The use of the words "far side" and "near side" in the past has led to confusion, because when joints are shown in section, all welds are equally distant from the reader, and the words "near" and "far" are meaningless. In the present system the joint is the basis of reference. Any joint the welding of which is indicated by a symbol will always have an "arrow side" and an "other side.""*

22.6
Welding Symbols. An enlarged drawing of the approved welding symbol is shown in Fig. 22.7, along with explanatory notes that indicate the proper locations of the marks and size dimensions necessary for a complete description of a weld.

The arrow is the basic portion of the symbol, as shown in Fig. 22.8(a). It points toward the joint where the required weld is to be made, as in Fig. 22.8(b).

---
*Extracted from ANS (ASA) Z32.2.1-1949.
†Based on ANS Y32.3-1959.

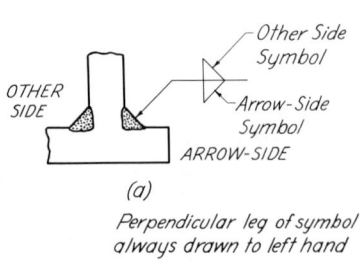

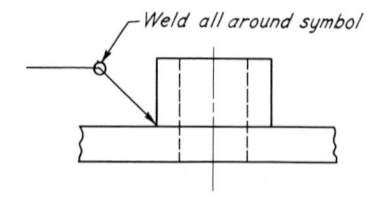

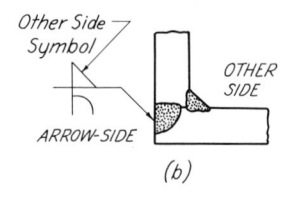

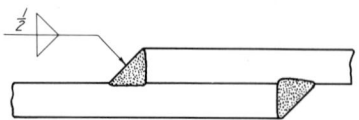

FIG. 22.9. Location of welding symbols.

FIG. 22.10. Weld-all-around symbol.

FIG. 22.11. Method of specifying the size of weld.

FIG. 22.12. Dimensioning a weld.

FIG. 22.13. Dimensioning a weld.

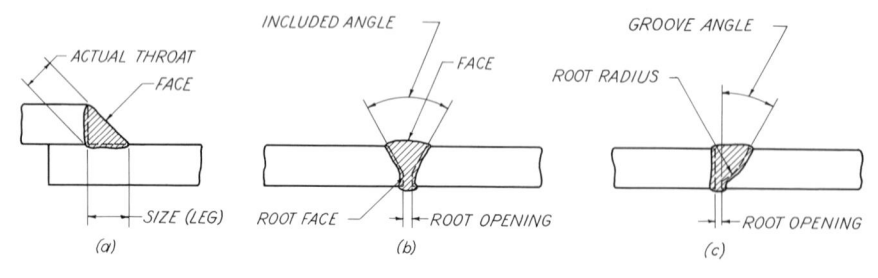

FIG. 22.14. Welding terms.

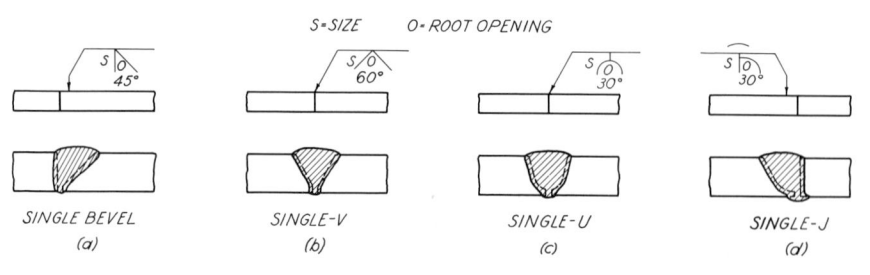

FIG. 22.15. Single-groove welds and symbols.

If the weld is on the arrow-side, the symbol indicating the type of weld is placed below or to the right of the base line, depending on whether that line is horizontal or vertical (Fig. 22.9). If the weld is located on the other-side, the symbol should be above or to the left.

To indicate that a weld is to be made all around a connection, as is necessary when a piece of tubing must be welded to a plate, a weld-all-around symbol, a circle, is placed as shown in Fig. 22.10.

The size of a weld is given along the base of the arrow, at the side of the symbol, as shown in Fig. 22.11. If the welds on the arrow-side and the other-side of a lap joint are the same size, only one dimension should be given (Fig. 22.12). If they are not the same size, each dimension should be placed beside its associated symbol (Fig. 22.13).

The welding terms associated with the specification of the size of welds are illustrated in Fig. 22.14.

Figure 22.15 shows the common types of single-groove welds and the related symbol for each. The symbols for double-groove welds are illustrated in Fig. 22.16.

22.7
Gas and Arc Welding Symbols. To satisfy the need for a standard group of symbols that could be understood in all manufacturing plants, the American Welding Society recommended in 1940 a set of conventional symbols so designed that each symbol resembled in a general way the type of weld it represented. Figure 22.17 shows a condensed table of symbols taken from ANS (ASA) Y32.3-1959. The symbols shown are the same as those first proposed by the American Welding Society.

22.8
Resistance Welding. Figure 22.18 shows the symbols for the four principal types of resistance welding. The method of specifying resistance welds differs from the methods used for arc and gas welds. In the former, the strength of a weld is given in units instead of size, and the symbols do not show the form of the weld. The strength of spot and projection welds is given in units of pounds per weld. The strength for seam welds is given in units of pounds per linear inch.

22.9
Welded Machine Parts. Many machine parts often can be constructed of welded rolled shapes at a much lower cost than if they were cast. This is due to the fact that the cost of the preparation of patterns is completely eliminated, less material is required, and labor costs are lower. A welded part is sometimes more desirable for a particular mechanism, because steel is stiffer, stronger in tension, and more resistant to fatigue stresses and sudden impact. Also, aside from the production of new parts, welding can be used to make a machine part to replace a broken cast

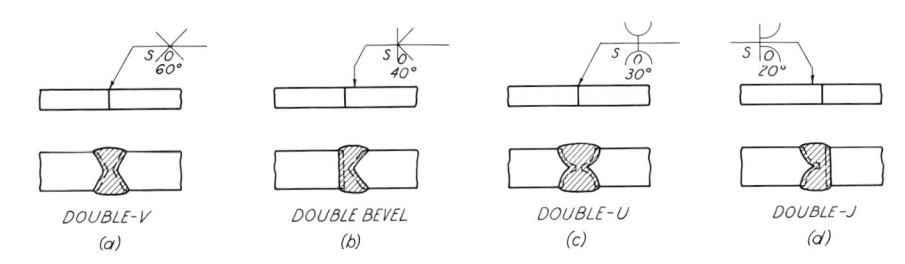

FIG. 22.16. Double-groove welds and symbols.

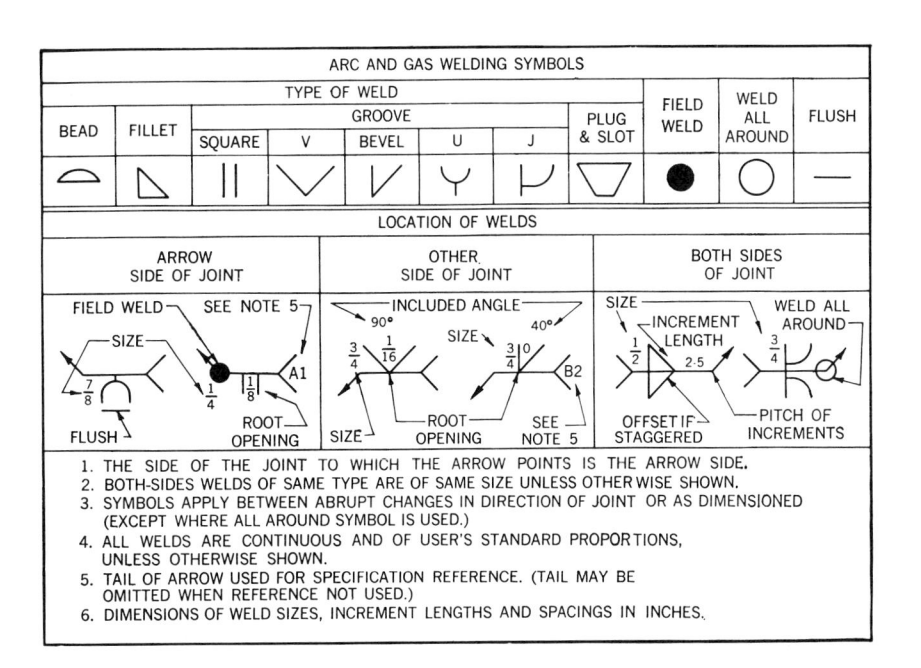

FIG. 22.17. American National Standard arc and gas welding symbols.*

*Based on ANS(ASA) Y32.3-1959.

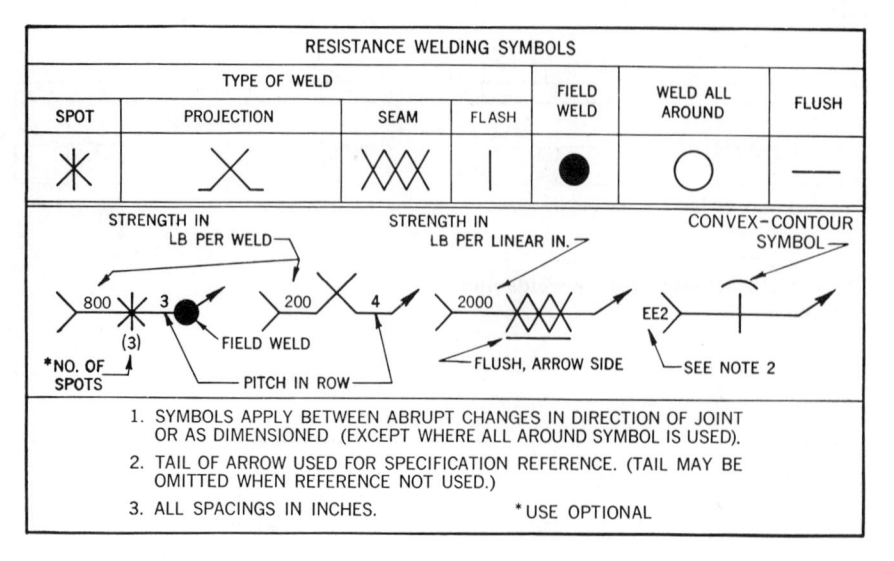

FIG. 22.18. American National Standard resistance welding symbols.*

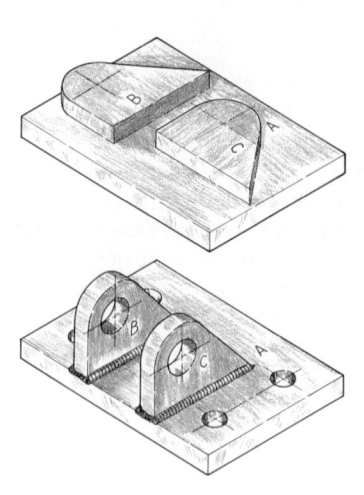

FIG. 22.19. Bracket-welded design.

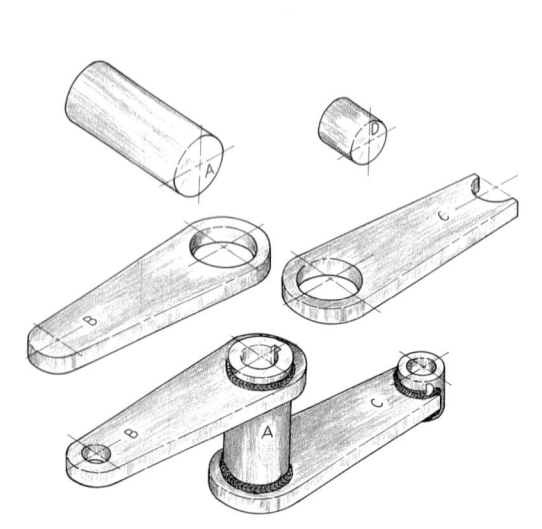

FIG. 22.20. Link-welded design.

*Based on ANS(ASA) Y32.3-1959.

part when it is necessary to place a machine back in operation in the shortest possible time. Figure 22.19 shows a part that is constructed of plates. Figure 22.20 shows the construction of a link using plates and round bar stock.

As previously stated, a designer is limited only by his own ingenuity. Parts of all shapes and sizes may be produced of readily available rolled forms. Simple bearings, levers, cranks, clevises, gear arms, and even cams can be quickly and easily made.

PROBLEMS

Two problems offering experience in the preparation of welding drawings are given in Figs. 22.21 and 22.22. Others may be had by redesigning many of the cast parts, (given at the end of the chapter on multiview drawing and in some of the other chapters) in such a way that they may be made of welded steel shapes. The student will find in these problems an opportunity to exercise some of his own ingenuity.

1. Prepare a welding drawing of the bracket shown in Fig. 22.21.

2. Prepare a welding drawing of the caster bracket shown in Fig. 22.22. The length of the tubing is $2^{11}/_{16}$ in.

3. Make a two-view orthographic drawing of the object shown in Fig. 22.2. The dimensions are to be assumed. The plates are $3/8$ in. thick. Show the correct specification for each type of weld.

4. Make a three-view detail drawing of the bracket shown in Fig. 22.19. The dimensions are to be assumed. Show the correct specifications for the welds.

5. Make a two-view detail drawing of the link shown in Fig. 22.20. The dimensions are to be assumed. Show correct specifications for the welds.

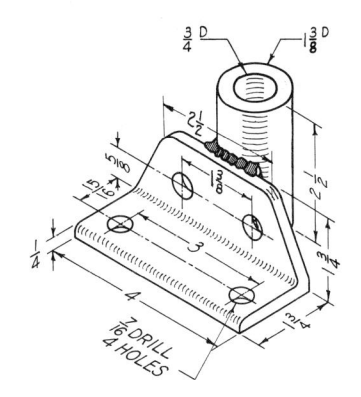

FIG. 22.21. Bracket.

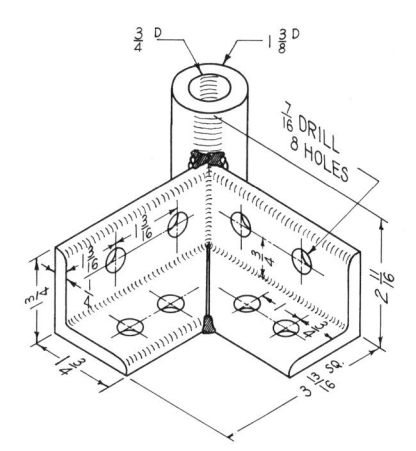

FIG. 22.22. Caster bracket.

It is impractical to make innumerable individual measurements in producing parts that are needed in considerable number, say from one-hundred to a million or more. To manufacture parts in such quantities, using measurement methods applicable to a few units, would be costly. Furthermore, the parts would not be consistently interchangeable. To produce low-cost interchangeable parts without making repeated measurements, jigs and fixtures are used as described in the chapter that follows. Many of the parts shown on the wheel assembly above were mass produced with the aid of jigs and fixtures.
(*Courtesy Ford Motor Company*)

Tool Design and Tool Drawings

23.1
Jigs and Fixtures. In general, it might be said that jigs and fixtures are devices for holding work while various machining operations are being performed. Such devices play an important role in the present quantity production of interchangeable parts, for their use greatly reduces the amount of labor required in performing accurate machining operations. However, the advantage that may be gained in the form of lower labor cost in the assembly of units having parts that are interchangeable may be just as important.

Although there are some people who use the terms denoting these devices interchangeably, there is a definite difference between a jig and a fixture that is quite generally recognized. Specifically, a jig is a work-holding device that is capable of controlling the path of the cutting tool. Since it is not fastened to the machine, a jig may be moved around so that several holes may be drilled, tapped, or reamed in their proper locations as established by the position of the drill bushings. Although it is usual for the work to be held by the jig, there are cases where the jig may be clamped on the piece. A well-designed jig should permit the work to be quickly inserted and removed.

A fixture, as the name implies, is fixed or fastened to the table of the machine to locate and hold the work securely in a definite position. Either the cutting tool is moved into position for the operation or the table is moved under the tool. A fixture does not guide the cutting tool. Fixtures are used for such operations as milling, honing, broaching, grinding, and welding.

The three factors that must be considered and evaluated when determining whether or not the cost of making a jig or a fixture will be justified are (1) the number of parts to be produced, (2) the saving in labor cost, and (3) the possibility that the device may be needed for making replacement parts at a later time. Using simple arithmetic, one can compute and compare the cost of producing one unit in the conventional manner against making the part using a jig or fixture. Knowing the cost of the jig or fixture, the number of units to be produced, and the savings per unit, it will not be difficult to arrive at a decision. Generally, the use of the device should result in a definite saving of time and labor.

More could be given here relating to the economic problems surrounding the use and design of jigs and fixtures but it would be beyond the scope of this chapter, which

513

is intended primarily to cover the preparation of the necessary drawings for the production of these devices.

23.2
Jig Borers. Jig borers are provided with accurate lead screws and special measuring devices that make possible the accurate location and boring of holes. Their use greatly reduces the cost of making jigs since the usual layout work with scriber and punch is not required. It is a common practice in many shops to use a jig borer or its equivalent to machine pieces in small lots rather than go to the expense of making jigs.

23.3
Principles of Design. There are seven items or principles of design that must be remembered and observed in designing a jig. None should be completely ignored. These items are as follows:

1. The jig must ensure accuracy within the limits required for interchangeability.

2. The work must go into the jig handily and must be located accurately.

3. The work must be clamped into the jig securely even though the ease with which it can be removed is of prime importance.

4. The jig must be designed to be foolproof or, in other words, designed in such a way that the operator cannot put the work into the jig in an incorrect position.

5. The design must provide ample clearance for chips.

6. The jig must be strong and rigid without having undue weight.

7. The design must incorporate any needed safety features.

23.4
Design of Jigs and Fixtures. A successful jig and fixture designer must have full knowledge of the production methods and be a person who is able to exercise considerable ingenuity in selecting the best-suited combination of methods for positioning and clamping as well as the means for quick loading and unloading.

When the designer has decided on the type of drill jig needed and has given general consideration to the preceding seven principles, he is ready to decide how he will position the work, clamp it, select the style and size of bushings, and choose the particular features of the jig body that are necessary to accommodate the work and satisfy the practices of good design. In some cases the designer will have a wide choice in the type of jig that can be used for a particular piece.

When deciding on the general design, the designer must make certain that the method of clamping will be positive and that the clamp will be sufficiently strong to hold the work firmly. In addition, he must decide on the best position and placement of locating pins, rest pads, stops, or V-blocks in the drill jig body and assure himself that the work will be properly located in the jig.

Since the jig body is usually moved over the surface of the machine table to perform machining operations, it should have contacting feet that have all been carefully finished off in one operation to be level. Levelness and perpendicularity are important factors in the production and use of jigs. Jig and fixture bodies may be either cast, fabricated, or built up of welded parts. Since elaborate drill jigs can be built up quickly using standard angles, channels, tees, plates, and bushings at a surprisingly low cost, a designer or draftsman should always have a set of standard tables at hand.

The shape of the piece on which the

operations are to be performed, previous machining, and certain specific features of the design as related to mating parts are deciding factors in determining the method of location that it will be best to employ. The designer must select a method that will ensure that each workpiece loaded into the jig will be located exactly in the same manner and in a definite position.

Location surfaces are used to locate the work. Location surfaces for registry may be a single surface, the surface of a pad, the surface of some fixed special attachment, or possibly two finished surfaces of the jig that are at right angles to each other. To establish location, a finished surface on the workpiece is placed against a finished surface of the jig or in some cases an unfinished surface of the workpiece may be placed against the finished locating surface. Sharp corners between locating surfaces should be avoided because they are hard to keep clean. Locating surfaces should always be fixed, the only moveable surfaces being those on the clamping device. The use of pins as locators is particularly suited for use with a single locator. They may be easily located and accurately installed. As used, a surface of the workpiece is held against either a pin and a location surface of the jig or against two or three pins through the use of some form of clamping. Pins that have been hardened and ground are generally better for locating than are finished flat surfaces since they may be adjusted for wear and are easier to keep clean. V-blocks are often parts of devices that are intended to serve both as locators and as clamps (Fig. 23.15). They should not be used where there is a chance that they will mar the machined surfaces of the workpiece. When a V-block is to serve as a backstop and is used principally as a locator, it is usually best to make it as a separate piece and attach it to the body of the jig by means of screws and dowel pins.

The most dependable means to foolproof a device and to prevent spoilage is by placing locating pins and blocks to receive the workpiece only when it has been correctly placed. When the jig or fixture has been incorrectly loaded, the pins and blocks should prevent the workpiece from slipping fully into position.

23.5

Types of Jigs. There are a number of types of jigs and fixtures that have been developed and are suitable for a wide range of work. Four types of jigs are shown in Fig. 23.1.

The plate jig is the simplest form of jig and is usually made when only a few pieces are to be produced. The essential parts are the plate, locating pins, and drill bushings. In the case of the jig shown in (*a*), the jig is clamped to the workpiece when the thumbscrews are tightened. Some other types of plate jigs are clamped directly to the part to be drilled by means of C-clamps. Simple jigs of the plate type are often called *template jigs*.

A diameter jig is shown in Fig. 23.1(*b*). With the drill bushing located in an adjustable bracket, a hole may be drilled perpendicular to the axis of a cylindrical workpiece at any specified location falling within the range of the adjustment. Another type of diameter jig is shown in Fig. 23.20.

The screw bushing of the channel jig shown in (*c*) serves as a clamp. The channel in the base positions the workpiece.

A leaf jig is identified by its hinged cover or leaf that is swung open to load or unload the jig [Fig. 23.1(*d*)]. Various methods are used to lock the leaf. Jigs of this type are suitable for complicated pieces of work of irregular contour. Their design permits fast loading and unloading.

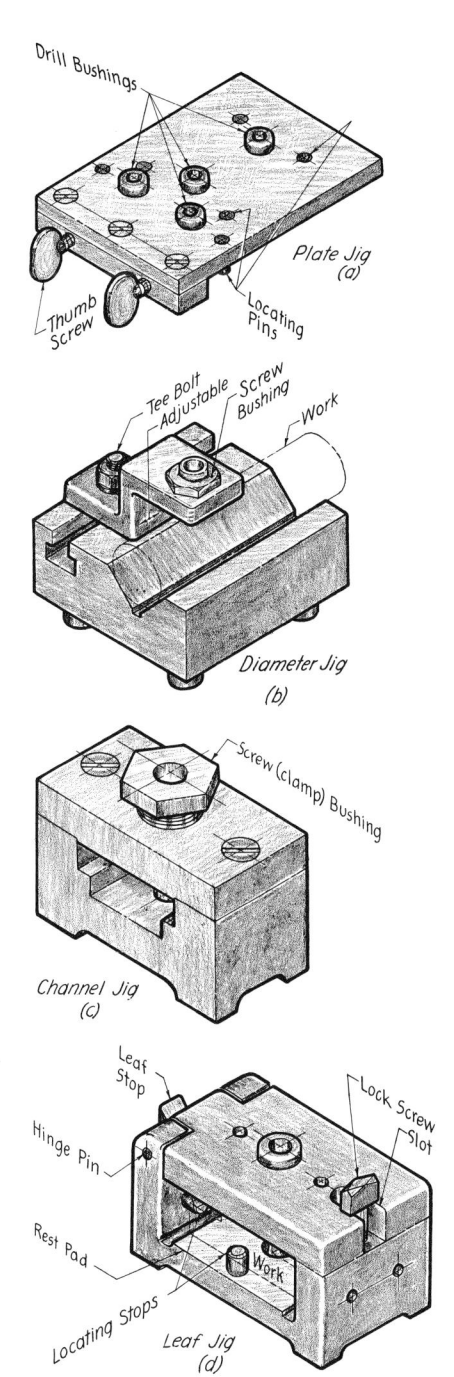

FIG. 23.1. Several types of jigs.

The design of an open jig is such that screws, wedges, or cam devices are depended on to clamp and hold the workpiece firmly while the needed operations are being performed.

A box drill jig is generally used when it is necessary to drill holes in two or more sides of a piece.

A tumble jig designed for drilling holes that are diametrically opposite in the hub of a gear is shown in Fig. 23.21.

The drawing for a simple jig for drilling a jacket tube is shown in Fig. 23.2. The work, shown in phantom line, is usually drawn in red, while the jig itself is drawn in black. In preparing the drawing, the visibility of the lines of the jig itself are as they would be if the work were not in place. This treatment of visibility along with showing the piece to be drilled in red is universal practice.

23.6

Parts for Jigs and Fixtures. When preparing the drawings for a jig or fixture every effort should be made to specify standard parts, washers, locating pins, rest buttons, rest pads, T-slot nuts, jig

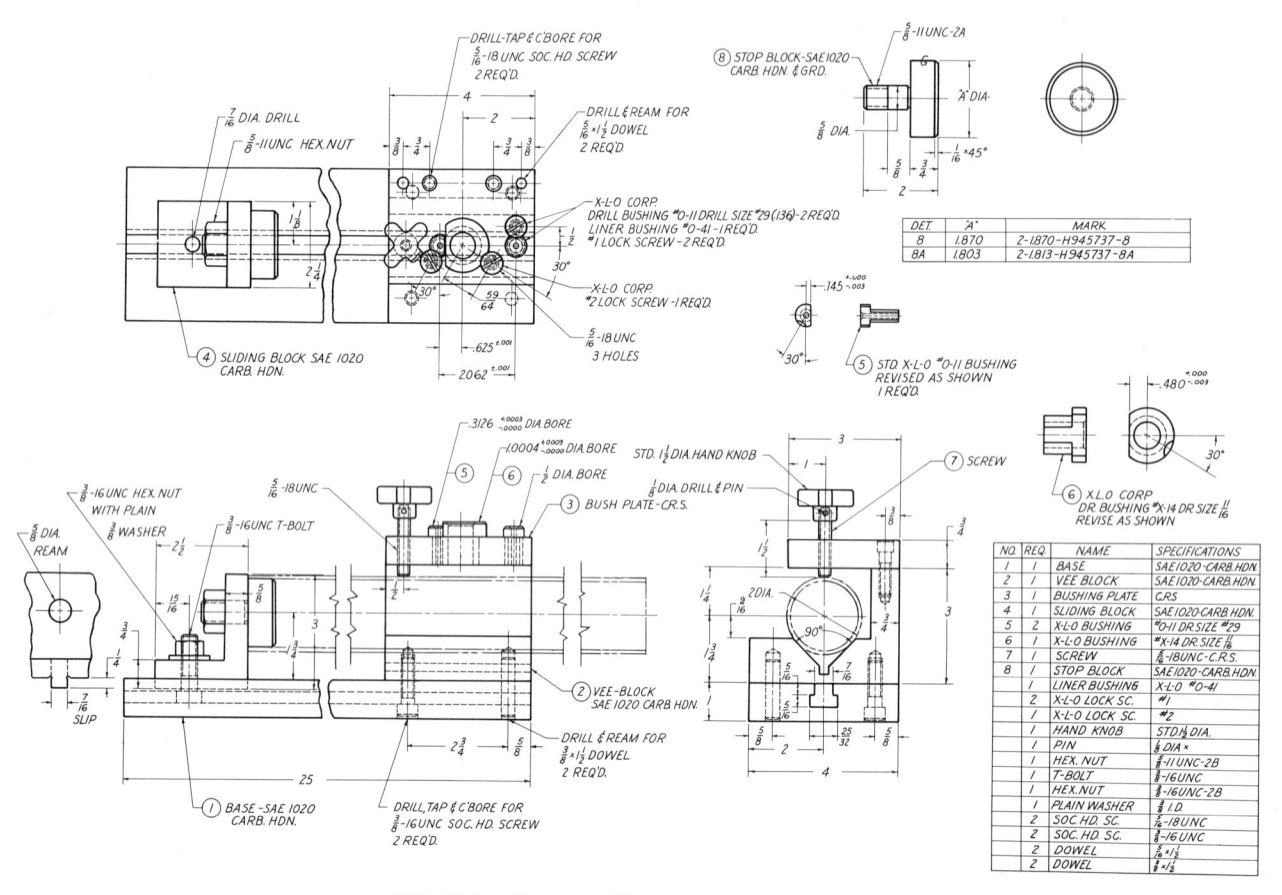

FIG. 23.2. Jig for drilling a jacket tube (*Courtesy Ross Gear Division of TRW Inc.*).

legs, straps, cams, knob screws, and clamps. The use of ready-made units makes it possible to produce a needed device at a lower cost. For some small parts, jig and fixture bodies may be obtained in varied standard arrangements. One can determine what parts can be purchased by consulting the catalogs of dealers and manufacturers (Fig. 23.3).

Spherical washers are often used under clamping nuts or knobs instead of standard plain washers because they permit a compensating adjustment for any misalignment due to the irregularity of an unfinished surface and, being ground and hardened, are less likely to wear. However, plain washers, if hardened and ground, serve just as well in most cases (Fig. 23.4).

Rest buttons, as the name implies, are used to support the workpiece for the machining operation. They are pins made of extremely hard tool steel that is wear resistant. Their use may eliminate the expense of machining a large flat surface. In addition, rest buttons reduce the possibility of trouble with chips, since they raise the workpiece sufficiently to provide needed clearance (Figs. 23.3 and 23.5).

When it is known that one series of workpieces will vary in one or more dimensions from another series, adjustable stop screws (jack screws) are used in place of rest buttons. Their use is also recommended whenever a satisfactory fit can be obtained between the workpiece and fixture at less expense by an adjust-and-try method than would be possible by producing rest buttons of exact size. There are several types available (Fig. 23.6).

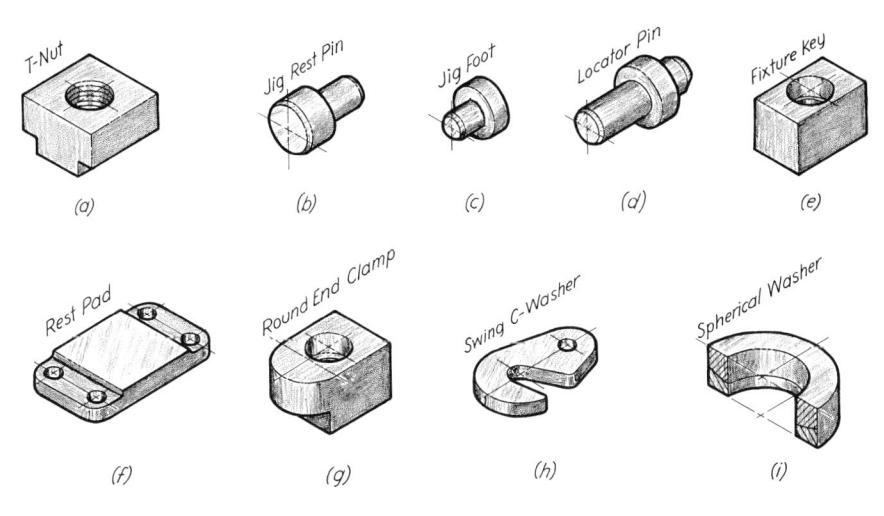

FIG. 23.3. Some standard parts.

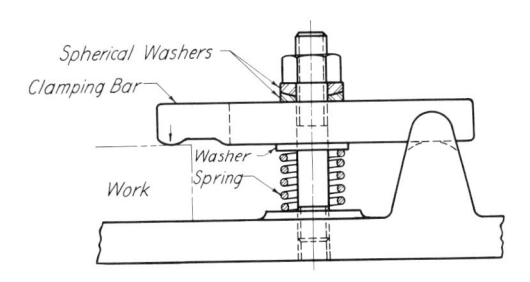

FIG. 23.4. Use of a spherical washer.

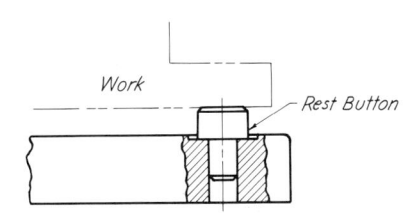

FIG. 23.5. Use of a rest button.

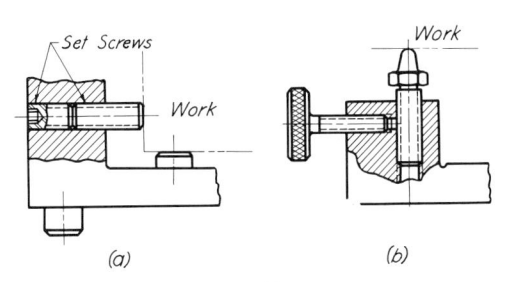

FIG. 23.6. Adjustable stop screws (jack screws).

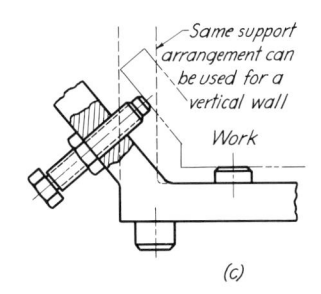

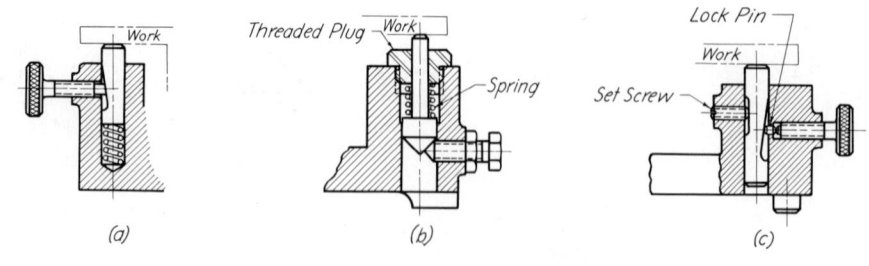

FIG. 23.7. Adjustable stop pins.

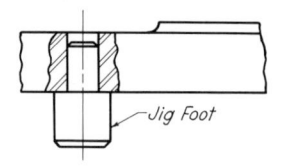

FIG. 23.8. Jig foot.

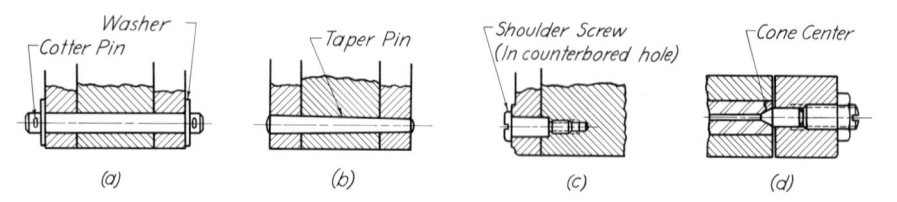

FIG. 23.9. Types of hinges.

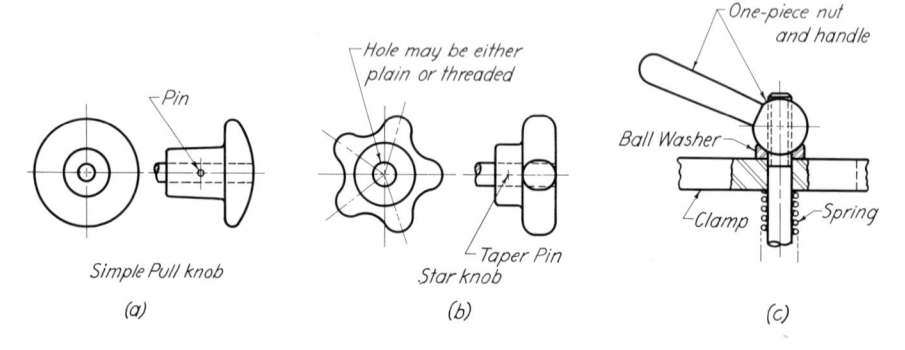

FIG. 23.10. Types of knobs and handles.

Adjustable stop pins (jack pins) are used when there is marked variation between individual workpieces that are rough castings or forgings (Fig. 23.7). Their use permits the operator to adjust each support separately as required. Adjustable stop pin devices should not be used at points where they will receive more or less direct pressure from a cutting tool.

Fig. 23.8 shows one type of jig foot that is commonly used.

A hinge in the simplest form involves the use of a plain pin, as shown in Fig. 23.9(a). Other types of hinges are the taper pin hinge, shoulder screw hinge, and conical point hinge. See Fig. 23.9(b), (c), and (d).

When a drill jig lid is a separate part of a jig and is not a swinging lid, care should be exercised in its design to make certain that it will be impossible for the operator to put it on in the wrong way.

Knobs and handles in a variety of forms are widely used on jigs and fixtures to facilitate hand operation of a clamping device (Fig. 23.10). Standardized knobs and handles should be used wherever possible.

Standard ANS drill bushings are of five different styles: plain (headless), head (shoulder) type, renewable-fixed type, slip type (removable), and liner. Each of these is shown in Fig. 23.11. They are available for all drill sizes (lettered, numbered, and fractional) in each of the five styles and may be purchased in as many as eight different lengths. See ANS B5.6–1962. Jig bushings also may be thought of as being either press fit, renewable fixed, renewable slip, screw, or special. A special bushing should not be used unless unusual circumstances make the use of a standard bushing impossible.

Press-fit bushings, headless and shoulder type, are forced permanently into place and it is not expected that they be replaced during the useful life of the jig [Fig. 23.11(a), (b), and (g)]. Press-fit bushings are used when there will be a limited production of a part. Ordinarily, the shoulder type is preferred over the plain headless form. However, when the holes to be drilled are so close that shoulder-type bushings cannot be used or when it is desirable to have the tops of bushings flush with the plate, the plain headless form must be used.

Renewable bushings, both the fixed and the slip type, are for use in a three-part arrangement with a liner and lock screw [(d), (e), and (h)]. They are used either where a bushing is to be more or less fixed but will wear out and must be replaced or where it is necessary that several bushings be interchanged in using the same jig. In general, it is intended that a fixed renewable bushing remain in place until it is worn out. Slip bushings can be pulled out to permit a secondary operation that requires a different inside diameter, as is the case when a drilling operation is to be followed by reaming, tapping, counterboring, and so forth. The use of the lock screw prevents their slipping upward and rotating. Slip bushings have knurled heads to facilitate their removal. A liner bushing (outer sleeve) used in combination with a slip bushing is permanently installed (pressed) into a jig. Slip bushings are interchangeable in a given size of fixed liner.

In the case of light work, where a soft metal is to be drilled, screw bushings are frequently specified for simple and inexpensive jigs [Fig. 23.11(i)]. Their use may be feasible if the screw bushing can provide sufficient holding effect and the requirement for accuracy can be satisfied. When considering their use, a designer must remember that any eccentricity between the thread and the drill hole of the bushing will result in holes being drilled off-center.

Special bushings should be used only when a standard bushing cannot meet the special conditions of a design, such as when two holes are so close together that standard bushings would interfere with each other [Fig. 23.11(f)].

23.7

Clamps and Clamping. Some form of clamping device is employed on nearly all jigs and fixtures. Their designing is an important part of a tool designer's work and in general commands a great deal of thoughtful attention on his part. Good design makes possible the rapid handling of the work; faulty design may lead to spoiled pieces. In general, the choice of a clamping device is dependent on the workpiece itself. Ordinary work of uniform shape usually requires only some form of simple clamp; complex castings, forgings, and parts of rather irregular shape require more intricate clamping devices that must be carefully designed. Sometimes it is difficult to make a choice from among the many types now employed and frequently one type may be as satisfactory as another. In making a choice the following points must be observed.

1. The workpiece must be held rigidly and accurately in position when under vibration or heavy pressure.

2. The clamping must be positive and pressure should be applied only to those surfaces of the workpiece that can withstand the stress that will be induced.

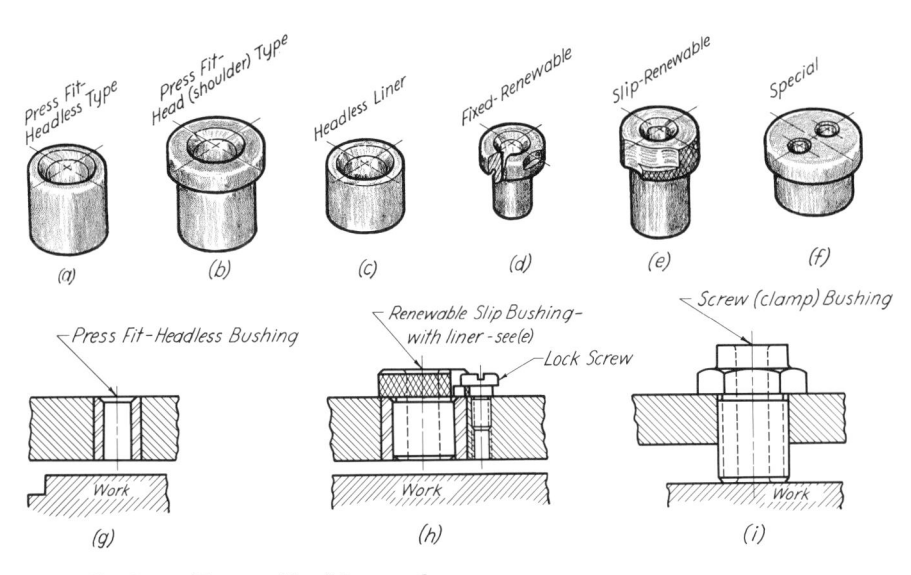

FIG. 23.11. Types of bushings and their placement.

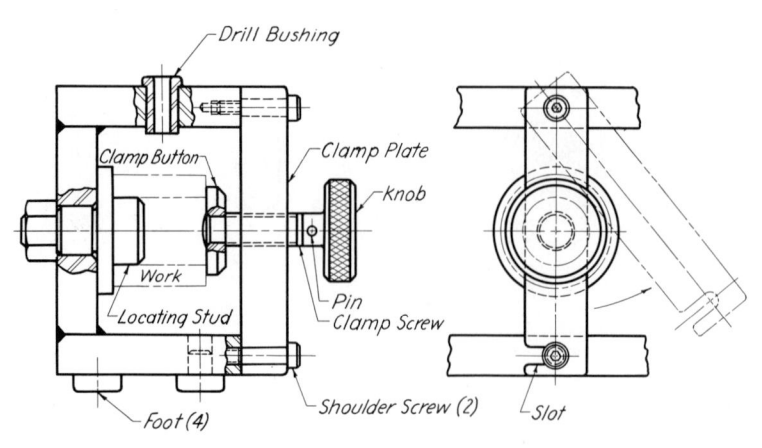

FIG. 23.12. Screw clamp.

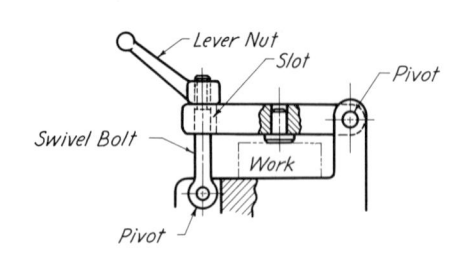

FIG. 23.13. Bolt type lever clamp.

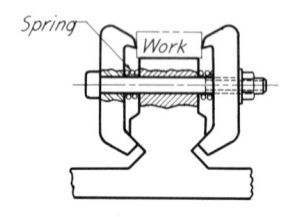

FIG. 23.14. Wedge clamp.

3. The clamp must not produce any noticeable distortion of the workpiece that could in turn lead to inaccuracy in the location of drilled holes.

4. The clamp must not mar the surface of the workpiece.

5. The clamp must permit easy loading and unloading in as short a time as possible to ensure maximum production at the lowest labor cost. The design must allow the operator to locate the workpiece quickly and accurately in proper position.

6. The clamp design must ensure safety of operation.

Although there are numerous and varied forms of clamps, all types incorporate one or more of the following basic elements: (1) screw, (2) hook, (3) wedge, (4) cam, (5) toggle, and (6) rack and pinion. Several methods of clamping will be discussed in the following paragraphs. One may obtain more detailed information and a more complete presentation of methods in the books listed in the bibliography of this text.

Screw clamps are quite commonly used because they are capable of providing adequate force with very little tendency to loosen under vibration. Since the action of a simple screw clamp is relatively slow, numerous combination devices have been developed as adjuncts to the screw to speed up clamping action (Fig. 23.4). Figure 23.12 shows a type of screw latch clamp that is quite commonly used.

Lever clamps are frequently used for drill jigs. This style of clamp holds the workpiece in the jig through pressure from one or more bearing points (Fig. 23.13).

Since so-called simple wedge clamps are time consuming to use, wedge elements are usually combined with screws and springs or levers in order to avoid the requirement for extra tools that might be mislaid and to speed up the clamping action. Figure 23.14 shows a pinch clamp employing a pair of wedges.

Figure 23.15(a) shows a clamp with a cam handle. In (b), the circumference of the cam contacts the locator (V-block) as shown. This design provides for the quick application and release of pressure.

23.8
Fixtures. Fixtures are designed for varied uses. They may be classified as vise, boring, milling machine, tapping, lathe, grinding, broaching, honing, welding, or checking fixtures. Most readers should be familiar with the principle of the vise. Checking fixtures, as the name implies, are used to check accuracy of production. Figure 23.16 shows a special milling machine fixture that is designed to hold a cover while a keyway is being cut. A boring fixture is shown in Fig. 23.22. The drawing presented has been prepared as a drawing exercise and is not to be thought of as an example of an industrial drawing.

23.9
Tool Drawings. When the product drawings for a structure or mechanism have been completed by the engineering department, they are released to the production division, where a tool routing sheet and a worksheet are prepared by a process engineer. A

routing sheet lists needed manufacturing operations in proper sequence and specifies which tools and machines are to be used. It also gives information for checking production accuracy and may specify the type of inspection instruments. The worksheets contain detailed information concerning the manufacturing processes.

In some cases, clearance specifications between mating parts may be given when critical situations are known to exist. These sheets furnish information needed by the tool designer and tool draftsman and ensure that current machine-shop and production practices will be followed.

The drawings for making the holding devices and special tools needed for the various operations are known as *tool drawings*, and they are prepared by the

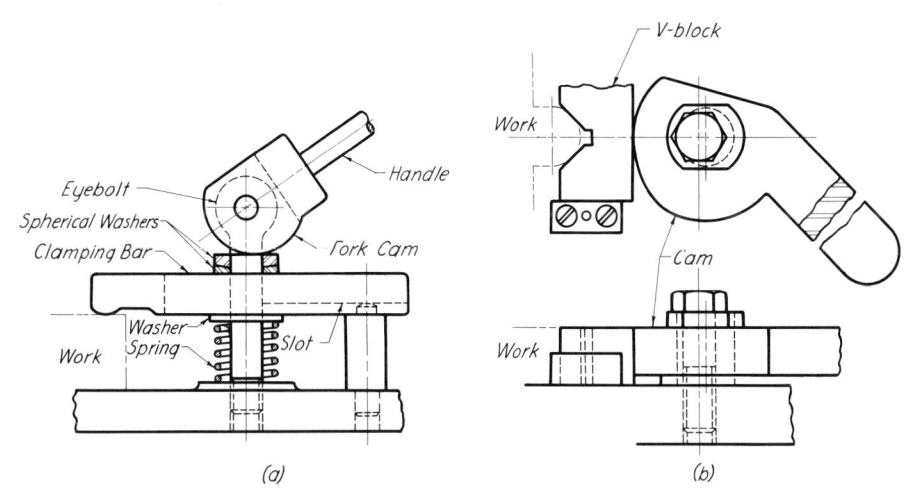

FIG. 23.15. Cam clamps.

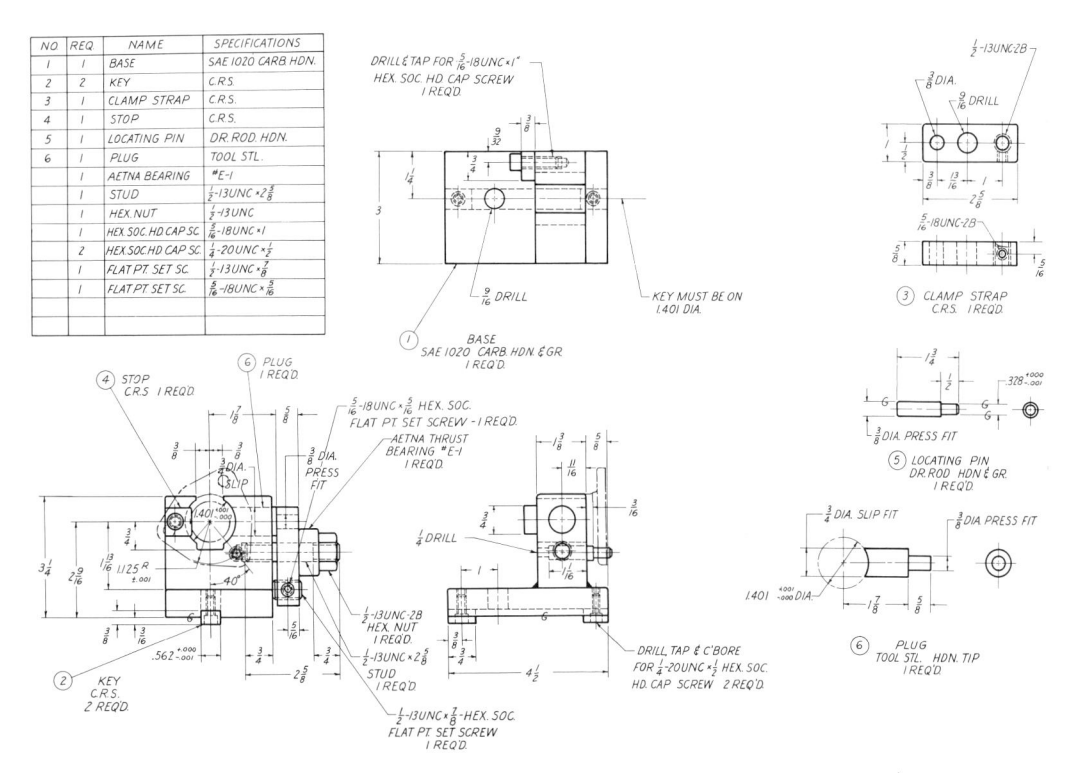

FIG. 23.16. Milling machine fixture for cutting a keyway (upper cover) (*Courtesy Ross Gear Division of TRW Inc.*).

tool engineering branch of the production division. Along with the routing sheet and worksheet, the tool designer and tool draftsman must have catalogs at hand that furnish information about standard parts and devices that may be purchased ready-made in standard arrangements.

In the planning stage of the development of a jig or fixture, freehand sketches may be used by the designer to integrate his thoughts and record information on standard parts. Such sketches assist the designer in preparing the accurate design layouts that are needed, particularly for complicated situations and where different tool draftsmen will be assigned the task of preparing the working drawings.

The tool draftsman starts with an outline of the workpiece traced in red using phantom lines. Then he draws the outline assembly around the workpiece using black lines (Fig. 23.2). Where a black line of the assembly drawing coincides with one of the red lines of the workpiece, the black line is drawn over the phantom red line. In other words, on tool drawings the black lines are given precedence over the red ones. The practice of showing the workpiece in red and the outline of the jig or fixture in black permits easy reading of the drawing by enabling the reader to distinguish quickly between the workpiece and the jig or fixture holding it. An assembly layout may show locating dimensions and toleranced dimensions for critical conditions.

After the design assembly layout has been completed and approved, prints are made for the use of the tool draftsman, who is to make the detail drawings. The draftsman or group of draftsmen under a squad leader prepares drawings for all nonstandard and altered standard parts, placing several detail drawings on each detail sheet, as space will permit without overcrowding. Each detail drawing is identified by the same part number shown for it on the assembly layout. In addition to showing the part number in a small circle, it is customary to letter, just below the drawing, the part name, part material, and number required for one unit (Fig. 23.16). In the case of relatively simple jigs and fixtures, the parts are dimensioned, where possible, directly on the layout so that the layout becomes a working drawing. Those parts that cannot be dimensioned conveniently on the layout are detailed in an open space adjacent to the layout (Fig. 23.16). Of course, additional sheets may be used if necessary.

The title given to each detail sheet must be identical with that given on the assembly drawing, except the word DETAILS replaces the word ASSEMBLY. With the assembly layout sheet being No. 1, it is good practice to number the detail sheets 2, 3, 4 and so forth, and to show the total number of sheets of the set on each drawing in the space provided in the title block. This practice makes it possible to determine whether or not all of the drawings of a set are at hand when they are being checked or used in the shop by the toolmakers.

Part numbers for all parts are placed on the assembly layout in "balloons" ($\frac{3}{8}$-in. circles) (Fig. 23.16). The leaders should be straight lines that need not be parallel. Only for added clearness should they be drawn with a change in direction. It is good practice to arrange the "balloons" in either a horizontal or a vertical alignment.

The tool draftsman must have a knowledge of standard machine and tool parts and he must be familiar with the ANSI Y 14 Drafting Standards. The drafting standards are extensive and may be purchased in sections as needed. See Appendix, ANSI Standards. In addition to the ANSI drafting standards, it is customary to adhere to supplementary company standards that have been prepared to secure conformity in manufacturing and filing.

Generally, base-line dimensioning is used to ensure accuracy in locating and boring holes in jigs. While it is the usual practice to use either the top or left edge, any finished surface may be a base line. The advantages of base-line dimensioning are that (1) each dimension is independent, (2) the possibility of cumulative errors in a series of dimensions is avoided, (3) the toolmaker is relieved of any trigonometric calculations, and (4) the work can be laid out better on a jig-boring machine.

The number, identifying name, and number required per unit are given for each part in the stock list. For designed parts, the material and size of stock are listed. Standard parts may be further identified and specified by giving their catalog numbers.

The title block contains all of the information usually given in title blocks on ordinary machine drawings but additional spaces are provided for recording other pertinent items of information, such as model number, operation number, tool number, machine number, and, if needed, department number.

23.10
Dies and Die Drawings. Since standard die-sets may be found in manufacturing catalogs in different styles and sizes, it is the usual practice of tool designers to analyze the workpiece carefully and then select a suitable die-set on which the required punches and dies can be mounted.

A standard die-set has three principal parts, namely, the punch holder (upper shoe), die holder (lower shoe), and guideposts. Other parts of a standard combination are the shank and guidepost bushings. The shank provides for fastening the punch holder to the ram of the press. The guideposts ensure accurate alignment of the punch with the die under all conditions (Fig. 23.17).

Specific information on die design may be found in the several books listed in the bibliography. It is recommended that one consult the handy reference book, titled *Practical Design of Manufacturing Tools, Dies, and Fixtures,* that was prepared under the direction of the Society of Manufacturing Engineers.

The fundamental press-work operations involving the use of punches and dies are (1) plain blanking, (2) piercing, (3) bending or forming, (4) drawing, (5) coining, and (6) assembling. Die assembly drawings usually show three or four views of the assembled die and the same general procedure is followed in their preparation as for jig and fixture drawings except for a modification of the theoretical arrangement of the views as shown in Fig. 23.18. In this illustration, the front view (front elevation) shows both of the main members (punch and die) in working position. The plan view of the lower shoe (die holder) is in the position of a top view directly above the front view. Aligned horizontally with this latter view is the plan view of the upper shoe (punch holder) shown as it would be seen looking upward from below. This is done so that the diemaker has a plan of the actual layout from which to work and to conserve space. The front view, always in section, shows the die as it would be seen from the front of the press and the views of the upper and lower shoes show all parts attached as they would be when in operation. Small part-section views and auxiliary views are used when needed. If a side view is necessary, it should be drawn in section. The assembly drawing should give general information and show the important dimensions needed by the diemaker, such as the shut height of the die, shrank diameter, the type and size of press, and the press stroke. On the die assembly drawing, each component part is numbered as shown in Fig. 23.19.

When it is necessary to detail a designed die, it is the usual practice to place the

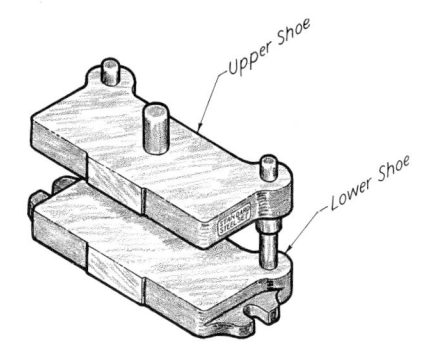

FIG. 23.17. A typical die set.

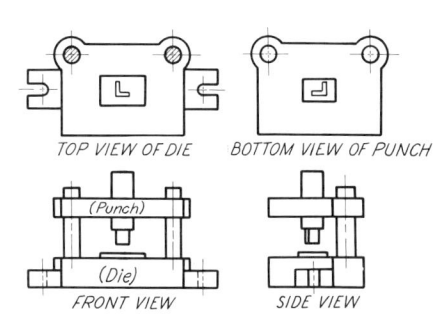

FIG. 23.18. Arrangement of views for a punch and die drawing.

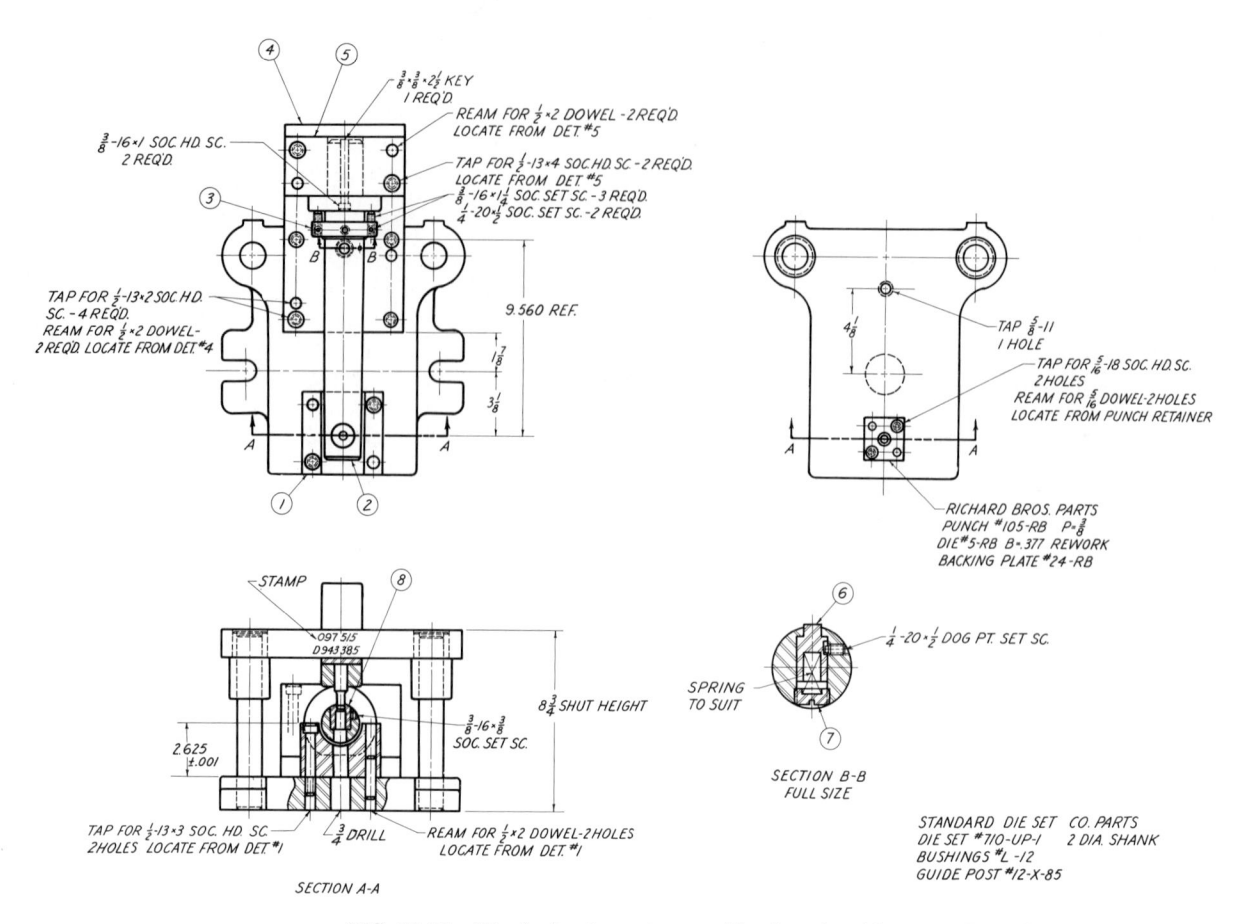

FIG. 23.19. Die design layout assembly drawing (*Courtesy Ross Gear Division of TRW Inc.*).

details on sheets separate from the assembly drawing.

A material list should be given on the die assembly drawing. This should show the number of each part and specify the rough material size.

PROBLEMS

1. Prepare the necessary drawings for the drill jig shown in Fig. 23.20. This jig has been designed for drilling a sleeve.

2. Prepare the necessary drawings for the tumble jig shown in Fig. 23.21. The jig has been designed to drill two diametrically opposite holes in the hub of a spiral bevel gear. See also Fig. 23.12.

3. Design a jig for drilling the plunger shown in Fig. 17.49.

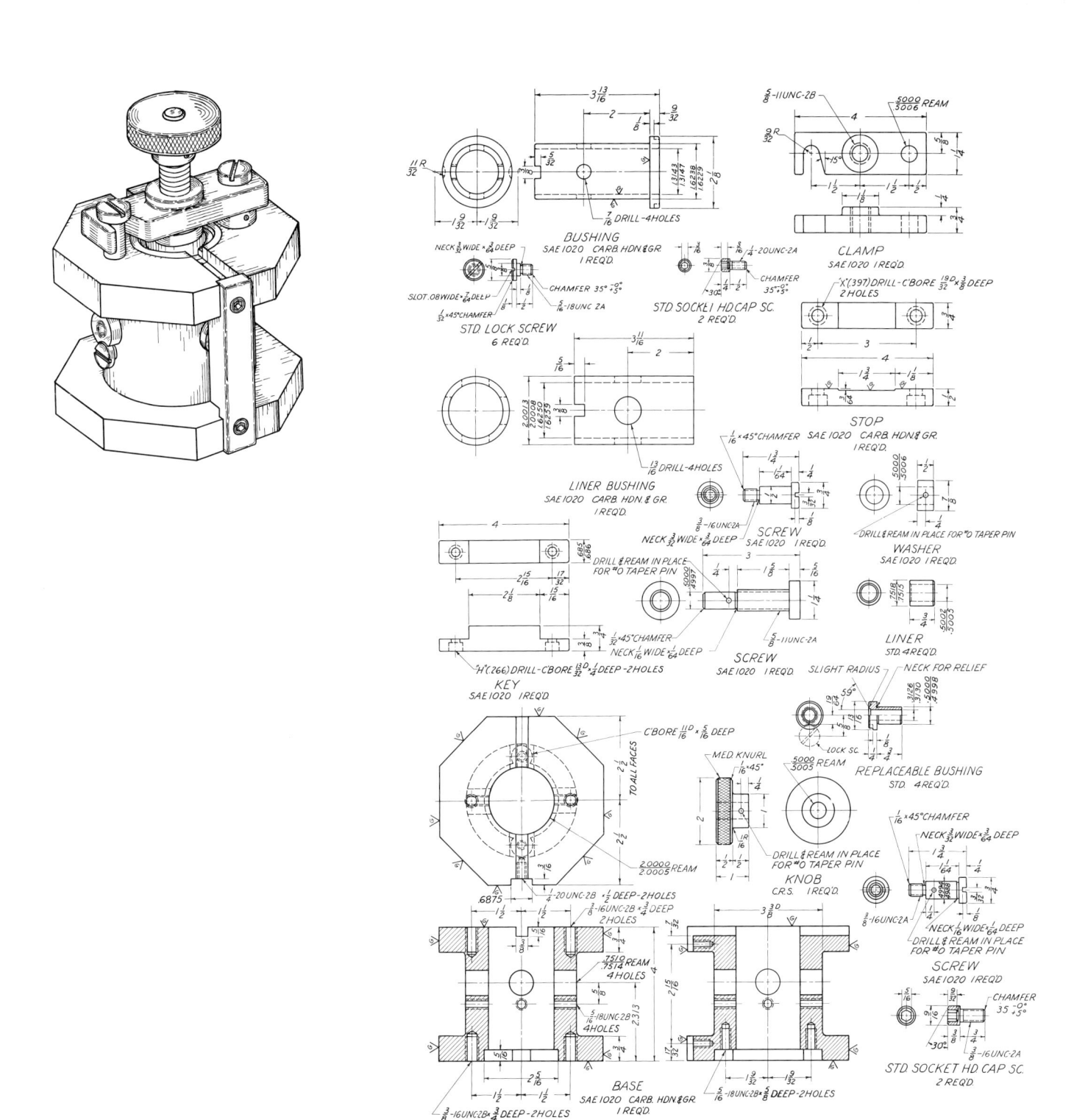

FIG. 23.20. Drill jig, milling, grinding fixture (*Courtesy Ross Gear Division of TRW Inc.*).

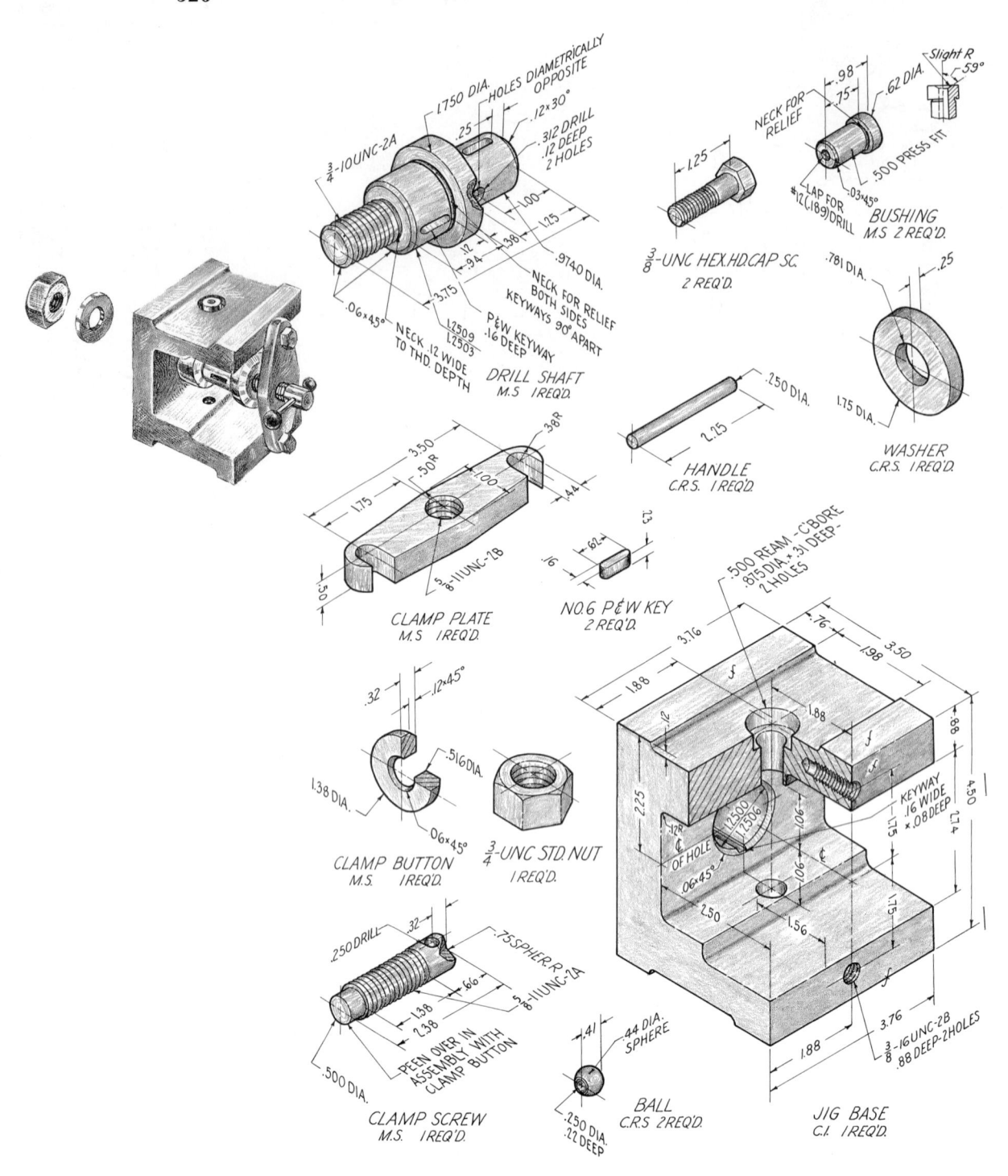

FIG. 23.21. Tumble jig (*Courtesy Fairfield Mfg. Co.*).

CHAP. 23 / TOOL DESIGN AND TOOL DRAWINGS 527

4. Design a fixture for milling the slot in the adjusting screw shown in Fig. 17.40.

5. Design a fixture for the ⅛-in. sawcut in the torch holder shown in Fig. 16.94.

6. Prepare the necessary drawings for the boring fixture shown in Fig. 23.22.

PART NO.	NAME	MATERIAL	NO. REQ'D
1	HOLDER	C.R.S	1
2	CLAMP STRAP	C.R.S	1
3	CLAMP	C.R.S.	1
4	CLAMP SCREW	C.R.S	1
5	PLUG	BRASS	1
6	THUMB SCREW	C.R.S.	1
7	REST BUTTON	TOOL STEEL	2
8	BUSHING	TOOL STEEL	1
9	PIN	DRILL ROD	1

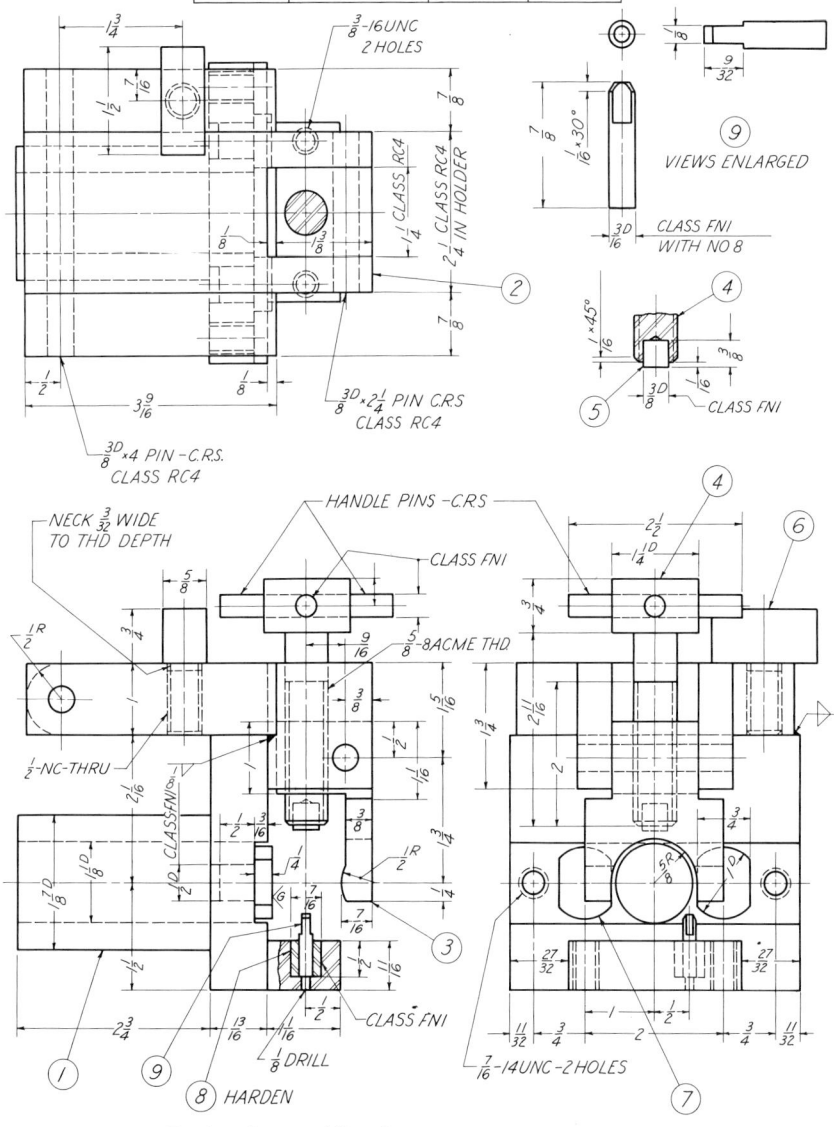

FIG. 23.22. Boring fixture (*Courtesy Ross Gear Division of TRW Inc.*).

TRS Tetrahedral Research Satellite ERS-1 (Solar Cell Degradation Experiments)
(*Courtesy TRW Systems Group*)

Electronic Drawings*

24.1

Introduction. Different kinds of drawings are needed in the design, manufacture, and use of electronic equipment (Fig. 24.1). The preparation of these drawings, particularly schematic and connection diagrams, requires a working knowledge of specialized symbolic forms and conventions. These conventions vary somewhat according to the product and the field of application, which, broadly speaking, may be classified as communications and commercial equipment, military, scientific research, or industrial control.

Engineering sketches are prepared first to show the layout of a proposed system or circuit or the features of existing equipment. Finished drawings are then made by a draftsman who follows the instructions given in the sketch. Usually, many details are left to the draftsman's discretion; however, it is the engineer's responsibility to make sure that the final work is correct and complete. In all instances, electronic drawings should be prepared in accordance with the relevant technical standards and specifications so that they will be acceptable for the particular applications.

24.2

Electronic Drawings and Diagrams. The most specialized work in electronic drafting concerns the preparation of symbolic diagrams. In contrast to mechanical drawings, which represent objects, symbolic diagrams impart technical information in abstract form. Since these diagrams are intended to show the function of a system or a circuit they lack intrinsic dimensions and, in general, do not show physical details of the parts.

Important examples of these specialized drawings are as follows: block diagrams, which show the overall organization of a

*Prepared by George Shiers, Santa Barbara City College.

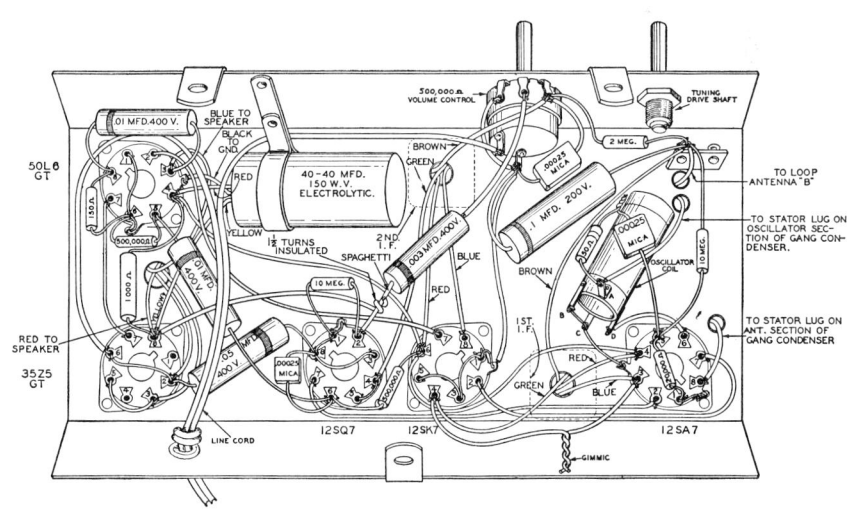

FIG. 24.1. Pictorial diagram (*Courtesy Allied Radio Corp.*).

529

system; schematic diagrams, which show the component parts and electrical details of a circuit; and connection diagrams, which show the wiring and connections between the component parts of an assembly. Other drawings and artwork are needed in the design and processing of printed circuits.

All these drawings are interrelated with the physical assembly and with each other. In many instances further material, such as lists, tables, and charts, may be needed to supplement assembly drawings and electronic diagrams, particularly for production breakdowns, test procedures, and service manuals.

24.3
Graphical Standards. Technical publications dealing with standardized engineering practices are available to guide the engineer and draftsman in the preparation of electronic diagrams. These standards have been established by technical committees representing professional societies, trade associations, government agencies, and various manufacturers and users. The most useful standards for electronic purposes are those that concern graphical symbols, letter symbols, reference designations, abbreviations, color codes, and electrical diagrams, as given in the following list.

ANSI—American National Standards Institute, Inc.
   Y14.15—Electrical Diagrams
   Y32.2—Graphical Symbols for Electrical Diagrams
   Z10.1—Abbreviations for Scientific and Engineering Terms
   Z10.5—Letter Symbols for Electrical Quantities
   Z32.13—Abbreviations for Use on Drawings

EIA—Electronic Industries Association
   GEN-101—Color Coding for Numerical Values
   GEN-102—Preferred Values
   REC-108—Color Coding

IEEE—The Institute of Electrical and Electronics Engineers, Inc.
(These publications were formerly issued by The Institute of Radio Engineers, Inc.)
   51 IRE 21.S1—Standards on Abbreviations of Radio-Electronic Terms
   54 IRE 21.S1—Standards on Graphical Symbols for Electrical Diagrams
   57 IRE 21.S1—Standards on Letter Symbols and Mathematical Signs
   57 IRE 21.S2—Standards on Reference Designations for Electrical and Electronic Equipment
   57 IRE 21.S3—Standards on Graphical Symbols for Semiconductor Devices

MIL—U.S. Government Printing Office
   MIL-STD-12 —Abbreviations for Use on Drawings
   –15 —Electrical and Electronic Symbols
   –16 —Electrical and Electronic Reference Designations
   –122—Color Code for Chassis Wiring for Electronic Equipment
   –283—Letter Symbols for Electrical and Electronic Quantities

NEMA—*National Electrical
   Manufacturers Association*
   IC-1959—Industrial Control

NMTBA—*National Machine Tool
   Builders' Association*
   Electrical Standards for Industrial
   Equipment
   Machine Tool Electrical Standards

These and related standards have been developed in the interest of clear documentation and accurate terminology. Their use promotes efficient engineering methods leading to economies in time, materials, and labor. An acquaintance with these standards, therefore, forms an essential part of the background of engineers, draftsmen, technicians, and supervisors engaged in the electronics industry.

24.4
Graphical Symbols. A graphical symbol is a geometrical design that represents an electronic device or component part in a circuit. Most symbols are composed of two or more basic elements, each of which represents a functional part of the device. Some commonly used electronic symbols are shown approximately full-size, with their letter designations, in Fig. 24.2.

Graphical symbols should be drawn in proportion to one another and with clear details so that the significance will be unmistakable. Symbol templates are widely used for drawing schematic diagrams. Printed designs on adhesive sheets (appliqués) are also employed, particularly for ink work and drawings prepared for publication. These drafting aids save time, avoid tedious construction of individual symbols, and promote uniformity.

24.5
Reference Designations. Component designations, such as R1, C3, etc., are added to each symbol to indicate the class of

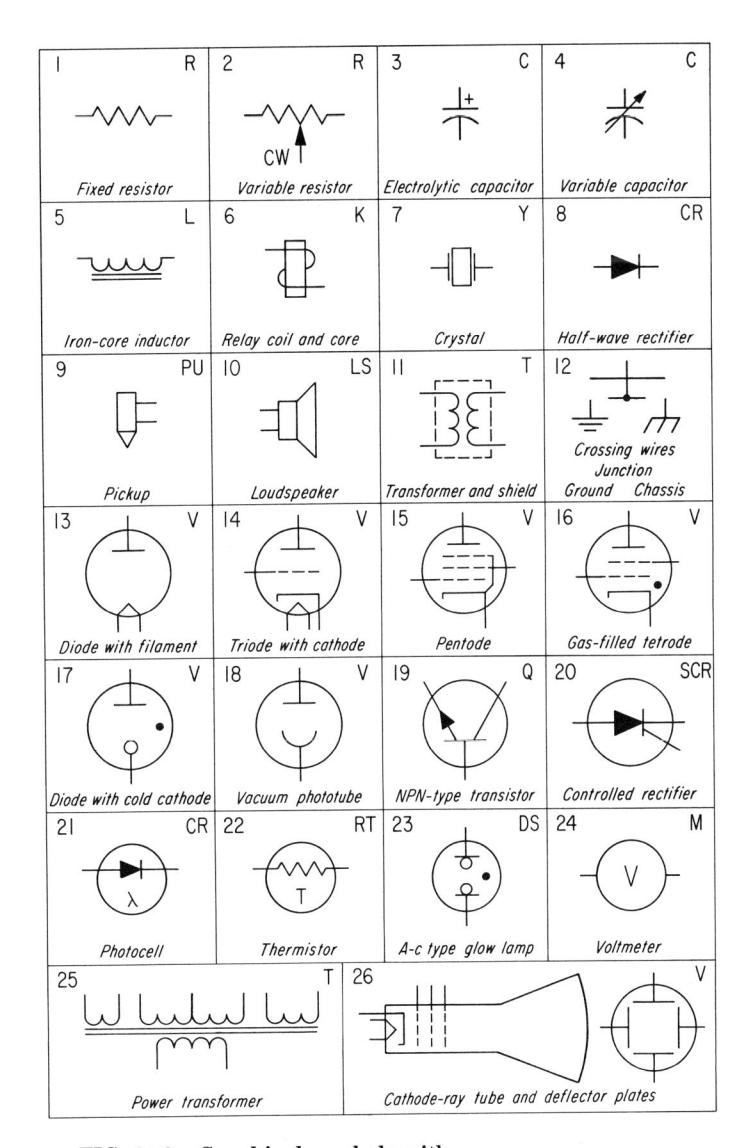

FIG. 24.2. Graphical symbols with reference designations.

component and its position in a circuit. These designations are assigned during the development stages of a product and usually appear as component markings on the actual equipment.

Other designations or symbol references may be required in a drawing to show the part value, type, electrical rating, or specific characteristics of a component. Examples are 15K, for a 15,000-Ω (ohms) resistor, where $K = 1000$; 6.8 MH (or mH), for a coil with an inductance of 6.8 millihenries; 2/400, as applied to a 2-μF (microfarad-MF) capacitor with a maximum working rating of 400 V (volts) dc; and 5–25, as applied to the range in micromicrofarads ($\mu\mu$F, or MMF) of an adjustable capacitor.

The following examples are with reference to Fig. 24.2.

Item 2. The letters CW indicate the direction of the slider when the shaft is rotated clockwise. An arrowhead may be used instead.

Item 3. The plus sign indicates a polarized capacitor, such as an electrolytic type.

Item 4. The arrowhead signifies variability.

Item 5. Parallel lines indicate a magnetic core.

Item 11. Broken lines signify a shield or screen, either electrical or magnetic, or a mechanical enclosure. A broken line that connects two or more symbols also denotes a mechanical linkage.

Item 12. Crossing lines that are not connected are drawn straight; a loop or saddle at the crossover point is not necessary. The junction dot is optional and may be eliminated provided the junction is obvious. Connections to a ground point or to a chassis or frame are distinguished by different symbols.

Item 15. Grids in electron tubes are numbered starting with the one nearest the cathode. A suppressor grid (No. 3) may be connected to the cathode internally, as shown, or to a separate pin in the tube base.

Item 16. Gaseous tubes are distinguished from high-vacuum devices by a solid dot conveniently located in the symbol, as shown.

Item 19. For *PNP*-type transistors the arrowhead on the emitter is reversed.

Item 21. Conductive type of photocell employing a semiconductor. "Lambda" signifies light sensitivity.

Item 22. The letter T denotes temperature sensitivity.

Item 24. Meter function is shown by an appropriate letter designation.

24.6

Data Sheets. Manufacturers' data sheets, technical bulletins, and product manuals contain full particulars of each class of device. These publications, such as tube, diode, transistor, and rectifier handbooks, should be consulted for basing diagrams, lead arrangements, socket and terminal connections, polarities, part codings, and the like.

24.7

Block Diagrams. Rectangular and other symbols in block diagrams may represent integral parts of a system, self-contained units, complete circuits, or single functional stages, according to the purpose of the drawing. The blocks are customarily located and joined with flow lines so that the overall progression is from left to right. Auxiliary items, such as power sources, are placed below the major blocks. In general, all blocks should be drawn the same size, with other symbols in proportion, and arranged in an orderly manner with equal spacings between adjacent blocks and flow lines.

The lines to each block also follow a similar sequence: input on the left, output on the right, with auxiliary lines usually at the bottom. In more complex drawings, where the flow paths may be somewhat circulatory, the symbols should be located to preserve the most logical sequence in the clearest possible manner with a minimum of crossovers.

Two representative block diagrams are shown in Fig. 24.3. In the computer system diagram (A) the blocks are drawn large enough to accommodate the lettering. The paths for control signals and data are distinguished by different line symbols, and a legend is furnished accordingly. The flow directions are indicated by arrowheads, which may be placed either on or beside the lines.

The control system diagram (B) includes some special block-type symbols, also some lettering adjacent to the symbols. Graphical symbols may be used in block diagrams, particularly for auxiliary items, such as antennas, grounds, switches, and various input and output devices.

24.8
Schematic Diagrams. A schematic diagram shows the electrical functions of a circuit without regard to the physical layout of the actual parts. Circuit components, wiring devices, and the interconnections are represented in a schematic by graphical symbols. Suitable part designations and other lettering must be furnished for reference. These diagrams are used in designing and developing circuits, in manufacturing and testing a product, and for installing and servicing complete equipment.

Part of a complex schematic, shown in Fig. 24.4, illustrates how a large amount of circuit data can be presented in an orderly manner. In laying out this kind of diagram, care is required during the planning stages to ensure proper distribution of the parts and to avoid undue crowding, wasted space, or excessive crossovers. The finished diagram should show the circuit in a logical sequence proceeding from left to right, as for block diagrams.

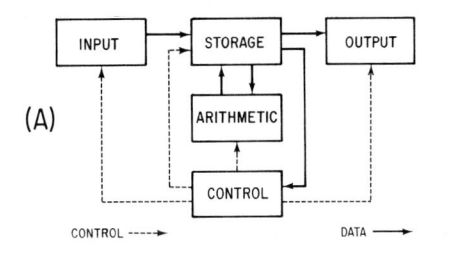

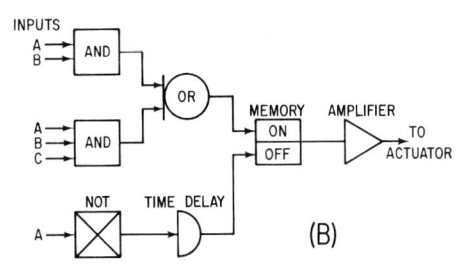

FIG. 24.3. Typical block diagrams. (A) Computer system, (B) Control system with special symbols. (From G. Shiers, *Electronic Drafting* (Englewood Cliffs, N.J.: Prentice-Hall, Inc.))

24.9
Schematic Projection. Most electronic circuits consist of several functional blocks, or stages. Each stage normally contains an active device, such as a tube or transistor, and the associated circuit components. Usually, stages are connected in cascade, whereby the output from one stage is fed to the input of the succeeding stage. In general, the symbols representing a single stage are grouped together. Each stage requires the four following basic connections: signal input and output, power supply line, and common line.

Using *horizontal* projection, stages are located between the power bus line and the common line, as shown in Figs. 24.4 and 24.6. When the *vertical* method of projection is used, the power bus is omitted and the circuit layout is arranged somewhat differently with the power sup-

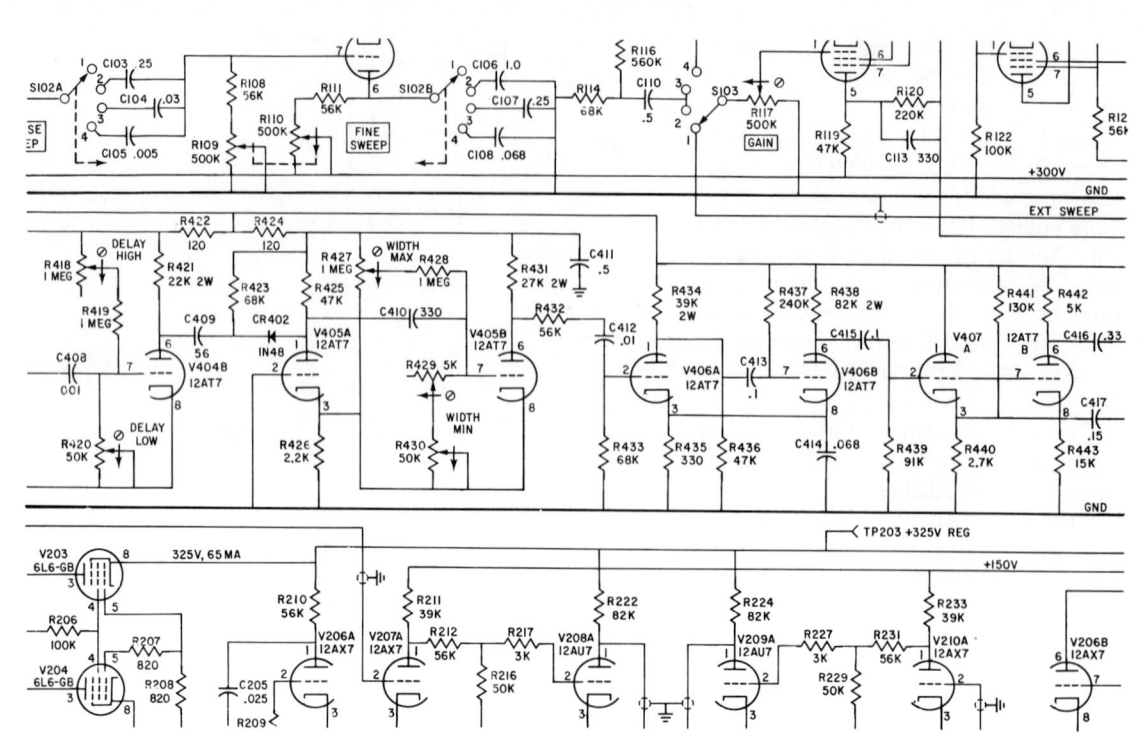

FIG. 24.4. Part of a complex drawing showing a typical schematic pattern. (From G. Shiers, *Electronic Drafting* (Englewood Cliffs, N.J.: Prentice-Hall, Inc.))

ply lines located vertically between the stages, as shown in Fig. 24.5. In both methods the diagram may be *complete*, showing all bus lines and common circuit paths (Fig. 24.6); or these lines may be isolated, with terminating arrowheads and designations to show the respective connections (Fig. 24.5). As a rule, horizontal projection is commonly used for military and some industrial applications, whereas the vertical projection method is favored for most commercial and radio communication equipment.

24.10

Circuit Analysis. In the early stages of electronic design suitable components are selected and connected to achieve a certain result. An engineering sketch, such as Fig. 24.5, is drawn to show the proposed circuit. Component types and values may be given in this sketch or in a separate parts list. With the parts mounted on a temporary base, or "breadboard," the circuit is then tested and modified as may be required. As soon as the circuit features have been established a finished schematic is drawn from the engineering data.

The first step in laying out a schematic diagram is to analyze the circuit sequence and electrical details so that the technical requirements and data are clearly understood. Major elements common to all schematic diagrams that should be recognized are as follows: (1) graphical symbols;

(2) symbol grouping; (3) flow paths for signals and power; (4) operating functions; and (5) reference designations, electrical values, and similar identities.

It may be helpful to mark up a sketch temporarily in order to show the preferred symbol grouping, as indicated by the broken lines in Fig. 24.5. In this diagram the functional blocks are marked ①–⑦. Flow paths for the signal ⑧ and the operating power ⑨ are shown, also mechanical linkage ⑩ between the variable capacitors, which actually consist of two units in a common assembly.

Symbols may be divided where they refer to a multifunction device, such as a dual-triode, multicircuit switch, or a multiple-contact relay. Symbols for each part of a device, with suitable references, are placed in the respective circuit paths. Clarity is improved, and drafting time is saved by the elimination of long lines and the reduction of crossovers.

Figure 24.4 shows the use of split symbols where each half of tubes V405, 406, and 407 are drawn apart to allow space for the interstage circuits. These sections may be located anywhere in a diagram, as for V206 in the bottom circuit. This diagram also shows the omission of tube heaters, again in the interest of simplicity and clarity. Conventionally, tube heaters and associated items, such as low-voltage pilot lamps, are drawn as subcircuits below the main part of a diagram.

24.11

Modular Layouts. Because of the abstract nature of the data and the "dimensionless" form, schematic diagrams are best laid out according to a modular plan. Cross-section or quadrille paper with eight rulings per inch is suitable for developing most diagrams. Symbol sizes, symbol locations, and the needed drawing areas can be estimated or specified easily and accurately in terms of grid units with this method. If necessary, a large diagram

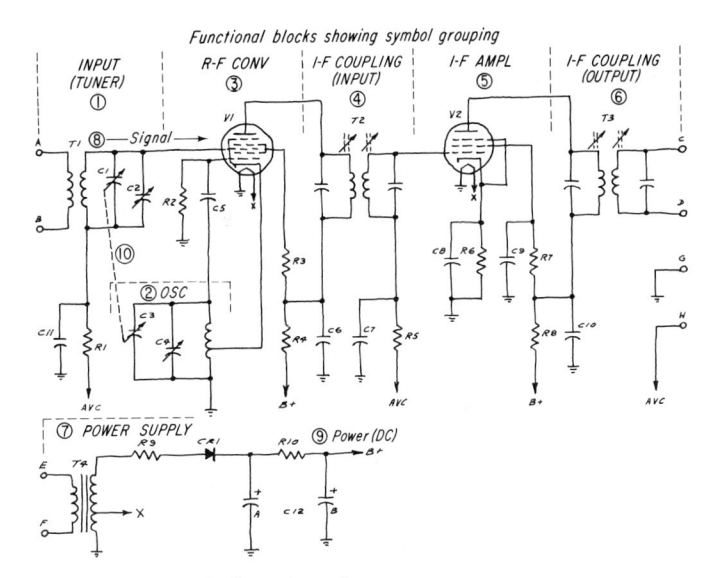

FIG. 24.5. Typical engineering sketch, marked up to show symbol grouping. (From G. Shiers, *Electronic Drafting* (Englewood Cliffs, N.J.: Prentice-Hall, Inc.))

may be broken down into sections containing several stages. Each section may then be developed separately in trial layouts, revised, and fitted together ready for the final drawing.

24.12

Trial Layouts. Figure 24.6(A) is an example of a trial layout, with typical spacings in grid units marked on each axis. The shaded areas represent spaces for required lettering. The solid dots denote tube pin numbers. Symbols should be aligned on common grid lines but staggered if required to permit adequate lettering. Common layout faults to be avoided are also shown. These consist of lines too close to symbols (B), (C), (D), and (G); symbols too close (E), (F), and (J); inconsistent symbols (E); insufficient lettering space (H); and symbols off-center (J).

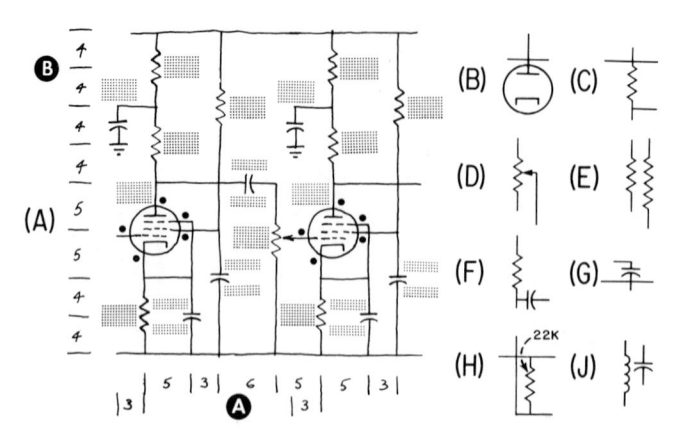

536 PART V / DESIGN AND COMMUNICATION DRAWING IN SPECIALIZED FIELDS

FIG. 24.6. Trial layout. (A) Preliminary layout for a two-stage amplifier showing typical spacings, (B) through (J) layout errors to be avoided. (From G. Shiers, *Electronic Drafting* (Englewood Cliffs, N.J.: Prentice-Hall, Inc.))

The grid units shown in Fig. 24.6 represent typical dimensions suitable for most schematic layouts. Thus, lengthwise: four–six units for a capacitor, eight units for a resistor or inductor, and nine or ten units between the plate and cathode connections of a tube, or between the emitter and collector connections of a transistor. Horizontal spacings will depend on the specific circuits, symbol arrangements, amount of lettering, and the method of projection.

Sufficient space should be allotted for auxiliary circuits, such as filters, and for switches, terminal blocks, connectors, and the related lettering. If the lettering size corresponds with the grid scale it will be in proportion to the symbols. Complex diagrams containing several hundred symbols, or other diagrams designed for a compact space, as in equipment manuals, can be drawn to a smaller *scale*, such as $1/10$ in., with lettering to correspond. Using a modular plan and trial layout as described, a finished diagram may be drawn to an enlarged or reduced scale by selecting a suitable grid background.

24.13
Placement of Designations. The parts in a schematic diagram have to be identified for descriptive purposes, cross references, circuit testing, and parts replacement. Numbers should be assigned in sequence from left to right and top to bottom. Lettering should be placed close to and, where possible, centered on the respective symbol.

Typical forms of reference designations and their locations are shown in Fig. 24.7. Several conventions are given, as follows: (A) part designation, R41; ohms value, 1800; wattage rating, 10; type, wire-wound (WW); (B) terminal numbers; (C) lead colors, T3; (E) terminal markings, C29; test point voltage, TP3; relay K12 coil resistance, 500 Ω.

24.14
Drawing Notes. Repetitious lettering in schematic diagrams may be avoided if items with common characteristics are

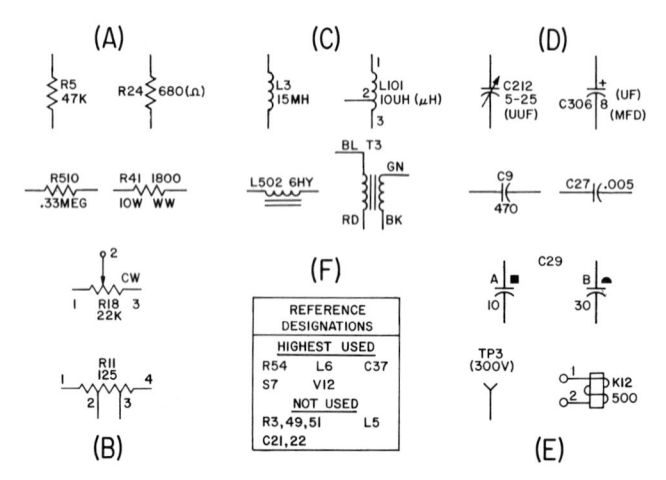

FIG. 24.7. Reference designations. (From G. Shiers, *Electronic Drafting* (Englewood Cliffs, N.J.: Prentice-Hall, Inc.))

explained in the general notes. Typical examples are as follows: (1) All resistors are half-watt except where specified. (2) Capacitor values given decimally are in microfarads; all others are in micromicrofarads. (3) All tolerances are ±10%, except where specified. (4) Components marked with an asterisk (*) apply only to Model No. *XYZ*.

Other significant data, such as control settings, meter types, test conditions, and calibration procedures, are generally included in these notes, along with explanation of special symbols or critical values. Test points, test voltages, and waveform pictures may be given as supplementary references in the body of the diagram. A reference table [see Fig. 24.7(F)], is generally furnished for the more complex diagrams. Such a table shows the extent of part numbering and any numbers in a sequence that are not used or that have been deleted through revisions. Since lettering is an important part of symbolic diagrams, all notations should be carefully compiled and checked to ensure clarity and completeness and to avoid ambiguity.

24.15
Industrial Schematics. Because most industrial control circuits contain electrical devices that frequently serve specialized functions, these diagrams may have to be laid out somewhat differently from the more usual radio, television, or instrument schematics. Typical examples of the different symbols required for industrial diagrams are those that denote circuit breakers, solenoids and actuators, timers, rotary machines, power tubes, relays, contactors, and special-purpose switches. The approved graphical symbols for these devices (some of which are alternative forms) are given in the respective standards. A few of these symbols are shown full-size in the numbered blocks in Fig. 24.8.

Several variables, particularly time, motion, and sequence, are involved in most industrial processes. Other factors, such as heat, light, color, weight, size, thickness, and alignment, may enter into the control or operation of equipment and the treatment of materials. Consequently, industrial schematics, or elementary diagrams, as they are also called, should be laid out in a logical sequence according to the functions of the individual circuits.

24.16
Control Circuit Layouts. The type of circuit format commonly used for industrial

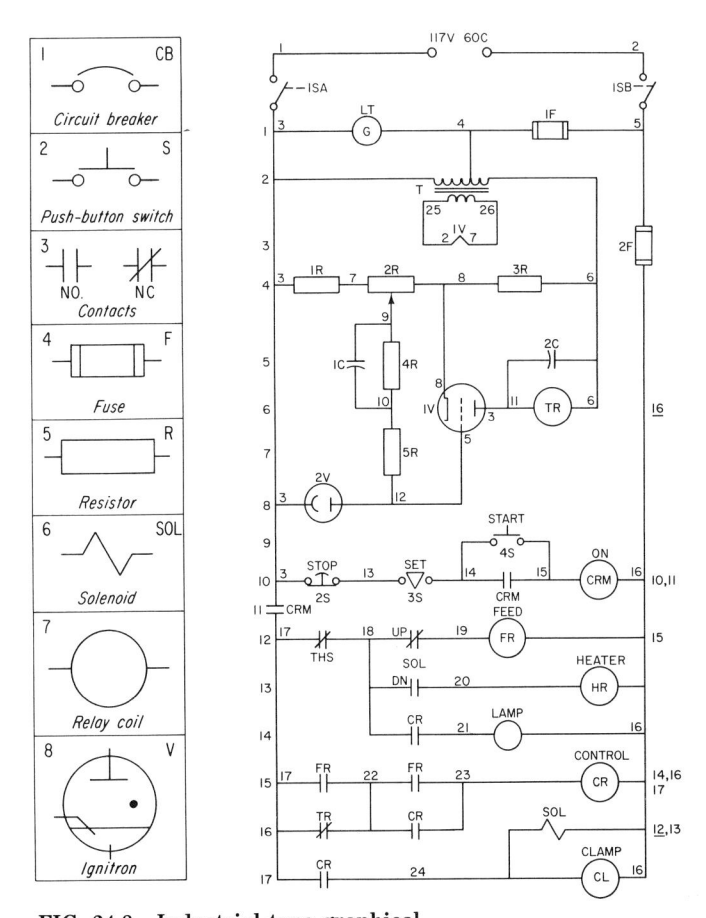

FIG. 24.8. Industrial-type graphical symbols and a typical elementary diagram of an industrial control circuit.

diagrams is shown in Fig. 24.8. Because of the layout, with individual circuits drawn between vertical supply lines, this is sometimes referred to as a *ladder diagram*. The power source is placed at the top with the circuits that follow located more or less in the order in which the operating sequence progresses.

As will be seen, contactor and relay coils and the associated contacts are separated, and the symbols for them are drawn in the circuits where they functionally belong. Circuit lines are evenly spaced in the interest of neatness and clarity. Similarly, symbols are evenly located and staggered to permit lettering.

Usually, all control devices are connected to the left-hand bus, while operating coils, lamps, solenoids, etc., are connected to the right-hand common line. In some layouts, the control circuits and the power circuits may be separated and drawn as two diagrams on the same sheet. Industrial diagram layouts may be prepared according to the modular principles previously described in Sec. 24.11.

24.17
Industrial Designations. Although basically serving the same purpose, the method of designating components in industrial diagrams differs somewhat from communications practice. Device designations are comprised of a standard letter or letter sequence that denotes the part and its particular function. Thus, with reference to Fig. 24.8: TR—timing relay; CRM—control relay master; FR—feed relay; CR—control relay; and SOL—solenoid. Other variations to be found include ET—electron tube; P—potentiometer; RH—rheostat; and SS—selector switch. Two or more similar devices are differentiated by prefix numbers, for example, 1V, 2V, 1R, and 2R. Component types and values may be given within a symbol, for example, 1200 for a resistor value in ohms; or G for a lamp with a green jewel.

The positions of component parts in a diagram are given with reference to the circuit "level," which is identified by a number on the left-hand side. Thus, the solenoid on level 16 in Fig. 24.8 has associated contacts, which are shown on levels 12 and 13. The UP contact is normally closed, as denoted by the slant line in the symbol, and by the underlined reference number. The other numbers adjacent to the wire lines identify individual wires. Corresponding numbers are marked on the wires in the equipment, as discussed in Sec. 24.20.

24.18
Connection Diagrams. A drawing that shows the wiring between components is known as a connection, or wiring, diagram. A similar drawing showing the external connections between self-contained units is referred to as an interconnection diagram. These drawings are used for original wiring and assembly, circuit tracing, equipment installation, testing, and maintenance.

The best method of presenting wiring and connection data depends on the wiring method, type of equipment, and the purpose of the drawing. The most common types of connection diagrams are presented in Fig. 24.9. Separate line diagrams are not needed for all equipment; sometimes a wiring list provides the necessary information. Again, the wiring may be superimposed on a plan view of the assembly, or it may be shown in a pictorial view (Fig. 24.1).

24.19
Wires and Cables. Particulars concerning wire types and sizes are frequently included with connection data. Typical examples of wires and cables with the respective graphical symbols are shown in Fig. 24.10.

Stranded conductors are used for most chassis wiring. The wire size may be specified by the number of strands and the strand size or by the equivalent American Wire Gauge. For example, 7/30 (22) signifies a conductor with seven strands of No. 30 gage equivalent in cross-sectional area to a solid wire, size AWG 22. These conductors are usually covered with a thermoplastic insulating material, such as polyvinyl chloride (PVC), in single colors or with a colored stripe, as shown in Fig. 24.10(A).

A solid conductor of bare tinned copper (BTC) wire is generally used for rigid bus bars or for short connections (jumpers) between adjacent terminals. The other types shown in Fig. 24.10 are a twisted pair (B), shielded cable (C), multiconductor cable (D), and a coaxial cable (E). The outer metallic braids serve as shields to minimize radiation or interference.

24.20

Wire Coding. Wire markings are necessary for original wiring inspection, testing, and troubleshooting. These markings may consist of insulation colors or number–letter sequences stamped on or attached to the wires. Such identities are given by code in line diagrams. Wire grades may be designated by a code letter that denotes type of insulation, voltage rating, temperature limits, etc.

The standard color code universally employed for electronic applications consists of color markings and their numerical equivalents. This code, with the two-letter abbreviations, is as follows: 0, black (BK); 1, brown (BN); 2, red (RD); 3, orange (OR); 4, yellow (YL); 5, green (GN); 6, blue (BL); 7, violet (VI); 8, gray (GY); and 9, white (WH). A single-letter code is sometimes used, as shown in Fig. 24.13(B).

Wire-coding methods are based on the need to identify specific wires; circuit function; wire size, type, and number; wire destination; and terminal connection. In the case of multicolored wires, for example, a code such as 14–22–A would signify a brown wire (1) with a yellow tracer (4), size 22, segment A. A two-section code showing the wire destination and the wire details, such as R7/3–C20/6, would signify a blue wire (6), size 20, type "C," connected to terminal 3 on resistor R7.

24.21

Wiring Methods. Basic methods for interconnecting components within a self-contained assembly are as follows: direct or point-to-point wiring; grouped or cable-form wiring; and printed circuits. These methods may be combined in a single assembly.

An example of point-to-point wiring will be seen in Fig. 24.1, where small parts are suspended by their leads and other wires take the shortest route between terminals. This type of wiring, which can be visually traced quite easily, is suitable for simple assemblies and special circuits that operate at high frequencies.

In other applications, particularly military, industrial control, scientific research, and high-grade commercial equipment, all parts must be individually mounted with the wiring properly secured. Usually, small parts are grouped together on component

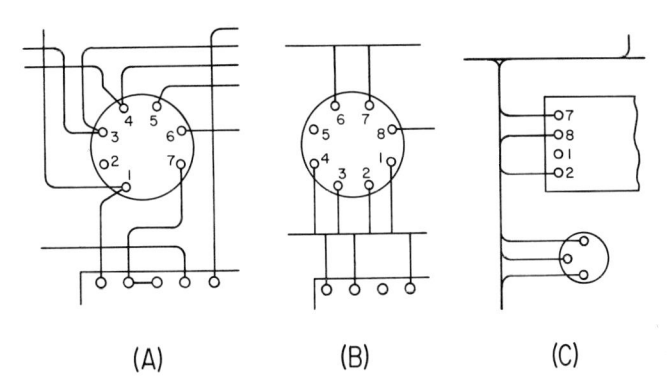

FIG. 24.9. Basic line diagrams. (A) Point-to-point, (B) baseline, (C) trunk-line or highway. (From G. Shiers, *Electronic Drafting* (Englewood Cliffs, N.J.: Prentice-Hall, Inc.))

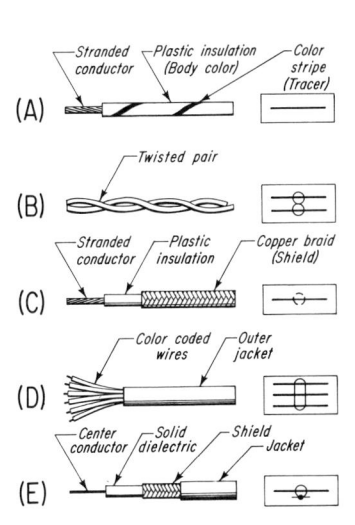

FIG. 24.10. Typical wires and cables with symbols. (From G. Shiers, *Electronic Drafting* (Englewood Cliffs, N.J.: Prentice-Hall, Inc.))

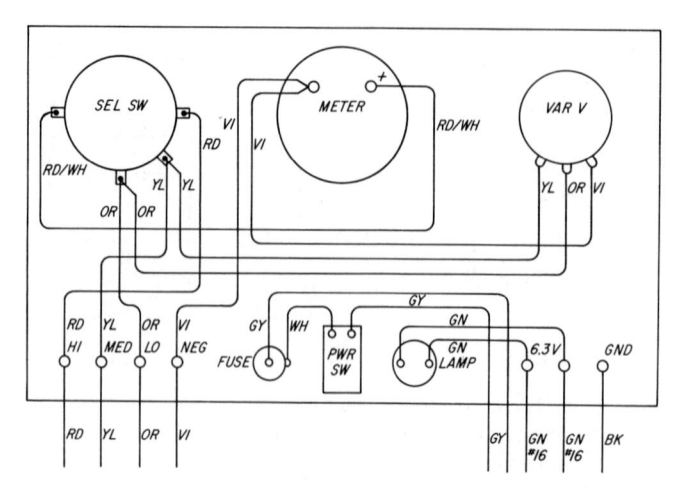

FIG. 24.11. Point-to-point wiring diagram of a panel layout. (From G. Shiers, *Electronic Drafting* (Englewood Cliffs, N.J.: Prentice-Hall, Inc.))

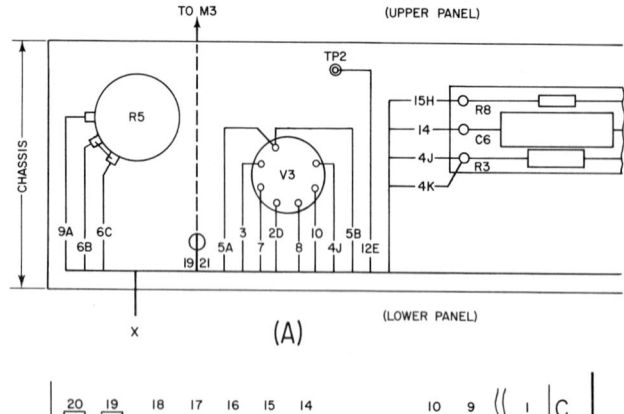

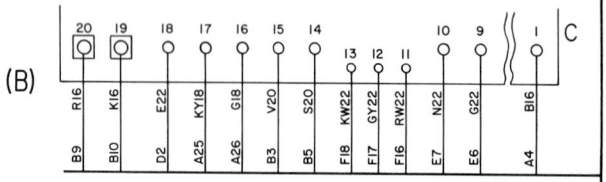

FIG. 24.12. Typical baseline diagrams, (A) partial chassis wiring, (B) terminal-strip interconnections. (From G. Shiers, *Electronic Drafting* (Englewood Cliffs, N.J.: Prentice-Hall, Inc.))

boards, with the wires tied in bundles or cableforms. These wiring assemblies, also called cable harnesses, are usually prefabricated on a wiring jig. Wire markings are essential in order to distinguish the wires and trace the connections.

24.22

Connection Diagram Layouts. The component parts in a connection diagram are represented in simplified outline by blocks or pictorial symbols. Sufficient detail should be included to enable the reader to identify the parts and the terminations. Graphical symbols may also be used. Although these drawings need not be done to scale, the layout should be in approximate agreement with the assembly, with similar placement of terminals, connections, and identifying features. These diagrams should be developed using a modular layout, as described in Sec. 24.11.

To reveal every component, perpendicular surfaces, such as the sides of a box-type chassis, are turned 90° and developed in the major plane. Connection diagrams therefore present a plan view of the wiring in which the turned surfaces are normally placed adjacent to the respective edges. Connections to certain components, such as multigang switches, may require a detailed view or a supplementary view of the part. If necessary, a symbol may be divided for clarity. In such instances, the sections should be suitably aligned and properly labeled, with specific references given to clarify the views.

24.23

Point-to-point Diagrams. In a point-to-point diagram, each wire is shown by a separate line. These diagrams show the wiring side of an assembly, such as for the back view of a control panel presented in Fig. 24.11. The wire lines are spaced apart for clarity and to permit lettering and therefore do not necessarily represent the actual wire routing. Wires, connections, and component parts must be suitably identified. Other references should correspond with panel or chassis markings, terminal numbers or letters, and schematic designations.

24.24
Baseline Diagrams. A connection diagram may be simplified if the wire lines from the components are terminated into common base lines. These lines, drawn horizontally and vertically between component symbols, may or may not represent the routing of the actual wires.

Figure 24.12(A) is a base-line diagram, which partially shows the wiring between a potentiometer (R5), a tube socket (V3), a component board, a test point, and related items. The wire identities showing wire numbers and segments, for example, 5A, 5B, and so on, are inserted in the wire lines. The actual connections would be given in a wiring list, which would also specify other wire details, such as wire type, size, length, and type of terminations.

The diagram shown in Fig. 24.12(B) refers to the terminal wiring on a chassis designated "C." In this example, the wire coding includes wire size, color, and destination or address, for example, a red (R) wire, size 16, on terminal 20, is connected to terminal 9 on chassis "B." The other end of this wire would be designated C20 (R16) in the diagram and marked accordingly.

24.25
Highway Diagrams. In another type of connection diagram the feeder lines from the component terminals are merged into a single trunk line, or highway. The routing for each lead should be indicated by a slant line, as shown in Fig. 24.13(A), or by radial turnoffs, as shown in (B).

Since the wire identities are lost by grouping, a code number is required to show the destination. With reference to

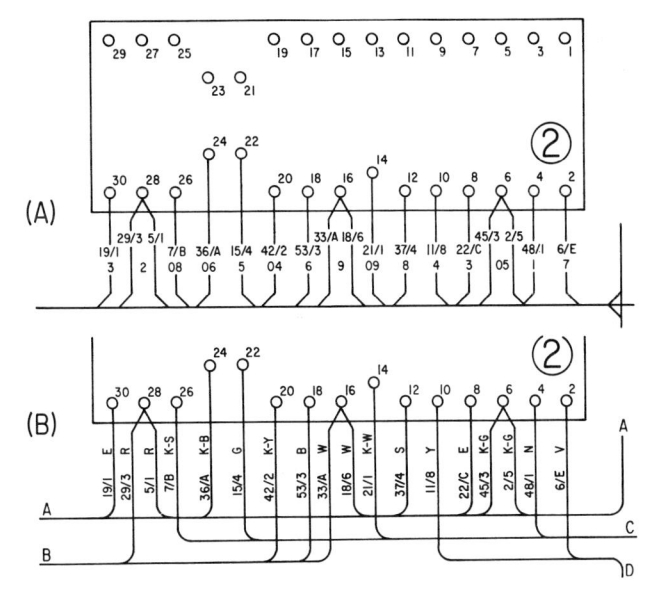

FIG. 24.13. Typical trunkline or highway diagrams showing a component board and associated wiring, (A) single trunk, (B) separate highways. (From G. Shiers, *Electronic Drafting* (Englewood Cliffs, N.J.: Prentice-Hall, Inc.))

Fig. 24.13(A), for example, the lead connected to terminal 2 on item 2 is designated 6/E(7), which signifies a violet wire (7), which is connected at the other end to terminal E on item 6. Such items, for example, component boards, tube sockets, switches, connectors, and so on, may be arbitrarily numbered, as shown, or they may be designated according to the class of item using standard letter symbols (such as V5, TB2, etc.) which agree with the schematic references.

Figure 24.13(B) shows separate highways for associated wires, a method that may be preferred because it facilitates circuit tracing. Thus, highway A carries wires from left to right to terminals 30, 24, 12, 8, and 6; also wires to the right from terminals 28, 16, and 6. These (and perhaps other wires) are carried upward to other parts of the drawing, a fact that is not specifically shown in (A).

24.26
Printed Circuits. Savings in space and weight and other advantages may be realized if conventional wiring is replaced by a "printed circuit." Such a circuit may be produced by depositing a conductive pattern on a dielectric base, by stamping or etching copper foil, or by special processes, which may include the formation of circuit components with the conductive pattern.

A suitable grade of insulating material, such as phenolic stock with copper foil bonded to the sheet, is used for general applications. Glass, ceramic, and synthetic dielectrics are used for special purposes. Typically, the circuit pattern is reproduced on the foil by photographic means, followed by an etching process. A large-scale black-and-white drawing showing the pattern in silhouette is prepared as a master layout. A photographic negative is made from this artwork.

In the usual construction, components are mounted on the plain side of the board, opposite the etched pattern. Component leads are inserted through holes or eyelets in the conductor pattern, the connections being made either by hand soldering or by dipping the wiring side of the assembled board in a bath of molten solder.

24.27
Conductor Patterns. Conductor patterns must be compatible with various mechanical and electrical requirements, notably, size, shape, and layout of the board; circuit connections; and electrical values. Adequate contact areas at the terminal points and interconnections must be incorporated in the design. Several basic conductor shapes are shown in Fig. 24.14. Conductor patterns should be drawn solid black with clean edges, free-flowing lines, and smooth contours. Fillets should be provided at junctions and land areas.

A conductor width of .031 in. is commonly used for general-purpose boards where the current is not more than a few hundred milliamperes. The spacing between conductors depends on the working voltage; .062 in. is usual where the peak voltage difference does not exceed 300 V. Conductor locations and spacings are also governed by electrical factors, such as capacitance, intercircuit coupling, shielding, and other requirements, which may be critical in certain designs.

24.28
Printed-circuit Layouts. Quadrille or cross-section paper is ideal for sketching printed-circuit layouts. The pattern can be drawn freehand in pencil, using the grid lines, with the divisions representing a suitable scale. Terminal pads should preferably be located on standard .1-in. intersections, with increments of .025 in., according to the space requirements and the component dimensions.

At this stage the objective is to develop connecting paths as short and direct as possible without any crossovers. Component parts may have to be reoriented or interchanged to provide access for every conductor. When an obstruction is unavoidable, however, a jumper or insulated wire is used as a bridge at the crossover point. Several sketches are generally needed before a feasible pattern can be established.

24.29
Printed-circuit Artwork. Master layouts for printed-circuit work are made to an enlarged scale, which may range from 2:1 to 20:1, depending on the size of the part and the intricacy of detail. This enlargement facilitates drawing and improves the accuracy of the final full-size copy. Accurate locations of the terminals and other

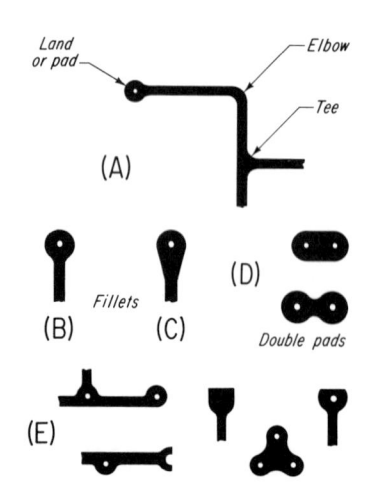

FIG. 24.14. Basic conductor shapes for printed circuits. (From G. Shiers, *Electronic Drafting* (Englewood Cliffs, N.J.: Prentice-Hall, Inc.))

center points are essential because land areas, pads, edge-connector strips, and so on, must match the holes and cutouts in the board. One major dimension, placed outside the board area, should be given for reference.

Some important details of master layouts are shown in Fig. 24.15. If component designations, part symbols, and other lettering are given on the master drawing they will appear in copper on the board. Such markings, sometimes alternatively printed or silkscreened on the board, are valuable service aids. Other markings, for example, hole centers and cutouts, may be needed for experimental models, hand assemblies, and small-quantity productions.

Plastic drafting film, glass cloth, and similar materials with good dimensional stability are preferred for master layouts. The drawing may be done in black India ink or with adhesive drafting aids. These aids, or appliqués, especially developed for printed-circuit work, consist of black tapes and precut matching shapes, such as elbows, tees, junctions, and pads, as shown in Fig. 24.14. In another method, the surface of a specially prepared film may be scribed and stripped to produce either a positive or negative master.

Separate drawings are required for double-sided boards, silkscreen lettering stencils, and for making press tools and

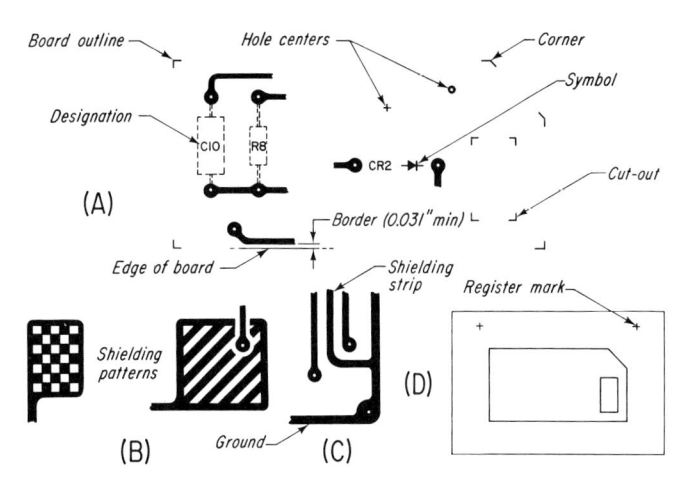

FIG. 24.15. Printed circuit artwork, (A) master layout details, (B) shielding patterns, (C) shielding strips and ground, (D) overlay and register marks. (From G. Shiers, *Electronic Drafting* (Englewood Cliffs, N.J.: Prentice-Hall, Inc.))

jigs used in quantity productions. In such cases, each drawing is aligned by means of register marks, as shown in Fig. 24.15(D), to ensure satisfactory matching of the important features. Printed-circuit artwork must be accurately and skillfully prepared because, unlike other technical drawings, the qualities of the drawing will be fully reproduced in the finished product.

PROBLEMS

Suitable layouts for the following problems should be developed freehand on opaque cross-section paper. Finished drawings should be made on plain vellum with a cross-section paper beneath it to serve as a grid background. Templates with appropriate cutouts should be used for drawing symbols. Some of the problems should be finished with adhesive drafting aids and in India ink in order to provide acquaintance with these techniques. The publications listed in Sec. 24.3 should be consulted when selecting symbols and designations.

1. Draw a block diagram representing the circuit of the chassis shown in Fig. 24.1. Letter the blocks as follows: (1) pentagrid converter; (2) IF (intermediate-frequency) amplifier; (3) detector, AVC, audio amplifier; (4) power amplifier; and (5) half-wave rectifier. Include

graphical symbols for the antenna (to block 1) and the loudspeaker (from block 4). Show block 5 as an auxiliary circuit, and include the power line.

2. Draw a schematic diagram of Fig. 24.5. Use horizontal projection and a $\frac{1}{8}$-in. grid scale.

3. Make a schematic diagram of the control panel wiring shown in Fig. 24.11.

4. Draw a schematic diagram to correspond with the parts and circuit of the chassis shown in Fig. 24.1. Use a symbol similar to item 11 of Fig. 24.2 with separate variable tuning cores for the IF transformers. The connections are as follows: blue-plate, red-B plus, green-grid, white-return, or common-line. The antenna and oscillator sections of the tuning capacitor (not shown) are ganged. The line switch and the volume control also are ganged. Use vertical projection, as shown in Fig. 24.5, and a $\frac{1}{8}$-in. grid scale.

5. Make a schematic diagram of the "400" series circuit shown in the middle level of Fig. 24.4. Show the circuit from V404B up to the grid of V407A. Renumber all symbols starting from 1 for each class. Include all designations and appropriate notes. Use horizontal projection and a $\frac{1}{10}$-in. grid scale.

6. Redraw the timing circuit (1V, 2V, from the input to level 8) shown in Fig. 24.8, using horizontal projection and a suitable scale. Show a double-wound transformer, similar to item 25 in Fig. 24.2 with two separate secondary windings, instead of T. Show a linecord terminated by a 3-pin plug, with the third pin grounded. Use zig-zag resistor symbols. Capacitor designated 2C is an electrolytic type. Relay TR has two sets of contacts: single-pole, normally open; single-pole, double-throw. Include a terminal block with five terminals suitably numbered and identified for these connections.

7. The underside view of a small chassis ($7 \times 5\frac{1}{4} \times 2$ in.) is shown in Fig. 24.16. This unit includes a power supply consisting of power transformer T; full-wave vacuum rectifier $V1$, type 5U4-GB; filter choke L; triple-unit electrolytic filter capacitor $C1$; 5-W resistor $R1$; and part of the circuit shown in Fig. 24.4. This circuit contains tube V406 ($V2$) and the associated components from C412 to pin 2, V407. With reference to Fig. 24.4, the respective component designations are C2–C412 through C5–C415 and R2–R433 through R8–R439. Chassis connections are made via a 10-wire terminal strip (TB).

Make a connection diagram to correspond with the circuit described, and the following connections. Use either the point-to-point or the baseline method. (Note: Component board connections are denoted thus: (T)–top, (B)–bottom.)

TB1-T9-V2/4-V2/5. TB2-T10-V2/9. TB3-C2(B). TB4-T7-C4(B)-chassis lug (ground). TB5-R1B-LB-C1B. TB6-R7(T)-R1A-C1C. TB7-R8(T). TB8 (spare). TB9-T1. TB10-T2. T3-V1/8. T4-LA-C1A. T5-V1/2. T6-V1/4. T8-V1/6.

8. Make a working sketch of a schematic to correspond with the circuit given in Problem 7. Use quadrille paper with eight divisions per inch. Include all designations and part values (in addition to those shown in Fig. 24.4) as follows: Power transformer primary, 1, 2; 5-V heater winding, 3, 4 (center tap), 5; 325-0-325-V secondary, 6, 7 (center tap), 8; 6.3-V heater winding, 9, 10. L, 20H; C1A, C1B, 20 mF; C1C, 10 mF; R1, 1800 Ω, 5-W, wire-wound. Show a divided terminal block with the power line input on the left and the other connections on the right.

9. A printed-circuit board with the required land areas and strip connections is shown in Fig. 24.17. Make a master layout drawing of this board twice full size to suit a conductor width of .031 in. A minimum clearance of .050 in. should be maintained between conductors and between a conductor and the edge of the

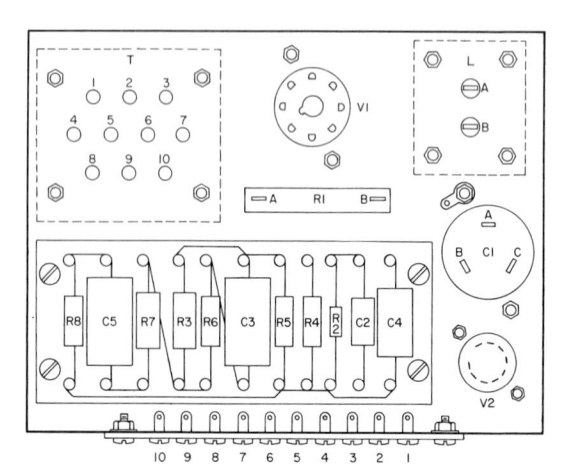

FIG. 24.16. Chassis assembly.

board. Land dimensions in inches are ID, .040; OD, .110. The strip connector widths of .10 in. should be maintained for .20 in. All tolerances on the conductor pattern are ±0.015 in. The connections are as follows: A-1-5-9, B-2-4-12-14, C-8-10-19, D-17, E-13-20, 3-15-16-18, and 6-7-11. The grid pattern and land numbers are for reference only.

10. Make a working sketch of a schematic to correspond with the printed circuit given in Problem 9. The components are as follows (terminal connections are with reference to Fig. 24.17):

R1, 9-10; R2, 5-6; R3, 16-17; R4, 14-15; R5, 1-2. C1, 7-8; C2, 3-4. Transistors are *PNP*-type: $Q1$, base 18, emitter 20, collector 19; $Q2$, base 11, emitter 13, collector 12. Label the strip connections as follows: *A*, negative 15 V; *B*, output; *C*, trigger; *D*, positive; *E*, ground.

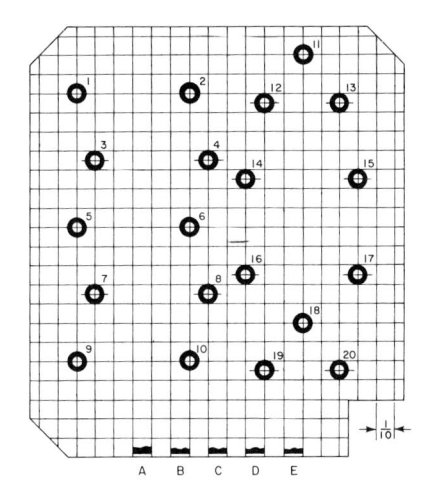

FIG. 24.17. Printed circuit board.

The detail drawing of a member in a steel structure must be clear and concise to enable the men in the shop to do their work efficiently without error.
(*Courtesy American Institute of Steel Construction, Inc.*)

Structural Drawings*

25.1

Although structural drawings are prepared in accordance with the general principles of projection, they differ somewhat from machine drawings in certain practices. These differences, which have gradually developed due to the type of raw material used and methods of fabrication, have become established drawing room customs that are recognized universally throughout the industry and must be understood and adhered to by every prospective structural engineer.

Steel structures vary widely and include almost everything fabricated from rolled shapes and plates.

Fabrication consists in shearing, flame cutting, punching, bending, forging, and machining, then fitting and aligning the parts, and finally permanently fastening the assembly by bolting, riveting, or welding. Although small roof trusses and girder bridges may be assembled as complete units in the shop, the size of most structures makes necessary the fabrication of subassemblies and shipment in knock-down form.

Sections of the principal shapes (angles, I-beams, channels, wide-flange sections, and plates) are shown in Fig. 25.1.

---

* Prepared in collaboration with R. S. Green, Ohio State University, and M. T. Ward, American Bridge Company.

The dimensions of the various standard shapes and other available information required by a structural detailer are given in structural steel handbooks published by different manufacturers and by the American Institute of Steel Construction.

25.2

Equipment of a Structural Draftsman. The equipment needed by a structural draftsman is the same as for any other line of industrial drafting, with a few additions. Smaley's tables of trigonometric functions and logarithms and Smaley's tables of slopes and rises are a necessity. A copy of the structural handbook published by the American Institute of Steel Construction must be readily available for constant use.

Some companies furnish each draftsman with a book that gives drawing room

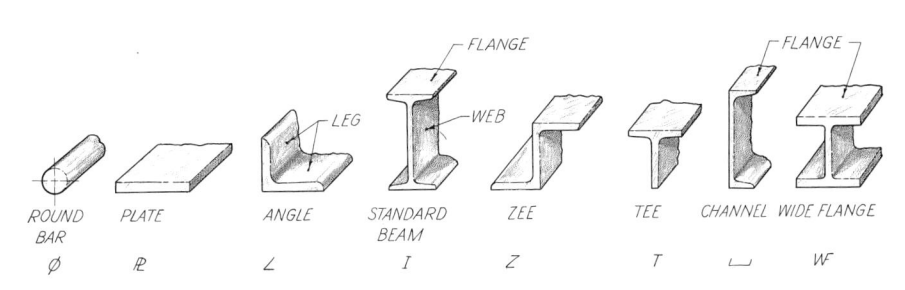

FIG. 25.1. Structural shapes.

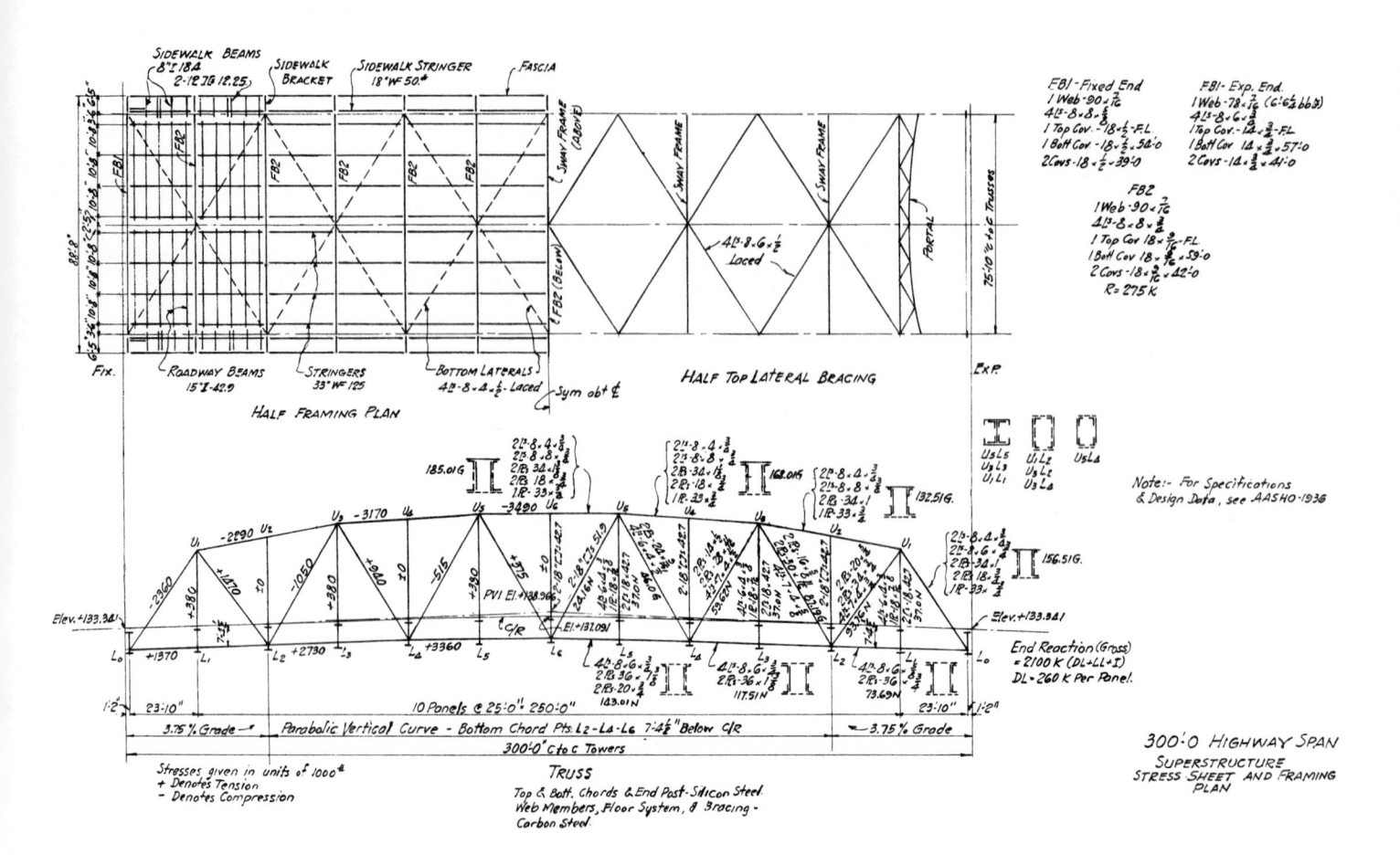

FIG. 25.2. Stress sheet.

standards. Included are typical drawings illustrating the arrangement of views, approved dimensioning practices, and notes for various types of structures. Some information also may be given about plant equipment.

It is suggested that the structural draftsman in training obtain a copy of the latest edition of the AISC text, *Structural Steel Detailing*. Mastery of the instructions in this excellent text should qualify one who is starting in this field to do acceptable work in structural detailing with any structural steel fabricator.*

25.3

Classes of Structural Drawings. Most of the large steel fabricators maintain a design office and a detailing office. The former prepares design drawings and es-

---

*Structural Steel Detailing, New York: American Institute of Steel Construction, Inc., 1966.

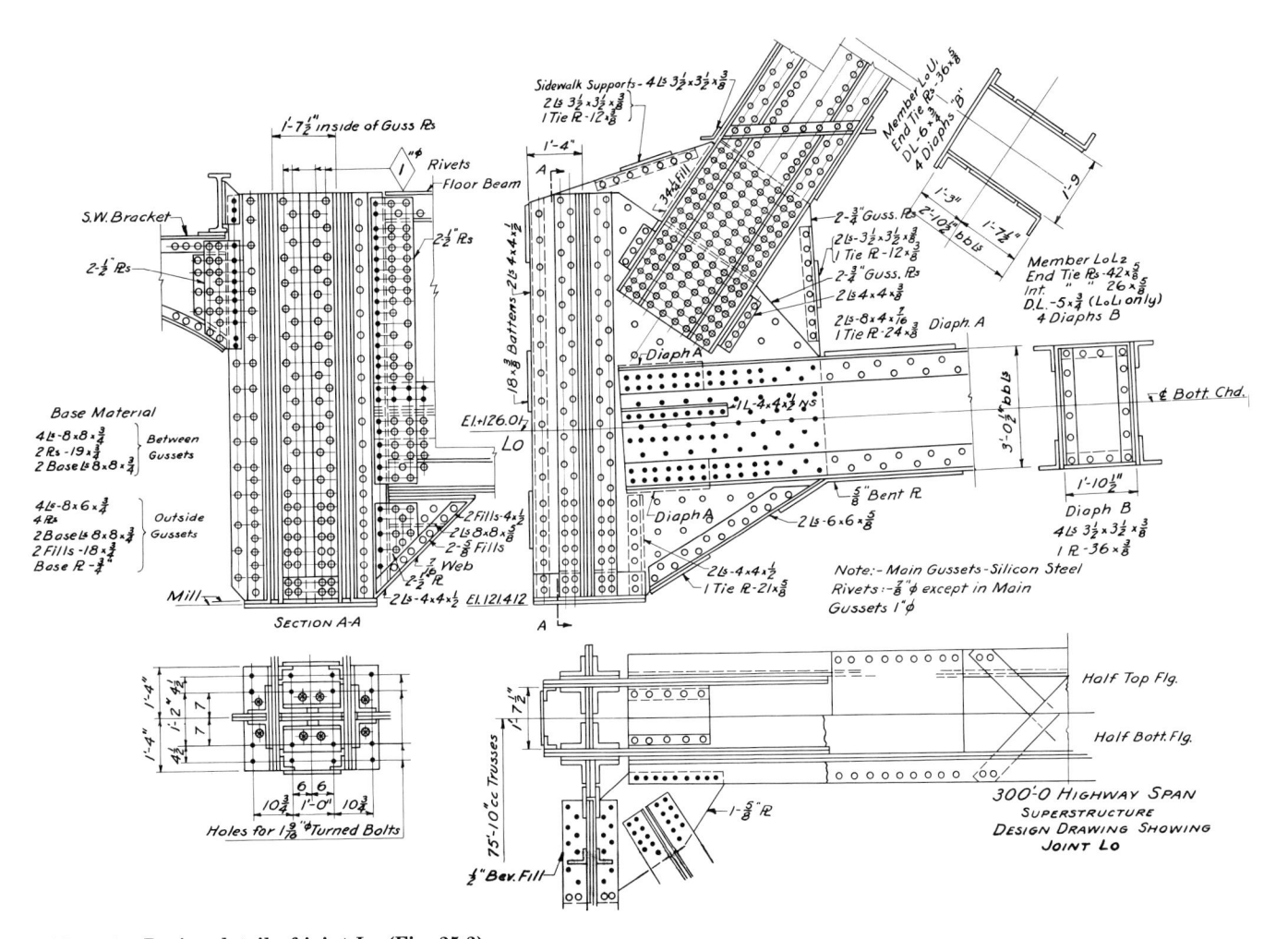

FIG. 25.3. Design detail of joint L₀ (Fig. 25.2).

timates costs in the preparation of bids and frequently serves in a consulting capacity on designs furnished by a customer. The detailing office, which is usually located at the fabricating plant, orders material and prepares shop and erection plans from the design sheets.

Design drawings usually are line diagrams showing the shape of a structure, the principal dimensions, structural sections, and in some cases the stresses to be used in detailing the connections. Figure 25.2 is an example of a design drawing.

For the use of the layout man a set of design drawings may contain elaborate design details, showing the type of connections, thickness of gusset plates, and the number of rivets. Figure 25.3 is the design detail for joint L_0 of the truss shown in Fig. 25.2. Design drawings of this type, however, are furnished only for important or complicated structures. Quite often the design of connections becomes a detailer's task.

A set of specifications covering special conditions, unit stresses, materials to be used, and so forth, is considered as part of the design information.

Shop detail drawings show all of the information necessary for shop fabrication.

Erection plans, which are prepared primarily for use in the field, consist of line diagrams giving dimensions, shipping marks, and notes in sufficient detail to guide the erector in assembling the parts to complete the finished structure.

25.4
Layouts. The first step in the development of structural steel detail drawings is the drawing of the layout sheets. These are intermediate drawings that are used only in the drafting room of the fabricating shop. Layouts are used for ordering material, obtaining early approval of details, and coordinating the work of the several draftsmen who may be employed on the project. As a general rule, layouts are made only when the complexity of the work demands a carefully scaled picture. For example, layouts would be necessary for all types of skewed work and for truss joints. Layouts may be drawn to any appropriate scale, but usually the detail drawing and layout scales are the same. They usually are made on bond paper that is thin enough to permit blueprinting. Layouts are not completely dimensioned, but the layout man may indicate any dimensions he wishes to be used.

Figure 25.4 is a layout of the cross frame of a deck-girder bridge. The detailer takes layouts of this kind, in addition to the design drawings for the project, and completely details the structure.

25.5
Detail Drawings. The making of the detail drawing is the final step in the process of creating structural steel working drawings. These drawings must be clear and concise, to enable men in the shop to do their portion of the work efficiently. To ensure accuracy, a thorough check of all arrangements and dimensions is made in the drafting room by a checker.

Parts to be riveted together in the shop are detailed in their assembled positions in the structure, instead of being detailed individually, as is the practice for machine work. Figure 25.5 is a detail drawing of a cross frame. It describes each plate and main member and shows the relations of the various elements of the structure to one another. When the structure is too large to be completely assembled in the shop and shipped in one piece, an assembly or erection diagram becomes necessary.

The scales in general use are not large enough to permit direct scaling of dimensions. One of the scales most commonly used in structural work is $\frac{3}{4}$ in. = 1 ft. Often structural members are too long to be drawn to scale and yet be contained on the sheet of drawing paper. In this event, the transverse dimensions and the details are drawn to one scale and the longitudinal dimensions are shortened or drawn to a smaller scale.

Structural steel drawings incorporate a few practices of projection that differ from other types of work. In all structural work the view of the structure that corresponds to the front view in a machine drawing is termed the *elevation* of the structure. The view that corresponds to the top view in a machine drawing is called the *plan view* of the structure. The view below the cross frame in Fig. 25.5 is a plan view of the lower-chord member and is not a bottom view. Likewise, the two views at the bottom of the sheet in Fig. 25.3 are not bottom views of the joint but are sectional views looking downward. The left view shows the location of the anchor bolts and

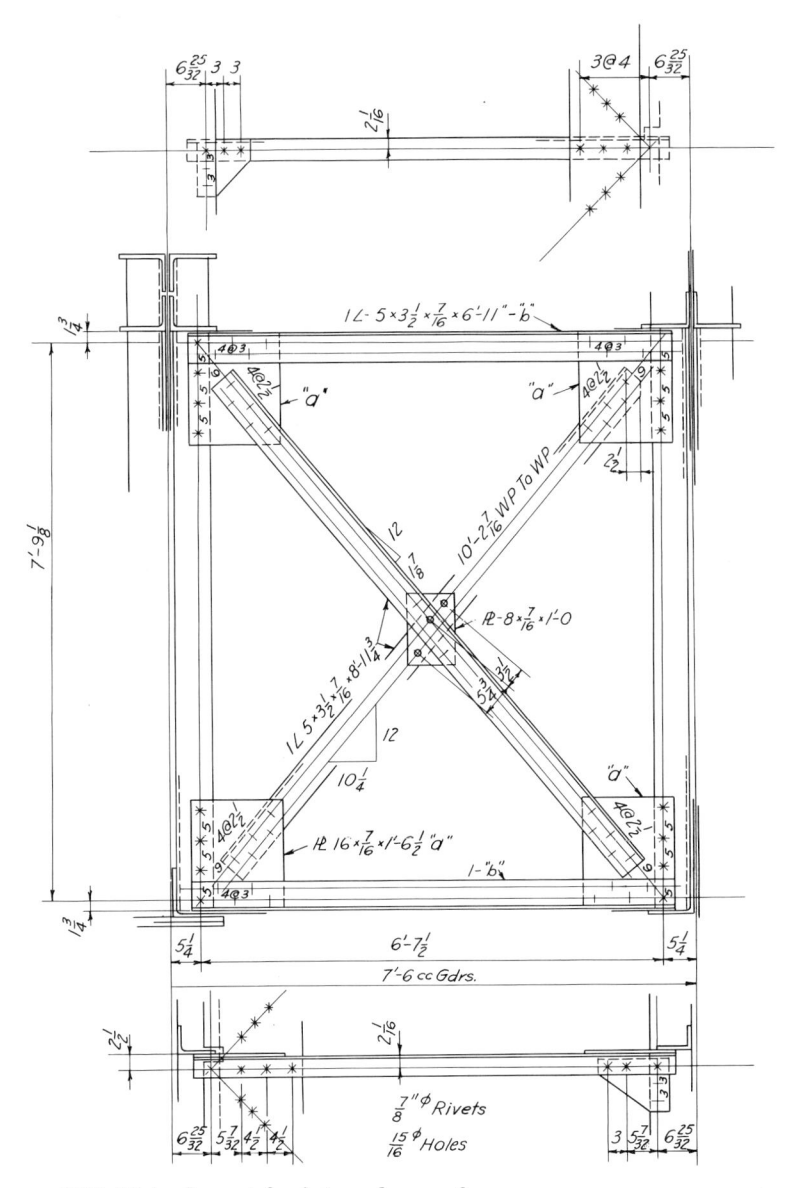

FIG. 25.4. Layout for internal cross frame.

the right view shows both the top and the bottom of the member L_0–L_1 where it frames into the joint. Shopmen prefer the use of bottom sections because the elevation of a piece, while being fitted, corresponds to the elevation on the drawings. Any fitting or inspection of the bottom is more easily accomplished by looking down than by crawling under and looking upward.

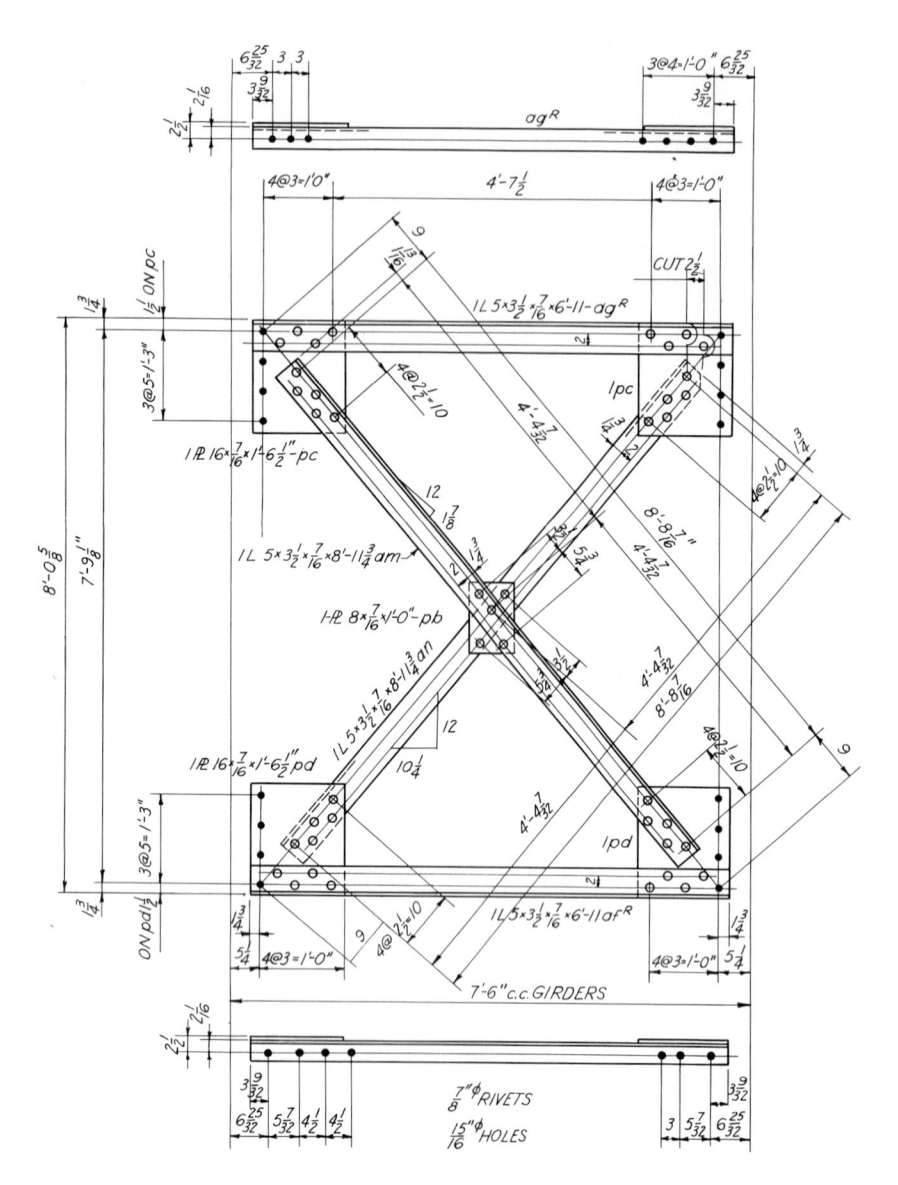

FIG. 25.5. Detail drawing of a cross frame.

Angular dimensions on structural drawings are shown as slopes that are expressed in inches per foot. A slope triangle is a right triangle constructed with its hypotenuse on the gage or working line whose slope is to be shown. The longer of the two legs is always given as 12 in., and the length of the shorter leg determines the slope. These slope triangles are not drawn to scale but are constructed any convenient size (Fig. 25.5).

Structural drawings are currently made in pencil on translucent bond paper. Pencil work requires particular care on the part of the draftsman to make his lines black enough to blueprint clearly. The outlines of the structural members should be wider than the gage lines and dimension lines because the contrast makes the blueprints easier to read.

Pencil tracings on special cloth or ink tracings on cloth are required by certain customers.

25.6
Structural Definitions and Notations.

$'$ = foot or feet
$''$ = inch or inches
ϕ = diameter
= pound or pounds
∠ = angle
I = I-beam
⌙ = channel
WF = wide-flange section

Anchor bolt. A bolt used to fasten steel girders, columns, trusses, and so on, to masonry.

Beam. A horizontal structural member (usually an I-beam or WF beam).

Bearing plate. A plate used under the end of a truss, beam, or girder, to increase the bearing area.

Chip. To chip off projecting parts with a chisel (pneumatic chisel).

Clearance. A general term applying to an opening or space between two adjacent pieces, without which interference would result (Fig. 25.11).

Column. A general term for a vertical member supporting beams or trusses.

Countersink. The operation of chamfering the edges of a hole to receive the conical head of a bolt, rivet, or screw.

Detail. To prepare a working structural drawing. (Working drawings are called details.) (Fig. 25.5).

Driving clearance. The distance from the center of a rivet to the nearest obstruction that would interfere with the driving of the rivet.

Edge distance. The distance from the center of a rivet or hole to the edge of the member (Fig. 25.11).

Erection diagram. An assembly diagram drawn to aid the erector in placing members of the structure in their proper positions.

Fabrication. The shop work of converting rolled shapes to complete structural members.

Field clearance. Minimum distance between unfinished edges that abut when erected at the site. Usually $\frac{1}{2}$–$\frac{3}{4}$ in.

Field rivet. A rivet driven into the structure at the site of construction.

Filler. A plate or washer used to fill up space between two surfaces.

Flame cut. To cut by hand or by a machine-guided oxyacetylene torch.

Flange. A general term for the outstanding part of a member (Fig. 25.1).

Gage. The distance from the back of an angle or channel to the center line of a row of rivets, or the distance between the center lines of two rows of rivets (Fig. 25.16).

Gage line. The center line of a row of rivets (Fig. 25.16).

Girder. A horizontal member built up of plates and angles.

Grip. The combined thickness of members connected by a rivet.

Gusset plate. A connection plate used to connect several members of a truss (Fig. 25.11).

Layout. A preliminary scale drawing made in the detailing department prior to detailing, for the purpose of ordering material and coordinating the work of the several detailers (Fig. 25.4).

Leg. The name for either of the two flanges of an angle (Fig. 25.1).

Line diagram. A drawing in which each member is represented by a single line (Fig. 25.2).

Pitch. The center-to-center longitudinal distance between adjacent rivets (Fig. 25.16).

Plate. A flat piece of structural steel having a rectangular cross section (Fig. 25.1).

Punch. To make a hole by forcing a nonrotating tool through the material.

Ream. To enlarge and finish a punched hole, using a rotating fluted cutter.

Rivet. A cylindrical rod of steel that is used to fasten together members of a steel structure. It has one head formed when manufactured; the other is formed after the rivet is in position.

Shape. The structural term for rolled steel having any cross section (except a steel plate) (Fig. 25.1).

Shop clearance. Minimum distance between unfinished abutting edges of members assembled in the shop. Usually $\frac{1}{4}$ in.

Shop drawing. A working drawing

made for the shop. Commonly called a *detail* drawing (Fig. 25.5).

Slope. The inclination of a line designated by a slope triangle expressed in inches of rise to a base of 12 in. (Fig. 25.5).

Span. The center-to-center distance between the supports of a beam, girder, or truss.

Staggered rivets. Rivets spaced alternately in parallel rows (Fig. 25.16).

Stitch rivets. Rivets spaced at intervals along a built-up member to cause the component parts to act as a unit.

Stress sheet. A drawing having a line diagram on which are recorded the stresses in the main members of a structure (Fig. 25.2).

Truss. A rigid framed structure, in the form of a series of triangles, which acts as a beam (Fig. 25.15).

Web. The thin portion between the flanges of a member (Fig. 25.1).

Weldment. Any welded assembly or subassembly.

Working point. The point of intersection of working lines (usually gage lines) (Fig. 25.15).

25.7

Sizes of Standard Members. The following structural specifications and abbreviations are those adopted by the American Institute of Steel Construction.

Plates. Width (in inches) × thickness × length. (Pl 15 × $\frac{3}{8}$ × 1'-10.) If it is a connection plate on a truss, cross frame, and so on, which is fabricated in the shop, the specification will be followed by the letters *pa, pb, pc,* or *pd,* and so on, which indicate the location of the plate. (Pl 15 × $\frac{3}{8}$ × 1'-10 *pa.*)

Angles—equal legs. Size of leg × size of leg × thickness × length. (∠ $3\frac{1}{2}$ × $3\frac{1}{2}$ × $\frac{3}{8}$ × 7'-6.)

Angles—unequal legs. Size of leg shown × size of outstanding leg × thickness × length. (∠ 4 × 3 × $\frac{5}{16}$ × 24'-7.)

I-Beams. Depth of I-weight per foot × length. (12 I 31.8 × 15'-4.)

Channels. Depth of [-weight per foot × length. (10[15.3 × 15'-10.)

Wide-flange sections. Depth of WF-weight per foot × length. (24WF74 × 12'-6.)

25.8

Detailing Information. The type of rivets and their treatment are indicated on structural drawings by the American National Standard conventional symbols shown in Fig. 25.6.

The holes for field rivets are indicated in solid black on a drawing, while shop rivets are shown by open circles having the same diameter as the rivet head (Fig. 25.7). Rivets should be drawn with either a drop pen or a bow pencil. In practice, the circles representing rivets are often drawn freehand on pencil drawings.

25.9

Location of Dimension Lines. Since shopmen are never permitted to scale a draw-

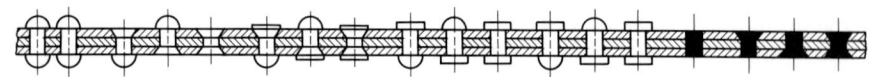

FIG. 25.6. Conventional symbols for rivets.

ing, all dimensions must be placed in such a manner that they will be easily understood. Principal dimensions are generally obtained from the design sheets; other dimensions necessary for detailing are found in tables or are determined by the detailer.

Dimensions for rivet spacing, minor location and size dimensions, and so on, are placed close to the view, while the longer dimensions, such as overall lengths, are placed farther away so that extension lines will not cross dimension lines (Figs. 25.8–25.10).

Dimension figures are generally placed above continuous (unbroken) dimension lines, which are made narrow and black. These lines usually should be placed off the view, but oftentimes added clarity may be obtained by putting a few dimensions in an open area on the view itself. Dimension lines ordinarily should not be placed less than $3/8$ in. apart or closer to the view than $1/2$ in. All of the above rules for the location of dimension lines may be modified to suit the available space (Fig. 25.9).

25.10
Dimensions and Notes in Structural Detailing.

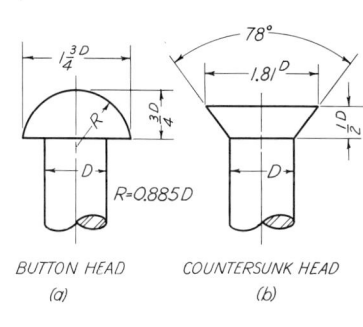

FIG. 25.7. Dimensions of rivet heads.

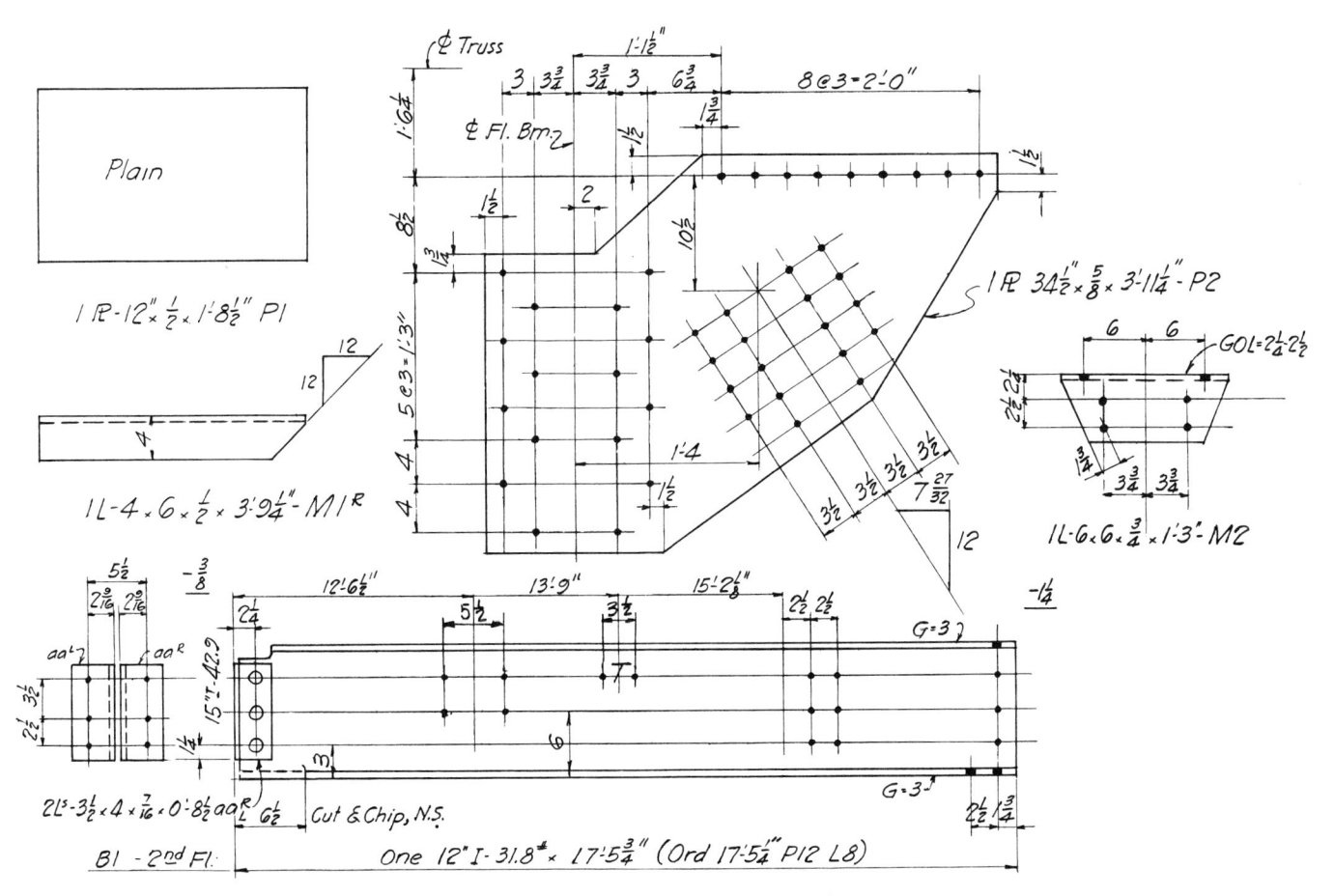

FIG. 25.8. Structural dimensioning.

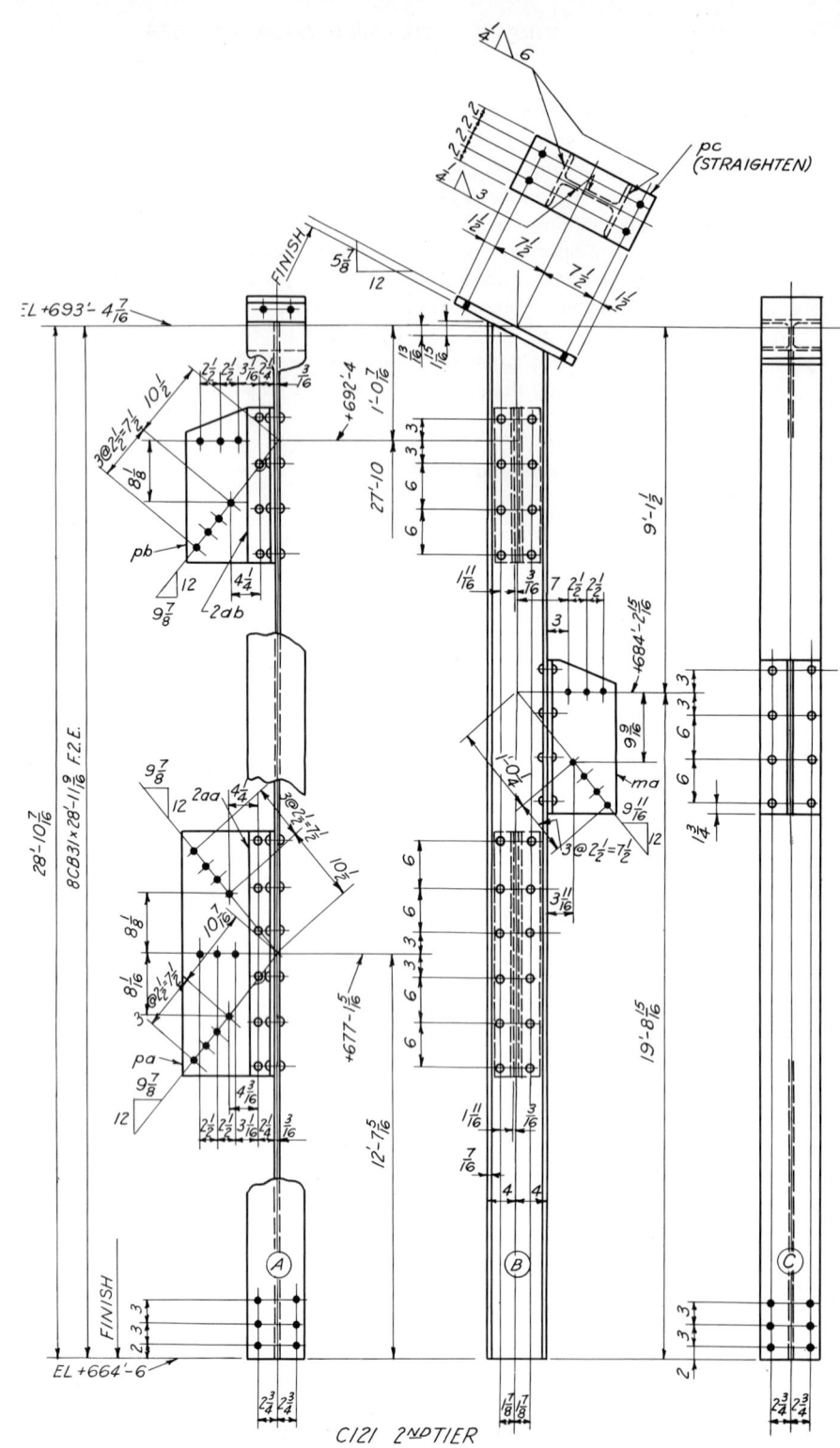

FIG. 25.9. Dimensioning a column (*Courtesy American Bridge Co.*).

CHAP. 25 / STRUCTURAL DRAWINGS 557

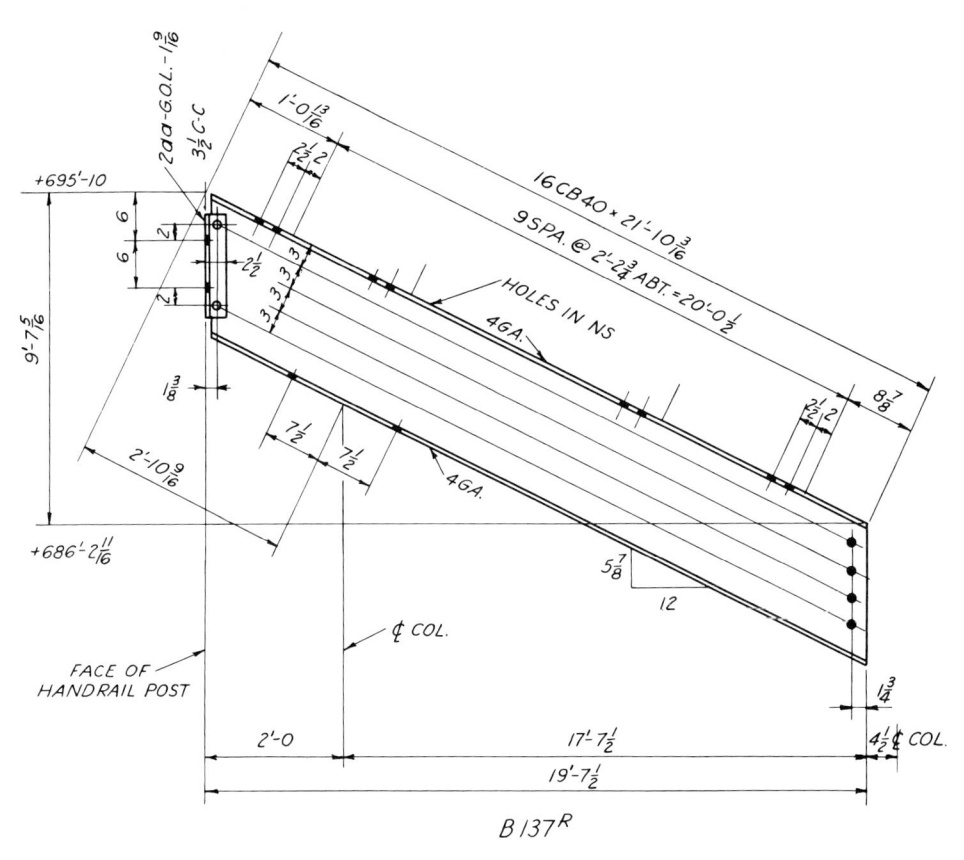

FIG. 25.10. Structural dimensioning (*Courtesy American Bridge Co.*).

1. Figures may be compressed without reducing their height, in order to place them in a limited space between arrowheads.

2. Figures can be placed to one side, with a leader to the dimension line, if the available space is very small.

3. Figures and notes must read from the bottom and the right side of the sheet because shopmen are accustomed to reading from these positions (Fig. 25.8).

4. For dimensions less than 1 ft, the inch marks (") may be omitted (Fig. 25.10).

5. With the exception of widths of plates and depths of sections, all dimensions of 1 ft or more are expressed in feet and inches (Fig. 25.8).

Correct	Incorrect
¼	0¼
9	0'-9"
10	10"
1'-0	12"
2'-3¼	2'-03¼"
4'-0¼	4'¼"

6. Usually, dimensions for rivet spacing are given in multiples of ⅛ in. or,

preferably, $\frac{1}{4}$ in. It is not desirable to use multiples of $\frac{1}{16}$ or $\frac{1}{32}$ in., except in rare cases.

7. Decimals found in tables should be converted to fractions to the nearest $\frac{1}{16}$ in. (except for machine-shop drawings for gears, shafts, and so forth).

8. To avoid complications that arise when corrections are made, dimensions shown on one view should not be repeated on another.

9. Rivets and holes are located by dimensions from center to center (Fig. 25.8).

10. Edge distances are frequently omitted, unless they are necessary to ensure clearances with connecting parts. (The shopmen understand that the distances on opposite edges are to be made equal.)

11. Dimensions *always* should be given to the center lines of I-beams and to the backs of angles and channels. (See Sec. 25.6, "gage" definition.)

12. When three or more rivet spaces for a line of rivets are equal, they should be dimensioned as a group (4 @ 3 = 1'-0). Staggered rivets are dimensioned as though they were on one gage line (Fig. 25.8).

13. Since a workman must use a rule or tape to lay off angles, a slope triangle should be shown to give the inclination of a working line (Fig. 25.10).

14. A man in the shop never should be compelled to add or subtract to obtain a necessary dimension.

15. A general note is usually placed on a detail drawing giving painting instructions, size of rivets, size of open holes, reaming instructions, and so on.

16. Members that are shipped separately for field erection are given a shipping mark of a letter and number that appears on the detail drawing and on the erection plan (Fig. 25.8).

17. The size of a member is indicated by a specification (in the form of a note) parallel to it (Fig. 25.8).

18. The width of a plate is always given in inches (Fig. 25.8).

25.11

Procedure for Making a Layout of a Gusset Plate. The general procedure for making the layout of a gusset plate that connects two members of a roof truss to the bottom chord member is given in Fig. 25.11. Each member is composed of two angles.

Step 1. Calculate the slopes of the diagonal members and draw in the working lines (Fig. 25.11). Use a scale of $1\frac{1}{2}$ in. = 1 ft or 3 in. = 1 ft. (Ordinarily the working lines will be gage lines.)

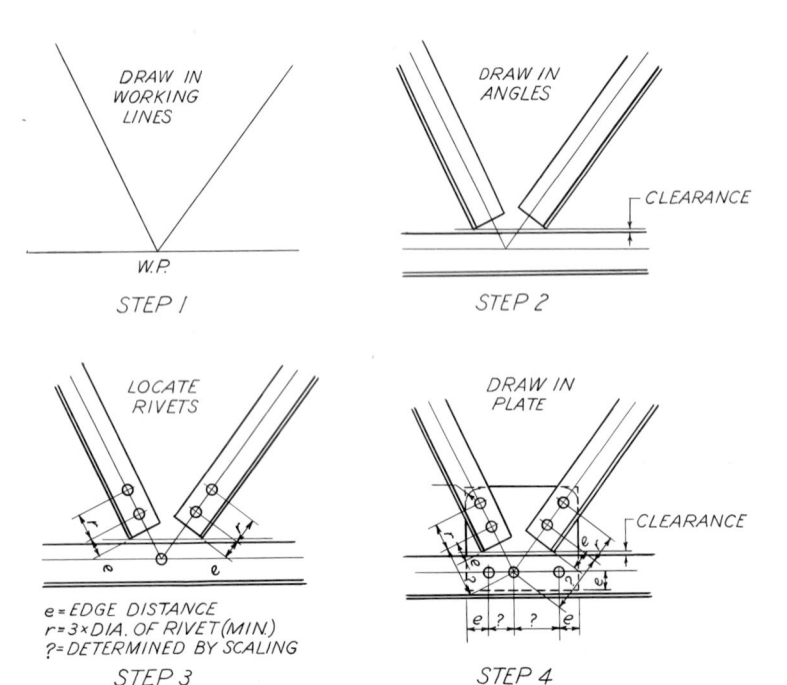

FIG. 25.11. Steps for making layout of gusset.

Step 2. Determine the correct dimensions and gages (Fig. 25.16) and draw in the lines representing the outstanding and perpendicular legs of the angles on the proper sides of the working lines. Draw in the clearance line at a preferred distance above the bottom chord angle and cut the diagonal angles perpendicular to their axes so that the corners fall on the clearance line.

Step 3. Locate an initial rivet in each diagonal at the desired edge distance from the sheared edge of the member. Since it is customary in structural drawing to give the distance from the working point to the first rivet to the nearest $\frac{1}{4}$ in., it usually will be found necessary to change either the edge distance or the clearance to meet this requirement. Locate the remaining rivets in each diagonal, using minimum spacing (3 × diameter of rivet), so that the plate will not be larger than is absolutely necessary.

Step 4. Draw in the edges of the gusset plate, after giving some consideration to the factors involved in an economical treatment of the design. The points to be observed are as follows: (1) Allow not less than minimum edge distance e from the center of each rivet to the nearest edge of the plate (Fig. 25.12). (2) Allow no corners of the plate to project beyond the angle. (3) Design the plate so that there will be a minimum number of cuts, for each cut increases the labor cost. (4) Make at least two edges parallel at a distance apart equal to a standard plate width, so that unnecessary cuts and material waste may be avoided.

The shorter dimension usually is considered to be the width and the longer dimension, the length. If the longer dimension is across the plate between parallel sides, however, it should be given as the width, because the plate may be cut from a long plate of that width. The length dimension usually is given to the nearest $\frac{1}{4}$ in. The dimensions of a plate are always those of a rectangle from which the plate may be cut.

Dia. of Rivet	Extreme Minimum "e"	Usual Minimum "e"	Preferred
$\frac{3}{8}$	$\frac{9}{16}$	$\frac{3}{4}$	$\frac{3}{4}$
$\frac{1}{2}$	$\frac{3}{4}$	1	1
$\frac{5}{8}$	$\frac{15}{16}$	$1\frac{1}{8}$	$1\frac{1}{4}$
$\frac{3}{4}$	$1\frac{1}{8}$	$1\frac{1}{4}$	$1\frac{1}{2}$
$\frac{7}{8}$	$1\frac{5}{16}$	$1\frac{1}{2}$	$1\frac{3}{4}$
1	$1\frac{1}{2}$	$1\frac{3}{4}$	2

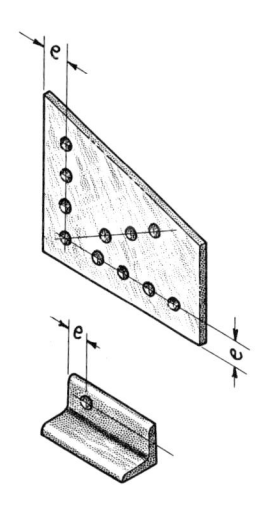

FIG. 25.12. Edge distance "e."

25.12
Machine-shop Work. The structural detailer will occasionally be called on to prepare detail drawings for castings for bridge shoes and roadway expansion joints and at times drawings for complicated gearing and shafting for movable bridges. Regular machine drawing practices apply, the principal difference being that bridge machinery in general is ponderous with single castings often weighing 10 or 15 tons.

25.13
Structural Welding. Since a large portion of structural work is either partially or completely welded, a working knowledge of the use of welding symbols (Chapter 22) is a requirement for a structural draftsman (Fig. 25.13).

Sizes and location of welds are usually given on the design drawing, but very

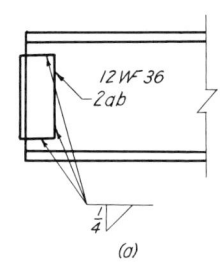

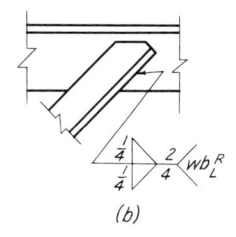

FIG. 25.13. Welded connections.

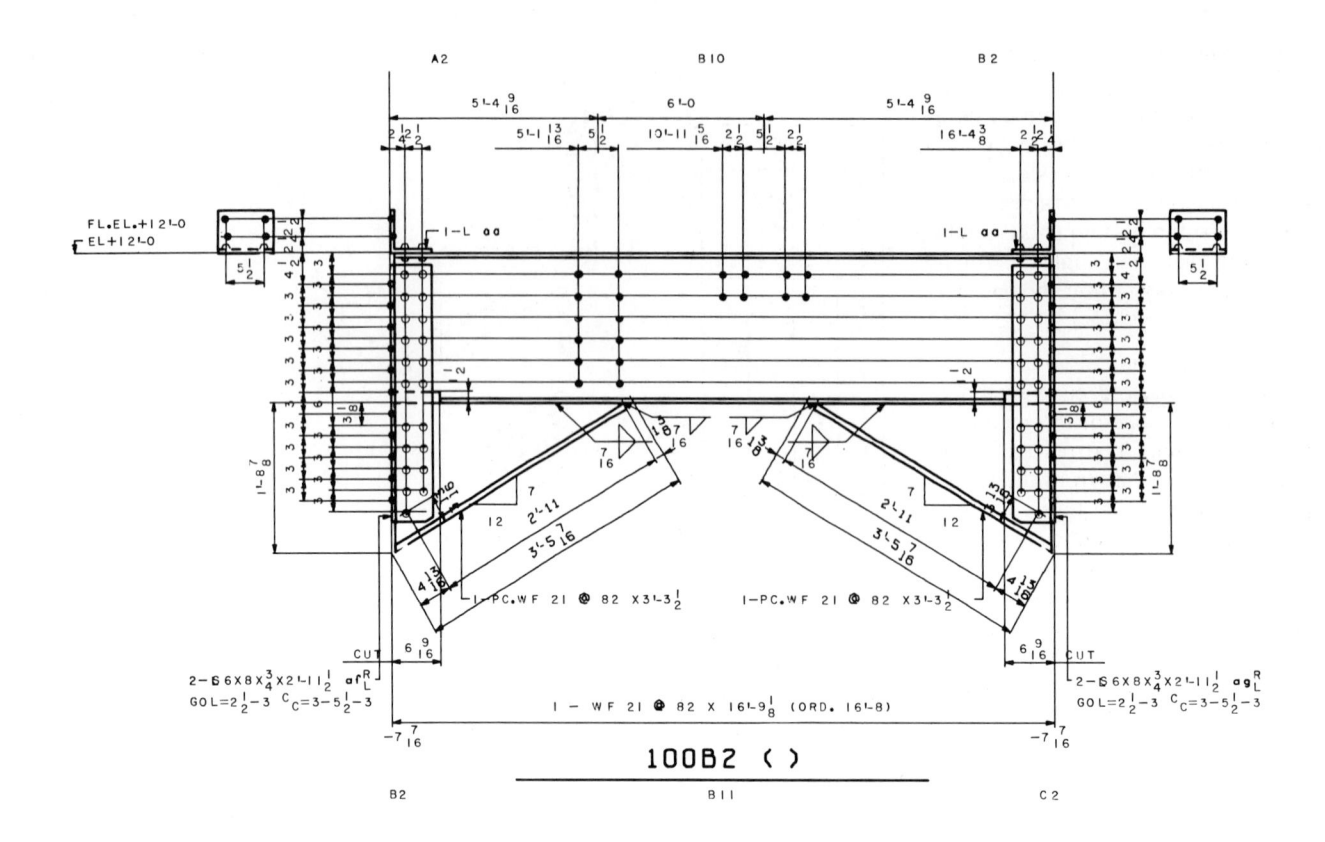

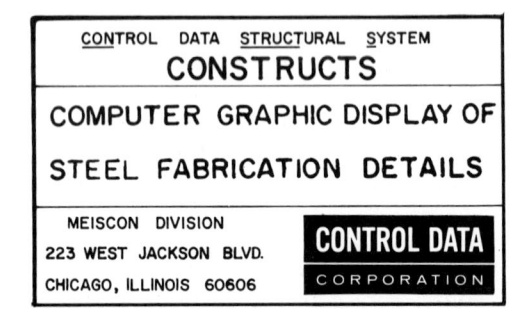

FIG. 25.14. A structural drawing prepared on a plotter. This drawing was made using the CONSTRUCTS System of automated drafting. (*Courtesy Meiscon Division, Control Data Corporation*)

often connections and minor details are left to the detailer.

25.14
Computer-plotter-prepared Structural Drawings. Programming systems have been prepared to produce complete shop (detail) drawings for the structural steel fabricating industry by automated drafting methods. See Chapter 18. At present, these systems will make shop drawings of beams, columns and bracing for most types of steel building frames. The Control Data Corporation (CDC) CONSTRUCTS System, which has been under constant development, now contains all of the specifications of the American Institute of Steel Construction and recognizes the standard practices for fitting and connecting structural steel shapes to carry the design loads indicated on the engineer's design drawings. The drawing shown in Fig. 25.14 was made using the Control Data Structural System.

In the application of programming systems that have been developed to prepare shop drawings to fabricate different types of structural members, a technician fills out an input form utilizing information furnished on the structural design drawing. This information, in turn, is fed into a computer for computation of the dimensions necessary for the fabrication of each structural member in a building framing plan.

The output from the initial run of the program is a complete set of tabulated computations and information. This print-out should be inspected for obvious errors. At this time, if there is a special reason, the person making the check may introduce nonstandard treatment of connections of members.

A second run through the computer produces a magnetic tape with the drafting instructions needed to direct the off-line plotter that will prepare the drawings.

PROBLEMS

The following problems are intended to furnish experience in the preparation of layouts and to emphasize the principles of structural drawing.

1. Make a pencil layout, plan, and elevation of joint A, Fig. 25.15. Follow carefully the steps outlined in Sec. 25.11 for making a layout of a gusset plate. The following requirements must be observed:
   Use $\tfrac{3}{4}$-in. ϕ rivets.
   Make the minimum allowable clearance between members $= \tfrac{1}{4}$ in.
   Use minimum rivet spacing $= 3 \times$ diameter of rivets.
   Use the preferred edge distance given in the table in Fig. 25.12.

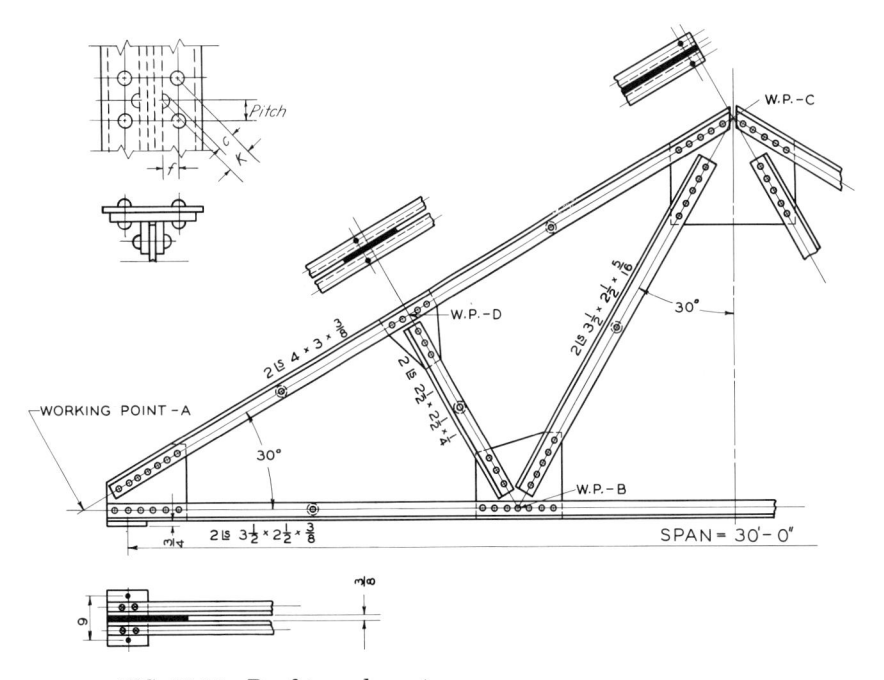

FIG. 25.15. Roof truss layout.

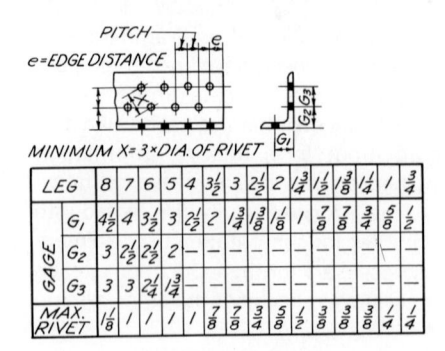

FIG. 25.16. Gage distances.

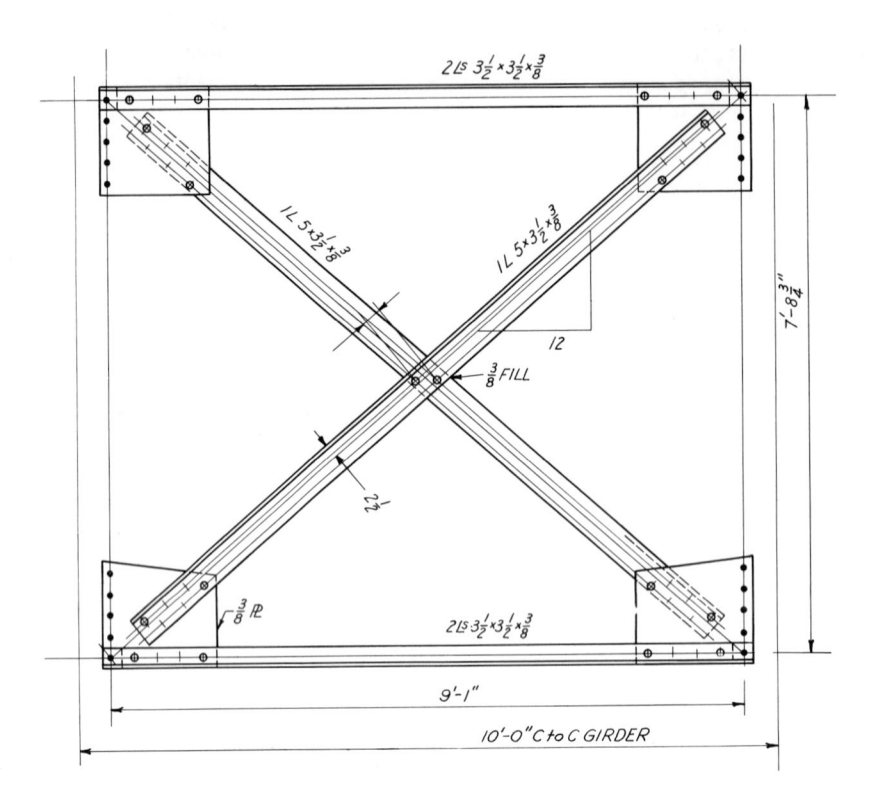

FIG. 25.17. Layout of interior cross-frame for 100 ft. railroad deck girder span.

Use standard gage distances, as given in the table in Fig. 25.16.

Make the width of the plate equal to the width of a standard plate. The variation of plate widths is by inches.

The bearing plate is a $9 \times \frac{3}{4} \times 1'\text{-}0$ steel plate. The rivet pitch in the plan view should be equal to the pitch of the rivets in the vertical leg, and they must be so located that the distances c, f, and k are equal to or exceed the minimum values for these distances for a $\frac{3}{4}$-in. rivet as given in structural handbooks. The minimum value of f for a $\frac{3}{4}$-in. rivet is $1\frac{1}{4}$ in.; the minimum value of k is $1\frac{3}{4}$ in.; and the minimum value of c is $1\frac{1}{4}$ in. These three values represent minimum driving clearance for a $\frac{3}{4}$-in. rivet.

The holes for the anchor bolts are $\frac{13}{16}$ in. in diameter. Letter the correct specifications for the gusset plate.

2. Make a pencil drawing of the cross frame shown in Fig. 25.17. The following requirements must be observed:

Use $\frac{7}{8}$-in. rivets.

Use a minimum rivet pitch of $2\frac{1}{2}$ in.

The elevation of the cross frame is the only view that is required.

Use standard gage and preferred edge distances, as shown in Figs. 25.12 and 25.16.

Use Fig. 25.5 as a model for the placing of complete dimensions.

The open holes are spaced at $3\frac{1}{2}$-in. pitch.

A touch of the electric "pencil" to the face of the tube signals the computer to begin the task of changing the roof lines. The attractive young designer in the photograph is attempting to arrive at a satisfying exterior design for a proposed residence. During the coming decade, computers and plotters will be widely used for preparing plans for commercial buildings. Floor plans will be laid out by plotters directed by computers. Other plans will be drawn by plotters operating off-line. Plotters will come to be recognized for what they really are—ordinary automated drafting machines operating under human direction. Practices and techniques of representation will not change to any great extent and designers and draftsmen operating plotters will find it necessary to have both a deep and broad knowledge of basic drawing.
(*Courtesy of International Business Machines Corp.*)

Architectural Drawings*

26.1

Introduction. The principles of architectural drafting are the same as those for other technical drawing work, except that the application of these principles requires special methods, symbols, and conventions. Architectural drawings of a building include floor plans, elevations, sections, and details sufficiently descriptive to permit the construction of the building according to the architect's ideas.

Although the architect and the architectural draftsman work hand-in-hand in the preparation of a set of plans for a structure, there is a wide gap between the experience and knowledge that each possesses. The architect may be his own draftsman, but the draftsman cannot be his own architect. The draftsman's function, therefore, is to assist in the execution of the architect's ideas. The architect must know not only how to prepare accurate working drawings, but he must also understand the best uses of buildings from the economic and social points of view; he must know business administration so that he may understand the financial and legal transactions incident to modern building construction; he must develop a sense of proportion and a knowledge of pleasing form and color through the study of the history of architecture; he must be familiar with the mechanical trades, such as plumbing, heating, electricity, and other engineering features, that have such an important bearing on the safety and durability of a structure.

26.2

Preliminary Studies. Before the architect or draftsman is required to draw the plans and elevations or the working drawings of the house, the owner and architect should have reached certain conclusions about the general design or style of the house, the kind of material to be used, the size, and the approximate cost of the proposed structure. Although it is impossible to give an accurate schedule of costs at this point, the following is an indication of the relative percentage of the cost of materials, labor, and land involved in building the average home.

Cost of materials	45.40%
Construction labor	29.80%
Overhead and profit	12.20%
Cost of land	12.60%
	100.00%

Following is an outline that the architect

---

*Prepared by William J. Hornung, Director of Long Island Technical Institute.

may prepare for further development by himself or his draftsman after consulting with the owner.

Design for Two-Level Stone Masonry and Frame House

Rooms—Main Floor

1. Living room with fireplace.
2. Dining room.
3. Kitchen.
4. Storage and heater room.

Rooms—Second Floor

5. Two bedrooms with closets.
6. Bathroom.
7. Terrace or sun deck.

Type of Construction

8. Concrete footings; masonry wall construction for first floor; frame walls for second floor; redwood siding.
9. Double-hung frame windows; six lights for each frame.
10. Flat canvas deck roofs, insulated.
11. Heating: one-pipe hot-water; recessed convectors.
12. Sewage disposal: septic tank and leaching pool.
13. Provide for future breeze-way and one-car garage.

26.3

Preliminary Sketches. In many instances the architect will prepare for himself or submit to the draftsman a freehand sketch of the plan showing the arrangement of rooms and indicating the approximate size of each room (Fig. 26.1). From this sketch the draftsman will prepare a preliminary drawing to a scale of $\frac{1}{8}'' = 1'\text{-}0''$. Of course, certain considerations and adjustments must be made as far as the arrangement and general dimensions of rooms are concerned, because the scale drawing will never quite work out in exact accordance with the preliminary rough sketch. When good circulation and a suitable arrangement of rooms are obtained, the draftsman will then lay out the $\frac{1}{4}$-in. scale drawing of the main-floor plan.

26.4

Presentation Drawings. The primary purpose of presentation drawings is to give the owner a general, realistic picture of the proposed structure. Presentation drawings may be made in several ways. One method is to prepare a perspective view of the exterior of the building, rendered in pencil, ink, or color. Walks, shrubbery, or trees that may surround the building are included. With the rendered perspective it is customary to show the main-floor plan giving the names and sizes of rooms in order that the client may study the room arrangement. A rendered perspective drawing is shown in Fig. 26.2(*a*) and (*b*).

In place of rendered perspectives, actual scale models of the proposed buildings are finding favor with many architects. The model is made in the drafting room, using paper and cardboard cut to size and glued together, forming an exact replica of the proposed building. The

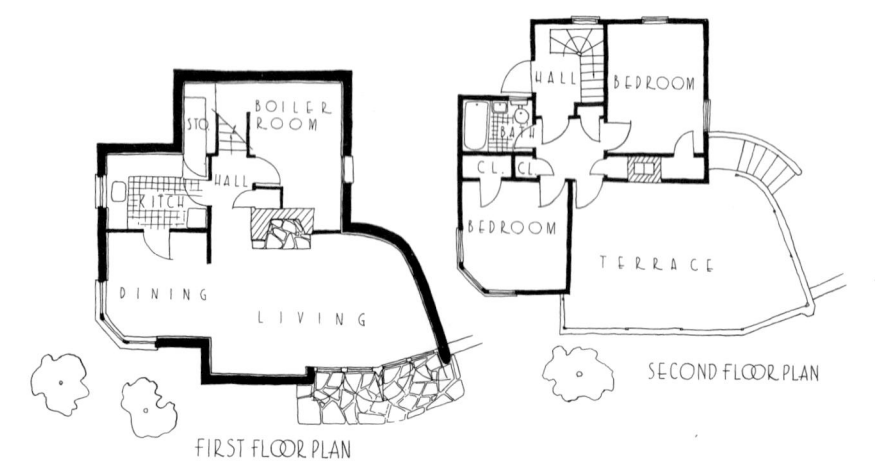

FIG. 26.1. Preliminary sketches.

CHAP. 26 / ARCHITECTURAL DRAWINGS 567

(a)

(b)

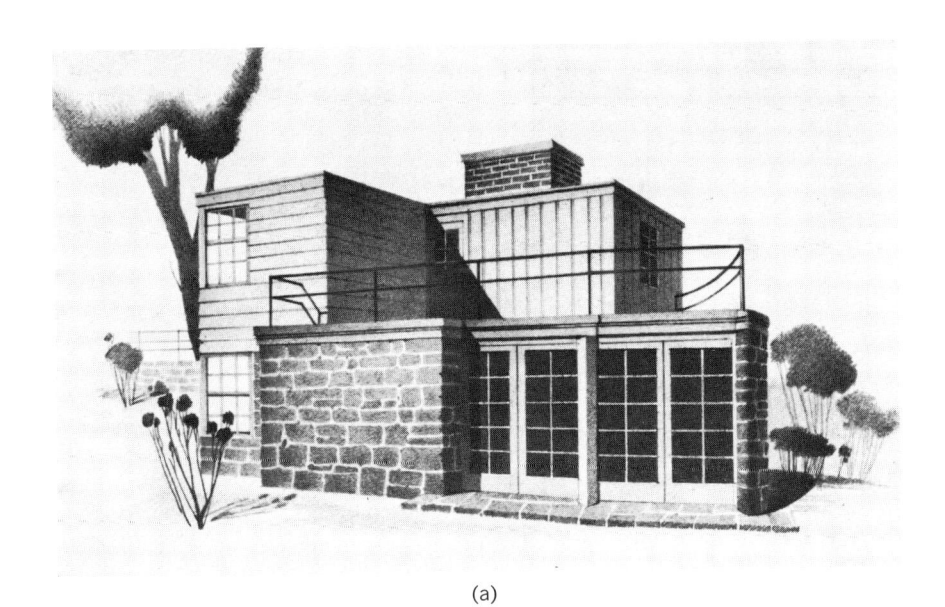

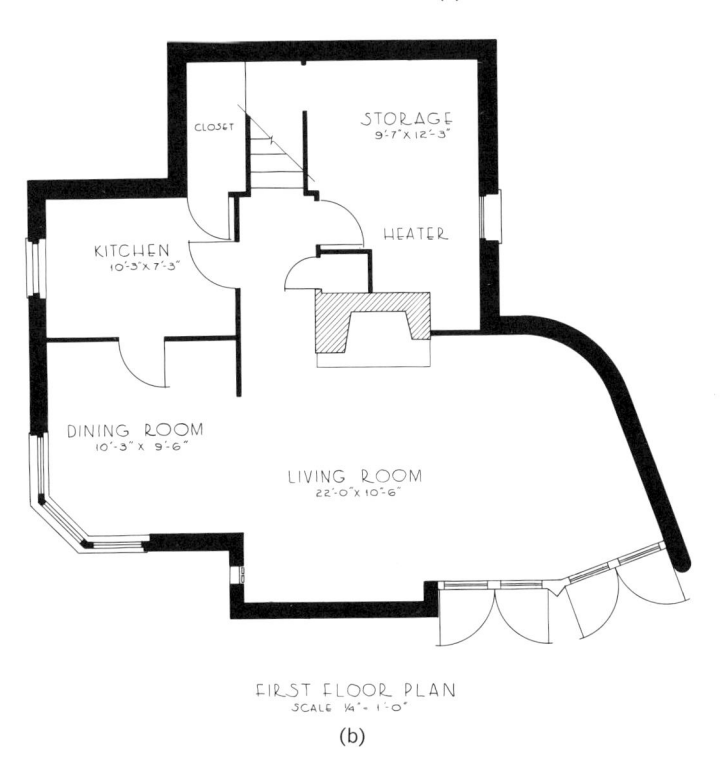

FIG. 26.2. **Presentation drawing.**

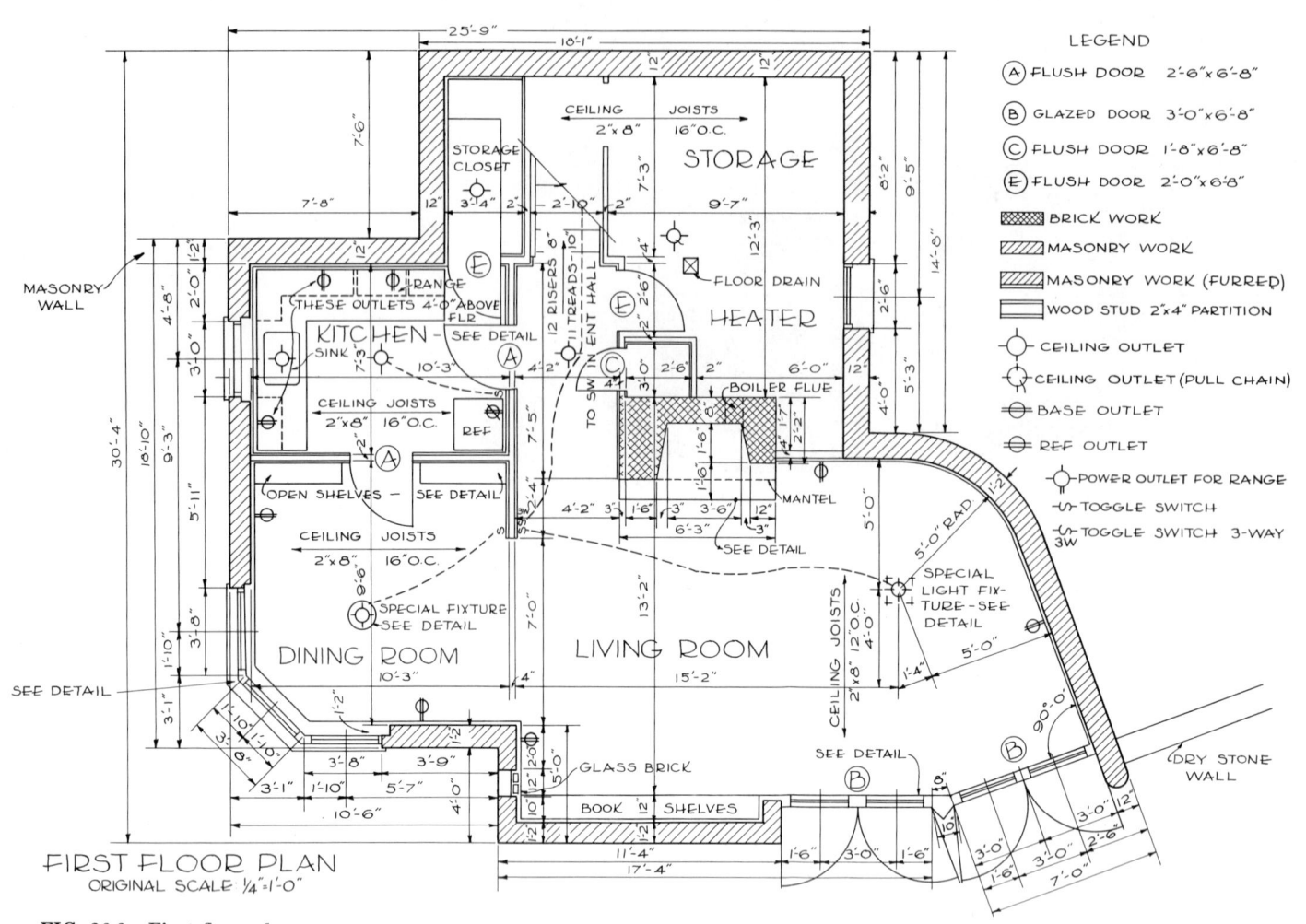

FIG. 26.3. First-floor plan.

effect of shrubbery, trees, hedges, and grass can be attained by colored sponges, sawdust, and sand. Such models are of great value to both architect and client because they can be viewed from all angles and their proportions can be studied more accurately.

26.5
Working Drawings. A set of working drawings consists of all of the drawings that are necessary for the contractor to erect the building. The set is composed of the plans, elevations, sections, details, and the lettered notes that assist in the interpretation of the drawings. In addition to the working drawings, the contractor also receives written instructions called *the specifications*. These specifications cover all the features that are not shown on the blueprints, such as the quality and quantity of the materials and the methods to be used in the construction or the manner in which the work is to be

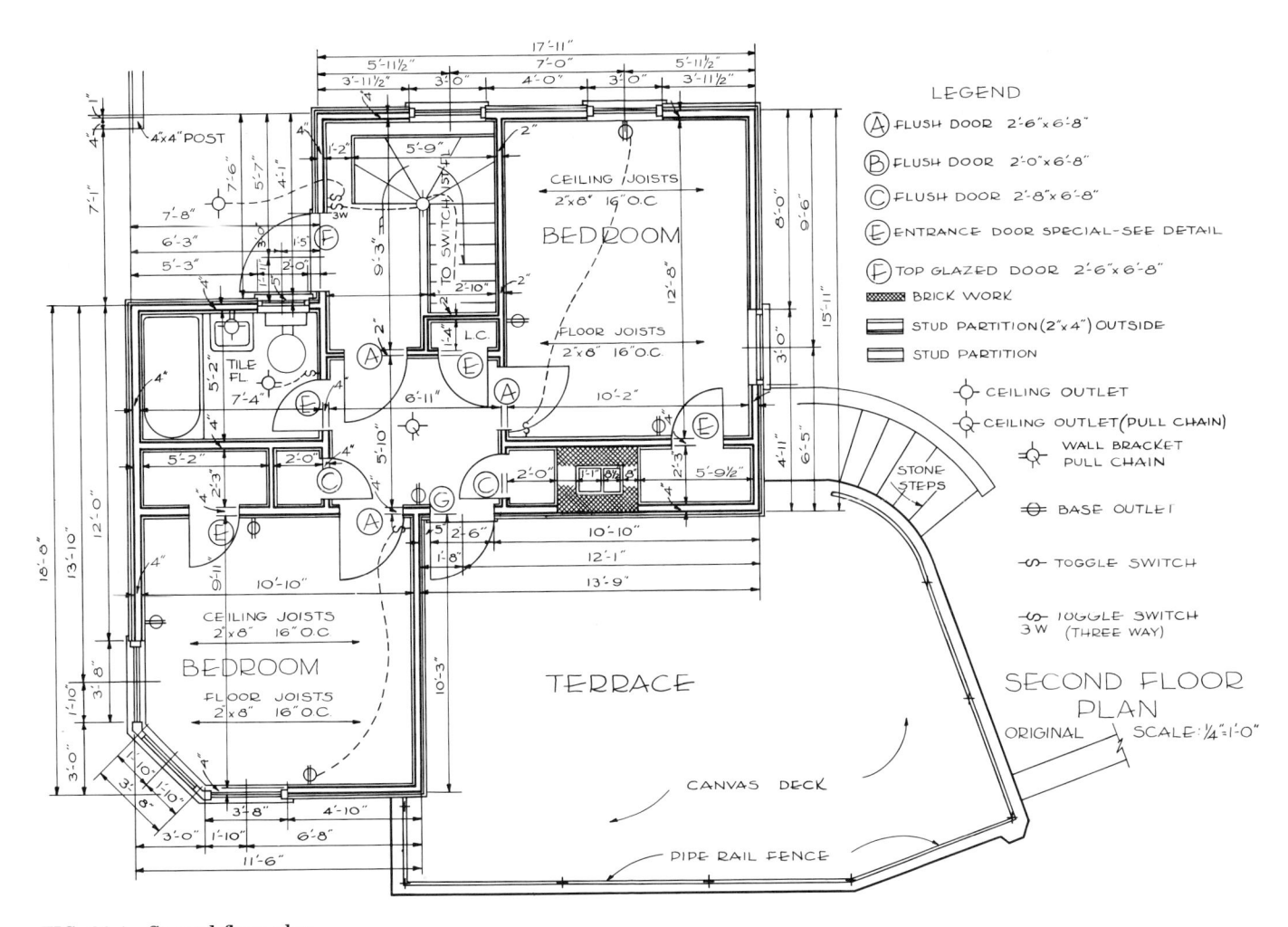

FIG. 26.4. Second-floor plan.

conducted. Like the plans, the specifications are indispensable to the builder. They are typed and accompany a set of working drawings.

26.6
The Plans. When a set of working drawings is prepared, the main-floor plan is generally drawn first, as in Fig. 26.3. This plan is a horizontal cut taken through the building at a level halfway up the windows. Its purpose is to show the builder the location of both outside and inside walls, their thicknesses, lengths, and the materials of which they are constructed. The location of windows and doors, stairs, fireplace, and other data pertaining to electrical outlets, fixtures, floor finishes, and the direction and sizes of overhead floor joists are indicated.

From the main- or first-floor plan the outlines of other floor plans are traced, such as the basement or foundation plan, the second-floor plan (Fig. 26.4), or the roof plan. Since many drawings are needed in the erection of a building, it is quite common to use a separate sheet for each plan. Special details that apply to the particular drawing are included.

26.7

The Elevations. The primary purpose of the elevation drawings (Figs. 26.5 and 26.6) is to give the builder the height dimensions of doors, windows, floor-to-floor heights, ridge heights, chimney height, and the finished-grade level in relation to the finished-floor level. On the elevations are also indicated the type of outside wall finishes, roof finishes, and the style of doors and windows. In many cases two elevation drawings, front and side, are sufficient to give the necessary information, but it is advisable to draw the four elevations of the building when each elevation has a distinct feature that cannot be clearly shown on other drawings.

26.8

The Plot Plan. One of the functions of a plot plan is to locate the house on the lot so that the builder knows where to begin. When a tract of land is intended for a home development site it is generally the practice to lay in public utilities, such as sewerage disposal systems, water, gas, and electricity. This necessitates a pattern of streets and avenues with sidewalks forming blocks. A block is generally un-

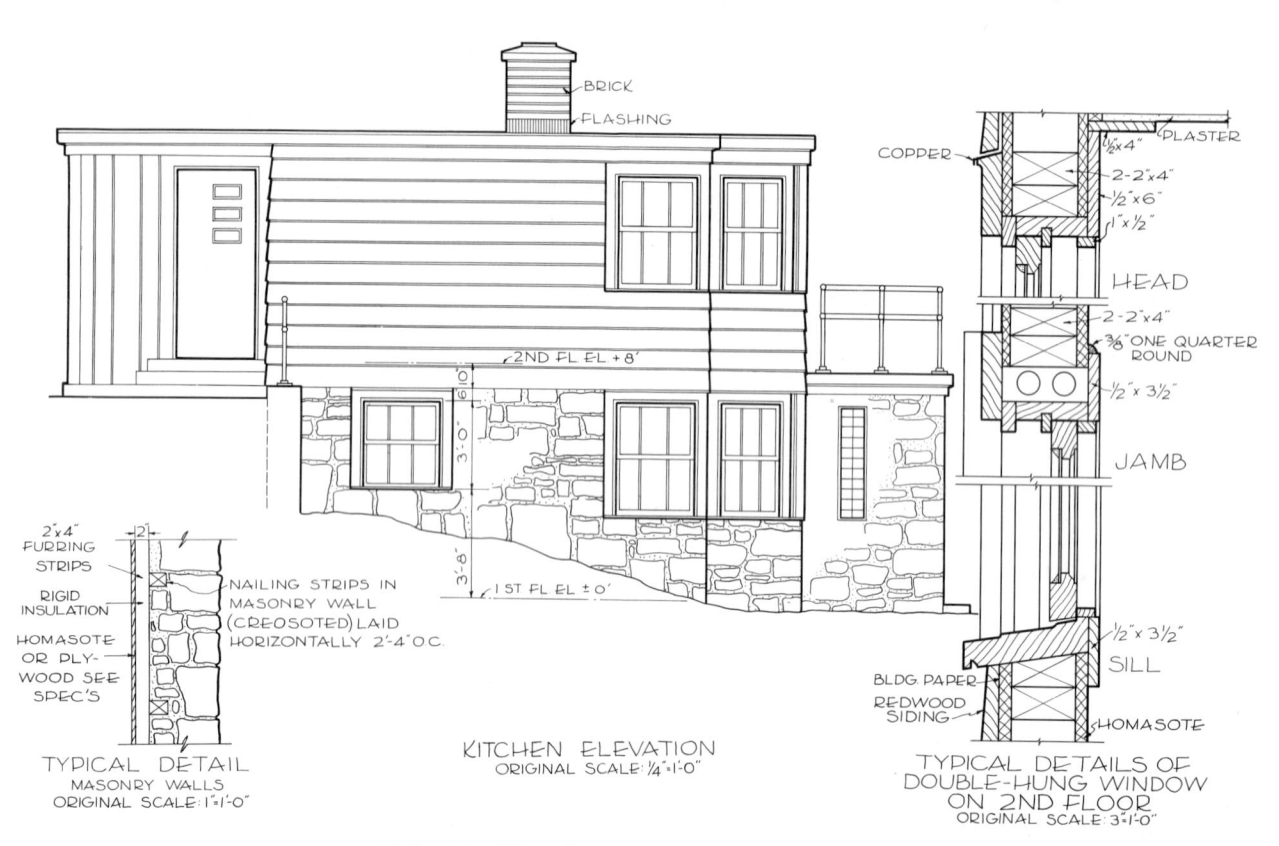

FIG. 26.5. Elevation.

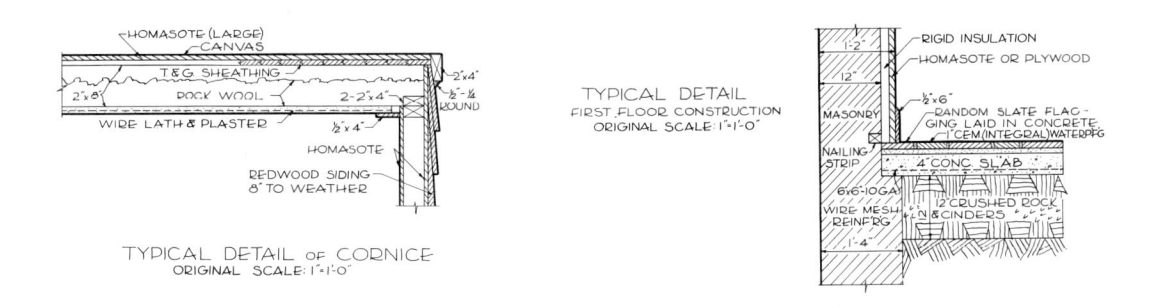

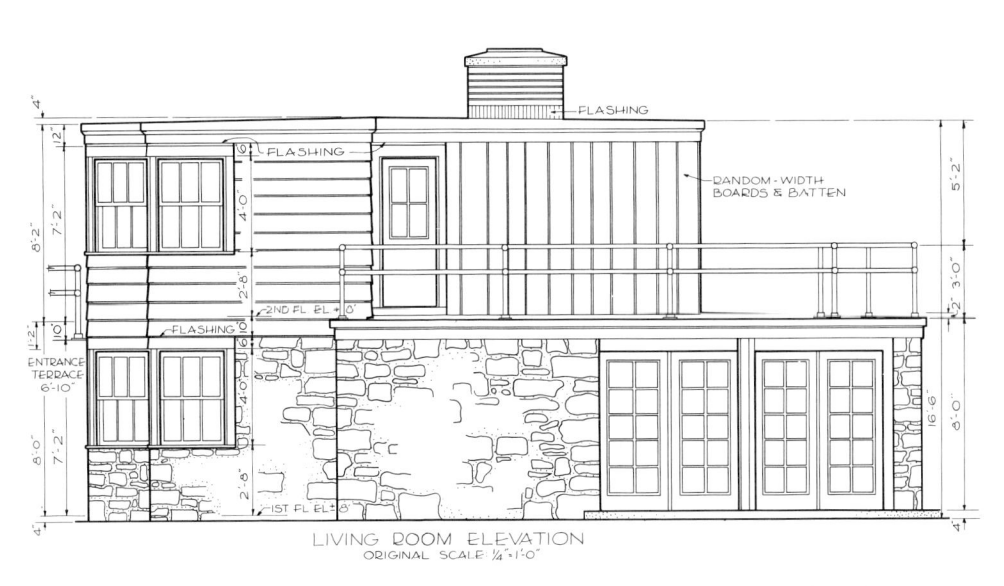

FIG. 26.6. Elevation.

derstood to mean an area of land rectangular in form bounded by streets and avenues. Each block, in turn, is subdivided into lots of the same or varying sizes (Fig. 26.7). Local building regulations frequently call for certain restrictions on the "frontage" or the distance that must be maintained between the street and the location of the house on the lot. In such cases the plot plan must show the exact location of the house on the lot. In unrestricted areas a landowner may build his house without defining the location of

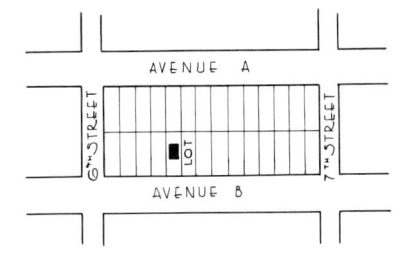

FIG. 26.7. Rectangular block bounded by streets and avenues subdivided into lots.

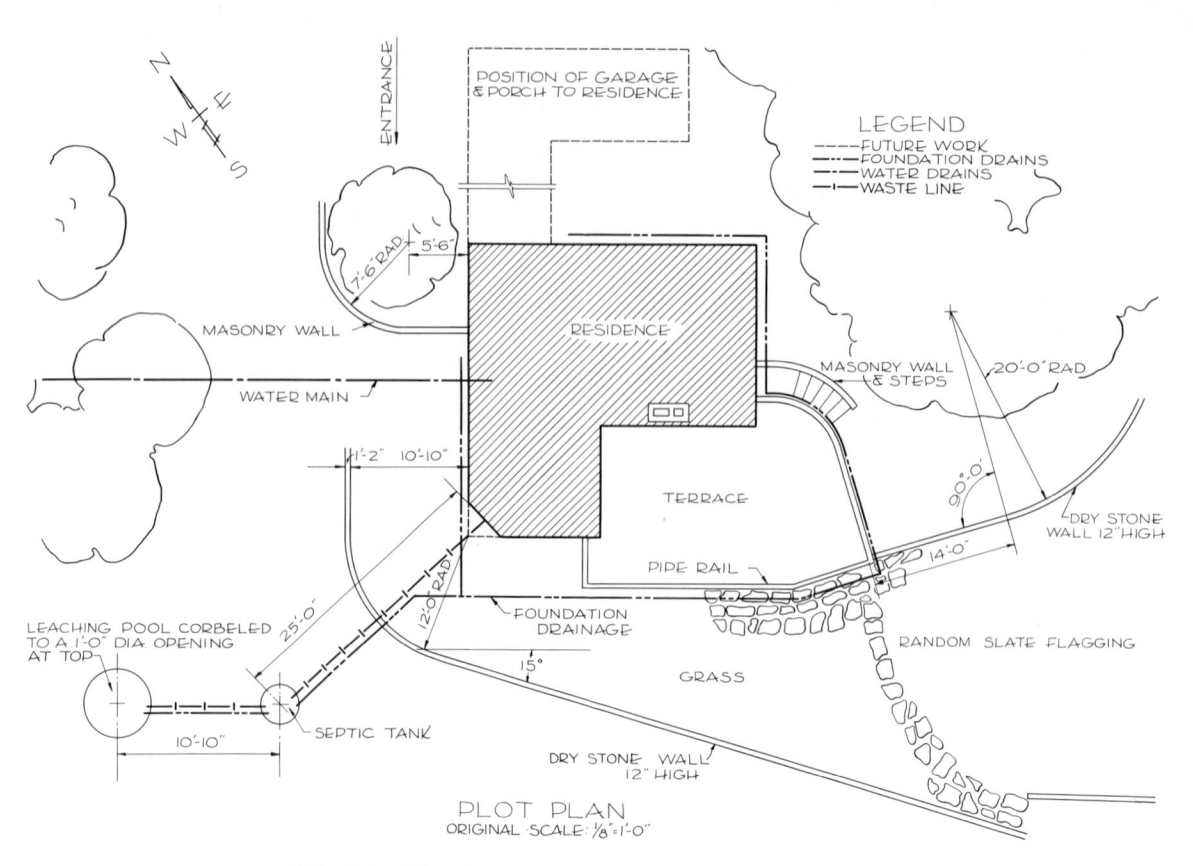

FIG. 26.8. Plot plan.

the house on the land, as shown in Fig. 26.8. Plot plans also show where sewer, water, gas, and drainage lines are located. If driveways and walks are to be built, they must also be shown. Shrubbery, existing trees, and the points of the compass are included on a finished-plot plan.

26.9
Sections. In addition to the plans and elevations, "part sections" are often used to clarify the drawings further. These "part sections" (Fig. 26.9) are often shown on the same drawing with the elevations, but generally are of larger scale.

The longitudinal or cross section is intended to show the interior construction and architectural treatment. It is a cut taken on a vertical plane through the center of the building. This cutting plane need not be continuous but may be staggered to include as much information as possible. Longitudinal or cross sections, as shown in Fig. 26.10, are of definite value to the builder. They show him the construction of the building from the footings to the roof rafters. The type of outside-wall construction is represented by its symbols; floor and ceiling joists are clearly shown and their sizes given; partition walls, stairs, fireplace, and interior-wall finishes can be indicated. Important height dimensions given from finished floor to finished ceiling are a definite aid in understanding the construction. On longitudinal sections cellar-floor constructions can also be indicated with dimensions and specifications so that in many instances larger details are not required.

26.10
Wall Sections. On smaller construction it is often desirable to draw a "wall section" in place of the longitudinal or cross section so that all the necessary height dimensions and the construction can be shown. Wall sections are drawn to scales of $\frac{1}{2}''$,

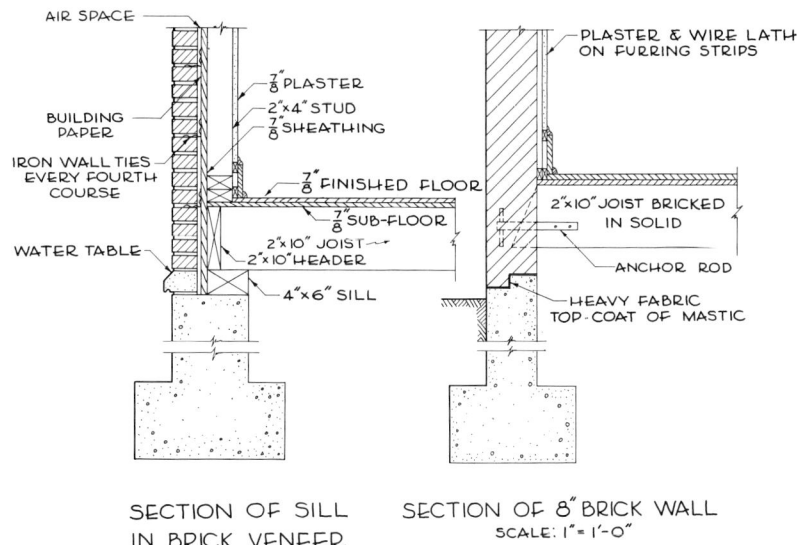

FIG. 26.9. Part sections.

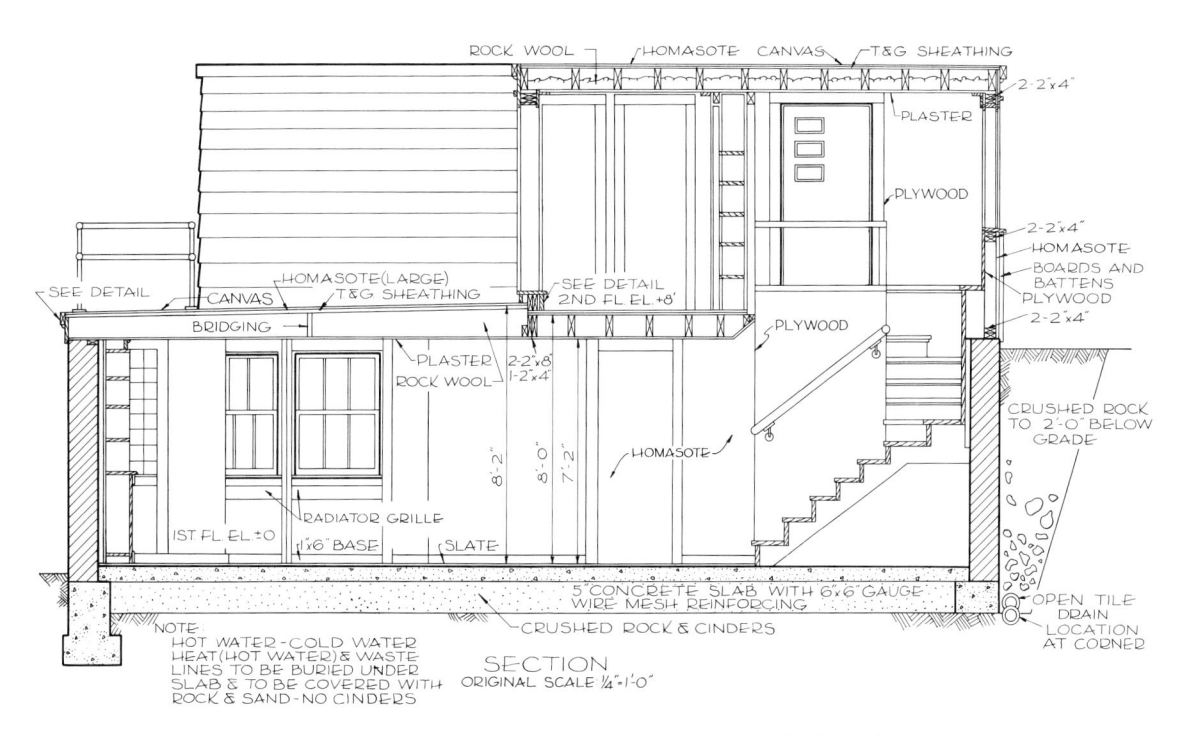

FIG. 26.10. Longitudinal section.

$\frac{3}{4}''$, or $1'' = 1'-0''$. A wall section such as that shown in Fig. 26.11 gives the depth of the footing below grade and the dimensions of the footing and the foundation wall. The 4-in. concrete floor on 6-in. cinder fill on earth is understood to be typical throughout. The section includes a window located by dimension above the finished-floor level, and the height and type is shown. The method of spanning the window opening by a precast reinforced concrete lintel is indicated. The section further shows a built-up roof properly flashed to the wall. The exterior and interior wall finish can be represented by symbols and notes.

26.11
Details. A set of working drawings is never quite complete without the large-scale detail drawings. Large-scale details are made when other drawings cannot describe the construction clearly. They are drawn to a scale of full size, half size, $3'' = 1'-0''$, $1\frac{1}{2}'' = 1'-0''$, $1'' = 1'-0''$, $\frac{3}{4}'' = 1'-0''$, or $\frac{1}{2}'' = 1'-0''$. Typical details, such as that shown for the small house (Fig. 26.12), include the elevation of the fireplace wall in the living room, special lighting fixtures, entrance door details, and other details, which can be clearly described but cannot be shown on other drawings at smaller scales. For larger buildings many additional detail drawings must be prepared, as illustrated in the window detail in Fig. 26.13. To be able to prepare good detail drawings the draftsman needs much experience in the use of trade literature, catalogs, and books dealing with the principles of construction. It might be well to mention here that in order to draw complex details the draftsman is largely dependent on manufacturers' information and previous similar drawings.

26.12
Special Features. In present-day building

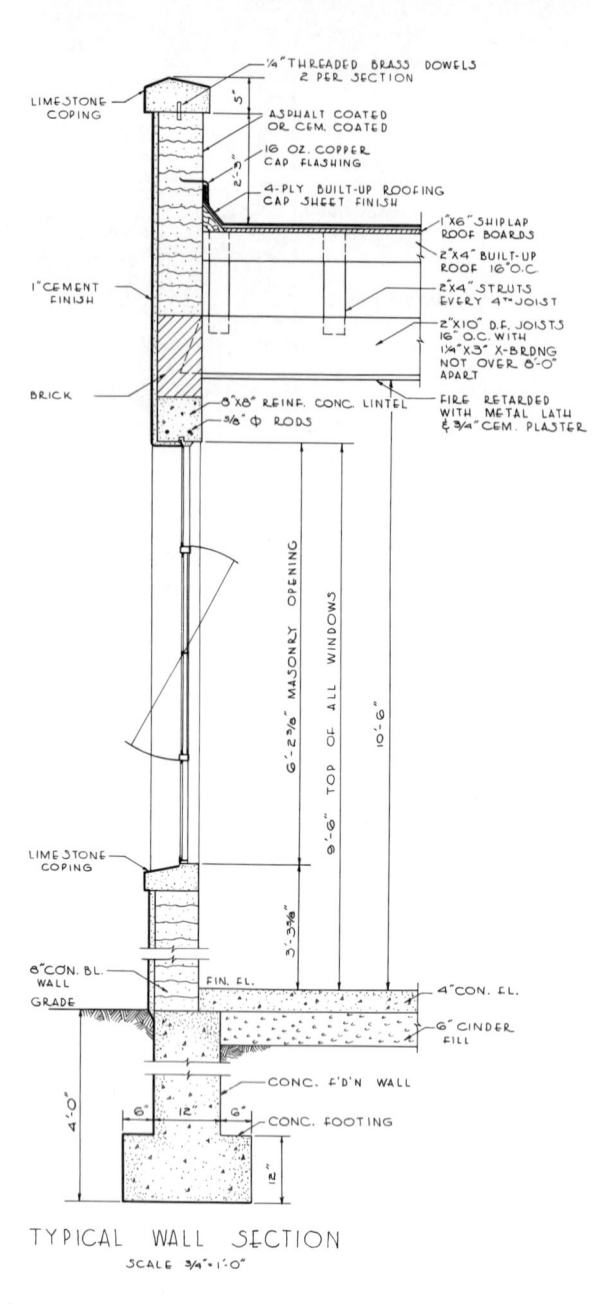

FIG. 26.11. Wall section.

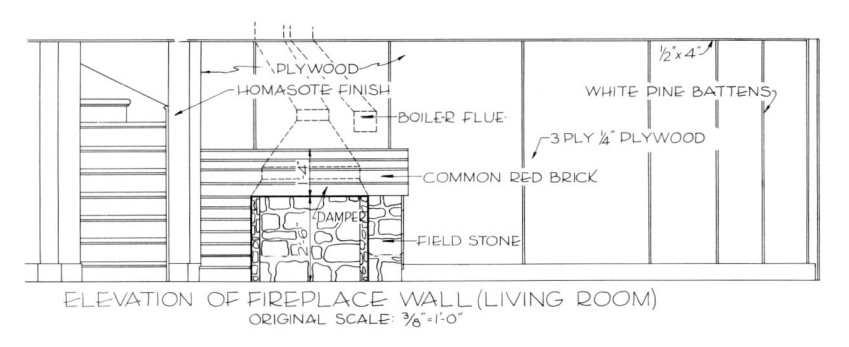

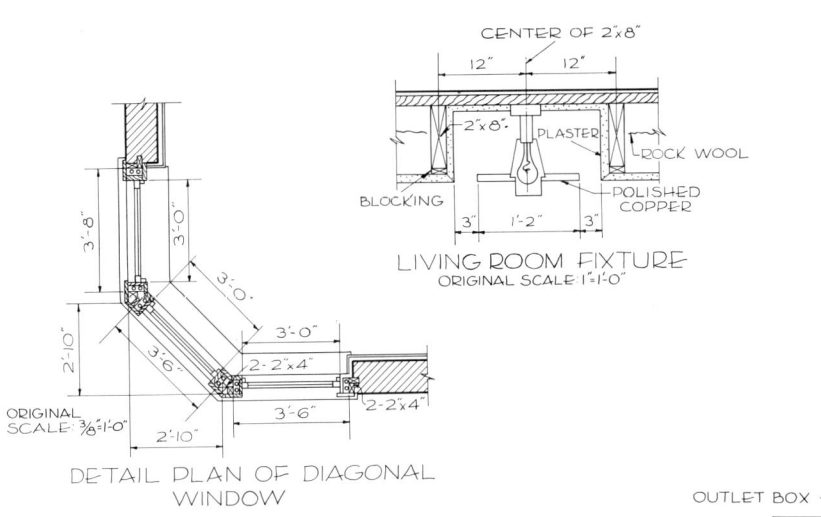

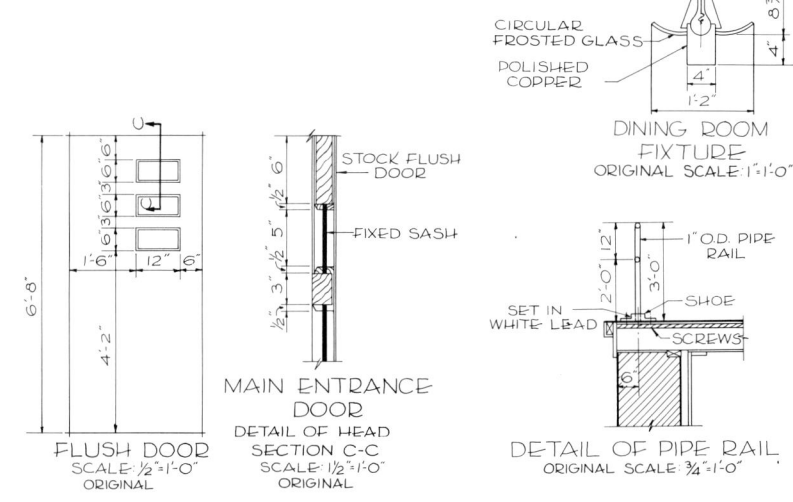

FIG. 26.12. Typical details.

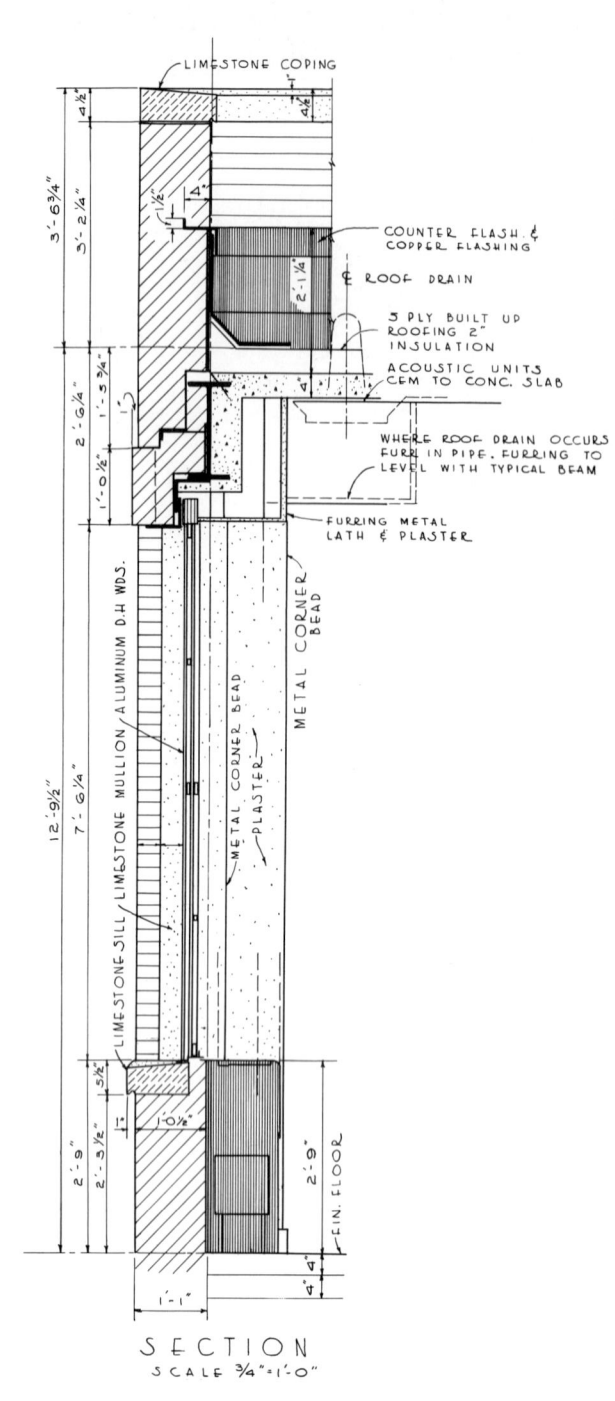

FIG. 26.13. Window detail.

construction, many parts that are used are manufactured by firms specializing in one particular item. As an example, wood sash details vary with different manufacturers. The architect gets scale details from the makers and draws his building to conform. Figure 26.14 shows a detail of a double-hung window and a table of cellar-window and picture-window sizes as supplied by the manufacturer. Other items, such as stair parts, doors, railings, fans, radiators, heating equipment, and many other special features, are always planned from drawings supplied by the manufacturers.

26.13
Symbols. The working drawings for a structure are composed largely of symbols and conventions representing manufactured items and materials. For example, in a plan a foundation wall made up of concrete block has a symbol of crosslines and dots. This symbol is universally understood to mean concrete blocks. The symbol for concrete is represented by small triangles, circles, and dots, representing crushed stone or gravel, sand, and cement. All architects, draftsmen, and builders understand these symbols that form a language of lines and correlate thought in the trade. Many symbols for materials have been standardized by the American National Standards Institute to facilitate understanding. Some of the new materials that have been added to the building industry in recent years have not as yet been standardized. When such materials are used on drawings a key to the materials must be included with the work. Figure 26.15 shows materials and conventions that have been standardized.

26.14
Dimensioning. Dimensioning of the working plans and elevations is governed primarily by knowledge of building construction. Dimensions must be so placed

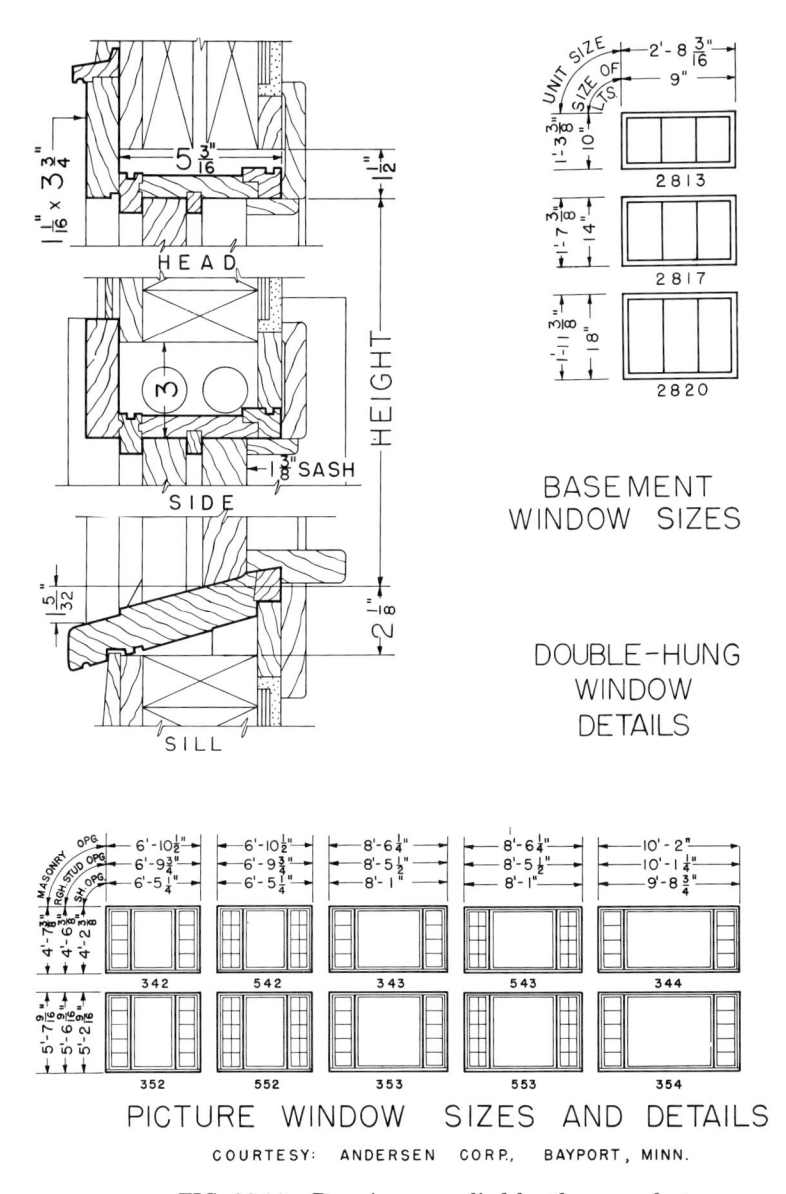

FIG. 26.14. Drawings supplied by the manufacturer.

that they are most convenient for the workman. On plans it is desirable to show dimensions around the outside of the plan whenever possible. Inside dimensions are generally those locating partitions, columns, beams, doors, or other openings. Dimensions on frame plans are given from the outside faces of studs on exterior walls

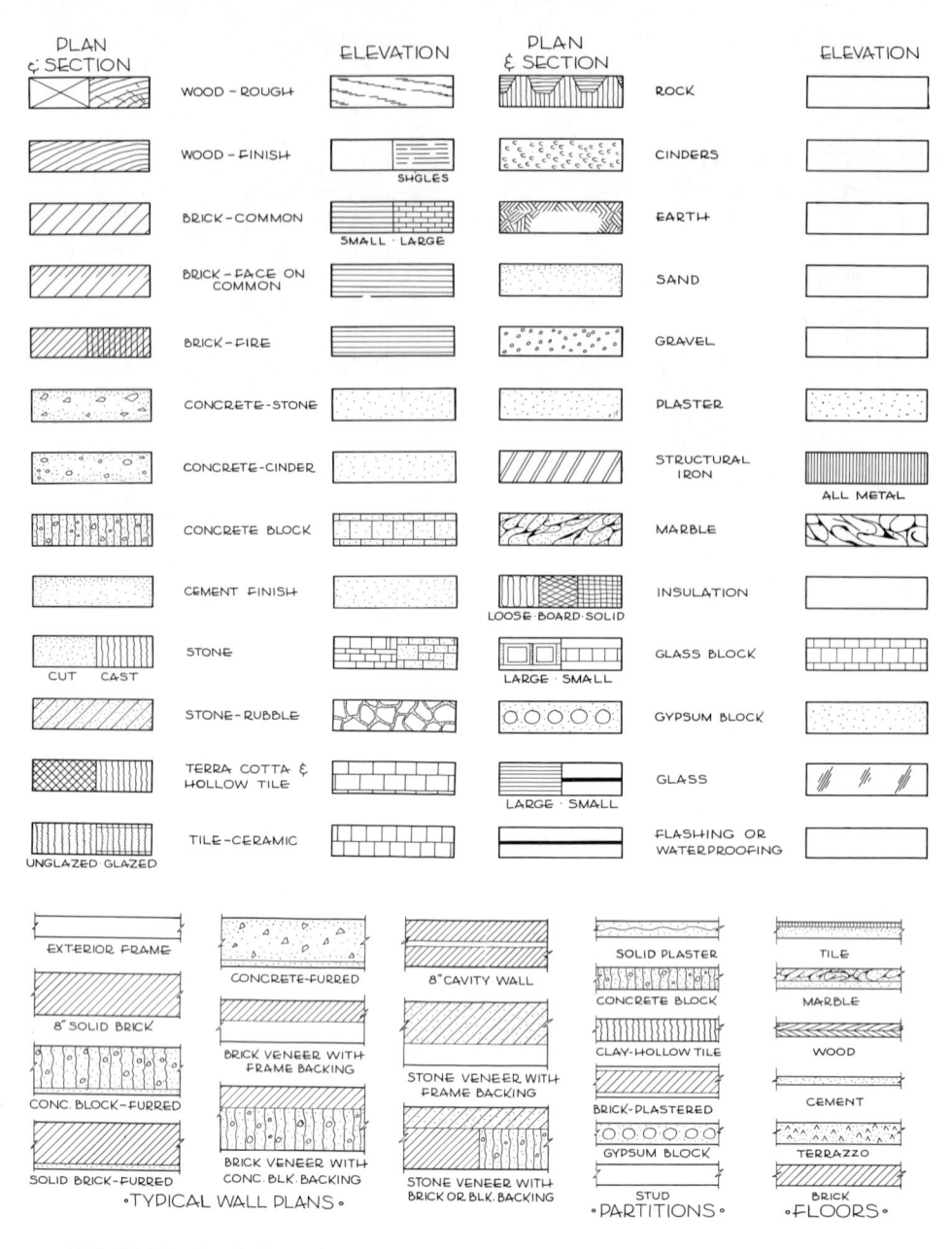

FIG. 26.15. Symbols and conventions.

to the center line of the window or door opening. Stud partitions may be located to the center of the partition or to the stud face. On masonry, outside-wall dimensions are given from the outer face of the wall to the opening of the window or door, then across the opening. Masonry-wall openings, such as doors and windows, may also be dimensioned to the center line of the opening. The elevations or cross sections must give the height or vertical dimensions of floors, windows, beams, roofs, and chimney. The plans in Figs. 26.3 and 26.4 and the elevations and cross section in Figs. 26.5, 26.6, and 26.10 should be carefully studied by the student before he attempts to place dimensions on a drawing.

26.15
Special Notes. In addition to the written specifications furnished the contractor, special notes are lettered on the drawings to clarify the work. Builders are apt to overlook a point mentioned only in the specifications, but because they are using the drawings constantly they will be sure to see a reference or note on the drawing of the part in question. It is also common practice to use "schedules"—notes laid out in tabular form. The finish schedule shown in Fig. 26.16 gives finish treatments of rooms, floors, and ceilings. Door schedules and window schedules are also commonly used on drawings so that the work will be better understood by the tradesmen.

26.16
Lettering. The lettering on drawings is as important as the plans of the building, because without lettered explanatory notes, titles, and dimensions, the plans could hardly be understood. The single-stroke architectural letter shown in Fig. 26.17 is typical of that used by the architect. The style is closely related to the old

FINISH SCHEDULE						
ROOM	FLOOR	BASE	WAINSCOT	WALLS	CEILING	TRIM
SALES	CONCRETE	WOOD PAINTED	PLASTER PAINTED		PLASTER PAINTED	WOOD PAINTED
TOILETS	CERAMIC TILE	CERAMIC TILE	CERAMIC TILE	PLASTER PAINTED	PLASTER PAINTED	WOOD PAINTED
STORAGE	CONCRETE	NONE	MASONRY CLEANED UNPAINTED		CEMENT PLASTER UNPAINTED	WOOD PAINTED
SERVICE ROOMS	CONCRETE	NONE	MASONRY PAINTED		CEMENT PLASTER PAINTED	WOOD PAINTED
NOTE: FOR COLOR OF PAINT AND NUMBER OF COATS SEE SPECIFICATIONS							

FIG. 26.16. Finish schedule.

Roman form. It is becoming increasingly evident that single-stroke uppercase architectural letters are gaining favor over the lowercase form and the trend is toward letters that resemble more closely the mechanical style of letter used in previous chapters of this text. In large architectural firms where many draftsmen are em-

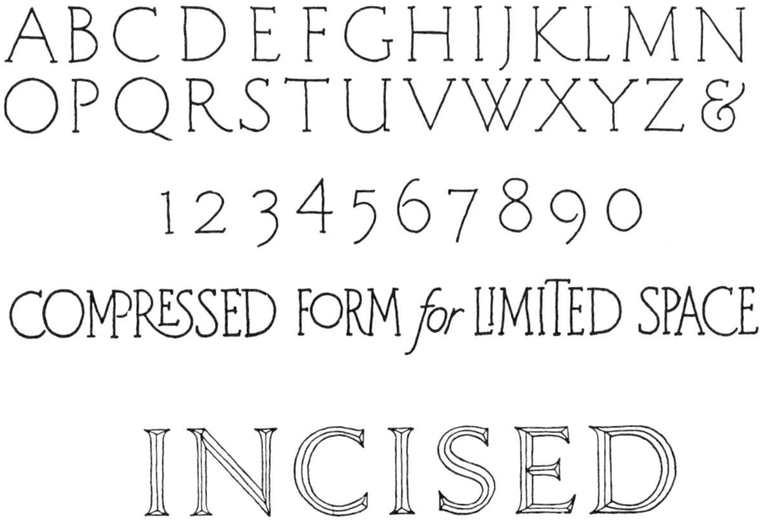

ABCDEFGHIJKLMN
OPQRSTUVWXYZ&
1234567890
COMPRESSED FORM for LIMITED SPACE
INCISED

FIG. 26.17. Architectural lettering.

ployed, mechanical guides are used for lettering in order to minimize individuality of style of the draftsman and to make the drawings more consistent in character. Another type of lettering the architect is called on to execute is the *incised* or the old Roman style that is used when letters are cut into stone, bronze, or other material used in connection with design (Fig. 26.17).

PROBLEMS

The following problems permit the student to prepare the necessary working drawings for building construction and introduce him to the study of architectural design. The problems may be modified or amplified by the teacher to the particular students' needs.

1. Draw the first-floor plan of a small house similar to the one represented in Fig. 26.3. The student may modify the plan or create one of his own design. It is advisable first to prepare rough, freehand thumbnail sketches of the plan to study room arrangements, window locations, and space for furniture. Have the instructor check preliminary sketches, and then proceed to draw a $\frac{1}{8}$-in. scale plan. After studying the plan again, proceed with the final $\frac{1}{4}'' = 1'-0''$ scale plan and dimension it completely. Check Fig. 26.3 for conventional representations of windows, doors, fireplace, stairs, fixtures, and material symbols.

2. Draw the foundation plan of the house to a scale of $\frac{1}{4}'' = 1'-0''$. Indicate concrete footings, foundation walls, footing for chimney, lally columns, if any, and windows. Completely letter and dimension the plan.

3. Draw the remaining two elevations of the house shown in Figs. 26.5 and 26.6. Refer to the plans in Figs. 26.3 and 26.4. Use a scale of $\frac{1}{4}'' = 1'-0''$. Particular attention should be given to the conventional representations of windows on the elevation and the important height dimensions.

4. Draw the detail of a window used in the plan of your own design showing the head section, jamb, and sill, to a scale of either $1\frac{1}{2}'' = 1'-0''$ or $3'' = 1'-0''$. Refer to window detail of Fig. 26.13 or 26.14. Indicate the rough openings and sash openings. These dimensions can be secured from manufacturers' catalogs.

5. Draw the front elevation to the plan drawn in Problem 1, to a scale of $\frac{1}{4}'' = 1'-0''$. Make preliminary sketches of the elevation and have them checked by the instructor before proceeding with the scale drawing. Check Figs. 26.5 and 26.6 for correct window conventions in elevation and symbols for exterior treatment. Place the necessary height dimensions on your drawing.

6. Draw a side elevation for the plan drawn in Problem 1, to a scale of $\frac{1}{4}'' = 1'-0''$. Heights, such as floor, grade, ceiling, and roof, may be projected from the front elevation. Make use of the plans for location of windows and doors.

7. Make the framing plans of the house of your design. Trace the outline of the foundation plan in Problem 2, and select joist sizes from standard tables on "Joist Spans and Sizes." Double the floor joists where partitions run parallel to the joists. Study the framing around stairwell and chimney openings.

8. Draw a longitudinal cross section through the house of your design. Use a scale of $\frac{1}{4}'' = 1'-0''$. Refer to plans and elevations for lengths and heights. Take section through stair and fireplace if possible. Use Fig. 26.10 for reference. Indicate all material by proper symbol and dimension section completely.

9. To a scale of $1\frac{1}{2}'' = 1'-0''$, draw a wall section showing the footing, foundation wall, sill construction, window-in-wall section, and cornice construction. Show all necessary dimensions. Refer to Fig. 26.11 for methods of dimensioning.

10. Draw any details necessary to clarify fully the working drawings completed. For suggestions about the type of details, refer to Fig. 26.12.

A highway route plan and profile. See Fig. 27.12. Program systems have been developed to produce civil engineering plans for highway, sewer, and drainage construction. The route plan and profile sheet shown was produced on a CalComp 702 in less than twenty-five minutes. All of the lines and lettered information were generated, except the title block at the bottom. The keypunch operator interprets the field notes and punches the required information into cards. This information is then fed into the computer to produce a magnetic tape which contains the needed drafting instructions. Johnson and Anderson, Inc. started to develop their system in late 1967. Their initial success encouraged further work towards the complete system that they now use to make their drawings at much less cost than by manual methods. To improve the total system further, they modified their method of taking field notes and changed the graphic read-out procedure. Increased efficiency is expected in the near future. (*Courtesy Johnson & Anderson, Inc., Consulting Engineers, Pontiac, Michigan*)

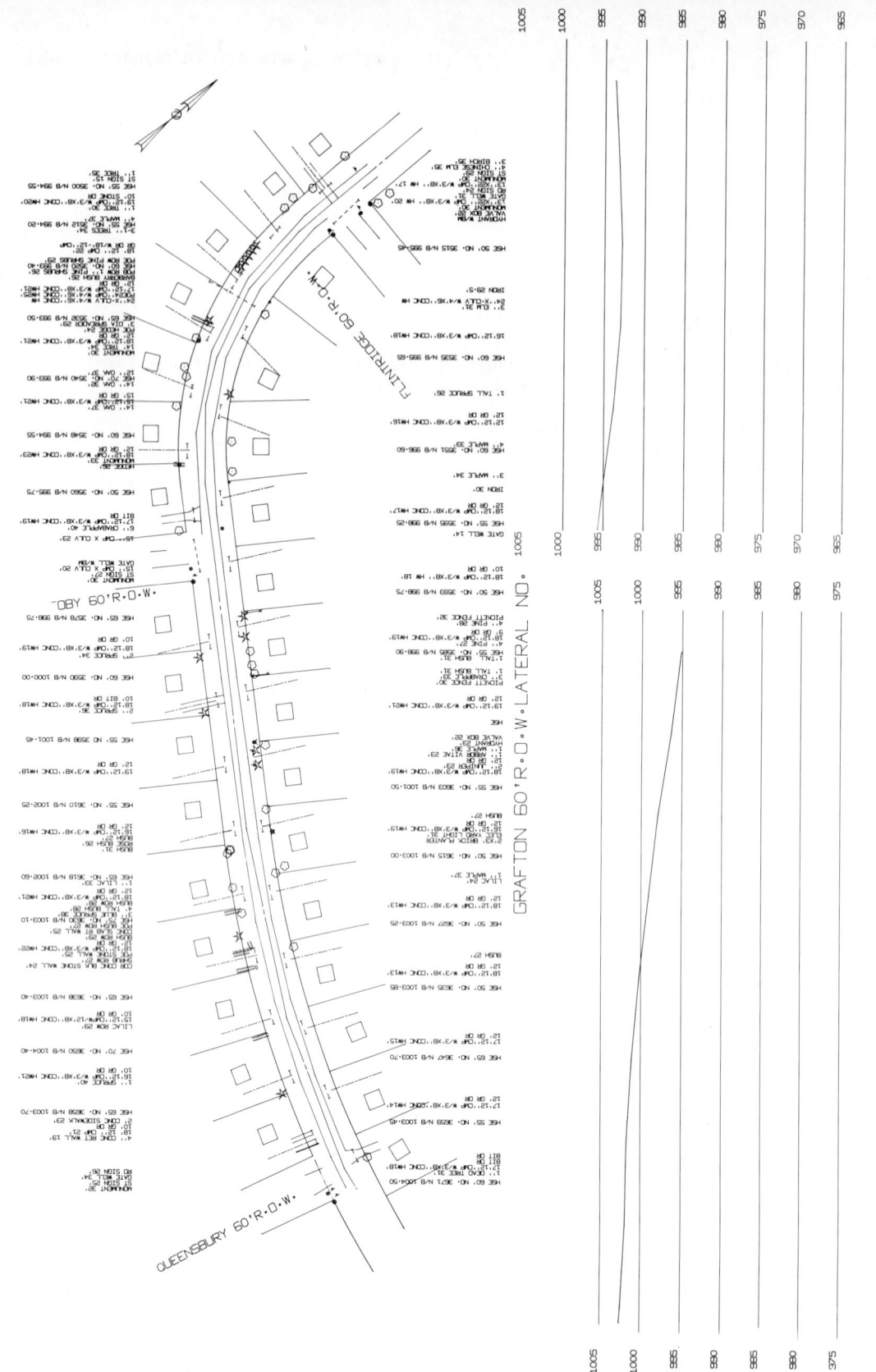

Topographic and Engineering Map Drawings

27

27.1
Map Drawing. A map is a drawing that represents a portion of the earth's surface area. Since it usually represents a relatively small part and the third dimension (the height) is not shown except in some cases by contour lines, a map may be thought of as a one-view orthographic projection (Fig. 27.1). Various forms of maps have been devised to satisfy different requirements. Land maps, plats, and so on, which fulfill their purpose by revealing only the natural and man-made features along with imaginary division lines and geometrical measurements, show only two dimensions. Others, such as topographical maps, show three dimensions, by representing height by means of contours.

27.2
Classification of Maps. Maps of interest to the engineer may be grouped for study in four general classes, in accordance with their purpose and method of preparation. The recognized classes are (1) topographical, (2) cadastral, (3) engineering, and (4) aerial photographic.

27.3
Topographic Maps. Topographic maps, although they are drawn to a relatively small scale, contain much detail. All natural features, such as lakes, streams, forests, fields, mines, and so on, and important permanent man-made creations, such as buildings, bridges, and houses, may be represented if necessary to fulfill the purpose of a map. Topographic maps, prepared by the United States Geological Survey to a scale of approximately 1 in. to a mile ($1/_{62,500}$), naturally do not contain very much detail (Fig. 27.2). The form of

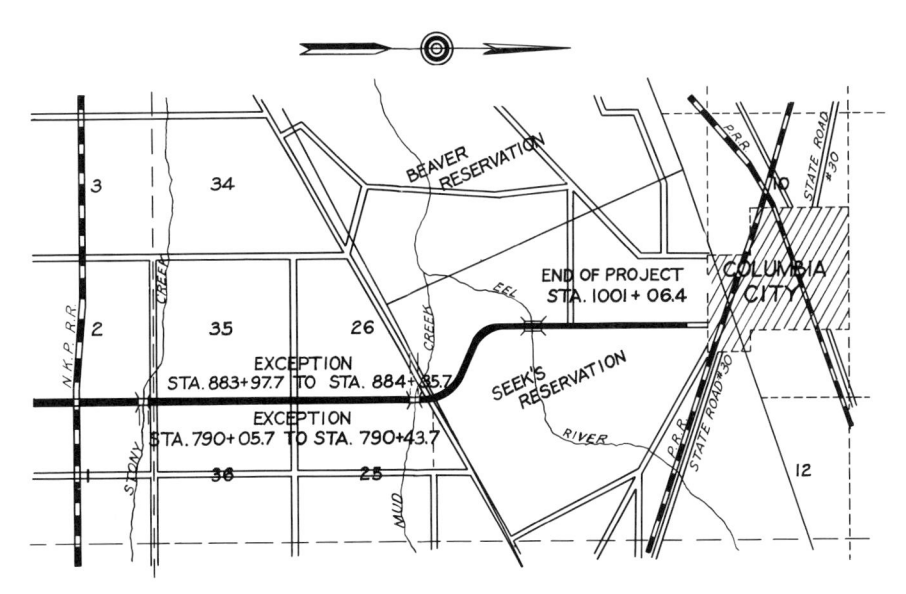

FIG. 27.1. A section from an engineering map.

583

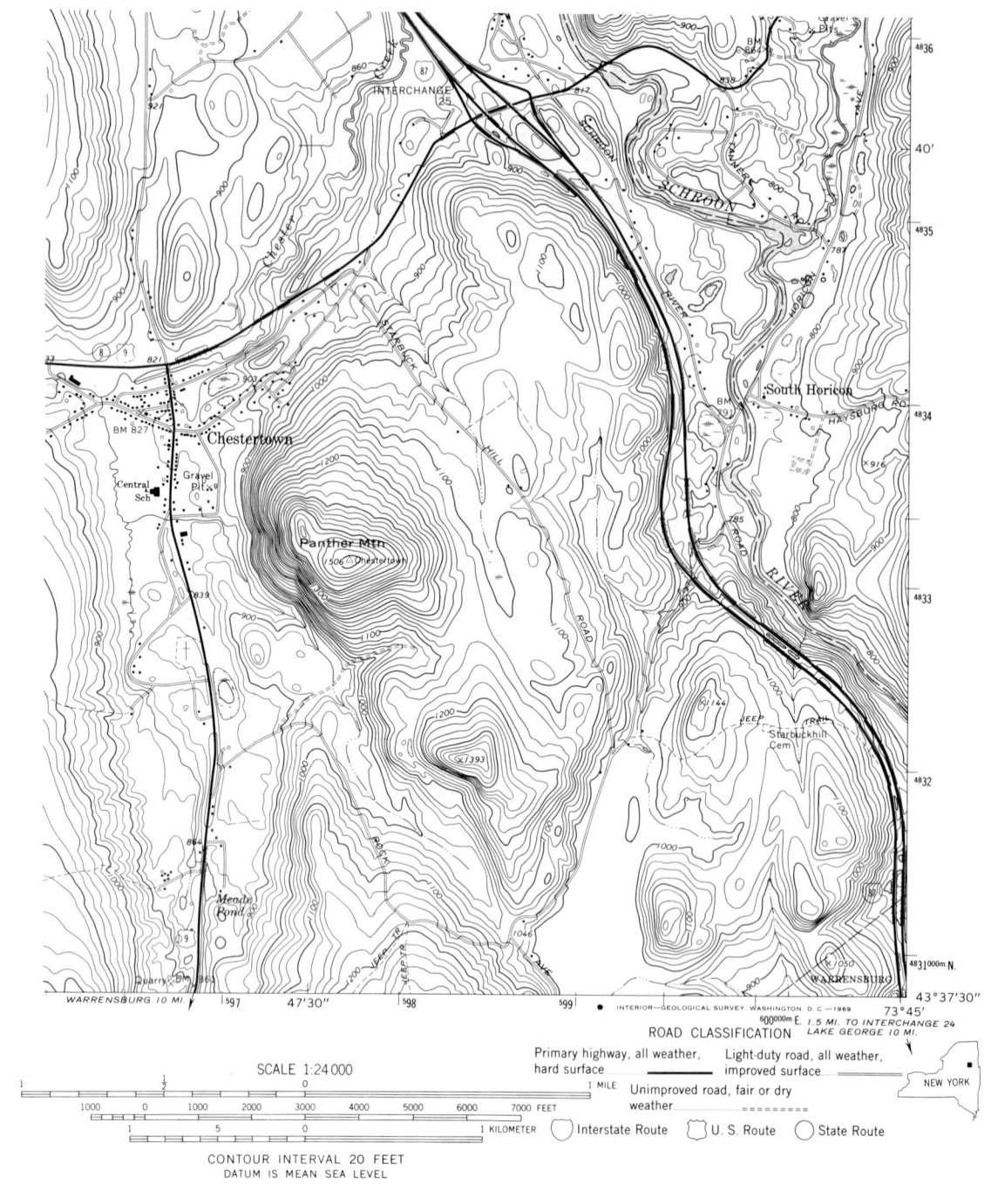

FIG. 27.2. Typical map prepared by the U.S. Geological Survey.

the surface of the ground is represented by contour lines. Any one contour line passes through points of the same elevation and closes either on the map or beyond its limits. Closed contour lines represent either a hill or a depression. Figure 27.6 shows a topographic map.

27.4
Cadastral Maps. The major portion of this group consists of city plats, city development maps, town maps, county maps, and maps prepared to show ownership (particularly for the purposes of governmental control and taxation). These maps, although they show practically no detail, must be accurate and for this reason are drawn to a large scale. Property lines, political boundaries, and a few important features, such as streams, roads, and towns, may be given on township and county maps, to enable a reader to identify particular locations.

27.5
Engineering Maps. Working maps prepared for engineering projects are known as engineering maps. They may be drawn for either reconnaissance or construction purposes. They usually are made to a large scale and accurately show the location of all property lines and important features. On maps of a topographic nature, practically all natural and man-made features along a right-of-way or on a site are shown, and the form of the surface of the ground is indicated by means of contours.

27.6
Plats of Land Surveys. A plat of a tract of land should contain a complete description of the land surveyed. It should show the lengths and bearings (or included angles) of the bounding sides and division lines, the included acreages, the locations of the monuments, and the names of the owners of the adjoining

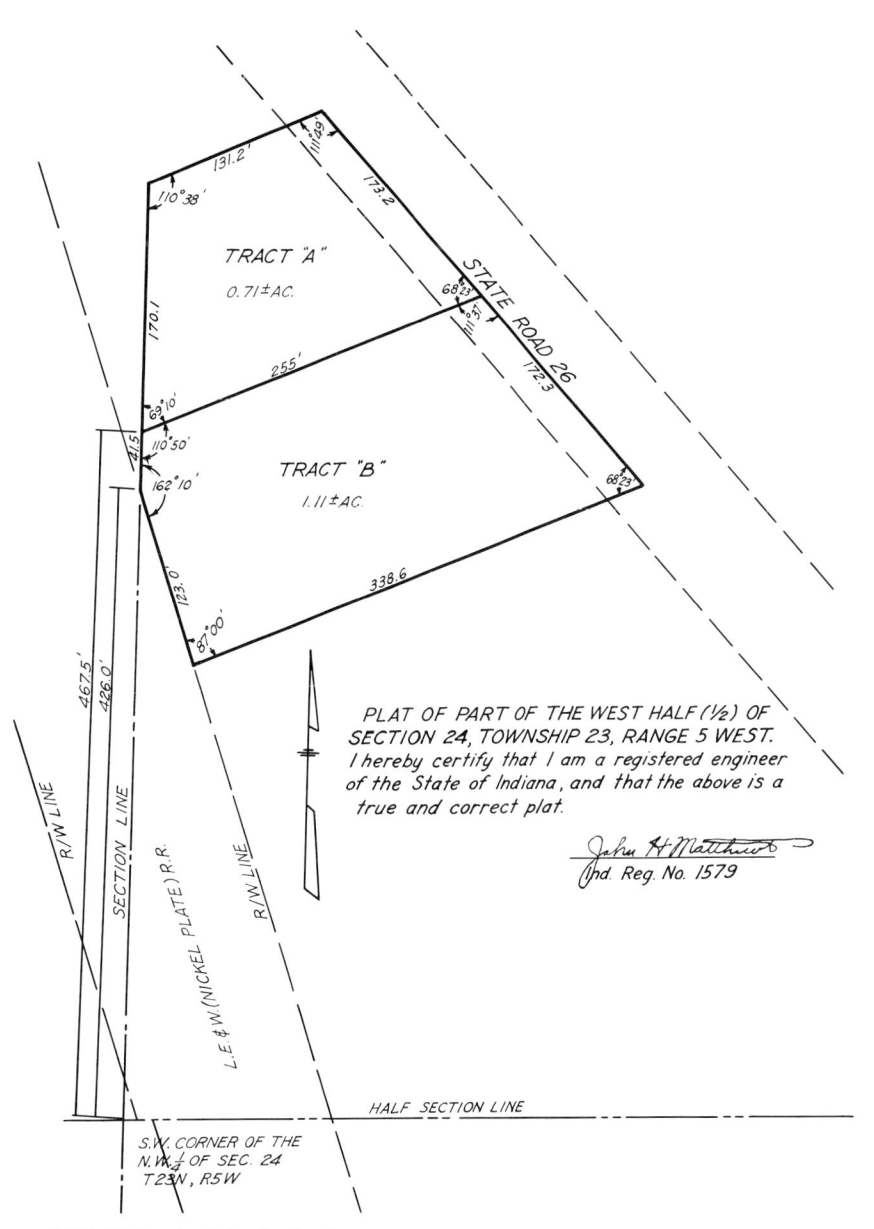

FIG. 27.3. A plat of a land survey.

properties. Figure 27.3 shows a plat of a typical land survey. Note that a clear, concise title is lettered in the large open area. A certification of the survey is generally required by law. In most states, a plat must bear the seal of a licensed surveyor.

27.7
Subdivision Plats. A plat of a real-estate development should show the measurements and angles of the survey of the whole tract of land, the sizes of the included lots, the widths of the streets and drives, and the locations of all monuments. Plats of subdivisions must be complete and accurate, since they are filed as public records in the county recorder's office. Sufficient information must be given to enable a surveyor to locate the corners of any lot with precision when

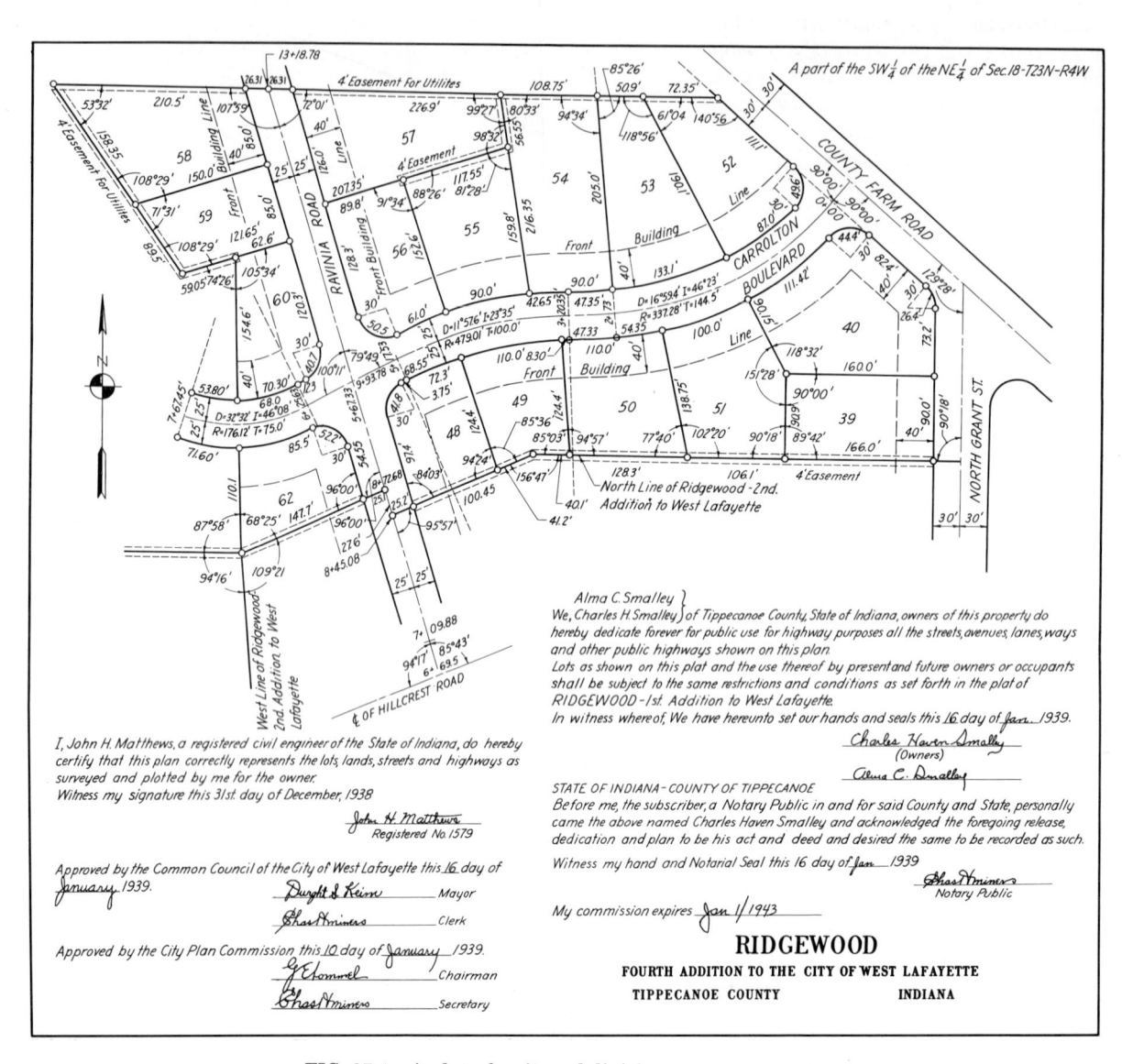

FIG. 27.4. A plat of a city subdivision.

making a resurvey at a later date. Figure 27.4 is a plat of a city subdivision.

27.8
Plats and Partial City Maps. Plats made from subdivision plats or city maps are prepared by the engineering departments of cities and public utilities. The purpose of these partial maps is to record special information concerning such things as proposed improvement projects, the location of lines of transportation, and the location of existing and proposed water mains, sewers, and so on. It is not necessary for such a map to contain all the information given on the subdivision plat from which it is made. The locations of monuments and angles generally are not shown. The widths of streets and the sizes of lots may or may not be shown, depending on the usefulness of such information. A few important buildings may be indicated for the sake of aiding the reader in orienting himself. Figure 27.5 shows the proposed locations of water mains and fire hydrants in a portion of a city.

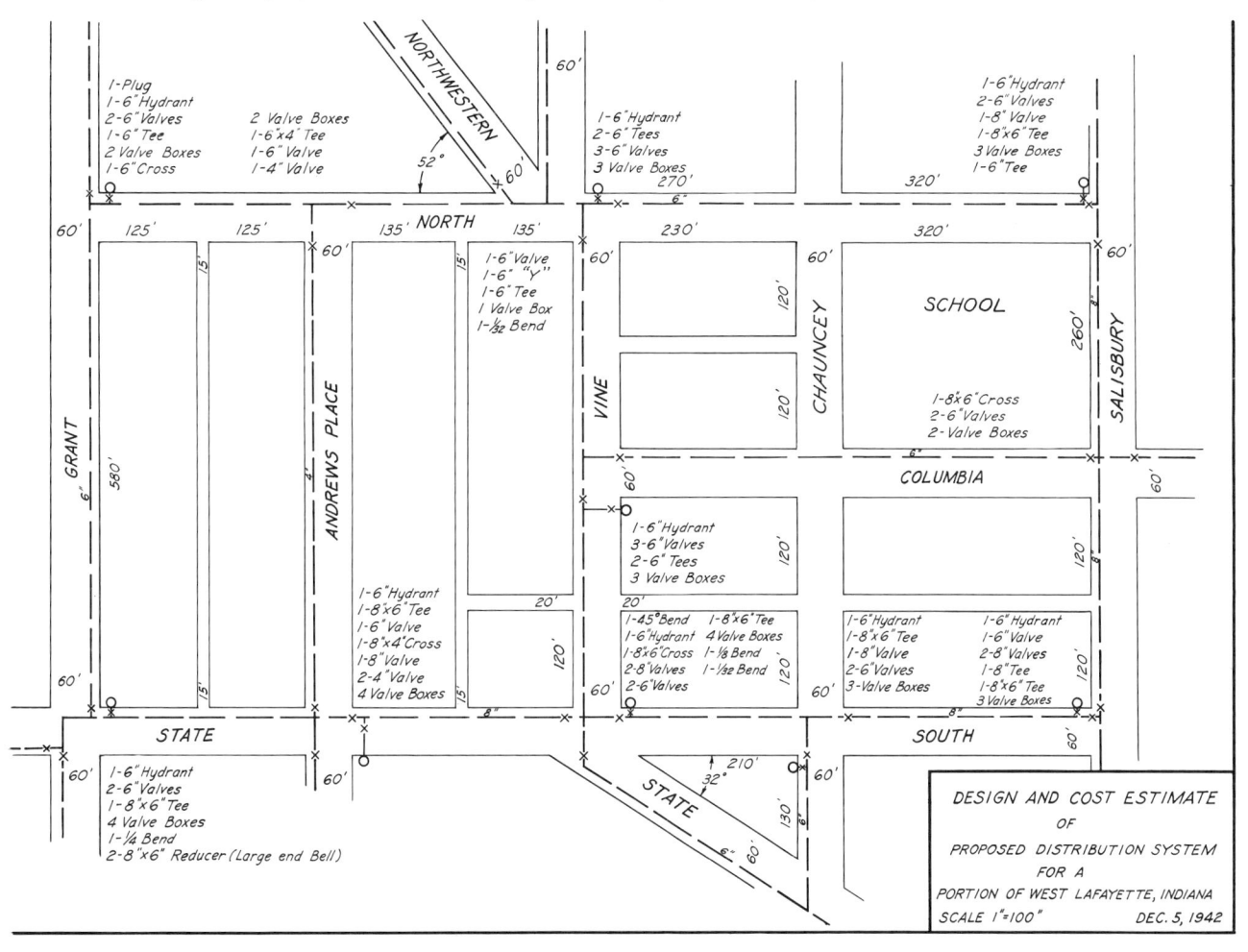

FIG. 27.5. A plat or partial city map showing the proposed location of water mains and fire hydrants.

27.9

Topographic Drawing. As previously stated, a topographic map is a reproduction, to scale, of a small area. On a complete topographic map, the natural and artificial features are represented by recognized conventional symbols and the form of the ground is shown by contours. Excessive detail should be avoided, and only necessary surface features should be shown. All names and required notes should be lettered in a position where they can be easily read; a complete title should be lettered, in the lower-right-hand corner. Ordinarily, single-stroke Reinhardt lettering is preferable on topographic maps prepared solely for construction projects, while vertical modern Roman is more desirable on finished maps where effect and pleasing appearance are important. Figure 27.6 shows a topographic map.

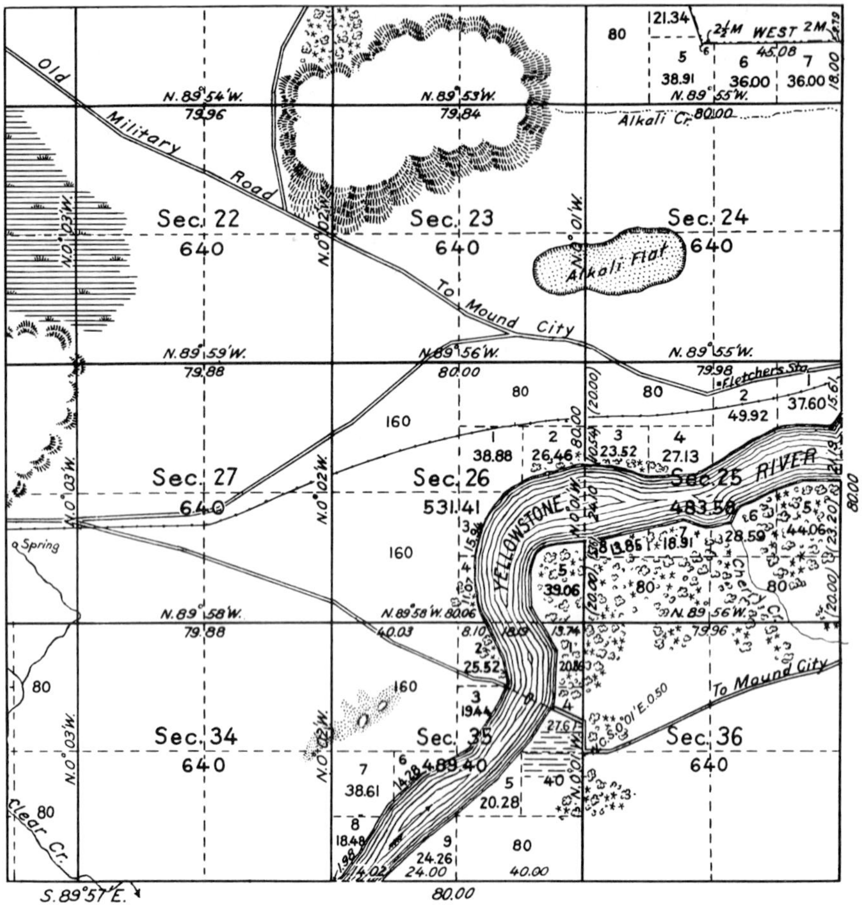

The scale to be used for a topographic map depends on the size of the area and the amount of the detail that must be shown. Scales range from 1 in. = 100 ft to 1 in. = 4 miles. Maps prepared by the United States Geological Survey (U.S.G.S.) are usually drawn to 1:62,500, which is almost 1 in. to a mile.

27.10

Use of Standard Topographic Symbols (U.S.G.S.). Recognized signs and symbols are used to represent the natural and artificial features on a topographic map. Many of these symbols have been designed to bear some pictorial resemblance to the feature or object represented and, for convenience, may be grouped as follows: (1) physical features (buildings, highways, railroads, and so on); (2) ground formations (elevations and depressions); (3) water-surface features (rivers, lakes, and streams); and (4) vegetation growths (grass, trees, and cultivated crops).

Conventional symbols used by the United States Geological Survey for representing the works and structures of man are shown in Fig. 27.7. Symbols for natural land formations, water features, and vegetation growths, both natural and cultivated, are shown in Figs. 27.8–27.10.

27.11

The Drawing of Symbols. Topographic symbols are drawn either freehand or mechanically, depending on the character of the features to be represented. For exam-

FIG. 27.6. A topographic map. (A portion of a map taken from a manual prepared by the U.S. Department of the Interior.)

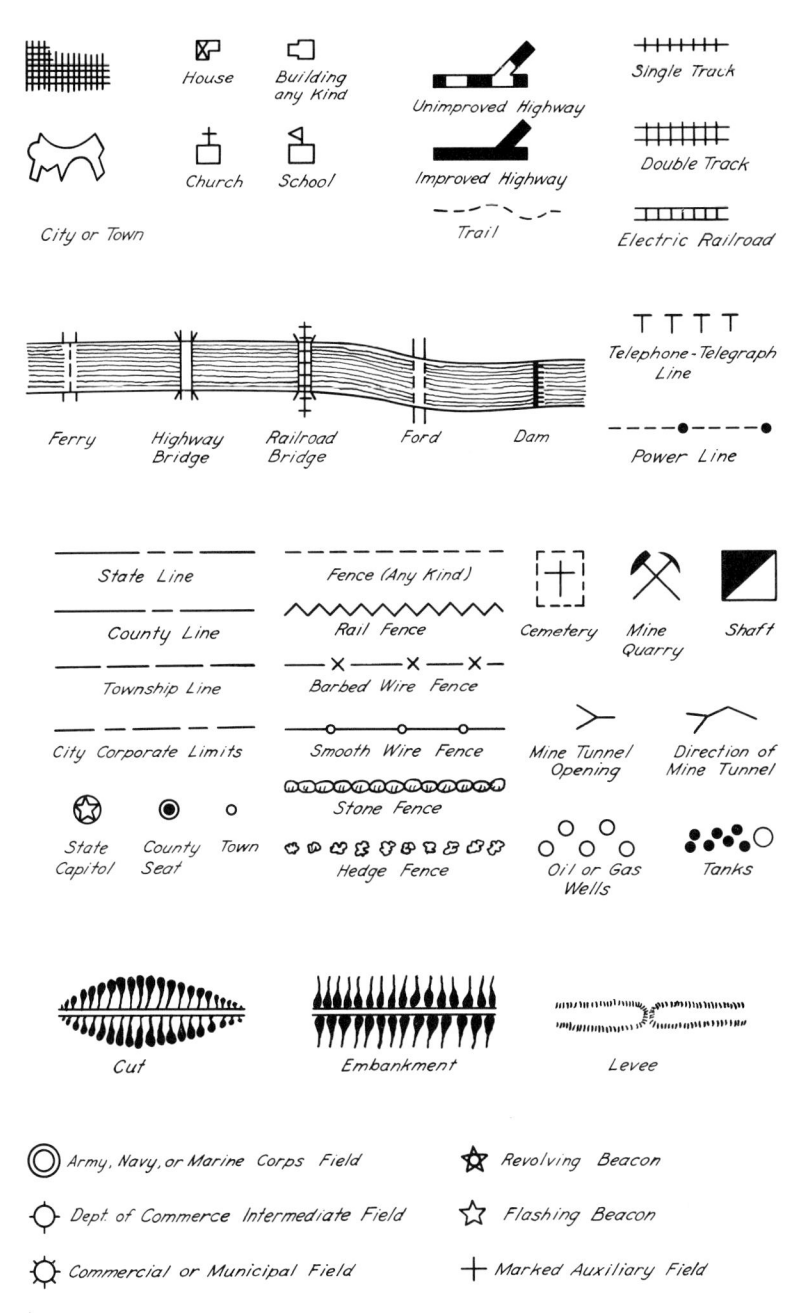

FIG. 27.7. Standard symbols for works and structures (*From Standard Symbols*, published by the U.S. Geological Survey).

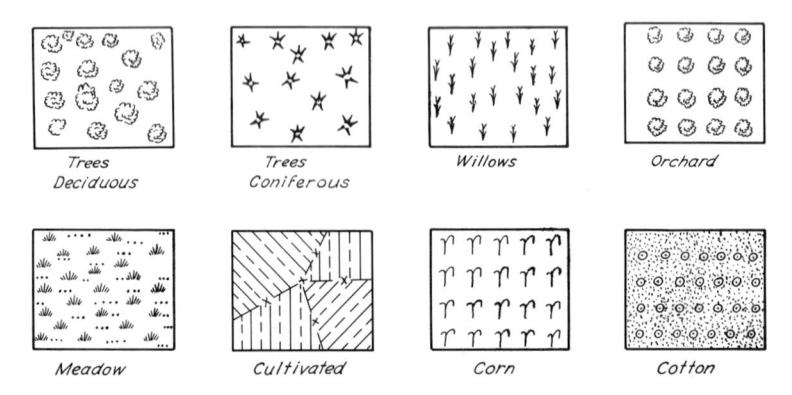

FIG. 27.8. Relief (natural land formations).

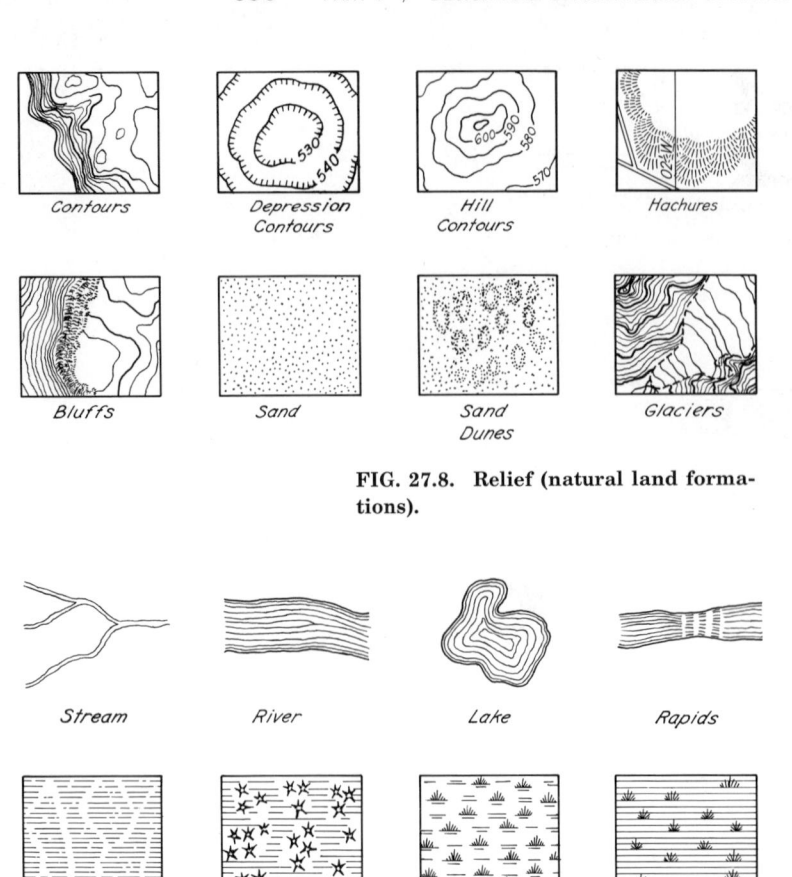

FIG. 27.9. Hydrographic symbols.

FIG. 27.10. Vegetation symbols.

ple, the symbols representing natural features are drawn freehand, while those representing artificial works are drawn mechanically. See Figs. 27.7–27.10. On topographic maps prepared for engineering projects, the symbols are drawn in India ink. When colors are used, as in finished maps, the artificial features (buildings, bridges, railroads, and so on) are drawn in black, the contours in brown, the water features in blue, and vegetation growths in green.

Although the size of symbols may vary somewhat with the size of the map, they are never to scale but are always exaggerations. The usual mistake of the beginner is to draw symbols too large or too close together. Either fault produces a disagreeable appearance and tends to attract the reader's attention away from more important features. The symbols representing prominent features are made to stand out from those of lesser importance by being drawn slightly larger and with heavier lines.

The beginner should study carefully the symbols as given in the various illustrations, so he will not miss some of the essential points in their construction. For instance, he should note that the symbol for a tree (Fig. 27.10) is composed of separate lines, irregularly located, and not of one closed line drawn without lifting the pen. The symbols for grass, corn, and other vegetation should be placed with the bases of the tufts and stocks parallel to the lower borderline.

27.12

The Drawing of Water Lines. Water lining, used to indicate water surfaces, is done entirely freehand with an ordinary lettering pen. The starting line (shoreline) should be fairly heavy, and each successive line should decrease in width until the center of the body of water is reached. See Fig. 27.9. The line next to the shoreline should be drawn parallel to it throughout its entire length, and the space between should be equal to the width of the shoreline. The spacing between succeeding lines should increase gradually to the center, but the change should be so slight that no marked increase will be noticeable. Each added line should show fewer of the small irregularities of the shoreline, the last few following only the prominent ones.

If several bodies of water are to be indicated on the same map, a good way to obtain uniformity is to draw all the shorelines first, then all the lines next to the shorelines, and so on, working back and forth from one body of water to another until the representations are completed. Excessive waviness gives these lines an unnatural appearance and should be avoided.

27.13

Contour Lines. A contour line is a line through points of the same elevation on the surface of the ground. Theoretically, the contour lines on a map may be thought of as the lines of intersection of a series of horizontal planes and the ground surface. In practice, the imaginary planes are equally spaced vertically so that the contour intervals will be equal and the horizontal distances between contours on a map will indicate the steepness of the rise or descent of the surface. The closer together they are, the greater the slope and, conversely, the farther apart they are, the less the slope. An arrangement of contour lines that close indicates either a hill or a depression. The case, whatever it is, usually can be determined by reading the values of the elevations of the contours. Usually each fifth contour is drawn heavier than the others and has a break in it where its elevation above a datum plane is recorded. If a U.S.G.S. bench mark is used, the datum plane will be at mean sea level.

The selection of the contour interval (vertical distance between contour planes) for a topographic survey is determined by the nature of the ground forms and the purpose for which the map will be prepared. For instance, if the area is relatively level, a 1- or 2-ft interval probably would be desirable, while, if the area is rugged, an interval of 50 or even 100 ft might be used.

Contour lines are plotted from survey notes made in the field. In the case of small areas, the usual method for locating contours is to divide the area into squares and take level readings at every intersection and at intermediate points where a pronounced change in slope takes place (Fig. 27.11). On the assumption that the slope of the ground is uniform between two points, the contours are sketched in by interpolating between the readings to

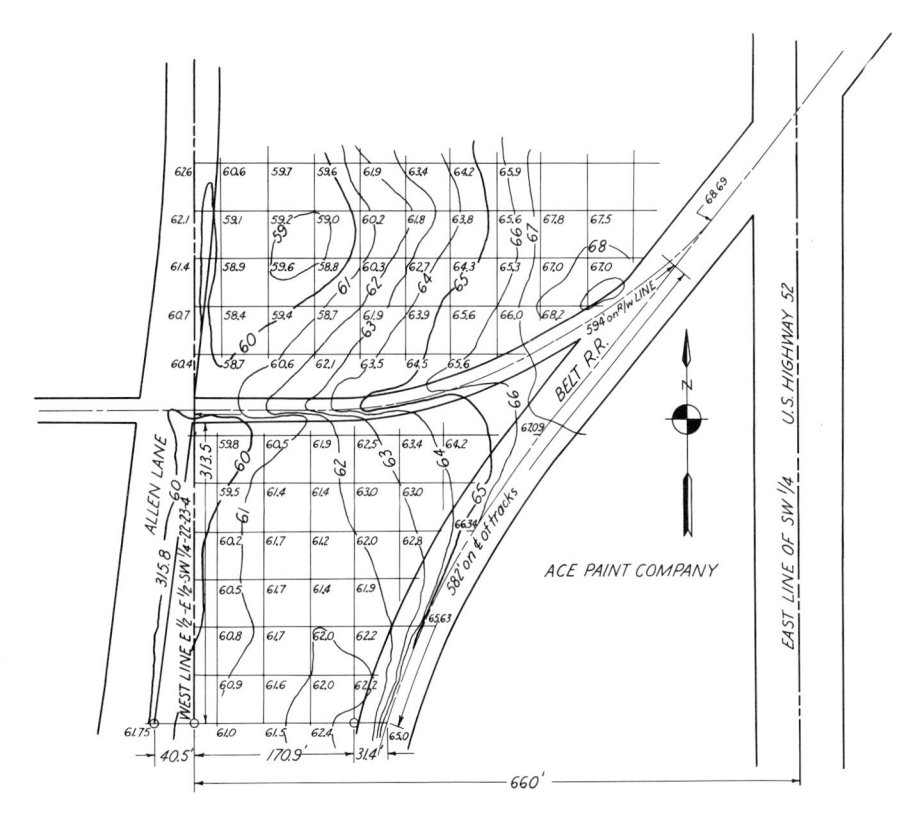

FIG. 27.11. A contour map of a small area.

FIG. 27.12. A sheet showing a plan and profile of a proposed highway project. This drawing was prepared manually. It is suggested that this drawing be compared with the one at the beginning of the chapter. It can be observed that the drawing prepared by the plotter shows all needed information.

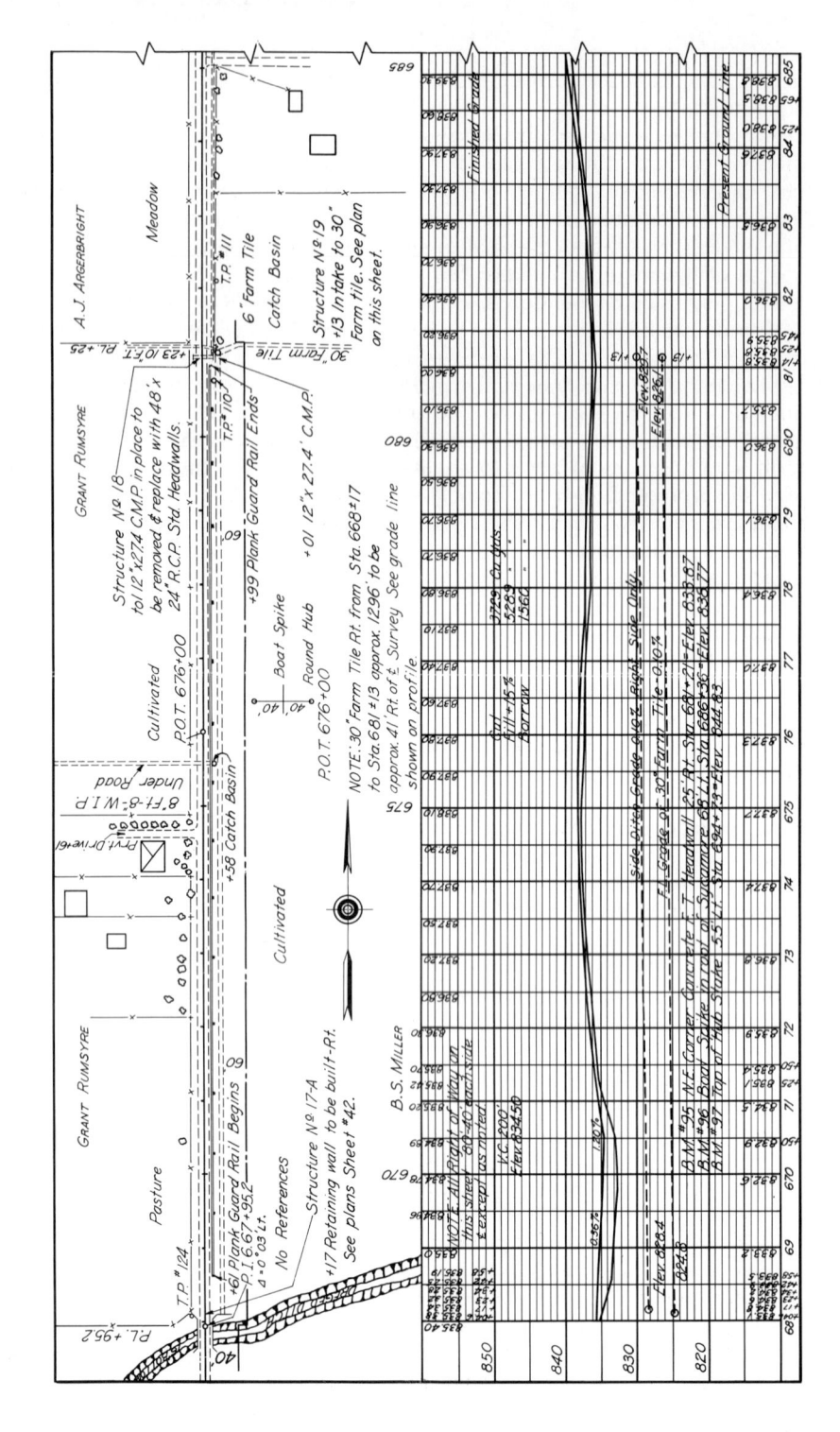

establish the points at which the contours cross the survey lines. The interpolation may be done by eye or by calculation.

Frequently, contours are determined from level readings taken along known lines or from stadia survey notes. When extreme accuracy is necessary and the land is fairly level, contours are established by finding and locating points directly on each contour.

27.14
Profiles. The profile of a line is prepared to show the relative elevation of every point on the line. Theoretically, it may be thought of as a view showing the line of intersection of a vertical plane through the line and the ground surface. Figure 27.12 shows a plan view and a profile of a section of a proposed highway project. Profiles are plotted to an exaggerated vertical scale, in order to magnify the relative differences in elevations of points along the line. When the plan and profile are on the same sheet, as in the illustration, the horizontal scale for the profile should be the same as the scale for the plan view ($1'' = 100'$) and the vertical scale should be 10 or 20 ft to the inch, depending on the amount of vertical exaggeration needed to emphasize surface irregularities. In deciding on the vertical scale to be used, a draftsman should determine the range of elevations and then should make his selection so that the heavy horizontal lines represent full feet at regular intervals, such as 820, 830, 840, and so on. In cases where it is impossible to plot a profile within the range of the grid, it is permissible to break the profile at a heavy vertical line and start again at a lower level. When the line is broken in this way, however, it is necessary to indicate the changed range of elevations by lettering in the new values for the heavy horizontal lines to the right of the "break line."

Profiles are drawn by plotting elevations computed from level readings taken at regular intervals on the ground and at points where the ground changes in slope. Since the slope between adjacent points is assumed to be uniform, a profile consists of a series of straight lines joining successive points.

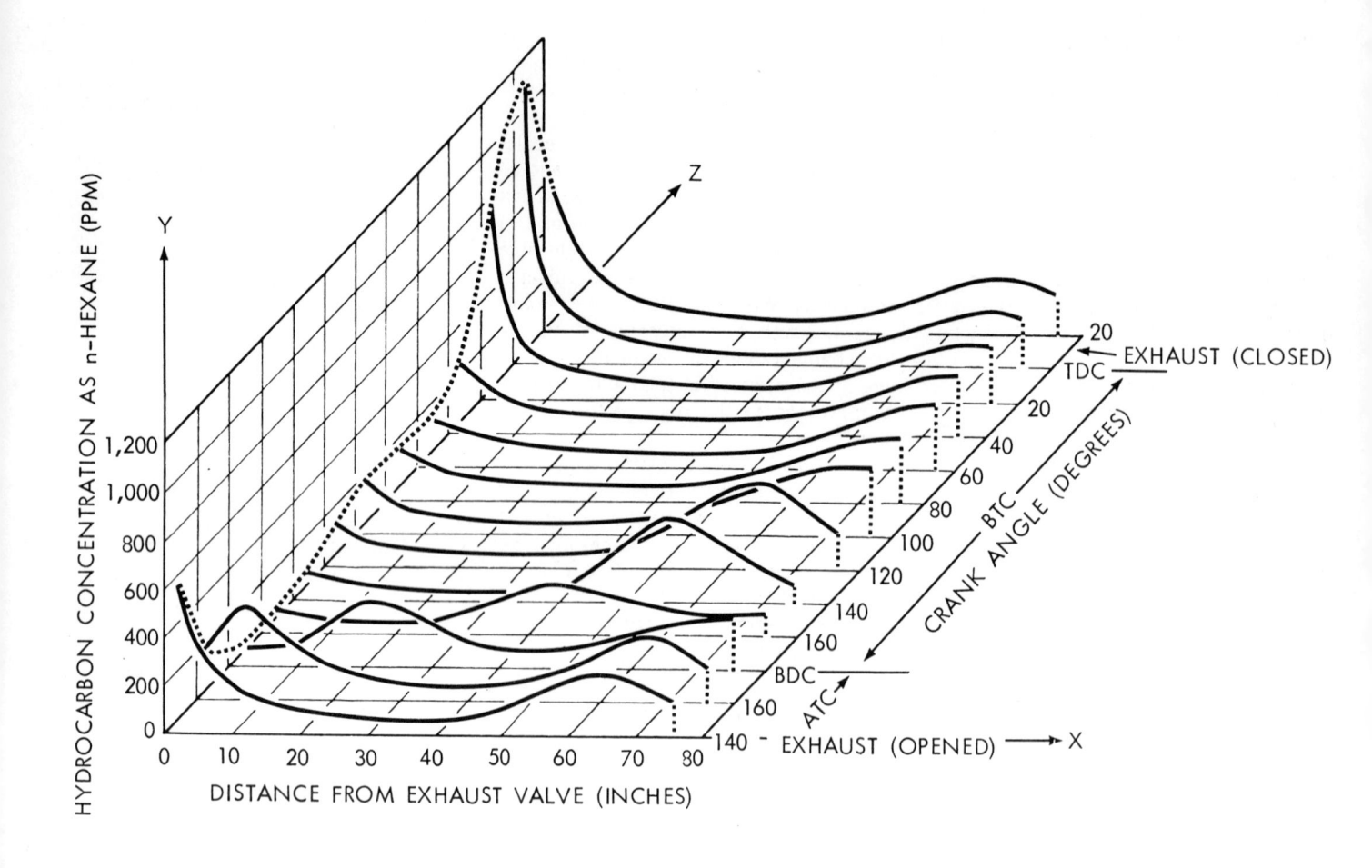

A three-dimensional graph. The curves above show the hydrocarbon concentration in the exhaust pipe as functions of crank angle and distance from the exhaust valve. Distance from the exhaust valve is plotted along the X-axis; engine crank angle, beginning with the time the exhaust valve opens, along the Z-axis; and hydrocarbon concentration is plotted along the Y-axis. Three dimensional charts are used to show the relationship among three variables. Their construction is based upon pictorial projection.
(Courtesy General Motors Corp.). Reprinted from the General Motors Engineering Journal with permission.

Graphic Methods for Engineering Communication and Computation

A: GRAPHS AND CHARTS

28.1

Introduction. A properly designed graphical representation will convey correlated data and facts to an average individual more rapidly and effectively than a verbal, written, or tabulated description, because a visual impression is easily comprehended and requires less mental effort than would be necessary to ascertain the facts from complex tables and reports (Figs. 28.1 and 28.22). It is because of this that diverse kinds of graphs and charts have been developed to present scientific, statistical, and technical information. Note how quickly the relationship presented by the line graph in Fig. 28.2 can be interpreted.

Engineers, even though they are concerned mainly with technical graphs, should be familiar also with the popular forms, for every industrial concern frequently must prepare popular types of graphs in order to strengthen their relationship with the public.

It is impossible to treat exhaustively the subject of graphical representation in a single chapter. Only a few of the most common forms used to analyze economic, scientific, and technical data can be discussed in detail. Many of the principles followed in the construction of engineering graphs, however, apply to the other types.

Those who are interested in the application of graphical methods for the analysis of experimental data and for problem solving will find full coverage of graphical calculus, arithmetic, and algebra; network charts; and empirical equations, in the author's text *Basic Graphics for Design, Analysis, Communications, and the Computer*. The presentation of these more specialized fields has been considered to be beyond the scope of this particular book.

As much drafting skill is required in the execution of a graph as in making any other type of technical drawing. Good appearance is important and can be achieved only with the help of good lettering and smooth, uniform, and properly contrasted lines.

28.2

Classification of Charts, Graphs, and Diagrams. Graphs, charts, and diagrams may be divided into two classes in accordance with their use and then further subdivided according to type. When classified according to use, the two divisions are, first, those used for strictly scientific and technical purposes and, second, those used for the purpose of popular appeal.

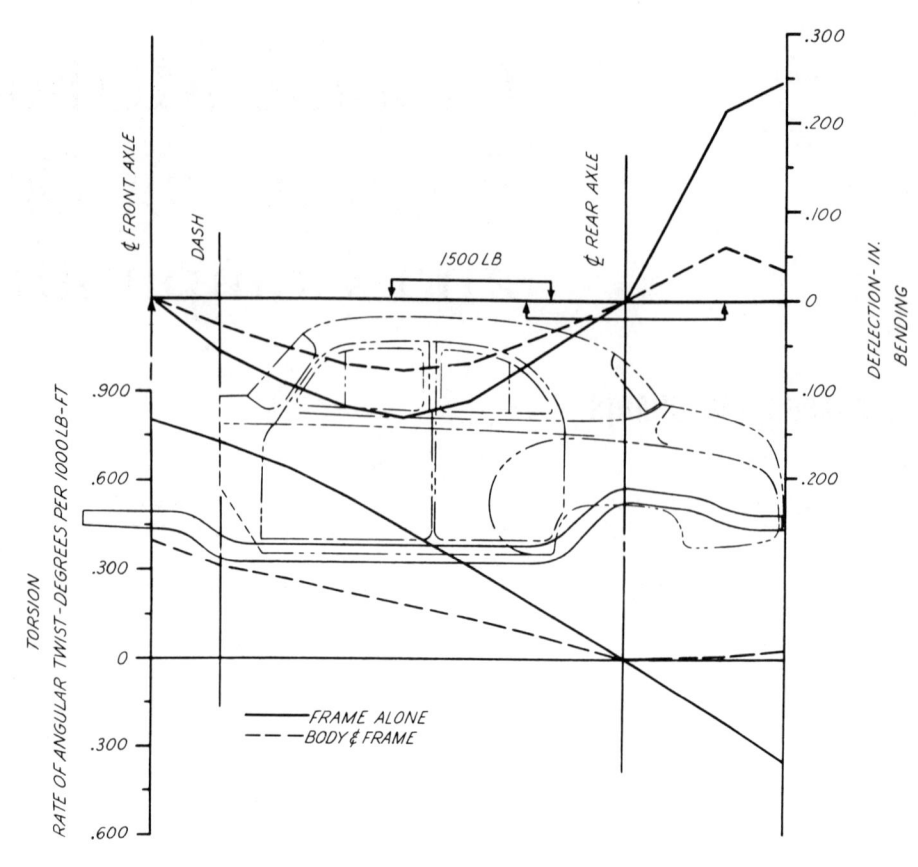

FIG. 28.1. An engineering graph (*Courtesy General Motors Corp.*). Reprinted from the General Motors Engineering Journal with permission.

The classification according to type is as follows:

1. Rectilinear charts
2. Semilogarithmic charts
3. Logarithmic charts
4. Barographs and area and volume charts
5. Percentage charts
6. Polar charts
7. Trilinear charts
8. Alignment charts (nomographs)
9. Pictorial charts

28.3

Quantitative and Qualitative Charts and Graphs. In general, charts and diagrams are used for one of two purposes, either to read values or to present a comparative picture relationship between variables. If a chart or graph is prepared for reading values, it is called a *quantitative* graph; if prepared for presenting a comparative

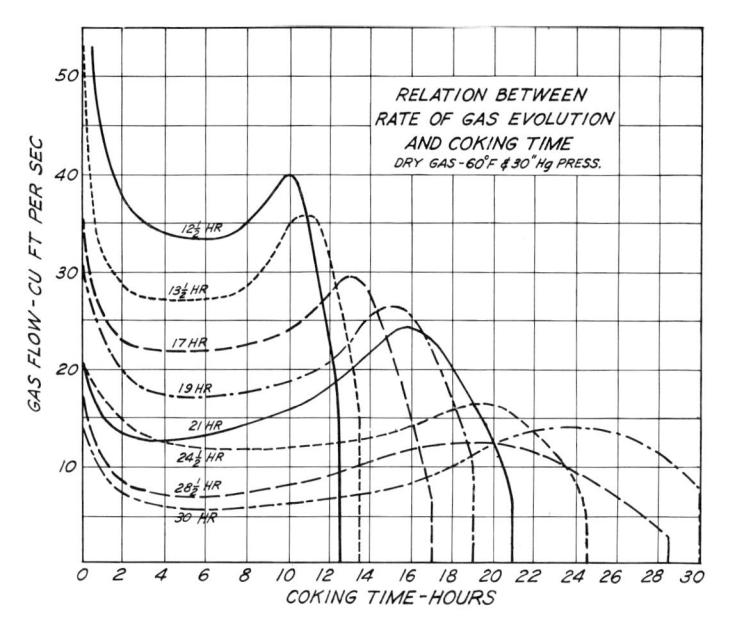

FIG. 28.2. An engineering graph prepared for publication (*Courtesy Blast Furnace and Steel Plant Magazine*).

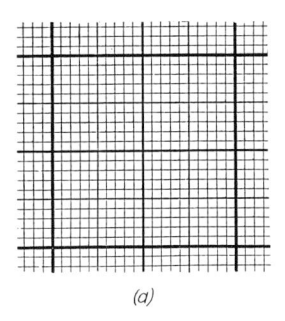

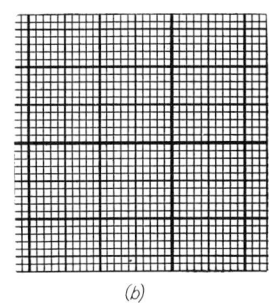

FIG. 28.3. Types of graph paper.

relationship, it is called *qualitative*. Obviously, some charts serve both purposes and cannot be classified strictly as either type. One of these purposes, however, must be predominant. Since a number of features in the preparation depend on the predominant purpose, such purpose must be determined before attempting to construct a graph.

28.4
Ordinary Rectangular Coordinate Graphs. Most engineering graphs prepared for laboratory and office use are drawn on ruled, rectangular graph paper and are plotted in the first quadrant (upper-right-hand), with the intersection of the X (horizontal) axis and Y (vertical) axis at the lower left used as the zero point or origin of coordinates. The paper is ruled with equispaced horizontal and vertical lines, forming small rectangles. The type most commonly used for chart work in experimental engineering is $8\frac{1}{2} \times 11$ in. and is ruled to form $\frac{1}{20}$-in. squares [Fig. 28.3(*a*)], every fifth line being heavy. Another type of paper frequently used, which is suitable for most laboratory reports in technical schools, has rulings that form 1-mm and 1-cm squares [Fig. 28.3(*b*)]. Other rulings run $\frac{1}{10}$, $\frac{1}{8}$, or $\frac{1}{4}$ in. apart. Ordinarily the ruled lines are spaced well apart on charts prepared for reproduction in popular and technical literature (Fig. 28.2). The principal advantage of having greater spacing between the lines is that large squares or rectangles tend to make the graph easier to read. Ready printed graph papers are available with various rulings in several colors.

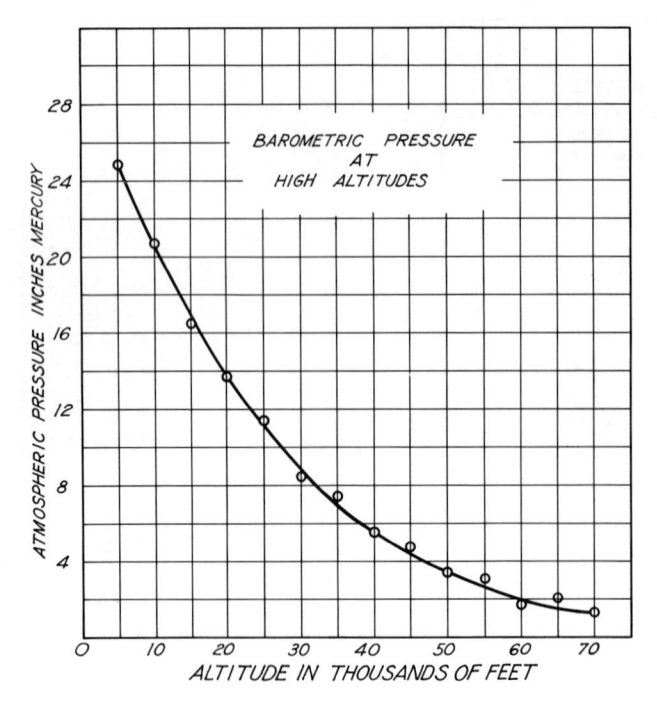

598 PART V / DESIGN AND COMMUNICATION DRAWING IN SPECIALIZED FIELDS

FIG. 28.4. Rectangular graph.

Ordinary coordinate line graphs are used extensively because they are easily constructed and easily read. The known relationship between the variables is expressed by one or more continuous lines, which may be straight, broken, or curved.

The graph in Fig. 28.4 shows the approximate barometric pressure at different heights above sea level.

A graphical representation may be drawn easily and correctly if, after the required data have been assembled, careful consideration is given to the principles of curve drawing discussed in the following sections.

28.5

The Determination of the Variables for Ordinate and Abscissa. The independent variable, the quantity arbitrarily varied during the experiment, usually is chosen for the abscissa (Fig. 28.5). Certain kinds of experimental data, however, such as a stress–strain diagram (Fig. 28.6), are plotted with the independent variable along the ordinate.

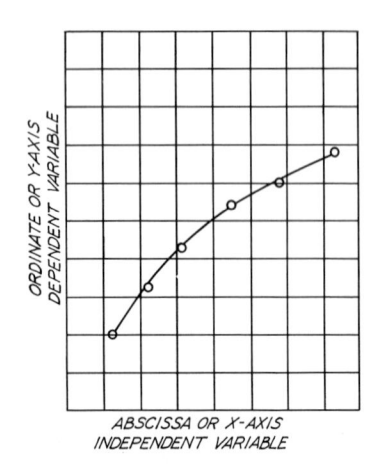

FIG. 28.5. Independent and dependent variables.

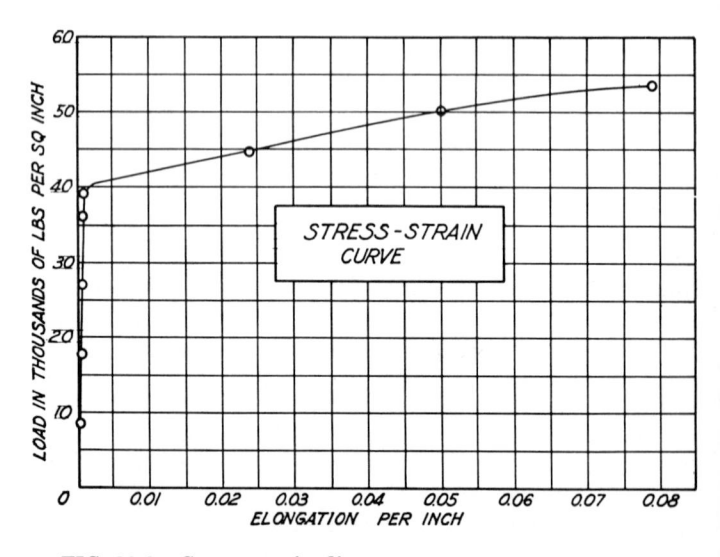

FIG. 28.6. Stress-strain diagram.

28.6
The Selection of Suitable Scales. The American Society of Mechanical Engineers in a standard for engineering and scientific graphs recommends*:

(a) Very careful consideration should be given to the choice of scales since this has a controlling influence on the slope of the curve. The slope of the curve, as a whole and also at intermediate points, provides a visual impression of the degree of change in the dependent variable for a given increment in the independent variable. Creating the right impression of the relationship to be shown by a line graph is, therefore, probably controlled more critically by the relative stretching of the vertical and horizontal scales than by any other feature involved in the design of the graph.

(b) The range of scales should be chosen to insure effective and efficient use of the coordinate area in attaining the objective of the chart.

(c) The zero line should be included, if visual comparison of plotted magnitudes is desired.

(If the chart is quantitative, the intersection of the axes need not be at the origin of coordinates. If it is qualitative, however, both the ordinate and abscissa generally should have zero value at the intersection of the axes, as in Fig. 28.2).

(d) For arithmetic scales, the scale numbers shown on the graph and space between coordinate rulings should preferably correspond to 1, 2, or 5 units of measurement, multiplied or divided by 1, 10, 100, etc.

(Other units could be used except for the fact that they create situations wherein it becomes difficult to interpolate values.

*These statements were abstracted from the *American Standard for Engineering and Scientific Graphs for Publication* (ANS Z15.3-1943).

For example, one square should equal one of the following.)

0.01	0.1	1	10	100	etc.
0.02	0.2	2	20	200	etc.
0.04	0.4	4	40	400	etc.
0.05	0.5	5	50	500	etc.
etc.	etc.	etc.	etc.	etc.	etc.

(e) The horizontal (independent variable) scale values should usually increase from left to right and the vertical (dependent variable) from bottom to top.

28.7
Locating the Axes and Marking the Values of the Variables. On graphs prepared for laboratory reports and not for publication, the axes should be located 1 in. or more inside the border of the coordinate ruling (Fig. 28.7). When selecting the scale units and locating the axes, it should be remembered that the abscissa may be taken either the long way or short way of the coordinate paper, depending on the range of the scales.

Concerning the numbers, the ASME standard recommends the following:

The use of many digits in scale numbers should be avoided. This can usually be accomplished by a suitable designation in the scale caption.

Examples:

PRESSURE, MM OF HG $\times 10^{-5}$;
RESISTANCE, THOUSANDS OF OHMS.

The numbers should read from the bottom when possible (Fig. 28.7). For the sake of good appearance, they never should be crowded. Always place a cipher to the left of the decimal point when the quantity is less than one.

Usually, only the heavy coordinate lines are marked to indicate their values or distance from the origin, and, even then, the values may be shown only at a regular

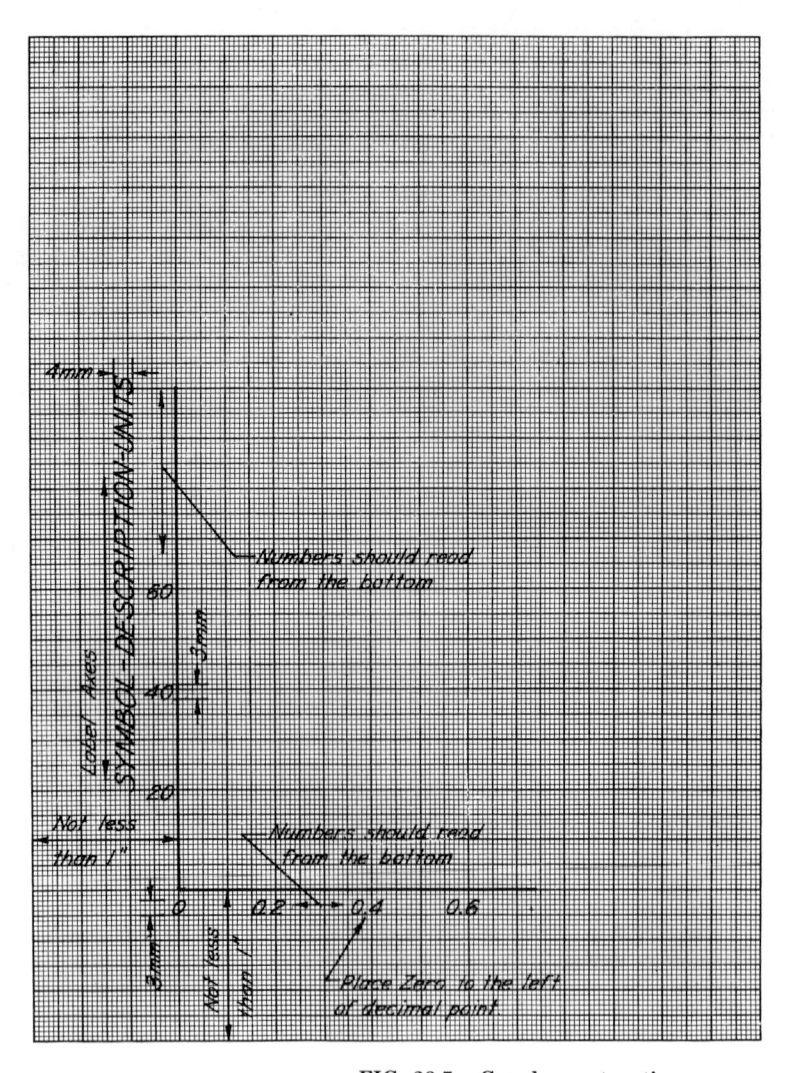

FIG. 28.7. Graph construction.

of the graph, unless it is desirable to place some at the right or along the top.

28.8
Indicating Plotted Points Representing the Data. If the data represent a set of experimental observations, the plotted points of a single-curve graph should be marked by small circles approximately 0.1 in. in diameter (Fig. 28.9). The following practice is recommended: open circles, filled-in circles, and partially filled-in circles (○ ● ◐) rather than crosses, squares, and triangles should be used to differentiate observed points of several curves on a graph. Filled-in symbols may be made smaller than those not filled in.

Mathematical curves are frequently drawn without distinguishing marks at computed positions.

28.9
Drawing a Curve. Since most physical phenomena are continuous, curves on engineering graphs usually represent an average of plotted points (Fig. 28.10). Discontinuous data should be plotted with a broken line, as shown in Fig. 28.11.

It is preferable to represent curves by solid lines. If more than one curve appears on a graph, differentiation may be secured by varied types of lines; but the most important curve should be represented by a solid one. A very fine line should be used for a quantitative curve if values are to be read accurately. A heavy line ($\frac{1}{40}$-in. width) is recommended for a qualitative curve. It should be observed in Figs. 28.10 and 28.11 that the curve line does not pass through open circles.

For ordinary qualitative graphs, the ASME standard proposes:

(a) When more than one curve is presented on a graph, relative emphasis or differentiation of the curves may be secured by using different types of line, i.e., solid, dashed, dotted, etc. A solid

selected interval (Fig. 28.7). The numbers should be placed to the left of the Y-axis and just below the X-axis.

When several curves representing different variables are to appear on the same graph, a separate axis generally is required for each variable (Fig. 28.8). In this case, a corresponding description should be given along each axis. The axes should be grouped at the left or at the bottom

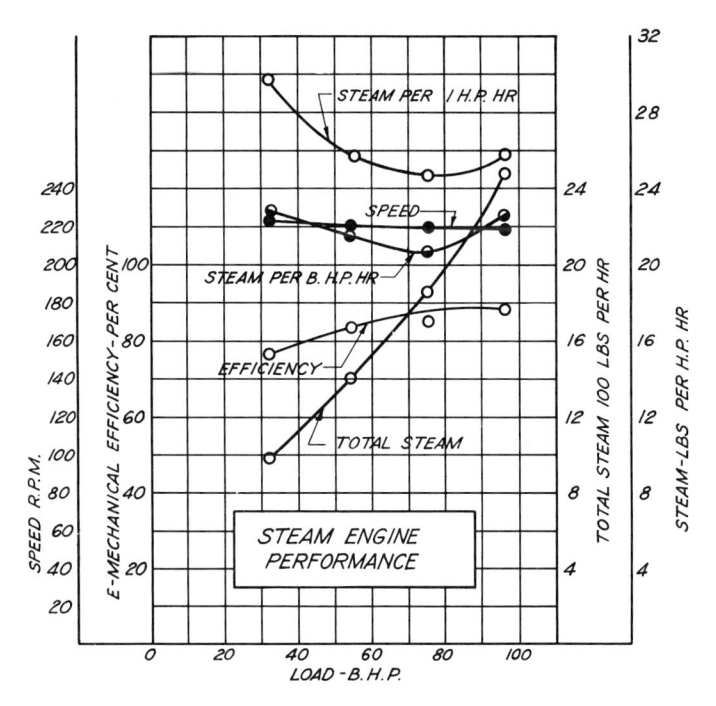

CHAP. 28 / GRAPHIC METHODS FOR ENGINEERING COMMUNICATION AND COMPUTATION 601

FIG. 28.8. Representation of several curves on a graph.

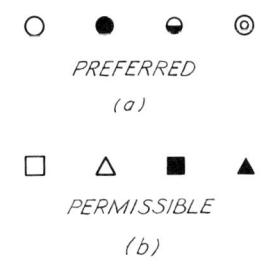

FIG. 28.9. Identification symbols.

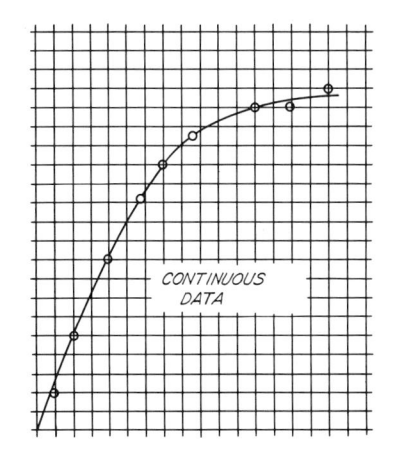

FIG. 28.10. Continuous curve.

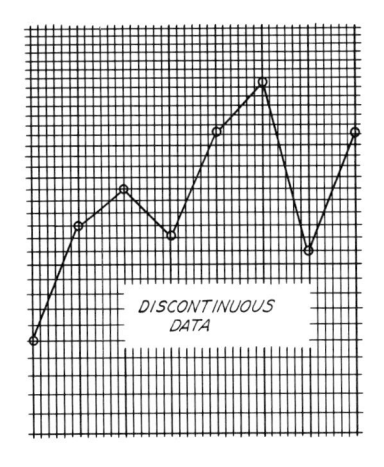

FIG. 28.11. Discontinuous data.

line is recommended for the most important curve.

(b) When more than one curve is presented on a graph, each should bear a suitable designation.

(c) Curves should, if practicable, be designated by brief labels placed close to the curves (horizontally or along the curves) rather than by letters, numbers or other devices requiring a key (Fig. 28.8).

28.10
The Labeling of the Scales. Each scale caption should give a description of the variable represented and the unit of measurement. The captions on engineering graphs frequently contain an added identifying symbol, such as

N-EFFICIENCY-PERCENT
P-OUTPUT-HP

All lettering should be readable from the bottom and right side of the graph (not the left side). When space is limited, standard abbreviations should be used, particularly for designating the unit of measurement. To avoid confusing the reader, the draftsman should use only recognized word contractions.

28.11
Titles, Legends, Notes, and So On. The title of a graph should be clear, concise, complete, and symmetrical. It should give the name of the curve, the source of the data, the date, and other important information (Fig. 28.12). It should be so placed that it gives a balanced effect to the completed drawing (Fig. 28.2). In addition to the title, a wiring diagram, pictorial diagram, formula, or explanatory note is

often necessary to give a clear picture of the nature of the experiment. For example, if there is any great irregularity in the plotted points or a condition that may have affected the values as shown by the data, a note of explanation should be given. A legend or key is sometimes included to explain a set of curves in greater detail.

In commercial practice, alcohol is often used to clear a rectangular area of coordinate lines in order that the title may be printed in an open space.

28.12
Procedure for Making a Graphical Representation in Ink

1. Select the type of coordinate paper.
2. Determine the variables for ordinate and abscissa.
3. Determine the scale units.
4. Locate the axes and mark the scale values in pencil.
5. Plot the points representing the data. [Many draftsmen ink the symbol (○ ●) indicating the points at this stage.]
6. Draw the curve. If the curve is to strike an average among the plotted points, a trial curve should be drawn in pencil. If the curve consists of a broken line, as is the case with discontinuous data, the curve need not be drawn until the graph is traced in ink.
7. Label the axes directly in ink.
8. Letter the title, notes, and so on. The title should be lettered on a trial sheet that can be used as a guide for lettering directly in ink on the graph.
9. Check the work and complete the diagram by tracing the curve in ink.

28.13
Logarithmic Graphs. Logarithmic coordinate graphs are constructed on prepared paper on which the parallel horizontal and parallel vertical rulings are spaced proportional to the logarithms of numbers (Fig. 28.13). This type of graph has two principal advantages over the ordinary coordinate type. First, the error in plotting or reading values is a constant percentage, and, second, an algebraic equation of the form $y = ax^b$ appears as a straight line if x has a value other than zero. The exponent b may be either plus or minus.

The equation for a falling body, $D = \frac{1}{2}gt^2$, is represented in Figs. 28.13 and 28.14. A practical application of interest to engineers is in the design of drop hammers. In this equation, based on uniform accelerated motion, t represents time in seconds and D the distance traveled in t seconds by a freely falling body with no initial velocity. Observe that the plotted points form a parabolic curve on ordinary

FIG. 28.12. A title.

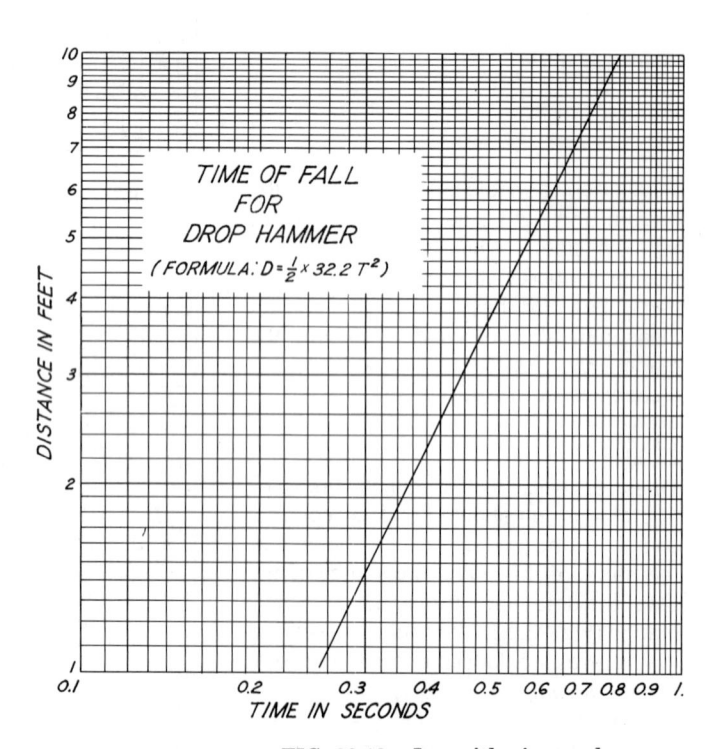

FIG. 28.13. Logarithmic graph.

coordinate graph paper and a straight line on logarithmic paper. To draw the line on the graph in Fig. 28.13, it is necessary to calculate and locate only two points, while in Fig. 28.14, several points must be plotted to establish the location of the corresponding curved-line representation. The line on Fig. 28.13 has a slope of 2:1, because the exponent of t is 2. Therefore, the line could be drawn by utilizing one point and the slope, instead of plotting two points and joining them with a straight line.

Log paper is available with rulings in one or more cycles for any range of values to be plotted. Part-cycle and split-cycle papers may also be purchased.

28.14
Semilogarithmic Graphs. Semilogarithmic paper has ruled lines that are spaced to a uniform scale in one direction and to a logarithmic scale in the other direction (Fig. 28.15). Charts drawn on this form of paper are used extensively in scientific studies, because functions having values in the form of geometric progressions are represented by straight lines. In any case, the main reason for the use of semilogarithmic paper is that the slope of the resulting curve indicates rate of change rather than amount of change, the opposite being true in the case of curves on ordinary coordinate graph paper. Persons who are interested may determine the rate of increase or decrease at any point by measuring the slope. A straight line indicates a constant rate of change. In commercial work this form of paper is generally called "ratio paper," and the charts are known as "rate-of-change charts."

As previously stated, the choice of a type of graph paper depends on the information to be revealed. Curves drawn on uniform coordinate graph paper to illustrate the percentage of expansion or contraction of sales, and so on, present a misleading picture. The same data plotted on

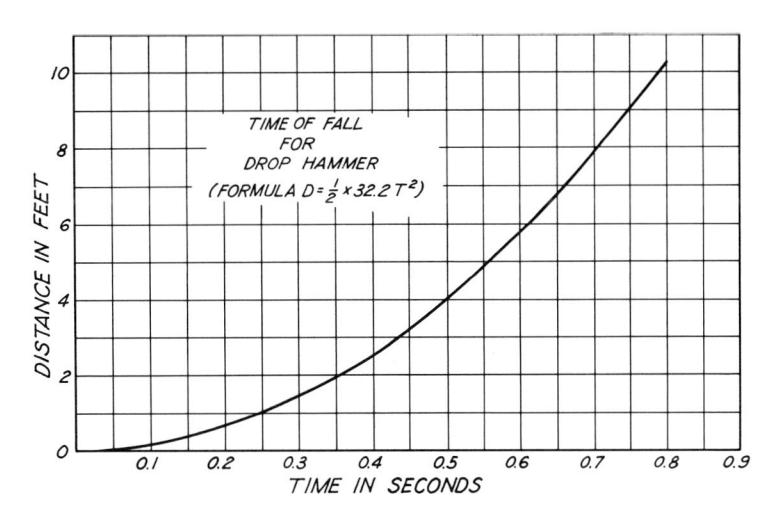

FIG. 28.14. Coordinate graph.

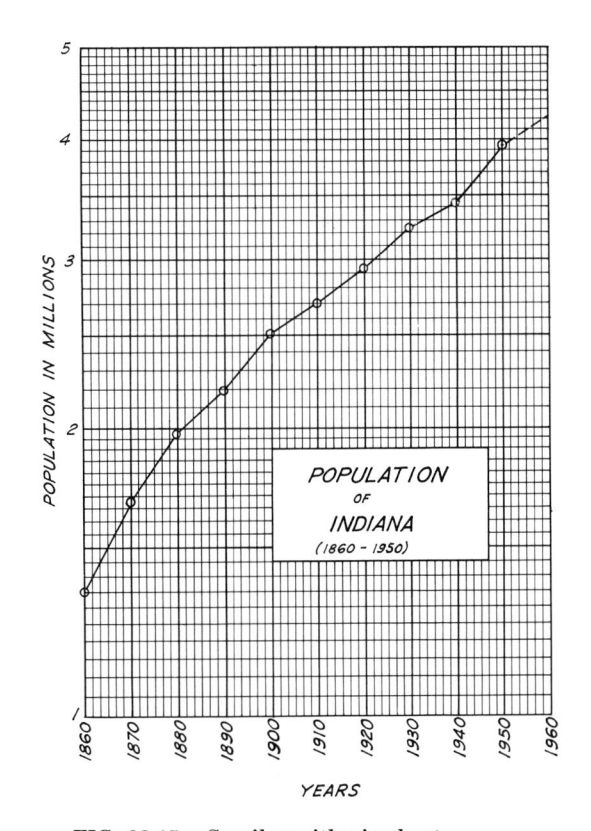

FIG. 28.15. Semilogarithmic chart.

semilogarithmic paper would reveal the true rate of change to the business management. For this reason, semilogarithmic paper should be used whenever percentage of change rather than quantity change is to be shown. In scientific work, when the value of one variable increases in a geometric progression and the other in an arithmetic progression, this form is valuable.

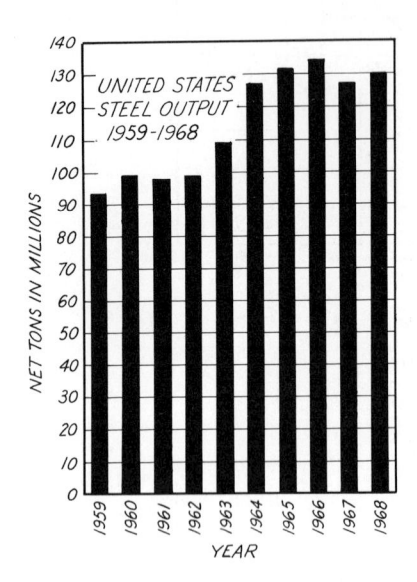

28.15
Bar Charts. Bar charts or barographs are used principally in popular literature covering economic and industrial surveys. They are a simple diagrammatic form giving a pictorial summary of statistical data and can be easily understood by the average person. Logarithmic and uniform coordinate graphs are less suited for this purpose, because few people know the procedure for reading curves or understand their picture qualities.

Whenever values or quantities are illustrated, as in Fig. 28.16, by consecutive heavy bars whose lengths are proportional to the amounts they represent, the resulting representation is called a *bar chart*.

The bars on this type of diagram may be drawn either horizontally or vertically, but all should start at the same zero line. Their lengths should be to some fixed scale, the division values of which may be given in the margin along the bottom or left side of the graph. When it is necessary to give the exact values represented, the figures should be placed along each bar in a direction parallel to it. To place the values at the end gives the illusion of increasing the length of the bars. Usually, the names of the items are lettered to the left of the vertical starting line on a horizontal chart and below the starting line on a vertical chart.

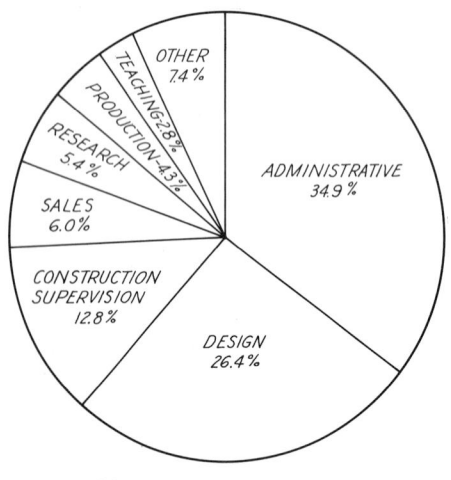

28.16
Area (Percentage) Charts. An area diagram can be used profitably when it is desirable to present pictorially a comparison of related quantities in percentage. This form of representation illustrates the relative magnitudes of the component divisions of a total of the distribution of income, the composition of the population, and so on. Two common types of the various forms of area diagrams used in informative literature are illustrated in Figs. 28.17 and 28.18. Percentages, when represented by sectors of a circle or subdivisions of a bar, are easy to interpolate.

The pie chart (Fig. 28.17) is the most popular form of area diagram, as well as the easiest to construct. The area of the circle represents 100% and the sectors represent percentages of the total. To make the chart effective, a description of each quantity and its corresponding percentage should be lettered in its individual sector. All lettering should be completed before the areas are cross-hatched or colored if this is to be done. The percentage bar chart shown in Fig. 28.18 fulfills the same purpose as the pie chart. The overall area of the bar represents 100%. Note

FIG. 28.16. A bar chart.

FIG. 28.17. A pie chart.

that each percentage division is cross-hatched in a different direction. The descriptions may be placed on either side of the bar; the percentages should be on the bar or at the side.

28.17
Polar Charts. Certain types of technical data can be more easily plotted and better represented on polar coordinate paper. Polar charts are drawn by self-recording instruments, polar diagrams, and plotted polar curves representing various kinds of scientific data are very common. Polar curves are used to represent the intensity of diffused light, intensity of heat, and so on. The polar chart in Fig. 28.19 gives, in terms of candlepower, the intensity of light in two planes.

28.18
Trilinear Charts. Trilinear charts are used principally in the study of the properties of chemical compounds, mixtures, solutions, and alloys (Fig. 28.20). Basically this is a 100% chart the use of which, owing to its geometric form, is limited to the investigation of that which is composed of three constituents or variables. Its use depends on the geometric principle that the sum of the three perpendiculars from any point is equal to the altitude. If the altitude represents 100%, the perpendiculars will represent the percentages of the three variables composing the whole.

The ruling can be accomplished conveniently by dividing any two sides of the triangle into the number of equal-percentage divisions desired and drawing through these points lines parallel to the sides of the triangle.

28.19
Chemical Engineering Charts. Figure 28.21 shows a type of flow chart that must

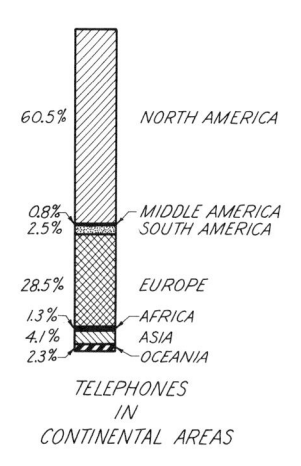

FIG. 28.18. Percentage bar chart.

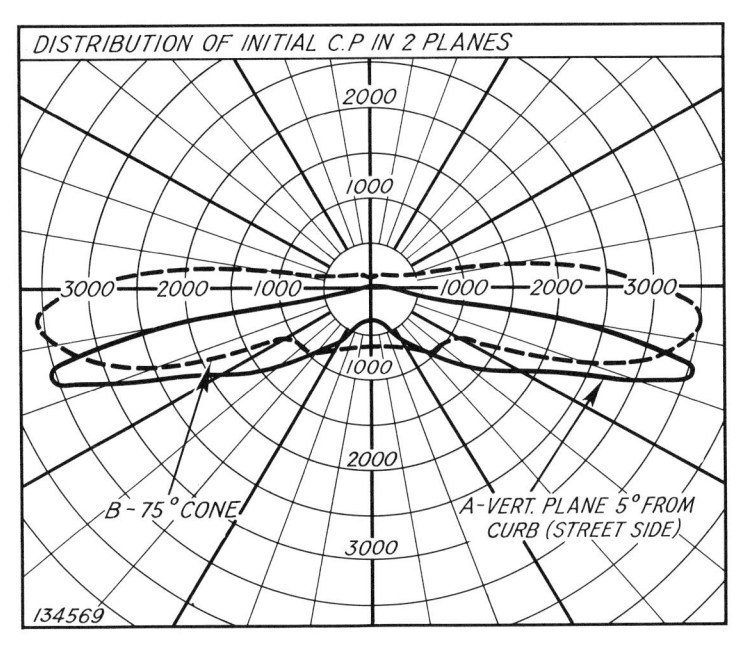

FIG. 28.19. Polar chart (*Courtesy General Electric Co.*).

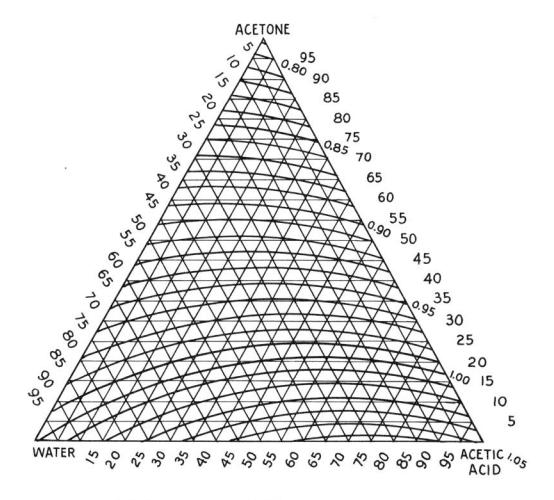

FIG. 28.20. Trilinear chart (*Courtesy American Chemical Society*).

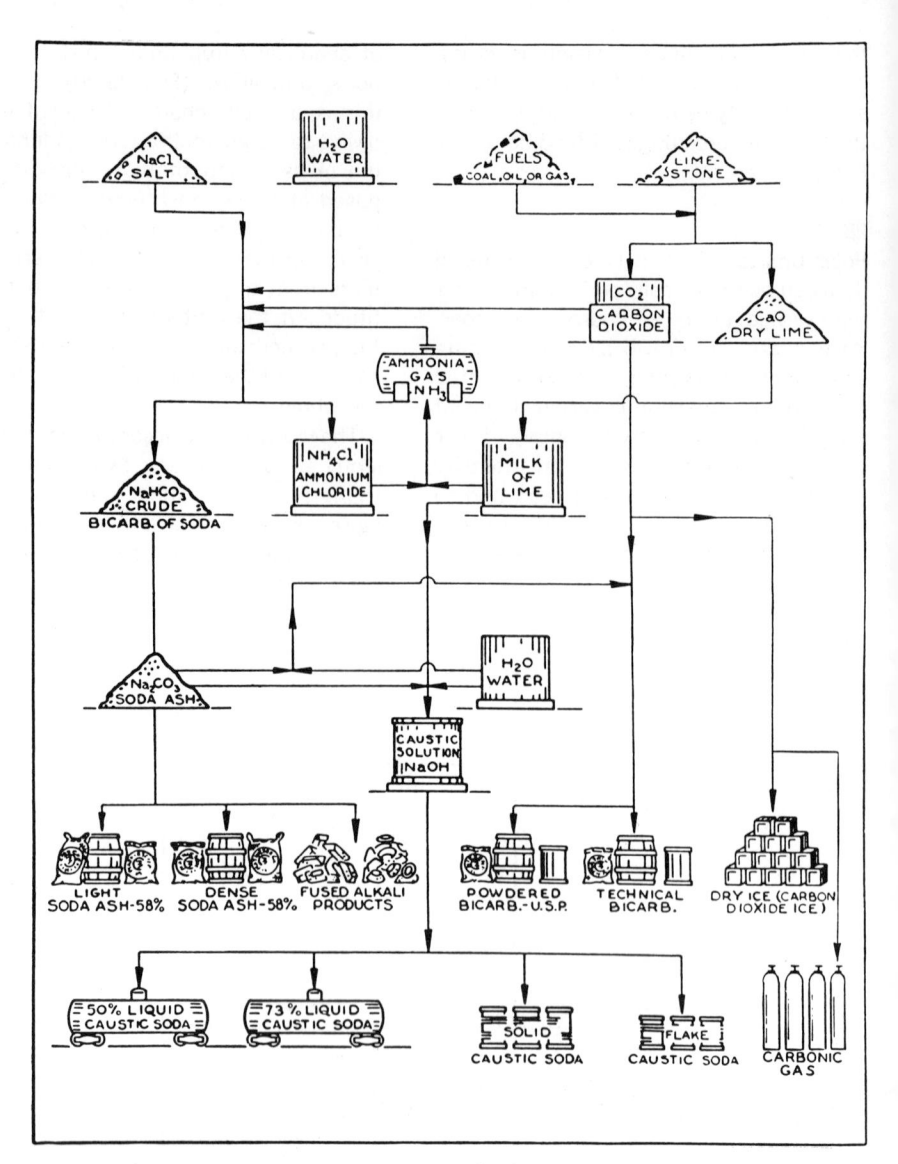

FIG. 28.21. Flow chart of ammonia-soda operations (*Courtesy Chemical Industries Magazine*).

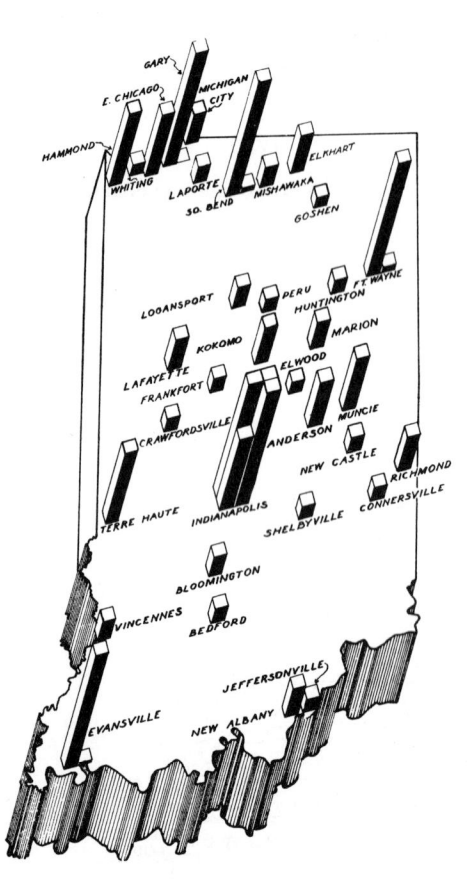

FIG. 28.22. Population chart (*Courtesy Indiana State Planning Board*).

be prepared frequently by chemical engineers in industrial practice.

28.20
Pictorial Charts. Pictorial charts are quite generally used to present data in reports prepared for nontechnical readers. Usually, such charts present comparisons of populations (Fig. 28.22), expenditures, costs, and so forth. Stacks of silver dollars may represent expenditures; sizes of animals can represent livestock production; and human figures can present employment data.

B: EMPIRICAL EQUATIONS

28.21
Empirical Equations. In all phases of engineering work considerable experimentation is done with physical quantities, and the engineer (or engineering technologist) in his work is usually the person most concerned with the behavior of quantities in relation to one another. Often it is known that the subject of the experiment obeys some physical law which can be expressed by a mathematical equation, but the exact equation is unknown. Then, the person performing the experiment is faced with the task of finding an equation to fit the data that has been obtained. The three articles that follow discuss means of arriving at an equation from a graphical study of the data. An equation determined in this manner is an *empirical equation*. Since the unknown law may be quite complex, a single empirical equation to fit the whole range of data may not exist. However, in the majority of such cases a series of the various empirical equations with limited coverage (parameters) can be found.

28.22
Equations of the Form: $y = a + bx$. If the plotted points, representing the data, lie in what appears to be a straight line when plotted on rectangular coordinate paper, the equation of the data is a linear or first degree equation of the form: $y = a + bx$, where b is the slope of the line and a is the y-intercept ($x = 0$).

After it has been decided that the relationship between quantities is linear, the next step is to draw the best average straight line that will be representative of the data (see Fig. 28.23). This line, extended if necessary to the y-axis, establishes the y-intercept ($x = 0$) which will be the value of a in the equation. The slope can be determined from any two points along the line. However, for accuracy the points should be selected as far apart as possible. The value of b is expressed as

$$b = \frac{y_2 - y_1}{x_2 - x_1}$$

Thus, for the line in Fig. 28.23, having selected two points as illustrated,

$$b = -\frac{3-1}{6-3} = -\frac{2}{3} \text{ (slope)}$$

With the slope now known and the value of a having been read directly on the y-axis as 5, the equation of the line can be written as

$$y = 5 - \frac{2}{3}x$$

If it is not reasonable to include $x = 0$ in the plot of the data, then a pair of simultaneous equations are set up using two points on the line:

$$y_1 = a + bx_1$$
$$y_2 = a + bx_2$$

This system can then be solved for a and b.

28.23
Equations of the Form: $y = ax^b$. If the data plots very nearly in a straight line on logarithmic graph paper, the equation of the data is a power equation of the form: $y = ax^b$. Power equations of this type, where one quantity varies directly as some power of another, appear as either parabolic or hyperbolic curves when plotted on rectangular coordinate paper, depending upon whether the exponent is positive or negative. For positive values of b (except for unity) the curves are parabolic; negative values produce hyperbolic curves.

When the equation is placed in logarithmic form and rewritten as: $\log y = \log a + b \log x$, it is now in the same form as the equation of a straight line. In this case, when $x = 1$ then $y = a$ because log $1 = 0$.

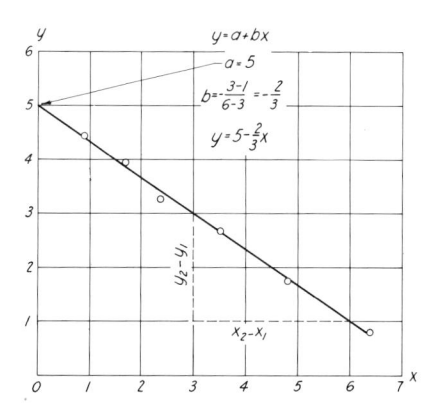

FIG. 28.23. Determination of empirical equations of the form $y = a + bx$ (first degree).

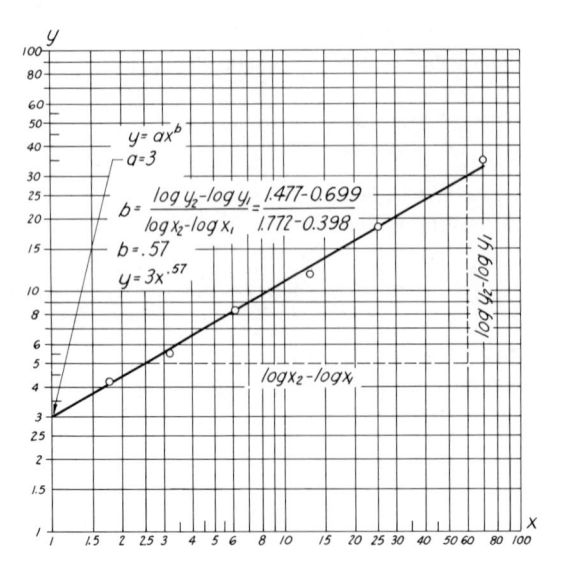

FIG. 28.24. Determination of empirical equations of the form $y = ax^b$ (power).

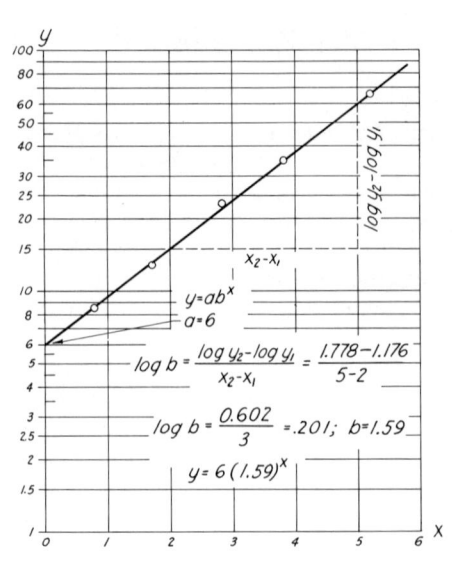

FIG. 28.25. Equations of the form $y = ab^x$.

Hence, after the data has been plotted (y vs. x) on logarithmic paper as in Fig. 28.24, a representative (average) straight line should be drawn. The line extended to the y-axis establishes a at the y intercept ($x = 1$). The value of a can be read directly, since the spacing is logarithmic. As before, two points along the line are used in the equation that follows to determine b:

$$b = \frac{\log y_2 - \log y_1}{\log x_2 - \log x_1}$$

For the two points selected along the line in Fig. 28.24,

$$b = \frac{1.477 - 0.699}{1.772 - 0.398} = .57$$

Thus, the equation is $y = 3x^{.57}$.

If $x = 1$ is not included in the plot of the data, then one may resort to a pair of simultaneous equations

$$\log y_1 = \log a + b \log x_1$$
$$\log y_2 = \log a + b \log x_2$$

In solving for a (also b) the solution gives the value for log a. The real value of a (and b) must be found in log tables.

28.24
Equations of the Form: $y = ab^x$. If the data plots as a nearly straight line on semilogarithmic graph paper (Fig. 28.25), the equation of the data is an exponential equation of the form: $y = ab^x$. This equation may be rewritten as: log y = log $a + x$ log b, which once again is in the same form as the equation of a straight line. In this case, when $x = 0$ then $y = a$.

With the data for the exponential equation plotted directly on semilogarithmic graph paper, one must again draw the most representative line along the path of the plotted points. This line extended to the y-axis ($x = 0$) determines the value of a. Again, two points must be selected along the line and their coordinates substituted in the equation

$$\log b = \frac{\log y_2 - \log y_1}{x_2 - x_1}$$

Then, with the logarithm of the value of b known, the real value of b as needed for the equation can be determined from log tables.

For the two points selected for the line in Fig. 28.25

$$\log b = \frac{1.778 - 1.176}{5 - 2} = \frac{0.602}{3} = .201$$

Hence,

$$b = 1.59$$

With the value of a read on the y-axis as 6, the formula for the data may be written as: $y = 6(1.59)^x$.

If $x = 0$ is not included in the plot of the data, then one must solve the simultaneous equations

$$\log y_1 = \log a + x_1 \log b$$
$$\log y_2 = \log a + x_2 \log b$$

Then, since the solution gives both a and b in terms of logarithms, log tables must be used to determine the real values of a and b.

When natural logarithms are available, the equation $y = ab^x$ may be changed to $y = Ae^{mx}$. This latter equation, in turn, may be written as: $\ln y = \ln A + mx$, which is still the equation of a straight line. The value of A can be determined as before at $x = 0$, and

$$m = \frac{\ln y_2 - \ln y_1}{x_2 - x_1}$$

where the value of m is found directly.

When $x = 0$ is not included, the equations to be used are

$$\ln y_1 = \ln A + mx_1$$
$$\ln y_2 = \ln A + mx_2$$

C: ALIGNMENT CHARTS

28.25

Alignment Charts (Nomographs). The purpose of alignment charts is to eliminate many of the laborious calculations necessary to solve formulas containing three or more variables. Such a chart is often complicated and difficult to construct, but if it can be used repeatedly, the labor involved in making it will be justified. In the commercial field, these charts appear in varied forms, which may be very simple or very complicated (Fig. 28.26).

Briefly stated, the simplest form of alignment chart consists of a set of three or more inclined or vertical scales so spaced and graduated as to represent graphically the variables in a formula. The scales may be divided into logarithmic units or some other types of functions, depending upon the form of equation. As illustrated in Fig. 28.27, the unknown value may be found by aligning a straightedge to the points representing known values on two of the scales. With a scale or triangle so placed, the numerical value representing the solution of the equation

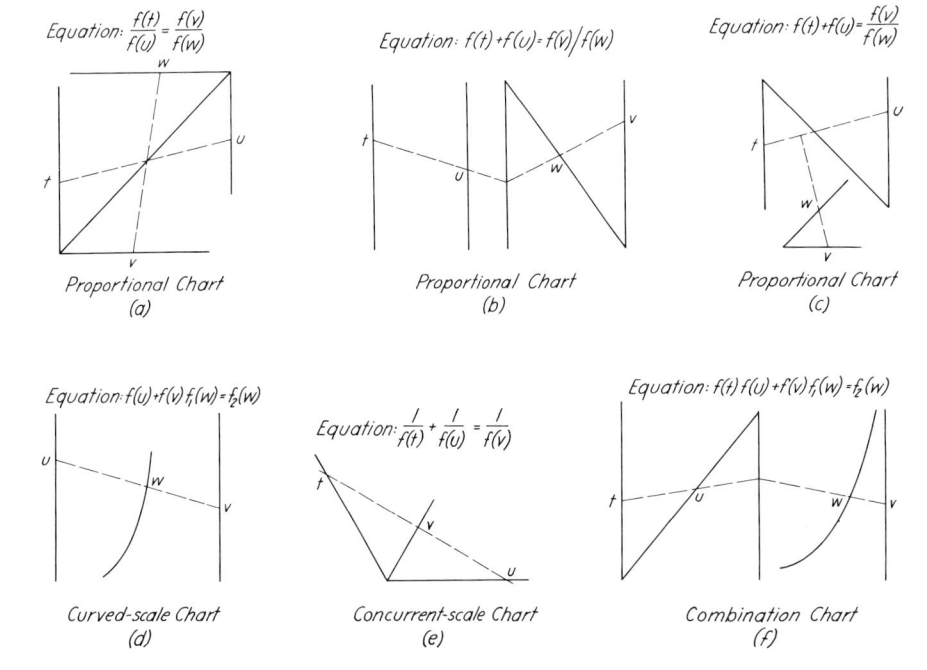

FIG. 28.26. Some common chart forms.

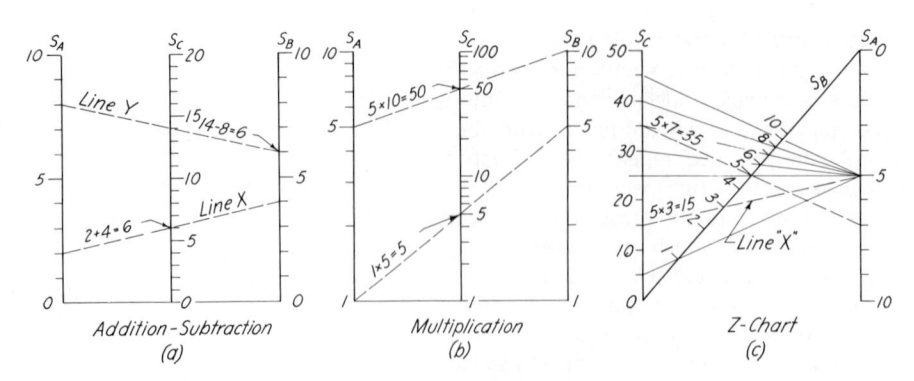

FIG. 28.27. Parallel-scale and Z-charts.

(a) Addition-Subtraction; (b) Multiplication; (c) Z-Chart

can be read on the third scale at the point of intersection.

Since alignment charts in varied forms are being used more and more by engineers and technologists, it is desirable that students studying in the fields dealing with the sciences have some knowledge of the fundamental principles underlying their construction. However, in any brief treatment, directed toward a beginner, it is impossible to explain fully the mathematics involved in the construction of the many and varied types (Fig. 28.26). Therefore, our attention here must be directed toward an understanding of a few of the less complicated straight-line forms with the hope that the student will gather sufficient knowledge to construct simple charts for familiar equations (Fig. 28.34).

28.26
Forms of Alignment Charts. Examples of some of the forms that alignment charts may have are shown in outline in Fig. 28.26. Examples of forms of proportional charts are illustrated in (a), (b), and (c). Miscellaneous forms are shown in (d), (e), and (f). One may obtain information needed for the construction of proportional type charts, concurrent scale charts, four-variable N-charts, and charts having a curved scale from any of the several books on nomography that are listed in the bibliography of this text.

28.27
Construction of Alignment Charts. In this limited study, the explanation for the constructions will be based on the principles of plane geometry. The two forms to be considered for formulas are the parallel-scale chart and the Z-chart, also called an N-chart (Fig. 28.27).

Without giving thought at this time to the geometry underlying the construction of alignment charts and to the selection of scales, the methods that might be used to construct simple charts for graphical addition and subtraction and graphical multiplication and division might well be considered [see Fig. 28.27(a) and (b)].

A parallel-scale alignment chart of the type shown in (a), prepared for the purpose of making additions and subtractions, could be constructed as follows:

Step 1. Draw three vertical straight lines spaced an equal distance apart.

Step 2. Draw a horizontal base line. This line will align and establish the origins (0) of the three scales.

Step 3. Using an engineer's decimal scale, mark off a series of equal lengths on scales S_A and S_B. Start at the base line in each case. Mark the values of the graduations upward on both scales starting with 0 at the base line.

Step 4. Mark off on the S_C scale a series of lengths that are half as long as those on scales S_A and S_B. Number the graduation marks starting at the base line.

In using this chart to add two numbers, say 2 and 4, one may align the ruling edge of a triangle through 2 on the S_A scale and 4 on the S_B scale, then, read their sum at the point where the edge of the triangle crosses the S_C scale (see line X). To subtract one number from another, say 8 from 14, the edge of the triangle should be placed so as to pass through 8 on scale S_A and 14 on S_C. The difference, read on the S_B scale, will be 6 as shown by line Y.

If logarithmic scales are used for this form of chart as in (b) instead of natural scales as in (a), a chart for multiplication and division results, for the log of the product of two numbers is equal to the sum of the logs of the factors. Thus, by a method of addition a product can be obtained.

Necessary information for the construction of logarithmic scales is given in Sec. 28.29.

A Z-chart (also called an N-chart), which will give the product of two numbers, is shown in (c). For example, if line X is assumed to represent the edge of a triangle so placed as to pass through 5 on the S_A scale and 3 on the S_B scale, it can be seen that $3 \times 5 = 15$.

A simple Z-chart that has been prepared solely for straight multiplication will have outside vertical scales of uniform spacing. The length of the scales and the spacing of the graduation marks can be arbitrarily determined as long as the chart will fit on the paper that is available and provided that the graduations cover the desired range in each case. The two vertical scales begin with 0 (zero) value at opposite ends of the diagonal scale so that the values of the graduations read in increasing magnitude upward on one scale and downward on the other.

28.28
Definitions. Before starting a discussion on the construction of scales, it is necessary that the student have an understanding of the meaning of the following terms and expressions that are commonly used when constructing alignment charts for solving equations:

Constant. A quantity whose value remains unchanged in an equation.

Variable. A quantity capable of taking values in an equation. A variable is designated by some letter, usually one of the latter letters of the alphabet.

Function of a variable. A mathematical expression for a combination of terms containing a variable, usually expressed in abbreviated form as $f(x)$ which is understood to mean "function of x." An equation usually contains several functions of different variables, such as $f(r) + f(s) = f(t)$; or $f(u) \cdot f(v) = f(w)$.

Functional modulus. A proportionality multiplier that is used to bring a range of values of a particular function within a selected length for a scale. For instance, with the upper and lower limits of a function known and a definite length L chosen for the scale, the value of the functional modulus (m) can be found by dividing L by the amount of the difference between the upper and lower limits of the function. The scale equation for determining m may be written

$$m = \frac{L}{f(u_2) - f(u_1)}$$

where $f(u_2)$ and $f(u_1)$ are the upper and lower limits.

Scale. A graduated line that may be either straight or curved. When the graduation marks are equally spaced, that is, when the distance between marks is the same for equal increments of the variable as the variable increases in magnitude, the scale is known as a uniform scale. When the lengths to the graduation marks are laid off to correspond to scale values of the function of a variable, the scale is called a functional scale.

28.29
Construction of a Functional Scale. Let it

be supposed that it is necessary to construct a functional scale, 5 in. in length, for $f(u) = u^2/2$ with u to range from 0 to 10. It will be found desirable to make the necessary computations by steps and to record the scale data in tabular form (Fig. 28.28).

Step 1. Record the values of u in the table.

Step 2. Compute the values of the function.

Step 3. Determine the functional modulus m.

Step 4. Multiply the recorded values of the function by the functional modulus.

In this case and in many other cases, the functional modulus may be chosen by inspection. For this problem, the over-all length (L) of the scale will be 5 in. when $m = 0.10$. If the scale equation is used to determine the functional modulus then

$$m = \frac{L}{f(u_2) - f(u_1)} = \frac{5}{(10^2/2) - 0}$$

$$= \frac{5}{50} = 0.10$$

All that now remains to be done to construct the scale is to lay off the computed distances along the line for the scale and mark the values at the corresponding interval points (Fig. 28.29).

Although a logarithmic scale might be constructed in this same manner, much time can be saved by using the graphic method shown in Fig. 28.30 for subdividing the scale between its end-points. To apply this method to a scale that has already been laid off to a predetermined length with the end-points of the range (say 1 to 10) marked, the steps of the construction are as follows:

Step 1. Draw a light construction line through point 1 making any convenient angle with the scale line.

Step 2. Using a printed log scale, mark off points on the auxiliary line.

Step 3. Draw a line through the 10 point on the construction line and the 10 point on the scale, then, through the remaining points draw lines parallel to this line through the 10's. These will divide the scale in proportion to the logarithms of numbers from 1 to 10.

28.30
Parallel-scale Charts for Equations of the Form $f(t) + f(u) = f(v)$. An alignment chart that is designed for solving an equation that can be set up to take this form will have three parallel functional scales that may be either uniform or logarithmic depending upon the equation. More information will be presented later concerning parallel-scale charts with logarithmic

u	0	1	2	3	4	5	6	7	8	9	10
u^2	0	1	4	9	16	25	36	49	64	81	100
$u^2/2$	0	0.5	2.0	4.5	8.0	12.5	18.0	24.5	32.0	40.5	50.0
$m(u^2/2)$	0	0.05"	0.2"	0.45"	0.80"	1.25"	1.80"	2.45"	3.20"	4.05"	5.00"

FIG. 28.28. Table.

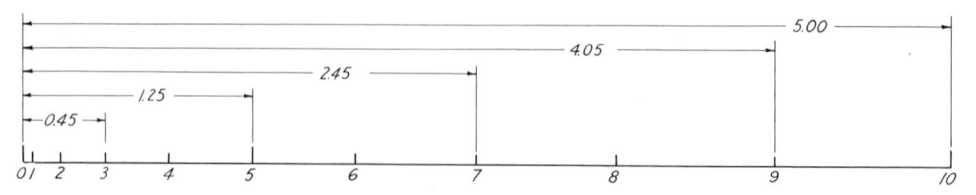

FIG. 28.29. Functional scale for $u^2/2$.

CHAP. 28 / GRAPHIC METHODS FOR ENGINEERING COMMUNICATION AND COMPUTATION 613

scales. In this section, attention will be directed to charts having scales with uniform spacing.

Before one can start constructing the chart, he must determine by calculation certain necessary information. First, he must determine how the scales are to be graduated, and second, he must calculate the ratio for the scale spacing.

To be competent to design parallel-scale charts, one must have a full understanding of the geometric basis for their construction. The explanation to follow is associated with the line layout in Fig. 28.31. Three parallel scales S_A, S_B, and S_C are shown with the origins t_0, u_0, and v_0 on line AB. Line (1) and line (2) are drawn parallel to AB through points v and u respectively on the isopleth. By similar triangles (shown shaded);

$$\frac{L_t - L_v}{a} = \frac{L_v - L_u}{b}$$

Now if

$$m_t = \frac{L_t}{f(t) - f(t_0)}$$

then

$$L_t = m_t[f(t) - f(t_0)]$$

When the function of t_0 is zero, the equation becomes

$$L_t = m_t f(t)$$

Similarly, when v_0 is zero,

$$L_v = m_v f(v)$$

and, when u_0 is zero,

$$L_u = m_u f(u)$$

Substituting these values;

$$\frac{m_t f(t) - m_v f(v)}{a} = \frac{m_v f(v) - m_u f(u)}{b}$$

Collecting terms,

$$m_t f(t) + \left(\frac{a}{b}\right) m_u f(u)$$

$$= \left(\frac{a}{b}\right) m_v f(v) + m_v f(v)$$

$$= m_v \left(1 + \frac{a}{b}\right) f(v)$$

But $f(t) + f(u) = f(v)$ only if the coefficient of the three terms are equal, therefore,

$$m_t = \left(\frac{a}{b}\right) m_u = \left(1 + \frac{a}{b}\right) m_v$$

and,

$$\frac{m_t}{m_u} = \frac{a}{b} \qquad \text{Eq. (1)}$$

Now since

$$m_t = \left(1 + \frac{a}{b}\right) m_v$$

and

$$\frac{a}{b} = \frac{m_t}{m_u}$$

Then,

$$m_t = \left(1 + \frac{m_t}{m_u}\right) m_v$$

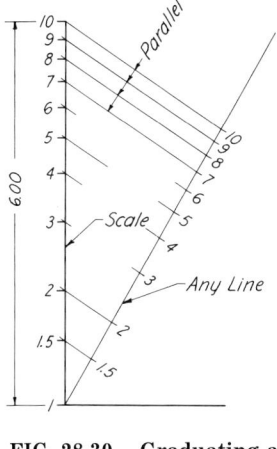

FIG. 28.30. Graduating a log scale.

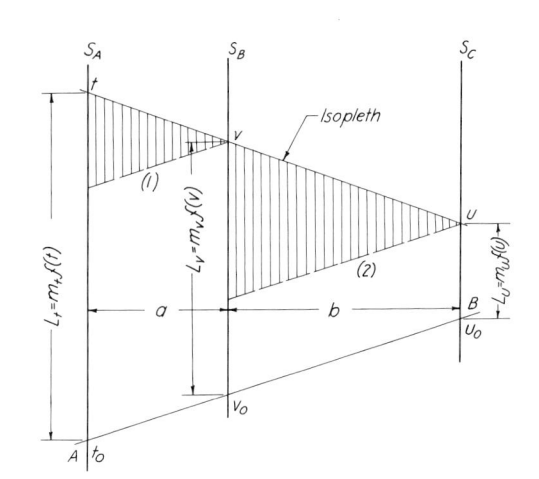

FIG. 28.31. Geometric basis for construction of parallel-scale alignment charts.

$$m_v = \frac{m_t}{\left(1 + \dfrac{m_t}{m_u}\right)}$$

and finally,

$$m_v = \frac{m_t m_u}{m_t + m_u} \qquad \text{Eq. (2)}$$

Now suppose that it is desired to construct a chart having the form of $t + u = v$ and that t is to have a range from 0 to 10 and u from 0 to 20 (Fig. 28.32). It has been determined that the scale lengths should be 6 in.

Then

$$m_t = \frac{6}{10.0} = \frac{6}{10} = 0.6;$$

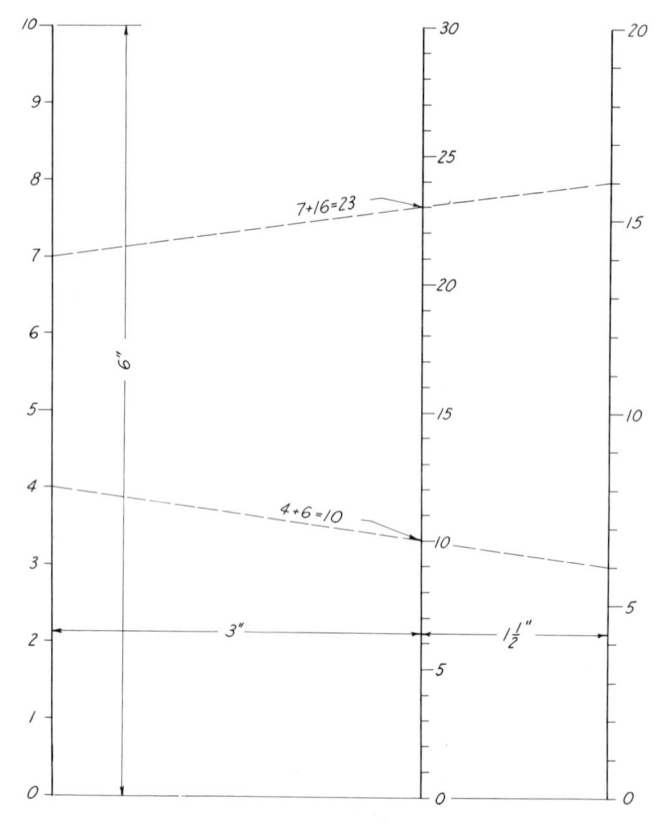

FIG. 28.32. Alignment chart for equation of the form f(t) + f(u) = f(v).

$$m_u = \frac{6}{20.0} = \frac{6}{20} = 0.3$$

and,

$$m_v = \frac{m_t m_u}{m_t + m_u} = \frac{0.6 \times 0.3}{0.6 + 0.3}$$
$$= \frac{0.18}{0.90} = 0.20 \qquad \text{Eq. (2)}$$

To determine the ratio of the scale spacing:

$$\frac{m_t}{m_u} = \frac{a}{b} = \frac{0.6}{0.3} = \frac{2}{1} \qquad \text{Eq. (1)}$$

For convenience, distance a between scales can be made 3 in. Distance b must then be $1\frac{1}{2}$ in. to satisfy the proportion of 2 to 1. The total width of the chart will be $4\frac{1}{2}$ in.

Since in this particular case the modulus for each of the scales is in full tenths and the scales are to be uniformly divided, an engineer's scale may be used to mark off the scales of the chart. With other conditions, it would be necessary to prepare either a table such as the one shown in Fig. 28.28 or to divide the line between its end-points using a geometric method.

28.31
Parallel-scale Charts for Equations of the Form $f(t) \cdot f(u) = f(v)$. Equations of this form may be rewritten so as to take the form $f(t) + f(u) = f(v)$ by using logarithms for both sides of the equation. For example, suppose that it is desirable to prepare a chart for $M = Wl$, a formula commonly used by designers and engineers. In this equation, M is the maximum bending moment at the point of support of a cantilever beam; W is the concentrated load; and l is the distance from the point of support to the load.

GIVEN:
$$M = Wl$$

REWRITTEN:
$$\log M = \log W + \log l$$

CHAP. 28 / GRAPHIC METHODS FOR ENGINEERING COMMUNICATION AND COMPUTATION **615**

Another example would be the formula for determining the discharge of trapezoidal weirs.

GIVEN:

$$Q = 3.367 L h^{3/2}$$

REWRITTEN:

$$\log Q = \log 3.367 + \log L + 1.5 \log h$$

In this last equation, Q is discharge in cubic feet per second; L is the length of the crest in feet (width of weir); and h is the observed head (depth of water).

For the purpose of our discussion, the formula $P = I^2 R$ will be used where P is power in watts; I is current in amperes; and R is resistance in ohms (Fig. 28.33). It has been determined that I must vary from 1 to 10 amp and R from 1 to 10 ohms. A chart of this type might be used to determine the power loss in inductive windings. The length of the scales is to be 5 in.

The steps for the construction are as follows:

Step 1. Write the equation in standard form.

$$\log P = 2 \log I + \log R$$

Step 2. Determine the moduli m_I and m_R for the outside scales.

$$m_I = \frac{5}{2 \log 10 - 2 \log 1} = \frac{5}{2} = 2.5$$

$$L_I = 2.5 (2 \log I) = 5 \log I$$

$$m_R = \frac{5}{\log 10 - \log 1} = \frac{5}{1} = 5$$

$$L_R = 5 \log R$$

Step 3. Determine m_P and L_P for the P-scale.

$$m_P = \frac{2.5 \times 5}{2.5 + 5} = \frac{12.5}{7.5} = \frac{5}{3}$$

$$L_P = \frac{5}{3} \log P$$

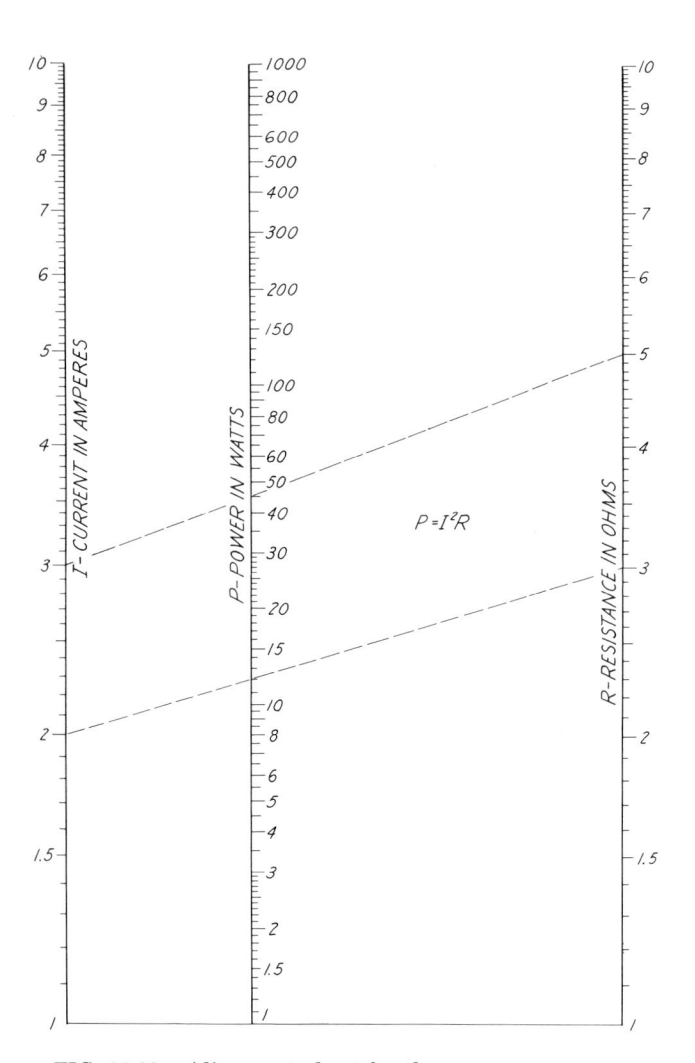

FIG. 28.33. Alignment chart for the equation $P = I^2 R$.

Step 4. Determine the ratio for the spacing of the scales.

$$\frac{m_I}{M_R} = \frac{2.5}{5} = \frac{1}{2} \text{ (ratio)}$$

Step 5. Draw three vertical lines 1 in. and 2 in. apart and add a horizontal base line. By using these selected values, the ratio for spacing will be maintained and the chart will have good proportion.

Step 6. Graduate the scales for I and R using the method shown in Fig. 28.30. In this particular case, both logarithmic scales will be alike and will range from 1 on the base line upward to 10.

Step 7. Graduate the P-scale. By substituting values in the equation, it will be found that P will range from 1 w to 1000 w; therefore, the scale will be a three-cycle logarithmic scale, and the graphic method may be used for locating the graduation marks.

Figure 28.34 shows another parallel-scale alignment chart. This particular one could be used to determine the volume of a cylindrical tank when the diameter and height are known.

The formula for the volume of a cylinder, as given in the illustration, may be rewritten as

$$\log V = \log (\pi/4) + 2 \log D + \log H$$

Suppose that it has been decided, as in this case, that both the diameter (D) and the height (H) are to vary from 1 ft to 10 ft, and that the length of the two outside scales is to be 6 in. For the moment, the constant term $\log (\pi/4)$ can be ignored, for it can be accounted for at a later time by shifting the V-scale for the volume upward until it is in the position for furnishing a correct reading for a particular value as computed using the formula.

The moduli can be determined as previously explained.

$$m_D = \frac{6}{2 \log 10 - 2 \log 1} = 3$$

and

$$L_D = 3(2 \log D) = 6 \log D$$

$$m_H = \frac{6}{\log 10 - \log 1} = 6$$

and

$$L_H = 6 \log H$$

$$m_V = \frac{m_D \times m_H}{m_D + m_H} = \frac{3 \times 6}{3 + 6} = \frac{18}{9} = 2$$

and

$$L_V = 2(\log V)$$

Scale spacing ratio:

$$\frac{m_D}{m_H} = \frac{3}{6}$$

For convenience, the scales can be spaced at 2 in. and 4 in., giving a chart that is a square in form.

The scales for D and H may be gradu-

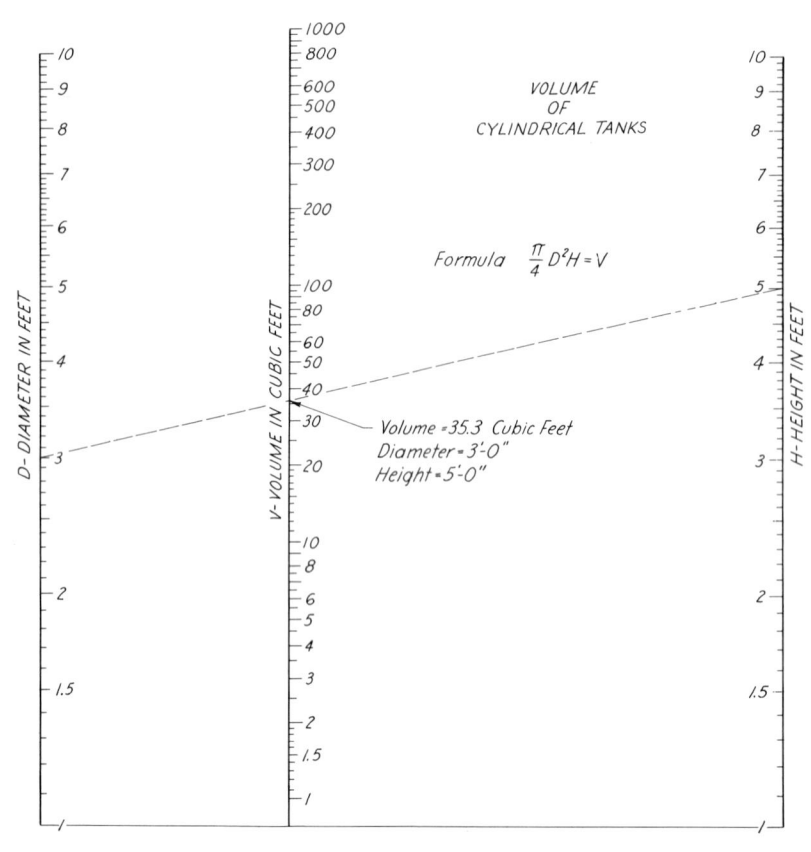

FIG. 28.34. Alignment chart for $V = (\pi/4)D^2H$ (volume of a cylinder).

CHAP. 28 / GRAPHIC METHODS FOR ENGINEERING COMMUNICATION AND COMPUTATION 617

ated by using the graphical method illustrated in Fig. 28.30. The scale for V will be a three-cycle scale with a 6-in. range of length between the 1 and 1000 values. Since the value of V at the base line must result from the substitution in the equation of the values of 1 and 1 for the other two scales, the resulting value of 0.7854 cu ft is the volume at the base line. The most convenient procedure to follow in graduating the V-scale is to start with the 0.7854 value at the base line. By so doing, the constant term, $\log \pi/4$, is taken into account. Should one desire to determine the distance to be laid off along the V-scale from the base line to the 1, it will be found to be equal to two times the difference between the logs of the numbers in this particular case, for the value of m_v is 2.

28.32
Three-Scale Alignment Chart—Simplified (Graphical) Construction. After the student has acquired a thorough understanding of the theory of alignment charts, which includes a full knowledge of the geometric basis underlying their construction, he will be in a position to simplify his construction work and make it purely graphical through the use of tie-lines. Of course, this can only be done after the chart form has been identified, the equation converted, and the ranges for the variables (as needed) have been decided upon. The use of tie-lines to locate check points on the third scale of a three-scale alignment chart is shown in Fig. 28.35.

GIVEN:
$$M = \frac{wl^2}{12},$$

the equation for the bending moment (maximum) of a beam, having a uniformly distributed load and fixed at both ends. In this equation, w is the load in pounds per foot of length and l is the span in feet.

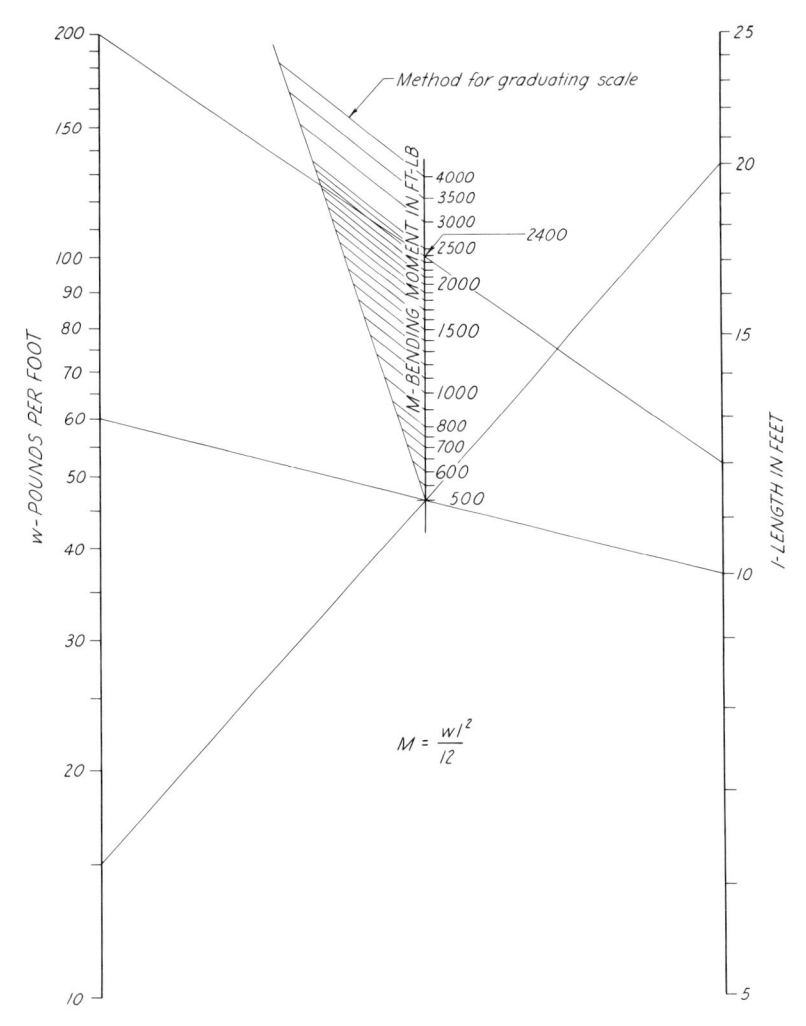

FIG. 28.35. Alignment chart—simplified construction.

It was decided that the alignment chart would fulfill most needs if w had limits from 10 to 200 lb per ft and l had limits from 5 to 25 ft.

EQUATION REWRITTEN:

$\log w + 2 \log l = \log M + \log 12$

The steps for the construction of the chart, with only minor calculations that may be performed mentally, are as follows:

1. Draw two vertical lines (say 5 in. long) at any convenient distance apart.

2. Graduate the w-scale (left-hand line) from the lower point 10 to the uppermost point 200. (In this case, use was made of the method shown in Fig. 28.30 to locate the scale values between 10 and 200.)

3. Graduate the l-scale, with the lower point as 5 and the point at the top of the scale as 25. (Scale values located as in Step 2.)

4. Using a value of 10 for l and 500 for M yields $w = 60$ for the tie-line from the 60 value on the w-scale to the 10 value on the l-scale. Again, with $l = 20$ and $M = 500$, w is found to be 15 for the second tie-line through $M = 500$. The intersection of these two tie-lines is a check point on the third vertical scale, a point that establishes not only the position of the scale line but the 500 value as well.

5. Locate a second check point on the M-scale by drawing a third tie line. In this case it was found to be convenient to use $w = 200$ and $l = 12$ to yield $M = 2400$.

6. Graduate the M-scale as shown (read Sec. 28.29).

28.33
Graphical Construction of a Z-Chart. A simplified graphical construction may be employed to construct a Z-chart (N-chart) such as the one shown in Fig. 28.36, for the equation $V = 2.467Dd^2$ which gives the volume of a torus, a solid taking the form illustrated in Fig. 4.61. The given equation was considered to be so arranged that the vertical V- and D-scales would be uniformly graduated. The d-scale on the diagonal representing a variable to a

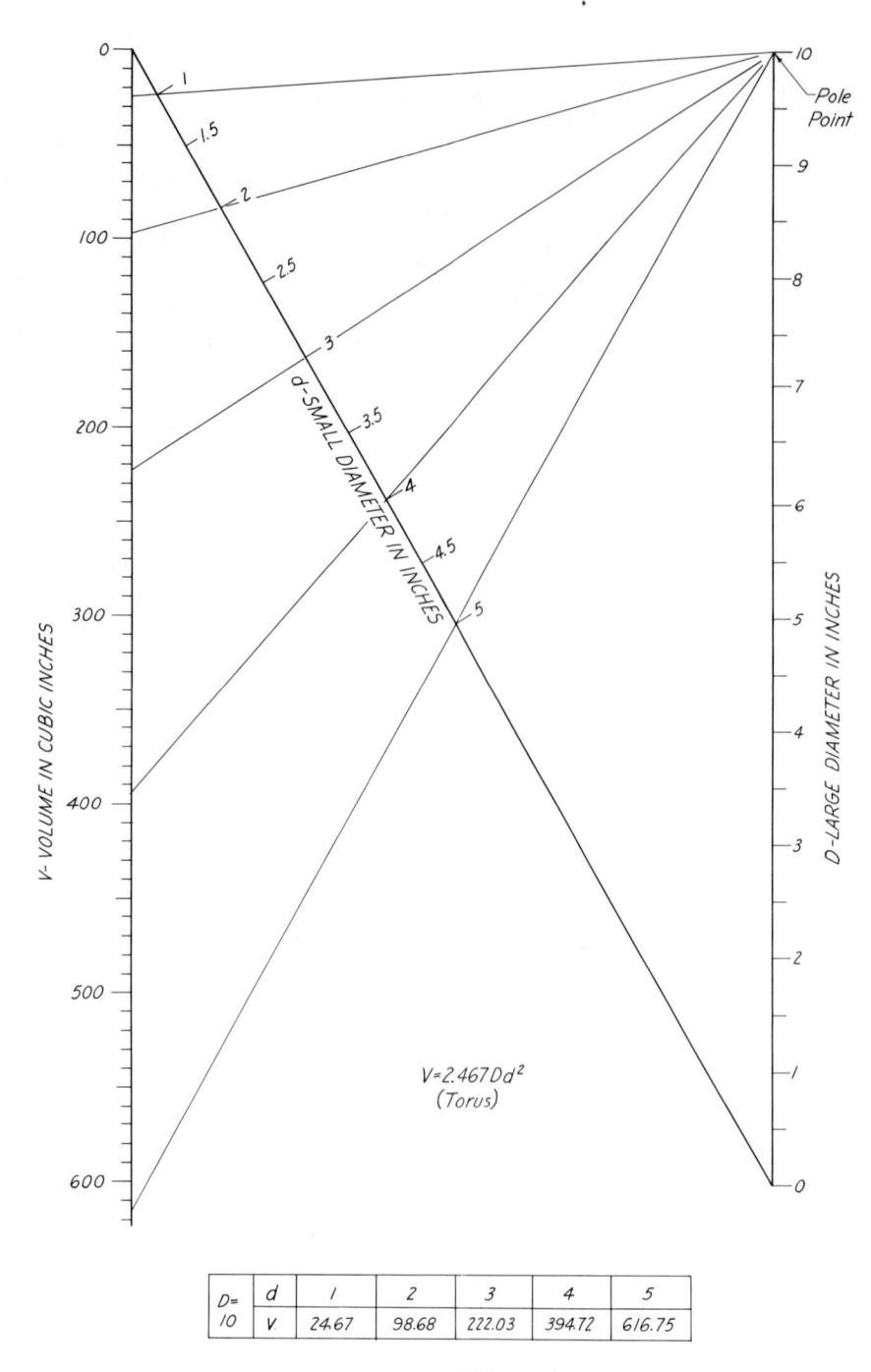

$D=$	d	1	2	3	4	5
10	V	24.67	98.68	222.03	394.72	616.75

FIG. 28.36. Chart for equation $V = 2.467Dd^2$.

CHAP. 28 / GRAPHIC METHODS FOR ENGINEERING COMMUNICATION AND COMPUTATION   **619**

power, is nonuniformly graduated. For this form of chart, one should recall that the vertical scales begin at zero and run in opposite directions (see Sec. 28.27). The diagonal connecting these two zero points completes the usual N-shape.

The steps in making the construction are as follows:

Step 1. Draw the scale lines for the variables V and D at any convenient distance apart, in this case 3.50 in. Then, lay off the D-scale to some selected length, say 6 in., and locate the zero point of V-scale opposite the 10 of the D-scale.

Step 2. Graduate the V-scale uniformly, being certain that the range is sufficient to make possible a full reading when using the maximum values of the other scales.

Step 3. Graduate the D-scale for the selected range of values, in this case from 0 to 10 in.

Step 4. Graduate the d-scale by selecting one convenient value of D and substituting it repeatedly in the original equation, each time with a different value of d which is to be marked on the diagonal scale. In so doing, values of V are found that establish the ends of tie-lines from the pole point (10) selected on the D-scale. For example, when the values 10 and 1 are substituted for D and d, respectively, in the given equation, V is found to be 24.67 cu in. With this known, a tie-line drawn from the pole to 24.67 on the V-scale, will locate d = 1 on the diagonal scale. The volumes for a range of d from 1 to 5 in. are shown in the table below the illustration. These values were used to draw the tie-lines shown.

28.34
Four-variable Relationship—Parallel-scale Alignment Chart. A four-variable parallel-scale alignment chart may be constructed for an equation of the form $f(t) + f(u) + f(v) = f(w)$ when the equation has been rewritten as follows:

$$f(t) + f(u) = f(k)$$
$$f(k) + f(v) = f(w)$$

When rewritten in this form, the four-variable chart can then be constructed as two three-scale nomographs with the k-scale common to both. The k-scale, which serves as a pivot line in using the chart, need not be graduated but it must be remembered that it does have a modulus and does represent a function in both equations.

In Fig. 28.37, a four-variable alignment chart is shown for the addition of num-

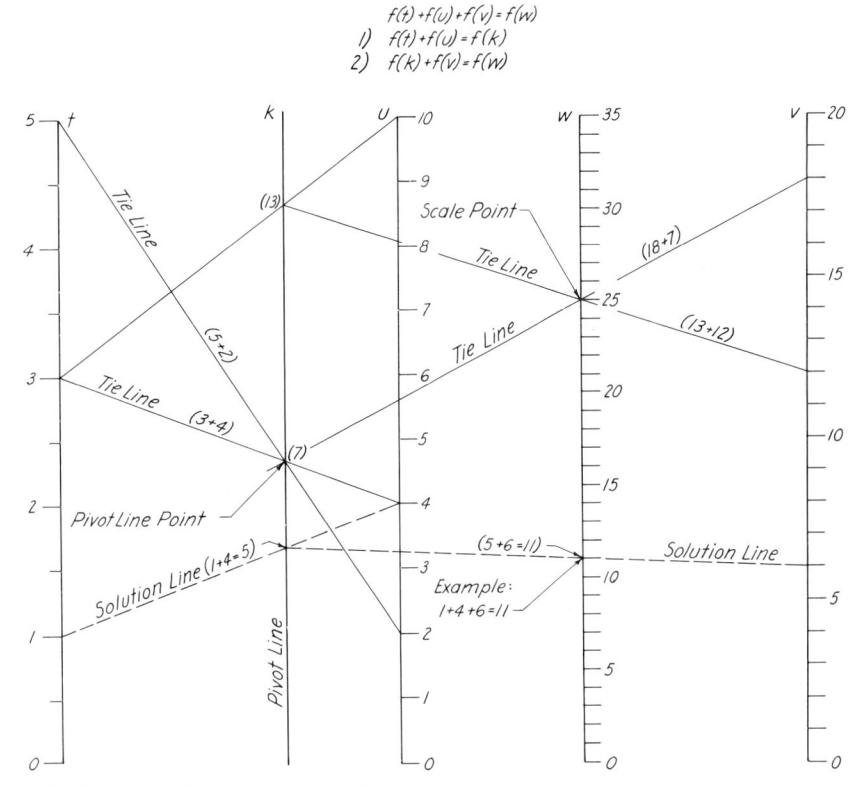

FIG. 28.37. Alignment chart for the equation $f(t) + f(u) + f(v) = f(w)$.

bers. For this particular construction, it was arbitrarily decided that t should have a range from 0 to 5, u from 0 to 10, and v from 0 to 20. The procedure for the construction of this chart is as follows:

Step 1. Draw the vertical lines (stems) for the t- and u-scales at any convenient distance apart and, by means of the engineer's scale or graphically, graduate t from 0 to 5 and u from 0 to 10.

Step 2. Draw the two intersecting tie-lines between the t and u scales that determine the position of the pivot line k at their point of intersection (7). Intersecting tie-lines could have been drawn from other graduation marks along the t and u scales as long as the sum of the values at the ends of one of the selected tie-lines equals the sum of the values at the ends of the other tie-line intersecting it.

Step 3. Draw a third tie-line to locate another check point along the pivot line k. In this case, the tie-line was drawn from 3 on the t-scale to 10 on the u-scale to locate the mark for 13 on the k-scale.

Step 4. Decide upon the best location for the v-scale, then draw the stem line and graduate it uniformly from 0 to 20.

Step 5. Using the 7 and 13 value marks that have now been established on the k-scale, draw the two tie-lines (18 + 7 = 25 and 13 + 12 = 25) that will determine the location of the w-scale at their point of intersection as well as the position of the 25 graduation mark.

Step 6. Draw the w-scale and graduate it from 0 to 35, the 35 value representing the largest sum obtainable from the use of the t-, u-, and v-scales as they have been graduated for this particular chart.

The procedure for finding the sum of the numbers 1, 4, and 6 is illustrated by the broken lines extending between the scales. First, a straightedge can be laid across the t- and u-scales through the 1 and 4 values, as shown, to determine the position on the pivot line (k) that the graduation mark would have that represents their sum, in this case 5. Then the straightedge should be shifted so that its edge will pass through the 5 position on the pivot line and the graduation mark for the 6 value on the v-scale. The sum of the three given numbers can then be read as 11 on the w-scale.

The four-scale alignment chart, shown in Fig. 28.38, for the computation of simple interest, may be easily constructed once the equation $I = PRT$ has first been written in the logarithmic form of

$$\log P + \log R + \log T = \log I,$$

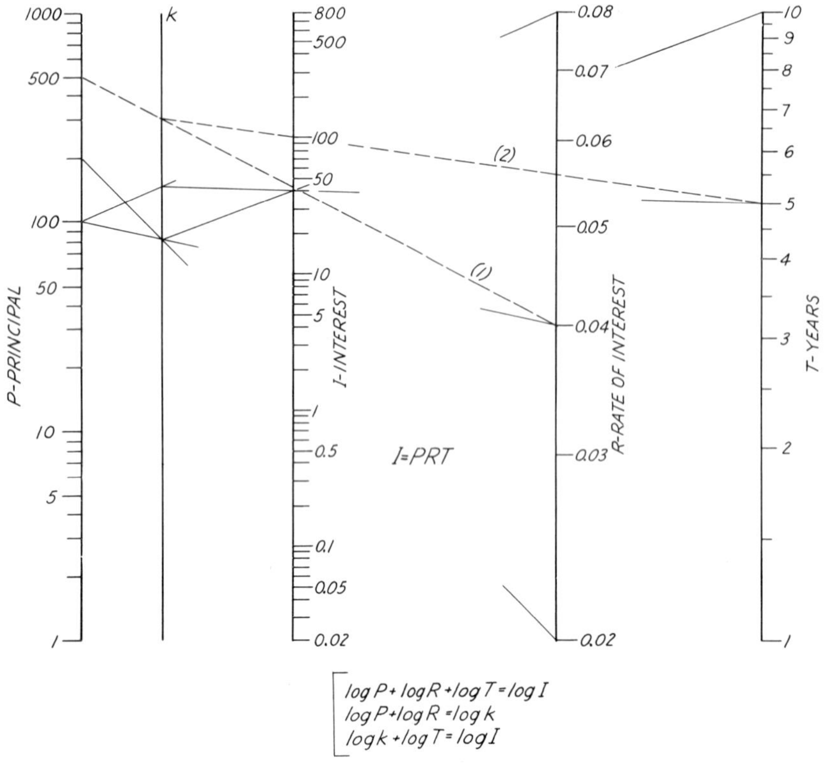

$$\begin{bmatrix} \log P + \log R + \log T = \log I \\ \log P + \log R = \log k \\ \log k + \log T = \log I \end{bmatrix}$$

FIG. 28.38. Alignment chart for the equation $I = PRT$.

and, then rewritten as

$$\log P + \log R = \log k \qquad (1)$$

and

$$\log k + \log T = \log I \qquad (2)$$

The equation as first rewritten is in the form of $f(t) + f(u) + f(v) = f(w)$ and as arranged in (1) and (2) in the form of

$$f(t) + f(u) = f(k)$$
$$f(k) + f(v) = f(w)$$

Now, since equations (1) and (2) have the same form as those for the previous problem, the alignment chart for the equation $I = PRT$ is constructed similarly except that logarithmic scales must be used in this case in place of natural (uniformly divided) scales. As before, tie-lines were used to position the k and I scales and to locate needed check points. The procedure for reading the chart is illustrated by the broken lines, numbered (1) and (2).

The reader is urged to follow through the construction of the alignment chart for the equation $I = PRT$ mentally, step by step. At the start, however, he must recognize that the k-scale belongs first to the PRk chart and then to the kTI three-scale chart that together make the complete chart for the four variables P, R, T, and I.

PROBLEMS

Technical Graphs and Charts

The following problems have been designed to emphasize the fundamental principles underlying the preparation and use of technical graphs and charts.

1. Determine the values for the following equations, as assigned, and plot the curve in each case for quantitative purposes.

Parabola	$Y = 4x^2$, x from 0 to 5
Ellipse	$Y^2 = 100 - 2x^2$
Sines	$Y = \sin x$, x from 0° to 360°
Cosines	$Y = \cos x$, x from 0° to 360°
Logarithms	$Y = \log x$, x from 1 to 10
Reciprocals	$Y = 1/x$, x from 1 to 10

2. The freezing temperatures for two common antifreeze solutions for various compositions are given opposite.

Prepare a chart for these data, mainly quantitative in character, from which the required per cent volume can be read for any desired freezing temperature. Use the type of paper shown in Fig. 28.3(b).

3. Approximate barometric pressures at different heights above sea level are given opposite. Prepare a qualitative chart for the given data on rectangular coordinate paper.
Note that the curve would be straight on semilogarithmic paper.

PRESTONE		DENATURED ALCOHOL	
% by vol.	Temp. °F	% by vol.	Temp. °F
10	25	10	25
20	16.5	20	17.5
25	11	25	14
30	5	30	5
35	−3	35	−1
40	−12	40	−11
45	−25	45	−18
50	−38	50	−25
55	−47	55	−32
		65	−45

H-ALTITUDE IN MILES	B-BAROMETRIC PRESSURE, IN. OF Hg
0	29.92
1	24.5
2	20.0
3	16.2
4	13.45
5	11.0
6	8.9
7	7.28
8	5.95
9	4.87
10	4.0

4. Data on rate of growth are frequently plotted on semilogarithmic paper, because the slope of the curve then represents the rate of growth. On semilogarithmic paper, plot the data for the enrollment in a university.

Year	Enrollment
1941	5,745
1942	5,831
1943	5,906
1944	6,238
1945	6,984
1946	7,313
1947	6,011
1948	5,112
1949	4,838
1950	4,621
1951	10,221
1952	11,320
1953	10,210
1954	10,101
1955	9,871
1956	9,211
1957	9,071
1958	9,647
1959	10,101
1960	10,456
1961	11,132
1962	11,656
1963	12,231
1964	12,910
1965	13,621
1966	14,222
1967	15,011
1968	15,976
1969	16,211
1970	18,013

Place the vertical axis 1 unit from the left edge and the horizontal axis at the extreme bottom of the page ruling. Letter in an appropriate title.

Also draw the curve of the general trend and enter on the chart, just below the title, what the enrollment would be in 1975 if the same rate of growth is maintained.

5. In a hydraulics laboratory, the construction of a quantitative curve that would give the weight of water contained in tubes of various diameters and lengths was desired. This was accomplished by filling tubes of known diameters with water to a depth of 1 ft and observing the weight of water thus added. The water was kept at a temperature for maximum density and the following data were obtained:

D = Diameter of tube in inches	W = Weight of 1-ft column of water
2	1.362
2½	2.128
3	3.064
3½	4.171
4	5.448
4½	6.895
5	8.512
5½	10.299
6	12.257
6½	14.385
7	16.683
7½	19.152
8	21.790

On a sheet of graph paper [Fig. 28.3(b)], plot the above data. Place the axes 3 cm in from the edges. Letter the title in any convenient open space.

6. Owing to uncontrollable factors, such as lack of absolute uniformity of material or test procedure, repeated tests of samples of material do not give identical results. Also, it has been observed in many practical situations that

a. Large departures from the average seldom occur.
b. Small variations from average occur quite often.
c. The variations are equally likely to be above average and below average.

The foregoing statements are borne out by the accompanying data showing the results of 4,000 measurements of tensile strength of malleable iron.

On a sheet of coordinate graph paper [Fig. 28.3(a) or (b)] prepare a graph showing frequency of occurrence of various strength values as ordinates and tensile strength as abscissa. Draw a smooth symmetrical curve approximating the given data.

Range of tensile strength values in pounds per square inch	Number of observations
Under 45,000	0
45,000–45,999	1
46,000–46,999	2
47,000–47,999	3
48,000–48,999	6
49,000–49,999	20
50,000–50,999	232
51,000–51,999	376

Range of tensile strength values in pounds per square inch	Number of observations
52,000–52,999	590
53,000–53,999	740
54,000–54,999	771
55,000–55,999	604
56,000–56,999	383
57,000–57,999	184
58,000–58,999	60
59,000–59,999	20
Over 60,000	8
	4000

7. On a sheet of paper of the type shown in Fig. 28.3(b), using India ink, plot a curve to represent the data given opposite. (Note: For *stress-strain diagrams*, although the load is the independent variable, it is plotted as ordinate, contrary to the general rule as given in Sec. 28.5. Figure 28.6 shows a similar chart. In performing tests of this nature, some load is imposed before any readings of elongation are taken.

It is suggested that the label along the abscissa be marked "Strain, 0.00001 in. per in." then fewer figures will be required along the axis.

Stress, pounds per square inch	Strain, inches per inch
3,000	0.0001
5,000	0.0002
10,000	0.00035
15,000	0.00054
20,000	0.00070
25,000	0.00090
30,000	0.00106
32,000	0.00112
33,000	0.00130
34,000	0.00140

8. Make a vertical multiple bar chart showing the enrollment at _____ University from 1961 to 1970. Obtain data from Problem 4.

9. Make a semilogarithmic graph showing the enrollment of your school for the last 20 years.

PROBLEMS

Alignment Charts

The following problems have been designed to emphasize the fundamental principles underlying the preparation and use of alignment charts.

10–21. Prepare an alignment chart for the given equation. Chart scales should have a sufficient number of division marks to enable the user to obtain some reasonably accurate results (readings). In each problem the range for two of the variables has been given. The range of the third variable must make possible the use of the full range of each of the other two variables.

10. Construct an alignment chart for the multiplication of numbers from 1 to 100 (read Sec. 28.27 and study Fig. 28.27).

11. Construct an alignment chart of the form $t + u = v$. Let t vary from 0 to 10 and u from 0 to 15 (read Sec. 28.30 and study Fig. 28.32).

12. Construct an alignment chart for determining the area of a triangle. The student is to determine for himself the range for each of the scales.

13. Construct an alignment chart for determining the volume of a cylinder. The diameter is to range from 1 to 5 in. and the height from 1 to 10 in. The volume is to be in cubic inches (read Sec. 28.31).

14. Make an alignment chart for determining the volume of a paraboloid, $V = 1/8\pi ab^2$, where a is the length (measured along the axis) and b is the diameter of the base. Let a vary from 1 to 20 in. and b from 1 to 10 in.

15. Construct an alignment chart for the maximum bending moment at the point of support of a cantilever beam, formula $M = Wl$. W is the concentrated load at the end of the beam and l is the distance from the point of support to the load (read Sec. 28.31). Let W vary from 100 to 1000 lb and l from 10 to 20 ft. M will be in ft-lb.

16. Make an alignment chart for the discharge of trapezoid weirs, formula $Q = 3.367Lh^{3/2}$. Q is discharge in cubic feet per second; L is length of crest in feet (width of weir); and, h is the head (depth of water). Let L vary from 1 to 10 ft and h from 0.5 to 2 ft (read Secs. 28.31 and 28.32).

17. Make an alignment chart for the formula $P = I^2R$ as explained in Sec. 28.31. Let I vary from 1 to 20 amp and R from 1 to 10 ohms.

18. Make an alignment chart for the formula $R = E/I$ where E is the electromotive force in volts; I is current in amperes; and, R is resistance in ohms. Let R vary from 1 to 20 ohms and I from 1 to 100 amp (read Secs. 28.31 and 28.32).

19. Make an alignment chart for the formula $I = bd^3/36$ where I is the moment of inertia of a triangular section; b is the length of the base in inches; and d is the depth of the section (altitude of triangle). Let b vary from 1 to 10 in. and d from 1 to 10 in. (read Secs. 28.31 and 28.32).

20. Make an alignment chart for the formula $M = wl^2/8$ where M is the bending moment in foot-pounds, w is the load in pounds per foot, and l the length of span in feet. Let w vary from 10 to 200 lb per ft and l from 5 to 25 ft (see Fig. 28.35).

21. Make an alignment chart (Z-chart) for the equation for the volume of a right circular cylinder, $V = \pi r^2 h/144$, where V is the volume in cubic feet, r is the radius of the base in inches and h is the height in feet. Let r vary from 0 to 20 in. and h from 0 to 20 ft.

June 11, 1963 M. A. FAGET ETAL 3,093,346
SPACE CAPSULE

Filed Oct. 16, 1959 4 Sheets—Sheet 4

INVENTORS
M.A. FAGET   W.S. BLANCHARD, JR.
A.J. MEYER, JR.   A.B. KEHLET
R.G. CHILTON   J.B. HAMMACK
C.C. JOHNSON, JR.
BY
ATTORNEYS

A patent drawing showing the sequence of events from launch to landing.

Patent Office Drawings

29.1

A person who has invented a new machine or device, or an improvement for an existing machine, and who applies for a patent is required by law to submit a drawing showing every important feature of his invention. When the invention is an improvement, the drawing must contain one or more views of the invention, alone, and a separate view showing it attached to the portion of the machine for which it is intended.

Patent drawings must be carefully prepared in accordance with the strict rules of the U.S. Patent Office. These rules are published in a pamphlet entitled *Rules of Practice in the United States Patent Office,* which may be obtained, without charge, by writing to the Commissioner of Patents, Washington, D.C.

In the case of a machine or mechanical device, the complete application for a patent will consist of a petition, a "specification" (written description), and a drawing. An applicant should employ a patent attorney, preferably one who is connected with or regularly employs competent draftsmen capable of producing well-executed drawings that conform with all of the rules. Ordinary draftsmen lack the skill and experience necessary to produce such drawings. Two sheets of drawings for a patent for a radiation protection system are shown in Figs. 29.1 and 29.2.

Several U.S. Patent Office publications that are available to the general public have been listed in the bibliography.

29.2
Rules. The following rules (49–55) are quoted verbatim from the pamphlet, *Rules of Practice in the United States Patent Office:*

> 49. The applicant for a patent is required by law to furnish a drawing of his invention whenever the nature of the case admits of it.
>
> 50. The drawing may be signed by the inventor or one of the persons indicated in rule 25, or the name of the applicant may be signed on the drawing by his attorney in fact. The drawing must show every feature of the invention covered by the claims, and the figures should be consecutively numbered, if possible. When the invention consists of an improvement on an old machine, the drawing must exhibit, in one or more views, the invention itself, disconnected from the old structure, and also in another view, so much only of the old structure as will suffice to show the connection of the invention therewith.
>
> 51. Two editions of patent drawings are printed and published—one for office use, certified copies, etc., of the size and

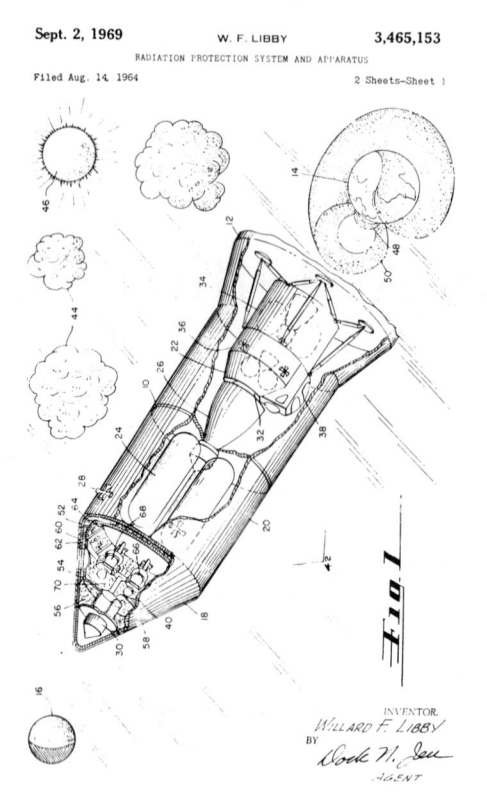

628 PART V / DESIGN AND COMMUNICATION DRAWING IN SPECIALIZED FIELDS

FIG. 29.1. The patent drawing showing a radiation protection system. See also Fig. 29.3.

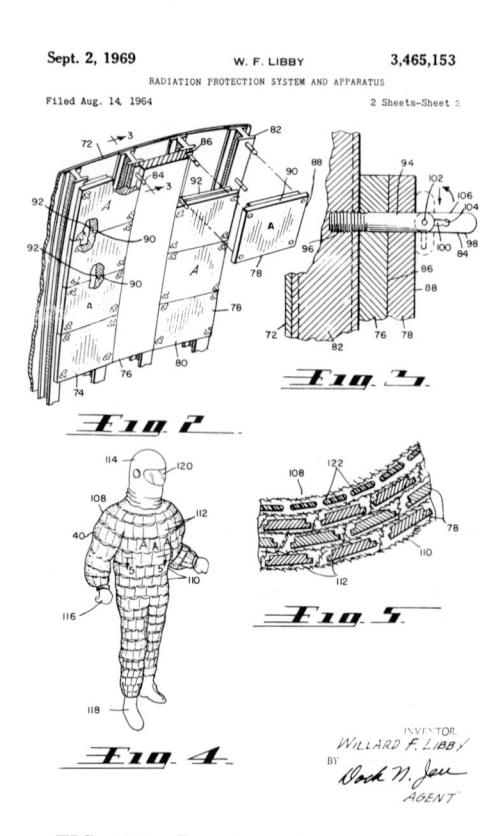

FIG. 29.2. Drawings showing the details that are related to the claims.

character of those attached to patents, the work being about 6 by $9\frac{1}{2}$ inches; and one reduction of a selected portion of each drawing for the Official Gazette.

52. This work is done by the photolithographic process, and therefore the character of each original drawing must be brought as nearly as possible to a uniform standard of excellence, suited to the requirements of the process, to give the best results, in the interests of inventors, of the office, and of the public. The following rules will therefore be rigidly enforced, and any departure from them will be certain to cause delay in the examination of an application for letters patent:

(*a*) Drawings must be made upon pure white paper of a thickness corresponding to two-sheet or three-sheet Bristol board. The surface of the paper must be calendered and smooth. India ink alone must be used, to secure perfectly black and solid lines.

(*b*) The size of a sheet on which a drawing is made must be exactly 10 by 15 inches. One inch from its edges a single marginal line is to be drawn, leaving the "sight" precisely 8 by 13 inches. Within this margin all work and signatures must be included. One of the shorter sides of the sheet is regarded as its top, and measuring downwardly from the marginal line, a space of not less than $1\frac{1}{4}$ inches is to be left blank for the heading of title, name, number, and date.

United States Patent Office

3,465,153
Patented Sept. 2, 1969

1

3,465,153
RADIATION PROTECTION SYSTEM AND APPARATUS
Willard F. Libby, Los Angeles, Calif., assignor to McDonnell Douglas Corporation, Santa Monica, Calif., a corporation of Maryland
Filed Aug. 14, 1964, Ser. No. 389,734
Int. Cl. G21f 1/12, 3/02, 7/00
U.S. Cl. 250—108   16 Claims

My present invention relates generally to astronautics, the science of space flight, and more particularly to a system and apparatus and method for the protection of astronauts from the hazards of suddenly encountered radiation fields of extreme intensity in space.

Manned space flights have now been successfully achieved by both the United States and the Soviet Union. Such flights will be followed by manned space probes including lunar and interplanetary missions for the manned exploration of the Moon, Mars and Venus. The manned space program of the United States is directed towards manned exploration first of the moon and then initially only of the two planets Mars and Venus of the solar system since all of its other planets appear to be barren and lifeless. These and other probes will, of course, eventually lead to interstellar journeys over vast distances to other stellar systems for the purpose of conducting explorations aimed at discovering new worlds which are susceptible to colonization by the human race.

2

by using a greater number of stages are offset by the additional complexity involved, and it is very difficult to increase the propellant-weight ratio much beyond a certain value in the present concepts of vehicle systems.

The only feasible alternative remaining is to reduce the inert weight which is not useful for propulsion in the vehicle system so that a greater payload weight can be obtained without the need to increase initial launch weight of the vehicle system. This is an important consideration since any unnecessary inert weight in the various stages of the vehicle system imposes a heavy, additional demand on required engine thrust which is functionally related to launch weight. In a large, three stage booster system to be used on a lunar flight, for example, any change in weight of the final stage will be reflected in a similar change in the total launch weight multiplied, however, by a growth factor which may easily number in the hundreds.

In undertaking manned, space exploration missions, the astronauts may be exposed to radiation fields of high intensity in space. Biological damage is done by the ionization produced by radiation and high energy charged particles which pass through the tissues of the astronauts. A lethal action arises when the radiation dosage is excessive such that changes in living cells result in their death when they attempt division. Of course, extremely high radiation dose rates which may be lethal to an astronaut after a relatively short exposure period are encountered except rarely in ordinary

FIG. 29.3. A portion of the first of six sheets of specifications (petition) for the radiation protection system illustrated in Figures 29.1 and 29.2. Copies of patents may be purchased from the Patent Office (50¢ each)

(c) All drawings must be made with the pen only. Every line and letter (signatures included) must be absolutely black. This direction applies to all lines, however fine, to shading, and to lines representing cut surfaces in sectional views. All lines must be clean, sharp, and solid, and they must not be too fine or crowded. Surface shading, when used, should be open. Sectional shading should be made by oblique parallel lines, which may be about one-twentieth of an inch apart. Solid black should not be used for sectional or surface shading. Free-hand work should be avoided wherever it is possible to do so.

(d) Drawings should be made with the fewest lines possible consistent with clearness. By the observance of this rule the effectiveness of the work after reduction will be much increased. Shading

(except on sectional views) should be used only on convex and concave surfaces, where it should be used sparingly, and may even there be dispensed with if the drawing be otherwise well executed. The plane upon which a sectional view is taken should be indicated on the general view by a broken or dotted line, which should be designated by numerals corresponding to the number of the sectional view. Heavy lines on the shade sides of objects should be used, except where they tend to thicken the work and obscure letters of reference. The light is always supposed to come from the upper left-hand corner at an angle of 45°.

(e) The scale to which a drawing is made ought to be large enough to show the mechanism without crowding, and two or more sheets should be used if one does not give sufficient room to accomplish this end; but the number of sheets must never be more than is absolutely necessary.

(*f*) The different views should be consecutively numbered. Letters and figures of reference must be carefully formed. They should, if possible, measure at least one-eighth of an inch in height, so that they may bear reduction to one twenty-fourth of an inch; and they may be much larger when there is sufficient room. They must be so placed in the close and complex parts of drawings as not to interfere with a thorough comprehension of the same, and therefore should rarely cross or mingle with the lines. When necessarily grouped around a certain part they should be placed at a little distance, where there is available space, and connected by lines with the parts to which they refer. They should not be placed upon shaded surfaces, but when it is difficult to avoid this, a blank space must be left in the shading where the letter occurs, so that it shall appear perfectly distinct and separate from the work. If the same part of an invention appears in more than one view of the drawing, it must always be represented by the same character, and the same character must never be used to designate different parts.

(*g*) The signature of the applicant should be placed at the lower right-hand corner of each sheet, and the signatures of the witnesses, if any, at the lower left-hand corner, all within the marginal line, but in no instance should they trespass upon the drawings. The title should be written with pencil on the back of the sheet. The permanent names and title constituting the heading will be applied subsequently by the office in uniform style.

(*h*) All views on the same sheet must stand in the same direction and must, if possible, stand so that they can be read with the sheet held in an upright position. If views longer than the width of the sheet are necessary for the proper illustration of the invention, the sheet may be turned on its side. The space for heading must then be reserved at the right and the signatures placed at the left, occupying the same space and position as in the upright views and being horizontal when the sheet is held in an upright position. One figure must not be placed upon another or within the outline of another.

(*i*) As a rule, one view only of each invention can be shown in the Gazette illustrations. The selection of that portion of a drawing best calculated to explain the nature of the specific improvement would be facilitated and the final result improved by the judicious execution of a figure with express reference to the Gazette, but which must at the same time serve as one of the figures referred to in the specification. For this purpose the figure may be a plan, elevation, section, or perspective view, according to the judgment of the draftsman. All its parts should be especially open and distinct, with very little or no shading, and it must illustrate the invention claimed only, to the exclusion of all other details. (See specimen drawing.) When well executed it will be used without curtailment or change, but any excessive fineness or crowding or unnecessary elaborateness of detail will necessitate its exclusion from the Gazette.

(*j*) Drawings transmitted to the office should be sent flat, protected by a sheet of heavy binder's board; or should be rolled for transmission in a suitable mailing tube, but should never be folded.

(*k*) An agent's or attorney's stamp, or advertisement, or written address will not be permitted upon the face of a drawing, within or without the marginal line.

53. In reissue applications the drawings upon which the original patent was issued may be used upon the filing of suitable permanent photographic copies thereof, if no changes are to be made in the drawings.

54. The foregoing rules relating to drawings will be rigidly enforced. A drawing not executed in conformity

thereto may be admitted for purposes of examination if it sufficiently illustrates the invention, but in such case the drawing must be corrected or a new one furnished before the application will be allowed. The necessary corrections will be made by the office, upon applicant's request and at his expense.

55. Applicants are advised to employ competent draftsmen to make their drawings.

The office will furnish the drawings at cost, as promptly as its draftsmen can make them, for applicants who cannot otherwise conveniently procure them.

REPRODUCTION OF DRAWINGS

VI

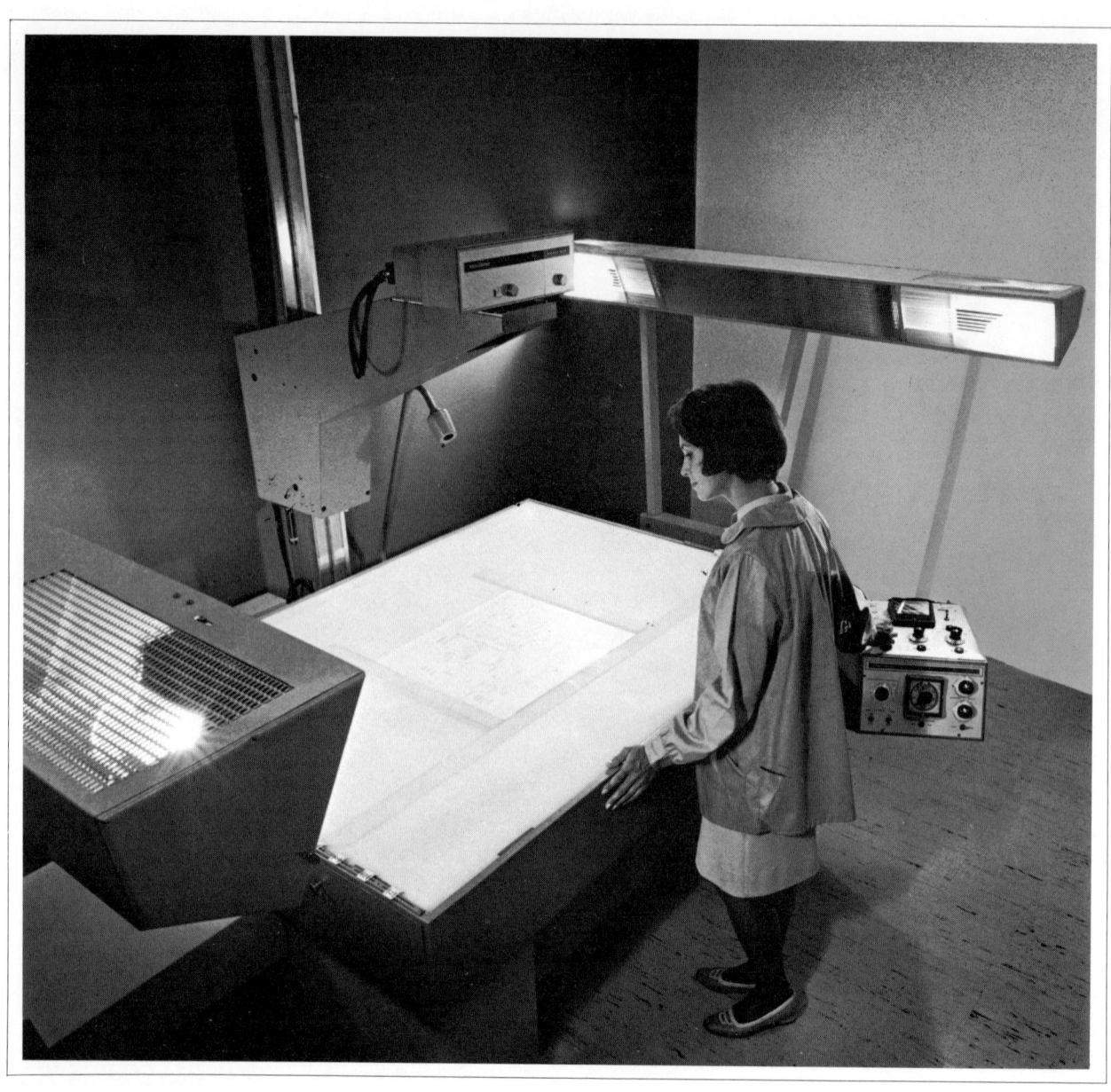

Recordak Micro-File Machine. The Micro-File Machine (Model MRG-1) shown above has been designed to simplify the microfilming of engineering drawings, white prints, blue prints, specifications, and other types of technical documents. With built-in automatic controls and other operating conveniences, it is easy to use. (*Courtesy Eastman Kodak Company*)

Reproduction and Duplication of Engineering Drawings

30

30.1
Usually it is necessary to duplicate a set of drawings of a machine or structure, one or more copies being made for the office and extra copies for interested persons connected with the home organization or an outside cooperating firm. Sometimes many sets are required. Under modern production methods, the various parts of a machine or structure may be produced in numerous departments and plants that are located miles apart. Each of these departments must have exact copies of the original drawings. To satisfy this demand, several economical processes have been devised.

The various processes may be grouped in accordance with the general similarity in methods. The mechanical processes form a group that includes mimeographing, hectographing, and printing; the photochemical processes, using reflected light, include photography and photocopying; the photochemical processes, requiring transmitted light, include blueprinting, Ozalid printing, Van Dyke printing, and so on. A few processes, such as photolithography, are combinations of methods.

30.2
Blueprints. A blueprint may be considered a photographic copy of an original drawing in that the process is similar to that of photography. A piece of sensitized paper is exposed to light transmitted through a negative (tracing) and then is developed in water to bring out the image. The negative is a transparent sheet of paper or transparentized cloth on which the image of the original drawing has been traced with opaque lines. The printing paper is a white paper that has been coated with a solution of ammonia citrate of iron and ferrocyanide of potassium. When the paper is exposed through the tracing, a chemical action takes place wherever the light is able to reach the sensitized surface. In the first bath of clear water, the coating is washed away from the parts of the surface protected by these lines, exposing the original surface of the paper against a developed blue background. The contrast between the blue background and white lines may be intensified by dipping the print in an oxidizing solution of potassium bichromate in water, after which the print must be rinsed thoroughly in clean water to avoid stain marks.

Notations and changes can be made on a blueprint by lettering and drawing with an alkaline solution strong enough to bleach out the blue compound. Although a solution of sodium hydroxide (caustic

635

soda) is best for this purpose, ordinary sodium bicarbonate (baking soda) in water, may be used.

Since a good print with clear white lines against a uniform brilliant blue background can be obtained only by proper timing of the exposure, it is well to make one or two trial (part) prints on small scraps of blueprint paper before making the final print. If the background is a pale blue, the trial print was underexposed and the time of exposure should be increased; if the trial print has a scorched appearance with indistinct lines against a very dark blue background, the print was overexposed and the time of exposure should be decreased.

30.3
Typed Material. In preparing a typewritten original for printing, a "soft record" ribbon should be used and the sheet should be "backed" with a piece of carbon paper so that the typed characters will be on two sides. Troublesome smearing can be somewhat reduced by spraying the sheet (both sides) with "fixative."

30.4
Blueprint Machine. For a large quantity of prints some form of continuous machine is desirable. On such a machine the paper unwinds continuously from a roll, as the tracings are "fed in" with the inked sides up. The exposure is made as the tracing passes upward in contact with a glass cylinder containing a bank of arc lights. Some machines are equipped with a washer and drier, thus allowing the prints to be made in one operation (Fig. 30.1), but these are so expensive that only firms making a great number of prints daily find them a worthwhile investment. Small firms have found it much cheaper to have their prints made by commercial printing concerns, of which there are at least one or two in every fairly large industrial city.

30.5
Brown Prints. A negative brown print is made on so-called Van Dyke paper, a thin printing paper with a yellowish-green sensitized surface that turns to a light bronze on exposure and a deep brown when washed in water. To intensify a developed brown print and make it permanent, it is "fixed" in a solution of sodium hyposulphite and again washed in water. If the print is to be used for making positive prints, it should be made by exposing with the tracing reversed so that the inked lines are toward the Van Dyke paper. A reversed negative will print faster and will produce sharper lines if it has been transparentized by rubbing the back with a specially prepared oil (white Vaseline in benzine).

A positive brown print, having brown

FIG. 30.1. Continuous printing machine with washer and drier (*Courtesy C. F. Pease Co.*).

lines on white background, is made on brown-print paper by using a brown-print negative as a substitute for the original tracing. Prints showing a change may be made without altering the original tracing if the part to be changed is "blocked out" on the negative print and drawn in on the positive print.

30.6
Blue-line Prints. A positive blue-line print, having blue lines on a white background, may be made on regular blueprint paper by exposing with a brown-print negative in the place of the original tracing. Such prints may also be made from an original tracing, if a paper coated with a solution of gum arabic, ammonia citrate of iron, and chloride of iron is used. When the print is developed in solution of ferrocyanide of potassium, the coated surface turns blue where it has been protected from light and remains white where it has been exposed. The print must be washed thoroughly in water when it is taken from the developer.

An advantage offered by blue-line prints is that alterations may be more easily indicated and read on a white background. Furthermore, if the prints are made on blueprint paper using a negative print, the original tracing is protected against wear.

30.7
Ozalid Prints. Ozalid prints, depending on the type of Ozalid paper used, show black, blue, or maroon lines on a white background. The prints are exposed in the same manner as for other contact processes. They are developed in controlled dry ammonia vapor and, since no liquid solution is used with this process, a finished print will be an undistorted exact-scale reproduction of the original tracing.

Ozalid printer–developer units, such as the one shown in Fig. 30.2, produce finished prints in two simple steps without

FIG. 30.2. Ozalid printing machine (*Courtesy General Analine and Film Corp.*).

any auxiliary apparatus. No washing, fixing, rinsing, or drying is required.

An Ozalid duplicate tracing, which is known as an *intermediate,* may be made on either Ozalid sepia-line papers (single- and double-coated), Ozalid sepia-line cloth, or Ozalid foil. Since each of these types of intermediate materials is translucent, an intermediate on any one type may be used in place of the original tracing to produce drawing room and shop prints. The use of intermediates makes it possible to file away the original drawing where it will not be damaged or smudged and will be safe from fire. The intermediate can be used for all reference work and may be altered when design changes become

FIG. 30.3. Bruning 255 (BW) diazo printing and developing machine (*Courtesy Charles Bruning Company, Inc.*).

purposes. As a matter of interest an intermediate will often make a much better print than an original tracing.

30.8
Black and White (Diazo) Prints (BW). Positive black-line prints may be made direct from an original tracing by using a specially prepared black-print paper. When developed, the sensitized surface turns black where it has been protected and remains white where exposed. Only two steps are required to obtain a fully developed print, exposure and development. This method of printing is similar to that used for making blueprints, except that the print is developed by a solution in a special developing unit on top of the printer (Fig. 30.3). Black and white prints are more desirable than blueprints, because of their greater legibility and the fact that they can be made in only two steps, whereas blueprints require five.

Colored-line (red, brown, or blue) prints having a white background may be made in the same machine. An appropriate paper must be used for each color.

30.9
Duplicate Tracings. A duplicate tracing may be produced on a special waterproof reproduction cloth. A negative brown print is used, and the cloth is exposed in a regular blueprint machine. The sensitized surface of this waterproof cloth turns black where exposed to light and remains transparent where protected. A few industrial firms produce "dupe" tracings, of original pencil drawings. This is done by photographing a drawing and using the negative in exposing the cloth. To obtain a satisfactory negative, careful consideration must be given to the weight of the pencil lines. Full directions for making duplicate tracings may be secured from almost any large commercial distributor of drawing supplies. In view of the fact that "dupe" tracings from original pencil

necessary. Changes may be made and obsolete detail removed with a corrector fluid and the new lines, dimensions, and notes may then be added. A second intermediate may then be made from the first one. The use of changed intermediates makes retracing unnecessary when rather extensive alterations in design become desirable. Also, the valuable original can remain untouched in the file for record

drawings eliminate all possible errors that might result from ink tracing and cost only a fraction of the price of the latter to produce, this method eventually should become widely adopted.

30.10
Photocopies. Photocopies (photostat prints) are direct photographic reproductions made from original drawings or printed matter by using an automatic machine equipped with a large camera that focuses an image directly on a sensitized paper. After being properly exposed, the print is washed and dried within the machine. Copies may be made to any scale of reduction or enlargement.

Although photocopies made from original drawings are brown prints with white lines on a dark background, positive prints having dark lines on a white background may be made by rephotographing brown-print photocopies.

This method is used extensively for preparing drawings for engineering reports and, occasionally, for changing the scales of related drawings so that they may be combined.

A photostat machine is shown in Fig. 30.4.

30.11
Translucent Masters—Photographic Method. Translucent masters, or so-called intermediates, may be made on photographic paper or cloth, using photographic processes (Eastman Company). Intermediates may be made, either to safeguard valuable originals or for the purpose of replacing worn or soiled drawings. Oftentimes, masters will produce better prints than original tracings, because line intensity is increased. This, in turn, permits faster printing speeds, which lead to a saving of time and money.

Frequently, an original may require a change, or it may contain material that should not appear on the finished print.

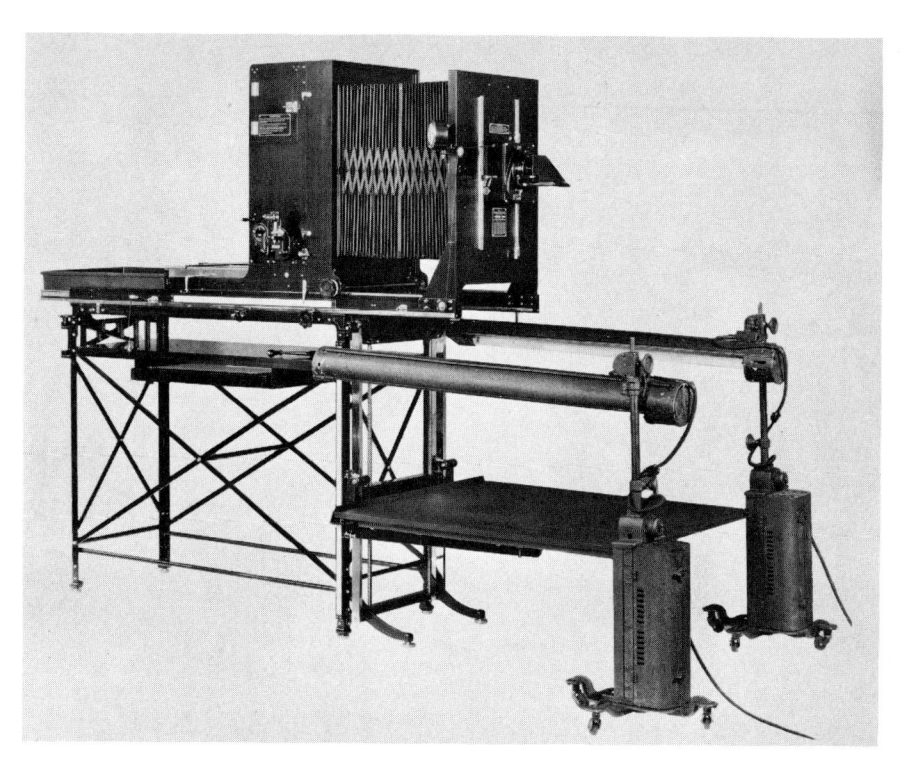

FIG. 30.4. A photostat machine (*Courtesy Photostat Corp.*).

An altered print may be produced by first making an intermediate print on which unwanted lines, figures, and notes can be removed and the new material added in ink or pencil. Prints made directly from the altered intermediate bear all of the added changes without showing the unwanted material. Drafting time has been saved for use on the other tasks, and the original tracing remains untouched for record purposes. This method of alteration may be used to delete portions of an original that might be so confidential that it should not be reproduced.

30.12
Reproduction of Worn or Mutilated Tracings. Worn or mutilated tracings that have reached a stage where it is difficult

FIG. 30.5. Transmitting drawings and sketches electronically. (*Courtesy Xerox Corporation*).

to make readable prints may be reproduced photographically rather than by hand tracing at a great saving in time and money. If desired, the scale may be changed. By taking advantage of the special types of film now available for this purpose, the intensity of the pencil lines can be increased to give a reproduction with clear and sharp lines. Stains and discolorations may be eliminated by using a proper filter on the camera or by opaquing.

30.13
Xerox Prints. Xerox prints are black and white positive prints that can be made in considerable number, if needed, at very little expense. The process employs a selenium-coated electrostatically charged plate that may be reused. After the image of the original has been projected onto the plate, a negatively charged powder, which will adhere to the positively charged areas (lines) of the image, is applied over the plate. Then, by means of a positive electrical charge, the powder is transferred to the paper and permanently fixed (baked) onto the surface as the last step in the process.

30.14
Long-distance Xerography (LDX). Long-distance xerography networks, utilizing microwave, coaxial cable, or special telephone line, provide a practical means for transmitting and receiving electronically any form of communication, typed or drawn, across a plant area or across the continent. The high-speed, high-capacity facsimile transmission and receiving equipment consists of an LDX scanner and LDX printer. These units are shown in Fig. 30.5. The document scanner on the sending end converts images to video transmission signals. At the receiving end the printer electronically restores the transmitted images and produces a black-on-white copy of the original document, sketch, or drawing. The system is easy to use. The original is simply inserted into the feed slot of the scanner.

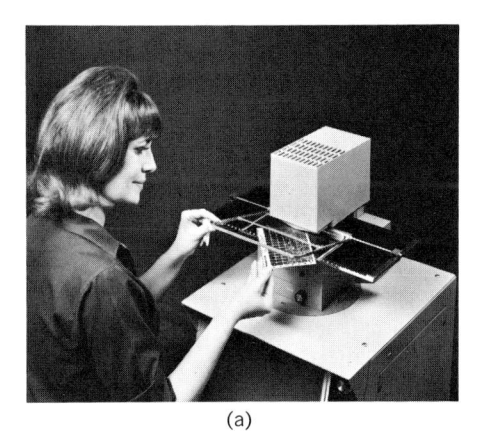

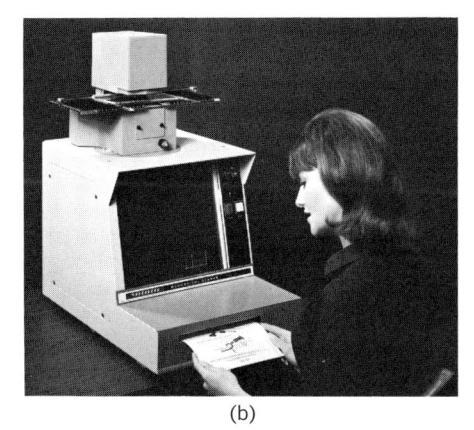

FIG. 30.6. The Recordak Magnafiche Reader shown above is a combination film reader and facsimile printer. (*Courtesy Eastman Kodak Company*).

It is returned to the operator in seconds. The scanner senses colors without exposure adjustment.

30.15
Microfilming Drawings. The practice of microfilming drawings is increasing rapidly, as many companies are giving more attention to their reproduction methods and are being forced to save filing space. Some companies have found that a microfilming program will reduce their storage space requirements by as much as 75%.

Reduction in filing space is made possible largely because obsolete drawings may be removed from the files and destroyed after they have been microfilmed.

Of equal importance is the protection offered when microfilm prints can be filed away in fireproof vaults. Since lost original tracings may be quickly replaced by first making enlarged printing intermediates, it can be said that microfilming offers a form of insurance both against careless loss through handling and from fire.

The three sizes of film in general use today are the 16mm, 35mm, and 70mm. Although the most common size is the 35mm, the 16mm is often used for small drawings. One large corporation uses 70mm for tracings as large as 37×50 in. Tracings, which may be as large as 54 in. $\times$ 20 ft, are microfilmed in sections, and related negatives are filed together so that prints can be made at a later time should the need arise.

Microfilm negatives may be cut and filed individually in envelopes marked with the same number given the tracing. Negatives are made for subsequent revisions, thus permitting the destruction of unnecessary and outdated tracings.

An engineer may obtain any needed information concerning the progressive development of a part or mechanism by viewing the negative on a microfilm reader or by using a portable projector (Fig. 30.6). When a full-size print, a reduced-scale print, or an intermediate is needed, either can be quickly made by enlargement on paper or cloth by using the negative, mounted on an aperture card, in a microfilm printer designed for printing from microfilm.

30.16
Combining a Line Drawing With a Photograph of a Part or Mechanism. The use

of photography in the preparation of assembly drawings of simple unit mechanisms has become increasingly popular because a photograph is readily understood by a relatively inexperienced person. By referring back and forth between the line drawing showing the assembly and the picture, it is possible for one to gain a full understanding of the mechanism in much less time than would be possible without the photograph.

The first step in the preparation of a photographic assembly drawing is the making of a halftone enlargement of the piece of equipment using an orthotype film. Then a positive intermediate is made from the original line drawing, and a window is cut into it at an open spot to accept the halftone positive. From this layout, consisting of a line drawing, a bill of material, a title block, and a halftone, a positive film intermediate is made that can be used to make needed prints on a direct-process machine.

At times, it has been found desirable to present a photographic representation on a line drawing showing a single part.

30.17
Use of Glass Cloth. Glass cloth, which has been a rather recent development, is a translucent drawing material that is dimensionally stable. It is similar to vellum and can be rolled for ease in handling, shipping, or storing. It has an excellent drawing surface for either pencil or ink.

Because drawings made on glass cloth will remain unvaryingly accurate, its use has opened the door to shortcut methods, which save both layout time and floor space. In the aircraft industry, it has made possible a more accurate production of templates, dies, and form blocks at a distinct saving in time and money, because its use eliminates shop layouts by hand, camera photography, and other expensive and complicated reproduction methods that have been used in the past. The use of glass cloth for the reproduction of layouts eliminates the necessity for a detailed checking that a hand-scribed layout requires.

In practice, the original full-scale drawing on glass cloth and the photosensitized template or tool stock are exposed together in a large contact printer. Development is simple, in that only a moist sponging is required with a developer. All work may be done under daylight, but not in sunlit areas.

The only drawing that need be prepared by the drafting room for use through final production is the original drawing on glass cloth.

30.18
Reproductions from Layouts on Metal Sheets. A reproduction may be made of a layout prepared on metal plate or other opaque material by the reflex contact method. The original, if prepared on metal, is drawn directly in pencil or ink on a working surface that has been prepared by spraying it with a white-matte, loft board surfacer. The special vinyl base film that is used for the intermediate is unique, in that the light that passes through it from the back during exposure strikes the prepared surface of the metal plate and is then reflected to the emulsion. For this reason one must be certain that the emulsion side of the film has been placed in contact with the front side of the plate when preparing for the exposure. After exposure, the film is removed and immersed in a developer for a few minutes and then fixed in hypo and washed.

The resulting negative may be used for making positive prints on cloth or paper or for making positive prints on metal, as desired. Prints on metal may be needed as copies for subcontractors or for use as templates if the original layouts have been prepared full-size.

30.19
Industrial Practice in Automobile-body Design. In automobile-body design, full-sized drawings of each year's models are made on the painted surface of a large sheet of aluminum. The drawings are carefully laid out with instruments directly on the painted surface; then the lines are scratched in. A detail drawing, such as one showing the details of a doorpost on a particular model, is made by tracing directly from the aluminum sheet. Aluminum is used because a body-design drawing for a model must be prepared 2 or 3 years in advance of the production date and the medium on which it is prepared must be strong enough to withstand constant wear and rough treatment. Furthermore, a drawing on an aluminum sheet is not affected by weather changes.

Appendix

CONTENTS

Graphical Symbols for Electrical Diagrams 647
Graphical Electrical Symbols for Architectural Plans 648
Graphical Symbols for Plumbing Fixtures 649

TABLE		
1	Standard Conversion Table	650
2	Unified–American Thread Series	651
3	Unified–American Special Threads	652
4	American National Standard Acme and Stub Acme Threads	652
5	Buttress Threads	652
6	American National Standard Wrench-Head Bolts and Nuts—Regular Series	653
7	American National Standard Finished Hexagon Castle Nuts	654
8	American National Standard Set Screws	655
9	American National Standard Machine Screws	656
10	American National Standard Cap Screws	657
11	American National Standard Plain Washers	658
12	American National Standard Lock Washers	658
13	American National Standard Cotter Pins	659
14	American National Standard Machine Screw and Stove Bolt Nuts	659
15	American National Standard Small Rivets	660
16	American National Standard Square and Flat Keys	661
17	American National Standard Plain Taper and Gib-Head Keys	662
18	American National Standard Woodruff Keys	663
19	Pratt and Whitney Keys	664
20	American National Standard Taper Pins	665
21	American National Standard Wrought-Iron and Steel Pipe	666
22	American National Standard Malleable-Iron Screwed Fittings	667
23	125-lb American National Standard Cast-Iron Screwed Fittings	668
24	American National Standard Pipe Plugs and Caps	669
25	American National Standard Cast-Iron Pipe Flanges and Flanged Fittings	670
26A	American National Standard Running and Sliding Fits	671
26B	American National Standard Locational Clearance Fits	673
26C	American National Standard Locational Transition Fits	675

26D	American National Standard Locational Interference Fits	676
26E	American National Standard Force and Shrink Fits	677
27A	Single-Row Radial Bearings—Type 3,000	678
27B	Radax Bearings—Type 30,000	679
28A	Shaft Mounting Fits for SAE or A.B.E.C.-1 Standard Bearings	680
28B	Housing Mounting Fits for A.B.E.C.-1 and A.B.E.C.-2 Bearings	681
29	Twist Drill Sizes	682
30	Standard Wire and Sheet-Metal Gages	683
31	Trigonometric Functions	684
32	Table of Chords	685
	Abbreviations and Symbols	686
	American National Standards	687
	Bibliography of Engineering Drawings and Allied Subjects	689

GRAPHICAL SYMBOLS FOR ELECTRICAL DIAGRAMS

AMPLIFIER General	DEVICE, VISUAL SIGNALING Annunciator	MICROPHONE
ANTENNA General	ELEMENT, THERMAL Thermal Cutout, Flasher	PATH, TRANSMISSION General
Loop	Thermal Relay	Crossing, Not Connected
ARRESTER General Multigap	or	Junction Junction, Connected Paths Pair
BATTERY Multicell		Assembled Conductors; Cable Coaxial
BREAKER, CIRCUIT General	FUSE General	2-Conductor Cable Grouping Leads
CAPACITOR General	Fusible Element	or
COIL Blowout (Broken line not part of symbol) Operating	GROUND HANDSET General	RECEIVER General Headset
	INDUCTOR WINDING General or	RECTIFIER General
CONNECTOR Female Contact Male Contact	LAMP Ballast Lamp Incandescent	REPEATER 1-Way RESISTOR General
CONTACT, ELECTRIC Fixed ° or Locking Nonlocking Rotating Closed or Open or	MACHINE, ROTATING Basic Generator Motor Wound Rotor Armature Winding Symbols 1-Phase 2-Phase 3-Phase Wye 3-Phase Delta	SWITCH General Single Throw Double Throw Knife THERMOCOUPLE Temperature-Measuring TRANSFORMER Magnetic Core Shielded
CORE Magnetic (General) Magnet or Relay		
COUPLER, DIRECTIONAL General		

*ANS Y32.2–1954.

GRAPHICAL ELECTRICAL SYMBOLS FOR ARCHITECTURAL PLANS

GENERAL OUTLETS

Ceiling	Wall	
○	-○	Outlet
Ⓑ	-Ⓑ	Blanked Outlet
Ⓓ		Drop Cord
Ⓔ	-Ⓔ	Electric Outlet; for use only when circle used alone might be confused with columns, plumbing symbols, etc
Ⓕ	-Ⓕ	Fan Outlet
Ⓙ	-Ⓙ	Junction Box
Ⓛ	-Ⓛ	Lamp Holder
Ⓛ$_{PS}$	-Ⓛ$_{PS}$	Lamp Holder with Pull Switch
Ⓢ	-Ⓢ	Pull Switch
Ⓥ	-Ⓥ	Outlet for Vapor Discharge Lamp
Ⓧ	-Ⓧ	Exit Light Outlet
Ⓒ	-Ⓒ	Clock Outlet (Specify Voltage)

CONVENIENCE OUTLETS

⇁⊖ Duplex Convenience Outlet
⇁⊖$_{1,3}$ Convenience Outlet other than Duplex 1=Single, 3=Triplex, etc
⇁⊖$_{WP}$ Weatherproof Convenience Outlet
⇁⊖$_R$ Range Outlet
⇁⊖$_S$ Switch and Convenience Outlet
⇁⊖$_{[R]}$ Radio and Convenience Outlet
▲ Special Purpose Outlet (Des. in Spec.)
⊙ Floor Outlet

SWITCH OUTLETS

S   Single Pole Switch
S$_2$ Double Pole Switch
S$_3$ Three Way Switch
S$_4$ Four Way Switch
S$_D$ Automatic Door Switch
S$_E$ Electrolier Switch
S$_K$ Key Operated Switch
S$_P$ Switch and Pilot Lamp
S$_{CB}$ Circuit Breaker
S$_{WCB}$ Weatherproof Circuit Breaker
S$_{MC}$ Momentary Contact Switch
S$_{RC}$ Remote Control Switch
S$_{WP}$ Weatherproof Switch
S$_F$ Fused Switch
S$_{WF}$ Weatherproof Fused Switch

SPECIAL OUTLETS

○$_{a,b,c,etc}$
⇁⊖$_{a,b,c,etc}$
S$_{a,b,c,etc}$

Any standard symbol as given above with the addition of a lower case subscript letter may be used to designate some special variation of standard equipment of particular interest in a specific set of architectural plans.

When used they must be listed in the Key of Symbols on each drawing and if necessary further described in the specifications.

PANELS, CIRCUITS, AND MISCELLANEOUS

■ Lighting Panel
▨ Power Panel
── Branch Circuit; Concealed in Ceiling or Wall
── Branch Circuit; Concealed in Floor
---- Branch Circuit; Exposed
↘ Home Run to Panel Board. Indicate number of circuits by number of arrows.
    Note: Any circuit without further designation indicates a two-wire circuit. For a greater number of wires indicate as follows: ─///─ (3 wires) ─////─ (4 wires), etc.
━ Feeders. Note: Use heavy lines and designate by number corresponding to listing in Feeder Schedule.
▭▭▭ Underfloor Duct and Junction Box. Triple System.
    Note: For double or single systems eliminate one or two lines. This symbol is equally adaptable to auxiliary system layouts.
Ⓖ Generator
Ⓜ Motor
Ⓘ Instrument
Ⓣ Power Transformer (Or draw to scale.)
⋈ Controller
Isolating Switch

AUXILIARY SYSTEMS

▫ Pushbutton
Buzzer
Bell
◇ Annunciator
◁ Outside Telephone
▷◁ Interconnecting Telephone
◁▷ Telephone Switchboard
Ⓣ Bell-Ringing Transformer
Ⓓ Electric Door Opener
F▷ Fire Alarm Bell
F Fire Alarm Station
⊠ City Fire Alarm Station
FA Fire Alarm Central Station
FS Automatic Fire Alarm Device
W Watchman's Station
W Watchman's Central Station
H Horn
N Nurse's Signal Plug
M Maid's Signal Plug
R Radio Outlet
SCI Signal Central Station
Interconnection Box
Battery
----- Auxiliary System Circuits
    Note: Any line without further designation indicates a 2-wire system. For a greater number of wires designate with numerals in manner similar to ----- 12-No. 18W-3/4"C., or designate by number corresponding to listing in Schedule.
□$_{a,b,c}$ Special Auxiliary Outlets.
    Subscript letters refer to notes on plans or detailed description in specifications.

APPENDIX **649**

GRAPHICAL SYMBOLS FOR PLUMBING FIXTURES

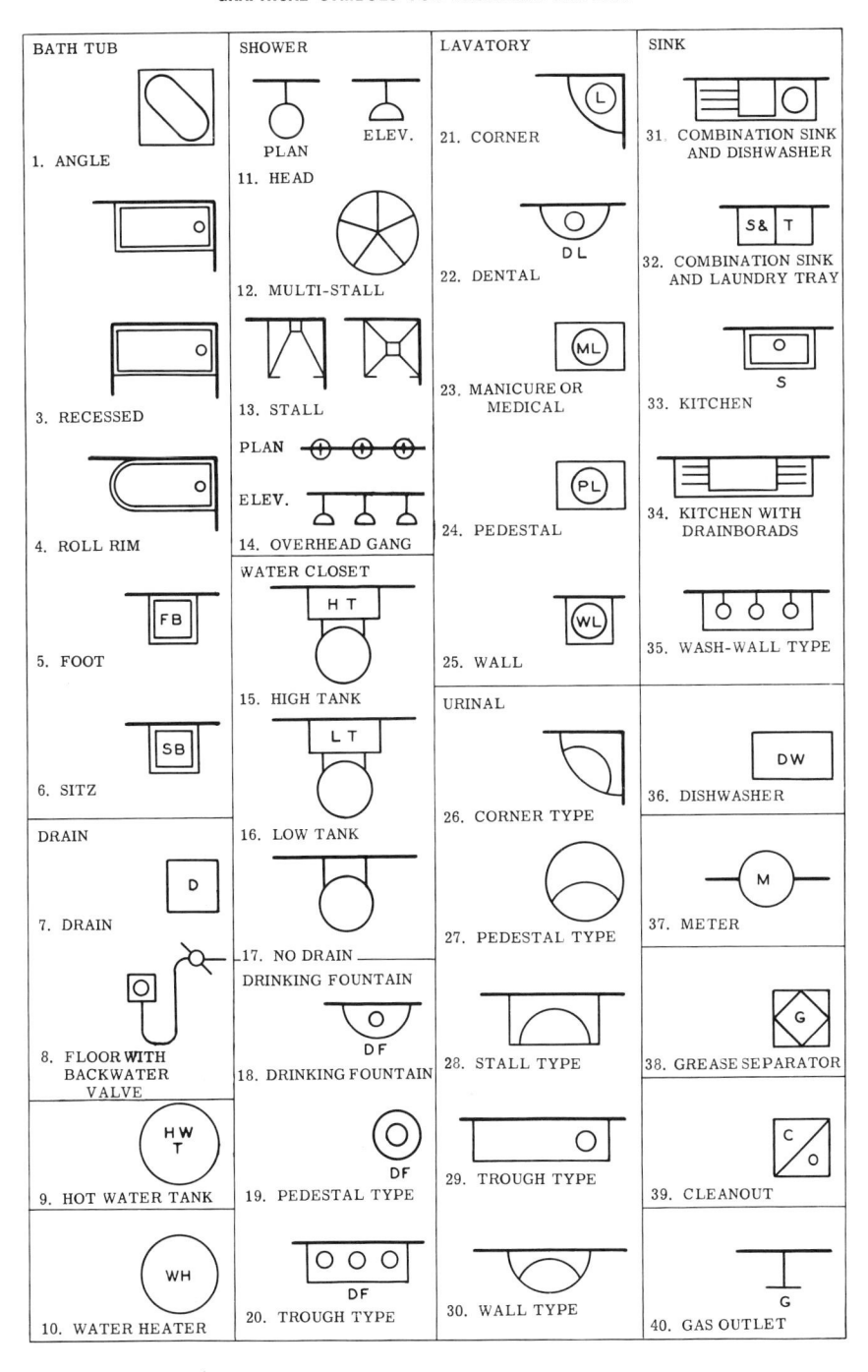

BATH TUB	SHOWER	LAVATORY	SINK
1. ANGLE	11. HEAD (PLAN, ELEV.)	21. CORNER	31. COMBINATION SINK AND DISHWASHER
3. RECESSED	12. MULTI-STALL	22. DENTAL	32. COMBINATION SINK AND LAUNDRY TRAY
4. ROLL RIM	13. STALL	23. MANICURE OR MEDICAL	33. KITCHEN
5. FOOT	14. OVERHEAD GANG (PLAN, ELEV.)	24. PEDESTAL	34. KITCHEN WITH DRAINBOARDS
6. SITZ	WATER CLOSET	25. WALL	35. WASH-WALL TYPE
DRAIN	15. HIGH TANK	URINAL	36. DISHWASHER
7. DRAIN	16. LOW TANK	26. CORNER TYPE	37. METER
8. FLOOR WITH BACKWATER VALVE	17. NO DRAIN	27. PEDESTAL TYPE	38. GREASE SEPARATOR
9. HOT WATER TANK	DRINKING FOUNTAIN	28. STALL TYPE	39. CLEANOUT
10. WATER HEATER	18. DRINKING FOUNTAIN	29. TROUGH TYPE	40. GAS OUTLET
	19. PEDESTAL TYPE	30. WALL TYPE	
	20. TROUGH TYPE		

TABLE 1
Standard Conversion Table

4ths	8ths	16ths	32nds	64ths	To 4 places	To 3 places	To 2 places
				1/64	.0156	.016	.02
			1/32		.0312	.031	.03
				3/64	.0469	.047	.05
		1/16			.0625	.062	.06
				5/64	.0781	.078	.08
			3/32		.0938	.094	.09
				7/64	.1094	.109	.11
	1/8				.1250	.125	.12
				9/64	.1406	.141	.14
			5/32		.1562	.156	.16
				11/64	.1719	.172	.17
		3/16			.1875	.188	.19
				13/64	.2031	.203	.20
			7/32		.2188	.219	.22
				15/64	.2344	.234	.23
1/4					.2500	.250	.25
				17/64	.2656	.266	.27
			9/32		.2812	.281	.28
				19/64	.2969	.297	.30
		5/16			.3125	.312	.31
				21/64	.3281	.328	.33
			11/32		.3438	.344	.34
				23/64	.3594	.359	.36
	3/8				.3750	.375	.38
				25/64	.3906	.391	.39
			13/32		.4062	.406	.41
				27/64	.4219	.422	.42
		7/16			.4375	.438	.44
				29/64	.4531	.453	.45
			15/32		.4688	.469	.47
				31/64	.4844	.484	.48
					.5000	.500	.50
				33/64	.5156	.516	.52
			17/32		.5312	.531	.53
				35/64	.5469	.547	.55
		9/16			.5625	.562	.56
				37/64	.5781	.578	.58
			19/32		.5938	.594	.59
				39/64	.6094	.609	.61
	5/8				.6250	.625	.62
				41/64	.6406	.641	.64
			21/32		.6562	.656	.66
				43/64	.6719	.672	.67
		11/16			.6875	.688	.69
				45/64	.7031	.703	.70
			23/32		.7188	.719	.72
				47/64	.7344	.734	.73
3/4					.7500	.750	.75
				49/64	.7656	.766	.77
			25/32		.7812	.781	.78
				51/64	.7969	.797	.80
		13/16			.8125	.812	.81
				53/64	.8281	.828	.83
			27/32		.8438	.844	.84
				55/64	.8594	.859	.86
	7/8				.8750	.875	.88
				57/64	.8906	.891	.89
			29/32		.9062	.906	.91
				59/64	.9219	.922	.92
		15/16			.9375	.938	.94
				61/64	.9531	.953	.95
			31/32		.9688	.969	.97
				63/64	.9844	.984	.98
					1.0000	1.000	1.00

TABLE 2
Unified–American Thread Series*

Nominal size diameter		COARSE (NC) (UNC) Threads per inch	Tap drill†	FINE (NF) (UNF) Threads per inch	Tap drill†	EXTRA-FINE (NEF) (UNEF) Threads per inch	Tap drill†
.060	0	—	—	80	3/64	—	—
.073	1	64	No. 53	72	No. 53	—	—
.086	2	56	No. 50	64	No. 50	—	—
.099	3	48	No. 47	56	No. 45	—	—
.112	4	**40**	No. 43	48	No. 42	—	—
.125	5	40	No. 38	44	No. 37	—	—
.138	6	**32**	No. 36	40	No. 33	—	—
.164	8	**32**	No. 29	36	No. 29	—	—
.190	10	**24**	No. 25	**32**	No. 21	—	—
.216	12	24	No. 16	28	No. 14	32	No. 13
.250	¼	**20**	No. 7	**28**	No. 3	32	No. 2
.3125	5/16	**18**	F	**24**	I	32	K
.375	3/8	**16**	5/16	**24**	Q	32	S
.4375	7/16	**14**	U	**20**	25/64	**28**	Y
.500	½	**13**	27/64	**20**	29/64	**28**	15/32
.5625	9/16	**12**	31/64	**18**	33/64	24	17/32
.625	5/8	**11**	17/32	**18**	37/64	24	19/32
.6875	11/16	—	—	—	—	24	41/64
.750	¾	**10**	21/32	**16**	11/16	**20**	45/64
.8125	13/16	—	—	—	—	**20**	49/64
.875	7/8	**9**	49/64	**14**	13/16	**20**	53/64
.9375	15/16	—	—	—	—	**20**	57/64
1.000	1	**8**	7/8	**12**	59/64	**20**	61/64
1.0625	1 1/16	—	—	—	—	18	1
1.125	1 1/8	**7**	63/64	**12**	1 3/64	18	1 5/64
1.1875	1 3/16	—	—	—	—	18	1 9/64
1.250	1 ¼	**7**	1 7/64	**12**	1 11/64	18	1 13/64
1.3125	1 5/16	—	—	—	—	18	1 17/64
1.375	1 3/8	**6**	1 13/64	**12**	1 19/64	18	1 5/16
1.4375	1 7/16	—	—	—	—	18	1 3/8
1.500	1 ½	**6**	1 21/64	**12**	1 27/64	18	1 29/64
1.5625	1 9/16	—	—	—	—	18	1 ½
1.625	1 5/8	—	—	—	—	18	1 9/16
1.6875	1 11/16	—	—	—	—	18	1 5/8
1.750	1 ¾	**5**	1 35/64	—	—	16	1 11/16
2.000	2	**4½**	1 25/32	—	—	16	1 15/16
2.250	2 ¼	**4½**	2 1/32	—	—	—	—
2.500	2 ½	**4**	2 ¼	—	—	—	—
2.750	2 ¾	**4**	2 ½	—	—	—	—
3.000	3	**4**	2 ¾	—	—	—	—
3.250	3 ¼	**4**	3	—	—	—	—
3.500	3 ½	**4**	3 ¼	—	—	—	—
3.750	3 ¾	**4**	3 ½	—	—	—	—
4.000	4	**4**	3 ¾	—	—	—	—

*ANS B1.1–1960.
Bold type indicates Unified threads. To be designated UNC or UNF.
Unified Standard—Classes 1A, 2A, 3A, 1B, 2B, and 3B.
For recommended hole-size limits before threading see Tables 38 and 39, ANS B1.1–1960.
† Tap drill for a 75% thread (not Unified–American Standard).
Bold type sizes smaller than ¼ in. are accepted for limited applications by the British, but the symbols NC or NF, as applicable, are retained.

TABLE 3
Unified–American Special Threads* (8-Pitch, 12-Pitch, and 16-Pitch Series)

Nominal size diameter		Threads per inch			Nominal size diameter		Threads per inch		
.500	½	—	**12**	—	1.750	1¾	**8**	**12**	**16**
.5625	9/16	—	**12**	—	1.8125	1 13/16	—	—	**16**
.625	5/8	—	**12**	—	1.875	1⅞	**8**	**12**	**16**
.6875	11/16	—	**12**	—	1.9375	1 15/16	—	—	**16**
.750	¾	—	**12**	**16**	2.000	2	**8**	**12**	**16**
.8125	13/16	—	**12**	**16**	2.0625	2 1/16	—	—	**16**
.875	⅞	—	**12**	**16**	2.125	2⅛	**8**	**12**	**16**
.9375	15/16	—	**12**	**16**	2.1875	2 3/16	—	—	**16**
1.000	1	**8**	**12**	**16**	2.250	2¼	**8**	**12**	**16**
1.0625	1 1/16	—	**12**	**16**	2.3125	2 5/16	—	—	**16**
1.125	1⅛	**8**	**12**	**16**	2.375	2⅜	—	**12**	**16**
1.1875	1 3/16	—	**12**	**16**	2.4375	2 7/16	—	—	**16**
1.250	1¼	**8**	**12**	**16**	2.500	2½	**8**	**12**	**16**
1.3125	1 5/16	—	**12**	**16**	2.625	2⅝	—	**12**	**16**
1.375	1⅜	**8**	**12**	**16**	2.750	2¾	**8**	**12**	**16**
1.4375	1 7/16	—	**12**	**16**	2.875	2⅞	—	**12**	**16**
1.500	1½	**8**	**12**	**16**	3.000	3	**8**	**12**	**16**
1.5625	1 9/16	—	—	**16**	3.125	3⅛	—	**12**	**16**
1.625	1⅝	**8**	12	**16**	3.250	3¼	**8**	**12**	**16**
1.6875	1 11/16	—	—	**16**	3.375	3⅜	—	12	16

*ANS B1.I–1960. Bold type indicates Unified threads (UN).

TABLE 4
American National Standard Acme and Stub Acme Threads*

Nominal size diameter		Threads per inch	Nominal size diameter		Threads per inch
.250	¼	16	1.250	1¼	5
.3125	5/16	14	1.375	1⅜	4
.375	⅜	12	1.500	1½	4
.4375	7/16	12	1.750	1¾	4
.500	½	10	2.000	2	4
.625	5/8	8	2.250	2¼	3
.750	¾	6	2.500	2½	3
.875	⅞	6	2.750	2¾	3
1.000	1	5	3.000	3	2
1.125	1⅛	5			

* ANS B1.5 and B1.8–1952.

TABLE 5
Buttress Threads* (Suggested combinations of diameters and pitches)

Nominal size diameter				Associated pitches (tpi)						
.500	.5625	.625	.6875	20	16	12				
.750	.875	1.000	—	—	16	12	10			
1.125	1.250	1.375	1.500	—	16	12	10	8	6	
1.750	3.000	2.250	2.500	—	16	12	10	8	6	5	4
2.750	3.000	3.500	4.000	—	16	12	10	8	6	5	4

* ANS B1.9–1953.

APPENDIX 653

TABLE 6
American National Standard Wrench-Head Bolts and Nuts—Regular Series*

		BOLT HEADS				NUTS				
		Width across flats	Height of head			Width across flats	Thickness			
							Regular		Jam	
BOLT DIAMETER Nominal size		Unfinished and semifinished square and hexagon†	Unfinished square	Unfinished hexagon	Semifinished hexagon	Unfinished hexagon, semifinished hexagon and hexagon jam	Unfinished square and hexagon	Semifinished hexagon and hexagon slotted	Unfinished hexagon	Semifinished hexagon
.250	1/4	3/8 sq. / 7/16 hex.	11/64	11/64	5/32	7/16	7/32	7/32	5/32	5/32
.3125	5/16	1/2	13/64	7/32	13/64	1/2	17/64	17/64	3/16	3/16
.375	3/8	9/16	1/4	1/4	15/64	9/16	21/64	21/64	7/32	7/32
.4375	7/16	5/8	19/64	19/64	9/32	11/16	3/8	3/8	1/4	1/4
.500	1/2	3/4	21/64	11/32	5/16	3/4	7/16	7/16	5/16	5/16
.5625	9/16	13/16	—	—	23/64	7/8	31/64	31/64	5/16	5/16
.625	5/8	15/16	27/64	27/64	25/64	15/16	35/64	35/64	3/8	3/8
.750	3/4	1 1/8	1/2	1/2	15/32	1 1/8	21/32	41/64	7/16	27/64
.875	7/8	1 5/16	19/32	37/64	35/64	1 5/16	49/64	3/4	1/2	31/64
1.000	1	1 1/2	21/32	43/64	39/64	1 1/2	7/8	55/64	9/16	35/64
1.125	1 1/8	1 11/16	3/4	3/4	11/16	1 11/16	1	31/32	5/8	39/64
1.250	1 1/4	1 7/8	27/32	27/32	25/32	1 7/8	1 3/32	1 1/16	3/4	23/32
1.375	1 3/8	2 1/16	29/32	29/32	27/32	2 1/16	1 13/64	1 11/64	13/16	25/32
1.500	1 1/2	2 1/4	1	1	15/16	2 1/4	1 5/16	1 9/32	7/8	27/32
1.625	1 5/8	2 7/16	1 3/32	—	—	2 7/16	—	1 25/64	—	29/32
1.750	1 3/4	2 5/8	—	1 5/32	1 3/32	2 5/8	—	1 1/2	—	31/32
1.875	1 7/8	2 13/16	—	—	—	2 13/16	—	1 39/64	—	1 1/32
2.000	2	3	—	1 11/32	1 7/32	3	—	1 23/32	—	1 3/32
2.250	2 1/4	3 3/8	—	1 1/2	1 3/8	3 3/8	—	1 59/64	—	1 13/64
2.500	2 1/2	3 3/4	—	1 21/32	1 17/32	3 3/4	—	2 9/64	—	1 23/64
2.750	2 3/4	4 1/8	—	1 13/16	1 11/16	4 1/8	—	2 23/64	—	1 37/64
3.000	3	4 1/2	—	2	1 7/8	4 1/2	—	2 37/64	—	1 45/64

* ANS B18.2.1-1965; ANS B18.2.2-1965.
Thread-bolts: coarse thread series, class 2A.
Thread-nuts: unfinished; coarse series, class 2B: semifinished; coarse, fine, or 8-pitch series.
† Square bolts in 1/4-1 1/2 in. sizes (nominal) only.

TABLE 7
American National Standard Finished Hexagon Castle Nuts*

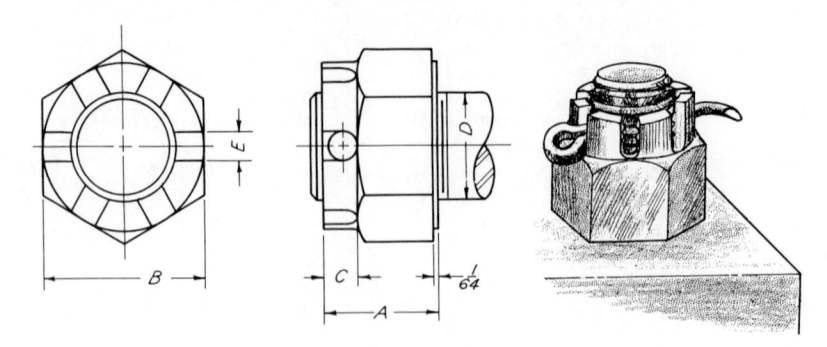

Nominal size diameter D		Threads per inch UNC	UNF	Thickness A	Width across flats B	Slot Depth C	Width E	Diameter of cylindrical part (min)
.250	¼	20	28	9/32	7/16	.094	.078	.371
.3125	5/16	18	24	21/64	½	.094	.094	.425
.375	⅜	16	24	13/32	9/16	.125	.125	.478
.4375	7/16	14	20	29/64	11/16	.156	.125	.582
.500	½	13	20	9/16	¾	.156	.156	.637
.5625	9/16	12	18	39/64	⅞	.188	.156	.744
.625	⅝	11	18	23/32	15/16	.219	.188	.797
.750	¾	10	16	13/16	1⅛	.250	.188	.941
.875	⅞	9	14	29/32	1 5/16	.250	.188	1.097
1.000	1	8	12	1	1½	.281	.250	1.254
1.125	1⅛	7	12	1 5/32	1 11/16	.344	.250	1.411

* ANS B18.2.2–1965.
   Thread may be coarse- or fine-thread series, class 2B tolerance; unless otherwise specified fine-thread series will be furnished.

TABLE 8
American National Standard Set Screws*

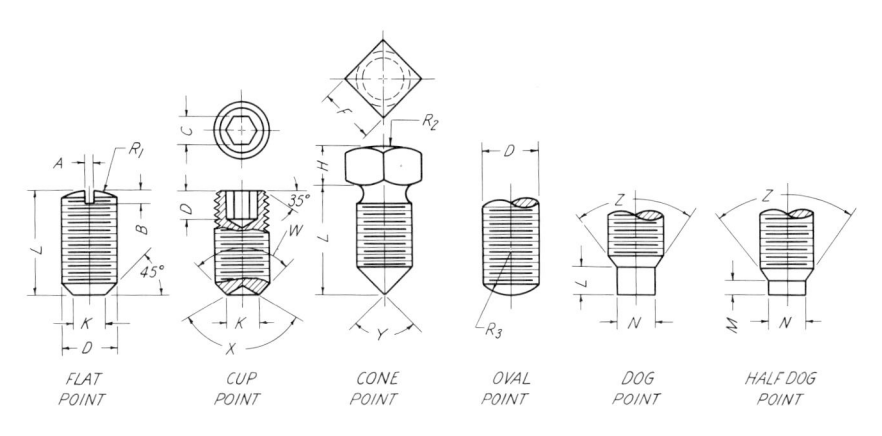

FLAT POINT | CUP POINT | CONE POINT | OVAL POINT | DOG POINT | HALF DOG POINT

Nominal size diameter D		Slotted headless			Hexagonal socket (min)		Square-head (F-max)			Cup and flat (K-max)	Cone	Oval	Full- and half-dog (N-max)			
		A	B	R_1	C	D†	F	H	R_2	K W X	Y	R_3	L	M	N	Z
.125	5	.023	.031	.125	1/16	.050	—	—	—	.067		.094	.060	.030	.083	
.138	6	.025	.035	.138	1/16	.050	—	—	—	.074		.109	.070	.035	.092	
.164	8	.029	.041	.164	5/64	.062	—	—	—	.087	$Y=118°\pm 2°$	.125	.080	.040	.109	
.190	10	.032	.048	.190	3/32	.075	.1875	9/64	15/32	.102	$Y=90°\pm 2°$	.141	.090	.045	.127	
.216	12	.036	.054	.216	3/32	.075	.216	5/32	35/64	.115		.156	.110	.055	.144	
.250	1/4	.045	.063	.250	1/8	.100	.250	3/16	5/8	.132		.188	.125	.063	.156	
.3125	5/16	.051	.078	.313	5/32	.125	.3125	15/64	25/32	.172		.234	.156	.078	.203	
.375	3/8	.064	.094	.375	3/16	.150	.375	9/32	15/16	.212		.281	.188	.094	.250	$Z=100°$-$110°$
.4375	7/16	.072	.109	.438	7/32	.175	.4375	21/64	1 3/32	.252		.328	.219	.109	.297	
.500	1/2	.081	.125	.500	1/4	.200	.500	3/8	1 1/4	.291	$W=80°$-$90°$ (Draw as 90°)	.375	.250	.125	.344	
.5625	9/16	.091	.141	.563	1/4	.200	.5625	27/64	1 13/32	.332	$X=118°\pm 5°$	.422	.281	.140	.391	
.625	5/8	.102	.156	.625	5/16	.250	.625	15/32	1 9/16	.371	When L equals nominal diameter or less, $Y=118°\pm 2°$.	.469	.313	.156	.469	
.750	3/4	.129	.188	.750	3/8	.300	.750	9/16	1 7/8	.450	When L exceeds nominal diameter, $Y=90°\pm 2°$.	.563	.375	.188	.563	
.875	7/8	—	—	—	1/2	.400	.875	21/32	2 3/16	—		—	—	—	—	
1.000	1	—	—	—	9/16	.450	1.000	3/4	2 1/2	—		—	—	—	—	
1.125	1 1/8	—	—	—	9/16	.450	1.125	27/32	2 13/16	—		—	—	—	—	
1.250	1 1/4	—	—	—	5/8	.500	1.250	15/16	3 1/8	—		—	—	—	—	
1.375	1 3/8	—	—	—	5/8	.500	1.375	1 1/32	3 7/16	—		—	—	—	—	
1.500	1 1/2	—	—	—	3/4	.600	1.500	1 1/8	3 3/4	—		—	—	—	—	

* ANS B18.6.2-1956; ANS B18.3-1961.
† Dimensions apply to cup and flat-point screws 1 diam in length or longer. For screws shorter than 1 diam in length, and for other types of points, socket to be as deep as practicable.

TABLE 9
American National Standard Machine Screws*

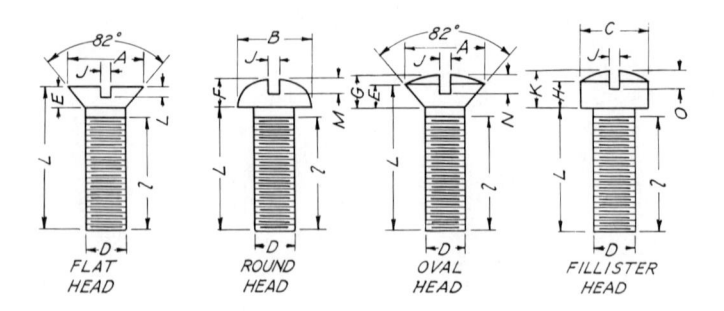

Size (Number) and Threads per Inch			Standard Dimensions (Max)												
Nominal size diameter D	Thread Coarse	Thread Fine	Head diameter A	B	C	Height dimensions E	F	G	H	K	Slot width J	Slot depth L	M	N	O
.060	0	—	80	.119	.113	.096	.035	.053	.056	.045	.059	.023	.015	.039	.030	.025
.073	1	64	72	.146	.138	.118	.043	.061	.068	.053	.071	.026	.019	.044	.038	.031
.086	2	56	64	.172	.162	.140	.051	.069	.080	.062	.083	.031	.023	.048	.045	.037
.099	3	48	56	.199	.187	.161	.059	.078	.092	.070	.095	.035	.027	.053	.052	.043
.112	4	40	48	.225	.211	.183	.067	.086	.104	.079	.107	.039	.030	.058	.059	.048
.125	5	40	44	.252	.236	.205	.075	.095	.116	.088	.120	.043	.034	.063	.067	.054
.138	6	32	40	.279	.260	.226	.083	.103	.128	.096	.132	.048	.038	.068	.074	.060
.164	8	32	36	.332	.309	.270	.100	.120	.152	.113	.156	.054	.045	.077	.088	.071
.190	10	24	32	.385	.359	.313	.116	.137	.176	.130	.180	.060	.053	.087	.103	.083
.216	12	24	28	.438	.408	.357	.132	.153	.200	.148	.205	.067	.060	.096	.117	.094
.250	¼	20	28	.507	.472	.414	.153	.175	.232	.170	.237	.075	.070	.109	.136	.109
.3125	⁵⁄₁₆	18	24	.635	.590	.518	.191	.216	.290	.211	.295	.084	.088	.132	.171	.137
.375	⅜	16	24	.762	.708	.622	.230	.256	.347	.253	.355	.094	.106	.155	.206	.164
.4375	⁷⁄₁₆	14	20	.812	.750	.625	.223	.328	.345	.265	.368	.094	.103	.196	.210	.170
.500	½	13	20	.875	.813	.750	.223	.355	.354	.297	.412	.106	.103	.211	.216	.190
.5625	⁹⁄₁₆	12	18	1.000	.938	.812	.260	.410	.410	.336	.466	.118	.120	.242	.250	.214
.625	⅝	11	18	1.125	1.000	.875	.298	.438	.467	.375	.521	.133	.137	.258	.285	.240
.750	¾	10	16	1.375	1.250	1.000	.372	.547	.578	.441	.612	.149	.171	.320	.353	.281

* ANS B18.6.3–1962.

Thread length—screws 2 in. in length or less are threaded as close to the head as practicable. Screws longer than 2 in. should have a minimum thread length of 1¾ in.

TABLE 10
American National Standard Cap Screws*

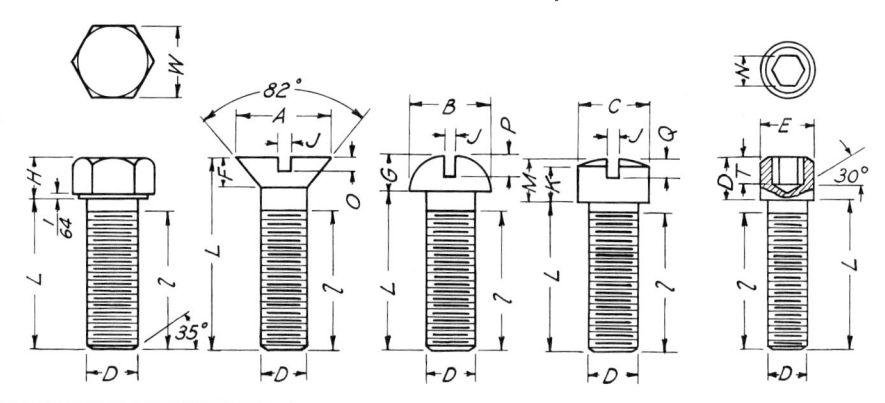

Nominal size diameter		Head diameter A	B	C	E	W	Height dimensions F av	G	H nom	K	M	Slot width J	Slot depth O	P	Q	Socket dimensions N min	T min
.250	¼	.500	.437	.375	⅜	7⁄16	.140	.191	5⁄32	.172	.216	.075	.068	.117	.097	3⁄16	.120
.3125	5⁄16	.625	.562	.437	7⁄16	½	.177	.245	13⁄64	.203	.253	.084	.086	.151	.115	7⁄32	.151
.375	⅜	.750	.625	.562	9⁄16	9⁄16	.210	.273	15⁄64	.250	.314	.094	.103	.168	.142	5⁄16	.182
.4375	7⁄16	.8125	.750	.625	⅝	⅝	.210	.328	9⁄32	.297	.368	.094	.103	.202	.168	5⁄16	.213
.500	½	.875	.812	.750	¾	¾	.210	.354	5⁄16	.328	.413	.106	.103	.218	.193	⅜	.245
.5625	9⁄16	1.000	.937	.812	13⁄16	13⁄16	.244	.409	23⁄64	.375	.467	.118	.120	.252	.213	⅜	.276
.625	⅝	1.125	1.000	.875	⅞	15⁄16	.281	.437	25⁄64	.422	.521	.133	.137	.270	.239	½	.307
.750	¾	1.375	1.250	1.000	1	1⅛	.352	.546	15⁄32	.500	.612	.149	.171	.338	.283	9⁄16	.370
.875	⅞	1.625	—	1.125	1⅛	1 5⁄16	.423	—	35⁄64	.594	.720	.167	.206	—	.334	9⁄16	.432
1.000	1	1.875	—	1.312	1 5⁄16	1½	.494	—	39⁄64	.656	.803	.188	.240	—	.371	⅝	.495
1.125	1⅛	2.062	—	—	1½	1 11⁄16	.529	—	11⁄16	—	—	.196	.257	—	—	¾	.557
1.250	1¼	2.312	—	—	1¾	1⅞	.600	—	25⁄32	—	—	.211	.291	—	—	¾	.620
1.375	1⅜	2.562	—	—	1⅞	2 1⁄16	.665	—	27⁄32	—	—	.226	.326	—	—	¾	.682
1.500	1½	2.812	—	—	2	2¼	.742	—	15⁄16	—	—	.258	.360	—	—	1	.745

*ANS B18.3-1961. ANS B18.6.2-1956.

Bold type indicates products unified dimensionally with British and Canadian standards.

Basically, threads may be coarse, fine, or 8-thread series; class 2A for plain (unplated) cap screws.

Minimum thread length will be $2D + ¼$ in. for lengths up to and including 6 in.

Socket-head cap screws—thread coarse or fine, class 3A. Thread length: coarse, $2D + ½$ in.; fine, $1½D + ½$ in.

TABLE 11
American National Standard Plain Washers (Type A)*

Washer Size Nominal		LIGHT-SAE (N = NARROW)			STANDARD-PLATE (W = WIDE)		
		A ID	B OD	H Thickness	A ID	B OD	H Thickness
.250	¼	.281	.625	.065	.312	.734	.065
.312	5/16	.344	.688	.065	.375	.875	.083
.375	⅜	.406	.812	.065	.438	1.000	.083
.438	7/16	.469	.922	.065	.500	1.250	.083
.500	½	.531	1.062	.095	.562	1.375	.109
.562	9/16	.594	1.156	.095	.625	1.469	.109
.625	⅝	.656	1.312	.095	.688	1.750	.134
.750	¾	.812	1.469	.134	.812	2.000	.148
.875	⅞	.938	1.750	.134	.938	2.250	.165
1.000	1	1.062	2.000	.134	1.062	2.500	.165
1.125	1⅛	1.250	2.250	.134	1.250	2.750	.165
1.250	1¼	1.375	2.500	.165	1.375	3.000	.165
1.375	1⅜	1.500	2.750	.165	1.500	3.250	.180
1.500	1½	1.625	3.000	.165	1.625	3.500	.180

*ANS B27.2–1965.

Plain washers are specified as follows: ID × OD × thickness — .375 × .875 × .083 PLAIN WASHER.

TABLE 12
American National Standard Lock Washers (Selected Sizes)

Washer Size Nominal		REGULAR (LIGHT)			EXTRA-DUTY (HEAVY)		
		C ID (Min)	D OD (Max)	T Thickness (Min)	C ID (Min)	D OD (Max)	T Thickness (Min)
.250	¼	.255	.489	.062	Same	.535	.084
.312	5/16	.318	.586	.078	as for	.622	.108
.375	⅜	.382	.683	.094	regular	.741	.123
.438	7/16	.446	.779	.109	lock	.839	.143
.500	½	.509	.873	.125	washers	.939	.162
.562	9/16	.572	.971	.141		1.041	.182
.625	⅝	.636	1.079	.156		1.157	.202
.750	¾	.763	1.271	.188		1.361	.241
.875	⅞	.890	1.464	.219		1.576	.285
1.000	1	1.017	1.661	.250		1.799	.330
1.125	1⅛	1.144	1.853	.281		2.019	.375
1.250	1¼	1.271	2.045	.312		2.231	.417
1.375	1⅜	1.398	2.239	.344		2.439	.458
1.500	1½	1.525	2.430	.375		2.638	.496

*ANS B27.1–1965.

Lock washers are specified by giving nominal size and series (⅜ regular lock washer).

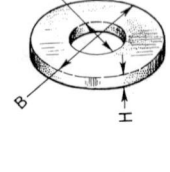

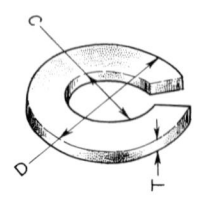

APPENDIX **659**

TABLE 13
American National Standard Cotter Pins

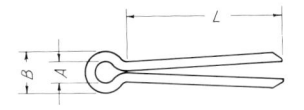

PIN DIAMETER			EYE DIAMETER		*Drill Size Recommended Hole/Diameter*	*Clevis Pin or Shaft Diameter*
Nominal	Max	Min	A—Inside	B—Outside		
.031	1/32	.032	.028	1/32	1/16	3/64—.0469	1/8
.047	3/64	.048	.044	3/64	3/32	1/16—.0625	3/16
.062	1/16	.060	.056	1/16	1/8	5/64—.0781	1/4
.078	5/64	.076	.072	5/64	5/32	3/32—.0938	5/16
.094	3/32	.090	.086	3/32	3/16	7/64—.1094	3/8
.125	1/8	.120	.116	1/8	1/4	9/64—.1406	1/2
.156	5/32	.150	.146	5/32	5/16	11/64—.1719	5/8
.188	3/16	.176	.172	3/16	3/8	13/64—.2031	—
.219	7/32	.207	.202	7/32	7/16	15/64—.2344	—
.250	1/4	.225	.220	1/4	1/2	17/64—.2656	—

* ANS B5.20–1958.

For shafts up to 5/8 in. diam select a cotter pin that is approximately equal to one-fourth of the shaft diameter. For larger shaft sizes use a cotter pin that is from one-fourth to one-sixth of the shaft diameter.

TABLE 14
American National Standard Machine Screw and Stove Bolt Nuts

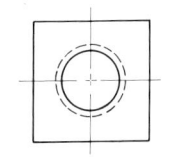

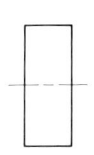

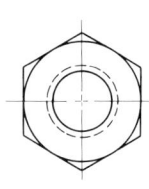

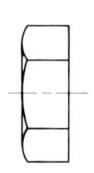

	NOMINAL SIZE												
DIAMETER	0	1	2	3	4	5	6	8	10	12	1/4	5/16	3/8
Across flats (nominal)	5/32	5/32	3/16	3/16	1/4	5/16	5/16	11/32	3/8	7/16	7/16	9/16	5/8
Across corners (min) Hexagonal	.171	.171	.205	.205	.275	.344	.344	.378	.413	.482	.482	.621	.692
Across corners (min) Square	.206	.206	.247	.247	.331	.415	.415	.456	.497	.581	.581	.748	.833
Thickness (nom)	3/64	3/64	1/16	1/16	3/32	7/64	7/64	1/8	1/8	5/32	3/16	7/32	1/4

* ANS B18.6.3–1962.
Dimensions in inches.
Square nuts—Threads are UNC, Class 2B.
Hexagonal nuts—Threads are UNC or UNF, Class 2B.

TABLE 15
American National Standard Small Rivets*

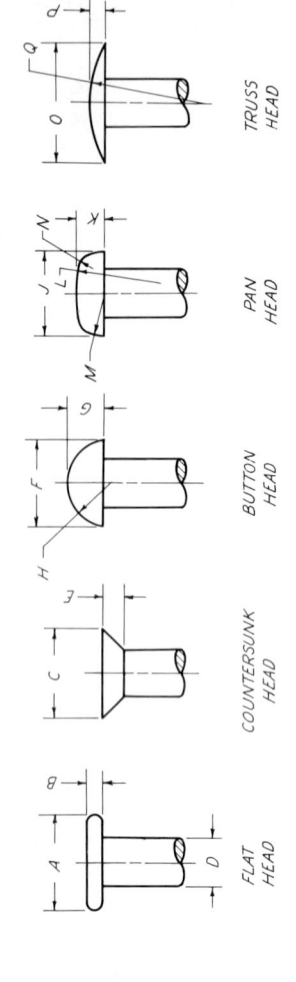

		FLAT		CSK.		BUTTON			PAN					TRUSS		
Rivet diam D		Diam A max	Height B max	Diam C max	Height E	Diam F max	Height G max	Rad H	Diam J max	Height K max	Rad L	Rad M	Rad N	Diam O max	Height P max	Rad Q
.062	1/16	.140	.027	.118	.027	.122	.052	.055	.118	.040	.217	.052	.019	—	—	—
.094	3/32	.200	.038	.176	.040	.182	.077	.084	.173	.060	.326	.080	.030	.226	.038	.239
.125	1/8	.260	.048	.235	.053	.235	.100	.111	.225	.078	.429	.106	.039	.297	.048	.314
.156	5/32	.323	.059	.293	.066	.290	.124	.138	.279	.096	.535	.133	.049	.368	.059	.392
.188	3/16	.387	.069	.351	.079	.348	.147	.166	.334	.114	.641	.159	.059	.442	.069	.470
.219	7/32	.453	.080	.413	.094	.405	.172	.195	.391	.133	.754	.186	.069	.515	.080	.555
.250	1/4	.515	.091	.469	.106	.460	.196	.221	.444	.151	.858	.213	.079	.590	.091	.628
.281	9/32	.579	.103	.528	.119	.518	.220	.249	.499	.170	.963	.239	.088	.661	.103	.706
.313	5/16	.641	.113	.588	.133	.572	.243	.276	.552	.187	1.070	.266	.098	.732	.113	.784
.344	11/32	.705	.124	.646	.146	.630	.267	.304	.608	.206	1.176	.292	.108	.806	.124	.862
.375	3/8	.769	.135	.704	.159	.684	.291	.332	.663	.225	1.286	.319	.118	.878	.135	.942
.406	13/32	.834	.146	.763	.172	.743	.316	.358	.719	.243	1.392	.345	.127	.949	.145	1.028
.438	7/16	.896	.157	.823	.186	.798	.339	.387	.772	.261	1.500	.372	.137	1.020	.157	1.098

* ANS B18.1-1965.
The length of a rivet is measured from the underside (bearing surface) of the head to the end of the shank except in the case of a rivet with a countersunk head. The length of a countersunk-head rivet is measured from the top of the head to the end of the shank.

TABLE 16
American National Standard Square and Flat Keys*

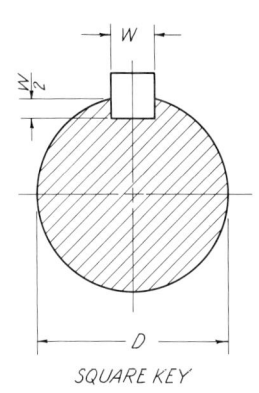

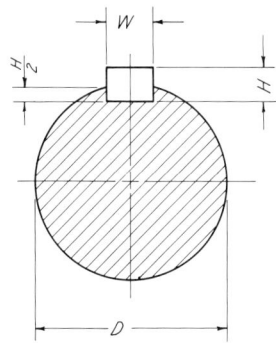

SQUARE KEY

FLAT KEY

SHAFT DIAM NOMINAL		Square Stock W	Rectangular Stock W × H	SHAFT DIAM NOMINAL		Square Stock W	Rectangular Stock W × H
Over	To (Inclusive)			Over	To (Inclusive)		
5/16	7/16	3/32	—	1 3/4	2 1/4	1/2	1/2 × 3/8
7/16	9/16	1/8	1/8 × 3/32	2 1/4	2 3/4	5/8	5/8 × 7/16
9/16	7/8	3/16	3/16 × 1/8	2 3/4	3 1/4	3/4	3/4 × 1/2
7/8	1 1/4	1/4	1/4 × 3/16	3 1/4	3 3/4	7/8	7/8 × 5/8
1 1/4	1 3/8	5/16	5/16 × 1/4	3 3/4	4 1/2	1	1 × 3/4
1 3/8	1 3/4	3/8	3/8 × 1/4	4 1/2	5 1/2	1 1/4	1 1/4 × 7/8

* ANS B17.1–1967.
All dimensions given in inches.

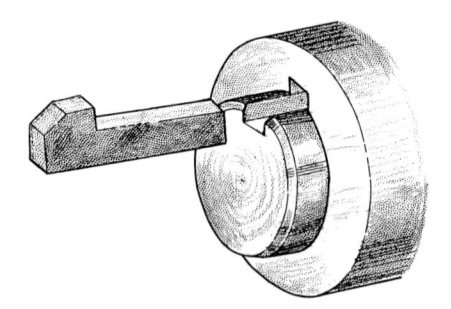

TABLE 17
American National Standard Plain Taper and Gib-Head Keys*

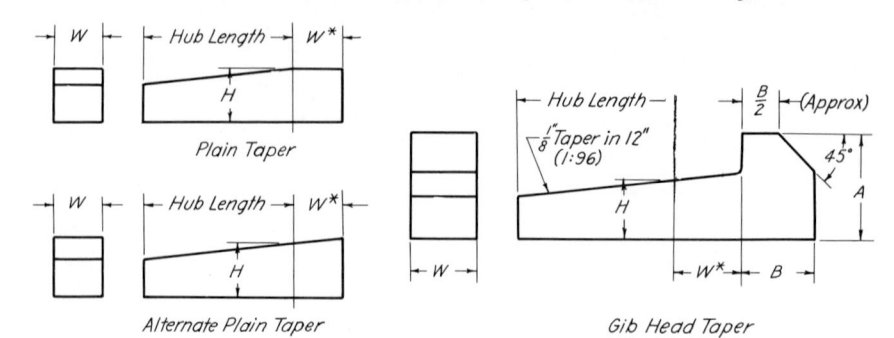

Plain and Gib Head Taper Keys Have a 1/8" Taper in 12"

SHAFT DIAM NOMINAL		PLAIN TAPER AND GIB-HEAD KEYS SQUARE AND RECTANGULAR		GIB-HEAD			
				SQUARE		RECTANGULAR	
Over	To (Inclusive)	Square Type $W = H$	Rectangular Type $W \times H$	Head Height A	Length B	Head Height A	Length B
5/16	7/16	—	—	—	—	—	—
7/16	9/16	1/8	1/8 × 3/32	1/4	1/4	3/16	1/8
9/16	7/8	3/16	3/16 × 1/8	5/16	5/16	1/4	1/4
7/8	1 1/4	1/4	1/4 × 3/16	7/16	3/8	5/16	5/16
1 1/4	1 3/8	5/16	5/16 × 1/4	1/2	7/16	7/16	3/8
1 3/8	1 3/4	3/8	3/8 × 1/4	5/8	1/2	7/16	3/8
1 3/4	2 1/4	1/2	1/2 × 3/8	7/8	5/8	5/8	1/2
2 1/4	2 3/4	5/8	5/8 × 7/16	1	3/4	3/4	9/16
2 3/4	3 1/4	3/4	3/4 × 1/2	1 1/4	7/8	7/8	5/8
3 1/4	3 3/4	7/8	7/8 × 5/8	1 3/8	1	1	3/4

* ANS B17.1–1967.
For locating position of dimension H.
For longer sizes see standard.
All dimensions given in inches.

TABLE 18
American National Standard Woodruff Keys*

Key No.	Nominal Size $A \times B$	Height of Key C_{max}	D_{max}	Distance Below Center E	Depth of Keyseat In Shaft $+.005$ $-.000$
202	1/16 × 1/4	.109	.109	1/64	.0728
202.5	1/16 × 5/16	.140	.140	1/64	.1038
203	1/16 × 3/8	.172	.172	1/64	.1358
204	1/16 × 1/2	.203	.194	3/64	.1668
302.5	3/32 × 5/16	.140	.140	1/64	.0882
303	3/32 × 3/8	.172	.172	1/64	.1202
304	3/32 × 1/2	.203	.194	3/64	.1511
305	3/32 × 5/8	.250	.240	1/16	.1981
403	1/8 × 3/8	.172	.172	1/64	.1045
404	1/8 × 1/2	.203	.194	3/64	.1355
405	1/8 × 5/8	.250	.240	1/16	.1825
406	1/8 × 3/4	.313	.303	1/16	.2455
505	5/32 × 5/8	.250	.240	1/16	.1669
506	5/32 × 3/4	.313	.303	1/16	.2299
507	5/32 × 7/8	.375	.365	1/16	.2919
605	3/16 × 5/8	.250	.240	1/16	.1513
606	3/16 × 3/4	.313	.303	1/16	.2143
607	3/16 × 7/8	.375	.365	1/16	.2763
608	3/16 × 1	.438	.428	1/16	.3393
609	3/16 × 1 1/8	.484	.475	5/64	.3853
610	3/16 × 1 1/4	.547	.537	5/64	.4483
707	7/32 × 7/8	.375	.365	1/16	.2607
708	7/32 × 1	.438	.428	1/16	.3237
709	7/32 × 1 1/8	.484	.475	5/64	.3697
710	7/32 × 1 1/4	.547	.537	5/64	.4327
806	1/4 × 3/4	.313	.303	1/16	.1830
807	1/4 × 7/8	.375	.365	1/16	.2450
808	1/4 × 1	.438	.428	1/16	.3080
809	1/4 × 1 1/8	.484	.475	5/64	.3540
810	1/4 × 1 1/4	.547	.537	5/64	.4170
811	1/4 × 1 3/8	.594	.584	3/32	.4640
812	1/4 × 1 1/2	.641	.631	7/64	.5110
1008	5/16 × 1	.438	.428	1/16	.2768
1009	5/16 × 1 1/8	.484	.475	5/64	.3228
1010	5/16 × 1 1/4	.547	.537	5/64	.3858
1011	5/16 × 1 3/8	.594	.584	3/32	.4328
1012	5/16 × 1 1/2	.641	.631	7/64	.4798
1208	3/8 × 1	.438	.428	1/16	.2455
1210	3/8 × 1 1/4	.547	.537	5/64	.3545
1211	3/8 × 1 3/8	.594	.584	3/32	.4015
1212	3/8 × 1 1/2	.641	.631	7/64	.4485

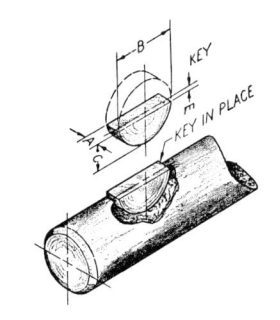

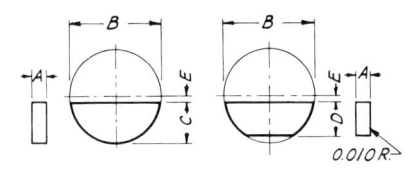

* ANS B17f-1967.

All dimensions in inches. Key numbers indicate the nominal key dimensions. The last two digits give the nominal diameter in eighths of an inch and the digits preceding the last two give the nominal width in thirty-seconds of an inch.

Examples: No. 204 indicates a key 2/32 × 4/8 or 1/16 × 1/2.
No. 808 indicates a key 8/32 × 8/8 or 1/4 × 1.

663

TABLE 19
Pratt and Whitney Keys

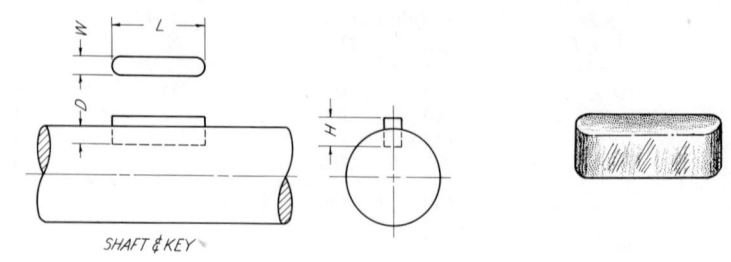

Key No.	L*	W	H	D	Key No.	L*	W	H	D
1	1/2	1/16	3/32	1/16	22	1 3/8	1/4	3/8	1/4
2	1/2	3/32	9/64	3/32	23	1 3/8	5/16	15/32	5/16
3	1/2	1/8	3/16	1/8	F	1 3/8	3/8	9/16	3/8
4	5/8	3/32	9/64	3/32	24	1 1/2	1/4	3/8	1/4
5	5/8	1/8	3/16	1/8	25	1 1/2	5/16	15/32	5/16
6	5/8	5/32	15/64	5/32	G	1 1/2	3/8	9/16	3/8
7	3/4	1/8	3/16	1/8	51	1 3/4	1/4	3/8	1/4
8	3/4	5/32	15/64	5/32	52	1 3/4	5/16	15/32	5/16
9	3/4	3/16	9/32	3/16	53	1 3/4	3/8	9/16	3/8
10	7/8	5/32	15/64	5/32	26	2	3/16	9/32	3/16
11	7/8	3/16	9/32	3/16	27	2	1/4	3/8	1/4
12	7/8	7/32	21/64	7/32	28	2	5/16	15/32	5/16
A	7/8	1/4	3/8	1/4	29	2	3/8	9/16	3/8
13	1	3/16	9/32	3/16	54	2 1/4	1/4	3/8	1/4
14	1	7/32	21/64	7/32	55	2 1/4	5/16	15/32	5/16
15	1	1/4	3/8	1/4	56	2 1/4	3/8	9/16	3/8
B	1	5/16	15/32	5/16	57	2 1/4	7/16	21/32	7/16
16	1 1/8	3/16	9/32	3/16	58	2 1/2	5/16	15/32	5/16
17	1 1/8	7/32	21/64	7/32	59	2 1/2	3/8	9/16	3/8
18	1 1/8	1/4	3/8	1/4	60	2 1/2	7/16	21/32	7/16
C	1 1/8	5/16	15/32	5/16	61	2 1/2	1/2	3/4	1/2
19	1 1/4	3/16	9/32	3/16	30	3	3/8	9/16	3/8
20	1 1/4	7/32	21/64	7/32	31	3	7/16	21/32	7/16
21	1 1/4	1/4	3/8	1/4	32	3	1/2	3/4	1/2
D	1 1/4	5/16	15/32	5/16	33	3	9/16	27/32	9/16
E	1 1/4	3/8	9/16	3/8	34	3	5/8	15/16	5/8

* The length L may vary but should always be at least $2W$.

TABLE 20
American National Standard Taper Pins*

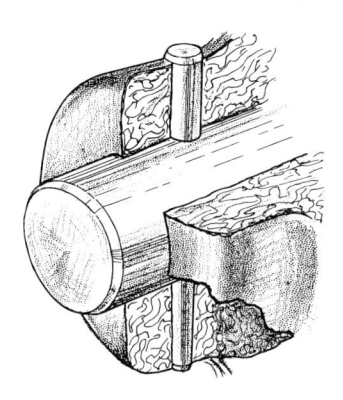

Number of Pin†	Diam at Large End		Maximum Length L	Approx. Shaft Diam‡	Drill Size‡
00000	.094	3/32	1	.250	No. 47 (.0785)
0000	.109	7/64	1	.312	No. 42 (.0935)
000	.125	1/8	1	.375	No. 37 (.1040)
00	.141	9/64	1¼	.438	No. 31 (.1200)
0	.156	5/32	1½	.500	No. 28 (.1405)
1	.172	11/64	2	.562	No. 25 (.1495)
2	.193	—	2½	.625	No. 19 (.1660)
3	.219	7/32	3	.750	No. 12 (.1890)
4	.250	1/4	3	.812	No. 3 (.2130)
5	.289	—	3	.875	1/4 (.2500)
6	.341	—	4	1.000	9/32 (.2812)
7	.409	—	4	1.250	11/32 (.3438)
8	.492	—	4	1.500	13/32 (.4062)

* ANS B5.20–1958.
† For Nos. 7/0, 6/0, 9, and 10 see the standard. Pins Nos. 11–14 are special sizes.
‡ Suggested sizes; not American National Standard.

Drill size is for reamer. The small diameter of a pin is equal to the large diameter minus $0.02083 \times L$, where L is the length.

TABLE 21
American National Standard Wrought-Iron and Steel Pipe*

	STANDARD WEIGHT						HEAVY			
							Nominal wall thickness			
						Nominal wall thickness	*Extra heavy*		*Double extra heavy*	
Nominal size	Outside diameter (all weights)	Threads per inch	Tap drill sizes†	Distance pipe enters fitting	Wrought iron	Steel	Wrought iron	Steel	Wrought iron	Steel
⅛	.405	27	11/32	5/16	.069	.068	.099	.095	—	—
¼	.540	18	7/16	7/16	.090	.088	.122	.119	—	—
⅜	.675	18	19/32	7/16	.093	.091	.129	.126	—	—
½	.840	14	23/32	9/16	.111	.109	.151	.147	.307	.294
¾	1.050	14	15/16	9/16	.115	.113	.157	.154	.318	.308
1	1.315	11½	1 5/32	11/16	.136	.133	.183	.179	.369	.358
1¼	1.660	11½	1½	11/16	.143	.140	.195	.191	.393	.382
1½	1.900	11½	1 23/32	11/16	.148	.145	.204	.200	.411	.400
2	2.375	11½	2 3/16	¾	.158	.154	.223	.218	.447	.436
2½	2.875	8	2⅝	1 1/16	.208	.203	.282	.276	.567	.552
3	3.500	8	3¼	1⅛	.221	.216	.306	.300	.615	.600
3½	4.000	8	3¾	1 3/16	.231	.226	.325	.318	—	—
4	4.500	8	4¼	1 3/16	.242	.237	.344	.337	.690	.674
5	5.563	8	5 5/16	1 5/16	.263	.258	.383	.375	.768	.750
6	6.625	8	6⅜	1⅜	.286	.280	.441	.432	.884	.864
8	8.625	8	—	—	.329	.322	.510	.500	.895	.875

* ANS B36.10–1959; ANS B2.1–1960.
  All dimensions in inches.
† Not American Standard. See ANS B36.10–1950 for sizes larger than 8 in.

APPENDIX **667**

TABLE 22
American National Standard Malleable-Iron Screwed Fittings*

Nominal pipe size	Center to end, elbows, tees and crosses A	Length of thread B_{min}	Center to end 45° elbows C	Width of band E_{min}	Inside diameter of fitting F_{min}	Inside diameter of fitting F_{max}	Metal thickness G	Outside diameter of band H	Center to male end elbows, tees J	Center to male end and 45° elbows K	Length of external thread L_{min}	Length of reducing couplings M	Port diameter male end N_{max}	Center to end inlet T	Center to end outlet U	End to end V	Length of straight couplings W	Thickness of ribs of couplings
⅛	.69	.25	—	.200	.405	.435	.090	.693	1.00	—	.2638	—	.20	—	—	—	.96	.090
¼	.81	.32	.73	.215	.540	.584	.095	.844	1.19	.94	.4018	1.00	.26	—	—	—	1.06	.095
⅜	.95	.36	.80	.230	.675	.719	.100	1.015	1.44	1.03	.4078	1.13	.37	.50	1.43	1.93	1.16	.100
½	1.12	.43	.88	.249	.840	.897	.105	1.197	1.63	1.15	.5337	1.25	.51	.61	1.71	2.32	1.34	.105
¾	1.31	.50	.98	.273	1.050	1.107	.120	1.458	1.89	1.29	.5457	1.44	.69	.72	2.05	2.77	1.52	.120
1	1.50	.58	1.12	.302	1.315	1.385	.134	1.771	2.14	1.47	.6828	1.69	.91	.85	2.43	3.28	1.67	.134
1¼	1.75	.67	1.29	.341	1.660	1.730	.145	2.153	2.45	1.71	.7068	2.06	1.19	1.02	2.92	3.94	1.93	.145
1½	1.94	.70	1.43	.368	1.900	1.970	.155	2.427	2.69	1.88	.7235	2.31	1.39	1.10	3.28	4.38	2.15	.155
2	2.25	.75	1.68	.422	2.375	2.445	.173	2.963	3.26	2.22	.7565	2.81	1.79	1.24	3.93	5.17	2.53	.173
2½	2.70	.92	1.95	.478	2.875	2.975	.210	3.589	3.86	2.57	1.1375	3.25	2.20	1.52	4.73	6.25	2.88	.210
3	3.08	.98	2.17	.548	3.500	3.600	.231	4.285	4.51	3.00	1.2000	3.69	2.78	1.71	5.55	7.26	3.18	.231
3½	3.42	1.03	2.39	.604	4.000	4.100	.248	4.843	—	—	—	—	—	—	—	—	—	—
4	3.79	1.08	2.61	.661	4.500	4.600	.265	5.401	5.69	3.70	1.3000	4.38	3.70	2.01	6.97	8.98	3.69	.265
5	4.50	1.18	3.05	.780	5.563	5.663	.300	6.583	6.86	—	1.4063	—	4.69	—	—	—	—	—
6	5.13	1.28	3.46	.900	6.625	6.725	.336	7.767	8.03	—	1.5125	—	5.67	—	—	—	—	—

* ANS B16.3–1963.
For use under maximum working steam pressures of 150 lb per sq in.

TABLE 23
125-lb American National Standard Cast-Iron Screwed Fittings*

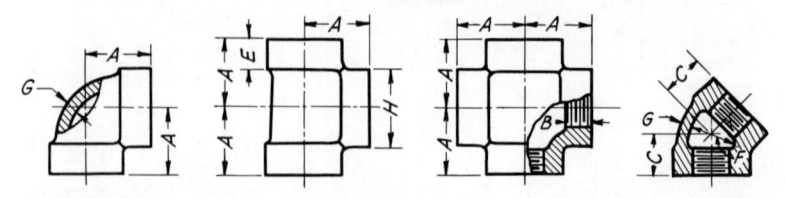

Nominal pipe size	Center to end, elbows, tees, and crosses A	Length of thread B_{min}	Center to end, 45° elbows C	Width of band E_{min}	Inside diameter of fitting F_{min}	F_{max}	Metal thickness G_{min}	Outside diameter of band H_{min}
¼	.81	.32	.73	.38	.540	.584	.110	.93
⅜	.95	.36	.80	.44	.675	.719	.120	1.12
½	1.12	.43	.88	.50	.840	.897	.130	1.34
¾	1.31	.50	.98	.56	1.050	1.107	.155	1.63
1	1.50	.58	1.12	.62	1.315	1.385	.170	1.95
1¼	1.75	.67	1.29	.69	1.660	1.730	.185	2.39
1½	1.94	.70	1.43	.75	1.900	1.970	.200	2.68
2	2.25	.75	1.68	.84	2.375	2.445	.220	3.28
2½	2.70	.92	1.95	.94	2.875	2.975	.240	3.86
3	3.08	.98	2.17	1.00	3.500	3.600	.260	4.62
3½	3.42	1.03	2.39	1.06	4.000	4.100	.280	5.20
4	3.79	1.08	2.61	1.12	4.500	4.600	.310	5.79
5	4.50	1.18	3.05	1.18	5.563	5.663	.380	7.05
6	5.13	1.28	3.46	1.28	6.625	6.725	.430	8.28
8	6.56	1.47	4.28	1.47	8.625	8.725	.550	10.63
10	8.08	1.68	5.16	1.68	10.750	10.850	.690	13.12
12	9.50	1.88	5.97	1.88	12.750	12.850	.800	15.47

* ANS B16.4–1963.
All dimensions in inches.

TABLE 24
American National Standard Pipe Plugs and Caps*

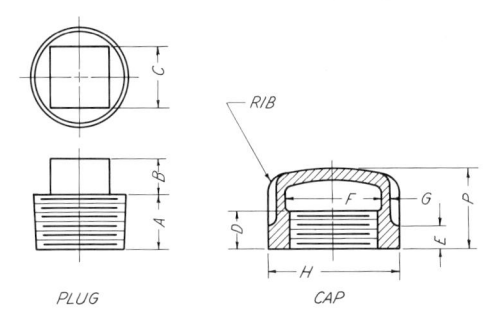

Nominal pipe size	PLUG Length of thread A_{min}	PLUG Height of square B_{min}	PLUG Width across flats C_{nom}	CAP Length of thread D_{min}	CAP Width of band E_{min}	CAP Inside diameter of fitting F_{max}	CAP Metal thickness G	CAP Outside diameter of band H_{min}	CAP Height P_{min}	CAP Thickness of ribs
⅛	.37	.24	9/32	.25	.200	.435	.090	.693	.53	—
¼	.44	.28	⅜	.32	.215	.584	.095	.844	.63	—
⅜	.48	.31	7/16	.36	.230	.719	.100	1.015	.74	—
½	.56	.38	9/16	.43	.249	.897	.105	1.197	.87	.105
¾	.63	.44	⅝	.50	.273	1.107	.120	1.458	.97	.120
1	.75	.50	13/16	.58	.302	1.385	.134	1.771	1.16	.134
1¼	.80	.56	15/16	.67	.341	1.730	.145	2.153	1.28	.145
1½	.83	.62	1⅛	.70	.368	1.970	.155	2.427	1.33	.155
2	.88	.68	1 5/16	.75	.422	2.445	.173	2.963	1.45	.173
2½	1.07	.74	1½	.92	.478	2.975	.210	3.589	1.70	.210
3	1.13	.80	1 11/16	.98	.548	3.600	.231	4.285	1.80	.231
3½	1.18	.86	1⅞	1.03	.604	4.100	.248	4.843	1.90	.248
4	—	—	—	1.08	.661	4.600	.265	5.401	2.08	.265
5	—	—	—	1.18	.780	5.663	.300	6.583	2.32	.300
6	—	—	—	1.28	.900	6.725	.336	7.767	2.55	.336

* ANS B16.3–1963.
† The outside radius of top of cap is equal to $3 \times F$.

TABLE 25
American National Standard Cast-Iron Pipe Flanges and Flanged Fittings*

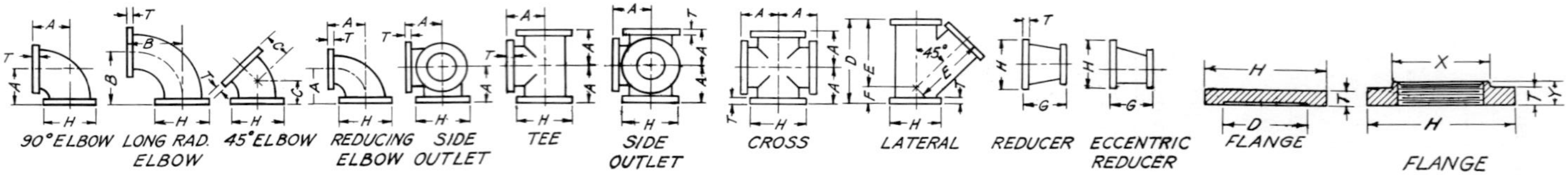

Nominal pipe size D	Center to face, elbow tees, etc. A	Center to face, long radius elbow B	Center to face, 45° elbow C	Face to face, lateral D	Center to face, lateral E	Center to face, "Y" and lateral F	Face to face reducer G	Diameter of flange H	Thickness of flange T	Diameter of hub X	Length of hub Y	Diameter of holes in flanges	Number of bolts for flanges	Diameter of bolts for flanges	Length of bolts for flanges	Diameter of bolt circle
1	3½	5	1¾	7½	5¾	1¾	—	4¼	7/16	1 15/16	11/16	⅝	4	½	1¾	3⅛
1¼	3¾	5½	2	8	6¼	1¾	—	4⅝	½	2 5/16	13/16	⅝	4	½	2	3½
1½	4	6	2¼	9	7	2	—	5	9/16	2 9/16	⅞	⅝	4	½	2	3⅞
2	4½	6½	2½	10½	8	2½	5	6	⅝	3 1/16	1	¾	4	⅝	2¼	4¾
2½	5	7	3	12	9½	2½	5½	7	11/16	3 9/16	1⅛	¾	4	⅝	2½	5½
3	5½	7¾	3	13	10	3	6	7½	¾	4¼	1 3/16	¾	4	⅝	2½	6
3½	6	8½	3½	14½	11½	3	6½	8½	13/16	4 13/16	1¼	¾	8	⅝	2¾	7
4	6½	9	4	15	12	3	7	9	15/16	5 5/16	1 5/16	¾	8	⅝	3	7½
5	7½	10¼	4½	17	13½	3½	8	10	15/16	6 7/16	1 7/16	⅞	8	¾	3	8½
6	8	11½	5	18	14½	3½	9	11	1	7 9/16	1 9/16	⅞	8	¾	3¼	9½
8	9	14	5½	22	17½	4½	11	13½	1⅛	9 11/16	1¾	⅞	8	¾	3½	11¾
10	11	16½	6½	25½	20½	5	12	16	1 3/16	11 15/16	1 15/16	1	12	⅞	3¾	14¼
12	12	19	7½	30	24½	5½	14	19	1¼	14 1/16	2 3/16	1	12	⅞	3¾	17

* ANS B16.1–1967.
For use under maximum working pressures of 125 lb per sq in.

TABLE 26A-1*
American National Standard Running and Sliding Fits

Limits are in thousandths of an inch. Limits for hole and shaft are applied algebraically to the basic size to obtain the limits of size for the parts. Symbols H5, g5, etc., are hole and shaft designations used in ABC system.

Nominal Size Range (Inches)† Over To	CLASS RC 1 Limits of Clearance	CLASS RC 1 Standard Limits Hole H5	CLASS RC 1 Standard Limits Shaft g4	CLASS RC 2 Limits of Clearance	CLASS RC 2 Standard Limits Hole H6	CLASS RC 2 Standard Limits Shaft g5	CLASS RC 3 Limits of Clearance	CLASS RC 3 Standard Limits Hole H7	CLASS RC 3 Standard Limits Shaft f6	CLASS RC 4 Limits of Clearance	CLASS RC 4 Standard Limits Hole H8	CLASS RC 4 Standard Limits Shaft f7
0–0.12	.1 / .45	+.2 / 0	−.1 / −.25	.1 / .55	+.25 / 0	−.1 / −.3	.3 / .95	+.4 / 0	−.3 / −.55	.3 / 1.3	+.6 / 0	−.3 / −.7
0.12–0.24	.15 / .5	+.2 / 0	−.15 / −.3	.15 / .65	+.3 / 0	−.15 / −.35	.4 / 1.12	+.5 / 0	−.4 / −.7	.4 / 1.6	+.7 / 0	−.4 / −.9
0.24–0.40	.2 / .6	+.25 / 0	−.2 / −.35	.2 / .85	+.4 / 0	−.2 / −.45	.5 / 1.5	+.6 / 0	−.5 / −.9	.5 / 2.0	+.9 / 0	−.5 / −1.1
0.40–0.71	.25 / .75	+.3 / 0	−.25 / −.45	.25 / .95	+.4 / 0	−.25 / −.55	.6 / 1.7	+.7 / 0	−.6 / −1.0	.6 / 2.3	+1.0 / 0	−.6 / −1.3
0.71–1.19	.3 / .95	+.4 / 0	−.3 / −.55	.3 / 1.2	+.5 / 0	−.3 / −.7	.8 / 2.1	+.8 / 0	−.8 / −1.3	.8 / 2.8	+1.2 / 0	−.8 / −1.6
1.19–1.97	.4 / 1.1	+.4 / 0	−.4 / −.7	.4 / 1.4	+.6 / 0	−.4 / −.8	1.0 / 2.6	+1.0 / 0	−1.0 / −1.6	1.0 / 3.6	+1.6 / 0	−1.0 / −2.0
1.97–3.15	.4 / 1.2	+.5 / 0	−.4 / −.7	.4 / 1.6	+.7 / 0	−.4 / −.9	1.2 / 3.1	+1.2 / 0	−1.2 / −1.9	1.2 / 4.2	+1.8 / 0	−1.2 / −2.4
3.15–4.73	.5 / 1.5	+.6 / 0	−.5 / −.9	.5 / 2.0	+.9 / 0	−.5 / −1.1	1.4 / 3.7	+1.4 / 0	−1.4 / −2.3	1.4 / 5.0	+2.2 / 0	−1.4 / −2.8
4.73–7.09	.6 / 1.8	+.7 / 0	−.6 / −1.1	.6 / 2.3	+1.0 / 0	−.6 / −1.3	1.6 / 4.2	+1.6 / 0	−1.6 / −2.6	1.6 / 5.7	+2.5 / 0	−1.6 / −3.2

* Tables 26A-1 through 26E are extracted from ANS B4.1-1967.
† For diameters greater than those listed in Tables 26A-1 through 26E see Standard.

TABLE 26A-2
American National Standard Running and Sliding Fits

Limits are in thousandths of an inch. Limits for hole and shaft are applied algebraically to the basic size to obtain the limits of size for the parts. Symbols H8, e7, etc., are hole and shaft designations used in ABC system.

Nominal Size Range Inches Over To	CLASS RC 5 Limits of Clearance	CLASS RC 5 Standard Limits Hole H8	CLASS RC 5 Standard Limits Shaft e7	CLASS RC 6 Limits of Clearance	CLASS RC 6 Standard Limits Hole H9	CLASS RC 6 Standard Limits Shaft e8	CLASS RC 7 Limits of Clearance	CLASS RC 7 Standard Limits Hole H9	CLASS RC 7 Standard Limits Shaft d8	CLASS RC 8 Limits of Clearance	CLASS RC 8 Standard Limits Hole H10	CLASS RC 8 Standard Limits Shaft c9	CLASS RC 9 Limits of Clearance	CLASS RC 9 Standard Limits Hole H11	CLASS RC 9 Standard Limits Shaft
0–0.12	.6 / 1.6	+.6 / −0	−.6 / −1.0	.6 / 2.2	+1.0 / −0	−.6 / −1.2	1.0 / 2.6	+1.0 / −0	−1.0 / −1.6	2.5 / 5.1	+1.6 / 0	−2.5 / −3.5	4.0 / 8.1	+2.5 / 0	−4.0 / −5.6
0.12–0.24	.8 / 2.0	+.7 / −0	−.8 / −1.3	.8 / 2.7	+1.2 / −0	−.8 / −1.5	1.2 / 3.1	+1.2 / −0	−1.2 / −1.9	2.8 / 5.8	+1.8 / 0	−2.8 / −4.0	4.5 / 9.0	+3.0 / 0	−4.5 / −6.0
0.24–0.40	1.0 / 2.5	+.9 / −0	−1.0 / −1.6	1.0 / 3.3	+1.4 / −0	−1.0 / −1.9	1.6 / 3.9	+1.4 / −0	−1.6 / −2.5	3.0 / 6.6	+2.2 / 0	−3.0 / −4.4	5.0 / 10.7	+3.5 / 0	−5.0 / −7.2
0.40–0.71	1.2 / 2.9	+1.0 / −0	−1.2 / −1.9	1.2 / 3.8	+1.6 / −0	−1.2 / −2.2	2.0 / 4.6	+1.6 / −0	−2.0 / −3.0	3.5 / 7.9	+2.8 / 0	−3.5 / −5.1	6.0 / 12.8	+4.0 / 0	−6.0 / −8.8
0.71–1.19	1.6 / 3.6	+1.2 / −0	−1.6 / −2.4	1.6 / 4.8	+2.0 / −0	−1.6 / −2.8	2.5 / 5.7	+2.0 / −0	−2.5 / −3.7	4.5 / 10.0	+3.5 / 0	−4.5 / −6.5	7.0 / 15.5	+5.0 / 0	−7.0 / −10.5
1.19–1.97	2.0 / 4.6	+1.6 / −0	−2.0 / −3.0	2.0 / 6.1	+2.5 / −0	−2.0 / −3.6	3.0 / 7.1	+2.5 / −0	−3.0 / −4.6	5.0 / 11.5	+4.0 / 0	−5.0 / −7.5	8.0 / 18.0	+6.0 / 0	−8.0 / −12.0
1.97–3.15	2.5 / 5.5	+1.8 / −0	−2.5 / −3.7	2.5 / 7.3	+3.0 / −0	−2.5 / −4.3	4.0 / 8.8	+3.0 / −0	−4.0 / −5.8	6.0 / 13.5	+4.5 / 0	−6.0 / −9.0	9.0 / 20.5	+7.0 / 0	−9.0 / −13.5
3.15–4.73	3.0 / 6.6	+2.2 / −0	−3.0 / −4.4	3.0 / 8.7	+3.5 / −0	−3.0 / −5.2	5.0 / 10.7	+3.5 / −0	−5.0 / −7.2	7.0 / 15.5	+5.0 / 0	−7.0 / −10.5	10.0 / 24.0	+9.0 / 0	−10.0 / −15.0
4.73–7.09	3.5 / 7.6	+2.5 / −0	−3.5 / −5.1	3.5 / 10.0	+4.0 / −0	−3.5 / −6.0	6.0 / 12.5	+4.0 / −0	−6.0 / −8.5	8.0 / 18.0	+6.0 / 0	−8.0 / −12.0	12.0 / 28.0	+10.0 / 0	−12.0 / −18.0

TABLE 26B-1
American National Standard Locational Clearance Fits

Limits are in thousandths of an inch. Limits for hole and shaft are applied algebraically to the basic size to obtain the limits of size for parts. Symbols H6, h5, etc., are hole and shaft designations used in ABC system.

Nominal Size Range (Inches) Over–To	CLASS LC 1 Limits of Clearance	CLASS LC 1 Hole H6	CLASS LC 1 Shaft h5	CLASS LC 2 Limits of Clearance	CLASS LC 2 Hole H7	CLASS LC 2 Shaft h6	CLASS LC 3 Limits of Clearance	CLASS LC 3 Hole H8	CLASS LC 3 Shaft h7	CLASS LC 4 Limits of Clearance	CLASS LC 4 Hole H10	CLASS LC 4 Shaft h9	CLASS LC 5 Limits of Clearance	CLASS LC 5 Hole H7	CLASS LC 5 Shaft g6
0–0.12	0 .45	+.25 −0	+0 −.2	0 .65	+.4 −0	+0 −.25	0 1	+.6 −0	+0 −.4	0 2.6	+1.6 −0	+0 −1.0	.1 .75	+.4 −0	−.1 −.35
0.12–0.24	0 .5	+.3 −0	+0 −.2	0 .8	+.5 −0	+0 −.3	0 1.2	+.7 −0	+0 −.5	0 3.0	+1.8 −0	+0 −1.2	.15 .95	+.5 −0	−.15 −.45
0.24–0.40	0 .65	+.4 −0	+0 −.25	0 1.0	+.6 −0	+0 −.4	0 1.5	+.9 −0	+0 −.6	0 3.6	+2.2 −0	+0 −1.4	.2 1.2	+.6 −0	−.2 −.6
0.40–0.71	0 .7	+.4 −0	+0 −.3	0 1.1	+.7 −0	+0 −.4	0 1.7	+1.0 −0	+0 −.7	0 4.4	+2.8 −0	+0 −1.6	.25 1.35	+.7 −0	−.25 −.65
0.71–1.19	0 .9	+.5 −0	+0 −.4	0 1.3	+.8 −0	+0 −.5	0 2	+1.2 −0	+0 −.8	0 5.5	+3.5 −0	+0 −2.0	.3 1.6	+.8 −0	−.3 −.8
1.19–1.97	0 1.0	+.6 −0	+0 −.4	0 1.6	+1.0 −0	+0 −.6	0 2.6	+1.6 −0	+0 −1	0 6.5	+4.0 −0	+0 −2.5	.4 2.0	+1.0 −0	−.4 −1.0
1.97–3.15	0 1.2	+.7 −0	+0 −.5	0 1.9	+1.2 −0	+0 −.7	0 3	+1.8 −0	+0 −1.2	0 7.5	+4.5 −0	+0 −3	.4 2.3	+1.2 −0	−.4 −1.1
3.15–4.73	0 1.5	+.9 −0	+0 −.6	0 2.3	+1.4 −0	+0 −.9	0 3.6	+2.2 −0	+0 −1.4	0 8.5	+5.0 −0	+0 −3.5	.5 2.8	+1.4 −0	−.5 −1.4
4.73–7.09	0 1.7	+1.0 −0	+0 −.7	0 2.6	+1.6 −0	+0 −1.0	0 4.1	+2.5 −0	+0 −1.6	0 10	+6.0 −0	+0 −4	.6 3.2	+1.6 −0	−.6 −1.6

TABLE 26B-2
American National Standard Locational Clearance Fits

Limits are in thousandths of an inch. Limits for hole and shaft are applied algebraically to the basic size to obtain the limits of size for the parts. Symbols H9, f8, etc., are hole and shaft designations used in ABC system.

Nominal Size Range (Inches) Over To	CLASS LC 6 Limits of Clearance	CLASS LC 6 Hole H9	CLASS LC 6 Shaft f8	CLASS LC 7 Limits of Clearance	CLASS LC 7 Hole H10	CLASS LC 7 Shaft e9	CLASS LC 8 Limits of Clearance	CLASS LC 8 Hole H10	CLASS LC 8 Shaft d9	CLASS LC 9 Limits of Clearance	CLASS LC 9 Hole H11	CLASS LC 9 Shaft c10	CLASS LC 10 Limits of Clearance	CLASS LC 10 Hole H12	CLASS LC 10 Shaft	CLASS LC 11 Limits of Clearance	CLASS LC 11 Hole H13	CLASS LC 11 Shaft
0–0.12	.3 / 1.9	+1.0 / 0	−.3 / −.9	.6 / 3.2	+1.6 / 0	−.6 / −1.6	1.0 / 3.6	+1.6 / 0	−1.0 / −2.0	2.5 / 6.6	+2.5 / 0	−2.5 / −4.1	4 / 12	+4 / 0	−4 / −8	5 / 17	+6 / −0	−5 / −11
0.12–0.24	.4 / 2.3	+1.2 / 0	−.4 / −1.1	.8 / 3.8	+1.8 / 0	−.8 / −2.0	1.2 / 4.2	+1.8 / 0	−1.2 / −2.4	2.8 / 7.6	+3.0 / 0	−2.8 / −4.6	4.5 / 14.5	+5 / 0	−4.5 / −9.5	6 / 20	+7 / −0	−6 / −13
0.24–0.40	.5 / 2.8	+1.4 / 0	−.5 / −1.4	1.0 / 4.6	+2.2 / 0	−1.0 / −2.4	1.6 / 5.2	+2.2 / 0	−1.6 / −3.0	3.0 / 8.7	+3.5 / 0	−3.0 / −5.2	5 / 17	+6 / 0	−5 / −11	7 / 25	+9 / −0	−7 / −16
0.40–0.71	.6 / 3.2	+1.6 / 0	−.6 / −1.6	1.2 / 5.6	+2.8 / 0	−1.2 / −2.8	2.0 / 6.4	+2.8 / 0	−2.0 / −3.6	3.5 / 10.3	+4.0 / 0	−3.5 / −6.3	6 / 20	+7 / 0	−6 / −13	8 / 28	+10 / −0	−8 / −18
0.71–1.19	.8 / 4.0	+2.0 / 0	−.8 / −2.0	1.6 / 7.1	+3.5 / 0	−1.6 / −3.6	2.5 / 8.0	+3.5 / 0	−2.5 / −4.5	4.5 / 13.0	+5.0 / 0	−4.5 / −8.0	7 / 23	+8 / 0	−7 / −15	10 / 34	+12 / −0	−10 / −22
1.19–1.97	1.0 / 5.1	+2.5 / 0	−1.0 / −2.6	2.0 / 8.5	+4.0 / 0	−2.0 / −4.5	3.0 / 9.5	+4.0 / 0	−3.0 / −5.5	5 / 15	+6 / 0	−5 / −9	8 / 28	+10 / 0	−8 / −18	12 / 44	+16 / −0	−12 / −28
1.97–3.15	1.2 / 6.0	+3.0 / 0	−1.2 / −3.0	2.5 / 10.0	+4.5 / 0	−2.5 / −5.5	4.0 / 11.5	+4.5 / 0	−4.0 / −7.0	6 / 17.5	+7 / 0	−6 / −10.5	10 / 34	+12 / 0	−10 / −22	14 / 50	+18 / −0	−14 / −32
3.15–4.73	1.4 / 7.1	+3.5 / 0	−1.4 / −3.6	3.0 / 11.5	+5.0 / 0	−3.0 / −6.5	5.0 / 13.5	+5.0 / 0	−5.0 / −8.5	7 / 21	+9 / 0	−7 / −12	11 / 39	+14 / 0	−11 / −25	16 / 60	+22 / −0	−16 / −38
4.73–7.09	1.6 / 8.1	+4.0 / 0	−1.6 / −4.1	3.5 / 13.5	+6.0 / 0	−3.5 / −7.5	6 / 16	+6 / −0	−6 / −10	8 / 24	+10 / −0	−8 / −14	12 / 44	+16 / −0	−12 / −28	18 / 68	+25 / −0	−18 / −43

APPENDIX **675**

TABLE 26C
American National Standard Locational Transition Fits

Limits are in thousandths of an inch. Limits for hole and shaft are applied algebraically to the basic size to obtain the limits of size for the mating parts. "Fit" represents the maximum interference (minus values) and the maximum clearance (plus values). Symbols H7, js6, etc., are hole and shaft designations used in ABC system.

Nominal Size Range (Inches) Over To	CLASS LT 1 Fit	CLASS LT 1 Hole H7	CLASS LT 1 Shaft js6	CLASS LT 2 Fit	CLASS LT 2 Hole H8	CLASS LT 2 Shaft js7	CLASS LT 3 Fit	CLASS LT 3 Hole H7	CLASS LT 3 Shaft k6	CLASS LT 4 Fit	CLASS LT 4 Hole H8	CLASS LT 4 Shaft k7	CLASS LT 5 Fit	CLASS LT 5 Hole H7	CLASS LT 5 Shaft n6	CLASS LT 6 Fit	CLASS LT 6 Hole H7	CLASS LT 6 Shaft n7
0–0.12	−.10 +.50	+.4 −0	+.10 −.10	−.2 +.8	+.6 −0	+.2 −.2							−.5 +.15	+.4 −0	+.5 +.25	−.65 +.15	+.4 −0	+.65 +.25
0.12–0.24	−.15 +.65	+.5 −0	+.15 −.15	−.25 +.95	+.7 −0	+.25 −.25							−.6 +.2	+.5 −0	+.6 +.3	−.8 +.2	+.5 −0	+.8 +.3
0.24–0.40	−.2 +.8	+.6 −0	+.2 −.2	−.3 +1.2	+.9 −0	+.3 −.3	−.5 +.5	+.6 −0	+.5 +.1	−.7 +.8	+.9 −0	+.7 +.1	−.8 +.2	+.6 −0	+.8 +.4	−1.0 +.2	+.6 −0	+1.0 +.4
0.40–0.71	−.2 +.9	+.7 −0	+.2 −.2	−.35 +1.35	+1.0 −0	+.35 −.35	−.5 +.6	+.7 −0	+.5 +.1	−.8 +.9	+1.0 −0	+.8 +.1	−.9 +.2	+.7 −0	+.9 +.5	−1.2 +.2	+.7 −0	+1.2 +.5
0.71–1.19	−.25 +1.05	+.8 −0	+.25 −.25	−.4 +1.6	+1.2 −0	+.4 −.4	−.6 +.7	+.8 −0	+.6 +.1	−.9 +1.1	+1.2 −0	+.9 +.1	−1.1 +.2	+.8 −0	+1.1 +.6	−1.4 +.2	+.8 −0	+1.4 +.6
1.19–1.97	−.3 +1.3	+1.0 −0	+.3 −.3	−.5 +2.1	+1.6 −0	+.5 −.5	−.7 +.9	+1.0 −0	+.7 +.1	−1.1 +1.5	+1.6 −0	+1.1 +.1	−1.3 +.3	+1.0 −0	+1.3 +.7	−1.7 +.3	+1.0 −0	+1.7 +.7
1.97–3.15	−.3 +1.5	+1.2 −0	+.3 −.3	−.6 +2.4	+1.8 −0	+.6 −.6	−.8 +1.1	+1.2 −0	+.8 +.1	−1.3 +1.7	+1.8 −0	+1.3 +.1	−1.5 +.4	+1.2 −0	+1.5 +.8	−2.0 +.4	+1.2 −0	+2.0 +.8
3.15–4.73	−.4 +1.8	+1.4 −0	+.4 −.4	−.7 +2.9	+2.2 −0	+.7 −.7	−1.0 +1.3	+1.4 −0	+1.0 +.1	−1.5 +2.1	+2.2 −0	+1.5 +.1	−1.9 +.4	+1.4 −0	+1.9 +1.0	−2.4 +.4	+1.4 −0	+2.4 +1.0
4.73–7.09	−.5 +2.1	+1.6 −0	+.5 −.5	−.8 +3.3	+2.5 −0	+.8 −.8	−1.1 +1.5	+1.6 −0	+1.1 +.1	−1.7 +2.4	+2.5 −0	+1.7 +.1	−2.2 +.4	+1.6 −0	+2.2 +1.2	−2.8 +.4	+1.6 −0	+2.8 +1.2

TABLE 26D
American National Standard Locational Interference Fits

Limits are in thousandths of an inch. Limits for hole and shaft are applied algebraically to the basic size to obtain the limits of size for the parts. Symbols H7, p6, etc., are hole and shaft designations used in ABC system.

Nominal Size Range (Inches) Over To	CLASS LN 1 Limits of Interference	CLASS LN 1 Hole H6	CLASS LN 1 Shaft n5	CLASS LN 2 Limits of Interference	CLASS LN 2 Hole H7	CLASS LN 2 Shaft p6	CLASS LN 3 Limits of Interference	CLASS LN 3 Hole H7	CLASS LN 3 Shaft r6
0–0.12	0 / .45	+.25 / −0	+.45 / +.25	0 / .65	+.4 / −0	+.65 / +.4	.1 / .75	+.4 / −0	+.75 / +.5
0.12–0.24	0 / .5	+.3 / −0	+.5 / +.3	0 / .8	+.5 / −0	+.8 / +.5	.1 / .9	+.5 / −0	+.9 / +.6
0.24–0.40	0 / .65	+.4 / −0	+.65 / +.4	0 / 1.0	+.6 / −0	+1.0 / +.6	.2 / 1.2	+.6 / −0	+1.2 / +.8
0.40–0.71	0 / .8	+.4 / −0	+.8 / +.4	0 / 1.1	+.7 / −0	+1.1 / +.7	.3 / 1.4	+.7 / −0	+1.4 / +1.0
0.71–1.19	0 / 1.0	+.5 / −0	+1.0 / +.5	0 / 1.3	+.8 / −0	+1.3 / +.8	.4 / 1.7	+.8 / −0	+1.7 / +1.2
1.19–1.97	0 / 1.1	+.6 / −0	+1.1 / +.6	0 / 1.6	+1.0 / −0	+1.6 / +1.0	.4 / 2.0	+1.0 / −0	+2.0 / +1.4
1.97–3.15	.1 / 1.3	+.7 / −0	+1.3 / +.7	.2 / 2.1	+1.2 / −0	+2.1 / +1.4	.4 / 2.3	+1.2 / −0	+2.3 / +1.6
3.15–4.73	.1 / 1.6	+.9 / −0	+1.6 / +1.0	.2 / 2.5	+1.4 / −0	+2.5 / +1.6	.6 / 2.9	+1.4 / −0	+2.9 / +2.0
4.73–7.09	.2 / 1.9	+1.0 / −0	+1.9 / +1.2	.2 / 2.8	+1.6 / −0	+2.8 / +1.8	.9 / 3.5	+1.6 / −0	+3.5 / +2.5

APPENDIX 677

TABLE 26E
American National Standard Force and Shrink Fits

Limits are in thousandths of an inch. Limits for hole and shaft are applied algebraically to the basic size to obtain the limits of size for the parts. Symbols H7, s6, etc., are hole and shaft designations used in ABC system.

Nominal Size Range (Inches) Over–To	CLASS FN 1 Limits of Interference	CLASS FN 1 Standard Limits Hole H6	CLASS FN 1 Standard Limits Shaft	CLASS FN 2 Limits of Interference	CLASS FN 2 Standard Limits Hole H7	CLASS FN 2 Standard Limits Shaft s6	CLASS FN 3 Limits of Interference	CLASS FN 3 Standard Limits Hole H7	CLASS FN 3 Standard Limits Shaft t6	CLASS FN 4 Limits of Interference	CLASS FN 4 Standard Limits Hole H7	CLASS FN 4 Standard Limits Shaft u6	CLASS FN 5 Limits of Interference	CLASS FN 5 Standard Limits Hole H8	CLASS FN 5 Standard Limits Shaft x7
0–0.12	.05 / .5	+.25 / –0	+.5 / +.3	.2 / .85	+.4 / –0	+.85 / +.6				.3 / .95	+.4 / –0	+.95 / +.7	.3 / 1.3	+.6 / –0	+1.3 / +.9
0.12–0.24	.1 / .6	+.3 / –0	+.6 / +.4	.2 / 1.0	+.5 / –0	+1.0 / +.7				.4 / 1.2	+.5 / –0	+1.2 / +.9	.5 / 1.7	+.7 / –0	+1.7 / +1.2
0.24–0.40	.1 / .75	+.4 / –0	+.75 / +.5	.4 / 1.4	+.6 / –0	+1.4 / +1.0				.6 / 1.6	+.6 / –0	+1.6 / +1.2	.5 / 2.0	+.9 / –0	+2.0 / +1.4
0.40–0.56	.1 / .8	+.4 / –0	+.8 / +.5	.5 / 1.6	+.7 / –0	+1.6 / +1.2				.7 / 1.8	+.7 / –0	+1.8 / +1.4	.6 / 2.3	+1.0 / –0	+2.3 / +1.6
0.56–0.71	.2 / .9	+.4 / –0	+.9 / +.6	.5 / 1.6	+.7 / –0	+1.6 / +1.2				.7 / 1.8	+.7 / –0	+1.8 / +1.4	.8 / 2.5	+1.0 / –0	+2.5 / +1.8
0.71–0.95	.2 / 1.1	+.5 / –0	+1.1 / +.7	.6 / 1.9	+.8 / –0	+1.9 / +1.4				.8 / 2.1	+.8 / –0	+2.1 / +1.6	1.0 / 3.0	+1.2 / –0	+3.0 / +2.2
0.95–1.19	.3 / 1.2	+.5 / –0	+1.2 / +.8	.6 / 1.9	+.8 / –0	+1.9 / +1.4	.8 / 2.1	+.8 / –0	+2.1 / +1.6	1.0 / 2.3	+.8 / –0	+2.3 / +1.8	1.3 / 3.3	+1.2 / –0	+3.3 / +2.5
1.19–1.58	.3 / 1.3	+.6 / –0	+1.3 / +.9	.8 / 2.4	+1.0 / –0	+2.4 / +1.8	1.0 / 2.6	+1.0 / –0	+2.6 / +2.0	1.5 / 3.1	+1.0 / –0	+3.1 / +2.5	1.4 / 4.0	+1.6 / –0	+4.0 / +3.0
1.58–1.97	.4 / 1.4	+.6 / –0	+1.4 / +1.0	.8 / 2.4	+1.0 / –0	+2.4 / +1.8	1.2 / 2.8	+1.0 / –0	+2.8 / +2.2	1.8 / 3.4	+1.0 / –0	+3.4 / +2.8	2.4 / 5.0	+1.6 / –0	+5.0 / +4.0
1.97–2.56	.6 / 1.8	+.7 / –0	+1.8 / +1.3	.8 / 2.7	+1.2 / –0	+2.7 / +2.0	1.3 / 3.2	+1.2 / –0	+3.2 / +2.5	2.3 / 4.2	+1.2 / –0	+4.2 / +3.5	3.2 / 6.2	+1.8 / –0	+6.2 / +5.0
2.56–3.15	.7 / 1.9	+.7 / –0	+1.9 / +1.4	1.0 / 2.9	+1.2 / –0	+2.9 / +2.2	1.8 / 3.7	+1.2 / –0	+3.7 / +3.0	2.8 / 4.7	+1.2 / –0	+4.7 / +4.0	4.2 / 7.2	+1.8 / –0	+7.2 / +6.0
3.15–3.94	.9 / 2.4	+.9 / –0	+2.4 / +1.8	1.4 / 3.7	+1.4 / –0	+3.7 / +2.8	2.1 / 4.4	+1.4 / –0	+4.4 / +3.5	3.6 / 5.9	+1.4 / –0	+5.9 / +5.0	4.8 / 8.4	+2.2 / –0	+8.4 / +7.0
3.94–4.73	1.1 / 2.6	+.9 / –0	+2.6 / +2.0	1.6 / 3.9	+1.4 / –0	+3.9 / +3.0	2.6 / 4.9	+1.4 / –0	+4.9 / +4.0	4.6 / 6.9	+1.4 / –0	+6.9 / +6.0	5.8 / 9.4	+2.2 / –0	+9.4 / +8.0

TABLE 27A
Single-Row Radial Bearings—Type 3000*

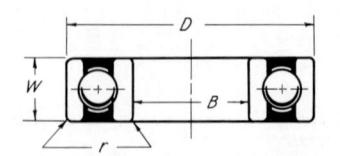

See table below for explanation of letters

Bearing No.	Bore B mm	Bore B in.	Diameter D mm	Diameter D in.	Width W mm	Width W in.	Balls Diam	Balls No.	Radius r†
3200	10	.3937	30	1.1811	9	.3543	7/32	7	.025
3300	10	.3937	35	1.3780	11	.4331	1/4	7	.025
3201	12	.4724	32	1.2598	10	.3937	.210	8	.025
3301	12	.4724	37	1.4567	12	.4724	9/32	7	.04
3202	15	.5906	35	1.3780	11	.4331	.210	9	.025
3302	15	.5906	42	1.6535	13	.5118	5/16	7	.04
3203	17	.6693	40	1.5748	12	.4724	9/32	8	.04
3303	17	.6693	47	1.8504	14	.5512	11/32	7	.04
3204	20	.7874	47	1.8504	14	.5512	5/16	8	.04
3304	20	.7874	52	2.0472	15	.5906	13/32	7	.04
3205	25	.9843	52	2.0472	15	.5906	5/16	9	.04
3305	25	.9843	62	2.4409	17	.6693	13/32	8	.04
3206	30	1.1811	62	2.4409	16	.6299	11/32	9	.04
3306	30	1.1811	72	2.8346	19	.7480	15/32	8	.04
3207	35	1.3780	72	2.8346	17	.6693	7/16	9	.04
3307	35	1.3780	80	3.1496	21	.8268	17/32	8	.06
3208	40	1.5748	80	3.1496	18	.7087	15/32	9	.04
3308	40	1.5748	90	3.5433	23	.9055	19/32	8	.06
3209	45	1.7717	85	3.3465	19	.7480	15/32	10	.04
3309	45	1.7717	100	3.9370	25	.9843	21/32	8	.06
3210	50	1.9685	90	3.5433	20	.7874	15/32	11	.04
3310	50	1.9685	110	4.3307	27	1.0630	23/32	8	.08
3211	55	2.1654	100	3.9370	21	.8268	1/2	11	.06
3311	55	2.1654	120	4.7244	29	1.1417	25/32	8	.08

*For radial or combined loads from either direction where thrust is to be resisted by a single bearing and is not great enough to require use of angular contact type.

†Radius r indicates maximum fillet radius in housing or on shaft, which bearing radius will clear.

Pages 140–143 from Vol. I, *New Departure Hand Book*.

TABLE 27B
Radax Bearings—Type 30,000*

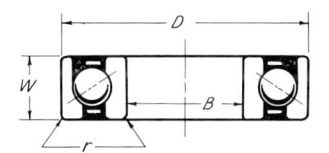

See table below for explanation of letters

Bearing No.	BORE B mm	BORE B in.	DIAMETER D mm	DIAMETER D in.	WIDTH W mm	WIDTH W in.	BALLS Diam	BALLS No.	Radius r†
30204			47	1.8504	14	.5512	$1\tfrac{1}{32}$	10	
30304	20	.7874	52	2.0472	15	.5906	$\tfrac{3}{8}$	10	
30404			72	2.8346	19	.7480	$\tfrac{9}{16}$	8	.04
30205			52	2.0472	15	.5906	$1\tfrac{1}{32}$	11	.04
30305	25	.9843	62	2.4409	17	.6693	$\tfrac{7}{16}$	10	.04
30405			80	3.1496	21	.8268	$\tfrac{5}{8}$	9	.06
30206			62	2.4409	16	.6299	$\tfrac{3}{8}$	12	.04
30306	30	1.1811	72	2.8346	19	.7480	$\tfrac{1}{2}$	10	.04
30406			90	3.5433	23	.9055	$1\tfrac{1}{16}$	9	.06
30207			72	2.8346	17	.6693	$\tfrac{7}{16}$	12	.04
30307	35	1.3780	80	3.1496	21	.8268	$\tfrac{9}{16}$	11	.06
30407			100	3.9370	25	.9843	$\tfrac{3}{4}$	9	.06
30208			80	3.1496	18	.7087	$\tfrac{1}{2}$	12	.04
30308	40	1.5748	90	3.5433	23	.9055	$\tfrac{5}{8}$	11	.06
30408			110	4.3307	27	1.0630	$1\tfrac{3}{16}$	10	.08
30209			85	3.3465	19	.7480	$\tfrac{1}{2}$	13	.04
30309	45	1.7717	100	3.9370	25	.9843	$1\tfrac{1}{16}$	11	.06
30409			120	4.7244	29	1.1417	$\tfrac{7}{8}$	10	.08
30210			90	3.5433	20	.7874	$\tfrac{1}{2}$	14	.04
30310	50	1.9685	110	4.3307	27	1.0630	$\tfrac{3}{4}$	11	.08
30410			130	5.1181	31	1.2205	$1\tfrac{5}{16}$	10	.08
30211			100	3.9370	21	.8268	$\tfrac{9}{16}$	14	.06
30311	55	2.1654	120	4.7244	29	1.1417	$1\tfrac{3}{16}$	12	.08
30411			140	5.5118	33	1.2992	1	10	.08
30212			110	4.3307	22	.8661	$\tfrac{5}{8}$	14	.06
30312	60	2.3622	130	5.1181	31	1.2205	$\tfrac{7}{8}$	12	.08
30412			150	5.9055	35	1.3780	$1\tfrac{1}{16}$	10	.08

*Single-row angular contact; provide maximum capacity for one-direction thrust loads. Mounted two bearings opposed for combined loads or thrust from either direction.

†Radius r indicates maximum fillet radius in housing or on shaft, which bearing radius will clear.

Page 143 from Vol. I, *New Departure Hand Book*.

TABLE 28A

Shaft Mounting Fits for SAE or A.B.E.C.-1 Standard Bearings*

BEARING AND BORE NUMBERS	BEARING BORE Diameters Max.	BEARING BORE Diameters Min.	SHAFT REVOLVING Diameters Max.	SHAFT REVOLVING Diameters Min.	Expected Fit Loose or Tight	Expected Fit Tight	Theoret. Fit Loose	Theoret. Fit Tight	SHAFT STATIONARY Diameters Max.	SHAFT STATIONARY Diameters Min.	Expected Fit Max. Loose	Expected Fit Min. Loose	Theoret. Fit Loose	Theoret. Fit Tight
34	.1575	.1572	.1576	.1573					.1573	.1570				
35	.1969	.1966	.1970	.1967	.0001L	.0003	.0002	.0004	.1967	.1964	.0004	.0000	.0005	.0001
36	.2362	.2359	.2363	.2360					.2360	.2357				
37	.2756	.2753	.2757	.2754					.2754	.2751				
38	.3150	.3147	.3151	.3148	.0001L	.0003	.0002	.0004	.3148	.3145	.0004	.0000	.0005	.0001
39	.3543	.3540	.3544	.3541					.3541	.3538				
8006	.2362	.2359	.2363	.2360					.2360	.2357				
8007, 8102	.2756	.2753	.2757	.2754	.0001L	.0003	.0002	.0004	.2754	.2751	.0004	.0000	.0005	.0001
8008, 8103	.3150	.3147	.3151	.3148					.3148	.3145				
8009	.3543	.3540	.3544	.3541	.0001L	.0003	.0002	.0004	.3541	.3538				
8011	.4331	.4328	.4333	.4330	.0000L	.0004	.0001	.0005	.4329	.4326	.0004	.0000	.0005	.0001
8013	.5118	.5115	.5120	.5117	.0000L	.0004	.0001	.0005	.5116	.5113				
8014	.5512	.5509	.5514	.5511	.0000L	.0004	.0001	.0005	.5510	.5507	.0004	.0000	.0005	.0001
8016	.6299	.6296	.6301	.6298	.0000L	.0004	.0001	.0005	.6297	.6294	.0004	.0000	.0005	.0001
8026	1.0236	1.0232	1.0239	1.0235	.0000L	.0006	.0001	.0007	1.0233	1.0229	.0006	.0000	.0007	.0001
N.D. 8-6	.2362	.2359	.2363	.2360					.2360	.2357				
N.D. 8-7	.2756	.2753	.2757	.2754	.0001L	.0003	.0002	.0004	.2754	.2751	.0004	.0000	.0005	.0001
N.D. 8	.3150	.3147	.3151	.3148					.3148	.3145				
N.D. 10-9	.3543	.3540	.3544	.3541	.0001L	.0003	.0002	.0004	.3541	.3538				
N.D. 10	.3937	.3934	.3939	.3936	.0000L	.0004	.0001	.0005	.3935	.3932	.0004	.0000	.0005	.0001
N.D. 12-11	.4331	.4328	.4333	.4330	.0000L	.0004	.0001	.0005	.4329	.4326				
N.D. 12	.4724	.4721	.4726	.4723	.0000L	.0004	.0001	.0005	.4722	.4719				
N.D. 13	.5118	.5115	.5120	.5117					.5116	.5113				
N.D. 15	.5906	.5903	.5908	.5905	.0000L	.0004	.0001	.0005	.5904	.5901	.0004	.0000	.0005	.0001
N.D. 16	.6299	.6296	.6301	.6298					.6297	.6294				
N.D. 17	.6693	.6690	.6695	.6692	.0000L	.0004	.0001	.0005	.6691	.6688	.0004	.0000	.0005	.0001
N.D. 20	.7874	.7870	.7877	.7873	.0000L	.0006	.0001	.0007	.7871	.7867	.0006	.0000	.0007	.0001
N.D. 25	.9843	.9839	.9846	.9842	.0000L	.0006	.0001	.0007	.9840	.9836	.0006	.0000	.0007	.0001
0	.3937	.3934	.3939	.3936					.3935	.3932				
1	.4724	.4721	.4726	.4723	.0000L	.0004	.0001	.0005	.4722	.4719	.0004	.0000	.0005	.0001
2	.5906	.5903	.5908	.5905					.5904	.5901				
3	.6693	.6690	.6605	.6692	.0000L	.0004	.0001	.0005	.6691	.6688	.0004	.0000	.0005	.0001
4	.7874	.7870	.7877	.7873	.0000L	.0006	.0001	.0007	.7871	.7867	.0006	.0000	.0007	.0001
5	.9843	.9839	.9846	.9842	.0000L	.0006	.0001	.0007	.9840	.9836	.0006	.0000	.0007	.0001
6	1.1811	1.1807	1.1814	1.1810	.0000L	.0006	.0001	.0007	1.1808	1.1804	.0006	.0000	.0007	.0001
7	1.3780	1.3775	1.3784	1.3779	.0001T	.0007	.0001	.0009	1.3776	1.3771	.0007	.0001	.0009	.0001
8	1.5748	1.5743	1.5752	1.5747	.0001T	.0007	.0001	.0009	1.5744	1.5739	.0007	.0001	.0009	.0001
9	1.7717	1.7712	1.7721	1.7716	.0001T	.0007	.0001	.0009	1.7713	1.7708	.0007	.0001	.0009	.0001
10	1.9685	1.9680	1.9689	1.9684	.0001T	.0007	.0001	.0009	1.9681	1.9676	.0007	.0001	.0009	.0001
11	2.1654	2.1648	2.1659	2.1653	.0001T	.0009	.0001	.0011	2.1649	2.1643	.0009	.0001	.0011	.0001
12	2.3622	2.3616	2.3627	2.3621					2.3617	2.3611				
13	2.5591	2.5585	2.5596	2.5590	.0001T	.0009	.0001	.0011	2.5586	2.5580	.0009	.0001	.0011	.0001
14	2.7559	2.7553	2.7564	2.7558					2.7554	2.7548				
15	2.9528	2.9522	2.9533	2.9527	.0001T	.0009	.0001	.0011	2.9523	2.9517	.0009	.0001	.0011	.0001
16	3.1496	3.1490	3.1501	3.1495	.0001T	.0009	.0001	.0011	3.1491	3.1485	.0009	.0001	.0011	.0001
17	3.3465	3.3457	3.3471	3.3464	.0002T	.0012	.0001	.0014	3.3458	3.3451	.0012	.0002	.0014	.0001
18	3.5433	3.5425	3.5439	3.5432										
19	3.7402	3.7394	3.7408	3.7401	.0002T	.0012	.0001	.0014						
20	3.9370	3.9362	3.9376	3.9369										
21	4.1339	4.1331	4.1345	4.1338	.0002T	.0012	.0001	.0014	4.1332	4.1325	.0012	.0002	.0014	.0001
22	4.3307	4.3299	4.3313	4.3306					4.3300	4.3293				

* The "*theoretical fits*" given in this table are those that could result if the shaft diameters and bearing bores were to vary the full limits of their respective tolerances. Actually, bearing bores are ground uniformly close to the minimum limit, and investigation by the Annular Bearing Engineers Committee has proved that well over 95% of actual installations result in the "*expected fits*" given here. Reproduced with permission from Vol. I, *New Departure Hand Book*.

TABLE 28B
Housing Mounting Fits for A.B.E.C.-1 and A.B.E.C.-2 Bearings*

BEARING AND BORE NUMBERS			BEARING OUTER DIAM.		HOUSING STATIONARY				HOUSING REVOLVING			
Series			Diameters		Diameters		Expect. Fit		Theoret. Fit		Diameters		Expect. Fit		Theoret. Fit	
Lgt.	Med.	Hvy.	Max.	Min.	Max.	Min.	Min. Loose	Max. Loose	Tight	Loose	Max.	Min.	Tight	Loose	Tight	Loose
	34		.6299	.6295	.6303	.6298					.6298	.6293				
	35, 36		.7480	.7476	.7484	.7479					.7479	.7474				
	37, 38		.8661	.8657	.8665	.8660	.0000	.0005	.0001	.0008	.8660	.8655	.0002	.0002	.0006	.0003
	39		1.0236	1.0232	1.0240	1.0235					1.0235	1.0230				
	8102, 8103		.8661	.8657	.8665	.8660					.8660	.8655				
	8006, 7 & 8		.9449	.9445	.9453	.9448	.0000	.0005	.0001	.0008	.9448	.9443	.0002	.0002	.0006	.0003
	8009		1.1811	1.1807	1.1815	1.1810					1.1810	1.1805				
	8011, 8013		1.2598	1.2593	1.2603	1.2597	.0000	.0007	.0001	.0010	1.2597	1.2591	.0003	.0003	.0007	.0004
	8014, 8016		1.3780	1.3775	1.3785	1.3779	.0000	.0007	.0001	.0010	1.3779	1.3773	.0003	.0003	.0007	.0004
	8026		2.0472	2.0466	2.0479	2.0473	.0000	.0010	.0001	.0013	2.0472	2.0464	.0004	.0004	.0008	.0006
	N.D. 8-6, 8-7, 8		.9453	.9449	.9457	.9452	.0000	.0005	.0001	.0008	.9452	.9447	.0002	.0002	.0006	.0003
	N.D. 10-9, 10		1.1028	1.1024	1.1032	1.1027	.0000	.0005	.0001	.0008	1.1027	1.1022	.0002	.0002	.0006	.0003
	N.D. 12-11, 12		1.2603	1.2598	1.2608	1.2602	.0000	.0007	.0001	.0010	1.2602	1.2596	.0003	.0003	.0007	.0004
	N.D. 13		1.1816	1.1811	1.1821	1.1815					1.1815	1.1809				
	N.D. 15		1.3785	1.3780	1.3790	1.3784	.0000	.0007	.0001	.0010	1.3784	1.3778	.0003	.0003	.0007	.0004
	N.D. 16		1.4966	1.4961	1.4971	1.4965					1.4965	1.4959				
	N.D. 17		1.7328	1.7323	1.7333	1.7327					1.7327	1.7321				
	N.D. 20		1.8509	1.8504	1.8514	1.8508	.0000	.0007	.0001	.0010	1.8508	1.8502	.0003	.0003	.0007	.0004
	N.D. 25		2.0477	2.0472	2.0482	2.0476					2.0476	2.0470				
0			1.1811	1.1807	1.1815	1.1810	.0000	.0005	.0001	.0008	1.1810	1.1805	.0002	.0002	.0006	.0003
1			1.2598	1.2593	1.2603	1.2597	.0000	.0007	.0001	.0010	1.2597	1.2591	.0003	.0003	.0007	.0004
2	0		1.3780	1.3775	1.3785	1.3779	.0000	.0007	.0001	.0010	1.3779	1.3773	.0003	.0003	.0007	.0004
	1		1.4567	1.4562	1.4572	1.4566					1.4566	1.4560				
3			1.5748	1.5743	1.5753	1.5747	.0000	.0007	.0001	.0010	1.5747	1.5741	.0003	.0003	.0007	.0004
	2		1.6535	1.6530	1.6540	1.6534					1.6534	1.6528				
4	3		1.8504	1.8499	1.8509	1.8503	.0000	.0007	.0001	.0010	1.8503	1.8497	.0003	.0003	.0007	.0004
5	4		2.0472	2.0466	2.0479	2.0471	.0000	.0010	.0001	.0013	2.0472	2.0464	.0004	.0004	.0008	.0006
6	5		2.4409	2.4403	2.4416	2.4408	.0000	.0010	.0001	.0013	2.4409	2.4401	.0004	.0004	.0008	.0006
7	6	4	2.8346	2.8340	2.8353	2.8345	.0000	.0010	.0001	.0013	2.8346	2.8338	.0004	.0004	.0008	.0006
8	7	5	3.1496	3.1490	3.1503	3.1495	.0000	.0010	.0001	.0013	3.1496	3.1488	.0004	.0004	.0008	.0006
9			3.3465	3.3457	3.3473	3.3463	.0000	.0012	.0002	.0016	3.3466	3.3456	.0005	.0004	.0009	.0009
10	8	6	3.5433	3.5425	3.5441	3.5431					3.5434	3.5424				
11	9	7	3.9370	3.9362	3.9378	3.9368	.0000	.0012	.0002	.0016	3.9371	3.9361	.0005	.0004	.0009	.0009
12	10	8	4.3307	4.3299	4.3315	4.3305					4.3308	4.3298				
13	11	9	4.7244	4.7236	4.7252	4.7242	.0000	.0012	.0002	.0016	4.7245	4.7235	.0005	.0004	.0009	.0009
14			4.9213	4.9203	4.9223	4.9211	.0001	.0015	.0002	.0020	4.9214	4.9202	.0006	.0005	.0011	.0011
15	12	10	5.1181	5.1171	5.1191	5.1179	.0001	.0015	.0002	.0020	5.1182	5.1170	.0006	.0005	.0011	.0011
16	13	11	5.5118	5.5108	5.5128	5.5116					5.5119	5.5107				
17	14	12	5.9055	5.9045	5.9065	5.9053	.0001	.0015	.0002	.0020	5.9056	5.9044	.0006	.0005	.0011	.0011
18	15	13	6.2992	6.2982	6.3002	6.2990					6.2993	6.2981				
19	16		6.6929	6.6919	6.6939	6.6927	.0001	.0015	.0002	.0020	6.6930	6.6918	.0006	.0005	.0011	.0011
20	17	14	7.0866	7.0856	7.0876	7.0864	.0001	.0015	.0002	.0020	7.0867	7.0855	.0006	.0005	.0011	.0011
21	18	15	7.4803	7.4791	7.4815	7.4801	.0001	.0018	.0002	.0024	7.4804	7.4790	.0007	.0007	.0013	.0013
22	19	16	7.8740	7.8728	7.8752	7.8738					7.8741	7.8727				
		17	8.2677	8.2665	8.2689	8.2675	.0001	.0018	.0002	.0024	8.2678	8.2664	.0007	.0007	.0013	.0013
	20		8.4646	8.4634	8.4658	8.4644					8.4647	8.4633				
	21	18	8.8583	8.8571	8.8595	8.8581	.0001	.0018	.0002	.0024	8.8584	8.8570	.0007	.0007	.0013	.0013
	22		9.4488	9.4476	9.4500	9.4486	.0001	.0018	.0002	.0024	9.4489	9.4475	.0007	.0007	.0013	.0013

*The housing fits given in this table are those which would result if the bearing diameters and housing bores were to vary the full allowable limits. Actually, bearing diameters are ground uniformly close to the maximum and with housings properly bored, fits well within the limits given will be obtained in practice. Reproduced with permission from Vol. 1, *New Departure Hand Book*.

TABLE 29
Twist Drill Sizes*

| \multicolumn{4}{c|}{NUMBER SIZES} | \multicolumn{2}{c}{LETTER SIZES} |

No. size	Decimal equivalent	No. size	Decimal equivalent	Size letter	Decimal equivalent
1	.2280	41	.0960	A	.234
2	.2210	42	.0935	B	.238
3	.2130	43	.0890	C	.242
4	.2090	44	.0860	D	.246
5	.2055	45	.0820	E	.250
6	.2040	46	.0810	F	.257
7	.2010	47	.0785	G	.261
8	.1990	48	.0760	H	.266
9	.1960	49	.0730	I	.272
10	.1935	50	.0700	J	.277
11	.1910	51	.0670	K	.281
12	.1890	52	.0635	L	.290
13	.1850	53	.0595	M	.295
14	.1820	54	.0550	N	.302
15	.1800	55	.0520	O	.316
16	.1770	56	.0465	P	.323
17	.1730	57	.0430	Q	.332
18	.1695	58	.0420	R	.339
19	.1660	59	.0410	S	.348
20	.1610	60	.0400	T	.358
21	.1590	61	.0390	U	.368
22	.1570	62	.0380	V	.377
23	.1540	63	.0370	W	.386
24	.1520	64	.0360	X	.397
25	.1495	65	.0350	Y	.404
26	.1470	66	.0330	Z	.413
27	.1440	67	.0320		
28	.1405	68	.0310		
29	.1360	69	.0292		
30	.1285	70	.0280		
31	.1200	71	.0260		
32	.1160	72	.0250		
33	.1130	73	.0240		
34	.1110	74	.0225		
35	.1100	75	.0210		
36	.1065	76	.0200		
37	.1040	77	.0180		
38	.1015	78	.0160		
39	.0995	79	.0145		
40	.0980	80	.0135		

* Fraction-size drills range in size from one-sixteenth—4 in. and over in diameter—by sixty-fourths.

TABLE 30
Standard Wire and Sheet-Metal Gages*

GAGE NUMBER	(A) BROWN & SHARPE OR AMERICAN	(B) AMERICAN STEEL & WIRE CO.	(C) PIANO WIRE	(E) U.S. ST'D.	GAGE NUMBER
0000000	.6513	.4900	—	.5000	0000000
000000	.5800	.4615	.004	.4688	000000
00000	.5165	.4305	.005	.4375	00000
0000	.4600	.3938	.006	.4063	0000
000	.4096	.3625	.007	.3750	000
00	.3648	.3310	.008	.3438	00
0	.3249	.3065	.009	.3125	0
1	.2893	.2830	.010	.2813	1
2	.2576	.2625	.011	.2656	2
3	.2294	.2437	.012	.2500	3
4	.2043	.2253	.013	.2344	4
5	.1819	.2070	.014	.2188	5
6	.1620	.1920	.016	.2031	6
7	.1443	.1770	.018	.1875	7
8	.1285	.1620	.020	.1719	8
9	.1144	.1483	.022	.1563	9
10	.1019	.1350	.024	.1406	10
11	.0907	.1205	.026	.1250	11
12	.0808	.1055	.029	.1094	12
13	.0720	.0915	.031	.0938	13
14	.0641	.0800	.033	.0781	14
15	.0571	.0720	.035	.0703	15
16	.0508	.0625	.037	.0625	16
17	.0453	.0540	.039	.0563	17
18	.0403	.0475	.041	.0500	18
19	.0359	.0410	.043	.0438	19
20	.0320	.0348	.045	.0375	20
21	.0285	.0317	.047	.0344	21
22	.0253	.0286	.049	.0313	22
23	.0226	.0258	.051	.0281	23
24	.0201	.0230	.055	.0250	24
25	.0179	.0204	.059	.0219	25
26	.0159	.0181	.063	.0188	26
27	.0142	.0173	.067	.0172	27
28	.0126	.0162	.071	.0156	28
29	.0113	.0150	.075	.0141	29
30	.0100	.0140	.080	.0125	30
31	.0089	.0132	.085	.0109	31
32	.0080	.0128	.090	.0102	32
33	.0071	.0118	.095	.0094	33
34	.0063	.0104	.100	.0086	34
35	.0056	.0095	.106	.0078	35
36	.0050	.0090	.112	.0070	36
37	.0045	.0085	.118	.0066	37
38	.0040	.0080	.124	.0063	38
39	.0035	.0075	.130	—	39
40	.0031	.0070	.138	—	40

* Dimensions in decimal parts of an inch.
(A) Standard in United States for sheet metal and wire (except steel and iron).
(B) Standard for iron and steel wire (U.S. Steel Wire Gage).
(C) American Steel and Wire Company's music (or piano) wire gage sizes. Recognized by U.S. Bureau of Standards.
(E) U.S. Standard for iron and steel plate. However, plate is now generally specified by its thickness in decimals of an inch.

TABLE 31
Trigonometric Functions

ANGLE	SINE	COSINE	TAN	CO-TAN	ANGLE
0°	0.0000	1.0000	0.0000	∞	90°
1°	0.0175	0.9998	0.0175	57.290	89°
2°	.0349	.9994	.0349	28.636	88°
3°	.0523	.9986	.0524	19.081	87°
4°	.0698	.9976	.0699	14.301	86°
5°	.0872	.9962	.0875	11.430	85°
6°	.1045	.9945	.1051	9.5144	84°
7°	.1219	.9925	.1228	8.1443	83°
8°	.1392	.9903	.1405	7.1154	82°
9°	.1564	.9877	.1584	6.3138	81°
10°	.1736	.9848	.1763	5.6713	80°
11°	.1908	.9816	.1944	5.1446	79°
12°	.2079	.9781	.2126	4.7046	78°
13°	.2250	.9744	.2309	4.3315	77°
14°	.2419	.9703	.2493	4.0108	76°
15°	.2588	.9659	.2679	3.7321	75°
16°	.2756	.9613	.2867	3.4874	74°
17°	.2924	.9563	.3057	3.2709	73°
18°	.3090	.9511	.3249	3.0777	72°
19°	.3256	.9455	.3443	2.9042	71°
20°	.3420	.9397	.3640	2.7475	70°
21°	.3584	.9336	.3839	2.6051	69°
22°	.3746	.9272	.4040	2.4751	68°
23°	.3907	.9205	.4245	2.3559	67°
24°	.4067	.9135	.4452	2.2460	66°
25°	.4226	.9063	.4663	2.1445	65°
26°	.4384	.8988	.4877	2.0503	64°
27°	.4540	.8910	.5095	1.9626	63°
28°	.4695	.8829	.5317	1.8807	62°
29°	.4848	.8746	.5543	1.8040	61°
30°	.5000	.8660	.5774	1.7321	60°
31°	.5150	.8572	.6009	1.6643	59°
32°	.5299	.8480	.6249	1.6003	58°
33°	.5446	.8387	.6494	1.5399	57°
34°	.5592	.8290	.6745	1.4826	56°
35°	.5736	.8192	.7002	1.4281	55°
36°	.5878	.8090	.7265	1.3764	54°
37°	.6018	.7986	.7536	1.3270	53°
38°	.6157	.7880	.7813	1.2799	52°
39°	.6293	.7771	.8098	1.2349	51°
40°	.6428	.7660	.8391	1.1918	50°
41°	.6561	.7547	.8693	1.1504	49°
42°	.6691	.7431	.9004	1.1106	48°
43°	.6820	.7314	.9325	1.0724	47°
44°	.6947	.7193	.9657	1.0355	46°
45°	.7071	.7071	1.0000	1.0000	45°
ANGLE	COSINE	SINE	CO-TAN	TAN	ANGLE

TABLE 32
Table of Chords*

DEGREES	0′	10′	20′	30′	40′	50′
0	.0000	.0029	.0058	.0087	.0116	.0145
1	.0174	.0204	.0233	.0202	.0291	.0320
2	.0349	.0378	.0407	.0436	.0465	.0494
3	.0523	.0553	.0582	.0611	.0640	.0669
4	.0698	.0727	.0756	.0785	.0814	.0843
5	.0872	.0901	.0930	.0959	.0988	.1017
6	.1047	.1076	.1105	.1134	.1163	.1192
7	.1221	.1250	.1279	.1308	.1337	.1366
8	.1395	.1424	.1453	.1482	.1511	.1540
9	.1569	.1598	.1627	.1656	.1685	.1714
10	.1743	.1772	.1801	.1830	.1859	.1888
11	.1917	.1946	.1975	.2004	.2033	.2062
12	.2090	.2119	.2148	.2177	.2206	.2235
13	.2264	.2293	.2322	.2351	.2380	.2409
14	.2437	.2466	.2495	.2524	.2553	.2582
15	.2610	.2639	.2668	.2697	.2726	.2755
16	.2783	.2812	.2841	.2870	.2899	.2927
17	.2956	.2985	.3014	.3042	.3071	.3100
18	.3129	.3157	.3186	.3215	.3243	.3272
19	.3301	.3330	.3358	.3387	.3416	.3444
20	.3473	.3502	.3530	.3559	.3587	.3616
21	.3645	.3673	.3702	.3730	.3759	.3788
22	.3816	.3845	.3873	.3902	.3930	.3959
23	.3987	.4016	.4044	.4073	.4101	.4130
24	.4158	.4187	.4215	.4243	.4272	.4300
25	.4329	.4357	.4385	.4414	.4442	.4471
26	.4499	.4527	.4556	.4584	.4612	.4641
27	.4669	.4697	.4725	.4754	.4782	.4810
28	.4838	.4867	.4895	.4923	.4951	.4979
29	.5008	.5036	.5064	.5092	.5120	.5148
30	.5176	.5204	.5232	.5261	.5289	.5317
31	.5345	.5373	.5401	.5429	.5457	.5485
32	.5513	.5541	.5569	.5596	.5624	.5652
33	.5680	.5708	.5736	.5764	.5792	.5820
34	.5847	.5875	.5903	.5931	.5959	.5986
35	.6014	.6042	.6069	.6097	.6125	.6153
36	.6180	.6208	.6236	.6263	.6291	.6318
37	.6346	.6374	.6401	.6429	.6456	.6484
38	.6511	.6539	.6566	.6594	.6621	.6649
39	.6676	.6703	.6731	.6758	.6786	.6813
40	.6840	.6868	.6895	.6922	.6950	.6977
41	.7004	.7031	.7059	.7086	.7113	.7140
42	.7167	.7194	.7222	.7249	.7276	.7303
43	.7330	.7357	.7384	.7411	.7438	.7465
44	.7492	.7519	.7546	.7573	.7600	.7627
45	.7654	.7680	.7707	.7734	.7761	.7788

Chord AB is tabulated

* Tabulated values are chord lengths of arcs of unit radius subtending the specified angles.
Use multiples for accuracy.

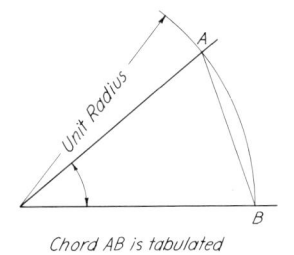

ABBREVIATIONS AND SYMBOLS*

alternating current	AC	lateral	LAT
aluminum	AL	long	LG
American Standard	AMER STD	longitude	LONG.
approved	APPD	linear	LIN
average	AVG	machine	MACH
Babbitt	BAB	malleable iron	MI
ball bearing	BB	material	MATL
brass	BRS	maximum	MAX
Brinell hardness number	BHN	meter	M
bronze	BRZ	miles	MI
Brown & Sharpe	B & S	millimeter	MM
cast iron	CI	miles per hour	MPH
center line	CL or ℄	minimum	MIN
center to center	C to C	minute (angular measure)	′ or MIN
centimeter	CM	minute (time)	MIN
chemical	CHEM	outside diameter	OD
circular	CIR	pattern	PATT
circular pitch	CP	phosphor bronze	PH BRZ
copper	COP	piece	PC
cold-rolled steel	CRS	pitch	P
counterbore	CBORE	pitch diameter	PD
countersink	CSK	plate	PL
cubic	CU	pound	# or LB
cubic inch	CU IN	pounds per square foot	PSF
cubic foot	CU FT	pounds per square inch	PSI
cubic yard	CU YD	Pratt & Whitney	P & W
cylinder	CYL	quantity	QTY
degree	DEG or °	radius	R or RAD
diameter	DIA	required	REQD
diagonal	DIAG	revolution per minute	RPM
diametral pitch	DP	right hand	RH
direct current	DC	round	RD
drawing	DWG	round bar	φ
drawn	DR	screw	SCR
detail drawing	DET DWG	second (time)	SEC
effective	EFF	second (angular measure)	″
electric	ELEC	section	SECT
engineer	ENGR	Society of Automotive Engineers	SAE
external	EXT	square	SQ
fabricate	FAB	square inch	SQ IN
fillister	FIL	square foot	SQ FT
finish	FIN.	standard	STD
foot	′ or FT	steel	STL
gallon	GAL	steel casting	STL CSTG
galvanized iron	GI	thousand	M
grind	GRD	ton	TON
harden	HDN	thread	THD
hexagon	HEX	traced	TR
horsepower	HP	volt	V
hour	HR	watt	W
impregnate	IMPREG	weight	WT
inch	″ or IN.	Woodruff	WDF
inside diameter	ID	wrought iron	WI
internal	INT	yard	YD
left hand	LH	year	YR

*Only those abbreviations that are commonly used on engineering drawings have been given in the list above. These have been selected from the long and comprehensive list given in ASA Z32.13–1950. The professional draftsman should have this standard close at hand for use when needed.

AMERICAN NATIONAL STANDARDS*

A few of the more than 500 standards approved by the American National Standards Institute are listed below. Copies may be obtained from the ANS Sales Department at 1430 Broadway, New York, N.Y. 10018.

B1.1-1960	Unified and American Screw Threads for Screws, Bolts, Nuts, and Other Threaded Parts
B1.5-1952	Acme Screw Threads
B1.8-1952	Stub Acme Screw Threads
B1.9-1953	Buttress Screw Threads
B2.1-1960	Pipe Threads
B2.4-1966	Hose Coupling Screw Threads
B4.1-1967	Preferred Limits and Fits for Cylindrical Parts
B5.10-1963	Machine Tapers, Self-Holding and Steep Taper Series
B5.15-1960	Involute Splines, Side Bearing
B5.20-1958	Machine Pins
B16.1-1967	Cast-Iron Pipe Flanges and Flanged Fittings, Class 25, 125, 250, and 800 lb
B16.3-1963	Malleable-Iron Screwed Fittings, 150 lb
B16.4-1963	Cast-Iron Screwed Fittings for Maximum WSP of 125 and 250 lb
B16.5-1968	Steel Pipe Flanges and Flanged Fittings
B16.9-1964	Steel Butt-Welding Fittings
B17.1-1967	Shafting and Stock Keys
B17.2-1967	Woodruff Keys and Keyseats
B18.1-1965	Small Solid Rivets
B18.2.1-1965	Square and Hex Bolts and Screws
B18.2.2-1965	Square and Hex Nuts
B18.3-1961	Socket Set Screws and Socket-Head Cap Screws
B18.4-1960	Large Rivets
B18.5-1959	Round-Head Bolts
B18.6.2-1956	Hexagon-Head Cap Screws, Slotted-Head Cap Screws, Square-Head Set Screws, and Slotted Headless Set Screws
B36.1-1956	Welded and Seamless Pipe (ASTM A53-44)
B36.2-1956	Welded Wrought-Iron Pipe
B36.10-1959	Wrought-Iron and Wrought-Steel Pipe
B48.1-1933	Inch-Millimeter Conversion for Industrial Use
B94.6-1966	Knurling
Y14.1-1957	Size and Format
Y14.2-1957	Line Conventions, Sectioning, and Lettering
Y14.3-1957	Projections
Y14.4-1957	Pictorial Drawing
Y14.5-1966	Dimensioning and Notes
Y14.6-1957	Screw Threads
Y14.7-1958	Gears, Splines, and Serrations
Y14.8- —	Castings (In preparation)
Y14.9-1958	Forgings
Y14.10-1959	Metal Stampings
Y14.11-1958	Plastics
Y14.12- —	Die Castings } (In preparation)
Y14.13- —	Springs, Helical and Flat }

*Formerly the ASA and USASI Standards.

Y14.14-1961	Mechanical Assemblies
Y14.15-1966	Electrical and Electronics Diagrams
Y14.16- —	Tools, Dies, and Gages (In preparation)
Y14.17-1966	Fluid Power Diagrams
Y14.18- —	Drawings for Optical Parts
Y14.19- —	Engineering Drawings for Photographic Reproduction ⎫ (In preparation)
Y14.20- —	Extruded Products Drawings ⎭

GRAPHICAL AND LETTER SYMBOLS

Y10.2-1958	Hydraulics (Letter)
Y10.4-1957	Heat and Thermodynamics (Letter)
Y10.7-1954	Aeronautical Sciences (Letter)
Y10.9-1953	Radio (Letter)
Y10.10-1953	Meterology (Letter)
Y10.11-1959	Acoustics (Letter)
Y10.12-1961	Chemical Engineering (Letter)
Y10.14-1959	Rocket Propulsion (Letter)
Y10.15-1958	Petroleum Reservoir Engineering and Electric Logging (Letter)
Y10.16-1964	Shell Theory (Letter)
Y10.17-1961	Guide for Selecting Greek Letters Used as Letter Symbols for Engineering Mathematics (Letter)
Y15.2-1960	Time-Series Charts, Manual of Design
Y32.2-1962	Electrical Diagrams (Graphical)
Y32.3-1959	Welding (Graphical)
Y32.4-1955	Plumbing (Graphical)
Y32.7-1957	Use on Railroad Maps and Profiles (Graphical)
Y32.10-1967	Fluid Power Diagrams (Graphical)
Y32.11-1961	Process Flow Diagrams in Petroleum and Chemical Industries (Graphical)
Y32.12-1960	Metallizing Symbols (Graphical)
Y32.17-1962	Nondestructive Testing Symbols (Graphical)
Z10.1-1941	Abbreviations for Scientific and Engineering Terms (Letter)
Z10.3-1948	Mechanics for Solid Bodies (Letter)*
Z10.6-1948	Physics (Letter)*
Z10.8-1949	Structural Analysis (Letter)*
Z32.2.3-1953	Pipe Fittings, Valves, and Piping (Graphical)*
Z32.2.4-1949	Heating, Ventilating, and Air Conditioning (Graphical)*
Z32.2.6-1956	Heat-Power Apparatus (Graphical)*
Z32.13-1950	Abbreviations for Use on Drawings (Graphical)*
Z15.3-1943	Engineering and Scientific Graphs for Publications

*Y is the new letter assigned to standards for abbreviations, charts and graphs, drawings, graphical symbols, and letter symbols. The Z will be changed to Y as the standards are revised and reaffirmed.

BIBLIOGRAPHY
OF ENGINEERING DRAWING AND ALLIED SUBJECTS

Aeronautical Drafting and Engineering

Anderson, N. H., *Aircraft Layout and Detail Design,* 2nd ed., New York: McGraw-Hill.
Katz, H. H., *Aircraft Drafting,* New York: Macmillan.
LeMaster, C. A., *Aircraft Sheet Metal Work,* Chicago: American Technical Society.

Architectural Drawing

Hornung, W. J., *Architectural Drafting,* Englewood Cliffs, N.J.: Prentice-Hall.
Muller, E. J., *Architectural Drawing,* Englewood Cliffs, N.J.: Prentice-Hall.
Ramsey, C. G., and H. R. Sleeper, *Architectural Graphic Standards,* New York: Wiley.

Blueprint Reading

Bush, G. F., *Reading Engineering Drawings,* New York: Wiley.
DeVette, W. A., and D. E. Kellogg, *Blueprint Reading for the Metal Trades,* Milwaukee: Bruce.
Dick, A. A., *Blueprint Reading,* New York: Ronald.
Dwight, C., *Blueprint Reading in the Machine Industries,* New York: McGraw-Hill.
Heine, G. M., and C. H. Dunlap, *How to Read Electrical Blueprints,* Chicago: American Technical Society.
Hornung, W. J. *Blueprint Reading,* Englewood Cliffs, N.J.: Prentice-Hall.
Lincoln Electric Co., *Simple Blueprint Reading,* Cleveland.
Norcross, C., *Aircraft Blueprints and How to Read Them,* New York: McGraw-Hill.
Owens, A. A., and B. F. Slingluff, *How to Read Blueprints,* New York: Holt.
Spencer, H. C., and H. E. Grant, *Blueprint Language of the Machine Industries,* New York: Macmillan.
Thayer, H. R., *Blueprint Reading and Sketching,* New York: McGraw-Hill.
Weir, J. J., *Blueprint Reading,* New York: McGraw-Hill.

Castings

Campbell, H. I., *Metal Castings,* New York: Wiley.
Morris, J. L., *Metal Castings,* Englewood Cliffs, N.J.: Prentice-Hall.

Catalogs (Instruments)

Alteneder, Theo., and Sons, Philadelphia, Pa.
Boston Gear Works, Inc., Chicago, Ill. (Gears, etc).
Crane Co., Chicago, Ill. (Pipe Fittings)
Elliott, B. K., Co., Pittsburgh, Pa.
Eugene Dietzgen Co., Chicago, Ill.
Frederic Post Co., Chicago, Ill.
Keuffel & Esser Co., Hoboken, N.J.
New Departure, Bristol, Conn. (Ball-Bearing Handbook)
Timken Roller Bearing Co., Canton, Ohio. (Roller Bearings)

Computer Graphics Films

DAC-1 (color), General Motors Corporation, Public Relations Staff, Film Library, Detroit, Michigan 48202.
Graphic Data Processing, International Business Machines Corp., available through local IBM representative.
Sketchpad, Lincoln Laboratories, Massachusetts Institute of Technology, Lexington, Massachusetts.

Computers–Data Processing Systems

Bernstein, Jeremy, *The Analytical Engine,* New York: Random House.
Englebardt, S. L., *Computers,* New York: Pyramid.
Fetter, W. A., *Computer Graphics in Communication,* New York: McGraw-Hill.
Hagg, J. N., *Comprehensive Fortran Programming,* New York: Hayden.
International Business Machines Corp., *1620 Drafting System.*
———, *Introduction to Data Processing Systems.*

Lohberg, Rolf and Theo Lutz, *Electronic Brains,* New York: Sterling.
Thornhill, R. B., Engineering Graphics and Numerical Control, New York: McGraw-Hill.

Descriptive Geometry

Johnson, L. O., and I. Wladaver, *Elements of Descriptive Geometry,* Englewood Cliffs, N.J.: Prentice-Hall.
Paré, E. G., R. O. Loving, and I. L. Hill, *Descriptive Geometry,* 2nd ed., New York: Macmillan.
Slaby, S. M., *Three-Dimensional Descriptive Geometry,* New York: Harcourt.
Street, W. E., *Technical Descriptive Geometry,* New York: Van Nostrand.
Warner, F. M., and M. McNeary, *Applied Descriptive Geometry,* 5th ed., New York: McGraw-Hill.
Watts, E. F., and J. T. Rule, *Descriptive Geometry,* Englewood Cliffs, N.J.: Prentice-Hall.
Wellman, B. L., *Technical Descriptive Geometry,* 2nd ed., New York: McGraw-Hill.

Descriptive Geometry Problems

Paré, E. G., and others, *Descriptive Geometry Worksheets,* New York: Macmillan.
Wiedhaas, E. R., *Applied Descriptive Geometry Problems,* New York: McGraw-Hill.

Die Casting

Chase, H., *Die Castings,* New York: Wiley.

Electrical Drawing

Baer, C. J., *Electrical and Electronic Drawing,* New York: McGraw-Hill.
Bishop, C. C., C. T. Gilliam, and others, *Electrical Drafting and Design,* 3rd ed., New York: McGraw-Hill.
Carini, L. F. D., *Drafting for Electronics,* New York: McGraw-Hill.
Kuller, K. K., *Electronics Drafting,* New York: McGraw-Hill.
Mark, D., *How to Read Schematic Diagrams,* New York: Rider.
Raskhodoff, N. M., *Electronic Drafting Handbook,* New York: Macmillan.
Shiers, G., *Electronic Drafting,* Englewood Cliffs, N.J.: Prentice-Hall.
———, *Electronic Drafting Techniques and Exercises,* Englewood Cliffs, N.J.: Prentice-Hall.
Van Gieson, D. W., *Electrical Drafting,* New York: McGraw-Hill.

Engineering Design

Alger, J. R., and C. V. Hays, *Creative Synthesis in Design,* Englewood Cliffs, N.J.: Prentice-Hall.
Buhl, H. R., *Creative Engineering Design,* Ames, Iowa: Iowa State University Press.
Dixon, J. R., *Design Engineering,* New York: McGraw-Hill.
Edel, D. H., *Introduction to Creative Design,* Englewood Cliffs, N.J.: Prentice-Hall.
Hill, P. H., *Design Projects and Notes for Engineering Graphics and Design,* New York: Macmillan.
Wellman, L. B., *Introduction to Graphical Analysis and Design,* New York: McGraw-Hill.
Woodson, T. T., *Introduction to Engineering Design,* New York: McGraw-Hill.

Engineering Graphics

Black, E. D., *Graphical Communication,* New York: McGraw-Hill.
Earle, J. H., *Engineering Design Graphics,* Reading, Mass.: Addison-Wesley.
French, T. E., and C. J. Vierck, *Engineering Drawing,* 10th ed., New York: McGraw-Hill.
Giesecke, F. E., and others, *Technical Drawing,* 5th ed., New York: Macmillan.
Hammond, R. H., and others, *Engineering Graphics,* New York: Ronald.
Hoelscher, R. P., and C. H. Springer, *Engineering Drawing and Geometry,* 2nd ed., New York: Wiley.
Hornung, W. J., *Mechanical Drafting,* Englewood Cliffs, N.J.: Prentice-Hall.
Levens, A. S., *Graphics in Engineering and Science,* New York: Wiley.
Luzadder, W. J., *Basic Graphics for Design, Analysis, Communications, and the Computer,* Englewood Cliffs, N.J.: Prentice-Hall.
———*Fundamentos de Dibujo Para Ingenieros,* 2nd ed., Mexico, D.F.: Compañia Editorial Continental.
———*Graphics for Engineers,* India: Prentice-Hall.
———*Technical Drafting Essentials,* 2nd ed., Englewood Cliffs, N.J.: Prentice-Hall.

Rule, J. T., and S. A. Coons, *Graphics,* New York: McGraw-Hill.
Schneerer, W. F., *Programmed Graphics,* New York: McGraw-Hill.

Engineering Graphics Films (See Text Films)

Engineering Graphics Problems

Earle, J. H., *Engineering Graphics and Design Problems* (Series 1, 2 and 3), Reading, Mass.: Addison-Wesley.
Giesecke, F. E., and others, *Technical Drawing Problems,* 3rd ed., New York: Macmillan.
Johnson, L. O., and I. Wladaver, *Engineering Drawing Problems,* Englewood Cliffs, N.J.: Prentice-Hall.
Levens, A. S., and A. E. Edstrom, *Problems in Mechanical Drawing,* New York: McGraw-Hill.
Luzadder, W. J., K. E. Botkin, and F. H. Thompson, *Problems in Engineering Drawing,* 6th ed., Englewood Cliffs, N.J.: Prentice-Hall.
———, K. E. Botkin and C. J. Rogers, *Engineering Graphics Problems for Design, Analysis and Communications,* Englewood Cliffs, N.J.: Prentice-Hall.
———, and R. E. Bolles, *Problems in Drafting Fundamentals,* Englewood Cliffs, N.J.: Prentice-Hall.
Spencer, H. C., and I. L. Hill, *Technical Drawing Problems,* New York: Macmillan.
Vierck, C. J., and R. I. Hang, *Engineering Drawing Problems,* New York: McGraw-Hill.

Graphical Representation and Computation

Davis, D. S., *Empirical Equations and Nomography,* New York: McGraw-Hill.
Douglass, R. D., and D. P. Adams, *Elements of Nomography,* New York: McGraw-Hill.
Levens, A. S., *Nomography,* 2nd ed., New York: Wiley.
Lipka, J., *Graphical and Mechanical Computation,* New York: Wiley.
Robinson, A. H., *Elements of Cartography,* New York: Wiley.

Handbooks

American Institute of Steel Construction, *Steel Construction,* New York.
Crocker, S., *Piping Handbook,* 4th ed., New York: McGraw-Hill.
Kent, W., *Mechanical Engineer's Handbook,* 12th ed., New York: Wiley.
Knowlton, A. E., *Standard Handbook for Electrical Engineers,* 9th ed., New York: McGraw-Hill.
Le Grand, R., Ed., *New American Machinist's Handbook,* New York: McGraw-Hill.
McNeese, D. C., and A. L. Hoag, *Engineering and Technical Handbook,* Englewood Cliffs, N.J.: Prentice-Hall.
Marks, L. S., *Mechanical Engineers' Handbook,* 6th ed., New York: McGraw-Hill.
Oberg, E., and F. D. Jones, *Machinery's Handbook,* 17th ed., New York: Industrial Press.
O'Rourke, C. E., *General Engineering Handbook,* 2nd ed., New York: McGraw-Hill.
Perry, J. H., *Chemical Engineers' Handbook,* 4th ed., New York: McGraw-Hill.
Wilson, F. W., Ed., *Tool Engineers' Handbook,* 2nd ed., New York: McGraw-Hill.

Jig and Fixture Design

Colvin, F. H., and L. L. Haas, *Jigs and Fixtures,* 5th ed., New York: McGraw-Hill.
Hinman, C. W., *Die Engineering Layouts and Formulas,* New York: McGraw-Hill.
Jones, F. D., *Jig and Fixture Design,* New York: Industrial Press.

Kinematics—Machine Design

Faires, V. M., *Design of Machine Elements,* 3rd ed., New York: Macmillan.
Hinkle, R. T., *Kinematics of Machines,* Englewood Cliffs, N.J.: Prentice-Hall.
Lent, D., *Analysis and Design of Mechanisms,* Englewood Cliffs, N.J.: Prentice-Hall.
Maleev, V. L., *Machine Design,* 3rd ed., Scranton, Pa.: International.
Norman, C. A., E. S. Ault, and I. F. Zarobsky, *Fundamentals of Machine Design,* New York: Macmillan.
Spotts, M. F., *Design of Machine Elements,* 2nd ed., Englewood Cliffs, N.J.: Prentice-Hall.

Lettering

De Garmo, E. P., and F. Jonassen, *Technical Lettering,* New York: Macmillan.

Machine Drawing

Svensen, C. L., *Machine Drawing,* 3rd ed., New York: Van Nostrand-Reinhold.

Map and Topographic Drawing

Sloane, R. C., and I. M. Montz, *Elements of Topographic Drawing,* 2nd ed., New York: McGraw-Hill.

Numerical Control

International Business Machines Corp., *Automatic Programming of Machine Tools,* Poughkeepsie, N.Y.

Patent Drawing

Publications of U.S. Government Printing Office, Washington, D.C.:
Guide for Patent Draftsmen
Manual of Classification
Patent Laws
Patents and Inventions, an Information Aid for Inventors
Rules of Practice of the U.S. Patent Office

Pattern Design

Hall, B. R., and H. E. Kiley, *Pattern Design,* Scranton, Pa.: International.

Perspective

Lawson, P. J., *Practical Perspective Drawing,* New York: McGraw-Hill.
Turner, W. W., *Simplified Perspective,* New York: Ronald.

Pipe

Crocker, S., *Piping Hand Book,* 4th ed., New York: McGraw-Hill.
Day, L. J., *Standard Plumbing Details,* New York: Wiley.
Thompson, C. H., *Fundamentals of Pipe Drafting,* New York: Wiley.

Sheet-Metal Work

Atkins, E. A., *Practical Sheet and Plate Metal Work,* New York: Pitman.
Frazer, R. H., and O. Berthiaume, *Practical Aircraft Sheet-metal Work,* New York: McGraw-Hill.
Norcross, C., and J. D. Quinn, *How to Do Aircraft Sheetmetal Work,* New York: McGraw-Hill.
O'Rourke, F. J., *Sheet-metal Pattern Drafting,* New York: McGraw-Hill.

Shop Practice

Begeman, M. L., *Manufacturing Processes,* 4th ed., New York: Wiley.
Boston, O. W., *Metal Processing,* 2nd ed., New York: Wiley.
Doyle, L. E., *Metal Machining,* Englewood Cliffs, N.J.: Prentice-Hall.
———, J. L. Leach, J. L. Morris, and G. F. Schrader, *Manufacturing Processes and Materials for Engineers,* Englewood Cliffs, N.J.: Prentice-Hall.
Marek, C. T., *Fundamentals in the Production and Design of Castings,* New York: Wiley.
Stieri, E., *Fundamentals of Machine Shop Practice,* Englewood Cliffs, N.J.: Prentice-Hall.
Young, J. F., *Materials and Processes,* 2nd ed., New York: Wiley.

Sketching

Katz, H., *Technical Sketching and Visualization for Engineers,* New York: Macmillan.
Turner, W. W., *Freehand Sketching for Engineers,* New York: Ronald.
Zipprich, A. E., *Freehand Drafting for Technical Sketching,* 3rd ed., New York: Van Nostrand-Reinhold.

Slide Rule

Arnold, J. N., *The Slide Rule,* Englewood Cliffs, N.J.: Prentice-Hall.

Structural Drafting

American Institute of Steel Construction, *Structural Steel Detailing,* New York.
Bishop, C. T., *Structural Drafting,* New York: Wiley.
Lothers, S. E., *Design in Structural Steel,* Englewood Cliffs, N.J.: Prentice-Hall.

Technical Dictionary

Tweney, C. F., and L. E. C. Hughes, *Chamber's Technical Dictionary,* 3rd rev. ed., New York: Macmillan.

Technical Illustration

Gibby, J. C., *Technical Illustration,* Chicago: American Technical Society.

Thomas, T. A., *Technical Illustration,* New York: McGraw-Hill.

Text Films

Engineering Drawing, 7 films, 6 strips, New York: McGraw-Hill.

Engineering Drawing, 16 films. Purdue University.*

Tool Design

Cole, C. B., *Tool Design,* Chicago: American Technical Society.

Donaldson, C., and G. H. LeCain, *Tool Design,* 2nd ed., New York: Harper & Row.

Doyle, L. E., *Tool Engineering, Analysis and Procedure,* Englewood Cliffs, N.J.: Prentice-Hall.

Jeffries, W. R., *Tool Design,* Englewood Cliffs, N.J.: Prentice-Hall.

Welding

Lincoln Electric Co., *Simple Blueprint Reading,* Cleveland.

———, *Procedure Handbook of Arc Welding Design and Practice,* Cleveland.

Morris, J. L., *Welding Processes and Procedures,* Englewood Cliffs, N.J.: Prentice-Hall.

———, *Welding Principles for Engineers,* Englewood Cliffs, N.J.: Prentice-Hall.

*These films are available on a rental basis or they may be purchased from Audio-Visual Center, Memorial Center, Purdue University, West Lafayette, Indiana 47907.

INDEX

Abscissa, variables for, 598
Acme threads, 332, 337
Addition of forces, 198–200
Adjustable stop pins, 518
Adjustable stop screws, 517
Adjustment plates, 73
Airbrushes, 282–283
Air-cushion vehicles, 184
ALGOL, 435
Aligned views, 107, 108
Alignment charts, 609–621
    construction of, 610–611
    definitions, 611
    forms of, 610
    three-scale, 617–618
Alternate positions, 111
American-British unified thread, 328
American Institute of Steel Construction, 547
American National Standard Preferred Limits and Fits for Cylindrical Parts, 369–370
American National Standards Institute, 36, 37–38, 320, 530
    on bolts and nuts, 337–338
    on conventional breaks, 110–111
    on limit dimensions, 369
    on line symbols, 46
    on pipe thread, 492–493
    thread symbols, 331–333
    welding symbols, 509, 510
American Society of Mechanical Engineers, 599, 600–601
American Standards Association, 1
Ames lettering instrument, 8, 10
Angle bracket, dimensioning, 359, 360
Angles:
    between a line and a plane, 194–195
    between two intersecting oblique lines, 195–196
    between two nonintersecting lines, 195

Angles (*cont.*)
    to bisect, 51–52
    constructing:
        chord method, 53–54
        to a given angle, 53
        tangent method, 53
    convenient, 128
    dihedral, 169, 170
        between two planes, 196–197
    in isometric drawing, 255
    projection of, 93–94
        oblique, 266
    protractor, 27
    to trisect, 52
Angular dimensioning, 360, 379
Angular perspective, 273, 274–276
    sketches in, 297
Angular tolerances, 374, 376, 377
Arches, elliptical, 73
Archimedes' spiral, 69
Architects' scales, 35, 36–37
Architectural drawings, 565–580
    detail, 574
    dimensioning, 576–579
    elevations, 570
    lettering, 579–580
    notes, 579
    plans, 567–570
    plot plan, 570–571, 572
    preliminary sketches, 566
    preliminary studies, 565–566
    presentation, 566–567
    sections, 571–572
        wall, 572–574
    special features, 574–576
    symbols, 576
    working, 567
Arcs:
    circular, 57–59
        to approximate a curve with, 61

Arcs (*cont.*)
    dimensioning, 360
    having an inaccessible center, 60
    to lay off approximate length of, 62
    to lay off a specified length, 62
    tangent, 57
Arc welding, 505, 509
Area charts, 604–605
Areas, meaning of, 99
Areo threads, 344
Arrowheads, 355, 356
Arrow-side welds, 507
Artist's pencils, 27
Assembly drawings, 392, 397, 400–401
    diagram, 402–404
    exploded pictorial, 402, 403
    installation, 401–402
    outline, 402
    working, 397
Asymptotes, 68
Automated drafting, 445–460, 560
Automated photodraft systems, 461–463
Automobile-body design, 453, 456
    industrial practice in, 643
Auxiliary planes, 163
Auxiliary views, 163, 183, 237–238
    bilateral, 168, 169
    constructing, 169
    curved lines in, 168, 170
    dihedral angles, 169, 170
    line of intersection, 172–173
    partial views and, 165, 169–171
    primary, 163–173
    principal views and, 171, 172
    projection of a curved boundary, 168–169
    secondary, 173–175
    symmetrical, 166–167, 168
    true length of a line, 173
    types of, 163–166
    unilateral, 167–168

INDEX

Auxiliary views (*cont.*)
  unsymmetrical, 166
  use of, 163
Axes:
  horizontal:
    perpendicular to the frontal plane, 104
    perpendicular to the profile plane, 104
  isometric, 259
  locating, 599–600
  receding, 267
  vertical, revolution about, 103–104
Axonometric projection, 79, 250–263
  angles, 255
  circle, 255–259
  circle arcs, 255–259
  coordinate construction method, 254–255
  dimetric, 260–263
  division of, 250–252
  isometric, 252–253, 261–263
  isometric axes, 259
  isometric scale, 252
  isometric sectional views, 259–260
  nonisometric lines, 253–254
  trimetric, 261–263

Ball bearings, 487–488
Bar charts, 604, 605
Barch-Payzant pens, 8, 9
Base circles, 479
Baseline diagrams, 541
Base-line dimensioning, 363
Beam compass, 40
Bearing of a line, 189–190
Bearings, 487–488
  ball, 487–488
  roller, 487–488
Bevel gears, 484
Bilateral auxiliary views, 168, 169
Bilateral tolerances, 373
Bill of materials, 397–400
Bisect:
  an angle, 51–52
  a straight line, 51
Bits, 436
Black and white prints, 638
Block diagrams, 532–533
Blue-line prints, 637
Blueprint machines, 636
Blueprints, 44–45, 635–636
Boeing Company, The, 459
Boltheads, 339
  violations of true projection, 106
Bolts, 344, 345
  American National Standard on, 337–338
Boring, 314, 316, 317
Boundaries:
  curved, projection of, 168–169
  elliptical, plotting, 95–96
Bow pencils, 41

Bow pens, 41
Bow's notation, 202–203
Braddock lettering triangles, 8–9, 10, 25
Breaking down method, 99
Breaks, conventional, 110–111
Brilliant points, 284
Broaching, 319–320
Brown prints, 636–637
Build-up method, 132, 136
Bushings, 518–519
Buttress threads, 337
Bytes, 437

Cabinet drawings, 267
Cables, 538–539
Cadastral maps, 585
CalComp plotters, 478
Calipers, 322
  inside, 133
  outside, 133
Cam clamps, 521
Cams, 484–485
  design of, 486–487
  disc, 485
Capital letters:
  inclined, 12–15
  vertical, 12–15
Caps, large and small in combination, 18, 19
Cap screws, 340
Cartesian coordinates, 467–468
Castings, 311–312
  die, 313
  machined, 321
Cast-iron pipes, 494–495
Center lines, 97
  parallel lines about, 52
Channels, 472
Charts, 595–606
  alignment, 609–621
    construction of, 610–611
    definitions, 611
    forms of, 610
    three-scale, 617–618
  area, 604–605
  bar, 604, 605
  chemical engineering, 605–606
  classification of, 595–596
  definitions, 611
  flow, 606
  parallel-scale, 612–617
  pictorial, 606
  pie, 604
  polar, 605
  population, 606
  qualitative, 596–597
  quantitative, 596–597
  semilogarithmic, 603
  trilinear, 605
  Z-, 618–619

Chemical engineering charts, 605–606
Chemical engineering drawings, 404
Chemistry templates, 30
Chord method to construct an angle, 53–54
Circle arcs:
  in isometric drawing, 255–259
  oblique projection, 266
Circles, 60–63
  base, 479
  concentric method to construct an ellipse, 64
  definition of, 452
  dividing into equal parts, 34
  finding center through three given points not in a straight line, 57
  involute of, 68
  in isometric drawing, 135, 255–259
  large:
    drawing, 40
    sketching, 128–130
  to lay off approximate length of the circumference of, 61–62
  line tangent to:
    at a given point on the circumference, 60
    through a given point outside the circle, 60
    two given, 61
  oblique projection, 266
  in perspective, 274, 278–279
  sketching, 128–130
  tangent, 57
Circuits:
  analysis of, 534–535
  control layouts, 537–538
  electronic computer design, 444
  printed, 542
    artwork, 542–543
    layouts, 542
Circular arcs, 57–59
  to approximate a curve with, 61
  dimensioning, 360
  having an inaccessible center, 60
  to lay off approximate length of, 62
  to lay off a specified length, 62
Circular pipes, 225
Circular pitch, 482
City maps, partial, 587
Civil engineering drawings, 404–405
Civil engineers' (chain) scales, 35, 36, 37
Clamping, 519–520
Clamps, 519–520
  cam, 521
  Y-, 72
Clearance fits, 370, 373
Clockwise revolution, 104
Cloth:
  glass, 642
  tracing, 29
COBOL, 435

Column dimensioning, 556
Communication drawings, 391–434
　alterations, 395–396
　assembly, 392, 397, 400–401
　　diagram, 402–404
　　exploded pictorial, 402, 403
　　installation, 401–402
　　outline, 402
　　working, 397
　bill of materials, 397–400
　checking, 401
　chemical engineering, 404
　civil engineering, 404–405
　corrections, 395–396
　design, 391
　detail, 393–394
　electrical engineering, 404
　forge-shop, 396
　machine, 391–393
　machine-shop, 396–397
　one-view, 394
　parts list, 397–400, 402
　pattern-shop, 396
　record strips, 394–395
　sketches, 391
　subassembly, 397
　title, 394, 400
　　contents of, 395
　title blocks, 394–395
　working, 393, 395
Compass, 39
　beam, 40
　using, 39–40
Compass lead:
　shaping, 39
　sharpening, 39
Composition in lettering, 9–11
Compressed letters, 7, 8
Compression springs, 346, 347
Computer Graphics in Communication
　(Fetter), 459
Computers, 435–445
　in automobile-body design, 453–456
　communicating with, 438
　design programs, 443
　electronic circuit design, 444
　graphics, 438–440, 443–445
　　input-output systems, 444–445
　languages of, 435, 436–437, 473
　output, 438
　plotter-prepared structural drawings, 561
　programming, 472
　storages, 437–438
　time-shared services, 472–475
　use of, 435–436
Concentric circle method to construct an
　　ellipse, 64
Concentricity, tolerance for, 376, 377
Conductor patterns, 542
Cones, 243

Cones (*cont.*)
　intersection of, 233–234, 239–240, 241–242
　oblique, 224
　　intersection of, 241
　points where a line pierces, 231–232
　right, 222
　　truncated, 223
　surface shading on, 284
Conic sections, 62–63
Connection diagrams, 538
　layouts, 540
Consecutive dimensions, 359
CONSTRUCTS System, 560
Continuous curves, 601
Contour lines, 591–593
Control circuit layouts, 537–538
Control statements, 453
Convenient angles, 128
Conventional breaks, 110–111
Conventional practices, 105–112
Conventional representation, 111–112
Convergent projection, 81
Converging projectors, 81
Coons, Professor, 444–445
Coordinate construction method, 254–255
Coordinate graphs, 603
Coordinates, Cartesian, 467–468
Coordinate tolerancing, 378
Cope, the, 311
Coplanar forces, 199, 201, 203–204
Counterboring, 315
Counterclockwise revolution, 104
Countersinking, 316
Counterweight system, 73
Couplings, 495
　force, 202
　threads for, 493
Creative sketching, 305
Creative thinking, 291–310
Cross frames, 551, 552
CRT plotting systems, 456–457
Cumulative tolerances, 374
Curved boundaries, projections of, 168–169
Curved lines:
　in auxiliary views, 168, 170
　parallel, about a curved center line, 52
Curved outlines, 96
Curves, 600–601
　to approximate with tangent circular
　　arcs, 61
　continuous, 601
　dimensioning, 363
　flexible, 27, 28
　French, 41
　involute, 68
　irregular, 42
　parabolic:
　　to construct through two given
　　　points, 66
　　to locate the directrix of, 67

Curves (*cont.*)
　　to locate the focus of, 67
　space, 96
　reverse (ogee), 59–60
　　tangent to three given lines, 60
　tooth, 479–480
Cutting-plane lines, 93
Cutting planes, 145, 150, 152
Cutting tools, 316
CV point, 271
Cycloidal system, 479, 480–481
Cycloids, 68–69, 480
Cylinders, 243
　to develop, 217–219
　dimensioning, 360, 361
　intersection of, 232–233, 238–240, 241
　oblique, 219, 220
　surface shading on, 284
Cylindrical parts, limit dimensions, 371–372

Dashed lines, 93
Data sheets, 532
Da Vinci, Leonardo, 126, 292
Dead center, 314
Decimal dimensioning, 357
Decimal scales, 38–39
　reading, 39
Decimal system, 36
　in dimensioning, 356–357
Degree composite system, 482
Descriptive geometry, 185–197
　angle between a line and a plane, 194–195
　angle between two nonintersecting lines,
　　195
　bearing of a line, 189–190
　dihedral angle between two planes, 196–
　　197
　distance between two parallel planes, 196
　edge view of an oblique plane, 191–192, 193
　parallel lines, 187–188
　perpendicular lines, 189, 190
　piercing point of a line and a plane, 193–
　　194
　point view of a line, 190–191
　principal lines of a plane, 191, 192
　projection:
　　of a plane in space, 186–187
　　of a point, 185–186
　　of a straight line, 186
　shortest distance between two skew lines,
　　197
　shortest distance from a point to a line,
　　191
　true length of a line, 188
　　oblique, 188–189
Designations:
　industrial, 538
　placement of, 536
　reference, 531–532, 536

INDEX 697

Detail drawings, 320–321
  communication, 393–394
Developments, 215–228
  frustum of a pyramid, 221, 222
  oblique cone, 224
  oblique cylinder, 219, 220
  oblique prisms, 217, 218
  practical, 216
  right cone, 222
    truncated, 223
  right cylinder, 217–219
  right pyramid, 221, 222
  right truncated prism, 216–217
  sphere, 227–228
  transition pieces, 224, 243
    approximately developable surface, 223–224, 226–227
    connecting a circular and a sphere pipe, 225–226
    connecting rectangular pipes, 224–225
    connecting two circular pipes, 225
    triangulation method, 223–224, 226–227
  true-length diagrams, 220–221
  true length of a line, 219–220
Diagram assembly drawings, 402–404
Diagrams, 529–530
  baseline, 541
  block, 532–533
  classification of, 595–596
  connection, 538
    layouts, 540
  displacement, 486
  flow, 449–450
  highway, 541–542
  ladder, 538
  point-to-point, 540–541
  schematic, 533
  stress-strain, 598
  true length, 220–221
Diametral pitch, 482
Diazo prints, 638
Die casting, 313
Die drawings, 523–524
Dies, 523–524
Digital drafting systems, 445–449
Dihedral angles, 169, 170
  between two planes, 196–197
Dimension figures, 356
Dimensioning:
  angle, 360, 379
  angle bracket, 359, 360
  architectural drawings, 576–579
  areas to avoid, 361
  base-line, 363
  circular arc, 360
  a column, 556
  contour principle of, 358
  curves, 363
  cylinders, 360, 361

Dimensioning (*cont.*)
  decimal, 357
  decimal system in, 356–357
  a dovetail slot, 365
  fractional, 356
  gears, 483
  a half-section, 366
  holes, 361, 363
  keyslots, 364
  keyways, 364
  knurls, 365
  in limited spaces, 361
  location, 354, 363
  machined cylinders, 361
  notes, 367–368
  pictorial, 267–268
  a piece with a spherical end, 361
  practices, 355–356
  procedure in, 354
  profile, 367
  slots, 364, 365
  tapers, 365
  theory of, 353
  threads, 335–336
  tongue, 365
  true-position, 378–381
    the maximum metal condition, 380–381
  weld, 508
Dimension lines, 355
  location of, 554–555
  structural, 554–555
Dimensions, 452, 453
  angular, 360
  consecutive, 359
  from datum, 367
  horizontal, 362
  limit, 369–371
    basic hole system, 372
    basic shaft system, 372–373
    for cylindrical parts, 371–372
    tolerance, 373–378
  oblique, 362
  out of scale, 367
  parallel, 358
  on piping drawings, 499
  placing, 354–355
  reference, 359
  selection of, 357–367
  size, 353–354
  structural, 555–558
  vertical, 362
Dimetric drawing, 261
Dimetric projection, 260–263
Directrix of a parabolic curve, 67
Disc cams, 485
Displacement diagrams, 486
Ditto lines, 111
Dividers, 40
  adjusting, 40

Dividers (*cont.*)
  proportional, 29
  use of, 40–41
Double-curved surfaces, 71, 215
Double-groove welds, 509
Dovetail slots, dimensioning, 365
Draft, 312
Drafting:
  automated, 445–460, 560
  essential equipment, 25
Drawing equipment, 25–60
Drill presses, 315–316
Drop pencils, 27, 28
Drop pens, 27, 28
Dryseal pipe threads, 493–494

Eckhart, L., 261
Edco pens, 8, 9
Electrical engineering drawings, 404
Electric pencils, 564
Electrodes, 72
Electronic circuit design, 444
Electronic drawings, 529–545
  baseline diagrams, 541
  block diagrams, 532–533
  cables, 538–539
  circuit analysis, 534–535
  conductor patterns, 542
  connection diagrams, 538
    layouts, 540
  control circuit layouts, 537–538
  data sheets, 532
  drawing notes, 536–537
  graphical standards, 530–531
  graphical symbols, 531
  highway diagrams, 541–542
  industrial designations, 538
  industrial schematics, 537
  modular layouts, 535
  placement of designations, 536
  point-to-point diagrams, 540–541
  printed circuits, 542
    artwork, 542–543
    layouts, 542
  reference designations, 531–532, 536
  schematic diagrams, 533
  trial layouts, 535–536
  wire coding, 539
  wires, 538–539
  wiring methods, 539–540
Electronics Engineers, Inc., 530
Electronics Industry Association (EIA), 467, 472, 530
Electro symbol templates, 30
Elevation drawings, 570, 571
Ellipses, 49, 63–65
  to construct:
    concentric circle method, 64

Ellipses (*cont.*)
    foci method, 63
    four-center method, 64
    parallelogram method, 64–65
    trammel method, 63–64
  sketching, 130
  tangent to:
    at any given point from a given point outside, 65
Elliptical arches, 73
Elliptical boundaries, plotting, 95–96
Elliptical lunar orbits, 74
Empirical equations, 607–609
End view—dolly block, 72
Engineering geometry, 51–74
Engineering maps, 583, 585
Engineers' decimal scales, 36
Epicycloids, 69, 480
Equilateral hyperbola, constructing, 68
Equilateral triangle, constructing, 54
Equilibrants, 200
Equilibrium, forces in, 200–201, 204
Erasers, 294
  soft, 125
  use of, 42
Erasing machines, 27–29
Erasing shields, 42
Exploded pictorial assembly drawings, 402, 403
Extended letters, 7, 8
Extension lines, 355
Extension springs, 347

F pencils, 125
Fasteners, 337–345
Fetter, William A., 459
Fillets, 312
  representation of, 108–110, 300
Finish marks, 356
First-angle projection, 80–81
Fits, 370
  clearance, 370, 373
  force, 371
  interference, 370, 373
  locational, 371
  transition, 370
Fittings, 495
  flanged, 495
  screwed, 495
  specifications, 496
  welded, 495
Fixtures, 320, 513–514, 520
  design of, 514–515
  parts for, 516–519
Flanged fittings, 495
Flanges, 495
Flasks, 311
Flatness, tolerance for, 375, 376

Flat springs, 348
Flaws, 382
Flexible curves, 27, 28
Flow charts, 606
Flow diagrams, 449–450
Foci method to construct an ellipse, 62
Focus of a parabolic curve, 67
Force fits, 371
Forces, 198
  addition of, 198–200
  coplanar, 199, 201, 203–204
  couples, 202
  in equilibrium, 200–201, 204
  moment of, 202
  noncoplanar, 204–205
  in opposite directions, 199
  parallel, 201–202, 204
  parallelogram of, 199
  simple load-bearing frame, 205–208
  simple load-bearing truss, 208
Ford Motor Company, 453–456
Forge shops, 313
  communication drawing, 396
Forging drawings, 313
FORTRAN, 435
Foundry, the, 313
Four-center method to construct an ellipse, 64
Fractional dimensioning, 356
Fractions:
  guide lines for, 10
  lettering, 10, 18
French curves, 41
Frontal plane, revolution about a horizontal axis perpendicular to, 104
Frustum of a pyramid, 221, 222
Functional scales, construction of, 611–612

Gas turbine engines, 248
Gas welding, 509
Gate, the, 311
Gears, 479–482
  bevel, 484
  dimensioning, 483
  helical, 483
  standard involute spur, 482–483
  terms, 481–482
  working drawings of, 484
Generatrix, 215
Geometric construction, 73
Geometric objects, 215
Geometric shapes, 70
Geometric solids, 71, 215
Geometric surfaces, 215, 228–229
Geometric tolerancing, 374, 375
Gib-head keys, 342
Glass box method of obtaining views, 84–86
Glass cloth, 642

GM DAC-1 system, 439, 440–442
Gothic lettering, 19, 20
Gothic numerals, 20
Graph papers, 597
Graphs, 595–606
  classification of, 595–596
  coordinate, 603
  logarithmic, 602–603
  procedure for making representation in ink, 602
  qualitative, 596–597
  quantitative, 596–597
  rectangular coordinate, 597–598
  semilogarithmic, 603–604
  three-dimensional, 594
Grinding machines, 317–319
Ground lines, 270–271
Guide lines, 22, 23
  devices for drawing, 8–9
  for fractions, 10
  lettering, 8–9, 22, 23
Gusset plates, layout of, 558–559

Half-section dimensioning, 366
Half views, 106
Hand reaming, 316, 317
Handles, 518
Helical gears, 483
Heli-lifted classrooms, 293
Helix, the, 69–70
Henry tank pens, 8
Hexagon, regular, 55
Highway diagrams, 541–542
Highway interchange, 74
Highway route plan, 582
Hinges, 518
Hole system, basic, 372
Holes:
  dimensioning, 361, 363
  for pins, 106
  radially arranged, 107, 108
  representation of, 101
Honing, 319
Horizon:
  plane of, 270
  position of the object in relation to, 271–272
Horizon line, 270
Horizontal axis:
  perpendicular to the frontal plane, 104
  perpendicular to the profile plane, 104
Horizontal dimensions, 362
Horizontal lines, 88, 188
  drawing, 32–33
  sketching, 129
Horizontal planes, 103–104
Horizontal projection, 533
Hydrographic symbols, 590

Hyperbola, 63, 67–68
  to construct, 67–68
  equilateral, 68
Hypocycloids, 69, 480

IBM 1620 Data Processing System, 449
IBM 1620 drafting system, 449–450
IBM 1620 plotter, 449
IBM 2250 display unit, 442–443
Idea sketches, 295, 296, 303–305
Illustromat 1100, 457–458
Inclined letters:
  capital, 12–15
  lowercase, 17
Inclined lines, 88, 188, 276–277
  drawing, 33–34
  making an angle with an oblique line, 35
  sketching, 129
Inclined numerals, 15–16
Industrial designations, 538
Industrial illustration, 279–285
  design, 281–282
  shading methods, 282–283
    surface, 283–285
  technical drawings, 279–281
Industrial schematics, 537
Ink bottle filler, 43
Ink bottle holder, 43
Inking pens, 12
Ink lines, 44
Installation assembly drawings, 401–402
Institute of Electrical and Electronics
    Engineers, Inc., 530
Instruction manuals, 402
Instruments:
  set of, 26–27
  special, 27–29
  standard set of, 26
  use of, 25–50
Interference fits, 370, 373
Intermediates, 637, 639
Intersections, 228–242
  auxiliary views, 237–238
  of a cone, 233–234, 239–240, 241–242
  of a cylinder, 232–233, 238–240, 241
  line of, 172–173, 195–196, 228–229
  of an oblique cone, 241
  of an oblique plane, 232–235
  of a paraboloid, 241
  piercing point, 229–230
    line-projecting plane, 230, 232, 236, 239
  of a prism, 235–236, 237, 241–242
  projecting planes, 230–231
  of a pyramid, 236, 237
  run-out, 109–110
  of a sphere, 234–235
  surfaces, 96, 244–246
  treatment of unimportant, 106–107
  of two planes, 232

Invisible lines, 91, 97
  omission of, 93
  treatment of, 91–92
Involute:
  of a circle, 68
  of a polygon, 68
Involute curves, 68
Involute spur gears, 482–483
Involute system, 479–480
Irregular curves, 42
Isometric axes, 259
Isometric drawings, 253
  angles in, 255
  circle arcs in, 255–259
  circles in, 135, 255–259
Isometric projection, 252–253, 261–263
Isometric scale, 252
Isometric sectional views, 259–260
Isometric sketching, 134–135, 296

Jig borers, 514
Jigs, 320, 513–514, 525, 526
  design of, 514–515
  parts for, 516–519
  template, 515
  types of, 515–516
Joints:
  riveted, 345, 346
  threads for, 493
  weld, 506

Keuffel & Esser photomechanical system,
    461–463
Keys, 342
  gib-head, 342
  heavy duty, 342
  light duty, 342
  Pratt and Whitney, 342
  square, 342
  Woodruff, 342–343
Keyslots, dimensioning, 364
Keyway, 521
Keyways:
  cutting, 320
  dimensioning, 364
Knobs, 518
Knurling, 314–315
Knurls, dimensioning, 365

Ladder diagrams, 538
Land surveys, 585–586
Languages of the computer, 435, 436–437,
    473
Lapping, 319
Large-bow sets, 26–27
  using, 39–40

Lathes, 314–315
Lay, 382, 383
  symbols, 384
Layouts:
  connection diagram, 540
  control circuit, 537–538
  of gusset plates, 558–559
  for internal cross frame, 551
  metal sheet reproductions, 642
  modular, 535
  printed-circuit, 542
  roof truss, 561, 562
  structural, 548, 558–559
  trial, 535–536
Leaders, 355
Lead of a screw thread, 329
Left-hand threads, 329
Legends, 601–602
Leroy device, 19
Leroy pens, 8, 9
Lettering:
  architectural drawings, 579–580
  compressed letters, 7, 8
  extended letters, 7, 8
  freehand technical, 7–23
    capital letters, 12–15
    composition, 9–11
    fractions, 10, 18
    general proportions of letters, 7
    Gothic, 19, 20
    guide lines, 8–9, 22, 23
    large caps and small caps in
        combination, 18, 19
    lowercase single-stroke, 16–18
    mechanical devices, 19
    Modern Roman, 19, 21
    numerals, 10, 15–16
    pencils, 7–8
    pens, 7–8
    Reinhardt letters, 7
    single-stroke letters, 7, 16–18
    slope lines, 8–9
    stability, 11
    technique of, 11–12
    templates, 19
    titles, 18–19
    uniformity in, 9, 11
  general proportions of letters, 7
  styles of, 6
Limit dimensions, 369–371
  basic hole system, 372
  basic shaft system, 372–373
  for cylindrical parts, 371–372
  tolerance, 373–378
Line drawing, combining with a photograph,
    641–642
Line of intersection, 172–173
Line-projecting planes, 230, 232, 236, 239
Line reamers, 316
Line symbols, 46

Lines:
  alphabet of, 47
  analysis of, 89, 90
  angle between a plane and, 194–195
  bearing of, 189–190
  center, 97
    parallel lines about, 52
  contour, 591–593
  curved:
    in auxiliary views, 168, 170
    parallel lines about, 52
  cutting-plane, 93
  dashed, 93
  definition of, 452
  dimension, 355
    location of, 554–555
    structural, 554–555
  ditto, 111
  dividing proportionally, 53
  extension, 355
  ground, 270–271
  guide, 22, 23
    devices for drawing, 8–9
    for fractions, 10
    lettering, 8–9, 22, 23
  horizon, 270
  horizontal, 88, 188
    drawing, 32–33
    sketching, 129
  inclined, 88, 188, 276–277
    drawing, 33–34
    making an angle with an oblique line, 35
    sketching, 129
  ink, 44
  of intersection, 172–173, 195–196, 228–229
  invisible, 91, 97
    omission of, 93
    treatment of, 91–92
  meaning of, 88–89
  measuring, 276
  nonintersecting, angle between two, 195
  nonisometric, 253–254
  oblique, 88, 188
    angle between two intersecting, 195–196
    inclined lines making an angle with, 35
    true length of, 188–189
  parallel, 52, 94–95, 187–188
    drawing, 34
  parting, 312
  pencil:
    drawing, 32
    inking over, 44
  perpendicular, 189, 190
    drawing, 34–35
  perspective projection, 272
  piercing point with a plane, 193–194
  point piercing a cone, 231–232
  point view of, 190–191
  precedence of, 93
  principal, of a plane, 191, 192

Lines (cont.)
  profile of, 593
  projection of, 86–88
  reverse curves tangent to three, 60
  shortest distance from a point to, 191
  sketching techniques, 125–126
  skew, shortest distance between two, 197
  slope, devices for drawing, 8–9
  solid, 93
  straight:
    to bisect, 51
    dividing into equal parts, 52
    projection of, 186
    sketching, 126–128
    to trisect, 51
  tangent to a circle:
    at a given point on the circumference, 60
    through a given point outside the circle, 60
    two given, 61
  through a given point and the inaccessible intersection of two given lines, 53
  true length of, 100, 173, 188, 209, 219–220
    oblique, 188–189
    by revolution, 101–102
  vertical, 88, 188
    drawing, 33
    sketching, 129
Live center, 314
Locational fits, 371
Location dimensioning, 354, 363
Locking devices, 343–344
Lock washers, 343
Logarithmic graphs, 602–603
Log scales, 613
Lowercase letters:
  inclined, 17
  single-stroke, 16–18
Lunar orbits, elliptical, 74
Lunar Surface Vehicles, 290

Machined casting, 321
Machine drawings, classes of, 391–393
Machine elements, 479–489
  bearings, 487–488
  cams, 484–485
    design of, 486–487
    disc, 485
  gears, 479–482
    dimensioning, 483
    standard involute spur, 482–483
    terms, 481–482
    working drawings of, 484
  welded, 509–510
Machine screws, 340
  commercial lengths, 340–341
Machine shops, 313
  communication drawing, 396–397
  structural, 559

Machine tools, numerically controlled, 464–478
  computer-assisted programming, 472
  equipment, 465–467
  manual tape preparation, 468–472
  programming process, 468–472
  time-shared computer services, 472–475
  use of Cartesian coordinates, 467–468
Macro subdrawings, 453
Manufacturing illustration, 281
Manufacturing processes, 320–321
Map drawing, 583–593
  cadastral, 585
  classification of, 583
  contour lines, 591–593
  engineering, 583, 585
  partial city, 587
  plats of land surveys, 585–586
  profiles, 593
  subdivision plats, 586–587
  symbols, 588–590
  topographic, 583–585, 588–590
  water lines, 590–591
Mariner 3, 280
Maximum metal condition (MMC), 380–381
Measurements:
  to lay off, 38–39
  in sketching, 133
Measuring instruments in sketching, 133
Measuring lines, 276
Measuring points, 277–278
Measuring tools, 321
Mechanical engineers' scales, 35, 36, 37
Metal sheet reproductions, 642
Metric scales, 35, 37
Microfilming drawings, 641
Microinches, 382
Micrometers, 133, 322
Milling machines, 316, 318
Minigap system, 306
Missiles, 283
Modern Roman lettering, 19, 21
Modern Roman numerals, 21
Modular layouts, 535
Moment of a force, 202
Multiple revolution, 104–105
Multiple-start threads, 329
Multiview drawing, 83–101
  definition, 83
  principles of, 86
Multiview projection, 272–273
Multiview sketching, 125–133

National Electrical Manufacturers Association (NEMA), 531
National Machine Tool Builders' Association (NMTBA), 531
National Standards Institute, 1
Natural methods of obtaining views, 83–84

Needle point, adjustment of, 39
Nibs, shaping, 46
Nomographs, 609–610
Noncoplanar forces, 204–205
Nonintersecting lines, angle between two, 195
Nonisometric lines, 253–254
Notes, 452, 601–602
   architectural drawings, 579
   dimensioning, 367–368
   electronic, 536–537
   placement of, 357–367
   shop, 368
   structural, 555–558
Numerals:
   Gothic, 20
   lettering, 10, 15–16
   Modern Roman, 21
Numerically controlled machined tools, 464–478
   computer-assisted programming, 472
   equipment, 465–467
   manual tape preparation, 468–472
   programming process, 468–472
   time-shared computer services, 472–475
   use of Cartesian coordinates, 467–468
Nuts, 339, 344, 345
   American National Standard on, 337–338

Objects:
   geometric, 215
   revolution of, 102–103
Oblique cones, 224
   intersection of, 241
Oblique cylinders, 219, 220
Oblique dimensions, 362
Oblique drawing, 264, 265
Oblique lines, 88, 188
   angle between two intersecting, 195–196
   inclined lines making an angle with, 35
   true length of, 188–189
Oblique planes:
   edge view of, 191–192, 193
   intersection of, 232–235
   true shape of, 192–193
Oblique prisms, 217, 218
Oblique projection, 79, 80, 81, 251, 263–269
   angles, 266
   circle arcs, 266
   circles, 266
   conventional treatment, 268–269
   drawing, 264, 265
   pictorial dimensioning, 267–268
   principle of, 263–264
   reduction of measurements, 267
   rules for placing an object, 265–266
   sectional views, 267
   use of a basic plane, 264–265
Oblique sketching, 136, 137, 296
Oblique surface, true shape of, 105

Octagon, to construct, 55–56
Offset method to construct a parabola, 66
Offsets, 363
Ogee (reverse) curves, 59–60
   tangent to three given lines, 60
One-plane projection, 79
One-point perspective, 299
One-view drawings, 394
Ordinates, variables for, 598
Orthographic drawings, 96–98
Orthographic projection, 77–79, 81
Orthographic views, 261–263
Other-side welds, 507
Outline assembly drawings, 402
Overlay sheets, 300–303
Ozalid prints, 637–638

Paper:
   fastening, 32
   placing, 32
   tracing, 29
Parabola, 63, 65–67
   to construct, 65
      offset method, 66
      parallelogram method, 66–67
      tangent method, 65–66
Parabolic curves:
   to construct a curve through two given points, 66
   to locate the directrix of, 67
   to locate the focus of, 67
Paraboloid, intersection of, 241
Parallel dimensions, 358
Parallel forces, 201–202, 204
Parallelism, tolerance for, 376, 377
Parallel lines, 52, 94–95, 187–188
   drawing, 34
Parallelogram method:
   to construct an ellipse, 64–65
   to construct a parabola, 66–67
   forces, 199
Parallel perspective, 273–274
   sketches in, 297
Parallel planes, distance between two, 196
Parallel projection, 77–79, 81
Parallel-scale charts, 612–617
Partial views, 106
   auxiliary views and, 165, 169–171
Parting lines, 312
Parts list, 397–400, 402
Patent office drawings, 626–631
Pattern shops, 312
   communication drawing, 396
Pencil lines:
   drawing, 32
   inking over, 44
Pencils, 29
   artist's, 27
   bow, 41

Pencils (*cont.*)
   conical point, 31
   degrees of hardness, 29
   drop, 27, 28
   electric, 564
   F, 125
   lettering, 7–8
   obtaining proportions by, 297, 298
   pointing, 29–31
   sharpening, 29, 126
   sketching, 126
   thinking with, 294–296
   using, 32
   wedge points, 31
Pencil shading, 299–300
Pens:
   Barch-Payzant, 8, 9
   bow, 41
   dirty, 44
   drop, 27, 28
   Edco, 8, 9
   Henry tank, 8
   holding, 12, 42
   inking, 12
   Leroy, 8, 9
   lettering, 7–8
   ruling, 28, 29
      cleaning, 44
      faults in handling, 43
      sharpening, 45–46
      use of, 42–44
   speedball, 8, 9
   Wrico, 19
Pentagon, to construct, 55
Perpendicularity, tolerance for, 375–376
Perpendicular lines, 189, 190
   drawing, 34–35
Perspective:
   angular, 273, 274–276
      sketches in, 297
   one-point, 299
   parallel, 273–274
      sketches in, 297
Perspective projection, 77, 251, 269–279
   angular, 273, 274–276
   circles, 274, 278–279
   inclined lines, 276–277
   lines, 272
   measuring lines, 276
   measuring points, 277–278
   multiview, 272–273
   nomenclature, 270–271
   object in relation to the horizon, 271–272
   parallel, 273–274
   picture plane, 269, 270, 271
   station point, 269, 271
   types of, 273
   vanishing points, 276–277
Perspective sketching, 296–299
Phillips heads, 344, 345

Photocopies, 639
Photodraft systems, automated, 461–463
Photograph, combining with a line drawing, 641–642
Photostat machines, 639
Pictorial charts, 606
Pictorial dimensioning, 267–268
Pictorial drawing, 249–288
    divisions of, 249
Pictorial sketching, 133
Picture plane, 269, 270, 271
Pie charts, 604
Piercing points, 229–230
    line-projecting plane, 230, 232, 236, 239
    with a plane, 193–194
Pins:
    adjustable stop, 518
    holes for, 106
    taper, 343
Pipes:
    cast-iron, 494–495
    circular, 225
    rectangular, 224–225
    square, 225–226
Piping, 490–503
    drawings, 497–498
        dimensions on, 499
    fittings:
        flanged, 495
        screwed, 495
        specification, 496
        welded, 495
    materials, 491
    models, 499–502
    sizes, 494–495
    special, 491–492
    steel specification, 494
    symbols, 499, 500
    threads:
        American National Standard, 492–493
        for couplings, 493
        drawing, 494
        dryseal, 493–494
        for joints, 493
        specification of, 492–493
    unions, 496
    valves, 496–497
    wrought-iron specification, 494
Pitch, 329
    circular, 482
    diametral, 482
Planers, 317
Planes:
    angle between a line and, 194–195
    auxiliary, 163
    cutting, 145, 150, 152
    dihedral angle between two, 196–197
    frontal, revolution about a horizontal axis perpendicular to, 104
    of the horizon, 270

Planes (*cont.*)
    horizontal, 103–104
    intersection of two, 232
    line-projecting, 230, 232, 236, 239
    oblique:
        edge view of, 191–192, 193
        intersection of, 232–235
        true shape of, 192–193
    parallel, distance between two, 196
    picture, 269, 270, 271
    piercing point of a line and, 193–194
    principal lines of, 191, 192
    profile, revolution about a horizontal axis perpendicular to, 104
    projecting, 78–80, 230, 231, 232, 236, 239
    in space, 186–187
    surface, true-shape projection of, 103
    true shape of, 209
    true size of, 209
    use of a basic, 264–265
Plans:
    architectural, 567–570
    plot, 570–571, 572
Plates:
    adjustment, 73
    spline, 73
Plats:
    of land surveys, 585–586
    subdivision, 586–587
Plot plans, 570–571, 572
Plotted points, 600
Pointers, 355
Points:
    analysis of, 89, 90
    brilliant, 284
    CV, 271
    definition of, 452
    lines through and the inaccessible intersection of two given lines, 53
    measuring, 277–278
    piercing, 229–230
        line-projecting plane, 230, 232, 236, 239
        with a plane, 193–194
    plotted, 600
    projection of, 185–186
    shortest distance to a line, 191
    station, 269, 271
    vanishing, 276–277
    where a line pierces a cone, 231–232
Point-to-point diagrams, 540–541
Point view of a line, 190–191
Polar charts, 605
Polishing, 319
Polygon:
    to construct, 56
    involute of, 68
    string, 202–203
    to transfer, 54
Population charts, 606
Position tolerancing, 374–375, 378

Practical Design of Manufacturing Tools, Dies, and Fixtures, 523
Practical developments, 216
Pratt and Whitney keys, 342
Presentation drawings, 566–567
Principal (front) views, 91, 92
    auxiliary views and, 171, 172
Printed circuits, 542
    artwork, 542–543
    layouts, 542
Prisms, 71
    intersection of, 235–236, 237, 241–242
    oblique, 217, 218
    right truncated, 216–217
    surface shading on, 284
Production machines, special, 321–323
Profile dimensioning, 367
Profile of a line, 593
Profile plane, revolution about a horizontal axis perpendicular to, 104
Profile tolerancing, 377
Programming:
    complex, 471
    computer-assisted, 472
    process of, 468–472
    simple, 471
Projection, 77–82
    of angles, 93–94, 266
    axonometric, 79, 250–263
        angles, 255
        circle, 255–259
        circle arcs, 255–259
        coordinate construction method, 254–255
        dimetric, 260–263
        division of, 250–252
        isometric, 252–253, 261–263
        isometric axes, 259
        isometric scale, 252
        isometric sectional views, 259–260
        nonisometric lines, 253–254
        trimetric, 261–263
    convergent, 81
    of a curved boundary, 168–169
    first-angle, 80–81
    horizontal, 533
    isometric, 252–253, 261–263
    of lines, 86–88
    oblique, 79, 80, 81, 251, 263–269
        angles, 266
        circle, 266
        circle arcs, 266
        conventional treatment, 268–269
        drawing, 264, 265
        pictorial dimensioning, 267–268
        principle of, 263–264
        reduction of measurements, 267
        rules for placing an object, 265–266
        sectional views, 267
        use of a basic plane, 264–265

Projection (*cont.*)
  one-plane, 79
  orthographic, 77–79, 81
  parallel, 77–79, 81
  perspective, 77, 251, 269–279
    angular, 273, 274–276
    circles, 274, 278–279
    inclined lines, 276–277
    lines, 272
    measuring lines, 276
    measuring points, 277–278
    multiview, 272–273
    nomenclature, 270–271
    object in relation to the horizon, 271–272
    parallel, 273–274
    picture plane, 269, 270, 271
    station point, 269, 271
    types of, 273
    vanishing points, 276–277
  planes, 78–80, 230, 231, 232, 236, 239
    in space, 186–187
  of a point, 185–186
  scenographic, 77
  schematic, 533–534
  sketching, 125
  a space curve, 96
  of a straight line, 186
  of surfaces, 89
  systems of, 81
  third-angle, 80–81
  true-shape of a plane surface, 103
  vertical, 533–534
  violations of true, 106
Projectors, 80
  converging, 81
  parallel, 81
Proportional dividers, 29
Protractor angles, 27
Purdue Riefler sets, 26
Pyramids, 71
  frustum of, 221, 222
  intersection of, 236, 237
  right, 221, 222
  surface shading on, 284

Quadruped machines, 504
Qualitative charts, 596–597
Qualitative graphs, 596–597
Quantitative charts, 596–597
Quantitative graphs, 596–597

Radial distances, marking off, 129
Radially arranged features, conventional treatment of, 107
Radially arranged holes, 107, 108
Radial ribs, 107

Radial spokes, 107
Reaming, 314
  hand, 316, 317
  line, 316
Receding axis, 267
Recordak Manafiche Readers, 641
Recordak Micro-File Machines, 634
Record strips, 394–395
Rectangular coordinate graphs, 597–598
Rectangular pipes, 224–225
Re-entry vehicles, 447
Reference designations, 531–532, 536
Reference dimensions, 359
Regular hexagon, 55
Regular octagon, 55–56
Regular pentagon, 55
Regular polygon, 56
Reinhardt letters, 7
REMAPT, 473
Research satellites, 162
Resistance welding, 509, 510
Rest buttons, 517
Reverse (ogee) curves, 59–60
  tangent to three given lines, 60
Revolution, 101–105
  clockwise, 104
  counterclockwise, 104
  horizontal axis:
    perpendicular to the frontal plane, 104
    perpendicular to the profile plane, 104
  of an object, 102–103
  simple (single), 103
  successive (multiple), 104–105
  true length of a line by, 101–102
  true-shape projection of a plane surface, 103
  vertical axis perpendicular to the horizontal plane, 103–104
Revolved triangles, 35
Rhomboids, 135
Ribs:
  radial, 107
  in section, 154
Right-hand threads, 329
Riser, the, 312
Riveted joints, 345, 346
Rivets, 344, 345, 346
Rocket control system, 281
Roller bearings, 487–488
Roof truss layout, 561, 562
Roughness, 381–382
  height, 382, 383
  width, 382
  width cutoff, 382, 383
Rounds, 312
  representation of, 108–110
  sketches, 300
Ruled surfaces, 215
Rules of Practice in the United States Patent Office, 627–631

Ruling pens, 28, 29
  cleaning, 44
  faults in handling, 43
  sharpening, 45–46
  use of, 42–44
Run-out intersections, 109–110

Satellite-friction experiment, 390
Satellites, 185, 528
  research, 162
Scales, 35–39, 599
  architects', 35, 36–37
  civil engineers' (chain), 35, 36, 37
  decimal, 38–39
    engineers', 36
    reading, 39
  functional, construction of, 611–612
  labeling of, 601
  log, 613
  mechanical engineers', 35, 36, 37
  metric, 35, 37
  reading, 38
  of reduction, 37
Scenographic projection, 77
Schematic diagrams, 533
Schematic projection, 533–534
Schematics, industrial, 537
Screwed fittings, 495
Screws, 344, 345
  adjustable, 517
  cap, 340
    commercial lengths, 340–341
  machine, 340
    commercial lengths, 340–341
  set, 341–342
Screw threads, 327–337
  Acme, 332, 337
  American-British unified, 328
  American National Standard conventional symbols, 331–333
  buttress, 337
  detailed representation, 329–331
  dimensioning, 335–336
  identification symbols, 335
  lead, 329
  left-hand, 329
  multiple-start, 329
  pitch, 329
  right-hand, 329
  in section, 333–334
  sketches, 300
  square, 331, 332, 336
  stubb Acme, 337
  Unified and American classes, 334–335
  Unified and American series, 334
Second position, the, 84–86, 87
Sectional views, 143–162
  auxiliary, 152
  broken, 143, 146–147

Sectional views (*cont.*)
    conventional, 152–154
    cutting planes, 145, 150, 152
    full, 143
    half, 143, 145–146, 154–155
    lining, 149–150, 151
    material symbols, 155
    oblique projection, 267
    outline, 150, 151
    phantom, 149
    practices, 151–152
    removed (detail), 147–149
    revolved, 147, 148
    ribs in, 154
    spokes in, 153
Section drawings, 571–572
    wall, 572–574
Semilogarithmic charts, 603
Semilogarithmic graphs, 603–604
Set screws, 341–342
Shading, 282–283
    pencil, 299–300
    surface, 283–285
Shaft system, basic, 372–373
Shapes, 316–317, 318
    geometric, 70
Shop notes, 368
Shop processes, 311–323
Shop terms, 323–325
Simple load-bearing frames, 205–208
Simple load-bearing trusses, 208
Simple (single) revolution, 103
Single-curved surfaces, 215
Single-stroke letters, 7
    lowercase, 16–18
Size dimensions, 353–354
Sketching, 291–310
    in angular perspective, 297
    architectural drawings, 566
    circles, 128–130
    communication drawings, 391
    creative, 305
    design in, 295, 305–307
    determining proportions, 297–298
    ellipses, 130
    horizontal lines, 129
    idea, 295, 296, 303–305
    inclined lines, 129
    isometric, 134–135, 296
    large circles, 128–130
    materials, 125, 307
    measurements in, 133
    measuring instruments in, 133
    mechanical methods of, 133–134
    multiview, 125–133
    oblique, 136, 137, 296
    of parts for the purpose of replacement
        and repair, 132
    perspective, 296–299
    pictorial, 133

Sketching (*cont.*)
    projections, 125
    proportions, 130–132, 135–136
    rounds, 300
    screw threads, 300
    showing mechanisms exploded, 303
    steps in, 131
    straight lines, 126–128
    technique of lines, 125–126
    titles, 133
    value of, 125
    vertical lines, 129
Sketching pencils, 126
SKETCHPAD, 444–445
Skew lines, shortest distance between two, 197
Sliding triangles, 35
Slope lines, devices for drawing, 8–9
Slots, dimensioning, 364, 365
Slotted guides, 72
Society of Automotive Engineers Congress, 282
Society of Manufacturing Engineers, 523
Solid lines, 93
Solids, geometric, 71, 215
Space, projection of a plane in, 186–187
Spacecraft, 280
Space curves, projecting, 96
Space stations, 76
Speedball pens, 8, 9
Spheres, 227–228
    intersections of, 234–235
    surface shading on, 285
Spherical washers, 517
Spiral of Archimedes, 69
Spline plates, 73
Spokes:
    radial, 107
    sectional, 153
Springs, 345–348
    compression, 346, 347
    extension, 347
    flat, 348
    tension, 346
    torsion, 347–348
Sprue, the, 311
Spur gears, involute, 482–483
Square, to construct, 54–55
Square and Hexagon Bolts and Nuts, 337
Square keys, 342
Square pipes, 225–226
Square threads, 331, 332, 336
Stability in lettering, 11
Standard stock forms, 313
Standards, graphical, 530–531
Stand molds, 312
Station point, 269, 271
Steel pipes:
    sizes, 494–495
    specification, 494

Stock forms, standard, 313
Stop pins, adjustable, 518
Stop screws, adjustable, 517
Straight lines:
    to bisect, 51
    dividing into equal parts, 52
    projection of, 186
    sketching, 126–128
    to trisect, 51
Straightness, tolerance for, 375
Stress sheets, 549
Stress-strain diagrams, 598
String polygon, 202–203
Structural drawings, 547–562
    classes of, 548
    computer-plotter-prepared, 561
    definitions, 552–554
    detail, 548–552
    detailing information, 554
    dimensions in, 555–558
    equipment, 547–548
    layouts, 548, 558–559
    location of dimension lines, 554–555
    machine-shop work, 559
    notations, 552–554
    notes, 555–558
    sizes of standard members, 554
    welding, 559–561
Stubb Acme threads, 337
Studs, 339–340
    commercial lengths, 340–341
Subassembly drawings, 397
Subdivision and Mapping System (SAMPS), 434
Subdivision plats, 586–587
Successive (multiple) revolution, 104–105
Superfinishing, 319
Surfaces:
    analysis of, 89, 90
    approximately developable, 223–224, 226–227
    characteristics, 382–383
    double-curved, 71, 215
    geometric, 215, 228–229
    intersecting, 96, 244–246
    oblique, true shape of, 105
    plane, true-shape projection of, 103
    projection of, 89, 103
    quality, 381–382
    ruled, 215
    shading, 283–285
    single-curved, 215
    tangent, treatment of, 94
    texture, 381, 383
    warped, 215
Symmetrical auxiliary views, 166–167, 168

Tangent arcs, 57
Tangent circles, 57

Tangent circular arcs, to approximate a curve with, 61
Tangent method:
   to construct an angle, 53
   to construct a parabola, 65–66
Tangent surfaces, treatment of, 94
Tape preparation, manual, 468–472
Taper pins, 343
Tapers, dimensioning, 365
Template jigs, 515
Templates, 19, 27–29, 30
   chemistry, 30
   electro symbol, 30
   tilt-hex drafting, 30
   tooling, 30
Tension springs, 346
Tetrahedral Research Satellite, 528
Thinking, creative, 291–310
Third-angle projection, 80–81
Threads:
   Acme, 332, 337
   American-British unified, 328
   American National Standard, 492–493
   areo, 344
   buttress, 337
   for couplings, 493
   drawing, 494
   dryseal, 493–494
   for joints, 493
   left-hand, 329
   multiple-start, 329
   right-hand, 329
   screw, *see* Screw threads
   specification of, 492–493
   symbols, 331–333
Three-dimensional graphs, 594
Three-scale alignment charts, 617–618
Tilt-hex drafting templates, 30
Time-shared computer services, 472–475
Title blocks, 394–395
Titles, 601–602
   communication drawing, 394, 400
   contents of, 395
   lettering, 18–19
   sketching, 133
Tolerances, 373–378
   angular, 374, 376, 377
   bilateral, 373
   for concentricity, 376, 377
   coordinate, 378
   cumulative, 374
   for flatness, 375, 376
   of form, 374–375
   geometric, 374, 375
   for parallelism, 376, 377
   for perpendicularity, 375–376
   position, 374–375, 378
   profile, 377
   for straightness, 375
   unilateral, 373

Tongue, dimensioning, 365
Tool design, 513–527
   principles of, 514
Tool drawings, 513–527
Tooling templates, 30
Tooth curves, 479–480
Topographic maps, 583–585, 588–590
Torsion springs, 347–348
Tracing, 44–45
   duplicate, 638–639
   mutilated, 639–640
   worn, 639–640
Tracing cloth, 29
Tracing paper, 29
Tracked air cushion research vehicles, 2
Tracked-Air-Cushion-Vehicle (TACV), 82
Trammel method, to construct an ellipse, 63–64
Transition fits, 370
Transition pieces, 224, 243
   approximately developable surface, 226–227
   connecting a circular and a square pipe, 225–226
   connecting rectangular pipes, 224–225
   connecting two circular pipes, 225
Translucent masters, 639
Trapezoid, dividing the area into equal parts, 56–57
Trial layouts, 535–536
Triangles, 33
   Braddock lettering, 8–9, 10, 25
   constructing:
      equilateral, 54
      given its three sides, 54
   dividing the area into equal parts, 56–57
   equilateral, constructing, 54
   revolved, 35
   sliding, 35
   testing for nicks, 33
   vector, 199
   Wrico, 28
Triangulation method, 223–224, 226–227
Trilinear charts, 605
Trimetric projection, 261–263
Trisect:
   an angle, 52
   a straight line, 51
True-length diagrams, 220–221
True-length of lines, 100, 173, 188, 209, 219–220
   oblique, 188–189
   by revolution, 101–102
True-position dimensioning, 378–381
   the maximum metal condition, 380–381
Try sheet, testing a trial line on, 43
T-squares, 32–33
   manipulating, 32
Tubing, special, 491–492
Typed material, 636

Underwater Production System, 214
Unilateral auxiliary views, 167–168
Unilateral tolerances, 373
Unions, 496
United States Geological Survey, 588
U. S. Government Printing Office, 530
Unsymmetrical auxiliary views, 166

Valves, 496–497
Vanishing points, 276–277
Variables:
   for abscissa, 598
   for ordinates, 598
   values of, 599–600
Vector geometry, 197–209
   Bow's notation, 202–203
   components, 200
   forces, 198
      addition of, 198–200
      coplanar, 199, 201, 203–204
      couples, 202
      in equilibrium, 200–201, 204
      methods, 197–198
      moment of, 202
      noncoplanar, 204–205
      in opposite directions, 199
      parallel, 201–202, 204
      parallelogram of, 199
      simple load-bearing frame, 205–208
      simple load-bearing truss, 208
      string polygons, 202–203
Vector triangle, 199
Vegetation symbols, 590
Vela LV-Nuclear Detection Satellite, 352
Vertical axis, revolution about, 103–104
Vertical dimensions, 362
Vertical letters:
   capital, 12–15
   lowercase, 18
Vertical lines, 88, 188
   drawing, 33
   sketching, 129
Vertical numerals, 15–16
Vertical projection, 533–534
Views:
   aligned, 107, 108
   auxiliary, 163–183, 237–238
      bilateral, 168, 169
      constructing, 169
      curved lines in, 168, 170
      dihedral angles, 169, 170
      line of intersection, 172–173
      partial views and, 165, 169–171
      primary, 163–173
      principal views and, 171, 172
      projection of a curved boundary, 168–169
      secondary, 173–175
      symmetrical, 166–167, 168
      true length of a line, 172–173

Views (*cont.*)
    types of, 163–166
    unilateral, 167–168
    unsymmetrical, 166
    use of, 163
  choice of, 91, 92
  half, 106
  interpretation of adjacent areas of, 99–100
  isometric sectional, 259–260
  line analysis, 89, 90
  methods of obtaining, 83
    glass box, 84–86
    natural, 83–84
  oblique sectional, 267
  orthographic, 261–263
  partial, 106
    auxiliary views and, 165, 169–171
  point analysis, 89, 90
  principal (front), 91, 92
    auxiliary views and, 171, 172
  sectional, 143–162
    auxiliary, 152
    broken, 143, 146–147
    conventional, 152–154
    cutting planes, 145, 150, 152
    full, 143
    half, 143, 145–146, 154–155
    lining, 149–150, 151
    material symbols, 155
    oblique projection, 267
    outline, 150, 151
    phantom, 149
    practices, 151–152
    removed (detail), 147–149

Views (*cont.*)
    revolved, 147, 148
    ribs in, 154
    spokes in, 153
  selection of, 90–91
  surface analysis, 89, 90
  terminology, 87
  visualizing an object from, 98–99

Wall sections, 572–574
Warped surfaces, 215
Washers:
  lock, 343
  spherical, 517
Water lines, 590–591
Waviness, 382
  height, 382, 383
  width, 382
Welded fittings, 495
Welding, 505–511
  arc, 505, 509
  gas, 509
  machine parts, 509–510
  processes, 505–506
  resistance, 509, 510
  structural, 559–561
  symbols, 507–509, 510
  working drawings, 506–507
Welds:
  arrow-side, 507
  classification of, 506
  dimensioning, 508
  double-groove, 509

Welds (*cont.*)
  other-side, 507
  types of, 506
Westinghouse Electric Corporation, 478
Wire coding, 539
Wires, 538–539
Wiring methods, 539–540
Woodruff keys, 342–343
Working drawings:
  architectural, 567
  assembly, 397
  communication, 393, 395
  of gears, 484
  of welded parts, 506–507
Worm, 484, 485
Wrench, 72
Wrico outfits, 19
Wrico pens, 19
Wrico triangles, 28
Wrought-iron pipes:
  sizes, 494–495
  specification, 494

Xerography, 640–641
Xerox prints, 640
X-Y plotters, 50

Y-clamps, adjustable, 72

Z-charts, 618–619